THE MAINSTREAM OF
CIVILIZATION

Fifth Edition

Stanley Chodorow
University of California, San Diego

MacGregor Knox
University of Rochester

Conrad Schirokauer
The City College of The City University of New York

Joseph R. Strayer

Hans W. Gatzke

THE MAINSTREAM OF
CIVILIZATION

HBJ **Harcourt Brace Jovanovich, Publishers**
San Diego   New York   Chicago   Austin   Washington, D.C.
London   Sydney   Tokyo   Toronto

Fifth Edition

ISBN: 0-15-551579-9

Library of Congress Catalog Card Number: 88-80637

Printed in the United States of America

Preface

Writing a history of civilization is an almost foolhardy enterprise. But it is easier to do if you have done it before, as the authors of the first four editions of this history, Joseph R. Strayer and Hans W. Gatzke, noted dryly in their preface to the previous edition. We, their successors, had not done it before. But we did have the robust framework that the original authors left to us. We have done our best to preserve that framework while adding, in our rewriting, many things of our own.

Following the "mainstream of civilization" requires a gradual shift of geographic focus from the Mediterranean to Europe, and ultimately to the entire globe. It demands descriptions of the major civilizations east and south of Europe, from Byzantium and Islam to India, China, and Japan. And as the mainstream flows toward the present, the need to understand that present dictates an ever more detailed analysis and narrative. We have sought in that narrative to combine clarity with at least some of the complexity revealed in the historical evidence. We have attempted to convey to readers the texture and flavor of past civilizations and the astonishing variety of human possibilities and accomplishments. We have emphasized the interrelationships of all spheres of life, from politics and warfare to economics, art, scholarship, and religion. We have suggested at least some of the differing ways in which contemporaries and historians have understood the past. Above all, we have tried to explain that past, to explain historical change. Why and how have states, institutions, and ideas risen, flourished, and crumbled into dust? Why did events happen as they did, and not otherwise?

Writing history is a contentious business. That is one of its attractions. As our narrative moves toward the present it inevitably touches on issues that arouse passionate debate, and not only among historians. We have tried to address those issues honestly, as we see them. We hope and trust that what we have written will provoke readers to further exploration, discussion, and—yes—even debate. The human past is too intriguing and too weighted with consequences for the present to leave exclusively to academic professionals. It is and should be the common property of all literate individuals.

This book inevitably draws heavily upon the publications, contributions, and advice of other scholars. Our format precludes detailed references to our sources, but we have sought wherever possible to hint at our major debts in the "suggestions for further reading" that follow each chapter. We owe special thanks to Conrad Schirokauer, City College of the City University of New York, for his contribution of Chapters 6 and 15. For their perceptive comments and criticisms, we thank

Stanley Engerman, University of Rochester; Benton H. Fatherree, Hinds Junior College, Raymond Campus; William B. Hauser, University of Rochester; Tina Isaacs; Brenda Meehan-Waters, University of Rochester; Williamson Murray, Ohio State University; Thomas X. F. Noble, University of Virginia, Charlottesville; David S. Sefton, Eastern Kentucky University; Robert Westbrook, University of Rochester; Mary Young, University of Rochester; and Perez Zagorin, University of Rochester. All have helped to make this book better, but they bear no responsibility for sins of omission or commission and errors of fact or judgment, which belong to the authors alone.

Finally, we owe a very great debt to the late Hans W. Gatzke. Despite the increasingly debilitating effects of a tragic illness, he oversaw with tact and consideration the transition from one "team" of authors to the next. He set an ambitious goal for the new team: a major revision and recasting of the book. He shaped the plan for that revision, and suggested a number of the new themes that we have attempted to emphasize. He read many of the rewritten chapters with warm encouragement and a critical eye. To his memory, and to that of the late Joseph R. Strayer, we thankfully dedicate this fifth edition.

Stanley Chodorow / MacGregor Knox

Contents

List of Maps

Introduction

History is the story of the human past. It is also the only available introduction to the human future. The first critically thinking historian, Thucydides the Athenian, implied as much in introducing his history of the great war between the two rival Greek cities of Athens and Sparta in the fifth century B.C. Thucydides addressed his history to those "who want to understand clearly the events which happened in the past and which (human nature being what it is) will, at some time or other and in much the same ways, be repeated in the future." He added that his book was "not a piece of writing designed to meet the taste of an immediate public, but was done to last for ever."

No modern historian would dare make the latter claim. "For ever" is a length of time beyond human grasp, and the mass-market tastes of the immediate public now have a weight that Thucydides the aristocrat would have roundly condemned. But Thucydides' book, the most penetrating historical work of the ancient world, has nevertheless survived for 2,400 years, and has probably enjoyed more readers in the last three centuries than in its entire previous existence. And Thucydides' perception that human affairs follow patterns visible to the trained eye has remained the fundamental argument for studying history.

The future is by definition unknowable and unpredictable; events are unique, and never repeat themselves precisely. But they often follow patterns. Individuals are unique, and are free to make their own history. That freedom gives the unfolding of history its element of suspense. But individuals also band together to create societies. Those societies have structures—languages, religions, intellectual traditions, artistic styles, and political, social, economic, and military institutions—that constrain individuals in the ways they can make history, that limit the range of thoughts and actions open to them. Those historical structures operate in consistent ways that the mind can analyze. Historical situations separated by centuries and continents have similarities, and sometimes develop according to a similar logic. Historical analogies—the comparison between one set of historical structures or events and another—are powerful if treacherous tools for probing future possibilities.

Historical analysis faces inevitable limitations. Evidence about the past is always incomplete. Politics, warfare, religion, philosophy, and art have left more traces than has everyday life. The leisured few loom far larger in the surviving sources than the experiences and aspirations of the sweat-soaked many. Men appear more frequently than women. Societies with writing have left far more behind them than those without. Twentieth century technology—aerial photography, radiocarbon dating, precise chemical analysis, meticulous archaeological technique—has disclosed much about voiceless societies and groups, and has broadened our knowledge even of societies that left extensive literatures. Textual analysis and source criticism—close scrutiny of the style, content, context, purposes, and reliability of surviving texts—have deepened our understanding of the written sources. The fragmentary nature of the evidence transmitted from the past nevertheless limits the historian's ability to see clearly and to draw valid conclusions. And in the nineteenth and twentieth centuries, the written record has swollen exponentially with the coming of mass literacy and the creation of immense bureaucracies. Too much evidence rather than too little is the affliction of the historian of the recent past.

Worse, the historian's own values inevitably color and sometimes drastically distort both the selection of evidence and the analysis of ideas and events. The past is the indispensable key to the present, but the present can also crush the past. Crusading religions and combative secular ideologies such as nationalism or Marxism-Leninism tend to alter history to fit preconceived dogma. Traumatic experiences such as wars, revolutions, or economic catastrophes tend to impel the historian to seek escape in a largely imaginary and far more pleasant past, or to rewrite the recent past as a one-way street leading with deterministic inevitability to the cataclysmic present. And historians, although their calling should lead them to take the long view, sometimes fall victim to passing fads. The historian's only defenses against ideological distortion and trendiness are the search for detachment and the passionate commitment to the verifiable evidence that has distinguished the best historical writing from Thucydides onward.

For history, if painstakingly and honestly written, offers to those who pursue it a sense of the probabilities, of the range of outcomes inherent in a given historical situation. Historical knowledge can teach us how the world works.

But it is also indispensable in a second way. History is memory. Historical knowledge is self-knowledge. It tells us how our world, our own society, and we as individuals got to where we are. Memory can give pleasure, but is also decisive in our lives. For the individual, memory is the essential component of identity. For society, the "collective memory" or knowledge of the society's past and shared values is equally indispensable. It is part of the glue that binds society together. When a society suffers collective amnesia, when it loses its historical consciousness, the values formed through that society's history inevitably erode. That decay undermines the society's political, social, and intellectual cohesion, and may threaten its survival.

In the empires, city-states, monarchies, and tribal polities of the past and in the single-party dictatorships of the present, religion, custom, political indoctrination, and force have usually sufficed to maintain cohesion. But our own civilization has over the last three centuries evolved a historically unique concept: laws that guarantee the rights of the ruled against the rulers, the rights of individuals against the state. Those laws have provided an unprecedented measure of freedom for individuals to worship as they please, to follow their economic interests, to pursue private happiness. The victories of rights against the state in the seventeenth and eighteenth centuries and of representative democratic government in the nineteenth century marked an immense leap forward in human freedom and economic dynamism. But that freedom has also carried with it the possibility that its heirs might one day lose it, through forgetfulness of the sacrifices and struggles that had secured it and through ignorance of its historical uniqueness and potential fragility. Historical knowledge can guard against that outcome as no other knowledge can.

History as the History of Civilization

If our present comes from our past, what is the shape of that past? The readers of this book, by the fact that they read the English language, are heirs to a tradition that stretches back to the first millennium B.C., to the Greeks on the one hand and to the Hebrew authors of the Old Testament on the other. That *civilization*—a term coined in the eighteenth century and derived from the Roman word for city, *civitas*—is the civilization of the West, the civilization of Europe.

Civilization above all means cities, a human institution less than 10,000 years old. Cities require a highly developed peasant agriculture to feed them, architects and laborers to erect them, artisans to people them, bureaucrats to organize and tax them, soldiers to defend them, rulers to rule them, and religious or communal myths and customs to engender loyalty to the existing order. Cities mean a degree of social stratification, of differences between the high and the low, unknown in the hunter-gatherer or cattle-herding nomad societies that preceded them. Cities mean *literacy, organization,* and *specialization* of work. And the degree of literacy, organization, and specialization affects the density of population a given civilization can support and the character and attainments of that civilization. The Greek city-states were capable of efforts and achievements far surpassing those of the Scythian nomads to the north and of the ramshackle Persian empire to the east.

Cities have meant the intensified development of religion, philosophy, technology, art, and literature. The great religions, from those of ancient Egypt and Mesopotamia through Hinduism and Buddhism to Christianity and Islam, were urban creations presiding over urban civilizations—even though Islam achieved its early successes through the swords of desert warrior nomads. Philosophy, the quest for the principles and realities underlying human knowledge and existence, was an offshoot of religion that first arose in the Greek cities and in the urban civilizations of China and India. Technological advance, from improvements in tools and weapons to the building of fortifications, roads, and aqueducts, was a precondition and consequence of the rise of cities. Highly developed art, from architecture and sculpture to ceramics and painting, has been the mark of urban civilizations. And writing, invented for the tax accounting of the bureaucrats and the records of the city priesthoods, eventually made possible the flowering of poetry, drama, history, and science.

Cities have meant common values that bind the inhabitants together, that induce them to accept the sacrifices—often without immediate or apparent compensating benefits—which specialization and organization impose. Those values can derive from a variety of sources. The great religions, the modern ideologies that claim to grasp the meaning and destination of history, the cult of the nation-state, and the sense of duty toward the community that is the "civic religion" of democracies have all provided the myths and values needed to sustain urban civilization. Those myths and values have in turn been related to the type of civilizaton they spring from and support.

Finally, cities have meant conflict as well as achievement. Hunter-gatherers and nomads raid their neighbors for booty, women, slaves, and cattle. All adult males are by definition warriors. But in urban civilizations, specialization of work extends to warfare, to the creation of hereditary warrior castes or of standing armies and navies that in time of war command the entire resources of the state. Urban civilizations, by virtue of literacy, organization, and specialization, are capable of a violence far more systematic and long-lasting than that of their predecessors. Externally, that violence has resulted in the formation of *state systems,* of highly competitive groups of rival states. In such systems, as the greatest of Greek philosophers, Plato, bitingly remarked, "What most people call peace . . . is just a name; in fact there is by nature an everlasting undeclared war of all against all." And even within the city walls, fierce conflicts between rival groups among the ruling few or between the few and the downtrodden many have frequently broken the peace.

The history of civilization must thus seek to analyze the gradual increase of literacy, organization, and specialization over the last three millennia. Such a history must be a political history, for politics is the key to understanding the nature, growth, and collapse of *states*—the large-scale political units whose character, success, or failure has been a matter of life or death for the inhabitants of all known civilizations. A history of civilization must be an economic and social history, for economic and social relationships shape politics, and are in turn shaped by politics. A history of civilization must be a history of art, literature, and ideas—for art, literature, and ideas define and reflect the systems of shared beliefs without which no civilization is possible. Above all, a history of civilization must seek to analyze the interconnections of politics, economics, and ideas that determine the character, development, and fate of civilizations.

And as seen from the late twentieth century, the history of human civilization as a whole centers on the history of the West, the history of Europe. For Europe's civilization, although at first merely one of the world's major traditions, spread outward after 1492 to dominate the entire globe. That outcome was nevertheless not foreordained, for Europe started late. The earliest civilizations arose as early as 3,000 B.C. in the great river valleys of Egypt, Mesopotamia, India, and China. The first recognizably Western

civilization only appeared after 1,000 B.C. in the Greek city-states of Greece, Asia Minor, southern Italy, and Sicily. The Greeks borrowed much from their predecessors to the east and south, including the alphabet they took from their Phoenician rivals. But the Greeks were unique. In the space of little more than three centuries—the sixth through fourth centuries B.C.—they invented the Western traditions of philosophical, historical, and scientific inquiry. They created the concept of individual freedom. They laid the foundations of Western literature. They made Western civilization self-conscious, inquiring, and *historical.* And in the fourth century B.C., the immense conquests of Alexander of Macedon, heir to a half-barbarian kingdom on Greece's northern border, spread Greek civilization—and Greek-ruled cities named Alexandria—from Egypt to the borders of India.

The successors of Alexander, the Romans, dominated the entire Mediterranean basin for five centuries. In art and literature they borrowed much from the Greeks. In law, statecraft, and military organization they were bold and ruthless innovators who solved brilliantly the problem that had perplexed the Greeks: how to create large-scale and long-lasting political units that ruled over citizens and noncitizens alike. The only contemporary civilization that rivalled the brilliance of Rome and the extent of Rome's power was China, which experienced a merciless unification in the same centuries as the Roman conquest of the Mediterranean.

Roman legions, Roman roads, Roman cities, and Roman laws civilized Europe as far east as the great river barriers of the Rhine and the Danube and as far north as the wild borders of Scotland. Rome provided the political order within which a new religion, which blended the Hebrew traditions of the Old Testament with the philosophical conceptions of the Greeks, could spread and prosper. In the fourth century A.D., that new religion, Christianity, became the official religion of the empire. By that point Rome was near collapse. Interrelated and mutually reinforcing pressures from within and without brought the empire down: bloody civil wars, brigandage and piracy, economic decay, plague epidemics, loss of intellectual self-confidence and social cohesion, and vastly increased barbarian pressure on the Rhine-Danube frontier.

In the fifth century A.D., Rome fell to waves of invaders, as the pitiless Huns on their shaggy steppe ponies drove the warlike Germanic tribes across Rome's crumbling borders. The western half of the empire collapsed. The unity of the Mediterranean basin was gone. A Greek-speaking remnant of the empire centered on Byzantium survived in the east for another thousand years, but had small influence on developments in the west. In the seventh and eighth centuries A.D., the Arabian tribes, under the green banner of their new religion, Islam, conquered the eastern Mediterranean and swept across northern Africa to Spain. Those conquests further divided Rome's inland sea—between the heirs of Greece, Rome, and Jerusalem and the heirs of the prophet Mohammed. The *ancient world*, the Greco-Roman civilization of the Mediterranean basin, had ceased to exist.

The new *medieval* civilization that eventually arose in western Europe after the eighth century was thus thrown back on its own resources. It saved only a fragment of its Roman inheritance, as Rome had been only a part of the ancient world. And the new rulers of western Europe, the Germanic peoples, had never been part of that world. They only gradually assimilated the fragments of Latin literature and Roman law that Rome had left behind. They were slow to blend with the Latin peoples they had conquered. They and their subjects were equally slow to absorb Christianity. But the fusion over some six centuries of those disparate ethnic and intellectual elements ultimately produced a distinctive European civilization.

Once its fundamental character was set, medieval Europe developed rapidly. It eagerly received lost Greek texts, decimal numbers, and algebra from its neighbors, the more highly developed Arabs and Byzantines. Many of its basic institutions and ideas, such as universities and representative assemblies, originated in the twelfth and thirteenth centuries. Its centers were in the north, in the triangle bounded by the formerly Roman cities of Paris [*Lutetia Parisiorum*], Cologne [*Colonia*] and London [*Londinium*], and in north Italian cities such as Florence, Bologna, and Padua. Its periphery, from Sicily, Spain, and Ireland to Scandinavia, Poland, and Bohemia, developed more slowly. And beyond that periphery Western influence almost ceased. Byzantium remained apart: Greek in language, despotic in politics, and Orthodox rather than Catholic in religion. Byzantium's influence dominated the southern and eastern Slavic peoples that had moved into eastern Europe as the Germanic peoples moved west. Byzantium likewise inspired the embryonic Russian state, until Mongol conquerors subjugated Moscow and Kiev in the thirteenth century and forced them to face eastward for more than 200 years.

South and east of Byzantium lay the civilizations of Islam, which began to close themselves to new ideas just as Europe was beginning its ascent. Still further east lay the great civilizations of India, China, and Japan. Each had characteristic values—religious in India, scholarly and bureaucratic in China, military and bureaucratic in Japan. All three had on occasion borrowed from their neighbors, but they nevertheless tended toward self-absorption and the perfection of existing modes of thought rather than the acquisition of new knowledge. India suffered Moslem conquest, constant wars, and crushing taxation. China after the sixteenth century showed little interest in exploration or seaborne trade. Japan, which had borrowed much from China, fiercely walled itself off after 1600. And after pioneering efforts—gunpowder, rockets, firearms, crucible steel, iron smelting with coke—none of the eastern civilizations developed a tradition of scientific inquiry and technological innovation rivaling that of the West.

By the fifteenth century, medieval Europe had begun to break out of its original mold, and out of its narrow and rain-sodden peninsula off the Eurasian landmass. Since the twelfth century, Europeans had shown an insatiable scholarly curiosity about distant lands, and a thirst for trade and booty. Europeans had given evidence of a precocious fascination with machinery—from clocks and windmills to ships and cannon—rarely seen to the south and east. European scholars had begun to lay the groundwork for the seventeenth-century scientific revolution that immeasurably increased humanity's mastery over nature, and transformed its view of its place in the universe.

In the last decade of the fifteenth century, Europeans leapt across the globe—the Spaniards to the New World in 1492 and the Portuguese around Africa to India in 1498. Europe's new seaborne empires—the empires of the *early modern* age of Western expansion—soon dominated the fringes of Africa and Asia, and conquered three newly discovered continents: North America, South America, and Australia.

Then came two further revolutions within Europe itself. The collapse of the French monarchy in 1788–89 opened 25 years of revolution and war that spread the democratic ideas of the French revolutionaries and the notion of nationalism—the political religion of the nation-state—eastward across Europe. Simultaneously, an industrial revolution that transformed humanity's power over nature and over its own existence began in Britain. Those twin revolutions—of mass politics and nationalism, and of engine-powered machines and economic freedoms—have been the driving forces of the *modern* era in which we still live. They transformed Europe and the world. For the first time in history, one civilization brought all others into increasingly direct contact with it, and forced its rivals to emulate it or go under.

Those rivals ultimately maintained or reasserted their independence—within the framework of the worldwide state system that Europe established—by adopting Western ideas and techniques. The world has not become one; mortal rivalries between states, religions, ideologies, and cultures continue to rend it. But for good or ill, a recognizably Western global civilization has taken shape, bound together by an accelerating revolution of science and technology, an ever-expanding world market, and a thickening web of mass communications. That is the present which a history of civilization must seek to explain.

THE MAINSTREAM OF
CIVILIZATION

1
The Origins of Civilization: The Ancient Middle East to ca. 500 B.C.

*H*uman beings have long been interested in their past. But for most peoples the remote past has been very difficult to recover. A few undated monuments, small collections of ancient utensils and ornaments, groups of often contradictory legends were all that was available. As recently as two hundred years ago—or about the time of the American Revolution—western scholars knew almost no history before that of the classical age of Greece (*ca.* 500 B.C.). True, there was some understanding of the historical passages of the Hebrew scriptures, and some awareness that the colossal monuments along the Nile were the remnants of a very early Egyptian civilization. But little attention was given to these evidences of the existence of preclassical societies.

Just at this time, however, the excavations at Pompeii began, and the discoveries made there gave a tremendous impetus to the development of the science of archaeology. During the past two centuries it has become clear that thousands of years before the Greeks there were highly developed civilizations in many parts of the Old World. About the year 1800, archaeologists and historians began to reconstruct the long and fascinating history of ancient Egypt. More recently, in the nineteenth and twentieth centuries, they uncovered many other civilizations—notably in Mesopotamia, in India, and on the island of Crete—whose existence had not been known before.

Although great cities long unknown have been unearthed and whole libraries and archives discovered, the pace of new excavations continues unabated. Historians of the preclassical civilizations must be constantly prepared to revise their interpretations in the light of new evidence.

PREHISTORY TO
ca. 3500 B.C.

The study of the evolution of the modern human species is a fascinating subject fraught with controversies because the fossil record is incomplete, and anthropologists and archaeologists are continually making new finds that change our understanding of existing evidence. The record of development is difficult to trace until about 2 million years ago, during the geological period called the Pleistocene, which began about 3 million years ago. At that time, a creature, called *Australopithecus* (Apeman), occupied a wide range in the temperate areas of Africa and Southwestern Asia. *Australopithecus* was bipedal and had a brain capacity of 700 cc (compared to gorillas with a brain capacity of 585 cc average and chimpanzees with 470 cc). The big question about the new creature is whether it used tools. The answer, not yet pinned down by research, determines whether one should call *Australopithecus* a hominid. Although scientists have observed chimpanzees fashioning implements for desired goals, hominids are distinguished by having a tool kit. They make tools according to standard models and carry them from job to job.

The earliest animal recognized by all to be a hominid is *homo erectus*, which had a geographical range even wider than *Australopithecus*. *Homo erectus* appears to have originated in Africa, and its remains have found from western Europe to China (Peking Man) and Indonesia (Java Man). The major finds date from 350,000 years ago and are associated with tools that are crude but of standard form and that do not vary from one region to another.

The next stage of human evolution appeared about 60,000–55,000 years ago and is called Neanderthal Man *(homo sapiens neanderthalensis)*, after one of the earliest sites where its remains were found. Neanderthal hunted big game and lived in caves. It may have practiced a primitive animism (belief in spiritual beings, often seen as inhabiting inanimate objects, that affected human life), and it certainly had developed a society willing and able to maintain invalided individuals for long periods of time.

Modern Man *(homo sapiens sapiens)* emerged about 40,000 years ago, during the last ice age, and for a long time it coexisted with the Neanderthal species. The earliest known occurrence of the modern species is from Cro-Magnon in France, and he is called Cro-Magnon Man.

The Culture of Early Man

Cro-Magnon Man lived, like the Neanderthals, as hunters of big game, and he too found shelter primarily in caves. These peoples lived by hunting and by gathering seeds, roots, and fruits. They followed the herds of rhinoceros, mammoth, bison, and other game, and collected whatever vegetable food was available where they happened to be. Nonetheless, the new species definitely created a higher culture than Neanderthal Man had. The Cro-Magnon tool kit was more advanced than that of the Neanderthals. *Homo sapiens sapiens* used a greater variety of tools and was able to put a better edge on them than Neanderthal had, and the new species also was the first to put handles on its tools. In addition, by 30,000 years before the present, Cro-Magnon communities were painting elaborate scenes on the walls of caves and making sculptures, both probably meant to perform sympathetic magic by representing the successful hunt that they hoped for.

Although no evidence connects sex roles or other characteristics of human culture with this economic revolution, it is fascinating to speculate on the profound effect that the development of hunting may have had on the future of human society. It may be that the development of the hunting economy created the basis for the differentiation of the roles of males and females in the society of early man. The first hominids were gatherers, just as their progenitors had been, and all members of the community were equally engaged in collecting nuts, fruits, roots, and other plant foods. Once the species began to hunt large animals, the basic economy was divided into male and female realms. Hunting was a male activity. The men went out as cooperative bands to hunt animals that could not be killed by single men; in this way men learned to communicate effectively and to work together. Gathering then became a female activity carried out near the settlement. This differentiation of sex roles was still observable among the hunter-gatherer peoples discovered by anthropologists during the nineteenth and early twentieth centuries.

After the end of the last glaciation about 30,000 years ago, Cro-Magnon Man extended its range in relation to the shrinking ice sheets. Between 30,000 and 10,000 years ago, the land bridges from continent to continent disappeared slowly, and *homo sapiens sapiens* followed the herds into nearly all the continents. Among the regions of human habitation, Europe and the Mediterranean Basin were somewhat special. These regions provided a rich and comfortable environment for human life. They were rich in animal and plant life and in the stone needed for high quality tools. Later, they would prove to be among the most favored human habitats on earth, for they combined abundant natural resources with an extensive system of communication based on the Mediterranean Sea and great, slow-moving rivers.

The culture of Early Man, from *homo erectus* to *homo sapiens sapiens*, is called Paleolithic, or Old Stone Age, Culture (400,000–10,000 years ago). The economy of Paleolithic peoples was bound by the provisions of nature, but these were relatively abundant. The hunters and gatherers developed a tool kit not only of stone, but also of bone and other materials. By the end of the Paleolithic period they were able to use virtually everything an animal carcass had to offer. The camps of late Paleolithic peoples contain a central, often paved, fireplace and no indication of shelters. Archaeologists conclude that the families in the little bands built small shelters of organic materials— sticks, sod, and hides.

There is also evidence from these sites that the inhabitants practiced some "management" of wild herds. Where the refuse of hunting camps contain predominantly the bones of young animals, archaeologists conclude that the people practiced some form of herding, which permitted them to cull the flocks. This impression is strengthened by the finds of dog skeletons in the camps. About 20,000 years ago, the hunters either domesticated dogs and used them in handling the wild herds or, what is less likely, men and dogs had formed a symbiotic relationship by then.

Notwithstanding these signs that paleolithic hunter-gatherers were engaged in proto-pastoralism, it is clear that they did very little to manipulate nature. Old Stone Age Man did not domesticate food animals to create a truly pastoral way of life. The true domestication of nature happened when human communities developed agriculture, which included animal as well as plant husbandry, about 10,000 years ago.

Agriculture and the New Stone Age

The evidence for the first practice of agriculture comes from village sites in Southwest Asia, especially in the upper valleys of the Tigris and Euphrates rivers and in eastern Asia Minor (modern Turkey). At Jericho, the city made famous by the Hebrew Bible, a fortified agricultural village existed about 6000 B.C.

Art of the Old Stone Age: Harpoon, Dart thrower of reindeer antler, Venus of Willendorf.

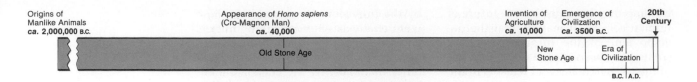

Origins of Manlike Animals ca. 2,000,000 B.C.		Appearance of *Homo sapiens* (Cro-Magnon Man) ca. 40,000	Invention of Agriculture ca. 10,000	Emergence of Civilization ca. 3500 B.C.	20th Century
		Old Stone Age	New Stone Age	Era of Civilization	
				B.C.	A.D.

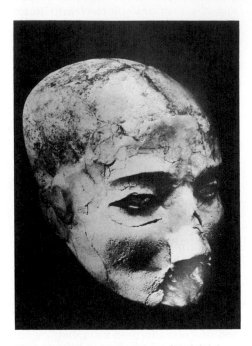

Human skull from the ruins of Jericho (*ca.* 7000 B.C.). The inhabitants of this city developed the art of "portraiture" by modeling the features in plaster and inlaying the eyes with shell in an attempt to reconstruct the face of the dead man.

These villages were fully agricultural in that they had domesticated both animals and plants, but the first agriculturists did not know how to make pottery, seriously limiting their ability to store as well as to cook their produce. The first farmers cultivated wheat, barley, and other grain crops and kept sheep, goats, and cattle. They used dogs to guard their flocks and kept cats to defend their stored grain from rodents. The communities were large by the standards of the hunter-gatherer societies; the villages could contain several hundred people.

In contrast to hunter-gatherer communities, agricultural communities did not need all their members to spend all their time producing food. At peak periods, such as sowing and harvesting, all in the village would be engaged in farm work, but between busy periods a significant portion of the population could engage in other activities. Some people became specialists in crafts such as weaving, pot and tool making, and house building. Consequently, the agricultural revolution produced a revolution of technology and the arts. The new society produced a wide variety of buildings, implements, and goods. The villagers also engaged in active trade. They exchanged stone that was good for tools and materials, such as amber, that was used for art or personal ornamentation. The tool kit of these communities was extremely large and beautifully crafted of polished stone, and archaeologists have given it the name Neolithic, or New Stone Age, Culture to distinguish it from the crude culture of the hunter-gatherers.

Language and Language Groups

Just as those individuals who could manipulate rocks and other materials to make effective tools had an advantage over those who could not, so those who could communicate by language had a definitive social advantage that contributed to their own and their offsprings' survival. Language is a kind of technology that provides storage for the techniques of survival and for ideas. Language cannot be separated from culture, or culture from it.

Modern linguists have developed two methods for classifying languages. The first is genetic: some languages are related to one another by similarity of words and syntax because they developed from a common language. The

Romance languages and the Turkic languages form families, and scholars can create family trees of such language groups. The second way to classify languages is by type (typological classification). For example, languages can be classified by grammatical structure, which may bring together languages from more than one language group. German and Latin share many grammatical characteristics. Both are part of the large language group called Indo-European, but they are members of different families within that group. During the last 25 years, linguists have looked for those grammatical characteristics common to all languages, which many think must stem from the aboriginal language of mankind. Perhaps *homo erectus*, the earliest hominid to have a culture, had a single language, which spread with him throughout the world.

Whether a single, aboriginal language ever existed, the far-flung migrations of *homo sapiens* created the conditions for linguistic diversity very early in the history of culture. There are literally thousands of languages now spoken. They can be divided into large groupings or phyla, but linguists still carry on lively disputes about the relationships of a great many individual languages. In many cases, the relationships among the languages in the phyla are uncertain, but many languages have no known relatives. In Europe, for example, Basque may represent the language of the population that preceded the Indo-Europeans. In Japan, Ainu is unrelated to the Japanese languages and to all others known. The Ainu people are also racially distinct from Mongolian peoples.

The distribution of related languages and the occurrence of isolated

Origins of Agriculture   6000 B.C.

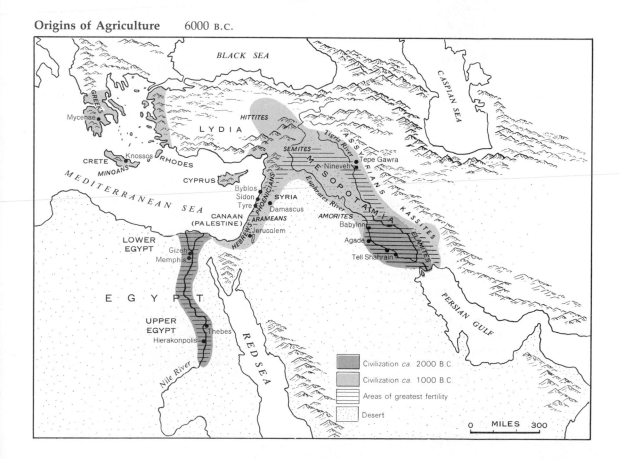

languages reveal something of the prehistoric migrations of peoples. The Indo-Europeans (Celts, Germans, Slavs, Armenians, Persians, Aryans) appear to have come from the region north of the Black Sea between the Danube and the Volga rivers. About 2000 B.C. they broke out of this area and migrated westward. The Italic tribes moved into Italy, and the Greeks moved into the Balkans and around the Aegean Sea. In Asia Minor, the Hittites maintained a great empire between 1800 and 1200 B.C. By 1000 B.C., the Celts (Gaelic speakers) controlled most of Europe. Not long afterward, the Germanic and Slavic peoples migrated into Scandinavia as well as northern and eastern Europe.

During the same period of migration, Indo-Europeans moved into India and Southeast Asia. The Kassites invaded Mesopotamia about the middle of the 1700s B.C., and about the same time Sanskrit-speaking peoples, the Aryans, conquered parts of India. In the Indus River Valley, the Aryans founded an advanced civilization, called Harappan from one of the first sites excavated. Harappan civilization had developed independently about 2300 B.C. in agricultural villages that had been founded a few centuries earlier throughout the Indus River Valley and along the Ravi and Sutlej rivers, tributaries of the Indus. The Harappans used polished stone tools, but they also worked copper and bronze. Their craftsmen were exceptionally skilled, and their beads and seals were widely traded. The Harappan towns maintained a lively commerce with Mesopotamia, and there is evidence that the Harappans built ocean-going vessels as well as river boats.

The Harappan civilization spread over an area larger than modern Pakistan, and scholars think that it may have been politically unified. The Harappans created uniform weights and measures and used writing, although scholars have not been able to decipher the 2,000 or so inscriptions so far found by archaeologists. The decline of the civilization coincided with the beginnings of the Indo-European invasions about 1750 B.C. The invaders absorbed much of Harappan civilization and made it part of a new civilization that developed later in the Ganges River Valley.

THE ORIGIN OF CIVILIZATION

Although in everyday speech we often use the words culture and civilization loosely, it is useful in starting a discussion of the origins of civilization to define them with some precision. A culture is a body of knowledge, skills, and beliefs that can be passed down from one generation to another in a community. The knowledge and techniques of tool making, pottery making, and farming are parts of a culture. The beliefs in spirits and gods and the knowledge of how to appease them are parts of a culture.

In the culture of the neolithic farmers, as in that of the hunter-gatherers, the body of skills and knowledge that governed a community's way of life was passed down by word of mouth from one generation to another. Consequently, the limits of human memory and the way individual members of the community perceived and did things affected the character and limited the amount of what was transmitted. The sum of cultural knowledge remained relatively constant, and its character changed only slightly over the generations.

It is correct to say that all civilizations are cultures, but the opposite is not true. A civilization is a culture that has an urban political organization and a medium for the preservation and communication of knowledge, skills, and beliefs. A civilization possesses a material and political organization that permits it to exercise power over an extensive area and to reach out effectively to regions beyond its control. It also possesses a body of knowledge, skills, and beliefs unlimited by the capacity of the human memory. A civilization is inconceivable without writing and a library. This institution preserves the records necessary for maintaining control over complex commercial, political, and social activities. It is both the repository and the basis of intellectual invention.

The word "civilization" comes from the Latin adjective *civilis,* having to do with a city. The creation of cities was not merely a matter of enlarging the old agricultural villages, but required the establishment of an internal social and political organization. Cities were a new type of community; they were centers of political order and power and of religious worship, and they had a population both larger and more specialized than that of agricultural villages. The large urban market created a demand for the best products of the human imagination and encouraged both invention and specialization on a different order than in the agricultural villages.

Writing was invented by the Sumerians, who were also the first people to build cities in Mesopotamia—the valleys of the Tigris and Euphrates rivers. About 3500 B.C., the Sumerians began using symbols to represent first numbers and then words. The Sumerians may have invented the new skill in order to keep track of their complicated commercial transactions, and for hundreds of years, it was used only for the limited purposes of commerce. It seems strange to say that this recording of business dealings is the birth of civilization, but it did permit the Sumerians to conclude complicated transactions that would have been impossible without the written record, and complexity is the hallmark of civilization.

Until recently, prehistorians have held that civilization began in Mesopotamia ("between the rivers") and spread from there both west and east, into Europe and to China by way of India. It has even been argued that Central American civilization developed through the influence of the Middle East. The Norwegian adventurer Thor Heyerdahl showed that the Egyptians could have influenced the peoples of Central America directly when he sailed a replica of an ancient Egyptian papyrus boat across the Atlantic from the Mediterranean to Central America.

Using a cross-dating method based on the Sumerian and Egyptian king lists, which were made for religious reasons, early twentieth-century archaeologists wrote a history of Mediterranean civilization. The method rests on the principle that when a datable Egyptian object (datable because it can be associated with one of the kings in the datable king list) is found at a certain level of a site, the archaeologist would know the date of that level and could construct a relative chronology of all the layers uncovered at the site. On the basis of this method, scholars thought that civilization spread as a result of diffusion from Southwest Asia. They argued that Middle Eastern sea-traders took civilization across the Mediterranean to Crete and Greece and to Spain. From these places, it was transmitted north to Britain and northern Europe and into the Balkans and Central Europe.

What Middle Easterners are supposed to have taught the Europeans is the technique of building with large stones. Archaeologists have seen the megaliths found in Europe, such as the tombs built with huge stones in Greece, Malta, and Brittany and the monuments like Stonehenge in England, as evidence that the peoples who built ziggurats in Mesopotamia and pyramids in Egypt taught the advanced technology of civilization to the Europeans. Archaeologists have also seen European pottery decorated with cuneiform markings as proof that the European communities were under the influence of Sumeria, which developed this form of script made by incising wedges on wet clay. Similarly, they ascribed the development of copper and then bronze (copper-tin alloy) metallurgy in Europe to Middle Eastern influence.

There are many problems in the cross-dating method. It relies on foreign objects (which often may have been heirlooms treasured for generations); the layers at most sites are disturbed and difficult to read; and the supposed diffusion did not bring urban life to the western Mediterranean. But, also, modern scientific techniques, such as carbon dating, have upset the traditional view. European sites are as old as, in some cases older than, those in the Middle East. The pottery and metallurgy in the Balkans and Central Europe, which are called Old Europe by archaeologists, were made in communities older than those in Spain, Crete, and Greece, which were supposed to have been the source of the European styles and technology. It now appears that the flow of influence was, at least in some periods, in the opposite direction, although the effect of contact between Old Europe and the Middle East cannot be judged on the basis of what is now known, and it is best to treat the two regions independently.

THE PROTO-CIVILIZATION OF OLD EUROPE

The remarkably advanced culture of Old Europe, which can be traced back to about 5000 B.C., was not a true civilization. The people of Old Europe did not build cities and did not use writing, so far as we know. It was a culture that was based on large agricultural villages, that used symbols, and that practiced metallurgy. Therefore, it is best called a proto-civilization.

Old Europe   6000–3500 B.C.

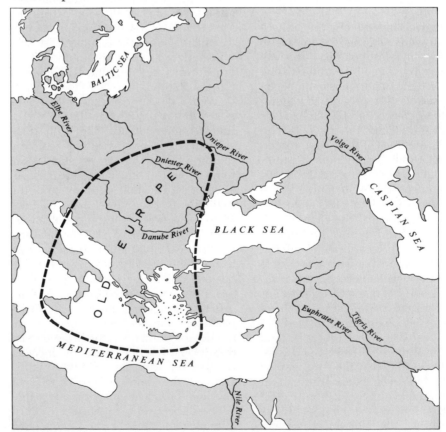

The agricultural economy of Old Europe came from Mesopotamia, where it first developed, but it was in Central Europe that it first became the basis of an advanced culture. The climate of Europe is unstable, and the environment is difficult. To plant and harvest in the Balkans, communities had to clear dense forests, while praying that the powers in control of the environment would be kind. Stormy weather and drought, which ruin crops and cause famine, are common in that part of the world.

Although the Europeans began to use copper very early, their basic tool kit was made of stone, some of it transported from distant quarries. Their use of special stones and of metal from the eastern Mediterranean suggests that the culture maintained a large commercial network. The villages cultivated wheat, barley, and other grains, and herded sheep, goats, and cattle. In its earliest stages the culture practiced *swidden* agriculture, in which the villagers cleared fields, used them for several years, and then, having exhausted the soil, moved on to other sites. Over the generations, sites might eventually be reused.

The success of this sort of agriculture, which was also practiced in China during the early phase of its agricultural revolution, supported a steadily growing population and thus allowed the formation of new village communities. In time, the number of villages grew so large that they could not easily find new lands to clear. The farmers then developed means for maintaining the fertility of the soil. For example, they learned to return their refuse to the ground and to leave a portion of the land fallow each year. These improvements in agricultural technique permitted the communities to settle sites permanently.

In the unpredictable environment of Europe, the village communities became inventive. By about 5000 B.C. the villages of the region were building granaries for long-term storage of food and had developed an advanced pottery. The pottery served both practical and religious purposes—although the villagers certainly considered religious activities practical, because they placated the gods of the environment.

In fact, the whole life of the people of Old Europe was permeated by religion, and their system of belief was much more advanced than the belief in magic that is evident in the cave paintings of Cro-Magnon Man 25,000 years earlier. The early hunter-gatherers of the caves had performed rites of magic to ensure the success of their hunting. They painted pictures of successful hunts, apparently thinking that the pictures actually affected the outcome of the hunt by describing beforehand what would take place in the fields and forests. The farmers of Old Europe certainly believed in the efficacy of magic, but they also had religion, a system of belief in one or more powers that created and controlled the world.

Fertility was the main concern of these people. They depended upon the regular cycle of the seasons, so they sought protection from the climatic disasters that ruin crops and kill animals. Their villages contained shrines and clay models of shrines, and their pottery bore pictures and symbols meant to be charms against the fury of nature.

They expressed their concern about fertility in many ways. One of their deities was a bird goddess, the layer of the universal egg. She was both painted on pottery and represented in figurines, sometimes realistically, but usually abstractly. Normally, her image was rather abstract, and archaeologists once thought that the commonly found form represented a human female with steatopygia (the outsized development of the buttocks). Now, they know that the figure was the bird goddess, with the universal egg ready to be laid.

The people of Old Europe were also fascinated by snakes. The periodic shedding of their skin and the mysterious way they move made people think of snakes as representing the world's turning and the cycle of the seasons. The universal snake, often depicted in abstract form as a spiral, became a common motif in European art and was later used by the Minoans in Crete.

The bull, the toad, the cross (which in Old Europe and in the hieroglyphs of Egypt represents life), and various representations of water, as rain and as river or ocean, convey the beliefs of people who depended on nature. It is now possible to link some aspects of Minoan and Greek mythology—such motifs as the bull born of a woman and the bird-goddess aspects of Hera, the queen of the gods in the Greek pantheon—with the motifs found in the culture of Old Europe. Old Europe was apparently one of the sources of the civilizations of the eastern Mediterranean.

Many pottery vessels from the villages in Central Europe and the Balkans bear signs that look very much like the cuneiform writing developed in Mesopotamia. Until recently, archaeologists assumed that these signs represented the illiterate copying of Sumerian script by the European villagers, but carbon dating has shown that the "writing" of Old Europe is earlier than the Mesopotamian development. No one has yet understood the signs on the pots, so presently no one can say whether they represent language. The exact nature of the connection between Old Europe and Sumeria is, therefore, still a mystery. However, it can at least be said that the flow of influence at the time when civilization began to develop in the Middle East was certainly not in only one direction, even though who taught what to whom continues to be one of the great questions of modern archaeology.

THE CIVILIZATION OF MESOPOTAMIA, *ca.* 3500–1500 B.C.

As noted earlier, village agriculture developed first in the upper valleys of the Tigris and Euphrates where the water necessary for cultivation came from rainfall. Along the Nile and in lower Mesopotamia precipitation was insufficient to support agriculture, and, when the idea of farming spread into these regions during the fourth millennium B.C., the people there had to develop new methods to use the water provided by the yearly flooding of the river.

In both places, the earliest agriculturalists had to harness the rivers, preserving the water of the floods and distributing it through irrigation. These tasks required much larger and better organized communities than those that farmed the rain-watered uplands. The use of the river required an intricate system of reservoirs to catch flood water and of canals to distribute it. The consequences of a failure to perform these operations adequately were very severe—widespread famine. This difficult and chancy environment forced the farming communities to develop cities and a literate culture—civilization.

The Dominance of Woman in Old Europe

Much new material on the mythical imagery of Old Europe has emerged during the ten-year interval [1972–82]. . . . The new discoveries have served only to strengthen and support the view that the culture called *Old Europe* was characterized by a dominance of woman in society and worship of a Goddess incarnating the creative principle as Source and Giver of All. In this culture the male element, man and animal, represented spontaneous and life-stimulating—but not life-generating—powers. . . .

The persistence of the Goddess worship for more than 20,000 years from the Paleolithic to the Neolithic and beyond, is shown by the continuity of a variety of a series of conventionalized figures. Her specific aspects of power such as life-giving, fertility-giving, and birth-giving are extremely long lasting. [The Greek goddesses Hekate and Artemis, goddesses of the moon, are survivals of the Great Mother Goddess of pre-Indo-European culture.]

From Marija Gimbutas, *The Goddesses and Gods of Old Europe,* 2nd ed. (Berkeley: Univ. of California Press, 1982), pp. 9–10.

Ancient Egypt and Mesopotamia

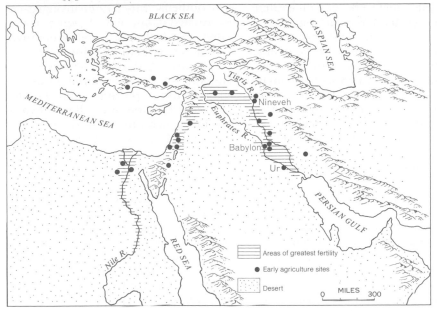

Around 4000 B.C., at places like Ur, Tell Shahrain, and Tepe Gawra, the people of Mesopotamia built mud-brick towns that are striking for their size and for their focus on an impressively large central temple, which was furnished with equipment that took skill and time to make. The picture that emerges from excavation of these sites is of a large town physically centered on a holy precinct and socially centered on its priesthood. Next to farming, propitiation of the divine powers that controlled the environment was the most important activity of the community. The elaborate arrangements needed to ensure a livelihood from the flood plains enhanced the religious consciousness of the communities.

The sites of settlement in Mesopotamia had continuous existence for hundreds of years—in some there are twelve or more layers of settlement—so the course of development can be followed closely. The temples were progressively enlarged and were built on large rectangular platforms, which rose above the town. Between about 3500 and 3100 B.C., the townspeople began to use cylindrical seals, which were used to mark goods exchanged in the commercial system of the valley. Toward the end of this period, the towns erected true ziggurats—stepped platforms—in the place of the older temples. These immense works were of stone and became the dominant feature of the first cities. At about the same time, the Sumerians began using copper and silver vessels and started producing larger-than-life sculptures, both signs of their wealth.

But the development of pictographic writing outshines the architectural and artistic achievements of these fourth-millennium communities. This technique for recording information was first used to keep temple accounts, which indicate that the priests ran a system to redistribute the resources of the community in order to support people—such as soldiers, administrative personnel, artisans, merchants, and the priests themselves—who did important work, but were not personally engaged in the production of food. It is clear from the records that the towns had developed into complex social organizations controlled by the temple personnel. The use of written accounts suggests that the supply of these organizations had become too intricate and extended to be maintained by the power of memory alone.

About 3000 B.C. this society began to change rapidly. Apparently, the towns succeeded so well in exploiting their environment that they began to achieve substantial wealth, which is revealed by the occurrence of an increasing number of metal tools and personal ornaments. The engraved cylindrical seals bear pictures of chariots and boats, which indicates the importance of war and transport, and there is also ample evidence that the Sumerian communities were now being ruled by kings. Kingship was a new type of leadership.

The kings may have originally been the head priests, whose power increased and changed as the communities grew into prosperous cities. Some archaeologists think that royal power originated in sacred functions and rituals, in which the kings took the lead. While it is certain that the kings were considered sacred in Sumeria, as in every other society in which kings have dominated the political organization, other archaeologists think that royal power derived from the rise of warfare.

Because the early cities were wealthy, they were subject to the attacks of the poor tribes from the hills and deserts. Moreover, the growth of wealth created a market for a wide variety of goods, which in turn created the need for raw materials. This economic development would have made the cities increasingly dependent on regions that could supply materials, and cities often tried to extend their control over these areas, by war if necessary. During the third millennium, the cities of Mesopotamia were periodically destroyed and, as a result, fortified either because they needed to defend themselves from poor neighbors or because they had become aggressive toward their neighbors. In both cases, the war leader became a dominant figure in the society. Royal tombs and mosaic representations of warfare led by the king found at Ur are striking records of that power.

Ziggurat at Ur (*ca.* 2250 B.C.).

During the Early Dynastic Period in Sumeria, between about 3000 B.C. and 2370 B.C., each of the small city-states that dotted Mesopotamia was ruled by a king. These small urban communities were effective in organizing the floodplain agriculture, in developing bronze and other metallurgy, and in building impressive temples. Eleven of these cities have been discovered—all of them the seats of royal dynasties and all engaged in a turmoil of alliances and wars. One cannot speak of the separation between urban and rural in this period because the life of the cities was based on agricultural activity carried out by their populations, but certainly the growth of nonagricultural crafts and commerce gave a hint of things to come, when the people of great urban settlements would become almost wholly engaged in such pursuits.

About 2370 B.C., Sargon of Agade—the king of the Semitic Akkadians—united the whole region of south Mesopotamia. It appears that over time Sargon and his successors extended their control to Elam in the north and all the way to eastern Asia Minor in the northwest. The Akkadians were the first to use writing for purposes besides commerce and temple accounts. In the remains of their cities archaeologists have found a treasure of literary works that represent the first written record of an ancient people's religious ideas and historical consciousness.

The power of the Akkadians was broken about 2200 B.C. by raiders from the Zagros Mountains to the east, who founded a new dynasty, called the Third Dynasty, at Ur, which had been one of the principal cities of the Akkadian empire. For the next century and a half, the kings of Ur dominated lower Mesopotamia, while the other sections of Sargon's domain went their own ways. During this period, the Sumerians developed their pictographic writing into the abstract form called cuneiform, which was more compact and versatile than the earlier type of script. The technology, art, and architecture of the Third Dynasty make

Dilmun

As the excavations in Mesopotamia added to our knowledge of ancient civilization there, scholars noticed rare mentions of Dilmun, a powerful, civilized state that played an uncertain role in the history and culture of the region. During the 1950s and 1960s, Geoffrey Bibby, an English archaeologist, went looking for Dilmun. He found it in an unlikely place.

For almost two and a half millennia Dilmun was in literal truth a lost civilization, lost as Assyria and Egypt and Babylonia never were, as even the Hittite Empire and Minoan Crete and the Sumerians were not lost. . . . [In an Assyrian inscription, deciphered in 1861, King Sharru-kin, the Sargon of the Hebrew prophet Isaiah, says] "I brought under my sway Bit-Iakin on the shore of the Bitter Sea as far as the border of Dilmun," and he adds that "Uperi, king of Dilmun, whose abode is situated like a fish, 30 double-hours away in the midst of the sea of the rising sun, heard of the might of my sovereignty, and sent his gifts."

On the desert island of Bahrain, Bibby discovered round seals. A few such seals had previously been found at Ur in Mesopotamia and at Mohenjo-Daro in the Indus Valley, Bibby reports the stirrings of discovery:

As I smoked my pipe in the Bahrain diggings, and attempted to recall these facts [the earlier reports on the round seals], two further points presented themselves. For the first, that the presence of identical seals at Ur and Mohenjo-Daro proved that there had been contact between India and Mesopotamia at the time of the Indus Valley civilization. And for the second, that the round stamp-seals were "foreign" both in India and in Mesopotamia. In both cases they formed less than one percent of the total seals found. The rest were cylindrical in Mesopotamia, square in India.

If they were "foreign" in India and Mesopotamia, was it possible that they were "native" to Bahrain? Had it been travelers from Bahrain, merchants perhaps, who had lost the thirteen round seals in Ur and the three in Mohenjo-Daro?

The continuing excavations showed that Bahrain was indeed the center of Dilmun, a great commercial civilization that had linked India with the Middle East for over a thousand years, from Sargon of Agade to Sargon the Assyrian.

From Geoffrey Bibby, *Looking for Dilmun* (New York, 1969), pp. 27, 37, 163.

Hammurabi (*ca.* 1765 B.C.).

it the classical period of Sumerian civilization.

Just before 2000 B.C., the influence of Ur was broken by new raids of Elamites and Amorites, mountain peoples from the north and east of Mesopotamia. The Amorites were another Semitic people. About 1990 B.C. they founded the first dynasty of Babylon, just up the river from Agade, the center of Sargon's power. Under their king Hammurabi (*ca.* 1792–1750 B.C.), the Amorites, who are often called the Babylonians, recreated the empire of the Akkadians.

Hammurabi is famous for having issued the first code of law. Actually, his code was the culmination of earlier codifications by Sumerian kings. The importance of Hammurabi's comprehensive law book was that it provided a uniform and understandable set of

regulations for the peoples under his domination. The published regulations became the basis for economic and social innovation because knowledge of the law made it possible for merchants and subordinate officials of the state to act independently and to plan ahead.

The Babylonians also produced the first known mathematics. They solved rather complicated problems in arithmetic and geometry, and they had some understanding of algebra. Their system of numbers used both base 10 (decimal) and base 60 (sexagesimal). The modern 60-minute hour and the 360-degree circle are vestiges of their system of measurement.

Like the older agricultural peoples, the Babylonians studied the heavens, because successful agriculture depended on a knowledge of the seasons. The movements of the sun and moon had long been followed—there is evidence of this in the art of Old Europe— but the Babylonians succeeded in tracking the regular movements of the planets also. Another vestige of Babylonian civilization is astrology, which bases its predictions on planetary movements.

This civilization was not limited to a tiny elite in Babylonian society. The publication of Hammurabi's law code indicates that literacy was widespread, for otherwise the code would not have been of much use. During Hammurabi's reign, Akkadian and cuneiform writing became the medium of commerce and culture throughout the empire. Because of the development of a common Mesopotamian culture and of numerous economic ties, Babylonian civilization survived the political collapse brought about by the invasion of the Kassites from the east about 1595 B.C.

This invasion destroyed the First Babylonian Dynasty and put the Kassites, an Indo-European people whose exact origins are unknown, in control of southern Mesopotamia. The new tribe maintained control of the region for 400 years, and Babylon did not again become an important political center until the seventh century B.C.

A Babylonian boundary stone (*ca.* thirteenth to tenth century B.C.), showing an example of cuneiform writing.

EGYPTIAN CIVILIZATION

The Pre-Dynastic Period
ca. 3800–3100 B.C.

Nine hundred miles to the southwest of Mesopotamia another river, the Nile, provided opportunities for irrigated agriculture. The Nile flows south to north for over 600 miles, and its annual floods deposit fertile soil over its flood plains. In the south (Upper Egypt), the band of fertility is rarely more than ten miles wide, but in the north (Lower Egypt) the river forms a large triangular delta, which is swampy and fertile.

The first agricultural villages in Egypt date from the early fifth millennium B.C., and the implements used by the first farmers show the influence of places like Jericho, where agriculture had begun at least a thousand years earlier. The influence of the northerners was crucial, but the Egyptians preserved important aspects of their own pre-agricultural culture. One of the most characteristic features of Egyptian civilization was its independence and the durability of its indigenous elements. At various points in their history, the Egyptians received new technologies from abroad, but they absorbed these into a culture that diverged little from its ancient course.

The history of Pre-Dynastic Egypt—which might also be called pre-civilized Egypt—has been divided into several broad periods, representing the development of pottery and other implements. During the last of these periods, from about 3800 B.C. to 3100 B.C., the pace of development quickened. The development began in Hierakonpolis (Greek for "City of the Falcon"; the Egyptians called the place Nehken), a very large community in Upper Egypt supported by flood-plain agriculture, but dominated by the manufacture of pottery and other fine goods.

Hierakonpolis became the first capital of the unified Egypt, but in 3800 B.C. political development in the Nile Valley had not progressed very much. The town, which is presently being excavated by an international team of archaeologists, rested on high ground above the flood plain. Enough has been discovered to give an outline of the developments that led to the foundation of the First Dynasty about 3100 B.C.

During the first centuries of the fourth millennium B.C., the town grew to between, 2,500 and 10,000 people. Throughout the settlement, archaeologists have found kilns and pottery "factories," some of them spreading over 1200 square yards. The factories produced two types of pottery—a coarse ware tempered with straw and a fine ware called Plum Red Ware. The latter required firing in high temperatures, and the cliffs near the site have natural wind tunnels that were used as kilns for the fine ware. The town also produced stone mace heads, which were a specialized product used by rulers of the Nile Valley to symbolize their political authority.

Most of the dwellings in Hierakonpolis were rectangular and built of mud

Pre-dynastic Egyptian pottery jar decorated with gazelles and ostriches.

brick. The houses were usually crowded together, but some seem to have had gardens around them. This suggests that the society of the town was large, wealthy, and specialized enough to support an elite class. The cemetery confirms this, for the excavators have found large tombs, along with normal-sized ones similar to those found elsewhere in the valley. The elite, probably a merchant elite, dominated this society in life and in death.

The power of Hierakonpolis rested on its commercial pottery works, but its survival depended on agriculture. The agricultural economy began to decline after about 3500 B.C., when the climate became drier, turning the savannah—grassland and sparse woods—into desert. The population was forced to move closer to the river, and, while the town continued to exist, the kilns and cemetery were abandoned.

In the period that followed this climatic change, the old elite appears to have used its wealth to establish control over the new villages founded near the river. But the tendency toward independence that this social organization encouraged was countered by the need for cooperation to control the flood waters. This is the period in which large irrigation projects were begun and in which the ruling elite built palaces, temples, and walled towns. They began to use the symbols of royal authority—particularly the crown and mace—and conflict among the fortified villages became common. The history of Egypt between 3500 and 3100 B.C. was a confusion of war and cooperation during which the country was dominated by petty kings. Yet there is also evidence of active trade with the Mesopotamian centers of civilization.

The power of the local kingdoms reached a critical level about 3200 B.C., and for a century after that wars were a constant feature of life in the valley. During this time, the rulers of Hierakonpolis, which had retained enough wealth to become one of the royal centers, began again to use the

old cemetery and created a necropolis (city of the dead), which represented the politics and society of the living. The burial ground was laid out along a dry stream (wadi), which was symbolically the Nile.

In the last century of the Pre-Dynastic Period, 3200–3100 B.C., each king struggled to unify the whole valley, which by now was recognized by the Egyptians themselves as being divided into two regions, Upper and Lower Egypt. About 3100 B.C., Narmer of Hierakonpolis (who was known in Egyptian legend as Menes; his actual name means catfish) succeeded in reaching this goal. Narmer may have been building on the success of his predecessor Scorpion, but, for the Egyptians, Narmer was the first pharaoh, the founder of the first dynasty.

The cemetery of Hierakonpolis also represents Narmer's achievement. It is divided into sections representing the two halves of the united Egypt, with the tombs of the southern section built of mud brick in the manner of Upper Egypt and those of the northern part of stone in the style of Lower Egypt. A particularly large tomb, lying on the border between the two sections, may be that of Narmer's predecessor Scorpion. Its position symbolizes the importance of unification.

Dynastic Egypt, ca. 3100–333 B.C.

Our view of the history of unified Egypt rests on the work of a third century B.C. priest named Manetho, who wrote a history of his country in Greek. He grouped the kings into 30 dynasties from the legendary Menes—now identified as Narmer—to the last native Egyptian pharaoh, Nectanebo II, who died in 343 B.C. After the discovery of the Rosetta Stone in 1799 by Napoleon's conquering army, the original and much older Egyptian sources became available. The stone is a tablet with parallel texts in Greek and hieroglyphics and, therefore, provides the key to deciphering the ancient script. Modern historians count 31 dynasties

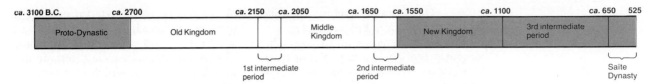

ca. 3100 B.C.	*ca.* 2700		*ca.* 2150	*ca.* 2050	*ca.* 1650	*ca.* 1550	*ca.* 1100	*ca.* 650	525
Proto-Dynastic	Old Kingdom			Middle Kingdom		New Kingdom		3rd intermediate period	

1st intermediate period   2nd intermediate period   Saïte Dynasty

and usually use the Egyptian instead of the Greek names for the kings, but Manetho's idea of dividing Egyptian history into dynasties still holds. Egyptian history is further broken into long historical periods—the Early Dynastic Period (*ca.* 3100–2700 B.C.), the Old Kingdom (*ca.* 2700–2150 B.C.), the Middle Kingdom (*ca.* 2050–1650 B.C.), and the New Kingdom (*ca.* 1550–1100 B.C.). Between these kingdoms there were periods of political disorder, and after the New Kingdom, Egypt was dominated by a series of Middle Eastern empires.

The full unification of the northern and southern kingdoms took about 400 years (3100–2700 B.C.), during which the foundations of Egyptian civilization were also laid. This is the period of the first two dynasties, sometimes called the Proto-Dynastic or Early Dynastic period. The success of these kings provided both the resources and the peace necessary for rapid cultural development.

The Pre-Dynastic cemetery at Hierakonpolis, which dates back to about 3800 B.C., already contained artifacts that were later considered to be characteristic of Egyptian civilization. For example, the arrangement of the cemetery as a necropolis, in which many of the tombs were covered with wooden or reed houses, already represented an early stage in the development of the cult of the dead, which later dominated Egyptian religion. In addition, some tombs from this early period contained pots with writing-like signs on them. These symbols may actually be primitive writing, but archaeologists do not yet understand them. The excavators have also found painted scraps of a papyrus-like plant in the tombs. The use of papyrus for keeping written records, instead of stone or clay tablets as in Mesopotamia, provided the Egyptians with a cheap, easy-to-use writing material and greatly expanded their ability to create and distribute lengthy written works.

Under the first dynasties, the pace of cultural advance quickened. The primitive attempts to manage the Nile floods had shown that the river could be the source of great agricultural wealth, but its potential could not be developed until a single authority governed all the projects along the river. The unification therefore greatly increased the material wealth of Egyptian society, which depended not only on the organization of large-scale irrigation and flood-control projects, but also on the accurate timing of these activities. The Egyptian priests, closely associated with the king, developed their precise calendar about the time of the unification.

To the Egyptians, the land of the Nile Valley belonged to the gods. The pharaoh, under whose authority the river was harnessed, was the divine representative of the gods on earth; he made the land produce its wealth. This belief also made the priesthood a powerful force in the society.

The idea that the gods controlled the environment, which was common in all agricultural societies, had, already at the beginning of the fourth millennium B.C. in towns like Hierakonpolis, led the Egyptians to concentrate their religious contemplation on the boundary between the visible world of society and the invisible world of the gods. This was the boundary between life and death, and the interaction between these two worlds was represented in the belief that, like the cycle of seasons, the life of a person cycled through life and death—from birth to death to rebirth.

The formal activities carried out at the junctures between these states of existence were like the activities carried out in agriculture. Just as the most important act of the agricultural cycle was the collection and preservation of seed for next year's planting, so the most important moment of a person's life was the preparation for life after death, through which one would pass to rebirth. Part of this belief was that the successful completion of the cycle required that the body of the dead person be preserved, and the ancient cemetery at Hierakonpolis contains evidence of primitive mummifying. It is therefore no surprise that one of the most striking aspects of Egyptian culture was the cult of the dead and that the holy book of Egypt was the Book of the Dead. It is not surprising either that the community should take the great-

est care to provide the king, whose centralized authority and divinity guaranteed the success of agriculture, with a safe and effective passage from life into death.

The contrast with Sumerian civilization is illuminating. While the Sumerians first used writing to keep the temple accounts and records of commerce, the Egyptians appear to have used it first in connection with the cult of the dead. This is particularly so if the first Egyptian script is represented by mysterious incising found on the pots buried at Hierakonpolis. Likewise, the engineering skills of the Sumerians, celebrated in the biblical story of the tower of Babel (which was a ziggurat), were developed in the building of temples, while the skills of the Egyptians came to fruition in the construction of tombs. In fact, one feature of Egyptian society is that the tombs are by far the most impressive and technically advanced buildings, so that, by contrast, the "palaces" of the great men were unimposing. It appears that for the Egyptians the transient world of the living was of slight value compared with the eternal world of the dead.

The cult of the dead led the Egyptians to build the principal architectural achievements of their civilization—the pyramid tombs. The first one was built at Saqqara by Zoser (Djoser in Egyptian), the first or second pharaoh of the third dynasty (ca. 2600 B.C.). It was a stepped pyramid surrounded by an enclosure and out-buildings—a palace for the dead king. Later, the pharaohs built a series of smooth-sided pyramids. About a century after Zoser, Cheops (Khufu in Egyptian) had the Great Pyramid of Giza built for himself and his queen. This tomb covered an area of 194 square yards and rose over 400 feet. It contained more than 2,300,000 two-and-a-half-ton blocks of stone, transported to the site from a great distance.

According to the Greek historian Herodotus (fifth century B.C.), whose work is among the most important sources for Egyptian history and who

---

Egyptian Religion   Fourteenth century B.C.

Morality and the Last Judgment in the Book of the Dead.

Hail to you, ye gods. . . . Behold, I came to you without sin, without evil, without wrong. . . . I gave bread to the hungry, water to the thirsty, clothing to the naked, and a ferry to him without a boat. I made divine offerings for the gods and food offerings for the dead. Save me! Protect me!

■ ■ ■

Monotheism in the hymn to the sun god (Aton). This was written during the brief period when King Akhnaton (1375–1358 B.C.) was trying to establish the cult of a single sun god.

How manifold are thy works!
They are hidden before men.
O sole God, beside whom is no other,
Thou didst create the earth according to thy heart. . .
Thou didst make the distant sky in order to rise therein,
In order to behold all that thou hast made
While thou wast yet alone.
Shining in thy form as living Aton,
Dawning, glittering, going afar and returning.
Thou makest millions of forms
Through thyself alone.

From James H. Breasted, *The Dawn of Conscience* (New York: Scribner's, 1934), pp. 259, 284–85.

Ramses II, ruler of the Egyptian Empire at its height, built this temple to Amon at Karnak. Below is a colossal statue of Ramses at Karnak. At his knees is his queen, Nefertari.

could be considered the first anthropologist, it took 20 years to complete the Great Pyramid. Archaeologists estimate that 4,000 stonemasons worked throughout the building period and that the unskilled labor of hauling the stone and lifting the blocks into place, which would have been done in the seasons when agricultural work was light, engaged crews of up to 100,000 men. No better representation could be found of the Egyptians' view of the passage from life to death than the building of Cheops' pyramid.

The geographical features that made unification and centralization of authority in Egypt so important—the control of the whole lower course of the Nile (about 500 miles long)—also made the maintenance of centralization difficult. After the period of unifica-

tion, the kings of the third dynasty built up a large bureaucracy to administer the country. The government divided the territory of the kingdom into districts, called *nomes*, each of which had a royal vizier (*nomarch*) to govern it.

When the government was strong, this system worked well, but weakness at the center gave opportunity, and sometimes made it necessary, for the local leaders to act independently. The reasons for replacement of one dynasty by another are not usually clear, but some evidence suggests that often weakness in the central government permitted political turmoil out of which a strong nomarch or royal bureaucrat emerged to found a new dynasty.

One sign of the effect of this governmental system is that after the Old

Ceremonial axe of victory over the Hyksos showing the pharaoh Ahmose smiting an enemy.

Kingdom the kings ceased building the great pyramidal tombs. This was not because the Egyptians no longer believed in the cult of the dead, but because power was more widely distributed in the state than it had been. The nomarchic system had provided the kings with the means of controlling the nation, but it also provided local governors with power bases. This dichotomy of the system helps to explain why the history of the Egyptian state was both tumultuous and amazingly stable. There was always a class of able men ready to enter a contest for control of the central authority, but they came to it well schooled in the techniques and ideology of the centralized state.

Between the great periods of Egyptian history, the Old, Middle, and New Kingdoms, there were periods of weakness or subjugation. After the Old Kingdom collapsed with the end of the sixth dynasty, the century from *ca.* 2150 to 2050 B.C. was a period of internal strife, until the country was finally reunited by the kings of the eleventh dynasty, who founded the Middle Kingdom. From *ca.* 1650 to 1550 B.C., after the end of the Middle Kingdom, the country was under the domination of the Hyksos, a people of unknown origin who gained control of the Nile delta and eventually formed a new dynasty themselves. But the Hyksos kings—called the Shepherd Kings, which suggests that they ruled a nomadic people—were never absorbed into Egyptian society, and Ahmose (1570–1546 B.C.) the native ruler of Thebes, in Upper Egypt, finally expelled them. Ahmose, the first king of the eighteenth dynasty, founded the New Kingdom.

During the period of this kingdom Egypt had more contact with the world around it than ever before. From the south came a rich trade in gold and ivory, and the kings campaigned in the Sudan, perhaps to protect that trade. During the eighteenth dynasty, the Egyptians conquered parts of Southwestern Asia, and cuneiform documents have been found at Egyptian sites dating from this period. Egyptian expansion coincided with that of the Hittites, an Indo-European people (their language was related to modern Armenian) who built a great empire in Asia Minor between about 1800 and 1200 B.C. Egyptian influence in Asia lasted until the middle of the twelfth century B.C.

The effect of this foreign contact may be revealed in the new religious cult of Akhenaton (1379–1362 B.C.). He abandoned the old gods in favor of Aton, who was represented by a sundisk and whom he considered his father. Akhenaton built a new capital city at Amarna and developed a new theology to support his religion. But this experiment ended shortly after Akhenaton's death, and his successor Tutankhaton (1361–1352 B.C.) gave up the cult four years into his reign. It was then that Tutankhaton changed his name to Tutankhamen and returned to the old capital at Thebes, where the cult of Amon dominated. Under this young pharaoh, royal officials undertook major building projects in the capital, and the furnishings of his tomb, which is famous because it was discovered intact, seem to represent his return to the old religion.

In the eleventh century B.C., the New Kingdom collapsed when powerful families from the delta region replaced the Theban dynasties. This shift of power to the north shows the effects of the imperial period, when Egypt became involved in the affairs of Asia and the delta region became the frontier between old Egypt and its subject territories. The new dynasties themselves represented foreign elements. From the tenth to the eighth century, Libyans who had been settled in military camps in the western delta formed new dynasties and dominated the country. Then the center of power shifted to the other frontier of Egyptian power, the Sudan. From the late eighth to the middle of the seventh century, Kushites from Nubia in the Sudan held

The Egyptian and Hittite Empires   *ca.* 1450 B.C.

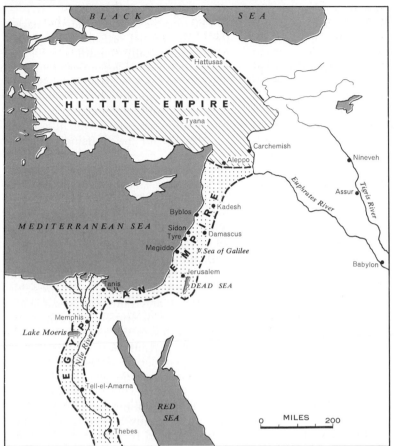

Akhenaton, from a pillar statue in the temple of Aton.

sway. Finally, from the seventh to the fourth century, the Persians dominated the Nile Valley

During this last period, Egypt was constantly buffeted by events beyond its borders, and native Egyptian rulers were only able to establish an independent state for short periods. Among the foreign events that affected Egypt in this period, the conflict between the Persians and Greeks around the turn of the fifth century B.C. caused many Greek mercenaries and settlers to come to the Nile Valley. During the period from the eleventh to the fourth century, Egypt was conquered repeatedly, so that it would have been hard to recognize the finality of the Macedonian conquest led by Alexander the Great in

333 B.C. As it turned out, a Greek dynasty, the Ptolemies, ruled Greece from the death of Alexander in 326 until the Roman conquest in 30 B.C.

Egyptian Civilization

Egypt was an urban society based on the agricultural wealth of the Nile Valley. The civilization seems to have been founded by a merchant elite in the region of Hierakonpolis toward the end of the fourth millennium B.C. The unification of Nilotic towns during the first dynasties permitted the society to achieve control of the river and produced a society in which religion and administrative skills were highly valued. This was not a society based on the values of small, free farmers—as would be the case in Greece, Rome, and other later civilizations. It was a civilization based on the conformist, regulated life of the bureaucracy.

By the time of the Middle Kingdom (*ca.* 2050–1750 B.C.), the bureaucratic class was fully formed. The scribes, as the civil servants were called, established a scholastic system that permitted talented men of quite humble origins to rise in the state service. They also created a literary culture, which provided a basis for a form of education that we call classical—an education in language and rhetoric—and which expressed the values and ideology of the educated elite.

The religious sensibility of the society was realized in the development of a large priestly class. The pharaoh was the head of all the cults, but the priesthoods of the various gods actually carried out the cults. It is difficult to assess the relative status of the priests and scribes, but apparently the scribes stood higher than priests. Scribes were exempt from the levy of troops and of labor, while priests, at least those of the lower ranks, were not.

During the New Kingdom, the growth of the Asian empire and the conquest of the Sudan gave increased importance to the military elite. The pharaohs received military educations and were supported by a professional officer class, which represented a new, third element in the upper classes of society. It seems that many pharaohs took wives from leading military families.

Although the first pharaohs appear to have come out of the merchant elite, merchants played little role in the mature civilization of Egypt. Independent merchants were restricted to local markets and low-cost wares. The most important trade was a state activity controlled by the priests, perhaps because the temples were so richly endowed that they were the suppliers of the market. The three segments of the upper class—the scribes, the priests,

and the military—controlled the wealth of the society.

The upper classes provided a market for a substantial artisan class, which was economically "middle-class," but not made up of independent entrepreneurs. The upper-class families supported the woodworkers, metalworkers, artists, and others within their own households, and there was little if any free market for the craftsmen's goods.

All these classes of the society were but a veneer on the great mass of peasants, whose labor provided the basis for the whole society. The peasants lived in villages and had their own plots, but the agricultural wealth of society rested not on the independent cultivation of the small farmers, but on the great state water projects that made all agriculture in the valley possible. The kings and nomarchs organized a labor draft, or corvée, at each of the crucial times in the agricultural cycle, and the peasants formed the core of these great labor forces. Members of the artisan and priestly classes also had to join the force. During the periods of the year when the agricultural work was light, many peasants must have supplemented their incomes by working on the pyramids or other great building projects of the kings and upper classes. The peasantry also provided the manpower for the armies.

The Hebrew Bible publicized the role of slaves in Egyptian society, but it gives a false impression. Mostly, slaves were foreign prisoners of war, and they constituted a small segment of the society. Upper-class families generally had one or two household slaves, and the pharaohs had slave labor forces in the state mines and on some construction projects, but the agricultural wealth of the society rested on the labor of the free peasants in the corvée.

The remains of Egyptian civilization show that it was a society that was highly regulated and traditional, careful about preserving the ideas and artistic styles of the past. They also show that, while men dominated the society, women were not entirely subjected. Although marriage was, as in other ancient societies, a contract between the husband—or husband's family—and father of the bride, the law seems to have given women the same rights to divorce and make contracts as it did to their husbands. The male priesthood was balanced by a female one of great importance, and the equal treatment of men and women in the cult of the dead suggests that women were viewed as significant members of society.

Egyptian civilization, although affected by foreign influences at many points during its long history, maintained a remarkable amount of its distinctive, indigenous character. Although it is now clear that the history of Mediterranean and Middle Eastern civilization is more complex than was once thought, it remains true that Egypt had an enormous influence on the culture of other Mediterranean societies.

THE ERA OF SMALL KINGDOMS, *ca.* 1250–750 B.C.

Between about 1150 and 750 B.C. there were no great imperial powers in the Levant, and several small kingdoms were able to flourish. Among these were the Phoenician city-states, which played a significant role in the Mediterranean trade, and the Canaanite and Hebrew kingdoms of Palestine.

The Phoenicians were people of mixed ethnic background who occupied the cities of the eastern Mediterranean seaboard. These cities had survived the invasions of the sea peoples and of Semitic nomads, such as the Hebrews and Aramaeans. By about 1100 B.C., Phoenician ships were common along the Mediterranean trade routes abandoned by earlier civilizations, and for the next three centuries they controlled Mediterranean commerce.

The Phoenicians built their great commercial empire not only by trading with established cities, but also by settling colonies in the western Mediterranean regions. These colonies, such as Carthage near modern Tunis in North Africa, exploited the regions near them and supplied raw materials for Phoenician industry. The sailors who maintained commercial contact with these settlements became famous. They regularly sailed through the Straits of Gibraltar to get tin for bronze manufacture from Cornwall, Brittany, and even Ireland. Egyptian sources suggest that they sailed all the way around Africa, a feat that would not be repeated until the fifteenth century A.D., and some scholars think that they may even have sailed to the Americas.

The largest of the Phoenician cities was Tyre, but the oldest was Byblos, which was famous for the manufacture of writing materials. The Greek word for book, *biblion,* stems from the name of this old city. The Phoenicians also helped to refine and to spread the West Semitic alphabetical system of writing. This was a great advance over Egyptian hieroglyphics and Sumerian cuneiform because it used simple-to-draw and

Small Kingdoms of the Levant   *ca.* 800 B.C.

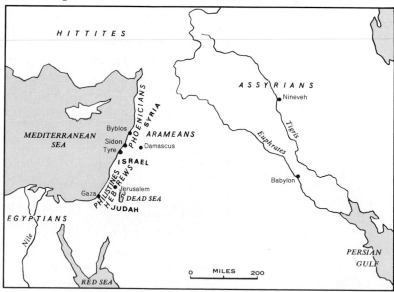

easily recognizable symbols (letters) for sounds. The Phoenician alphabet consisted of 22 letters and was the basis of all three of the major alphabets now used in the western world: the Hebrew, the Greek, and the Latin, which we use. The Greek alphabet, in turn, was the basis of the Cyrillic alphabet used in Russia and parts of eastern Europe, and an Aramaic version of the West Semitic script formed the basis for the writing systems of India.

About 750 B.C., the Phoenician cities came under the domination of the Assyrian Empire and began a rapid decline. At the time of the Assyrian conquest, leading merchant families migrated from Tyre and other cities to the western colonies. Thereafter, Carthage became the center of the Phoenician, or Punic, world until the Romans destroyed it in 146 B.C.

Between about 1200 and 400 B.C., the Hebrews, a minor group related to the Canaanites, developed a religion

Phoenician	Greek	Roman
⟁	A	A
⇁	B	B
⋀	Γ	G
⊲	Δ	D
⤳	E	E
⅄	[Y]	F
⌁	Z	Z
⧖		H
⤳	I	I
Y	K	[K]
∠	Λ	L
⨆	M	M
⇂	N	N
○	O	O
⊃	Π	P
⊘		Q
⊿	P	R
W	Σ	S
✕	T	T
	Y	U,V
	X	X
	Ω	

Typical letters of the alphabet in Phoenician, Greek, and Roman forms. The final Greek letter, omega, is pronounced like the Roman long *o*.

The Hebrews

Were the Hebrews unique? Did they develop a religion completely new to the world? Modern scholarship has revealed the debt this creative people owed to their neighbors in the Middle East. From Mesopotamian precedents, the Hittites developed the suzerainty treaty—a covenant between conqueror and conquered.

The [suzerainty] convenant is regularly spoken of as that which the sovereign gave to his vassal—it is the sovereign's covenant. . . . In the desert, [the Hebrews] . . . had no status in any social community large enough to ensure their survival. Therefore, they were formed into a new community by a covenant whose text we have in the Decalogue. . . . Contrary to the usual procedure, the Israelites did not bind themselves by oath to obey Moses as their leader. Instead, following the form of suzerainty treaties, they were bound to obey certain stipulations imposed by Yahweh Himself. . . . In effect, then, each clan became a vassal of Yahweh by covenant—and at the same time bound to each other in a sacred truce.

From George E. Mendenhall, "Covenant Forms in Israelite Tradition," *The Biblical Archaeologist* 17 (1954), pp. 57, 63–64.

that was unique among ancient peoples: it was monotheistic. The Hebrews also created a sacred scripture that chronicled the relationship between the people and their God, Yahweh, and these books have helped the Hebrews maintain their identity down to the present day. Unlike other ancient peoples, they resisted absorption by the waves of conquerors that passed over Southwest Asia.

The Hebrew scriptures (known to Christians as the Old Testament) are a collection of books written between about 1000 and 150 B.C. At the beginning of this period the twelve tribes that united under the first Hebrew king, Saul (*ca.* 1000 B.C.) began to form their historical traditions into a coherent history that would solidify the union. They traced the origins of the tribes to the twelve sons of Jacob (also called Israel), who was the grandson of Abraham, a man who according to tradition had migrated into Palestine from Ur in Mesopotamia. The Hebrews called themselves Israelites from this descent from Jacob-Israel.

Many, if not all, of the tribes had been among the foreigners who lived in Egypt during the New Kingdom, and their traditions said that a great leader Moses (whose name is Egyptian) had led them out of Egypt into the Sinai Desert. Moses gave the tribal groups a law, the Ten Commandments, which was then elaborated in the book of Deuteronomy ("the second law"). After this formative period under Moses, about 1200 B.C., the Hebrews invaded Palestine under Joshua.

It is unknown how many of the tribes participated in this conquest, which took about two centuries to complete. About 1000 B.C. the tribes in the confederation united under King Saul, who was appointed by a religious leader named Samuel, who not long after this designated David (r. *ca.* 1000–960 B.C.) as Saul's successor. King David completed the conquest of the Canaanites and the Philistines (who lived in the southern coastal district near Gaza) and built his capital at Jerusalem. David's son and successor Solomon (r. *ca.* 960–930 B.C.) reaped the benefits of these successes. He was able to establish lucrative trading and diplomatic relations with his neighbors, and he built a great royal palace and temple to Yahweh in Jerusalem. But Solomon's strong rulership raised opposition among the tribes, and after his death, the ten northern tribes seceded to form the Kingdom of Israel under another dynasty. The two southern tribes remained loyal to the house of David in the Kingdom of Judah. These two kingdoms were subjected to repeated conquests by three successive empires that dominated Mesopotamia

and the eastern seaboard of the Mediterranean between about 750 and 333 B.C.

THE NEW AGE OF EMPIRES, *ca.* 750–333 B.C.

The Assyrian Empire, ca. 750–612 B.C.

The Assyrians were a Semitic people that occupied territory in the highlands of the upper Tigris Valley and were always among the first to feel the effects of new invasions from the north. By the end of the eleventh century B.C., they had developed a powerful professional army, and, after 900 B.C., they terrorized and conquered their neighbors. By about 750 B.C., the Assyrians

Semite prisoner inscribed on a relief at the temple of Luxor (perhaps dating from the period of Hebrew residence in Egypt).

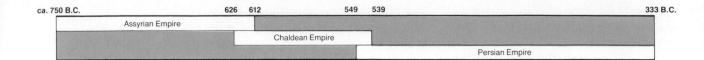

had the whole of Mesopotamia in their control and then swiftly conquered Syria, the Phoenician cities, the kingdoms of Israel and Judah, and, finally, Egypt.

From their capital city of Nineveh, the Assyrians ruled by terror, killing and enslaving large portions of their subject populations. Under their rule, the ten northern tribes of the Hebrews were destroyed, and only the two southern ones in the kingdom of Judah, which was an Assyrian dependency, maintained their identities.

The Assyrians maintained their empire for over 100 years, but were not numerous enough to garrison their vast territories. Moreover, the systematic cruelty of the rulers made it impossible for them to control subject peoples except by force of arms. About 613 B.C., the Babylonians rebelled against them and were joined by other conquered peoples. Nineveh fell in 612

The Assyrian Empire   *ca.* 700 B.C.

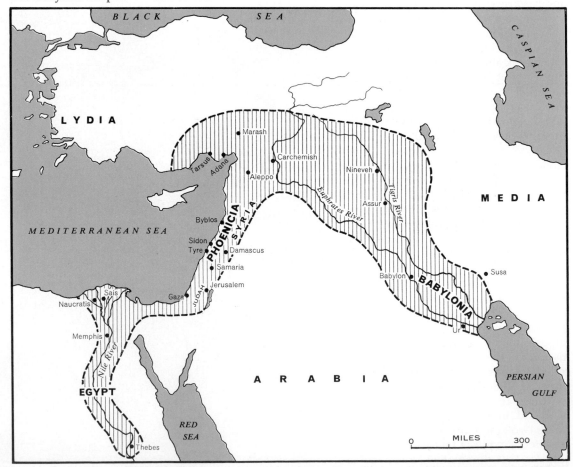

B.C., and the Assyrian empire collapsed overnight.

The Chaldean Empire, ca. 626–539 B.C.

The leaders of the rebellion against the Assyrians were the Chaldeans of Babylon, who, after the fall of Nineveh, constructed an empire of their own. In 587 B.C., the Chaldean king Nebuchadnezzar overran Judah, which had joined a anti-Chaldean coalition led by Egypt, and destroyed Solomon's temple in Jerusalem. To control the population of the conquered kingdom, Nebuchadnezzar carried off the leading citizens to Babylon. The so-called Babylonian Captivity lasted until the fall of Babylon in 539 B.C. Although the Hebrew prophets saw the fall of Babylon as divine punishment for the Chaldeans' treatment of the people of God, the ac-

An alabaster relief showing an Assyrian king on a hunt.

The Persian Empire   *ca.* 500 B.C.

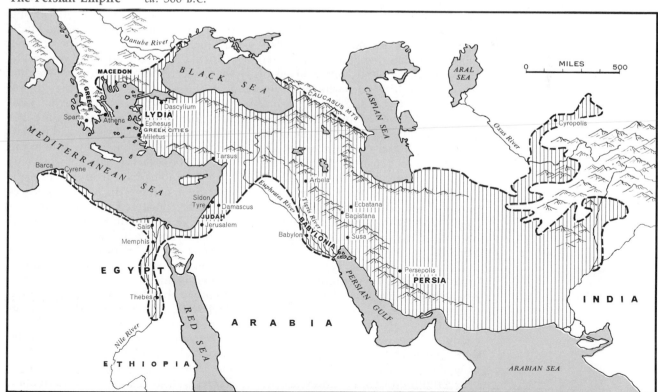

Lydians paying tribute to the Persian emperor Darius I.

tual cause of the fall was the rise of Persia.

The Persian Empire, ca. 549–333 B.C.

The Persians occupied a high plain east of Mesopotamia, where they herded sheep and raised horses. They lived in a loose tribal federation with the Medes and other neighbors. In 549 B.C., Cyrus, an able military leader, established himself as king and unified the various peoples tightly under his leadership. From his seat north of the fertile crescent, Cyrus led his forces first against Asia Minor, which he conquered in 543 B.C., thereby gaining access through the Greek cities of the western coast (Ionia) to the rich trade and high culture of the Aegean. In 539 B.C., he conquered the Chaldean Empire and added Mesopotamia, Syria, Palestine, and the Phoenician cities to his power. His son conquered Egypt in 525 B.C.

Cyrus created a new type of empire in his territories. He permitted the subject peoples to exercise a large measure of autonomy under the careful supervision of his government. Each of the conquered peoples kept its own customs and religion and its special form of government. For example, the Hebrews returned to Judah and were permitted to reestablish their kingdom and to rebuild their temple. In each territory, a Persian governor and garrison kept the peace and supervised the collection of taxes. Rebellion against this lenient system was met with severe military measures.

The Persian imperial system influenced the later Greek and Roman empires, but the Persians also left a strong mark on the later religions of the Mediterranean. The Persian upper classes followed the teachings of the sixth-century prophet Zoroaster, who taught that the world is under two divine powers, one good and one evil. These two powers were engaged in a battle that would last 6,000 years, and human beings were free to join one side or the other. Those who allied themselves with the god of good would go to paradise (a Persian word), while the others would be consumed in eternal fire. Although Zoroastrianism did not spread much beyond Persia, it influenced the religions of the Middle East through the Persian imperial system and gained immense historical importance. The Hebrews absorbed the concepts of the devil, hell, paradise, and the last judgment from Zoroastrianism.

Persian power was first checked by the Greeks in 490 B.C., and, after a serious defeat by the Greeks in 479 B.C., Persia ceased to be the dominant power in the Mediterranean. Nonetheless, the Persian Empire survived in the Middle East until Alexander the Great conquered it in 333 B.C. In the third century A.D., after a long period during which Hellenistic successors of Alexander ruled Persia, a native Persian dynasty that was deeply devoted to Zoroastrianism rose to recreate the empire. This new empire lasted until the Arabs destroyed it in A.D. 637.

Among all these people of the Middle East, the Hebrews were perhaps the most important, not because they created a great empire or advanced civilization more than others, but because through their religion and scriptures, they transmitted the civilization of the Middle East to the West. For 2,000 years before Europeans discovered early civilization through archaeology, they knew and had absorbed the basic characteristics of that civilization through the Hebrew tradition, which was one of the cornerstones of western civilization. The Greeks created another of the cornerstones of that civilization; they are the subject of the next chapter.

Persian gold cup (fifth century B.C.).

Suggestions for Further Reading

General

On the geography of human habitation, see L. Febvre, *A Geographical Introduction to History* (1924). There are excellent maps, with explanatory notes, for this and other chapters, in *The Times Atlas of World History*, ed. G. Barraclough (1978). For an overview of prehistory, see G. Clark, *World Prehistory in New Perspective*, 3rd ed. (1977). W. Howells reviews our understanding of human evolution in *Mankind in the Making* (1959), and *The Evolution of the Genus Homo* (1973). On the Old Stone Age, see K. P. Oakley, *Man the Tool-maker*, 4th ed. (1958), and F. Bordes, *The Old Stone Age* (1968). On the Neolithic and the origins of agriculture, see P. Singh, *The Neolithic Cultures of Western Asia* (1974);

J. Mellaart, *Catal Huyuk: A Neolithic Town in Anatolia* (1967); and P. J. Ucko and G. W. Dimbleby, eds., *The Domestication and Exploitation of Plants and Animals* (1969). On the spread of the agricultural revolution, see J. G. D. Clark, *Prehistoric Europe: the Economic Basis* (1971). On the dating of ancient civilizations, see C. Renfrew, *Before Civilization* (1979). For surveys of Old Europe, see S. Piggott, *Ancient Europe, from the Beginnings of Agriculture to Classical Antiquity* (1965), and C. Renfrew, *The Emergence of Civilization: The Cyclades and the Aegean in the Third Millennium B.C.* (1972). On the culture of Old Europe, see M. Gimbutas, *The Goddesses and Gods of Old Europe*, 2nd ed. (1982).

Mesopotamia

A. L. Oppenheim, *Ancient Mesopotamia* (1964), and H. W. F. Saggs, *The Greatness That Was Babylon* (1962), are detailed surveys of Mesopotamian history. For an appreciation of life in the valleys, see J. Hawkes, *Life in Mesopotamia, the Indus Valley and Egypt* (1973), and

G. Contenau, *Everyday Life in Babylon and Assyria* (1954). S. N. Kramer has translated original Sumerian documents in *History Begins at Sumer* (1959) and *The Sumerians* (1963). For the history of Dilmun, see G. Bibby, *Looking for Dilmun* (1969).

Egypt

On early Egyptian civilization, see W. B. Emery, *Archaic Egypt* (1961). There are two good surveys of dynastic Egypt. Of them, A. H. Gardner, *Egypt of the Pharaohs* (1961), is the more factual, and J. A. Wilson, *The Culture of Ancient Egypt* (1956), the more interpretative. For a study of Egyptian monuments, see I. E. S.

Edwards, *The Pyramids of Egypt* (1975). H. Frankfort, *Ancient Egyptian Religion* (1958), largely replaces older standard works on this subject, and P. Montet, *Everyday Life in Egypt in the Days of Ramses II* (1958), is the counterpart of Contenau's book on Babylon.

Syria and Palestine

Informative studies on the non-Hebrew peoples of Syria-Palestine can be found in E. Anati, *Palestine before the Hebrews* (1963); J. Gray, *The Canaanites* (1964); D. B. Harden, *The Phoenicians* (1962); and R. A. H.

Macalister, *The Philistines* (1913). Among the best of the many books on the Hebrews, see J. Bright, *A History of Israel* (1959); W. F. Albright, *The Biblical Period from Abraham to Ezra* (1963); and A. Lods, *Israel* (1932).

Assyrians, Chaldeans, and Persians

The general histories of Mesopotamia mentioned above treat the Assyrians and Chaldeans. For studies of the Persians and their subjects, see R. N. Frye, *The*

Heritage of Persia (1963), and A. T. Olmstead, *A History of the Persian Empire* (1959).

2
Greek Civilization

Greece is a rugged land. On the mainland peninsula, rocky mountains enclose fertile plains, and mountains rise directly from the Aegean Sea to form countless islands and the craggy promontories of Asia Minor. Geography made it difficult to unify the peninsula, much less the scattered islands and settlements on the coast of Asia Minor (Ionia), so no Greek state could achieve the wealth and power of the great Middle Eastern empires.

Yet, the small city-states of Greece produced a remarkable civilization that became one of the foundation stones of western civilization. Settled around the excellent harbors, cosmopolitan communities encouraged artists and intellectuals to absorb the science of the Middle East. Greek thinkers developed principles and rules for the use of reason in the pursuit of knowledge, and the legacy of Greek science is the idea of method, rather than specific findings. From early work on the nature of the world, the Greeks evolved the approach called philosophy and finally logic, which was the tool used by philosophers to discover the truth about things. Western science, ethics, political thought, aesthetics, and literary criticism all derive from the Greeks.

The paradox of Greek history and civilization is that it was the achievement of a minority. This was a culture created by a few men in a few leading cities, and it did not affect the life of men living very far beyond the shadow of the walls of these cities. Boeotia, only 30 miles from Athens, was notorious among the Greeks as the home of dull, ignorant, blundering yokels. Yet, the Greeks shared a common language, worshipped common gods, and competed against one another at great festivals, such as the Olympic Games. The best harbors were usually not near the best farming land, so that the cosmopolitan traders of the seaports had to interact with the rural populations of the fertile inland plains. Geography as well as language and religion encouraged trade and cultural interaction.

THE BRONZE AGE

Greek civilization began during the Bronze Age, roughly the second millennium B.C. The hardness of bronze makes it excellent for the manufacture of all sorts of implements, and it can be cast in a multitude of shapes. The workability of bronze permitted production of a wider variety of tools than had been possible with stone, and because it could easily be reworked, experimentation was also relatively easy. In addition, the process of manufacturing metal implements was much faster than the making of stone tools, and the metal tools were more uniform in quality and type.

The metal revolution increased trade and, consequently, intercultural contact. During the late Stone Age, communities sometimes imported good stone—particularly obsidian (volcanic glass)—for tools, but these were special implements and the trade that made them possible was not an important feature of the Stone Age economy. In contrast, metallurgy relies on rarely occurring natural resources, and few communities could engage in it without establishing stable and frequent commercial relations with distant places. Because successful trade required societies to produce commercial goods, the introduction of metal brought about an economic revolution in the eastern Mediterranean. Further, the international economy produced many wealthy societies that supported a professional class of craftsmen and artists. These societies traded artistic tastes and ideas as well as material goods, which increased the pace of cultural development.

CRETE AND MYCENAEAN GREECE

Greek culture owes much to the civilization of Crete, an island that stretches for over 150 miles across the entrance to the Aegean Sea. In such stories as those of a fabulously rich King Minos—from whose name the civilization of Crete is called Minoan—and of Perseus's defeat of the bull-man Minotaur, Greek mythology preserved the memory of Minoan influence.

Minoan civilization developed after about 2000 B.C., when many communities on the island grew into rich cities whose economies were based on trade. In 1900 A.D., the English archaeologist Arthur Evans discovered a magnificent palace at Knossos on the northern coast of the island. This center, the capital of the legendary King Minos, flourished from 2000 to 1400 B.C., when it was destroyed.

Minoan commerce was so widespread and complex that it required the

Opposite: Gold Mycenaean funeral mask (*ca.* 1500 B.C.).

Above is a seal stone impression of the earliest form of Minoan writing, from which Linear A developed. Below is a Linear A tablet. At bottom is a Linear B tablet.

keeping of written records, and the Minoans developed a distinctive script to accomplish this task. They recorded contracts, sales, and bills of lading on clay tablets in a script that archaeologists call Linear A to indicate that it is the first of two scripts used by the Minoans and that it was written in lines. This script has not been fully deciphered—in part because we do not know what language the Minoans spoke—but it is clear that it is a syllabic script, in which the symbols represented syllables instead of whole words as in pictographic writing. However, the contents of the "documents" can often be guessed because the Minoans used pictographs in the margins as a quick reference index to their contents.

Toward the end of the Knossan period Linear A was replaced by Linear B, a change that suggests that new people gained power in the Minoan centers. For a long time, this script was totally mysterious, but in 1954 the Englishman Michael Ventris used the techniques of cryptography to show that it represents an archaic form of Greek. The script can now be partly understood. Like Linear A, it was used primarily to record commercial documents and communal laws.

This discovery that Greeks gained prominence in the Minoan cities undermined an old theory that the Greeks caused the downfall of the civilization of Crete about 1400 B.C. The palace at Knossos burned about that time, and archaeologists had speculated that the Greeks caused the destruction. At first, it was thought that Linear B repre-

sented the culture of the conquerors, but now, after discovering that other Minoan centers were destroyed at about the same time and that there is no evidence that the civilization recovered from the destruction, it is thought that the Greeks arrived earlier and were, together with the natives, victims of the disaster.

Recent excavations on the Greek mainland show that by the sixteenth century B.C., long before the fall of the Minoan centers, the Greeks had developed a sophisticated Bronze Age civilization that was influenced by the Minoans. Linear B tablets have also been found at Greek sites. This Greek society is called Mycenaean, from Mycenae the home city of the Homeric hero Agamemnon.

The evidence of destruction and rebuilding in many Mycenaean sites shows that the princely families were often in conflict. This was the heroic age, when independent leaders dominated political and economic life. The myths of later times rested on stories of these legendary men and women, who led their people out of barbarity and formed a civilization strongly influenced by, but distinct from, the Minoans.

Mycenaean Greek civilization was, like Minoan, based on cities, each controlled by a princely family. The towns were typically centered on the palace of the ruling family, which sat on high ground, and the city held sway over a territory with a radius of six to nine miles around the high point. The broken geography of Greece, with its small fertile valleys cut off from one another

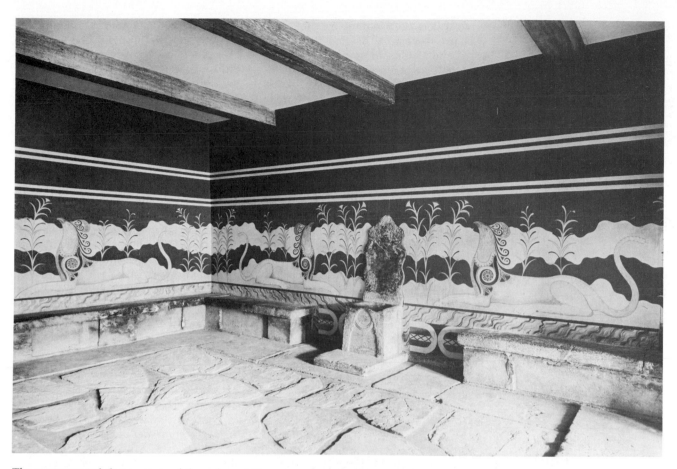

The reconstructed throne room of the palace at Knossos.

by rugged mountains, encouraged this pattern of small, independent, princely states.

The palaces were built around the megaron, a large room with a big central hearth. The center of the room rose two stories, while around the walls an interior balcony provided space for living quarters. The megaron was usually entered through a covered porch and was surrounded by corridors that also opened off the porch. One could not get directly from the megaron to the corridors. Along the outside of the corridors were workshops and storerooms; the palace was a place of residence, government, and industrial and commercial activity. The palace compound was walled, and the porch, through which entry to the whole was gained, was fortified.

One assumes that the royal and aristocratic clans protected their women carefully. As will be noted later, classical Greek families significantly restricted the activities of their women. In such families, women were kept at home and trained to run the household. But the tablets found in Mycenaean sites, which mostly pertain to commercial activities, show that outside the leading families women played a large role in the economy. The tablets list 40 female occupations, most of them connected with textile manufacture and sale. Sometimes, craftswomen mentioned on the tablets have names that indicate that they were refugees who were supporting themselves by their craft. It is also clear that certain crafts were associated with specific towns; women in these occupations were called such names as the "Tinwasian weavers," "Aswian flax-workers," and "Milesian spinners." A few aristocratic women served in the priesthoods and occupied prominent places in the community, and these female priesthoods had female helpers and servants, some of whom exercised control over the considerable wealth of the temples they served. A few tablets name prominent secular women, who appear to have been free of the control of any male relative (*sui generis*).

The centralized and fortified society of Mycenaean Greece rested on military and commercial activities. One of the striking features of the sites is that, unlike Minoan cities, the Mycenaeans did not build religious shrines, and there is little evidence of what Mycenaean religion was like. The commer-

cial economy is also not fully understood, but we know that Greek traders brought home raw materials, particularly metals, for the workshops of the princely compounds.

The excavations in Crete and Greece indicate that before the destruction in 1400 B.C. the Minoans had taken on the Greeks as partners in their trade. It seems that the men of Crete introduced the Greeks to their markets and either developed Linear B themselves or gave the Greeks the impetus to do so. Linear B was Greek-Minoan and represented the importance that the Greeks had gained in Minoan society and commerce. It also represented the influence of the Minoans on Greek civilization. Later Greek writing, which was based on the alphabet that is still used, reflected a new influence, the Phoeni-

The Aegean World   *ca.* 1500–146 B.C.

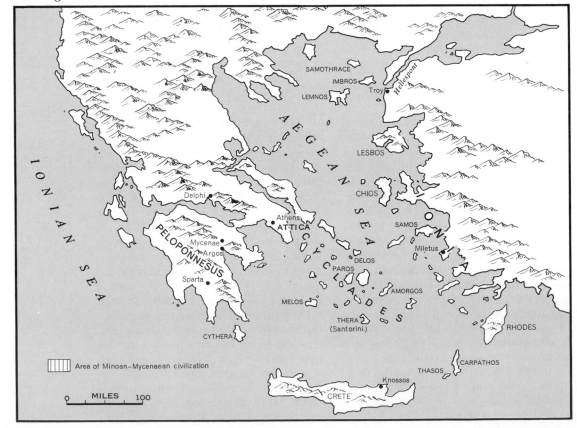

cian, but this influence was exerted only after the collapse of Minoan civilization.

The collapse of Crete's cities was sudden and widespread, and there have been many theories propounded to explain it. As noted earlier, it was once thought that the Greeks themselves were the cause. However, the archaeological evidence points to natural disaster. Many of the buildings had cracked foundations, and there is little evidence of fire, which is commonly associated with invasion and siege. The evidence points to earthquake as the cause of the collapse, and earthquakes are still common in the region. Then, in 1966, American oceanographers found a layer of volcanic ash in the floor sediments of the eastern Mediterranean and were able to show that in the early fifteenth century B.C., a volcanic island about 160 kilometers north of Crete blew up. This explosion, which was something like the recent explosive eruption of Mount St. Helens in the state of Washington, was the most violent eruption ever recorded, and the collapse of Minoan civilization is now blamed on the tidal waves and earthquakes caused by this event.

THE SEA PEOPLES, THE TROJAN WAR, AND THE DORIANS

After the disaster, the mainland civilization of the Mycenaeans survived as the heir of the Minoans for about 200 years. The Greeks became known as traders and mercenaries throughout the eastern Mediterranean. The petty kings of Greece fought one another and made short-lived alliances. The mythological story of the Seven Against Thebes is based on one of these confederations, and the epics of the Trojan War are based on another. Scholars now think the war against Troy occurred during the two decades after 1200 B.C., but at one time historians thought the war was purely legendary, the product of the imagination of the

eighth-century B.C. poet Homer, whose epics *The Iliad* and *The Odyssey* recount the story of the war and its aftermath.

Nineteenth-century scholars saw little historical value in the Homeric stories, except as evidence about the state of Greek society and religion at some date before the classical period. Then in 1870, Heinrich Schliemann, a German businessman, convinced that there actually had been a siege of Troy, began excavations on a mound near the Dardanelles in Asia Minor that was the traditional site of Troy. To the astonishment of the scholarly world, he found layer after layer of ancient settlements, one of them a large fortified city that had been destroyed around 1200 B.C. and another older and very rich town that had fallen earlier (about 1800 B.C.). Schliemann thought the older town was the Troy of legend, but it is more probable that the city that had fallen around 1200 B.C. was the city of Priam and Hector.

Next, Schliemann went to southern Greece and dug at Mycenae, the legendary home of the Greek leader Agamemnon. There, he found a royal palace and evidence of a surprisingly advanced Bronze Age civilization whose roots went back at least to 1800 B.C. The picture of Mycenaean society and civilization rests on the work of Schliemann's successors.

The world in which the Trojan War took place was dominated by a phenomenon called the Sea Peoples. The settled civilizations of the eastern Mediterranean found themselves under constant threat of raids, and their records contain notices of several great sea battles. Prehistorians used to think that the Sea Peoples were new invaders to the area and argued a great deal about who they might have been. They now think that the era of the Sea Peoples was caused by military and social conditions within the region itself. The raiders were established residents of the Mediterranean who took to piracy when the great powers—the Egyptians, the Hittites, and the Minoans—

The earliest representation of Homer, on a fourth-century B.C. coin.

no longer appeared so formidable. Many of these pirates were Mycenaean Greeks, and during the thirteenth century B.C., they expanded Mycenaean influence and power into the eastern Mediterranean.

Normally, the Mycenaean adventurers operated in small bands led by kings, but occasionally these groups joined in great expeditions led by the principal eastern Mediterranean powers. For example, about 1286 B.C., Greeks fought on both sides of a critical battle between the Hittites and Egyptians. But they also formed great federations of their own. In 1233 B.C., they joined in a grand alliance with Sicilians, Sardinians, Lycians, and others against the pharaoh Merneptah. The era of military confederation was brought to a close in two grand naval battles—one against the Egyptians in about 1187 B.C. and another against the Hittites five to ten years later. These confrontations were won by the Egyptians and Hittites, who considered them wonderful victories against formidable opponents.

Later Greek mythology reached back to memories of the last part of the era of the Sea Peoples, and two events stood out in their history—the Trojan War and the invasion of the Dorians. In the cities that sent contingents to fight Troy, stories of the contest were passed from generation to generation, and in the eighth century B.C., the poet Homer drew on many of these stories to create his two epic poems on the war, *The Iliad* and *The Odyssey*. *The Iliad* tells the story of the war itself, and *The Odyssey* tells of the long journey by which one of the Greek leaders, Odysseus, returned home to Ithaca. The stories of many others who returned were also passed down and represented in later works of literature, history, and drama.

In the historical memory of the Greeks, the end of the Trojan War marked an epoch. The fifth-century B.C. historian Thucydides noted that, "After the Trojan War Greece was in a state of constant movement and was being settled in a way that left her no peace to grow strong again." The returning forces had learned new ways, and while they were away, many of the kings had been displaced by usurpers. Thucydides says that there were civil wars in most cities and that losers in these struggles left to found new cities. In Thucydides' mind these internal troubles were connected with the coming of new peoples, who, he says, controlled the Peloponnesus by about 80 years after the war. His association of the two series of events is probably based on their coincidence and on the violence that accompanied both.

The newcomers were Dorians, and the Mycenaeans recognized them as cousins, Greeks who had lived somewhere to the north of the Greek peninsula. The Dorian migration coincided with the end of the era of the Sea Peoples. The destruction of some cities, like Pylos in Messenia, might be connected with this new incursion, but in most places the Dorians apparently settled peacefully. They did not bring much new technology or religious practice with them, and we can only tell that new Greeks had arrived by the later evidence provided by localized writings in their dialect. The use of iron, the practice of cremation burial instead of inhumation (burial in the ground), the beginnings of pottery decorated with geometric designs, and new types of weapons, such as the broadsword, all came from non-Greek sources, rather than with the Dorians.

THE DARK AGES AND ARCHAIC GREECE, *ca.* 1150–500 B.C.

After the decline of the Mycenaean world, Greek society entered a new phase. The number and size of cities diminished, and the ruling class of Mycenaean society was replaced by local aristocracies little given to adventure and great deeds. During the period from the late twelfth to the eighth century B.C., the Greeks produced no written records and little art and architecture of significance. Historians call the period the Dark Ages and usually blame the decline of literacy, wealth, and urban life on the Dorian invasions. The archaeological evidence does not support this conclusion.

Though it did not produce great art or engage in widespread commerce, Greek society of the Dark Ages was very stable. For hundreds of years, the local aristocracies patronized minstrels and poets who preserved the cultural traditions going back to the heroic times of the Sea Peoples. Over the generations, the stories were slowly shaped to present universal themes of human life as the Greeks saw them. The relationship of human and divine and of men and women, the elements of the best and worst human characters, the limitations of human wisdom and knowledge, the basic principles and problems of moral and social life were all major themes of the oral poems. This maintenance of cultural memory shows both that the troubles of the Dark Ages had not been severe enough to cause a break in the cultural tradition, and that, whatever happened during that time, the communities were stable.

The sign that the Dark Ages was coming to an end was the revival of trade toward 800 B.C. Several cities on the eastern mainland and on the western coast of Asia Minor—the area called Ionia—emerged as commercial centers. Miletus and eleven other Greek cities maintained a trading port in the Nile Delta, and Miletus itself had a string of trading posts along the shores of the Black Sea.

The latter part of the Dark Ages was also a period of active colonization. The historical tradition represented in the passages from Thucydides, quoted earlier, suggests that one cause of colonial expansion was civil strife in the late Mycenaean cities, but the main impetus came much later, when the revival of the economy caused a growth of population that upset the social balance of many cities. The successful commercial cities became crowded, and few of them possessed enough agricultural territory to support a large population. The population pressure and the search for new markets encouraged groups to settle new areas. Greek pio-

Greek and Phoenician Colonization and Trade   *ca.* 750–550 B.C.

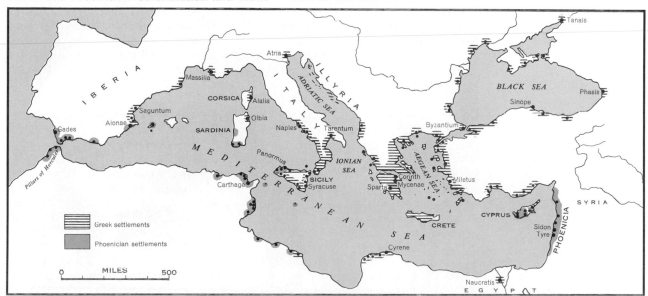

neers went into the Black Sea and into the western Mediterranean. Wherever they went they founded cities modeled on the communities they had left, and the colonies maintained cultural and religious ties with the mother cities. At places like Byzantium on the Bosporus and Phasis on the eastern shore of the Black Sea, Syracuse and Palermo in Sicily, Tarento and Naples in southern Italy, and in towns along the eastern coast of Spain, the colonists exploited the coastal districts of the Mediterranean Basin and increased both the wealth and influence of Greek civilization.

In the late seventh century B.C., coined money was invented in Asia Minor, probably in the kingdom of Lydia, and this innovation gave impetus to the growth of trade. For a long time, the value of goods had been gauged against specific weights of gold and silver, but most trade had been based on barter. Coins were small standardized pieces of precious metal stamped to show who had struck them and who, therefore, guaranteed their weight and fineness.

These standardized pieces could be used repeatedly, and they made a new kind of trade possible. Before the invention of money, merchants had to trade one good or product for another and had to transport their new possessions from one market to another. For example, it was common for a merchant, setting out with the goal of buying luxury goods in a distant city, to engage in a series of barters all along the route to the distant port. He would start off the series by selling his home goods in a nearby city, then would transport the goods he got in that trade to another city along his route, barter again, and repeat the process all along the way. The interim trades were necessary both to pay for his travel and

Scene from a Greek vase (*ca.* 550 B.C.) showing merchants weighing produce. As trade routes multiplied, Greek merchants and producers of wine and oil prospered.

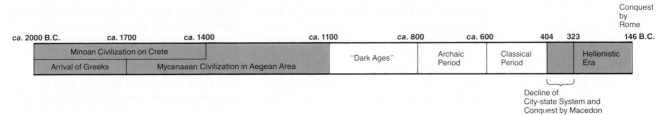

because the products were often bulky and perishable and could only be transported a short distance. The use of money changed this system, although the practice of trading along a route continued because it was profitable. Now, merchants could accumulate the profits, travel more quickly than before, and, when desirable, go directly from home to the place where the goods they wanted were to be found.

But coinage had another, specifically cultural, significance. From early times, Greeks had been interested in value and had sought objects the possession of which would show their personal value. In the many contests—athletic, poetic, and dramatic—the winners, and sometimes all competitors, received awards that signified the value of the man. An example is the golden fleece, which occurs in Greek mythology and is a sign of royalty. Whoever possessed the fleece bore the mark of a king. In the story of the Argonauts, Jason had to obtain the fleece before he could sit on the throne he claimed. Coined money was also a sign of wealth and value, and "Money makes the man" was a very old Greek saying. The signs and inscriptions which identified issuers of coins made them symbols of the issuers' value in society, and it is not surprising that, eventually, emperors and kings claimed for themselves the exclusive right to coin money. Even today, the federal government of the United States retains a similar right, against the states and all other governmental and nongovernmental authorities, as a symbol of its authority.

The introduction of money occurred in the period of Greek civilization called the Archaic, from 800 to 500 B.C. It is an immensely important historical period, for the Greeks resumed writing, formed new political institutions, and began to develop the intellectual techniques of philosophical and scientific inquiry.

THE DEVELOPMENT OF CLASSICAL GREEK CIVILIZATION

The Rebirth of Civilization

The economic revival of the eighth century B.C. brought the Greeks, particularly those of Ionia, into renewed contact with the old established civilizations of the eastern Mediterranean. The influence of these civilizations produced profound changes in Greek society. During that time, Greeks of Ionia adapted the Phoenician alphabet for writing Greek and, thereby, recreated civilized life in the Greek world. The new literacy served the interests both of commerce and of poetry.

The economic and social revival transformed the small cities that survived during the Dark Ages. The growth of international trade led to the establishment of enclaves of foreign merchants in many cities, and the urban population became much more varied than it had been. The commercial classes grew powerful enough to challenge the authority of the local aristocracy, and the people who came to buy and sell goods also brought new ideas and traditions with them.

Homer's great epics of the Trojan War, *The Iliad* and *The Odyssey* represent the new commercial network, for he brought together many legends that had been preserved in once isolated communities. Homer stood near the beginning of a new literary and artistic movement. Not long after the composition of the Homeric epics, Hesiod, a small landowner in Boeotia, wrote long didactic poems describing the origins of the gods and the life of the farmer. On the Aegean island of Lesbos, the first famous woman poet, Sappho, composed lyric poems that became well known throughout the Greek world. In the Peloponnesus, where the old, aristocratic-military society remained strongest, the Spartan commander Tyrtaeus composed martial songs to inspire his men. Communities in every part of the Greek world, from Sicily to the Black Sea, produced poets, but Ionia was the center of this new civilization.

During the seventh century B.C., the cities rebuilt and enlarged their public buildings. Architects developed the characteristic shape of the Greek temple in this period. It became an oblong building framed by pillars with sculptured figures on the doorposts and along the upper walls. Early Greek sculpture owed much to the Egyptians, but by the sixth century B.C., the Greeks had developed new ways to represent the human figure. They learned to depict figures in frontal view, which the Egyptians did not do, and they showed increasing interest in the natural beauty of the human body. During this period, the traditional geometric designs painted on pottery—a style that developed after the fall of the

Mycenaeans—was replaced by realistic scenes of human activities.

The City-State

When the Dorians arrived in Greece, they lived in a society ruled by kings. After they settled, their society gradually changed. The kings lost some of their authority, becoming first among equals within the aristocratic class. During the Dark Ages, the communities coalesced into the *poleis* or city-states. Although these urban states differed from one another in many ways, they shared two basic characteristics. Each *polis* controlled the countryside around it, including in many cases subordinate villages, and each concentrated political authority in the city.

In the early days, the society of the *polis* was based on the aristocratic clans, which had formed during the Dark Ages. Each clan included the extended noble family and its household servants, but beyond that it had the support of citizens from all classes. The noble clan supported lesser families by protecting them in disputes, lending them money, and helping them make marriages, and in return the families gave the clan political allegiance. These associations of patrons and clients were the participant units in social, economic, and political life. The society of the *polis* in the Dark and Archaic Ages was vertically organized, rather than horizontally by economic or social class.

Each clan (*genos* in Greek) had its own religious life, some of it devoted to ancestor cults, some to cults of one or another of the gods, and some to a special role in the religious ceremonies of the community. The *gené* claimed to descend from heroes or gods, and this gave them special religious functions within the community. Justice was a matter of negotiation between families, and, in any case, judicial action had strong religious overtones because the gods were the ultimate judges of right.

In the noble clans the notion of family and of succession developed. The

The Greek Cities

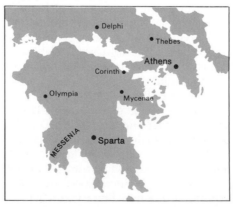

clans were highly aware of family relationships and of who had the right to participate in the religious ceremonies with which each *genos* was associated. Further, the aristocracy was defined by its wealth, and, particularly, by the display of wealth. Such displays demonstrated the value or honor of the aristocratic family and assured its place in society. From this concern for visible signs of value, the custom of giving awards for all sorts of activities originated.

Men controlled the *gené*, but because the *genos* was fundamentally a family institution, women were also important. Sappho of Lesbos reveals that young girls in the mid-seventh century B.C. were educated in groups under a female choral leader. Sappho herself may have been one of them. In these groups, girls may have written poetry extolling female relationships—such as Sappho wrote, perhaps as models for her charges. A girl's formal education consisted primarily in literary work and music, which was closely connected with literature; one presumes that the girls learned the household arts at home.

During the seventh century B.C., changes in the economic and social life of the *poleis* gave rise to political changes. The aristocracy throughout Greece was drawn into commerce by the development of the trade in olive oil and wine. In the commercial cities, merchants found large markets for these products, but only the large landlords had the economic wherewithal to produce them because it takes years to develop vineyards and olive orchards. The peasant farmers continued to grow grain, but the new agricultural exports undermined their prosperity because the wealth generated by trade in oil and wine permitted the upper classes to import cheap grain from Egypt and Sicily, which depressed the economy of local farmers. This produced not only a widening gulf between rich and poor, but also a conflict of values. The traditional social values of good citizenship in the Greek cities rested on the ideal of

the citizen as a yeoman farmer, but this class was ruined by competition with the great landowners and commercial classes.

At the same time, there was a change in the military practices of the Greeks. The Mycenaeans and their successors of the Dark Ages had fought in disorganized armies based on the principle that each man was an independent agent of the state. Battles were melees in which the individual soldiers of one side fought against their individual counterparts of the other side. In such fighting, speed and agility were all-important, and Greek warriors wore light armor and carried spears and short swords.

Beginning about the middle of the eighth century B.C., warriors began to wear heavy pieces of armor to protect themselves. Gradually, they added greaves to protect their shins, plate corslets to protect their upper bodies, a closed helmet, and a large round shield (*hoplon*). By about 675 B.C., warriors were using all these elements of armor together, but it was not until about 650 B.C. that the heavily armed men (called hoplites from the name of the shield) were organized into a new formation, the phalanx, for battle. In the phalanx, the men lined up in a tight formation several rows deep and fought as a coordinated and well-disciplined troop. The object of the line's attack was to push the opposing phalanx off the field. In the line, each man's shield, held on the left arm, protected both his own left side and the right side (and weapon hand) of his neighbor. The man on the right end was relatively vulnerable, and there was a tendency for the line to swing around toward the right as the end man moved to protect his right flank.

The new military system had important social effects. The ancient, heroic, form of battle had emphasized the leadership of the aristocratic warriors. The armies had consisted of small bands of lightly armed peasant-warriors led by their noble patrons. The new formation had a leveling effect and drastically reduced the importance of individual prowess. All citizens who owned a certain amount of land (five acres in the fifth century B.C.) served in the hoplite phalanx, and all in the phalanx had the same basic role. Order and discipline had replaced heroism and self-assertion, and ordinary citizens acquired the status that goes with important military function.

The Rise of the Tyrants

These economic, military, and social changes coincided, roughly, with the rise of a new type of political leadership, tyranny, which spread in the *poleis* during the seventh century B.C. The history of Greek tyranny is not very clear. In the first place, the meaning of the word "tyranny" cannot be pinned down. It is not a Greek word, and it was probably borrowed from Lydia, a kingdom in Asia Minor, where the king was called "tyrant." If the term was foreign, then the Greeks may have used it to describe a leader who did not rule within the traditional political system of the *polis*. That system was an oligarchy in which a few leading nobles controlled the state. The hereditary kingship had survived, but the king's functions are not well known, and his authority was not much greater than that of the aristocratic clans. By contrast, the tyrant arrogated all political power to himself. He stood outside and above the old social and political fabric of the state.

There is a good deal of controversy over the origins of tyranny. Some historians think it rested on the development of the hoplite system; others argue that the tyrants came to power as representatives of the pre-Dorian underclass that still existed throughout mainland Greece in the seventh century B.C. The fifth-century B.C. historian Thucydides, who was the first historian to be concerned with the causes of historical events, thought the tyrants arose because of the growth of wealth, and many modern historians agree with him.

There is something to be said for all of these ideas, except the hoplite theory. The earliest tyrants rose to power before the hoplite phalanx developed, and while tyrants certainly benefited from the social changes engendered by the new military system, they did not come into being because of it. The notion that the tyrants may have represented the pre-Dorian Greeks is supported by some of their actions. In many cities, the tyrants rearranged the political structure giving more power to pre-Dorian tribes—that is, groups of clans that performed political, religious, and military functions within the state. In some cases, the tyrants seem to have come from such tribes. Likewise, there is little doubt that the tyrants benefited from the economic changes of the period. In many cities, the growth of commerce led to conflict between aristocrats who had joined the commercial revolution and those who remained landed gentry. These groups had conflicting economic interests and were soon in a contest for control of the *polis*. In the turmoil, the tyrant seized power, often with the support of the ordinary citizens, whose livelihoods depended on the maintenance of peace.

The tyrants were usually experienced politicians, some of them very capable rulers, who used the lower classes as the basis for their power. Typically, the tyrant tried to weaken the land-owning aristocracy and to bring about reforms that favored the urban commercial classes. Nonetheless, the tyrants were unable to solve the social problems caused by economic change, and few of them remained in power for long. After a long history of political order under aristocratic rule, the Greek communities were suspicious of tyranny because it was not a traditional form of political authority and it concentrated power in the hands of a single man. In the long run, the ancient idea that the community is the source of authority and should be self-governing reasserted itself, and in Greek political thought the tyrant was seen as a usurper, who was at best a necessary evil to be tolerated until social conditions permitted a return to normality.

The Lawgivers

Tyranny was not the only response to the social and political troubles of the seventh and sixth centuries B.C. This was also the age of the lawgivers. The peaceful existence of any community depends on how well its citizens know the traditional laws. In the early *poleis*, the communities were small and stable, and everyone learned the customs and law through oral tradition. Epic poetry, which preserved the historical traditions of the communities, also served to inculcate social values and the basic structure of the legal system through the examples of the heroes.

The economic and social changes of the Archaic period introduced new ideas and new economic activities that made much of the body of ancient custom outmoded. Commerce produced innovations and social relations unknown to the traditional law, so that even conservative aristocratic clans supported men who sought to reform the laws. Moreover, commerce brought new people to the cities, foreign merchants and craftsmen who wanted to take advantage of its markets and who did not know its customary law.

Early codes were rigid and severe; the word *draconian* is still a memorial to the harsh laws of the Athenian Draco (621 B.C.). Later lawgivers were less severe and more concerned with the welfare of the poor. For example, about 590 B.C. Solon of Athens established laws that reduced the burden of debt on small farmers and prohibited enslavement for debt. The Solonic code survived a period of tyranny to form the basis of a new Athenian constitution at the end of the sixth century. Other cities had experiences similar to that of Athens.

It is difficult to overestimate the importance of this movement to introduce written law codes. The codes helped to form a new basis for social order in the cities and changed the nature of social and political development. Before the codification movement, the law had changed through a subtle and hidden process that took place as it was passed down in oral tradition from generation to generation. Now, legal change became a conscious and public activity because the written law could only be reformed by the formal act of rewriting it.

The codes provided a foundation for the commonweal; citizens could feel a part of a community by giving their allegiance to its laws. In the *polis*, loyalty to the city was paramount. The community was now embodied in its law code, its market, and its public buildings. The city became a republic, in the sense that *res publicae*, the communal affairs, became the dominant concern of the citizens. One of the features of the *polis* was that it could be governed in a variety of ways. It could have a monarchical, aristocratic, or popular (democratic) constitution. The noun "politics" and the adjective "political" derive from the communal life of the *polis*, which was intensive, whatever the form of its constitution.

The economic and communal center of the *polis* was its market place, the *agora*. In the *agora*, the population did its daily business and kept abreast of everything that affected the life of the city. Here, young men followed their teachers and exhibited their abilities and characters. Here, politicians argued over issues of public concern. Here, artisans and artists found their clients and audiences. Here was the heart of the classical Greek city.

Although most *poleis* rested their power on the hoplite phalanx, maritime powers also used citizen levies for their fleets of oared warships, and, because sailors needed little personal equipment, the naval powers had the advantage of being able to use citizens of virtually every economic class. The increasing importance of public life and of citizen levies had the natural effect of increasing the political participation

This stele informed the Athenians of the Law Against Tyranny in 336 B.C.: "Should anyone, in an attempt at absolute power, rise up against the people or try to overthrow the democracy of Athens—whoever kills him shall be blameless."

of ordinary citizens. Consequently, during the sixth century B.C. the power of the general assembly of citizens increased in most cities. In many cities, the officials, or governing council, were elected by the assembly, while in others the aristocracy controlled state offices.

The community of the *polis* was conscious of its unity and its role in the nurturing of its members. In 399 B.C. when the people of Athens, sitting as a jury, condemned the philosopher Socrates to death for corrupting his stu-

dents, he refused to take the opportunity to escape from the city because, he said, the city had been the parent of his character, and he owed it obedience. Two generations later, Aristotle wrote a work on politics in which he argued that human beings are by nature social animals, so that the social and political world of the *polis* is the necessary environment of a fully human life. These ideas helped to cultivate a sense of civic duties among the Greeks and explain their willingness to perform public functions.

The Society of the Polis

During the classical period (fifth century B.C.), the constitutions of the *poleis* differed, but their societies—except for Sparta's, which will be discussed later—were very similar. Athens is a convenient model, both because it was the greatest Greek city and because we know most about it. The citizens ran the *polis*. Only Athenian males over 17 years old whose father had been a citizen and whose mother was the daughter of a citizen could be citizens. From the age of 7 to 14, a boy would be educated with his peers in the palaestra, where he learned wrestling and other physical arts, and the gymnasium, where he practiced those arts with older boys and men. When a boy with the correct parentage reached 17, he was enrolled in a *deme*, one of the districts of the city.

As a citizen, the young man had the right and obligation to serve on the jury, in the assembly, and in the hoplite phalanx. He could hold public office, own land, and receive free corn distributions when they were made. Finally, the wealthy citizen was obligated and privileged to perform "liturgies." These were public functions of the greatest importance—organizing and paying for the festivals, putting on poetic, musical, and dramatic performances, and taking command (and financial responsibility) for a trireme, the principal warship of the Athenian

Greek vase of the late sixth century B.C. depicting a foot race. The vase was awarded to the winner of the race at the Panathenaic festival in Athens.

navy. Citizens took pride in performing these time-consuming and expensive services.

About one-half of the Athenian population consisted of citizens, their wives, and daughters. The other half was made up of metics and slaves, mostly the former. Metics were foreigners more or less permanently resident in Athens. They controlled manufacturing, banking, and commerce. They were subject to a head tax, could not own a house or land, and had only restricted access to the courts. All metics had citizen patrons who offered them legal protection and often participated in their economic activities. Metics could serve as rowers in the fleet, where they shared the benches with poor citizens, and, in times of trouble, they could join the forces defending the city. One measure of the status of metics is that the premeditated murder of one was equivalent to the unpremeditated murder of a citizen. Both crimes led to exile.

Slaves were common in Greek society, and families of even modest means owned them. Most families had one or two to help with farming or craft work. Wealthy families might have many, some serving in the household, some as pedagogues (guardians of the young boys of the family), and some as craftsmen and small businessmen connected with the economic activities of the family. Some of the latter could live independently and even build up enough money to buy their freedom. Freedmen became metics. A few wealthy men kept slave crews that they rented out to individuals and the state. Some of the slaves in the state's silver mines at Laurium were leased from private citizens. All in all, slavery supported the life of the upper and middle classes, and the evidence shows that slaves in Athens ran away fairly frequently, but never revolted, as they did in Sparta and, later, in Rome. Although the idea put forward by Plato and Aristotle that the Greeks looked down on people who earned their living is certainly inaccurate, it appears that they did consider labor for wages to be slave's work and, therefore, degrading.

Where did women fit in Athenian society? The wives and daughters of the upper- and middle-class citizens were closely protected. Women were viewed as wanton and dangerous and much more prone to sexual desire than men. Therefore, families put restrictions on their women, who mostly stayed in the household and only went out with escorts, usually trusted male slaves. Men put great value on the preservation of the family's integrity, which meant that women had to be controlled and adultery laws strict.

Virtually all women were married; in Athens, there were only 40 priestesses. In the marriage ceremony, the father of the bride said, "I give you this, my daughter, for the procreation of legitimate children," apparently meaning the correct number and gender of children as well as children whose fatherhood was known and correct. Most men wanted two sons (in case one died) and a daughter, and they could order that unwanted children be exposed.

Most girls married between 14 and 18 years of age, and, typically, their husbands were twice their age. Brides came with a portion of their fathers' estates, the dowry, which was managed by the husband, but would have to be returned in case of divorce. Under Athenian law, women could get divorces, but the law favored men, for whom divorce was relatively easy. The wealthy metics, of whom there were many, treated their wives and daughters in the same way as citizens. Among the poor citizens and metics, women shared the burdens of making a living and, as in the Mycenaean period, practiced some crafts.

Marble grave relief of a girl with pigeons (*ca.* 450 B.C.).

Classical Greek Religion

The religion of Mycenaean Greece appears to have been based on family cults, perhaps derived from ancient

Athena, goddess of wisdom, protector of the home and the citadel, is shown in this bronze statue in military dress (*ca.* seventh century B.C.).

fertility rites. Contact with the Minoans of Crete and with other civilized peoples of the eastern Mediterranean introduced the Mycenaeans to the developed ideas of universal gods and contributed to the growth of a pantheon. The collective memory of the heroic age of the late Mycenaean period added legendary heroes to the unseen world of the gods. Mythological figures like Herakles, Theseus, and Medea were never fully divine, but constituted a link between the worlds of man and the gods. The shrine of Apollo at Delphi continued to declare men to be heroes down to the fifth century B.C.

By the time of Homer, the gods were seen as a family of twelve major divinities who lived on Mount Olympus. In classical Greek religion, as later in Roman religion, the gods of the developed pantheon absorbed the place-gods, which had been revered by agricultural peoples since prehistoric times. These absorptions of ancient divinities caused each local manifestation of the pantheonic god to be somewhat distinct from other manifestations. For example, the Apollo of Delphi was different from the Apollo revered on the Aegean island of Delos.

In the pantheon, Zeus was the ruler of the gods and wielder of the thunderbolt; his sister and wife, Hera, was goddess of women and marriage. Each of the gods held sway over one or two particular human activities: Ares was god of war; Athena was goddess of wisdom; Demeter was goddess of the harvest; Apollo was god of music and poetry (later also the sun god); his twin sister Artemis was goddess of the hunt; Haephastos was god of smithing and metal crafts. Each city and many special shrines in the countryside had divine patrons. Athena was revered in Athens. Artemis was the protectress of Sparta. Delphi on the mainland and the island of Delos had shrines dedicated to Apollo. At these shrines, the god spoke to pilgrims through priestesses; the priestess went into a trance, and, while she was in that state, the god spoke through her voice.

After the development of the *polis*, the community took over the practice of religion and transformed it into a civic function. Religious festivals and devotion became one of the focal points of communal life, so that people reaffirmed their sense of community by participating in the cult. But this transformation of religion created problems. First, it centralized both the practice and the ideas of religion, and, in bringing together the traditions and stories of the gods, it revealed a great confusion of contradictory and inconsistent mythological stories. Educated Greeks were troubled by these inconsistencies; the philosopher Socrates was charged with blasphemy and the corruption of the young because he posed questions about how the gods were to be understood. Second, when the sacrifices and other religious practices became a function of the community, they lost much of their emotional power. Early Greek religion had been based on the family cults and was one of the most important ways in which the cohesiveness of the clan was expressed. In the practice of family religion, people got a powerful sense of belonging to a group. The civic religion of the classical *polis* consisted of formal rituals that no longer appealed to the emotions of individuals. Religion had ceased to engender group feelings. As the cities grew, and society became less personal, people needed a sense of belonging to help them maintain a sense of identity. The failure of the civic religion to provide this identity was one of the reasons why foreign mystery cults became popular in Greece during the classical period. Those initiated into them became part of a select group, differentiated from the rest of society by the secret knowledge and beliefs.

THE PERSIAN WARS, 499–479 B.C.

Athens and Sparta

The revived commercial success of the Greeks made them known to all the powers of the eastern Mediterranean, and, in the middle of the sixth century B.C., it made them the object of conquest. Soon after Cyrus the Great created the Persian Empire by consolidating his power in the Middle East, he moved against the wealthy Greek cities of Ionia. By about 540 B.C., he had conquered them and had become a threat to the Greeks of the Aegean and the mainland. Resistance to the Persians depended on the cooperation of Sparta and Athens, the two mainland cities that had emerged as leaders among the Greek city-states. But cooperation was not easy, for Sparta and Athens were at opposite poles of the Greek political system.

Much has already been learned about Athens. Although it controlled a prosperous agricultural district, its pri-

A procession recorded in marble at the Parthenon (fifth century B.C.). The paraders on their way to the Acropolis carry jars containing sacrificial gifts.

mary sources of wealth were its silver mines at Laurium and its trade. By the late sixth century B.C., Athens had gained dominance over the trading communities of the Aegean.

During the sixth century B.C., Athens went through a period of tyrants who relied on the political support of ordinary citizens and undermined aristocratic power. After the last tyrant was overthrown in 510 B.C., the popular leader Cleisthenes put through basic constitutional reforms. He divided the citizens into ten tribes, so organized that each tribe was a cross section of the whole population, rich and poor, rural and urban. From each tribe, 50 citizens were chosen by lot to serve on the Council of Five Hundred, which prepared business for the assembly of

Pericles on Athens and Sparta

This oration, inserted by the Greek historian Thucydides in his *History of the Peloponnesian War*, does not give Pericles' exact words, but it does express admirably the pride of the Athenians in their city and its form of government.

We are called a democracy, for the administration is in the hands of the many and not of the few. But . . . the claim of excellence is also recognized, and when a citizen is in any way distinguished, he is preferred to the public service, not as a matter of privilege, but as the reward of merit. . . . Our city is thrown open to the world, and we never expel a foreigner or prevent him from seeing or learning anything of which the secret, if revealed to an enemy, might profit him. . . . In the matter of education, whereas the Spartans from early youth are always undergoing laborious exercises which are to make them brave, we live at ease, and yet are equally ready to face the perils which they face. . . . For we are lovers of the beautiful, yet simple in our tastes, and we cultivate the mind without loss of manliness. . . . Such is the city for whose sake these men fought and died; . . . and every one of us who survive should gladly toil on her behalf.

From Pericles' Funeral Oration, in Thucydides, *The History of the Peloponnesian War*, trans. by B. Towett in Francis R. B. Godolphin, ed., *The Greek Historians* (New York: Random House, 1942). Vol. I, pp. 648–50.

all citizens. The assembly held legislative power in the state, as had long been the case. The chief civilian and military officers were elected by the people, but these offices were not paid and were open only to the wealthy. Thus, the new constitution created a mixed government in which there was a balance of power between ordinary and aristocratic citizens. Athenian political life was hurly-burly; virtually every citizen took a deep interest in issues of policy. In the Athenian *agora*, argument became an art and education an instrument of political and social leadership. The citizen had a commitment to personal participation; he owed the state the best products of his intellect and judgment.

Sparta had a different history and grew into a different kind of state. It occupied a fertile plain in the Peloponnesus and, by the early seventh century B.C., had gained domination over its neighbors. About 650 B.C., one of the communities in its shadow rebelled and fought a ferocious 50-year-long war that almost destroyed the Spartan state. During this bitter struggle, Sparta evolved from an aristocratic city-state into a military regime. The entire male population of the *polis* was transformed into a standing army, and the society and economy of the state were organized to support this military force.

The population of Sparta and its dependencies, a state called Lacedaemon, was divided into three classes. The Spartan male citizens (fewer than 10,000 men) had full political rights and enjoyed full equality among themselves. The free citizens of subject communities managed their own affairs, but had no say in the affairs of the ruling city. The serfs or *helots* worked the lands that supported the professional citizen-army.

The lives of the citizens were rigidly regulated. Boys left home at the age of 7 to begin military training. They entered the service at 20 and were then allowed to marry, but they could not live with their wives until they were 30. They lived in barracks for ten years and remained liable for military service until they were 60. By 500 B.C., Sparta controlled most of the Peloponnesus, either directly or through a system of alliances called the Peloponnesian League. It is not surprising that Sparta and Athens found it difficult to cooperate against the Persians.

The Defeat of Persia

In 499 B.C., the Ionian cities rebelled against the Persians, and Athens sent a fleet to assist them. The rebellion failed, and King Darius of Persia dispatched an army to punish the Athenians. This force came across the Aegean by ship and landed north of Marathon, where a narrow passage between the sea and the hills led to Athens. In 490 B.C., a small Athenian army defeated the Persian force at Marathon, and this humiliation caused the Persian king to plan a full-scale invasion of Greece.

Darius died before he could carry out his plan, but his successor Xerxes turned his attention to the Greek project in 480 B.C. He crossed the Dardanelles with over 100,000 men and marched down the Greek peninsula. The small cities in his path quickly declared their neutrality and left the task of defending Greece to Athens and the Peloponnesian League.

The Spartans and their allies formed the backbone of the resistance to Xerxes' army. A small, disciplined Spartan force led a composite army of about 6,000 men to a narrow pass at Thermopylae and held it, while the Athenians led a composite fleet against the Persian fleet off the coast. The Persians were supplying their large army by sea and defeat of their fleet would force them to withdraw from the peninsula. But the sea battle was indecisive, and the heroic stand of the Spartans ended in disaster; the entire force was wiped out. The Greek alliance withdrew to the Isthmus of Corinth and the Bay of Salamis, and the Athenians abandoned their city to the Persians, who looted and burned it.

The taking of Athens was a false victory. Under the leadership of a far-

The Persian Wars   499–479 B.C.

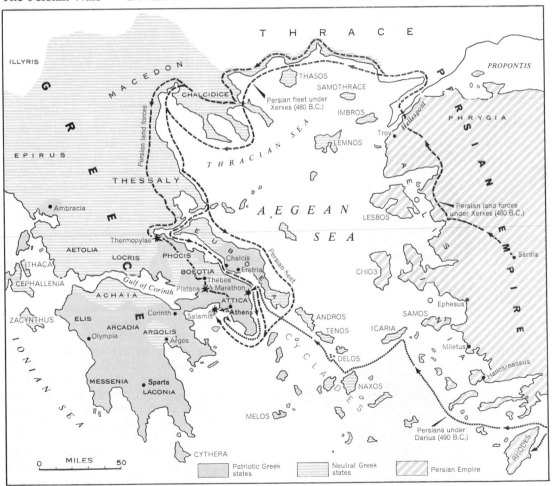

sighted politician named Themistocles, the Athenians had used the income of their silver mines at Laureum to build a fleet much larger than any city of its size would normally need. Themistocles recognized that the conquest of Greece, even of the mainland, would depend on naval power to control the hundreds of islands and inlets and supply the occupying forces. His strategy paid off when the Greek fleet, two-thirds of which was Athenian, defeated the Persian navy in the Bay of Salamis and cut off supplies to the Persian army. Soon after this battle, the Greek army led by Sparta defeated the Persians at Plataea (479 B.C.), and, later in the year, the Greek fleet utterly destroyed the Persian navy off the coast of Asia Minor.

The Persian war took on a historical significance for the Greeks like the American Revolution did for Americans. Athenians in particular took the success as proof of the moral and cultural superiority of their social and political system. From the rich variety and constant arguments of the *agora* had come a sound and successful policy and lasting naval power. For a long time, the citizens were committed to Cleisthenes's democratic constitution.

The Athenians recovered very rapidly from the Persian occupation. During the two or three generations before the Persian War, Athenian merchants had taken over from Miletus and the Ionian cities—then under Persian domination—the position of principal Greek commercial power. The naval successes of 479 B.C., based on the program of Themistocles, gave Athens domination of the Aegean and permitted it to bring the newly independent cities of Ionia into its economic and political power.

THE AGE OF ATHENIAN DOMINATION AND THE PELOPONNESIAN WAR, 478–404 B.C.

The Classical Civilization of Greece

When the Athenians returned to their ruined city, they undertook a massive program of rebuilding. The multitude of construction projects made the city a mecca for architects, artists, and craftsmen from all over the Greek world. Athens became the center of Hellenic civilization; the celebration of its renewed vigor provided festivals that served as institutional support for poets, dramatists, and other men of literature and art. The glory of education was evident in the new Athens, and teachers became important figures in the life of the *agora*.

The art of the new city adorned imposing public buildings and temples. Greek sculptors had achieved the ability to represent the forms of living things in great detail, and the sculpture of fifth-century Athens was a representation of ideal nature. Greek artists projected their perceptions of the world around them onto the image of the gods. In their works, the gods appear

Head of a Spartan warrior believed to be King Leonidas, who commanded the Greek force at Thermoplyae (early fifth century B.C.).

as ideal human beings. For the Greeks of the fifth century B.C., there was no antagonism between the real and the ideal. Life in this world at its best could be beautiful and satisfying, and the artists sought to depict such a life.

The crowning achievement of classical Greek art, and of the rebuilding of Athens, was the temple of the Parthenon* dedicated to Athena, the patron goddess of the city. The Parthenon stands on the crest of the Acropolis, the hill that dominates Athens. Though it is almost as large as a football field, the Parthenon's basic qualities are har-

*The Parthenon served as a place of worship for over 2,000 years; it was a temple to Athena, then a Christian church, and finally a mosque. It was almost intact until it was blown up in a minor war 300 years ago. Today only the outer row of columns is standing, though many of the sculptures were saved.

mony and proportion. Its sculptures were executed by Phidias, the greatest sculptor of his day, whom Pericles, the political leader of Athens in the middle of the century, put in charge of planning the new city. The program of reliefs along the side of the temple represented the people of the city in their processions, athletic contests, and military exercises. Thus, the sculptures did not distinguish the religious from the secular; or, to put it another way, the noblest and best secular activity also had religious significance.

The planners of the new city also built an outdoor amphitheater into the side of the Acropolis, and Athens became a center for a new performance art, the drama. For centuries, the Greeks had celebrated religious festivals by performing ancient stories. A single speaker told a story, and a cho-

The Parthenon at Athens.

Sophocles, popular fifth-century playwright.

rus responded to him at appropriate moments. During the fifth century B.C., Athenian poets turned these rituals into full-fledged drama by adding other speakers. The city held contests for the new dramatists in connection with the festival of Dionysus (god of wine). Each playwright submitted three plays, tragedies, using themes drawn from traditional legend and mythology. The works of three of these writers—Aeschylus (525–456 B.C.), Sophocles (496?–406 B.C.), and Euripides (480?–406? B.C.)—stand at the beginning of the western tradition of drama, and they are still performed today. Other festivals were devoted to comedy, and the most famous of the comic dramatists was Aristophanes (448?–380? B.C.), whose plays are also still performed and remain very funny even though his work was often topical, referring to specific events and personalities about which we know little or nothing.

The development of the *polis* focused the Greeks' attention on the natural world, of which political and historical life were part. Through their involvement in the life of the *polis*, men became interested in worldly matters. During the sixth century B.C., the Greeks began to pay attention to the precise chronology of their history and to develop a formal, conscious way of thinking about the nature of things. They were the first to develop both a historical consciousness and the formal approach to knowledge that came to be called philosophy—the love of wisdom.

The basis of chronology was the Olympiad, the four-year cycle of games held in honor of Zeus. The first historian to write narratives of past events was Herodotus of Halicarnassus (*ca.* 480–420 B.C.), who spent some time in Athens. He wrote a history of the Persian War and of the peoples of the Middle East. It would not be wrong to call Herodotus the first anthropologist. He cataloged the characteristics of all the peoples then known to the Greeks. Herodotus was followed by the Athenian Thucydides (*ca.* 460–*ca.* 395 B.C.), who wrote a history of the war between Athens and Sparta (431–404 B.C.), in which he had served as a general. Thucydides introduced the idea of causation into historical writing. He did not just recount events and celebrate heroes, but he sought to explain the causes of the war and of the defeat of Athens. Modern historians have long argued about which of these two writers is the first true historian.

From the Egyptians and Babylonians, the Greeks learned the rudiments of astronomy and mathematics, which came to them as practical pursuits, but which they turned to purely intellectual ends. For the Greeks, astronomy and the science of numbers raised basic questions about the nature of the world, and by the sixth century B.C. Greek thinkers had begun to propound

Thucydides on Writing History

Thucydides was the first historian to recognize his dependence on his sources and the first to think of his history as a work of "science" that would teach universal truths about human behavior.

With reference to the narrative of events [in his history], far from permitting myself to derive it from the first source that came to hand, I did not even trust my own impressions, but it rests partly on what I saw myself, partly on what others saw for me, the accuracy of the report being always tried by the most severe and detailed tests possible. My conclusions cost me some labor from the want of coincidence between accounts of the same occurrences by different eye-witnesses, arising sometimes from imperfect memory, sometimes from undue partiality for one side or the other. The absence of romance in my history will, I fear, detract somewhat from its interest; but if it be judged useful by those inquirers who desire an exact knowledge of the past as an aid to the interpretation of the future, which in the course of human things must resemble if it does not reflect it, I shall be content. In fine, I have written my work, not as an essay which is to win the applause of the moment, but as a possession for all time.

Thucydides, *The Peloponnesian War* (New York: Modern Library, 1951), pp. 14–15.

theories to explain such phenomena as physical objects, time, and change. Thinkers were fascinated by the relationship between numbers and real objects and were led to ask whether numbers themselves are real. During the fifth century B.C., Athens attracted many intellectuals, and it became fashionable among the upper classes to support teachers and thinkers as well as artists and architects. In this intellectual activity was the beginning of philosophy.

In the later fifth century B.C., Athens produced a thinker who changed the way both the Greeks and all who have been influenced by them think about the world. This was Socrates (469–399 B.C.), who developed a method for finding the truth about things. He asked simple questions, each derived from the answer to the one before, which led by stages to a true knowledge of something. In fact, he used this method usually to show that what his contemporaries commonly thought about something was false, but that it was possible to work toward a true knowledge of it. This practice made him popular with the young aristocrats who followed him in the *agora*, but the point of Socrates' argument was antidemocratic. Democracy rested on the notion that ordinary citizens had the knowledge and wisdom necessary to carry out the affairs of state. Socrates spent his adult life undermining that notion. The danger of such views was particularly apparent to his contemporaries at the end of the fifth century B.C. In 411 and 404 B.C., Athens was controlled by oligarchies that imposed reigns of terror. In 401 B.C., an aristocratic faction tried once more to replace the democracy with an oligarchy. In this atmosphere, Socrates was accused of corrupting the youth of the city—that is, its young aristocrats—and in 399 B.C. the jury of citizens condemned him to death.

Socrates left no written works, but his pupil Plato (426–347 B.C.) immortalized him in a series of dramatic dialogues. Scholars think that Plato's earli-est dialogues accurately represent his teacher and give us a picture both of his character and of his deep concern for questions of ethical and political behavior. In the later dialogues, the character Socrates became a mouthpiece for Plato himself. Plato used the Socratic method to analyze the nature of reality and of the *polis*. He developed the notion that true reality was not what could be seen and touched, but the ideas that gave form to these worldly things. He founded a school in Athens, the Academy, which was the first institution of learning in western civilization.

His successor as head of the Academy, Aristotle (384–322 B.C.), took the next step in the methodical approach to knowledge. He created logic, the method of rational thought that under-

The Trial of Socrates

Plato, in his dialogue *The Apology*, reported the trial of Socrates. In this passage Socrates explains why he cannot change his ways.

Suppose . . . you said to me "Socrates, we shall disregard Anytus and acquit you, but only on one condition, that you give up . . . philosophizing. If we catch you going on in the same way, you shall be put to death." . . . I should reply, "Gentlemen, . . . I owe a greater obedience to God than to you; and so long as I draw breath and have my faculties, I shall never stop practicing philosophy and exhorting you and elucidating the truth for everyone that I meet." I shall go on saying . . . , "My very good friend, you are an Athenian and belong to a city which is the greatest and most famous in the world for its wisdom and strength. Are you not ashamed that you give your attention to acquiring as much money as possible, . . . and give no attention or thought to truth and understanding and the perfection of your soul? . . . Wealth does not bring goodness, but goodness brings wealth and every other blessing, both to the individual and to the State." Now if I corrupt the young by this message, the message would seem to be harmful. . . . And so, gentlemen, I would say, "You can please yourselves . . . whether you acquit me or not; you know that I am not going to alter my conduct, not even if I have to die a hundred deaths."

From Plato, *The Last Days of Socrates*, trans. by Hugh Tredennick (Baltimore: Penguin Books, 1959), pp. 61–62.

Socrates, statuette from the Hellenistic period.

Plato (426–347 B.C.),
Socrates' pupil.

lies the main branches of human thought and knowledge, and he made contributions to virtually every field— ethics, politics, physics, botany, zoology, the study of poetry and other forms of literature, and many more.

The Athenian Empire

During the struggle against the Persians, the Greek cities of the Aegean had formed the Delian League, and Athens had gained the leading position in this alliance. In 478 B.C., the members of the league met on Delos, the headquarters from which the league took its name, to plan for the future defense of the Aegean, because the Persians remained a threat. From this meeting emerged a plan according to which each member of the league would contribute an annual quota of ships or money. Athens, which had by far the largest naval force, dominated the parley and won the right to name the league's admiral and to control its treasury, which was kept on Delos. In time, the league's navy became almost exclusively Athenian—the great majority of other members just contributed money—so that the league became an instrument of Athenian power. Gradually, more and more member cities became mere dependencies of Athens, and the transfer of the treasury to Athens in 454 B.C. was symbolic of the transformation of the league into an Athenian maritime empire.

The Athenians viewed their empire as necessary and honorable. It was necessary because Athens had been dependent on foreign grain since the time of Solon; it grew only about one-third of its food supply. Hence, its survival depended on control of the seas and of suppliers abroad, and, furthermore, its commercial economy also benefited from the imperial system. At the same time, the Athenians did not hesitate to admit that the empire contributed to the honor of the city (in the same way that wealth and its display gave honor to the individual citizen).

While Athens built its empire, the Spartans and their allies in the Peloponnesian League had strengthened their ties, and, although they did not compete directly with Athens for control of the Aegean, the Peloponnesian League became a countervailing force to the Athenians. Between 454 and 431 B.C., most cities outside of the two leagues had to decide to become associated with one of them, and the Greek world became divided between two great empires, dominated by Sparta and Athens, respectively.

Aristotle (384–322 B.C.), pupil of Plato and organizer of Greek thought.

Athenian Politics

By the middle of the fifth century B.C., the population of Athens had grown to about 100,000, of which only 20,000 men were citizens with full political rights. The old constitution, which had been created to organize the life of a Greek city-state, was inadequate for an imperial capital, and political unrest was common.

In fear of a revival of tyranny, the reformers of the late sixth century B.C. had created the institution of ostracism. By majority vote the citizens could exile any person for ten years. The citizens voted by writing a name on a pottery shard (*ostraka*) and depositing it on the pile. Archaeologists have discovered "factories" that produced these shards, pre-printed by the political enemies of one or another prominent person. Therefore, the constitution tilted political power to the lower classes, and the threat of ostracism made demagogy—that is, playing to the crowd—necessary for pursuing a successful political career. A long political career was virtually impossible.

It is remarkable that some men survived the dangerous shoals of Athenian politics and that one in particular maintained his power for over 30 years. From 463 to 429 B.C., Pericles was the dominant figure, and he was annually elected to the generalship for the last 15 years of this period. It was he who led Athens during the period of aggressive imperialism.

The Peloponnesian War, 431–404 B.C.

After the Persian War and the decline of Persian power in the Mediterranean, the two great confederations, the Delian League under Athens and the Peloponnesian League under Sparta, coexisted uneasily. Their competition was intensified by their economic dependence on one another and by their constitutional differences. On the one hand, the cities of the Peloponnesus provided agricultural surplus and a market for the commercial economy of Athens and its dependencies. On the other hand, cities with conservative aristocratic constitutions tended to ally themselves with Sparta, while democracies sided with Athens, and each side tried to intervene in the politics of uncommitted cities to bring them into line with its own constitution.

War broke out between the two leagues in 431 B.C. The principal contemporary historian of the war, Thucydides, believed that it was inevitable. As he saw it, the imperialist policies of Athens under Pericles threatened Sparta, and, finally, Sparta had to go to war to preserve its position. The imme-

A four drachma coin from Athens showing Athena and her owl (*ca.* sixth century B.C.).

Ostraka, or broken pieces of pottery, on which citizens wrote the names of those they wished to ostracize from Athens (*ca.* 470 B.C.). The names on these pieces are Themistocles, who was later recalled, and Cimon.

Pericles, from a Roman copy of a Greek bust of the fifth century B.C.

diate causes of the war were a quarrel between Athens and Corinth over the colonies of Corcyra and Poteidaea and the decision by Athens to exclude merchants of Megara from Athenian markets. By themselves, these actions did little damage to Corinth or its ally Sparta, but they gained significance as part of a long series of imperialist actions by Athens.

The strategies of both sides reflected the nature of their economies and armed forces. Pericles' war plan was to abandon the Athenian rural areas, concentrate the population inside the city walls, and rely on his navy to harass the enemy and to keep the sea lanes open. The Peloponnesian League had only small naval forces—mostly Corinthian—and Pericles could be confident that his city could be supplied by sea. But in the second year of the war (429 B.C.) a plague broke out in Athens, perhaps as a result of the crowded conditions. It killed a considerable portion of the population, including Pericles himself. Afterwards, no leader was able to build the kind of political power that Pericles had enjoyed, and the city was unable to maintain a consistent policy or plan of action. Nonetheless, the Athenians were successful enough to force Sparta to make peace in 421 B.C.

The hope of this truce was undermined by the unstable politics of Athens itself. Politicians sought support by promising a new, victorious war with Sparta, and such promises soon led to a reopening of hostilities. In the new conflict, the Athenians took greater and greater risks as competing politicians tried to secure their own positions by bold military action. The culmination of this course was a disastrous attack on Syracuse between 415 and 413 B.C., which nearly destroyed Athenian naval power. Further losses forced Athens to surrender to Sparta in 404 B.C. Spartan domination of Greece did not last long. By 370 B.C., Athens and many other cities had managed to make themselves independent, and Sparta was too weak even to defend the Peloponnesus.

THE GREEK WORLD IN THE FOURTH CENTURY B.C.

In 404–403 B.C., Sparta had placed its agents in cities throughout Greece, but almost immediately many of the cities asserted their independence and threw out the Spartans and their local allies. In the meantime, the Persians again became involved in Greek affairs. The Greek victory over Persia in 479 B.C. had freed Greece and the Ionian cities from Persian power, but the Persians still controlled most of Asia Minor; they had a provincial capital at Sardis, less than 100 kilometers from the Ionian coast. Shortly after the Peloponnesian War, the Persians were again interfering in Greek politics, and Persian power was a factor in Greek politics throughout the fourth century B.C.

In Greece, Sparta struggled to maintain its hegemony while in Boeotia, Ionia, and elsewhere new leagues of cities were formed to counter Spartan power. In 395 B.C., Thebes (the leading city of the Boeotian League), Athens, Argos, and Corinth joined in a war against Sparta. Both sides appealed to Persia, who finally gave support to the Spartans. In 388 B.C., King Artaxerxes II of Persia (r. 404–359/58 B.C.) proposed a peace treaty that would preserve the Peloponnesian League and Sparta's power while guaranteeing autonomy to all the other Greek cities. This grant of autonomy would undermine the anti-Spartan leagues by preventing leading cities like Thebes and Athens from creating powerful, unified leagues under their authority. The final text of the treaty recognized some existing subordinations of cities. A second new feature of the treaty was that it imposed a common peace. Until that time, treaties had sealed the peace between two states or leagues. This peace covered all the cities of Greece, and, thereafter, most treaties attempted to establish a common peace.

Between 385 and 378 B.C., Sparta outraged Greek opinion by intervening forcefully in the affairs of several cities, and in 378 B.C. Athens formed the Second Sea League. The cities in the new league stood on an equal footing consistent with the treaty of 388 B.C., but by the middle of the century Athens had asserted its authority and subordinated some of its allies. Through the middle of the century, Greece was divided into several leagues, of which the most important were the Peloponnesian League, the Second Sea League, and the Boeotian League. Greek politics was a maelstrom of alliances, wars, and peace conferences; Persia's interference affected the outcome of most conflicts. Then, in the early 350s B.C., Philip II of Macedon (r. 359–336 B.C.) began an aggressive policy of expansion. Macedon was a landlocked pastoral kingdom north of Thessaly in central Greece. By 354 B.C., Philip had gained access to the Aegean, and in the next decade he pushed east into Thrace and west into Epirus. In the late 340s B.C., he controlled Thessaly.

In all these activities, Philip threatened the major Greek cities. His move into Thessaly was of great concern to the Boeotians, who sought allies against him. Once established in central Greece, he became a major participant in the affairs of the great shrine of Delphi, which was administered by an ancient league of the Greek cities. In Thrace, he threatened Athens, which had to control the Bosporus and Propontis to ensure the safety of its grain fleet. The Athenians were wholly dependent on grain from the Black Sea, which was shipped south once a year in great fleets of around 200 ships. Philip's move west also alarmed the Persians, but notwithstanding the opposition of Athens and Persia, he was able to gain control of the Propontis, and in 340 B.C. he seized the grain fleet opening war with Athens. In the next two years, Philip campaigned against the Athenians and their allies, and in 338 B.C. decisively defeated them.

The treaty ending the war was dictated by Philip, but he could not completely have his way. The Athenians still had the largest fleet in the Aegean, and, while the Second Sea League was disbanded by the treaty, Athens held on to some of its overseas possessions. In many Greek cities, Philip installed garrisons to preserve the common peace he had imposed. From this point on, Greece was dominated by the Macedonians, although its cities remained independent and continued their habit of arranging constantly changing alliances. The Macedonians kept a close eye on events and intervened when it suited their interests; otherwise, they left the Greeks to their political games.

Alexander the Great, 336–323 B.C.

Philip was assassinated in 336 B.C., and his 20-year-old son Alexander succeeded him. The young king was conceited, overbearing, undisciplined, temperamental, charming, and brilliant. His soldiers idolized him.

Alexander set out to complete his father's plan to unify all of Greece and to lead a Greek-Macedonian army against the Persians. In 334 B.C., he crossed the Hellespont with an army and began a career of conquest during which he proved himself to be one of the premier military geniuses in history. He defeated a Persian force in Asia Minor, then proceeded to Syria and defeated a new army led by the Persian king himself (333 B.C.). The next year Alexander invaded Egypt, where he founded the city of Alexandria, destined to become one of the great cities of the Mediterranean world. Following ancient tradition, the Egyptian priests declared Alexander to be the son of the god Amon, and Alexander made this claim to divinity part of his political propaganda.

After gaining control of the eastern Mediterranean, Alexander defeated the remnants of the Persian army and declared himself king of Persia. This victory opened the East to him, and he marched north through the Transoxiana into Turkestan, on the eastern boundary of the Persian Empire. From this crossroads of the Eurasian continent, he led his army south into the Indus Valley in the northwest corner of

Greek coin bearing the likeness of King Philip, conqueror of Athens.

India. Alexander campaigned in northwestern India in 327–326 B.C. and succeeded in forcing the rulers of this region into alliance with him. He built at least two Greek cities there and planned to expand his conquest, but his army mutinied, and he had to turn back.

Alexander's military conquests were the basis of a bold plan to build a Greek empire. Throughout his dominions, the young king established Greek colonies and encouraged his garrisons and colonists to marry into the local populations. In these new centers, of which Alexandria in Egypt was only the most successful, Greek language and culture became the imperial culture. Alexander hellenized the upper classes of the eastern seaboard of the Mediterranean, Egypt, Mesopotamia, Persia, and northwest India, and, for 800 years, Greek culture unified the Middle East without supplanting the native cultures that continued to flourish among the peasants and urban lower classes.

Alexander himself did not live to know how successful his plan was. He

Idealized statue of Alexander, probably the work of an artist of Pergamum in Asia Minor.

Alexander's Empire 336–323 B.C.

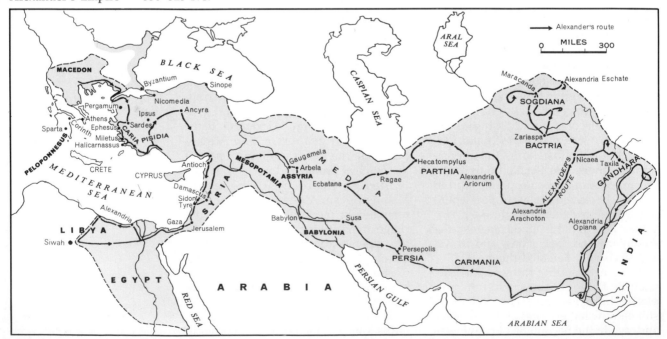

died of a fever in 323 B.C., at the age of 33. The political unity based on his military successes quickly disintegrated. His Macedonian generals fought to gain control of the various regions, and soon these men called themselves kings. The Alexandrian empire was therefore succeeded by a number of independent Greek kingdoms that maintained control over the native populations. Macedon, under Antigonus, continued to dominate the Greek peninsula, but its power over Asia Minor and the Balkans steadily declined. In Egypt, Ptolemeus established himself as king in Alexandria, which developed into a city of a million people. Situated in the Nile Delta, Alexandria profited from the international trade that Alexander's conquests had opened up, and it became a leading center of Greek culture. Its library was world famous.

The old Persian territories fell to Seleucus, who controlled a vast territory stretching from the Mediterranean to the Indus Valley. Beyond the Hindu Kush, the Seleucids could not maintain Alexander's conquest, and, after a war with the new Maurya dynasty of the Ganges Valley, the northwest corner of the Indian subcontinent became part of the first Indian empire. Nonetheless, the treaty that ended the war became the basis for a friendly trade relationship between the Seleucid kingdom and India, and this preserved contact between the Mediterranean Basin and India.

THE HELLENISTIC ERA, 323–*ca.* 30 B.C.

The political disunity that followed Alexander's death did not interfere with the functioning of a great Greek cultural commonwealth. All the successor states were dominated by Greeks and by natives who imitated the Greek way of life. Throughout the east, peasants and the urban lower

The Partitioning of Alexander's Empire   *ca.* 300 B.C.

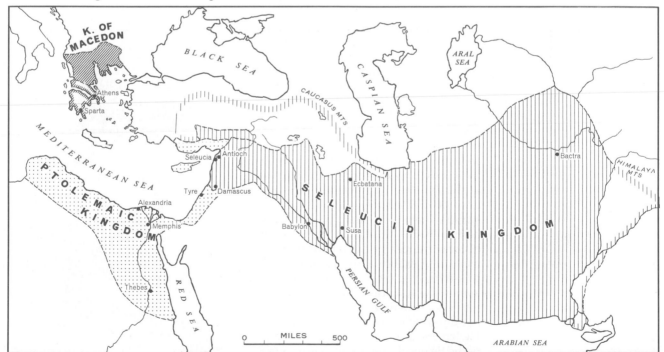

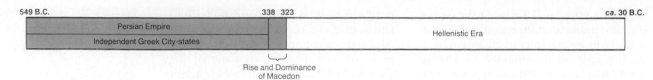

| 549 B.C. | | | 338 323 | | ca. 30 B.C. |

Persian Empire

Independent Greek City-states

Hellenistic Era

Rise and Dominance
of Macedon

classes held fast to their native cultures and languages, but scholars, administrators, and businessmen all used Greek and were guided, to a significant degree, by Greek ideas and customs. This era of Greek influence in the eastern Mediterranean and throughout the Middle East is known as the Hellenistic period, from the name the Greeks gave to themselves—Hellenes. Politically, it ended in 30 B.C., when Rome annexed Egypt, the last nominally independent Hellenistic state. But the cultural unity of the Hellenistic world lasted far longer; it was broken only after the Arabs conquered Syria and Egypt in the seventh century A.D. The influence of Hellenistic civilization survived even that conquest.

Hellenistic culture flourished especially in Egypt. Alexandria, the emporium of the eastern Mediterranean Basin and base for trade with India, was the wealthiest city in the world. Its ruling family, the Ptolemies, encouraged artists and scholars and built, next to the palace, a magnificent temple to the Muses (called the Museum) for the study of the arts and sciences. The famous library stood next to the Museum. Scholars from all parts of the Hellenistic world came to Alexandria, which soon rivaled Athens as a center of Greek culture. But Alexandria was more than a Greek city. Native Egyptians made up most of its population, and in its streets one could hear virtually all the languages of the ancient world. There were more Jews in Alexandria than in Jerusalem, and the city became the center of Hellenistic Judaism. In Alexandria the Hebrew Bible was translated into Greek, and this version of the scriptures became the Christian Old Testament.

Alexandria was by far the largest Hellenistic city, but Antioch, the capital of the Seleucid Empire, was also a great city and trade center. In the west, the isle of Rhodes and city of Pergamum (near the site of ancient Troy) prospered as transshipment points for goods headed for the Aegean and Black Seas, respectively, and Pergamum attracted a group of very able artists. Dozens of other Hellenistic cities took part in commercial, intellectual, and artistic activity.

Art and Literature

Hellenistic art naturally differed from Greek art of the fifth century B.C.; it had lost the serenity and self-confidence of the sculpture and architecture of that period. Hellenistic art was emotive, depicting the pathos of human

Old Peasant Woman. **Sculpture from the Hellenistic era is more emotional and realistic than art of the fifth century** B.C.

life. Occasionally, it sought to impress by mere size, as in the gigantic statue that stood astride the harbor of Rhodes or the Mausoleum at Halicarnassus. But at its best it created works that still impress us with their beauty and power. The Winged Victory of Samothrace, the Venus of Milo, and the Dying Gaul of Pergamum are sculptures probably better known than the great statues of the Parthenon. Hellenistic art became increasingly realistic. Paintings, mosaics, and statues depicted everyday life with precision, and, while such works are not great art, they are immensely helpful to historians. They show men and women as they were, and life as it was actually lived.

The literature of the age is not as well known as the art. Some Hellenistic poets were very good, but often their work is buried in a mass of mediocre followers. Theocritus (fl. *ca.* 270 B.C.) wrote good lyric poetry concerning pastoral subjects, the *Idylls*, but so many followers imitated him that it is difficult to recognize his originality. Apollonius (*ca.* 295–215 B.C.), who may have been head librarian at Alexandria, wrote an epic in the tradition of Homer, the *Argonautica*, which has some excellent parts, but, again, later poets repeated his work *ad nauseum*. Perhaps the most important writer of the period was Menander (*ca.* 342–292 B.C.), a dramatist who wrote comedies that have amused audiences for 2,000 years. His work had a great influence on Roman comedy, and, through them, his plots influenced Shakespeare and inspired modern musical comedy.

Alexandria was also the place where literary scholarship was born. Aristarchus of Samothrace (head of the Alexandria library *ca.* 180–*ca.* 145 B.C.) was a literary scholar who produced editions of Homer, Hesiod, Pindar, and other great poets of the Archaic and classical ages and wrote a great many commentaries on ancient literature. All educated Alexandrians memorized Homer, and a common parlor game involved guests taking turns telling a

The Winged Victory of Samothrace.

story using only lines and half-lines from the Homeric epics.

Science

Many scholars would say that the most striking achievements of the Hellenistic age were in science. Hellenistic scientists performed some remarkable experiments and developed theories that foreshadowed the discoveries of the sixteenth and seventeenth centuries after Christ. In medicine and other sciences, Hellenistic writers gathered all the knowledge and lore of the past and added observations and findings of their own. Therefore, their work is of supreme importance both for the advances they made and for the transmission to later ages of Babylonian, Egyptian, and classical Greek knowledge.

The Hellenistic thinkers who made these advances considered science to be philosophical speculation on the nature of the universe and, therefore, connected to other fields of philosophy and to religion—all of them ways of finding out about the visible and invisible world. Herophilus (4th–3rd century B.C.) was a great anatomist in Alexandria. He discovered the nervous system and came very close to proposing a theory of circulation of the blood, but his work did not affect the practice of contemporary medicine. Aristarchus of Samos (b. *ca.* 320 B.C.) was the astronomer who first proposed that the planets revolve around the sun. His work influenced Copernicus in the sixteenth century, but because Aristarchus thought that the planets followed circular orbits, his theory did not explain the data of observation, and his immediate successors abandoned his idea. Eratosthenes (second half of 3rd century B.C.), who was another head of the Alexandrian library, wrote poetry, history, and literary commentaries, but he is best known as a great mathematician who very accurately calculated the circumference of the earth.

Most of this brilliant work sank into oblivion—it was a long time before anyone used Eratosthenes' calculation to plan a circumnavigation of the earth— because men continued to use the older scientific treatises of Aristotle. His doctrines remained the standard explanation of natural phenomena throughout the Roman and much of the medieval period. The first to take up Hellenistic science were Moslem scholars, and it was through them that it reached the West in the thirteenth century.

The most important exception to this rule was mathematics, which had immediate practical use. Euclid (fl. *ca.* 300 B.C. in Alexandria) created a coherent system of geometry out of the scattered theorems and proofs of centuries of work, and his work has been studied carefully from his day to ours. Archimedes of Syracuse (278?–212 B.C.) worked out the basic problems of mass and motion. He also perfected the theory of machines, such as the compound pulley. Because his work was important in everyday life, and particularly in the construction of war machines, it entered the mainstream of Mediterranean civilization. However, his theoretical work was soon forgotten. When his works were rediscovered by Europeans in the thirteenth century, they became one of the foundations of the scientific revolution.

Philosophy and Religion

Hellenistic philosophy and religion reacted to the conditions of life in what seemed to contemporaries to be a worldwide society. No longer was life circumscribed within the tiny city-state of the classical period. Hellenistic people were part of a culture that stretched from the western Mediterranean to India, and their lives could be affected by events unforeseen and never fully understood. In such a world, individual effort seemed useless, and Hellenistic philosophy and religion responded to the need of people to find meaning in their actions and lives.

The three most popular schools of philosophy of the period emphasized private virtues and self-discipline, not civic participation. Stoicism, founded on the thought of Zeno of Citium (fl. *ca.* 300 B.C.), propounded a universal law, which bound all men. Since all men were subject to this law, all were brothers. Everyone from slave to king must do his duty in the position in which he found himself. Power and wealth, human desires and affections, were dangerous distractions. Public office was not to be sought, though it might be one's duty to accept it. The ideal existence was that of a private citizen, unaffected by political and other events. Epicureanism, based on the philosophy of Epicurus (341–270 B.C.), held that the wise man should seek pleasure, which stemmed from right conduct, serenity of mind, and moderation in all things. Because political ambition and pursuit of wealth caused more pain than they were worth, the wise man avoided strong attachments to family, friends, or state. Cynicism stemmed from the thought of Antisthenes (b. *ca.* 440 B.C.) who taught in the gymnasium called the Cynosarges in Athens. The Cynics doubted the possibility of any true knowledge and saw no sense in trying to save a world trapped in hopeless ignorance. For them, the wise man should not worry about wealth and power; he should find peace of mind by withdrawing from worldly concerns.

Philosophy was an occupation of the upper classes, and of a small portion even of them. Ordinary people sought solace in the spiritual satisfactions of the mystery cults. These cults absorbed much from the cultures submerged under Hellenistic civilization and traveled throughout the Hellenistic world. They were eclectic religions that borrowed easily from one another and from older religious traditions of the Mediterranean and Middle East. Each was based on elaborate and secret ceremonies and a claim that initiates, who went through ritual purification of their sins, would be introduced to the mystery that held the key to communion with the god of the cult. Especially popular were the Dionysian rituals from the Greek cities, Isis worship from Egypt, and the cult of the Great Mother from Asia Minor. The cult communities were small, mystic cells that offered their members a sense of security and personal worth and a promise of eternal life of the soul, in contrast to the feelings of helplessness and the harshness of Hellenistic life. The cults did not reach out to the world, but, like the philosophical schools, they turned inward and provided an escape from senseless reality.

The Fall of the Hellenistic States

The Hellenistic states were never militarily strong, and most were weakened by the cultural diversity and internal dissensions of their populations. The Seleucid Empire soon lost Bactria and Persia, and in 167 B.C. the Jews, led by the Maccabees, regained their independence. When Rome became the dominant power in the Mediterranean about 200 B.C., it was easy for it to annex the Hellenistic states one by one. Rome had effective control of the eastern Mediterranean by 146 B.C., and with the seizure of Egypt in 30 B.C., it had acquired all of Alexander's empire except Persia.

But while the political framework of Hellenistic civilization rapidly eroded and finally collapsed, its influence remained. The Romans greatly admired Hellenistic culture and borrowed heavily from it. Greek continued to be the language of the upper classes in the Middle East, and Athens and Alexandria became the culture centers of the Roman Empire. It also influenced Moslem culture, which absorbed Hellenistic populations during the seventh century, when the Arabs created a great Mediterranean and middle eastern empire. In a sense, Hellenistic civilization never ended, though its sphere of influence began to shrink after A.D. 500. In Greece, Asia Minor, and the Levant, it gradually and imperceptibly changed into Byzantine culture, and Byzantine culture only ended after the fall of Constantinople in A.D. 1453.

The Greeks were creators of a new vision of the world. In their science, arts, and literature, they focused on the natural world and on human behavior. The idea that logical thinking could produce a true knowledge of the world, ethics, and politics led to the foundation of traditions of scientific, historical, and literary scholarship and of politics that continue to flourish in our civilization. Further, in the political life of the *poleis*, the Greeks gained a unique consciousness of social and political organization. They were the first to think about the constitution of the state and to compare different constitutions. They were also the first to make constitutional ideology a basis of foreign policy. The attempts of Athens and Sparta to impose their constitutions on their allies were entirely new in their day, and the connection between alliance and constitution was not made again until the nineteenth century. In the twentieth century, it has been one of the principal features of American foreign policy.

Suggestions for Further Reading

General

J. B. Bury, *A History of Greece*, rev. ed. R. Meiggs (1975), is the most comprehensive history of the ancient Greeks. A. A. Andrewes, *The Greeks* (1967), and F. J. Frost, *Greek Society* (1972), are interpretive works. Complete texts of all the Greek writers are available in the *Loeb Classical Library*. For Herodotus and Thucydides, see Herodotus, *The Persian Wars*, trans. G. Rawlinson (1942), and *The Histories*, trans. A. de Sélincourt (1954); Thucydides, *The Peloponnesian War* (1951).

The Mycenean Era and Dark Age

On Bronze Age and Minoan civilization, see E. Vermeule, *Greece in the Bronze Age* (1964), and L. R. Palmer, *Mycenaeans and Minoans* (1965). See also A. E. Samuel, *The Mycenaeans in History* (1966). For the period of the Trojan War, see D. L. Page, *History and the Homeric Iliad* (1959).

The Greek World from 800 to 500 B.C.

A. R. Burn, *The Lyric Age of Greece* (1960), presents a detailed history of the politics and literature of Archaic Greece. See also M. I. Finley, *The World of Odysseus* (1954). On the Greek cities of Ionia and of Sicily and Italy, see J. M. Cook, *Greeks in Ionia and the East* (1962), and A. G. Woodhead, *Greeks in the West* (1962). On the political development of Greece in this period, see H. Michell, *Sparta* (1952); A. A. Andrewes, *The Greek Tyrants* (1965); W. G. Forrest, *The Emergence of Greek Democracy* (1966); and A. Lintott, *Violence, Civil Strife and Revolution in the Classical City: 750–330 B.C.* (1982). In general, see R. Sealey, *A History of the Greek City States, 700–338 B.C.* (1976).

The Fifth Century B.C.

Studies of the Persian Wars include A. R. Burn, *Persia and the Greeks* (1962), and C. Hignett, *Xerxes' Invasion of Greece* (1963). On Athens in the Golden Age, see C. A. Robinson, *Athens in the Age of Pericles* (1959); V. Ehrenberg, *From Solon to Socrates* (1968); and W. R. Connor, *The New Politicians of Athens* (1971). On the economic life of the period, see M. I. Finley, *The Ancient Economy* (1973), and K. D. White, *Greek and Roman Technology* (1984). For a comprehensive history of the Peloponnesian War, see B. W. Henderson, *The Great War Between Athens and Sparta* (1927); D. Kagan, *The Origins of the Peloponnesian War* (1969); *The Archidamian War* (1974); and *The Peace of Nicias and the Sicilian Expedition* (1981).

Social History

For the social history of Greece, see the studies in M. I. Finley, *Studies in Ancient Society* (1974); S. B. Pomeroy, *Goddesses, Whores, Wives and Slaves: Women in Classical Antiquity* (1975); M. Balme, "Attitudes to Work and Leisure in Ancient Greece," *Greece and Rome* 31 (1984) 140–52; J. C. Billigmeier and J. A. Turner, "The Socioeconomic Roles of Women in Mycenaean Greece," *Women's Studies* 8 (1981) 3–20; E. S. Stigers, "Sappho's Private World," *Women's Studies* 8 (1981) 47–63; S. G. Cole, "Could Greek Women Read and Write?" *Wom-en's Studies* 8 (1981) 129–55. For a general study of Athenian society in the classical age, see J. W. Roberts, *City of Sokrates* (1984).

Art, Literature, and Drama

For a thorough history of Greek literature, see G. Murray, *The Literature of Ancient Greece* (1956), and A. Lesky, *A History of Greek Literature* (1966). For an introduction to Greek art, see J. Boardman, *Greek Art* (1964), and G. M. A. Richter, *A Handbook of Greek Art* (1974).

Alexander the Great and the Hellenistic Era

The principal ancient sources on Alexander the Great are the Anabasis of Alexander by Flavius Arrian and a much later biography by Plutarch, of which there are many editions. For good modern histories of Alexander and his period, see A. R. Burn, *Alexander the Great and the Hellenistic World* (1947), and U. Wilcken, *Alexander the Great* (1932). For the Hellenistic period, see M. I. Rostovtzeff, *Social and Economic History of the Hellenistic World* (1941), and W. W. Tarn and G. T. Griffith, *Hellenistic Civilization* (1952). On the social and economic significance of Hellenistic piracy, see J. J. Gabbert, "Piracy in the Early Hellenistic Period: A Career Open to Talents," *Greece and Rome* 33 (1986) 156–63.

3

Rome and the Unification of the Mediterranean World

*A*fter the death of Alexander the Great (323 B.C.), a new power rose to prominence in the Mediterranean world. This was Rome, a city near the western coast of south central Italy. From the standpoint of the traditional powers in the eastern Mediterranean—Greece, Macedon, Asia Minor, and Persia—the rise of Rome was entirely unexpected. But Rome, a small city facing the western Mediterranean, succeeded in unifying the entire Mediterranean Basin under its government. Having conquered Greece, the Romans came under the influence of its civilization, and Roman intellectuals and artists preserved Greek philosophy, science, and art for later civilizations. The Roman Empire also became the milieu in which Christianity, one of the great world religions, came into being. From the Romans themselves later civilizations received a magnificent legal system. This system and the constitutional framework of Roman government became one of the principal bases of western government and law.

The people of Rome belonged to a group of Indo-European tribes, later called Latins, that migrated from central Europe into the Italian peninsula about 2000 B.C.—that is, about the same time that Minoan civilization was becoming an important influence in the eastern Mediterranean. The Italian peninsula is a narrow land shaped like a boot and divided lengthwise by a mountain chain, the Apennines, which is a spur of the Alps. In Roman times, the peninsula was heavily forested. In the northeast, the Lombard plain is drained by the Po River and its tributaries, which flow east to the Adriatic Sea. Along the western coast is a long, low territory through which several rivers, the Arno and the Tiber being the most important, flow west from the mountains to the Tyrrhenian Sea. In the south, there are more plains, some of them quite high. This is a region of excellent harbors. Lying only a few miles off the toe of the boot is Sicily, a large island. The dominant feature of the island is a high plain that supplied

Opposite: The lid of a bronze container from Praeneste, in Latinum (fourth century B.C.). The handle represents two warriors carrying a slain comrade.

69

Etruscan sarcophagus (third century B.C.) showing the deceased couple reclining on a couch and pouring libations as if at their own funeral banquet.

grain to many parts of the ancient world.

THE ORIGINS OF ROME

Foundations

By 1000 B.C., the Italian tribes, which included the Latins, had settled most of the peninsula and had begun the task of clearing the forests and developing its agricultural potential. Soon after 800 B.C., new commercially minded civilizations developed in the north and south. In the north, the Etruscans built fortified hill towns in the Lombard plain, in the Apennines, and along the western coastal region down to Campania, the plain inland from the Bay of Naples. In the south, colonists from Greece founded many cities and established control over the Italic tribes in their neighborhoods. The Greeks also settled the coast of Sicily.

The Etruscans were instrumental in the early history of Rome. They appear to have been non-Indo-European na-tives of the Italian peninsula, who in-dependently developed a high civiliza-tion. Modern scholars cannot identify them completely because they have not been able to decipher Etruscan writing. The Etruscans evolved an exotic and powerful artistic tradition in painting, terra-cotta, bronze, and precious met-als. Their political organization was, like Mycenaean and classical Greece, based on independent city-states. Through trade they came into contact with the Greeks and Phoenicians, and their culture was influenced by these eastern civilizations.

One feature of Etruscan society makes them stand out among the an-cient peoples of the Mediterranean. They held women in high repute. Their funerary art—which is mostly what survives—shows men and women as equals, and because of the prominence and freedom of women in their society, the Greeks considered the Etruscans decadent. Like other societies of the time, Etruscan society was aristocratic. Thus, it was based on the family, and, for the Etruscans, the importance of the family made the union between men and women significant and gave honor to both partners.

Rome originated as an Etruscan-type city during the late seventh or early sixth century B.C. There is now some controversy about whether the coalescing of the city was done by the Etruscans themselves or by local villagers trying to protect themselves against Etruscan expansion. One sign that the latter was the case is that the Indo-European Romans did not treat women as did the Etruscans. But whatever the origins of Rome, the Etruscans did eventually gain control of the city and its region, and throughout the sixth century B.C., an Etruscan dynasty, the Tarquins, ruled from Rome. About 510 B.C. (Romans later fixed the date as 509, but it remains uncertain), the local aristocracy ousted the Tarquins and established a republic controlled by the aristocratic families, the patricians.

The Republican Constitution

The new constitution was carefully wrought to prevent the rise of a new king or a tyrant. Two elected magistrates, the consuls, held chief executive power, while other officials, also elected in twos or threes, managed the treasury and presided over the legal system. The important magistrates held office for only one year at a time. In an emergency, the constitution allowed for the establishment of a dictator, who could hold authority only until the crisis had passed. In no case could a dictator rule for more than six months.

The electorate of citizens—as in Greece, only males were citizens—was organized as an assembly, which in turn was based on the centuriate, the system of military organization, probably going back to the Etruscan kings. In its original form, the centuriate was made up of a series of units of 100 men. Under the Republic, the citizens were organized into voting centuries of ir-

regular size. This was an important new feature because it gave the patricians control of the assembly.

The assembly was divided into five classes based on wealth, and each class had a certain number of centuries. The wealthiest class had 80 centuries, the four lower classes had, in total, 90 centuries. However, there were classes in the assembly outside the five main ones. The equestrians (men of the first class of wealth who served in the cavalry), artisans (who were of the second class), and even proletarians (landless men who were not in any class) had centuries in the assembly, but again the numbers were tilted toward the upper class. The equestrians had eighteen centuries, the artisans two, and the proletarians one. In practice, the equestrians voted with the first class, and together they held the majority— 98 centuries out of 193. The assembly elected the magistrates, had legislative power and the right to declare war, and sat as the ultimate court of appeal in capital cases.

In normal times, the patricians governed this small Republic. Only they could be elected to the magistracies, and they controlled the assembly not only through the centuriate system, but also through a client system, in which the patrician families gave economic and other support to small farmers and city people in return for political loyalty. In addition, the patricians formed a council of former magistrates, the Senate (from *senex* meaning elder), which wielded great authority in matters of state. In fact, until the late fourth century B.C., it seems that no act of the assembly was executed by the magistrates until the Senate had approved it.

Nonetheless, the plebeians—the common citizens—gradually gained important concessions from the patricians. About 450 B.C., the plebeians forced the ruling class to issue a written code of law, the Twelve Tables. This transition from unwritten law—always controlled by the aristocratic families—

Etruscan kitchen utensils: a water bottle and a spoon.

to written law had already taken place in many Greek cities, and, in Rome as in Greece, it made the mass of citizens more secure. Later, the plebeians won the right to elect their own magistrates, the tribunes, to represent their interests. Still, until the last century of the Republic's existence (*ca.* 130–30 B.C.), the Senate remained the dominant force in Roman political life.

This was a small, regulated world. The constitution, which was not written down, but was carefully preserved in the memory of the Senate and people, operated as an extension of society, rather than as an impersonal legal system. The Senate's influence over the elected officials rested on class and family ties, as well as on the normal pattern of a political career. Every patrician who rose to office, and it was the mark of a successful career and life to serve a term as consul, would for most of his career exercise political authority and influence through participation in the Senate. As a result, the debates in the Senate usually determined policy and attracted more attention from contemporaries than the actions and pronouncements of the magistrates or the assembly.

Roman government also united military and civilian government. As with the aristocracy of Greece, military leadership was one of the ancient functions of the Roman aristocracy, going back to the time of the kings, and neither the Romans nor anyone else in the ancient world thought to separate these two aspects of government. But the Romans did begin the process that has led to the modern view that military and civil functions differ and should be separated. While the consuls were the commanders-in-chief of the army, their military authority was valid only outside the city limits. Thus, in Rome, where policy was made by the Senate and magistrates, civil government held sway. The Romans did not want the army to interfere in the governmental process and prevented it by ending military discipline at the city walls. In the field, the citizen-soldier was a sol-

dier subject to the strict discipline of the order of battle, but, in the city, he was a citizen free to voice his opinion on matters of state and to vote as he wished. Because the consuls held office, both as magistrates and generals, for only one year, no one could build up political authority based on military authority.

During the fifth century B.C., the offices of state became fixed. From the beginning, the consuls had had assistants, called *quaestors*, who were generally up-and-coming young men of the patrician class. By the middle of the fifth century, the quaestors had become independent magistrates, elected by the assembly. In 421 B.C., there were four quaestors, two in charge of the public treasury and two assisted the consuls in handling military finances. A little earlier, by about 435 B.C, two *praetors* had been established. These officials were responsible for the administration of justice. One handled the cases of citizens and governed the city when the consuls were away. The other handled the cases of foreigners. Each year, the new praetors would issue edicts describing the kinds of cases they would hear, and these edicts became, along with the Twelve Tables and assembly legislation, the basis of Roman law. After centuries of evolution, the edicts became fixed as long legal codes issued annually with only minor changes. By that time, in the first century B.C., the law of the edicts was the pride of Rome.

The successful patrician followed a career regulated by the constitution. The able young aristocrat could be elected quaestor at the age of 25. At 30, he was eligible for election as praetor, and at 35, he could stand for the consulship. One could serve in these offices more than once, but in 342 B.C. the assembly passed a law prohibiting anyone from holding an office, particularly the consulship, within ten years of the last time he had held it. This law, similar in intent to the limitation of American presidents to two terms, soon became totally impractical because Rome became engaged in long campaigns to conquer Italy. In 325 B.C., to get around the law, the Senate permitted a consul to continue as general after his term expired, not by permitting his reelection, but by making him *pro consule,* an officer who acted *for* or *as* the consul. In time, the proconsulate became a major part of the power structure of the state.

The Republic had been founded on the rebellion against the Tarquins carried out by the patricians, and it was entirely in the control of the patricians. But the plebeians did not accept this situation calmly. Under the kings, the ordinary citizens could seek royal protection against aristocratic aggression, and the natural competition between the king and aristocracy often made the king a sympathetic hearer of complaints. Under the Republic, the aristocrats were unchecked, and Roman society, always rough, became rougher still. The powerful often used their positions to coerce their neighbors or get advantages for themselves. The wealthy were not content with their riches. They wanted more, and morality played no role in their economic actions. The small farmer was subject to economic pressures from his wealthier neighbors and, often, to physical attacks aimed at forcing him to become a client or simply at getting control of his land. Neither the city nor the countryside was a quiet, well-ordered world, where life and property were safe.

For the small man, this difficult world was made nearly impossible by the control that the patricians had over the state. The plebeian stood before a patrician judge, very likely related to his opponent by blood, marriage, clientage, or politics. Furthermore, under the kings and in the first decades of the Republic, the law was unwritten, and, consequently, it was controlled by the magistrates and their class. It was what they said it was. This situation brought forth a great prolonged struggle between the two orders.

The plebeians made a first advance about 470 B.C., when they forced the patricians to set up the tribunes as plebeian officers. An assembly of plebeians elected the tribunes to guard the interests of the order, and it was a tribune who first proposed the writing down of the law in the late 450s B.C., leading to the creation of the Twelve Tables. This great success was followed by another. In 446 B.C., the old prohibition of intermarriage between patricians and plebeians was ended. Even

Plebeian Reforms

Enslavement for debt was a constant threat to the poorer peasants of the ancient world. In this passage, the Roman historian Livy (59 B.C.– A.D. 17) shows how the plebeians gained constitutional safeguards against enslavement for debt by refusing to fight in a time of emergency.

An old man suddenly presented himself in the Forum. . . . Though cruelly changed from what he had once been, he was recognized, and people began to tell each other, compassionately, that he was an old soldier who had once commanded a company and served with distinction. . . . "While I was on service," he said, "during the Sabine War, my crops were ruined by enemy raids, and my cottage was burnt. Everything I had was taken, including my cattle. Then, when I was least able to do so, I was expected to pay taxes, and fell, consequently, into debt. Interest on the borrowed money increased my burden; I lost the land which my father and my grandfather had owned before me, and . . . I was finally seized by my creditor and reduced to slavery. . . ."

The man's story . . . caused a tremendous uproar, which spread swiftly from the Forum through every part of the city. . . .

On top of this highly critical situation, came the alarming news . . . that a Volscian army was marching on Rome. . . . For [the plebeians] it seemed like an intervention of providence to crush the pride of the Senate; they went about urging their friends to refuse military service. . . . [One of the consuls then issued] an edict, to the effect that it should be illegal . . . [to] imprison a Roman citizen. . . . As a result of the edict, all "bound" debtors who were present gave their names on the spot, . . . and in the ensuing fight with the Volscians no troops did more distinguished service.

From Livy, *The Early History of Rome,* trans. by Aubrey de Sélincourt (Baltimore: Penguin Books, 1960), pp. 113–16.

though patrician families were slow to accept marriages with plebeians, the new openness had a great effect in the long run.

But the most important issue was eligibility for the magistracies. The plebeians wanted to hold offices that had military authority, but the patricians put up a fierce resistance. About 444 B.C., a compromise was worked out under which a military tribunate was established. Each year, the Senate decided whether circumstances warranted the granting of military authority to the three military tribunes or the two consuls; with these decision makers, the choice was never in doubt. In addition, the patricians controlled the assembly, which elected the military tribunes, and no plebeian actually held the office until 400 B.C., when a difficult campaign made it absolutely necessary to choose the best qualified men, regardless of order.

By then, plebeians had finally begun to break down the barrier to election to the regular magistracies. In 421 B.C., they became eligible for election to the quaestorship, although the patricians still controlled the assembly. The struggle for the consulate lasted until 367 B.C., when plebeians became eligible for the highest office and, consequently, the military tribunate was abolished. Under the new law, one consul was to be patrician and one plebeian, but no plebeian was actually elected until 340.

The extraordinary length of these struggles gives an idea of the conservatism of the Roman community and state. The struggles lasted for generations, and, throughout, the patricians remained bitterly opposed to sharing power. Every concession resulted from the necessities connected with war— first, wars for survival of the new Republic and, later, wars of expansion over strong enemies. The tradition of aristocracy was extremely strong in Rome. It was a community created and governed by a small class of men who considered themselves best among the citizenry. As the best men, they had the obligation to govern and protect, and they had the right to maintain and build up their own positions. For, as they saw it, on the maintenance of patrician power depended the prosperity of the Roman state, which benefited all citizens.

THE GROWTH OF ROMAN ITALY, *ca.* 500–265 B.C.

Rome's prosperity rested on an agricultural economy, and one of the city's continuing characteristics was the long persistence of rural values. In this respect, the culture of Rome was similar to that of Sparta, and Rome also developed a strong military tradition based on an army of citizen-farmers. This development was a response to competition among the city-states of central and northern Italy.

When the Republic was founded, Rome controlled a territory of about 300 square miles, an area with a diameter of under 20 miles. The soil of this region was only moderately fertile; Rome was famous for its malarial marshes. Thus, Rome's wealth had to be founded on a wider territory.

Around the city, in Latium, were other Latin and Etruscan communities which the Etruscan kings of Rome had dominated, and the Republic inherited this domination. Beyond this small circuit, the city was surrounded by Etruscans, Latins, and other Italic communi-

Cities of the Latin League   *ca.* 400 B.C.

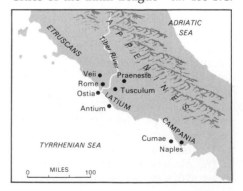

Independent Roman Kingdom	Etruscan Dominance	Rome Conquers Italian Peninsula	Punic Wars	Rome Conquers Entire Mediterranean Area

ties and tribes. Southern Italy was under the power of the Greek colonies founded centuries earlier.

About 496 B.C., the Latin cities immediately around Rome formed a league and rebelled against the Republic. The Romans recognized that the Latin League was a powerful opponent and that they needed its support against other, particularly Etruscan, neighbors. So instead of waging a war against the League, Rome made treaties with it. Latins and Romans were given rights in each others' courts, and the cities promised to give assistance to each other. As a result, the Romans were able to create a powerful armed force, and the alliance was able to expand its domination over central Italy. Colonies of Latin and Roman military veterans were established in conquered territories to maintain the power of the alliance.

The settlement with the Latin League had long-term effects on Roman policy toward other peoples. The Greek city-states jealously guarded entry to the citizenry and always remained under the power of a small and exclusive community of men. In the treaty with the Latins, Rome had taken a step toward opening its citizenship to outsiders, and, in time, this became a feature of the Roman Empire. Ultimately, Rome became a city-state with the citizenry and the power of an empire.

Not long after the reaffirmation of the Latin League, Etruscan power was weakened by the invasion of new peoples, the Celts, in northern Italy. The Celts began their incursions around 450 B.C. and, during the next century, conquered the Etruscan cities in the Lombard plain. About 400 B.C. the Romans took advantage of the invasions to challenge Etruscan power in central Italy. Between *ca.* 405 and 396 B.C.,

Rome and its Latin allies besieged the Etruscan city of Veii, and, when it finally fell, the balance of power between the Romans and Etruscans was permanently altered in favor of the Romans. By the middle of the fourth century B.C., the Etruscans' power was completely broken, and their culture was being subsumed into that of both the Romans and the Celtic conquerors. But before this, the Celts threatened Rome.

The Celts were iron-using Indo-Europeans who spread out from the regions just north of the Alps beginning in the sixth century B.C. In successive waves of migration and conquest, they gained control of most of the European continent from Spain to western Russia. The Galatians in central Asia Minor were Celts. The branch of these peoples that moved into Italy in

This head of a statue of Hermes (*ca.* 500 B.C.) was part of a group of terra-cotta figures that adorned the roof of a temple of Apollo in Veii. It became a spoil of war when Veii fell to beseiging Romans in 396 B.C.

the fifth century B.C. was the Gauls, and after they had conquered the Lombard plain, they pressed south into the peninsula. About 390 B.C., they defeated a Roman army, and Rome was abandoned to the conquerors. Only the citadel of the city held out. But the new conquerors had reached the southern limits of their expansion and, after sacking the city, they returned north.

Recovery from this disaster took about a generation, and Roman expansion only restarted in the 360s B.C., when Roman armies again went on the

Early Italy   *ca.* 275 B.C.

Roman territory *ca.* 326 B.C.

Rome and its allies at the start of the Second Punic War, 218 B.C.

offensive. By about 350 B.C., Rome had completed its conquest of the Etruscans by annexing southern Etruria, and it then turned its attention to the Italic tribes. These tribes occupied the Apennines and plains of south-central Italy, and, with the decline of Greek power during the fourth century B.C., they had expanded their spheres of influence. They spoke Oscan, a language related to Latin in about the same way as French is related to Spanish or Italian. The most powerful of the Italic tribes were the Samnites who controlled much of south-central Italy, including the plain of Campania.

The Romans had to put off an attack on this dangerous competitor for a generation because of a great rebellion among the Latin allies. Between *ca.* 340–338 B.C., Rome fought the Great Latin War, and, after defeating the coalition of Latin cities, it dissolved the Latin League and made the citizens of the Latin cities citizens of Rome. From this time on, opening Roman citizenship to conquered peoples in Italy became a possibility often taken. It expanded Roman manpower, and gave newly or recently conquered peoples a stake in Roman politics and fortunes.

About 325 B.C., the Romans turned on the Samnites and waged a long series of wars against them. The Samnites allied themselves with the remnants of Etruscan power and forced Rome into a two-front war, in which Rome lost most of the early battles. But in the long run, Rome's superior military organization and its tight control over its allies gave it victory. It was during these difficult campaigns that the Romans had to find a way to prolong the military service of its consuls. By 290 B.C., Samnite power was broken, and after a little mopping up, Rome controlled virtually all of Italy except for the Gallic cities in the Po Valley and the Greek city-states in the south.

The conquest of the Greek cities in Italy was tied to the intervention of King Pyrrhus. After the end of the Samnite Wars, some Greek cities allied themselves with Rome; others sought protection by allying with Epirus, the partially Hellenized kingdom on the eastern shore of the Adriatic. About 280 B.C., King Pyrrhus of Epirus came over to the peninsula to support his allies and to establish his own power. He won many battles, but he lost the war. In one of his victorious battles, he lost so many men that his victory was nearly as bad as a defeat, and his name now stands for a disastrous victory, the pyrrhic victory. By 265, the Greek city-states had accepted Roman hegemony.

Through all these wars, the Romans developed both a first-rate military system and an ethos of never giving up. The military system was based on the legion, the infantry unit of about 4,300 men, which was subdivided into smaller units for maneuverability. The officer corps was made up of young patricians, although wealthy plebeians also served in it after the expansion of plebeian power, and it was led by the consuls. With its many subdivisions, the legion was a highly flexible unit. As a whole, it was a large force of disciplined soldiers. Divided up into its constituent units, it could be deployed in a wide variety of formations. The small units could be closely controlled by their officers, and the chain of command leading up to the legionary commander made it possible to coordinate the fighting of the whole. It was the best army of the ancient world.

The Romans' ability to come back from defeat, which became a hallmark of the Roman character, rested on the subjection of Rome's dependencies and on the successful maintenance of its alliances. Rome controlled a rich agricultural territory that supported a large population, and it therefore had a superiority in manpower over all the enemies it faced. Even the strongest states of the Mediterranean world could not withstand the steady pressure that Rome could exert.

ROMAN EXPANSION OVERSEAS, 264–146 B.C.

When it acquired control of the Greek cities of southern Italy, Rome inherited

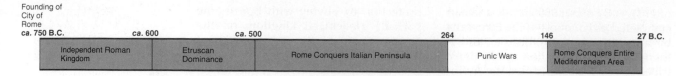

Founding of City of Rome ca. 750 B.C.	ca. 600	ca. 500		264	146	27 B.C.
Independent Roman Kingdom	Etruscan Dominance	Rome Conquers Italian Peninsula		Punic Wars	Rome Conquers Entire Mediterranean Area	

their ancient conflict with Carthage for control of Sicily and the western Mediterranean. Carthage was an old Phoenician colony on the coast of north Africa (near present-day Tunis). Like the earlier struggle between Sparta and Athens, this one was also between a land and a sea power. By the third century B.C., Carthage had become the greatest naval power in the Mediterranean, whereas at the beginning of the wars Rome had no navy. The series of wars between Rome and Carthage are called the Punic Wars (from *Poenicus* meaning Phoenician).

The Punic Wars, 264–146 B.C.

The First Punic War began in 264 B.C., only a year after Rome completed the conquest of southern Italy. The object of this contest was Sicily, but, to win it, Rome had to build a fleet and learn the arts of naval warfare. It developed a type of ship that would allow its men to use their infantry skills through tactics that permitted them to board enemy ships. But the sea took its toll. After some early victories, Rome lost three fleets in storms. Yet, with great sacrifice, the Romans built a fourth fleet, which defeated the Carthaginians off western Sicily. In 241 B.C., Carthage surrendered Sicily to Rome.

After this defeat, Carthage expanded its power into Spain, where there were rich mines and farmlands. Once the city acquired and developed this new province, it again came into conflict with Roman interests. For more than a thousand years, southern Gaul (France) and Spain had been important in Mediterranean trade, and, naturally, Rome had established itself there. Carthaginian power in Spain was therefore a greater threat than just the resurgence of an old enemy. The immediate cause of the Second Punic War was a

Carthaginian attack in 218 B.C. on a Spanish city allied with Rome.

This war might have been fought in Spain, or even in north Africa, but for the brilliance and daring of the Carthaginian general Hannibal. At the beginning of the war, Hannibal marched through southern Gaul and crossed the Alps with a large army that included 50 war elephants. For the first two years of the war, the Romans tried to hem in Hannibal's army, always avoiding a decisive battle. Then, in 216 B.C., two inexperienced consuls decided to confront him, and at Cannae, on the eastern side of the peninsula south of Naples, Hannibal inflicted one of the worst defeats Rome ever suffered. Nearly 70,000 Roman soldiers died; 10,000 Roman prisoners-of-war were sold into slavery. For 13 years after Cannae, Hannibal ravaged the Italian countryside defeating one Roman army after another. Although he threatened Rome itself once, the loyalty of Rome's allies in central Italy forced him to spend most of his time in the south, where he found support among the Italic peoples. But the Romans controlled the sea, and Hannibal could not get reinforcements from Africa. For a long time, the two sides were stalemated.

The deadlock was broken when the Romans sent a first-rate general, Scipio Africanus, into the field. Scipio first took the war to Spain and conquered the peninsula for Rome. He then invaded North Africa itself, and Hannibal had to leave Italy to defend Carthage. After a difficult campaign, Scipio finally defeated Hannibal in 202 B.C. at Zama, a few miles from Carthage and imposed a harsh treaty on the city. Carthage ceded Spain to Rome; it had to pay a heavy war indemnity; and its fleet was henceforth limited to ten ships.

Symbol of Sicily, found in Ostia, chief port of Rome. The symbol's three legs correspond to the three points of Sicily.

Fifty years after these events, Carthage had again recovered some of its wealth, but was no longer a military threat. Nonetheless, Romans remembered the desperate war against Hannibal, and the question whether Carthage should be destroyed had remained a political issue, endlessly debated by the Roman Senate. Finally, in 146 B.C., Rome moved against Carthage. The city fell after a six-month siege, and every inhabitant was either killed or enslaved. The city was razed, its fields sown with salt, and its territory made into a Roman province. However, most of North Africa remained quasi-independent under native rulers who were clients of Rome.

Rome and the Hellenistic East

While Roman expansion in the western Mediterranean proceeded from strategic purposes, it is difficult to find a convincing geopolitical explanation for the growth of Roman power in the eastern Mediterranean. Rome was drawn into eastern affairs by degrees, as one eastern state after another asked for its assistance. Once intervention began, it was difficult to withdraw, and, of course, the great wealth of the East was attractive. But Rome moved hesitantly and repeatedly refused to annex defeated states, making them independent client kingdoms instead.

Rome's first experience in the East was its war with King Pyrrhus of Epirus during the 270s B.C. Later, during the Second Punic War, the Macedonians gave support to Hannibal, and

Roman Plundering   167–146 B.C.

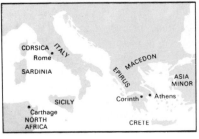

Rome defeated them in order to isolate the Carthaginians. In addition, the successor states to Alexander's empire—Ptolomaic Egypt, Seleucid Persia, Macedon, the leagues of cities in Greece, and the small kingdoms in Asia Minor—were in constant competition with one another and constantly called on Rome for assistance. But every peace imposed by Rome collapsed, and Rome became more and more deeply entangled in the political morass.

Exasperation made the Romans brutal. In 167 B.C., they plundered Macedon and Epirus and sold thousands of their inhabitants into slavery. They punished Corinth for disobedience by destroying it and selling much of its population into slavery, and they plundered Athens and sent thousands of its young men to Italy as slaves. By the late 140s B.C., Macedon had become a Roman province; the Greek cities were under Roman control; Asia Minor had become a Roman protectorate; and Egypt and Syria, although they remained independent, could not act in foreign affairs without Roman approval.

THE CONSEQUENCES OF EXPANSION

Economic, Social, and Political Change

By 146 B.C., Rome had become the capital of a great Mediterranean empire. Wealth poured into Rome on a scale never before seen in the Mediterranean world. The upper classes, which controlled Roman government, benefited most from the spoils of imperialism, and the difference of wealth between rich and poor grew to be monumental. In the old days of the city-state, the differences of wealth had not been so wide, because the estates of the aristocrats had not been very much larger than the farms of the yeomen, and all were prosperous. The economic effects of empire transformed the Roman

This third-century B.C. coin bears one of the few known contemporary portraits of Hannibal. The elephant appears on the reverse.

Scenes from everyday life in first-century Rome. Top: (Left) Grain from African colonies is being unloaded. (Right) A goldsmith practices his trade. Below: A stooped farmer takes his produce to market.

economy. The small farmers of the Italian countryside could not compete with the cheap grain from Sicily and Spain and became dependent on the noble families. The senatorial families bought out the ruined farmers and turned their vast estates to the production of wine and olive oil for export. Consequently, Roman Italy became substantially dependent on the provinces for food staples.

These economic changes resulting from imperialism created social and political changes. By the middle of the second century B.C., many of the ruined farmers who had once formed the backbone of the Roman population had moved to the city to form a new element in Roman life—the urban mob. The new urbanites at first retained their traditional client relationships with the noble families of their old districts, but ambitious politicians were able to woo the mob by offering people more than their traditional patrons offered. In the 140s B.C., politicians used promises of land reform to win power. In time, the mob became a fickle electorate, and Roman politics lost its stability.

Imperialism also increased the importance of the commercial classes, called "equestrians" because they had once formed a class whose members could supply their own horses for cavalry service. In general, equestrians were less wealthy than senators, but there was overlap between the two groups. Most equestrians were landowners as well as merchants. After the formation of the empire, the equestrians derived new political and economic power both from the growth of trade and from the imperial tax system. Conquered peoples had to pay taxes, but the Roman government did not set up a bureau to collect them. Rather the government sold the right to "farm" taxes in the various provinces. Companies of equestrians formed to bid on

these contracts, and the winners then went out and collected enough to cover the contract price and to make a profit. Tax collectors are never popular, but the businessmen who collected Roman taxes (called publicans) earned the special hatred of their victims.

Naturally, taxes fell heaviest on the provincial populations, but the Romans' lenient attitude toward the granting of citizenship and analogous rights won the support of many important provincials. Following the model of Italy, the territories were organized around cities, usually built up on the basis of the native towns. In these communities, the Roman governors permitted the local aristocracy to manage political and economic affairs, and those who served on the town councils were awarded Roman citizenship. In this way, the leaders of the conquered peoples became loyal Roman men. Native Romans looked down on them, but legally these people were the equals of citizens in the capital.

Finally, imperialism made slavery a major feature of Roman life. The conquests produced many prisoners of war, who, according to the common practice of the ancient world, were sold into slavery. The role of slaves in the Roman economy is hard to assess. As had been the case in classical Greece, most slaves seem to have been household servants and assistants to craftsmen. The conquest of the Greek states of the eastern Mediterranean also produced many slaves who were highly educated or skilled in rare crafts. As Rome extended its power over the East, many of the leading Roman families acquired Greek slaves as guardians and teachers for their children, and these men had a great influence on Roman civilization. As in other societies of the ancient world, the Romans also used slaves in dangerous and unhealthy jobs, such as mining. There were also some manufacturing activities carried out by slaves, although there was little large-scale manufacturing in the ancient economy. There is controversy over whether the labor

forces on the great landed estates were slave or free, but certainly the senatorial families had a great many slaves. In fact, all but the poorest families owned slaves.

The familiar relationships between masters and their household slaves led to the growth of a tradition of manumission, the freeing of slaves. Many Romans manumitted their slaves in their wills, and a significant number of slaves also managed to buy their freedom. The freedman was considered to be specially obligated to the family of his former master, and wealthy families had cadres of freedmen who provided various services and contributed to the family treasury.

Unlike the cities of Greece, Rome admitted freed slaves as citizens. Freedmen could not serve in the army, but they could become rowers in the fleet. Their children were full citizens of the state. The long process of creating the empire brought hundreds of the thousands of slaves to Italy, and the practice of manumission became very common, so that by the end of the republican period (end of the first century B.C.), many Roman citizens traced their descent from foreign slaves. This condition was extremely unusual in the ancient world, and it strengthened Rome. Although Rome did not give full citizenship to everyone, and spent decades in struggles with conquered peoples that wanted citizenship, its liberal practices tied the majority of those it had defeated to its constitution and laws and reduced the incidence and severity of rebellion and strife.

Governing the Provinces

The growth of empire affected the Roman political system not only by bringing about social and economic change, but also by expanding the responsibilities of government. The constitution designed to regulate the life of a small city-state now had to govern vast territories populated by foreign peoples. Under normal conditions, the consuls served as generals as well as

Expansion of the Roman Republic Beyond Italy   First Century B.C.

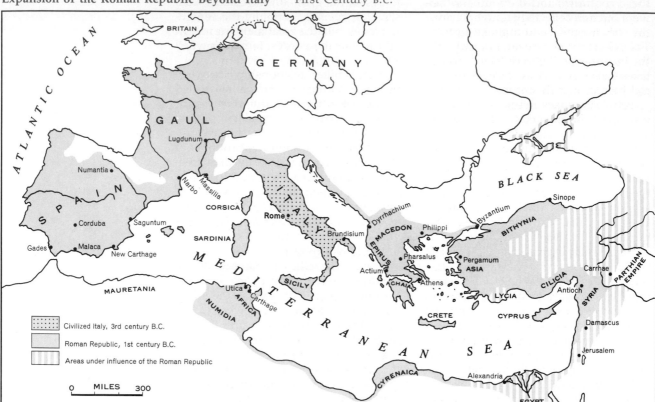

heads of the civilian government, but during the period when the empire was being built, the armies were often active in several theaters of war at once and needed extra military leaders. This was the necessity that led to the creation of the proconsular authority. Because most provinces had military garrisons, it became common to unite provincial administration with military command in the persons of the proconsuls. Thus, the separation of military and civilian power that was one of the distinctive features of Roman government was not exported to the provinces.

The possession of military power made it possible for an unscrupulous proconsul to enrich himself at the expense of the provincials, and, in 149 B.C., the Romans established a special court to try corrupt governors. This action shows that the Romans were concerned to provide good provincial government, but the court soon became useful to Roman politicians. A man who served as proconsul could be sure that his political enemies would sue him for corruption when he returned home. In this way, the governance of the provinces affected Roman politics, while the existence of the special court complicated the political lives of leading Roman citizens.

The Roman provinces were not all treated the same way. Some of the older ones had only token, peacekeeping garrisons, and their governors were primarily civilian officials. Recently conquered provinces, or those threatened by enemies of Rome, had military governments. In general, the Roman governors had very small staffs and left local affairs to native leaders.

The local aristocracies tended to become Romanized. They learned Latin, gave their sons a Roman education, and built Roman-style houses and public buildings. The provincial upper classes thus served as a link between the Romans and the mass of the native populations, which preserved much of their linguistic and cultural traditions. Some provincial city-states had complete autonomy, although they were bound to maintain a close alliance with Rome. Elsewhere, Roman governors intervened only when it was necessary or profitable. In North Africa and in some parts of the Middle East, the Romans permitted the old kingdoms to continue as client kingdoms. The kings had control over internal affairs, but had to act consistently with Roman foreign policy and to get Roman permission for any arrangement of the succession to the throne. Though Roman provincial government was self-interested, it was generally less burdensome than that of previous conquerors, and it kept the peace. Under the Romans, the Mediterranean Basin enjoyed a period of extraordinary peace, the *Pax Romana* (Roman Peace), and prosperity.

Literary, Artistic, and Religious Change

Even before the eastern wars, educated Romans had known and been influenced by Greek culture, but the great influx of thousands of Greeks and others from the Hellenized East after the campaigns literally transformed Roman civilization. Many artists, philosophers, and craftsmen came as slaves and worked their influence within and through the great families. Greek became the second language of the educated person, and Greek forms of poetry, literature, and art became dominant.

These cultural changes did not happen without controversy. Conservative Romans viewed the imitation of conquered foreigners as an undermining of traditional Roman culture and values. For them, Rome had achieved greatness because of its political and cultural virtues, and the newfangled artistic movement was tantamount to admitting to a cultural inferiority. Others were enthusiastic Hellenizers and even went so far as to denigrate the old Roman cultural tradition. Most people held a balanced view on all this, but the disagreement between the proponents of the two extreme positions ran deep and had repercussions in politics. Conservatives were sure that it was Hellenization that caused the rise of the urban mob and other undesirable political changes in Rome.

In the period after the eastern conquests, Roman artists imitated Greek models. In fact, many Greek sculptures are only preserved in Roman copies of this period. in architecture, too, the Greek style replaced the native Roman about 200 B.C. It is difficult to find examples of Roman art and architecture that do not show Greek influence.

This is also true of literature. Although the Romans certainly wrote poetry before the conquest of Greece, one of the first long poems written in Latin was a translation of the *Odyssey*. The Romans also enjoyed Greek drama, and the first Roman plays were written in Greek. Later the leading playwrights wrote in Latin, but based their plays on earlier works of Hellenistic authors. Menander, the late fourth-century B.C. writer of comedies, had a particularly great influence, and many early Roman comedies are essentially paraphrases of his works. As in drama, the first Romans who wrote histories wrote them in Greek (around 200 B.C.). About 168 B.C., Cato, the senator perhaps most responsible for bringing about the destruction of Carthage and a strong opponent of Greek influence in Roman culture, wrote the first major historical work in Latin. As a writer, Cato wanted to raise Latin prose up to the Greek level. But perhaps the best account of Rome's rise to power in the Mediterranean was that of Polybius (*ca.*

202–120 B.C.), a Greek who spent considerable time as a hostage in Rome. While he admired Roman power, as a historian he imitated Thucydides rather than a Roman model.

In religion, like the Greeks before them, the Romans had formed a pantheon that had absorbed the local gods of the Italian peoples they had conquered. After the conquest of Greece, the Romans amalgamated their pantheon with the Greek one. They identified the twelve gods of Olympus with their own divinities, although the correspondences were not perfect. But the main effect of the formation of the empire on Roman religion was the introduction of the mystery religions.

Although these religions entered Rome in the second century B.C., they did not become a major influence on Roman religious life until after the end of the republican period (after 30 B.C.). Traditional Roman religion was controlled by the aristocracy through the control of the priesthoods, and, so long

This fresco found in a villa on the outskirts of Pompeii depicts initiation rites of a Dionysian mystery cult, but they are rendered in such a way as to make precise interpretation difficult for the outsider.

as the senatorial class maintained its dominance of society and politics, the traditional civic religion held sway. However, it is certainly true that by the second century B.C. this old religion had lost much of its grip on the Roman population, and Hellenizers were often attracted to the new cults that came to Rome with Hellenistic civilization.

In contrast to these ways in which the Greeks affected Romans, Roman jurisprudence showed only slight Greek influence. From early in their history, the Romans had become convinced that their special contribution to human civilization was law and government. After the codification of the law in the Twelve Tables, Roman law was written, and, therefore, over time it built up into an impressive body of legislation. Much of this legislation had to do with constitutional questions, such as whether plebeians would be eligible for election to the magistracies, but that was not the whole content of the law in which the Romans took such pride.

The edicts issued by the praetors contained rules about bringing cases to their courts, primarily defining the types of cases the judges would entertain. Because each new praetor reissued the edict pertaining to his court, the legal remedies available to citizens and foreigners grew and changed to reflect changes in the society and economy of the city and empire. In their courts and edicts, the praetors responded to the demands of litigants, who tried to persuade the courts to accept new claims, remedies, and procedures. Thus, the Roman legal system was created by the clamor of litigants, and it was flexible and expansive in dealing with the myriad legal disputes of an imperial society.

Notwithstanding the central role of the praetors, the Roman legal system was not centralized and professional like modern legal systems. When a complainant brought a case to the praetor, the magistrate did not hear the case; he only decided whether the claim was actionable. If it was, then the praetor appointed a private citizen, invariably from the patrician or, at least, the wealthy and educated, class, to decide the case. The judge delegate could hear the case in almost any way he wanted—there were no established rules of procedure or evidence—but his handling of the case had to meet the high standards of the praetor. A judge who mishandled a case, either through incompetence or prejudice, was subject to severe penalties.

Litigation was a part of everyday life, and patricians had to be trained to handle it, as magistrates, judges, and litigants. In practice, some men became known as legal experts and were called on to advise judges delegate, litigants, and even the praetors when necessary. From the first century B.C. on, the legal specialists produced an increasing number of commentaries on the praetorian edicts and treatises on various aspects of the law. Nonetheless, it does not appear that there was ever a legal profession as such. Patricians and other wealthy men did not engage in work for pay, although they would doubtless receive some value, political or pecuniary, for assisting their co-citizens; the practice of law was merely one of the attributes of the cultured gentleman.

Just as conquered cultures did not contribute much to Roman law, they contributed little to the organization and strategy of the Roman military system. In large part, the cultural identity of the Romans was maintained against the flood of Greek civilization by Romans' consciousness of their distinctive role in the history of law and by their successful military tradition.

THE COLLAPSE OF THE REPUBLIC, 146–59 B.C.

The Society of the Late Republic

Although many Romans, like Cato, clung to the ancient values of the farmer-citizen, by the middle of the

Founding of
City of
Rome
ca. 750 B.C.   *ca.* 600   *ca.* 500   264   146   27 B.C.

| Independent Roman Kingdom | Etruscan Dominance | Rome Conquers Italian Peninsula | Punic Wars | Rome Conquers Entire Mediterranean Area |

second century B.C. Roman society was nothing like what it had been in the early days of the Republic. The influx of foreigners had changed the society of the capital city, and out in the countryside imperialism had wrought a social and economic revolution. Italian agriculture had become specialized in olive oil and wine, which required a great deal of capital and the ability to wait for trees and vines to mature. They also required effective commercial networks, because they were grown only as money crops, principally for export. Only the great landowners had the capital and the commercial contacts.

The collapse of the small-farm economy was gradual but inexorable. The upper classes were the principal beneficiaries of the conquests and brought home great wealth. Because land was the only stable and permanent form of wealth, the enriched upper-class landholders sought to buy whatever land they could put their hands on. Like all aggressive entrepreneurs, they did not wait for small holders to make up their minds to sell. Whenever possible, the great men worked to subordinate the small men. They lent them money to plant, not, as of old, because of the patron-client relationship, but so that when they defaulted because of a bad harvest, sickness, or other disaster, they could seize the land. Often, the impatience of the large landowners led them to help disaster along. From later times, there is evidence of great men permitting their flocks to destroy the crops of lesser neighbors or sending their crews to break irrigation ditches at crucial times of the year. The life of the small farmer, who was, according to Roman ideals, the backbone of the state, became nearly impossible during the late third and early second centuries B.C.

The result was a steady concentration of land and wealth in the hands of the upper classes. Thousands of small farmers were driven out of the countryside and came to Rome, sometimes seeking redress (from the very people, or their relatives, who were depriving them), sometimes seeking a livelihood to replace the one of their ancestors. The population of Rome swelled with unhappy, unemployed, or underemployed masses, living in unhealthy tenements. Poor and wretched as these people were, they were citizens, and many conservative politicians saw them as symbols of the tragedy of Rome.

The Gracchi

In the 140s B.C., the leaders of this conservative political movement were Tiberius and Gaius Gracchus, grandsons of the great Scipio who had defeated Carthage. For them, the yeoman farmer was the foundation of Rome's greatness and the only way to save the state was to institute land reform that

A funerary relief showing a man and his wife, a portrait of an ancestor, and an attribute of the man's profession (first century B.C.).

would return the urban mob to their farms. They could never bring the majority of the senatorial class over to their position because this was the group that had most benefited from the decline of the small farmers.

In 133 B.C., Tiberius Gracchus was elected tribune of the people and immediately proposed legislation, opposed by the Senate, to redistribute public land. The law would not have deprived the senatorial families of their estates, but the public lands were also controlled by these families under very favorable, long-term leases. The conflict over the law precipitated a political and constitutional crisis because it raised questions about the powers of the Senate and the tribunes. Not only did the law hurt the senators' interests, but it also violated the ancient constitutional principle that laws opposed by the Senate would not be pushed through. The Senate persuaded another tribune to veto the law, and Gracchus in an unprecedented move had the man voted out of office. To ensure that his program would be carried through, Gracchus then ran for a second term as tribune, which violated the old custom and threatened the power of the Senate in a direct way. If a man could hold office indefinitely, then the old order of the state, which checked popular power, would be destroyed. To meet the threat, a group of senators led their clients in a riot, during which Tiberius Gracchus was lynched.

Ten years later, Gaius Gracchus overcame senatorial opposition to follow his older brother as tribune. He revived his brother's legislation on land reform and was able to establish colonies of small farmers on state land. Recognizing the need for a wide political base, Gaius sought the support of the urban mob by such measures as instituting a grain dole—the people could purchase grain from the state at half price. He sought the support of the equestrians by increasing their role in government, particularly by giving them control over the juries that heard cases of corruption in tax collecting and other governmental activities. Finally,

he responded to the old complaint of the Italian allies, particularly of the Samnites, that though they had contributed much to Rome's success, they had never received full rights as citizens. Gaius' proposal to give Roman citizenship to the allies defeated him. His own political supporters were split on the issue, and during the conflict over it, Gaius, like his brother before him, was murdered.

Marius and Sulla

The conflicts generated by the Gracchi weakened the political fabric of the Roman Republic. The relationships among the Senate, the tribunes and assembly, and the equestrians were no longer stable, and no one sociopolitical element could carry out its policy without meeting strong opposition. Nonetheless, the end of the Republic resulted not from internal political conflict, but from the rise of independent military power, and this development was itself a consequence of Rome's imperialism.

In 107 B.C., Rome was engaged in a difficult war with a former ally in North Africa, and, in desperation, the citizens elected an ambitious equestrian from rural Italy named Marius as consul. Marius was already famous as a general, and he quickly brought the African war to a successful conclusion. In 104 B.C., Marius was called on again to meet a new threat. New Indo-European tribes, the Germans, had come out of the northern European forests to invade Gaul and finally to threaten northern Italy. They had defeated the Romans several times before, and Marius was reelected consul five years in a row (104–100 B.C.), while the crisis lasted.

However, unprecedented as it was, the constitutional change represented in the elections of Marius was not the most important change that he effected. In order to maintain an armed force sufficient to meet the German threat, he broke the ancient connection between ownership of land and military service. He recruited landless

A coin minted in 137 B.C. celebrates the private ballot. A Roman is shown dropping a stone tablet into a voting urn.

men. In the old system, the state did not have to pay its armies because soldiers supported themselves. Now, Marius had to find a way to reward his men. He did it by distributing booty won from the enemy and by settling his soldiers on lands in conquered territory. The effect of the new system was twofold. First, Marius created an army that was loyal to its general, because he was the source of its reward for service. Second, army service became an attractive career for the poor and dispossessed, who could look forward to receiving a new start on the land as the reward for service. The first beneficiaries of this new career were the poor of Rome and Italy, but in time, they were replaced by provincials and finally by barbarians, men who came from beyond the borders of the Roman Empire to seek their fortunes in service to it. In sum, the Roman army was professionalized and became progressively independent of the civilian government that it was supposed to serve. It also became independently aggressive because the soldiers' rewards, booty, and land, depended on successful conquest.

Sulla, dictator of Rome from 82 to 79 B.C.

After 100 B.C. Marius remained politically prominent, but he was unable to maintain total dominance. In 90 B.C., the Italian allies, who had sought citizenship for centuries and almost received it under Gaius Gracchus, finally rose in a great rebellion against the Romans. This was the so-called Social War (that is, war with the allies—*socii* in Latin), and Marius again took military command. But it was one of his former officers, Sulla, who emerged from the two years of conflict as the most prominent figure in Roman politics. Sulla was consul (88 B.C.) when the Romans ended the war by granting full citizenship to the Italians. At this time, Mithridates, king of a small Hellenistic state in Asia Minor was trying to recreate a Hellenistic empire, and in 88 B.C. he had given the signal for a massacre of 80,000 Romans in the Greek cities along the west coast of Asia Minor.

Although he was consul, Sulla had to march on Rome to prevent Marius from getting the command against Mithradates. In 87 B.C., Sulla was able to march against Mithradates, but it took three years of hard campaigning to put down the rebellion. This long absence from Rome gave Sulla's enemies an opportunity to deprive him of his command and, therefore, of his political position, and in 83 B.C. he again marched on the city to save his authority. The Marian military reforms provided Sulla with an army that was absolutely loyal to him and that even supported his subversion of the constitution. In 82 B.C., Sulla was named dictator, to resolve a crisis he himself had created, and he began a reform of the Roman state. Sulla proscribed thousands of his enemies—that is, he put a price on their heads and confiscated their property. He then distributed the confiscated property among his veterans. He established his supporters in the Senate and tried to weaken the constitutional powers of the tribunes and the popular assembly. By 79 B.C., Sulla had completed his reforms, and he retired from public life; he died the following year.

New Leaders:
Pompey, Crassus, and Cicero

As a result of the Marian military reforms and of the model of Sulla's career, the chief object of a political career in Rome became a provincial military command. The command gave its holder the opportunity to gain both great wealth from the provincial administration and control of a loyal army. In the years after Sulla's retirement, one of his officers, Pompey, emerged as the leading general. Unlike Sulla, however, Pompey had some respect for the constitution, and he never fully dominated Roman politics as his predecessor had done.

Pompey's chief rival was Crassus, who had made a fabulous fortune in questionable real estate operations in Rome. In 71 B.C., while Pompey was putting down a rebellion in Spain, Crassus, who was not much of a general, defeated a dangerous slave rebellion led by the former gladiator Spartacus. The potential conflict between the two generals was avoided when both were elected consul for the year 70 B.C.

In the following years, a third man, Cicero, emerged as a political leader. Cicero was from the equestrian class and came from the same town as Marius. None of his ancestors had served in the magistracies, so he was that unusual figure in Roman politics, the "new man." But he parlayed his extraordinary skill as a lawyer and orator into a distinguished senatorial career. In fact, Cicero became *the* orator, the model for all successors down to the present day. He wrote treatises on rhetoric and philosophy that not only set the basic rules of public speaking, but also set a new standard of Latin prose. From soon after his death, Cicero's work became the staple diet of every student of the Latin language.

Cicero rose to prominence after he successfully prosecuted a spectacularly corrupt provincial governor named Verres, and, throughout his political career, he tried to maintain his political independence. Nonetheless, when a political choice had to be made, Cicero supported Pompey. His connection with Pompey was strengthened when he was consul in 63 B.C. and put down a conspiracy, led by Catiline, to seize control of the state while Pompey was in the East. Cicero published the brilliant speeches he made against these malefactors.

Pompey had gone to the East in response to a new rebellion. In 83 B.C., Sulla had left Mithradates in power in order to get back to Rome quickly, and, in 74 B.C., Mithradates rebelled again. This time the Romans knew that the threat to their power was serious, and they made provision for stable military

Bust of Pompey showing him late in life.

Electioneering in Rome in the Last Days of the Republic

Quintus Cicero to his brother when the latter was running for consul in 64 B.C.

I have said enough about gaining friends, now I should speak of acquiring popular support. The people like to be called by name, flattered, be courted, receive favors, hear about you, feel that you are working for the public good. . . . You must flatter endlessly; this is wrong and shameful in ordinary life, but necessary in running for office. . . . Be in Rome and in the Forum and ask for support. . . . See that you and your friends give parties, widely and to many voting groups. . . . Make it possible for men to see you at any time, day or night. . . .

Let the voters say and think that you know them well, that you greet them by name, that you are generous and openhanded. . . . If possible accuse your competitors of having a bad reputation for crime, vice or bribery. . . . Remember that this is Rome, a city made up of many peoples, in which plots, lies and all kinds of vices abound. You must suffer much arrogance, many insults, much ill-will and the pride and hatred of many people.

Translated from Dante Nardo, *Il Commentariolum Petitionis* (Padua: Liviana, 1970), pp. 213, 215.

Bust of Julius Caesar showing him at the time of his assassination.

command in the East. Pompey was permitted to remain there for more than a decade and was commissioned to create a new imperial system throughout the eastern Mediterranean. By the time he returned to Rome in 62 B.C., he had created a new Roman province in western Asia Minor, made Syria into a province, and put the rest of the East under new client kings. The Jewish kingdom of Palestine was one of these vassal kingdoms.

When he returned to the capital, Pompey found that the Senate was unwilling to ratify all of these arrangements and to keep the promises he had made on its behalf. In the political struggle that ensued, he allied himself to a powerful urban politician named Gaius Julius Caesar.

The Rise of Caesar, 59–44 B.C.

Caesar was the scion of an ancient patrician family who had won huge popularity and, while doing so, had piled

up huge debts. This gave Crassus, who had been unable to maintain his power after his consulship, a chance to reassert himself politically. He paid the young man's debts and helped him win an enthusiastic following and rapid political advancement. In 60 B.C., Caesar was able to bring Pompey and Crassus together to form a triumvirate, the so-called First Triumvirate. This alliance elected Caesar as consul for the year 59 B.C., and he saw to it that Pompey's arrangements in the East were ratified and that Pompey's veterans were properly rewarded with land. He also distributed land to his own urban supporters.

Caesar's personal reward was a military command, but the one he got was not nearly so promising as the eastern command that had made Pompey's reputation. Caesar took command of Gaul, which was the weak link in the provinces of the western Mediterranean. The Romans controlled only a narrow strip of territory along the coast, Transalpine Gaul, which linked Cisalpine Gaul (Gaul on the Italian side of the Alps) with the important province of Spain. North of Transalpine Gaul, Gallic and German tribes were in constant conflict, and these conflicts threatened the Roman province. Stabilizing this province was a necessary task, but unrewarding because the Gallic tribes had neither the wealth nor the splendor of the enemies of the East.

In 58 B.C., Caesar received a five-year proconsular command in Gaul; the term was later extended to ten years. The command included both Cisapline Gaul and Transapline Gaul. Immediately, Caesar undertook a campaign to pacify the tribes north of Transalpine Gaul, but as he moved north, he met new enemies. In the end, he conquered the whole of Gaul and made two expeditions to Britain, where his Gallic opponents often took refuge with their Celtic allies. He also crossed the Rhine several times to push back the Germans. He commemorated these campaigns in a book, *Commentaries on the Gallic War*, which has become

Caesar in Gaul   58–49 B.C.

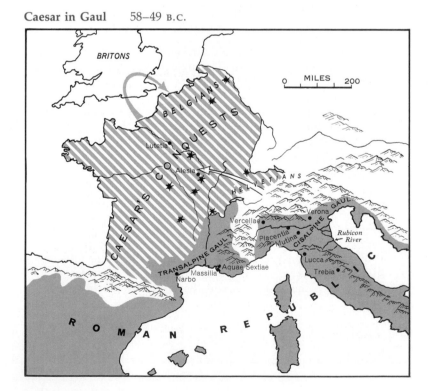

a model of terse Latin prose and which helped establish his fame as a general and administrator.

Crassus also received a military command through the triumvirate and led an army against the Parthians, as the Romans called the Hellenistic successors of the Persian empire. In 53 B.C., the Parthians destroyed Crassus's army and Crassus himself was killed. This ended the First Triumvirate and left Pompey and Caesar as Rome's leading political figures. Pompey was now back in Rome, while Caesar was pacifying the new province of Gaul. The two leaders had already been drifting apart when Crassus died.

Caesar and Pompey

In 52 B.C., Pompey was elected sole consul to combat mob violence in Rome, and this extraordinary power put him in a better position than Caesar. Yet, so long as Caesar had his command and a fiercely loyal army, Pompey could not be secure. Therefore, he tried to deprive Caesar of his command. This attempt failed when Caesar's friends in Rome blocked it, but it was clear that the two men were now permanent enemies. The Senate tried to arrange a settlement according to which both men would give up their commands. When Caesar refused to agree to this, the Senate ordered Pompey to march against him.

Caesar's outstanding characteristic as a general was his ability to act swiftly, and he did so now. On March 1, 49 B.C., he crossed the tiny Rubicon River, which was the border between Cisalpine Gaul and Rome's home country, and opened civil war against Pompey. The Senate had been convinced that Pompey could raise an army quickly, but few of his veterans were settled in Italy, and he had to flee to the East, leaving Rome and the remnants of its Senate to Caesar. Most Senators followed Pompey to Greece. After a year of indecisive fighting, which mostly went in Pompey's favor, Caesar defeated him at Pharsalus in 48 B.C.

Pompey escaped to Egypt, but the Ptolomaic king ordered him executed to gain Caesar's favor. For the next three years, Caesar and his lieutenants campaigned against Pompey's supporters in Spain, North Africa, and the East. By 45 B.C., Caesar was master of the Roman state.

Caesar in Power, 48–44 B.C.

Caesar was named dictator in 48 B.C., but while this title was republican, many in Rome knew that the political reality had changed dramatically. Caesar also kept the *imperium*, military power, and, therefore, was *imperator* (from which the word *emperor* derives), the supreme military commander. Thus, he united military and civil au-

Richly embossed helmet of an aristocratic warrior of Gaul, at the time of Julius Caesar's conquest.

The Murder of Caesar   44 B.C.

The *Lives*, written by the Greek historian Plutarch around A.D. 100, supplies valuable information on Greek and Roman history, particularly on the confusing years of the late Republic. As may be seen from this passage, Plutarch's *Lives* served as a source of Shakespeare's play *Julius Caesar*.

When Caesar entered, the senate stood up to show their respect to him, and of Brutus's confederates, some came about his chair and stood behind it. . . . Tillius, laying hold of his robe with both his hands, pulled it down from his neck, which was the signal for the assault. Casca gave him the first cut in the neck. . . . Those who were not privy to the design were astonished, and their horror and amazement at what they saw were so great that they durst not fly nor assist Caesar, nor so much as speak a word. But those who came prepared for the business enclosed him on every side. For it had been agreed that they should each of them make a thrust at him, and flesh themselves with his blood; for which reason Brutus also gave him one stab in the groin. Some say that he fought and resisted all the rest, shifting his body to avoid the blows, and calling out for help, but that when he saw Brutus's sword drawn, he covered his face with his robe and submitted, letting himself fall . . . at the foot of the pedestal on which Pompey's statue stood. . . .

From Plutarch, *The Lives of Noble Grecians and Romans*, trans. by John Dryden, rev. by Arthur Hugh Clough (New York: Modern Library, n.d.), pp. 892–93.

A coin commemorating the death of Caesar. One side bears the portrait of Brutus; the other side shows the assassins' daggers flanking the cap of liberty.

thority not as the consuls had under the Republic, but as Sulla had 35 years earlier. Caesar's power rested not on election to civilian office, but on his military command.

As soon as he was in power, Caesar began reforms similar to those of Sulla and Pompey. He settled his veterans on government land and tried to end corruption in the provincial administrations. He enlarged the Senate and even seated some provincial nobles in it, but the full incorporation of provincials in Roman government and society was still far in the future. He reformed the calendar, adopting the Egyptian year of 365 days with the addition of an extra day every four years to keep it synchronized with the solar year.

The various reforms seem to have gained him support in Italy and the provinces, where Romanization now proceeded quickly, but the old senatorial class continued to oppose him. Caesar had permitted many scions of the old families to retain their positions, but the conciliatory political strategy failed. For these men the new government was a direct challenge to their ancient rights and an unconstitutional usurpation of power, and their dissatisfaction led to a conspiracy under the leadership of Brutus and Cassius. The conspirators assassinated Caesar in the Senate House on the Ides of March (March 15), 44 B.C.

It is difficult to assess Caesar's goals or achievements. He was not in power long enough to see whether he intended to set aside the ancient republican constitution or to try, like Sulla, to reform it. Whatever his intent, his death created a political crisis in which any hope that the Republic would be restored was lost.

CIVIL WAR AND THE SECOND TRIUMVIRATE, 44–30 B.C.

The death of Caesar created a chaotic political situation in Rome. Mark An-

tony, Caesar's chief lieutenant, gained the support of the veterans and much of the mob. Brutus had hoped for a revival of senatorial government, but the old system had broken down completely, and he and his co-conspirators found themselves without substantial support. Octavian, Caesar's grandnephew and adopted heir, was a frail 18-year-old, and perhaps for this reason he received support from Cicero and other senators who thought they could control him. But when Octavian had established himself sufficiently, he suddenly switched sides and joined Mark Antony and another of Caesar's former lieutenants, Lepidus, in a second triumvirate. The three led an army on Rome in late 44 B.C. and received full power for five years from the assembly.

The new Triumvirs began their rule with a bloody proscription against their opposition. Like Sulla before them, they distributed the confiscated property of the proscribed among their soldiers and gained the support of a new class of land owners. Cicero, a personal enemy of Antony, was forced to commit suicide. Brutus and Cassius had escaped to Macedonia, and the Triumvirs pursued them there as soon as they were in control of Rome. In 42 B.C., they defeated and killed the conspirators, but they offered good terms to their army and so quickly ended the first part of the civil war.

Following this victory, the three men had to deal with each other. They divided the empire among themselves. In this arrangement, Antony came out on top. He had the largest army and held both Gaul and the East. But in time Octavian was able to force Lepidus into retirement, gaining control of a double portion. Meanwhile, Antony became entangled in a love affair with Cleopatra, the queen of Egypt, and he began to lose support. He also opened a war with the Parthians and weakened his forces without gaining anything. In the meantime, Octavian consolidated his control over Italy, and in 32 B.C. was ready to move against Antony. He secured a decree removing Antony from his command and prepared his forces. After about a year of skirmishing, the two sides met in a great naval battle at Actium, on the Adriatic coast of Greece, in 31 B.C. Octavian's fleet, commanded by the capable Agrippa, defeated Antony and Cleopatra decisively. The two fled to Egypt, where first Antony and then Cleopatra committed suicide.

This battle ended the wars that followed Caesar's death. Octavian was without rivals in the Roman world, and on January 13, 27 B.C., he proclaimed the restoration of the Republic. This restoration was the beginning of the Roman Empire.

While the Empire became the political ideal of the western Europe during the Middle Ages, the Republic left a legacy that eventually supplanted that ideal. Born in opposition to the tyrannical kingship of the Tarquins and creator of a legal system that in principle treated all citizens as equals before the law, the Roman Republic became the symbol of political freedom for thinkers of the Italian Renaissance sixteen centuries later. In this idealized image, the Republic inspired political reforms and intellectual renewal.

Suggestions for Further Reading

General

There are many reliable texts devoted to Roman history. Among the best are H. H. Scullard, *History of the Roman World from 753 to 146 B.C.*, 3rd ed. (1961); F. B. Marsh, *History of the Roman World from 146 to 30 B.C.*, 3rd ed. (1961); and H. H. Scullard, *From the Gracchi to Nero: A History of Rome from 133 B.C. to A.D. 68* (1975).

For a shorter work, see A. E. R. Boak, *A History of Rome to A. D. 565*, revised by W. G. Sinnigen (1977). A very rich sampling of selections from ancient Roman sources is collected in the first volume of N. Lewis and M. Reinhold, eds., *Roman Civilization* (1951).

The Etruscans and the Roman Republic

On the Etruscans, see R. Bloch, *The Etruscans* (1958); and H. Hencken, *Tarquinia, Villanovans and Early Etruscans* (1968). O. J. Brendel, *Etruscan Art* (1978), is excellent. L. Bonfante uses Etruscan funerary art to reveal Etruscan society in "Etruscan Couples and their Aristocratic Society," *Women's Studies* 8 (1981) 157–87. R. Bloch, *The Origins of Rome* (1966), and H. H. Scullard, *The Etruscan Cities and Rome* (1967), treat the early history of Rome. On the early conquests see E. T. Salmon, *Samnium and the Samnites* (1967), and *Roman Colonization under the Republic* (1969). Two works treat the development of Rome's overseas empire, R. M. Errington, *The Dawn of Empire* (1972), and E. Badian, *Roman Imperialism in the Late Republic* (1968). On the social history of the period, see the studies by M. I. Finley, *Studies in Ancient Society* (1974), and P. A. Brunt, *Social Conflict in the Roman Republic* (1971).

The Roman Empire

On the transition from the Republic to the Empire, see L. R. Taylor, *Party Politics in the Age of Caesar* (1949). R. Syme, *The Roman Revolution* (1939), a classic, offers an exciting account of the social as well as the political changes wrought by Augustus. For a detailed social history of the late republican period, see T. Frank, *Life and Literature in the Roman Republic* (1930). On Cicero, see D. Stockton, *Cicero* (1971), and the best biography of Caesar is M. Gelzer, *Caesar, Politician and Statesman* (1968).

On the early Empire, see F. B. Marsh, *Founding of the Roman Empire* (1927), and M. Hammond, *The Augustan Principate in Theory and Practice* (1933). For the second century, see M. Hammond, *The Antonine Monarchy* (1959). For comprehensive histories of Roman literature, see J. W. Duff, *A Literary History of Rome to the Close of the Golden Age*, 3rd ed. (1963), and *A Literary History of Rome in the Silver Age*, 3rd ed. (1964).

4
The Roman Empire
27 B.C.—A.D. 476

*R*eturning in triumph to Rome after his victory at Actium, Octavian showed himself to be careful and cautious. He had learned the lessons of Caesar's assassination. He was a young man of 32 who had already had 14 years of experience in politics and war. He was quite willing to conciliate the upper classes by preserving old institutions, and that was the meaning of his declaration of January 27 B.C. that the Republic had been restored. He was able to preserve the forms of republican government—to permit the election of consuls and rely on the Senate and even, from time to time, to call a meeting of the assembly.

Nonetheless, Octavian still held the *imperium,* supreme military command, and had loyal armies behind him. Also, because the civil war had decimated the senatorial class, he could remake the state within the old constitution. He reestablished the Senate by introducing his supporters into it, and he exercised civilian power by taking the position of *Princeps,* or First Citizen, in the ancient deliberative body. In the Senate, the Princeps spoke first on any issue, and, when he was Octavian, his speech decided the issue. For this reason, the period of Octavian and his immediate successors is called the Principate.

In 27 B.C., the Senate voted to bestow the title *Augustus* on Octavian. This word had several layers of meaning. It was a title used of gods as well as men, and a person called *augustus* was looked upon with awe and reverence. In this new political usage, the title emphasized that Octavian was the beneficent protector of the state. Henceforth, Octavian used the title as a name; it was a masterstroke of propaganda, which enhanced his authority while avoiding the violations of constitutional principles that the senators had seen in Caesar's dictatorship.

Relief of a figure
thought to be Horace
(fragment of a marble
frieze, Greco-Roman
period).

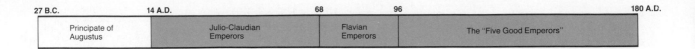

27 B.C.	14 A.D.		68	96		180 A.D.
Principate of Augustus	Julio-Claudian Emperors		Flavian Emperors		The "Five Good Emperors"	

THE PRINCIPATE OF AUGUSTUS, 27 B.C.–A.D. 14

Augustus's Social Program

The theme of Augustus's policy was restoration. He reestablished peace in Rome and the Empire. Although it was a sham that the old republican distribution of power had been restored, he did govern through the traditional magistracies and Senate. It was merely that, as *Princeps* and *Imperator*, everything went his way. He also undertook a restoration of traditional Roman religion and morals. He prohibited the practice of mystery cults, which were becoming increasingly popular. He passed legislation to restore the family and encourage people to have children. All in all, he projected a thoroughly conservative image designed to link him with the hallowed past of Cato, Cicero, and other heroes of the Republic.

Augustus's legislation favoring the family reveals a great deal about the position of women in Roman society. In its law and ethos, this was a patriarchal society. In law, women were subject to their fathers or the male head of their families, the *paterfamilias*. Every woman was supposed to have a guardian and could only make important decisions, such as to marry or buy and sell property, with the approval and assistance of the guardian. The Roman ideal of womanhood combined these civilized and urbane characteristics with survivals of ancient values. The Roman woman was expected to spin and weave and perform all the household chores. In legend and funerary inscriptions, women who had produced many children were held in high honor. Of course, while upper-class women were taught the household arts, slaves actually performed them,

and Roman women practiced both contraception and abortion. Augustus was much concerned about the failure of upper-class women to produce children.

Nonetheless, we know of several women who rose to prominence in Roman society and whose guardians are never mentioned. Upper-class Roman women often became important patrons of the arts and literature and sometimes played a role in politics. We know of some who were excellent businesswomen. In practice, most women seem to have had considerable freedom to manage their own affairs. A study of Cicero's wife, Terentia, shows that she managed her own substantial property holdings by herself and even kept knowledge of what she was doing from her husband. Therefore, Augustus may have been freeing women from an old law that no longer had much strength when he ruled that women who had three children would no longer need a guardian.

Also women could divorce their husbands, although the law said that only the man could divorce and then only for certain grave reasons. Yet, the freedom of women to divorce stemmed from their real social and legal condition. Formally, the act of marriage was a handing over of the bride from father to husband, but it was possible in law, and apparently it was common in practice, for the father to retain legal authority over his daughter. This arrangement gave the woman considerable freedom, for while she lived in her husband's house, she could continue to appeal to her father or brothers (whoever was at the time *paterfamilias* of her own family) against actions of her husband. The artful playing of one authority figure off against another must have been one of the basic lessons taught young girls at their mothers' knee. When divorce did occur, the children stayed with the father.

As in every society, the laws that hemmed in or liberated upper-class women had little effect on the lower classes. Lower-class women shared their husbands' burdens of eking out a living. They tended shops, worked fields, and ran their households. They were subject to the legal power of their fathers and husbands, but in the daily struggle for existence their subordination had little meaning.

The Organization of Imperial Government

Governance of the provinces continued to be a problem. Augustus retained the supreme proconsular authority, and all provinces in which military garrisons were stationed were governed by his military lieutenants. The tax revenues of these provinces were used to support the armies that patrolled them. Yet, Augustus appointed senators to govern thoroughly pacified provinces, and, ironically, the Senate controlled the richest, most Romanized, territories.

The backbone of Augustus's power was the army, which contained 25 legions of about 6,000 men each and an equal number of auxiliary units made up of provincial troops. Under Augustus, the armies were kept at very near full strength; he had about 250,000 men under arms at all times. Soldiers served for 20 years and received large cash bonuses and land upon retirement; they were completely loyal to their commander-in-chief.

Augustus permitted local provincial authorities to carry out most of the functions of government. He continued the old practice of permitting semi-independent client kingdoms on the fringes of the Empire to control their internal affairs. In Judea, King Herod ruled one of these kingdoms.

The development of local autonomy was encouraged throughout the Em-

pire. In Gaul, Augustus's government encouraged the transformation of old tribal centers into Romanized cities, from which the surrounding territory was governed. The Romans made large investments in these places, putting up public buildings and introducing Roman culture, and they made a great effort to Romanize the tribal aristocracy. In some provinces, this practice of founding cities took on the aspect of a modern development plan. In Spain and North Africa, the Romans planted cities wherever they wanted to develop the agricultural economy. In the eastern Mediterranean, the ancient city-states were permitted to govern themselves under Roman supervision. Consequently, the Empire was a world of city-states under a centralized government in Rome.

The Golden Age of Latin Literature

The Augustan restoration provided the environment for the highest development of Latin literature. Although Greek culture remained a powerful influence on all Roman civilization, Augustus and his lieutenants, particularly Maecenas, encouraged and patronized a group of writers and poets whose literary culture was rooted in the late republican period. As noted in the last chapter, Cicero had achieved great fame as an orator and essayist on many subjects, and his prose became a standard not only for Latin, but for later languages as well. Caesar's history of the Gallic campaigns, set a standard for the sparse style of the man of action. The leading historian of the period was Livy (59 B.C.–A.D. 17), who produced a monumental history of Rome from its origins to Augustus. Most of this work is lost, but enough remains to show that Livy faithfully served Augustus's interest in the restoration of Roman values by celebrating the virtues of Roman character.

The poets of the late Republic had avoided politics. Catullus (87–54 B.C.) wrote wonderful love poetry in the

Augustus issued these coins to proclaim the submission of Egypt and Armenia to Roman power.

Contemporary bust of Cicero, the great orator of the first century B.C.

B.C.), and Vergil (70–19 B.C.) all wrote poems reflecting on the horrors of civil war and the ethical problem of basing a new society on it. But they and others, such as Ovid (43 B.C.–A.D. 18), also wrote love poetry, pastoral idylls, and works with mythological themes. Ovid's life story is illustrative of what Augustus was trying to do and how it affected the arts. Ovid was a friend of Horace and Propertius, but unlike them he never wrote poems extolling the ancient Roman virtues so dear to the *Princeps*. In A.D. 8, after the publication of his *Ars Amatoria* (The Art of Love), Augustus banished him to a small town on the western shore of the Black Sea, where he died ten years later. Augustus had found his poem, and perhaps his behavior, to lack the high moral character that the Augustan program sought to reinstill in Roman life.

Of the poets of the early Empire, Vergil was the greatest. He was born near Mantua in the Lombard plain, and, after receiving his education in Cremona, Milan, and Rome, he returned to his ancestral farm. In 41 B.C., the farm was confiscated by the government to settle the soldiers who had defeated Brutus and Cassius (the assassins of Julius Caesar) at Philippi, and Vergil moved to the Campania. There, he was patronized by one of Augustus' lieutenants, Maecenas, who also patronized Horace, Propertius, and other artists. In the 30s B.C., Vergil published two poem cycles dealing with rural life before Augustus asked him to compose a work glorifying Rome and Augustus' achievement.

For the last eleven years of his life, Vergil worked on a great epic, the *Aeneid*, which told of the origins of Rome and made a clear analogy between Aeneas as the legendary founder of the city and Augustus as its refounder. But the poet could not accept the Augustan propaganda that Rome's greatness rested on its moral superiority. Aeneas, Augustus's prototype, was unable to follow the course of action that he himself recognized to

lyric style. Lucretius (99–55 B.C.), perhaps the greatest poet of the republican period and the most original of all Latin authors, wrote a great work, *De rerum natura* (Concerning the nature of things), which expressed the values of Epicurean philosophy. This was a new synthesis of the old Hellenistic philosophy, but Lucretius was too speculative and abstract to appeal to the Romans, who prided themselves on being practical and down-to-earth. He had little influence and no successors as a philosophical poet.

The poets of the early Empire also wrote much that was apolitical, but they also contributed to the Augustan program. When they wrote political poems, they showed themselves to be more ambivalent than the historians about the Augustan achievement. Horace (65–8 B.C.), Propertius (*ca.* 50–*ca.* 16

be morally right. When, at the end of the poem, Aeneas killed his enemy, who lay helpless at his feet, the hero violated the precept that one should "war down the proud, spare the weak." This final act of violence permitted the founding of Rome, but the new city could not claim superiority over all others on the basis of a superior moral character.

THE SUCCESSORS OF AUGUSTUS, A.D. 14–68

Because Augustus had retained the forms of the republican constitution, there were no rules about succession to the Principate. Nonetheless, Augustus made it clear that his successor must be from his own family, the Julians, so that during the last two decades of his reign intrigue was a constant companion of the imperial family. From A.D. 14, when Augustus died, until A.D. 69 the Julian line continued in power, even though the emperors were often incompetent or paralyzed by suspicion and fear. Yet, the imperial government continued to flourish.

Augustus himself was succeeded by Tiberius, an able administrator and general who had been embittered by the old emperor's continual refusal, until all other possibilities had been tried, to name him as successor. Tiberius came from a distinguished senatorial family, the Claudians, but many senators resented him and intrigued against him. It did not help that he had high standards for his administrative assistants and removed many incompetent or dishonest scions of senatorial families from the civil service. Within his own family, the struggle over the succession led to several suspicious deaths, and fearful for his own life, he eventually left Rome for Capri, an island in the Bay of Naples. In his absence, Rome seethed with intrigue, and hearing of it Tiberius ordered the execution of many officials and senators on charges of treason. Everyone was relieved when he died in A.D. 37.

Tiberius's successor, Caligula, was worse. He had won the hearts of Romans as a young boy, and people expected great things from him. But Caligula was insane, and his whimsical cruelty and lack of sense in military affairs finally led the palace guard (the

A family portrait.
Above right:
Claudius
(*ca.* A.D. 50).
Right: Agrippina,
Claudius' wife, with
her child Nero.

Nero as emperor.

Vespasian, founder of the Flavian dynasty.

inces, and equestrians still handled most of the Empire's financial affairs, but Claudius's system became the basis of the imperial bureaucracy.

Claudius's good sense and ability did not extend to his family arrangements. He married his niece Agrippina, an evil woman who finally poisoned him so that her son from a previous marriage could succeed him. This was Nero, who came to power in A.D. 54. In the beginning, Nero acted under the guidance of his tutor Seneca, a philosopher and literary writer of high standing, and Burrus, the master of the palace guard, but in A.D. 62, after the death of Burrus, Seneca retired, leaving the young emperor under evil influences. Three years later Seneca was implicated in a plot against the emperor, who ordered him to commit suicide.

Nero was a megalomaniac who fancied himself a poet and artist. It was rumored that he himself had set the great fire in Rome in A.D. 64 to serve as a brilliant backdrop for a recitation of his poetry. This is certainly false, but one outcome of the fire was that Nero blamed it on the tiny community of Christians that had formed in the city, and he ordered them killed. Christian tradition says that St. Peter lost his life in this early persecution.

In his last years, Nero became fearful of plots and in addition to ordering Seneca's suicide, he condemned to death his mother, the poet Lucan, and the brilliant general Corbulo, who had defended the eastern frontier against the Parthians. He also executed many senators and confiscated their wealth. Consumed with the intrigues, Nero paid no attention to the administration and army, and, in A.D. 68, the legions scattered throughout the Empire rebelled. Nero was quickly overthrown and committed suicide. Thus ended the succession within Augustus's family. What followed was a brief civil war as the main segments of the army competed to raise their generals to the imperial power.

elite corps of the army) to conspire to put him to death. His reign lasted four difficult years.

For a short time after the death of Caligula, the Senate tried to reassert its authority and even to restore the Republic in fact as well as in name. But for a century real power had resided in the army, and soon the palace guard that had done away with Caligula found another to take his place. He was Caligula's uncle Claudius, a scholarly and sickly man of 51 who had survived the intrigues by cultivating the image of a harmless fool. Claudius turned out to be a more capable ruler than anyone had expected. He initiated the conquest of Britain and continued the ancient Roman practice of extending citizenship, which won the support of provincials. As an administrator, he established four bureaus, each headed by a freedman of the imperial family (usually a Greek). Senators still commanded armies and governed prov-

27 B.C.	14 A.D.	68	96	180 A.D.
Principate of Augustus	Julio-Claudian Emperors	Flavian Emperors	The "Five Good Emperors"	

THE EMPIRE AT ITS HEIGHT, A.D. 69–180

The troubles of A.D. 68–69 revealed the real weakness in the Augustan constitution. The army was the source of all power, and it was loyal to its commander. So long as the emperor was an able and popular figure he held the loyalty of all the armed forces, and unity was preserved. When the emperor was weak, as was the case with the later Julians, the armies looked to their local commanders to provide them with the leadership that guaranteed success and the rewards of service. After the death of Nero, legions put up their own candidates for the imperial power; in one year, there were four "emperors." From this civil strife, Vespasian, the commander of the eastern legions emerged victorious. Vespasian was a self-made man, and after him there was a series of emperors who had risen through the ranks of the army. They were men who had much experience in the affairs of the Empire and knew the provinces well. They represented a new upper class, which rose from service to the imperial government instead of from ancient aristocratic roots.

Under these men, the Empire and imperial government reached their high points. In A.D. 96, a distinguished, elderly senator named Nerva succeeded to the imperial throne. He recognized the problem he would have with the succession and adopted an able commander, Trajan, as his successor. This practice of adopting an able man as heir and successor continued for four more generations and produced, starting with Nerva, the "five good emperors." These men were excellent and wise administrators, and under them the Empire prospered in peace.

Yet, much of what the second-century emperors did also made the Empire more fragile than it had been.

Imperial Administration

The letters between the emperor Trajan and Pliny the Younger, his representative in one of the provinces of Asia Minor, suggest that imperial administrators, however severe, were generally more concerned with achieving justice than with following the letter of the law.

Pliny to Trajan

. . . Having never been present at any of the trials of the Christians, I am unacquainted with the method and limits to be observed either in examining or punishing them. Whether any difference is to be made on account of age, or no distinction allowed between the youngest and the adult; whether repentance admits to a pardon, or if a man has been once a Christian it avails him nothing to recant . . . .

In the meanwhile, the method I have observed . . . is this; I interrogated them whether they were Christians; if they confessed it I repeated the question twice again, adding the threat of capital punishment; if they still persevered, I ordered them to be executed.

Trajan to Pliny

The method you have pursued, my dear Pliny, in sifting the cases of those denounced to you as Christians is extremely proper. It is not possible to lay down any general rule which can be applied as the fixed standard in all cases of this nature. No search should be made for these people; when they are denounced and found guilty they must be punished; with the restriction, however, that if the party denies himself to be a Christian, and shall give proof that he is not (that is, by adoring our Gods) he shall be pardoned on the ground of repentance . . . .

From Pliny, *Letters*, trans. by William Melmoth, rev. by W. M. L. Hutchinson, The Loeb Classical Library (Cambridge, MA: Harvard University Press, 1953), pp. 401, 407.

Trajan (*ca.* A.D. 100).

The most important change was in the military system. Under Augustus and his immediate successors, the frontier armies had been mobile and had protected the borders by making forays across them. In the second century, the legions were gradually settled in permanent camps behind fixed fortified frontiers. In northern Britain, the emperor Hadrian built a wall across the island to keep out northern tribes. Along the Rhine and Danube frontier, the Romans built a line of fortress camps and watchtowers. The static armies that manned these fortifications had to be much larger than the mobile ones, and from the second century on the armed forces absorbed an increasing share of the Empire's economic wealth.

Just as the new defensive system was successful but potentially burdensome and difficult to maintain, so the second-century economy had a shallow health. Throughout its history, the Roman economy was predominantly agricultural, but peace made possible an uninhibited trade that increased wealth while encouraging the various parts of the Empire to specialize in crops that could be sent to market. Earlier, Sicilian grain had pushed Italian agriculture into the production of olives and wine. Now, Egyptian and North African grain competed successfully with the Sicilian crop, and Gallic wine with Italian. The parts of the Empire became increasingly interdependent, making them increasingly susceptible to any disturbance of the

The Roman Empire at Its Height   A.D. 117

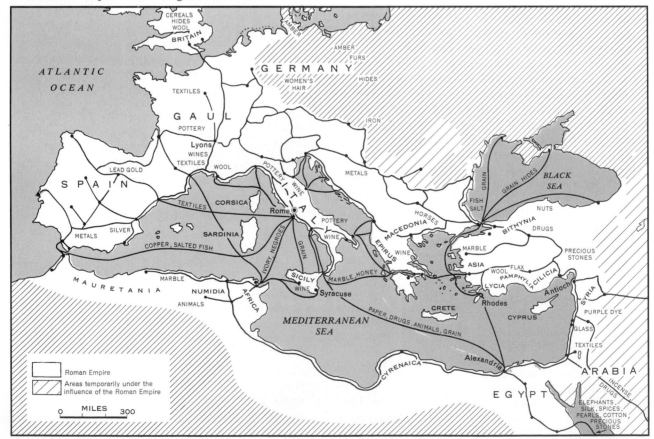

imperial peace. During the second century, it all worked well, but a multitude of troubles erupted in the next century.

THE CRISIS OF THE THIRD CENTURY

Political and Military Weakness

The last of the "good emperors," Marcus Aurelius (r. 161–80), found it necessary to spend a great deal of his time away from Rome. Trier, a city close to the Rhine-Danube border of the European provinces, became a rustic second capital. The problem that occupied Marcus was renewed unrest among the Germanic tribes across the border.

The new trouble was partly the fault of the Romans themselves. By establishing a static defensive line and ending forays across the border to keep the peoples there off balance and weak, the Romans had permitted the Germanic tribes to gather strength. Moreover, they had contributed to that strength by developing an active trade with the tribal groups living close to the frontier and by encouraging the consolidation of tribal groups. Both in trade and in diplomacy, the Romans found it easier to deal with large confederations than with a multitude of small tribes. Through these processes of peaceful coexistence, the Germans, even those living far from the frontier, were drawn into the sphere of Roman civilization and wealth.

From the end of the second century on, the northern border defenses came under continual pressure, which strengthened the position of local commanders. Under attack, but not engaged in a great war, the border armies looked to their immediate commanders for leadership rather than to the emperor. So long as the emperors chose competent and experienced successors who could control their lieutenants in the field, the tendency toward divisiveness was held in check. But when Marcus Aurelius ended the practice of adopting an heir and passed the impe-

The emperor Marcus Aurelius (160–180) entering Rome in triumph (detail from the column of Marcus Aurelius in Rome).

rial power on to his incompetent son Commodus (r. 180–92), a rift appeared between the central government and the border armies. When Commodus was assassinated, the events of A.D. 68–69 were repeated. The various segments of the army put up their generals as candidates for the imperial seat. Out of the strife, Septimius Severus (r. 193–211) emerged to establish a new dynasty, which ruled from 193 to 235. The brief civil war changed the balance of power in Roman government. Although the emperors had always risen to power through the army, the civilian government still set policy and commanded the legions. From 193 on, the army determined the policy of the government. Septimius is reported to have advised his son to assure for himself the affection of the army and count for little the views of other subjects.

When the last of the Severi was assassinated in 235, the powerful border armies took hold of the Empire. Be-

Roman Military Weakness   Late Second Century

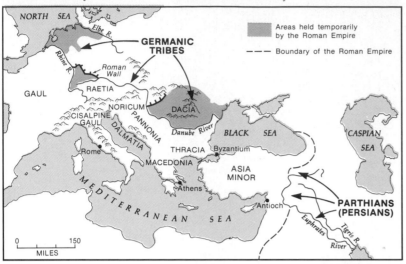

Roman soldier fighting on the Danube frontier (A.D. 108–109).

tween 235 and 285, the armies created and destroyed 26 emperors and at least as many unsuccessful contenders for the throne. The political involvement of the armies was in part the result of their isolation from Roman society and civilian government. A series of military reforms over the centuries had produced a professional army that was out of touch with the civilian population. The soldiers were inclined to concern themselves only with their own interests and to see the emperor, acting through his lieutenants in the field, as the guarantor of their well-being. After Marcus Aurelius had settled the Danube and eastern frontiers, the imperial system was able to keep the peacetime army well supplied and happy. But under the stress created by the local attacks of the people living beyond the borders, the system broke down. The number of demands on the emperor's attention went up sharply, and even if the emperor was competent and energetic, he could not hope to meet this demand. Consequently, the troops naturally looked to their own immediate commanders for the rewards of service, which these commanders could only deliver if they controlled the whole state.

The involvement of the border armies in the civil wars drew them off the frontiers into the provinces themselves and weakened the Empire's defenses. When Septimius Severus died in 211, he was in northern Britain, where he was engaged in pacifying the Caledonian tribes that had been raiding the British province from Scotland. His sons quickly ended the war without fully solving the problem because they had to return to Rome to establish themselves as the heads of government. On the Danube, the Germans, pushed back by Marcus Aurelius in the 170s, reasserted themselves soon after Septimius's death, and they seem to have been better organized than Marcus's foes had been. The attacks now came from large confederations of tribes. To the north, in the region of the lower Rhine Valley, a group of related tribes formed a confederation called the Franks. To the south, along the upper Rhine, the confederation of the Alemans emerged, and, to the east, along the lower Danube, the Goths formed from tribal groups that appear to have migrated southeast from southern Scandinavia. The Goths were even able to assemble a pirate fleet in the eastern Mediterranean.

In the East, the Parthians, who had also attacked the Empire during the reign of Marcus, renewed their pressure after 224, when the anti-Hellenistic Sassanid dynasty overthrew the old Hellenistic state. The new Persian shahs plundered the eastern provinces of the Empire and defeated the emperors who went to fight them. In 260, the emperor Valerian was defeated and captured; he apparently died as a slave in the Persian court.

Third-century tomb relief showing an affluent banker and two struggling Roman laborers. The Roman economy was weakened by this gap between the wealthy few and the poor masses.

Economic and Political Problems

By the third century, the principal problem of Roman government was the maintenance of the army. In 212, the emperor Caracalla issued a law that made all free men in the Empire citizens and thus liable to certain taxes and eligible for military service. Virtually the whole return from taxes went to supply the vast border armies, and, in fact, most taxes were paid in kind—that is, in grain or other produce instead of in coin—at stations along the famous military roads that had been built throughout the Empire. From these collection points, the goods moved out to the borders. In addition, the state had become the principal buyer of agriculture surplus, and the beneficiaries of this market were the great landowners. With their tax exemptions, these men did not have to give their grain to the government, but could sell it for profit. The government bought the produce to supplement the supplies it collected from less privileged farmers, and the great landowners enlarged their already huge fortunes.

The government also dominated other sectors of the economy. Many staple goods were manufactured in state factories, including all weapons and most of the clothing used by the armies. The goods were sent through the extensive government transport system that virtually monopolized large-scale shipping. Since the government organized and subsidized the provisioning of the major cities, independent merchants were largely restricted to dealing in a few widely available, and not very valuable, raw materials like timber, wool, and flax, and in the tools and implements used in everyday life. Merchants also dealt in luxury items like spices, jewelry, and fine wines, but this was a limited trade that was not an important part of the basic economy. Most of the traders in luxury goods were orientals, like Syrians and Jews, who had connections with the eastern Mediterranean cities through which these goods passed, some of them from as far away as India and China.

Greek and Roman merchants traveled freely in the stable world of the first two centuries A.D. Their ships could average more than one hundred miles a day (detail from a sarcophagus from Ostia, second or third century A.D.).

The Romans were not interested in the invention of labor-saving devices. The crane pictured here required the work of many slaves to operate the treadmill (detail from a tomb relief, first century A.D.).

The civil wars put enormous stress on this government-dominated economy. There was repeated disruption and rampant inflation. Now, the armies were competing for tax revenues as well as for the imperial throne, and the provincials found themselves liable to multiple demands for taxes—demands always backed by military force.

The principal victims of the crisis were the provincial aristocrats who governed the multitude of towns in the Empire, for the whole system of tax collection and government rested on these people. Under the Roman system, local municipal governments, run by a council (curia) made up of the leading men of the town, collected taxes, maintained roads and bridges, and did all the other business of government in their districts. Every man whose property amounted to a certain value was obligated to serve as a curialis of his municipium, and, with his colleagues, he was personally responsible both for carrying out governmental functions and for collecting taxes. In normal times, the curia merely organized the performance of these duties by the town's population and gained all the benefits of privilege, but, during the civil wars, the economic and political stresses ruined so many people that curiae often could not get either the performance of public functions or the requisite tax revenues out of their communities. Then, the personal liability of the council members became a very heavy burden.

In these circumstances, many men, whose families had once held their positions as curiales to be the sign of their economic and social success, tried to escape from their obligations by retiring to their country estates. As a result, the governments of a large percentage of the provincial towns collapsed, and the communities were left disorganized and without even the protection that the curiae could provide in the difficult conditions. At various times, the imperial government, momentarily functioning well, tried to reestablish the municipal governments, but the constant strife undermined these efforts.

Not all curiales escaped their obligations by withdrawing to the country. The imperial government itself provided another avenue of escape. Imperial civil servants were exempt from curial service, and, during the third century, a great many local aristocrats sought appointment to the bureaucracy from the succession of competing emperors. As a result, the bureaucratic class grew immensely, to the detriment of municipal government. Moreover, the continual civil war and rapid coming and going of emperors kept the bureaucracy in constant turmoil, ripped by shifting loyalties and competing claims. With each new emperor the supporters and civil servants of the last one were purged, though some people managed to survive the changes of regime.

Municipal Services in the Greco-Roman Cities

What are today regarded as the municipal services *par excellence* are not very frequently mentioned in antiquity . . . . The first duty of the *astynomi* [controllers or *curiales* of the towns] was the care of roads and bridges, both in the city itself and in its territory. They had to prevent encroachments on the public highway; the . . . law laid down minimum widths for country roads, thirty feet for a main road, twelve feet for a byroad. They had to remove obstructions; shopkeepers were allowed to display their wares outside their shops, but not in such a manner as to block the traffic. They had to prevent rubbish being tipped into the streets . . . . Landowners and householders were responsible . . . for the paving of the roads on which their property fronted, and the *astynomi* had to enforce this obligation . . . . Another care of the *astynomi* was drainage. Progressive cities had a regular system of drains, running under the streets, which carried off both surface water and sewage . . . . For their water-supply all ancient cities relied to some extent on wells and rain-water cisterns, and it was the duty of the *astynomi* to see that the owners of these kept them in good order.

From A. H. M. Jones, *The Greek City*, (New York: Oxford University Press, 1940), pp. 212–13.

IMPERIAL SOCIETY

What was life like during these centuries of Roman Peace followed by decades of civil war? Even during the height of Roman power and prosperity, it was not really very peaceful. In the countryside, the populace was made up of peasants and shepherds. For the most part, people lived in small villages, many of them wholly owned by upper-class landlords. The world outside the villages was very dangerous, inhabited by various desperate people who made their livelihood by robbery and thought nothing of murdering. Many villages had watchtowers, and virtually all posted guards. Where farmsteads were away from a village, it was an accepted principle that it should be situated well off the road and fortified with walls and watchtowers. The Romans had no police force, particularly in rural areas, and their armed forces took note only of major insurrections.

At the bottom of the social hierarchy were the shepherds, who worked for others, peasants and great landowners, and lived a difficult life away from the protection of even the small, weak peasant villages. In the pastures where he watched his sheep and goats, accompanied by his powerful mastiffs, bands of rustlers roamed, and the shepherd always had to be on his guard. In the village, he lived with others of his class in the most rundown section, which was often referred to as the Shepherds' Quarter.

The peasants, by far the largest class in the Empire, were not much better off than the herders. Many, if not most, peasants farmed as tenants of the great landowners and constantly battled the landlord's bailiffs and accountants. These men, unfettered by any moral conscience or control by their employers, sought to get as much as they could from the tenants. If their harsh exactions were particularly successful, they might gain profit beyond what they earned from their masters. In the few records of the Empire that still exist, mostly from the papyri of the Egyptian province, there is ample evidence of the bitter conflict between peasants and their landlords. At times, the bailiffs were physically attacked by desperate villagers, who felt, justifiably, that they were being ruined by the high rents and exactions.

There is some evidence of a small rural middle class of prosperous farmers and villagers, but most peasants who owned their own plots were no better off than the tenant farmers. Plots were likely to be small and poor (there are records of people owning one-sixth of an olive tree and one-tenth of a small house), and powerful, upper-class neighbors were a constant threat. In most cases, the big men did not hold large, contiguous estates, but many scattered parcels, and they did whatever they could to force the small men in their neighborhood off the land, so that they could enlarge and consolidate their enormous estates. The extant records show farmers complaining that powerful neighbors had turned animals into the fields, ruining their crops, or had sent work crews to harvest their carefully tended crops. Only rarely did such incidents come to the attention of authorities; much of the time, the farmers could not defend their farms and had to sell or abandon them to the great landowners.

If a powerful neighbor did not ruin the small, independent farmer, then the state might. Romans assumed that taxes would be paid by the rural populations on the basis of their production. Furthermore, many upper-class holders obtained tax exemptions, which increased the burden on the peasants. With the enormous growth of the defensive armies, the taxes grew to be a crushing burden, and from time to time the government had to relax it or whole districts would be deserted as farmers gave up and migrated to the cities.

Rural housing was extremely inadequate. Although the evidence is spotty, it shows that overcrowding was the norm. There might be 25 people, related more or less closely, living in a house, and in Egypt abandonment of unwanted children was common. The infant was left on the village dung-heap (and carried the designation ''of the dung-heap'' throughout life), where a well-to-do family might pick it up to be raised as a slave. The general picture of life in the provinces of the Empire was one of endless struggle and deprivation. The inadequacy of transportation isolated regions from one another, so that a poor harvest meant starvation, even if another, not too distant, locale had good crops.

Wealth and talent flowed to the cities, whose populations looked down on rural villagers. The rents, taxes, and food produced in rural districts went to the cities, and often the rape of the countryside was so effective that rural districts starved, while the local townsmen lived comfortably. With few exceptions, such as the famous biographer Plutarch (*ca.* 46–*ca.* A.D. 120), the great landowners lived in the cities, where they had magnificent houses and gardens. In addition, the best craftsmen left the peasant villages for the city, so that only simple items were available in the country. Rural folk relied on peddlers from the city for things that required skill and good materials to make.

The houses and gardens of the great might take up a substantial part of the territory of a city; one-third of Rome's area was occupied by great estates. Beside the rich neighborhoods, about one-quarter of the area was devoted to public buildings. Elsewhere in the city the population lived in dense neighborhoods, usually organized in blocks. The density of the larger Roman cities has been calculated to have been about 200 people per acre. This compares with 140 per acre in Paris in 1856. Today in Europe, 150 per acre is considered dense and 250 per acre a slum. In such a community, people spent as much time as possible in the streets, and it is often said that only the existence of the public areas made the Roman cities bearable for the majority of their populations. The publicness of

A Roman vegetable stall and its owner.

life left people with little privacy and led to frequent mob disturbances. Every incident instantly drew a crowd, so that life fluctuated between quiet and violence with a bewildering quickness. A person was never far from violence.

In distribution of property ownership, the cities were not different from the countryside. The blocks and multistory tenements in which most urbanites lived were owned by the great men, who often let them down terribly. Indeed the buildings were badly built and often collapsed. Cicero wrote to a friend about two of his buildings that fell down; he decided to rebuild in the hopes that he could get a good return on the investment. The triumvir Crassus made a fortune in Rome through real estate. He built up his holdings by creating a private fire brigade. When a building went up in flames, Crassus's men would arrive, strike a deal for the property, and then put the fire out.

The city populations formed block associations, and the census was taken on the basis of these. The associations, centered in the corner cafe, took care of

This marble relief pictures a small Italian city as it looked in the days of the early Caesars. Blocks of two- and three-story tenements are enclosed by the ancient town wall. At the right, the country villas of the wealthy, with their gardens and colonnades, sprawl across the nearby hillsides.

all sorts of business. They helped families struck by a disaster, functioned as burial societies, and organized youth athletic clubs, which competed with one another during the festivals. There were also associations of the different trades. People engaged in the same craft or trade—butchers, booksellers, cobblers, and so forth—lived in the same quarters, so that buyers knew where to go to find the market in the goods they wanted. Tradesmen competed, but not fiercely. For the most part, they cooperated. Their associations functioned much as the block associations did and also lobbied government officials for and against measures that affected the trade. In fact, clubs and organizations were ubiquitous in city life. They were formed to support shrines, promote athletics, and dozens of other purposes. The foreigner entering a city always knew to go to the shrine set up by his countrymen who lived in the city. There, he would find assistance. In a few instances, cities set up official bureaus in other cities with which they had substantial trade.

The two great cities were Rome and Alexandria, which approached a million inhabitants. Antioch and Carthage (which continually recovered from Roman depredations) came next with populations of several hundred thousands. Then there was a precipitous fall-off. There were about six cities with populations of 75,000, and a great mass of cities of about 20,000. Finally, there were the cities that were urban centers only in name. There were hundreds of "cities" founded in North Africa as its rich lands were brought into production. Each of these towns was a *municipium*, with all the rights and privileges of a city to rule over its district and exercise control over local affairs, but in reality they were agricultural villages. In Rome, North Africans were considered countryfolk and were the butt of jokes.

In country and city, the average Roman struggled for subsistence. The gulf between rich and poor was extreme in the imperial period, with only a small middle class to hold the economic center. Virtually all wealth was in land and loans; senatorial families did not participate much in the commercial activities of the small merchant class. A man could make 6 percent on his loans, which doubled his worth every dozen years. With their vast holdings in land, the rich could afford to wait on the growth of their fortunes.

The depredations of the third century made life more difficult for everyone, but it is remarkable how stable the basic social and economic patterns remained. Notwithstanding the continued growth of the great estates, peasant agriculture remained the backbone of the imperial economy, and notwithstanding the troubles in the cities, the curial class remained strong.

The local municipal aristocracies constituted the largest class of educated people in the Empire, and their education was remarkably similar from one end of the Roman world to the other. The Greek East was linguistically and culturally different from the Latin West, but these differences were narrowed by education. Greeks did not study Latin unless they were interested in pursuing military or legal careers— all official documents sent to the East were accompanied by a Greek translation—but, in the first and second centuries, all educated westerners mastered Greek. The disruptions of the third century, which increased the provincialism even of the upper classes by weakening the imperial economy and concentrating everyone's attention on local crises, seem to have contributed to the breakdown of this universal system of education in Greek. By the fourth century, many translators were at work translating the corpus of Greek philosophy, science, and theology into Latin.

The aristocracy was a thin, homogeneous veneer on an Empire of very different peoples. Although the characteristics of society, described earlier, varied little throughout the Empire, imperial society was a patchwork of ethnic societies. Because Latin and Greek were virtually the only written languages (Syriac and Hebrew were

rare exceptions) and the only ones taught in schools, it is difficult to tell the strength of native languages and cultures in the Empire. However, it seems that the peasant populations remained un-Romanized and continued to speak their own ancestral languages. Several dialects of Celtic (from which modern Gaelic and Breton derive) were spoken in Gaul and Britain, and several native cultures continued to thrive in Asia Minor. Syriac and Coptic (the Egyptian language) continued to be spoken in the East. Modern Albanian probably derives from the language spoken by the ancient Illyrians, and Thracian, the language of tribes living in the southern Balkans, still survived in the fourth century.

Thus, there were two or more layers of culture in most parts of the late Empire. On one side, the imperial government and the classes that served it saw a great territorial Empire united by the Mediterranean and by a network of roads that provided inland communications for state services and armies. The education, institutions, and tastes of the governing classes were remarkably homogeneous; theirs was the culture known as Greco-Roman civilization. On the other side, most of the Empire's populations maintained their pre-Roman customs and languages, even while the imperial economy and government greatly affected their lives.

Even though the upper classes were culturally unified, they were socially highly stratified. Under the Empire, with its vast imperial bureaucracy and many subject peoples, Romans had developed a love of honorific titles to distinguish their social and governmental positions. The crisis of the third century enhanced this affection for honorifics. They became the distinguishing marks of the municipal aristocrats who eagerly joined the imperial service. In the late third century, the highest class, the senators, bore the title *clarissimi* (most distinguished), while the high judges of imperial courts were called *eminentissimi* (most eminent) and their immediate subordi-

A Roman girl with a writing tablet is depicted in this fresco from Pompeii (*ca.* A.D. 70).

nates, *perfectissimi* (most excellent). The prestige ascribed to these titles became diminished as many people acquired them, because the emperors often rewarded faithful service with high status. In the late third century, about 500 senators were *clarissimi*, but by the middle of the sixth century, several thousand claimed the title. The same thing happened to other titles, and there was a proliferation of new titles— for example, *spectabiles* (nobles) and *viri illustri* (illustrous men). Such titles also defined the privileges accorded to their holders.

There were middle-class titles also, but these defined obligations rather than privileges. At the top of the middle classes were the *curiales,* the heavily burdened members of the municipal councils. The imperial government was constantly tampering with the laws dealing with this class in order to maintain its numerical and economic strength. The superintendents of state factories, which dominated the industrial economy of the Empire, were substantial men and received appropriate titles. They ranked above merchants, who had low status and, even when they were successful, only rarely rose into the class of *curiales.* On the whole, merchants were on the same level as the simple craftsmen, who worked in the state factories.

THE RISE OF CHRISTIANITY

The principal religious development of the late ancient world was the spread of Christianity. Originating as a religion profoundly antagonistic to many of the values of Roman society and politics, by the late fourth century, Christianity had become the predominant religion of the Empire. It became one of Rome's greatest legacies to the medieval and modern worlds.

Christianity developed from Judaism at a time when that ancient religion was in ferment. There was a basic division in the Jewish community between those who had been Hellenized during the long rule of the Seleucids and Ptolemies and those who retained their Semitic culture. The translation of the Hebrew Bible into Greek, which was done in Alexandria in the second century B.C., was symbolic of this division. In addition, Judaism was broken into a variety of religious sects that vied for religious and political leadership in Judea.

Until 4 B.C., this conflict took place in a semiautonomous client state of Rome, of which the last king was Herod the Great (r. 37–4 B.C.). When the Romans took over direct administration of the kingdom, they had to deal with the religious and social turbulence directly, and it increased. The Jews believed that the Romans stood in the way of their historical destiny as a nation, and fanatical sects agitated constantly against the conquerors. Most of the time the majority of the Jewish population accommodated itself to Roman rule, but sometimes the small radical sects stirred up widespread rebellions against the imperial administration, which was often insensitive to Jewish religious feelings.

The first major rebellion took place at the very beginning of Roman provincial rule. In 4 B.C., the Romans, following good adminstrative practice, instituted a census. The Hebrew Bible prohibited the numbering of the people of God, and the Jews rebelled. After the Romans put down this upheaval, resistance among the Jews was reduced to guerrilla warfare until A.D. 66, when a new great rebellion occurred. It took the Romans four years of very hard fighting to put down this insurgence, and afterward they tried unsuccessfully to destroy the Jews' sense of identity by destroying the city of Jerusalem and its temple. The last great Jewish rebellion took place in 135, and after it the Romans tried to solve the Jewish problem by forcing many of them to emigrate to other parts of the Empire. During this series of troubles, the Romans crucified thousands of Jews as subversives and conceived a strong dislike for Jews, whose religion caused so much trouble.

Between about A.D. 26 and 29, Jesus of Nazareth created his tiny movement in Judea. His earliest followers were Semitic Jews from the Galilee, a district of the ancient kingdom of Samaria that had been formed after the reign of Solomon (r. *ca.* 960–930 B.C.), but like all Jews, Jesus looked on Jerusalem as the center of Judaism, and in A.D. 29 he led his people there.

Religious figures like Jesus were common in Judea at that time, and they made both the Romans and the Jewish leaders nervous because they often became the focal points for anti-Roman agitation or insurgency. As a result, Jesus fell under suspicion when he arrived in the environs of Jerusalem, and soon he was arrested and executed by the Romans. Crucifixion was the penalty Romans reserved for insurgents.

After Jesus's death, his followers scattered, but they were eventually reunited, apparently by Peter (one of the earliest members of the sect), in Jerusalem. There, the Romans seem to have left them alone, but other Jews persecuted them. If the sect grew at all, it did so modestly and slowly, and only among other Semitic Jews. Then, the conversion of a Hellenized Jew named Saul changed the circumstances of the sect.

Saul, who changed his name to Paul after his conversion, preached the message of Jesus to the huge community of Hellenistic Jews. These people had assimilated into Hellenistic society and migrated to many of the great cities of the eastern Mediterranean. In those places, they had attracted many gentile "fellow travelers," who came to prayer services and learned something about Jewish religion without actually becoming Jews. It was among these hybrid communities that Paul and his assistants worked.

By the time Jerusalem was destroyed A.D. 70, Hellenistic Christianity had spread to Antioch, Alexandria, Rome, and many smaller cities. The Christians formed small communities—much like the usual urban associations. They met for common worship—which focused on a ritual meal modeled on the last supper of Jesus—in the houses of their richest members, and they organized works of charity on behalf of their poorest members. These communities seem to have had little formal structure. They were led by elders (presbyters), who organized the worship and social activities of the congregations. The basic beliefs of the Christians derived from the Jews, but the Christians profoundly altered Jewish beliefs so that they appealed to all people, not just to Jews. The Jews believed that a Messiah (one anointed by God) would come to establish the kingdom of God on earth, defeating all the enemies of Judea. The Christians believed that Jesus was the Messiah, but that he came not to lead Israel to the final conquest over their enemies, but to save mankind as a whole. For the Christians, Jesus was the incarnation of God—the Son of God—with the mission of giving mankind an opportunity to recover from the sin Adam had committed in the Garden of Eden (*Genesis* 3). Through his death, Jesus had redeemed man from the sin of Adam, and to be saved through Jesus one only had to believe that this was true.

In its first century and a half of existence, Christianity was just one of a multitude of cults in the Empire. Augustus had failed to drive out the mystery cults, which had become very popular about the time of Jesus. To many Romans, Christianity was such a cult. Like the mystery cults, the new religion emphasized individual religious experience and a personal, emotional, and intimate contact with the deity. Like them, it offered communion with the deity in this life, and union with the deity after death. The cults commonly used sacraments, ritual actions that prepared the initiated for communion with the god, and had a theology, or body of doctrine, that explained the mystery by which the death of their particular divine hero had conquered death itself. In these things too, Christianity appeared similar to the cults.

Hellenistic Christianity had developed in the context of this profusion of cults, and it absorbed ideas and practices from them, probably introduced by new Christians who previously had belonged to another cult. However, the new religion had several advantages over its rivals. First, it rested on the rich and ancient Judaic heritage, which provided it with a strong sense of identity.

Second, the beliefs of the Christians derived from a particular way of interpreting the Bible, and this method also gave the new religion a means of integrating new ideas into a body of inherited truth. For example, Christians interpreted the biblical prophecy of the Messiah as referring not to a ruler who would lead Israel to worldly triumph, but as a suffering servant who would conquer death by dying himself. This interpretation made it possible for Christians to continue to believe in Jesus after his execution, and it was consistent with the beliefs of many mystery cults. Therefore, many pagans who had experience in the cults found Christianity congenial and attractive.

Third, the Christians inherited from the Jews an intense feeling of exclusiveness. This was evidenced in their absolute refusal to honor the Roman gods or other cults and in the careful relationship they maintained with the imperial government. The religion was always adamant in its refusal to render unto Caesar what was due to God. This attitude made Christianity more of a community than a cult.

Finally, Christianity evolved by responding to the religious ideas of the Greek peoples of the Empire—the people the Christian preachers were trying to convert. Despite its Judaic origins, the religion that emerged in the New Testament was greatly influenced by Hellenistic beliefs and ideas. Christianity was both ancient and modern, and what became orthodox Christianity was a Greco-Roman religion.

The specialness of Christianity gave it advantages and disadvantages in its relations with the Roman state. Everyone in Roman society believed in the existence of the unseen world of the gods—or god in the case of the Jews

and Christians—and in the connection between this world and the world of human affairs. To ensure the favor of the divine powers, which was necessary for the welfare of the state, it was essential that the community perform its sacrifices, and, in order for these to be efficacious, every member of the community had to participate. The Jews had stood aside from these sacrifices for centuries, but the Romans tolerated the exclusiveness of Jewish monotheism. They recognized that the Jews were following an ancient cult and had always been tolerant of such traditions. Some Roman officials, such as Pontius Pilate, governor of Judea from A.D. 26 to 36, liked to bait the Jews, but on the whole they were left in peace.

The Christians were a different matter. Although their religion had originated as a Jewish sect, they made strenuous efforts to distinguish themselves from the Jews, particularly after the Jewish rebellion of A.D. 66–70, and by the second century the majority of Christians stemmed from the gentile population. Consequently, the Christian community did not constitute a distinct ethnic minority following an ancient religious tradition, and the Christians' refusal to participate in the civic cults was not tolerated. Before the end of the first century Roman law made it a capital offense to be Christian, and for generations people circulated rumors that Christians engaged in immoral rituals during their secret communions.

The popular and official suspicion of the Christians increased during the third century, when the attack of Germans and Persians made Romans feel a special need of divine favor. In 250, the emperor Decius ordered all his subjects to perform the sacrifices and to obtain certificates showing that they had done so. This order constituted an official persecution of the Christians. In most places, the authorities did not strictly obey the emperor's order, and Christians were either able to ignore the order or to get certificates through offi-

Symbol of Christianity, incorporating the Greek letters chi and rho (the monogram for Christ that forms the shape of the cross) and alpha and omega (meaning beginning and end).

96 A.D.	180	284	305
The "Five Good Emperors"	Century of Disorder	Diocletian	

cial connivance. But a few Christians made a public show of their refusal to perform their duty and were executed. When Decius was killed by the Germans in 251, the persecution ended completely, to be revived in 257, when the emperor Valerian wanted new prayers for success against the Persians. When Valerian was captured by the Persians in 260, official persecution virtually disappeared for 40 years.

In this period, the Christian communities grew rapidly and came to exercise a large influence in many towns. As municipal administrations disintegrated under the pressure of the civil wars, many of the functions of government, particularly care for the poor and the settlement of disputes, were left to private associations, such as the Christian communities. The Christian congregations had evolved an internal organization, directed by bishops, that made it possible for them to perform these social functions well, and, as they became important in the towns, they gained adherents. The bishops became increasingly visible and respected in the urban communities.

It was the optimism and complacency generated by these two generations of growth that made the persecution of 303 so traumatic. This was the Great Persecution of later Christian tradition, and it lasted until 311. To understand its place in Roman, as opposed to Christian, history, we must turn to the reign of the emperor Diocletian.

THE RESTORATION OF ORDER: THE REIGN OF DIOCLETIAN, 284–305

The prolonged political and military crisis of the third century disrupted, but did not destroy, the Roman army and bureaucracy, and the potential for recovery remained. Aurelian (r. 270–75) began the work of restoration by stopping the civil wars and starting the shoring up of the border defenses. This work was carried on by his successors, even though the armies continued to make and unmake emperors frequently. In 284, this process raised the Illyrian general Diocletian to power, but, unlike his predecessors, Diocletian managed to hold on to the imperial power and to restore the Empire's internal stability.

To achieve this success, Diocletian broke with custom in several ways. He abandoned Rome as his official residence and ruled from cities close to the frontiers. From these seats, he rebuilt the frontier fortifications and enlarged the army, but he broke it into smaller units and separated military command from the supply and payment of the troops. These reforms hindered the rise of independent commanders who

Diocletian and his coemperor stand in front, embracing each other; the two Caesars stand behind them (St. Mark's Cathedral, Venice).

The Administrative Divisions of Diocletian   Third and Fourth Centuries

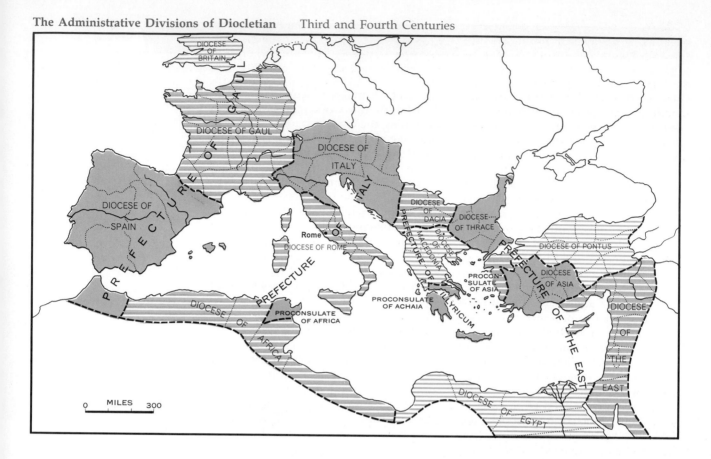

could count on the support of large armies.

The emperor balanced these changes in the field armies with changes in the highest level of command. Diocletian recognized that the military problems of the Empire could not be solved by a single centralized leadership, and he therefore divided the supreme command. He began by associating Maximian with himself as co-emperor—both men took the title Augustus. Later he created two assistant emperors who were designated as heirs of the imperial title; they were each called Caesar. Diocletian's dominant personality and power kept the potential for conflict in this new arrangement in check.

In addition to dividing imperial authority, Diocletian reorganized the administrative structure of the Empire. He increased the number of provinces from 50 to 100 and combined the prov-

inces into 13 dioceses. This reorganization of the provinces had a great effect on the populations of the Empire. The new provincial administrations were more effective than the old, and they absorbed some of the functions once left to the municipal councils. Nonetheless, the curial class remained a very important element of the administration, and Diocletian and his successors tried to close off the avenues by which its members were escaping their obligations. These attempts ultimately failed, and in the early fifth century the *curiae* began to be replaced by imperial officials. In the East, this development took place about the end of the fifth century.

As part of his effort to stabilize the society of the Empire, Diocletian issued a series of laws that created a caste system. Sons had to follow their fathers in their occupations and professions. Farmers, tenant and free, were required to remain on the land they had occupied when the last census, done in the 290s, was taken, and sons had to be registered with the authorities who kept the census. Other occupations, such as bakers and sailors, also became hereditary castes. For centuries, the census had been taken periodically by Roman authorities and had served as the basis of the tax system and for other administrative purposes. Now, it was kept current by officials who had to maintain the new caste system, but it soon was used by the emperor's financial administrators as well. Each year the chief financial administrators of the government reassessed the levy on the basis of the census, and this annual attention to the tax system had the effect of increasing both the efficiency and the importance of the system. The civil wars had damaged the old state economy, which rested on state-run industries as well as on taxes, and taxes were now more important than ever before as a source of funds for the government's activities. This reliance on tax revenues combined with the existence of an efficient method of assessing taxes led to a doubling of the tax rate between 324 and 364.

In economic affairs, Diocletian tried to stop the inflationary spiral that had resulted from the constant wars by reforming the currency, and, when this did not work, he issued a decree fixing prices on many goods. This policy failed completely, even though the penalty for transgressing the edict was death.

While Diocletian's administrative and military reforms had lasting effects, his solution to the problem of succession did not work for long. In 305, he himself retired and forced his associate Maximian to do the same. The two Caesars succeeded to the imperial power. By 316, when Diocletian died, the dynastic ambitions of these men had ruined his system. After more than ten years of war, Constantine, the son of Maximian's Caesar, emerged as sole emperor (r. 324–37). Like Diocletian, Constantine preferred to rule the

Empire from the East, and he built a new capital on the site of the ancient Athenian colony at Byzantium on the Bosporus. This city was dedicated in 330 and was later renamed Constantinople. In the West, Milan had already replaced Rome as the principal seat of government, because it was a better place from which to direct the defense of the western frontiers.

THE CHRISTIANIZATION OF THE EMPIRE, 313–390

Constantine dramatically changed the status and condition of the Christians. Early in his struggle for power, he became convinced that the pagan god—

Constantine's Religious Beliefs

The official policy of the Empire after 312 was toleration, as shown in a letter sent in the name of both Constantine and his coemperor to the governor of Bithynia in 313.

. . . **we resolved to make such decrees as should secure respect and reverence for the Deity; namely, to grant both to the Christians and to all the free choice of following whatever form of worship they pleased, to the intent that all the divine and heavenly powers that be might be favorable to us and all those living under our authority.**

■ ■ ■

But Constantine showed stronger personal convictions in a letter written only a year later to the governor of Africa, dealing with the problem of schism in that province.

Since I am assured that you are also a worshipper of the supreme God, I confess to your Excellency that I consider it absolutely wrong that we should pass over in insincerity quarrels and altercations of this kind, whereby perhaps the supreme divinity may be moved not only against the human race, but even against me myself, to whose care He has entrusted rule over all earthly affairs . . . . For then, and only then, shall I be able truly and most fully to feel secure . . . when I shall see all men, in the proper cult of the Catholic religion, venerate the most holy God with hearts joined together like brothers in their worship.

From *Great Problems in European Civilization*, ed. by K. M. Setton and H. R. Winkler (Englewood Cliffs, N.J.: Prentice-Hall, 1954), pp. 75, 79.

the Unconquered Sun—worshipped by his family was identical to the Christian god that had helped him win a crucial battle at the Mulvian Bridge, just to the north of Rome (312). In 313, Constantine issued an edict of toleration of Christianity and forced his colleague in the East to confirm the decree. Issued at Milan it is often called the Edict of Milan.

The motives for Constantine's new religious policy will never be fully known, but it is clear that personal conversion played a role. Although he was not baptized until 337 on his deathbed, the leaders of the Christian church came to his support immediately after

he issued the edict of toleration, and he began immediately to take an active part in the affairs of the Christians. The role of the Christians changed suddenly, even though only a small minority of the Empire's population was Christian. At this time, the population was perhaps 10 percent Christian in the East, and about 5 percent in the West. But the movement was strong in the cities, and during the previous two generations leading families had joined it. Moreover, the churches had become well organized and could provide immediate and effective support for the emperor.

Although Constantine did not make Christianity the state religion—which would have been politically suicidal—he provided the religion with the means to grow and prosper. He permitted the churches to become corporations and, therefore, to hold property under Roman law. Many of the private houses in which Christian communities had met were deeded to the corporation and became churches. Because Christianity had spread through the cities of the Empire, each city already had a chief Christian official called the bishop. Constantine authorized bishops to act as judges in disputes brought to them by their parishioners. With this sort of social and legal status, the church grew rapidly toward becoming the majority religion in the Empire.

Reliance on the Christian church led Constantine to concern himself with the problems of the Christian movement. These problems stemmed from theological disputes on the one hand and from the consequences of the earlier persecutions on the other. From the wide variety of ethnic and social groups in which Christian preachers made conversions came many competing religious ideas and beliefs. The arbiters of the inevitable disputes were the bishops, but these men represented their local churches and, therefore, were often unable to agree on doctrine among themselves. In many disputes, the problem was the existence of competing traditions within the various

Colossal head of Constantine, from his basilica in Rome (*ca.*** 320).**

congregations. Each congregation had learned its Christian beliefs from its founder and had passed these beliefs down from generation to generation. Local variations of doctrine were often introduced in this process and produced disunity in the Christian movement.

The bishops who governed the churches founded directly by Jesus's followers, the apostles, offered a solution to this problem. They claimed that the traditions handed down in their churches came most directly from Jesus himself and should take precedence over the traditions of other churches. The bishops of Jerusalem, Antioch, Alexandria, Ephesus, and Rome, among others, could make this claim. But the bishops of these churches did not agree on all points either, and while the doctrine of apostolic tradition narrowed the focus of disputes, it did not end them.

There was also controversy, particularly in the churches of North Africa, about how Christians had responded to the most recent series of persecutions. On one side, followers of Donatus (the Donatists) claimed that the only true Christians were those who had resisted the imperial government without compromise. On the other side, the majority of bishops and church members forgave accommodation as the only reasonable act under the circumstances. This dispute seriously disrupted the African churches, because the Donatists refused to recognize the legitimacy of priests who either had themselves avoided confrontation with the imperial authorities or had been ordained (made priests) by bishops who had. The North African church was in turmoil for generations because of this conflict.

Constantine relied on the Christian god to guarantee his success and had an interest in ending these disputes. In 314, he summoned the bishops of Africa and the West to a council at Arles to deal with the Donatist dispute. The council decided against the Donatists, establishing the doctrine that the effi-

cacy of the sacraments was independent of the personal character of the priest. This decree established the principle that the legitimacy of a priest was legal in nature. Henceforth, a priest could continue to serve the altar so long as the ecclesiastical authorities recognized his legal right to do so, and the people could not reject him because they considered him unworthy. This meant that obedience to the church became a legal obligation.

The theological disputes were primarily a problem in the East, where a welter of religious and philosophical traditions affected the way individual Christians viewed their god. The main dispute concerned the precise relationship between Jesus's human and divine natures. Constantine could not intervene in this controversy until after he unified the imperial power in 324, but he acted immediately after that. In 325, he held a new council of over 300 bishops at Nicaea. Constantine himself presided over the council's sessions, and it is considered the first ecumenical—that is, universal—council of the church. Nicaea confirmed that Jesus was both man and God and began the development of the Christian creed. Even though the creed was not fully enunciated until the council of Chalcedon in 451, it is called the Nicene Creed.

The council also established two important principles of ecclesiastical organization—first, that a council of bishops held the supreme authority in deciding matters of Christian doctrine and church law, and, second, that the emperor, as the supreme secular ruler, had an important role to play in church affairs. The first of these principles gave the church a means of settling disputes and contributed to its ability to survive as a universal institution. The second undermined the New Testament attitude that the Christian's obligation to Caesar was distinct from and often in conflict with his obligation to God.

With the exception of Julian (r. 361–63), the emperors of the fourth century

The declining creativity and technical skill of the artists of the late Roman Empire can be seen in the Arch of Constantine in Rome (312–315).

adhered to the Christian religion and remained embroiled in its affairs. Nonetheless, there remained strong opposition to it in the conservative senatorial class—whose members linked their adherence to the old pagan cults with their support of the ancient rights of the Senate. The conflict with the conservative senators came to a head later in the fourth century and issued in a complete victory for the Christians. In 390, the emperor Theodosius I made Christianity the official religion of the Empire.

However, the challenge to Christianity mounted by the educated pagans had a lasting effect. In responding to their arguments against Christian beliefs and claims, the North African bishop Augustine (354–430) formulated what became the basic Christian view of what it means to be a Christian and how Christianity fits into human history. In his *Confessions* (written in the 390s), Augustine explored the meaning of his own conversion, and his conception of this event became the accepted view of how God saves the human soul from dying a meaningless death. In *The City of God*, he constructed a Christian theory of history and formulated a Christian approach to understanding human society. In many other works, Augustine established the foundations of western Christian theology.

During the fourth and fifth centuries, the church also developed as an institution. Bishops appointed priests and deacons to help in the governance of their churches, and many lesser orders of officials were created. The bishop had complete authority over all his subordinates and over the property owned by his church. Yet, the international church had little organization. The emperor could call a council to solve questions of doctrine, but the universal church had no way of its own to resolve disputes.

The old idea that those churches founded by the apostles took precedence over others held some promise for creating an accepted order for the church, but the apostolic churches often disagreed among themselves. To resolve such disputes, the leading apostolic churches made further claims based on the status of their founders. Alexandria claimed to have been founded by Paul; Antioch and Rome could claim to have been co-founded by Peter and Paul. It was Rome that capitalized on these claims by propounding the Petrine Doctrine. This doctrine rested on passages of the New Testament (principally Matthew 16: 18–19) that indicated that Jesus had chosen Peter to be the leader of the apostles. Since tradition said that Peter had ended his life in Rome and that he had been head of the Roman church, the bishops of Rome claimed to have inherited his primacy, and they appropriated the title pope (*papa* meaning father), which had been widely used by bishops, for themselves. Pope Leo I (r.

St. Augustine on the City of God

Accordingly, two cities have been formed by two loves: the earthly by the love of self, even to the contempt of God; the heavenly by the love of God, even to contempt of self. The former glories in itself, the latter in the Lord. For the one seeks glory from men, but the greatest glory of the other is God, the witness of conscience. . . . In the one, the princes and the nations it subdues are ruled by the love of ruling; in the other, the princes and the subjects serve one another in love, the latter obeying, while the former take thought for all. The one delights in its own strength, represented in the persons of its rulers; the other says to its God: "I will love Thee, O Lord, my strength." And therefore the wise men of the one city, living according to man, have sought for profit to their own bodies or souls, or both, and those who have known God "glorified him not as God, neither were thankful, but became vain in their imaginations, and their foolish heart was darkened. . . . " For they were either leaders or followers of the people in adoring images, "and worshipped and served the creature more than the Creator." But in the other city there is no human wisdom, but only godliness, which offers due worship to the true God, and looks for its reward in the society of the saints, of holy angels as well as holy men, that God may be all in all.

From St. Augustine, *City of God*, in *Basic Writings of St. Augustine*, ed. by Whitney J. Oates, Vol. II, p. 274. Copyright 1948 by Random House, Inc. Reprinted by permission.

440–61) was the first to enunciate the complete doctrine, and in the West, where Rome was the only apostolic see, the doctrine was gradually accepted. In the East, the great episcopal powers—particularly Antioch, Alexandria, and Constantinople—never accepted the doctrine.

Throughout the late imperial period, Christianity remained primarily a religion of the cities. It made very slow progress in the countryside among the peasants. As a religion formed by educated Greeks, it did not appeal strongly to the illiterate classes, and it took a long time for Christians to develop a strategy and means for successfully proselytizing the vast agricultural population of the Empire.

The church of Santa Sabina, built in 425, incorporates the characteristics of a Roman basilica—a long, rectangular nave divided from two side aisles by rows of pillars.

THE EMPIRE IN THE FOURTH AND FIFTH CENTURIES

The Fourth Century

Constantine's decision to move the capital of the Empire to Byzantium shows that he saw both problems and opportunities in the East. The problems arose from the danger posed by the Persian Empire, which had again become aggressive in the fourth century. However, the new Roman capital was strategically placed and very well protected. It sat on a promontory jutting out into the Bosporus, so that it could control the entry to the Black Sea and the Balkans and could be strongly defended by sea walls and a short land wall. From Constantinople, the emperors could take advantage of the great wealth and manpower of the eastern provinces, which were both the richest and the most populous parts of the Empire.

The threat of the Persians was balanced by renewed pressure by the Germans on the Rhine-Danube frontier. Here, the Roman armies began to have serious problems of manpower, and the imperial government had to expand the use of foreign troops. From very ancient times, the Roman legions had been supplemented by auxiliary troops of provincials, but this distinction meant little after the grant of universal citizenship in 212. Now, the Romans enlisted German tribal units to make up the deficiencies in their armies. They made pacts with German kings according to which their tribes could settle on Roman territory in return for forming a military buffer against other Germans. The tribes enlisted in this way were called *foederati* (allied or confederated peoples), and by the latter part of the fourth century these confederates constituted the bulk of the Roman army in the West. Consequently, German kings and military leaders became generals in the Roman armies and large numbers of Germans became at least partially Romanized. *Foederati* were less important in the

East, where native Roman manpower was sufficient.

In the long run, this process of Romanization smoothed the transition to a new society after the collapse of imperial power in the West, but in the short run—during the fourth century—it made the border uncertain and unstable. While the federated Germans learned something of the Roman system, they did not break relations with their fellow Germans on the other side of the border. In times of peace, there was considerable commerce and interchange among all Germanic peoples.

In order to maintain their system of defense the Romans had to play tribes off against one another, which was at best a chancy business. In the second half of the fourth century the frontier broke down repeatedly. Franks,

Alemans, Burgundians, Lombards—all peoples whose names live in the political geography of modern Europe—pressed into the Empire, were driven back, and came again. Then came the massive influx of the Visigoths toward the end of the century.

The Goths had troubled the Empire for a century and a half, but the imperial armies had kept them back, and they had settled in the southern plains of western Russia (the Ukraine). In the course of their migrations, they had divided into two large groups, the Ostrogoths and the Visigoths. In 375, these two peoples were suddenly overrun by the Asiatic Huns.

The Huns were nomadic people from Central Asia. Normally, these peoples lived in small bands that migrated constantly over a large territory

The Late Roman Empire   *ca.* A.D. 395

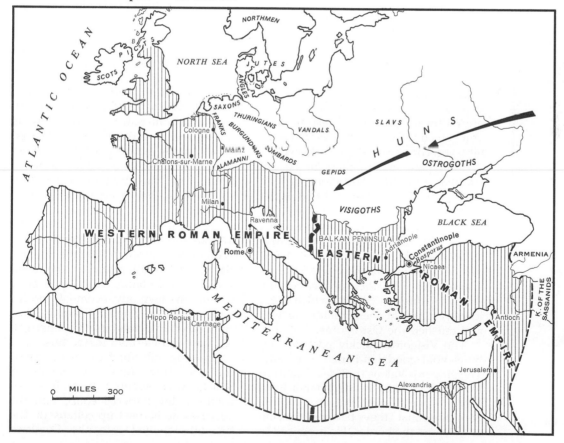

Silver commemorative plate depicting
Theodosius and his two sons (*ca.* 388).

Stilicho the Vandal general in
the service of Rome.
Although he is a barbarian,
he wears Roman clothing
(panel of an ivory diptych,
ca. 410).

following the growth of pasturage for
their flocks. Through centuries of this
life, they had become expert horsemen,
and they had acquired most of the
equipment necessary for cavalry warfare, such as the horseshoe and the
stirrup. A strong leader occasionally
united these bands, and once unification gained momentum, it was irresistible. The consolidated tribes forced all
in their path to join them or be destroyed, and the civilizations on the
edges of their vast territories soon felt
the effects of the movement. The Huns
were an excellent example of such a
movement. In the mid-fourth century,
they attacked China and, driven back,
turned west, where there was little resistance. In 375, they arrived in the
southern Russian plains, which were
ideally suited to their military tactics,
and crushed the Ostrogoths.

The Visigoths quickly packed their
household goods and tried to escape.
The emperor Valens (r. 364–78) permitted them to settle inside Roman territory in present-day Bulgaria on the
condition that they become *foederati*
and defend the border. He promised to

supply them for the defense, but did
not honor this commitment, and the
Visigoths soon renounced their allegiance and abandoned the border.
They began systematically plundering
the provinces to the south, toward
Constantinople, and the emperor led
an army against them. The war ended
in 378 in a pitched battle at Adrianople,
at which the Goths decisively defeated
the Romans and killed Valens. But the
victors had no program or goal and
spent the next year aimlessly pillaging
Greece and the provinces to its north.
This threat was ended by Theodosius I
(r. 379–95), who managed to resettle
the Visigoths as *foederati* along the
lower Danube. This was the same
Theodosius who made Christianity the
official religion of the Empire, and
while he ruled, the Germans were kept
in check. In the meantime, the Huns
continued to move west and soon settled in the Hungarian plain, the only
extensive natural grasslands in Europe.

The End of the Empire in the West

Soon after the death of Theodosius, the
Visigoths broke out again. An ambitious king, Alaric, had united them and
now tried to gain control of the Balkans, which he failed to do because he
was unable to take the fortified cities.
In 407, Alaric led his people out of the
Balkans toward Italy, which was defended by the Romanized Vandal
Stilicho, who had been a lieutenant of
Theodosius. To meet the new threat,
Stilicho stripped troops from the Rhine
frontier and left its defense to Frankish
foederati, who failed to hold the line. He
also paid no attention to the commander in Britain, who, apparently
seeking his own advancement, led his
army across the English Channel. Britain was left to defend itself against Caledonian and German marauders.

So long as Stilicho lived, Alaric
could not break into Italy, but in 408
Stilicho was executed through an intrigue in the imperial court, and the
defenses he had set up collapsed. The
Visigoths moved into the Lombard

The Germanic Migrations   Fourth to Sixth Centuries

plain and marched on Rome, which they took in 410. The destruction was negligible, but the incident made a greater impression on contemporaries than any other event of the late imperial period.

Alaric did not intend to remain in Rome. He needed land for his people, which Rome, surrounded by marshes, could not provide. So the Visigoths moved south and gathered a fleet for transport to the rich territory of North Africa, which had a wetter climate then than it does now. But Alaric died and the fleet was destroyed by a storm. The Goths turned about and headed for Gaul. Finally, they settled in southern Gaul and established a kingdom, which eventually extended into Spain.

The death of Stilicho was the beginning of the collapse of Roman authority in the West. Stilicho's own tribe, the Vandals, with which he apparently had little contact, moved off the northern frontier and migrated to Spain, ravaging a swath through Gaul as they progressed. Then, under a young king, Gaiseric (r. 428–77), they crossed into North Africa in 428 and began a conquest of the old Roman provinces. Augustine, bishop of Hippo, died in 430 as Gaiseric besieged his city. Once settled, the Vandals built a fleet and disrupted the shipping essential to the provisioning of Italy. They even attacked Italy itself many times and "vandalism" became a common term for wanton destruction.

Head of a barbarian found in Gaul, probably representing one of the Helvetian (Swiss) peoples.

Meanwhile, the Franks, a large confederation living along the lower Rhine, migrated into northern Gaul and established themselves after being thrown back several times. The Burgundians moved through the Jura Mountains and the Alps into the east-central part of the province. Then the Huns reappeared. After they had shattered the Ostrogoths in southern Russia, they had formed a loose confederation of Huns, Slavs, and Germans. In 433, this confederation was consolidated by a charismatic king, Attila. His troops served the Romans as mercenaries against the Germans—in one battle they nearly obliterated the Burgundians—but in the 440s, he turned to plundering the Empire. He pillaged the Balkans as far as the walls of Constantinople and then turned west to Gaul. In these campaigns, Attila's troops earned a reputation for slaughter and rapine, and he earned the appellation "the scourge of God." He was finally turned back in 451 in western Gaul and, on his retreat, he came into northern Italy. In 452, he sacked the great city of Aquileia, whose refugees fled into the swamps and islands at the head of the Adriatic Sea. The villages they founded eventually grew into Venice. At this moment, Pope Leo I led an embassy to Attila's camp to persuade him to leave the peninsula alone, and when Attila did in fact retreat, Leo got the credit. But it is likely that since the Hunnish troops were exhausted and sick—Italy was a malarial region—Attila's decision was independent of the pope's intervention. The king died in 453.

By the 470s, among the western territories of the Empire, only Italy remained under its direct governance. The western emperor was a puppet of Orestes, the Empire's German commander-in-chief. In 476, Orestes was overthrown, with his emperor, by a rebellion of the troops led by another German, Odoacar. The new military chief did not enthrone an emperor. Instead, he had himself elected king by the German troops and made Italy into a Germanic kingdom. In Gaul and Spain, the kings of the Franks, Visigoths, and Burgundians were also establishing independent kingdoms.

These kingdoms were recognized by the emperor in Constantinople, but recovery of the old provinces became the constant goal of the emperor. In the late 480s, Emperor Zeno commissioned the Ostrogothic king Theodoric, who had been raised in Constantinople, to reconquer Italy. The remnants of the Ostrogoths had been settled along the Danube as *foederati* and had thrived there. Theodoric entered Italy in 489 and within four years had killed Odoacar and established the Ostrogothic kingdom of Italy. The history of this and the other Germanic kingdoms will be taken up in the next chapter.

ROMAN CULTURE DURING THE MIGRATIONS

The eastern provinces survived the Germanic and Hunnish invasions virtually untouched, and the Persian

---

Capella on Geographic Zones

Martianus Capella's work, from which the following was taken, was written in the early fifth century. It was one of the typical encyclopedic digests of the late Empire. Note that Capella, and the scholars he quoted, knew that the world was round.

The round world may be divided into five zones or bands of different characteristics. Of these, great excesses of heat or cold force three to be abandoned. The two zones which touch either end of the earth's axis, dominated by terrible cold, are deserted because of frost and snow, while the middle zone, baked by flames and breath-taking heat, scorches all living things that come near. The two other zones, tempered by the breath of life-sustaining air, offer a habitation to living things. These zones, curving around the sphere of the earth, go around both the upper and the lower hemisphere. . . . Those who live opposite us are called "antipodes." . . . For when we roast in summer, they shiver with cold; when spring here begins to cover the fields with flowers, there worn-out summer is passing into sleepy autumn.

From Martianus Capella, *De nuptiis philologiae et Mercurii* (Leipzig: Tuebner, 1866), Book VI (on Geometry), p. 252.

threat did not disrupt imperial territories in this period. During the fifth century, the East became the bedrock of the Empire, and the now old Hellenistic culture continued undisturbed on its course (see pp. 177–79).

In the West, a sophisticated Latin culture continued to exist until about 425. People were aware of the danger of invasion by the barbarians, but they continued to write books of philosophy, theology, and history and kept up an active correspondence with one another. This was the period in which Augustine converted and began writing his seminal works. It was the time when Ambrose, a well-educated man who rose high in the imperial service, became bishop of Milan, the principal western capital, and exerted a wide influence in Christian circles. It was Ambrose who led the final assault on the cultured paganism of the upper classes.

This was also an important time in the history of the papacy. Pope Damasus (r. 366–84) made progress in advancing the claims of Rome to universal primacy, and he commissioned Jerome to translate the Bible into Latin. A Latin translation of most of the sacred text, made in North Africa, was already available, but it was faulty. Jerome's work became the standard, or vulgate, text in the Middle Ages.

The literary culture depended on communication among the small coterie of educated men. A great deal of the literature of the period was written in the form of letters, and even books were often written in response to the requests of friends. The invasions and migrations disrupted the community of *literati*, though not everywhere at the same time. The Vandals virtually destroyed the Latin culture of North Africa, but the decline was gradual in most regions. In Spain, the Visigoths, who had been converted to an unorthodox Christian belief while still in Russia, persecuted orthodox Christians, but did not suppress Roman culture. In Gaul, the literary culture dwindled during the later fifth century as the migrations of the Franks and Burgun-

Silver-gilt spear mount made for a barbarian warrior, found in a tomb in northern France (*ca.* fourth century).

dians forced the old provincial aristocracy to retire to the isolation of their estates. In Italy, the establishment of Odoacar's and Theodoric's kingdoms did not permanently affect the life of the educated elite, and Theodoric found highly educated Romans to serve his government. In general, one of the surprises of the history of the fall of the Empire in the West is that the old governing classes fared quite well.

The Roman Empire provided medieval government with a political model that gave impetus to the consolidation of royal power that eventually led to the creation of the European nation-states. The authority of this model also helped make Roman law, which had been perfected during the imperial period, a primary source of European law. Imperial Roman law supported strong central government, and it is no surprise that when it was rediscovered in the eleventh century the kings seized on it as a source of authority for their programs of centralization. But the most important legacy of the Roman Empire was the imperial church. By the end of the fourth century, Christianity had become the imperial religion, and the emperors had provided the church with a strong institutional structure based on the imperial government. In this new form, the church became the principal preserver of Roman civilization for the West. The preservation of Greco-Roman philosophy, education, theology, and art can be attributed to early Christian writers because their work was itself preserved within the durable institutions of the church—monasteries, episcopal churches, and the papacy. The works of pagan writers of the late classical period were mostly lost because of the destruction of pagan institutions and libraries.

Suggestions for Further Reading

General

For a general history of the later Roman Empire, see H. M. D. Parker, *History of the Roman World from A.D. 138 to 337* (1935), and M. Grant, *The Climax of Rome* (1968). The classic social and economic history of the Empire is M. Rostovtzef, *The Social and Economic History of the Roman Empire*, rev. ed. (1957). See also, R. Mac-Mullen, *Roman Social Relations* (1974). M. I. Finley, *The Ancient Economy* (1973), and *Studies in Ancient Society* (1974), are also excellent. On social stratification and the legal system in the imperial period, see P. Garnsey, *Social Status and Legal Privilege in the Roman Empire* (1970). On women in Roman society, see S. B. Pomeroy, *Goddesses, Whores, Wives, and Slaves* (1975), and T. Carp, "Two Matrons of the Late Republic," *Women's Studies* 8 (1981), 189–200.

For the frontier provinces, see F. Millar, *The Roman Empire and its Neighbors* (1968), and, on provincial administration, see G. H. Stevenson, *Roman Provincial Administration* (1939). E. N. Luttwak, *The Grand Strategy of the Roman Empire* (1976), analyzes the military approaches the emperors took to defend the Empire's borders. On the cities, see F. F. Abbott and A. C. Johnson, *Municipal Administration in the Roman Empire* (1926), and A. H. M. Jones, *The Cities of the Eastern Roman Provinces* (1937). For an interesting attempt to reconstruct Roman tax policy and its social and economic consequences, see W. Goffart, *Caput and Colonate: Towards a History of Late Roman Taxation* (1974). F. Millar, *The Emperor in the Roman Empire 31 B.C.–A.D. 337* (1977), is a massive study of the role of the emperor in Roman government and life. For a general intellectual history of late antiquity, see H. Marrou, *History of Education in Antiquity* (1948).

Christianity

On the rise of Christianity, see J. Lebreton and J. Zeiller, *The Emergence of the Church in the Roman Empire* (1962), and R. L. Fox, *Pagans and Christians* (1986), which puts Christianity in the context of Roman religion. On this subject, see also T. R. Glover, *The Conflict of Religions in the Early Roman Empire* (1960); R. Mac-

Mullen, *Paganism in the Roman Empire* (1981); and J. Ferguson, *The Religions of the Roman Empire* (1970). On the persecutions, see W. H. C. Frend, *Martyrdom and Persecution in the Early Church* (1967). The world of late Roman religion is illumined by Peter Brown, *Religion and Society in the Age of Saint Augustine* (1969), and *Society and the Holy in Late Antiquity* (1982). On Constantine, see R. MacMullen, *Constantine* (1969), and J. Eadie, ed., *The Conversion of Constantine* (1971), which surveys opinion about the emperor's motivation. The best biography of St. Augustine is Peter Brown, *Augustine of Hippo* (1967). Augustine's *Confessions* and *City of God* have been published in many editions.

The Fall of the Empire in the West

E. Gibbon's monumental, *The Decline and Fall of the Roman Empire*, ed. J. B. Bury (1886–1900), has been the classic treatment of the subject since 1776. As a general history, it should now be supplemented with A. H. M. Jones, *The Later Roman Empire, 284–602*, 3 vols. (1964). For a history of the third-century crisis and Diocletian's reestablishment of stability, see R. MacMullen, *Roman Government's Response to Crisis A.D. 235–337* (1976), and S. Williams, *Diocletian and the Roman Recovery* (1985). In *The End of the Ancient World* (1931), F. Lot attributed the fall to economic causes. For a recent survey of the invasions, see L. Musset, *The Germanic Invasions* (1975). Most recent studies have focused on specific aspects of the German migrations. See M. Todd, *The Northern Barbarians, 100 B.C.–A.D. 300* (1976); E. A. Thompson, *The Early Germans* (1965), *The Visigoths in the Time of Ulfilas* (1969), and *Romans and Barbarians: The Decline of the Western Empire* (1982). For contrast, see R. Van Dam, *Leadership and Community in Late Antique Gaul* (1985).

5
The Germanic Kingdoms in the West

*I*n 476, when the western Roman emperor was supplanted by his commander-in-chief, no one in the Empire really thought that an epochal event had taken place; no contemporary of the event would have spoken of the "fall of the Roman Empire." Thus, when historians say that the new Germanic kingdoms that formed in the western half of the Empire were "successors of the Roman Empire," they are using hindsight. To contemporaries, the division of the eastern and western parts of the Empire, stemming from Diocletian's reforms, was only a practical solution to the problems of governing the immense imperial territories. People conceived of the Empire as a unified state, and, therefore, the fall of the western emperor did not appear to be a decisive event. For the time being, the Empire had only one emperor instead of two.

Moreover, the end of the western imperial court made less of an impression on western Romans than one

This fragment from the crown of the Lombard king Agilulf shows the king being greeted in the cities he conquered (early seventh century).

might suppose. This was true, first, because westerners had become used to German domination of the army and of the western court and, second, because most of the German kings asked the emperor in Constantinople for confirmation of their right to rule part of his territory. These actions confirmed the ideas that the Empire was still whole and that the political developments that took place after 476 were just one more phase in the long history of the Empire.

However, the settlement of the Germans soon began to affect the cultural unity of the Empire. To a large extent, the Germans retained their own culture and languages. Their society remained tribal even in the midst of the imperial society that they ruled. By the late sixth century, it was clear that there would be no reunification with the East, and

as the Germans settled into the old provincial society, new vernacular languages and new forms of culture—the beginnings of medieval civilization—began to evolve. The old Roman aristocracy served its new masters and gradually lost touch with eastern, Greek culture. The breakdown of the homogeneity of upper-class culture, which had been a striking characteristic of the Empire for centuries, accelerated from the end of the fifth century.

THE GERMAN "SUCCESSOR STATES" IN EUROPE

In the sixth century, four major Germanic kingdoms were founded on the European territories of the Roman Empire. The Visigoths had been settled in southern Gaul and Spain since the

The Germanic Kingdoms *ca.* 500

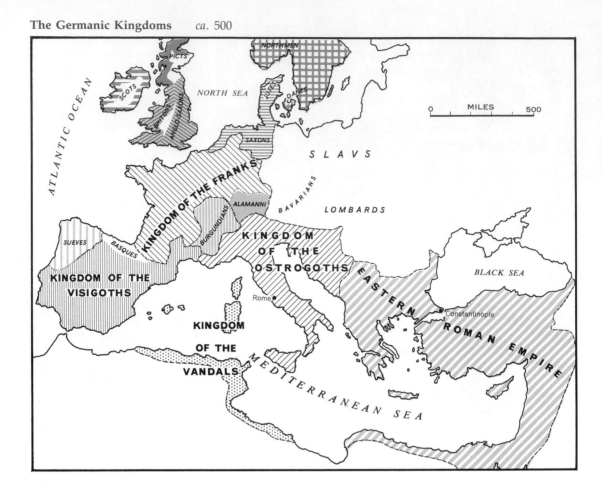

420s and 430s. This was the oldest of the kingdoms. In the early 490s, King Theodoric (r. 493–526) had led the Ostrogoths to Italy at the command of Emperor Zeno I in Constantinople, but when he seized control of the province in 493, the king effectively established an independent kingdom. Clovis (r. 481–511) consolidated his authority among the Franks in the early 480s and had established a Frankish kingdom in Gaul—driving out the Visigoths—by the time of his death in 511. The Angles and Saxons, peoples from southern Scandinavia, had begun settling in Britain in the 440s. By the sixth century several Anglo-Saxon kingdoms were established on the island, and the provincial population had migrated into Cornwall and Wales, and to Ireland.

Among these peoples, the Goths were already Christians when they invaded the imperial territories. They had been converted by missionaries from Constantinople during the fourth century. However, the effect of the conversion on their relations with their Roman subjects was complicated because they had received an unorthodox form of Christianity and were in conflict with the imperial church. In contrast, the Franks and Anglo-Saxons came to the imperial lands as heathens, and their conversion to orthodox Roman Christianity took on great significance not only because it was a foundation for their integration into the old Roman society, but also because it set them at odds with the unorthodox Goths.

Nonetheless, the Goths and Burgundians, who had also been converted to unorthodox Christianity, absorbed Roman civilization readily and preserved much of the Roman way of life. As they settled in Italy and the old western provinces, they lost some of their identity as peoples, and their kingdoms had no staying power. During the sixth century, the Ostrogothic kingdom of Italy and the Vandal kingdom of North Africa were destroyed by the Eastern Roman Empire, while the Visigoths and Burgundians in southern Gaul were conquered by the Franks. In contrast, the northern German kingdoms—the Franks and the Anglo-Saxons—absorbed relatively little of Roman civilization, but created strong kingdoms that became the strongest states in medieval Europe.

A glance at a modern map will illustrate this difference between the northern and southern Germanic kingdoms. Italy and Spain have retained their old Roman names; they did not become East Gothia and West Gothia. But the Franks imposed their name on Gaul, which became France, while the Angles imposed theirs on Britain, which became known as England.

The Settlement of the Germans

One of the puzzles of the age of invasions is how the Germans were settled among the existing Gallo-Roman population. The sources, principally the law codes issued by German kings, indicate that the German soldiers received a portion—half or two-thirds—of the lands of the provincials, and historians have generally supposed that this meant that they actually expropriated the properties. If the Germans did get land, then they would have become farmers, and most depictions of Germanic society in the new kingdoms portray it as a society of yeoman farmers.

But such wholesale expropriation would have raised much more protest than is evident in the Roman sources of the period. Recently, historians have suggested that the division referred to in the sources did not pertain to land but to tax revenues. It appears that the German tribes settled as armies under ancient rules about the settlement of Roman armies. In those rules, the provincials owed hospitality, consisting of quarters and revenues, to the troops. In an extension of those laws, the Germans received houses on Roman lands, but, more important, they took over the revenues that had been due to the Roman state. Furthermore, it appears that the division was not between Germans and Romans, but between the German king and his men. In most places, the king received one-third of the tax revenues, his men two-thirds. In general, the king's share came from the great landowners whose own income stemmed from tenant and servile farmers. Thus, the old Gallo-Roman aristocracy had a special relationship with the new rulers. This system supported the Germans as the Roman armies had been supported, and for the natives it only changed the recipients of the taxes they paid.

It was only gradually that the Germans became actual landowners. Some of this process must have resulted from intermarriage, but war was the most important cause. In the incessant civil wars that plagued the Germanic kingdoms during the sixth century, the kings deprived their enemies of their land rights and redistributed them to their supporters. Gallo-Romans as well as Germans were involved in the wars, and when the provincials were on the losing side, they lost not their rights to taxes, but their land. Hence, the winners received property rights among their rewards. By these gradual processes, the German armies were integrated into the rural society of the European provinces.

The Visigothic Kingdom of Spain

The oldest of the Germanic kingdoms was Visigothic Spain. In the early fifth century, the Visigoths had settled in southern Gaul, but they soon gained control of Spain. After 507, the expansion of the Frankish conquest restricted their power to the Iberian peninsula, except for the neighboring province of Septimania. Even before the migrations, the Visigoths had absorbed some Roman culture through their church, even though it was considered heretical by the imperial Church. In addition, southern Gaul and Spain had been the most thoroughly Romanized of the western provinces. Yet, during most of the sixth century the Visigothic kings were at odds with the Romanized provincial population because of their religious differences.

By the 580s, religion had become a point of contention within the royal family and Visigothic aristocracy, and when King Recared I (r. 586–601) came to power, he converted to orthodox Christianity. To settle doctrinal disputes and organize a new, unified Spanish church, Recared held a series of church councils, which stimulated intellectual activity in the kingdom and produced legislation that had a lasting influence on western Christendom. In the seventh century, Spain was one of the principal centers of Christian intellectual life in the West.

The Visigothic kings preserved much of the old Roman administrative structure and seem to have thought of themselves as rulers within the Empire, rather than as heads of a separate kingdom. Wherever the Germans settled they had to deal with the social and legal differences between themselves and the subject population. To reconcile the two populations, the kings issued a series of law codes designed to preserve the distinctiveness of the two legal systems while simultaneously making clear to everyone what the provisions of each system were. During the 480s, Burgundian and Visigothic kings published parallel codes of Roman law and Germanic law written in Latin. The Roman law was a vulgarized version of the system that the emperor Justinian's lawyers would later describe in the *Corpus Iuris Civilis* (see p. 180), but the codes served the

courts well. In the Visigothic kingdom, Alaric II (r. 484–507) issued the *Lex Romana Visigothorum* (The Roman Law of the Visigoths) which combined Roman and Visigothic law. The Visigothic part of the code recorded ancient customary law, but the influence of Roman law and culture is evident in it. The roughly contemporary *Lex Romana Burgundionum* showed the same influence and performed the same function. These codes preserve the most important record of how the settlement of the Germans in the Roman provinces was accomplished.

Throughout the seventh century, the Visigothic kingdom suffered from disputed successions to the throne and aristocratic rebellions. By the time the Moslems crossed the Strait of Gibraltar in 711, the kingdom was too divided and weak to resist, and it collapsed immediately after the invaders defeated a royal army. A small population of Christians took refuge in the northern hills of Asturias and Galicia and established small kingdoms there. The rest of the peninsula became part of the vast Arab empire that had begun to form during the 620s.

The Ostrogothic Kingdom of Italy

The Ostrogothic kingdom of Theodoric was in many ways the most successful of all the barbarian realms in the West. Theodoric had been raised in Constantinople and was a Roman citizen. He had even held the office of consul before Zeno commissioned him to reconquer Italy. He found Italy ruined by decades of war and misgovernment, and he subsidized public works and revived agriculture and trade. He also tried to stabilize the relations among the new Germanic kingdoms by making a series of marriage alliances. He himself married a Frankish princess; he married his sister to the king of the Vandals, his two daughters to the Visigothic and Burgundian kings, and a niece to a Thuringian king.

In his own kingdom, he tried to preserve Roman civilization and all that he

A German king (left) and his bishop. From an early manuscript copy of Alaric's code of law.

could of Roman government by engaging men of the leading Roman families as advisers and ministers. Two of these, Cassiodorus (*ca.* 490–580) and Boethius (*ca.* 480–524) are giant figures in the intellectual history of Europe. Cassiodorus was a man renowned for learning. After serving the king as secretary for many years, he retired to his estate where he wrote *An Introduction to Divine and Human Readings,* a compendium of the classical learning intended to serve as the basis for Christian education. This book was a major contribution to the preservation of classical culture for posterity.

Boethius was a philosopher who undertook to translate all the works of Plato and Aristotle into Latin. Boethius finished translations of two of Aristotle's introductory treatises on logic and wrote some basic mathematical treatises. These works were used throughout the Middle Ages and until the twelfth century were the primary works on logic available in the West. Further, in his *Tractates,* Boethius showed how logic could be applied to problems of Christian theology, which helped ensure the survival of logic as a branch of medieval learning. But Boethius never completed his task because he became a victim of the suspicion and tension between Roman and Ostrogothic Christians at a time when the Ostrogoths feared a Byzantine invasion. In 522, he was accused of treason and condemned to death. While imprisoned, he wrote his most famous work, *The Consolation of Philosophy,* in which he engages in a dialogue with Lady Philosophy, who leads him from his despair to "that true contentment which reason allied with virtue alone can give." This little book remains influential as an argument for the superiority of spiritual over material values.

Theodoric's kingdom did not long survive his death. The emperor Justinian's invading army arrived in 536, and

Gold coin of Theodoric, Ostrogothic king of Italy in the early sixth century.

The tomb of Theodoric in Ravenna, Italy.

Theodoric's successor was unable to organize any resistance. After suffering a series of defeats, the Goths replaced the line of Theodoric with a new dynasty that struggled for 20 years against the Byzantine army. This war devastated the peninsula. Rome's population declined by perhaps 90 percent, although the size of its population at any given time can only be roughly estimated. Other cities were repeatedly besieged and plundered by both sides. The endemic plague that struck the Mediterranean region in the 540s and continued until the 570s also took its toll. The province that the Byzantines finally won in the 550s was a ruined district and easy prey for new invaders.

These entered the scene in 568; they were the Lombards, a northern Germanic people that was among the least Romanized of all the Germans. They had been mercenaries in Italy about 552 and now came back on their own account. By 572, they controlled most of the peninsula. Competition among the leading Lombard aristocrats prevented the rise of a strong king, but Italy was now divided between the enclaves of Byzantine power and a group of Lombard duchies.

The Rise of the Franks

The Franks appeared during the chaotic third century, when they made raids deep into Gaul, as far as Spain. At the beginning of the fifth century, when Stilicho withdrew the legions from the Rhine to fight the Visigoths, he made the Franks *foederati*. But instead of protecting the frontier the Frankish kings occupied northern Gaul and permitted the Vandals, Suevi, and Alans to sweep through the province to Spain. The Vandals eventually crossed over to North Africa; the Suevi settled in present-day Portugal; the Alans settled in Spain, but some joined the Vandals when they crossed to Africa. The Franks controlled both sides of the Rhine and were divided into two large confederations of tribes—the Ripuarian Franks on the east bank of the Rhine and the Salian Franks on the right. They were often in conflict with one another.

The constant warfare among the Frankish kings was finally ended by Clovis, who succeeded to a tribal kingship among the Salians in 481. He was then 15 years old and a scion of a royal family that claimed descent from the legendary Merovech; the kings of the line are called Merovingians. The family's capital was at Tournai. Clovis (r. 481–511) soon started to consolidate power among the Salian tribes and then slowly unified all the Franks under his kingship, while expanding

Caesar Conquers Gaul

56 B.C.	*ca.* 486 A.D.	751	987	1328
Roman Gaul	Merovingian Dynasty	Carolingian Dynasty	Capetian Dynasty	

Frankish territory. In 486, he destroyed a Roman principality, the "kingdom of Soissons." In 496, his army annihilated the Alemanni, which permitted the Franks to expand eastward, back into Germany. In 507, Clovis defeated the Visigoths in a great battle, which led to the conquest of most of southern Gaul. He could not reach the Mediterranean because Theodoric prevented it by occupying Provence and helping the Visigoths hold on to Septimania. This province along the Mediterranean coast of Gaul remained culturally and politically allied with Catalonia in Spain throughout the Middle Ages.

The Franks settled in the depopulated north of Gaul, and the Roman provincial population put up little resistance to them. The orthodox Christian community favored the heathen Franks over the heretical Christian Visigoths and Burgundians, who had settled in the western Alps and adjacent districts. In fact, the bishops of Gaul were encouraged to think that Clovis might convert to Roman Christianity, and this kept them from stirring up rebellion. Around 498, the king finally did convert, along with about 3,000 of his men, and in a single stroke he gained a decisive advantage for himself. He was the only Catholic ruler among the Germanic kings, and he received the support of the episcopate and their flocks. At the end of his life, Clovis was the most powerful Germanic king in Europe, and, like his contemporaries in Burgundy and the Visigothic kingdom, he issued a great law code (usually dated 507–11), the *Lex Salica.*

When Clovis died in 511, his four sons divided the kingdom. They conquered the Burgundians in 534. Two years later, they took Provence and reached the Mediterranean, opening their kingdom to trade with the Byzantine Empire, with which they were allied against the Ostrogoths. They also expanded Frankish power in Germany, where they conquered Thuringia in 531.

However, within Gaul the brothers fought one another constantly, until in 558 only Chlotar I remained. He reunited the kingdom for the last three years of his life, but when he died, the kingdom was again divided among his four sons. Most of these men died young, leaving women as regents for their infant sons, and there was continual internecine warfare in the kingdom until 613, when Chlotar II (r. 584–629), a grandson of Chlotar I, established himself as sole ruler. But the long struggle had taken its toll on royal power. To win support the kings had given away large tracts of land and rights to the nobility, and by 613, the kingdom was controlled not by the monarchy, but by the main aristocratic families. Under Chlotar's only son Dagobert (r. 629–39), when there was no competition for the kingdom, the royal family made a modest recovery, but the future belonged to the great noble families.

The first century of Merovingian rule was chronicled by Bishop Gregory of Tours (538–94), who wrote the famous *Ten Books of Histories.* Clovis' conversion to orthodox Christianity had earned him and his heirs the steady support of the bishops, most of whom came from the old provincial aristocracy and had great authority both with the Franks and the Gallo-Roman landowners. Gregory, who was representative of this class, admitted that Clovis was treacherous and told the story of how on one occasion Clovis bewailed his lack of relatives "not because he grieved at their death but with the cunning thought that he might perhaps find one still alive whom he could kill."

Childeric, father of Clovis and an early king of the Franks, from a signet ring found in his tomb. His long hair and his spear are signs of royal authority.

The Morals and Faith of the Early Franks

ca. 575

Ragnachar was then king at Cambrai, a man so unrestrained in his wantonness that he scarcely had mercy for his own near relatives. . . . Clovis came and made war on him, and he saw that his army was beaten and prepared to slip away in flight, but was seized by his army, and with his hands tied behind his back, he was taken with Ricchar his brother before Clovis. And Clovis said to him: "Why have you humiliated our family in permitting yourself to be bound? It would have been better for you to die." And raising his ax he dashed it against his head, and he turned to the brother and said: "If you had aided your brother he would not have been bound." And in the same way he smote him with his ax and killed him. . . . These kings were kinsmen of Clovis, and their brother, Rignomer by name, was slain by Clovis's order at the city of Mans. When they were dead Clovis received all their kingdom and treasures. And having killed many other kings and his nearest relatives, of whom he was jealous lest they take the kingdom away from him, he extended his rule over all the Gauls. . . . For God was laying low his enemies every day under his hand, and was increasing his kingdom, because he walked with an upright heart before Him, and did what was pleasing to His eyes.

From Gregory of Tours, *History of the Franks*, trans. and annot. by E. Brehaut (New York: Columbia University Press, 1916), pp. 48–50.

Yet, Gregory still summed up Clovis' career by saying: "God was laying low his enemies every day under his hand, and was increasing his kingdom, because he walked with an upright heart before Him, and did what was pleasing to His eyes." The good bishop was equally complimentary of Clovis' grandson King Guntram (r. 561–93), of whom the best that could be said was that he murdered somewhat fewer people than his brothers did. "One would have taken him," Gregory says, "not only for a king, but for a priest of the Lord."

The decline of royal power after Dagobert left the way open for aristocratic families. The greatest prize was the position of mayor of the royal palace, originally the official who managed the king's private affairs. But the Franks did not distinguish between private and public, so that the mayor also controlled the functioning of the royal government. After Dagobert, when the kings were increasingly incompetent and ineffectual, the mayor was the real king.

By 700 the kingdom of Clovis had been split into an eastern, largely Germanic kingdom called Austrasia, a western, more Latinized kingdom named Neustria, and a weak southern kingdom of Burgundy. Southwest Gaul (Aquitaine) and southeast Germany (Bavaria) were practically autonomous. In each of the major parts of the kingdom there was a mayor of the palace who was constantly threatened with rebellion among his own supporters and with competition from his rival mayors. The endemic wars that had been fought among the sons and grandsons of Clovis were continued among the mayors of the palaces.

Out of these struggles one family emerged to reunite the whole Frankish kingdom and to strengthen it so that it became the cradle of a new western European civilization. This family—the Carolingians, named from its most famous member, Charles the Great or Charlemagne (from Latin Carolus Magnus)—gained control of the Austrasian mayorality in the early seventh century. Under Pippin of Heristal it defeated an alliance of the Neustrians and Burgundians at the Battle of Tertry in 687, so that Pippin unified the mayoral position for the whole kingdom. By the time Pippin died in 714, the Frankish kingdom was again the most powerful of the successor states in the West.

The Anglo-Saxons in Britain

The Germans who settled the province of Britain did not create a united kingdom. The Angles and Saxons, who were hardly distinguishable linguistically or culturally, came in tribal groups, each founding its own kingdom. In the Midlands, Angles founded the kingdoms of Mercia, Norfolk, and Suffolk. North of the Humber River, other Angles founded Deira centered on York and Bernicia further north. In the south, the Saxons formed several small kingdoms—Sussex, Essex, and Wessex. The kingdom of Kent, facing the Gallic coast, is associated in tradition with the Jutes, but this people has not been identified, and historians now consider the peculiarities of the society in Kent to have been the result of its close trade links with the Continent.

The Celtic population that had occupied Britain under the Romans retreated to the west after failing in a heroic struggle to stop Anglo-Saxon settlement. The legend of King Arthur stems from this struggle. He was a military leader, not a king, whose authority was based on the remnant of the old Roman military system that the Celtic population had preserved. At the beginning of the sixth century, he led a final Celtic resistance to the Germans in which he lost his life, but the war did stop the Anglo-Saxon advance for about a generation.

The Celtic population established itself in Cornwall, Wales, and Ireland. A small group crossed to Brittany, where a form of Gaelic is still spoken. The Celtic emigrants took with them the remnants of Roman civilization that they had preserved after Roman government had collapsed in Britain, and this tradition was destined to play a large role in the cultural history of Europe. In their new regions, Celtic society was based on clans, extensive kindreds and retainers under the authority of a clan head. In Scotland, where some Celts settled, this social organization persisted into the modern period.

In the Anglo-Saxon territories, some of the smaller kingdoms were absorbed by their neighbors, and by the middle of the seventh century the Anglo-Saxon kingdoms formed a heptarchy. In the south were Kent, Wessex, Sussex, and Essex; in the Midlands were Mercia and East Anglia (the combination of Norfolk and Suffolk); and in the

The Anglo-Saxon Kingdoms of England
Seventh Century

north was Northumbria (the unified kingdoms of Bernicia and Deira). A kind of weak union of the kingdoms existed through the recognition of a senior king called the *bretwalda*, whose function is hard to discern, though it was probably to mediate disputes and organize common defensive actions if necessary. England was not truly unified until the tenth century.

But the Anglo-Saxons shared a language, religious tradition, and material culture. When they were converted to Christianity, the church grew as a unit, crossing the boundaries of the kingdoms, although local bishops were appointed by their kings and were loyal to them. Much of our knowledge of early Germanic society stems from

The helmet (reconstructed from fragments) of a seventh-century Anglian king. From the Sutton Hoo treasure, one of the great archaeological discoveries of this century, found under the untouched funeral mound of an early Anglian king.

English sources, particularly Anglo-Saxon law and literature.

GERMANIC SOCIETY

The Germans had originated in Scandinavia and northern continental Europe and were a large group of related peoples who spoke similar, although not identical, languages. The Slavs can also be counted among these peoples because, notwithstanding their considerable linguistic differences, Germans and Slavs are virtually indistinguishable in the archaeological record.

The Romans first encountered these peoples in the forests of northern Gaul and Germany, and our earliest sources relating to them are Julius Caesar's *Gallic Wars* and Tacitus's *Germania*. The former is based on Caesar's campaigns against German tribes that had settled in Gaul, which he had conquered during his proconsular tenure (58–49 B.C.; the book covers 58–52 B.C.). The latter

work was an armchair ethnography based on reports Tacitus received from his father-in-law, Agricola, who had served in Germany. He wrote the *Germania* early in the reign of the emperor Trajan (r. A.D. 98–117). Of the two, Tacitus's is the more reliable work, but both were profoundly shaped by theories of societal evolution then popular among educated Romans, who had long been interested in history, both their own and that of subject peoples. The principal source of these theories was Posidonius (*ca.* 135–51 B.C.), a Greek born in Syria, who had written an account of the evolution of the Celts from the comfortably safe distance of Rhodes, where he was head of the Stoic school.

Based on the works of Caesar and Tacitus and the early Germanic law codes and literature, historians have tried to reconstruct a picture of the original Germanic culture. Archaeology shows that this effort is bound to be fruitless. From very early times, the peoples who came to be called Germans were influenced by Celts and, probably, by the Greeks. By the time we hear of them, the Germans had a pantheon strikingly similar to, though more primitive than, that of the Medi-

Bust of a young German warrior, of the type the Romans fought. The soldier wears a necklace believed to have magic power.

terranean peoples. Certainly, the origins of this collection of gods goes back to the same Indo-European sources as those of the Greeks and Italic tribes—as the Indo-European languages descend from a common language—but there is no way to tell what in the German religious culture stems from the common source, what is original to them, and what is borrowed from other peoples.

The same can be said of their material culture. To the archaeologists, Germanic villages of the first century A.D. look virtually identical to those of the Gauls and Slavs. They all had similar tool kits and agricultural practices, and all of them had absorbed some Roman culture, with which they had contact long before Roman imperialism brought them to bay. Under direct Roman influence, these societies were changed so that their original characteristics are nearly impossible to discern.

It appears that there was a significant difference between the eastern and western Germans. The easterners, mainly Goths settled on the plains of southern Russia, were converted to Christianity in the later fourth century. A biography of an early Gothic saint tells us of a society of small agricultural villages dominated by elders and rarely affected by the doings of central authorities, which appear to have been weak. The Gothic communities protected their members—as is shown by the story of the saint, whom the community tried to protect against external demands for pagan sacrifice—and generally resisted outside influence. It was a community in which everyone knew everyone else throughout life, foreigners were suspect and usually driven off, and social relations were organic, that is, regulated by the villagers' sense of community and by lifelong personal relationships rather than by law. It is impossible to say anything about the law of these communities, for it is a lost oral tradition.

The western Germans, living closer to the Roman Empire along the Rhine

and upper Danube, had evolved a tribal society dominated by kings by the time the Romans came into contact with them. In this society, the tribal community appeased the gods through the kings, whose authority rested on a claim that they descended from the gods. For example, the Anglo-Saxon kings claimed descent from Woden (or Odin, god of war and poetry that celebrated feats in war). Their connection with the gods gave the kings great authority, but it also made them responsible for the fortunes of the tribe. When the military or agricultural luck of the tribe went bad, the king was blamed, and a run of bad luck could result in his being deposed in favor of another member of the royal family, who also had the blood of the gods in him.

The royal leadership of confederated tribes (the *foederati*) had the support of the Roman authorities and, by a process hard to trace, the Germans absorbed some Roman ideas of political power. By the time the Germans began to settle the European provinces as conquerors, their kings had benefited from Roman support and from the centralizing effects of migration and warfare.

Although life beyond the imperial borders was based on the agricultural village, much as early Roman society had been, the *foederati* lived as an army supported by the provincial population. Nonetheless, the army was a Germanic community within late Roman society, and this community was what is called a status society. Every man had a worth determined by birth, wealth, and actions. A man could improve his status by economic success, by creating a strong family, and by acting honorably. The members of a man's immediate family benefited from his status, and their actions affected the man's reputation in turn. Good service in war, successful trading, and a good marriage all had an effect on the status of an individual and his kin. Marriage was of the greatest importance to families, which controlled it carefully. Sons and daughters married whomever their

An artifact of the migration period. Ostrogothic gilt bronze buckle with jewels (sixth century). The style is Germanic.

parents chose for them, so it is no surprise that conflict between parents and children over marriages was a constant theme of German myth and literature. In this respect, German society was similar to Greek and Roman society.

When a person's status was decreased because someone insulted or injured him in some way, he had to recover his honor. The success of all of his affairs, of all of his dealings with others, depended on it. The natural way to recover honor and status was the blood feud, but the law provided a peaceful means of settlement, and the community had a great stake in making the law work. In a small society, a feud

The crown of King Recceswin of the Visigoths (*ca.* 660).

would inevitably spread as one man and his family after another was touched by it; so the Germanic community is seen in early medieval literature as surrounding the disputants, encouraging—even forcing—them to settle their differences according to the law.

The alternative to violence in the settlement of disputes was compensation, which is found in all known societies. The principle of compensation was essentially the same as that of the modern law of damages: An injury had a value, and if the perpetrator paid his victim for the injury, then the *status quo ante* was considered reestablished, and the parties and community could return to normal life. The kings stood behind the system of compensation, and they codified it in their earliest law codes.

Even though the Germans recognized the sacral role of the king, they considered the law to be the most important social institution. The king had the law in his breast because it was put there by the gods, from whom all principles and rules of justice stemmed. The king was, therefore, in an anomalous position. He was a member of the community, subject to its laws, but he stood outside of it, in communion with the gods. The definition of royal power and the constitutional relationship between the king and his people became a persistent problem in European political thought.

It is usually said that the most important social units in Germanic society were the families or kin groups. There is no doubt that these were important units, but recent scholarship has shown that families, whether nuclear families or extended kindreds, were not the basic units of German social life. As is shown by the law pertaining to the occupation of vacant land in a community, neighbors were as important as kin. Also, the law of compensation shows that the role of the kindred was not all encompassing.

The *Lex Salica*, published in the early sixth century, said that no one could occupy a vacant farm unless all the neighbors consented. The objection of even one neighbor was enough to invalidate occupation. However, this rule only held if the new occupant was not a legitimate heir of the former holder. The neighbors could not prevent the son, daughter, or other heir of a man from succeeding to his freehold. What was the intent of this legislation? Principally, it stemmed from the late Roman tax system, which treated estates and villages as fiscal units and imposed the tax burden on the whole unit. When a piece of land became vacant, the main concern of the community of the unit was to find someone who would take up the previous holder's share of the tax burden. Otherwise, it would fall on them. Both the Roman and German law recognized the right of heirs to succeed to the holding, and to its burdens, but both recognized also that, failing heirs, the neighbors had the right to determine the members of their community. Thus, the world of the German, like that of the Greek or Roman, was circumscribed by his neighbors as much as or more than by his kindred. The seventh-century B.C. Greek poet Hesiod expressed the point neatly when, speaking of the call for help when one was threatened, he said, "If any trouble arises in your place, neighbors come as they are, but relatives dress for the journey."

This picture of a society of farmers regulated by the taxing authority of the Empire and later by the German kings, most of whom tried to preserve imperial administration, is balanced by the revelations of the law of compensation. When a man committed a crime, he had to pay his victim. If he did not have the wherewithal to do so, the law specified that he could call on his family to help. In any case, the compensation had to be paid. The first ones obligated to help the criminal were his immediate family, his father and brothers. If together they could not pay the whole amount, then the man could call on his paternal and maternal relatives to the third degree—that is, all those

descended from his grandparents. If that failed, the man's life was forfeit, which usually meant that the victim or his family could seize the perpetrator and either enslave or kill him. The former seems to have been most common, since the enslaved criminal (called a *thrall* in Old German) is a common character in early Germanic literature. But before giving himself up to his victim, the man could seek support from his neighbors—who might help out because they wanted him to continue as a bearer of the communal burdens.

These regulations show the importance of the family and kindred. A man's life might depend on such relationships or he could find himself ruined by the actions of a cousin. But they also show that the kindred played a limited role in everyday life. The kindred recognized by law was not the grand one extending to distant cousins, and even the narrow one defined by the law was not an economic or social unit. It only served a social purpose when the law required. Nonetheless, men sometimes found themselves seriously endangered by that legal construct, and the early Frankish law permitted a man to renounce his kinship with certain of his relatives, so that he could not be called on to pay for their rambunctiousness. Once he had renounced them, he could not inherit from them, but that may have been of little importance if the disowned relatives were constantly paying for scrapes.

By backing a man up when he had to pay compensation, by providing him with support in court, and by standing with him in times of trouble, the neighbors and kin made it possible for him to function in society. For example, a man's promise to come to court and to obey its judgment or honor a settlement was guaranteed first by his family and then by his community, because the members of these groups, particularly the kin, would have to stand in his place should he default. Consequently, no one would trust a person who was kinless or without a suite of neighbors; he could do no business, and no one would accept his suit for marriage.

Long before the foundation of the successor kingdoms, the Germans had

come under the influence of Roman law in its vulgar form—as opposed to the learned law of the imperial law schools—and the law of the early codes reflects this influence. It is difficult to tell what was Germanic and what was Roman in them. The gradual amalgamation of these two legal traditions created the foundations of the European legal systems, just as the gradual union of Latin and the Germanic tongues produced the European languages.

To a large extent, the communal organization of the Germans was determined by military organization. The men of the villages constituted units of the army, and their relationship with the king was therefore that of soldier to general as well as man to sacral king. But it would be wrong to suppose that the military relationship was a formal one. Rather, it was personal; the man owed a personal loyalty to his king. At the highest level, the aristocratic associates of the king formed a coterie around him, called the *comitatus*. They fought with him, counseled him, and drank with him. His mead hall was the center of his and their world. (Mead is a strong wine made from honey.) Each nobleman had his own coterie of soldiers from the neighborhood of his estate, and these men related to him as he did to the king, so that the army was built up of personal groups focused on the king.

Women in Germanic Society

During the Middle Ages, it was sometimes said that a man had married *more germanicorum*, according to the custom of the Germans. That custom consisted of making a marriage by abducting and raping a woman; the act of sexual intercourse made the marriage. The medieval Church looked on marriage as an act of consent between the man and woman, but it did not consider the marriage valid until they had had sexual intercourse. So the *more germanicorum* lived on in the genteel tradition of canon law. But did the Germans make their marriages in that way? Not

---

Early Medieval Marriage

Among the early Germanic peoples, marriage was not a union of two people in love, but one of the normal commercial relationships among families. The marriage was a contract, as is shown by the following quotation from the laws of Ine, an Anglo-Saxon king of the seventh century.

If anyone buys a wife and the marriage does not take place, he [the bride's guardian] shall return the bridal price and pay [the bridegroom] as much again, and he shall compensate the trustee of the marriage according to the amount he is entitled to for infraction of his surety.

Marriage was virtually the only type of "executory" contract in the German communities—that is, it was the only agreement that would be carried out in the future—and it required a person beside the parties to guarantee that it would be executed. Here, the bride's guardian broke the contract and had to pay.

A passage from Ethelbert's laws (written before A.D. 604), illuminates another aspect of Anglo-Saxon marriage.

If a man forcibly carries off a maiden [he shall pay] 50 shillings to her owner, and afterwards buy from the owner his consent. If she is betrothed to another man, 20 shillings shall be paid as compensation.

Women were not owned in Germanic society—unless, of course, they were slaves—but they had guardians, who were usually men of their family. They could do nothing without the consent and action of their guardians, and men treated them almost as if they were chattels. Marriage was a commercial agreement between a man and his wife's guardian, and the second law is aimed at preserving the value of the marriage to the guardian if a man deprives him of it by abducting the girl. In law, the girl had little to say about who she married, but early medieval literature contains stories about women who were married off without their consent. The common view was that such actions led to trouble. Only in the twelfth century did church law, which controlled marriage, begin to require that both the man and woman consent of their own free will to a marriage for it to be valid.

Texts quoted from A. M. Lucas, *Women in the Middle Ages* (New York: St. Martin, 1983), pp. 63–64.

usually. The so-called German custom was one of the ways a marriage could be made among the Germans; if a man violated a woman, his neighbors and family considered him married.

The normal mode of marriage was no different among the Germans than among the Greeks and Romans. The man and his family made a deal with the woman's family. The literary evidence suggests that the man usually took an active role in finding a bride, but that the woman was subject to the will of her father or male relatives. Probably, in the average marriage, the man was substantially older than the woman.

This picture of women's plight was somewhat ameliorated by the value of women in the Germanic kingdoms. For the purposes of legal actions, such as the receipt or payment of compensation, kin groups were bilateral, that is, the relatives of the mother counted as much as those of the father, and women inherited almost equally with their male siblings. Under the *Lex Salica*, the property that came to a marriage with the woman went back to her family if she died without heirs. If a couple had no heirs, the property that they had acquired during their marriage was divided equally between the wife's and husband's families.

Because the society of the Germanic kingdoms was a composite of Roman and Germanic elements, it had a complex attitude toward women. The Church reflected Greek and Roman attitudes and viewed women as weak and dangerous. They were weak because they were seen as prone to giving in to sexual desire and dangerous because they could lead men to licentiousness. The Germans had a more pragmatic view of women. Tacitus reports that they expected women to share the burdens of making a living and, generally, gives the impression that the Germans wanted their women to take an active role in society and the family. Further, he says that the Germans looked on women as having a special holiness, so that people sought

out their advice. Among some Germanic peoples it seems to have been common for a new king to marry his predecessor's wife. In Sweden, the kings were said to derive their charismatic power from the goddess Freya, and people may have thought that this power flowed through the queen to her husband. In general, German society was built up from personal relationships, and from the villages to the aristocrats surrounding the king, women played crucial roles. Because kin groups were bilateral, husband and wife stood side by side in the family.

THE GROWTH OF CHURCH INSTITUTIONS

The Bishops and Clergy

By the second century, the Christian communities—which were independent, but still maintained active communication with one another—had evolved a hierarchical organization that persists in developed form to this day. The highest official of each church was the bishop, whose authority corre-

Two Ostrogothic brooches. The one at left is made of gold inlaid with emerald and garnet and marks the zenith of the Ostrogothic style; the one below, made after the defeats of 552–553, is poor in quality and crudely decorated.

sponded in extent with the Roman administrative unit centered on the *civitas* or city. Under Diocletian (r. 284–305), these administrative territories were reorganized as dioceses, which were still centered on cities, and the Church's organization changed to reflect the new arrangement. The units of episcopal authority are still called dioceses.

From an early date, the bishop was assisted by various officials. Presbyters (priests; the word means elders) ministered to the spiritual needs of the community. Deacons assisted in nonspiritual functions, such as the maintenance of its houses of worship and of any other property the community acquired. The deacons also distributed alms to the poor in the community. Lesser officials—exorcists, cantors, readers, and others—performed a host of functions that are indicated by their titles. As a group, these officials constituted the bishop's *familia*, his family or household.

The position of the bishop rested on a theory that was first propounded by Bishop Irenaeus of Lyons (*ca.* 180). Although the New Testament was the most important source of Christian revelation, Christians believed that some of Jesus's teachings had not been included in the 27 documents of their sacred book. His other teachings had been passed down from the apostles, and they were considered an important part of the Christian faith. It was in this tradition that Church leaders found the means to settle disputes about the meaning of certain passages in the Bible.

Irenaeus used this idea of an oral tradition to develop a theory of episcopal authority according to which the bishops, as the heads of the churches directly or indirectly founded by the apostles, were the successors of the apostles. According to this theory, the bishops were the recipients, preservers, and interpreters of the authoritative Christian tradition.

As already noted (see pages 118–119), this theory, which was soon accepted, gave the bishops of the churches founded by the apostles themselves, the "apostolic" churches, a claim to superior authority because they could claim to have preserved the tradition in a direct and, therefore, reliable line of succession. Unfortunately the bishops of these churches were often in conflict about central points of doctrine, so that there was a need for a refinement of Irenaeus's theory.

This version of the theory ranked the authority of a bishop according to the importance of the apostle who had founded his church, thus becoming the basis of the claims of universal primacy made by the Roman bishops. They argued that they inherited the authority of Peter, who had been chosen by Jesus as prince of the apostles. This argument is the Petrine doctrine (see p. 120). The claim by the Roman bishops to the title pope (*papa* meaning father), which had commonly been applied to all bishops in the second and third centuries, was part of the campaign to get their claims recognized. Except when it was convenient to do so, the eastern bishops did not recognize papal claims, but, in the West, where Rome was the only apostolic see, the popes slowly gained prestige and authority. The pontificate of Gregory I (r. 590–604) was crucial in this development.

Gregory, a Roman aristocrat, was educated for service in the imperial bureaucracy that Justinian had reconstructed in Italy. But as a young man, he turned away from secular service to become a monk. He did not remain withdrawn from the world of affairs for long. Although the clerical leadership of the diocese had always been in the hands of old men who had progressed slowly through the papal bureaucracy, Gregory rose quickly to prominence. He was elected pope in 590, when he was 50.

When Gregory became pope, his principal tasks were the conversion of the Lombards and the restoration of the papal finances. Trained in government, he rebuilt the ecclesiastical hierarchy, which had been severely damaged by the Gothic wars of the mid-sixth century. This work consisted in combining poor bishoprics with others to form strong ones, establishing new bishoprics where none had existed, and reorganizing and restaffing the papal bureaucracy. Gregory combined his practical talents with a powerful intellect, and he produced writings of lasting value to the Church. His letters to subordinates enunciated with great clarity the basic principles of ecclesiastical organization, and his commentary on the biblical Book of Job set out the standards for Christian pastoral work. These and other writings gave permanence to his achievements as leader of the Church; to this day, he is the first and greatest guide to priests, bishops, and popes who seek to understand and carry out their duties.

Gregory also played an important role in the affairs of churches throughout the old western provinces of the Empire, and he fostered the spread of Christianity throughout the Germanic world. When the Visigothic king Recared I converted to orthodox Christianity, he looked to the pope to assist in the construction of a new ecclesiastical organization. Gregory thus became the godfather of a reform movement that produced legislation of lasting importance in Church law. He also encouraged the intellectual activity that soon made Spain one of the principal heirs of Roman civilization.

About 595, Gregory saw Anglo-Saxon slaves in Rome, and this event apparently reminded him that Britain had once been part of the Roman world. He decided to send missionaries to the new rulers of the province, and, in 597, the Roman monk Augustine (not the same man as the great Christian writer, who lived 354–430) arrived in Kent with a small entourage. Here, as with Recared in Spain, Gregory was the source of advice and authority, and he wrote many letters in which he instructed the missionaries about how to deal with the Germans. The missionaries wanted to know how to deal with pagan shrines and customs, and Gregory advised that they should try to incorporate them as much as possible into the Christian practices they were introducing. Thus, some pagan rituals, such as the blessing of the fields during the planting season, were absorbed by the English church. The local priest led the procession and performed the blessing in the name of Christ. Likewise, many of the old pagan shrines were taken over as Christian churches, so that the new religion supplanted the old in the most important venerated places. Gregory's letters on these matters became a kind of handbook for missionaries and increased the authority of the popes as the source of Christianity among the Germans.

Gregory's missionaries to the Germans had competitors. During the late sixth century, Irish monks were preaching among the Germans of northern Europe, having already established themselves in northern Britain a generation before the arrival of Gregory's mission in the south of the island. The Irish had an ambivalent attitude toward the popes and were often in conflict with them. The Irish church, cut off from Rome by the Anglo-Saxon invasions, had developed independently for a century and a half. The tension increased under Gregory because he supported a new kind of monasticism that was very different from Irish monasticism.

Western Monasticism

Christian monasticism originated in Egypt during the later third century. It was a profession for simple laymen. The monk withdrew from the world, so that he could live as a Christian, safe from sin. Although the New Testament contains passages that encourage withdrawal (Mark 10:21–25; Romans 13:14; 1 Corinthians 6:13–20), the monastic movement grew spontaneously, without encouragement from the church hierarchy. In the mid-third century—at a time when eastern and western Roman society was disturbed by constant civil strife and frequent persecution of Christians—members of village communities in Egypt escaped into the desert wilderness. (It is important to understand that in the ancient and medieval worlds a desert was not a hot, barren waste, but rather a place where men did not live, a wilderness.) Not all of the people who went to the desert were Christians—several other Middle Eastern religions also encouraged withdrawal—but many were, and Christianity soon became the dominant religion of the desert. The earliest Christian monks engaged in such practices as fasting, vigils, the wearing of rough and irritating clothing (such as hairshirts), the deliberate avoidance of baths (which they associated with the immoralities of the Roman public baths), and celibacy. Their asceticism was not aimed at mere self-torture, but represented a rejection of the material life of Roman civilization. In place of prosperity and comfort, they practiced poverty and self-deprivation. In rejection of family life, which was so important in Roman society, they practiced celibacy.

The leading figure among these "desert fathers" was Anthony (251–356), a man of exceptional sanctity, austerity, and longevity (which accounted for the accumulation of his reputation). He and his fellow monks were hermits, who lived alone in huts and caves. Those living in a district might look after one another in an informal way and might gather for worship on special holidays, but they were essentially independent and alone. Just after the beginning of the fourth century, perhaps at the time when Constantine issued his edict of toleration of Christianity (313), a disciple of Anthony, Pachomius founded the first monastic community in Egypt. The cenobitic monasticism (life in a *cenobium* or community) of Pachomius became the dominant form within a few generations.

To live as Anthony did required an iron constitution and will, for the hermit's life was harsh, and he alone had to repress the urge to leave the straight and narrow path. Many men who went to the desert had a good, but not a strong, will and fell away from Anthony's example. Pachomius's chief concern was to provide for such men. He drew up a rule for his monastic community that took into account the needs and abilities of normal people. Moderation and organization were the main characteristics of the Pachomian regimen. He also emphasized common worship of the monks, thus combining asceticism with the sacramental system of the Church. Therefore, episcopal control was a feature of early cenobitic monasticism because only the bishops could ordain the priests needed to administer the sacraments in the monastic community.

The idea of monasticism arrived in the West around 340, when Athanasius, patriarch of Alexandria and the first biographer of Anthony, was in Italy as an exile from his native land. One of the earliest western monasteries was founded on the island of Lerins, near Marseilles, toward the end of the fourth century. The fame of Lerins was established by one of its earliest abbots, John Cassian (d. 429), who had spent time in Pachomius's community. Under John, Lerins became the fount of monastic ideology in the West. He pre-

One of the desert fathers, St. Simon Stylites lived atop a pillar for 40 years (from a sixth-century reliquary casket).

served the monastic ideals of the Egyptian monks in two important books. The first, the *Institutes,* presented the rules of Pachomius's monastery, and the second, the *Collations,* contained sayings of the desert fathers that John thought would inspire and instruct his monks.

But the independent monastic house represented by Lerins was not the only type in the West. About 20 years after Athanasius's sojourn in Europe, Bishop Martin of Tours founded a Pachomian-type monastery in his church. Martin served both as abbot of the monastery and as bishop of the diocese, and the monks functioned as his episcopal *familia.*

This union of monasticism with the regular hierarchy of the Church became a model of ecclesiastical organization in the West. Monk-bishops became common in the European and North African churches. The great Augustine of Hippo was one of those who founded a monastery in his episcopal church.

Martin of Tours also pioneered the use of monks as missionaries. Although Christianity had made rapid progress among the inhabitants of the cities, it spread slowly in rural areas, and Martin found the monks to be effective in bringing these areas into the Church. Nonetheless, the monastic houses founded by bishops did not become the most active missionaries in rural Europe. By a strange development, the Celtic monks from Ireland and northern Britain became famous in this occupation. To understand how this came to be, it is necessary to give a brief history of the Celtic church.

The Celtic population of Roman Britain had been partly Christianized during the third and fourth centuries, so that the Celtic church was already a strong institution when the Anglo-Saxons invaded in the later fifth century. Even before these events, Celtic missionaries had begun to work beyond the Roman borders. The most famous of these missionaries was the monk Ninian, who prepared in Rome and Tours for his mission (*ca.* 397) among the Picts of Galloway (southwestern Scotland). But the movement he represented was interrupted for a generation by the Germanic invasions and was not revived until about 440, when Patrick (d. 461) began to preach among the Celts of Ireland. Patrick was a monk who also was said to have spent time on the Continent, perhaps at Lerins, and in twenty years of missionary work he founded the Irish church.

The organization of this new church was very different from the organization of the church in the old Roman provinces. After the collapse of Roman government in Britain, the ancient structure of Celtic society, which was based on clans, had reemerged in Britain, and this social pattern was transferred to Wales and Ireland, when the Celtic population migrated there. The organization of the Celtic church rested, therefore, on clans rather than on cities, and it was generally the monastery under its abbot, rather than the bishop's diocese, that formed the chief administrative unit. Each monastery served the spiritual needs of a single clan, and the abbot was a clan leader. The bishop, whose duties were wholly sacramental, was a subordinate official in the Celtic monastery.

Celtic monasticism was based on the Pachomian tradition, but Celtic monks had a penchant for extreme asceticism. They also developed a zeal for missionary work, which may have been the legacy of men like Ninian and Patrick. By 565, the Irish monk Columba had founded a monastery on the island of Iona in the Irish Sea. From this house the conversion of the Picts was continued and the conversion of the Angles of Northumbria was begun. In Britain, the Irish founded the famous monastery of Lindisfarne, and soon thereafter Irish monks were wandering on the Continent, where they were instrumental in the spread of Christianity among the rural population, both German and Gallo-Roman. Between 585 and 615 Columbanus, a monk from

A Northumbrian cross (*ca.* 700).

St. Benedict giving his Rule to his monks. This eighth-century drawing is the oldest known representation of St. Benedict.

Iona, became famous as a missionary in the Frankish kingdom. He founded Luxeuil, which with its 600 monks was the monastic metropolis of the kingdom. He then traveled on to Italy, where he founded Bobbio, between Genoa and Pavia. These houses and the daughter houses founded from them became major centers of education and culture.

The great age of Celtic monasticism was between 550 and 650, and it had a powerful effect in the western Christian world. But Celtic monasticism clashed with the basic values of Roman society. Unlike the eastern population, which supported monasticism, even of the unruly desert kind, westerners considered asceticism to be irrational and suspect. The monks rejected the conservatism, conformity, and social order that were valued in Rome and the Romanized provincial centers. This clash of values slowed the spread of

monasticism in the West, but westerners who favored monasticism gradually introduced reforms that made monastic life acceptable to Romans.

Augustine wrote a rule for the monks of his monastery, and Bishop Caesarius of Arles (*ca.* 470–542) wrote one for nuns. These were short and relatively well-organized, but they assumed that the communities for which they were written would exist within the official hierarchy and live under the direction of a bishop. Yet, even in the West, most monastic communities were not governed by bishops, and there was still a need for a monastic constitution sufficient to the requirements of independent communities. This need was filled by the Italian Benedict of Nursia (*ca.* 480–543). After an experience among the disorderly and unregulated hermits in the valley of Subiaco, east of Rome, Benedict founded a monastery at Monte Cassino between Naples and Rome. There he wrote a rule that was profoundly influenced by John Cassian's works, but was a masterpiece of simplicity and comprehensiveness. Benedict's rule eventually became the basis of virtually all monastic life in the West, and he is considered the "father of western monasticism."

The main features of Pachomian monasticism were communal worship and the three monastic values of poverty, chastity, and obedience. Communal worship, the *opus Dei* (work of God), was also the central feature of the Benedictine monasticism, but the success of Benedict's rule rested on four new elements that he introduced. First, his rule was a constitution that consisted of general regulations, rather than specific rules and examples. As a result, it could be adapted to a wide variety of conditions. Second, Benedict enhanced the authority of the abbot. He was elected by the community, but consecrated by the local bishop. Therefore, he held a divinely ordained power that put him above his monks, in the position of an intermediary between them and God. Third, to the usual vows of poverty, chastity, and obedience, Benedict added another—the vow of stability. This was a vow not to leave the monastery without the abbot's permission, which increased both the abbot's disciplinary powers and the community's solidarity. Finally, the Benedictine rule required the monks to do manual labor, so that the community would be economically self-sufficient.

Benedict did not mention intellectual labor in his rule, but the life of the monastery required it. The *opus Dei* required that the monks know how to read, which in turn required the maintenance of a library and a scriptorium to copy books. Although the monks of Benedict's own time learned to read and write in secular schools or at home, the decline of the old Roman nobility and of the towns caused a decline in literacy even among the aristoc-

racy, and monasteries soon had to maintain their own schools for novices. Within a century of Benedict's death, monasteries were the principal intellectual centers of Europe.

Benedict's rule became known in Rome after 580, when Monte Cassino was destroyed by the Lombards and the refugee monks fled to the capital. One of those attracted to the new monasticism was the future Pope Gregory I, who gave up a promising career in the imperial administration to found a Benedictine monastery on land owned by his family in the city. After he became pope, Gregory wrote a work called the *Dialogues*, in which he recounted the life of Benedict and spoke of his work. With the force of Gregory's support behind it, Benedictine

---

St. Benedict on the Authority of the Abbot

This excerpt illustrates the firm yet reasonable discipline that St. Benedict sought to instill in western monasteries.

Whenever any weighty matters have to be transacted in the monastery let the abbot call together all the community and himself propose the matter for discussion. After hearing the advice of the brethren let him consider it in his own mind, and then do what he shall judge most expedient. We ordain that all must be called to council, because the Lord often reveals to a younger member what is best. And let the brethren give their advice with all humble subjection, and presume not stiffly to defend their own opinion. Let them rather leave the matter to the abbot's discretion, so that all submit to what he shall deem best. As it becometh disciples to obey their master, so doth it behove the master to dispose of all things with forethought and justice.

In all things, therefore, every one shall follow the Rule as their master, and let no one rashly depart from it. In the monastery no one is to be led by the desires of his own heart, neither shall any one within or without the monastery presume to argue wantonly with his abbot. If he presume to do so let him be subjected to punishment according to the Rule.

From the *Rule of St. Benedict*, trans. by Cardinal Gasquet (London: Chatto and Windus, 1925), pp. 15–16.

A self-sufficient monastery. Its produce included fish bred in the *vivarium* shown in the foreground. A *vivarium* was often taken as a symbol of a monastery. The fish represented the monks—note their faces.

monasticism spread slowly until it supplanted all other rules by the end of the ninth century.

From the beginning, monasticism attracted women as well as men. The rule of Caesarius had been written for communities of women, though it served as well for men. Women were also attracted to St. Benedict's rule. From the seventh century, there are many biographies of holy women who withdrew from society to live as nuns. The women of these stories rejected the controlling influence of their families and often escaped an unwanted marriage by running away to a monastery. In most cases in this period, women's communities were attached to and under the protection of men's, and some monastic houses had both men and women in them. In the biographies of women saints, it often happened that a holy man helped the subject escape secular life, and a spiritual relationship formed between the two that paralleled the married state both had rejected.

The Conversion of the Germans

Following the lead of Martin of Tours and the Irish monks, Gregory used monks as troops in his battle to convert the Germans, particularly the Lombards and Anglo-Saxons, and to spread Christianity to the isolated villages of the European countryside that had escaped the attention of urban churches. As noted earlier, in directing this effort, Gregory formulated a policy for dealing with the pagan beliefs of the German population. He counseled compromise with, rather than harsh rejection of, superstition and pagan practices. Therefore, his missionaries tried to adapt some of these old beliefs and practices to Christianity, so that many practices of the medieval and modern Church can be traced to pre-Christian paganism. The compromise sped up the conversion process and the policy of compromise became established in the church.

Yet, the rapidity of the conversion of the Germans stemmed more from their own religious tradition than from Gregory's policy and the talent of his missionaries. Throughout the process of conversion, the Germans continued to view their kings as intermediaries between the divine and human worlds, so that when the kings gave their allegiance to a new god, the great bulk of their people immediately followed suit. In the case of the Franks, the conversion of Clovis brought virtually the whole people into the Church.

In Anglo-Saxon England, the process took longer because the country was not unified. The Irish monks had been working in the north for a generation, but their influence had not penetrated south of the Humber River. When in 597 the Roman monk Augustine convinced King Ethelbert of Kent, who was married to a Christian princess from the Frankish royal family, to convert, Ethelbert's people followed their king into the new religion. But Ethelbert's rivals in other kingdoms resisted conversion, and for 50 years the struggle between Christianity and paganism was part of the political rivalry within and among the Anglo-Saxon kingdoms. By the 660s, Christianity was triumphant in England.

The centrality of the king in the German conversions and the persistence of the view that the king was an intermediary between man and God brought the Old Testament, with its stories of consecrated kings, to the fore in European Christianity. Christian intellectuals in the Germanic kingdoms used the Hebrew scriptures as a source for a Christian ideology of political authority. On its side, the Church exerted a great influence on German society and culture. In general, it was the source and avenue of the flow of Greco-Roman civilization to the Germans, and, in particular, it affected German legal ideas in profound ways.

Old German law had no notion of a corporation, but that was what the Church was in Roman law, and, therefore, it took for granted rights and privileges that the Germans had never considered. In German society, only the members of the community could own land, and the law specified who succeeded to land after the death of its holder. Moreover, persons unattached to kin or community had no standing in law, for they had no one to guarantee their conduct or stand surety for them should the need arise. After the conversion, the Church and its clergy had to be integrated into this society of family men and women, and it took bold innovation on the part of the kings to accomplish this. On the Continent, the acceptance of Roman law and customs meant that the Church could own land and its clerics were recognized members of the community. The Visigoths, Ostrogoths, Franks, and other Germanic peoples settled in the old Roman provinces simply accepted the *status quo*. In England, the Church had left with the Celtic population, and Ethelbert of Kent had to find a way to enlarge the concept of community to include the clerics of his new religion. Almost immediately after the conversion, he issued, under the Church's influence, a written law code in Anglo-Saxon which, in addition to setting down Kentish law, assigned a value to the clergy for purposes of compensation. Thus, clerics were integrated into the society of the kingdom.

The problem of land ownership took longer to solve. During the 630s, the Anglo-Saxon kings created a new form of landholding based on the possession of a written charter instead of on the witness of family and neighbors. Under normal circumstances, a dispute over land was decided by the opinion

Religious carving from Niederdollendorf, probably depicting the symbols of Thor.

of neighbors and family members about who had the right to the land under the law. But the Church had no property rights under the law because all such rights stemmed from a person's membership in a family through which the rights had passed. The new form of property right, called *bookland* because it rested on possession of a charter or book—that is, a written instrument—gave the Church rights in land. Only the king could issue a charter because law flowed from God through the king, and the new property rights constituted a giving of law to the Church. If a man wanted to give land to the Church, he "booked" it by getting a charter from the king. He then handed the charter over to the Church, which could produce the document if its rights were ever challenged. This great innovation in property law became one of the foundations of modern society.

Thus, the Christian Church played a central role in the formation of a new civilization. It became one of the principal institutions in which Roman and Germanic ideas and ways of life came together to form medieval European civilization. And the Church did not cease to play this role after the period of the successor kingdoms. It remained a source for change and innovation throughout the Middle Ages and continued to be a central institution of European society until the nineteenth century.

The breakdown of Roman political authority and the transformation of Roman civilization in the West was in strong contrast with what happened in the East. In China, India, and Byzantium, the civilizations of the past remained largely intact, even though political changes took place. In those civilizations, religion, language, cultural tradition, and political ideology continued along their ancient tracks, and newcomers were absorbed into the dominant culture without deflecting it from its course or changing its nature. Only in the Middle East, where a new religion, Islam, came into being, was there a cultural transformation similar to that in the West. Like the Europeans, the Arabs were heirs of Greco-Roman civilization, and like them they reshaped that tradition to fit their new religion. But Islamic civilization preserved much more of the ancient tradition than the Europeans did, and it added valuable new material to that tradition. In the twelfth century, Islamic civilization became an important source of new knowledge and ideas for the westerners. The next chapters look at the civilizations of the East.

Suggestions for Further Reading

General

For general histories of the Germanic invasions and studies of early Germanic society, see the works cited at the end of Chapter 4. On the relations between the old Roman population and the Germans, see S. Dill, *Roman Society in Gaul in the Merovingian Age* (1926), and W. Goffart, *Barbarians and Romans, A.D. 418–584: The Techniques of Accommodation* (1980). F. Lot, *The End of the Ancient World and the Beginning of the Middle Ages* (1931), is still a good survey of the successor kingdoms. J. M. Wallace-Hadrill, *The Barbarian West, 400–1000* (1952), is an excellent brief survey. A series of new studies gives a close look at several of the kingdoms: T. Burns, *The Ostrogoths* (1984); C. Wickham, *Early Medieval Italy: Central Power and Local Society 400–1000* (1981); E. James, *The Origins of France: From Clovis to the Capetians 500–1000* (1982); and P. J. Geary, *Before France and Germany* (1987). The most important source for the history of the Franks is Gregory of Tours, whose work has been published as *The History of the Franks* (1974, and other editions). For the history of the Anglo-Saxons, see Bede, *The Ecclesiastical History of England* (many editions). F. M. Stenton, *The Anglo-Saxons*, 2nd ed. (1947), is an excellent general history. On the Visigoths, see Thompson's *The Goths in Spain* (1969); P. D. King, *Law and Society in the Visigothic Kingdom* (1972); and R. Collins, *Early Medieval Spain: Unity in Diversity 400–1000* (1983).

Germanic Society

The picture of Germanic society has been altered by the study of A. C. Murray, *Germanic Kinship Structure* (1983). See also E. A. Thompson, *The Early Germans* (1965). The best modern studies of the early Germanic idea of kingship are J. M. Wallace-Hadrill, *Early Germanic Kingship in England and on the Continent* (1971); P. H. Sawyer and I. N. Wood, ed., *Early Medieval Kingship* (1977); and H. A. Myers (with H. Wolfram), *Medieval Kingship* (1977), which covers the whole subject up to the late Middle Ages. M. McCormick, *Eternal Victory: Triumphal Rulership in Late Antiquity, Byzantium, and the Early Medieval West* (1986), shows how Roman imperial ideas of rulership survived in early Germanic kingship. Much of what is known of early Germanic society derives from study of the law codes: see K. F. Drew, *The Burgundian Code* (1949) and *The Lombard Laws* (1973), and T. J. Rivers, *Laws of the Alamans and Bavarians* (1977). On the condition of women in the early period, see S. Wemple, *Women in Frankish Society: Marriage and the Cloister 500–900* (1981), and S. M. Stuard, ed., *Women in Medieval Society* (1976). There is a chapter on the early medieval household in D. Herlihy, *Medieval Households* (1985). See also J. Chapelot and R. Fossier, *The Village and House in the Middle Ages* (1985).

The Early Church

For a comprehensive history of the early Church, see K. Baus and H. Jedin, *History of Church History*, Vol. 1 (1965), and J. Danielou and H. Marrou, *The Christian Centuries*, Vol. 1 (1964). Both of these works give ample treatment of the growth of ecclesiastical institutions. On the development of Christian liturgy, see J. A. Jungmann, *The Early Liturgy to the Time of Gregory the Great* (1959), and G. Dix, *The Shape of the Liturgy* (1960). The standard study of Gregory the Great's pontificate is still F. H. Dudden, *Gregory the Great*, 2 vols. (1905), but for a modern appreciation of his achievement against the background of the early medieval papacy, see J. Richards, *The Popes and the Papacy in the Early Middle Ages 476–752* (1979). On the formation of the Papal State, see T. F. X. Noble, *The Republic of St. Peter: The Birth of the Papal State 680–825* (1984). On early monasticism, see P. Rousseau, *Pachomius* (1985) and *Ascetics, Authority and the Church in the Age of Jerome and Cassian* (1978), and C. H. Lawrence, *Medieval Monasticism: Forms of Religious Life in Western Europe in the Middle Ages* (1984). For translations of early saints' lives, see H. Delehaye, *The Legends of the Saints* (1962), and E. S. Duckett, *The Wandering Saints of the Early Middle Ages* (1958). For an interpretation of the monastic ideal, see P. Brown, *Society and the Holy in Late Antiquity* (1982). The Rule of St. Benedict has been published in many editions.

6
India and China in Antiquity

*C*ivilization in South and East Asia developed later than in Mesopotamia and Egypt but well before Greece and Rome. India and China resemble each other in their antiquity, their duration, and the vast geographical extent of their cultural influence, but in many essential respects they represent a study in contrast. Furthermore, even though India, unlike China, did share in a broad and diffuse Indo-European heritage, it developed a civilization as distinct from those to the West as it was from that of China. Contact between the various civilizations is a fascinating and occasionally important historical theme, but the primary interest of Indian and Chinese civilizations, as of their western counterparts, lies in their intrinsic importance in the past and present history of the globe, the enduring value of their cultural achievements, and in the wealth of material they offer for the study of the comparative history of civilization.

INDIA

The Indian subcontinent, stretching from the frosty Himalayan Mountains to the tropical beaches of the south, is a vast area inhabited by peoples with strong regional and local traditions. In the course of time, sufficient unity developed so that we can speak of an Indian civilization, but within that civilization there has always been great diversity. The interplay of the factors making for one or the other is a major theme of Indian history.

As we have seen, civilization in India dates to the third millenium B.C. when a sophisticated culture flourished, centered in the Indus River Valley. Over a territory of half a million square miles, some 300 sites have been investigated, most of them near rivers whose waters sustained agriculture and provided transportation. The most impressive sites are those of Mohenjo-Daro and Harappa, the former a city of 25,000–30,000 inhabitants. Laid out on grids and capped by citadels, these two cities were complete with granaries and advanced drainage stystems, and the presence of separate industrial areas points to class differentiation. Small square seals found as far away as Sumerian Mesopotamia attest to a flourishing commerce. These seals were probably used by merchants to mark their wares. Some are decorated with real or imaginary animals; others bear abstract symbols, including the Greek cross and the swastika. Written inscriptions on the seals have not been deciphered, although the script is generally considered to be in a Dravidian language. The technological repertoire of the cities included wheel-made pottery, cotton spinning, and metallurgy. The impressive bath at Mohenjo-Daro, similar to water tanks in later Hindu temples, may attest to the importance of religion, but no actual temples have been uncovered from this period.

Environmental factors such as devastating floods, a shift in the course of the Indus River, and exhaustion of soil fertility may have accounted for the

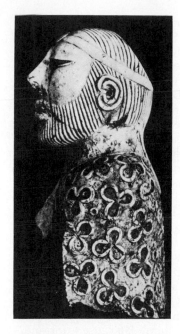

Statuette of a man, perhaps a priest, wearing an ornamental robe, from Mohenjo-Daro (*ca.* 2500 B.C.).

demise of this civilization. A decline in social organization followed, as mirrored in later city planning. By the time the crude Aryan tribal peoples entered the subcontinent, the old civilization was gone, leaving in its wake impoverished localized cultures.

Early Aryan–Indian Society

The Aryans began to enter India in substantial numbers through the Hindu Kush mountains around 1500 B.C. They were tribal peoples related to the inhabitants of Iran, and they spoke Sanskrit, an Indo-European language which became the classic language of India. They were a vigorous, indeed tumultuous and warlike people, not unlike the Greeks. Originally pastoral, as time passed they also turned to agriculture. They gradually achieved dominance first in the Indus Plain, then in North India. After 1000 B.C. there were also Aryan incursions into the region beyond the Vindhaya Mountain Range, which separates North from South India. Although ultimately

Opposite: Capital on a column erected by Asoka to commemorate the Buddha's preaching of the First Sermon in Sarnath.

157

North Indian culture profoundly influenced the South, the various southern regions never lost their cultural or linguistic identity. Today, South India continues to be dominated by peoples speaking Dravidian languages belonging to a different linguistic family from that of the Indo-European tongues of the North.

In the beginning the Aryans were divided into warriors, priests, and commoners, but as they settled down their social organization became more complex. There developed what became India's classic division of society into four social orders (*varnas*). Most likely, the warriors (*kshatriyas*) originally had pride of place, but the classic order ranks priests (*brahmans*) first with warriors second. Other Aryans were included in the third varna, that of the *vaishyas*, a term later used for merchants and cultivators. Members of these three orders were entitled to full membership in society as symbolized by the sacred thread granted to boys in an induction ceremony. This status was denied to the dark-skinned conquered people who formed the fourth order, the *shudras*, who were reduced to serfdom and forced to perform menial tasks. Still further down in social status were those whose work was considered polluting: attendants at cremation grounds, those who worked with animal carcasses, leather workers, and others. Later they were known as "untouchables," beyond the pale of Aryan society.

As political integration proceeded and Aryan influences spread, the interaction between India's various communities grew in complexity and extent. The process by which major components of North Indian culture were spread is frequently termed "Aryanization," but the influence was not all one way. The varna system did not operate everywhere in the same way, and another institution, the *jati* (caste) made for a diversity of lifestyles and beliefs even within the same locality. The jatis were endogamous (intermarrying) groups which shared a common religious heritage, traditional values, dietary rules, and, characteristically, a common occupation. It was the jati to which they belonged that gave men and women their basic sense of community and determined the essential pattern of their lives. Like membership in a family, membership in a jati was a matter of birth; a person could no more change his jati than he could his family. To be expelled from one's jati and become an outcast was the worst possible fate, for no other jati would accept such a person.

Although the tendency was for the jati to be grouped under the major varna, the fit was often imperfect. By preserving the traditions and identities of numerous groups, the jati system contributed to Indian pluralism while, at the same time, it reinforced social differentiation. Although much has changed in the long course of history, the existence of over 3,000 jatis attests to the continuing significance of this institution in India today.

Religious Developments

The success of the brahmans (priests) in gaining first place in the social hierarchy suggests the importance of religion in early India. Like other Indo-European peoples, the Aryans worshipped a number of gods—some being more important than others. As the civilization grew in complexity and sophistication, the old rituals and formulas no longer met everyone's religious needs, and there appeared a tendency toward abstract thought and a posing of such ultimate questions as those concerning the nature of being and nonbeing, questions which were to be central to India's loftiest religious and philosophical discourses.

These religious concerns were expressed in the *Upanishads*, a group of religious treatises of the eighth and seventh centuries B.C. The *Upanishads* contain the religious speculations of teachers working in the traditions of the *Rig Veda*, an ancient collection of hymns handed down orally from generation to generation and written down in its present form around 600 B.C. Since the *Upanishads* do not stem from a single source, they contain diverse ideas, but they do agree on one central theme: that the invisible but essential "soul" within each of us *(Atman)* is identical with the world-soul *(Brahman)*, the underlying reality of the world. Failure to realize this truth condemns people to be prisoners of their illusions and chains them to an unending cycle of birth and rebirth. Death provides no relief, for it is merely a stage, an interlude between lives. Release comes only when the individual Atman is rejoined with the Brahman, attainable only after comprehension is achieved through disciplined effort, meditation, and/or various spiritual and yogic exercises.

The individual fate of those who do not attain release is governed by the law of *karma,* according to which every action brings forth a reaction, not only in this life but also in the next. Thus a person who has led a good life but still falls short of the perfection needed for release will at least enjoy a favorable rebirth, but a wicked person might come back as a pig, a goat, or even an insect. In later Indian thought various theories were advanced to account for the operation of karma. Different behavioral conclusions were drawn (for instance, it reinforced a tendency toward vegetarianism), but the concept of karma itself was accepted as a basic truth not only by ordinary folk but by all traditional Indian thinkers and holy men.

Most of the era's men of religion stayed within the Vedic tradition, but there were some important exceptions. One was Vardhamana Mahavira (*ca.* 540–468 B.C.), the founder of Jainism, a religion that teaches nonviolence and is centered on the belief that everything is animated. Even more influential was Gautama Siddharta (*ca.* 563–483 B.C.), also known as Sakyamuni, who achieved religious illumination and became the Buddha, the "Enlightened One." He then spent the remainder of

Vedic Hymns

ORIGINS OF THE FOUR *VARNA*

When they [the gods] divided the Man,
  into how many parts did they divide him?
What were his mouth, what were his arms,
  what were his thighs and feet called?

The brahman [priest] was his mouth,
  of his arms were made the warrior.
His thighs became the vaisya [merchants and cultivators],
  of his feet the sudra [servants] was born.

The moon arose from his mind,
  from his eye was born the sun,
from his mouth Indra and Agni [the war god and the fire god],
  from his breath the wind was born. . . .

HYMN OF CREATION

Then even nothingness was not, nor existence,
There was no air then, nor the heavens beyond it.
What covered it? Where was it? In whose keeping?
Was there then cosmic water, in depths unfathomed?

Then there was neither death nor immortality,
nor was there then the torch of night and day.
The One breathed windlessly and self-sustaining.
There was that One then, and there was no other. . . .

But, after all, who knows and who can say
whence it all came, and how creation happened?
The gods themselves are later than creation,
so who knows truly whence it has arisen?

Quoted in A. L. Basham, *The Wonder That Was India* (London: Sidgwick and Jackson, 1954; New York: Macmillan, 1968), pp. 241, 247–248.

his life sharing his insights with others. His disciples renounced the world, took vows of chastity and poverty, and formed communities of monks and nuns. The idea of monasticism had such deep appeal to people of religious vocation that it spread not only to regions east of India but also west to the Middle East.

At the core of the Buddha's teachings were the Four Noble Truths: that

The Buddha was first not pictured in human form; his presence here is indicated by the tree in the upper left corner (detail from a pillar at Sanchi, first century B.C.).

does not involve a substance but rather it is like the passing of a flame from one lamp to another until it is finally extinguished. The state of Nirvana, which literally means "extinguished," was the ultimate goal.

Another major difference between the orthodox Vedic traditions and Buddhism was that Buddhism rejected the hereditary claims of the brahmans. For Buddhists, birth did not determine worth. This attitude naturally appealed to merchants, warriors, and others offended by the pretensions of the priesthood. As Buddhism developed it acquired other features which enhanced its appeal and won it patronage. Its greatest Indian patron was the third emperor of the Mauryan Empire.

The Mauryan Empire 321–181 B.C.

In a gradual process over many centuries, tribes and tribal confederations were formed into more complex political organizations. By mid-sixth century B.C. there were 16 kingdoms that we know by name. The largest of these was the Magadhan state, which from its base in the eastern Gangetic Plain expanded to create an empire in North India. In the meantime, India's northwest became part of the great Achaemeneid Empire of Persia, which was destroyed by Alexander the Great in the fourth century B.C. When the power of Alexander's empire receded, the Magadhan state, under the Mauryan dynasty, took its place. The Mauryans then expanded until they ruled over the entire Indian subcontinent, except for the extreme south.

The empire had a complex administrative structure. It built public works (especially roads and irrigation facilities), maintained an army, and collected taxes. Theoretically, all land belonged to the emperor. Cultivators paid about a third of their crop in taxes, and were charged for the use of government water. There were also numerous levies on merchants and craftsmen, many of whom lived in Pataliputra (modern Patna), a cosmo-

life is suffering; that the cause of suffering is carving or desire; that to stop the suffering the desire must be stopped; that this is accomplished through the Eightfold Path (right views, right intention, right speech, right action, right livelihood, right effort, right mindfulness, and right concentration). Like his contemporaries the Buddha taught that salvation lay in release from reincarnation, but he denied the existence of a soul and taught that what we think of as the self is merely a temporary aggregate of the material body, the sensations, perception, predisposition, and consciousness. It is a momentary cluster of qualities lacking any underlying unity. Transmigration, in this view,

politan city whose bazaars offered goods from places as far away as China, Mesopotamia, and Asia Minor.

Much of the empire's success has traditionally been ascribed to Kautilya, the author of the *Arthashastra* (Treatise on Material Gain), India's prime text on practical politics and administration. It contains a good deal of sound, practical advice (for instance, that officials should be selected on the basis of merit and that the king should devote himself to his tasks), but it also offers frank counsels of expediency. A notorious example is its advice to the ruler that he employ spies to inform him of what is happening in the state and also to spread propaganda for him.

Emperor Ashoka (r. 269–232 B.C.) is perhaps India's most famous ruler. Converted to Buddhism, Ashoka did much to advance the religion. He sponsored a great Buddhist council, sent out missionaries, and erected numerous stupas, Buddhist reliquary mounds. The largest of these, that at Sanchi,

The Buddha (detail of a relief from Gandhara, second century A.D.).

The Mauryan Empire   *ca.* 250 B.C.

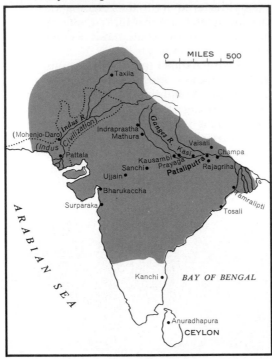

exceptionally strong ruler to organize a political machine and inspire the wide loyalty needed to maintain as huge and disparate a domain as that of the Mauryas, a domain with few economic or institutionalized political bonds that might have made for a more permanent union.

Political Division 180 B.C.–A.D. 320

The next 500 years in India were complicated politically, but it was a period of cultural brilliance, economic growth, and increased contacts with other cultures.

A succession of many foreign peoples into India was a major source of the period's instability. We have already noted the invasion of Alexander the Great; the ultimate legacy of Greek interest in India was the formation of a number of Indo-Greek states, some of which issued bilingual coins. However, the most successful people to inhabit India during this period were the Kushans, who entered the subcontinent from Central Asia in the first century A.D. and created an empire that lasted until 240. The Kushan empire was the only one ever to straddle the Hindu Kush and Baluchi Hills and become a major power in both Central Asia and India. Most of the lucrative trade along the silk route passed through the Kushan empire in the north while, at the same time, maritime trade flourished in the south. Hoards of Roman coins found in South India, beyond the borders of the Kushan empire, substantiate the complaint of Pliny the Elder that the trade was causing a gold drain in Rome.

The Kushans were converted to Buddhism and they eventually spread their new faith to Central Asia and to China. Under the Kushans the first statues of the Buddha appeared, executed in an Indo-Roman style that spread to the east. The growth of Buddhist art was only one of a number of ways in which Buddhism was gradually transformed and its appeal broadened. Another major development was

stands 56 feet tall and was later encased in sandstone and supplied with a beautifully carved railing and gateways. The lion column he erected to commemorate the Buddha's first sermon has become a symbol of India, adopted in the twentieth century to decorate the state seal of the Republic of India. In his patronage of Buddhism, Ashoka has been compared to Emperor Constantine and his support of Christianity in Rome, but the Indian monarch also maintained religious tolerance throughout his far-flung empire. In the edicts he had inscribed on rocks and special pillars, he displayed the imperial paternalism appropriate to a universal ruler. "I consider my work to be the welfare of the whole world," he proclaimed in one edict.

A half century after Ashoka's death, the Mauryan Empire was in collapse. Its last ruler was assassinated by a general who had to content himself with ruling over a much diminished state in central India. It would have taken an

the growth of worship and devotionalism, with the recognition of a number of Buddhas and *bodhisattvas*, beings who, on the threshold of Nirvana, postpone their own salvation in order to help others. Such figures attracted the pious veneration of the common folk even as Buddhist theorists developed subtle and profound doctrines that supplied spiritual and intellectual nourishment to those who dedicated their lives to the religious quest. These developments coalesced to constitute Mahayana Buddhism, and it was largely in this form that the religion spread from the Kushan empire to East Asia, while the older Theraveda (or Hinayana) form prevailed to the south.

Running parallel to the changes in Buddhism were changes that transformed the traditional Vedic religion into Hinduism. With Hinduism, as in Buddhism, worshipers felt the need for divine beings that were accessible to them, and there developed a rich pantheon of gods and deities even as Hindu saints and philosophers pointed

A stone relief of an amorous couple from a sculptured cave temple at Karli, A.D. 100.

to an ultimate unity underlying all diversity. Of the three main Hindu deities—Brahma (The Creator), Vishnu (The Preserver), and Siva (The Destroyer but also a Creator)—the latter two became the main wings of Hinduism, inspiring sects which gained a vast number of devoted adherents who regarded their gods as representative of the Absolute. Vishnu was believed to have appeared in nine incarnations. His ninth incarnation was as the Buddha suggesting that Buddhism was simply part of a greater Hindu whole. Vishnu was also incarnated as Rama, hero of India's great epic, the *Ramayana*, and as Krishna, an important figure in the Hindu pantheon.

It is as Krishna that Vishnu appears in the *Bhagavad Gita (The Song of the Lord)*, which was inserted into the great and much older epic, *The Mahabharata*. In the *Gita* Krishna appears as the charioteer and friend of a warrior named Arjuna, who, greatly distressed to see friends and relatives lined up in the enemy ranks as a battle is about to begin, lays down his bow. But Krishna urges him to perform his sacred duty *(dharma)* as a warrior, telling him that everyone has a social role that must be fulfilled, and as long as one fulfills his dharma without attachment, he will not incur bad karma.

There are other subtle and profound concepts in the *Gita*, the most widely studied and revered Hindu text. One that fits in well with India's system of castes and social orders is the concept that people's *dharma* differs according to their social group, and that salvation lies in everyone's following his *dharma* without regard for self-benefit. The basic idea that different duties and lifestyles pertain to different groups of people was also involved in the theory of the four stages of life, which were prescribed as the ideal for members of the upper three varnas. First came the stage of the earnest student, diligently following the instructions of his teacher. Next came the phase of the householder, with all the joys and responsibilities of an active secular life. Love and pleasure *(kama)*, as well as material gain *(artha)*, were among the accepted goals of life. However, there came a time to retire from the active life of the householder and to partially withdraw into the forest to meditate. This was followed by the final stage, that of the ascetic wandering free from all human bonds, concerned only with the soul's liberation. Many, indeed most, householders did not actually end their lives in this manner, but it had its attractions in a land which honored ascetics and respected the religious quest.

The Guptas, ca. 325–550

Like the Mauryan Empire, that of the Guptas was based in the Gangetic Plain. From there they expanded west to the Punjab, northwest to Kashmir, east to Bengal, and established themselves as a presence in the south. However, the south was not fully incorporated into the empire; defeated rulers were largely reinstated in their lands as tributaries. There were also rulers in distant places such as Sri Lanka who, in theory, accepted Gupta overlordship and sent the emperor gifts, but who were well beyond the range of its authority.

The dynasty reached its greatest height of well-being under Chandra Gupta II *(ca.* 375–415), even though it had not attained its geatest geographical extent. The account of Faxian (Fa Hsien), a Chinese monk who visited India at this time, testifies to the safety

---

The Ends of Man

Some say that dharma [virtue] and material gain are good, others that pleasue and material gain are good, and still others that dharma alone or pleasure alone is good, but the correct position is that the three should coexist without harming each other.

From *Sources of Indian Tradition*, ed. by Wm. Theodore de Bary and others (New York: Columbia University Press, 1958), p. 213.

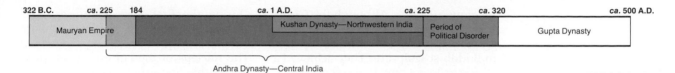

322 B.C.   ca. 225   184   ca. 1 A.D.   ca. 225   ca. 320   ca. 500 A.D.

| Mauryan Empire | Kushan Dynasty—Northwestern India | Period of Political Disorder | Gupta Dynasty |

Andhra Dynasty—Central India

of travel and the general prosperity of the realm. He tells of cities with fine mansions, and that in Pataliputra (Patna) there were "houses for dispensing charities and medicine." He also reports, optimistically, that no one in the kingdom killed animals, drank intoxicating liquor, or ate onion or garlic—no one except "wicked men" who had to warn others of their approach by striking a piece of wood so they could avoid contamination.

It was a time of prosperity and, at least at court, luxury, for there were great feasts with drink served in ruby cups or cups in the shape of dancing peacocks. The quantity and quality of Gupta coins attest to the importance of commerce. India's trade with China and Southeast Asia was on the increase and trade with the West remained significant. Merchant and artisan guilds prospered. The fiscal basis of the state included a land tax and various supplemental levies. There was also a government monopoly on salt and metal mines. Once again, as under the Mauryans, there was a complex administrative hierarchy and a strong network of government agents and spies.

The last great Gupta emperor was Skandagupta (455–67), who repelled the Hunas (Huns) who invaded India from Central Asia. After his reign, however, the dynasty went into decline. The throne was weakened by succession disputes, a recurrent problem in India where there were no clear rules of primogeniture (succession by the eldest son). In the end, the state was unable to withstand repeated attacks from the Huns.

The Gupta period is celebrated less for its political achievements than for its cultural brilliance. India's greatest playwright, Kalidasa, most probably served at the court of Chandra Gupta II. There were notable advances in mathematics and astronomy. The numerals later introduced into Europe by the Arabs and consequently known as Arabic numerals were actually Indian in origin, as was the decimal system. In 499 an Indian astronomer calculated the value of *pi*, determined that there are 365.3586805 days in a year, and argued that the earth is round, that it revolves around its own axis, and that lunar eclipses occur when the earth's shadow falls on the moon. However, these theories were disputed by other astronomers. As elsewhere, astronomy remained firmly wedded to astrology.

Along with a flourishing literary and intellectual culture, the visual arts also reached new excellence. The most lasting achievements were made under

The Gupta Empire   *ca.* A.D. 400

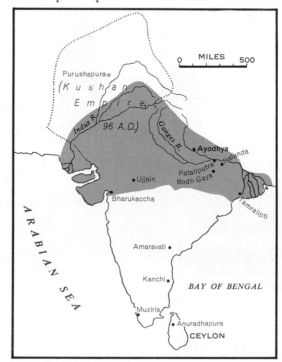

religious auspices. Although the Gupta rulers generally favored Hinduism, Gupta artists created their masterpieces in Buddhist sculpture. They achieved a classic style not only in the sense that it served as a touchstone for later artists, but also in that it achieved a perfect balance between the transcendental and the human in idealized figures representing the Buddha. India's finest wall paintings also date from this period, although they were produced in the south, beyond the bounds of the empire. These are the world famous Buddhist caves at Ajanta, which are decorated with secular as well as religious scenes and constitute a narrative art of the highest quality.

South India

The fact that both of India's great empires were based in the north should not obscure the contributions of the south to the development of Indian civilization. Inscriptions began to appear in South India in the second century B.C. and a century earlier in Sri Lanka.

During the first three centuries A.D. anthologies of poetry were compiled in Tamil, a major Dravidian language. The nucleus of the culture which produced this literature was a little south of modern Madras. The early Tamil poems describe a complex culture of farmers and townspeople—over 100 towns are mentioned, as are numerous occupations. Politically the Tamil-speaking area was long divided between three competing states until the Pallavas (roughly 315–800, with their highpoint around 600) achieved dominance. Over the centuries the Tamil and other southern cultures were deeply influenced by Sanskrit culture without, however, loosing their identities. The interaction between the southern cultures and those of the north forms a major theme in the study of South India.

The Spread of Indian Culture

By the middle of the sixth century, Indian influence had spread far beyond the subcontinent. It was a gradual and

A view of the temple of Angkor Wat, built in the twelfth century by the king of Cambodia.

The Spread of Buddhism   Sixth Century B.C. to Sixteenth Century A.D.

Map: The Spread of Buddhism. Labels include: MONGOLIA, GOBI DESERT, MILES 0–1000, AFGHANISTAN, Indus River, Ganges River, ORIGIN OF BUDDHISM 6TH C. B.C., 250 B.C., 1ST C. B.C., 1ST C. A.D., Yellow River, CHINA, Yangtze River, 16 C. A.D., 4TH C. A.D., KOREA, 6TH C. A.D., JAPAN, JAPAN SEA, EAST CHINA SEA, PACIFIC OCEAN, SOUTH CHINA SEA, BURMA, 6TH C. A.D., SIAM, INDO-CHINA, 7TH C. A.D., 2ND C. A.D., MALAYA, 7TH C. A.D., JAVA, BAY OF BENGAL, 1ST–2ND C. A.D., 250 B.C., INDIAN OCEAN.

selective process of cultural diffusion. The peoples of Southeast Asia did not have Indian culture forced upon them. Local rulers, impressed by the achievements of Indian civilization and valuing the power of Indian knowledge and religion, selected and adapted certain Indian institutions to their own distinct cultural patterns.

The influence of India was deep and permanent in all regions of Southeast Asia, with the exception of the Philippines and North Vietnam. The figures of Borobudur, the great eighth-century Buddhist monument in Indonesia, clearly show the influence of Gupta sculpture, and elsewhere South Indian influences were also much in evidence. In later centuries, the temples at Pagan in Burma and the magnificent structures in the jungles of Cambodia (Kampuchea) were to attest to the appeal of Hinduism, as well as Buddhism. The largest religious building in the world is Angkor Wat in Cambodia. Dedicated to Vishnu, this Hindu temple was built in the first half of the twelfth century. It is a walled complex measuring some 1500 by 1300 meters and is surrounded by a moat 200 meters wide—just as the world, in Indian eyes, is surrounded by the ocean. The balustrades in the first interior section are in the shape of nine-headed snakes, referring both to an ancient snake cult and to Vishnu's rainbow, the magic bridge which leads to heaven. Relief carvings on the wall portray stories of Rama and Krishna, the two most prominent incarnations of Vishnu.

Although Angkor Wat was built much later than the period we are concerned with here, it symbolizes the enormous influence of Hinduism in the lands to India's east. Yet it was the influence of Buddhism that was to be the more lasting; to this day it is the dominant religion of the Southeast Asian mainland and Sri Lanka. As a proselytizing religion of great force, Buddhism also spread from India through Central Asia to China, where it eventually made a great impact.

CHINA

Archeologists have uncovered a number of Neolithic cultures in China, but it was in the Shang period (*ca.* 1600–1027 B.C.) that the first real civilization emerged. As in India, the first substantial cities appeared in the north from which the first states grew. A good indication of Shang organizational power was its ability to mobilize the manpower needed to build a wall estimated at 2,385 feet long, 60 feet wide, and 30 feet high surrounding an early capital city. It has been calculated that this wall took 10,000 laborers working 330 days a year, 18 years to complete.

With the Shang, China entered the bronze age. The finest products of the period are bronze vessels unsurpassed in their artistry, as befitted their use in solemn sacred rites. Many such vessels have been found, along with jades and other precious objects, in Shang tombs of the rich and powerful. The remains of people buried alive have also been found in these tombs. In one case, a chariot was discovered, complete with horse and driver; in others, entire entourages accompanied the deceased in death. The victims were non-Shang barbarians, captured in war and reduced to slavery, who were believed to accompany the dead on a journey to the afterworld.

Of more permanent influence was the development of the Chinese system of writing during this period. The earliest Chinese characters were pictograms (stylized pictorial representations) and ideograms (visual representations of a thing or concept), but most characters were more complex, consisting of an element that indicated a category of meaning and another that functioned as a phonetic indicator. Unfortunately, the pronunciation of the language later changed so that today the phonetic element is not necessarily a reliable guide to pronunciaton. The early characters were used to inscribe oracle bones and tortoise shells used for divination. Command of the written language was the prized possession of a privileged group, and full literacy, until modern times, remained the possession of an elite minority who prided themselves in working with their brains rather than with their hands.

While the written language was associated with the perpetuation of social distinctions, it helped to overcome geographical barriers, for people who spoke mutually unintelligible languages could still communicate with each other in writing, particularly after the form of characters was standardized in 221 B.C. Thus today, even though Cantonese and Mandarin speakers cannot converse with each other, they can communicate in writing and they can read the same books and journals. Similarly, scholars in Korea, Japan, and Vietnam acquired a command over China's literary culture even though they were unable to speak Chinese.

When the Shang were overthrown by the Zhou (Chou)* around 1027 B.C., at first there was no break in cultural continuity since the Zhou represented a variant of Shang culture. They even produced bronze vessels very similar to those of their predecessors. However, the inscriptions on the vessels, as well as the decorations and artisitic effects

A ceremonial vessel in the form of an elephant (Shang dynasty).

*This text uses the *pinyin* system of romanization, followed in parentheses by Wade-Giles. An exception to this is some common geographical names which appear in their earlier customary forms.

gradually changed, indicating a process of secularization which transformed them into treasured family heirlooms. At the same time, burial practices changed, and the immolation of humans and animals in the tombs of the powerful became increasingly rare.

The Zhou did not attempt to govern the area they conquered directly, but invested members of the royal house, favored adherents, and allies with the authority to rule over more than a hundred separate territories, which these men were free to administer without interference from the Zhou king. These subordinate rulers received ranks later systematized into a hierarchical order. They were obliged to render military service and tribute. In practice these positions were hereditary under a system of primogeniture, but with each generation the succession to a local lordship had to be legitimized by formal royal investiture. Some of these Zhou arrangements resembled those of the feudal system which later developed in Europe and Japan.

We are inadequately informed about the political structure of local village life or the economic relations between those who cultivated the soil and their rulers. However, we can learn something from the folk poetry included in the *Book of Songs*, which was compiled around 600 B.C. and was later accepted as one of the classics of Confucianism. Some songs show ordinary people at work: the men clearing weeds from the fields, plowing, planting, and harvesting; the girls and women gathering mulberry leaves to feed the silkworms, making thread, carrying food out to the fields for their men. There is much about the staple crop, millet—both the eating variety and that used for brewing. We hear about wheat, barley, and rice, and men building a house, stamping down the earth between planks to make the walls. There are joyful celebrations of granaries full of grain and references to men gathering thatch for their roofs. Mention is made of lords' fields and private fields, and a "bailiff" is referred to, but the details of the sys-

Chinese calligraphy. Left: a rubbing from one of the ten "Stone Drums," an example of the Great Seal style of writing, which evolved in the latter part of the Zhou dynasty. Right: a rubbing from a stone inscription of the Han dynasty, inscribed in the Official Style.

tem remain hidden. There are also poems of complaint against the government. One compares tax collectors to big rats. Another tells of the hardships of military service, men constantly on the march, day and night without rest, living like rhinoceroses and tigers. Sometimes a soldier survives the dangers of war and returns home only to find that his wife has given him up for dead and married another. Among the most appealing in their freshness and the innocence of their language are the love poems, for this was a time when girls and young women were not yet restricted by the rules of etiquette from free expression of their longing for their sweetheart or their wish to be married.

The Age of Philosophers

As the bonds which tied the lords to the Zhou king weakened, there was an erosion of power so that by the ninth

Bronze wrestlers (Zhou dynasty).

Ancient symbol *Yi*, which stands for "changes." One of the five Confucian classics is the *Classic of Changes*.

century B.C. the Zhou kings were unable to prevent the local rulers from fighting each other. Nor could they check the incursions of non-Chinese barbarians from beyond the pale. It was to evade the latter that in 771 B.C. the capital was moved from Shaanxi (Shensi) east to the Luoyang (Loyang) region. After this move the Zhou "king" nominally continued to reign for another 500 years, until 256 B.C., but actually he exercised no military, political, or economic power. China was now divided among competing states. During the aptly named "Warring States Period" (403–221 B.C.) the competition between the states became increasingly more desperate and ruthless. With strong states subduing and annexing the weaker, the number of states diminished. The successful states grew ever bigger and more formidable until the process reached its logical conclusion and only one huge state remained.

The Chinese States at the Time of Confucius   *ca.* 500 B.C.

Confucius (*ca.* 551–*ca.* 479 B.C.), a contemporary of the Buddha, lived relatively early in this period of accelerating change. Distressed by the disintegration of the political and moral order, he sought to put the world back together again and hoped to find a ruler who would implement his ideas. When this failed, he turned to teaching. Confucius saw himself not as a creator but as one who merely transmitted the traditional wisdom and values of civilization. He was a creative transmitter who understood the tradition in terms suitable for his own age and thereby revitalized and transformed old values. A good example is his redefinition of nobility as a quality acquired through virtue and wisdom, not through birth. For Confucius, the ideal man is humane, wise, and courageous. He is motivated by virtue, and the ultimate virtue is *ren* (*jen*), a term sometimes translated as "benevolence" or "humaneness," but for which there is no exact English equivalent. *Ren* is the ground for all other virtues, the condition of being fully human in dealing with others. The written Chinese character for *ren* consists of the symbols for "man" and "two."

Morality and the achievement of social harmony were at the core of Confucius' concerns. He urged the need for people to observe the *li*, a term meaning sacred ritual, ceremonial, and propriety, as well as good manners. The *li* were part of the precious heritage of antiquity, imbued with an aura of sacred reverence. When performed with true sincerity, life is truly human and civilized. When everyone follows the *li* and carries out his social role with genuine devotion, harmony will ensue. There will then be no need for coercion, no need for laws or punishments. Of crucial importance to achieve this was the initiative of the ruler who, by following the advice of a perfectly virtuous minister, could make government benevolent and win over the people.

Among the virtues and *li* emphasized by Confucius were those related to the family. He placed special importance on filial piety, the wholehearted obedience a child owes a parent. The obligations toward a father have priority over those owed a state: a son should not turn in his father for stealing a sheep. The relationship between father and son formed one of the classic Five Relationships of Confucianism. The others were ruler/minister, husband/wife, elder/younger brother, friend/friend. They entail reciprocal obligations between people of superior and inferior status and illustrate the importance of the family. Even the two which are not familial were thought of in family terms: the ruler/minister relationship was compared to that between father and son, while that between friends is analogous to that between elder and younger brother. The Confucian view of society was thus paternal and hierarchical.

Confucius and his followers also believed there was only one valid and true, eternal way. The Way was open to all, but only the morally and intellectually cultivated could understand it. The idea that there might be a number of legitimate ways to live one's life and conduct affairs was foreign to the Chinese who, at that time, had no contact with other highly developed and literate civilizations that were radically different from their own.

Confucius' ideas were not widely accepted for many centuries, but ultimately he proved to be one of the world's truly seminal thinkers. His person became a model to be emulated by later Confucians. As he appears in the *Analects*, discourses written by his disciples, he was a man of moderation: gentle but firm, dignified but not harsh, respectful but at ease. One passage gives an account of his intellectual and spiritual progression, culminating at the age of 70 when he was able to follow his heart's desires without transgressing against morality. The Confucian sage personified these characteristics and perfected his moral wisdom to the point that he automatically did what was right.

Confucius on Government

Zi-gong asked about government. Confucius said "Sufficient food, sufficient armament, and sufficient confidence of the people." Zi-gong said, "Forced to give up one of these, which would you abandon first?" Confucius said, "I would abandon the armament." Zi-gong said, "Forced to give up one of the remaining two, which would you abandon first?" Confucius said, "I would abandon food. There have been deaths from time immemorial, but no state can exist without the confidence of the people."

Analects 12:7. From *A Source Book in Chinese Philosophy* by Wing-tsit Chan (Princeton, N.J.: Princeton University Press, 1963), p. 39, with Wade-Giles transcription changed into *pinyin* here and in all boxes.

Confucius was only the beginning of Confucianism. There were many issues he left unsettled, and his philosophy permitted various interpretations. His later followers, such as Mencius and Xun Zi, further developed his teachings, partly in response to challenges from other schools, such as that founded by Mo Zi (Mo Tzu) *ca.* 470–391 B.C.), who taught the practicality of universal love. Mencius (371–289 B.C.) is famed for his view that human nature is fundamentally good but that this goodness has to be cultivated and nourished. Xun Zi (Hsün Tzu) 298–238 B.C.) is associated with the opposite view, that people are naturally selfish but nevertheless have the potential to become good. Although for different reasons, education was of essential importance for both men. Consistent with these positions, Mencius stressed the need for benevolence in government, while Xun Zi more readily accepted the need for laws and punishment. Mencius is also famous for developing the older idea of the mandate of Heaven, according to which a dynasty ruled only as long as it ruled properly. When a regime lost the mandate, rebellion was justified, and an evil ruler forfeited the right to rule.

While Confucians put a premium on social harmony, the thinkers known as

Zhuang Zi (also called Zhuang Zhou)

Once Zhuang Zhou dreamt he was a butterfly, a butterfly flitting and fluttering around, happy with himself and doing as he pleased. He didn't know he was Zhuang Zhou. Suddenly he woke up and there he was, solid and unmistakable Zhuang Zhou. But he didn't know if he was Zhuang Zhou who had dreamt he was a butterfly, or a butterfly dreaming he was Zhuang Zhou. Between Zhuang Zhou and a butterfly there must be *some* distinction! This is called the Transformation of Things.

The fish trap exists because of the fish; once you've gotten the fish, you can forget about the trap. The rabbit snare exists because of the rabbit; once you've gotten the rabbit, you can forget the snare. Words exist because of meaning; once you've gotten the meaning, you can forget the words. Where can I find a man who has forgotten words so I can have a word with him?

From *Chuang Tzu: Basic Writings,* trans. by Burton Watson (New York: Columbia University Press, 1946), p. 45 and p. 140, respectively.

Daoists (Taoists) sought to understand the eternal order of the universe. Daoism deals with the unconditioned, unnameable source of all reality that transcends being and nonbeing by standing above and beyond all distinctions. The first great Daoist classic, the *Dao De Jing (Tao Te Ching)* or *Lao Zi (Lao Tzu),* is cryptic, paradoxical, and highly suggestive. Among its themes there is a preference for the negative over the positive, nothing over something, weak over strong, nonaction over action. It teaches silence is more meaningful than words and ignorance is superior to knowledge; in sum, "Those who know do not speak; those who speak do not know." This view of the limitation of language is shared by Zhuang Zi (Chuang Tzu), author of the second great Daoist classic that bears his name. Zhuang Zi had a keenly developed sense of paradox, as when he argues for the usefulness of the useless: when the able-bodied young men of the village are marched off to war, it is the hopelessly deformed hunchback who stands by the side of the road

Divine seal of Lao Zi used in Daoist magic.

waving them off. Another theme he pursues is the relativity of everything.

The Unification of China

During the period from 771 B.C. to 221 B.C., momentous and rapid changes took place in all areas of human activity. Warfare is a good example. No longer were battles fought by gentlemen in chariots; now most of the fighting was done by foot-soldiers, peasant conscripts commanded by professional officers. Armies grew enormously. Some are said to have numbered a million men, although that may be an exaggeration.

Armies had to be fed and supplied. To support the forces, an increase in agricultural production was achieved by reclamation projects, irrigation, and technological changes, including the introduction of iron. There were also changes in management and administration as states adopted systems of taxation and labor services. Land became a commodity to be bought and sold. Commerce increased along with the size of states and the development of roads. Metallic currencies appeared, replacing the cowrie shells used earlier. Among the items of trade were various kinds of textiles, metals, woods, bamboo, jade, and regional specialties. Urban centers grew and expanded until they required new city walls.

Social change was inseparably linked to military, economic, and political change. Merchants and generals were not the only new professionals. It took a skilled diplomat to steer a state through the treacherous waters of international relations, someone with an eloquent voice to win a debate. Faced with internal and external challenges, rulers tended to pay more attention to a man's competence than to his pedigree. Old families declined and new ones grew in importance.

Faced with a world of disturbing and baffling change, many Chinese turned for guidance to what they perceived to have been a much better past, but some, such as Han Fei Zi (Han Fei Tzu, d. 233 B.C.), held that new problems demanded new and drastic solutions. These so-called Legalists stressed the rationalization of administration, the improvement of managerial techniques, and the strict enforcement of punitive laws. Their theories which were applied by the state of Qin (Ch'in) unified China in 221 B.C.

The Qin was located in the west of North China, the same region from which the Zhou had conquered North China. This area was economically able to support a strong military and political apparatus, and it was well situated strategically, protected by mountains whose passes were easy to defend and yet provided access to the east. It was something of a buffer region between the Chinese and various warlike tribal peoples. Making the best of this situation, the Qin toughened its armies by fighting the tribesmen. At the same time it drew on the administrative and technological expertise developed in the more sophisticated, centrally located states. Under Legalist influence the state was divided into districts governed by a centralized bureaucracy and financed by a direct tax on the peasantry. A system of mutual responsibility was introduced, with harsh penalties for criminals and those who failed to report a criminal. Everything was designed to make the state wealthy, strong, and disciplined.

The First Empire: Qin and Han

The unification of China by the Qin was the beginning of some four hundred years of imperial rule even though the Qin Dynasty (221–207 B.C.) itself barely survived the first emperor, Qin Shihuangdi (Ch'in Shih Huang-ti). He and his Legalist advisor, Li Si (Li Ssu) applied to the whole domain the policies first enacted in the state of Qin, including the division of the state into administrative districts governed by a bureaucracy. The integration of the realm was also furthered by a program

of road building, the issuance of a standard official coinage, the standardization of weights and measurements and of the script, and the suppression of scholars and writings critical of the new order. Qin hostility toward Confucianism was reciprocated in kind with the result that once Confucianism prevailed, the Qin acquired the most negative reputation of any Chinese dynasty.

The traditional image of cruelty and oppression may well be exaggerated, but it seems clear that the regime tried to do too much too fast. A physical expression of its ambitions were vast building projects, including the Great Wall, built to protect and separate China from barbarism. It was constructed by linking segments of walls previously erected by individual states. Although the present wall dates from the fifth century, the Qin wall was its ancestor.

A life-sized terra-cotta figure of an armored archer of the Qin dynasty. This is one of over 7,000 such figures unearthed from the tomb of the first emperor of China.

| ca. 1500 B.C. | 1027 B.C. | 221 B.C. | 202 B.C. | 220 A.D. |

Shang Dynasty   Zhou Dynasty   Han Dynasty

Qin Dynasty

After the death of its founder, the Qin soon disintegrated, but it left foundations on which the Former Han (202 B.C.–A.D. 8) and the Later Han (25–220) erected much more lasting edifices.

In many respects Han China was comparable to Imperial Rome. Both were great empires with powerful armies ranging far beyond the heartland: Han forces even crossed the Pamir Mountains. Both are celebrated for practical accomplishments, as in civil engineering: the Han maintained some 20,000–25,000 miles of highway radiating out from the capital. They also made advances in shipbuilding (the axial rudder), medicine, astronomy, and agriculture. Intellectually, both empires built on the achievements of their predecessors and were noted more for the synthesis of old philosophies rather than for producing strikingly new ones. Both also excelled in the writing of history. China's greatest historian was Sima Qian (Ssu-ma Ch'ien, *ca.* 145 B.C.-*ca.* 90 B.C.) whose *Records of the Grand Historian* is a literary masterpiece as well as a work of careful scholarship.

In China, as in Rome, it took great political ability to create and maintain a huge empire over a long period of time. But there was no counterpart in the Han to the Roman development of law. Instead, the Chinese relied on a bureaucracy staffed by men who shared a common education, a common fund of historical references, and a common set of largely Confucian values. To help mold these men there was an imperial university where, under the Later Han, some 30,000 students were studying mostly Confucian texts. Imperial Confucianism did not preclude the employment of pragmatic Legalist military and political policies,

The Han Empire   100 B.C.

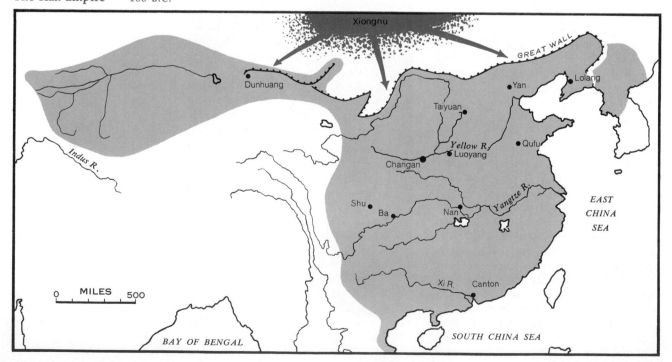

but it did provide the dynasty with legitimacy and could prompt ministers to faithful service. The Confucian ideal was one of unselfish public service, not unthinking compliance with the whims or policies of a ruler. Intellectual and political independece from the throne was also made possible because most officials came from families of notables that dominated the local power structure.

The system operated best when there was a balance between central and local power. Since the wealthy and powerful were also the most apt to evade taxes, the state had a stake in preventing an undue concentration of landownership, but attempts to limit the size of landholdings failed, as did the attempt to stabilize the price of grain through government purchases when it was plentiful and inexpensive and reselling it when grain became scarce. For its own finances, the government drew heavily on agriculture but also collected commercial taxes and operated salt and iron monopolies.

As in Rome, in weak hands the throne itself became a source of political instability as various groups maneuvered for influence and control. In the Han the families of imperial consorts became exceedingly powerful, and it was a member of one such family who, after serving as regent for a child emperor, overthrew the Former Han but did not succeed in establishing a lasting dynasty of his own. Instead, after a period of turmoil and fighting, a member of the imperial Han family established the Later Han in 25 A.D.

The Han established a Chinese presence in North Korea and North Vietnam, but the most challenging foreign policy problem was how to deal with the nomads who lived beyond the northern and northwestern frontiers. Nomadic peoples, like the Altaic speaking Xiongnu (Hsiung-nu), were formidable opponents because of their skill in warfare. For them war was merely a special application of the skills of horsemanship and archery they practiced every day in guarding their flocks. Their mobility was an asset in

Han earthenware tile.

defense as well as attack, for, traveling lightly with their flocks and tents, they could elude Chinese military expeditions and avoid destruction or control. Chinese measures to deal with these troublesome neighbors ranged from military suppression to conciliation by means of gifts and marriage alliances, so that the nomads would accept tributary status. Tributaries had to acknowledge Han supremacy but profited by an exchange of presents and the opportunity to trade. Much of this trade was conducted in markets along the borders. Chinese exports included lacquerware, ironware, bronze mirrors, and silk, which first reached Europe over the famous Silk Road. The Chinese also did whatever they could to foster disunity among the tribal peoples; "using barbarians against barbarians" became a permanent part of their foreign policy.

Pottery tile rubbing depicting hunters and peasants (Han dynasty).

China in Disunity, 220–589

Disrupted by internal strife, in fiscal trouble because of a shrinking tax base, and beset by foreign challenges, the Han came to an end in 220. Beginning early in the next century, a succession of nomadic peoples carved out states in North China. Some of these, notably the Northern Wei (386–534), attained a good measure of success, but none matched the Han in duration or extent. To enjoy their Chinese conquests, the nomads required a more sophisticated political system than the tribal organization they brought from the steppes. They had to rely on Chinese administrators who knew how to operate a tax system, keep records, and run a government. There was also a tendency for the nomads themselves to become more like the Chinese. This not only jeopardized their cultural heritage but also tended to alienate those nomads who had remained on the steppe.

Warfare and devastation in the north stimulated vast migrations to south China, especially into the Yangtze region, which underwent great economic development, foreshadowing the time when it would become China's rice bowl. Politically the south remained under Chinese control, but the southern states were unstable and weak. When reunification came, it was, as always, from the north.

When the Han fell, a whole civilization seemed to have collapsed. A spiritual and intellectual, as well as political vacuum was created. Some of China's most brilliant and talented men responded by turning to Daoism or to discovering new meaning in poetry, calligraphy, and painting. Others, both humble people and aristocrats, were attracted to Buddhism, which addressed itself more directly to human suffering than did any of the components of the native Chinese tradition. In the north, Buddhism also benefitted from the patronage of rulers who, as foreigners themselves, could sympathize with a foreign religion.

It took many long years for Buddhism to overcome its foreignness in China, years during which Buddhist missionaries patiently labored to translate and explain the Buddhist teachings. It was a formidable task to render the highly inflected Indian languages and discursive Indian writings into uninflected and terse Chinese, to find Chinese equivalents for concepts such as karma or Nirvana, and to bridge the gulf which separated Indian and Chinese perceptions of the meaning of life and the nature of the universe.

The greatest of the translators was a Central Asian, Kumārajīva, who, early in the fifth century, directed a staff of about 1,000 monks. In a vivid comment on the translator's predicament, he once compared his work to that of a man who chews rice and then gives it to another to swallow. By the end of the period of disunity, the labors of such men had made Buddhism palatable to the Chinese, but it was not until after reunification in 591 that they felt sufficiently familiar with the faith to develop it in ways of their own.

For a time Buddhism provided a link between China and India, yet there remained distinct differences between the historical-minded Chinese tradition and the focus in India on the ultimate.

The contrast between the two civilizations is also apparent in their different political histories. At the end of the sixth century, India was again politically fragmented, whereas China had entered one of its great ages of imperial unification.

Suggestions for Futher Reading

India

A gold mine of authoritative information is *A Historical Atlas of South Asia* (1978), ed. J. E. Schwartzberg, which contains historical essays and bibliographies. A. L. Basham, *The Wonder that Was India* (1954), is a lucid and balanced account of Indian civilization. S. Wolpert, *A New History of India*, 2nd ed. (1982), is a good survey, although stronger on modern India. A good compedium for intellectual history is *Sources of Indian Tradition* (1958), ed. W. T. de Bary et al. D. L. Eck, *Banaras: City of Light* (1982), is a multifaceted account of India's most holy city. On India's greatest playwright, see B. S. Miller, *Theater of Memory: The Plays of Kalidasa* (1984).

China

C. Blunder and M. Elvin, *Cultural Atlas of China* (1983), provides an unusually stimulating introduction to many aspects of Chinese history and civilization. Kwang-chih Chang, *The Archeology of Ancient China*, 4th ed. (1986), and *Shang Civilization* (1980), are authoritative as is *The Cambridge History of China*, Vol. 1, *The Ch'in and Han Empires 221 B.C.–A.D. 220* (1986). Also recommended are B. Watson, *Ssu-ma Ch'ien: Grand Historian of China* (1958), and three anthologies: *Sources of Chinese Tradition* (1960), by W. T. de Bary et al.; Wing-tsit Chan, ed., *A Source Book in Chinese Philosophy* (1963); and P. B. Ebrey, *Chinese Civilization and Society: A Sourcebook* (1981). A general survey is provided by C. Schirokauer, *A Brief History of Chinese and Japanese Civilizations*, 2nd ed. (1989), which includes suggestions for further reading.

Buddhism

A good place to begin reading about Buddhism and other religions is the *Encyclopedia of Religion* (1987), M. Eliade, general editor. For China, see *Buddhism in Chinese History* (1959), by A. F. Wright. Buddhist materials are also included in the source books listed above.

Reference

For recent studies see the *Bibliography of Asian Studies*, published annually by the Association for Asian Studies, Inc.

7

The Byzantine Empire and Civilization

*T*he collapse of the western Roman Empire caused little disruption in the eastern half, but after the West was lost to the Germans, the East gradually developed into another of the successors of the Empire, the Byzantine Empire. Between the seventh and the eleventh centuries, the Byzantine Empire and the European kingdoms had histories that were basically separate, but it is still difficult to understand the important events and movements in one region without reference to those in the other. This is true because the Christian church extended over both the eastern Empire and the Germanic kingdoms and because the imperial court in Constantinople continued for centuries to view the West as a part of its patrimony.

Throughout the classical period of Byzantine civilization, the eighth to the eleventh centuries, the Empire faced a constant set of problems. It had to cope with external enemies on two fronts—the Arabs in the east and in the Mediterranean and the Bulgarians in the north and west. The imperial government also had to cope with a persistent ecclesiastical controversy over iconoclasm. The controversy brought to the surface deep cultural divisions in the eastern Empire, and the contending elements seized on other issues great and small to express their differences. For centuries the Empire was troubled by dispute and hatred that rose to the surface in every significant event, and in many insignificant ones.

THE ORIGINS OF THE BYZANTINE EMPIRE

The changes that created the Byzantine Empire of the Middle Ages began in the fifth century. The principal change was from a military, Latin government and bureaucracy to a civilian, Greek one. In the Byzantine Empire, the old Hellenistic culture of the east reemerged as dominant after centuries of Latin rule.

During the fifth century, increasing numbers of hellenized Egyptians and

Opposite: Gold coin portraying Justinian on horseback. The coin was struck to commemorate the defeat of the Vandals in 535.

179

View of the interior of Hagia Sophia in Constantinople (532–37).

Syrians—long excluded from service in the institutions of the central government—made their way to Constantinople and into the imperial administration. This influx of hellenized easterners, which civilianized the imperial government, accelerated under Emperor Anastasius (r. 491–518). The great officials of his government—the financial wizards, advisers, and lesser administrators—were educated career civil servants from the east. In this period, Constantinople changed from being the capital city—the place of residence of the emperor and his government—and became the "ruling city," the community that dominated the cultural life of the eastern Empire. It replaced Rome as the intellectual and cultural center of the world and was often called New Rome.

The process of civilization coincided with renewed trouble on the eastern borders. Persia, under a revived Sassanid dynasty, attacked the eastern districts with great success, and the way the emperors met this threat is indicative of the way the focus of the Empire had shifted. Faced with the Persian threat, Emperor Zeno I (r. 479–91) did not create an army of German mercenaries—who were available in the Ostrogothic tribes—but of Isaurian troops from southern Asia Minor. Although Zeno's successor Anastasius reduced the influence of Isaurians both in the army and in the court, he too relied on armies recruited in the east.

The turn to the east also affected the religious policy of the emperors. The populations of the eastern provinces, although mostly Christianized, kept their ancient religious traditions alive in a number of unorthodox theologies. The commercial civilization of the east also provided a medium for the active exchange of religious ideas and provided a fertile ground for theological creativity. The emperors, who needed to preserve the unity of the Empire in the face of the constant threat of invasion, treated the religious groups leniently and even sought to reconcile

their ideas to the creeds that earlier ecumenical councils had enunciated. The Roman popes railed against these compromises and came to stand for conservatism in the church. Emperor Anastasius, in particular, refused to obey the commands of the Roman popes to condemn and destroy the various heretical sects that flourished in the eastern provinces. He looked on the religious differences as a political rather than a spiritual problem.

Anastasius left a full treasury and an efficient civil service, but the army reasserted itself after his death and installed as emperor a soldier from the Balkans, Justin I (r. 518–27). The long-term effect of this shift back to a military, Latin government was limited by the influence of Justin's nephew Justinian. This young man was educated in Constantinople by the court bureaucrats assembled by Anastasius, and he became thoroughly Byzantinized. He married Theodora, a courtesan from a family connected with the racing stables in the Hippodrome (the city stadium) and when he succeeded Justin in 527, he inaugurated a decade of exuberant cultural and political revival.

Justinian

Justinian (r. 527–65) was a reformer, who pursued the goal of restoring the Empire to its former glory. Among the first steps he took to accomplish this was the establishment of a commission to revise and codify the Roman law. The period from Augustus (r. 27 B.C.–A.D. 14) to A.D. 200 had been the golden age of Roman law, when a succession of great jurists had developed the system and its basic doctrines. After that period, legislation, judgments, and learned commentaries accumulated, and by Justinian's time a person could spend a lifetime reading the law without mastering all of it. Judges were often stymied in settling cases because both parties could cite good law.

Byzantine gold wedding ring (*ca.* fifth century).

Mosaic portraits of Justinian and Theodora, San Vitale, Ravenna (*ca.* 547).

Earlier emperors had tried to end the confusion in the legal system by commissioning codes, but none of these efforts—such as the code of Theodosius II, published about 480—succeeded because they did not deal with the whole corpus of legislation and legal commentary. Justinian's commission tried to weave a new fabric from the whole confusing tradition of the law. In 534, it produced a comprehensive code called the *Corpus Iuris Civilis* (the Body of Civil Law), which contains one of the most sophisticated legal systems ever created. It was symbolic of what Justinian hoped to achieve—a reunited, well-governed Empire.

Early in his reign, one great event almost put an end to this hope. In 532, mob violence erupted in Constantinople in response to the government's fiscal measures. The riots—called the Nika Riots because the mobs used the slogan *nika* (vanquish)—quickly turned into an attack on the hated ministers of the imperial administration. The extreme danger of the riots stemmed from the involvement of the Hippo-drome clubs, which had been established to organize the games in the stadium. In the 480s, Emperor Zeno had armed them as a militia when he feared an Ostrogothic attack on the city, so that they were extremely dangerous. Although normally competitive with one another, they now joined to loot and burn the city. It was said later that Justinian wanted to flee in this crisis, but that Theodora persuaded him to stay. The gamble paid off. The rebellion soon collapsed, and Justinian was left in power, in a city whose center was totally destroyed.

Despite the destruction, the outcome of the riots invigorated Justinian. In 533, he sent an army to North Africa to begin a reconquest of the western provinces. Africa was important as a grain producer, and it would serve as an excellent base for reconquering the European provinces. The general who led the troops was the brilliant Belisarius, who had participated in the suppression of the riots. He took Carthage in the first year of the campaign and, within a short time, destroyed the Vandal kingdom that

Gaiseric had established in 430. None-theless, the collapse of Vandal power stimulated the Moorish tribes to seek independence, and the Byzantine garrison did not really pacify the province until 548.

Belisarius, meanwhile, took Sicily in 535 and was in Rome a year later. However, after this initial success the general fell from favor and was retired, and the Ostrogoths began a long war of resistance. Unable to hold Rome, which was taken repeatedly by each side, the imperial government established its capital in Ravenna, a city on the Adriatic Sea that was well protected on the land side by extensive marshes. By 556, after 20 years of destructive war, most of Italy was ruled by a Byzantine official, the Exarch of Ravenna. But as we have seen Byzantine power was short-lived. In 568 new Germanic invaders, the Lombards, entered Italy and quickly overran most of it.

In Constantinople, Justinian devoted himself to rebuilding the city, and he did it on a magnificent scale befitting the city that ruled the world. He built baths, aqueducts and cisterns to supply the city with water, and new government buildings of all sorts. He also dedicated 25 churches in the city and its suburbs. The crowning achievement of this program was the new church of Hagia Sophia. The original church had been built by Constantine and had been reconstructed about 400. Now Justinian commissioned two Greeks, Anthemius of Tralles and Isidore of Miletus, to build a completely new kind of church, centered on a great dome. The church was completed in the amazingly short time of six years. Its dome rises 180 feet above the pavement and, with two half-domes on either side, covers an area 100 by 250 feet. The lateral thrust of these domes is enormous and required great exter-

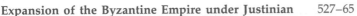

Expansion of the Byzantine Empire under Justinian   527–65

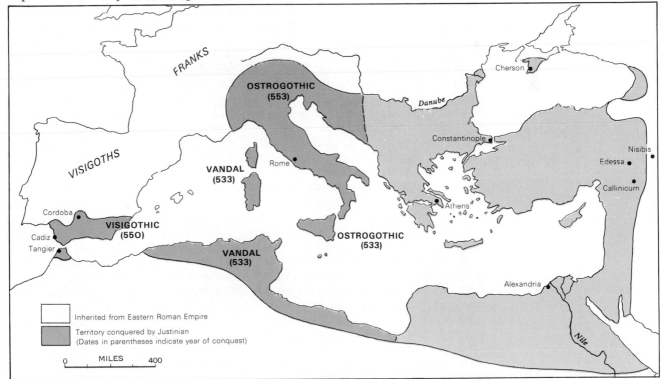

Hagia Sophia, built *ca.* 535. The minarets were added after the Ottoman Turks captured Constantinople in 1453.

nal buttresses, which make the church look from the outside like a great pile of masonry. But the interior is light and airy, and the interior surfaces of the domes were covered with brilliant mosaics.

The revival of conflict with the Persians and trouble in the Balkans ended the flamboyant spirit of the 530s. In 540, Shah Khusro I of Persia attacked the eastern provinces and took the great city of Antioch. He offered to sell it back to Justinian. At about the same time, Slavic tribes moved into the Balkans and destroyed Byzantine authority there. These developments deprived the Empire of two important regions: from the Balkan provinces it had drawn manpower, and from Syria commercial wealth. These military disasters also coincided with the beginning of an epidemic that hit Constantinople in 542 and recurred in the two following years. The disease then jumped from place to place around the Mediterranean Basin until the 570s.

In these circumstances, Justinian had to reduce the campaign in Italy to a holding action and had to cut the costs and building programs of the imperial government. He started to experiment with a series of innovative tax measures and to reorganize the military, which had now to work with smaller resources of money and manpower. The Byzantine commanders developed new, mobile tactics for small forces, and, in a major test, a new model army executed a brilliant campaign in 552, breaking the last Ostrogothic resistance in Italy. In the east, Justinian compensated for the lack of manpower by building a string of strategically placed fortifications, and he used diplomacy instead of force whenever he could.

By the 560s, he had achieved notable successes. He had held off Khusro I, defeated the Goths, pacified North Africa and strongly fortified it, and constructed an elaborate series of alliances along the Danube, which limited the effect of Slavic invasions. His subjects thought he never slept.

However, the strains produced by accomplishing all this showed. When Justinian cut costs by dismantling the ancient government transport system, farmers in the interior of Asia Minor went bankrupt. The system had been a market for fodder, and the farmers had become economically dependent upon it. Now, their market was gone, and they were too far from the coast to find another. This and other economic strains caused by the wars and by Justinian's earlier building program depleted the treasury, which was empty when he died in 565.

The crises also encouraged a concentration of power in the person of the emperor. Both to cut costs and because he was so successful, Justinian reduced the size of the imperial bureaucracy and took on much of the work of government himself. By the end of his reign, the emperor simply had too much to do, and the maintenance of Justinian's success would take even more attention than he had devoted to its achievement. After him, the delicate balance broke down quickly. The emperor Maurice (r. 582–602) was an able man, but he could not keep up with simultaneous disasters in all quarters. The Lombards had invaded Italy; the Danubian alliances disintegrated as new peoples, the Slavic Bulgars and the Altaic Avars (related to the Huns), pushed up to the border; the Persians became aggressive again.

From Eastern Roman to Byzantine Empire

Under Maurice's successor Phocas (r. 602–10), the Byzantine world collapsed. The Slavs and Avars conquered the Balkans and Greece. Asia Minor became a Persian province (satrapy), and the Persians carried out an anti-Christian campaign there. When Phocas died, the eastern part of the Empire consisted of the city of Constantinople. In the west, there were the marshlands around Ravenna and Rome, Apulia and Calabria in southern Italy, Sicily, and the North African provinces. Phocas's successor Heraclius (r. 610–41) thought of fleeing from Constantinople to North Africa and

trying to build a basis for reviving the Empire there.

But, largely through accident, Heraclius found himself trapped in Constantinople, and he had to commit himself to rebuilding Byzantine power from the city. The prospect cannot have looked promising. He spent more than a decade rebuilding the army and preparing for a long campaign. In 622, he sailed south to Ionia and began a war of attrition against the Persians. In four years of bitter fighting against superior forces, his troops broke Persian military strength and reconquered Asia Minor. He forced the population of the province to reconvert to Christianity. In 627, he took advantage of Persian military weakness to lead his army on a raid into the heart of Persia. After this, the Persian nobility turned on the shah Khusro II and assassinated him (628). By that time, Heraclius had reestablished Byzantine control of Syria, Palestine, and Egypt.

The effects of these wonderful successes were short-lived. While a small, well-trained army could win back the eastern provinces, a large, stationary, and costly army was needed to defend them. The Persian occupation and the long war had ruined the economy of the eastern provinces, and they could not support such a defensive apparatus. These provinces, which had been the richest in the Empire of Justinian and Maurice, were now a drain on the imperial fisc. At the end of his life, Heraclius had to watch a new eastern power, the Arabs, take away much of what he had won.

Nonetheless, Heraclius had reestablished the Greek world of the Mediterranean, and during the seventh century the region remained the heartland of Christendom. A significant east-west trade was revived, and eastern churchmen—such as the first great archbishop of Canterbury (England), Theodore of Tarsus (669–90)—played a large role in the western church. During this period, the emperors also exercised a great influence in the Roman church, where a large sector of the clergy was actually Greek-speaking. Rome had remained under the control of the Exarch of Ravenna even though the territory between the two cities had fallen to the Lombards. But the Exarch's role caused continual trouble because the imperial court often favored or at least condoned religious ideas considered heretical by the conservative papal court.

Heraclius started a dynasty and stabilized the succession to the imperial throne, but his heirs could not hold the Empire's borders. The Arab expansion, the progressive settlement of the Slavs in the Balkans, and the establishment of a Bulgar kingdom north of the Danube prevented a continuation of Heraclius's work. The Arabs built a fleet in the Mediterranean that challenged Byzantine naval supremacy and repeatedly attacked Constantinople itself between about 669 and 677. The city, nearly impregnable, stood against these assaults and was able to hold Asia Minor, but the provinces along the eastern seaboard of the Mediterranean were soon gone. By the end of the

seventh century, the Empire was nothing more than a Greek state centered in Asia Minor with outlying provinces in the Balkans, North Africa, Sicily, and Italy.

The Heraclian dynasty was brought to a bloody end in 711, when its last emperor was murdered in a palace rebellion. After six years of anarchy, a provincial administrator and general, Leo the Isaurian, established himself as Leo III and founded a new dynasty. Leo (r. 717–41) came to power at a critical moment and was uniquely qualified to meet the threat of a great land and sea siege of Constantinople by the Arabs (717–18). The new emperor was born in northern Syria and knew Arabic well. In his youth, his family had been forcibly transplanted to the Bulgarian border, and, therefore, he also knew that troubled region of the Empire.

Leo actually won the imperial throne with Arab assistance. Early in 717, the Arabs invaded the eastern province Leo governed, and he seems to have made a deal with them. If they

The Byzantine Empire   Seventh and Eleventh Centuries

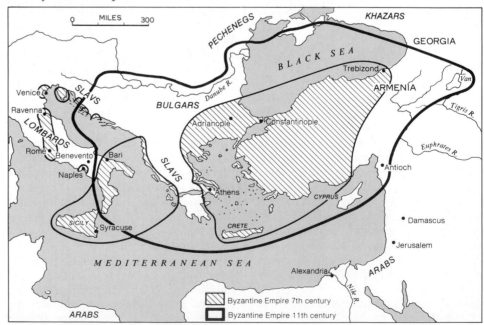

gave him support, he would try to seize the imperial government and would bow to their demands for territory or tribute. The Arabs withdrew, while Leo stormed the capital and won the imperial throne.

When the Arabs invaded again, Leo negotiated with them until he had gained the advantage, then he threw off his false mask and defeated them. The crucial moment in the defense of the capital came when the Bulgars arrived and destroyed the Arab besieging army. Shortly after this, Leo was able to defeat the Arab fleet. Thus, he began his reign as the savior of the capital city. He followed this triumph with a series of campaigns in eastern Asia Minor that halted the Arabs after 100 years of expansion.

Emperor Leo represented the landed aristocracy of Asia Minor against the court and bureaucracy that had held sway since Anastasius, and he carried out the most important reforms since Justinian. He commis-

sioned new Greek law codes, including an abridged and modernized Greek version of the *Corpus Iuris Civilis*. He regularized the system of administrative districts, called *themes*, which significantly improved government. He also instigated a new religious movement against the use of religious images (icons); the movement was called iconoclasm.

ICONOCLASM

In 726, nine years after he came to power, Leo destroyed a famous picture of Christ in the porch of his palace. The act caused riots in Constantinople and in the western parts of the Empire, but the armies and populations of the eastern provinces did not react. This difference of reaction suggests that Leo's stance was born in his own Syrian origins and that iconoclasm was a revolt of Semitic against Greco-Roman religious feelings.

Procession of saints and martyrs, Sant' Apollinare Nuovo, Ravenna (*ca.* 574).

The use of religious images for prayer and worship had grown to be part of Christianity in the Hellenistic world. The pagan Greeks had used idols in their worship, and Greek Christians had naturally used images in their religious life. Plato had said in one of his most famous dialogues, the *Symposium,* that the contemplation of beautiful objects led one to the contemplation of beauty itself, and the assimilation of Platonic thought into Christianity during the period from the second to the fifth centuries gave religious representational art a similar role in the practice of worship. The beautiful image of the divinity helped the worshipper rise from contemplation of the world to contemplation of the Maker of the world.

The Hebraic tradition ran exactly counter to the Greek in this matter. The second of the Ten Commandments stated unequivocally that men should make no images of the divine, and this anti-icon attitude prevailed in some Semitic Christian communities, as well as in Judaism and Islam. The use of images in the Greek churches of the Middle East, which by the eighth century were under the protection—usually benevolent—of the caliphate of Damascus, was always a sore point with the Arab conquerors. In 723, the caliph Yazid II, in a fit of unfriendliness toward Christians—following the failure of his great siege of Constantinople in 717–18—ordered the destruction of representational art of all kinds everywhere in his lands.

In Constantinople, the monks led the protest against Leo's destruction of the palace image of Christ. Monasticism had spread faster in the east than in the west, and in the east monasticism became so popular that by the eighth century people were concerned about the health of society, which was losing many of its best young people, men and women, to monasteries.

Eastern monasticism was dominated by the influence of Basil (329–79), who rose out of monasticism to become bishop of Caesaria in Syria. About 50 years after the foundation of Pachomius's community (see p. 148), he created from the Pachomian materials a carefully constructed constitution of monasticism, which balanced the life of the monks between worship and work and formulated the three basic values of monastic life—poverty, chastity, and obedience. By the time of Leo III, Basilian communities had been founded in the midst of the urban society of the eastern cities, where they made a great impression and soon began to play an active role in the affairs both of church and state.

The monasteries were able to play this role because they benefited from an attitude, strongly held by the eastern populations, that holy persons exercised divine authority. This attitude made the monastic life attractive to extraordinary men and women and gave the monks great authority among the people. The monasteries became wealthy as beneficiaries of pious gifts. Under the monastic rule, individual monks owned nothing, but the monastic communities could amass fabulous wealth.

How important the role of the monks could be was demonstrated during the conflict over the use of icons. Leo apparently viewed the opposition to iconoclasm as an attack on the *imperium* itself, and in 730 he issued an edict prohibiting the use of icons. In this decree he was essentially asserting the idea of Caesaropapism, which held that as the representative of Christ on earth the emperor had authority over religious as well as secular affairs. This theory of imperial authority was rooted in Constantine's assumption of responsibility for the disciplinary and doctrinal unity of the church in the councils of Arles (314) and Nicaea (325), and it contradicted the theory of papal authority, the Petrine doctrine (see p. 121), which held that the pope was the sole vicar of Christ.

That Leo saw the controversy in this way is not surprising. In developing an argument against iconoclasm, the monks had put forth a doctrine of separation of church and state that challenged a basic tenet of Byzantine society and government. Leo and his son Constantine V (r. 741–75) became antimonastic—Constantine fanatically so.

The complexity of the dispute increased when the monastic party appealed for support to the Roman popes, and Pope Gregory II (r. 715–31) condemned iconoclasm. The popes held to a tradition of separation of ecclesiastical and secular authority, which prohibited the emperor from pronouncing on doctrinal matters. Also, the Romans used icons. In 731, Leo punished the pope for his opposition by depriving the papacy of jurisdiction over the churches of Dalmatia (the coastal district of modern Yugoslavia) and southern Italy, which was a blow to the papal treasury. Consequently, jurisdictional and territorial interests were brought into the conflict.

Under Leo's able son Constantine V, the controversy over icons entered a new phase. Constantine, an intellectual and a connoisseur of art, developed a theological rationale for the iconoclastic position. He could cite early Christian writers—such as Eusebius, the biographer of Emperor Constantine I—who had said that the divine is not describable. From this, he argued that when a painter paints Christ, he paints either only the human form of God or both the human and divine. If it is the former, then the artist commits heresy by depicting Christ as only a human being. If it is the latter, then he commits heresy by giving the divine a worldly, and limiting, form. In his argument, the emperor assumed that the image was identical to the object depicted, and he said that the God-man Christ could only be represented in the sacrament of the Eucharist, when the bread and wine became his body and blood. Constantine called a council to Constantinople in 754, and, under his forceful guidance, the council fathers adopted his position on icons. Ironically, the emperor's opponents, the iconodules (lovers of images), found their intellectual champion in a Syrian Christian named Mansur, better known as John of Da-

mascus (d. after 746), who wrote the classic defense of icons, based on the idea that when God became man in Christ, it became possible to represent him in his incarnate form.

When the monks reacted to the council of 754 as they had to the edict of 730, Constantine responded by closing monasteries, drafting monks into the army, and forcing monks and nuns into marriage and into the professions of everyday life. However, the emperor recognized that there was a danger of serious political division between the eastern and western sections of the Empire, and he sought to prevent it by marrying his son and heir Leo to an Athenian, Irene, who was a supporter of icons. When Constantine died in 775, Leo IV moderated, but did not give up, the iconoclast effort. When Leo died in 780, leaving a 10-year-old son as his heir, the power of government passed to Empress Irene. Under her guidance, the government began to move slowly toward the restoration of images. In 784, Irene's government summoned a new council, which finally met in Nicaea in 787. Here, the first phase of iconoclasm was brought to an end, when the council reversed the decrees of 754 and confirmed the theory of John of Damascus.

An iconoclast whitewashing an image in a Byzantine church (from a ninth-century psalter). In 730 Leo III issued an edict forbidding the veneration of images. For a hundred years thereafter, icons, mosaics, and frescoes in churches were destroyed or whitewashed.

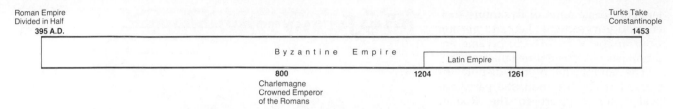

Roman Empire
Divided in Half
395 A.D.

Byzantine Empire

Latin Empire

800
Charlemagne
Crowned Emperor
of the Romans

1204

1261

Turks Take
Constantinople
1453

The council of 787 did not suppress iconoclasm; it only made the government and church officially orthodox. In the populations of the Empire, the old feelings about icons remained strong, and the army, which was primarily recruited in southern and eastern Asia Minor, was predominantly iconoclast. As a result, the imperial court had constantly to deal with the politics of the iconoclast controversy, and the stance of the court itself depended on the personal views of those in power. The final restoration of images came in 843, under Empress Theodora, who was regent for her young son Michael III. But the government proceeded very carefully. It was more than 20 years before major projects of restoring images in the churches of Constantinople were undertaken.

The decline of iconoclastic feeling in the Empire resulted from both demographic and cultural changes. Demographically, the expansion of the Arab Empire in Syria and the eastern parts of Asia Minor reduced the role of Semitic Christian communities in Byzantine affairs. Culturally, there was a revival of secular, Greek learning among the upper classes, which contributed to the spread of neo-Platonic ideas.

The iconoclast struggle began as a manifestation of the ethnic division in the Byzantine Empire, but it created political conditions in the Caesaropapist state that survived after the effects of ethnic diversity decreased. Iconoclasm brought out a deep religious controversy between the monks, who rejected secular influence in religious affairs, and moderate churchmen, who assented to the union of ecclesiastical and secular authority in the emperor. This conflict between moderates and radicals became a perennial problem in the politics of the Byzantine

Church. The heresy also contributed to the schism between the Greek and Latin churches.

THE BYZANTINE EMPIRE BETWEEN EAST AND WEST

When Leo III defeated the massive Arab invasion in 717, he did severe damage to the Arab fleet, but the Arab army—after heavy losses to the Bulgarian allies of the emperor—had made an easy retreat across Asia Minor. As a result, the Arabs were able to continue their raids into Byzantine territory throughout Leo's reign, and he spent much of his time leading armies to meet the threat. At the same time, the Slavs migrated steadily across the Danube frontier and settled in Macedonia and Greece. These peoples were heathens, and the regions they occupied were lost to the church as well as to the Empire.

In eastern Asia Minor, where the Islamic and Byzantine worlds met, Leo's reign was the heroic age of dashing aristocratic military leaders. Men on both sides formed the historical kernel of the heroic legends of both the Arabic and the Byzantine empires. The central governments of the empires only occasionally affected the events in these border provinces.

Leo III was a capable man; his son Constantine V (r. 741–75) was even more capable. Although the iconodules gave him a terrible name—the eponym "Coprynomus" ("dung name")—he was able to consolidate his eastern frontier. Yet, while the emperor was engaged in the east, the Lombards finally overthrew the Exarchate of Ravenna (*ca.* 750). Constantine ignored the loss, for he recognized that the maintenance of Byzantine power in

The Empires of Charlemagne and Byzantium   *ca.* A.D. 800

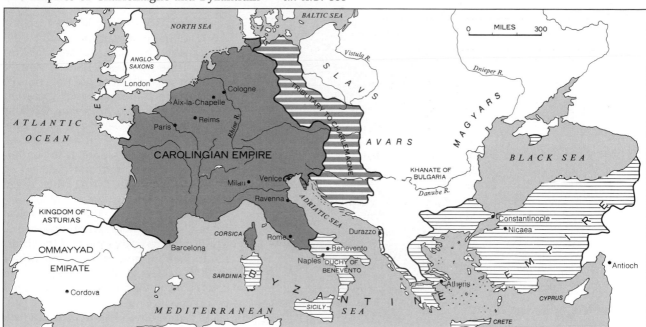

Italy was peripheral to the main interests of his government. However, the political change that Constantine's attitude represented was not immediately recognized by the pope. When the Lombards, having secured their rear by the capture of Ravenna, turned on Rome itself, Pope Zachary (r. 741–52) followed age-old custom in appealing to the emperor for help. Constantine ignored the appeal, and, finally, the pope turned to the Franks, who had much to gain by undertaking the protection of the papal church (see pp. 239–40). In 753, Zachary's successor made an alliance with the Frankish royal house that had momentous results for the history of western Europe.

In the second half of his reign, Constantine V devoted virtually all his attention to the Bulgars. They had begun to build a heathen empire, carved out of the Balkan provinces of the Empire. Constantine made nine campaigns against them, and he was remembered, even by his iconodule enemies, as a successful general. Unfortunately, his successors could not keep up the good work. His son Leo IV survived him by only five years and then Empress Irene, an exceptionally cruel woman, controlled the government for her son, Constantine VI. When, in his late twenties, Constantine VI finally tried to assert some independence, Irene had him blinded.

Although Irene was able to maintain herself in power after this and signed her official acts with the strange title "Irene Emperor," everywhere, except at court, people considered the Empire to be without an emperor (commander-in-chief). This political uncertainty produced significant effects. Soon after the death of Constantine VI, there were unsuccessful negotiations for a marriage between Irene and the Frankish king Charlemagne (Charles the Great). Then, on Christmas day 800, Pope Leo III crowned Charles Emperor of the Romans. This act appears to have been intended to resurrect the Roman Empire in the West.

While many in the Byzantine Empire must have shared the westerners' view that Irene was an illegitimate usurper of imperial authority, both the government and people in Constanti-

Early map of Constantinople (fifth or sixth century).

nople considered Charlemagne's coronation to be the preposterous act of a barbarian, who simply did not understand what it meant to be emperor. In the East, the emperor was viewed as the elect of Christ, not of the pope, and Christ had elected the emperor in Constantinople, not in Aix-la-Chapelle (Aachen). Charlemagne tried to pressure the Byzantines into recognizing him by seizing Venice, the Byzantine gateway to Europe, while the Byzantines, who were then militarily occupied by more immediate dangers, opened a long series of negotiations to get Venice back, protect their western borders from Frankish attack, and resolve the legal and political dispute over the imperial title. These talks finally produced a settlement in 813, the year before Charlemagne died. The treaty recognized him as Emperor *of the Franks*.

In Constantinople, the settlement of Frankish claims to the imperial title ended a schism that was serious because the Franks were so powerful. As far as the Byzantine court was concerned, Charlemagne gave up his claim to imperial authority when he relinquished his claim to the title Emperor of the Romans. That the view in the West was different did not concern the Byzantines because they expected the barbaric Franks to misunderstand the nature of the *imperium*. In fact, in the mind of the Byzantine court, the failure of the westerners to understand why they could not claim to be emperors confirmed that they were barbarians.

In the meantime, the last years of Irene's government were disastrous. The Arabs took advantage of the disarray in the Empire to invade Asia Minor in 798, reaching the Aegean. In the court, the government was paralyzed by competition among the leading officials. Irene ruined the treasury by trying to win popularity through a remission of taxes, and, not surprisingly, she was deposed in 802 by her minister of finance, Nicephorus, who became emperor himself.

Irene and Nicephorus (r. 802–11) were both unfortunate to rule during the reigns of the greatest king of the Franks, Charlemagne (r. 768–814), and the greatest caliph of Baghdad, Harun al-Rashid (r. 786–809). Harun seized every opportunity to make encroachments on the Empire, and his great campaign of 798 was only the most spectacular of his aggressions. During Nicephorus's reign, Charlemagne and Harun exchanged embassies, increasing the danger posed to Constantinople. After they died, their successors were occupied with internal political troubles in their realms, and their danger to the Empire decreased. Leo V (r. 813–20) was able to restore a measure of stability to the frontiers, but during his reign the first signs of an important socio-economic change in the Empire began to show.

The Byzantine army and navy were based on the conscription of peasant-soldiers from the administrative districts (*themes*) of Asia Minor. The interior provinces provided infantry troops, while the maritime regions supplied the fleet. Since the seventh century the emperors had pursued a policy of maintaining the prosperity of the yeoman class that provided the military manpower. When provinces were devastated by war, famine, or disease, the emperors repopulated them with communities of small farmers. Following a variation of the old policy of confederation that the emperors of the fourth century had used to defend the Empire's borders, the Heraclian and Isaurian emperors had invited tribal groups to settle internal provinces. This socioeconomic system gave the imperial armies amazing resilience. In the early ninth century, the devastations of the Bulgars and Arabs had ruined so many of the small farmers that the policy broke down. The rural aristocracy, which had served as the military leadership of the provincial districts, was able to create great estates by buying out ruined farmers, who became tenants or migrated to the cities. This process was slow, but in the long run it did significant damage to the Empire's economy and military system. It also gave the aristocratic generals new power, because their soldiers were now their tenants.

During the period of weakness in the first half of the ninth century, the Arabs made new incursions on Byzantine territories. They took Crete and for 135 years used it as a base for disrupting the Empire's shipping in the Aegean and the eastern Mediterranean. The imperial government sent four unsuccessful expeditions against the island before finally recapturing it in 961. North African Moors also began a conquest of Sicily in 827, and although a few Byzantine enclaves held out for a long time, the Moors controlled the island by 902. From Sicily, they were able to establish themselves in the Byzantine territories of southern Italy, and during the ninth century the imperial government was often trying to engage the Franks in an alliance to drive the Moors out of Italy. Inevitably, the negotiations concerning the alliance raised the question of the imperial title.

During the middle of the ninth century the imperial government was a shaky regency for Michael III (r. 842–67). The first regent was Michael's mother Theodora, who restored the images. The emperor's uncle Bardas pushed her aside in 856 and controlled the government until 866. Michael had reached majority, but he was an alcoholic and a homosexual. In the later years of his uncle's rule, Michael raised the Armenian Basil from the status of stable boy to that of co-emperor. Basil was a giant man, who had been raised in Macedonia and is known as the Macedonian. In 866, he murdered Bardas and took control of the government. A year later, when Michael went mad with alcohol and threatened him, Basil had him killed and succeeded as emperor.

Bardas deserves more than mere mention, for he accomplished a great deal while he was regent. He supported a renaissance of classical studies to which we owe the preservation of many ancient Greek literary and philosophical works. The center of this renaissance was Bardas's friend Photius, who became patriarch of Constantinople. Bardas refounded the secular university in Constantinople, while Photius reformed the education of the clergy. Photius, the most learned man of his age, composed a work called *Myriobiblion (The Library)*, a monumental compendium of history, philosophy, and theology. In the court school, he associated with two world-renowned scholars, Leo the Mathematician and Constantine the Philosopher. Leo, whom Bardas made the first rector of the new university, was invited to the court at Baghdad, which had an avid interest in mathematics and astronomy. Constantine became a missionary to the Slavs and created a script for writing Slavonic (see pp. 364–65). The university continued as a center of education, scholarship, and culture for two centuries.

Under Photius there was renewed conflict between the papacy and the patriarch of Constantinople. In 858, Pope Nicholas I, an intransigent and forceful man allied with Photius's enemies, investigated the way the patriarch had come to power, and during the inquiry he suggested that it was now time that the dioceses removed from Roman jurisdiction by Emperor Leo III, way back in 731, be restored. Photius replied that the emperor—who was the incompetent Michael III—could not see his way clear to do this.

Behind this request of Nicholas was not just a desire to get back long-lost territory and income. What was really at stake was a whole new sector of Christendom. The Slavs and Bulgars were ready to become Christians, and the Bulgarian khan Boris was negotiating with the Frankish Church and Constantinople about which church he should commit himself and his people to. Photius took action by sending missionaries to Boris and to Moravia, and in 864, Boris submitted to Constantinople, but the competition for the Slavs, to which the dispute over Photius's elevation was incident, continued for the next six years, until the Bulgarians were finally fully committed to the eastern church.

In the meantime, Nicholas found occasion to spell out for the emperor and his patriarch the full theory of papal authority, relying on the *Donation of Constantine*. This document came into existence sometime in the first half of the ninth century. It purported to record the donation of Rome and the western half of the Roman Empire that Constantine I (r. 312–37) made to Pope Sylvester I (r. 314–35) when the emperor moved his capital to the rebuilt city of Byzantium. This charter, which was not exposed as a forgery until 1440, was to play a great role in the political and constitutional history of western Europe, but the Byzantines always dismissed it. Photius replied to Pope Nicholas in a learned and elegant document that contradicted the Donation on every point. Photius argued that Constantine had taken spiritual as well as secular authority with him when he moved to Byzantium, and the patriarch, as the principal ecclesiastical official of the universal emperor, was the equal of the pope, at least.

Basil the Macedonian reversed Bardas's policy and deposed Photius, making rapprochement with the papacy possible, but Pope Nicholas had died, and his successor did not pursue the possibility. Despite many attempts, the Photian Schism between the eastern and western churches has not been ended to this day.

Basil was an anomaly among the medieval Byzantine emperors. He was an illiterate in one of the world's most literate societies. He was a man of towering physical stature and strength in a world that had often been dominated by court eunuchs. Yet, he founded a

The Donation of Constantine

Constantine tells how Pope Sylvester I cured him of leprosy. In gratitude Constantine accepts baptism and decrees

that the sacred see of blessed Peter shall be gloriously exalted above our empire and earthly throne. . . . And the pontiff who presides over the most holy Roman Church shall be the highest and chief of all priests . . . and according to his decision shall all matters be settled . . . for the worship of God or the confirmation of the faith.

We convey to the most blessed pontiff, our father Silvester, universal pope, both our palace [the Lateran] and likewise all provinces, places and districts of the City of Rome and Italy and of the regions of the West, . . . bequeathing them to the power and sway of him and his successors.

Wherefore we have perceived that our empire and the power of our government should be transferred to the regions of the East . . . for it is not right that an earthly emperor should have authority . . . where the head of the Christian religion has been established by the Emperor of heaven.

From the Donation of Constantine, as quoted in *Select Documents of European History*, ed. by R. G. D. Laffan (London: Methuen, 1930), Vol. 1, pp. 4–5.

dynasty that brought the Empire to its greatest cultural brilliance and prosperity.

THE MACEDONIAN PERIOD

Basil (r. 867–86) first set out to make an alliance with the Frankish king of Italy, Louis II, who called himself emperor, against the Moors, whose strongholds in southern Italy threatened Louis as well as the old Byzantine cities. But the alliance foundered on Louis's claims to the imperial title; so Basil proceeded largely alone. Under the great admiral Nicephorus Phocas, Byzantine forces made steady, though hard, progress in southern Italy, while the Moors consolidated their hold over Sicily. Also on his western front, he sent missionaries to the southern Slavs who had settled Dalmatia and Greece and established provincial administrations along the eastern coast of the Adriatic Sea, entering into close ties with Venice.

The emperor also devoted much effort to a series of eastern campaigns. Here too, Byzantine military fortunes were variable, but, overall, Basil's armies both regained strategically important territories and cities and kept the Arab armies at bay. He combined his land operations with naval attacks in the eastern Mediterranean and was able to maintain the upper hand against the Arab fleets. He defeated the pirates of Crete several times and may have occupied the island for a short time. In sum, Basil made an excellent start on one of the hallmarks of the Macedonian period, the reestablishment of the Empire's territorial integrity and of its military superiority against its traditional enemies.

Basil also introduced some important governmental reforms. He commissioned the writing of a manual of administrative practice, which became a guide to the bureaucracy until it was replaced by the great work of Emperor Constantine VII, Basil's grandson. He also commissioned the making of a new law code, because the iconoclastic

Interior view of St. Mark's cathedral, Venice. The mosaics were done by Byzantine artists (tenth century).

controversy and the accumulation of cases and learned treatises had cluttered and confused the law.

The brilliance of Basil's reign dulled after he began to lose his sanity in 879. In the remaining seven years of his life, the patriarch and other leading court figures controlled the government. This led to intensive palace intrigue, which ended when the mad old emperor was assassinated in 886— probably by friends of his 20-year-old son Leo. In contrast to his father, Leo V (r. 886–912) was a highly educated, scholarly man. He understood the governmental importance of the patriarchate and the seriousness of conflicts within the church. Consequently, he made his own younger brother, Stephen, patriarch and began a tradition of making the church not only a de-

Greek fire, a mixture of quicklime, petroleum, and sulfur that ignited when it came in contact with water, was introduced into the Byzantine navy after 675. It was a very effective weapon against the Arabs (detail from a fourteenth-century manuscript).

partment of state, but also an appendage of the imperial family.

Like his predecessors, Leo faced difficult military problems throughout his reign. In the eastern Mediterranean the Arab fleets had recovered and were doing great damage to the coastal cities and shipping of the Empire. Basil had favored the navy, and Leo continued the policy, making the navy the Empire's principal military force. However, in 911 the majority of the Byzantine fleet was lost in a great battle against the caliph's.

Meanwhile, the Bulgarian frontier was quiet. Khan Boris's conversion to Christianity had not wiped out paganism among his people, and the last years of Boris's reign were disturbed by religious conflict. In 889, Boris abdicated in favor of his eldest son Vladimir, a pagan, but a civil war broke out that lasted until 893, when Vladimir was overthrown by his Christian brother, Symeon. Symeon had been educated in Constantinople, but he

turned out nevertheless to be a fierce enemy of the Empire.

While he suffered mixed military fortunes, Leo carried out great administrative reforms. He established new Byzantine provinces in southern Italy and upper Mesopotamia, and he reorganized the *themes* (administrative districts) to strengthen them as the first line of defense against the constant raiding of the Arabs. He completed the legal code begun by his father and issued 113 edicts designed to reestablish good government in church and state. He regulated commerce through publication of the *Book of the Eparch*. He continued the tradition of Bardas and Photius—whose party he favored—by patronizing art and education, and Byzantine writers called him Leo the Wise.

The end of Leo's reign was troubled by a controversy over his fourth marriage. The religious and civil law prohibited a person from marrying a third time, unless it was absolutely necessary for the continuation of his family; fourth marriages were out of the question. By 905 Leo had gone through three marriages without a male heir, and when his mistress gave birth to a male in September of that year, legitimization of the child became imperative. Leo sought a dispensation from the legal prohibition and eventually forced the patriarch to give it. The action started a sharp debate in the Byzantine Church, which was especially significant because the two sides were led by exceptionally learned men, formerly friends, who argued the matter on the highest plane of theology and law.

After Leo's death in 912, his dissolute brother Alexander and his fourth wife competed for control of the regency for young Constantine VII, whose legitimacy remained in dispute. The competition brought the Bulgarian Symeon into the picture. He made claims on the imperial title for himself, and when he was denied, he started an incredibly destructive eleven-year war (913–24). In 919, the military commander Romanus seized control of the government, married the young emperor to his own daughter, and had himself crowned co-emperor with his son-in-law.

Romanus (r. 920–44) was able to create a great alliance against Symeon of Bulgaria, and when the old khan died in 927, the Bulgarian threat was contained. This success was matched by developments on the eastern frontier of the Empire. Right in the middle of the Bulgarian war, the eastern armies had made a brilliant campaign against the Arabs, and, after this, the Byzantines were on the offensive in the East. During Romanus's reign, the Empire established itself in Armenia and pushed into the Caucasus, the mountainous region between the Black and Caspian seas. In the north, Romanus fought a war against the Russians, which ended in a lasting treaty (945).

When Romanus was overthrown by his own sons, the mob in Constantinople demanded that Constantine VII be put on the throne. Constantine was then nearly 40 and had spent his life as a scholar. Still uneasy about the taint on his legitimacy, he took the title Porphyrogenitus ("born in the purple"— that is, as the legitimate heir).

During Constantine VII's reign (r. 944–59), the arts, literature, science, and crafts flourished under imperial patronage, and the period is considered the heart of the renaissance that had begun nearly a century earlier under Bardas and his friend Photius. Court scholars produced manuals of military strategy, law, philosophy, history, and theology. Much of this work was in the form of collections of snippets from the great works of the past, and since many of these originals are lost, we owe a great debt for preserving parts of them to the rather unoriginal work of the mid-tenth-century compilers. The emperor himself compiled a great work on the ceremony and ideology of the Byzantine court, which is the principal source of knowledge about these subjects. He is also famous for a book on the history and practice of imperial administration and diplomacy, which he wrote for his son Romanus II.

Constantine VII was not an innovative emperor. Following his grandfather Basil's example, he negotiated with the northern successors of Charlemagne, and in 949 the German king Otto I (r. 936–73) sent an embassy to Constantinople. The result of this negotiation was a proposed marriage between Romanus II and Otto's daughter, and the imperial government sent tutors to Otto's court to teach the young girl the Greek language and Byzantine manners. This marriage did not take place, because Romanus rashly married another, but the plan to link the German and the imperial houses was realized when Otto II (r. 973–83) married Theophano, daughter of Romanus II.

During the period from 959, when Constantine VII died, to 976, when his grandson Basil II succeeded to the throne, the growing power of the military aristocracy became apparent. Since the ninth century, when the policy of maintaining the strength of the yeoman class had broken down, the aristocracy had gained economic and political control of the provinces. In 963, the great naval commander Nicephorus Phocas (r. 963–69) seized power; he was succeeded by the aristocratic general John (r. 969–76). These men reestablished the soundness of the Byzantine military system and recovered territory lost in earlier reigns. But the idea that the emperor must be legitimate remained strong, and John's successor was the legitimate heir, Basil II, a strange person who is considered the greatest of the Byzantine emperors.

Basil II (r. 976–1025) never married and seems to have stayed away from women. Although he grew up in a court and society that had developed as high an appreciation of the cultured life as any before or since, Basil was totally uninterested in education, learning, and art. He was a man out of place, an ascetic; he was also a military genius.

He was remembered most for his campaigns against the Bulgarians. Like Constantine V in the eighth century, Basil went against the Bulgarians year after year, at one time repatriating 14,000 Bulgarian prisoners-of-war, all of whom had been blinded. He earned the title "the Bulgar Slayer." He also pacified the Russians with the help of a force of Varangian (Scandinavian) troops. The result of his wars and negotiations with the Kievan state was a treaty, concluded about 989, according to which the Russian prince of Kiev converted to Christianity and married a member of the imperial family. The Varangians became an elite imperial guard, and in the medieval Scandinavian sagas, service in the guard was considered a sign of high birth and great ability, for the emperor was said to accept only men who were from the best families and who had proven themselves. At the turn of the eleventh century, Basil was in the East, where he was as successful as he had been in the West. He campaigned successfully against the Arabs of Syria and moved forcefully into the provinces south of the Caucasus. In 1001, the caliph concluded a ten-year truce with him.

Basil's knowledge of the military, together with his experience of putting down two serious rebellions by the aristocratic class, led him to put some basic social reforms in place. As the rise of Nicephoras and John showed, the military aristocracy had become a dominant force in Byzantine society and politics. The process of consolidation of landed estates had eroded the ancient basis of Byzantine prosperity, the mass of small farmers. Moreover, the landed aristocracy had a strong instinct toward territorial independence and toward enmity to the central government. The reforms of the thematic system under Leo V at the beginning of the tenth century had strengthened the individual provinces and had given their leading aristocratic families strong power bases. Since that time, most of the serious rebellions had been fomented by the landed aristocracy. The destitution of the yeoman class also reduced the available manpower of the Empire, while it increased the economic and social distance between rich and poor.

Basil set out to stop the decline of the yeoman class. On January 1, 996, he issued a decree that required the great landholders to produce documentary proof that they had owned their land for at least 75 years. If someone occupied old government land, which could be shown from the excellent imperial archives, then he had to produce proof of ownership going back 1,000 years. This meant producing an authentic document that had been preserved in the family since the reign of Augustus (r. 27 B.C.–A.D.14)! With the support of the army and the populace, Basil was able to enforce this incredible legislation, and many great families were reduced to poverty. A few years later, he added to the burden of the rich landowners by requiring that they make up any deficit in the communal taxes assessed by the imperial government. The churches were the chief sufferers from this law, but the emperor ignored the clergy's protests and pleas for relief.

These measures halted the economic decline of the Empire for a generation, but during a single reign, even a long one, the power of the aristocracy could only be weakened, not broken. After Basil's death in 1025, his successors could not hold the line, and the great families recovered. Between 1025 and 1081, the civilian bureaucracy, which supported the legitimate Macedonian emperors, and the provincial military aristocracy competed fiercely for control of the Empire. The bureaucracy held power through most of this period, and it tried to weaken its enemies by reducing the size and undermining the strength of the army. When the Macedonian house died out in the middle of the century, the Empire's military system was in ruins, and the new imperial house ruled over a series of disasters.

During the same period, 1025–81, the external enemies of the Empire revived and made great inroads on the imperial territories. In the West, the Normans conquered southern Italy, driving out Byzantines and Arabs alike. To the north, the Patzinaks threatened the Danubian border. Most serious, in the East, the Seljuk Turks, who had come out of Central Asia to conquer the caliphate at Baghdad attacked the eastern provinces of the Empire (see pp. 229–30).

The Seljuks devastated large areas of Asia Minor in the 1060s, and under this pressure the aristocrat Romanus Diogenes seized control of the state. In 1071, he mustered what was left of the Byzantine army and met the Turks at Manzikert, where he suffered a disastrous defeat and was himself captured. When he ransomed himself by promising to pay a huge tribute to the Sultan, he found the civilian government had organized a coup d'etat, and the treaty with the Turks, which might have given the Empire some respite from invasion from the east, went by the boards. In the same year, the Normans

captured Bari on the west coast of southern Italy and were in a position to invade Greece.

During the next decade, rival claimants to the Byzantine throne made alliances with the Turks and Normans, hastening the process of conquest from east and west. In this crisis, the Ducas family, which had been supported by the bureaucracy, allied itself with the greatest of the aristocratic generals, Alexius Comnenus, who married a Ducas princess and became emperor in 1081.

Alexius (r. 1081–1118) was a brilliant politician. When he came to power, the Normans posed the greatest danger. They had crossed the Adriatic and were trying to conquer Epirus. Their

A Crusader's View of Byzantium

Odo of Deuil, the author of this piece, was a historian of the Second Crusade.

And then the Greeks degenerated entirely into women; putting aside all manly vigor, both of words and of spirit, they lightly swore whatever they thought would please us, but they neither kept faith with us nor maintained respect for themselves. In general they really have the opinion that anything which is done for the holy empire cannot be considered perjury. . . . When the Greeks are afraid they become despicable in their excessive abasement, and when they have the upper hand they are arrogant. . . .

Constantinople itself is squalid and fetid. . . . People live lawlessly in this city, which has as many lords as rich men and almost as many thieves as poor men. . . . In every respect she exceeds moderation, for just as she surpasses other cities in wealth, so too does she surpass them in vice. . . .

[The bishop of Langres] added that Constantinople is Christian only in name and not in fact . . . and that her emperor had ventured a few years ago to attack the [Crusader] prince of Antioch. . . . "Though it was his [the emperor's] duty to ward off the near-by infidels by uniting the Christian forces, with the aid of the infidels he strove to destroy the Christians."

From Odo of Deuil, *De profectione Ludovici VII in orientem*, trans. by V. G. Berry (New York: Columbia University Press, 1948), pp. 57, 65, 69.

leader, Robert Guiscard, wanted to be emperor himself. Therefore, Alexius made peace with the Turks and Patzinaks, granting them the territories they had conquered as vassals of the imperial throne. Then, he made an alliance with the Venetians, who since the tenth century had been building a great commercial and maritime power. The Venetians were to help the Byzantines in return for the right to trade freely in the imperial territories.

Meanwhile, since the 1070s the emperors had been appealing to the western European powers for help against the infidel Turks, who had conquered Jerusalem in 1077. Finally, in 1095, Pope Urban II succeeded in organizing a great crusade of western knights. This movement caused the Empire great grief. Alexius wanted to use the westerners to reconquer his lost territories, but he found the crusading army disorganized and led by headstrong men who wanted to establish independent Latin principalities in the Holy Land. Once the crusaders were established there, the Empire found

that it had yet another enemy in the East.

Like his military and diplomatic policies, Alexius's economic policy had ambiguous results. He restored the currency after it had deteriorated for decades, but he also doubled taxes, and the Byzantine population was severely oppressed by heavy taxation and the Venetian monopoly of trade. Late in his reign, Alexius tried to counter Venetian power by granting trading privileges to Venice's rival, Pisa, but this just made the Empire's commerce the object of competition among the great Italian cities. The emperor also tried to strengthen the army by increasing the number of imperial land grants made in return for military service. The end result of this practice was the growth in the number of large estates and the increase in the power of the provincial military aristocracy. Nonetheless, the bad consequences of these policies were not felt during Alexius's reign. Under him, intellectual and artistic life once again flourished. It was a period of scholarship, of the recovery of past learning rather than of the discovery of new ideas, but the work of preservation was important for later ages. Michael Psellus wrote a great history of the Empire, the *Chronographia*, and Alexius's own daughter, Anna, wrote an excellent history of his reign.

The struggle to restore the Empire was lost in the final 20 years of the twelfth century. The Byzantines had failed to free themselves from the commercial control of the Italians, and the rise of the provincial aristocracy resulted in the creation of provincial armies. Between 1181 and 1204, the Serbians created a Balkan empire and the Bulgarians reestablished their power. Meanwhile, the Normans rulers of southern Italy continued to aim at the imperial crown, and in the late 1180s, the German emperor inherited this goal when he married the heiress of the Norman kingdom.

The total collapse of the Empire came in 1204. Another great crusade,

A Byzantine View of the Crusaders

Anna Comnena, the author of this piece, was the daughter of the Emperor Alexius I.

Now he [the emperor] dreaded the arrival of the Crusaders, for he knew their irresistible manner of attack, their unstable and mobile character, and all the peculiar . . . characteristics which the Frank retains throughout; and he also knew that they were always agape for money, and seemed to disregard their truces readily for any reason that cropped up. . . . The simpler-minded Franks were urged on by the real desire of worshiping at our Lord's Sepulchre, but the more astute, especially men like Bohemund . . . had another secret reason, namely the hope that . . . they might by some means be able to seize the capital itself. . . . For the Frankish race . . . is always very hot-headed and eager, but when it has once espoused a cause, it is uncontrollable.

From Anna Comnena, *The Alexiad*, trans. by E. A. S. Dawes (London: Kegan Paul, 1928), pp. 248, 250.

The Latin Empire of Constantinople   1204–61

the fourth, had been assembled in Europe, and the Venetians were to ferry it to the Holy Land. But the westerners held a great anger against the Byzantines: the Venetians bore many grudges; the western church wanted to reunite the two churches; and the crusade's leaders resented the repeated attempts by Constantinople to assert its power over the Latin principalities in the East. Hence, it was rather easy for the Venetian Doge Dandolo to divert the crusaders to Constantinople in partial payment for the cost of transportation, which the crusaders could not afford. Constantinople fell to the crusaders in July 1204.

For the next 56 years, until 1261, Constantinople was the seat of a Latin emperor, but the Empire had really ceased to exist. In western Asia Minor, Byzantine resisters set up the Empire of Nicaea. To the east was the Sultanate of Iconium, a part of the old Seljuk state. In the northeastern sector of Asia Minor, the remnants of the Comneni dynasty established the Empire of Trebizond. To the west, Epirus became an independent Byzantine state, while Athens became the center of a Frankish duchy, and Venice controlled most of the major coastal cities with their territories. As a result, the Latins were under constant pressure, and in 1261 Michael VIII Paleologus (r. 1259–82) recaptured Constantinople and founded a new dynasty, which presided over the last two centuries of the Empire.

That the Empire survived as long as it did after 1261 is a testament to the diplomatic skills of the Paleologi. The Empire was constantly threatened from all sides. In the West, the successors of the Normans continued to seek the imperial crown, until foreign control of southern Italy and Sicily collapsed in 1282. After this, other western kings and lords repeatedly plotted with Byzantine dissidents and the heirs of the Latin emperors to retake Constantinople.

The great danger posed by the western powers led Emperor Michael VIII to treat with the pope about the unification of the churches because if the eastern church submitted to Rome the Latins would have no excuse for attacking the Empire. The act of union was celebrated at a great council in Lyon in

1274, but it raised a storm of protest in the East. People of every class and condition ended up in the imperial prisons.

Despite Michael's successes, the Byzantine Empire he restored was a minor state among those that had been established by the westerners and the Turks on the old territories of the Empire. Constantinople was the ruling city of a state exhausted both militarily and economically, and Michael's successors faced new enemies, the Serbs to the west and the Ottoman Turks to the east. In the fourteenth century, the Serbs established a powerful state, which occupied most of the Empire's Balkan provinces and controlled Bulgaria. At the same time, the Ottoman Turks conquered all of Asia Minor. By 1329, the Empire controlled only a few cities on the western edge of their former heartland, and the Turks sat directly across the Bosphorus from Constantinople.

The following decades were filled with civil wars and palace intrigues, while the Ottomans extended their conquests into Thrace and the territory of Thessalonica. By the end of the fourteenth century, the Ottomans had defeated the Serbs and their allies in several important battles and had Constantinople entirely surrounded. Then the Mongols, a people from eastern Asia, gave the Empire and eastern Europe a respite. Under Timur, they swept down on the Ottomans and crushed them in 1401. But the emperors could take no advantage of the good luck; the Empire was too weak. Although it took two generations for the Ottomans to recover from the disaster, Constantinople was in no better condition to resist them then than it had been earlier. In 1453, the Ottoman Sultan Muhammed II brought a powerful army, supported by artillery he had acquired from the West, against the city, and, after nearly two months of attacks and bombardment, he took it (May 29). The last emperor, Constantine XI, a capable man given an impossible situation to save, died in the fight-

ing. By 1461, the Turks had conquered all the outlying pockets of Byzantine power, and the Empire was no more.

BYZANTINE GOVERNMENT

The Byzantine Empire developed one of history's most extensive and elaborate bureaucracies. After Emperor Anastasius I (r. 491–518) established the dominance of civilians in the government, the bureaucracy grew steadily. Entry into the civil service rested on education, and the bureaucrats created a system of secular education that contrasted with the ecclesiastical education offered by the Byzantine Church.

The heart of the secular program was study of the classics of Greek literature, philosophy, and science. The student began by learning Greek grammar and by memorizing Homer's epics and other great works. Normally, this study was completed by the age of 14, and the student went on to study rhetoric, philosophy, and science. This system produced an elite of highly educated classical scholars. Although a small group of aristocratic families dominated the state offices by ensuring that their male children were properly educated for government service, any young man with a talent for learning could find a means to complete the academic program and get in.

The bureaucracy was divided into departments. The chancellor ran the section that took care of all state correspondence. The postmaster general was responsible for the extensive communications system of the Empire. The *Sacellarius* headed the financial offices. All of these principal officers, and many others too numerous to name, were supported by bureaucracies. The officers of the imperial household were mostly eunuchs, who could be trusted all the more because they could never usurp the imperial throne. There were eight chief offices reserved for eunuchs, each with his own bureaucracy. Missing from the government were the military officers, who stood outside and were in constant competition with the civilians.

The provinces or *themes* were run by military governors. At the beginning of the ninth century, there were 10 *themes*; by the end of the century, there were 26, and by the end of the twelfth twice that number. The emperors continually subdivided the *themes* to keep them from becoming power bases for the provincial military aristocracy. The emperor controlled the governors also by keeping tabs on the administration. The governors had financial officers under them, who reported directly to the imperial government. This system for maintaining control was supplemented by the extensive use of spies. The intelligence network was so pervasive that people were distrustful even of their friends.

The emperor was the center of the whole system of government. The Byzantines considered themselves to be the direct heirs of the Romans, and power was totally centralized in the hands of the emperor. In Roman and Byzantine law, the people held all power when there was a vacancy in the imperial office, but when they had elected a new emperor, they transferred the power to him.

Under the influence of Christianity, the emperor was viewed as the vicar of Christ on earth, head of the Byzantine Church as well as of the secular state (Caesaropapism). He appointed the patriarchs of Constantinople and other bishops, and he made both civil and ecclesiastical law in his statutes. There was no legal way to remove the divinely ordained emperor, but the same idea that made his power an emanation from God justified rebellion against him. A successful rebellion was a divine sign that it was time to change emperors, while an unsuccessful one was treason against God as well as the emperor.

To symbolize these ideas of divine autocracy, the Byzantines developed an incredibly elaborate court ceremony, which was patterned on the liturgy. Every appearance or act of the

The Pomp of the Byzantine Court

The Byzantine court was famous for the elaborate ceremony of all its functions, here a modern historian describes some of it on the basis of medieval handbooks.

The rigid rules of a quasi-liturgical ceremonial held an Emperor in their grip from the moment of his accession, and an imperial prince was compassed about by them from the cradle to the grave. . . . Constantine Porphyrogenitus [Emperor Constantine VII, 913–59], who himself compiled a *Book of Ceremonies* . . . counted his work as a necessary duty and explained its purpose: by following such a commendable order the imperial power would show itself in a better aspect and become raised to a higher dignity, thus filling foreigners and subjects alike with admiration. . . . The reception accorded to foreign guests and embassies was hedged about with a precisely regulated and ceremonious etiquette from the moment of their arrival in Constantinople. . . . An envoy's first impression of his reception by the Emperor must usually have been overwhelming. The foreigner was led into the Audience Hall of the palace through rows of imperial bodyguards with glittering arms and past the assembled throng of high dignitaries in rich vesture. One final curtain was drawn aside to expose the Emperor clad in his robes of state and seated on his throne. Golden roaring lions watched about the imperial throne and mechanical golden birds sang in a gilded tree. And while the envoy made the three prescribed prostrations, the throne was raised aloft to mark the unapproachability of the now yet more richly bedecked monarch.

From W. Ensslin, "The Government and Administration of the Byzantine Empire," *Cambridge Medieval History*, 2nd ed. (Cambridge: Cambridge University Press, 1967), Vol. 4.2, pp. 16–17, 51–52.

emperor was carried out according to a rigid program of ritual that emphasized the majesty of the imperial office. But the ceremonies also imposed a powerful restraint on the absolutist emperor himself. They contained the basic ideas about how the emperor ought to act and the values of justice and good government he ought to hold dear. Byzantine history is full of evil characters, palace revolutions, and other disasters, but Byzantine government was stable and consistent in both its theory and practice for longer than any other Mediterranean state.

BYZANTINE SOCIETY

The Empire had a double society—the society of Constantinople and the society of the provinces. During the classical age of Byzantine power from the eighth century to the twelfth century the city had a population of between 500,000 and 800,000, divided into three socioeconomic classes—the bureaucrats, the commercial class, and the poor. The commercial class was by far the largest, including the merchants, tradesmen, and small shopkeepers. The aristocracy of the civil service was small, but still numbered in the thousands, and, of course, it dominated the city. The poor class was an important element that may have numbered as many as 30,000.

Although the middle class was huge, its upper crust of merchants never evolved into a powerful force in society or the state. Until the eleventh century, the government rigidly controlled all commerce through guilds that restricted profits and regulated trade. When the system of governmental control broke down at the end of the eleventh century, the Venetians and other Italians replaced the native merchant class in Byzantine commerce. In general, middle-class families hoped that their sons would escape from commerce by entering either the military or bureaucracy, and many families castrated some of their sons in the hope that they would succeed as court eunuchs.

The breakdown of the government's control over trade coincided with the end of its control over the countryside. Until the late eleventh century, the government had been able to exploit rural districts to support Constantinople. It had kept food prices artificially

A Byzantine lady of rank (late fifth or early sixth century). Note her elegantly draped mantle and the snoodlike bonnet of the imperial type.

low, which made it possible for people with minuscule incomes to survive in the city. Aside from this support system, the emperor, the church, and the leading citizens of the city ran an extensive program of charities. The church preached charity, and giving to the poor became a regular part of the economic and social activities of upper classes. The city was filled with hospitals and charitable institutions of various kinds, which impressed foreign visitors very much. The poor were, in effect, a professional class, and there were even companies of beggars, which controlled the best stations in the city.

Nonetheless, the lower classes had it hard. With the end of the system of government control over the countryside, food prices rose sharply and conditions in the city deteriorated. Cloth goods of all types had always been expensive, so that most of the poorer classes were ill-clad. Housing was also grossly inadequate. Thousands of people slept in archways and any other sheltered spots they could find. Besides, the city was filthy. Refuse and sewage flowed or sat stagnant in the streets, and disease was endemic. Not surprisingly, the sale of perfumes and aromatic herbs was brisk, for the wealthy wanted to protect their homes from the smells of the streets. People also believed that the pleasant aromas were a guard against disease.

Although the late Roman and Byzantine law gave women substantial rights, Byzantine women were a shepherded class. Respectable women wore veils when they left home, and they were taught to approach guests in their homes diffidently. These restrictions led to many incidents of secret liaisons and tragic falls from respectability. In the lower classes, prostitution was a major problem. The owners of taverns and baths often ran brothels, and there were independent pimps. Historians estimate that at any given time there were thousands of prostitutes in the city.

Early Byzantine jewelry contained Hellenistic and Roman features. The clasp of this late sixth-century necklace, for example, is of a Hellenistic type, while the cylindrical slides between the pendants are a late Roman feature.

Out in the provinces, life was hard, but healthier than in Constantinople or Thessalonica, which with a population of about 200,000 was the second city of the Empire. Until the middle of the ninth century, the imperial government maintained the yeoman class by repopulating devastated districts and restricting the growth of great estates. By this process, the rural population became multicultural, and military officers, who had to muster, train, and lead the peasant-soldiers, were required to learn at least one vernacular language.

The yeomen farmers were settled in communes of from 50 to 500 people, depending on the quality of the land. Each family owned its own land in the village, and men had a way to escape from the limitations of rural life by en-

Women of the Byzantine Imperial Family

Imperial women played an important role in Byzantine affairs. They were well educated and often exercised great political power. Here is a description by Anna Comnenus, daughter of Emperor Alexius I (1081–1118), of her paternal grandmother Anna. The younger Anna wrote an excellent history of her father's reign.

[At the beginning of Alexius's reign] He [Alexius] really longed that his mother rather than himself should take the helm of the state. . . . Therefore in all daily business he did nothing, not even a trifling thing, without her advice. . . . When . . . Robert's [the Norman ruler of Italy] crossing in Epirus forced Alexius to leave the capital [he entrusted] his mother single-handed with the imperial government. . . . For my grandmother was so clever in business and so skilful in guiding a State, and setting it in order, that she was capable of not only administering the Roman Empire, but any other of all the countries the sun shines upon. She was a woman of wide experience and knew the nature of things. . . . To put it concisely, the situation was as follows, he indeed had the semblance of reigning but she really reigned—moreover she drew up laws, administered and directed everything; all her orders, written or unwritten, he [Alexius] confirmed by his seal or by word. . . . "

From Anna Comnenus, *The Alexiad*, trans. by Elizabeth A. S. Dawes (New York: Barnes & Noble, 1967), pp. 82, 83, 85–86.

tering the army or getting an education. Rural monasteries ran schools for talented young men, who could then enter the bureaucracy or the church.

The government added greatly to the natural vicissitudes of agricultural life. Taxes were collected by tax farmers, who bought the right to collect in a district. With the support of the government, these men were incredibly rapacious. They collected twice what was owed and had the right to imprison and flog those who could not pay, regardless of the reason. On Cyprus, the collectors set hungry dogs on delinquents. From the ninth century on, small farmers increasingly fell into debt and had to become unfree tenants of the great landlords of their districts. By this means the Empire's rural districts fell into the control of the provincial aristocracy, which set itself against the imperial government. By the late Byzantine period, the provinces were virtually independent of the central government, and the peasants were oppressed subjects of the local nobility. By that time, Constantinople relied on Italian merchants for its food and other supplies, and the city lived from crisis to crisis, while the countryside was devastated by invading armies.

Suggestions for Further Reading

General

The leading general histories of the Byzantine Empire are G. Ostrogorsky, *History of the Byzantine State*, 2nd ed. (1968), which focuses on political history, and *Cambridge Medieval History*, Vol. 4 (2 parts), ed. J. M. Hussey (1966–67), which contains excellent articles on all aspects of Byzantine history and culture. On the early period, see A. H. M. Jones, *The Later Roman Empire*, 2 vols. (1964). On Constantine, see the works cited in Chapter 4. P. Charanis treats Anastasius I in *Church and State in the Later Roman Empire* (1974). On Justinian, see J. W. Barker, *Justinian and the Later Roman Empire* (1966), and R. Browning, *Justinian and Theodora* (1971). On the Heraclian dynasty, see R. Jenkins, *Byzantium: The Imperial Centuries, A.D. 610–1071* (1966).

The Iconoclasm Controversy and Relations with the West

On Iconoclasm, see S. Gero, *Byzantine Iconoclasm during the Reign of Leo III* (1973), and *Byzantine Iconoclasm during the Reign of Constantine V* (1977). On Irene, see C. Diehl, *Byzantine Empresses* (1963). For a history of the Byzantine Church, see R. M. French, *The Eastern Orthodox Church* (1951), and G. Every, *The Byzantine Patriarchate (451–1204)*, 2nd ed. (1962). On the relations between East and West, see F. Dvornik, *Byzantium and the Roman Primacy* (1966) and *The Photian Schism* (1950); H. Pirenne, *Mohammed and Charlemagne* (1939); and C. Brand, *Byzantium Confronts the West: 1180–1204* (1968). For a history of the Bulgarians, see S. Runciman, *A History of the First Bulgarian Empire* (1930), and on eastern Europe, see F. Dvornik, *The Making of Central and Eastern Europe* (1949).

Byzantine Civilization

For a picture of classical Byzantine civilization, see A. Toynbee, *Constantine Porphyrogenitus and his World* (1973); J. M. Hussey, *Church and Learning in the Byzantine Empire, 867–1185* (1937), and *The Byzantine World*, 2nd ed. (1961); and S. Runciman, *Byzantine Civilization* (1933). On the economic life of Byzantium, see the articles in the *Cambridge Economic History of Europe*, Vol. 1 (1942). The classic study of Byzantine government is J. B. Bury, *The Imperial Administrative System in the Ninth Century* (1911). See Michael Psellus, *Fourteen Byzantine Rulers (Chronographia)*, trans. E. R. A. Sewter (1966), and *The Alexiad of Anna Comnena*, trans. E. R. A. Sewter (1969). D. Geanakoplos, *Byzantium: Church, Society, and Civilization Seen Through Contemporary Eyes* (1986), contains a large collection of sources.

End of the Byzantine Empire

On the capture of Constantinople by the Franks, see K. M. Setton, *A History of the Crusades*, Vol. 2 (1962). On the Latin period, see M. Angold, *A Byzantine Government in Exile: Government and Society under the Laskarids of Nicaea, 1204–1261* (1975). On the fall of the Byzantine Empire, see D. M. Nicol, *The Last Centuries of Byzantium, 1261–1453* (1972), and P. Wittek, *The Rise of the Ottoman Empire* (1938).

8
Islam and the Rise of the Arab Empire

*A*fter the middle of the seventh century, the counterweight to the Byzantine Empire in the eastern Mediterranean was the Arab Empire. The two great powers pummelled each other for centuries; the resilience of the Byzantines was matched stroke for stroke by the relentless attacks of the caliphs. Islamic civilization was another of the heirs of the Roman Empire, and, although its language was not one of those used by the upper classes of *Romania*, it absorbed a great deal of Greek culture, which it preserved for the Latin West. It is one of the ironies of the modern cultural consciousness of westerners that they view the Islamic world as alien while owing so much to it.

The new power faced by the Byzantines and Persians in the second quarter of the seventh century was Arab, but the religious, social, and political world of the Arab Empire was Islamic. It is important to understand the principal characteristics of that world, for they still affect the society and politics of the Middle East today.

Opposite: Mohammed and his followers (tenth-century manuscript illustration).

209

The holy Kaaba in modern Mecca is the most sacred Islamic shrine.

THE FORMATION OF THE ISLAMIC WORLD

The Creation of Islamic Religion

A great deal more is known about the origins of Christianity than of Islam. This is true primarily because Christianity arose from a literate society, while Islam was formed in a largely illiterate, nomadic culture. No substantial body of pre-Islamic Arabic literature exists in which the seminal ideas of the religion are apparent.

The home of Islam, the Arabian Peninsula, had for millennia been bounded by great imperial civilizations. The ancient civilizations had traded along the edges of the region. The Sumerians already knew of the spices available in Yemen and Oman in the south of the peninsula. The Romans controlled the north and northwest of the peninsula and traded down its western coast, and they called the southern area Arabia Felix (Arabia the Fortunate) because it was the source of rare goods like myrrh (the basis of incense), perfumes, and medicines. The Persians held the northeast, and their routes went down the east coast and through the Persian Gulf.

In Roman times, the rich, ancient Yemenite kingdom controlled the mid-point of the trade between East Asia and the Mediterranean and dominated the interior of the peninsula. During the third century, Yemen had strong competition from Abyssinia, on the African side of the Red Sea. The Romans mostly supported the Abyssinians, who gained the upper hand by the beginning of the fourth century.

In the fifth century, Egyptian missionaries converted Abyssinia to Christianity, and the Abyssinians imposed the religion on the Yemenites. Taking advantage of this, the Persians interfered in south Arabia, stirring up religious and political resistance to the Abyssinians. The Byzantines, who had inherited Roman interests supported the Abyssinians. Finally, in the 590s, the forces supported by Persia won out, at the time when the Persian armies were beginning their final assault on the Byzantine Empire.

Throughout their history, the southern Arabian kingdoms and northern imperial powers had tried to control the interior deserts in order to protect the trade routes, but no political organization in the desert ever lasted long. The nomadic Arab-Bedouins retained their independence and their ancient pagan culture, unaffected by the external political powers. Only the Christian bishops of Abyssinia made some progress, establishing bishoprics in the largest camps during the early seventh century. The influence of these men may have been a factor in the formation of a confederation of tribes that defeated Persia in 604 or 611—the date is uncertain. This battle meant little to the Persians, but for the Arabs it became a symbol of their strength in unity.

While the interior of the peninsula was an unorganized world of nomadic tribes, the coast had several important towns, which served as way stations along the trade route. They comprised many tribal units, which maintained their identity within the towns, so that the structure of the urban society was like a coalition of independent groups. Medina and Mecca were two of the most important of these towns. Their tribes participated in the international trade and cooperated in trying to control the Bedouin tribes in their vicinities. The independent role of the Arab traders increased as the great powers to the north weakened one another in constant war. At the beginning of the seventh century, this independent action, together with the experience of victory over the Persians, generated a kind of Arab ethnic movement in the peninsula. The coastal cities led the movement, and Mohammed, born about 570 into a leading Meccan tribe, became the principal figure in it.

About 610, Mohammed began to tell friends and relatives about religious experiences. About three years later, he began to speak of these revelations publicly, and a small following formed around him. Soon opposition and hostility also formed, which eventually drove him from Mecca.

The basic tenets of Mohammed's religion were that God is good and omnipotent; that he will judge all men on the last day and assign them to heaven (the garden) or hell (the fire); that man should be grateful to God and should worship him for making the world as it is; that God expects man to be generous with his wealth; and that Mohammed is the prophet of God to teach them and warn them about the last judgment. These precepts, while clearly influenced by the Jewish and Christian religions, were not copied directly from them. Rather, they arose from the social and economic conditions in Mecca, which had won control of the caravan route and was suffering from the ills of a successful commercial economy.

The leading merchants naturally objected to a teaching that urged all to be generous with the income of God's world, and they tried to get Mohammed's clan to silence him. But his kin protected him until about 619, when there was a change in its leadership. The new chief had become prosperous in commerce himself, and he was not inclined to continue to protect the prophet. He began by putting pressure on Mohammed to cease his preaching, and when Mohammed failed to find another protector in Mecca, he left for Medina, where he had powerful followers. This emigration took place in 622.

The journey to Medina, the *hegira* (journey), became the foundation of Islam. Moslems reckon their years from the *hegira*. (In English, the notation attached to dates is "A[fter] H[egira].") In Medina, Mohammed created an Islamic community, and his revelations established the rules by which such a community should live. He instituted dietary rules similar to those of the Jews, prohibited the drinking of wine, gambling, and usury (the charging of interest on loans). He set up a legal system that substituted arbitration for blood feud, prohibited infanticide, and regulated inheritance, so that the rights of orphans and widows were secure. He put limits on polygamy and divorce: no man could have more than four wives at one time, and a wife was not to be sent away penniless.

Soon after he settled in Medina, Mohammed and his followers began attacking Meccan caravans. By 628, this raiding had evolved into a constant, unexciting, warfare, but then Mohammed created a dramatic event. With about 1,500 followers, he joined the annual pilgrimage to the holy shrine of the Kaaba located in Mecca. The Meccans naturally barred the gates to him, and he opened negotiations with them. In these talks, his personal charisma saved a difficult situation. He worked out a compromise with the Meccans according to which he could return the next year, when the Meccans would evacuate their town for three days.

During the next year, Mohammed was able to incorporate local Bedouin tribes into the Islamic state of Medina, and when he returned to Mecca in 629, its leaders recognized the futility of resistance and submitted to him. After this, the Meccan tribes supplied much of the leadership of the Islamic state, although its administrative center remained in Medina.

The Christian View of Islam

John of Damascus, the famous defender of icons during the iconoclast controversy, was a subject of the Ommayyad caliphs and served in their government. In one of his works, he gave the Christian view of Islam, which he treated as a heresy rather than as a separate religion.

There is also the still-prevailing deceptive superstition of the Ishmaelites, the fore-runner of the Antichrist [a term John used for those who denied the divinity of Christ]. It takes its origin from Ishmael, who was born to Abraham from Hagar. . . . Until the times of Heraclius [610–41] they were, undoubtedly, idolaters. From that time on a false prophet appeared among them, surnamed Mame*th*, who, having casually been exposed to the Old and the New Testament and supposedly encountered an Arian monk, formed a heresy of his own. And after, by pretence, . . . he spread rumors that a scripture was brought down to him from heaven. Thus, having drafted some pronouncements in his book, worthy [only] of laughter, he handed it down to them in order that they may comply with it.

From John of Damascus, *On heresies,* ed. and trans. by D. J. Sahas, *John of Damascus on Islam* (Leiden, Brill, 1972), p. 133.

The Foundation of the Arabic Empire

War among the Bedouin tribes had been endemic until Mohammed was able to suppress it. In the first decades of the Islamic state, its leaders turned the militarism of the Arabs to the uses of the religion. In time, Islamic thinkers developed a religious rationale for the war that was fought for God—the *jihad.*

In 630, Mohammed led an army north against the Byzantine territories. He also condoned Bedouin attacks on the Persian Empire, which had been weakened by the victories of Heraclius and the murder of Shah Khusro II (628). Before his death in June, 632, Mohammed had also extended his influence into the Yemenite kingdom.

The prophet had made no provision

for succession to his authority. After his death there was a brief crisis that was resolved by the election of one of his earliest followers, Abu Bakr, as caliph (representative or vicar of the Prophet). Abu Bakr (r. 632–34) succeeded in maintaining the alliances in Arabia and of completing its unification.

Abu Bakr's successor Omar (r. 634–44) started the conquests that created a new empire. Damascus fell in 635, Jerusalem in 638, and all of Syria and Palestine were soon under the control of the Arabs. Jerusalem became the third holy city of Islam. In 637 the Bedouin alliance that had earlier attacked Persia took its capital, Ctesiphon, and soon the whole Persian Empire was ruled by Arabs. In 643, Arab raiders from Persia entered India for the first time. Meanwhile, Egypt was conquered between 640 and 642—although the Byzantines held on to Alexandria until 646—and Arab armies marched along the North African coast as far as Tripoli. In the Mediterranean an Arab fleet from the coastal cities of Palestine and Syria defeated the Byzantines and occupied Cyprus by the middle of the seventh century. The Arab navy kept constant pressure on Constantinople until Leo the Isaurian defeated it in 718.

The government of this new empire was a theocracy. Like Mohammed, the caliphs exercised both spiritual and secular authority; Islam recognized, and still recognizes, no distinction between the two types of authority. The central government controlled the new provinces through tribal colonies. Mohammed had tried unsuccessfully to suppress the tribal society of the peninsula to create a single Islamic society, but his successors used the old social units to control the conquered territories. Tribes settled in isolated communities from which military and administrative functions were carried out. Each of these centers had a governor appointed by the central government in Medina.

The Arabs retained their desert culture and did not mingle with the sub-

The Growth of the Islamic Empire   632–750

ject populations, which in many places were highly civilized. The conquerors came to view their empire as "a garden protected by our spears." When the caliphs needed to build fleets, it was the provincial populations that provided them and that served in the navy. Furthermore, the new imperial power, though a theocracy, did not enforce conversion to Islam. Non-Moslems had to pay a heavy land tax and could not serve in governmental positions, but they suffered no other disabilities.

The Islamic State

Mohammed's mission lasted from about 610 until his death in 632, and he continued to utter revelations to the end. His followers memorized his revelations—called *koran*—written down under the third caliph, Othman (r. 644–56) in a book, the *Koran*, the holy book of Islam.

The other part of the prophet's legacy was his practice (*sunna*) as head of the *umma*, the community of Islam, which formed a state. Mohammed's successors discussed the nature of his practice and the meaning of this or that action for the governance of the state. Memories of the *sunna* could not be written down in exact terms, so that discussion and dispute over them were continual.

From the beginning, the religious nature of the Islamic state has meant that religious disagreement nearly always has a political consequence, and vice versa. The first civil war in the *umma* led to the creation of the politico-religious parties that still dominate in the Islamic world.

The war originated from a long dispute over the succession to the caliphate. Omar, the second caliph, had confirmed that the electoral process was the proper way to determine the succession, but when a Persian slave murdered him in 644 the electors had a difficult choice. While all agreed that the succession must remain within the Hashimites, the clan to which the prophet had belonged (named for Mohammed's grandfather), this family, like all other powerful clans, was an extended community that included both direct descendants of Hashim and those who had married into the clan. In 644, the two leading members of the clan were Ali, Mohammed's cousin who had married the Prophet's daughter Fatima, and Othman, an Ommayyad who had married two of the Prophet's other daughters.

The decision went to Othman, a wealthy and urbane man, but he turned out to be unable to deal with the growing financial problems of the Empire, and Ali encouraged and exploited opposition to him. Othman was accused of violating the *sunna*, and in 656 he was murdered by Arab malcontents, among whom were some men of high standing connected with Ali's party.

The murder led to a civil war between Ali and Othman's relative, Mu'awiya, who was governor of Syria and demanded the blood revenge permitted by the Koran. After inconclusive skirmishing, the choice of the new ca-

Mohammed choosing Ali as his heir.

liph was handed over to two arbitrators, who found themselves divided. But some fanatical supporters of Ali withdrew from his host claiming that it was contrary to the Koran to arbitrate the dispute. Ali had the dissidents, called Kharijites ("those who withdrew or rebelled"), massacred, and in 658 a Kharijite murdered Ali. Mu'awiya was then able to get himself elected caliph and to persuade Ali's sons to acquiesce in the new regime. The new caliph moved the capital of the Islamic state to Damascus and did away with the elective principle in the caliphate.

The contest between Othman and Ali was the basis of an enduring division within Islam between the Shi'ites (the party of Ali) and the Sunnis. Ali's claim to the caliphate rested on his hereditary rights, but he also opposed his rival on religious grounds, claiming to be a stricter follower of the Koran and the *sunna* of the Prophet than Mu'awiya. The party of Mu'awiya responded that the Ommayyads preserved the truly orthodox *sunna*, and, its victory made the Sunnis the orthodox party of Islam. For their part, the Kharijites also developed distinctive religious veiws and remained a force in the Islamic world.

Even after the Ommayyads gained control of the caliphate, the *umma* remained a community divided and difficult to govern. Arabic society was tribal, and even Mohammed had failed to suppress the ancient tribal authority. The first caliphs seem to have recognized the permanence of tribal society, and they permitted, if they did not promote, the survival of tribal organization in the arrangements they made to garrison the newly conquered territories. They sequestered the troops in tribal camps, so that Arabs would not mix with the conquered populations. Significantly, this policy seems to have been first developed in Persia, which had been conquered by tribal armies under the aegis, but not under the control, of the Prophet and the caliphs. The armies in Persia were settled at Kufa and Basra in lower Mesopotamia,

and these camps soon became substantial tribal cities, like Mecca and Medina themselves.

While one can speak, therefore, of a *Pax Islamica* within which there developed a universal civilization and commerce, the Arab Empire did not achieve the degree of administrative and political unity that its predecessors the Roman and Persian Empires, or its contemporary the Byzantine Empire, achieved. Several causes contributed to the character of the Arab Empire, but the most important were probably geographical and social; in large areas of the Empire the tribal society worked best. The geography of the new Empire favored the nomadic, tribal society, which was privileged anyway under Islamic law, and made it difficult for a distant central government to establish a settled imperial system.

From the beginning of the Islamic movement, the Arabs regarded themselves as the people of God, and, under Islamic law, they enjoyed substantial privileges—freedom from taxation and the right to serve in the army and in government being the two most important. The persistence of the Arabian character of the state caused strains among the ethnic groups within the Empire. Every opponent of the caliphate could count on support from the oppressed or insulted *mawali*, the non-Arab converts to Islam.

THE OMMAYYADS

The Ommayyad dynasty (661–750) represented the victory of the Arab aristocracy of the cities over the Bedouins who had carried out the conquests under the theocracy of Medina. Under Mu'awiya and his successors, the conquests resumed, although at a slower pace than earlier. The new caliphs were interested in organizing and exploiting their territories, and this took time. Slight progress was made in Asia Minor, where the Hellenistic population led by the emperor in Constantinople put up stiff resistance. In the

Early Islamic calligraphy. Calligraphy was highly developed by Moslem artisans in part because of the religious proscription on representational art.

north, Arab armies reached the Caucasus Mountains between the Black and Caspian Seas and pushed into Samarkand, where they could control the route from central Asia to the Middle East and India. In India, the caliph's forces crossed the Indus River around 710 and succeeded in establishing a loosely governed territory in the Sindh (modern Pakistan). Within a generation the Arab governors had suppressed the local rulers and organized the region, including portions of the Punjab and Kashmir, into a province of the Empire. The Indians were then able to check further expansion, but it is clear from Indian sources that the Indians did not fully recognize the nature of the threat, for they knew virtually nothing of what had happened in the Middle East.

This push east was matched by one to the west. At the end of the seventh century, Arab armies moved westward from Tripoli, but they met stiff resistance from the Byzantine garrisons, supported by the Berber tribes of the North African desert. Carthage finally fell in 698, after the Byzantine fleet bringing reinforcements was defeated. In the aftermath of this success, the Berbers converted to Islam and joined the march west. Morocco was occupied within the next ten years. In 711, the Berber leader Tarik led a force across the Straits of Gibraltar (gib-al-Tarik, the rock of Tarik) into Visigothic Spain.

The Berbers or Moors attacked the Visigothic kingdom when it was disrupted by internecine war, so the conquest was relatively easy. Within a few months, Toledo, the capital, fell. Then, Arab reinforcements from North Africa came over and assisted in the capture of fortified cities, such as Seville, that had held out. After a brief period of consolidation, the new Islamic rulers controlled the entire peninsula, except

for a narrow band of territory along the southern foothills of the Pyrenees, where the Christian kingdom of Asturias held on to a precarious existence. In 720, the Moors and their allies crossed the Pyrenees into Septimania, which became a base for raids to the north. Throughout the eighth century, the Franks struggled to push the Moors back into the Iberian Peninsula.

Under the Ommayyad dynasty, the Arabs continued their lenient policy toward the religion and culture of the conquered peoples. They taxed non-Moslems heavily, but otherwise left them alone. Nonetheless, the pace of conversion to Islam accelerated during the seventh and eighth centuries. It is not clear why this happened. Perhaps the non-Arabs wanted to escape the taxes or to achieve a measure of power in the government of their territories.

The movement had two main effects. First, it created a fiscal problem, and the caliphs were constantly concerned about whether the new Moslems should pay taxes anyway. If they did not pay, the budget could not be balanced, so that most caliphs sought ways to keep up the payments. This caused dissent among the new converts and gave opponents of the government a ready audience. Second, the new converts usually attached themselves to Arab noblemen, seeking protection and support, and, therefore, the movement created a new society of clients coalesced around Arab leaders.

This development may have contributed to a peculiar feature of the Arab Empire—that the language of the Arab nomads won out over the languages of highly civilized subject peoples. The victory of Arabic was not difficult in Syria and Palestine, where the populations spoke related Semitic languages, but in Persia, Egypt, and North Africa, it was not to be expected. The Ommayyads encouraged the transition by making Arabic the official language of government, but the dominance of the language rested primarily on the Arabic intellectual and literary culture that began to develop during the Ommayyad period.

The most popular literary genre was poetry, which had been the principal form of literature in pre-Islamic Arabia. Ommayyad poets wrote romantic and satirical poetry, as well as odes to the good life. Among the poets there were Christians as well as Moslems, indicating the success of the caliphs' policy of toleration. The new imperial bureaucracy also developed Arabic into a language capable of meeting the prosaic needs of government. In order for Arabic, a language of the desert, to function as a language of officialdom, the educated bureaucrats had to enlarge its vocabulary and to give it a formal grammatical structure. The new grammar made the language more precise and regular than it had been and made it possible for foreigners to learn it quickly. The new Arabic language was also a good medium for theology, philosophy, and history, but the earliest

works of Islamic thinkers date only from the end of the Ommayyad period. Few of their works survive, but quotations from them were incorporated into later writings.

The Ommayyads also founded the tradition of Arabic architecture and decorative arts. In Damascus, they built a great mosque, a place of prayer, in a new form, influenced by the Roman basilica. The building had a long nave and side aisles and was copied elsewhere in the Empire. In Jerusalem, the dynasty built another great mosque on the rock sacred to the Jews, the Dome of the Rock, which was a building that enclosed a great central space under the dome. This structure exerted a substantial influence on the architects of other buildings in the Islamic world.

The dynasty also built desert palaces and developed a distinctive domestic architecture. The Ommayyads preferred to spend most of their time in hunting lodges and desert residences, and in time these attained impressive size and decoration, containing apartments, private mosques, baths, and formal gardens. In this period, the

The Great Mosque in Damascus, Syria, begun in the late seventh century.

The Dome of the Rock in Jerusalem. This mosque was built on the spot from which Mohammed was believed to have ascended to heaven.

an alien physical and cultural environment.

The Ommayyad caliphs had maintained the distinction between Arab and non-Arab (*mawali*), even after the actual power of government had long been in the hands of *mawali* secretaries and generals. By the eighth century, the *mawali* were a majority of the community of Islam, and the conditions were good for a major change in the caliphate.

THE ABBASID REVOLUTION

The Ommayyads made claims to orthodoxy, but they established a court that scandalized many Moslems. Damascus and the various desert palaces of the caliphs became centers of luxury that offended hardy Arab tribesmen and gave the *mawali* an opportunity for just complaint. Moreover, the Ommayyads associated with non-Moslems and copied Byzantine governmental institutions that were unfamiliar and suspect to men of the desert. The Ommayyads protected the large Christian and Jewish communities of Syria, and educated men of both communities served the caliphate, often in high positions. Their presence contributed to the secular image of Ommayyad government.

The Ommayyads faced almost continual financial crisis, and their measures to bring the budget under control generated opposition among the subject populations, which had become progressively Islamicized. Furthermore, despite a constant struggle to do so, the caliphs could not establish regular administrative control over the provinces. When provincial governors felt threatened, they often rebelled with the support of both tribal contingents and the local *mawali*. The leader of each rebellion justfied himself by making charges of heterodoxy against the caliph.

The endemic war with the Byzantines also caused opposition to the central government. Through a century of

opposition between town and country (desert) became established as a perennial feature of Islamic civilization. Under the Ommayyads, the urbanized populations of Syria and other regions adopted Arabic and created Arabic civilization, while paradoxically the Arabs themselves kept to the desert and held on to their ancient bedouin values. The great hunting lodges of the Ommayyads represented both worlds of the empire. They were symbols of the draw of the desert milieu, but they were also islands of urban comfort in

warfare, the balance of victories went to Constantinople, and the caliphs put enormous fiscal resources into the effort without winning either spoils or territory. Even though the caliphs' armies made progress to the east—leading to the establishment of Moslem states in the Transoxiana and in the Indus Valley—few of the Ommayyads could base their authority on a reputation as a great conqueror.

The main center of opposition to Damascus was in Iraq, the old heartland of the Persian Empire, but it was in the Persian province of Khurasan, on the plains south of the Oxus River, that the final rebellion of the Ommayyad period took place, in the aftermath of another in the series of civil wars among rivals in the Ommayyad clan. In 747, the victor in this war, Marwan II (r. 749–50), consolidated his power over the provincial governors, and the governor of Khurasan rebelled.

Detail from a portal of an Ommayyad palace in Syria (*ca.* 720).

The new rebellion united tribal and religious rivalries with the anti-Arab feelings of the *mawali*. Abu Muslim, an official of Persian descent, rose in the name of the Shi'ite *imam* Ibrahim, a descendant of Abbas (hence Abbasids), who had held a position in Kufa, the center of Shi'ism. After Ali's assassination, the sons of Ali had been able to establish themselves in Kufa, where the Yemenite tribesmen, who had a tradition of hereditary kingship, favored the rights of the house of Mohammed.

In 680, Ali's son al-Husain was murdered during a rebellion against the Ommayyads, becoming the first martyr of Islam. His descendants, inheriting his earthly role, came to be regarded as imams, divinely inspired leaders. A rebellion in the name of Ali's family in 685 added another element to the political religion of the Shi'ites. When the imam in whose name it was waged was killed, his followers claimed that he had only been hidden away by God and would come again when the time was right. This belief in the hidden imam, the *mahdi*, became part of Shi'ite theology.

By the late 740s, the missionaries of the Abbasid imams had created a community of believers in Khurasan, and Abu Muslim gathered it to his rebellion by declaring himself to be the servant of Ibrahim. The Ommayyads succeeded in imprisoning Ibrahim, who died in captivity, but they could not muster an army that could defeat Abu Muslim's forces. In November 749, Abu Muslim had Abu'l-Abbas, Ibrahim's brother, declared caliph in Kufa; in early 750, Abu defeated and executed Marwan.

The Abbasids are regarded as having brought about a revolution in Islam. Although they represented the old Arab leadership and claimed the caliphate as members of Mohammed's clan, the change of dynasty accelerated the integration of the *mawali*, particularly the Persians, into the society and politics of the *umma*. When the second Abbasid caliph, al-Mansur, built a new capital just a few miles from the old

Hunting scene woven into a seventh-century fabric.

Persian capital at a place called by the Persian name Baghdad, he completed the transition, not from an Arab to a Persian empire, but rather from an Arab to an Islamic one.

Al-Mansur (r. 754–75) relied principally on Persian servants, particularly Khalid b. Barmak, whose family continued in power until 803, and the new government was soon run by a Persian bureaucracy under a new official, called the Wazir or Vizier—a kind of prime minister. As a result, the court absorbed a great deal of the old Persian culture, and like the old Persian shahs, the caliphs became inaccessible within an elaborate palace community of officials and eunuchs.

Soon after they came to power, the Abbasids began to favor the Sunnis, turning away from their tradition of Shi'ism. They did this because the Sunnis constituted the majority of Islam and because Shi'ism was deeply divided. Early in its history, the dynasty had to face two Shi'ite rebellions.

THE ABBASID CALIPHATE

The first thing the Abbasids did was to carry out a systematic massacre of the Ommayyad clan, missing only one young boy. That boy, Abd al-Rahman, escaped to Spain, where he established an independent Ommayyad caliphate at Cordova. Thereafter, Spain remained permanently outside the political power of Baghdad.

Under al-Mansur progress was made in bringing the provinces, except Spain and the Maghrib (Tunisia, Algeria, and Morocco), back into obedience. In the Maghrib, the ancient Berber tribes reasserted their independence, as they had throughout the period of Roman domination, and they were able to resist all the forces sent by the central government.

In essence, gaining control over the provinces meant either forcing the provincial governors, the emirs, to give homage to the caliph or sending new, loyal governors to take their places.

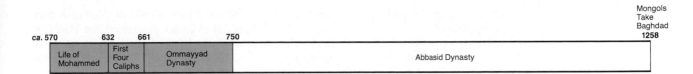

The finances of the central government depended on the power of the governors, because taxes were collected by them. Most rebellions began when an emir withheld tax revenues from the caliph's government.

On the whole, the move from Damascus to Baghdad reduced the competition between the caliphate and Constantinople, but in the later eighth century, the old conflict revived. The Byzantine emperors were still concerned with consolidating their eastern provinces and frontier, so endemic warfare continued in that region. Al-Mansur's son, al-Mahdi (r. 775–85), fought the Byzantines for years with considerable success, but his reign was also troubled by rebellions and by a resurgence of the Manichaeans.

The Manichaeans were followers of Mani, a Persian priest of the third century, who had combined the old Persian religion, Zoroastrianism, with Christianity. The result was a belief in two world powers, one of good and one of evil, locked in a titanic struggle for supremacy. The religion troubled both Islam and Christianity for centuries. Augustine, one of the greatest fathers of Latin Christianity, went through a Manichaean phase during his youth, and the sect reappeared in Europe in the late eleventh century. Al-Mahdi carried out terrible purges of the Manichaeans, but the majority of the people he purged were not members of the religion. The caliph seems to have used the Manichaean threat as an excuse for purifying Islam both of its religious enemies and of its caliph's enemies.

Al-Mahdi introduced Persian customs and ceremonies to the caliph's court. He spent most of his time in leisure, but the government was run, and run well, by his Persian Wazir and secretaries. Under him the court of Baghdad became a great center of art and entertainment.

Westerners became aware of the splendor of the Islamic court during the reign of Harun al-Rashid (r. 786–809). Al-Rashid was in contact with the Frankish king Charlemagne, from whom he received two embassies. In his turn, al-Rashid sent spectacular gifts (including an elephant) to Charlemagne. The purpose of these exchanges seems to have been the planning of a joint attack on Ommayyad Spain, but it never occurred. Al-Rashid carried out massive raids in Asia Minor, and his army reached the Aegean Sea in 798, when the Byzantine government was in confusion under Irene (see pp. 189–90).

Nonetheless, al-Rashid faced many difficulties. He had to recognize the *de facto* independence of the Maghrib, where he granted the governor an independent authority in return for a substantial annual payment to the caliph's treasury. The governor was also permitted to pass his position on to his heirs. Thus was born the Aghlabid emirate of North Africa, which became very aggressive toward Christendom a couple of decades later. In 827, Aghlabid forces began the conquest of Sicily. They attacked Rome itself in 846 and were a menace to the coastal cities of Italy throughout the ninth century.

Al-Rashid's government was run by the Barmakids, the Persian family that had risen to prominence under al-Mansur. These men sought to effect a settlement between the Abbasids and Shi'ites, and they encouraged active discourse on law, philosophy, and theology in the hope of finding a common ground for reconciliation. When the Shi'ites rebelled, the Barmakids were suspected of favoring them, and the family fell from power in 803. The event made a deep impression on contemporaries.

After al-Rashid's death (809), the Empire disintegrated politically. Khurasan became independent under a Persian dynasty (820). A rebel leader disrupted Azerbaijan (the region around the south shore of the Caspian Sea) and could not be defeated. Refugees from Spain, which was troubled by internecine conflict, took Crete from the Byzantines and held it for 135 years. These same people also stirred things up in Egypt. The spiritual authority of the caliphs was still recognized, except by their religious enemies, but their political power was rapidly diminishing to the point of their becoming merely one among many ruling dynasties.

However, al-Rashid's successors continued to support intellectuals, and their court remained the center of Islamic civilization. Al-Rashid's son, al-Ma'mun (r. 813–33) founded a university, the House of Wisdom, and built several observatories for the study of astronomy. In trying to reconcile the many strains of Islam, he encouraged religious thinkers to rely on Greek philosophy as a basis for a comprehensive dogmatic theology of Islam.

Toward the middle of the ninth century, the Turks appeared for the first time in the history of the Islamic world. The long experience of undependable armies, which had plagued their predecessors, led the caliphs to create a force of Turkish slaves, and thus the era of the slave armies began. The Turks were Asiatic tribes that had moved into Turkestan, the region north of the Transoxiana. During the 840s, the Turkish slave army grew to enormous size—some sources say 70,000 men—and caused such havoc in Baghdad that the caliph Mutawakkil (r. 846–61) built a new residence for the government and its troops at Samara, some distance from the city.

The Turks provided a force loyal to the caliph's family, but of course conflict within the family disturbed this relationship. In 861, Mutawakkil was killed by Turkish officers while he was trying to enforce his authority against one of his sons. The decade following his death was a period of anarchy. Eastern Persia broke away immediately upon Mutawakkil's death and remained independent until about 910. A Turkish officer, Tulun, who was provincial governor in Egypt and had with him a large slave army, seized control

Islam   *ca.* 888

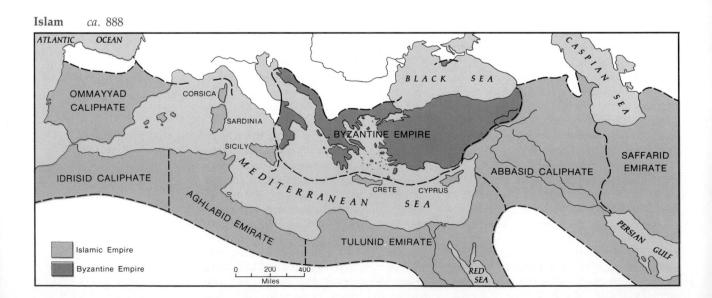

Early mosque and minaret,
Samara, Syria (*ca.* 850).

of the province in 871, and his family maintained itself there until 905. But these independence movements were not as great a threat as the slave revolt that broke out in southern Mesopotamia in 868.

As in other ancient societies, slavery was common in the Islamic world, and the Koran condoned it, while encouraging emancipation. In most places, slaves were used either as soldiers or as personal secretaries and servants, and the frequency with which one reads of freedmen suggests that many gained their freedom. In this respect, Islamic society was like those of Greece and Rome, where former slaves, while stigmatized, nevertheless could achieve successful careers. However, in the lower valleys of the Tigris and Euphrates, masses of black African slaves worked sugar plantations under horrible conditions, and it was they who rebelled in 868, starting a reign of terror. The caliphs were unable to crush the rebellion until 883.

The victory over the slaves signaled a period of recovery under the last able Abbasid caliph—al-Muktafi (r. 902–08). Under his successors the government became very unstable because of financial problems. The provinces, on which the system rested, were either too independent or too troubled to obey the central government's demands for the taxes. In 924, the government found it necessary to put a military officer, the Turk Mu'nis, in control, and he succeeded in transforming the government into a military dictatorship. Except for brief periods in the 930s, the caliphs were henceforth figureheads for an emirate in Baghdad itself.

The trouble that forced the civilian government to submit its authority to the army in 924 was caused by the rise of the Isma'ili movement, which had established an anti-caliphate in north Africa in 909.

THE ISMA'ILIS AND THE RISE OF FATIMID CALIPHS

The Isma'ili party was a splinter group of the Shi'ites. Al-Husain the first martyr of Islam, was a son of Ali by Fatima, and the imams of his line succeeded one another without incident for six generations, until Ja'far. He found reason to disinherit his eldest son and presumed heir Isma'il, who he said did not follow the tenets of Islam. Ja'far named his younger son Musa as next in line for the imamate. Although the question of succession became moot when Isma'il predeceased his father, a small party of Husainites held by Isma'il's right of succession and became the Seveners (that is, seven generations) or Isma'ilis. Musa succeeded as imam in 765, and his line lasted until the twelfth imam disappeared in Baghdad in the middle 870s. His followers, who were the main body of Husainites, were called the Twelvers. The Seveners believed that Isma'il was the *mahdi*, the hidden imam who would return to lead Islam into the true religion. In 909 a group of Isma'ilis seized control of North Africa. Once in power, they proclaimed the *mahdi*, in the person of Ubaid Allah al-Mahdi, as caliph in opposition to the Abbasids.

The ultimate goal of the Fatimid caliphs was to replace the Abbasids as as the true leaders of Islam. Ubaid's son, al-Ka'im (r. 934–46), built a fleet that terrorized the central Mediterranean. It attacked the coast of France and raided all over Italy. It also made a third attempt—the first two had been made unsuccessfully by Ubaid—to conquer Egypt as the first step in the progress toward Baghdad. The conquest was finally accomplished in 969 by al-Ka'im's grandson, al-Mu'izz (r. 953–75).

By 959, al-Mu'izz had control of almost all of North Africa to the Atlantic Ocean. The Ommayyads of Spain, who had extended their influence to the region, were confined to small enclaves near Gibraltar. During the first 15 years of his reign, al-Mu'izz also established the Fatimid military and administrative systems, which lasted into the fifteenth century. These accomplishments were the work of two of his ministers, neither of them native Arabs. His general was Jawhar, an Islamicized Greek slave, who led the conquest of North Africa and then of Egypt. Recognizing the strategic importance of a site in the Nile Delta and the danger posed by the Byzantines, now that they had recaptured Crete (961), Jawhar and al-Mu'izz built a new capital at Cairo, which soon became famous as one of the most beautiful cities in the Mediterranean world.

The architect of Fatamid fiscal and administrative policies was al-Mu'izz's wazir Ya'qub b. Killis, an Islamicized Jew from Baghdad, who served both al-Mu'izz and his successor al-'Aziz (r. 975–96). Through enlightened taxation and other measures, Ya'qub and his masters encouraged trade through Egypt and the Red Sea to East Asia and built a navy to protect Egyptian ports. Alexandria became, as it had been in Hellenistic and Roman times, one of the world's great emporia, and the new commercial powers in Italy—Amalfi, Venice, and Genoa—sent their merchants there to buy silks and spices for the growing European market.

The Fatimids reached out to the whole Mediterranean world to create their success and the brilliance of their court. Al-'Aziz was so much a part of that international world that he married a Christian, appointed Christians to high office, and permitted Jews and Christians to live without persecution or constraint. He also created a Turkish slave army in order to control the Berber troops that Jawhar had led to Egypt, but this led to great racial strife.

The ibn-Tulun Mosque in Cairo, Egypt (eighth century).

He died in 996 at the age of 41, and under his son Al-Hakim (r. 996–1021), who was then 13, the caliphate quickly declined.

Al-Hakim instituted a persecution of Jews and Christians and destabilized the government by executing one after another of the ministers and generals he appointed. He had the habit of going out secretly at night, and during one of these perambulations, in 1021, he disappeared. His body was never found.

Already under al-'Aziz the Fatimids' push to Baghdad had lost momentum. The resurgence of the Byzantines under Basil II presented a danger to Egypt and North Africa. The Fatimids had become increasingly conservative, and they had lost the support of fanatical Isma'ilis who held the territory between Egypt and Baghdad. Finally, the caliphate of Baghdad had become strong enough to resist the Fatimid threat, and the independent Turks were also too strong.

THE RISE OF THE TURKS

The Background of Turkish Power

The Turkish troops had asserted themselves at times of weakness during the ninth century, particularly in the 860s when they made and unmade caliphs at a rapid rate, but after 945 Turkish power was checked by the Buyids, a family from Azerbaijan that seized power in Baghdad and installed its own candidate as caliph.

The Buyids were Shi'ites who were aligned against the Isma'ili tradition and who did not supplant Sunni orthodoxy. They were rarely united themselves, and for most of the period of

Buyid domination the various provinces of Iraq and Persia were governed by competing scions of the Buyid clan.

The political competition that preoccupied the Buyid rulers engendered an era of peace for outsiders living within the caliphate. The Christians, principally members of sects considered heretical by both the Greek and Latin churches, became important in the cultural life of the caliphate. Through them Greek learning continued to exert a great influence on Arabic intellectual life. The Jews also enjoyed a period of peace and prosperity. During the tenth and eleventh centuries they were much better off in the provinces of the Baghdad and Ommayyad caliphates (the Middle East and Spain) than their coreligionists were in Europe. In the Islamic Empire, both Jews and Christians found employment as teachers and government functionaries during this period.

Buyid power was restricted to Iraq and the areas along the southern flank of the Caucasus. To the west, the Hamdanids controlled northern Syria and upper Mesopotamia, centered on the old city of Aleppo. This dynasty was historically important because it patronized artists and scholars. It also helped keep the Buyids in check. To the east, Persian dynasties like the Samanids of Khurasan, established themselves.

The Samanids were significant for many reasons. They encouraged the revival of Persian as a language of science and poetry, and under them court poets and writers created "New Persian" or Farsi. This language was written in the Arabic alphabet and borrowed many Arab words, but it was

The Eastern Islamic World

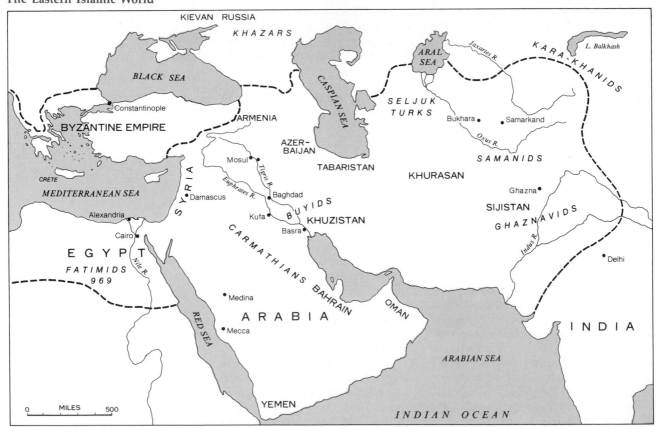

Persian and remains the language of Iran to this day.

The Samanids also had a great effect as the patrons of missionary activity among the Turkish tribes who lived beyond the Transoxiana. This conversion was of great historical importance because it made it impossible for the Samanids to resist the Turks when they began to migrate into the Transoxiana. The dynasty could not organize a holy war, a *jihad*, against fellow Moslems. Under attack from the Turks, Samanid power collapsed between 999 and 1004.

The Turkish Dynasty of Ghazna: Afghanistan and India

Still further east, in the region that is now Afghanistan, a Turkish military leader in service to the Samanids established another dynasty at Ghazna. The Ghaznavids, as they were called, rose to prominence on the ruins of Samanid authority, gaining control of the southern and eastern regions of Persia under the great ruler Mahmud (r. 998–1030). Mahmud was the patron of Firdawsi, the Persian poet whose great epic poem, the *Shah-nama*, is considered one of the masterpieces of Islamic Persian literature.

Mahmud's historical importance is based on his activities in India. The small Islamic principalities that had been established in the Indus Valley during the early eighth century had remained in place for three centuries without expanding their power or influence. They continued to be important in the trade between India and the Middle East, but the bulk of that trade now went by sea to Fatimid Egypt. Mahmud gained control of these states and used them as a basis for annual campaigns beyond the Indus.

These campaigns opened India to Moslem missionaries, and opened the Islamic world to a new cultural influence. Mahmud patronized Islam's greatest intellectual, al-Biruni (973–*ca.* 1050), who ranks with Aristotle in both the breadth of his interests and achievements and in the perceptive-

ness of his intellect. In Mahmud's court, al-Biruni fell under the influence of Indian culture, which shows in his works on mathematics and astronomy, and he took the opportunity of the Indian campaigns to write a book (*ca.* 1030) on India itself. This remarkable description remains an important source of knowledge about medieval India.

The Coming of the Seljuks

Mahmud pushed west as well as east. By the end of his reign he had gained control of Khurasan and was ready to make an attempt on Iraq, where the Shi'ite Buyids still held sway. But this plan to reunify the caliphate under Sunni power was ruined by the irruption of the Seljuk Turks.

The Seljuks, named for an early chieftain, were nomadic people who broke away from the main Turkish confederation that had taken control of the Transoxiana. In the 1020s, they moved into Khurasan and threatened Ghaznavid power there. Mahmud's son and successor, Mas'ud I (r. 1030–1040), tried to stop them, but in 1040 the Seljuks defeated him in a decisive battle. Persia was now open to them, and Ghaznavid power was limited to the territories that are now Afghanistan and the Punjab in India, which Mahmud had organized as a Moslem state.

The Seljuks now followed Mahmud's plan themselves. They invaded Iraq and occupied Baghdad in 1055. In the next decades, they established their own empire within Islam, setting up a new form of political power. The Seljuk rulers did not hold an emirate, which was technically a governorship under the authority of the caliph, but a sultanate, which was an independent political power loyal to the caliph.

Under the sultan Alp Arslan (r. 1063–72), the Seljuks took Jerusalem in 1071 and destroyed the Byzantine army at the battle of Manzikert, in Armenia, in the same year. From this battle, unlike the hundreds of others between the seventh and the eleventh centuries, the Byzantines did not recover, and their pleas for help from the West led to the great expedition of Frankish knights, the First Crusade (1096). Under Alp Arslan's successor, Malik-Shah (r. 1072–92), the Seljuks took Damascus (1076) and established a powerful empire in the Middle East. Although they stopped the advance of Fatimid power, they could not conquer Egypt, and the schism in Islam continued until the rise of the Ottoman Turks in the fifteenth century.

The Seljuks renewed the Persian influence in the caliphate. Having absorbed Persian culture through the Samanid missionaries, they encouraged the use of Persian as the language of high culture and soon used it themselves, even in everyday life. Malik-Shah left the organization of his empire to a Persian wazir Nizam al-Mulk (r. 1018–92), who was one of the greatest of the Islamic prime ministers.

Nizam and his sultan initiated a Sunni renaissance, after the long period of Shi'ite rule under the Buyids. In 1067, Nizam founded a great school of law, which became the intellectual center of Sunni Islam. One student of this school, unsatisfied with the formalism of the law, became the principal theologian of Islam. This was al-Ghazzali (1058–1111), who wrote a massive work in which he stressed the importance of prayer and charity. His ideas gained acceptance and became the basis of modern Sunni religion. One important aspect of al-Ghazzali's work was his opposition to philosophy. The revived religion that rested on his theology turned away from philosophical and scientific speculation about the created world to concentrate on the experience of the individual Moslem. Consequently, his influence was a counterweight to the main tradition of Moslem intellectual life, and the classical age of Islamic civilization is generally said to have ended about 1200 as a result of this turn inward.

It was also during the reign of Malik-Shah that a splinter group of Isma'ilis settled in the mountains of northern Persia around the fortress of Alamut, not far from modern Tehran. The leader of this people, Hasan-i Sabbah, had hoped to find support for an anti-Seljuk (and anti-Sunni) rebellion, but when he received no support, he organized a terrorist movement, sending his agents to kill government functionaries and even rulers throughout the caliphate. These were suicide missions, and orthodox Moslems thought the perpetrators of them ate *hashish,* Indian hemp, before committing themselves to action. From the name of the drug, the Moslems called the terrorists "Assassins." Hasan-i died in 1124, but his movement lived on, and for generations the Assassins were feared in the Islamic world.

After the death of Malik-Shah the Seljuk empire broke into blocks controlled by individual leaders. There were Seljuk states in Asia Minor, Khurasan, Kirman (southwest of Khurasan), and Iraq. These were too occupied with local problems to oppose the European invaders of Syria and Palestine, who arrived in the First Crusade in the late 1090s. As a result, the crusaders were able to establish a Latin kingdom of Jerusalem, which sustained itself for several generatons.

Saladin and the Recovery of the Mediterranean Lands

The counterattack against the Christians began under Zengi, the Turkish governor of Mosul on the upper Tigris River. Zengi recaptured Edessa in 1144—stimulating the call for a second crusade in Europe—and his son Nur al-Din (r. 1146–74) completed the work of confining the Latins to small enclaves on the coast. Nur al-Din was a remarkable ruler, who earned a reputation for good government and honest justice. Under him Kurdish leaders from Iraq became important men and one of these, Saladin, became a great conqueror. Saladin rose to prominence in the defense of Egypt against attack by the Franks. By 1169, he was in control of Egypt.

In a short time, Saladin brought Egypt into a state of peace and prosperity and expelled the Franks from Damietta. After Nur al-Din's death in 1174, Saladin was able to win out over rivals to succeed him in Mosul. Saladin benefited from the weakness of the Byzantines, who were defeated again by the Seljuks in 1176 and who were preoccupied by dynastic troubles after the death of Emperor Manuel in 1180. In 1187, Saladin invaded the Latin kingdom of Jerusalem and crushed its army. At the end of the campaign, the Christians held the fortress city of Tyre and a strip of coast between Acre and Jaffa. In Europe, there was a call for a third crusade.

Saladin earned a reputation for good government and courtly manners. He had established a loosely united empire that included North Africa, Egypt, and the coastal regions of the Middle East up to Armenia. His family, the Ayyubids (named after Saladin's father Ayyub), ruled this empire for 60 years after his death in 1193. Under the Ayyubids, Egypt remained prosperous, though not militarily strong, and became important to the commercial cities of Italy.

THE MONGOL INVASION

Seljuk rule in northern Persia and the Transoxiana lasted until the 1150s, when a new people appeared out of Asia. The Seljuk government of Khwarazm collapsed as a result of war with Oghuz tribesmen from the steppe. At the same time, the Ghaznavids were overthrown by Ghurids, tribesmen from the foothills of the Hindu Kush who had recently been converted. A new, Persian dynasty, using the old Persian title "shah," rose in Khwarazm and by the end of the twelfth century, it had secured itself in its province and driven the Ghurids back beyond the Indus. In the first dec-

ades of the thirteenth century this dynasty, which was Shi'ite, tried to seize Baghdad, but in the midst of this effort, the shah made a fatal error.

In 1218, the shah's men massacred a caravan of merchants from Central Asia, where the Mongols had created an empire of nomads, and the ruler of the Mongols, Chengis (Ghengis) Khan, went to war over the incident. The khan arrived in Transoxiana in 1220 and overran it, using Chinese engineers to take the fortified towns by siege. In two years of campaigning, he totally destroyed the Kwarazmite state; then he returned to Mongolia.

In the next generation, the Mongols entered a new phase of expansionism. They conquered Russia and invaded eastern Europe, reaching the Adriatic in 1241. Fourteen years later, the Mongol army, which was a composite of Mongol, Turkish, and even Armenian and Georgian troops, moved into Persia and the Middle East. It began the campaign by utterly destroying the Isma'ili Assassins, and then in 1258 marched on Baghdad. After the caliph failed to respond quickly enough to a preemptory demand to open the gates, the Mongol army stormed the city. It is hard to believe the contemporary reports of the carnage that followed. The Mongol army virtually destroyed the entire city and the most conservative estimate of the loss of life is 800,000. Only the Christians, some of whose coreligionists were in the besieging army, were spared. The Abbasid caliphate, weak and often challenged for centuries, came to an end. The last of the line surrendered to the Mongols in 1258 and disappeared.

By 1260, the Mongol army was in Syria, but any plans its leadership might have had to establish a western Mongol khanate were interrupted by the death of the Great Khan in Mongolia. Most of the Mongol army withdrew to the Caucasus to await the succession, and the Mamluk Turks, who had gained control of Egypt in 1250, organized an effective Moslem resistance. In late 1260, a Mamluk army routed the Mongol forces left in Syria at Ain Jalut, near Nazareth, and broke the momentum of the khan's conquest. The battle also made Mamluk Egypt the most powerful state in Islam, until the rise of Ottoman Turks in the fifteenth century.

ISLAMIC SOCIETY AND ECONOMY

Arabian society was tribal, and tribal social values continued to be strong long after the establishment of the Empire. To this day, nomadic tribes dominate the social world of the arid regions. Yet, the regions the Arabs conquered were urbanized, and the basic values of imperial society were urban, not pastoral. The cities of the Islamic world had no special legal status. They did not become unified communes as they did in the West. They were dominated, rather than governed, by their leading families, which were in constant competition with one another. These families created districts, often walled, and enlisted the support of the lower classes to act as henchmen.

But there was some governmental organization in the towns, as is suggested by the existence of urban services. The towns had elaborate water systems—since the supply of water is a constant problem in the Middle East—

and roads and fortifications were well maintained. The trades occupied specific quarters, centered on the main mosque, and there is evidence that the tradesmen in the various crafts were organized into something like guilds. But virtually nothing is known about these organizations.

The Islamic commercial system also gave the towns a special role. As economic centers, the towns naturally provided the major markets and supplied most manufactured goods. But the government established warehouses for the long-distance traders. Here, the caravans brought their goods, paid duties, and distributed the goods to local people. The long-distance trade was kept separate from the local market, which was controlled by the town's own merchants.

The needs of commercial transactions were met by financial instruments that later became very important in the West. Islamic merchants developed the letter of credit to transfer money from one end of the Arab Empire to the other. A merchant in one city would pay the bearer of a letter a sum of money, knowing that his own agent would be paid by the bearer's principal another time. So long as there was a stable commercial relationship, with goods flowing in both directions, the principals could assume that the accounts would remain even. The merchants also developed the promissory note that has become the modern bank check. In fact, the word "check" probably derives from Arabic.

Islamic society was ethnically mixed and was less racist than either Byzantine or western society. The Arabs intermarried with local populations, and migrating peoples constantly added new elements to the mix. Since most caliphs were the sons of slave or low-born wives of their predecessors, there was little room in Islamic society for the feelings of racial purity so common in Constantinople or the Germanic kingdoms.

This reference to the caliphs' wives leads to a discussion of the Islamic fam-

An Islamic coin (698–99), the first silver coinage struck of purely Islamic type. The inscription in the center of the coin reads: "There is no God but God alone; no one is associated with him." The insistence on God's oneness and the denial of an associate to him is directed against the Christians and their doctrine of the Trinity.

ily and the condition of women. The Koran permitted Moslems to have four wives, and the Islamic law accepted slave concubines. In practice, only the wealthy could afford several wives and concubines, but most men above the lowest class had at least one of each. Therefore, the Moslem household was large, made up of wives and concubines, the children of each, and household slaves. Most families had at least one or two slaves, and slavery was generally confined to the household, except for the Turkish slave armies and the slaves on the sugar plantations near Basra in southern Iraq.

The large Moslem households were ruled by men. Men had dominated the heroic society of the desert, where tribal chiefs led small groups in their struggle against nature. In the desert, life depended on the cohesive operation of the group—on centralized control and on the qualities of the leader. The constant tests of those qualities gave the leading males honor or shame, which affected the cohesiveness of the group and the respect it earned from competing groups. Later Islamic society continued to be principally concerned with the honor of men. Status, achieved through the respect he won from others, determined a man's every prospect—his opportunity for trade and his ability to marry well. Every slight or injury was a challenge to a man's honor and had to be avenged, so that he could recover his honor and maintain his place in society. Consequently, feud was endemic in Islamic society.

Central to a man's self-image was his control over his women. In Islamic law women and men had virtually the same rights, but in life men dominated women. If anyone approached a Moslem man's wives or women servants, he suffered a shame that he saw as damaging to his status. It was injurious even to mention a man's wife. Thus, women were closely protected and went out of the house veiled, so that other men could not see and perhaps seduce them.

The Moslem's Behavior around Women

Mohammed ordered women to cover their beauty, lest they become a cause of sin.

And let them [women] not display their beauty and ornaments except what [must ordinarily] appear thereof. And let them draw their garment over their bosoms and not display their beauty except in the presence of their husbands, or their own fathers, or their husbands' fathers, or their own sons, or their husbands' sons, or their own brothers, or their brothers' sons, or their sisters' sons . . . .

Koran 24:31

In his treatise (thirteenth century) about the duties of the *muhtasib*, the law enforcement official of the medieval Islamic town, al-Ukhuwwa tells the muhtasib how to regulate the relations between men and women. The passage is headed "Reprehensible conduct."

The muhtasib must prevent people from placing themselves in dubious situations and from incurring suspicion. He must be timely in his warning and not hasten to punish . . . . The muhtasib may not interfere with a man and woman standing conversing in a frequented street and where their conduct shows no sign of offence. In an unfrequented street and in cases of doubt he must forbid them to continue yet must not be in haste to punish, for the woman may be closely related to the man. He must warn the man to keep the women of his family out of dubious situations . . . . The muhtasib must visit the places where women congregate, such as the thread and cotton markets, the river-banks, and the doorways of the women's bath-houses. Any young men found there without lawful business must be punished by the muhtasib.

From *The Ma'alim al-Qurba*, ed. and trans. by R. Levy (London: Luzac, 1938), pp. 9–10.

Within the household, which was the center of social life, Moslem men formed the harem, the separate quarters for the women. The harem was a locked section of the house where all the women and children lived. The harem consisted of several competing "families" (women with their children), each woman struggling to win the favor of the head of the household for herself and her children. Young girls were instructed by their mothers

Moslem Values and the Behavior of a Prince

In the late eleventh century, Kai Ka'us Ibn Iskandar, ruler of a principality south of the Caspian Sea, wrote a treatise on how to be a prince for his son and heir. His advice gives a good picture of conventional Islamic social values, but it also contains advice to act expediently when necessary.

Much as you would not be parsimonious over kindly words, so also, if you have the means, do not begrudge your material largesse; men are more often beguiled by money than by words. Be on your guard against places of doubtful repute and flee from a companion who sets an evil example in conduct and thought. Do not of your own accord venture into dubious situations, and go only to places where, being sought, you may be discovered without shame. . . . The basis of all virtues consists of knowledge, discipline of the flesh, piety, truth, pure faith, innocuity, sympathy and modesty. As for modesty, although it is said "Modesty is part of faith," yet it may frequently happen that bashfulness is a misfortune to men. Do not therefore be so shamefaced as to cause failure or injury to your own interests. . . . Do not be over-hasty in shedding innocent blood, and regard no killing of Moslems to be lawful, unless they are brigands, thieves and grave-robbers or such whose execution is demanded by the law. . . . Yet do not neglect your duty where blood must rightfully be shed, for the general welfare demands it and out of remissness evil is born.

From *A Mirror for Princes: the Qabus Nama,* trans. by R. Levy (New York: Dutton, 1951), pp. 23, 30, 88.

which sexual jealousy had a central social role and created extremely difficult relations between the sexes.

But Islamic society also gave men and women the opportunity to rise from poverty and lowly status to wealth and power. Although there was an aristocracy, it was not so exclusive as its counterparts in the Byzantine Empire or western Europe. Men often took wives and concubines from families less well placed than themselves, and the children of these women had all the advantages that the husbands could provide. Further, the school system gave talented men the opportunity to gain entry into the bureaucracy, while the active commercial economy gave others the opportunity to get rich.

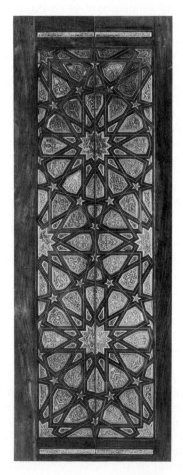

Islamic door with ivory panel (fourteenth century).

in the household arts and in sex, the better to win and keep the favor of their future husbands. Of course, women influenced their husbands or masters, but their power was always exercised within the harem.

The inaccessibility of women may have contributed to the commonness of homosexual relations among Moslem men. Islamic society was tolerant of homosexuality, but outsiders found it scandalous. While the percentage of men who were exclusively homosexual was probably no greater than in other societies, many Moslem men who had normal relations with women also had occasional relations with men. This was another feature of a society in

Islamic society was a society for self-made men.

ISLAMIC CIVILIZATION

Even though the Samanids encouraged a revival of ancient Persian literature and culture in the tenth century and even though the Seljuk Turks continued this policy, Islamic civilization was never Persian. The supporter of the first Abbasid, Abu Muslim, and his Persian successors in the government of Baghdad were committed to an Arabic, if not an Arab, *umma,* and they preserved the Ommayyad tradition of Arabic culture. This meant that the full integration of the *mawali* into the Islamic community did not lead to a revival of Persian culture, but rather to the creation of a new hybrid civilization.

There were many elements in the foundation of this new civilization. The acceptance of Arabic as the universal religious language unified the whole Islamic world in a single intellectual community, while the integration of non-Arab groups in the community introduced many intellectual traditions. The Arabs also possessed a cheap writing material—paper. The Chinese had used paper since about A.D. 100, but it did not become known to the Mediterranean Basin until 751, when some Chinese prisoners of war were in Samarkand in the Transoxiana. From there, it spread to Baghdad where a paper factory was founded in 793, and then to Egypt (900) and Spain (950). The Europeans got the invention from Spain, but as late as the thirteenth century, paper was rare, even in Christian Spain. As it did in Europe later, the use of paper quickened the spread of ideas and widened the circle of both readers and writers.

Islamic civilization borrowed ideas and intellectual traditions from other civilizations. It absorbed the philosophical and scientific traditions of Greece, the astronomical and medical science of Persia and its predecessors,

and the mathematics of India (from which came "Arabic" numerals, first used by Islamic writers in the late ninth century and still universally used today). The government of the caliphate was normally tolerant of minority ethnic groups that clung to their ancestral religions, and this attitude meant that these groups could contribute to Islamic civilization. The Syrian Christians were heirs of Greek civilization and had translated many important works into Syriac. Through this medium, Aristotle and other Greek authors were translated into Arabic and exerted an influence on Islamic philosophy and theology. When the western Europeans rediscovered Aristotle through contact with Islamic and Jewish scholars in Spain, Sicily, and the Latin kingdom of Jerusalem, they also received elaborate commentaries written by Moslem writers. The most important of these commentators were the physician and scientist Ibn Sina (or Avicenna, 980–1037) and the philosophers al-Kindi and Ibn Rushd (or Averroes, 1126–98).

Al-Kindi was an Arab, Ibn Rushd a Moor from Spain, Ibn Sina a Persian, but while people from all over the Islamic world participated in Arabic civilization, it was dominated by the Persians. The first great Islamic historian, Tabari (d. 923); the mathematician Omar Khayyam (d. 1123), who is known in the West for his poetry; the scientific thinkers, al-Biruni (d. *ca.* 1150) and Ibn Sina; and the first scholar of comparative religion, Shahrastani (d. 1153) were all Persians. After the reemergence of Persian culture under the Samanids and Ghaznavids during the tenth century, Persian poetry and literature revived and continued to be written under the Turks.

In the West, during the thirteenth century, the development of scientific thought centered on optics, and while this subject had roots in European thought and society, it was also rooted in the scientific tradition that the Europeans learned from the Moslems. Medicine was the primary science of Islam

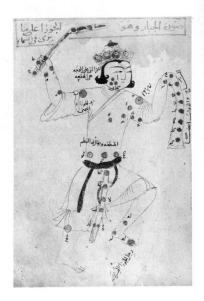

Representation of the constellation Orion in a fourteenth-century manuscript of a tenth-century Islamic astronomical treatise.

Arabic Anthropology

Al-Biruni was the Persian Aristotle, a universal genius who worked in virtually all the branches of human knowledge. He lived at the Ghazna court and followed his ruler on his campaigns in India. On the basis of this experience, al-Biruni wrote a great work on the Indians, describing their language, religion, and social customs. Here, he describes the Indian character.

. . . the Hindus believe that there is no country but theirs, no nation like theirs, no kings like theirs, no religion like theirs, no science like theirs. They are haughty, foolishly vain, self-conceited, and stolid. They are by nature niggardly in communicating that which they know, and they take the greatest possible care to withhold it from men of another caste among their own people, still much more, of course, from any foreigner. . . . Their haughtiness is such that, if you tell them of any science or scholar in Khurasan and Persis, they will think you to be both an ignoramus and a liar. If they travelled and mixed with other nations, they would soon change their mind, for their ancestors were not as narrow-minded as the present generation is. One of their scholars, Varahamihira, in a passage where he calls on the people to honour the Brahmans, says: "The Greeks, though impure, must be honoured, since they were trained in sciences, and therein excelled others. What, then, are we to say of a Brahman, if he combines with his purity the height of science?"

From *Alberuni's India,* ed. by E. C. Sachau (Delhi, 1964), pp. 22–23.

and, because eye diseases were so prevalent in North Africa and the Middle East, ophthalmology and optics were given much attention. Once Arabic medical works became available in Latin translations, during the later twelfth century, they became the basis of European medical study and science for centuries.

In both civilizations the study of medicine touched all the sciences. Clearly, physiology and pharmacology belonged to the study of medicine, but so did astronomy, physics, chemistry, botany, and optics. Arabic and European physicians were concerned both with the bodily humors (fluids) that they believed caused disease when present in improper proportions and with the astronomical powers they believed affected worldly events. Astrology was an ancient Babylonian science that had been kept alive by the successive civilizations of the Middle East and had been carried throughout the Mediterranean in Roman times. According to astrology, the stars exert a force that affects events on earth, and ancient and medieval physicians thought that the influence of the stars also caused disease. Christian writers, most notably Augustine (d. 430), condemned the belief as superstition, but in Islam it was considered to be a science. The influence of astrology grew in the West after western physicians began reading Arabic medical texts in the twelfth century.

The Mongol invasion seriously damaged the urban culture on which this brilliant civilization was based, and it coincided with other events and movements that injured Islamic intellectual life. The violence of the Mongol invasion and the conquest of Spain by the Christians, who by the thirteenth century had pinned the Moslems in the south reduced the two most active intellectual centers in the Islamic world. The victory of al-Ghazzali's theology constrained philosophical and scientific work. Ibn Rushd's work on Aristotle and on theology was meant as an answer to al-Ghazzali's school of thought, but it could not turn the tide. He argued that the truths of philosophy and religion were separate and separable, and he was condemned both in Islam and in Christendom, when his work became known there. The idea of the unity of truth was fundamental in both religions. Ibn Khaldun (1337–1406), one of the deepest thinkers of Islam, regarded all knowledge as religious.

With rare exceptions, such as Ibn Khaldun, there were few creative thinkers in Islam after about 1200. The civilization continued its life in those places, such as Egypt, that escaped either Mongol or Christian conquest, but it was a repetitive and derivative intellectual culture that persisted. Ironically, the heirs of medieval Arabic learning were the Europeans, for in Europe, the translations of Arabic works created an intellectual revolution in the twelfth and thirteenth centuries.

Suggestions for Further Reading

Islamic Religion

The basic source of Islamic religion is the Koran itself. A good translation is that of A. J. Arberry, *The Koran Interpreted* (1955). For a general history see the *Cambridge History of the Islam*, 2 vols. (1970), a collection of excellent articles on all aspects of the civilization. M. G. Hodgson provides both a survey and an interpretation of Islamic history and civilization in *The Venture of Islam*, 3 vols. (1974). J. J. Saunders, *A History of Medieval Islam* (1965); H. R. Gibb, *Mohammedanism: An Historical Survey* (1949); P. K. Hitti, *History of the Arabs*, 6th ed. (1958); B. Lewis, *The Arabs in History*, 4th ed. (1958); and F. Rahman, *Islam*, 2nd ed. (1979), are good brief surveys. B. Lewis published a large collection of sources in *Islam*, 2 vols. (1974).

The Arab Empire

On early Arabian history, see P. Crone, *Meccan Trade and the Rise of Islam* (1987). D. L. O'Leary, *Arabia before Muhammad* (1927), M. Rostovtzeff, *Caravan Cities* (1932), and B. Thomas, *Arabia Felix* (1932), are still valuable. For a modern appreciation of Mohammed, see H. N. Kennedy, *The Prophet and the Age of Caliphates* (1986); T. Andrae, *Mohammed, the Man and his Faith* (1952); and W. M. Watt, *Muhammad at Mecca* (1953), and *Muhammad at Medina* (1956). On the early conquests, see F. M. Donner, *The Early Islamic Conquests* (1981), and, for an appreciation of the military achievement, see J. Glubb, *The Great Arab Conquests* (1961). On the historical role of the Prophet's sayings and practices, see A. Guillaume, *The Traditions of Islam* (1924), and P. Crone and M. Hinds, *God's Caliph: Religious Authority in the First Centuries of Islam* (1986).

The standard history of the Ommayyad dynasty is J. Wellhausen, *The Arab Kingdom and its Fall* (1927), which also gives a detailed account of the Abbasid revolution. On the problem of conversion to Islam and the economic aspects of relations between Moslems and non-Moslems, see D. C. Dennett, *Conversion and the Poll-Tax in Early Islam* (1950). For specific regions of the Arab Empire, see P. K. Hitti, *A History of Syria* (1951); S. Lane-Poole, *A History of Egypt in the Middle Ages*, 3rd ed. (1924); W. M. Watt, *History of Islamic Spain* (1965); H. A. R. Gibb, *The Arab Conquests in Central Asia* (1923); and S. Lane-Poole, *The Story of the Moors in Spain* (1886). D. S. Richards, *Islam and the Trade of Asia* (1971), shows the shift in interest toward the East under the Abbasids. On the Turks, see W. Barthold, *Turkestan down to the Mongol Invasion*, trans. of 2nd ed. (1958); T. Rice, *The Seljuks in Asia Minor* (1961); and C. E. Bosworth, *The Ghaznavids* (1963).

Islamic Society and Civilization

For studies of Islamic society, see the work of Hodgson, cited previously and articles in the *Cambridge History of Islam*. The broadest treatment is R. Levy, *The Sociology of Islam* (1957); see also, W. M. Watt, *Islam and the Integration of Society* (1961). N. Abbot, *Two Queens of Baghdad* (1937), focuses on life in the Abbasid court. S. Goitein, *A Mediterranean Society*, 4 vols. (1967–80), is based on the discovery in Egypt of a treasure of Jewish documents, but, because the Jews were a well-assimilated minority, it reveals a great deal about the whole Islamic society and economy of the Middle East. See also, A. Udalvitch, *Partnership and Profit in Medieval Islam* (1967).

On Islamic civilization, see G. E. von Grunebaum, *Classical Islam, 600–1258* (1970) and *Medieval Islam: A Study in Cultural Orientation*, 2nd ed. (1953); see also, H. A. R. Gibb, *Arabic Literature*, 2nd ed. (1963); and the essays published in R. M. Savory, ed., *Islamic Civilization* (1976). On special topics, see R. Walzer, *Greek into Arabic, Essays on Islamic Philosophy* (1962); C. Elgood, *A Medical History of Persia* (1951); A. J. Arberry, *Revelation and Reason in Islam* (1957); and S. H. Nasr, *Science and Civilization in Islam* (1968). H. A. R. Gibb and H. Bowen, *Islamic Society and the West*, 2 vols. (1950), explore the impact of the West on Islam. For western views, see N. Daniel, *Islam and the West: The Making of an Image* (1960), and R. W. Southern, *Western Views of Islam in the Middle Ages* (1962). In general, see T. Arnold and A. Guillaume, eds., *The Legacy of Islam* (1931).

9

The Emergence of Western European Civilization

*B*yzantine civilization derived directly from its Roman predecessor, but, naturally, emphasized the Greek element in the old Roman culture. Islamic civilization cannot be said to have derived from the Roman, but it shared much with it. Greek culture had spread through the Middle East during the Hellenistic period, and this was the same culture that influenced Rome after it gained control of Greece in the 140s B.C. One could say that Islamic civilization was an amalgam of the Hellenistic and Persian civilizations, although other cultures of the Arab Empire contributed to it also. In Europe, another heir of classical Mediterranean civilization emerged after the settlement of the Germans and the end of Roman power. This was the product of the union of Roman and Germanic civilization—medieval Europe.

For a long time after the collapse of Roman government in the western provinces, people there—including the new German rulers—continued to view themselves as part of the empire. The Romanized provincial populations had become used to the military role of the Germans, both in the "Roman" army and as *foederati,* and the German rulers sought and received official Roman titles from the government in Constantinople. All this contributed to the impression that while things were different after the German kings took control, there was continuity.

Nonetheless, the transition to government by Germanic kings had great effects on European society and civilization. Although the early kings tried to preserve some of the Roman administrative system—particularly in Ostrogothic Italy—Germanic government was more personal than bureaucratic in character. This meant that the king's power derived from the personal loyalty of his men, so that he had to keep constantly on the move around the kingdom to show himself in person to his people.

The Christian Church was well established by the time of the invasions, and having developed in the pattern of the Roman administration, it was centered in the cities. By the late fourth century, the Latin Church was controlled by members of the educated elite, which also provided the bureaucrats of the imperial administration. The decline of the cities and the gradual disappearance of the Roman administration left the members of the Church hierarchy as the preservers and

Opposite: Charlemagne presents a model of his church at Aix-la-Chapelle (Aachen) to the Virgin (detail from a panel of the shrine at Aix).

237

continuators of Latin culture. But while the Church preserved Roman culture, the Germans changed the Church as they incorporated it into their society. As the Church and German states accommodated to one another, precedents were set that contributed much to the later relationship between church and state.

THE RISE OF THE CAROLINGIANS

By the early seventh century, the dynasty founded by Clovis (r. 481–511), the Merovingians, had declined, so that its kings no longer exercised real authority. Dagobert (r. 629–39) was the last Merovingian who ruled his kingdom. After him, the mayors of the palace (or palaces, since the kingdom was divided) governed, while constantly fighting with one another. That the Franks permitted degenerate kings to remain on the throne is an indication of how much they had absorbed Roman legal and political ideas.

The authority of the late Merovingians rested on an idea of kingship that combined Roman and Germanic elements. This idea preserved the old Germanic notion that the king is a special person who stands between the community and God, but it also contained the Roman idea that royal power can be described as a set of specific functions. This way of viewing king-

The Frankish Kingdom   *ca.* 700

ship permitted the further idea that someone else could perform these functions in the king's name. This was the basis of the authority held by the mayors of the palace.

The civil wars were ended when Pippin of Herstal, the mayor of the palace in the Austrasia since 680, won the battle of Tertry in 687 against the mayor of Neustria and Burgundy. By the time Pippin died in 714, he had restored the authority of the central government. His sons by his wife Plectrude had predeceased him, and he bequeathed his mayoralty to his two young grandsons, with Plectrude as regent. But the aristocracy, particularly in Neustria and Burgundy, took the opportunity to rebel, and Pippin's adult son by one of his concubines, Charles, was able to use the opposition to gain control. Charles (r. 719–41), a hard man and traditional war leader who earned the nickname Martel, the Hammer, continued his father's work.

Charles had not only to control the unruly aristocracy of the kingdom, but also to meet the challenge of Moorish expansionism from Spain. The Moslem Moors had conquered the Iberian peninsula in 711, and in 720, they captured Narbonne, the capital of the ancient Roman province of Septimania. It then became a base for raiding the Frankish kingdom. Aquitaine, a rich province in the southwest of Gaul, bore the brunt of Moorish attacks. For decades, the dukes of Aquitaine had been able to maintain their autonomy from the Merovingian government, but now, faced with annual raids, Duke Eudes had to compromise his independence by asking Charles for support. About 732, Charles defeated a large Moorish army near Poitiers; the Moors had hoped to plunder the rich church of Tours, which contained the shrine of St. Martin, the monk-bishop (see p. 149). From this time on, the Moors were on the defensive in southern Gaul.

Charles encouraged the missionary activities of the Irish and Anglo-Saxon monks who continued the work of Columbanus and his confreres (see pp. 149–50). Charles became closely associated with the greatest among them, Wynfrith, a monk from Wessex who had taken the Roman name Boniface after he visited Rome and won papal approval for his work. Boniface founded the monastery of Fulda in central Germany and was the most prominent churchman in the Frankish kingdom for over two decades.

It may have been through Boniface that Pope Gregory III (r. 731–41) approached Charles in 739 for help against the Lombards, who were then threatening Rome. The pope had turned to Constantinople for aid against the threat, but the emperor had ignored the plea. Papal-imperial relations were severely strained at that time by the iconoclastic controversy, and the Empire's military forces were fully occupied in wars against both the Ommayyad caliphate and the Bulgarians. But Charles would not help the pope. The Lombard king, Luitprand, had aided the Franks in their war against the Moors, and Charles had sent his son Pippin III to the Lombard court as a way of binding the two royal families together. There was nothing for Charles in an alliance with the papacy.

This policy was reversed 13 years later by Charles's son and successor Pippin III, called the Short (r. 741–68). During the 740s great changes had taken place in the Frankish kingdom. When Charles died in 741, his mayoralty devolved on his two sons, Pippin and Carloman. Like their father, these men supported Boniface in his effort to establish Benedictine monasticism in the kingdom, but it was a long time before that form of monasticism became dominant in the kingdom. In the eighth century, most monastic houses followed mixed rules, often the product of local tradition, that combined features of the Rule of Columbanus (Irish) with those of eastern rules that ultimately derived from those of Pachomius and Basil. Frankish monasticism existed in a bewildering variety

Gold fibula made of paste and stones (seventh century).

of forms. Shortly after they succeeded to the mayoralty, Pippin and Carloman summoned councils where Boniface tried to reform the monasteries and churches of the kingdom. Then, in 747, Carloman retired to a monastery, first in Rome and then at the rebuilt house at Monte Cassino. Pippin was left in control of the kingdom.

When Pippin and Carloman became mayors, no Merovingian sat on the throne. Although their father had been able to rule for a while without a king, the new mayors felt that they needed a king to establish their legitimacy. A search throughout the kingdom produced a distant relative of the royal family, and in 743 he was crowned as Childeric III. After Pippin became sole mayor, he decided to take the revolu-

The Carolingian Family Tree

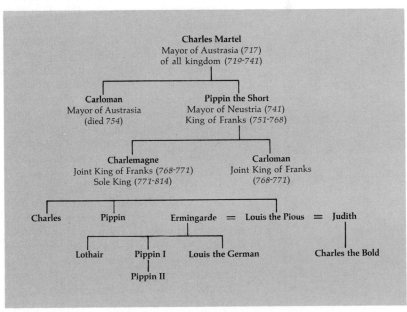

tionary step of transferring the royal power from this useless scion of Clovis to himself. In 751, he accomplished the transferral with the support of the nobility.

The replacement of the ancient dynasty was a tricky matter. Pippin lacked the divine character that the Germans attributed to their kings, for the Germanic king remained a divine figure, as he had been in pagan times, and the right to be God's minister on earth rested not on the exercise of power, but on hereditary right. Therefore, Pippin had to find a way to overcome the essential defect in his legitimacy. He did this by turning to the pope, with whom he had good relations through Boniface.

In 749 or 750, Pippin sent a questionnaire to Pope Zachary (r. 741–52) asking, "Was it right or not that the king of the Franks at that time had absolutely no power but nevertheless possessed the royal office?" Zachary answered that Pippin, who exercised royal authority, was indeed king, and in 751 the Frankish bishops anointed him after the manner of the Old Testament kings. This ceremony had originated in Spain, and the idea of it may have been brought to Gaul by refugees from the fallen Visigothic kingdom. It was an unprecedented act in the Frankish kingdom, but Pippin needed to shore up his legitimacy. The anointment symbolized that Pippin possessed the indwelling spirit of a king and was a true heir of the Merovingian authority.

The dealings between Pippin and Pope Zachary set the stage for a change in the Carolingians' attitude toward the war between the papacy and the Lombards. In the winter of 752–53, Zachary's successor, Pope Stephen II (r. 752–57), asked Pippin for help against Aistulf, the Lombard king. Pippin invited Stephen to his kingdom and in January 754 met him at Ponthion, a principal royal residence east of Paris on the Marne River. At the meeting, the king promised to help the pope, and in the spring he persuaded the nobles to support this new policy toward the papacy. The pope was in Francia throughout these events, and at Easter Pippin gave him promises that he would restore the territories of the papacy. In July at St. Denis, Stephen repeated the anointment of Pippin, this time also anointing his wife and sons, and named him *patricius Romanorum* (patrician of the Romans) as special protector of the Roman see. The anointment of Pippin's sons confirmed the new dynasty in its position.

During the next year or so, Pippin negotiated with Aistulf, but the talks failed to produce the result Pippin had promised to achieve, and in 755 the Frankish king invaded Italy. The campaign lasted into 756, when Pippin forced the Lombards to restore to the pope the lands of the Byzantine Exarchate of Ravenna, which they had conquered about ten years earlier. The restoration was recorded in a document, now lost, that was deposited in St. Peter's. It is often referred to as the "Donation of Pippin."

CHARLEMAGNE AND THE CAROLINGIAN RENAISSANCE

Pippin the Short died in 768, leaving the monarchy to his two sons, Charles and Carloman. These brothers did not get along well, and the Franks might have experienced another round of civil wars had not Carloman died suddenly in 771. Nonetheless, there had been enough enmity between the brothers to scare Carloman's widow and children into taking refuge with the Lombard king, Desiderius. When Desiderius renewed Lombard claims to the territory that Pippin had donated to the papacy, Charles had a double reason for action. He would honor his father's alliance with the papacy and remove competing claimants to the crown. He invaded Italy in 773 and within a year had conquered the Lombard kingdom. In 774 he took the crown of the Lombards for himself, and Carloman's widow and children disappeared.

Charles was a successful warrior king. Even during his lifetime he was known as Charlemagne, or Charles the Great. For 32 years (772–804), he led almost annual campaigns against the heathen Saxons on the northeastern border of his kingdom, finally bringing them into his power. His success was helped by missionaries whom he supported and who cemented his own alliance with the Church. In the southwest, Charlemagne continued his father's and grandfather's wars against the Moors. Between 778 and 801 he established a strong buffer territory along the southern flank of the Pyrenees— the Spanish March. During the campaign of 778, the Moors ambushed his vanguard as Charlemagne returned home, and the tragic story of that battle became the basis of one of the greatest medieval epics, *The Song of Roland*. On the eastern frontier, Charlemagne brought the Bavarians into his power in 787, and he established another buffer, the Ostmark (East March), between his territories and the restless Slavic tribes of eastern Europe. This march formed the core of what later became Austria. About 796, he crossed the eastern frontier and crushed the Avars, bringing home an immense treasure of gold. This campaign put him in touch with the western frontier of the Byzantine Empire.

These military successes were matched by the development of an effective internal government for his realm. Charlemagne followed his father and uncle in using councils and assemblies to govern his realm. The councils served all types of functions; through them, the king issued legislation for the Church, settled disputes, and administered his army. Performed in front of the assembled men of the kingdom, his actions were immediately known to those affected by them. The king also issued numerous capitularies (so named because they were divided into chapters, *capitula*), which regulated the administration of royal and ecclesiastical estates and dealt with myriad other functions of government.

The Golden Psalter, presented to Charlemagne by Pope Adrian I (*ca.* 780–795).

Charlemagne's Conquests and Empire   814

To implement these regulations, Charlemagne used the countship, a late Roman office that had combined military and civilian authority, and appointed counts throughout his territories. These men were royal officials, but the aristocrats who served as counts were never entirely dependent on the central government for their power. They could rely on their own ancient families and landed estates, so that even under the powerful Charlemagne they could not be trusted to be always loyal and responsible. As a result, he also instituted *missi dominici* (those sent by the king) as special representatives of his government. These men traveled a circuit checking up on the counts and other, lesser, royal officials.

The *missi* usually traveled in pairs, a layman and a cleric, and this represents another aspect of Charlemagne's rule: he concerned himself with ecclesiastical as much as with secular affairs. In this also, he was following in the footsteps of his father and grandfather. They had relied on churches to build up their authority, and under Charles Martel many bishoprics and abbeys were controlled by secular men who used the great wealth of the Church in support of the mayor. As kings, Pippin and Charles Martel claimed to be God's vicar, responsible for the ecclesiastical as well as the secular affairs of the realm.

The Carolingian Renaissance

Following the policy of his father and grandfather, Charlemagne sought to make the churches an effective support of his government. However, he found that the churches had developed independently of one another and differed greatly in liturgy and constitution. Monastic houses lived by many different rules, most of them local products. There were even differences of doctrine among the churchmen of the realm. Therefore, to ensure the peace of the Church and to make it an effective support of the monarchy Charlemagne had to undertake a great reform.

The reform movement was centered in the royal court at Aix-la-Chapelle (Aachen), the ancient Carolingian estate that had become Charlemagne's capital. Charlemagne became interested in reform very early in his reign and almost from the beginning began inviting intellectuals to his court. In 774, while he was in Italy after the defeat of the Lombards, he received a copy of the papal collection of canon law from Pope Adrian I (r. 772–95). In the 780s, the intellectual life of the court quickened as Charlemagne attracted an increasing number of scholars to his court. Charlemagne himself studied with these men, and they carried on the reform under his guidance and protection. The leader of the reformers was an Anglo-Saxon monk named Alcuin (*ca.* 735–804), who had come to Aix-la-Chapelle in 781 at Charlemagne's behest. Alcuin had been educated in York—at that time a great

A small bronze statue of Charlemagne or his grandson Charles the Bald. He wears a crown and carries an orb, symbol of royal power (ninth century).

intellectual center—and he stood in a line of scholars that led back to the Northumbrian monk Bede (*ca.* 672–735), one of the greatest scholars of the Middle Ages. Under Alcuin, Charlemagne's court became a center for ecclesiastical reform and an intellectual center of great historical significance.

The idea of the reform was to train a new generation of clerics for the Frankish church. Charlemagne would then spread the influence of the court by appointing these men to the principal bishoprics and abbeys of the realm. In addition, the court "school" would produce model texts on which the religious life of the kingdom could be based. Charlemagne had asked the pope for a sacramentary (which gave the order and content of the Mass) and a carefully prepared copy of the Benedictine Rule. The court scholars used these works to produce model texts, from which certified copies were made for churches throughout the realm. In this way, the king sought to standardize liturgical practice. The monastic reform based on certified copies of St. Benedict's Rule made some progress, but it was Charlemagne's son, Louis, who pursued it with vigor and who tried to impose the Rule on all monasteries of the realm in 816–17. Even so, monastic reform proceeded very slowly because the monasteries clung to their old ways.

Intellectually, the aim of Alcuin and his fellows was to rediscover and reestablish the intellectual tradition of Rome. For that reason, the new movement was a true renaissance, a rebirth of an old and almost dead civilization of the past. Bits and pieces of Roman civilization had survived in isolated places in England and Spain during the centuries of barbarian rule, but the Roman tradition had been debased and reduced in authority.

Alcuin himself was best known as a teacher, and he developed an educational curriculum based on that of Rome. He divided the seven liberal arts, which had been defined by late Roman writers, into two parts, the *trivium* and the *quadrivium*. The *trivium* consisted of grammar, dialectic (logic), and rhetoric. The *quadrivium* included arithmetic, geometry, astronomy, and music (which was thought to derive from the very structure of the universe). To provide an adequate grounding in Latin, Alcuin attracted the great Italian grammarian Peter of Pisa to Aix-la-Chapelle, where Peter produced new editions of the late Roman grammatical works. Paul the Deacon, another Italian, came to court to seek the release of his brother, whom Charlemagne had imprisoned, and stayed for a couple of years. He compiled a book of model sermons for pastors. Meanwhile, Alcuin undertook a new edition of Jerome's Latin translation of the Bible, which had become corrupted by numerous errors in the course of nearly four centuries of copying. The work was finished by his students after his death, and it made Jerome's translation, which had competed with an earlier version, the accepted one. Henceforth, it was the vulgate (*vulgatus* meaning common) Bible of Europe.

The reform inspired and led by Charlemagne continued throughout his reign, but three main legislative actions spurred it along, the issuance of Capitularies in 789, 802, and 811–13. The first of these contained a summary of the most important sections of the papal law book Charlemagne had received in 774 and a general statement of the aims of the reform. Its principal effect was to establish the idea that law was the basis of religious life—in other words, that religious life should be regulated by a coherent and unified body of written rules. Before 789, local custom, the product of communal practices and the personal preferences of the bishops who had governed the dioceses over the centuries, delineated the religious life of the kingdom's churches. The Capitulary of 802 reaffirmed the authority of the papal law book, and the legislation of 811–13 dealt with various aspects of the reform in detail. These regulations of Charlemagne's last years summed up the aims and the experience of nearly 40 years of reform activity.

This summary of Charlemagne's reform hardly does it justice. As part of its intellectual activity, the palace school produced numerous new editions of Roman works as well as new writings patterned on them. This great work of copying manuscripts was spurred on by Charlemagne himself, and it speeded up the development of a new form of Latin script. During the 780s (the exact date is unknown), he issued instructions to monasteries and cathedrals to copy old books. The scripts used in the Merovingian and early Carolingian period were difficult to read and full of peculiar abbreviations and letter forms. There was little regularity in scribal practice. This lack of uniformity and the difficulty of the scripts had contributed to the corruption of texts, because scribes often misread their exemplars. At some monasteries, particularly Corbie (north of Amiens), a clear book-script had begun to develop in the middle of the eighth century, and the new increased activity of book production brought it to perfection. For the first time, monastic writing operations (scriptoria) developed house styles, standardized ways of writing letters that were taught to the monastic scribes, and scholars can often date and place ninth-century manuscripts on the basis of their script.

The new script, called Caroline Minuscule, used few ligatures (connected letters that could become mysterious signs in the hands of artful or minimally competent scribes) and few abbreviations. The monastic scriptoria produced a large library of beautifully written copies of ancient texts. When the humanist scholars of fifteenth-century Italy began searching the libraries for works of classical literature, they found these Carolingian books and, because of their clarity and beauty, took them for ancient copies. In their zest for ancient civilization, they revived the Caroline Minuscule and established it as the script of scholarship and culture. This script continues to be used today. This book is printed in Caroline Minuscule.

The Coronation of Charlemagne as Emperor

After Charlemagne seized the Lombard crown in 774, Pope Adrian I gave him the title earlier conferred on his father, *patricius Romanorum* (patrician of the Romans). But he eventually came to make claims to spiritual authority that his father appears never to have contemplated. The sending out of clerics as *missi dominici* suggests these claims, as does the lead Charlemagne took in organizing the reform of the Frankish church. About 794, in the *libri Carolini* (Caroline Books), which condemned both iconoclasm and iconodulia, he asserted his position as "rector of the Christian people," a title that reminds one of Caesaropapism. Like Leo III in

Small letters and a bold, rounded design were characteristic of the elegant Carolingian handwriting, which is the basis of modern type (detail from a ninth-century manuscript).

Interior of the Palatine Chapel, Aix-la-Chapelle (Aachen).

his edict against icons and Constantive V in his iconoclastic treatise (see pp. 187–89), Charles, in the *libri*, participated in the theological debates of his age.

With the great treasure he had seized from the Avars in 796, Charlemagne built a "second Rome" at Aix-la-Chapelle. He imported craftsmen and materials from Italy to create a palace and church modeled on the Byzantine buildings at Ravenna. In this period, he also sent and received embassies to and from the caliph Harun al-Rashid (probably about their common enemies, the Moors in Spain). Already in the mid-780s, intellectuals at his court had begun to use the word *imperium* (imperial authority) to describe the authority Charlemagne exercised.

The use of this term may have had something to do with events in the Byzantine Empire. When Irene had her son Constantine VI blinded in 797, the westerners viewed the imperial throne as vacant. There were negotiations—or perhaps only talk of negotiations—about a marriage between Charlemagne and Irene, but nothing came of them. Then in 800 there were disturbances in Rome against Pope Leo III (r. 795–816), and the pope sent to Charlemagne, as the *patricius Romanorum*, for aid. Imbued as he was with his role as rector of the Christian

Gold coin bearing the likeness of Irene, empress in Constantinople from 797 to 802. She was the first woman to assume sole rule over the Byzantine Empire, taking the title of emperor. Her rule provided the pope with an excuse to crown Charlemagne emperor in 800 to fill the allegedly vacant throne.

people and reformer of the Church, he responded to this appeal by going himself to Rome to settle the dispute.

In late December 800 in Rome, Charlemagne called a council of churchmen to judge the dispute between Leo and his opponents. This meeting produced important precedents for the constitutional law of the Church because the assembled churchmen declared themselves unable to make the judgment. They told the king that the pope, as successor of St. Peter and the highest priest, could be judged by no one. This statement confirmed the hierarchical view of the Church implied by the Petrine doctrine, on which papal authority rested. To clear himself of the crimes that his opponents alleged against him, Leo was called upon merely to take an oath declaring his innocence. When he had accomplished this, the case was closed, and the statement of the council fathers became a legal recognition of the position of the pope in the Church.

A couple of days after these events, Charlemagne and his entourage went to St. Peter's church, which had been built by Constantine I, for the Christmas Mass. As Charlemagne rose from prayer at the altar, Leo placed an imperial crown on his head, and the people in the church uttered the traditional acclamation to the emperor. So began the conflict between Charlemagne and the eastern court about the imperial title (see pp. 190–92).

Charlemagne may have been uncertain about the meaning and usefulness of the imperial title. His biographer, Einhard, reports him saying that he would not have gone to church that Christmas day if he had known what Pope Leo would do. It is hard to believe that Leo tricked the king on that occasion, but he may have persuaded Charlemagne to go through with something that Charlemagne later regretted. As it was, Charlemagne did not actually use the title until 801, and in 806, he divided the empire among his three sons. This was a conventional thing to do for a Frankish king, but it was inconceivable to the imperial court in Constantinople, which was now convinced that Charlemagne did not understand the nature of imperial authority. Nonetheless, Nicephorus, who had seized power from Irene in 802, was in a difficult position, and he engaged Charlemagne in tortuous negotiations

The Coronation of Charlemagne   800

Now when the king upon the most holy day of the Lord's birth was rising to the mass after praying before the tomb of the blessed Peter the Apostle, Leo the Pope, with the consent of all the bishops and priests and of the senate of the Franks and likewise of the Romans, set a golden crown upon his head, the Roman people also shouting aloud. And when the people had made an end of chanting praises, he was adored by the pope after the manner of the emperors of old. For this was also done by the will of God. For while the said Emperor abode at Rome certain men were brought to him who said that the name of Emperor had ceased among the Greeks, and that there the Empire was held by a woman called Irene, who had by guile laid hold on her son the Emperor and put out his eyes and taken the Empire to herself. . . . Which when Leo the Pope and all the assembly of the bishops and priests and abbots heard, and the senate of the Franks and all the elders of the Romans, they took counsel with the rest of the Christian people, that they should name Charles king of the Franks to be Emperor, seeing that he held Rome the mother of empire where the Caesars and Emperors always used to sit.

From *Chronicle of Moissac*, trans. by J. Bryce, *The Holy Roman Empire* (New York: Macmillan and St. Martin's Press, 1911), p. 54.

that finally produced a treaty in 812, after Nicephorus had been overthrown. By this agreement, the Byzantines would address Charlemagne as Emperor of the Franks, while the Emperor of the Romans would remain in Constantinople. However, Charlemagne and his successors never used the title Emperor of the Franks.

Although Charlemagne divided his kingdom among his three sons, when he died in 814, only one son, Louis, still lived, and he inherited the magnificent realm alone. Louis also inherited the imperial title, which his sons and grandsons competed for and which continued to disturb relations with the eastern court.

THE DECLINE OF THE CAROLINGIANS AND NEW INVASIONS

The Disintegration of the Carolingian Kingdom

Louis (r. 814–40) was a capable man who succeeded a giant, and his reputation has suffered accordingly. It was not helped by his sobriquet "the Pious." He earned this name because he associated with churchmen and monks and because one of his first acts was to reform the morals of the royal court, which under his father had been a rather licentious place. Under his father, Louis had been king of Aquitaine, and he had formed an alliance with an energetic and forceful Aquitainian monastic reformer named Benedict of Aniane. When he became emperor, he brought Benedict to Aix-la-Chapelle and continued to pursue the reform of the Church and particularly of the monasteries. Like his predecessors, Louis held a series of councils at which reforms were put in place, and in 816–17 he and Benedict tried to impose the Benedictine rule on all monasteries in the realm. This regulation was ultimately successful, but many old monasteries held to their ancient rules for many years. Although he was an avid

reformer, Louis did not patronize scholars very much, and the pace of the renaissance started by his father slowed.

Louis pursued the same military and political policies as his father, but he faced problems that Charlemagne did not have. First, Louis came to power at the age of 36, and his three sons were virtually adults. In 817, he followed Charles's precedent and divided the kingdom among his sons, who became subrulers. This arrangement, which guaranteed the Carolingian succession, failed as a strategy for governing the vast domain. During the 820s, the sons began warring with each other and with their father. In 833, they defeated Louis, and his oldest son, Lothar, im-

Louis the Pious, son of Charlemagne. The words in the poem written across the portrait can also be read as a crossword puzzle, so that the letters in the cross and halo also form verses (*ca.* 840).

Lothair I in Roman dress seated on his throne (ca. 817).

prisoned him in the monastery of St. Medard of Soissons. Under Lothar's influence, the leading churchmen of the realm declared Louis unfit to rule and deposed him. After several months, some powerful nobles and churchmen returned to Louis's camp, and he was able to reestablish himself. But he had to do penance before the churchmen would recognize his kingship.

These wars and events greatly damaged the position of the royal house, principally because the aristocracy was able to play one king off against another and to gain for themselves royal lands and rights. The Church's humiliation of the emperor also caused significant damage by furthering greatly a trend toward the establishment of the Church's right to participate in the crowning of the emperor. Charlemagne himself had crowned Louis in 813. In 816, Louis was crowned by Pope Stephen IV (r. 816–17), who had

come to Reims. Then, in 824, the emperor sent his eldest son, Lothar, to Rome to be crowned by Paschal I (r. 817–24). Now the Church had set an important precedent by asserting its right to judge the fitness of the king.

After Louis's death in 840, his sons received their shares of the kingdom. Louis (r. 840–76) inherited Germany; he is called Louis the German. Charles (r. 840–77) inherited West Frankland; he became known as Charles the Bald. The eldest brother, Lothar (r. 840–55), held a middle kingdom that stretched from the Netherlands (Frisia) in the north through the region west of the Rhine (later called Lotharingia after Lothar's son, Lothar II) to Provence and Italy. He also received the imperial title. In theory, the three kings held joint power in one kingdom, but immediately after their father's death the three kings renewed the civil war with ferocity. In 842, Louis and Charles swore an oath of allegiance against Lothar. To ensure that the two armies understood the terms of the alliance, Louis took his oath in the Romance language that was then spoken by the West Franks, while Charles took his in Old German. The written record of Louis's oath is the earliest evidence of the Old French language.

The war that stemmed from this alliance ended in the Treaty of Verdun in 843, by which the Frankish kingdom was divided into three independent parts. Louis and Charles were supposed to recognize the superior authority of their brother, who retained the imperial title, but they usually treated him as an equal. Lothar spent much of his time trying to force his brothers to respect his authority. When Lothar died in 855, his kingdom was divided among his three sons. Lothar II (r. 855–69) received the northern portion; Charles (r. 855–63) got Provence; and Louis II (r. 855–75) was king of Italy and emperor. Lothar II died without a legitimate heir, and Charles the Bald seized Lotharingia. But the next year Louis the German drove him out, and in 870 with the Treaty of Mersen, the two brothers divided the region between themselves. The division was made according to the number of cities and bishoprics, rather than along some natural boundary, and from that point on West Frankland and East Frankland (France and Germany, respectively) have continued to struggle for control of the region (now called Alsace and Lorraine) into the twentieth century.*

The Viking and Magyar Invasions

These internal conflicts prepared the way for successful operations by new invaders. In 793, a raiding party of Northmen from Norway or Denmark had attacked the famous English monastery of Lindisfarne. Alcuin, at the Frankish court, heard about it and was shocked by the destruction of one of Europe's leading spiritual and intellectual centers. Within a few years, other raids had occurred, and at the end of his reign Charlemagne fortified the Frisian coast against these marauders. In 810 a large Danish force overran these defenses, but, shortly afterward, the Danish king was murdered, and the internal struggle for power kept the Danes occupied for several years.

Lorraine is the French form of Lotharingia.

Section from the Strasbourg Oaths, earliest examples of the dialects that became French and German. The oath was taken by Louis the German and Charles the Bald in 842, when they agreed to oppose their brother Lothair. The first paragraph gives the oath in French, taken by Louis, the second the same oath in German, taken by Charles. *The oath of Louis:* "For the love of God and the salvation of the Christian people and our common salvation, from this day forward, in so far as God gives me knowledge and power, I will succour this my brother Charles in aid and in everything, as one ought by right to succour one's brother, provided that he does likewise by me, and I will never undertake any engagement with Lothair which, by my consent, may be of harm to this my brother Charles."

The Division of Charlemagne's Empire

Invasions of the Northmen, the Moslems, and the Magyars   Eighth to Tenth Centuries

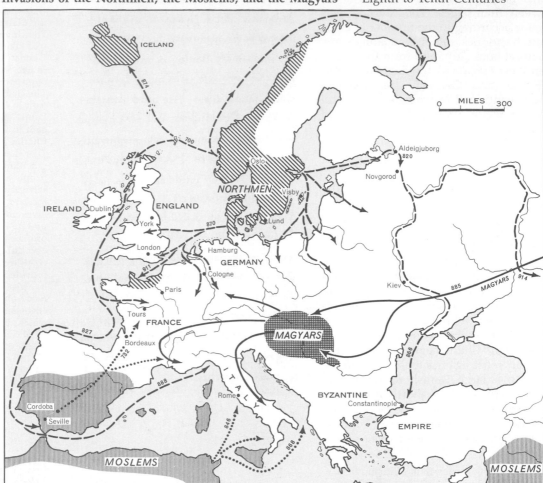

The new invaders mostly came in small bands and were not under the control of any of the Scandinavian kings. They were Vikings, "those who go abroad." Men of account in Scandinavian society were expected to spend some time at sea trading and raiding in order to establish themselves before settling down to the life of a northern farmer. As raiders, the Vikings were difficult to deal with. They came in their fast longboats and attacked their victims without warning.

The coastal districts were not the only regions threatened by the Viking bands. The broad, slow-moving rivers of northern Europe provided avenues for raids deep inland. In 834, a large

force came up the Seine and sacked Paris, while another went up the Elbe and destroyed Hamburg. In the succeeding decades, bands established themselves in Brittany and raided up and down the Atlantic coast. They even entered the Mediterranean and achieved the amazing feat of sacking Seville, in the heart of the powerful caliphate of Cordoba.

The character of the raids changed in the second half of the ninth century. The rise of a strong monarchy in Norway about 860 under Harald Finehair drove many aristocratic clans, opposed to royal power, to Iceland and England, and a large composite army grew in southern England. This force be-

Swedish drinking horn (*ca.* eighth century).

came known as the Great Army, and by the 870s it had destroyed several of the Anglo-Saxon kingdoms in England and threatened the rest. The crisis was met by Alfred (r. 871–99), king of Wessex, who spent most of his reign fighting the Great Army, finally forcing it to come to terms. After the war, large contingents of the Northmen settled in a band of territory in eastern England, and, in the tenth century, Alfred's successors brought this Danelaw (the area subject to Danish—that is, Scandinavian—law) under their control. Old Danish, which was closely related to Old Norse, was among the major linguistic contributors to the development of the English language.

Not all of the segments of the Great Army settled down after Alfred defeated it. Many bands went over to the Continent, and, using northwestern Gaul as a base, raided deep into Frankish territory. In 911, after a generation of warfare, the West Frankish king Charles the Simple (r. 898–922), great-great-grandson of Charlemagne,

made peace with Rollo, one of the major Viking leaders. Under the terms of the peace, Rollo converted to Christianity and became a vassal of the West Frankish king with the title of count, while Charles granted him the lands on which his men had settled. Rollo was bound to defend the kingdom from other Vikings, and his territory became known as Normandy.

These events were among the last of the Viking invasions, but before the end of the ninth century a new wave of invasions from the east had begun. The new invaders were the Magyars, the ancestors of the modern Hungarians. Linguistically, the Magyars do not belong to any known language group; the Finns are their only linguistic relatives. They entered history in 895, when the Byzantines set them upon the Bulgarians, thus introducing them into eastern Europe. In a short time, the Magyars had conquered the Hungarian plain and were raiding deep into Germany and Italy. During the first half of the tenth century, the Magyars were the scourge of Europe. In 955, Otto I of Germany defeated them near Augsburg, and after this they settled quietly in Hungary.

West Francia in the Ninth and Tenth Centuries

Charles the Bald of West Francia (r. 840–77) was much younger than his brothers, Lothar and Louis the German; he had not yet been born in 817, when Louis the Pious divided his kingdom among his three sons—Lothar, Louis the German, and Pippin. But Louis the Pious was fond of young Charles, and he made provisions for him in the western region of the empire. These grants were opposed by Louis's older sons, but he persisted, and after the death of Pippin (838) Charles became king of Aquitaine, leaving Pippin's son without an inheritance. He now had a kingdom equal to those of Lothar and Louis the German, but he had to contend with opposition from Pippin's son and supporters. Fur-

A rune stone (*ca.* ninth century) found in Scandinavia. The carving is distinctly viking: within an elaborate border are two panels, one showing a chieftain on a horse and the other, a viking ship on a voyage.

Remains of a viking ship at Osberg, Norway.

Viking animal head of carved wood used for a decoration on a sled, a wagon, or furniture (ninth century).

thermore, when Louis the Pious died, Charles had not been king of West Francia for long and had not built up much support of his own, as his brothers had in their parts of the empire. In the late 850s and early 860s, Charles faced rebellions of factions of the nobility and the invasion of Louis the German, who intervened in West Frankish affairs at the invitation of Charles's opponents. At the beginning of his reign, Charles followed Carolingian precedent by crowning his son Charles the Child as king of Aquitaine. When young Charles died in 866, he was succeeded by his brother Louis the Stammerer. However, the nobility of Aquitaine was virtually independent under the young kings, and Charles never visited the region after the mid-850s.

The developing independence of the nobility in Aquitaine was paralleled in a different way elsewhere in West Francia. During Charles's reign, the nobles formed factions around particularly powerful men. Charles himself contributed to this development by the efforts he made to win support. He favored certain nobles with offices (including abbacies) and lands, and in several cases individual noblemen held many countships and abbacies at once. This concentration of authority in the hands of a few great men created a counterforce to the king. So long as the leaders of the nobility remained loyal to Charles, he was strong, but when he did something to anger one or another of them, he faced a dangerous rebellion. At the beginning of his reign, he also made numerous grants to the churches of the realm in order to win over the bishops. Consequently, they too became potentially dangerous to the monarchy. Under Charles, the political power of the West Frankish monarchy declined.

Notwithstanding his political weakness, Charles revived the Carolingian renaissance, which had slowed under his father. He was a great patron of artists and commissioned some of the greatest art treasures of the early Middle Ages. In particular, he commissioned several illuminated bibles containing portraits of himself, which are important as indications of how Charles viewed his kingship. In the pictures, he was associated with the biblical kings as the vicar of God on earth. Thus, he was responsible for the spiritual as well as the temporal welfare of his people. This view was put forth

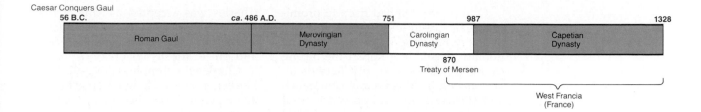

Caesar Conquers Gaul

56 B.C.		ca. 486 A.D.		751	987		1328
Roman Gaul		Merovingian Dynasty		Carolingian Dynasty	Capetian Dynasty		

870
Treaty of Mersen

West Francia
(France)

by the leading churchman in the realm, Archbishop Hincmar of Reims (r. 845–82). Hincmar had been a cleric at the court of Louis the Pious and became, as archbishop, one of the dominant figures of West Francia.

Charles was strong enough to achieve some notable successes. He was largely successful in defending the realm against the Vikings, and when he found it necessary or expedient to pay them off, his government, still based on the counts and *missi dominici*, could raise enormous amounts of silver from the country in a very short time. He also was able to reform the coinage, which could only have been achieved if he retained a considerable amount of authority. He continued the Carolingian practice of issuing capitularies.

When Charles the Bald died, he was succeeded by Louis the Stammerer (r. 877–79), whose mind was not much quicker than his speech. Louis secured his kingship by granting away yet more honors and offices to lay and ecclesiastical magnates. After this start, whether he could have built up his power will never be known because he died only 16 months after his coronation. The parties of nobles that had developed under Charles the Bald now contested the succession. Louis left two teenaged sons, Louis III and Carloman (another son, Charles, was born posthumously), and the aristocratic factions fought over whether one or both of these youngsters should succeed to the kingship. The Welf Hugh*, who had

*The Welfs were an old noble family that rose to prominence under Charles the Bald. In the eleventh century, they became dukes of Bavaria and remained involved in German and Italian politics for centuries.

risen to power under Charles the Bald, wanted only Louis III to succeed because he was sure that he could dominate a united kingdom through Louis. The other main party, led by Gauzlin, the head of the chancery, and Theudebert of Vermandois, wanted to divide the kingdom between the two sons. Gauzlin and Theudebert got their way by inviting Louis the German's son Louis the Younger to invade the kingdom. Of course, they had to pay off Louis the Younger to make him leave after they had succeeded in defeating Hugh's plan.

Louis and Carloman showed promise, but it was never realized. In 882, Louis won a major victory against the Vikings, but almost immediately afterward he died in a fall from his horse while chasing a girl. Carloman died two years later in a hunting accident. Charles the Simple, Louis the Stammerer's posthumous son, was only 5 years old in 884, so the West Frankish nobles invited Charles the Fat, Louis the German's youngest son and by then king of East Francia, to become king. Thus, for the next three years the Frankish kingdom of Charles the Great and Louis the Pious was ruled by a single man. However, the governments of West and East Francia remained independent because both were really in the hands of the nobles, and Charles the Fat was so ineffective as king that he was forced to abdicate in 887. In East Francia, the nobles elected Arnulf (r. 887–99), an illegitimate scion of a branch of the Carolingian line, as king. In West Francia, the nobles again passed over Charles the Simple, who was now 9 years old, and chose a non-Carolingian, Odo.

Odo (r. 887–98) had risen to prominence as a result of Charles the Bald's policy of building up the power of the nobility. His father, Robert the Strong (d. 866), had been one of Charles's favorites and had held many countships and abbacies. Odo had proved himself by defending the Paris region against the Vikings, and during his reign he continued to fight them. He also continued to rely on the nobility, particularly on his brother Robert, who succeeded Odo in Paris and became his heir when his son died in infancy. By the early 890s, Robert had become a *marquis,* a royal officer superior to all the counts in his region. This was a relatively new use of a title that had once designated a royal officer responsible for a march or border region. Other regions also had marquises, such as Burgundy, where Richard the Justiciar held sway. Thus, Odo continued and furthered the Carolingian policy of relying on the aristocratic counts as the basis of government, but the creation of the marquises strengthened a tendency for the kingdom to become a collection of semiautonomous duchies (the title duke began to be used by the greatest magnates during the tenth century). Nonetheless, Odo followed the old Carolingian practice of holding assemblies and took over the Carolingian chancery. Like Charles the Bald, he also relied on churchmen as advisers and members of his government, and he used lay abbacies to reward his supporters and maintain control over the wealthy monasteries. He gave his brother Robert four abbacies. Thus, Odo's reign did not create a sharp break with the past, even though he was not a Carolingian.

That Odo's kingship was only a brief interlude in the history of the Carolingian monarchy was indicated in 893, when nobles and churchmen opposed to Odo rebelled and had Charles the Simple, now 14 years old, crowned king. Odo dealt with the rebellion quickly, and Charles gave up the kingship and retreated to Lotharingia. But when Odo died on January 1, 898,

Charles was accepted as king. Odo's brother Robert was one of his principal supporters and received still more land and offices for his loyalty.

Charles the Simple (r. 898–922) can be seen as a weak king because he was so dependent on the noble factions. However, it seems that he was quite successful against the Vikings, and when he made the treaty with Rollo in 911 he was apparently dealing from some strength. In the same year, Charles became king of Lotharingia, where the nobles supported him instead of the new, non-Carolingian, East Frankish king, Conrad of Franconia. After this, Charles spent most of his time in Lotharingia, and the nobility in West Francia, particularly Robert, governed their territories almost independently. By 920, Charles's neglect of West Francia and the favoritism he showed certain Lotharingian nobles led to a rebellion orchestrated by Robert, who was elected king in 922. Charles met Robert in battle in June 923, and, although Robert was killed, his forces won the battle. About a month later, Ralph, son of Richard the Justiciar, was elected king, and shortly afterward, one of the other great men of the West Frankish realm, Herbert of Vermandois, captured Charles the Simple. Charles died in prison in 929.

Ralph (r. 923–36) concentrated on building up his power in Burgundy, his own patrimony, and continued the practice of giving lands and offices to great men elsewhere in the kingdom to ensure their loyalty. In fact, what he ensured was only their nominal recognition of his kingship. The most powerful nobleman in the kingdom was Hugh the Great, Robert's son, who held the Paris region and seven or more abbacies. When Ralph died, Hugh supported Charles the Simple's son, Louis IV, and received the title "Duke of the Franks" as a sign of his power within the kingdom. Louis IV (r. 936–54) had grown up in England, where his mother, sister of the king of Wessex, had gone after Charles was defeated in 923. Louis soon broke with

Hugh and other magnates and spent his reign in conflict with them. In the 940s, he made an attempt to seize Lotharingia, but Otto I (r. 936–73) of East Francia drove him back. After this, Louis tried unsuccessfully to reduce the power of Hugh the Great, sometimes calling on Otto I to help him. He might have succeeded had he not died in a fall from his horse in 954.

Louis's son, Lothar (r. 954–86), was the last Carolingian ruler of West Francia. When he ascended the throne, Hugh the Great was the most powerful man in the kingdom, but Hugh died in 956, leaving Lothar free to develop his monarchy. Lothar spent his reign in constant struggle with the nobles. He worked tirelessly to set them against one another and to undermine the great men by winning the loyalty of their subordinates. In the 950s, he tried to intervene in Lotharingia, but found that Otto I was too powerful. He tried again in the 970s, when Otto II (r. 973–83) was preoccupied with opposition in East Francia, but Otto was soon able to turn to Lotharingia, and he quickly reestablished his suzerainty there. Finally, Lothar invaded the region in 985, when Otto III (r. 983–1002) was still in his minority and the government was under the regency of his mother Theophano. As with Charles the Simple, Lothar's preoccupation with Lotharingia caused unrest in West Francia, but whether he could have overcome it and held onto Lotharingia will never be known because he died in 986.

Lothar was succeeded by his son, Louis V, who began his reign under the guidance of his mother and Hugh Capet, the oldest son of Hugh the Great. But Louis tried immediately to establish his independence and struggled against the great men of the realm. He died without heir in an accident in 987. Now, the West Franks elected Hugh Capet as king. Like Ralph before him, Hugh (r. 987–96) concentrated on building up his power in his own region, centered on Paris, and permitted the great men of the realm to rule their own principalities with little interference. He was content to have their recognition of his kingship. It has been said that he accomplished little, but that his reign was successful just because he succeeded in passing his crown on to his son, Robert. With the establishment of his family's hereditary right to the West Frankish throne, Hugh created a dynasty, the Capetians, that lasted until 1328.

THE RISE OF THE GERMAN EMPIRE

Henry I

The Otto who defeated the Magyars in 955 was the second of a new line of kings in East Francia, or Germany. The East Frankish Carolingian line died out in 911, with the death of Louis the Child, who had succeeded his father Arnulf in 899 at the age of 6. Instead of reuniting East and West Frankland by placing themselves under Charles the Simple, the easterners elected Duke Conrad of Franconia as king (r. 911–18). He spent the seven years of his reign vainly trying to assert his authority over the great men who had elected him, and, on his deathbed, he designated Duke Henry of Saxony as his successor. The magnates (great men), assuming that Henry would be no more successful than Conrad I in building royal power, elected him.

In 918, the fiscal condition of the royal house of Germany was dreadful. The magnates had gained control over the royal estates, which had been the economic basis of Carolingian power, to such a degree that when Conrad died, the royal fisc had diminished to 180 estates distributed about the kingdom. The Saxon dukes had been among the most successful usurpers of royal estates; only five royal estates still existed in Saxony. When Henry ascended the throne and added his family holdings to those of the royal house, the number of estates held by the German king jumped to about 600.

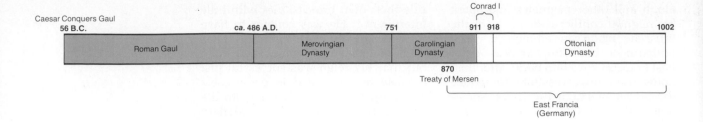

Henry I (r. 918–36) has the reputation of having ignored the affairs of the kingdom while continuing to strengthen his ducal power, which was the basis of his authority, but he actually gave considerable attention to his royal obligations. He pushed back the northern Slavs and began an eastward expansion of Germany that lasted for centuries. This expansion was not merely a conquest, but rested on missionary activity and colonization. Henry and his successors supported

missionaries in eastern Europe and the north and built new towns populated by Germans. Many of the major cities of Poland and Czechoslovakia were founded as German colonial settlements in the tenth and eleventh centuries.

Henry also developed a cavalry force to counter the fast-moving Magyars, and this troop inflicted the first defeat on the raiders in 933. Meanwhile, the king worked assiduously to force the dukes to recognize his authority. He forced the Swabians to accept his own nominee as duke; he made a marriage alliance between his family and that of the duke of Lorraine (Lotharingia); and he made a serious effort to regain control of the old royal estates. He also seems to have initiated a policy toward the episcopate and great monasteries that affected German politics and religion for centuries. He was certainly the best German king since Louis the German.

Otto I

When Henry died, his son Otto I (r. 936–73) became king by hereditary right, although formal election was held in accordance with the precedent of 911. Building on his father's success, Otto was able to establish a powerful monarchy. He continued his father's effort to bring the Slavs into the Church and to colonize the eastern frontier, and he supported the establishment of the bishoprics of Magdeburg and Prague as part of this effort. During the first five years of his reign, Otto faced several serious rebellions led by dukes, and, in putting them down, he gained control of the ducal

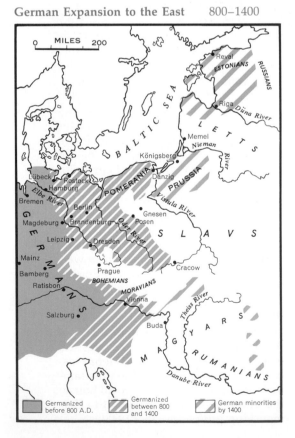

German Expansion to the East   800–1400

power in Bavaria, Swabia, and Lorraine. In 939, he annexed Franconia to Saxony. The general plan of these early successes was to establish members of his own family in the duchies, but he soon found that they too had a penchant for taking up local interests and rebelling. Therefore, he adopted Henry's idea of using the churches as a basis of royal authority.

To gain control of the churches, Otto had to assert his authority to appoint bishops and archbishops. This right had once been held by the Carolingians, but the dukes and other magnates had long ago usurped it. Otto successfully wrested it from these men, and his royal chapel became the training ground for clerics who later became loyal bishops. As he succeeded in appointing his own men to the episcopal churches, he granted land and rights to them, and, in turn, they became effective representatives of his power. The policy included assertion of control over the appointment of abbots in the richest monasteries, so that they too became agents of royal authority.

The policy gave Otto three main advantages. First, he made the best educated and ablest men in the kingdom loyal supporters of his monarchy. Second, the rule of celibacy was enforced among the higher clergy, though not among the lower, so that the bishoprics could not become dynastic powers. Third, Otto could rely on the bishops to act as a counterpoise to magnates in their districts and as direct supporters of royal authority. The success and importance of the program was demonstrated in 982, when Otto's successor, Otto II, campaigned in Italy with an army in which 76 percent of the troops were supplied from the lands of churches.

Otto I became the most powerful king in Europe, and his court, as the training academy of bishops and abbots, became a center of intellectual and artistic life. In 951, he seized an opportunity to marry the heiress to the throne of Italy—in part to prevent the king of Burgundy or one of his own

Ivory plaque showing Otto the Great offering a model of Magdeburg Cathedral to Christ (late tenth century).

dukes from marrying her—and this led him to revive the imperial title, which had been vacant since 924. But the pope was hostile to the idea, and a rebellion in Germany forced Otto to return home. During the next decade he was concerned with this trouble and with the threat of Magyar raids.

Germany and Italy at the Time of Otto the Great   962

Papal Coronation of
Otto the Great
962

Death of
Frederick II
1250

Napoleonic Reorganization
of the Germanies
1806

H O L Y   R O M A N   E M P I R E

In 961, a new pope, John XII (r. 955–64), appealed to Otto for aid against an Italian usurper, Berengar of Friuli, who claimed to be king of Italy, and Otto crossed the Alps a second time. After putting down Berengar, Otto again sought the imperial crown, and in 962 Pope John crowned him Emperor of the Romans. But relations between John and Otto soon deteriorated. As emperor, Otto wanted to assert the same rights in the papal church as he had in German bishoprics, and naturally John objected. In 963, Otto drove John from Rome and presided over a council that deposed John and elected a pope of Otto's liking. Otto controlled the election of two other popes during his reign, and these actions became important precedents in later debates over the relationship between the secular and ecclesiastical authorities.

From 962, Otto spent most of the remainder of his reign in Italy, trying to consolidate his position. He made good progress in the north, but could not extend his authority over the south. He did receive Byzantine recognition for his new title and achieved the long-sought alliance between the western and eastern imperial houses when he arranged the marriage of his son Otto II with the imperial princess Theophano.

Otto II (r. 973–83) spent most of his reign in Germany, where there were widespread rebellions against the monarchy. The magnates had been kept in line by Otto I, and they hoped to regain some of their power and independence under the new king. When Otto II died, the magnates achieved much of their purpose because Otto left an infant heir, Otto III (r. 983–1002). The government was run in his name by the queen mother Theophano and Otto I's widow Adelaide. While Otto III's authority was recognized immediately in Italy, the regents had to give up a great deal to achieve the same in Germany. As a result, the German dukes and magnates won a greater measure of autonomy than they had enjoyed since the days of Henry I. Young Otto III was raised in a Byzantinized court, and he dreamed of restoring the Christian empire of Constantine the Great, the first Christian emperor. He and his father were served by Gerbert, who was reputed to be the most learned man in Europe.

Gerbert (ca. 945–1003) was born in Aurillac in Aquitaine. He studied in Spain, where Christians were in contact with the Moslems, and learned some mathematics and astronomy. After his sojourn in Spain, he went to Italy where he met Otto I, who made him tutor of Otto II. From this period,

Ivory plaque showing Otto II, his wife Theophano, and their son Otto III kneeling before Christ (*ca.* 980).

The four provinces of Slavinia, Germania, Gallia, and Roma (left) paying homage to Otto III (right), from the Reichenau Gospels (tenth century). Note that Otto wears a Roman imperial costume, not a Germanic one.

he had a close relation to the East Frankish royal family. About the time Otto II became king, Gerbert went to Reims in West Francia to study logic with a famed teacher there, and he soon taught at the cathedral school in Reims. About 980, Gerbert returned to Otto II's court, and Otto appointed him abbot of the great Italian abbey of Bobbio, near Piacenza. But this did not work out because Gerbert tried to reform the financial system of the monastery, which was under the control of the local nobility. He returned to Reims, where he became involved in West Frankish politics, eventually supporting the house of Capet against the Carolingian, Charles of Lotharingia, brother of the last Carolingian king, Lothar. With Hugh Capet's support, Gerbert became archbishop of Reims in 991. But there was controversy over his appointment, and he eventually went back to Italy, where he received support from Otto III. Otto appointed him archbishop of Ravenna (from which position he was finally able to carry out the reforms at Bobbio) and then, in 999, pope.

As pope, Gerbert took the name Sylvester II to signify that Otto III and he were renewing the empire and the cooperation between the emperor and pope that had existed in the time of Constantine I and Sylvester I. As part of this work, Sylvester authorized the establishment of an independent archdiocese and Church hierarchy in Poland and crowned Stephen of Hungary king, both in 1000. He also brought King Olaf Tryggvason of Norway and his new church into the orbit of papal authority. But the dream of rebuilding the empire failed when Otto III died childless in 1002, and Sylvester died the next year.

Nonetheless, Gerbert's career was of the greatest importance in the culture of western Europe. He had united teaching and scholarship with service to the highest worldly authority, so that the attainment of learning appeared to be a viable road to success. Further, his connection with Spain opened up a world of knowledge then unknown in the West. Gerbert was credited with introducing Arabic numerals to Europe, which made work in mathematics easier. Roman numerals were poorly suited to scientific work of any kind. He also reorganized the study of logic, which provided the basis of intellectual work. Thus, this politically prominent intellectual stood at the beginning of a cultural revival that would eventually engender the renaissance of the twelfth century.

ANGLO-SAXON ENGLAND

Anglo-Saxon Culture

By the end of the seventh century the Anglo-Saxon kingdoms, the Heptarchy (seven kingdoms), were fully converted to Christianity and were politically stable. During the eighth century the kingdoms engaged in active trade with the Continent, and during the second half of the century the *bretwalda* or chief king among the seven kingdoms was Offa of Mercia (r. 757–96), whose reign marked a period of prosperity.

This was a period in which Charlemagne dominated Europe and was looked upon by other kings, including Offa, as a model. But after the fall of Spain to the Moors, England, not the Frankish kingdom, was the intellectual center of northern Europe. The English had inherited an intellectual and artistic tradition from the Irish monks who had converted the northern Angles during the sixth century. The Irish had preserved the remnants of Roman civilization when they were driven out of Britain by the Anglo-Saxon invaders. At the beginning of the eighth century, the Northumbrian monk Bede rose to prominence in England and began a tradition that eventually produced Alcuin and other intellectual leaders of early medieval Europe.

Bede wrote commentaries on many books of both the Old and New Testaments and was one of the founders of the medieval tradition of biblical commentary. He also wrote works on astronomy and introduced to the West a dating system, beginning from the birth of Christ, that had been created by a Greek writer of the sixth century. Bede's most important work was the *Ecclesiastical History of the English People,* a wonderfully written work that is the principal source of information about early Anglo-Saxon history. Yet, his greatest contribution was as a teacher. Bede's pupil Egbert became head of the cathedral school in York and then bishop of the city, and, under him, York became the intellectual capital of England. Egbert's student Aelbert succeeded him as archbishop, and Aelbert made his favorite student Alcuin head of the cathedral school. It was on a mission to Rome for Aelbert's successor that Alcuin met Charlemagne.

The eighth century was also important in the literary history of the English. As their world changed from the heroic, pagan society of the migrations to the settled, Christian society of the Heptarchy, English poets set down in writing some of the ancient stories they had told in the halls of the kings, aristocrats, and ordinary freemen for generations. The most important of the poems was *Beowulf,* an anonymous work which tells of a heroic king of premigration days in southern Scandinavia. The version of the poem we have stems from about A.D. 1000, but the earliest version was written about 725. The great battle poems *Maldon* and *Brunanburh* date from the ninth century, though they too received their final form in the tenth. In the last quarter of the ninth century, King Alfred the Great made Anglo-Saxon a language of cultural transmission. He himself translated Bede's history, and he ordered translations of works by Boethius and other important writers. He apparently also commissioned the writing of the *Anglo-Saxon Chronicle,* a history of events which was continued into the twelfth century.

Anglo-Saxon Government

After King Alfred defeated the Great Army of the Vikings, his successors carried on the work of conquering the

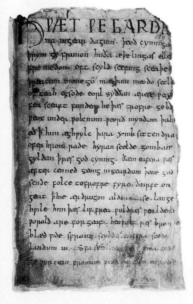

Page from the earliest manuscript of *Beowulf* (tenth century).

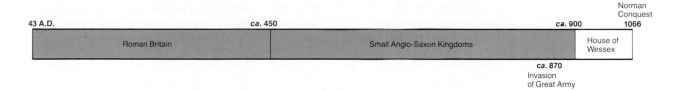

43 A.D.	ca. 450	ca. 900	Norman Conquest 1066
Roman Britain	Small Anglo-Saxon Kingdoms		House of Wessex

ca. 870
Invasion
of Great Army

Danelaw, virtually the whole eastern half of England. In the process, the Wessex royal house united the Anglo-Saxon kingdoms, and by 950 England was a unified kingdom. To secure their conquests, the kings supported a reform of the English church and introduced new institutions of local government. The church reform brought Benedictine monasticism to England and gave the bishoprics monastic constitutions. The clergy of English bishoprics were henceforth members of monasteries established in the cathedral churches. The new institutions of local government were so effective that they survived the Anglo-Saxon monarchy for centuries and even formed the basis of local government in the United States of America.

The tenth-century Anglo-Saxon kings divided the country into shires, or counties, and then subdivided the shires into smaller units called hundreds. Shires and hundreds were judicial as well as administrative units; the shire court met twice a year while the hundred courts met about once a month. For the most part, this was a rural organization. Fortified towns were organized as boroughs, which had courts of their own.

Although this system was similar to that established by Charlemagne, it differed significantly because the nobles never got control of the individual districts. Although the English king was surrounded by noble ealdermen (earls), each of whom had responsibility for several shires, the government of the shires came to be controlled by the king directly through his representatives. The system rested on the way the king managed his own estates, which were scattered throughout the realm. He managed these properties

through *reeves* or bailiffs, and gradually one of these was appointed chief reeve of the shire (shire reeve or sheriff) to supervise the others. When the shires became units of government, the sheriffs made the natural transition to head of the local government. The sheriff managed the collection of royal revenues and held the semiannual court.

England from Alfred the Great to Edgar

Powerful as the sheriff became, he never became independent of the king. Though he came to be counted among the nobility, he ranked beneath the great men, the earls, and the king could replace him if he failed to do his job loyally and efficiently. By the end of the tenth century, the English king had a representative in every part of the country. In contrast, the kings on the Continent grew weak and poor because they lost control of local government and revenues. By the eleventh century, England rivaled Germany as the most powerful kingdom in Europe.

MEDIEVAL SOCIETY: THE GROWTH OF FEUDAL INSTITUTIONS

Since the eighteenth century, historians have referred to medieval society as "feudal society." The term "feudal" was coined in the eighteenth century to describe a society based on the fief (*feudum* in Latin), a property held of the king or lesser lord in return for services, primarily military service. The fief was not owned by its holder, so that the services were not like Roman or modern taxes, which owners owe on their property, but was a grant for life. It was the physical element in a relationship between two men, lord and subordinate (eventually called a vassal), in which loyalty and mutual help were the most important elements. The fief provided support for the subordinate enabling him to serve his lord. In their full picture of feudal society, historians saw peasants, in their turn, as subject to the fiefholder, so that the whole of society, outside the cities, was subsumed in the feudal system. The vision of feudalism was of a military structure based on feudal tenures— that is, property rights that were less than ownership, but more than leasehold. According to this view, the feudal tenures, which included peasant holdings that were more precarious than those held by the lords, deter-mined the whole structure and character of rural society in the Middle Ages.

Modern studies have dispelled this view. Since the early 1950s, scholars studying specific regions of medieval Europe based on extant documents (many of them preserved in monastic archives), have shown that while fiefs existed, so did simple ownership of land. In these studies, medieval society appears as a complex structure, and it is no longer possible to speak of "feudal society." Nonetheless, feudal institutions, on which feudalism was supposed to have been based, did play a role in medieval society and can be said to be among the distinctive features of that society. Hence, it remains important to trace their origins and development.

Feudal institutions were primarily aristocratic. They affected the legal status, though not the life, of peasants. They were based on the notion of "tenure," a word that describes a right that one has to occupy land—by freehold (ownership), lease for a term of years, or villeinage. Villeinage was a hereditary tenure, but it was held at the will of a lord, who himself might hold the land as freehold or by some other tenure. For example, a friend of the king could receive land as a fief and grant parts of it to small farmers in villeinage. In the Middle Ages, many farms and mills, which also fell under this system, were subject to a chain of tenures: the holder held it by one tenure from a person who held it by another who held it from another and so on. In peasant villages, some families had freeholds, while others held their lands as tenants of the aristocracy. Every village also contained families that held no land, and, therefore, had no tenure. These persons were cottagers. They usually lived in a cottage that belonged to someone else; they had a small vegetable garden and supplemented their meager living by working for others. A person's legal status depended on the character of his tenure. Freeholders were freemen with full legal rights. Villeins were subject to the authority of those from whom they held their land in villeinage. Cottagers were subject to the authority of the lord of the village.

Feudal tenure was one of the many types of tenure, but the system that historians call "feudalism" included aspects of social and political relationships that had little to do with tenure. There were three main foundations of feudal institutions—the relationship between lord and vassal, the fragmentation of public power, and the devolution of public authority into private hands—each of which developed separately.

Vassalage derived from an old Roman institution, the commendation. In the late Roman period, one person could commend himself to another. The act created a legal relationship between them within which the superior owed protection to the inferior, while the inferior owed loyalty and assistance to the superior. The man who commended himself became the *fidelis* (faithful man) of his lord and took an oath of fealty to him. This was commonly the way in which a small farmer who faced ruin saved himself. He placed himself and his land in the hands of a great landowner. A second result of the act was the creation of a subject tenure—using a later term—by which the farmer held his land. Obviously, the subject tenure and the legal status of its holder were not things great men sought for themselves, and until the eighth century the subject relationship, which was then called vassalage, had a stigma attached to it. To be sure, the aristocrat owed allegiance to his king, but this relationship derived from the ancient relationship between the Germanic war leader and his warriors, which the Roman writers who heard of it had called the *comitatus*. The relationships of obedience and loyalty in the *comitatus* were honorable—the relationships of free men with their king.

During the eighth and ninth centuries, the institutions of the *comitatus* and vassalage gradually merged. In 757, the Duke of Bavaria was caught in a web of intrigue and treason and was forced to commend himself to King Pippin as a vassal. In 787, Charlemagne forced this same man to acknowledge his status as a royal vassal. As Charlemagne used this device to bring some of his overmighty subjects into his power—they were bound to him by an oath of fealty—the stigma of the status began to wear off.

Feudal tenure, which eventually came to be called the fief, derived directly from the Roman law of property. In Roman law, a person could grant land as a benefice, under which the grantee held the land on very favorable terms. Nonetheless, the grantor retained a proprietary right in the land. In Roman times, such grants were made for a definite period of time, but by the seventh century, under the Merovingians, they were usually made

Twelfth-century seal depicting a vassal giving homage to his lord.

The Ceremony of Becoming a Vassal

1127

This description comes from the period when feudalism was fully developed. It is very full because the leading men of Flanders had just accepted a new count after a disputed succession. Homage (the specific obligation of the vassal) is carefully distinguished from the more general obligation of fidelity. By the twelfth century it was assumed that most vassals had fiefs.

On Thursday, homages were done to the count. First, they did homage in this way. The count asked [the vassal] if he wished to become his man without reserve, and the latter answered: "I do." Then, joining his hands together, he placed them in the hands of the count, and they bound themselves to each other by a kiss. Then the man who had just done homage pledged fidelity . . . to the count in these words: "I promise on my faith to be faithful from now on to count William and to observe [the obligations of] my homage completely, in good faith, and without deceit." This he swore on the relics of the saints. . . . Finally, with a little stick that he held in his hand, the count gave investiture of fiefs to all those who had . . . promised security, done homage, and taken the oath.

From Galbert of Bruges, *De Multro Karoli comitis Flandriarum*, ed. by H. Pirenne (Paris, 1891), p. 89.

for the life of the grantee. By the tenth century, the fief had become hereditary. While the lord still granted it for life, he always granted it to the eldest son of the previous holder.

The original purpose of the benefice was to cement relations between grantor and grantee. Under Charles Martel and Pippin the Short, it became common for the granting of benefices and commendations—the making of the lord-vassal relationship—to be joined. The lord granted a benefice to his vassal as a way of providing the support that he owed the vassal. When this joining of the two institutions happened, a man could actually increase his wealth by becoming a vassal, and by the late ninth century a feudal hier-archy was beginning to emerge. Many men of the old aristocratic families, who held large tracts of land by free-hold, increased their economic stature by becoming vassals of the king and getting benefices. About the same time, the word "benefice" was giving way to a new term, "feudum" or fief.

The new institutions rested also on the ancient *comitatus* and, therefore, on the old Germanic ideas about the function of royal government. Eighth- and ninth-century vassals held fiefs principally for performing military service. The vassal was bound to serve in the royal army for a certain period— eventually 40 days per year. He served at his own expense, which meant that the fief was to provide the income

The life of a feudal knight: carrying a standard into battle (ninth century).

needed for the service and was normally of a size that would produce the requisite income. The smallest military fief—there were other kinds, but they became increasingly rare—was the knight's fief or, as it came to be called in English, knight's fee. Many fiefs were much larger than that and were valued according to the number of knightly soldiers they could support.

The concept of the knight's fee was not so different from the old Roman concept that people who owned a piece of land had an obligation to serve in the army. Remember that the Byzantine government tried to ensure the prosperity of yeoman farmers, so that it would have sufficient military manpower. The differences between that old system and the European feudal system were the nature of the rights by which fief-holders held their lands and the size of the holdings. The size of fiefs in Europe was much greater than that of yeoman farms in the Byzantine Empire because the western system was a feature of the aristocracy and supported a new sort of soldier. This was the heavily armed mounted soldier, who became part of an elite corps in the armies of medieval Europe. The regular force of armed yeomen continued to be the foundation of the medieval army, but the mounted knights—who were professional soldiers—became its special element.

The development of this new type of soldier rested on the introduction of new technology—the horseshoe and the stirrup. There is much controversy about when these implements came into use—the Huns had them in the fifth century—but, in Europe, the rise of the new soldier based on them occurred in the eighth century. The horseshoe made the horse a reliable military vehicle, and the stirrup gave a rider the support and leverage he needed to fight on horseback. Charles Martel and Pippin the Short built up troops of the new soldiers by expanding the vassalage-benefice system. As part of this effort, they forced churches and monasteries to grant benefices to

A feudal knight accompanying a travelling king (eleventh century).

royal vassals and thus brought the churches into the military system. If one asks why Henry I and Otto I were able to make bishops and abbots part of their governments, the answer is that for generations the churches had been supplying knights to the royal armies, and, therefore, the highest ecclesiastical officials were already part of the feudal aristocracy.

The distinction between military and governmental function, which is commonplace in modern societies, did not exist in early medieval society. It was assumed that the elite of the army, the king's companions, were part of his government. In this way, the new feudal hierarchy functioned much like the ancient *comitatus,* which also had combined military and governmental functions. The difference was that while the *comitatus* had been made up mostly of young men who lived with the king, and who ceased to play a role in royal government when they went home to their farms and estates, the members of the feudal hierarchy held land from the king and were part of his government at court or at home. This was true both because the fief-holders owed the king allegiance and assistance and because the nature of government had changed since the Germans settled the Roman provinces.

Mounted knights in battle
(from the *Book of St. Gall, ca.
925).*

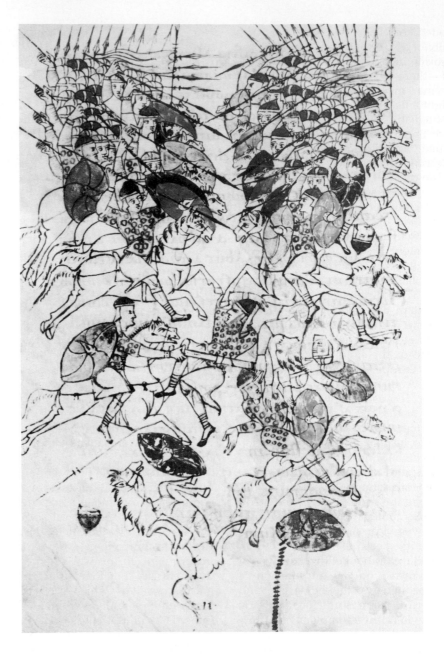

The governmental functions of early medieval kings were carried out from royal estates spread around the kingdom. Under Charlemagne the royal bailiffs and counts governed their districts from seats on royal estates; the income of the estates supported the functions of government. Consequently, the rights of government in each district were associated with specific properties and when these were granted away during the civil wars of the late Carolingians, the governmental powers went with them.

In France, the Viking invasions increased the fragmentation of governmental authority because the royal government was unable to meet the threat of the small bands of raiders. Local men organized the defense of their districts and arrogated governmental authority to themselves in the process. Some of these men held fiefs, others did not, but the fragmentation of public authority and its control by private—that is local—men was not a function of the growth of the feudal system. On the eastern frontier, by contrast, the large Magyar armies required a centralized defense against them, so that the threat they posed enhanced the role and power of the German kings and made it possible for Otto I to revive the *imperium* of Charlemagne.

Up to the end of the eleventh century, feudal institutions did not dominate the social or governmental life of any region of Europe, but in most regions there were some fief-holders scattered among those who held their estates by ancient freehold tenure. Many great men held estates under both systems. The rise of truly feudal states in England and the Latin kingdom of Jerusalem resulted from conquests to be treated later (see pp. 288–99).

Women in Early Medieval Society

The military society of the early medieval kingdoms was dominated by men, and feudal institutions and the social relations they engendered were fitted into this pattern. In the eighth and ninth centuries, when feudal tenure was held only for the life of the grantee, the king's male companions— and those of his chief vassals—earned their fiefs and their political power by showing their loyalty and demonstrating their ability. When most fiefs had become hereditary in the tenth century, they became the objects of dynastic strategy. Now, women became important in the social and political system because a lord's daughter could inherit the fief. Once this happened, the lord became concerned about his vassal's daughters, and the feudal relationship expanded to include the lord's power over the marriage of a potential heiress. The vassal could not give his daughter in marriage without the lord's approval, and an orphaned heiress became the ward of the lord, who could marry her to whomever he liked. Both of these provisions protected the lord's right to ensure that the right man entered the fief, so that the feudal duties would be properly and loyally carried out. Furthermore, marriage to an heiress became one way to enter the feudal hierarchy, and many men who achieved local power during the Viking period married women of the feudal aristocracy. The aristocracy of the central Middle Ages, the eleventh through thirteenth centuries, developed from such marriages.

Even after women became important for the maintenance of the feudal hierarchy, the law placed them in a subordinate position. A woman could not manage her own affairs: she could not buy or sell property on her own. Whatever she brought to a marriage was managed freely by her husband. She could not go to a law court without her husband or a male relative acting on her behalf. She could usually influence her family's decisions about marriage, but the power to decide resided with her father or her male relatives.

However, the realities of a woman's position and authority did not usually conform to the legal theory. In practice, the mistress of a feudal household was often left to run the affairs of the estate herself. Her husband was often at the royal court or, if he held many estates, visiting his other properties. In his absence, the mistress managed the large household and carried on the business of the estate. The bailiffs reported to her and took orders from her. She supervised the education of the children. If her husband was an important political figure, she often helped him maintain his position, which was hers also.

In the lower classes—as in all agricultural societies—women shared in the struggle to make a living. Peasant women generally had responsibility for the house garden and the animals— except the oxen or horses—and they helped with the harvesting. In towns, which were small and poor in the early Middle Ages, the wives of craftsmen managed the household and often helped sell their husbands' products. As in the upper classes, in the lower classes women shared the status and the work of their husbands.

Suggestions for Further Reading

General

On the rise of the Carolingians, see P. Geary, *Before France and Germany* (1988), and J. M. Wallace-Hadrill, *The Barbarian West, 400–1000* (1952). The best work on the Carolingian period is R. McKitterick, *The Frankish Kingdoms under the Carolingians* (1983). On the missionaries, see W. Levison, *England and the Continent in the Eighth Century* (1946), and C. H. Talbot, *Anglo-Saxon Missionaries in Germany* (1954), which treats the relationship between Pippin the Short and Boniface and provides a view of religious life in the eighth century. On Pippin's coronation, the most recent study is M. J. Enright, *Iona, Tara, and Soissons: The Origin of the Royal Anointing Ritual* (1985).

Charlemagne

The almost contemporaneous biography is Einhard, *Life of Charlemagne* (several editions, some with the later life by Notker). For a survey of the Frankish empire, see H. Fichtenau, *The Carolingian Empire* (1957), which emphasizes social conditions. D. Bullough, *The Age of Charlemagne*, 2nd ed. (1973), is a well-illustrated survey. For studies of Frankish institutions, see F. Ganshof, *Frankish Institutions under Charlemagne* (1968), and *The Carolingians and the Frankish Monarchy* (1971). On the economic history of the period, see R. Latouche, *The Birth of the Western Economy* (1961), and G. Duby, *The Early Growth of the Medieval Economy* (1974). For the different views of the Coronation of Charlemagne, see R. E. Sullivan, ed., *The Coronation of Charlemagne: What Did It Signify?* (1959). On the relations between the Franks and the papacy, see T. F. X. Noble, *The Republic of St. Peter: The Birth of the Papal State, 680–825* (1984). On the way people of the period lived, see P. Riché, *Daily Life in the Age of Charlemagne* (1978).

Later Carolingians

On Charles the Bald, see the studies in J. L. Nelson and M. T. Gibson, eds., *Charles the Bald: Court and Kingdom* (1981). On the ecclesiastical politics of the ninth century, see P. McKeon, *Hincmar of Laon and Carolingian Politics* (1978), and J. L. Nelson, "Charles the Bald and the Church in Town and Countryside," *Studies in Church History* 16 (1979) 103–18. On the Carolingian view of kingship, see W. Ullmann, *The Carolingian Renaissance and the Idea of Kingship* (1969). On the origins of the nobility, see the essays in T. Reuter, ed., *The Medieval Nobility* (1978). P. Sawyer, *The Age of the Vikings*, 2nd ed. (1971), gives a good picture of the Viking invasions. See also, J. M. Wallace-Hadrill, *The Vikings in Francia* (1975). On Viking civilization, see J. Brønsted, *The Vikings* (1960). C. A. Macartney, *The Magyars in the Ninth Century* (1930), is a scholarly study of the origins and wanderings of the Magyars.

The Carolingian Renaissance

On the origins of the Carolingian Renaissance, see M. L. W. Laistner, *Thought and Letters in Western Europe, 500–900* (1966); P. Riché, *Education and Culture in the Barbarian West* (1976); and L. R. Reynolds and N. G. Wilson, *Scribes and Scholars*, 2nd ed. (1974). For a survey of the Renaissance, see J. Broussard, *The Civilization of Charlemagne* (1969). On Charles the Bald as a patron, see R. McKitterick, "Charles the Bald (823–877) and his Library: The Patronage of Learning," *English Historical Review* 95 (1980) 28–47. K. J. Conant, *Carolingian and Romanesque Architecture* (1959); A. Grabar and C. Nordenfalk, *Early Medieval Painting: From the Fourth to the Eleventh Century* (1957); and J. Hubert, *Carolingian Art* (1970), give surveys of Carolingian art.

West and East Francia (France and Germany)

For an overview of the period in which the Carolingian dynasty ended, see R. S. Lopez, *The Tenth Century* (1959). On the history of West Francia (France) in the period, see E. James, *The Origins of France: From Clovis to the Capetians, 500–1000* (1982). For a general introduction to the history of the Ottonian empire, see G. Barraclough, *The Origins of Modern Germany* (1947); J. Fleckenstein, *Early Medieval Germany* (1978); and B. H. Hill, *The Rise of the First Reich: Germany in the Tenth Century* (1969). K. J. Leyser, *Rule and Conflict in an Early Medieval Society: Ottonian Saxony* (1979), provides a view of politics and social relations in tenth-century Germany.

Feudalism

On the growth of feudal institutions, see F. L. Ganshof, *Feudalism*, 3rd ed. (1964), which gives a good account of "classical feudalism" from the Carolingian period on. J. R. Strayer, *Feudalism* (1965), emphasizes political factors. For the role of feudalism in medieval society, see G. Duby, *Rural Economy and Country Life in the Medieval West* (1968), and G. Fourquin, *Lordship and Feudalism in the Middle Ages* (1976).

Women

For studies of women in early medieval society, see P. Stafford, *Queens, Concubines and Dowagers: The King's Wife in the Early Middle Ages* (1983); S. Wemple, *Women in Frankish Society* (1981); and S. M. Stuard, ed., *Women in Medieval Society* (1976), which is a collection of articles on the various roles played by women. See also, A. M. Lucas, *Women in the Middle Ages* (1983); E. S. Duckett, *Women and Their Letters in the Early Middle Ages* (1964); and M. Labarge, *A Baronial Household in the Thirteenth Century* (1965). On childrearing, see L. deMause, ed., *The History of Childhood* (1974).

10
Revival and Reform In Western Europe

*D*uring the late Carolingian period, much of what the early Carolingian rulers had achieved was lost. The central governments of France and Germany lost control of the nobility, which gradually coalesced around a few great men who created territorial principalities. The Church, which the early Carolingians had reformed and controlled, produced leaders who sometimes played the role of kingmakers. By the end of the Carolingian era, the Frankish kingdoms were fragmented into powerful duchies whose rulers recognized the king, while they acted as independent powers. The great lords usurped royal rights and gained control of royal estates, offices, the churches, and the monasteries of their regions. When they succeeded to the kingship, the Saxon dukes in Germany and the Capetians in France mounted their thrones as powerful ducal lords, and their first concern was the maintenance of their power in their own regions.

In France, the king remained the first among equals until the twelfth century. In Germany, the Saxon dukes made considerable progress toward the reestablishment of central government during the tenth century. A cornerstone of the policy of the Ottonians, as the Saxon kings are called after Otto I (r. 936–73), was the control and use of the Church. Otto asserted his authority to appoint bishops and abbots, and he granted these men rights, lands, and offices. His successors continued the policy, which created a powerful counterweight to the great magnates. Nonetheless, the Ottonians faced frequent rebellions, and the politics of the German kingdom were anything but tranquil.

Notwithstanding these facts, there was an improvement in security during the eleventh century, and from the second half of the century there was a

surge in all forms of human activity. Production and trade increased; cities grew and became important as social and economic centers; political, legal, and religious institutions grew stronger. At the same time, the intellectual tradition precariously preserved in the work of a few men like Pope Sylvester II (Gerbert of Aurillac) flowered into a great civilization, and the arts experienced a remarkable revival.

SOCIAL AND ECONOMIC DEVELOPMENT

The Agricultural Economy

The agricultural economy of the Middle Ages was based on village communities, many of which had been in continuous existence since Roman times. The agricultural practices and the social order of the villages rested on centuries of experience. The land of western Eu-

Tympanum of the church of St. Ursin at Bourges (twelfth century). This tympanum is unusual in its depiction of secular themes—the hunt and the labors of the months.

rope, which had once been heavily forested, had deep, rocky soil that could produce rich crops, but only if men cooperated in working it. The northern farmers had to use heavy plows that required large teams of oxen to pull them, and the cost both of the plow and the animals was too high for any one man. Moreover, several men had to tend the plow and team as it worked through the rocky soil.

The families of the village communities owned their own lands, or held lands by villeinage tenure (see p. 262), but the strips of land held by each family were part of common fields worked in concert by all. Individual families claimed the produce of their own strips when harvest time came. Obviously, some parts of the common fields produced more than others, and in most villages the families held strips scattered throughout the fields, so that all possessed some of the best land. But inevitably, good luck, good husbandry, or good marriages gave some families control of larger shares of productive land, while others fell into poverty. Every village had its leading members

The layout of a medieval village in Middle Ditchford, Gloucestershire, England, is still visible long after its desertion in the eleventh or twelfth century.

and its poor. However, in the social and economic environment of the medieval village, a run of bad luck, such as the untimely death of a husband or the failure of offspring or a disastrous legal suit, could change the fortunes of any family. All lived in fear of disaster.

In ancient times, the communities had learned to leave portions of the fields fallow to permit them to recover their nutrients. Cattle grazed on these unplanted fields, and their manure helped to replenish them. Nonetheless, medieval villages were perennially short of fodder for their animals. The pasturage, both on fallow fields and in nearby meadows (held in common), was almost always too small to provide sufficient hay to feed animals over the long European winters. In addition, the farmers could not supplement the supply of grass with grain feed because the planted fields yielded only about four grains for every one planted. (Modern American farms have yields of about twenty-five to one.) Consequently, the whole grain crop had to be saved for human consumption and for the next year's seed. The great feasts of late winter and early spring—which in pagan times had been connected with the fertility cults—permitted the agricultural community to get some use from animals that might die anyway because there was not enough fodder left at winter's end.

The usual diet was based on bread and cereals and had little meat in it. What meat the villagers ate—except at the great feasts—came from the common woods. The lords kept for themselves the right to hunt in the woods, but poaching was very common. The villagers were permitted to gather fuel, herbs, and mushrooms in the woods and to support herds of pigs; patches of woods were measured by the number of pigs they could support. The pigs were let loose to forage for acorns and roots, then rounded up once or twice a year for culling and slaughter.

From time immemorial the village communities were subject to the power of great landowners. The villages had mostly been settled on the Roman villas, which had been taken over by the new aristocracy of the German tribes. The lord held a part of the village's fields, controlled pasturage and woodland, and required the village community to work his domain. Members of the village were subject to different burdens of domainal obligation, and the process of sorting out who owed what kind of labor service was a constant occupation of the village and its lord.

The unit made up of the domain and village was called a villa or manor. In developing their manors into economically viable entities, the lords built mills, fish ponds, smithies, and other "industrial" works. The rights to use or hold these parts of the manor were arranged in a way similar to the holding of land. Millers and smiths held their respective manufactories from their lords and paid a rent in kind to them. The rights to take fish from ponds were similar to the rights the villagers held in the woodland or common pasture. As a whole, the manorial unit was not self-sufficient economically, but it was strong and productive.

The Agricultural Revolution of the Middle Ages

The regularity of economic and social development in the agricultural villages and their manors, which produced a common historical pattern across northern Europe, gives the system an image of conservatism. It is difficult to imagine how innovation would be introduced into such a stable social economy. But two features of medieval social and economic history actually promoted change. First, the settlement of new groups—the Germans, then their cousins the Vikings—disrupted the natural cycle of village life and introduced new ideas and new technology. Second, the lords increased their own wealth by encouraging peasants to reclaim old arable land and colonize new land, and these new villages were more open to innovation than the old.

The principal innovations in medieval agriculture were the use of the heavy wheeled plow, horsepower, and the introduction of three-field crop rotation to replace the ancient two-field rotation. These changes caused an increase of both the variety and quantity of crops grown, which, in turn, had important effects on the European diet.

The heavy wheeled plow had been used in a few places in late Roman times. It may have been an invention of the Celtic population of the northern provinces, but it has also been found in Germanic settlements. The Romans had brought their simple, unwheeled, light plows north with them from the Mediterranean lands, where these plows had performed adequately. It is actually better to plow the light southern soils with a scratch plow because the region is dry for most of the year and deep plowing, which exposes a good deal of soil, allows too much moisture to evaporate. But scratch plowing is inadequate for the heavy, moist soils of the north. The great advantage of the wheeled plow with a moldboard is precisely that it can cut deeply into the soil and turn it over to bring the nutrients to the surface. The plentiful rain of northern Europe makes water conservation unnecessary in normal years.

Like all important inventions, the heavy plow produced economic and social changes as its use spread throughout northern Europe during the ninth and tenth centuries. First, it was an expensive implement that required constant repair, because the receding glaciers had left rocks in the excellent soils through which it was

Illustration from an eleventh-century manuscript depicting plowing and sowing.

Horse in harness pulling a harrow (detail from a thirteenth-century manuscript illustration).

pulled, and the plowshare was often damaged. Villagers had to band together to buy and maintain their plow, and they needed smiths to keep it in good repair. Of course, the smiths did more than tend the village plow, and through their other activities, they contributed to the spread of iron implements for agriculture. Second, the heavy plow required an amount of animal power that no peasant could muster himself. Teams ranged in size, but teams of six to eight oxen were not uncommon. Such teams were put together from the animal resources of several families, and, therefore, not only the ownership of the plow, but also its use fostered cooperative agriculture. Third, the more powerful plow increased production from old lands and permitted the exploitation of new fields, so that food production climbed steadily from the ninth through the twelfth centuries.

A second great innovation of this period was the introduction of horses to replace oxen as the source of power. The advantage of horses over oxen is speed. The horse generates a bit less power than the ox, but pulls at twice the speed. The use of horses not only increased the amount of plowing done each season, but also permitted the teams to go out much further from the village before beginning their day's work than had been possible with oxen. The disadvantage of horse power is that the horse is a much more delicate creature—more susceptible to disease and injury—than the ox.

The change from oxen to horses rested on two technological advances— the use of the horseshoe and the development of a collar that would permit a horse to pull weight comfortably. The horseshoe had been in use for some time before the collar was invented. The Huns had had horseshoes, and the Carolingian cavalry had used them. The hooves of horses are quite fragile, and the moist, rocky ground of Europe causes both breakage and hoof rot. In Europe, therefore, the iron shoe transformed the horse into a reliable animal, for both transport and war. But until the invention of a collar, the horse could not pull wagons or plows of any great weight, because the old harnesses crossed the animal's windpipe. During the ninth century, a new collar, which rested on the horse's withers (the highest points of the shoulder blades), came into use, and the horse became a farm and team animal.

The horse revolution was not rapid because the animals were expensive to maintain, but it gradually spread over Europe during the eleventh century. It had two important effects. First, the use of horses for drawing wagons increased the efficiency of land transport, both for commerce and for military campaigns. This led to the growth of a land transport industry served by guilds of teamsters. It also led to a general improvement of the European road system and increased the commercial opportunities for some crossroads communities. Second, the increased speed of horse power permitted an expansion of arable land and contributed to the growth of food production. Oxen continued in use in old and poor settlements, but the use of horses often accompanied the aggressive agricultural expansion that steadily pushed back the medieval forest.

Finally, the northern European villages introduced a three-field rotation system. Since old villages, in which the distribution of land and the socioeconomic structure were based on the two-field system, must have been reluctant to make this change, it probably started in new settlements. The new system expanded the amount of land in production while preserving the old principle that land should be left fallow to recover. Now, two-thirds—instead of half—of the village fields were in production at any time. The system also encouraged the villagers to develop a new crop rotation because it provided them with two large fields to plant rather than one.

During the first year of the new cycle, the farmers typically planted one field in winter wheat, which they harvested in July; then they let the winter-wheat field rest until the following spring, when they sowed it with a summer crop. They harvested this crop in the fall, replowed the field and sowed it again in winter wheat. The other two fields were planted in the same way, but on a different cycle, so that in any year, one-third of the village's land was in winter wheat, one-third in summer grain, and one-third fallow. Over a three-year period, each field was rested for one and a half years. In many regions, the summer crop was a legume, such as soybean, which returns nitrogen to the soil, so that production increased even more than would be expected just from the extra amount of land kept in production.

The system was only usable where the even distribution of rainfall during the year permitted the growing of the summer crop and where village agriculture was possible. In the Mediterranean lands summer is a dry season during which no crop can be grown, and in Scandinavia the rocky soil and short growing season do not support large agricultural communities. Therefore, Mediterranean villages kept the two-field system, while most Scandinavian farming was done by individual homesteads, which preserved the independence and importance of free farmers and created a social and politi-

The Three-Field System

	Field A	Field B	Field C
First Year	FALLOW until the fall Sow wheat in the fall	Harvest wheat in July FALLOW from July until the spring	Sow oats in the spring Harvest oats in the fall FALLOW until the next fall
Second Year	Harvest wheat in July FALLOW from July until the spring	Sow oats in the spring Harvest oats in the fall FALLOW until the next fall	FALLOW until the fall Sow wheat in the fall
Third Year	Sow oats in the spring Harvest oats in the fall FALLOW until the next fall	FALLOW until the fall Sow wheat in the fall	Harvest wheat in July FALLOW from July until the spring

cal world different from that on the Continent.

Commerce and Industry

The political and economic crises of the late Roman period and the Germanic invasions had reduced both the size and the economic importance of European towns. The German kings used the cities as fortified centers of royal government, but they also used royal estates scattered throughout the country, so that cities ceased to have the central role they had had under the Romans. This was particularly true in northern Europe. In Italy, the Gothic wars of the sixth century devastated the cities, and they recovered very slowly. It was over two centuries before Italian cities began again to affect more than their own regions. In Spain, the Moslem conquest cut off the old cities—such as Valencia, Seville, and Granada—from the former European provinces of the Roman Empire. The slow progress of reconquest during the eleventh and twelfth centuries brought these communities back into contact with the West.

After the collapse of Roman power, international trade declined—though it did not end—and this commercial decline contributed to economic depression in the cities. During the sixth through eighth centuries, there was not enough commerce or governmental activity to encourage the recovery of urban centers. The towns became local market centers, but this function did not support a large population or sparkling cultural activity. The later Carolingians tried to revive international commerce. They invited Jewish merchant communities to emigrate from Italy to the northern cities and gave them privileges and protection. During the late ninth and tenth centuries, these merchants carried on an active trade with the Mediterranean and provided an economic outlet for the agricultural surplus produced by the great northern estates. The Jews had connections with Jewish communities

A peddler offering silver beakers (detail from a thirteenth-century manuscript).

in commercial centers throughout Italy and the Mediterranean. By following this policy, the kings stimulated the local market economy, which was now tied to an international trade network, and the great growth of the late Carolingian economy rested on the local markets.

Within the towns, the Jews settled in close-knit quarters and formed a distinctive cultural as well as commercial community. Jewish religious practice required that they live near the synagogue—the place of worship and study—and in buildings arranged around courtyards. On the sabbath, the Jew is not permitted to work, cook, carry anything, or handle money, but he can perform necessary functions within his own home. The rabbis defined the courtyard communities as "homes," so that the people in them could get along on Saturdays. The Jewish community also had a special legal status because it was under the protection of the king. In the tenth century, when the local lords gained control of most towns, the Jews remained in a separate status, forming a self-governing community under royal protection. The degree to which these communities helped the twelfth-century kings to regain control of the towns is not clear, but there are many similarities between the urban communities incorporated under royal law at that time and the old Jewish communities that existed within them.

The recovery of the Italian towns began around 800. Ravenna, the former capital of Byzantine power in Italy, had never been a great commercial center and had lost its administrative importance after the Lombards finally took it in 751. Venice was also Byzantine in this period and was the transit point for Byzantine commerce in western Europe. Its importance was demonstrated when Charlemagne seized it in order to put pressure on the imperial court to recognize him as emperor. During the next century Italian cities, particularly those in the Po Valley, grew slowly as the recovery in the Byzantine Empire increased trade with the eastern Mediterranean.

After the Fatimid caliphs conquered Egypt in 969 and reformed the Egyptian fiscal system to encourage trade, the recovery of Italian cities gathered speed. Amalfi (south of Naples), Venice, and Genoa were soon active trading partners of Egypt, and the new wealth spread to secondary markets in Italy and northern Europe. Italian commerce benefited in this period from the disruption of the northern routes between the Middle East and Europe, which went through Russia to the Baltic regions. New invaders continually blocked these ancient routes. As a result, from the later tenth century on, Italian merchants became common in Europe, competing with the small communities of Jews, and the beginning of a substantial Christian merchant class can be traced to this period.

The growth of the Italian cities was matched, though not to the same extent, in Flanders. Bruges, Ghent, St. Omer, Ypres, and other towns of that region grew as centers of both commerce and industry. Under its counts, Flanders achieved political stability very early, and the combination of internal security and productive farmlands encouraged both trade and the growth of population. But the trade was smaller both in volume and in value than the Italian trade. It involved mostly raw materials, particularly wool and wood, from England and Scandinavia.

Wool was the basic clothing material of western Europe, but to turn the raw wool into cloth took a great deal of work by specialists. The wool had to be cleaned and carded, spun into thread, woven, smoothed by shearing off the knots and rough spots, and dyed. These processes could be carried out by villagers, but the production of high quality, comfortable cloth required trained and experienced craftsmen. The market for good cloth developed as the rise of agricultural production created wealth, and Flanders, which was the principal market for wool, became

the center of industrialized textile production. The region became the most urbanized in medieval Europe; and, until the industrial revolution in the nineteenth century, the textile industry continued to be the most important industry in western Europe.

Outside of Italy and Flanders, medieval towns were small, and their commercial and population growth was slower and less spectacular than in those regions. Nonetheless, from the tenth century on, old towns all over Europe grew, and new ones were founded. The principal founders of new towns were the kings, who were trying to expand the commercial agricultural economy into the hinterland by establishing towns further and further up the rivers from the coastal ports. In England, the growth of the wool trade was an important result of this economic development. In Germany, the kings founded towns along the eastern frontier where the colonization efforts of Henry I and the Ottos were concentrated.

These innovations by the kings made many towns, particularly the new ones, directly subject to the monarchs, but at the beginning of the period of growth most towns were still subject to local feudal lords. Many urban centers had grown up around monasteries and were subject to the

Weaving became an important industry in the eleventh and twelfth centuries. Note that the upright loom was used instead of the horizontal loom, which was developed a century later (detail of a miniature painting from the eleventh-century manuscript of Rabanus Maurus).

A woman carding wool (detail from a twelfth-century manuscript illustration).

jurisdiction of the abbot and community of monks. Others formed around old, well-located villas and lived under the authority of the lord of the villa. This political fragmentation had a harmful effect on the commercial economy of the towns. The lords imposed taxes, tolls, and market fees to take advantage of the commercial wealth of their towns, and merchants who traveled from town to town repeatedly had to pay fees. The need to reduce the obstacles in the path of commerce was felt both by the merchant communities in the towns and by the kings, who benefited most from the long distance trade. At the end of the eleventh century, these two political powers joined to create conditions that favored trade and, therefore, themselves.

The device that permitted the towns and kings to escape the power of the local lords was the royal charter of incorporation. The merchants of a town appealed to the king for a charter that would give them the right to govern themselves as an independent corporation under royal law and protection.

The town would pay for the privilege to incorporate and would agree to pay taxes into the royal treasury, but the town fathers themselves—who were invariably the leading merchants—could arrange the collection of the taxes in a way that would not harm commerce.

By the early twelfth century, trial and error had produced a model charter, which was then copied repeatedly. Thereafter, the charter movement spread rapidly across Europe. Under a charter, a town achieved freedom from feudal obligations because the city fathers and kings recognized that freedom was a necessary condition for the growth of commerce and industry. A person who had lived in an incorporated city for one year and a day was freed from his former servile condition, and it became proverbial that "city air makes one free."

The new urban corporations were dominated by merchants, who had formed guilds to organize and control their commercial activities. The merchants' guildhall commonly doubled as the city hall. But other groups of urban craftsmen—such as butchers, weavers, and smiths—had also formed guilds to regulate their professions, and through their guilds, these people competed with the merchants for political power in the cities. Where industrial activities were very important, as in Flanders, the craftsmen's guilds had the economic and social power to win political power, and in the later Middle Ages the competition for power in these towns often led to riots and revolutions.

The Duke of Normandy and the Norman Church   1172

Although this document comes from the twelfth century, it repeats obligations laid on the Norman Church in the time of William the Conqueror.

The bishop of Avranches owes 5 knights, and another five from the fief of St. Philibert.
The bishop of Coutances, 5 knights
The bishop of Bayeux, 20 knights
The bishop of Sées, 6 knights
The bishop of Lisieux, the service of 20 knights
The abbot of Fécamp, the service of 10 knights
The abbot of Mont St. Michel, the service of 6 knights in the Avranchin and Cotentin and 1 knight in the Bessin
The abbot of St. Ouen of Rouen, the service of 6 knights [other abbots owe a total of 25 knights].

From Charles H. Haskins, *Norman Institutions* (Cambridge, Mass.: Harvard University Press, 1925), p. 8.

REFORM OF THE CHURCH

By the middle of the eleventh century many of the institutions in the Church had been secularized and were in need of reform. The German kings had been appointing bishops and abbots for over a hundred years, and this system had two effects. First, although the royal appointees were usually men of good character and high ability, they had a strong feeling of loyalty to the monarchy and were often involved in secular affairs. Second, the kings had granted lands and rights to the bishops, so that they had become part of royal government. Therefore, bishops were expected to do homage to the king and to take an oath of fealty to him.

The process of secularization also affected the parish churches and lesser monasteries. Before the Germans converted to Christianity, they had built private temples and shrines on their properties. After the conversion, the lords renewed the old practice by building private churches in the villages of their larger estates. Under Germanic law, those churches belonged to the lords, who, therefore, appointed the priests and collected the income. Church income consisted primarily of first fruits (an offering from the harvest) and tithes, a tenth of the produce of the land. As a result, the private churches were a part of the lords' estates and produced income, like the domain, leased land, and mill. Unlike the kings, the lords often appointed to these parish churches priests who were not educated for the priesthood and some who were serfs of the lord. Consequently, the spiritual and financial condition of many rural parishes was scandalous.

From the seventh century on, lords also established monastic houses on their lands. Here, the motivation seems to have been financial and dynastic. Particularly in England, but also on the Continent, the folk law of the Germanic communities determined who inherited a man's estate, and no one could alter those rules of succession. In effect, the family owned the estate rather than the head of the family, who was required to meet the military and financial obligations attached to it.

The creation of the Christian Church introduced a new element into this system of landholding and inheritance. As already noted (see p. 154), during the seventh century the kings created *book-*

Bronze figure of a monk writing on the tail of a monster, on which he is seated (from a cross or candlestick base, north German or English, *ca.* 1150).

land, a new form of landholding for the Church alone that was based on the royal charter. The new form of tenure, in addition to putting the Church on a firm economic foundation, gave new power to the heads of families. By 700, large landholders had recognized that by getting royal charters for part of their lands, they could free it from the constraints of folk law. This would permit them to sell it or to pass it on to favored offspring. They got these charters by establishing monasteries and asking the king for charters for land they would grant to the new houses. Because they controlled the houses, the lords could get the chartered lands back virtually any time. By the early eighth century, churchmen were complaining that aristocratic families were founding captive monastic houses in order to get charters for lands. As might be expected, the captive monasteries were rarely dedicated to the monastic life of contemplation and prayer.

Cluniac Monasteries   Tenth and Eleventh Centuries

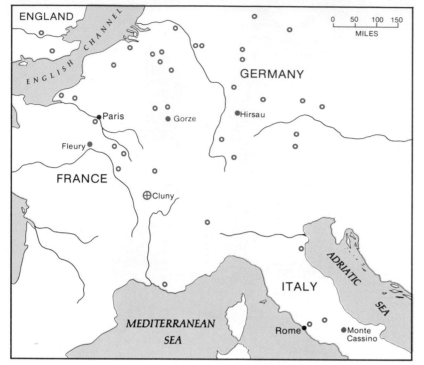

The immense growth of Cluniac monasticism had a secondary effect of extraordinary importance for the history of Europe. When the Cluniacs turned to the papacy for protection and privileges, they found that it was in dreadful condition. After Otto I was crowned emperor in 962, he had asserted his right to control the papal see in the same way that he controlled those in Germany. This assertion of imperial authority weakened the papacy, and within a short time, the papacy became an object of the competition of the leading families in the city of Rome. The emperors played a role when they could, but none could stay in Italy continuously to support the papacy against its enemies. The Cluniacs publicized the dismal condition of the primatial Church and called for a reform of its condition. Their concern was echoed by the best churchmen and finally won royal support from King Henry III of Germany (r. 1039–56).

Henry inherited the Ottonians' ideal of a royal church, but he had a strong commitment to reform. In 1046, after he had secured the throne, he marched to Rome to receive the imperial crown from the pope. In Rome, he found three claimants to the papal see, each of them a representative of one of the local aristocratic factions. In an action that recalled Otto I, Henry summoned a Church council, which deposed all three popes. He then installed a German as the legitimate successor of St. Peter, and this pope crowned Henry emperor. When Henry returned to Germany, the new pope died from mysterious causes, and the emperor appointed Bruno of Toul, who took the name Leo IX (r. 1049–54). Under Leo the Germans began a reform of the Roman church, which reestablished its spiritual leadership in Christendom.

The reformers of the Roman see held councils to legislate their program. They prohibited the buying and selling of ecclesiastical offices, clerical marriage, and interference by laymen in ecclesiastical affairs. They also sought

The problem of the monasteries was the first to be addressed by reformers. In 910, Duke William of Aquitaine asked the monk Berno to found a monastery on his estates at Cluny in Burgundy. Berno agreed to do so on the condition that William not interfere with the life or property of the monastery. William accepted this condition, and, to protect the new house in perpetuity, he arranged that when he died the monastery be put under the protection of the pope. The new house soon became famous, and other great men wanted it to sponsor similar foundations on their lands. Older houses also were inspired by Cluny and asked it to send monks to help reform them. By the eleventh century, under a series of remarkable and long-lived abbots, Cluny had become the hub of hundreds of reformed monasteries. It also inspired other reform movements among monasteries in Germany and England.

to gain control over the city of Rome. The architect of their political policies was a Roman monk named Hildebrand, who for two decades was the archdeacon of the Roman diocese. The archdeacon was responsible for the administration of the diocese and for its relations with local families.

The Investiture Controversy

The reformers had developed strong views about the role and structure of the Church, and these were set down by the German monk Humbert, who had come to Rome with Leo IX. According to Humbert, the Church was superior to secular authorities because it was responsible for the spiritual welfare of people, while the emperor and kings were only responsible for their material well-being. He said that the Church was to secular authorities as the sun is to the moon, implying that the secular rulers received their authority from the Church. It is no accident that the reformers cited such documents as the Donation of Constantine, the early ninth-century forgery that portrayed the emperor Constantine as having given his authority to Pope Sylvester I. Humbert further argued that Christ had established the Church as a hierarchical institution and that the pope, as successor of St. Peter, was at the top of the hierarchy.

Humbert's views of royal and ecclesiastical authority were not the only ones expressed from within the reform movement. The great north-Italian monastic reformer, Peter Damian, set forth a view that justified Henry III's participation in the reform and his actions in appointing the reform popes themselves. Damian argued that, like papal authority, royal authority derived from God (citing the example of the Old Testament kings and St. Paul's *Letter to the Romans* 13) and that, therefore, kings had a role to play in spiritual as well as secular government. The king could not perform the sacramental acts, such as giving communion or ordaining priests, but he was responsible

for the well-being of the Church. Only when the king, or a lesser secular lord, acted against the interests of the Church and people—by appointing evil or incompetent men or by seizing Church property—was the Church justified in resisting the participation of secular authority in ecclesiastical affairs. By this argument, Henry III's actions were fully justified; indeed, they were to be applauded.

Many reformers supported Peter's ideas, but eventually Humbert's gained the upper hand in papal circles. It was not long before problems arose between the papal and German courts. Henry III died in 1056 and left a boy of six, Henry IV, as his heir. The regents were under such pressure from rebellious magnates that they seized every opportunity to appoint loyal men to bishoprics and abbacies. These men were not always of the sort that the reformers would have liked appointed, and the papal court became increasingly estranged from the regents.

In 1059, Pope Nicholas II (r. 1059–61) issued new reform legislation that was a direct attack on the old practices of the German kings and emperors. He prohibited the investiture (installation) of priests and bishops by laymen, and he stated that henceforth the popes would be elected by the college of cardinals. This new electoral college represented the clergy of the diocese of Rome, because under ancient law, those clerics who had the right to say Mass in the churches of the Roman diocese were cardinals. By the eleventh century, there was a definite number of bishops, priests, and deacons "incardinated," and the reformers had used these positions to install their supporters in the Roman churches. Under Nicholas's legislation, the cardinals formed a college to elect the new pope. With small modifications, this is the electoral system still in use today. After 1059, the cardinals became increasingly important as officials of papal government. They were also used as ambassadors, or legates, to all the provinces of the Church.

Principles of Gregory VII   *ca.* 1075

This document was certainly drawn up in Gregory's circle, and probably by the pope himself. It expresses the views of those who were trying to increase papal power in both Church and state.

1. That the Roman church was founded by the Lord alone.
2. That only the Roman pontiff is rightly called universal.
3. That he alone can depose or reestablish bishops.
4. That his legate, even if of inferior rank, is above all bishops in council; and he can give sentence of deposition against them. . . .
12. That it is permitted to him to depose emperors. . . .
18. That his decision ought to be reviewed by no one, and that he alone can review the decisions of everyone.
19. That he ought to be judged by no one.
20. That no one may dare condemn a man who is appealing to the apostolic see.
21. That the greater cases of every church ought to be referred to him.
22. That the Roman church has never erred nor will ever err, as the Scripture bears witness.
23. That the Roman pontiff, if he has been canonically ordained, is indubitably made holy by the merits of the blessed Peter. . . .
24. That by his precept and license subjects are permitted to accuse their lords. . . .
27. That he can absolve the subjects of the unjust from their fealty.

From *Dictatus Papae Gregorii VII*, trans. by E. Lewis, *Medieval Political Ideas* (New York: Knopf, 1954), Vol. II, pp. 380–81.

reformers, which forced them to obey the papal decrees. In particular, they had to agree that the priests of their own private churches ought to be appointed and invested by the proper ecclesiastical authorities in accord with Church law. This position led the magnates aligned against Henry IV to divest themselves of the private churches on their estates. In some instances, the lords gave their churches to reformed monasteries, which then took the place of the lords in the old system. This was certainly an improvement, but soon the monasteries were also under attack for controlling churches. In other cases, the lords gave up the right to collect the income of the churches and to install priests, but kept a right of patronage that permitted them to nominate the priest. The bishop of the diocese almost always accepted this nomination, though disputes over the installation of priests were common. During the century from 1060 to 1160, virtually all the rural parish churches that had once belonged to the lords of the villages in which they were located became

During most of the 1060s, the government in Germany was in no position to challenge these decrees, but it effectively ignored them and continued to treat the Church as part of royal government. When Henry IV (r. 1056–1106) came of age in 1066, he continued this policy. Royal appointment and investiture of bishops was a cornerstone of Henry's political program. The act of investiture, during which the bishop took an oath of fealty to the king, guaranteed the relationship on which the king counted for support against his enemies.

Meanwhile, the aristocratic opponents of the king sided with the papal

Manuscript illustration of Gregory VII.

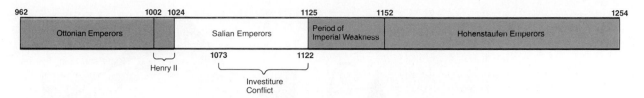

Church property, which was under the control of the local bishop.

In 1073, the archdeacon Hildebrand became Pope Gregory VII (r. 1073–85), and the reform movement entered a new phase. While his predecessors had been exercising diplomacy in trying to get first the regency government and then Henry IV to obey the reform decrees, Hildebrand had been engaged in the daily struggle to establish papal power in the city of Rome. He was a master of city politics and a committed reformer, but no diplomat.

At the beginning of his pontificate, Gregory reaffirmed the reform decrees, particularly emphasizing the prohibition of lay investiture. In June 1075, Henry IV decisively defeated his opponents in Germany and reasserted the ancient rights of the monarchy in ecclesiastical affairs. For Henry, the Church was the most important basis of royal power, and he had to control the appointments to its highest offices. At the end of 1075, Gregory threatened Henry with excommunication—which would prevent him from entering a church and prohibit all Christians from dealing with him—if he did not obey the papal decrees.

Henry reacted to this threat by summoning his loyal German bishops to a council where he and they prepared a letter attacking Gregory as a false pope and demanding that he give up his usurpation of the Roman see. Gregory responded by excommunicating and then deposing Henry, thus putting the ideas of Humbert into practice. The action caused a new rebellion of the German magnates, and, for a time, it looked as if Gregory and his supporters would succeed in making the deposition a reality. In January, Gregory traveled north to attend a great council in Germany, at which his action would be recognized. But while he stopped at the castle of Canossa in northern Tuscany, Henry suddenly appeared to beg forgiveness and absolution from the sentence of excommunication. As a pastor, the pope had no choice but to absolve him. However, by doing so, he removed the grounds on which he had deposed the king.

Officially, Henry was now an obedient son of the Church, and the rebellion in Germany quickly disintegrated. Gregory did not continue his journey north, and he lost the trust and support of many magnates in Germany who had counted on him to back up their rebellion. But the absolution at Canossa did not resolve any of the underlying issues between the pope and king. It only demonstrated the limited usefulness of excommunication as an instrument of political policy. When the continuing dispute over investitures led Gregory to excommunicate the king again in 1080, the action was largely ignored in Germany.

The controversy over investitures, which lasted for 47 years (1075–1122), changed the course of historical development in Italy and Germany and caused a revolution in the relationship between the ecclesiastical and secular authorities in Europe. The German kings invaded Italy several times and hindered the reestablishment of papal power in the peninsula. The popes fomented a series of rebellions in Germany that kept the kings off-balance for much of the period and hindered the development of a strong monarchy, which had been developing under the Ottonians and their successors.

In the meantime, both sides elaborated theories about the nature of secular and ecclesiastical authority. The papacy followed the argument laid out by Humbert, which made the Church

Henry IV before journeying to Canossa. Miniature from an early twelfth-century manuscript of the life of Countess Matilda of Tuscany. Henry, kneeling, asks Abbot Hugh of Cluny and Countess Matilda to intercede for him with Pope Gregory VII.

led by the pope the highest human authority because it was responsible for the highest human goal—salvation. The supporters of Henry followed Peter Damien in developing a theory of dual authority, which recognized the spiritual authority of the Church, but maintained that royal authority was also divinely ordained. The compromise that ended the investiture controversy in 1122 was based on this dualist theory, which became the dominant idea of authority in Europe. Henceforth, disputes between church and

state became a regular feature of European history, and the counterbalance of the two powers contributed to the development of the peculiarly western idea that both church and state have limited authority. No other civilization has recognized an independent spiritual authority.

The investiture controversy and its important political results were not the only outcome of the reform movement. The reformers strengthened the papal role in the Church, and by the late eleventh century papal legates were frequently seen in most parts of Europe. The reform also improved the education of priests and established the principle that no one who served the altar ought to be married. By the late twelfth century, married clerics were rare, except in Scandinavia, which was about 50 years behind the times.

Religious Life: New Monastic Orders

Finally, the reform of the hierarchy was accompanied by a religious fervor that affected all levels of society and led to a new reform of monasticism. Cluniac monasticism preserved the ancient idea that monks should be the poor of Christ, but it permitted the accumulation of wealth by the monasteries themselves. Over the two centuries of their existence, the Cluniac houses had grown into wealthy institutions, where "poor" monks lived in sumptuous surroundings. Cluny itself was the largest landowner in Burgundy. Within the monasteries, monks spent their days in common and individual prayer. St. Benedict had ordained that the monks should come together for communal prayer services, or offices, seven times a day. In the Middle Ages, people believed that God would listen to the prayers of holy men more than to those of ordinary folk, and the donors to monasteries expected, in fact demanded, that the monks pray for them in perpetuity. Over time, the prayers for patrons multiplied until the monks spent virtually all day in church. Cluniac liturgy became very elaborate, and the monasteries built large and ornate churches in which the monks used richly decorated implements and books.

From the middle of the eleventh century, perhaps influenced by the papal reform movement, some monks withdrew from Cluniac and other houses to live as hermits. Ecclesiastical authorities found these men troublesome because there was no way to know whether they were really living a holy life, so the bishops put pressure on them to form communities. In Italy, several communities were formed in which the monks lived solitary and ascetic lives of prayer and engaged in a minimum of common activity to support themselves. Peter Damian entered one of these houses, Fonte Avellana, as a young man and became its prior in 1043. He rose to prominence from this position. The most famous communities of hermits were the Charterhouse (La Grand Chartreuse), from which the Carthusian order stems, and Camaldoli, which also spawned an order.

The largest and most influential of the new orders was the Cistercian order, which followed the Benedictine Rule. About 1098, some monks withdrew to a desolate place called Cîteaux (Cisterciensis in Latin; the name means a marshy place) in Burgundy. These men wanted to live a very austere life. They wanted to renounce property not only for themselves as individuals, but also as a community, and they wanted to reemphasize the role of manual labor

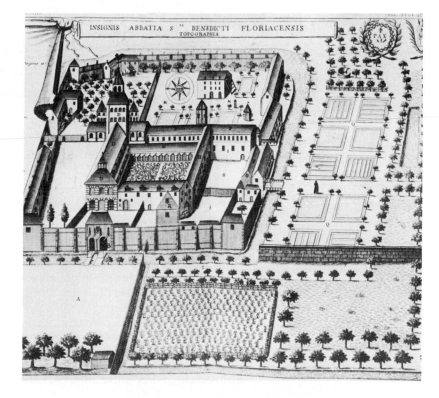

Seventeenth-century print of the ancient Benedictine monastery of Fleury in France.

INSIGNIS ABBATIA S. BENEDICTI FLORIACENSIS TOPOGRAPHIA

PAX

Cistercian Monasteries   Twelfth Century

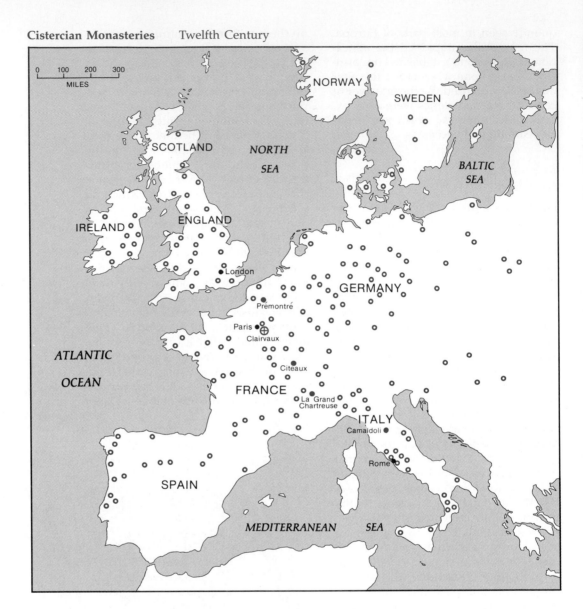

in the monk's life. The wilderness to which they withdrew was particularly harsh, requiring that they work hard just to survive. For several years the monks at Cîteaux struggled to maintain themselves, as the number of monks dwindled. Then, in 1112, when it appeared that the community would fail, a young man named Bernard (*ca.* 1090–1153) arrived with some relatives and friends to join the house. Bernard was a genius with extraordinary personal magnetism, and he soon attracted oth-

ers to Cîteaux. In 1115, he led a group of monks to found a daughter house of Cîteaux at Clairvaux, where he was abbot for the remainder of his life. In those four decades, the Cistercian order grew to over 350 houses, and Bernard became the leading personality in Europe. He wrote hundreds of letters and many commentaries on various books of the Bible. His influence was demonstrated when a former member of his community at Clairvaux, Eugene III, became pope in 1145.

In contrast to the Cluniac movement, the Cistercians were a true order. A multitude of abbeys had copied Cluny's Rule, and many had asked Cluny to send monks to reform them, but these houses were not subject to Cluny in any legal or institutional way. All the Cistercian houses were founded by members of one of the older houses. Clairvaux was a daughter house of Cîteaux; Clairvaux in turn had many daughter houses; and many of Clairvaux's daughter houses had daughter houses of their own. All of these monasteries had the same rule, but more than that, it was expected that the abbot of the mother house would visit each of its daughter houses once a year to make certain that the rule was being followed in every particular. Also, once a year all the abbots of the order gathered at Cîteaux for a general chapter at which the rule was reviewed and the cases of abbots who had been found wanting were heard. But, as the Cistercian order grew and the fame of its monks' holiness spread, its houses, like Cluniac houses before them, became the recipients of pious gifts. Within a generation, Cistercian houses were wealthy and were struggling with the dangers of wealth. By the middle of the twelfth century, Cistercian abbots played a large role in ecclesiastical and secular politics.

About the same time as the Cistercians came into being, other forms of religious life were also born. Cathedral churches had many priests, called canons, attached to them. These men performed the divine offices in the church and assisted the bishop in the management and pastoral work of the diocese. By the late eleventh century, many of the groups of canons had accepted a rule and become regular (from the Latin *regula* meaning rule). In many rural churches, small groups of canons followed suit. The canons lived much as the monks did, but their rule was different. It stemmed from a letter attributed to St. Augustine (354–430), rather than from the Rule of St. Benedict. In the early twelfth century, a

Cistercian monks shown living by their own labor. Illuminated capital letter from a manuscript of St. Gregory's *Moralia in Job,* written at the motherhouse of Cîteaux in the twelfth century.

German priest founded a house of canons regular at Prémontré, and from it he developed an order, the Premonstratensian order.

The movement affected women no less than men. For generations, convents had received widows and unmarried daughters of noble families, but now they began to receive women who might have married. The Cistercians created an order of Benedictine nuns who followed the same rule, though their houses were not founded in such desolate and difficult environments as the men's. There also developed orders of canonesses, who lived according to the same Augustinian rule as the canons, but did not, of course, perform priestly duties.

All these forms of monastic life were limited, for the most part, to individuals of the noble classes, but the reform movement also stimulated a religious movement among the lower classes. The twelfth century was the great age of the wandering preachers, powerful orators who went from village to village and town to town urging the population to live like the apostles. In a few cases, these preachers gained followings that lasted, such as Waldo, whose followers, both men and women, left everything behind to live a common life and aid in the conversion of others. The Waldensians formed small communities in many towns and villages and became a worry for the ecclesiastical authorities. The bishops became concerned about the orthodoxy of the preachers and their followers because these people had no formal training or

Urban's Speech at Clermont   1095

I exhort you . . . to strive to expel that wicked race [the Turks] from our Christian lands . . . Christ commands it. Remission of sins will be granted for those going thither. . . . Let those who are accustomed to wage private war wastefully even against believers go forth against the infidels. . . . Let those who have lived by plundering be soldiers of Christ; let those who formerly contended against brothers and relations rightly fight barbarians; let those who were recently hired for a few pieces of silver win their eternal reward. . . . The sorrowful here will be glad there, the poor here will be rich there, and the enemies of the Lord here will be His friends there. Let no delay postpone the journey . . . when winter has ended and spring has come . . . enter the highways courageously with the Lord going on before.

Adapted from Fulcher of Chartres, *History of Jerusalem*, trans. by M. E. McGinty (Philadelphia: University of Pennsylvania Press, 1941), p. 16. Fulcher was at Clermont and went on the First Crusade.

authority from the Church, and their message was often critical of the wealth and worldliness of the Church. The Waldensian movement lasted for centuries—never formally condemned, but never embraced either.

THE CRUSADES

Capital in the Cathedral of St. Lazarus at Autun showing the flight into Egypt.

When Byzantine military power collapsed after the battle of Manzikert in 1071 (see p. 199), the imperial court in Constantinople appealed to the pope and the western kings for assistance. While these leaders had little interest in saving territory for the eastern emperor, the Byzantine ambassadors played artfully on the outrage of Moslem control of the Holy City, which the Turks had taken shortly after Manzikert. In 1095, Pope Urban II (1089–99) seized the opportunity to assert papal leadership of all Christendom by proclaiming a crusade against the Turks. At a great council in Clermont, France, he preached a famous sermon urging the assembled knights to march east against the infidel. The effect of this speech was startling. Thousands took

the cross, which became the symbol of the crusader—the warrior who had dedicated himself to fight for Christ.

There were three background causes of this great surge of religious fervor. First, since the late tenth century, bishops had tried to protect their parishioners from the horrors of war by enforcing a truce in regard to certain groups in the population. The movement was called the Peace of God. It began in central France and was based on associations of knights who swore not to attack peasants, merchants, and churchmen. The bishops also tried to get the knights to observe a truce, the Truce of God, on feast days, but this attempt was far less effective than the Peace of God. The great lords supported the program because it helped them keep control over the lesser lords and knights. It also brought the knights into contact with churchmen, who endeavored to temper their rough ways. Gradually, the bishops spread the idea that the highest ideal of knighthood was to fight in the service of God. The Peace of God movement may also have been the foundation of the chivalric code of behavior, which was developed in the vernacular literature of the twelfth century.

Second, the Europeans had already become aggressive toward Moslem states closer to home and had developed the idea of holy war, an idea similar to the Moslems' idea of *jihad*. In Italy, northerners had become involved in the age-old struggle against the Moslems in southern Italy and Sicily. The leaders of this internal crusade were Normans, and by the middle of the century they had formed independent principalities in the south. The Norman leader Roger I (1085–1111) completed the reconquest of Sicily in 1091. The papal reformers allied themselves with these successful men and ultimately anointed their ruler as king (1130). In Spain, the collapse of the caliphate of Cordova in 1031 gave the Christian states on the southern flank of the Pyrenees the opportunity to begin operations against the several independent emirates that emerged in the peninsula. The Iberian crusade attracted men from France and other northern regions and made steady progress. Toledo, the former capital of the Visigothic kingdom, was taken in 1080, and by the thirteenth century only the emirate of Granada remained of Moorish Spain.

Third, during the reform movement and investiture controversy, many of the aristocracy sided with the reformers against the kings, who were trying to limit the autonomy of the magnates. Particularly in Germany, the leaders of the reform movement were magnates who saw that if the Church achieved independence of the king the monarchy would be weakened. As the leader of the reform, the pope had great authority among the lesser nobility who contributed to the fantastic response Pope Urban II got to his appeal for a crusade. After about a year of organizing, thousands of knights gathered in eastern France to march to Jerusalem. Significantly, no kings joined this parade.

In the meantime, thousands of lesser folk went eastward on their own, and, when they arrived at Constantinople, the emperor was horrified. He had expected an army, not a peasant mob, to help him reconquer Asia Minor, and the peasants were eating everything in sight in the vicinity of the city. To rid himself of this scourge, the emperor ferried the peasants across the Bosporus, where the Turks massacred them. Very few survived to join the march on Jerusalem later.

The main army was led by several great lords from France, and these men spent much time feuding while on the march. When the army arrived at Constantinople, it caused only a little less consternation than had the peasants. The western army of foot and mounted knights was disorganized and motley, totally unlike the Byzantine army. The emperor was also dismayed to find that the westerners had not come to serve him, but to make a raid across Turkish territory to Jerusalem. He gave up on

The Norman Conquest of Southern Italy   1130

them, and they set off to accomplish their aims.

In its trek eastward, the crusading army suffered from disease and lack of food. Further, it suffered heavy losses in two battles with the Turks, and its leaders continued to feud. When the troops arrived in the Levant, they broke into segments that attacked different targets. It is amazing that one part of the army actually succeeded in taking Jerusalem in 1099 and that the other parts also took major cities. By 1100, there was a string of crusader states stretching from Antioch in the north to the Dead Sea.

The condition of these states was always precarious, and the Moslem enemies occasionally made serious inroads against them. At these times calls went out to the West for fresh reinforcements, and European churchmen again preached the crusade. In the 1140s, Bernard of Clairvaux preached a crusade and succeeded in getting the kings of France and Germany to join it. King Louis VII of France (r. 1137–80)

Crusade Routes   1096–1270

Political boundaries are those of the middle of the twelfth century

- ····1——— First Crusade, 1096-99
- ····2·——— Second Crusade, 1147-49
- ····3 ——— Third Crusade, 1189-92
- ····4·——— Fourth Crusade, 1202-04
- ··L·· First Crusade of Louis IX, 1248-54
- ··LL·· Second Crusade of Louis IX, 1270

MILES
0 ——— 300

actually went all the way to Palestine, but he did not accomplish much there.

After Saladin retook Jerusalem in 1187, Church leaders preached a third crusade. The German and English kings led this army, which met a bad end. King Frederick I of Germany died in 1190 on the way to the Levant, and the English king Richard the Lionhearted came back to Europe after an inconclusive campaign and was captured by an enemy of his house in the eastern part of the German realm. The English had to collect a huge sum to ransom him.

These twelfth-century crusades, while primarily aimed at Palestine, also gave attention to the conquest of Egypt, where the Fatimid caliphs had established the richest and most powerful Moslem state. The attempts to attack the Nile delta were repeatedly thrown back, but they disrupted the lucrative trade that had grown up between Egypt and the Italian cities. Thus, when a fourth crusade was organized in 1202 and aimed specifically at Egypt, the Venetians, who had been contracted to provide transport, artfully diverted it to conquer a Byzantine port that competed with Venice. This action involved the crusaders in Byzantine dynastic competition, and soon they were on their way to Constantinople itself. They took the city in 1204 and established a Latin empire, which lasted until 1261 (see pp. 200–201).

THE RENAISSANCE OF THE TWELFTH CENTURY

The Intellectual Renaissance

Just as the Church reform of Charlemagne had been the basis of an intellectual and artistic renaissance, so the reform of the eleventh century stimulated a new cultural awakening. By the twelfth century, Europe was, as one contemporary observer put it, clothed in new churches. New intellectual activities also flourished.

The twelfth-century renaissance arose from several causes. The reformers of the Church sought to improve the education of clerics and encouraged the research and intellectual work necessary for attaining this goal. Old libraries were raided for precious books, which, once rediscovered, were copied and distributed to growing scholastic centers. The conflict with the German kings contributed to this research effort, for both sides tried to argue their cases on the basis of historical precedents and the writings of the fathers of the Church. But the old monastic and cathedral libraries were not the only institutions in which forgotten books were found. Increased contact with Islam in Spain, southern Italy, and Syria also had a great effect. After the initial wars of conquest, these countries became centers of intellectual exchange. In Spain, Jewish scholars provided Latin translations of Arabic works of philosophy and science, and similar work went on in Sicily and the eastern Mediterranean.

In philosophy, the rediscovery of Aristotle's advanced treatises on logic produced great excitement at the end of the eleventh century. Logic was a powerful tool for the discovery of new truths, for it gave one confidence in the inferences that could be drawn from observations of the real world. The Italian philosopher-theologian Anselm (1035–1109), who migrated to Normandy and was appointed archbishop of Canterbury in 1187, provided a striking example of the power of logic when he created the ontological argument for the existence of God. This proof rested on a definition of God as a being greater than which cannot be conceived, from which it followed by logical deduction that God exists (since otherwise one could conceive of a greater being).

Teachers of logic were swarmed by students, among whom was a prodigy named Peter Abelard (*ca.* 1070–1141). By about 1110, Peter had achieved fame in the schools and was writing works that stirred great controversy. Although Anselm and a few others had approached theological problems by using logic, the prevailing method in theological study was to collect the relevant passages from the Church fathers and present them as an answer to particular theological questions. Abelard was not the only one to see a great many contradictions in the patristic tradition, but he took a new step when he proposed a method for dealing with them. In the book *Sic et Non* (Yes and No), he asked a series of theological questions, then arranged the patristic texts on both sides of each question, and finally used logical analysis to make fine distinctions that would permit a reconciliation of the differences of opinion. The effect of this method was to call into question the opinions of the fathers, who were considered to have been inspired by God, and Abelard was condemned for his book.

Among the leading opponents of Abelard was Bernard of Clairvaux. The two men represented opposing sides of the twelfth-century renaissance. For Bernard, the purpose of intellectual work was to enhance spiritual experience, and this purpose imposed both form and limitation on the work. As the basis of divine revelation, the Bible must be the principal object of study, and study must consist in a contemplation of the meaning of the sacred text, which contained the whole truth about God and the created world. This was a mystical theology, a use of the rational capacity to attain the mystical experience of oneness with God. Many Cistercians and other monastic thinkers followed Bernard in developing this mode of theological discourse, which was mostly contained in sermons on biblical passages.

Abelard on Scholarship

. . . Investigation is the first key to wisdom: it is the kind of industrious and repeated inquiry which Aristotle, the wisest of all philosophers recommended to his students in saying: "It is difficult to solve problems with confidence unless they have been frequently discussed. It is not useless to express doubts about some matters." For through doubting we come to inquiry and through inquiry we discover the truth, as Truth Himself said: "Seek and you will find, knock and the door will be opened to you."

St. Bernard on Abelard

We have in France an old teacher turned into a new theologian, who in his early days amused himself with logic and who now gives utterance to wild imaginations upon the Holy Scriptures. . . .

There is nothing in heaven above nor in the earth below which he deigns to confess ignorance of: he raises his eyes to heaven and searches the deep things of God and . . . brings back unspeakable words which it is not lawful for a man to utter. He is ready to give a reason for everything, even for those things that are above reason. Thus he presumes against reason and against faith. For what is more unreasonable than to attempt to go beyond the limits of reason? And what is more against faith than to be unwilling to believe what cannot be proved by reason? . . .

And so he promises understanding to his hearers, even on those most sublime and sacred truths that are hidden in the very bosom of our holy faith. He places degrees in the Trinity, modes in the Majesty, numbers in the Eternity. . . . Who can endure this? . . . Who does not shudder at such new-fangled profanities?

Translated from *Sic et Non*, ed. by V. Cousin, *Ouvrages inédits d'Abélard* (Paris: Imprimerie royale, 1836), p. 104; translated from *Patrologia latina*, Vol. 182, cols. 1055–56.

to knowledge were compatible and consistent with one another. This was heady stuff for young men in the early twelfth century, and it drew them in droves to Abelard's and others' lectures. Bernard saw this movement as contrary to the true way to truth—which was through the monastic profession—and he viewed Abelard and his method as a dangerous influence on the young.

These two points of view represented two intellectual milieus, both of them popular and powerful in the twelfth century. The monastic orders were growing rapidly and attracting men of great ability and personal magnetism. The monks had both a special way of life and a special way of approaching knowledge, and they actively tried to influence others to follow them. They constituted a strong moral force in the political and social life of western Europe. Abelard and men like him set themselves up in cathedrals and cities. They occupied teaching positions within the old cathedral schools, which educated future clerics. The reform of the Church caused an expansion of the clerical orders by encouraging the establishment of more churches and the improvement of ecclesiastical administration, and the cathedral schools provided the educated men for these positions.

But the intellectual movement went beyond the confines of church schools. Abelard had sought a position in Paris, but the bishop there refused to permit him to teach in the cathedral school. In lieu of that, he taught under the aegis of a monastic house in the city, and hundreds came to hear his lectures. Other masters took advantage of the pool of students to set themselves up in Paris, which soon became the leading intellectual center in Europe. Not having the specific task of training clerics, these independent masters developed philosophical and scientific curricula that provided students with skills and knowledge useful to secular rulers, and it became common for educated men to enter the service of kings

For Abelard, the human mind, using logic to analyze sense perceptions of the created world, could create a knowledge of truth that was independent of revelation. Therefore, for him there were two sources of knowledge of God and the world, biblical and "scientific," and he believed the two ways

and great lords. The new class of educated bureaucrats, both in the Church and in the secular governments, provided an audience for intellectual work and gave continuing impetus to scholars in a great variety of subjects.

Abelard and his successors in Paris determined the method of scholarship, and his program of bringing order out of the chaos of patristic writings produced a new theology. In the 1150s, Peter Lombard, the master of the cathedral school in Paris (later bishop of the see), wrote a systematic treatment of Christian doctrine called the *Four Books of Sentences*, which became the basic textbook of theological study. By the late twelfth century there were so many masters teaching in Paris that they formed a separate guild or *universitas* (the Latin word for guild) to regulate their curricula and other business. The exact date when the guild was founded is unknown, but it had existed for some time by 1200.

The foundation of the guild of masters was the beginning of the modern university, an institution of higher learning based on the cooperative activities of teachers. In the early days of the new institution, which was subject to episcopal control, the masters established curricula, regulated competition amongst themselves, and set standards for admission to the guild. Students paid fees directly to the masters with whom they studied. The regular study of philosophy and theology, based on the rediscovered works of Aristotle and on Peter Lombard's *Sentences*, encouraged the development of systematic— or as it is called because of where it was produced "scholastic"—theology. In contrast to the mystical theologians, who continued to flourish, the scholastic theologians took a systematic approach to the Bible. In the late twelfth century, the Englishman Stephen Langton, then a professor at Paris but later archbishop of Canterbury (r. 1207–28), introduced the chapter and verse divisions into the biblical text. Once this was done, commentators could cite the text with precision, which contrib-

Medieval Schools and Universities   1100–1250

uted both to systematic study and to debate over the meaning of particular passages.

The new intellectual movement also affected legal studies. One of the great discoveries of the eleventh-century scholars was a copy of Justinian's *Corpus Iuris Civilis* (see p. 182). It is believed that the book was found during the 1070s in a library in Pisa. The copy was made in the sixth century, not long after the *Corpus* was issued by the emperor, and it created a revolution in medieval legal thinking. Justinian's code presented a coherent, sophisticated legal system, and it soon became the basis for a school of legal scholars formed in Bologna. These men reintroduced the idea that law was not just a collection of old legislation, but a logical system based on principles of justice. The discovery also provided a new basis for the development of secular law, which, because of the rediscovery of Justinian's code, could now gain strength from the grand tradition of Roman jurisprudence.

The Church also benefited from the discovery. Church law had begun to develop during the fourth century, after the emperor Constantine recognized the Church as a legal institution under Roman law. In its early development, Church, or canon, law was based on Roman law, just as the ecclesiastical administrative structure was based on the Roman diocese. During the centuries after the collapse of Roman authority in the West, the canon law absorbed elements of Germanic law—such as the notion of the private church—and developed independently. Now in the eleventh century, the influence of Roman law and institutions was felt again.

One aspect of this influence was the urge to form the canon law into a coherent system parallel to the Roman law, and about 1140, a canonist teaching at Bologna published a great, organized compilation of canon law that soon became the basis of a school of canonical jurisprudence. The canonist, Gratian, had found as he worked on this book that the church law contained contradictions, just as the passages of the Church fathers did. He applied the principles of Peter Abelard's rational method to produce a work whose coherence and comprehensiveness established a new standard for legal thought in the Church.

The excitement engendered by the rediscovery of Roman law and the new canonical jurisprudence made Bologna a great center of legal studies, and during the late twelfth century a university formed there. Unlike Paris, where the guild consisted of teaching masters, this guild was formed by the students. The student university established the curriculum of study and regulated the activities of faculty and students alike. It required masters to proceed in an orderly fashion through all the material to be studied in a course and would not let a master leave the city without posting a bond to ensure that he would return. Although the guild of masters eventually became the model for the western universities, the student university prevailed for a long time in schools of professional studies like law and medicine, in which the students were commonly in their thirties and already advanced in their educations.

The legal system based on the new work affected every province of Europe, since it was the jurisprudence of the universal church, and it had an enduring effect on all the western legal systems.

Romanesque and Gothic Art and Architecture

The reform movement of the eleventh and twelfth centuries coincided with an economic prosperity that gave Europeans the resources needed to replace old churches with grander buildings. During the early twelfth century many bishops and rich monasteries built great stone churches, which provided an opportunity for sculptors to accomplish large-scale artistic programs. There was a twelfth-century renaissance in art and architecture as well as in philosophy, theology, and law.

The patrons and their master masons, who actually designed and directed the building, tried to recreate the style that they associated with Roman building. This style—called, naturally, Romanesque—was based on the arch. The masons designed buildings that were shaped like a cross. The cruciform plan consisted of a nave with aisles on either side and a transept. Beyond the transept extended an apse (round or square). The ceiling was an arched vault that emphasized both the spatial volume of the building and the longitudinal sweep toward the altar, which was at the east end.

Some of these buildings were of immense size—the monastic church at Cluny had a vault about 160 feet high and was the largest church in Christendom until St. Peter's in Rome was rebuilt in the sixteenth century. The buildings were also marvelously ornate, although today it is difficult to see that in the remaining examples. The

Abbot Suger depicted in a stained-glass window at St. Denis (twelfth century).

exterior walls were whitewashed and presented a gleaming surface. The interior walls were covered with murals depicting the life of Christ and other biblical stories. These murals were the "books" of the unlearned. The capitals of the great pillars that held up the barrel vault were sculpted by highly skilled stonemasons, who produced a new artistic style, more naturalistic than the sculpture of the past, which had been strongly influenced by the abstract Byzantine style.

The European-wide building boom created a class of professional stonemasons, who traveled from site to site and eventually became organized into a guild. The cadre of craftsmen provided the basis for innovation because its members knew many buildings and developed an artistic consciousness that encouraged creativity. The church leaders who employed the masons also encouraged change because they often felt the urge to compete with their neighbors and wanted to create unique monuments to their piety.

In 1150 these inducements to innovation produced a completely new style in the monastic church of St. Denis near Paris. Abbot Suger (ca. 1091–1152) was a man of wide education and experience in national affairs. He had served as regent of the kingdom while King Louis VII was away on crusade, and, as abbot of St. Denis, he held a central place in the kingdom. St. Denis had for centuries been the burial place of the French kings. As a progressive and proud man, he encouraged his masons to innovate.

The aims of the new style were to solve a structural problem of the barrel vault, while finding a way to open the walls of the church with large windows. Suger wanted to flood his church with light, which emanated directly from God. The problem of the round arch is that it produces great outward pressure and requires very strong walls to contain that pressure. The walls of Romanesque buildings were exceptionally thick—twelve feet in some instances—and could not be weakened by large or numerous windows. Masons had already experimented with pointed arches and vaults, in which the thrust of weight

Left: barrel vault, church of St. Savin (eleventh century). Although no light could be admitted in the upper part of the nave, the vault could be covered with fine Romanesque painting. Center: groin vault, formed by the intersection of two barrel vaults, Mont-Saint-Michel (twelfth century). The walls could now be pierced with windows. Right: rib vault, Mont-Saint-Michel (late Romanesque). Ribs made it easier to design and build a groin vault, but the effect is still heavy.

was more nearly vertical and which, therefore, did not need massive walls. Suger's masons based the church at St. Denis entirely on these arches and were able to lighten the piers within the building and to enlarge the windows greatly.

The new building—in a style now called Gothic because men in the sixteenth century associated it with the "Gothic" Middle Ages—was flooded with light through windows of stained glass that were designed as illuminated murals, performing the same function as the wall paintings of older churches. The church at St. Denis also introduced a new style of sculpture—based on careful proportions, though still somewhat abstract. This new building transformed the architectural and artistic taste of patrons, although in some regions advanced Romanesque buildings continued to be built until the end of the century. For the remainder of the Middle Ages, Gothic was the dominant style, eventually developing an angular and ornate aspect that emphasized height and complex vaulting.

THE REVIVAL OF POLITICAL AUTHORITY

The economic and cultural revival of the eleventh and twelfth centuries resulted to a certain extent from a political revival that went back to the beginning of the eleventh century or earlier. In Germany, the Ottonian kings had begun the establishment of a strong monarchy that could maintain internal peace and support a push to the east that gradually brought the Slavic lands into the European civilization. In England, the unification under the tenth-century kings of Wessex provided the basis for ecclesiastical reform and the development of lasting institutions of local government. In the eleventh and twelfth centuries the growth of centralized political authority gained momentum.

The Creation of the Anglo-Norman State

About a century after they had been recognized as the rulers of northwestern France and had given their name to the province of Normandy, the Nor-

Left: early Gothic rib vault, Mont-Saint-Michel. Greater height and light are now being exploited. Right: rib vaulting on a grand scale, the nave of Chartres Cathedral (1194–1220). Great height and light have been achieved; the upper (clerestory) windows are larger and more useful than those at floor level.

mans were playing an important role in European history. In the eleventh century, they conquered southern Italy and participated in both the reconquest of Spain and the Levantine crusades. But their most important achievement was the conquest of England in 1066, for from that event stemmed the development of one of the most powerful nation-states in Europe.

England had been in the Scandinavian orbit since the late ninth century, when the Great Army of Vikings fought with King Alfred of Wessex for control of the island. Even after Alfred had defeated the Vikings, Scandinavians continued to view England as part of their world because so much of the country had been settled by Danes and other Scandinavians. Scandinavian interest in the island led, in the early eleventh century, to a new conquest by the Danish king Canute (r. 1016–35), who made the whole of England part of a vast Scandinavian empire. During Canute's reign, Edward, the son of the last Anglo-Saxon king, Ethelred the Ill-Counseled (r. 978–1016), lived in Normandy, the country of his mother

Emma, daughter of the duke of Normandy. When the Danish empire collapsed in 1042, Edward ascended the throne.

In England, the Danes had preserved the old Anglo-Saxon aristocracy, so that Edward (1042–66) found himself surrounded by well-established men who asserted a right to participate in the governance of the country. But the king was more comfortable with the Norman friends he had brought to England than with the Anglo-Saxon earls, and his reign was troubled by competition between these friends and the native aristocrats. The leader of the earls was Godwin of Wessex, who managed to get Edward to marry his daughter.

When Edward died without an heir in 1066, Godwin's son Harold claimed the throne by a weak hereditary right—through his sister the widowed queen—and by a strong political right—the support of the Anglo-Saxon aristocracy. Edward's cousin, Duke William of Normandy, also claimed the throne and prepared an invasion to pursue the claim. He landed on the English coast

England after the Norman Conquest   Late Eleventh Century

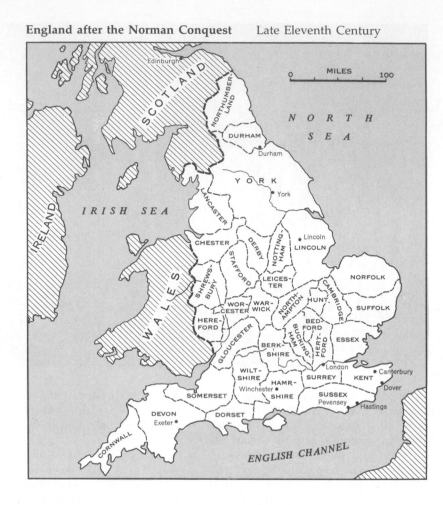

near Hastings in 1066 and was victorious over Harold and the Anglo-Saxon army in the decisive battle of Hastings. After the battle, William was able to gain control of the whole country in a remarkably short time.

As a conqueror, William was able to construct an almost entirely new political system in England. He displaced the great majority of the old Anglo-Saxon aristocracy and granted their lands as fiefs to his own men. Henceforth, all land was held by feudal tenure from the king, and those who held from him—the tenants-in-chief—granted some of their lands in fief to their own supporters. Within a few years, the conquerors created a feudal hierarchy in the country. Thus, under William all of England was feudalized,

and the kingdom became a model feudal kingdom.

Although William the Conqueror (r. 1066–87) and his men brought their Norman legal system with them to England, William claimed to be the rightful heir of King Edward. Therefore, he sought to preserve the old laws and governmental system of Anglo-Saxon England. England had a long tradition of written law codes, and William made himself the guarantor of those laws. Nonetheless, the Norman law—which was the law of the new aristocracy—also had strong support in the country, and there were many cases in which the two laws were in conflict. William's son Henry I (r. 1100–35) commissioned a new code that integrated the two legal systems.

Norman troops on horseback engaging Anglo-Saxon foot soldiers in battle (detail from the Bayeux tapestry, late eleventh century).

The death of Harold, as portrayed in the Bayeux tapestry.

By the reign of Henry I, the new monarchy had gained control over the main institutions of Anglo-Saxon government and society. William I and his two sons, William II (r. 1087–1100) and Henry I, took over the institutions of local government, which were based on the shire (or county) and the hundred, and they continued the system of sheriffs, who were now invariably Normans.

Under the Norman kings, England became the best governed and most politically unified kingdom in Europe. But England was only one part of the territory controlled by the Anglo-Norman kings. William I had remained duke of Normandy after he became king of England, and his sons continued to combine the two lordships, so that as dukes they now brought the power of England to bear on the politics of the French kingdom.

The Growth of Royal Power in France

Royal power developed slowly in France because there was strong opposition from the great lords. This was the legacy of the late Carolingian period. In the twelfth century, the Capetians, who had obtained the crown in 987, ruled over a kingdom comprising semi-autonomous duchies and counties. Through several long reigns the Capetians had consolidated their hold on the monarchy, but the main focus of their attention was always the building up of their own county. Yet, even though it was not effectively unified, the political condition of France was not chaotic in the twelfth century. The great lords had succeeded in gaining control of their territories, and merchants and students were able to travel regularly to the growing urban centers of the kingdom.

Only in the twelfth century, under King Louis VI (r. 1108–37), did the Capetians begin the work of building up their power over the other counts and dukes. The king succeeded in asserting control over many, though not all, of the episcopal churches and monasteries. Consequently, the papal reformers had to concern themselves with the investiture policy of the

Silver penny bearing the likeness of William the Conqueror.

French king as well as the German king, and there was a French investiture controversy similar to but shorter and less damaging than the one in Germany. The French controversy was settled in 1107, when Louis VI and Pope Paschal II (r. 1099–1118) forged a compromise that foreshadowed the Concordat of Worms, which settled the German controversy in 1122 (see p. 283). Further, the growth of towns gave the kings a chance to take advantage of the charter movement to make alliances with urban communities throughout the kingdom. Nonetheless, the process of consolidation lasted until the thirteenth century and will be followed in the next chapter.

Suggestions for Further Reading

The Medieval Economy

For a good general survey, see R. H. Bautier, *The Economic Development of Medieval Europe* (1971). On the agricultural economy of medieval Europe, see N. Nielson, *Medieval Agrarian Economy* (1976); G. Duby, *Rural Economy and Country Life in the Medieval West* (1968), and *The Three Orders: Feudal Society Imagined* (1980); and M. Bloch, *French Rural Society* (1966). The first three volumes of the *Cambridge Economic History of Europe*, ed. M. M. Postan (1952–66), contain excellent articles on agriculture, commerce, and industry. The second edition of Volume 1 is much improved over the first edition. See also R. Lennard, *Rural England* (1959). On the agricultural revolution, see the work of L. White, Jr., *Medieval Technology and Social Change* (1962), and J. Gimpel, *The Medieval Machine* (1976).

Urban Development

On the rise of the cities, see H. Pirenne, *Economic and Social History of Medieval Europe* (1937). F. Rörig, *The Medieval Town* (1967), and M. M. Postan, *The Medieval Economy* (1972), are very good on the towns. C. T. Smith, *An Historical Geography of Western Europe before 1800* (1978), is very good on the growth of the cities. F. Lane, *Venice: A Maritime Republic* (1973), is the best account of the rise of a major trading city. On England, see S. Reynolds, *An Introduction to the History of Medieval English Towns* (1977). There is also very interesting material in I. Agus, *Urban Civilization in Pre-crusade Europe*, 2 vols. (1965), which contains translations of rabbinical *responsa* (legal opinions). See also, J. W. Parkes, *The Jew in the Medieval Community: A Study of His Political and Economic Status* (1938). On life in the cities, see M. Girouard, *Cities and People: A Social and Architectural History* (1985); J. Gies and F. Gies, *Life in a Medieval City* (1969), which focuses on Troyes and the fairs of Champagne; and D. Nicholas, *The Domestic Life of a Medieval City: Women, Children, and the Family in Fourteenth-Century Ghent* (1985).

Ecclesiastic Reform

On the monastic background of the eleventh-century reform movement, see H. E. J. Cowdrey, *The Cluniacs and the Gregorian Reform* (1970). On the ideologies of the reform movement and German kings, see G. Tellenbach, *Church, State, and Christian Society in the Time of the Investiture Controversy* (1940). On the polemics of the investiture controversy, see I. S. Robinson, *Authority and Resistance in the Investiture Contest* (1978). For a survey of the reform, see R. W. Southern, *Western Society and the Church* (1976), and for the effect of the investiture controversy in Germany, see H. Fuhrmann, *Germany in the High Middle Ages c. 1050–1200* (1986). On Cluniac monasticism, B. Rosenwein, *Rhinoceros Bound: Cluny in the Tenth Century* (1982); N. Hunt, ed., *Cluniac Monasticism in the Central Middle Ages* (1971), and *Cluny under Saint Hugh (1049–1109)* (1967); and G. Constable,

Cluniac Studies (1980). For the English background of the monastic reform, see D. Knowles, *The Monastic Order in England* (1951). For a survey of the whole period, see C. N. L. Brooke and W. Swaan, *The Monastic World 1100–1300* (1974). On the conflict of values between Cluniac and Cistercian monasticism, see D. Knowles, *The Conflict between St. Bernard and Peter the Venerable* (1955). On the spirit of the new monasticism of the twelfth century, see J. Leclercq, *The Love of Learning and the Desire for God* (1961).

The Crusades

On the idea of the Crusade, see C. Erdmann, *The Origins of the Idea of Crusade*, trans. M. W. Baldwin and W. Goffart (1977), and J. Riley-Smith, *The First Crusade and the Idea of Crusading* (1986). A. C. Krey, *The First Crusade* (1921), gives a very good picture of the crusade from the accounts of eyewitnesses and participants. For a readable account, see S. Runciman, *A History of the Crusades*, Vol. 1 (1951). M. L. W. Baldwin, ed., *The First Hundred Years* (1955), Vol. 1 of *A History of the Crusades*, ed. K. M. Setton, is a collection of essays by leading historians of the crusades. On the Latin kingdoms in the Levant, see J. L. La Monte, *Feudal Monarchy in the Latin Kingdom of Jerusalem* (1932), and J. Prawer, *The*

World of the Crusaders (1972), which emphasizes the social and intellectual life of westerners in the Levant. On the conquest of Constantinople by the crusaders, see D. E. Queller, *The Fourth Crusade* (1977). The primary sources on the crusades have been published in many collections. See especially, E. Peters, ed., *The First Crusade* (1971), and J. Muldoon, ed., *The Expansion of Europe: The First Phase* (1977). For an enlightening view of the crusades, see F. Gabrieli, *Arab Historians of the Crusades* (1969). On the origins of the chivalric code, see C. S. Jaeger, *The Origins of Courtliness: Civilizing Trends and the Formation of Courtly Ideals, 923–1210* (1985).

Twelfth-Century Renaissance

On the renaissance of the twelfth century, see the classic work by C. H. Haskins, *The Renaissance of the Twelfth Century* (1927). This work has been brought up to date in R. Benson, G. Constable, and C. D. Lanham, eds., *Renaissance and Renewal in the Twelfth Century* (1982). For an interpretive study, see R. W. Southern, *The Making of the Middle Ages* (1953), and essays by the same author in *Medieval Humanism and Other Studies*

(1976). On Abelard and Bernard, see E. Gilson's *The Mystical Theology of St. Bernard* (1940), and *Heloise and Abelard* (1948). B. S. James, *St. Bernard of Clairvaux* (1957), focuses on Bernard the man. For a general study of twelfth-century theology, see M. D. Chenu, *Nature, Man, and Society in the Twelfth Century*, trans. J. Taylor and L. K. Little (1968). See also the works cited in Chapter 11.

Gothic Architecture

On the development of Gothic architecture, see E. Panofsky, trans., *Suger on the Abbey of St. Denis* (1946). E. Mâle, *The Gothic Image* (1913), is a classic study of Gothic art. For interpretive essays, see E. Panofsky, *Gothic Architecture and Scholasticism* (1951), and

O. von Simpson, *The Gothic Cathedral* (1956). On the social context, see G. Duby, *The Age of the Cathedrals: Art and Society, 980–1420*, trans. E. Levieux and B. Thompson (1981). For a study of the stonemasons, see J. Gimpel, *The Cathedral Builders* (1961).

England and France

On the creation of the Anglo-Norman state in England, see F. Stenton, *Anglo-Saxon England* (1947); D. A. Douglas, *William the Conqueror* (1964); and A. L. Poole, *From Domesday Book to Magna Carta*, 2nd ed. (1955). For histories of the growth of royal power in France, see J. Dunbabin, *France in the Making: 843–1180* (1985); E. M. Hallam, *Capetian France, 987–1328* (1980); J. B.

Henneman, ed., *The Medieval French Monarchy* (1973), which is a collection of articles; and G. Duby, *The Chivalrous Society* (1977). R. Fawtier, *The Capetian Kings of France* (1960), is still useful. Works on twelfth-century English history also contain much information on the French kingdom.

11

Medieval Civilization at Its Height

After 1150 western Europeans began to experience the results of the economic expansion and political consolidation of the eleventh and early twelfth centuries. Cities grew steadily and gained both political and economic power. International trade became an important factor in the economies of cities and kingdoms, and the peasant economy experienced a period of prosperity. The roads were full of travelers: merchants with their goods; students on their way to Paris, Bologna, or one of the other centers of learning; government agents on the business of their lords; peasants going to local markets. The general prosperity showed itself in buildings. Town after town and monastery after monastery built gigantic churches in the new Gothic style. Merchant guilds built spacious guildhalls. The great feudal lords built imposing stone castles. Most of the oldest medieval buildings still standing were built or begun in the twelfth century.

TOWNS AND TRADE

Long-distance Trade

The Mediterranean trade had never died out after the breakup of the Roman Empire, though it had gone through periods of decline and growth. The basis of that trade had been grain, first for Athens and then for Rome, but through much of the Middle Ages it

was principally luxury goods from the eastern Mediterranean. Even after it had lost northern Africa and Sicily, the Byzantine Empire, reduced as it was, could supply itself with grain from Asia Minor. Only after the thirteenth century, when Constantinople was cut off from its provinces, did the Empire again become dependent on Mediterranean trade for its food.

In the West, the Mediterranean trade, controlled by the Italians, brought in luxury goods from the Empire and Fatimid Egypt. Merchants from Venice, Pisa, and Genoa traveled north with their goods to trade in central Europe, which was rich in agricultural produce and raw materials. The patterns of this trade had been established by the Jews in the ninth century. As shown by the judicial opinions of the medieval rabbis, the Jewish communities kept in contact with each other, and Jewish families sent sons to distant towns to extend their trade. The basic problem was trust. A merchant had to be able to deposit goods and funds in a town and have knowledge of local markets and personalities. The placement of family members in important markets solved this problem.

Further, the merchants had to be able to travel, and the roads were dangerous. Yet, even in the tenth century, when Europe was divided among powerful local men and bands of robbers roamed its roads and forests, Jewish merchants were able to carry on an ac-

Opposite: The rose window of Amiens Cathedral (thirteenth century).

Medieval Trade Routes   Tenth to Twelfth Centuries

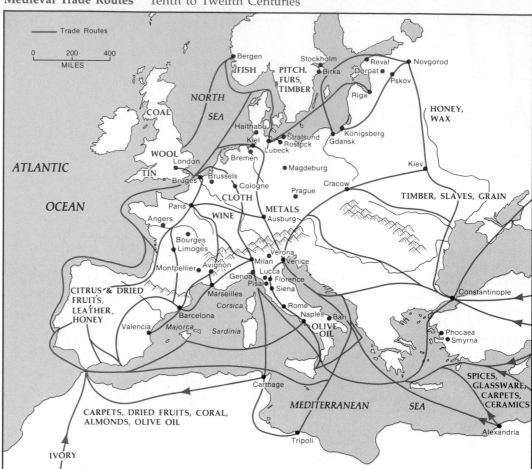

tive and profitable trade. The main reasons for this were that the kings supported them and that there was little robbers could do with the luxury items they might steal from a traveling merchant. Stealing from a merchant in the tenth century was a little like stealing a famous painting today. What was the robber to do with the prize? Rabbinical records show that merchants often got their goods back when the thieves tried to sell them.

Until the late eleventh century, the Jewish merchants were borrowers rather than lenders of money. The wealth of northern Europe was in agriculture, and the great landholders had little in which to invest their wealth. Jews borrowed the capital to finance their trade. This pattern changed about the time of the crusades. The crusaders, mostly knights with modest holdings, needed capital for their journey and turned to Jews and others, particularly monasteries, for funds. The loans were to be paid out of the annual proceeds of the borrowers' estates. From the middle of the twelfth century, the knights and their lords were investing in grandly fortified houses and stone castles, so they continued to need capital and continued to borrow. Monasteries also became borrowers when they began to build grand churches, and in the thirteenth century bishops were often concerned about the indebtedness of churches and monasteries in their dioceses.

By the middle of the twelfth century, European trade had been taken over by Christians. The Italians represented the peak of the merchant community of Europe, and they created new business practices to carry out their activities. They formed partnership companies in which a group of men invested various sums for a period of years. The documents of such companies specify the kind of business to be undertaken, the shares of individual investors, and the persons who had responsibility for carrying on the business. The partnerships dominated the most profitable trade, and the Italian cities built huge fleets, which made regular voyages each year to Constantinople, Alexandria, and Acre. The growth of this trade steadily increased the size of the fleets the merchant companies used to transport their goods, and by the end of the twelfth century the fleets were large enough to become the normal means of transporting the crusaders to the Holy Land.

After the Italians unloaded their purchases on their home docks, they transported them north over the Alps by pack train. Along the routes in the Po Valley, southern France, and southern Germany, towns grew up. But while these cities benefited from the trade, the goal of the pack trains was actually the great fairs held every year in Champagne. Located across the river valleys leading south to the Mediterranean and north to Paris, the English Channel, and western Germany, these fairs became the central market for all western Europe. Here, foreign merchants met bringing textiles and wool from the north to exchange for the Oriental goods brought over the Alps from Italy. Fine wine was another important trade good from early times. Merchants gradually developed the practice of settling their accounts when they met in Champagne, thus making the fairs the money market as well as the commodity market of the West.

Several factors combined to give merchants a special status in European society. Most people were resident in a

Money changers are portrayed in this stained-glass window at Le Mans Cathedral (thirteenth century).

particular community and derived their social status from that community. Status depended on one's obligations and subordination to others; the question was always, "Whose man are you?" The merchant traveled constantly, so that he was often in a place where he was no one's man. Further, the social relationships, based on power relationships, that constrained the lives of peasants and local lords were incompatible with the freedom necessary to carry on successful trade. The merchant had to be free to come and go and to manage his affairs as he saw fit. These realities of the business world contributed to the charter movement, which gave the cities independence from local feudal lords and created municipal corporations controlled by the merchants. As a privileged class,

An Early Medieval Merchant

When the boy had passed his childish years quietly at home [in Norfolk, England], he began to follow more prudent ways of life, and to learn carefully and persistently the teachings of worldly forethought. He chose not to follow the life of a husbandman but . . . aspiring to the merchant's trade, he began to follow the peddler's way of life, first learning how to gain in small bargains and things of insignificant price and thence . . . to buy and sell and gain from things of greater expense. For in his beginnings he was wont to wander with small wares around the villages and farmsteads of his own neighborhood, but in process of time he gradually associated himself by compact with city merchants. . . . At first he lived for four years as a peddler in Lincolnshire, going on foot and carrying the cheapest wares; then he traveled abroad, first to St. Andrews in Scotland and then to Rome. On his return . . . he began to launch on bolder courses and to coast frequently by sea to the foreign lands that lay about him. . . . At length his great labors and cares bore much fruit of worldly gain. For he labored not only as a merchant but also as a shipman . . . to Denmark and Flanders and Scotland; in all which lands he found certain rare wares, which he carried to other parts wherein he knew them to be less familiar and coveted by the inhabitants. . . . Hence he made great profit in all his bargains, and gathered much wealth in the sweat of his brow, for he sold dear in one place the wares which he had bought elsewhere at a small price.

From *Life of St. Godric of Finchale*, trans. by G. G. Coulton, *Social Life in Britain from the Conquest to the Reformation* (Cambridge: Cambridge University Press, 1925), pp. 415–17.

---

and made them satellites of their market economies. The villages were principally suppliers of raw materials and agricultural produce and purchasers of manufactured goods. In the fourteenth century, villagers began to manufacture some goods, such as cloth, and the cities tried either to stop this rural manufacture because it competed with the urban industry or to control and take advantage of it.

Over time, the long-distance trade, which was affected by events and economic and political changes beyond a city's control, shifted from city to city. For example, the English wool staple—the market in which merchants had to buy the wool and which possessed tax advantages—moved from city to city in Flanders, and in the past historians tended to view the loss of a staple as a sign that a city was in decline. But recent studies have shown that cities often continued to grow and prosper after they lost a staple. The growth of the regional market economy more than made up for the loss. Like the long-distance trade, regional prosperity rested on the improvement of the transportation system, which relied primarily on rivers and coastal transport, but which also benefited from the improvement of roads.

The kings helped too. Beginning in the early Middle Ages, kings became active founders of cities, which became marketplaces for local agricultural production. In eastern Germany, the cities were planted to consolidate the colonization efforts supported by the kings. In England, the kings built cities to extend the market economy up the rivers into the hinterland. In the twelfth century, the English kings maintained a special cadre of experienced town-builders to help merchants create new urban centers. The new foundations were economically connected with older ones downstream, and together the cities of a river basin or region formed the backbone of an active market economy. Overall, the process of urbanization was driven more by local and regional economic development

the merchants began to be accorded a special name—*bürger* in Germany, burgesses in England, and bourgeois in France, whence the collective term bourgeoisie.*

Local and Regional Trade

The prosperity of Europe in the twelfth and thirteenth centuries was based even more on the development of local and regional trade than on the long-distance trade. In the thirteenth century, towns all over Europe gained control over the villages in their vicinity

*All these terms derive from the German word *burg*, which meant first "fort" and then "walled town."

than by the growth of long-distance commerce.

Urban Society

The growth of the towns in the twelfth century and afterward stemmed from migration. The migrants to a city came from the region immediately around it and from districts in which it had substantial business. In the larger cities, some migrants came from smaller cities within their economic region, drawn to the bigger market and the opportunities of the most important town in the area. Persons who remained in a chartered town for a year and a day were considered free of any subject status they may have had where they came from.

The population of the towns was divided into merchants, craftsmen, and laborers. Everywhere, the merchants had led the effort to get a royal charter and controlled the town government. In most places, the guildhall of the merchants doubled as the city hall. The town was governed by an elected council and a mayor, who were almost always merchants. Below the merchants in the economic and social scale were the artisans—shoemakers, butchers, leather workers, and the like—who formed a large middle class. As in Roman cities, medieval artisans tended to live in quarters; buyers knew where to go to find the market in a particular good, and the more noxious trades, such as butchering and leather tanning, were located away from the main part of town. From the late eleventh century, earlier in some places, the independent artisans, who owned their shops, were organized into occupational guilds, which were very similar to the associations of craftsmen in Roman society. The guilds regulated the quality of products and controlled competition. They also served as mutual assistance societies for the families of members who became disabled or died.

Most guilds were local in nature, their power extending only to the city walls or into its suburbs, but a few were international. The teamsters served regional and international commerce and their loose organization extended over large areas. The stonemasons, employed in the many building projects from the mid-twelfth century on, formed a highly specialized craft that could not be supported in any one market, even a large one like Paris or London. The masons traveled from job to job and formed a loose guildlike

The Separation of the Jews

The *responsa* of the medieval rabbis reveal a great deal of the life of Jews in the Christian society of the European towns. Jewish religion and safety required a communal life. Here, an anonymous rabbi gives judgment in a case involving the living quarters of a town's Jews.

QUESTION   One of the home-owners in an alley exclusively inhabited by Jews wanted to sell, or lease, his courtyard to a non-Jew. May the other inhabitants of that alley legally restrain him from settling a non-Jew in their midst?

ANSWER   Since the inhabitants of an alley may legally restrain one another from settling a tanner in their midst, because of the objectionable odor of his craft, they may certainly do so in the case of a non-Jew. For a non-Jew, a violent man, would clearly inconvenience them, since they would have to be careful against his prying into their affairs, and perhaps even against stealing. Should the Jew nevertheless sell or rent his courtyard to a non-Jew, he would become liable to punishment by ban or stripes.

Translated by I. Agus, *Urban Civilization in Pre-Crusade Europe*, (New York: Yeshiva University Press, 1965), Vol. 1, pp. 131–32.

Medieval English minstrels, as depicted in marginal drawings in the Luttrell Psalter (*ca.* 1340).

organization. Both of these international guilds differed from the local ones by being made up of men who worked for others. Teamsters worked for merchants, and masons for wealthy patrons who wanted to construct stone buildings.

In the beginning, entry into a guild was relatively easy. Young boys—12 to 13 years old—were placed with a master craftsman as apprentices. In effect, the apprentice became a part of the master's family and was raised to the craft in the master's shop. After several years as an apprentice, doing all the simple, repetitive, and clean-up tasks of the trade, the youngster rose to the status of journeyman, still subject to the direction of the master, but now a craftsman in the shop. When his skills and character had reached full maturity, the journeyman could go out on his own as a member of the guild. This system worked well until the fourteenth century because most journeymen could expect to become masters in their turn. However, in the later Middle Ages, the system became restrictive, as guild membership tended to become hereditary, and then there began to be friction and conflict between the guild masters and their assistants. This development was probably caused by changes in the manufacturing practices of many crafts, which threatened the monopolies of the guilds.

But there was considerably more friction among the guilds themselves than among the segments of the manufacturing population. Most of these troubles concerned jurisdictional disputes similar to those found among trade unions today. For example, the harness of a horse contains both metal and leather: should it be made by leather workers, metalworkers, or both? In addition to such disputes, the guilds competed for influence in the town, and they often formed alliances to try to control the town's government.

At the bottom of the urban social order were the laborers, the proletariat.

Apprentices and journeymen were part of this class, but so were day laborers hired for the maintenance of the roads, bridges, and walls of the town. These people lived on casual and seasonal work, and their position was always precarious. They might be found working on a city project or helping out with the harvest in the immediate environs of the town. They lived poorly, but so long as the economy continued to grow, as it did from the late eleventh through the thirteenth centuries, they were a relatively peaceable segment of the urban population.

Urban Women

It is not easy to reconstruct the life of urban women of the Middle Ages. Presumably, women of the artisanal class worked with their husbands in running the shops, while also managing the extended family that included their own children, apprentices, and, sometimes, journeymen. In the lower classes, they were no less submerged in the struggle for survival than their husbands and brothers, though it is not clear what contribution they made to the economy of the proletariat. In the upper classes of the towns, women were expected to run the household and cater to their husbands. They were not so sheltered or restricted as they had been in ancient Greek society, but they had a special role.

That role is portrayed in a fourteenth-century book that a wealthy merchant of Paris wrote to instruct his young bride in the art of being a housewife. Public demeanor was important: the wife should not go out unaccompanied and should walk straight and calmly without looking around. Her eyes should be focused on the ground in the middle distance. She should be patient and calm when her husband became silly or difficult and should counsel him when he proposed to do foolish things. The writer also instructed his wife about managing the household, which in the case of a wealthy man meant managing the steward and servants. There was the food and wine to look after, and instructions were included about what to do when the wine was sour or bitter or muddy or the white wine was too red. The good man also gave his wife recipes for stews and spicy preserves of nuts, vegetables, and fruit.

The rearing of children was a function of women. Although some primitive methods of birth control were known, the birth rate was probably higher for upper-class women than for lower-class women both because upper-class women had better nutrition and health and because they did not nurse their own children. Upper-class infants were often "put out" to a wet nurse in a local village, although the infants of the bourgeoisie were usually wet-nursed in the family home; the wet nurse lived in. It is hard to tell whether the wives of artisans put out their infants, but it is unlikely. Probably, those able to do so felt that they had achieved a notable status in emulating those of the highest class. Male children became apprentices and lived with the families of their masters; female children were raised at home, where in preparation for marriage they learned to run a household.

At all levels of society, babies were delivered by midwives. These women also took charge of the newborn infant, rubbing its body with salt, cleansing its mouth with honey, and swaddling it. A thirteenth-century writer explained that swaddling was necessary because an infant's limbs were so "fluid" that they might become deformed unless closely bound. Writers of the same period urged women to put their babies in cradles, because the common practice of taking them to the parental bed resulted in many being suffocated during the night. The mother was regarded as the guardian of her children. She rocked the cradle, pre-chewed the food, played games, and taught the baby to speak. She was also the first instructor in religion and morals, and preachers spent much time trying to ensure that the women of their parishes did a good job in that task.

Poor single women were at the bottom of the social scale and had the most troubled existence. The poor widow was a commonplace in towns and villages and in folk tales. Her struggle to make ends meet was proverbial. Prostitution was very common, particularly in cities, and medieval governments frequently issued regulations concerning prostitutes. The principal subjects of these rules were sanitation, living conditions and even the hours kept by the prostitutes. One medieval theologian argued that prostitutes deserved their earnings just as others who provided labor, but he agreed with the common view that prostitution was evil and that prostitutes should give up their profession. Most churchmen found in prostitution a convenient symbol of the evils of worldly society.

Upper-class single women could escape from their predicament by entering monasteries, which were noble institutions not open to those of the lower classes. Many aristocratic widows took this route after they had discharged their duties to their children.

THE LIFE OF THE NOBILITY

From the late eleventh century on, Europe's unruly military aristocracy began to settle down to the regular political life of the developing medieval states. This was the world that produced the chivalric code that was promoted in a new literary genre, the romance, that was patronized by the royal families and high aristocracy. The code embodied the values of knighthood as they had been developed by the churchmen involved in the Peace of God movement of the previous century. The true knight was honorable and loyal to his lord, courteous to women, gentle with the poor and less fortunate, and a generous patron of the poets who created the romances. The code was universal, and though there were vast differences in wealth and station among the military aristocracy, from simple knight to king, all men of the class were seen as belonging to a single profession under a single code.

Young boys of the noble class began training for knighthood very early. By the time they were about seven, they were sent to the household of a great lord to learn the arts of war and the manners of their class. They immediately learned to ride a horse and began playing games with toy weapons soon after. From the time they were 12 or 13, training became serious, with frequent exercises on horseback and instruction in the use of weapons. In one common exercise, the boy rode with a lance against a target that would spin when hit off center. From the target were hung iron balls that would swing around after the boy as he went by. The event trained his eye and hand and taught him to avoid counter blows as he left an encounter.

In his later teens, the capable boy became a squire, the servant of a knight of the household. Under this tutelage, the squire continued to learn his craft, but his main function was to care for the horses, armor, and weapons. The time when a squire might become a knight was not fixed. Often it was when the lord needed men. Normally, it happened when the squire was in his early twenties. The cere-

mony was simple but meaningful. The young man knelt before his lord to pledge his fidelity. The lord took the young man's sword and hit him on each shoulder as a symbol of his entry into the rough world of the professional soldier. In the later Middle Ages, this ceremony could become quite elaborate, involving an all-night vigil in a chapel, special robes and armor, and ritual speeches, but in the twelfth and thirteenth centuries it was the simple act of admitting a well-trained man into the fraternity of knights.

Few inherited land and titles, and the majority of knights were landless. They were knights-errant who drifted through the feudal world. During the twelfth century, they were the main body of those who participated in tournaments, fought in wars, and went on the crusades. War was endemic, but it was not constant, and the knights-errant had their own economy based on the tournaments. During the season, from late spring to fall, great lords held tournaments every few weeks, and the knights-errant traveled from one to another. The events were melees, mock battles, and, although many men were seriously injured and killed in them, that was not their object. The economy of the tournament was based on the capture and ransom of opponents, and a good fighter could make a decent living in them. Many lords formed teams to participate in the tournaments, and these added to the verisimilitude of the contests, but, as in most medieval cavalry battles, the action was chaotic and rested on the exploits of individual men. Not surprisingly, the Church railed against tournaments and denied burial in consecrated ground to men who died in them.

The goal of all landless knights was to receive a fief from a lord or to marry an heiress, while the goal of heiresses, or their fathers, was to marry men with great inheritances. Most knights played out their careers as knights-errant until their bodies would no longer respond, and then they retired

Twelfth-century ivory chessmen from the Island of Lewis: Queen, King, and Bishop.

to positions as bailiffs or estate managers for the great men. As such, they were important men in the rural hierarchy, and many probably married the daughters of prosperous peasants, though no one knows for sure.

For most of the knightly class, home was a manor house or a motte and bailey castle. Manor houses were usually large timber structures surrounded by vegetable gardens and the fields of the local village. The holder of the manor had a domain within the village, which the villagers had to work for him. He also controlled the woods and open pastures, although the villagers commonly had the right to use them for some purposes, such as running a herd of pigs in the woods. The motte and bailey castle was a substantial establishment. The motte was a large mound from one to half a dozen acres in area surrounded by a wooden palisade. The bailey was the courtyard or open space adjacent to the motte and usually much larger in area. The bailey too was enclosed by a palisade. Depending on the terrain, the motte or both motte and bailey might be surrounded by a ditch or moat outside the palisade. In the center of the motte was the donjon or keep, a strong wooden tower without windows, though with slits through which defenders could shoot arrows. On the ground floor (and sometimes in cellars) were storage facilities and above were living quarters for the lord of the castle. The entry to the tower was on the second floor, so that there was no way in or out of the ground floor, and, in a crisis, the stair to the door could be pushed away. Except for the largest castles, the keep was the only building on the motte. All the buildings necessary for the normal life of the castle—barracks for the garrison, storehouses, stables, workshops, and the chapel—were in the bailey.

Only the greatest lords could afford to build stone castles, and these were planned much like the old motte and bailey forts. The Tower of London was the keep of a stone castle that William the Conqueror built shortly after winning control of England. From it, his garrison could ensure the loyalty of London and its surrounding area.

Life in the castle revolved around the affairs of its lord. Here, he held his court to decide disputes among his fiefholders and tenants. Here, he entertained the great men who passed through the neighborhood, if they were friends. When not on the tournament circuit, on campaign with the king, or at the king's court, the lord spent his time hunting and managing his estate. During the long winter's evenings he listened to professional storytellers and singers and played chess and other games. The men of this class tended to live hard: they were rough men in a rough society of professional soldiers, the perpetrators and victims of violence. They were avid to defend their rights and to seize those of weaker men. They also usually ate and drank too much, and many of them became quite fat, particularly after they no longer actively participated in wars or tournaments.

The women of this class were subject to their husbands, but they played a significant role in the life of the class. The mistresses of estates were often left alone to run them, and many were excellent managers. They had to deal with the bailiffs and tenants as much as or more than their husbands, depending on the political involvement of their men. In the case of the great families, the households supervised by the women were very large, including stewards, cooks, stablemen, servants, and the family's retainers. The women of these families often came from leading families themselves and were participants in the politics of the realm. They also were important patrons of the arts. They supported the musicians and singers who entertained the household and commissioned beautifully illuminated books of prayer, some of which made major contributions to the development of medieval painting. In law, women were subject to their husbands or male relatives. In literature, women were put on a pedestal and worshipped as figures of St. Mary, the mother of Jesus. But in practice they were capable managers and politicians who made important contributions to the welfare of their class.

THE MEDIEVAL CHURCH AT ITS HEIGHT

From the late twelfth century, the medieval Church developed into a highly

Contemporary mosaic portrait of Innocent III, from the old basilica of St. Peter in Rome.

bureaucratic institution of vast wealth and power. The first phase of this development was the growth of an ecclesiastical legal system that touched the lives of virtually every person in Christendom. The Church had jurisdiction over a great many types of cases that are now handled by secular courts. All cases having to do with marriage, sexual crimes, oaths and promises, and, of course, Church offices and property went to Church courts. The pope was the head of this legal system, and any litigant could appeal from his bishop to the papal court, which soon became the busiest in Europe. By the end of the twelfth century, the papal court handled thousands of cases each year, and its power was felt throughout the provinces of the Church.

The growth of legal business had a predictable effect on the character of those who entered the Church hierarchy. By the later twelfth century, training in the canon law school in Bologna became the avenue to advancement in the hierarchy, and virtually all the governments in Europe were served by men who had been trained there. Many of the judges who created the Common Law of England were trained as canon lawyers.

Under Pope Innocent III (r. 1198–1216), the authority of the Church reached its highest point. Innocent was a vigorous man, who became pope when he was only 37. He was able to force King John of England to accept his nominee for the archbishopric of Canterbury, and he protected John during the *Magna Carta* crisis in 1215. He also interfered in the politics of the French and Spanish kingdoms, asserting a right as the highest priest to judge kings and other secular rulers. His role in the civil war in Germany was decisive, and he took advantage of it to reassert papal control over the Papal States in central Italy.

Innocent also found that for the first time in centuries the Church was threatened by heresy. From the middle of the twelfth century churchmen had been concerned about the spread of heresy in the towns, and St. Bernard of Clairvaux had been asked to preach against heretics in western Germany. By Innocent's time, the sects had spread to Italy and southern France, and whole districts were affected. Many of the sects were merely anticlerical. They charged that priests were ignorant or immoral, and they urged their followers to avoid the masses of evil priests. Church law prohibited such independent actions by laymen, which amounted to taking the law into one's own hands. Other sects were theologically heretical. The most important of these were the Cathars, who derived from a Manichaean sect that had come to the West from the Byzantine Empire. These people believed that all material things were created by a god of evil, while spiritual things belonged to the world created by the god of good. The Cathars created a church of their own with a simple ritual and with leaders who were admired even by Catholics for their piety and goodness. Because they were especially numerous in the region of Albi in southern France, they are often called Albigensians.

Innocent sent missionaries to the Cathars, but when peaceful means failed to convert them, he proclaimed a crusade in 1207. The crusaders were recruited in northern France and led by Louis, son of the French king, and they waged a civil as much as a religious war. Because it was clear that the northerners aimed at conquering the south, many of the Catholic lords of the Albigensian region supported the heretics. The war was vicious. The northerners salted fields, making them unproductive for hundreds of years, and massacred all the citizens of Beziers before crushing the southerners. By 1215, the region had been incorporated into the French kingdom.

But the crusade did not root out all of the heresy. Many heretics continued to practice their rites in secret, and in order to discover and punish them, the Church developed a new court, the Inquisition. This court grew out of an

Detail from a page of Innocent's Register showing two wolves, one in friar's clothing, probably assisting in a heretical mass. The page deals with the Church's power to punish sinners.

old procedure of canon law in which the judge acted both as investigator and judge of a case. The judge was free to bring suspected criminals, or heretics, before his court, but because of very stringent rules of evidence, he practically had to get a confession in order to convict. This led to the use of torture, which was viewed as a legitimate means of extracting a confession from an alleged heretic. The establishment of the Inquisition had a long-term effect on European society, and it was exported to Latin America in the sixteenth century. It encouraged informers and false accusers, and in the hands of fanatical inquisitors, it could cause a reign of terror in a region. But overall the papacy supervised the inquisitors carefully and made sure that they followed canonical procedure and did not use their positions to terrorize people.

The thirteenth-century popes built their authority on the successes of Innocent III. In 1234, Gregory IX (r. 1227–41) published a great collection of papal judicial decisions that incorporated a large number of Innocent's decisions and his conciliar legislation and became one of the basic legal books of the Church. Gregory's successor Innocent IV (r. 1243–54) was one of Europe's greatest lawyers, and his influence was felt throughout Christendom. So long as the kings and emperors were challenged by opponents within their own realms, the papacy could influence the outcome of most disputes, but, as will be seen in the next chapter, in the 1290s the basic weakness of the papal position was revealed in a dispute with the French and English monarchs.

The Growth of the Mendicant Orders: The Franciscans and Dominicans

In the early years of the thirteenth century, at the same time that Pope Innocent III was preaching a crusade against the Cathars, two saintly men, the Italian Francis and the Spaniard Dominic, began movements that took a completely different approach to the problem of heresy. These men and their followers sought to win over the people who were attracted to heresy by simple preaching and by living exemplary Christian lives. It was to the credit of Pope Innocent that he recognized the value of the new preaching orders and gave them papal approval and support.

Francis (ca. 1182–1226) was the son of a wealthy merchant of Assisi. In early manhood, he suddenly gave up a life of wantonness to live as the apostles had. He gave all he owned to the poor and became a mendicant—a wandering beggar—preaching the Christian message as he imagined the apostles themselves had done.

Francis was a magnetic personality, who soon attracted others to his mission. These first Franciscans were simple men who could appeal as equals to the folk of the Italian cities and countryside. But the order changed rapidly. Many of those inspired by the spirit of Francis were scholars and professionals, and as they came to predominate in the order, it lost its simplicity. By the middle of the thirteenth century, one of the leading theologians of the age, Bonaventure, was minister general of the Franciscans, and the order had be-

come a powerful force throughout Christendom. Robert Grosseteste, the first rector of the University of Oxford, taught in the Franciscan house at the university, and the great scientist Roger Bacon was a member of the order.

Dominic (ca. 1170–1221) was a trained theologian, who approached the problem of heresy differently from Francis. He set out to create an order of mendicant preachers who would be highly trained to refute the arguments of the heretics. From the first, Dominic attracted intellectuals to his order, which developed a string of schools and became important in the universities. The great scholar of Aristotle, Albertus Magnus, became a Dominican in 1223, and his student Thomas Aquinas, the greatest theologian of the thirteenth century, became a Dominican in early manhood. The order also attracted the leading canonist of the early thirteenth century, Raymond of Peñafort, who wrote the Dominican constitution. It is the first constitutional document to recognize the principle of representation. Raymond also was responsible for making the great compilation of papal judicial opinions under Pope Gregory IX.

The Dominicans developed preaching into a science. They wrote manuals about it and discussed the ways to approach different audiences. Much of what we know about the popular beliefs of late medieval people comes from books by Dominicans who wanted their fellow preachers to be able to have the greatest possible effect on their listeners. But the Dominicans also became inquisitors. Their training in Christian doctrine and argument made them particularly excellent as judges of heresy. Some of these judges have given the Dominicans a bad name as oppressors, but as already noted the great majority of the inquisitors were shrewd and fair judges.

The two mendicant orders had a great effect on the life of the Church. Since both had been founded under the authority of the pope, they became

St. Francis strips off the garments he wore as a well-to-do young man and renounces all worldly goods. Painting by Giotto (1266?–1337), in the church of St. Francis at Assisi.

closely connected with the papacy and soon were seen by Europeans as agents of papal authority. The popes used Franciscans and Dominicans as legates, agents, and judges and gave them freedom to preach wherever they wished. This freedom conflicted with the right of bishops to control the priesthood in their dioceses, and by the middle of the thirteenth century many bishops were protesting to the pope that the mendicants were violating their rights. But the popes steadfastly supported the friars, who helped them gain the upper hand in determining what would happen in the dioceses.

ART, PHILOSOPHY, SCIENCE, AND LITERATURE

Gothic Art and Architecture

The general prosperity of the period was reflected in a burst of artistic and literary activity. It took vast sums of money to build a Gothic cathedral, and more cathedrals were built in the twelfth and thirteenth centuries than in any other period of European history. The money for these buildings did not come exclusively from the Church; kings and feudal lords and the wealthy classes of the cities contributed a great deal. Each church was a great artistic project involving an architectural program and a large collection of sculptures. By the thirteenth century, the towns were competing to build the largest and most spectacular cathedrals. If one city erected a handsome new cathedral, its neighbors strove to surpass it. The classic example of this competitiveness was Beauvais, whose town fathers decided to build the loftiest church in Christendom. For years their architects—master masons who were at the top of the guild of masons—struggled to overcome the technical difficulties of building an extremely high structure in stone. The work was finally finished in the mid-1250s, but 30 years later, in 1284, the nave collapsed, and the church stands today without most of its nave. Recent studies have shown that the collapse resulted from the effect of winds that progressively weakened the mortar on the slab-sided structure.

As the example of Beauvais shows, the architects of the era were trying to develop the basic principles of height and light embodied in the first Gothic church at St. Denis in Paris (see p. 295). They emphasized the vertical lines of the churches and steadily increased the size of the windows. In a small church like the royal chapel Sainte-Chapelle in Paris they were able to build the walls almost entirely of magnificent stained glass, supported by a few slender mul-

lions. Even in the larger churches, there was far more glass than stone at the upper (clerestory) level. The reduction of stone in the walls was compensated for by the addition of buttresses outside. These were built away from the wall of the church with arches flying in to support the wall laterally. Hence, they are called flying buttresses and are among the most characteristic features of the Gothic cathedral.

The sculpture programs of the churches were very extensive. The principal locales for sculpture were the portals, which were filled with hundreds of statues of Christ, the Virgin, the apostles, and the saints. The windows were also great art projects. They told stories or pointed a moral in brilliant colors that gave the church an ever changing illumination as the day proceeded. The portals and windows were pictorial books, the books of the illiterate, and they were highly symbolic and allegorical. Thus at Chartres the windows illustrate the continuity between the Old and New Testaments by portraying a prophet carrying an evangelist on his shoulders. But symbol and allegory were not the only type of Gothic art. The masons carved the capitals of pillars and adorned walls and roof with animals and plants, and these carvings are so realistic that they can be used to study the medieval flora and fauna of regions.

Technically, Amiens is perhaps the most perfect Gothic cathedral of all—the cathedral in which all the technical problems were solved. But many prefer the massive solidity of Notre Dame of Paris or the less uniform but more interesting cathedral of Chartres, with its powerful sculpture and glorious stained glass. As the Gothic style spread to England, Germany, and other countries, it produced remarkable buildings, not entirely like those in France, but beautiful and moving in their own right. Only in Italy was Gothic a relative failure. The Italians were imbued with Roman architectural ideas and built churches on the basilica model that they could still see in such

Two representations of the Visitation. Left: Romanesque façade of the abbey church of St. Pierre at Moissac (twelfth century). Right: Gothic façade of Reims Cathedral (late thirteenth century). The Romanesque work is linear and heavily stylized, like a manuscript illustraton. The Gothic sculpture is more naturalistic.

ancient buildings as Santa Maria Maggiore in Rome (fifth century).

Philosophy and Theology

The rediscovery of philosophy as a formal method of enquiry was the basis of the extraordinary advances made in theology, law, science, and many other fields. Dialectic, as logic was called in the Middle Ages, provided a formal system of thought that advanced these fields by making it possible to order their information and to infer new knowledge from what was known. Dialectic gave theologians, lawyers, and physicians confidence in their inferences and solidified the foundations on which their advances could rest.

In this scholastic period, the study of dialectic was spurred by the redis-covery of Aristotle's more advanced works on logic. Gerbert of Aurillac (Pope Sylvester II) had revived interest in the Old Logic, which was the elementary logical system contained in Aristotle's two elementary treatises, the *Categories* and *On Interpretation*, Porphyry's *Isagoge* (an introduction to Aristotle's *Categories*; Porphyry, a Greek writer, worked in Rome in the later third century), Cicero's *Topics*, and Boethius's commentaries on all of these books. The West knew the Greek works in translations made by Boethius. This was also the corpus known to the early twelfth-century philosophers, such as St. Anselm and Peter Abelard, who advanced the study of logic in their work.

In the later twelfth century, the westerners received the advanced works of Aristotle along with some commentaries by Arabic thinkers. The Arabs had also preserved Aristotle, and in the tenth century there was an active school of Aristotelian philosophers and logicians in Baghdad. The newly discovered treatises included Aristotle's *Prior Analytics*, *Posterior Analytics*, and the *Topics*, which were known collectively as the New Logic to distinguish it from the Old Logic. Much of the philosophical work of the thirteenth and fourteenth centuries was dedicated to the study of logic, in which philosophers focused on the study of language and how it works, and medieval authors made some major advances in the field.

However, philosophers were also concerned with a basic metaphysical problem, which had been generated by their study of logic. This was the problem of universals. The problem was raised by a passage in Porphyry's *Isagoge* in which he noted that it was not clear whether genera and species existed as real things or were only mental constructs that were useful in classifying observed individual entities. For example, do the terms "furniture" and "table" denote real things or are they only words used to classify all the actual tables that one sees in the world? This was a fundamental question that had the greatest significance for Christian thought. If only those things observed have reality, then how does one understand the reality of God? A problem of this sort had already arisen in the late eleventh century, when Lanfranc (archbishop of Canterbury 1070–89 and teacher of St. Anselm) and Berengar of Tours (d. 1088) waged a great controversy over whether Christ was really present in the bread and wine of the Eucharist. Berengar held that only the bread and wine existed as real objects, while Lanfranc used logic to argue that the body and blood of Christ were real in the bread and wine after the priest consecrated them. As the debate over this problem developed, thinkers like Lanfranc and Anselm, who believed that abstract nouns like "table" designate real things, came

to be known as realists, while those like Berengar, who attributed reality only to concrete, observable objects, were called nominalists (because they considered abstract nouns to be only names, *nomina*).

The realist-nominalist controversy reached a new stage in the thought of Peter Abelard (1079–1142). Peter tried to resolve it by concentrating on the distinction between a thing and the word that designates it. Thus, for him nouns describing universals (such as "table") are not mere words, as the nominalists said, nor are they things-in-themselves as the realists argued. Instead, they are concepts in the mind that have an objective reality derived from a process of mental abstraction. When one sees several tables, one discovers the concept "table" by a mental abstraction. This concept is real in a different way from the particular objects it embraces. The ecclesiastical authorities did not view this solution as satisfactory because it did not explain the reality of God. In Peter's system, God was real neither as a particular object nor as a mental abstraction. How, then, was God real? These criticisms led to the condemnation of Peter's thought as heretical in 1120, after which he was banished for a time to a monastery in the wilds of Brittany.

The new philosophical enquiries had been bound up with theology from the beginning, and the study of dialectic became the basis for the study of theology. For twelfth-century thinkers, philosophy and theology were virtually one and the same; philosophy was the servant of theology, which was the rational approach to the Christian revelation. By the late twelfth century, theology was considered the queen of the sciences, and philosopher-theologians had accepted realism and moved on to other metaphysical problems. These were raised when Christian Europe rediscovered Aristotle's metaphysical and scientific treatises, which came to the West with commentaries by Arabic writers.

Aristotle had described the world better than anyone before or after, but he had not known either the Jewish, Christian, or Islamic revelations. His description rested solely on observation and logical thought. Furthermore, Aristotle had held that the world was eternal, which directly contradicted the notion of the Creator-God. Arabic and Jewish philosophers had already confronted this problem of the differences between Aristotle and orthodox thought based on revelation. Some had simply ignored the differences, while others had tried to resolve them by explaining away certain features of Aristotle's thought. In his commentary on Aristotle's *Metaphysics,* the Arabic philosopher Averroës (Ibn Rushd, 1126–98) had proposed that there might be two truths, one known by reason through logical analysis and the other known by revelation. When his work was translated into Latin, along with the *Metaphysics*, it raised a storm in Europe, and in 1215 the Church banned the study of the *Metaphysics* and of Averroës's commentary. In 1231, Pope Gregory IX (r. 1234–41) appointed a commission of Christian scholars to review the works of Aristotle and his commentators and to purge them of error. Nonetheless, the university faculties continued to teach Aristotle—whom scholars of the age called, simply, "The Philosopher"— and the controversy over the two truths continued into the later thirteenth century, when Siger of Brabant (*ca.* 1240–81, perhaps as late as 1284) was still advocating the two ways to truth in his teaching at the University of Paris. Consequently, the reconciliation of Aristotle with Christian revelation was the great problem of thirteenth-century philosophy.

The man who achieved what most, though not all, philosophers and theologians considered the reconciliation was Thomas Aquinas (1225–74). He created a systematic explanation of the world that paralleled the structural perfection of the Gothic cathedral. In Thomas's work, reason and revelation—logic and the Bible—came together in a grand synthesis of the Christian world view.

St. Thomas Aquinas

Thomas was born in southern Italy, the son of a minor nobleman. He entered the Dominican order as a young man, and his intellectual brilliance was soon discovered. He studied at various Dominican houses until he was sent to Paris, where the Dominicans had a major center of study and where Dominicans had begun to become professors in the university. Thomas received his doctorate in theology at the remarkably young age of 27, in 1252, and was elected to a professorship at the university. Normally, a professorship lasted for three years, during which the holder gave a course based on Peter Lombard's *Sentences* (see p. 293). After

St. Thomas Aquinas, detail from the Crucifixion, by Fra Angelico (1387–1455). Although this representation was made two centuries after Thomas lived, it seems to accurately depict his large head and bearlike appearance.

the course was finished, the professor left the university for other teaching or ecclesiastical duties. Many professors became deans of cathedral chapters and bishops, some rose to the cardinalate and the papacy—such as Cardinal Robert of Courson (*ca.* 1160–1219) and Pope Innocent IV (r. 1243–54). Thomas Aquinas continued to teach at Dominican houses in Rome, Bologna, and Naples, and then he was recalled to a second professorship at Paris in 1268.

As a Christian, Thomas Aquinas argued that reason alone could only achieve a partial understanding of the universe. For complete understanding reason and revelation were both necessary, and he set out to show that the truths open to both faculties were consistent with one another. As Thomas saw it, the role of reason was to make deductions from the first principles laid down by faith in the revelations of God. Reason also acquired knowledge from the data of sense experience. In medieval thought, man stood at the top of the natural world and, therefore, between the natural and supernatural worlds. Reason was the human capacity that made man the highest worldly being and provided the means of connecting the natural and supernatural. That is why man has religion, which is not just a body or system of belief, but a body of knowledge about the material and spiritual universe.

Thomas's intellectual method represents the ultimate refinement of the scholastic analysis that began with the work of Peter Abelard in the first half of the twelfth century. Thomas built a vast structure of analysis concerning the nature of God, man, and the universe in which each of the broader topics is taken up in logical order. His *Summa Theologica* is divided into three parts, each subdivided into Questions, or general topics, totaling more than 600 for the whole treatise. Each Question is further broken down into Articles, or specific queries, beginning with "Whether. . . ." For example, Question 94 of the second part is entitled "Concerning Natural Law," and the fifth Article under this Question is headed, "Whether natural law can be changed?" The specific questions were answered through a series of opposing arguments: in the example, Thomas set forth all the arguments and authorities to support an affirmative answer (natural law can be changed) and then all the arguments and authorities to support a negative answer. He then proceeded to argue his own conclusion, reconciling the authorities on both sides—that is, showing that their contradiction of one another was only apparent. Among the authorities Thomas cited were the Church fathers and Aristotle, but the main burden of the argument is invariably borne by logical analysis.

The Reconciliation of Christian and Classical Philosophy

This extract from the *Summa Contra Gentiles* by St. Thomas Aquinas shows how a thirteenth-century scholar was able to use the ideas of Aristotle.

We have now shown that the effort to demonstrate the existence of God is not a vain one. We shall therefore proceed to set forth the arguments by which both philosophers and Catholic teachers have proved that God exists.

We shall first set forth the arguments by which Aristotle proceeds to prove that God exists. The aim of Aristotle is to do this in two ways, beginning with motion.

Of these ways the first is as follows. Everything that is moved is moved by another. That some things are in motion–for example, the sun–is evident from sense. Therefore, it is moved by something else that moves it. This mover is itself either moved or not moved. If it is not, we have reached our conclusion–namely, that we must posit some unmoved mover. This we call God. If it is moved, it is moved by another mover. We must, consequently, either proceed to infinity, or we must arrive at some unmoved mover. Now, it is not possible to proceed to infinity. Hence we must posit some prime unmoved mover.

From *On the Truth of the Catholic Faith. Summa Contra Gentiles*, trans. by A. C. Pegis (New York: Doubleday, 1955), p. 85

Thomas's vision of a unified understanding of God and the universe and his systematic presentation of that unity made his work exceptionally persuasive. It led to his early canonization and to his being considered, to the present day, the leading philosopher of Catholicism. In the twentieth century, there has been a revival of Thomism that has affected Catholic thought and teaching.

Yet, even in his own day, not all scholars shared Thomas's views. As a Dominican, Thomas was involved in the battle between the mendicants and the bishops, and this conflict affected the universities. The non-mendicant masters of Paris did not want the mendicants to teach and opposed their views in order to block their appointment to the faculty. But not all of the opposition was based on politics. The most eminent Franciscan theologian of the time, St. Bonaventura, was concerned about the extreme emphasis Thomas and his followers put on reason and about his reliance on Aristotle and other Greek philosophers. Bonaventura emphasized the will, following Augustine, who had believed his will to salvation was the basis of his own conversion and that will surpassed all others. For philosophers like Bonaventura, systematic and comprehensive knowledge of the world was less important than an understanding of the way man's will engendered God's act of salvation.

These scholarly disputes shook the confidence of intellectuals. Furthermore, Thomas's arguments were too technical and rational to have much influence on laymen. Thus, his work contributed to a distancing between the life of ordinary people and the doctrines of the Church, and this distancing increased the tendency toward the secularization of life observable in other spheres of activity.

The Revival of Science

Scientific knowledge had declined to such a low ebb in late antiquity and the early Middle Ages that the recovery in this field, which began in the eleventh century, was revolutionary. The first stirrings of the revolution took place in Salerno, an Italian city south of Naples, where scholars made contact with Arabic learning in medicine. This work reintroduced ancient Greek scientific thought and knowledge, which the Arabs had absorbed, but the ancient works were accompanied by important Arabic commentaries that extended the fields of inquiry. The work of translation was carried out in the kingdom of Sicily, which included southern Italy, and in Spain, where it involved Spanish Jews who had mastered Arabic and Latin as well as Hebrew.

Through the work of the translators, the first three sciences of the *quadrivium*—arithmetic, geometry, and astronomy—were transformed from elementary studies into the basic mathematical disciplines that are necessary for advanced scientific work. About 1126, the Englishman Adelard of Bath translated Euclid's *Geometry* and introduced the West to trigonometry through the works of the Arabic mathematician al-Khwarizmi. About 20 years later another Englishman, Robert of Chester, translated al-Khwarizmi's *On the Restoration and Opposition of Numbers*, which Arab scholars called The Book (*Al Gebra*), from which the advanced mathematics of algebra derives its name.

In astronomy the translation of the most exhaustive ancient work, Ptolemy's *Almagest*, vastly enlarged the traditional curriculum. This translation was done about 1160 in Sicily from a Greek manuscript that the Byzantine emperor had given to the king of Sicily. Working in Toledo, Gerard of Cremona made another translation of the work from Arabic, and his translation was preferred because the Arabs had corrected the original with their own observations. Gerard remained in Toledo for twelve years (*ca.* 1175–87), during which time the city became the chief center of translation. He himself translated more than 70 treatises into Latin,

A university lecture, as portrayed in a fourteenth-century Italian miniature. Attention to the lecturer is not undivided; several students are talking, and one is certainly asleep.

and together with other translators, he introduced the West to physics, optics, mechanics, biology, meteorology, and psychology. They translated most of the scientific works of Aristotle, along with Arabic commentaries on them.

By the early thirteenth century, Aristotle's works had become the basis of western science. Albertus Magnus (1193–1280) was the first to master the whole corpus of Aristotle. He wrote 21 large volumes, most of them devoted to commentaries on Aristotle's scientific treatises, and he was particularly concerned with the reconciliation of Aristotle's philosophy and Christian theology. But Albertus is best known as the teacher of Thomas Aquinas.

Oxford, England, was among the most important centers of science. The first rector of the University of Oxford, Robert Grosseteste (1168–1253), did important work in optics, which received special attention because of the view that light was an emanation of God. When he became bishop of Lin-

coln in 1235, Robert gathered a school of translators, which included several Jews, to translate scientific works. He designed an optical illusion for the new cathedral he built in Lincoln. The effect of the illusion is to make it seem that an aisle exists where there is only a wall. At Oxford, Robert's successor as the leading scientist was Roger Bacon (*ca.* 1220–92), who described eyeglasses, airplanes, self-propelled ships, and the process for making gunpowder. He also did crude experiments himself.

The works of these and many other scholars of the thirteenth century established the basis of the scientific revolution of the sixteenth century. Like the disputes over Thomas Aquinas's reconciliation of Aristotle and Christianity, the work of scholars like Robert Grosseteste and Roger Bacon raised serious questions about men's understanding of the world. While remaining faithful to the work of Aristotle, medieval scientists reintroduced the idea of scientific discovery and speculation.

Histories and Vernacular Literature

The great period of cathedral building was also a period of intense literary activity, both in Latin and the vernacular languages. The great monastic writers of the twelfth century, such as Bernard of Clairvaux, were brilliant stylists, whose Latin sparkled with expressive power and rhetorical flourishes. About the middle of the twelfth century, it became common for writers to collect their letters, which were consequently treated as a form of literature. Others wrote Latin poetry after the manner of the ancients, and among university students there grew up a tradition of satirical poetry that celebrated youth and its pursuits, particularly drinking and womanizing.

But the principal form of medieval Latin literature was history. Since Eusebius (early fourth century), Christians had been interested in history because they saw it as the working out of God's plan. In the early Middle Ages, Gregory of Tours and Paul the Deacon had written extensive histories of the Germanic peoples that had inherited Roman power in the West, and the Carolingian renaissance produced historians, like Einhard and Notker, who wrote biographies of the Carolingian kings. In the eleventh century, both sides in the investiture controversy used historical research to justify their positions, and many priests and monks wrote histories of their churches. Now in the twelfth century, kings began to patronize writers who would glorify their deeds and place them in their historical context. Men like Otto of Freising in Germany and Guillaume le Breton in France wrote connected narratives of the past. Counts and bishops also sought to have their acts recorded in local histories. Western Europeans were aware of the great changes they were bringing about, and they wanted them recorded for posterity.

Outside of the Latinate circle of monks and scholars, there was a flowering of vernacular literature. The Germanic peoples had possessed an oral literary tradition made up of stories that formed epic cycles. These were usually centered on some heroic figure, such as Charlemagne or the Celtic leader Arthur, that embodied the basic understanding of human life of early medieval society. From the eighth century, a few of the stories were written down—the Anglo-Saxon poem *Beowulf* (*ca.* 725) is an example—but from the beginning of the twelfth century an increasing number of the epics were written down. Shortly after the turn of the twelfth century, an anonymous poet wrote *The Song of Roland*, which was based on the cycle of stories about Charlemagne. *Roland* was an epic about an incident in Charlemagne's campaign against the Moors in Spain. About the middle of the century, a German poet wrote down the epic of the *Nibelungenlied* (Song of the Nibelungs), which rested on the story of Attila the Hun's destruction of the Burgundians in the mid-fifth century. But soon after the *Nibelungenlied* was written, literary style changed. The writers gave up the epic for the romance. Romances arose from chivalric society and told of the quest of knights for success. In the most profound romances, the knightly quest becomes the quest for spiritual salvation.

The new literary genre was created in France, but it soon spread throughout Europe. Its earliest patrons were the women of the family of King Louis VII of France (r. 1137–80), particularly his first wife Eleanor of Aquitaine and her daughter Marie of Champagne. The greatest of the early writers of romance was Chrétien de Troyes (*fl.* 1160–90), who wrote works of lasting fame and literary value. By the end of the century, German writers like Gottfried von Strassburg and Wolfram von Eschenbach were copying the style, and Wolfram's *Parzival* is one of the greatest works of the genre. Also in Germany, about 1200 an anonymous poet rewrote the *Nibelungenlied* as a romance. In England, the genre was popular for centuries and is represented by Sir Thomas Mallory's famous work on King Arthur and the knights of the Round Table.

In fact, most of the romances concerned the exploits of one or another of the knights of King Arthur. The plots follow a simple pattern in which the young man goes off to find adventure and finds a woman in the process. He then struggles to find a balance between the military calling of the knight and his love, which represents the settled life of the family. As the story progresses, he gives himself over too much to adventure or love, and he finds himself driven from Arthur's court as an imperfect knight. But, in the end, he finds the balance between the two poles of courtly life and gains readmittance to the court.

The romance may have grown out of the minstrel, or troubadour, tradition, which seems to have changed in the late eleventh century, when for the first time some of the minstrel songs were written down. The importance of this tradition in aristocratic culture is shown by the expectation that knights would be able to contribute to it. The properly educated knight learned to sing the old songs, and some, such as Eleanor of Aquitaine's grandfather William of Poitou, were accomplished poets. William was the first to write down his lyrics.

The troubadours promoted generosity and *courtoisie* as knightly virtues. The reasons are obvious: the poets lived on the patronage of the nobles. *Courtoisie*, from which the English word *courtesy* derives, implied gallantry, gentility, generosity, and the etiquette or manners conventional in the courtly life of the castle, where the roughness of the past had given way to refinement and delicacy. For the troubadours, passionate love ennobled both the man and woman, but more the man, so that romantic love became a part of the knightly ideology. Every man must love a woman, usually secretly, for through that love he will become a better man and knight. Since this was romantic love they were talking about, it was most often adulterous; marriage was a dynastic and political matter that had nothing to do with love.

The romantic mythology was embodied in Andreas Capellanus's book *The Art of Courtly Love,* written sometime between 1174 and 1186. Andreas systematized the romantic ideals in a set of rules, the first of which was "marriage is no real excuse for not lov-

The Rules of Courtly Love

Writing in the third quarter of the twelfth century, the cleric Andreas Capellanus described the nature of courtly love, the new ethos of upper-class society and of the romance literature with which it was enamored. In his work, Andreas imagined a Court of Love that would decide cases brought by forlorn lovers, and for this court he prescribed rules that would help it discern true love, some of which follow.

    I. Marriage is no real excuse for not loving.

    II. He who is not jealous cannot love.

    IV. It is well to know that love is always increasing or decreasing.

  VIII. No one should be deprived of love without the very best of reasons.

    X. Love is always a stranger in the home of avarice.

    XI. It is not proper to love any woman whom one would be ashamed to seek to marry.

 XIII. When made public love rarely endures.

 XIV. The easy attainment of love makes it of little value; difficulty of attainment makes it prized.

 XVI. When a lover suddenly catches sight of his beloved his heart palpitates.

 XIX. If love diminishes, it quickly fails and rarely revives.

 XXV. A true lover considers nothing good except what he thinks will please his beloved.

XXIX. A man who is vexed by too much passion usually does not love.

XXXI. Nothing forbids one woman being loved by two men or one man by two women.

From Andreas Capellanus, *The Art of Courtly Love,* trans. by J. J. Parry (New York: Norton, 1969), pp. 184–86.

ing." He even described a mythical "court of love" where cases involving lovers' rights against each other were decided, and he devoted a chapter to five typical cases.

In contrast to the literature of the nobility, which was full of fantasy and artificial *courtoisie*, the *fabliaux* were brief tales written in a realistic vein for a bourgeois audience. One of the main purposes of the *fabliaux* was to amuse, and the humor is crude and broad. Stock characters included monks and priests who were hypocritical and unscrupulous, the innkeeper who has a beautiful daughter and a deficiency of common sense, and the wealthy merchant who is sharp in trade and stupid in everything else. While in the romances women were on a pedestal, but did not participate directly in the dramatic action of the story, the women of the *fabliaux* were important characters and were portrayed as amoral or immoral. The heroes of these stories were usually wandering scholars or poor but quick-witted commoners who outwitted respectable people. Closely related to such stories were the fables, which added a moral to the story. In the fables, the characters were animals, representative of stock human types. The most famous cycles of fables were those known collectively as the *Romance of Reynard*, in which Reynard the Fox plays approximately the same role as the heroes of the *fabliaux*.

Dante

The greatest medieval poet, and one of the greatest poets of all time, was Dante Alighieri (1265–1321). He was one of the first serious writers to use the Italian language, which up to then had only been used in the *fabliaux* and other forms of popular literature, and he helped to establish the Tuscan dialect as the standard form of the Italian language. But he was also a student of philosophy, had studied the works of Aristotle and Thomas Aquinas, and was fully conversant with the Latin poetic tradition. He was born in Flor-

---

Dante's Divine Comedy

THE INSCRIPTION ON THE ENTRANCE TO HELL

Through me you pass into the woeful city
Through me you pass into eternal pain
Through me you go amid those lost forever.
Justice it was that moved my Great Creator;
Power divine and highest wisdom made me
Together with God's own primeval love.
Before me there was nothing save those things
Eternal, and eternal I endure.
All hope abandon, ye who enter here.

THE FINAL VISION

O grace abundant, through which I presumed
To fix my gaze on the eternal light
Which near consumes who dares to look thereon.
And in those depths I saw, bound up by love
Into one volume, all the universe. . . .
Here vigor failed the lofty vision, but
The will moved ever onward, like a wheel
In even motion, by the love impelled
Which moves the sun in heaven and all the stars.

From Dante, *Inferno,* canto 3; *Paradise,* canto 33, trans. by H. F. Cary (London: Bell, 1877).

---

ence, and as a young man he made a reputation as a lyric poet, but his greatest work was the *Divine Comedy*, an epic poem divided into three parts and 100 sections or *canzone*. He also wrote two notable Latin treatises, one defending his use of the vernacular, the other a strong plea for strengthening and preserving the empire.

Dante had a troubled and unhappy life. Deeply involved in Florentine politics, he was permanently exiled from the city in 1302. He wrote the *Divine Comedy* in exile. Like Thomas Aquinas, Dante was convinced of the unity and meaningfulness of all human experience. Thus, at least as a poet, he could put his own unhappy experience in the context of man's relationship with God. The *Divine Comedy* was the expression of this vision, which was played out on both the personal and historical levels.

In the *Comedy*, Dante imagines a journey through Hell, Purgatory, and Heaven to the beatific vision, the direct view of divinity. The journey was patterned self-consciously on the descent that Vergil's hero Aeneas made into the underworld, and Dante makes Vergil his guide through Hell, where the eternally damned exist, and most of Purgatory, where souls purge themselves of sin before ascending to Heaven. These sections of the poem are full of allusions to classical and contemporary poetry and history, and Dante places himself as poet alongside the greatest poets of western civilization. But the work also rests on a biblical pattern, and the journey it recounts takes place in the temporal context of the Christian liturgical calendar—specifically between Good Friday and Easter in the year 1300. One way of reading the poem is as a reenactment of the story of the exodus of the Jews from Egypt, which also was reflected in Christ's ministry. Finally, the work rests on the romance tradition of medieval litera-

ture, for Dante the pilgrim sets out on his quest guided by Beatrice, a young girl he had fallen in love with, but who had died before any real relationship could develop between her and the poet. The relationship thus became the model of the relationship between the knight and his lady that was at the center of all romances. It was Beatrice who sent Vergil and others to help the pilgrim. Thus, the poet united all the main cultural traditions of medieval thought and literature, just as Thomas Aquinas and others had reconciled and united pagan and Christian philosophy.

In the poem, Dante, in the middle of his life, finds himself in a dark wood, feeling that he has swum across a difficult passage. He is at the base of a mountain, but when he tries to climb it, he is driven back by animals that symbolize his sins. He then meets Vergil, who leads him down into Hell, which is the way man must approach

Dante and his guide, Vergil, visiting the circle of Hell to which usurers have been relegated (illustrated from a fourteenth-century Italian manuscript).

the truth. Augustine, when he pondered on his conversion to Christianity, had wondered at how he had turned away from God, but found God anyway. In Hell, Dante the pilgrim finds the sinners who did not ask forgiveness before death. Near the entrance are the ancients, who did not know the true God and are in a sort of limbo until the Last Judgment. Lower down are those who sinned against themselves, such as gluttons and those who loved beyond measure. Then come those who sinned against others—thieves, murderers, and such, and finally those who sinned against authority, Cassius and Brutus, the killers of Caesar (symbol of the Empire that Dante thought was necessary for the maintenance of peace and prosperity on Earth), and Judas, betrayer of Christ. The poet imagines these three figures in the mouth of Satan, the symbol of all sin as the one who sinned against God.

After this vision of deepest Hell, Dante and Vergil climb down the body of Satan, through the ice in which it is embedded, and, being in the center of the earth, turn around to climb up to the base of a mountain, Purgatory. They find themselves on the shore of a sea where reeds grow, and Dante, who had thrown away his belt during the descent through Hell, receives a reed as a new one. These acts symbolize how the pilgrim has given up power over himself and how God provides for his protection once he has done so. The man-made belt had prepared the pilgrim for the human quest; the natural belt (made by God) prepares him for the quest for the divine. In addition, the sense that the travelers have crossed to a new shore calls up the image of the Red Sea, the sea of reeds, and the exodus from Egypt. Now Dante the pilgrim is ready to climb the mount of Purgatory, on top of which he, like Moses on Sinai, will come into contact with divinity. In Purgatory, the sins are purged through suffering, and, in the reverse of Hell, the sinners first met are more heavily burdened than those at the top. In fact, the pilgrim finds that the climb gets easier as he approaches the top because he, along with those he meets, is shedding the weight of sin. At the top, he has a vision of the corrupt Church and of the figures of the last days. These figures, the Antichrist and his armies, will battle Christ and his forces, and after the battle time will end, and the victorious Christ will become the judge of the Last Judgment. After this vision, the pilgrim enters the Garden of Eden, having purged himself of sin and having left Vergil behind because the ancient poet cannot, without faith in Christ, achieve the perfection of sinlessness.

From the top of Purgatory, Dante enters Paradise, which is a spherical universe, the sphere symbolizing perfection and eternity (it neither begins nor ends). As he proceeds through the spheres, guided by St. Bernard of Clairvaux, he meets the saints of Christian history (including Thomas Aquinas) and learns about the structure of the universe. Here, medieval science plays a great role in the poem, as Dante incorporates contemporary views of physics into the work. Finally, the pilgrim achieves the beatific vision, the sight of "the love which moves the sun and all the stars." It is a vision of man, who was made in God's image, so that the way to God is found in human life, and the mystery of Augustine's conversion and of Dante's descent in order to ascend are explained. Men journey to God through the dark passages of human life, and the miracle of salvation is that such a passage leads to perfection.

In this great work, Dante brought together the whole western Christian tradition, and the poem was recognized as a classic almost immediately. But few of his readers had his breadth of vision or learning, and few accepted his optimistic view of the world. By the first years of the fourteenth century, secular and religious goals were seen to be in conflict, and increasing attention was being given to the secular.

Scene from a manuscript of *Romance of the Rose*. The lover enters the garden in which he will catch his first glimpse of the Rose.

Secularism in Art and Literature

The *Divine Comedy* was in many ways out of step with its times; the gradual growth of secular interests may be seen clearly in the art and literature of the later thirteenth century. For example, after 1270 there was a striking change in statues of the Virgin. In early Gothic sculpture she is the Queen of Heaven, majestic and dignified. In late Gothic sculpture she is a young girl, human and sympathetic, without the semidivine characteristics of the earlier period. In literature the break is shown by the difference between the two parts of a famous poem, *Romance of the Rose*.

The first part, written by Guillaume de Lorris in the 1230s, is an allegory of courtly love; the second part, written 40 years later by Jean de Meung, is a satiric encyclopedia. The first part respects the ethics and conventions of upper-class society; the second part attacks the fickleness of women and the greed of the clergy and gives brief summaries of the knowledge that every educated man was supposed to possess. No other poem was so popular during the later Middle Ages. It was copied and recopied in hundreds of manuscripts, and at the end of the fourteenth century Chaucer began an English translation of it. Nothing illustrates better the rise of a class of educated laymen, eager for worldly knowledge, suspicious of the clergy, and a little cynical about ideals of any kind. Such people could no longer be counted on to support the policies of the Church if those policies interfered with their interests or appeared tainted by secular concerns.

Suggestions for Further Reading

General

For a general history of the European economy, see the *Cambridge Economic History of Europe*, 3 vols. (1952–66). The first volume deals with agriculture; the second with commerce and industry; and the third with economic organization and policy. R. S. Lopez, *The Commercial Revolution of the Middle Ages* (1976), and C. Cipolla, *Before the Industrial Revolution*, 2nd ed. (1980), are good one-volume surveys based on recent scholarship. A. R. Bridbury, *Economic Growth: England in the Later Middle Ages* (1962), brings W. Cunningham, *The Growth of English Industry and Commerce* (1910), up to date, but the older work remains useful. P. Bois-sonade, *Life and Work in Medieval Europe* (1929), is also still valuable, but J. Le Goff, *Time, Work, and Culture in the Middle Ages* (1980), has given a modern perspective on many of the same issues. R. de Roover, *Money, Banking and Credit in Medieval Bruges* (1948), is a readable introduction to the operations of the Italian merchant-bankers in Flanders. A. Sapori, *The Italian Merchant in the Middle Ages* (1970), is an excellent general work; see also S. Thrupp, *The Merchant Class of Medieval London* (1948). On the Jewish merchants, see the work of I. Agus cited in Chapter 10.

Medieval Society

On the society of the towns, see the works cited in Chapter 10. U. T. Holmes, Jr., *Daily Living in the Twelfth Century* (1952), is a readable account based on the memoirs of a twelfth-century scholar. For a close look, see the studies of individual cities: C. N. L. Brooke, *London 800–1216: The Shaping of a City* (1975); G. Williams, *Medieval London* (1970); J. W. F. Hill, *Medieval Lincoln* (1948); P. Llewllyn, *Rome in the Dark Ages* (1971); R. Brentano, *Rome Before Avignon* (1974); D. Herlihy, *Medieval and Renaissance Pistoia* (1958); and P. Strait, *Cologne in the Twelfth Century* (1974).

An interesting primary source for the history of women is *The Goodman of Paris*, trans. E. Power (1928), a manual written in the fourteenth century by a bourgeois man for his young wife. For studies on women of all classes and conditions, see M. W. Labarge, *A Small Sound of the Trumpet: Women in Medieval Life* (1986), and M. C. Howell, *Women, Production, and Patriarchy in Late Medieval Cities* (1986). See also D. Herlihy, *Women in the Middle Ages* (1971); J. Ferrante, *Women as Image In Medieval Literature (1975);* and V. L. Bullough, *The Subordinate Sex: A History of Attitudes toward Women* (1973). D. Herlihy, *Medieval Households* (1985), places women in the context of medieval domestic life. E. Power's *Medieval Women* (1975), contains imaginative recreations of women's lives. For essays on childrearing, see L. deMause, ed., *The History of Childhood* (1974).

The life of the nobility is recounted in S. Painter, *William Marshal* (1933), and G. Duby, *William Marshal* (1985). See also, G. Duby, *The Chivalrous Society*, trans. C. Postan (1977), and J. Burke, *Life in the Castle in Medieval England* (1978). On the rise of the code of chivalry, see C. S. Jaeger, *The Origins of Courtliness: Civilizing Trends and the Formation of Courtly Ideals, 923–1210* (1985). On women of the aristocratic class, see M. W. Labarge, *A Baronial Household of the Thirteenth Century* (1965).

The Church at its Height

On the later medieval Church, see S. R. Packard, *Europe and the Church under Innocent III* (1927), and C. Edwards, *Innocent III: Church Defender* (1951). The best biography is H. Tillman, *Pope Innocent III* (1980). For an excellent study of Innocent's relations with England, see C. R. Cheney, *Pope Innocent III and England* (1967).

On the origins of heresy, see J. B. Russell, *Dissent and Reform in the Early Middle Ages* (1965), and R. I. Moore, *The Origins of European Dissent* (1975). On particular heretical movements, see S. Runciman, *The Medieval Manichee* (1947), which traces the history of the dualist heresy; E. W. McDonnell, *The Beguines and Beghards in Medieval Culture* (1954). On the crusade against the Cathars in southern France, see J. R. Strayer, *The Albigensian Crusades* (1971); W. L. Wakefield, *Heresy, Crusade and Inquisition in Southern France* (1974); and J. Sumption, *The Albigensian Crusade* (1978). On St. Francis, see P. Sabatier, *Life of St. Francis of Assisi* (1894), and O. Engelbert, *Saint Francis of Assisi,* 2nd ed. (1966), which has a good bibliography. Two important

works on the development of the Franciscan order are R. Brooke, *Early Franciscan Government* (1959), and M. D. Lambert, *Franciscan Poverty* (1961). The latter work traces the controversy over the Franciscans' claim that neither individual monks nor the order owned anything, even though they used property and goods. See in general, J. Moorman, *A History of the Franciscan Order* (1968). B. Jarrett's *Life of St. Dominic* (1924), is rather adulatory. P. Mandonnet, *St. Dominic and his Work* (1944), emphasizes the spirit and work of the Order. For a general history of the order in its early period, see W. A. Hinnebusch, *History of the Dominican Order* (1966).

Art, Philosophy, Science, and Literature

Works on the origins of the Gothic style of architecture and sculpture are cited in Chapter 10. P. Frankl, *Gothic Architecture* (1963), is the best treatment of Gothic art in the High Middle Ages. He traces the development of the style in all areas of Europe. See also the studies of individual cathedrals: A. Temko, *Nôtre-Dame de Paris* (1955), and A. E. M. Katzenellenbogen, *The Sculptural Program of Chartres Cathedral* (1959).

On medieval philosophy, see D. Knowles, *The Evolution of Medieval Thought* (1962), and the articles in R. L. Benson and G. Constable, eds., *Renaissance and Renewal in the Twelfth Century* (1982). On later medieval philosophy, see N. Kretzmann, A. Kenny, and J. Pinborg, eds., *The Cambridge History of Later Medieval Philosophy: From the Rediscovery of Aristotle to the Disintegration of Scholasticism, 1100–1600* (1982). On medieval logic, see A. Broadie, *Introduction to Medieval Logic* (1987), and D. P. Henry, *Medieval Logic and Metaphysics: A Modern Introduction* (1972). On Abelard and his influence, see D. E. Luscombe, *The School of Peter Abelard* (1969). The introduction of Aristotle and his Arabic commentators is covered in F. Van Steenberghen, *Aristotle in the West* (1955); R. J. Lemay, *Abu Ma`shar and Latin Aristotelianism in the Twelfth Century* (1962); and F. E. Peters, *Aristoteles Latinus: The Oriental Translations and Commentaries in the Aristotelian Corpus* (1968). On Thomas Aquinas, see the biography by J. A. Weisheipl, *Friar Thomas d'Aquino: His Life, Thought, and Work* (1974). On Thomism, see M. De Wulf, *Philosophy and Civilization in the Middle Ages* (1922). The best scholarly treatment of Thomas and his influence is E. Gilson, *History of Christian Philosophy in the Middle Ages* (1954). For the universities and their intellectual life, see G. Leff, *Paris and Oxford Universities in the Thirteenth and Fourteenth Centuries* (1968).

There are two monumental histories of medieval science: L. Thorndyke, *A History of Magic and Experimental Science,* 8 vols. (1923–58) and G. Sarton, *Introduction to the History of Science,* 3 vols. (1927–48). But the best history of medieval science is A. C. Crombie, *Medieval and Early Modern Science,* 2 vols. (1959). On the introduction of Arabic science in the twelfth century, see C. H. Haskins, *Studies in the History of Medieval Science* (1924); B. Stock, *Myth and Science in the Twelfth Century* (1972); and the works on the introduction of Aristotle cited above. In *Robert Grosseteste and the Origins of Experimental Science 1100–1700* (1953), Crombie argued that the scientific method developed long before Galileo. This view is not universally accepted. For a history of mechanics in the Middle Ages, see M. Clagett, *Archimedes in the Middle Ages,* 4 vols. (1964–80). J. Gimpel, *The Medieval Machine* (1976), treats the history of medieval technology. R. P. Multhauf, *The Origins of Chemistry* (1967), replaces all earlier studies.

On the historical writing of the Middle Ages, see S. Vryonis, Jr., *Readings in Medieval Historiography* (1968), which treats Latin, Byzantine, and Moslem historians. W. T. H. Jackson, *Medieval Literature* (1966), is a general treatment of medieval literature. P. Dronke, *Medieval Latin and the Rise of the European Love-lyric* (1968), is very useful. See also F. J. E. Raby, *A History of Secular Latin Poetry in the Middle Ages,* 2 vols. (1957). R. S. Southern, "From Epic to Romance," *Medieval Humanism and Other Essays* (1976), provides an interpretation of the literary history of the twelfth century in a brief essay. R. S. Loomis, *The Development of Arthurian Romance* (1963), is a good general introduction to the origins of the romance. For French literature, see U. T. Holmes, *A History of Old French Literature,* rev. ed. (1962). See also Holmes's *Chrétien de Troyes* (1970). For

Germany, see J. G. Robertson, *A History of German Literature* (1947). The best critical study of the vernacular literature of the twelfth and thirteenth centuries is E. Curtius, *European Literature and the Latin Middle Ages* (1963), which has excellent bibliographic materials. Many of the romances have been translated. F. Goldin provides ample collections of medieval lyrics in *Lyrics of the Troubadours and Trouvères* (1973), and *German and Italian Lyrics of the Middle Ages* (1973). See also Andreas Capellanus, *The Art of Courtly Love*, trans. J. J. Parry (1941).

There are many editions of Dante's *Divine Comedy* and other classics of medieval literature. See especially, C. Singleton, *The Divine Comedy*, 3 vols. (1970–75), which contains the original Italian, a facing-page translation, and commentary.

For a history of vernacular culture as a whole, see A. W. Ward and A. R. Waller, *The Cambridge History of English Literature*, Vol. 1 (1907), and E. Vossler, *Medieval Culture: An Introduction to Dante and His Times*, 2 vols. (1929).

12
The Rise of the Secular State

*T*he thirteenth century was the great age of the Church, when it successfully asserted its authority in political matters, influencing events in virtually every kingdom in Christendom. During this period, the ecclesiastical legal system was the largest and busiest in Europe and had jurisdiction in many important kinds of cases. Family law, oaths and promises, and litigation concerning the vast property of the Church were all subject to Church courts, and Church law influenced the secular law of all the European kingdoms. In addition, the pope and mendicant orders combined to check the spread of heresy, and the Inquisition assured that heresy remained only a minor problem. Finally, a remarkable group of scholars and theologians (mostly Dominicans and Franciscans) succeeded in reconciling Aristotle with the Christian faith and thus reduced the danger of intellectual heresy. By the middle of the thirteenth century there was little open dissent from orthodox doctrine in western Europe. Most people were honestly Catholic in belief; the few who were not found it expedient to pretend that they were.

THE EFFECTS OF ECONOMIC CHANGE

Yet, there were changes taking place in medieval society that would undermine the position of the Church and ultimately subordinate it to the secular state. The growth of trade and commercial activity caused a rise in prices that affected those who lived on fixed rents more than those who were actually involved in trade. The Church and many aristocratic landowners were the principal victims of inflation. In the Middle Ages, rents once set were fixed in perpetuity, so that lessors, with their fixed incomes, found themselves squeezed by rising prices. During the twelfth century, the great landholders had leased their lands to peasant farmers, and as prices rose the lessees gained the benefit. During the thirteenth century, the landlords took back their lands whenever possible and farmed them themselves, but then the small farmers suffered. They found themselves with small plots and could not take advantage of the good markets. Many had to work for their former landlords to make ends meet, and many migrated to the cities to improve their lot.

Aside from the struggle to raise the Church's income, ecclesiastical authorities had to deal with an increasingly urban society. The cities grew rapidly and there were too few parish priests to minister to the urban population. By the middle of the thirteenth century the Franciscans and Dominicans provided a good deal of the ministry in the cities, helping the diocesan priests, who soon discovered that the mendicants were strong competition for the loyalty and support of the people. The mendicants achieved a reputation for holiness, and people flocked to them for the sacraments and burial. They also gave them gifts that soon made the mendicant houses wealthy. The diocesan priests began to complain about the competition, which robbed them of income from fees and donations, and soon a serious dispute arose. The bishops claimed that only they could authorize priests to preach in their dioceses, while the mendicants claimed papal authority for their activities. In the end the papacy and the mendicants won this battle, but it caused a great deal of upheaval and weakened the prestige and effectiveness of the Church.

Prosperity created another problem for the Church. Wealth engendered pride and self-assurance, and business

Opposite: Medieval coins. Top to bottom: Florentine gold florin (thirteenth century); Venetian gold ducat (thirteenth century); obverse and reverse of a silver penny of Henry III of England (thirteenth century); gold agnel of Philip VI of France (fourteenth century). The gold coins were used for large-scale transactions; the silver, for wages and household purchases.

activity led to the spread of literacy. The Church strove, with some success, to give the wealthy a sense of social responsibility. It condemned flagrant profiteering and callous neglect of the poor, and many important charitable institutions—such as hospitals, which were for the homeless and destitute as well as the sick—were created in the thirteenth century. Nonetheless, the Church's social theology was at odds with a truly commercial society. It accepted the idea that a man who invested in a commercial enterprise was entitled to a return on the money he risked, but it denounced the lending of money for interest. As the medieval economy increasingly became a money economy, lenders became a prominent fixture, and many loansharks piled up large fortunes. That some of these left substantial endowments to charitable institutions when they died did not alter the fact that they did not obey the Church's economic doctrine. Gradually, western Europe was shifting to an economic system in which money was more important than inherited status. Concern over money made it hard for men to follow the teachings of the Church or to put the interests of the Church ahead of their own.

Churchmen themselves were affected by this new economy. Increasingly during the thirteenth century, ecclesiastics sought and received multiple offices, so that they would obtain the income needed to support themselves at the level they had come to expect. The papacy was the most important supporter of this system. The members of the papal curia could not be adequately supported on the fixed incomes of the traditional offices, so the popes gave them offices in local churches throughout Europe. A member of the curia might hold an office in one or more Italian bishoprics, one in England, and another in France. He would collect the income from all of them, but, of course, he never performed any of the functions of these various positions. Instead, he might appoint a substitute, to whom he would pay a low wage, but in most cases the far-flung offices just remained vacant. Bishops constantly complained about papal provisions of this sort, but the system survived all attacks. It was a device for meeting the economic needs of the papal see.

While the great landlords created short-term leases or took over production on their lands to take advantage of rising prices, these devices did not meet the needs of kings, princes, bishops, and popes, who had to govern as well as live comfortably. Sooner or later they had to supplement their ordinary income by taxes and fees. But when they did, they stirred up bitter resentment among their subjects and created conflicts among themselves over who had the right to tax.

The Church was especially vulnerable to criticism of its financial policies. The income tax on the clergy, first imposed by Innocent III, was levied more and more frequently, and at increasing rates, as time passed. Fees were imposed or increased for papal letters, legal documents, court costs, and confirmation of appointments to high offices in the Church. Both taxes and fees were derived, in the last analysis, from payments by laymen, so criticism was widespread. The Church was criticized for being too eager to raise money, too ready to give spiritual benefits in return for cash payments. The more zealous wing of the Franciscans urged that clergymen abandon all their property and lead lives of apostolic poverty, but the Franciscan Order itself was acquiring large amounts of property, even though it tried to disguise the fact by vesting title in trustees. When reformers became bishops and popes, they discovered that in the prevailing economic climate they could make no substantial changes in the Church's financial system. The situation cost the Church a great deal of prestige, as it became clear that as an organization it was no different from the rapacious secular governments of the period.

THE WESTERN MONARCHIES

The flowering of medieval civilization in the twelfth and thirteenth centuries was both the result and the stimulus of political consolidation and the growth of good government. Peace and prosperity were the necessary conditions for the building of great churches, the writing of literature, and the development of the schools, and it was the consolidation of power by the Anglo-Norman, French, and German kings that made these conditions possible. But the growth of civilization increased the demand for good government and the prosperity that resulted from it, for the renaissance of learning and the arts brought ever increasing numbers of people into its orbit. Consequently, in the late twelfth and early thirteenth centuries, rulers reorganized secular government. The greatest progress was made in England and France, but everywhere there was a push to create new institutions and to make laws that were more exact and more inclusive.

England under Henry II

Already under the Norman kings England had become the best governed and most politically unified kingdom in Europe. But England was only one part of the territory controlled by the Anglo-Norman kings. William I had remained duke of Normandy after he became king of England, and his sons continued to combine the two lordships. When Henry I of England died in 1135, he left a daughter, Mathilda, as heir. Mathilda was married to Count Geoffrey Martel of Anjou, with whom she had a young son, Henry. She claimed the English throne and the Duchy of Normandy for him.

These claims were countered by Stephen of Blois—the grandson of William I through his daughter Adele. After Henry I's death, a faction of the Anglo-Norman nobility favored Stephen because of their traditional enmity toward the Angevins. Stephen was able, therefore, to seize the English

throne. But his reign (1135–54) was troubled by almost constant civil war over the royal succession, until, toward the end of the reign, the two sides came to an agreement: Mathilda would permit Stephen to rule in peace, and Stephen, whose own son had just died, would declare Mathilda's son Henry to be his heir.

Meanwhile, young Henry had succeeded to the county of Anjou and married Eleanor of Aquitaine, the heiress of the duchy of Aquitaine, which was the largest and richest in the French kingdom. Thus, when Henry became King of England and Duke of Normandy in 1154, he united the larg-

Manuscript illumination of the coronation ceremony from a Coronation Order (text of the ceremony) written between 1272 and 1325. The king may be Edward II.

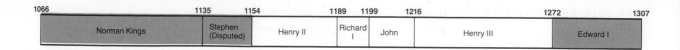

est state in Europe under his government. He soon added Brittany to an empire that included England and more than half of the kingdom of France.

England and France at the Time of Henry II   1154–89

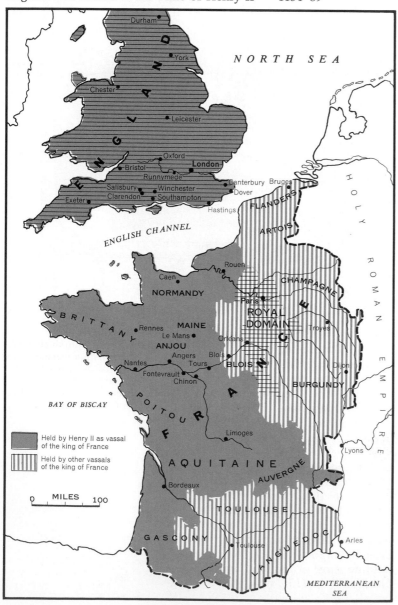

Held by Henry II as vassal of the king of France

Held by other vassals of the king of France

Henry II (r. 1154–89) was a brilliant king. He moved constantly through his vast realm keeping the barons in line, and he developed royal government in England to its highest potential. He spent the first few years of his reign settling the affairs of the kingdom after 20 years of civil war. He traveled around the country establishing his own men as sheriffs and knocking down castles that the barons had built without royal permission. In many places he found two claimants to fiefs because both Stephen and Mathilda had granted the estate to their supporters. In these cases, he issued a writ (a royal order) to the local sheriff instructing him to decide the issue of who had the best right to the fief.

The legal proceedings that these writs generated lasted years and were very complicated. Under Anglo-Norman law the question of right was decided in a trial by battle, but the courts were slow to get to the point of actually authorizing a battle. Consequently, in the early 1160s, Henry found that even though he had brought peace to England through military action, most of the disputes over land had not been been resolved. To speed things up—so that the peace would be secure—Henry issued legislation in 1164 that provided new remedies for those who claimed property.

The new actions contained three features that eventually transformed English law. First, the actions pertained only to the right to possess the disputed land. The king could not just change the procedure by which the question of right was tried, because people did not believe at that time that a king could change customary law. What Henry did instead was to allow the old process to go on, while his new writs instructed the sheriff to give A or B possession of the property until the final issue of who had the best right was decided. In practice, of course, once the sheriff had decided the issue of possession, the loser in the case gave up.

Second, the writs used an old, but rarely used, procedure—the jury trial. The idea of asking a jury to decide points of fact had been developed in the early Middle Ages as part of the inquest. For example, when the king wanted to know who owned which properties in a village and how much people owed to the lord of the village, he swore a jury of the leading men of the village and asked them a series of questions. The natural competition among neighbors worked within the jury to produce accurate information, for no one would let another understate his obligations or overstate his rights. Henry II put this procedure to a purely legal purpose. His writs ordered the sheriff to swear a jury of neighbors of the disputants to answer questions about who had the best right to possess the disputed property.

Third, the writs were "returnable." They were issued to a person who came to the king's court to complain that he had been unjustly deprived of possession of property. The complainant then took the writ and "returned" it to the sheriff of his shire, who as the principal royal official there acted for the king in the matter. This system put the king's law at the disposal of the people who had a case to bring, and it generated a huge number of cases. Many of these cases raised problems that no one had ever thought of, and,

when this happened, the cases were referred back to the king for decision. Thus a "case law" developed in the king's court and because this law was the same for the whole kingdom—as opposed to the customary law, which was only valid in the hundred or shire court that honored it—this law became known as the Common Law.

Henry II's sons, Richard (r. 1189–99) and John (r. 1199–1216), lacked his political skills. Richard was a warrior, who spent nearly his entire reign in war, either on the Third Crusade or fighting King Philip II of France (r. 1180–1223). He paid little attention to government and spent only ten months in England during his entire reign. Nonetheless, Henry's institutions continued to function smoothly during Richard's absences, showing how well he had designed and established them.

John, by contrast, was a poor soldier, but a shrewd administrator. Early in his reign, he lost Normandy, Anjou, and most of Aquitaine to the French king, and he spent the last twelve years of his reign trying to get them back. This meant that he needed money to field armies, and, because the armies were unsuccessful, he repeatedly asked the country to contribute to the war effort. He squeezed revenue from every source he could, imposing heavy fines and seizing the property of men he suspected of plotting against him. The repeated military failures and the repressive measures to which John resorted led to a baronial rebellion

Richard I spent much of his reign fighting in the Third Crusade or against Philip Augustus of France (detail from the effigy on his tomb, 1199).

Excerpts from Magna Carta   1215

We [John] have conceded to all free men of our kingdom, for us and our heirs forever, all the liberties written below, to be held by them and their heirs from us and our heirs: . . .

12. No scutage [redemption of military service] or aid [grant to the king] shall be taken in our kingdom except by the common counsel of our kingdom. . . .

14. And for obtaining the common counsel of the kingdom, for assessing an aid . . . or a scutage, we will cause to be summoned by our sealed letters the archbishops, bishops, abbots, earls and greater barons, moreover we will cause to be summoned generally by the sheriffs . . . all those who hold of us in chief [the other vassals] for a certain day . . . and place . . . and once the summons has been made the business shall proceed on the assigned day according to the advice of those who are present, even if all those summoned have not come. . . .

39. No free man may be seized, or imprisoned, or disposessed, or outlawed, or exiled . . . nor will we go against him or send against him except by the legal judgment of his peers and by the law of the land.

40. To no one will we sell, to no one will we deny or delay right and justice.

Translated from W. Stubbs, *Select Charters* (Oxford: Clarendon Press, 1921), pp. 294 ff.

---

ons and the great ecclesiastical lords, but it established the principle that English government was based on law and that the king had an obligation to govern according to the law.

Englishmen of all classes were attached to the laws and institutions that protected their rights. This was true, as was shown by the Magna Carta, even of the barons who might have been expected to view the king's aggressive development of royal government as a threat to their independence. Thus, the growing loyalty to the English state was loyalty to a system of government and law as much as it was loyalty to a dynasty. The king could not claim that he alone was working for the common welfare because his opponents could assert that they too were seeking the good of the "community of the realm" and could point to the Magna Carta as a body of law that embodied that good. Consequently, in England even bitter struggles between the king and nobility did not threaten the unity of the country; all sides were committed to unity and a vision of the state embodied in the law.

Henry III

This unusual political situation explains certain apparent contradictions in the reign of Henry III (r. 1216–72). Under Henry, royal officials strengthened the administrative and judicial institutions of the country. They created new types of general taxation and devised new writs for bringing more cases into the royal courts. In addition, the Church's condemnation of trial by ordeal (the use of hot iron or water to test the guilt or innocence of an accused man) at the Lateran Council of 1215 consolidated the authority of royal law. The ordeal was the preferred procedure of the customary courts; it was thought that judgment belonged to God, whose will was revealed in the ordeal. After 1215, the ancient inquest procedure, the jury trial—which Henry II had adapted as the procedure of the royal courts—spread to courts

against him in 1215. The result was the *Magna Carta* (Great Charter), a treaty that guaranteed the liberties of the barons. John signed it at Runnymede just outside London on June 15, 1215.

The charter contained 63 chapters covering a wide variety of subjects, but its main elements assured that the king would govern with the counsel of the barons. John promised not to demand tax aid without "taking counsel with the kingdom," which meant consulting the barons. Further, he promised not to convict any freeman of a crime without a trial by his peers and not to extort money for giving justice in his court. He also promised to consult with his vassals and bishops before he undertook major projects. The *Magna Carta* was intended only to protect the bar-

Henry III of England (1216–72) discusses the progress of a building (perhaps Westminster Abbey) with his architects. The workmen are raising materials to the masons with a windlass.

throughout the realm, which brought the courts of custom under royal justice. A court's status and character were determined by the procedure it used, so once trial by jury became the common form of procedure, private courts—the courts of barons, monasteries, and churches—began to die out.

These developments were summed up in a remarkable treatise on English law based on the work of Henry de Bracton, a royal judge. The final version, written in the 1250s, gave a clear, logical, and thorough explanation of the common law, using precedents and general principles. The writer of the treatise was greatly influenced by Roman law, which gave the work a comprehensiveness even though it rested on hundreds of individual cases to be found in the records of the royal courts. This achievement made the common law so coherent and self-sufficient that it has maintained its identity as a legal system up to the present even though it has absorbed influences from many sources.

Notwithstanding the development of common law under Henry III, there was constant conflict between the king and his barons. The barons were not trying to destroy the central government; they were trying to gain control of it to protect their status and to put into practice their political programs. They often found it expedient to claim that they were defending the realm against a foolish and spendthrift monarch.

Henry had inherited the throne as a young child, and his government was run by regents until he came of age in 1225. At that time, the barons persuaded him to reaffirm the Magna Carta by granting him a tax. This second issuing of the charter took place without a rebellion, and the version of 1225 was accepted by everyone as the law of the land. This was an auspicious beginning for the young king, and harmony prevailed until the 1240s when his policy raised opposition among the barons. Henry wasted money on vain attempts to reconquer the lost French territories; he filled bishoprics and secular offices with his French relatives and friends; and he allowed the pope to draw large sums of money out of England to fight his war against the Hohenstaufen rulers of Italy. Although modern nationalism did not exist at that time, the barons' opposition to Henry evinced many of the attitudes that would later be characteristic of nationalism. They had no interest in the French territories; they resented his French friends; and they saw no reason why the pious donations of Englishmen should be used to support the pope. The barons' opposition to foreign intruders and foreign entanglements was supported by most lesser landholders and by a surprising number of English clergymen.

Henry III's chronic shortage of money enhanced the power of the barons. Ordinary income from the royal domain was barely adequate for the maintenance of royal government during peacetime, and the Magna Carta made it difficult to raise additional revenues without the consent of the barons. If Henry wanted to wage war, he had to levy taxes. But after 1240 the barons constantly refused to grant any taxes. Nevertheless, Henry went ahead with an ambitious project to help the pope conquer Sicily, and the English clergy, under papal pressure, gave him some money, but not enough. By 1258 Henry was hopelessly in debt, and his foreign policy was a complete failure. In desperation, he appointed a committee of barons to reform the government.

The problem was really not the nature of the government, but its policies, and the baronial committee turned to making policy and appointing high officials to carry it out. Naturally, the committee soon split into factions, which the king exploited in his own interests. The barons had found it easy to agree to oppose Henry, but hard to agree on a positive policy of their own. Though the barons needed to unite, they were jealous of anyone who sought to lead them, and when the ablest of them, Simon de Montfort (the king's brother-in-law) gained control of the government, he found that the barons had deserted the cause. Henry's eldest son, Edward, was able to raise an army and to defeat and kill Simon in 1265, and Henry's authority was fully restored.

This episode was significant for two reasons. First, it set a pattern that was to be repeated in England many times during the next two centuries. Again and again the barons seized control of the state, only to split into factions and lose that control. Second, the struggle between Henry and the barons speeded up the development of the representative assembly in England. The two sides appealed to the community of the realm, defining it broadly to gain the support of the most powerful segments of society. They called assemblies and invited knights from the shires and representatives of the towns as well as great men and high churchmen. From the 1240s, these enlarged meetings of the king's court were called parliaments, and their representative nature made them symbols of the secular state that was forming under royal government.

The Growth of Constitutional Government

In the early thirteenth century, several elements in the practice and theory of government began to coalesce into constitutional or limited government. In the realm of theory, the Church developed some old Roman ideas of a corporation into a theory of ecclesiastical organization. The foundation of this development was the principle that "what touches all, ought to be approved by all," which was used to support the right of the clerical members of a church or monastery to participate in the affairs of the Church. About the same time, canon lawyers were discussing the problem caused by a vacancy in the chief office of a bishopric or monastery. The old law said that the bishop was the ruler of his church and the abbot ruler of his monastery, but who had that right during a vacancy? The Roman theory of the corporation provided the answer: the members of the church or monastery collectively exercised all powers until a new leader was installed.

These ideas were mirrored in the growth of municipal institutions. Under the royal charter, the town community as a whole was obligated to the king for taxes and services, such as maintenance of roads. Moreover, the introduction of the corporate idea led to the idea of representation. The officers of a corporation could act on its behalf and could represent it before others.

These ideas developed at about the same time that barons were asserting their right to participate in royal government. The most prominent assertion of that right was in England during the Magna Carta crisis, but it was being made in every kingdom. The right stemmed from the feudal law, which required the lord to consult with his vassals before acting in a way that would affect their welfare. The lord could not expect his vassals to give him loyalty and support if he refused to ask for their opinion about business that might lead to war or the expenditure of money.

The formation of legal communities affected many regions of Europe in the early thirteenth century. In many places, rulers called on barons and the representatives of towns to support them in governing. Pope Innocent III called together the barons and representatives of the towns of the Papal States when he was reorganizing them. The Spanish and Hungarian kings summoned similar meetings of the realm. But these institutions developed most successfully in England. King John called together barons and representatives of the shires to ask for contributions to his war effort in France. In the Magna Carta, the barons asserted their right to be consulted whenever important national business was in hand. The baronial rebellion of 1258–65 led to a significant step in the development of the assembly as a representation of the community of the realm.

The term that came to be used to describe these meetings was *parliament* (literally "talk-fest"), but they did not function as a separate branch of government until much later. The parliament was an enlarged meeting of the king's Council, which normally con-

sisted of the king's tenants-in-chief, the great men, both lay and clerical, who held fiefs directly from the king. Under feudal law, these men owed the king advice and counsel, and the king was bound to consult with them on the business that concerned them all, which was essentially all the business of the realm. At a parliament, this inner group was joined by other barons and great men, so that the actions taken by the king in parliament had the force of widespread support among the leading men of the kingdom. The parliament also functioned as a court, for those who came to them brought their cases, and it was in this expanded council that the king would hear important appeals. Again, the judgment rendered in the presence and with at least the tacit support of the parliament carried great weight, and this was important in a time when the king's justice was just one of the legal systems to which people could turn. Even today the House of Lords is the highest court in England, though cases are actually heard only by specially appointed "law lords."

It was useful to summon knights of the shires—country gentlemen who held local offices such as sheriff or tax collector—and representatives of the towns to the parliaments because these

The shield of Simon de Montfort (1208?–65).

men were naturally awed by the occasion and went home to report what had taken place. In the towns, the mayors and aldermen were wealthy merchants who found their government functions burdensome, but they, too, gained a sense of the importance of their burdens through the experience of the parliament.

Both Henry III and the baronial leader, Simon de Montfort, had tried to justify their policies by asking the counties to send knights to parliament. In 1265 Simon, in an effort to compensate for his loss of baronial support, took the additional step of asking the towns to send representatives. These precedents were not forgotten. In 1268, after Simon's death and the end of the baronial rebellion, Henry III summoned both knights and burgesses to a parliament. But the basic principles of constitutional government were established under Henry III's son, Edward I (r. 1272–1307). Edward was in constant need of money to fight wars against the Scots and the French, and he continually summoned parliaments to ask the barons and towns for financial support. In the first of these meetings, called in 1275, Edward followed precedent and summoned knights and burgesses, and after 1295 the practice of inviting representatives of the towns was established.

Constitutional government, based on the idea that government has limited authority and is subject to law, was ultimately based on the distinction between ecclesiastical and secular power. Once the Europeans had made that distinction, in the course of the investiture controversy (see pp. 281–85), they had accepted that neither kings nor popes held complete or unlimited authority. The growth of the new jurisprudence during the later twelfth century contributed to this view, for the lawyers had to define the relationship between the law and the law maker. When did the king or pope govern the law and when did it govern him? These were the basic questions of a constitutional system and in developing answers to them, the European lawyers, both in the Church and in the kingdoms, defined a system of limited government that was unique among the world's civilizations.

The Growth of Royal Power in France

Royal power developed more slowly in France than in England because there was strong opposition to centralization in France. In the twelfth century, the French king ruled over a kingdom made up of semi-autonomous duchies and counties. During the reigns of Henry II and Richard I of England, nearly half of these territories were ruled by a single man, who was in a position to counter the French king's pretensions.

The work of building the kingdom began under Louis VI (r. 1108–37). Louis's father, Philip I (r. 1060–1108), had named him Louis to recall the ancient glories of the French crown; Louis was the French form of Clovis and Ludovicus, the Merovingian and Carolingian ancestors. Louis VI took the implications of his name seriously. His father had concentrated on his demesne, the county of Paris, and issued very few charters to individuals or institutions outside the demesne. Louis increased the number of charters issued almost fourfold, from an average of three or four per year to about twelve a year, thereby increasing the role of the king in the affairs of bishoprics and monasteries throughout the realm. In addition, Louis asserted that all bishops who were not already under the protection of some great lord were to be under royal protection, and in the long run this assertion of authority led to a great increase in royal power. Bishops troubled by local magnates could call on the king, and the king, in acting on his promise of protection, extended his power both in theory and practice.

By constant pressure and attention to events, Louis took advantage of opportunities to add men to the number of his *fideles,* those who had taken an oath of fealty to him. He recognized that he could not assert, as had the Carolingians, that all men in the kingdom owed him an oath of allegiance, but he could extend the circle of his vassals and did so. In support of this effort, his chief adviser, Abbot Suger of St. Denis (abbot 1122–52), enunciated a theory of royal authority that harkened back to the Carolingian idea of kingship. In his biography of Louis, written shortly after the king's death, Suger asserted that all men were at least indirectly subject to the king. He imagined a feudal hierarchy in which lesser men were subject to Louis through the greater men who were the king's *fideles.* This was the line he had taken while Louis was alive and, though it was never accepted by the majority of the French nobility, it was the theoretical basis of Louis's constant press to expand the circle of those who gave homage to him. In addition, Suger asserted that the king was no man's *fidelis;* he was the man of St. Denis himself, the patron saint of the monarchy and the kingdom.

These ideas laid the foundation for the growth of royal power, but Louis made his greatest progress by attending to practical affairs. Toward the end of his reign he greatly expanded the radius of royal authority by marrying his heir Louis VII (r. 1137–80) to Eleanor of Aquitaine, heiress of the richest duchy in the kingdom. When young Louis succeeded to the throne, he made a grand procession to Aquitaine to demonstrate his authority. He was the first king to visit Bordeaux in 300 years. But the marriage produced only four daughters, and Eleanor, a strong and independent woman, led Louis into many difficulties. In 1147, he took her with him on the Second Crusade, and when on the journey she dallied with her cousin the Count of Toulouse, Louis decided to annul the marriage. He succeeded in getting the Church's judgment of annulment in 1152, and a

year later Eleanor married the king's most dangerous rival, Henry of Anjou, soon to be Henry II of England.

Louis VII continued the policies of his father, and Suger remained the chief adviser of the king until his own death in 1152. During Louis VI's reign, the abbot of Cluny had placed his abbey and its subordinate houses under the protection of the French king, because the local counts were disturbing the abbey's possessions. In 1166 and 1171, Louis VII took advantage of an appeal from the abbot to march into Burgundy. It was the first time a French king had visited the region since the middle of the tenth century. In arranging the affairs of Cluny, Louis established royal officers in an enclave in the duchy, and this became the basis for the expansion of royal authority there. By 1239, Burgundy was part of the royal demesne. He did the same in taking advantage of disputes over episcopal elections to interfere and assert his rights. By the end of his reign, half of the bishoprics of the kingdom were directly under royal protection and authority.

But the work of building royal power in France progressed slowly so long as Henry II and Richard I combined their holdings in France with the kingship of England. Henry and Richard held Louis VII and then his son Philip II (r. 1180–1223) at bay, most of the time refusing to do more than recognize them as their suzerain for the French lands. The shift of power finally came when John succeeded Richard in 1199. The events followed the pattern of extending royal power already established by Louis VI and Louis VII, when Philip got an opportunity to judge John. John had violated feudal law by mistreating one of his own vassals in France, and the injured baron appealed to John's overlord, Philip, who summoned John to his court. When John refused to come, Philip deprived him of his fiefs—Normandy, Anjou, Brittany, and most of Aquitaine—as a contumacious vassal.

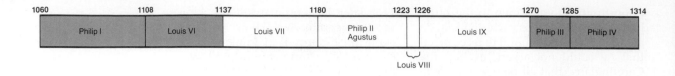

1060		1108		1137		1180		1223	1226		1270	1285		1314
Philip I		Louis VI		Louis VII		Philip II Agustus			Louis IX		Philip III	Philip IV		

Louis VIII

When Philip moved to take control of the territories in 1204, the barons there supported him against John, whose fiscal policies and arbitrariness had made many enemies.

Despite his trouble with Henry II and Richard I, Philip II was an exceptionally successful king. He inherited a monarchy that had an annual income of about 60,000 pounds and left one that collected 438,000 pounds per year. He accomplished this feat by developing new institutions to control the terri-

tories he won. Royal control rested on two principles: first, the king permitted the duchies and counties to keep their own laws and traditional institutions of government, and, second, he divided the territories up into small districts governed by men he sent from his court. Thus, Normandy continued to use Norman law and its court system remained intact, but it was divided into 13 administrative districts, each governed by a royal bailiff. Philip treated the bailiffs well when they performed well, and on the whole they demanded less from the people than the barons had. This made the king popular and helped strengthen Philip's hold on the kingdom. His system of governing through royal officials formed the model for all later governmental systems on the continent.

Philip was succeeded by his son Louis VIII (r. 1223–26), who had already been an active participant in government before his father's death and had been the leader of a crusade against heretics in southern France that resulted in the annexation of that region by the monarchy. But Louis's reign was too short to permit him to accomplish much, and it was left to Louis IX to continue the work of his grandfather.

St. Louis

As a result of the successes of his grandfather and father, Louis IX (r. 1226–70) was far more powerful than any combination of hostile French lords. He put down a few halfhearted rebellions early in his reign, and for the rest of his life his authority was never challenged. No one could oppose Louis's claim to rights or land. But Louis did not use his power arrogantly. He was imbued with the ideals of the

The Expansion of the Royal Domain in France   1180–1314

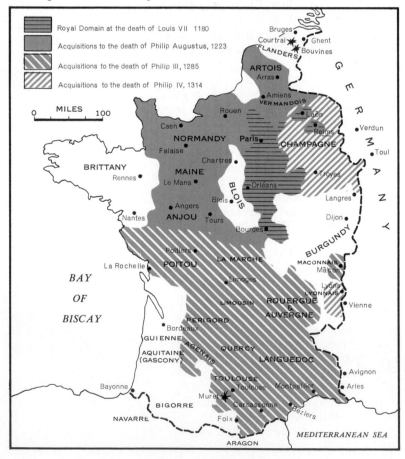

Christian ruler, which were based on the idea that the true king was good, generous, and conscientious. He settled the longstanding conflict with England, which stemmed from his grandfather's actions against John, by a generous treaty that gave the English king many coastal districts in Aquitaine. He kept faith with all men, even with Moslems. In France he submitted all disputed questions to the decisions of his courts and did his best to restrain the zeal of his administrative agents, who tended to exaggerate the extent of royal rights. Louis insisted that all in the kingdom observe his prerogatives and rights, but he also was scrupulous in observing those of others. No other medieval king had such a reputation for honesty and fair dealing.

Louis was pious, but he held the Church to the same standards as his subjects and made independent judgment of its claims. He refused to join Pope Innocent IV in the attack on the emperor Frederick II; he rejected demands of the French bishops that he punish all men who remained excommunicated for more than a year. He felt that, as a Christian king, he knew better than anyone else how to provide for the spiritual and material welfare of his people.

Louis's concern for law and justice led, naturally enough, to a strengthening of the royal judicial system. In France as in England, since time immemorial law had been a function of local communities, which passed down their customs from generation to generation. The customary law had its rules of procedure and substance (for example, its definition of who inherited property or what the penalty for theft would be), and the king did not interfere in this law. Royal justice concerned matters that people recognized as concerning the king's interests. This included litigation over royal lands and rights, over the obligations of subjects and towns (for example, to maintain bridges and roads), and over actions that could be construed as disturbances of the king's peace. Yet, as the king's power grew,

Statue of Louis IX, in the church of Mainville in Normandy.

the jurisdiction of royal law grew, and the theory of the Christian ruler seemed to give the king an almost universal authority. Nearly every crime could be seen as a violation of the king's peace, though normally the king left small matters to local community courts. During Louis's reign, the growth of royal authority led to the creation of one of the great institutions of the French monarchy, the Parlement of Paris. This was the king's own court, staffed with his closest advisers. It heard appeals from the decisions of his local administrative agents and, even more important, it heard appeals from the courts of his great feudal lords. By reviewing, and often reversing, the decisions of feudal courts, it established a legal basis for royal claims to supremacy over all subjects.

The king's local courts, headed by bailiffs and other administrative agents, were even more zealous than the Parlement in upholding royal

St. Louis as Described by Joinville

Jean de Joinville, a noble of Champagne, was a friend of St. Louis and went with him on his crusade of 1248.

This holy man loved God with all his heart, and imitated his works. For example, just as God died because he loved his people, so the king risked his life many times for the love of his people. . . . He said once to his eldest son: . . . "I beg you that you make yourself loved by the people of your realm, for truly, I would rather that a Scot came from Scotland and governed the people of the kingdom justly and well than that you should govern them badly. . . . " The holy king loved the truth so much that he kept his promises even to the Saracens.

A friar told the king . . . that he had never read that a kingdom was destroyed or changed rulers except through lack of justice. . . . The king did not forget this lesson but governed his land justly and well, according to the will of God. . . . Often in summer he went to sit down under an oak-tree in the wood of Vincennes, after hearing mass, and made us sit around him. And all those who had suits to bring him came up, without being hindered by ushers or other people. And he would ask them: "Does anyone here have a suit?" And those who had requests would get up. . . . And then he would call Lord Pierre de Fontaines and Lord Geoffroi de Villette [two of his legal experts] and say to one of them: "Settle this affair for me." And if he saw anything to correct in what they said on his behalf, he would do so.

From Jean de Joinville, *Histoire de Saint Louis,* ed. by N. de Wailly (Paris: Firmin Didot, 1874), pp. 11, 34.

rights. Since earlier kings had been too weak to enforce their theoretical claims, no exact boundary between the privileges of local lords and the rights of the monarch had ever been drawn. Thus on issues for which there were no clear precedents it was only natural that the bailiffs should rule in favor of the king. Louis did not take undue advantage of this situation; in fact, he and his Parlement often modified the more extreme claims of the bailiffs. But the net result was an increase in royal power, an increase that was cheerfully accepted by most people in the country. For the majority of the population, the king was a savior from the depredations of local lords, and he was viewed as the one who had suppressed disorder and brought about the peace that was the basis of prosperity.

Nonetheless, France was united only through the king and his bureaucracy. The provinces retained their customary law and privileges, and no one could have spoken of a French common law or of the "rights of Frenchmen." The creation of a singular French law had to wait until Napoleon in the first years of the nineteenth century.

As a Christian ruler, Louis was a zealous crusader. Jerusalem had been lost to the Moslems in 1187, and all efforts to recover it had failed. Armed expeditions had gained nothing, and a treaty that Emperor Frederick II had arranged, which gave the Christians control of the city, had lasted only a short time. In Louis's day, the Holy City was again in Moslem hands. These successive failures had somewhat dampened enthusiasm for overseas expeditions, but Louis felt that his responsibilities as a Christian king extended beyond the boundaries of his kingdom. He had a role to play in all Christendom. In 1248 and again in 1270 he led crusades to recover Jerusalem. The earlier expedition had some chance of success, but after a first victory Louis's army was cut off from its supplies and was forced to surrender. The second expedition was hopeless from the beginning, for Louis let himself be talked into attacking the outlying Moslem state of Tunis, which had been disturbing western shipping in the Mediterranean for centuries. Even if he had conquered the country, it would have done his cause little good; as it happened, he and many of his men died of fever soon after landing.

Louis IX was canonized during the 1290s, and his canonization was more than a personal tribute to a pious crusader; it completed the work of sanctifying the French monarchy. Louis's grandson, who insisted on the canonization as part of a general settlement of disputes with the papacy, was quite aware of the political value of the act.

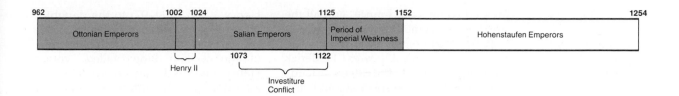

| 962 | | 1002 | 1024 | | 1125 | | 1152 | | 1254 |

Ottonian Emperors | Salian Emperors | Period of Imperial Weakness | Hohenstaufen Emperors

Henry II

1073 — Investiture Conflict — 1122

Louis's search for justice and order had been officially recognized by the Church, and it had created an almost inexhaustible reservoir of support for his dynasty. Some of his successors were evil and some were weak, but for centuries loyalty to the king was the strongest political force in France. The king stood as the symbol of unity and good government; he alone could override provincial differences and selfish local ambitions. France remained strongly Catholic, but loyalty to the Church began to take second place to loyalty to the state.

The Hohenstaufens in Germany

As the history of the Investiture Controversy showed, the building of royal power in Germany presented problems similar to those in France. When Henry I (r. 918–36) was elected to the throne, his power rested primarily on his own duchy of Saxony, and the task of building the monarchy depended on his being able to gain control over the other duchies. He and his son Otto I (r. 936–73) made great progress toward achieving this goal. But the building of a strong monarchy in Germany was difficult because in principle the king was chosen through an election by the dukes.

Henry I's predecessor Conrad I (r. 911–18) and Henry himself were elected by the dukes, and even though Otto I and his heirs inherited the crown, the formal election remained a part of the process by which a legitimate ruler was elevated. Whenever the direct line of male heirs failed—as in 1002, when Otto III died without heirs—the power of the electors became effective, and the result was that at certain periods of medieval German history there was considerable competition for the crown among the leading ducal families.

In the middle of the twelfth century, the Hohenstaufen* family emerged victorious from one of these periods of competition. In 1152, the Hohenstaufen Frederick I Barbarossa (r. 1152–90) became king and set out to reconstruct royal power, which had been weakened during the period of competition. Frederick I's political base was in Swabia, where he was duke, and he faced a difficult task to bring the other great dukes into line.

He began the job by extending his power not to the north, but to the south. He married the heiress of the kingdom of Burgundy, which had been a subordinate part of the German kingdom for several generations, and then in 1154 he went to Rome to receive the imperial crown. As emperor, he claimed authority over northern Italy, which could provide him with the tax revenues he needed to conquer or awe the German dukes. This strategy of basing his power on a collection of territories stretching south from Swabia to Rome worked well, and by the 1170s, Frederick was able to exercise real authority in Germany. In 1180, he deprived his principal rival, Henry the Lion, Duke of Saxony and Bavaria, of all his fiefs. The move anticipated the similar action by Philip II of France against John of England a little more than 20 years later. But while Philip was able to destroy John's power in France, Frederick could only temporarily affect Henry the Lion's position. In Germany, feudalism had not pro-

*The Hohenstaufen descended, in the female line, from Henry V. They took their name from their ancestral castle in Swabia.

Late twelfth-century gilded reliquary bearing the features of Frederick Barbarossa.

gressed so far as in France, and all the great lords combined feudal tenures with freeholds as the basis of their economic and political power. Frederick could not confiscate the extensive lands Duke Henry held in freehold, and, as a result, although the duke had to go into exile after he lost his fiefs, he remained the richest baron in Germany and a man whom Frederick and his successors would still have to contend with.

The strategy of basing German royal power on the position of the German king as emperor had its disadvantages. Frederick had to become involved in Italian affairs, and he married his son Henry VI (r. 1190–97) to the daughter of the king of Sicily in order to secure his southern flank. When the male line of the Sicilian kings failed, young Henry inherited that crown, and the attention and interests of the Hohenstaufens were split between north and south even more than before.

Henry VI died young in 1197, leaving only an infant heir, Frederick II (r. 1197–1250), and the inability of the heir to govern gave the German dukes the opportunity to reassert their right to elect a king. The result was a civil war in which the papacy became involved. The competition was between Henry VI's brother, Philip of Swabia, and Henry the Lion's son, Otto of Brunswick. Pope Innocent III asserted his right to judge between these men on the grounds that he would have to crown one of them emperor and had a right to decide which one was most fit to sit on the imperial throne. He supported Otto IV (r. 1197–1215), who became secure on the throne after Philip was murdered in 1208. But when Otto broke his promises to the pope in 1209 by invading the kingdom of Sicily, where Frederick ruled as a vassal of the papacy, Innocent switched his support to young Frederick, whom he thought he could control. The pope was determined to prevent the unification of northern and southern Italy under a single king, and to stop Otto he stirred up a rebellion in Germany in favor of Frederick. Otto had to return home in 1212, and in 1214, he invaded France, with the support of King John of England, in retaliation for Philip II's support of Frederick. At the great battle of Bouvines in Flanders, Philip decisively defeated the combined forces of England and Germany. In England, the defeat led to the Magna Carta crisis. In Germany, it cost Otto his crown, for he was deposed by an assembly of the magnates in 1215. Frederick was now in control, but the long civil war had weakened the monarchy in Germany, and the dukes were able to force concessions from the king.

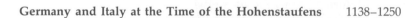

Germany and Italy at the Time of the Hohenstaufens   1138–1250

The Papal–Hohenstaufen Feud

In Germany and Italy the central government was far weaker than in England and France—a condition that Frederick II spent his life trying to correct. Though he failed, he came close enough to precipitate the last great struggle between the empire and the papacy.

Frederick II was by birth and upbringing an Italian. He spent a few years in Germany after becoming emperor, but he never felt at home there and never had much power over the German dukes. Apparently deciding that he could do nothing with Germany, at least until he had brought Italy fully under his power, he abandoned almost all authority to the princes. All he expected from Germany was a supply of soldiers for his Italian wars.

In Italy he followed exactly the opposite course. First, he eliminated all opposition in his hereditary kingdom of Sicily, transforming it from a feudal kingdom into a nearly absolute monarchy, and then he began to revive the old imperial claims to central and northern Italy. Thanks to the factional quarrels within and among the Italian towns, he was able to make substantial acquisitions of territory. Some of the northern Italian towns became so alarmed that they revived the Lombard League, which had fought Frederick I in the twelfth century, but Frederick crushed the league's forces at Cortenuova in 1237. For the moment he appeared to be in control of the whole Italian peninsula.

However, the papacy remained determined to keep Italy from falling into the power of any one master. The Church's strategy for maintaining its independence was to preserve the independence of the Papal States, stretching from Rome to Ravenna, and this could only be accomplished if Italy remained divided. No pope could believe that an emperor who ruled all Italy except the region around Rome would long respect Rome itself, and in

Portrait of Emperor Frederick II, from a manuscript of his treatise, *The Art of Hunting with Falcons.*

the history of the papacy there were many examples of imperial meddling in papal elections and affairs. Pope Innocent III, who had made Frederick II emperor, had kept the empire in turmoil rather than risk this danger; the policies he set appeared sound to his successors.

But the danger posed by Frederick was more than just political. His orthodoxy was somewhat suspect. He was a brilliant and inquisitive man who exchanged friendly letters with Moslem rulers, dabbled in science and magic, and was accused of writing a book called *The Three Imposters: Moses, Jesus, and Mohammed.* This charge was false, but it represented what people of the time thought of him. For his part, Frederick tried hard to convince the world that he was an orthodox ruler. He took the cross and went on crusade, and it was he who first condemned heretics to death by burning them at the stake. Yet, these actions raised more doubts than they settled. After taking the cross, he delayed leaving on crusade for many years and was excommunicated for violating his oath. When he did go, his strategy was to negotiate with the Moslems rather than fight them. This strategy produced a treaty that gave the Christians control of Jerusalem for a few years, but the pope condemned him anyway. Meanwhile, people thought that his persecution of heretics was designed to improve his political position.

When it became clear that Frederick intended to gain full control of the Italian peninsula, Pope Gregory IX (r. 1227–41) took drastic measures. He tried to hold a council in Rome to discuss the problem, but Frederick intercepted the fleet bearing many of the prelates and captured or drowned most of them, which did not improve his reputation for piety. Gregory's successor, Innocent IV (r. 1243–54), who was Europe's greatest lawyer and a man almost as able as his great namesake, Innocent III, called a council at Lyons in 1245. The council declared that Frederick had forfeited all his possessions

and that neither he nor any member of his family should ever again be permitted to rule in Germany or Italy. Innocent proclaimed a crusade against Frederick and imposed a tax on the clergy to pay for the armies to carry it out.

In Germany, the papal attack on Frederick destroyed the last vestiges of central government. The princes refused to obey either Frederick or an opposing line of rulers elected by the propapal faction. As a result, Germany became a loose confederation of states under the control of the princes who were free to accept or reject the policies made by the nominal ruler. No German emperor after Frederick exercised real authority, except in his own family possessions.

In Italy the issue was not decided so quickly. Frederick held on to most of the territory he had gained, but he never managed to build a strong government in the north. After his death in 1250, the towns of northern and central Italy asserted their independence, though the kingdom of Sicily remained loyal to his sons. The papacy might have been satisfied with this state of affairs, but it had been too badly frightened by Frederick to take any chances. So the popes carried on the war against the "viper brood" of the Hohenstaufen, refusing to relax until the hated family had been ejected from Sicily and Naples. They preached crusades, collected taxes from the clergy to cover their expenses, and sent cardinals out with armies to do battle with Frederick's heirs. And when they found that they could not do the job alone, the popes turned to England and France for help. The attempt to involve Henry III of England led to the baronial rebellion of 1258 and did not solve the pope's problem, but the approach to France was successful. St. Louis reluctantly permitted his brother, Charles of Anjou, to attempt the conquest of the kingdom of Sicily. Charles, aided by crusade privileges for his troops and crusade taxes, defeated the last Hohenstaufen ruler of Sicily in a

In 1241 Frederick's fleet captured (or drowned) two cardinals and a hundred bishops who were on their way to a council summoned by Gregory IX to depose the emperor. This manuscript illustration shows Frederick in the ship on the left, though actually he was not present. On the right, his soldiers attack the prelates in a ship bearing the papal ensign of the keys of St. Peters.

fast campaign in 1266. A grandson of Frederick II made a desperate attempt to regain the kingdom, but his forces were crushed in 1268, and the young man was executed. The papacy had finally attained its goal.

Loss of Prestige by the Church

But in winning this political victory, the papacy had lost moral prestige. People had had some doubts about the deposition of Frederick II—St. Louis had maintained a careful neutrality in the struggle—although the Church clearly had a case against him. Frederick was a controversial man, and he threatened the independence of the papacy. But Frederick's heirs were not very dangerous, and it seemed pure vindictiveness to harry them for two decades. Throughout this period, it was apparent that the Church was using its spiritual authority for its own political ends. It was difficult to distinguish the pope's actions from those of a secular prince. One could argue that if it was proper for the pope to tax the clergy to defend his territories, it was equally proper for a king to tax the clergy to defend his kingdom. This claim was the cause of the next great conflict between the papacy and secular rulers.

Moreover, the popes had won their victory over the Hohenstaufen only by creating political instability in both Germany and Italy, and in the long run this instability weakened the Church. No one in Germany was strong enough to protect the bishops, so they had to fight and intrigue to protect themselves. The German governments also could not act effectively against the heresies that sprang up in the fourteenth century and laid the foundation for Luther's revolt against the papacy in the sixteenth century. In northern and central Italy the absence of a central government encouraged the growth of powerful city-states that dominated the rural districts around them. Genoa and Venice, the towns that controlled the lucrative eastern trade, remained fairly stable and used their energy to establish colonies in the Aegean and, even (for Genoa) on the northern shores of the Black Sea. But the inland towns, even wealthy trading centers such as Florence and Pisa, were constantly plagued by factionalism that had its origins in the struggle between the papacy and Hohenstaufens. They were also constantly at war with one another. The situation was no better in the Kingdom of Sicily. Peter III of Aragon, who had married the daughter of the last Hohenstaufen king of Sicily, took advantage of a rebellion against the French ruler to seize Sicily in 1282. But Peter never acquired Naples and the mainland territories, which remained in the hands of a younger branch of the French royal family. However, this kingdom of Naples was torn by quarrels over the succession and was not able to help the papacy.

The state of affairs around Rome was especially precarious. The Roman nobility was trying to strengthen petty lordships in the region around the city; the small towns around Rome were striving for independence and territory, and Rome itself was disturbed by competition among the great families. The pope's position was almost impossible. He could either flee Italy and lose the prestige that was associated with Rome or stay and participate in the petty politics as a minor prince. Neither course would strengthen the papacy. In fact, the Church itself seemed to recognize the rise of the secular state and the decline of the Church during the thirteenth century. None of the great thirteenth-century popes became a saint, but several kings were canonized. And one of these saintly kings, Louis IX of France, probably exercised greater moral authority over the Europe of his day than did any churchman.

ENGLAND, FRANCE, AND THE PAPACY

In England and France the central government had grown very strong by the

Edward I of England (1272–1307) on his throne (illustration from a fourteenth-century manuscript).

end of the thirteenth century. Edward I of England had been the leading figure in the reestablishment of royal authority after the baronial rebellion of 1258–65, and he was determined to increase his power. Edward was a hard-working and intelligent ruler who selected good men to serve his government. He was also a man of terrifying rages—the dean of St. Paul's cathedral in London dropped dead of fright during a dispute with him—and few men dared to contradict him openly. Yet, he had learned that he had to retain the support of the propertied classes, both the aristocracy and the burgesses. In foreign policy, Edward sought to make himself supreme ruler of the British Isles. He avoided continental engagements and concentrated on the conquest of Wales and Scotland, which was a policy in harmony with the desires of the aristocracy. As a result, he controlled his administration and, unlike his father, was not dominated by a baronial council.

Edward succeeded in completing the conquest of Wales, which had been begun long ago by the barons of William the Conqueror. He replaced the last native prince of Wales with his own infant son, thereby creating a precedent that has endured to the present day. But Scotland proved more troublesome. Edward first tried to install a puppet king, but when his candidate proved less subservient than he had hoped Edward deposed him and tried to rule the country directly. However, Edward could not keep a large enough army in Scotland to suppress dissent, and the Scots rebelled, first under William Wallace and then under Robert Bruce. The rebellion was still raging when Edward died, and the Scots won their independence at Bannockburn in 1314.

Even though he tried to avoid continental engagements, Edward had to resist the attempt by the king of France to seize the duchy of Aquitaine, the last French holding of the English royal family.

Edward and Parliament

Edward's wars cost huge sums of money and kept him fully occupied—two reasons why he made greater use of Parliament than any of his predecessors. With all the important men of the realm, aristocrats and burgesses, present at meetings of Parliament, Edward could get their advice on policy, settle difficult legal cases, issue statutes, and obtain grants of taxes. Edward's statutes were so important in the history of common law that he earned the title the English Justinian.

Representatives of counties and towns came before the king in 1275, but for the next 20 years Edward summoned such representatives only sporadically. The essential element in Parliament was still the Council, composed of high officials, bishops, and barons. But in 1295 Edward summoned representatives of the realm to a very full meeting (the "Model Parliament"), and from that time on they were frequently present. Again, Edward could have probably done his business with the approval of the barons alone, but the full Parliament provided support from the knights and burgesses as well.

Edward probably could have done all this without Parliament, but it was more efficient to take care of everything at one time and in one place. Actions taken in Parliament had great prestige, so it was advantageous to obtain the sanction of Parliament for as many decisions as possible. Edward lost nothing by following this policy, for he controlled Parliament as effectively as he did every other branch of government. He could not have foreseen that he was building up a powerful institution that might some day develop a will of its own.

The representatives Edward summoned to Parliament had not yet joined in an organized body, and their role seems to have been largely passive: "to hear and to obey," as some of the early summonses put it. Such opposition as there was in Parliament came from the barons. In 1297, when Edward had pushed a new tax through at a very small meeting of the Council, the barons protested and forced the king to promise that in the future he would levy taxes only "with the common assent of the whole kingdom." This was not quite an admission that only Parliament could grant taxes, but it certainly implied that the assent of a large number of people was needed; and clearly the easiest way to obtain such assent was in Parliament. The barons had sought to avoid taxes by asserting the rights of other classes, and at the end of Edward's reign, when they petitioned the king for government reforms, they invited the representatives of both shires and towns to join them.

France under Philip the Fair

In France, which was less unified politically than England, the growth of royal power followed a different course. At the end of the thirteenth century, the French barons were still struggling to preserve their local rights of government and their exemptions from the authority of royal officials. Not particularly interested in controlling the central government in Paris, they simply wanted to keep it from interfering with their lands and their subjects. The chief problem of the French king was not to keep the barons from dominating his council, but to see that his orders were enforced in their lands.

The problem came to a head in the reign of Philip IV, called Philip the Fair (r. 1285–1314), the grandson of St. Louis. Like his grandfather, Philip was pious, upright in his private life, and imbued with a sense of the divine mission of the French monarchy. But he was narrow-minded where St. Louis had been magnanimous, and grasping where St. Louis had been merely firm. The number of bureaucrats grew enormously during his reign, and Philip encouraged them in their efforts to

Description of a Parliament

The medieval Parliament was a great concourse of people from the elite classes of English society. When the king did his business in Parliament, his acts were quickly known in the country and their effects were widely felt. Parliament was a display of royal majesty, an opportunity for the people to approach the king with their needs and complaints, and a palpable representation of the community of the realm. Here is a description of one of Edward I's Parliaments.

Close on seven hundred are [in the king's Great Hall at Westminster] . . . where at the end, surrounded by torches, sits King Edward I. . . . On his right is the Archbishop of Canterbury; on his left the Chancellor, William de Hamilton; below, some thirty members of the king's small council—his ministers and permanent official advisers. For reasons of comfort as well as in token of their dignity they sit upon great wool-sacks. . . . Close at hand are the justices of the Common Pleas, the Exchequer, and the King's Bench; their advice will be needed during the session to frame any statutes the king may propose. . . . Sitting apart are the ninety-five prelates of the realm, together with all manner of archdeacons and deans from the cathedral chapters. The king's business is not their business . . . But they know that if they do not attend parliament, . . . the barons and earls will almost certainly vote to tax [their lands]. . . . Beyond stand the barons, earls, and other magnates of the realm, clothed in stamped velvets of blue, red, or yellow, with cloaks of silk and cloth of Tars. Their arms and weapons they have been forbidden to bear in time of parliament by an ordinance of the king, whose special peace, protecting all coming to parliament, he means to enforce. . . . Toward the back of the hall, mingled with the barons, are the knights of the shire, clad in velvet doublets, well lined with rich furs; and beyond, awkward and uncertain in a group of nearly two hundred, the citizens and burgesses elected by the towns. . . .

Suddenly, the Bishop of London, clad in purple and scarlet, arises, and talking ceases as he opens with a prayer. The Archbishop of Canterbury follows with a sermon on the text, "How shall a court correct the ills of the whole realm, unless it shall first be itself corrected. . . ." How . . . can the king reform his realm when his subjects in parliament are reluctant to grant him money? This is the plain meaning of what the Archbishop has been saying.

From G. L. Haskins, *The Growth of English Representative Government* (New York: A. S. Barnes, 1960), pp. 10–12.

expand royal authority. He was willing to condone any expedient to break the power of a local ruler who tried to retain a semi-independent status. Lesser vassals could not resist, but the more powerful men were indignant. It is not surprising that Philip spent a large part of his reign warring with his greatest vassals, including the king of England (as duke of Aquitaine) and the count of Flanders. He gained some land from both, but he never took the rich textile cities of Bruges and Ghent from Flanders nor the flourishing port of Bordeaux from Aquitaine.

Philip the Fair had a harder time than Edward I raising money to pay for his wars. The French had never been subjected to a general tax, whereas the English had been afflicted with national taxes since the end of the twelfth century. Moreover, France was so divided that no central assembly like the English Parliament could impose a uniform tax on the whole country. Instead, royal agents had to negotiate with each region, and often with each lord or each town within each region. France was at least four times larger than England in both area and population, but it is doubtful whether Philip enjoyed any larger tax revenue than did Edward.

These difficulties in collecting taxes partly explain the military weakness of France during the next hundred years. They also explain why the French representative assembly, the Estates General, never became as powerful as the English Parliament. Philip was the first king to call representatives to a meeting at Paris, but he never asked them for a grant of taxes. He knew that the country at large would pay little attention to the decision of a central assembly, and the lack of any real power over taxation remained one of the chief weaknesses of the Estates General. Conversely, tax negotiations with local leaders and assemblies, though tedious, in the long run gave the ruler a free hand in imposing levies. It was easy to play one region off against another, or to threaten isolated areas that could not count on outside support. The royal bureaucracy was so persistent and skillful in conducting these negotiations that sooner or later it succeeded in breaking down most of the regional resistance to taxation.

Thus England was a strongly united country in which the king and the propertied classes cooperated in carrying out policies that they both approved. France was united more by the royal bureaucracy than by common interests, but the propertied classes of France were on the whole ready to trust the king on policy matters. And in both England and France some of the ideas that distinguish the modern sovereign state were beginning to appear: the welfare of the state was the greatest good; the defense of the realm was the greatest necessity; opposition to duly constituted authority was the greatest evil. As one of Philip's lawyers put it: "All men, clergy and laity alike, are bound to contribute to the defense of the realm." People who were beginning to think in these terms were not likely to be impressed by papal appeals and exhortations.

The Struggle with Boniface VIII

In the early 1290s, the cardinals had had great difficulty choosing a pope, and finally in 1294 they agreed on a most unlikely candidate, Peter Murrone, a hermit who lived on the slopes of Mount Vesuvius near Naples. As Celestine V, this unworldly man paid little attention to the complex papal government, and there were soon calls for his abdication. Before the end of the year, Celestine had abdicated, the only pope ever to do so, and the cardinals had elected one of the leading members of their college, who took the name Boniface VIII (r. 1294–1303).

Boniface was an able canon lawyer and a veteran of the political conflicts endemic to Italy. Sensing that a new type of secular authority in the western kingdoms was challenging papal authority more dangerously than the Hohenstaufens had, Boniface tried to reassert the superiority of ecclesiastical authority and the independence of the

Church. He made no claim that had not already been made by his predecessors, but the climate of opinion had changed. Many people now believed that their chief duty was to support their king rather than to obey the pope. As a result, Boniface was defeated in a head-on clash with the kings of England and France—a blow from which the medieval Church did not recover.

The issue was clear-cut: were the clergy to be treated as ordinary subjects of secular rulers, or were they responsible only to the pope? Specifically, could they be taxed for defense of the realm without the pope's consent? As already noted, the thirteenth-century kings could not run their governments without taxes, and they were always tempted to tap the resources of the Church. The popes themselves had provided precedents by imposing taxes on the clergy to support their political crusades, particularly against the Hohenstaufens, so, when Edward I and Philip the Fair drifted into war over Aquitaine in 1294, they both asked their clergy for a grant of taxes. They were outraged when Boniface prohibited these grants in 1296. Both kings stirred up public opinion against the clergy as disloyal members of the community, and both seized ecclesiastical property and forbade the transfer of money to Rome. Edward went further and virtually outlawed the English clergy. In the end, the harassed churchmen of both countries begged the pope to reconsider and remove his ban. Boniface did so, grudgingly but effectively, in 1298.

Worse was to follow. In 1301 Philip the Fair imprisoned a French bishop on a flimsy charge of treason and refused to obey a papal order to free him immediately. Boniface cited the old principle of canon law that clergy were not subject to secular courts. When Boniface threatened to punish the king and his agents, Philip called a great assembly at Paris (1302). This was the first meeting of what became the Estates General, and it brought together the three Estates or classes—the clergy, nobility, and bourgeoisie. The assembly gave

Pope Boniface VIII receives St. Louis of Toulouse, a grandnephew of St. Louis of France and son of Charles II of Naples. The representation of the pope corresponds to other pictures of him. Fresco by Ambrogio Lorenzetti, Siena (*ca.* 1330).

the king its full support and emphatically rejected any papal authority over France. When the dispute continued, Philip, through his minister, Guillaume de Nogaret, accused Boniface of immorality and heresy and appealed to a general council to condemn him. Local assemblies throughout France endorsed Philip's plan—the nobility and bourgeoisie enthusiastically, the clergy reluctantly but almost unanimously. Whatever pressure Philip exerted to get this response, he certainly had the support of the people, as subsequent events were to show. The people may not have believed all the charges, but they felt that the Church was corrupt and that the pope should not interfere with French internal affairs.

Assured of support at home, Philip now launched a very risky venture. In 1303 he sent Nogaret to Italy with a small force to join some of the pope's Italian enemies. Together they staged a surprise attack on Boniface's summer home at Anagni and succeeded in capturing him. They probably hoped to take Boniface back to France to await trial by a Church council, but they had no chance to put their plan into effect. The Italians had no great love for the

The Issue between State and Church

1302

Boniface VIII says in the Bull *Unam Sanctam:*

Both the spiritual sword and the material sword are in the power of the Church. But the latter is to be used for the Church, the former by her; the former by the priest, the latter by kings and captains, but by the assent and permission of the priest. The one sword, then, should be under the other, and temporal authority subject to spiritual power. . . . If, therefore, the earthly power err, it shall be judged by the spiritual power. . . . Finally, we declare, state, define and pronounce that it is altogether necessary to salvation for every human creature to be subject to the Roman pontiff.

■ ■ ■

One of Philip's ministers, speaking for the king, says:

The pope pretends that we are subject to him in the temporal government of our states and that we hold the crown from the Apostolic See. Yes, this kingdom of France which, with the help of God, our ancestors . . . created—this kingdom which they have until now so wisely governed—it appears that it is not from God alone, as everyone has always believed, that we hold it, but from the pope!

From *Select Documents of European History,* ed. by R. G. D. Laffan (London: Methuen, 1930), p. 117; from C. V. Langlois, *St. Louis, Philippe le Bel, et les derniers Capetiens directs* (Paris: Hachette, 1911), pp. 149–50.

pope, but they cared even less for the French. A counterattack by the people of Anagni and neighboring regions freed Boniface after a few days, but the shock of the experience damaged the pope's health—he was in his eighties—and he did not live long after these events.

Force had been used against earlier popes, and the Church had always been able to retaliate and to put the aggressor in a worse position than before. But after the assault at Anagni, the Church did not dare to react strongly. No one, either inside or outside of France, seemed disturbed by what had happened, and Nogaret remained Philip's favorite minister. It was now clear that the papal court would have to deal with the French

king, and after a brief attempt to remain independent of him, the college of cardinals elected a man who was at least acceptable to Philip, if not his own candidate. Clement V (r. 1305–14) yielded to Philip on everything and even declared that Philip had acted for good motives when he had seized Boniface. The power that Innocent III had bequeathed to his successors was thus all but gone.

The Popes at Avignon

When he was elected in 1305, Clement V set off for Rome from Bordeaux, where he had been archbishop, but he stopped in Avignon, a small city in the Rhone Valley, because he heard that the warring city-states of Italy made the Papal States unsafe. He apparently planned to continue on to Rome as soon as order was restored, but Avignon became Clement's permanent residence. The French king and French cardinals urged him to stay there, and political conditions remained unstable in Italy. Avignon became the seat of papal government for over 70 years.

The long exile in France (1305–78) is known in Church history as the Babylonian Captivity—an allusion to the original Babylonian captivity of the Jews in the sixth century B.C. In Avignon, the popes were in a small principality that was not subject to the French king, but they were certainly under his watchful eye and his power. The popes who succeeded Clement V at Avignon were not as subservient to the French kings as he had been, and many of them were excellent administrators. During the Avignon period, the papacy developed into the largest government in Europe, with an elaborate and powerful bureaucracy and a large income. But the pope was supposed to be the bishop of Rome, and there was a steady flow of criticism by Europe's leading intellectual and spiritual figures, who urged the popes to return to the Holy City. As successful as the papal government was in Avignon, the stay there was a scandal that damaged the prestige of the pope as the spiritual leader of Christendom.

Suggestions for Further Reading

Economy

On the economic changes that took place in the thirteenth and fourteenth centuries, see the works cited in Chapters 10 and 11. M. M. Postan, *Medieval Trade and Finance* (1973), is a general work. R. S. Lopez and I. W. Raymond, eds., *Medieval Trade in the Mediterranean World* (1955), contains much interesting source material. See also A. R. Lewis, *Naval Power and Trade in the Mediterranean* (1951), and *The Northern Seas* (1958). On the merchant class, see the works cited in Chapter 11 and E. M. Carus-Wilson, *The Medieval Merchant Adventurers*, 3rd ed. (1967).

England

W. L. Warren has written two excellent works on the Angevin kings in *Henry II* (1973), and *King John* (1961). See also, J. Gillingham, *Richard the Lionheart* (1978). A. L. Poole, *From Domesday Book to Magna Carta*, 2nd ed. (1955), provides an excellent general history. The most thorough treatment of Magna Carta is W. S. McKechnie, *Magna Carta* (1914), which studies the document chapter by chapter. For a shorter treatment, see J. C. Holt, *Magna Carta* (1965). On English history in the thirteenth century, see F. M. Powicke, *King Henry III and the Lord Edward*, 2 vols. (1947), and *The Thirteenth Century* (1953). For the later period, see M. McKisack, *The Fourteenth Century* (1959). The classic history of medieval common law is F. W. Maitland and F. Pollock, *The History of English Law*, 2 vols., rev. ed. by S. G. F. Milsom (1968). This work is brought up to date in J. H. Baker, *An Introduction to English Legal History*, 2nd ed. (1979). See also D. M. Stenton, *English Justice from the Norman Conquest to the Great Charter* (1964). A large collection of sources for the history of Common Law was published in J. H. Baker and S. F. C. Milsom, *Sources of English Legal History* (1986).

Constitutional Government

All the works on medieval England, cited above, contain much material on the growth of constitutional government. See also, J. E. A. Joliffe, *Angevin Kingship* (1955), which traces the growth of royal power in England and the development of the institutions of government through the twelfth century. On the idea of kingship in relation to law and political thought, see the classic by E. H. Kantorowicz, *The King's Two Bodies* (1957). For a survey of the institutions of constitutional government, see G. L. Haskins, *The Growth of English Representative Government* (1948); A. Marongui, *Medieval Parliaments: A Comparative Study* (1968); T. N. Bisson, *Assemblies and Representation in Languedoc in the Thirteenth Century* (1964); and F. L. Carsten, *Princes and Parliaments in Germany* (1959).

France

On France, see the works cited in Chapter 10, particularly J. Dunbabin, *France in the Making, 843–1180* (1985), and E. M. Hallam, *Capetian France, 987–1328* (1980). On Philip II Augustus, see A. Luchaire, *Social Life in France at the Time of Philip Augustus*, trans. E. B. Krehbiel (1912). On St. Louis (Louis IX), see J. R. Strayer, *The Administration of Normandy under St. Louis* (1932), and W. C. Jordan, *Louis IX and the Challenge of the Crusade* (1979). For a comprehensive history of Philip IV the Fair, see J. R. Strayer, *The Reign of Philip the Fair* (1980). On the conflict between Philip and Pope Boniface VIII, see C. T. Wood, ed., *Philip the Fair and Boniface VIII* (1967), which contains a selection of historians' work on the subject.

Germany

On the rise and fall of the Hohenstaufens, see G. Barraclough, *The Origins of Modern Germany* (1947); H. Fuhrmann, *Germany in the High Middle Ages, c. 1050–1200* (1985); J. B. Gillingham, *The Kingdom of Germany in the High Middle Ages* (1979); and J. Leuschner, *Germany in the Later Middle Ages* (1980). On Frederick Barbarossa, see M. Pacaut, *Frederick Barbarossa* (1969), and P. Munz, *Frederick Barbarossa: A Study of Medieval Politics* (1969), which takes the questionable view that Frederick was a "rational" politician whose every action was carefully calculated. The classic study of Frederick II is E. H. Kantorowicz, *Frederick II* (1931). T. C. Van Cleve, *The Emperor Frederick II* (1972), is also highly recommended. On the formation of the late medieval empire, see J. Bryce, *The Holy Roman Empire* (many editions) and C. Bayley, *The Formation of the German College of Electors* (1949).

Late Medieval Church and Boniface VIII

The classic work on the late medieval Church is A. C. Flick, *The Decline of the Medieval Church*, 2 vols. (1930). See also, F. Oakley, *The Western Church in the Later Middle Ages* (1979). On Boniface VIII, see T. S. R. Boase, *Boniface VIII* (1930).

13
Eastern Europe in the Middle Ages

*T*hroughout its history the German kingdom has been involved in eastern European affairs. World War I began in 1914 after a Serbian nationalist shot Prince Francis Ferdinand, the heir to the Austro-Hungarian throne. World War II began with Hitler's invasion of Poland, having earlier seized Czechoslovakia with the acquiescence of England and France. Of course, since World War II, Russia and the East European Bloc have played a major role in European and world affairs. The Germans have been involved in eastern Europe since the time of Charlemagne. During the 790s, he had conquered the Avars, centered in modern Hungary, and thereafter he maintained an interest in the regions across his eastern border. In the tenth century, the Ottonian kings pursued this interest by supporting a movement to colonize Slavic areas on the eastern frontier, and later kings constantly meddled in the affairs of the Slavic kingdoms and duchies. Consequently, the history of Slavonia, the vast region of eastern Europe stretching east to the Ural Mountains of Russia, north to the Baltic, and south to the Adriatic and Aegean seas is an important subject for a book on western civilization.

The civilized peoples of the Mediterranean first came into contact with the Slavs at the end of the fifth and beginning of the sixth centuries. Having originated in the north between the Vistula and Dnieper rivers, the Slavic tribes had followed the Germans into southern Russia and eastern Europe during the third century. But they did not appear on the borders of the Roman Empire until later, when the Germans had moved out of those regions toward the south and west. By the early sixth century, Lithuania, the Ukraine, central Russia, Poland, Bohemia, and Slovakia were Slavic regions, and Slavic tribes had moved south toward modern Yugoslavia. In this early period of migration, the Slavs were caught up in the movement of Turkic and Iranian peoples, such as the Avars and Sarmatians, who dominated Hungary and southeastern Europe in successive waves. But the Slavic tribes survived the collapse of these empires, and gradually the remnants of the Avars, Sarmatians, and others were absorbed into the Slavic culture.

The Romans fought the Slavs along the Danube frontier during the sixth century and settled some of them as *foederati* to help protect the frontier

against further incursions from the northern forests. But by the early seventh century, Constantinople was threatened by Slavic forces that accompanied the Avars. Emperor Heraclius (r. 610–41) dealt with the threat by settling the Slavic tribes in devastated provinces to the west. He also began the long process of Christianization, which eventually helped bring the Slavs into the fold of western civilization.

THE SOUTHERN SLAVS

Faced by the Avar empire in the Hungarian plain, Heraclius allied himself with the White Croats and Bulgars, peoples whose ancestors were not Slavs, but who had been slavicized during the migration into the Balkans. Heraclius helped the Bulgars free themselves from Avar power and persuaded the Croats to settle the old

For 60 years the Magyars made destructive raids deep into western Europe from their home on the Hungarian plain. In this illustration from the Book of St. Gall (ca. 925) they are shown attacking a city.

The Settlement of the Croats and Serbs   Seventh Century

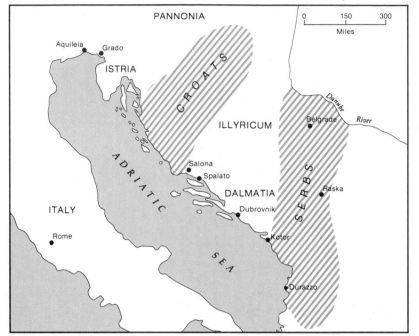

Roman provinces of Illyricum—the Dalmatian coast of modern Yugoslavia—and Pannonia. He also settled the Serbs in eastern Illyricum, from the coast around Kotor to the region of Pannonia around Belgrade. The whole region had been devastated by the Avars early in the seventh century, and it was empty. Sirmium, the capital of Pannonia, had ceased to exist. The Roman population had been Christian, but hardly a church or bishopric remained intact.

The Slavic settlers were pagans, and to ensure their loyalty, Heraclius sought to convert them. The Dalmatian coast and Istria were under the ecclesiastical jurisdiction of Rome, and the emperor therefore asked the pope to send missionaries to the Croats. After the Avar incursions, Pope Gregory I (r. 590–604) was concerned with the reestablishment of the Church in Illyricum, but it was his successor Honorius I (r. 625–38) who began the conversion of the new settlers by sending priests from Rome and Ravenna. Slowly, the missionaries reestablished

an episcopal system centered on Spalato, which inherited the metropolitan status from Salona, the old archiepiscopal see of the region. It was this ecclesiastical system that the emperor Leo III (r. 717–41) removed from Roman jurisdiction because the popes opposed his iconoclasm (see p. 189).

Meanwhile, Heraclius organized missions to the Serbs. Some of the missionaries for this effort came from Bari, the capital of Byzantine Apulia, but it appears that remnants of the old Christian population of the Roman province took the lead. The bishopric of Kotor may have survived the Avar invasions. But notwithstanding these early efforts, the conversion of the Serbs only succeeded in the ninth century. Recent archaeological discoveries show that the Serbs began building an extensive network of churches in the early ninth century.

Behind the Croats and Serbs came the Bulgars, who had been attacking the Danubian provinces of the Empire since the mid-fifth century. The Bulgars were probably a Turkic people who had settled in southern Russia among the Slavs and had become slavicized. They may have arrived in the region as part of the Hunnish horde that invaded in the 370s. In any case, they moved into the Danubian region of the Empire in the sixth and seventh centuries and became a major concern of the Byzantines during Heraclius's reign. Under the first known Bulgarian khan, Kurt or Kuvrat (r. 605–65), the Bulgars formed a state that the Byzantines called Great Bulgaria.

It was under the auspices of the Bulgarian khanate that Slavic tribes moved into Greece and established long-lasting independent communities in the mountainous central and northern regions, particularly around Thessalonika. Under pressure from the Persians and then the Arabs, the Byzantines could not reconquer these areas, and the Christian Greek population survived only in pockets within the areas of Slavic settlement. It was not until the later ninth century, after the Bulgarians had begun to accept Christianity, that the Byzantine government was able to conquer the Slavs of Greece and to begin converting them to Christianity. In time the Slavic peoples in Greece were not only fully christianized, but also assimilated into Greek culture. The Greek language was influenced very little by the Slavic peoples that occupied its territory for so many centuries.

MORAVIA AND THE CENTRAL EUROPEAN SLAVS

The Slavic settlements in Pannonia held an important geographical position. They lay across the rich trade routes of central Europe and were heir to the Roman culture of the region. As was to be expected, then, the central European Slavs were under constant pressure from their neighbors—the Germans to the west and north, the Avars to the east, and the Byzantines to the south. The communities seem to have formed a loose confederation of principalities centered on the revived towns of Sirmium and Belgrade, among others. The picture that emerges from the sources, which are not very good, is of a group of related petty princes who constantly jockeyed for position. It is a picture that would have fit the Franks before the rise of Clovis in the last decades of the fifth century (see p. 136). Among the most important of the rulers were those of Sirmium, which now carried the Slavic name Morava.

From early on, the Bavarians meddled in the affairs of the Slavs and sent missionaries to convert them, and after Charlemagne (r. 768–814) asserted his power over Bavaria, the Moravians and their neighbors came into his sphere of influence. Nonetheless, the Slavic tribes could maneuver for independence—and the maintenance of their ancient pagan culture—by playing the Germans off against the Avars. When Charlemagne crushed the Avars in 796, the Slavs of Pannonia were overwhelmed by German power.

Under this pressure, the Moravians and their neighbors formed centralized political communities. The small tribes united to preserve what they could of their political and cultural independence, and they soon found that though the Avars were no longer in the picture, the Byzantines were an equally good foil for the Germans. In the early ninth century, the Moravians led their Slavic neighbors, who were ruled by relatives of the Moravian prince, in an effort to carve out an independent Slavic state. The conflict between Byzantium and the Franks over Charlemagne's coronation as emperor helped them in this project.

Mounted warrior with a captive (detail from a gold vessel from the ninth century found in Sinicolaul, Rumania).

Charlemagne had to campaign against the Slavs in the first years of the ninth century, and he received the submission of the Slavic princes in 803. The defeated peoples included Bohemians, living north of the Danube in the valleys of the Carpathian Mountains, and Moravians from the south. But the Moravians, under their leader Mojimir, seem to have escaped the subjugation soon afterward, for when Louis the Pious, Charlemagne's son and successor, divided his empire among his own sons in 817, Moravia was not mentioned as going to Louis the German. Louis the Pious, with his son Louis, campaigned against the Slavs around 820, and the Slavic princes, including at least some from Moravia, submitted to him in 822. Thereafter, the Frankish monarchy made a major effort to solidify control over the region by sending missionaries to convert the Slavs. The Church was to be the agent of German power in central Europe.

The progress of the German missionaries was very slow. Mojimir managed to live at peace with the Franks,

and in 818 he himself agreed to convert, although he may not have carried out the promise until 822. The act of converting was a political matter, and Mojimir needed to convince the tribal chieftains of his realm that it was the right thing to do. In the meantime, he concentrated his attention on building up his state, unifying it politically and fortifying it militarily. In 817, a Bavarian geographer reported that Moravia had eleven fortified "cities," and archaeologists have recently confirmed the substance of this report.

Mojimir died about 845, and there was a brief pagan revival that aimed not only at leading the country back to its cultural roots, but also at establishing its independence from the Franks. To protect his interests, Louis the German intervened and put Mojimir's nephew Rastislav (r. 846–70) in power. However, Louis soon became engrossed in the conflicts with his brothers (see pp. 248–49), and the Moravian prince was free to go his own way. By about 850, Rastislav was the ruler of a virtually independent state that included most of the old province of Pannonia, and he exercised influence over Bohemia and the remnants of the Avars. To keep Louis off balance, Rastislav supported the king's son Carloman when he rebelled in the early 860s. Louis was so concerned about Rastislav's power that he sought an alliance with the Bulgarian khan Boris against him. With Louis and Boris threatening a two-pronged invasion, Rastislav himself needed an ally, and he eventually found it in Constantinople.

Before he turned to the Byzantine court, Rastislav asked Rome for help. He apparently thought that the key to the future of Moravia lay in freeing its ecclesiastical organization from the Germans, who were like a fifth column in the country. He hoped the pope would send a mission to set up an independent Slavic hierarchy subject directly to Rome, but Pope Nicholas I (r. 858–67) did not respond. Nicholas already had a difficult relationship with

Greater Moravia   Ninth Century

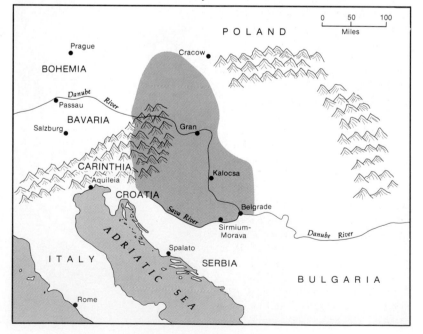

the Frankish monarchy and would not make it worse by interfering with the German mission in Moravia. Consequently, in 862 Rastislav sent an embassy to Byzantium.

In his request for assistance, Rastislav told the emperor Michael III (r. 842–67), "Our people has renounced paganism and is observing the Christian law, but we do not have a teacher to explain to us the true Christian faith in our own language in order that other nations even, seeing this, may imitate us. Send us therefore, Master, such a bishop and teacher, because from you emanates always, to all sides, the good law." The heart of this request was the assertion that Moravia, full of German missionaries, had no teacher of the faith who would create a Slavic church. Rastislav seems to have compromised with the conservative elements in his realm, who had led the anti-German movement of 845–46, by seeking to establish an independent church that would preserve native culture. The Germans, many of whom spoke Slavic, were trying to impose a Latin, Roman Church on the Slavic population, as it had been imposed on them centuries earlier.

No one doubted that Rastislav's request was really a plea for a political and military alliance, but to people at that time religion and politics were one. A Moravia allied with Byzantium would have a church allied with the patriarchate of Constantinople. As it turned out, the alliance produced little political result, but it greatly furthered the development of an independent, literate, Slavic culture.

The Mission of Constantine-Cyril and Methodius

The emperor had a man in his service perfectly suited to answer Rastislav's need. Constantine the Philosopher, as he was called, was then about 35 years old and teaching in an ecclesiastical college in Constantinople. He had been born in Thessalonika in 826 or 827, the son of a Byzantine military officer on

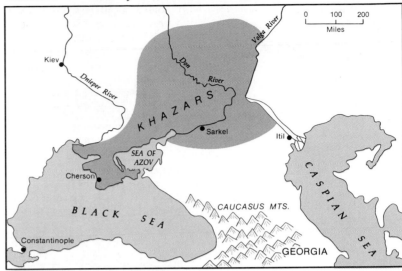

Constantine's Embassy to the Khazars   856

the staff of the provincial governor. As a young boy, after his father was killed fighting the Slavs, Constantine became the ward of Theoctistus, the *logothete* or prime minister of the Empire. Theoctistus brought him to Constantinople and put him in the court school, where he studied under Photius, the future patriarch and the most learned man in the Empire (see p. 193). Within a short time, Constantine earned a reputation for learning and linguistic ability. He had learned Slavic as a child in Thessalonika, and he may have learned Arabic as well. When he was about 28 years old, he succeeded his teacher Photius at the university. There is some evidence that the emperor sent him to Baghdad in 851 to debate religious questions with Moslem thinkers.

In 856, the Khazars, a Turkic people that had carved out an empire in southern Russia, asked the emperor to send a theologian to participate in a three-way debate among Christians, Moslems, and Jews. Such debates were always part of an effort to forge secular alliances, but everyone at that time thought that religious accommodation was an essential part of political alliance. Constantine had meanwhile entered a monastery, but he was retrieved, along with his brother,

Byzantine art exhibited
Christian influence and a
love of ornamentation.
Above: a tenth-century clasp
bearing the image of a saint.
Right: a reliquary cross
(probably twelfth century).

native speakers of Slavic. Their mission was carefully restricted to missionary activity; Rastislav's request for a bishop went unanswered. The government wanted to infiltrate Moravia, but it did not want to try to set up an ecclesiastical hierarchy in competition with the Germans. This might follow from a successful mission, but it involved very complicated politics with the western powers, including the papacy, which could claim jurisdiction over the central European Slavs. Heraclius had asked the papacy to undertake the conversion of the Slavs, so precedent appeared to be against aggressive Byzantine action on this front. Constantine was to challenge the Germans as a missionary, and the ecclesiastical consequences would be worked out later.

Before leaving for Moravia, the great philologist created an alphabet to make it possible to translate the sacred texts and formularies for the mass into Slavic. The alphabet—called the glagolitic—was not based on any existing one, but was unique and particularly well suited to the phonology of Slavic. The earliest works in Slavic were written in this script. Only much later was it replaced by an alphabet, now called Cyrillic, that was based on the Greek alphabet. In most western Slavic countries, the glagolitic alphabet was eventually replaced by the Latin alphabet, which is ill-suited to Slavic, and in the eastern Slavic countries it lost out to Cyrillic. It is now only used in certain isolated ecclesiastical institutions in Dalmatia and Montenegro (southern Yugoslavia).

Using the new script, Constantine and Methodius translated the basic liturgical works into Slavic. This meant that Slavic Christians—unlike westerners—used their own language in the Mass and other liturgical ceremonies, and from the beginning of his mission Constantine understood that he would have to defend his idea that the Slavs should use their native language in their religious practice. Conservative churchmen argued that only Hebrew, Greek, and Latin were accept-

Methodius, and sent to join the religious debate, while other officials dealt with secular matters. On the way, he stopped in the Black Sea region to learn Hebrew and Samaritan from Jews living there. Before he had returned from the embassy, he had translated most of a Hebrew grammar into Greek. When Constantine returned from Khazaria, he took a teaching post in one of the many ecclesiastical colleges in the city. He continued his studies of Hebrew and Samaritan and was often called upon to use his exceptional philological skills in interpreting inscriptions and texts in unknown languages and scripts.

His fame as a participant in multireligious debates and as a linguist made him the perfect man to carry out the mission Rastislav asked for. Further, Constantine and his brother were

able languages for the liturgy because these were the languages that Pilate had ordered used for the inscription on Christ's cross. Constantine characterized his opponents as disciples of Pilate.

Constantine and Methodius had used Byzantine liturgical works as the basis of the Slavic translations they made, but in Moravia, they found themselves in competition with Frankish missionaries, who apparently attacked their innovations as a foreign liturgy. To counter these assertions, the two brothers made a translation of a Greek liturgy based on the Roman practice. This liturgy was essentially the same as the western one introduced by the Germans, but being in Slavic it was more attractive to the natives than the Latin Mass. Nonetheless, the Byzantine missionaries continued to use many of the eastern formulas and prayers translated by the brothers, and many of these entered Slavonic church practice.

Throughout his work, Constantine was concerned with the establishment of principles of translation, and his translations had great consistency of style. He did not try to make a literal translation, but sought to render the Greek in a Slavic text that would capture the literary quality and texture of the original. In so doing, he created a literary language for the Slavs and showed himself to be a great poet in Slavic as well as in Greek. He had a genius for language, and his work not only gave the Slavs a literate culture, but also advanced their language as a vehicle for sophisticated thought.

The brothers left Moravia in 867, traveling south to Venice where they expected to take a ship to Constantinople. But Bardas had been murdered by Basil, and Photius had been deposed as patriarch (see pp. 193–94), and Constantine and Methodius found themselves deprived of their mentors in the capital. As a result, they accepted an invitation from the pope to go to Rome. There, they lived in a Byzantine monastery, of which there were several in the city, while waiting for news from home. In Rome, Constantine continued his intellectual work, but his health, which had been poor for many years, worsened. Perhaps despairing of ever returning to Constantinople, he joined the monastery and took the religious name Cyril. As a result, he is mostly known as St. Cyril.

The Results of the Mission

The 860s were momentous for the Byzantine mission to the Slavs. Although Constantine and Methodius did not bring the Moravians into the jurisdiction of the patriarchate of Constantinople, they profoundly influenced the Christianity of the country and left permanent vestiges of their work in Moravian liturgy and culture. In 864 Khan Boris of Bulgaria, who had been playing the Byzantines off against Rome, accepted baptism under the auspices of the emperor, and the Bulgarians became eastern Christians. Soon, the liturgical works of Constantine and Methodius were being introduced to Bulgaria. In the same period (864–66), Byzantine missionaries converted the Kievan Russians. This conversion did not endure, but for a while it looked as if all of Slavonia would convert to the Byzantine Church.

But the political future of Moravia was with the West. The Germans had looked upon these lands as satellites from early times, and the Carolingian kings actively pursued the goal of subjugating them, both politically and religiously. Rastislav was unable to withstand Louis the German, and in the late 860s he found himself challenged by his own princes. In 870, Rastislav's enemies captured him and turned him over to the Germans, who blinded him and put him away in a monastery. Immediately, there was another pagan revival, but it was soon put down by Sventopolk, Rastislav's nephew, who had been among the old leader's most formidable opponents. The new leader was supported by the Franks and carefully maintained his alliance with them, but Sventopolk also undertook to complete his uncle's work. In the first year of his reign in Morava, he asked the pope to send a bishop who would establish an independent Slavic hierarchy subject to Rome. Pope Adrian II (r. 867–72) sent Methodius, who had remained in Rome after his brother's death, and Methodius (815–85) became Archbishop of Moravia, with his seat in Morava.

Under Sventopolk (r. 870–94), Moravia reached its height. He reunited all the tribes in his region and then pushed out in all directions. He gained control of all of Croatia down to Istria and the Dalmatian coast and exerted influence over the Bohemians north of the Danube. Sventopolk also conquered the remnants of the Avar principalities to the east. Under him, Methodius constructed an independent Moravian church, spreading the Slavonic liturgy throughout the realm. The archbishop also did missionary work in Bohemia and Poland. The culmination of Sventopolk's policies was his coronation as king sometime between 880 and 885.

Throughout his reign, Sventopolk maintained reasonably good relations with the Germans. He had been on friendly terms with Arnulf of Carinthia before Arnulf became king of the East Franks in 887, and events soon solidified their alliance. About 890, the Magyars (Hungarians) appeared in Pannonia and began the raids that would make them the scourge of central Europe. At a meeting in 890, Arnulf gave Bohemia in fief to Sventopolk, probably in return for the Slavic king's help in defending Arnulf's realm from the marauding Hungarians. Sventopolk used the alliance to extend his power over Slovakia in the northern Hungarian plain, and he soon found it advantageous to ally himself with the Hungarians themselves. The result was that the last years of his reign were marred by invasions from Germany. In 892 and 893, Arnulf led armies into Moravia and devastated everything in sight. When Sventopolk died in 894, a civil war erupted between his young sons, and the Germans and Hungarians became involved in it. Moravia was an important buffer region between the two enemies, and both had an avid interest in its fate. Within a few years, the Hungarians had overrun Moravia and made it the base for their raids on Bavaria and Italy. Great Moravia had died with Sventopolk.

BOHEMIA

Bohemia was an ancient Slavic area centered on the castles of Prague, which straddled the Moldau River. The passes through the Carpathians and the river valleys below them had been crucial byways since paleolithic times. In prehistoric times, hunters had returned year after year to camps next to the migration routes of the great mammals—mammoths, rhinoceros, and buffalo. Later these routes became part of the Amber Road, the trade route through which amber—fossilized pine sap—was brought from the Baltic to the Mediterranean. Amber was a favorite jewelry item in neolithic and bronze-age cultures. Finally, the Car-

Bohemia   Eleventh to Twelfth Centuries

pathians were rich in minerals. Men had mined salt there since the paleolithic period, and the first users of metals in Europe, the Celts, had found their raw materials there and in the northern Alps.

The Bavarians had taken an interest in Bohemia and had asserted hegemony over the pagan Slavs of the region even before Charlemagne brought Bavaria into his power in 788. Thereafter, Bohemia was a constant concern of the Frankish monarchy. The Bohemians resisted Christianization, and the German missionaries began to make progress in the border areas only during the 820s. In the later ninth century, Bohemians were caught between the Germans and Moravians, but once the Hungarians destroyed the Moravian state, they fell completely under German domination. Henry I (r. 918–36) and his son Otto I (r. 936–73) encouraged German colonization in Bohemia, which enhanced the position of both Germany and Christianity in the country, but Otto was only able to establish a bishopric in Prague at the end of his reign, in 973.

Throughout the central Middle Ages the German kings kept Bohemia subjugated as a duchy and constantly interfered with the dynastic plans of the dukes. The agents of German power were usually the dukes of Bavaria, but virtually every king of the eleventh and

Buildings of the University of Prague. The tower dates from the fourteenth century.

twelfth centuries had at one time or another been personally involved in Bohemian affairs. To the best of their ability, the Bohemians played the central European powers—principally Germany, Poland, and Hungary—off against one another in a constant effort to gain some measure of independence. In 1158, the duchy became a kingdom when Emperor Frederick Barbarossa rewarded Vratislav II for assistance in his Italian campaign. In the fourteenth century, after the collapse of the Hohenstaufen monarchy (see p. 350), the kingdom of Bohemia fell to the Luxembourgs as a prize of the imperial crown. Emperor Henry VII of Luxembourg (r. 1309–13) gave Bohemia to his son John (r. 1313–46), who passed it on to his son Charles IV (r. 1346–74), who was elected emperor in 1347. It was Charles who, in 1348, founded the University of Prague as the first German university. The university became a center of the cultural struggle between Bohemians and Germans during the early fifteenth century. The Bohemian reformer John Hus studied and taught there. The Luxembourg king and emperor Sigismund (r. 1410–37) permitted the Council of Constance to burn Hus as a heretic in 1415 (see pp. 269–70), and Sigismund married his daughter Elizabeth to the Habsburg Albert II of Austria (emperor 1438–39). When Sigismund died without a male heir, this marriage was the vehicle through which Bohemia passed to the Habsburgs.

POLAND

Poland was the westernmost Slavic region of the North German Plain, the vast plain that stretches from the Atlantic to the Ural Mountains of Russia. Sitting in the middle of the plain, the country has no natural barriers to the east or west. On the south it is bounded by the Tatra Mountains, a branch of the Carpathians, and on the north by the Baltic Sea. As a result of its geography, this vast area, larger than any other European country, has suffered continual invasion and political instability. As a country, Poland arose from the unification of several tribal regions, which survived to become duchies in the kingdom. Throughout its history the regions have variously joined the federation, been subjected by a central monarchy, and broken away to ally themselves with foreign and domestic powers in competition with the central government. The political history of Poland is bewildering and can only be understood if one remembers that no natural features of the land provided protection from foreign interference or internal disunity. The periods of unity and strength were exceptions in the course of Polish history.

The first attempt to unify the tribes occurred in the early ninth century,

The Tyn Church (center) and Astronomical Clock (left) in Prague. The Tyn Church was founded in the fourteenth century by Germans living in Prague and became the main Hussite church.

when the ruler of the Polanians of Wielkopolska, centered on Poznan and Gniezno, established his hegemony over Kujawy, Malopolska, and Mazovia. This man, who was called Piast, is a semi-legendary person, but he succeeded in setting up a dynasty that divided its time between Gniezno and Cracow, the well-located city of the Vistulanians of Malopolska. Modern historians call this dynasty the Piast or Polanian. It dominated Poland from the time of Louis the Pious (r. 814–40) until 1370, when Kazimierz III the Great died.

The Ottonian policy of converting the Slavs and colonizing the eastern frontier of the German kingdom affected Poland as well as Bohemia. Shortly after he brought the Bohemians into obedience in 950, Otto I turned his attention to Brandenburg on the north-central border of Poland. In 961, he received papal permission to erect the see of Magdeburg as a missionary outpost to the Poles, and he began to encourage German migration into the area. Having observed the fate of Bohemia, which had been forcibly converted and made into a province of the German kingdom, Duke Mieszko I (r. *ca.* 963–92) sought baptism directly through the agency of the pope and by doing so was able to maintain some independence of the Germans. Nonetheless, Mieszko recognized the importance of good relations with the German monarchy, and he may have recognized the superiority of Otto III in 984, when Otto was an infant king under the regency of his mother. Mieszko also succeeded in gaining control over Pomerania, thus giving Poland an outlet to the Baltic.

Mieszko's son Boleslaw I the Brave (r. 992–1025) solidified the relationship with Otto III, who visited Gniezno in 1000 and established an independent bishopric there. This act, which shows that Otto envisioned an empire in which the Slavs would be substantial partners, ensured the ecclesiastical and political identity of the Poles. Boleslaw was a great conqueror, and he ex-

John Hus being led to the stake in 1415. He wears a fool's cap with pictures of the devil and the word *heresiarch* (leader of heretics).

tended the Polish state both east and west. In the west, he added Lusatia up to the Saal River (a tributary of the Elbe), and in the east he reached the Dnieper, incorporating Red Ruthenia and Kiev into his orbit. At the end of his life, Boleslaw won from the pope the grant of a royal crown (1025), but his successors were not always able to claim the title. It depended on the strength of the German monarchy. The next Polish king, Boleslaw II (r. 1058–79), took advantage of Henry IV's preoccupation with the rebellion connected with the Investiture Controversy (see pp. 282–83) to crown himself in 1076.

Notwithstanding the dependence of the Polish rulers on Germany, the establishment of an independent Polish diocese in Gniezno meant that Christianity spread from a Polish instead of a German center. As other parts of the realm received Christianity, Gniezno established bishoprics subordinate to

Poland in the Middle Ages

itself—Plock in Mazovia in 1076, Lubus in Lusatia in 1128, and Wolin in Pomerania in 1140. The progress of political unification under the Piasts continued until the end of the reign of Boleslaw III (r. 1102–38). Thereafter, the regions asserted their independence, and for 200 years the Piasts, as rulers of one substate or another, fought one another without any of them succeeding in recreating the large state Boleslaw III had assembled.

Polish Society

Our knowledge of early Polish society is slightly greater than of Moravian or Bohemian society. Little is known of the social structure of the Moravians, whose communities seem to have been dominated by princes of small substates, and the Bohemians appear to have been Germanized in their society and economy, if not in language and culture. The Piast princes presided over a community of nobles living on sizable estates settled with peasant villages. The villagers were freemen who paid rent and were obligated to provide troops to the ducal army. As in the West, the core of the Polish military system was the troop of mounted knights, but also like the western armies, the bulk of the army was made up of peasant foot soldiers. Hence, the peasants had not been reduced to servile status, which would have deprived them of their right and obligation to serve in the army as well as the wherewithal to do so.

But the eastern half of the German Plain, stretching from the Elbe River to the Urals, was very sparsely populated, and it seems that the Poles and other Slavic peoples had not learned the "modern" techniques of agriculture used by the Germans. Slavic peasants still were using the hook plough, a simple wooden implement that could not work the richest soils. Consequently, Slavic villages were confined mostly to areas of sandy soil, which did not produce much for the effort. When the Slavic lords came into contact with the Germans, through colonization or political interaction, they recognized the advantage of bringing Germans to their provinces. In the period of disunity, during the twelfth and thirteenth centuries, the Polish princes encouraged the massive immigration of German peasants, offering them very favorable terms.

Typically, colonization was carried out through locators, who were hired by the princes to bring communities of German peasants to their lands. The locator undertook to find hundreds of farmers in return for an estate and the headship in the village he would found. Each immigrant received a homestead and became a member of the community of the village. The locator had his larger estate and became the mayor of the village, presiding over its court, which heard the lesser cases. Important cases or charges of serious crime were heard by a district court headed by a representative of the prince. The village mayors attended the district court in the same way as the peasants attended the village courts.

To attract a sufficient number of settlers, the princes offered terms that included low rents, light labor duties—typically two to four days per year—and exemption from military service, except in defense of the district. Often, the rents were forgiven for the first ten to fifteen years to allow the villagers to make a good start in their new environment. The locators held a hereditary title to their estates and mayorality and so became village dynasts.

The extent of colonization differed greatly from region to region. In the early thirteenth century, the Piast prince Henry I of Silesia (r. 1231–38) undertook to bring to his province more than 10,000 Germans to settle 400 villages. His country became a patchwork of village communities under Polish or German law, and these communities held tenaciously to their culture. The Germans of Silesia were still distinct in the twentieth century.

The economic policy that led to the encouragement of colonization also led to the foundation and development of cities. Again, the Poles copied the Germans, giving their cities legal codes based on the law of Magdeburg. This law gave the cities substantial autonomy and freedom from feudal obligations, and during the mid-thirteenth century even older Polish towns like Poznan and Cracow were put under German law. As in the population of the countryside, the Piast princes

The Altneuschule in Prague is one of Europe's oldest synagogues.

sought to develop the towns through immigration. They encouraged the settlement of merchants from Germany and the Baltic, and several cities, including Gdansk (Danzig), Cracow, and Wroclaw, became members of the Hanseatic League, the confederation of Baltic trading cities that controlled northern commerce in the thirteenth and fourteenth centuries. The Polish princes also encouraged the immigration of Jews from Germany and Austria. In 1264, Boleslaw V of Cracow (r. 1243–79) issued a General Charter of Jewish Liberties, which ensured the legal rights of Jews. The charter permitted them to travel without restriction and to practice their religion without interference. Although some cities refused to allow Jews to become residents, Boleslaw's action established the foundation for the development of a wealthy and powerful Jewish community in Poland. In the later Middle Ages, the Jews acted as a separate community within the country, led by their own rabbis and secular leaders, who dealt directly with the princes and lesser lords and authorities.

The Reunification of Poland

Despite the long period of political disunity, Polish agriculture and trade made great strides, and in the late thirteenth century the country was potentially quite strong. The first Piast ruler to take advantage of this strength, Wladislaw I (r. 1306–33), started from Mazovia and slowly built up his state, taking advantage of a growing Polish nationalism engendered by Bohemian intervention. Led by the archbishop of Gniezno, the Poles sought to rid themselves of the foreigners who were associated with the German empire. By 1320, Wladislaw had recreated the Polish nation and was crowned king in Cracow, the first Polish king since Boleslaw II in the eleventh century. After this triumph, Wladislaw tried unsuccessfully to reconquer Kujawy and Pomerania held by the Teutonic

Knights, but he left a strong kingdom to his son Kazimierz III (r. 1333–70).

Kazimierz began his reign by consolidating his position. He made a truce with the Teutonic Knights and arranged a treaty with the Bohemian and the Hungarian kings. He paid the Bohemian king John of Luxembourg to give up his claim to Poland and agreed to arbitrate the status of Silesia. The arbitration went in favor of Bohemia, and Kazimierz renounced the province in 1339. When he finally made a formal peace with the Teutonic Knights in 1343, Kazimierz got Kujawy and gave up Pomerania, with its chief city Gdansk. In these actions, Kazimierz gave up a great deal, but he used the security gained to open new fronts. He challenged the Bohemians for Swidnica, west of Silesia, brought Mazovia to heel, and began a campaign for Red Ruthenia and the dukedom of Russia. In Red Ruthenia, he was challenging Lithuania and Hungary. By the end of his reign, Kazimierz had greatly enlarged the Polish state and earned the sobriquet "the Great."

Yet, Kazimierz was much more than a warrior king. In 1347, he issued a great codification of Polish law that became the basis for all legal reforms until the eighteenth century. At the same time, he created a royal bureaucracy to ensure the proper use of the laws. Through this new corps of royal officials, Kazimierz encouraged trade and constructed 50 fortresses to secure the country. Under his good government, Poland flourished, and many Polish towns were transformed by new building. In Cracow, the old wooden buildings were replaced by stone and brick ones built around a market square 200 yards on a side. By 1363, the new cathedral was completed and a new royal castle was under construction. The ancient St. Mary's church on the market square was being completely renovated, a project that would take 50 years to complete. In 1364, Kazimierz founded the University of Cracow, the first non-German institution in eastern Europe. He established chairs in the

Kazimierz III (from a seventeenth-century engraving).

arts, medicine, and law; the emphasis on the law, represented by eight professors, stemmed from his own deep interest in the subject.

In the same year as the foundation of the university, Kazimierz hosted a meeting of five kings and five dukes to discuss a new crusade against the Saracens in the eastern Mediterranean. The occasion of this congress was the visit of Peter of Lusignan, king of Cyprus, who was seeking support for a new crusade. The meeting demonstrated the prestige of Kazimierz, but it produced no crusade.

Kazimierz had many children, including several males, but only the females were legitimate. Early in his reign, Kazimierz arranged for the succession of King Louis of Hungary if he died without an heir. Immediately after Kazimierz's death, Louis seized the kingship and suppressed opposition among the Polish churchmen and nobility. The Piast dynasty was at an end. Louis ruled until his death in 1382, and his reign was a turning point in the history of the kingdom. In the first place, he was the embodiment of a new and long-lasting policy of alliance with Hungary. In the second place, he had no real interest in building a strong monarchy in Poland; it was enough that he sat on the throne. Consequently, Louis did not hesitate to keep the nobility happy by giving them royal rights and lands, and by the end of his reign he had severely weakened the monarchy. Further, Louis had no heir who might have had an interest in restoring what his father had ruined. By arrangement with the Polish nobility, he was succeeded by his younger daughter Jadwiga, who was only eleven years old in 1382. (His older daughter was married to the emperor Sigismund of Luxembourg who thereby inherited Hungary to add to his home kingdom of Bohemia.) Jadwiga was supposed to marry William of Habsburg, prince of Austria, but once her father was dead, the Poles refused to permit the German to marry his way into their kingship. Instead, they mar-

Cracow in 1493.

ried her to Jagiello of Lithuania, creating a union of the two states and establishing a new dynasty in the process.

LITHUANIA-POLAND

The Lithuanians were an ancient Baltic people related to the Latvians and Prussians. The Balts, as they have been called since the nineteenth century, were a group of Indo-European peoples distinct from the Germans and Slavs. Latvian and Lithuanian are the only surviving Baltic languages. The Baltic tribes settled very early in northwestern Russia and along the eastern shore of the Baltic Sea, perhaps as early as the third millennium B.C., but their history is virtually unknown until the thirteenth century, when the Teutonic Knights began conquering and forcibly converting them to Christianity.

The Teutonic Knights

The Order of St. Mary's Hospital in Jerusalem was one of several knightly orders founded in the Holy Land in the twelfth century. Their purpose was to hold back the Moslem enemy from the new Latin states of the Levant and to protect Christian pilgrims. The Order of St. Mary's was made up of German knights and eventually became known simply as the Teutonic Knights. When Saladin took Jerusalem in 1187, the Order left the Levant and returned to

Europe, looking for a crusade nearer to home. After a short sojourn in Transylvania in Hungary, they were invited by the north German lords to help in the subjugation and conversion of the Pomeranians and Prussians, who lived on the Baltic coast. They arrived in Prussia in 1226 and began operations two years later.

The Knights were highly organized and had created an advanced administrative system while in the Levant. They applied the methods of eastern crusading, based on the establishment of a string of impregnable fortresses and on the use of calculated cruelty, to their new task and systematically reduced the pagan Prussians. By the early fourteenth century, the Knights had created a powerful, well-run state in Prussia. Their center was in the fortress of Marienburg.

The drive of the Knights to extend their realm along the Baltic coast brought them into conflict with the Poles, who constantly struggled to open a Baltic port in Pomerania. Gdansk, the greatest port in the eastern Baltic, became the great commercial center of the north, and the Knights held it for most of its medieval history. In 1343, Kazimierz of Poland conceded it, with Pomerania, to the order.

Like their German neighbors to the west, the Knights encouraged German immigration to their realm. They too used locators to find and settle new villages in their thinly populated provinces, and large parts of their state became Germanized. To attract westerners, the Knights offered them privileges and low rents, and in the fourteenth century they encouraged Prussian and Slavic peasants to take up

The Teutonic State and Lithuanian Empire   Fourteenth Century

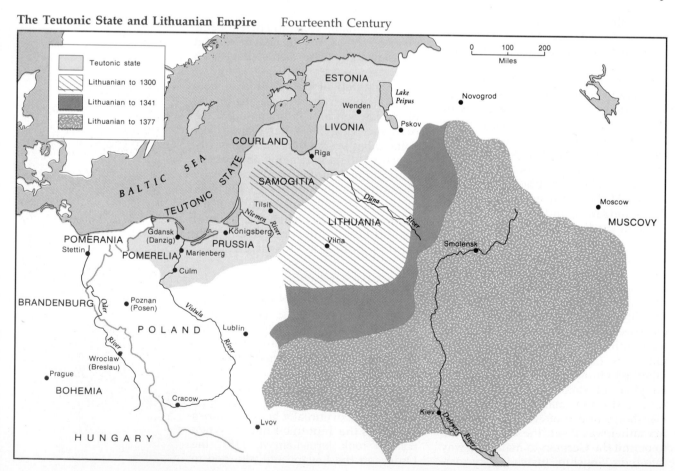

the advanced agricultural methods of the Germans and to become Germanized. Gradually, the Prussian language disappeared.

Beyond Prussia, the Knights conquered Courland, Livonia, and Estonia and forced the inhabitants to convert to Christianity. Though ostensibly devoted to crusading and to the Christian life, the Knights earned a reputation for viciousness in war and rapaciousness in economic affairs. Many critics have pointed out the discrepancy between their stated purpose and their behavior.

The Lithuanians

The Lithuanians appear to have formed a state in reaction to the pressure from the Teutonic Knights. Toward the middle of the thirteenth century, under their leader Mindaugas (d. 1263), the Lithuanian tribes united to resist the Knights. Part of the resistance was a devotion to the pagan gods, particularly Perkun, the god of thunder. The Lithuanians came to see themselves as the last bastion of the ancient religion, and they attributed their success to their gods. Under Mindaugas's successors, they extended their frontiers south and east into Russia, and in the first half of the fourteenth century Gedymin (r. 1316–41) created a powerful Grand Duchy centered on Vilna. Gedymin conquered all the land between the Baltic and the Black Sea, bringing the Russian principalities of Smolensk and Kiev into his state. During the fourteenth century, Lithuania was the greatest state of eastern Europe, and it was committed to paganism. To the Lithuanians, the Christian god was the German god.

In 1377, Jagiello (r. 1377–1434) inherited the Grand Duchy. He was 26, but had the perspicacity to see that he was in great danger, because Kazimierz had built a powerful state in Poland that was now united with Hungary, and the Teutonic Knights were at the height of their power. Knowing that the future of his duchy rested on his ability to make an alliance with one of the western powers and determined not to submit to the Teutonic Knights, Jagiello agreed to accept Christianity from the Poles in return for the hand of their queen Jadwiga. The Poles seized on this opportunity not only to bring a dangerous enemy into their fold, but also to counter the power of the Habsburgs to the south and the Teutonic Knights to the north. In 1386, Jagiello was baptized, married Jadwiga, and was crowned King of Poland.

Under Jagiello, the Poles and Lithuanians formed a single state, by far the largest and most powerful in eastern Europe. In 1413, the Polish and Lithuanian nobles made an agreement to settle all matters of dispute in a joint assembly. The Poles also got the right to participate in the election of the Grand Duke of Lithuania.

Palace of the Ancient Polish Kings in Cracow (photographed *ca.* 1890).

It is difficult to judge the internal stability and power of Poland-Lithuania because throughout the fifteenth century its neighbors were in disarray. The Luxembourgs of Bohemia were occupied with their cousins in Hungary and with the Habsburgs of Austria. The Ottoman Turks, who had appeared in southeastern Europe after taking Constantinople in 1453 (see p. 202) were distracted by the resistance of the remnants of the Empire and of the southern Slavic peoples. To the east, the Mongol Horde had disintegrated into independent tribal states, and the Russian principalities were small and weak. The Teutonic Knights were the only formidable enemy, and the Poles and Lithuanians fought them between 1409 and 1422, between 1454 and 1466, and between 1519 and 1521. Then suddenly the Reformation arrived in Prussia, and members of the Order deserted to the new religion. In 1525, the Knights ceased to be a secular power, though they have remained a Catholic service organization, with headquarters in Vienna, up to the present day.

Under the Jagiellonians, the Poles undertook the Christianization of Lithuania, which was thereby brought into western civilization. Beginning with Zbigniew Olesnicki, bishop of Cracow (r. 1423–55), Poland produced a remarkable series of politically active bishops who pursued the mission in Lithuania while serving the kings at home. With the support of the nobility and the Church, Jagiello refounded the University of Cracow, which had ceased to exist after the death of Kazimierz, and encouraged both cultural and economic life. Salt production, metal production, and trade increased under the Jagiellonians, as Poland became a major supplier of raw materials. With the collapse of the Teutonic Knights, the Poles finally gained control of Gdansk and had a direct outlet to the Baltic through which its goods could be shipped to western Europe. In the early fifteenth century, the kings were patronizing the arts and sciences; Copernicus (1473–1543) was trained at the University of Cracow and did his revolutionary astronomical work in East Prussia, which had become a fief of the Polish crown in 1525.

The fortunes of the Polish-Lithuanian state began to wane in the later sixteenth century. Moscow had succeeded in uniting the Russian principalities and had become aggressive toward its western neighbors. The last Jagiellonian, Sigismund II (r. 1548–72), was defeated on all fronts, and when he died, he was succeeded first by the prince of Transylvania and then by the king of Sweden. Poland-Lithuania was

The Rus

In 860 the Rus led a large coalition of Slavic tribes in an attack on Constantinople. Not only were the Byzantines surprised by the attack, but they also had no knowledge of the Rus and their allies. The earliest description of the Rus comes from Ahmed ibn-Fadhlan, an Arab traveler of the first half of the tenth century.

I saw the Rus, when they arrived to trade and camped at the River [Volga]. I have never seen [people] with more perfect bodies than they had. They were like palm trees, blonde, with ruddy cheeks, and white skin. They wore neither jacket nor caftan; but the man wore a *kisa* [a kind of robe], which he wrapped around one shoulder off to one side so that one of his arms protruded from it. And each of them had an axe, sword, and knife, from which he was inseparable. . . . And from his nails to his neck he had green trees, figures, and other things painted on his body.

As regards their women, each wears on her breast a little box, either of iron or silver, copper, gold, or wood, corresponding to the wealth and position of her husband. . . . And around their necks were chains of gold and silver. . . .

The *Rus dirhem* [monetary unit] is a grey squirrel [pelt] without fur, brush, front and back paws and head; and the same goes for sables. If something was missing, the monetary value of the skin was less. They also use them for trade transactions and they cannot be exported because they exchange them for wares. They do not have scales, only standard metal bars. They use a measuring cup for buying and selling.

From I. Spector and M. Spector, eds., *Readings in Russian History and Culture* (Palo Alto, CA.: Pacific Books, 1965), pp. 14–15.

ruled by the Swedish kings until the late seventeenth century.

RUSSIA

During the Middle Ages, Russia was a sparsely populated region through which migrating peoples passed continually. In the ninth century, Vikings came down the Dnieper River and settled at Kiev, which may already have been a trading center under the Khazars or even earlier. After the arrival of the Vikings under their leader Ruric, the Kievan state dominated Russia for centuries. The town was the center of a trade route over which eastern Mediterranean goods passed to northern Europe and Scandinavia. In the spring of 860, the Kievans led a coalition of Slavic tribes in a surprise attack on Constantinople. In typical Viking fashion, the attackers appeared under the sea walls of the city in 200 small ships. Shortly afterwards, the Byzantines were busy making an alliance with the Khazars of the Crimea—the embassy in which Constantine-Cyril and Methodius participated. By the late 860s missionaries had converted the Kievans, though as in so many other instances, the conversion engendered a pagan reaction. In this case, the reversion to paganism was virtually permanent, for Christian missionaries had to start from scratch when they reappeared in Kiev in the 980s. The Grand Prince of Kiev, Vladimir I (r. 980–1015), converted in 988 and began the permanent Christianization of Russia. As in the West, the conversion led to the codification of the Russian law. The church brought a literate culture to the Russians and required legislation to fit into the community's life, which was governed by customary law. The prince issued a statute that recorded the law for the benefit of the churchmen and provided a place for them in Russian society.

In the twelfth century, Kiev began to decline. The Italians had opened up new routes between Europe and the

The Grand Prince of Kiev Vladimir I.

eastern Mediterranean, and the nomadic Pechenegs had arrived in the Ukraine from central Asia. Their raids undermined the political power of the Kievan state. As a result, the center of power among the Russian principalities shifted to the north, and by the late twelfth century the prince of Suzdal ruled the strongest of many small principalities in Russia; Moscow was a new town founded about that time in his territory.

Alexander Nevsky and his family.

Alexander Nevsky

Throughout the first half of the thirteenth century the Russian city-states were threatened by Lithuanians, Swedes, and Prussians. After the arrival of the Teutonic Knights in Prussia, they became a great threat. One of the early heroes of the struggle against the Germans was Prince Alexander Nevsky of Novgorod. The Chronicle of Novgorod reports his great battle on the frozen Lake Peipus (here called Chud) of 1242 against the Knights and Prussians (men of Chud).

A.D. **1242.** *Knyaz* **[Prince] Alexander with the men of Novgorod and with his brother Andrei and the men of the Lower country went in the winter in great strength against the land of the Chud people, against the *Nemtsy* [German foreigners, the Teutonic Knights], that they might not boast, saying: "We will humble the Sloven race under us," for Pskov was already taken. . . . And when they came to their land, he [Alexander] let loose his whole force to provide for themselves. And Domash Tverdislavich and Kerbet were scouring [the country] and the *Nemtsy* and Chud men met them by a bridge; and they fought there, and there they killed Domash . . . and others with him, and others again they took with their hands, and others escaped to the troops of the *Knyaz*. And the *Knyaz* turned back to the lake and the *Nemtsy* and Chud men went after them. Seeing this, *Knyaz* Alexander and all the men of Novgorod drew up their forces by Lake Chud [Peipus] at Uzmen by the Raven's Rock; and the *Nemtsy* and Chud men rode at them driving themselves like a wedge through their army; and there was a great slaughter of *Nemtsy* and Chud men. And . . . God helped *Knyaz* Alexander. And the *Nemtsy* fell there and the Chud men gave shoulder, and pursuing them fought with them on the ice, seven *versts* [about four and a half miles] short of the Subol shore. And there fell of the Chud men a countless number; and of the *Nemtsy* 400, and fifty they took with their hands and brought to Novgorod.**

From B. Dmytryshyn, ed., *Medieval Russia: A Source Book, 900–1700* (New York: Holt, Rinehart and Winston, 1967), pp. 123–24.

Between 1237 and 1241, the Mongols conquered the disunified country. Earlier in the century, Chingis (Genghis) Khan (*ca.* 1167–1227) had unified the Mongol tribes on the borders of China and begun a western push across the steppes of Central Asia. When Chingis Khan died, his khanate was divided among his sons, but they continued his conquests in all directions. By 1234, one Mongol contingent had conquered Korea, while others pushed west into Russia. The western khanate took Kiev in 1240 and then pushed on into eastern Europe reaching the Adriatic Sea in 1242. But the leaders of the horde then turned back and settled their army in the lower Volga Valley. They permitted the Russian principalities to govern themselves, but demanded heavy annual tribute and insisted on regulating succession to the princely thrones. Another Mongol army crossed the Transoxiana into the Middle East, taking Baghdad in 1258 and Damascus in 1260. The Mamluk Turks of Egypt defeated the Mongols later in 1260 (see p. 230).

The Mongol conquest cut the Russians off from the West, but while the Mongol empire was intact, they had contact with the advanced peoples of the East. In the fourteenth century, when the empire broke into its constituent parts, Russia became isolated from both East and West, dealing mostly with the so-called Golden Horde—the Mongols living in the Volga region. Relations with the Golden Horde created conditions for the growth of autocracy in the Russian principalities. The Horde punished any transgression of its authority or failure to pay the tribute with extreme measures, destroying towns and massacring entire populations. To avoid such reprisals, the princes asserted absolute control over their populations. Hence, just when peasants in the West were beginning to gain freedom from the obligations of villeinage, Russian peasants were being bound in serfdom, tied to the soil to ensure the support of the nobles and the payment of the tribute.

During the fourteenth century, luck and the support of the highest religious authority made the principality of Moscow the strongest state in Russia. For several generations, there was only one surviving heir to the Muscovite throne when the reigning prince died, so that Moscow did not suffer the continual strife over succession that weakened other states. Moreover, the metropoli-

ca. 800		1241	*ca.* 1400	1613
	Kievan Russia	Mongol Regime	Rise of Muscovy and Creation of Russian Empire	

tan of Russia moved his seat to Moscow, giving the Muscovite princes an added measure of importance as the protectors of religion.

The Golden Horde soon came to rely on the prince of Moscow to manage its relationship with all Russians and gave him the title Grand Prince to symbolize his role. By the late fourteenth century, the Grand Prince had become the leader of the struggle to escape the Mongol yoke. In 1378, a Muscovite army defeated the Mongols, but it was a false beginning to national independence, for the Horde struck back and destroyed the city a few years later. During the fifteenth century, Moscow began to absorb neighboring principalities altogether, and, under Ivan III the Great (r. 1462–1505), it annexed the Republic of Novgorod, which controlled all of northern Russia. Now, the Grand Prince could challenge the Golden Horde, and, during the sixteenth century, the princes gradually conquered Mongol territories in the lower Volga region. At the same time, they were pushing west against Poland-Lithuania and claiming Kiev and its region as their patrimony. By the end of the century, Russia—which had begun as a tiny state of about 500 square miles—was the largest territorial empire in Europe.

The process of conquest and consolidation increased the power of the prince in his state. The peasants had lost all their rights earlier. By the sixteenth century, most nobles had also lost their independence and were servants of the crown. The greatest men in the land could be put to death on the mere suspicion of disloyalty, and bishops and metropolitans who contradicted the wishes of the sovereign were sent into exile. Under Ivan the Great, the growth of autocracy was represented in a new title. Ivan married Zoe, the niece of the last Byzantine emperor,

and began to think of himself as successor of the Caesars and to style himself Autocrat and Sovereign of All Russia. He also occasionally used the title "tsar" (a Russian form of Caesar), but this title did not become official until the reign of Ivan IV the Terrible (r. 1533–84). Ivan the Terrible was a great conqueror who was also one of the bloodiest tyrants in history. He massa-

The Church of the Savior at Novgorod (twelfth century). This is an early example of what became a typical style of ecclesiastical architecture in Russia.

The Growth of the Grand Principality of Moscow   1300–1584

Grand Principality of Moscow ca. 1300

Acquisitions to 1462

Acquisitions to the death of Ivan III, 1505

Acquisitions to the death of Ivan IV, 1584

cred nobles and townspeople on the smallest of pretexts and killed his own son in a fit of rage.

Despite its growth, Muscovy remained a backward, unwesternized country. During the fourteenth century, Poland-Lithuania, a Roman Catholic power, kept Russia cut off from Europe. In addition, the bulk of Rus-

sian peasants were still farming the poor soils of the north by primitive methods and had not opened up the rich black-earth districts of the Ukraine. Russia was also far behind its western neighbors in intellectual activities, in science and technology as well as in scholarship and literature. Only after 1600 did the Russians begin to over-

Part of the dowry of the marriage of Byzantine Princess Sophia to Ivan the Great was the right to adopt the Byzantine two-headed eagle as the tsar's royal coat of arms.

The Court of Ivan the Terrible

In 1553 the Englishman Richard Chancellor visited Moscow. He had been seeking a northern passage to China and, failing, went to Moscow where he was received by Tsar Ivan. His description of the city and court follows.

The [city of] Moscow itself is great: I take the whole town to be greater than London with the suburbs: but it is very rude, and stands without all order. Their houses are all of timber, very dangerous for fire. There is a fair castle, the walls whereof are of brick, and very high: . . . the Emperor [Tsar] lies in the castle, wherein are nine fair Churches, and therein are religious men. Also there is a Metropolitan with diverse Bishops. . . .

The Emperor's or Duke's house neither in building nor in the outward show, nor yet within the house is so sumptuous as I have seen. It is very low built in eight squares, much like the old building of England, with small windows, and so in other points.

. . . I came into the Council chamber, where sat the Duke himself with his nobles, which were a fair company: they sat round about the chamber on high, yet so that he himself sat much higher than any of his nobles in a chair gilt, and in a long garment of beaten gold, with an imperial crown upon his head, and staff of crystal and gold in his right hand, and his other hand half leaning on his chair. . . .

From B. Dmytryshyn, ed., *Medieval Russia: A Source Book, 900–1700* (New York: Holt, Rinehart and Winston, 1967), p. 188.

come these great obstacles to economic and cultural development.

HUNGARY

Hungary has already appeared at several points in this history, but it deserves some attention of its own. The country was unique in the European geography in that it was a true prairie, a flat grassland bordered on the north, south, and west by mountainous regions. By contrast, the much vaster North German Plain was a densely forested area only gradually cleared for farming.

Into the Hungarian plain came one Asian people after another. It was ideally suited to the horse cultures of the Asian steppes, and the Huns, Avars, and Magyars all made it the center of their short-lived empires. The last of these peoples arrived in the late ninth century, and their descendants are still there. For the first 60 years after their appearance in Europe, the Magyars occupied themselves with destructive raids deep into the western countries. As already seen, they contributed to the collapse of the Moravian state, and their armies marched through Germany into France. Then, in 955 Otto I of Germany defeated a large Hungarian army on the Lechfeld, near Augsburg, and the raiding came to an end. The newcomers settled down on their plain and began the slow process of building a permanent state.

Ivan the Terrible (from a seventeenth-century engraving).

The last Byzantine emperor, Constantine XI, and his consort. After the fall of Constantinople, Ivan III began to think of Russia as the successor of the Roman and Byzantine empires.

As with other people of eastern Europe, the westerners and Byzantium took an active interest in what was happening in Hungary, and the primary agents of that interest were missionaries. The work of Constantine-Cyril and Methodius did not affect the Hungarians because they were not within the Slavic linguistic and cultural orbit, but Rome and Constantinople vied for their religious adherence. In 975, Geza (r. 972–96), the great-grandson of the first known Hungarian chieftain, Arpad, accepted baptism from western missionaries. His son Stephen (r. 996–1038) brought about the Christianization of the country and with the help of the papacy established its ecclesiastical hierarchy. In 1000, Stephen won from the pope the right to crown himself king, making the kingdom a fief of the papacy. This move consolidated the political achievements of his predecessors and ensured Hungary's independence from its German and Slavic neighbors. Stephen was canonized in 1083.

The history of the Arpad dynasty (907–1301) was one of constant strife between rival claimants of the crown.

Very few Arpad kings received their inheritance or ruled without challenge. In the twelfth century, the kings followed the practice of other east European rulers and brought in settlers to occupy their sparsely populated lands. They used locators to settle Germans in northern and central Transylvania and brought Szekels, a related Finno-Ugric people, into eastern Transylvania. These colonies formed free communities under special legal status and were governed by a *voivode* or provincial governor.

In 1241, Hungary was overrun by the Mongols, who devastated the country and razed the cities. Overall, the population of the central plain suffered a 60 percent loss, and in some areas the whole population was killed or ran away. After the Horde retreated back to Russia, King Bela IV returned from hiding in Dalmatia and began to rebuild the kingdom. But the invasion had so disrupted the country that he could not fully reunite it; many local lords asserted their independence although they continued to recognize the titular suzerainty of the crown. After the death of Bela's son, Ladislav IV (r.

Mongols attacking Liegnitz in 1241 (from a miniature painting of 1353).

1272–90), the nobility had to search for a male member of the Arpad dynasty, finally finding Andrew III (r. 1290–1301) in Italy. Andrew proved to be a good king, but he died without an heir, and the nobles had to find a king from a new dynasty.

The competitors for the Hungarian throne were Charles Robert of Anjou, Wenceslas of Bohemia, and Otto of Bavaria. Although Wenceslas was able to win the crown, uniting under his kingship Bohemia, Poland, and Hungary, he was assassinated in 1306, and Charles Robert succeeded him in 1308. Charles (r. 1308–42), whose mother was an Arpad, was a scion of the royal house of Naples, which Charles of Anjou, the brother of Louis IX of France, had conquered in 1266. Still a boy when he was elected, he grew up in Hungary.

The period of the reigns of Charles Robert and his son Louis (r. 1342–82) was one of prosperity in eastern Europe, and Hungary flourished along with Bohemia and Poland. In this period, the Hungarians realized the full potential of the gold mines in the Transylvanian Alps, and the king received about 40 percent of the production. With that wealth they patronized the arts, built grand buildings in the cities, and added to their kingdom. With his great independent wealth, Louis was willing to give away rights and privileges to the nobility, which naturally remained loyal to him. In 1370, after the death of Kazimierz of Poland, Louis was elected king of Poland, and he followed the policy of liberality to the nobles in that kingdom also.

But the glory of the house of Anjou died with Louis. He left two daughters, Maria and Jadwiga, who inherited Hungary and Poland respectively. As was already seen, Jadwiga's marriage to Jagiello of Lithuania instituted a new dynasty and a lasting union with Lithuania. Maria was married to Sigismund of Luxembourg, who had himself crowned king of Hungary in 1387. But the success of Sigismund—he became emperor in 1411 and king of Bohemia

Matthias I, the last native king of Hungary (from a seventeenth-century print).

in 1419—did not lead to the establishment of a new dynasty. When Sigismund died, he left only a daughter, who was married to Albrecht of Habsburg, who was accepted as king in Hungary. But Albrecht died in 1439, and the nobility turned to Wladislaw Jagiello of Poland. When Wladislaw was killed in battle against the Ottomans in 1444, the country accepted Albrecht's posthumous son Ladislav (r. 1444–57), but the real governor of the country during his reign was the great general Janos Hunyadi. Hunyadi led the fight against the Ottomans until his death in 1456 and was then succeeded as general by his son Matthias Corvinus, who was elected king after the death of Ladislav. Matthias (r. 1457–90), the last native king of Hungary, was a man of exceptional ability. He held off the Ottomans and other enemies of the kingdom, rebuilt the cities, and created a huge collection of art, jewelry, and manuscripts. Using the wealth of his gold mines and what he squeezed from the peasants, Matthias brought Silesia, Bohemia, and lower Austria into his control. But after Matthias died in 1490, the external provinces fell away, and the kingdom weakened under a succession of Jagiellonian kings. The close alliance with Poland remained, but both kingdoms were weak, and the Habsburgs were able to assemble their empire in eastern Europe.

Suggestions for Further Reading

Slavic Migrations and Cultures

On the early Slavic migrations and culture, see F. Graus, "Slavs and Germans," in *Eastern and Western Europe in the Middle Ages,* ed. G. Barraclough (1970). All the essays in this book are useful. In general, see F. Dvornik, *The Making of Central and Eastern Europe* (1949), and A. P. Vlasto, *The Entry of the Slavs into Christendom* (1970). Dvornik's *Byzantine Missions among the Slavs* (1970), is extremely useful for the settlement and conversion of the Croats and Serbs and for the mission of Constantine-Cyril and Methodius. I. Boba, *Moravia's History Reconsidered* (1971), made the case that the Moravia was centered on Sirmium/Morava south of the Danube. On the history of the Bulgars, see R. E. Sullivan, "Khan Boris and the Conversion of Bulgaria: A Case Study of the Impact of Christianity on a Barbarian Society," *Studies in Medieval and Renaissance History* 3 (1966), 55–139, and, from the Byzantine perspective, R. Browning, *Byantium and Bulgaria* (1975).

Bohemia

Both Dvornik and Boba have much to say about the early medieval history of Bohemia. See also A. H. Hermann, *A History of the Czechs* (1975). Because of its close connection with Germany, comprehensive histories of medieval Germany have a good deal of information about Bohemia.

Poland and Lithuania

N. Davies, *God's Playground: A History of Poland*, 2 vols. (1982), sets a new standard. *The Cambridge History of Poland*, 2 vols., ed. W. Reddaway (1941, 1950), remains useful. For the late Piast period, see P. W. Knoll, *The Rise of the Polish Monarchy: Piast Poland in East Central Europe 1320–70* (1972). On Lithuania, see C. R. Jurgela, *History of the Lithuanian Nation* (1948), which historians consider flawed. O. Halecki, *The Borderlands of Western Civilization* (1952), is useful on Lithuania. See also J. R. Koncius, *Vlautas the Great, Grand Duke of Lithuania* (1964). *Baltic History*, ed. A. Ziedonis, W. L. Winter, and M. Valgemäe (1973), contains several articles of interest. On the Hanseatic League, see P. Dollinger, *The German Hansa* (1970).

The Teutonic Knights

F. L. Carsten, *The Origin of Prussia* (1954), is the best work on the state created by the Teutonic Knights. For a general history of the Order, see C. Krollmann, *The Teutonic Order in Prussia* (1938), and K. Gorski, "The Teutonic Order in Prussia," *Medievalia et Humanistica* 17 (1966). See also W. Urban, *The Baltic Crusade* (1975), which treats the Knights' conquest of Livonia and Estonia. For a broader view of the northern crusades, see E. Christiansen, *The Northern Crusades* (1980).

Russia

For a comprehensive survey of Russian history, see G. Vernadsky and M. Karpovich, *A History of Russia,* 5 vols. (1943–69). N. V. Riasanovsky, *A History of Russia,* 4th ed. (1984), and G. Vernadsky, *Russia at the Dawn of the Modern Age* (1959), are good one-volume surveys. See also F. Nowak, *Medieval Slavdom and the Rise of Russia* (1930). On the first entry of the Russians into Mediterranean history, see A. A. Vasiliev, *The Russian Attack on Constantinople in 860* (1946). On the Mongols in Russia, see G. Vernadsky, *The Mongols and Russia* (1953), and on the rise of Moscow, see J. Fennell, *Ivan the Great of Moscow* (1961). J. Blum, *Lord and Peasant in Russia from the Ninth to the Nineteenth Century* (1961), is an excellent study of social history. There is also a great deal of social history in D. H. Kaiser, *The Growth of Law in Medieval Russia* (1980). On the Khazars, see D. M. Dunlop, *The History of the Jewish Khazars* (1954).

Hungary

For a brief survey of the history of Hungary, see D. Sinor, *A Short History of Hungary* (1959), and C. A. Macartney, *Hungary: A Short History* (1962). On the early period of Magyar settlement, see C. A. Macartney, *The Magyars in the Ninth Century* (1930). On the Ottoman threat, see P. Coles, *The Ottoman Impact on Europe* (1968).

Richard II, from the portrait
by Beauneven of
Valenciennes (1398) in
Westminster Abbey.

14
The End of the Middle Ages

The fourteenth and fifteenth centuries were a time of confusion and chaos in the West. Decade after decade everything seemed to go wrong: economic depression, war, rebellion, and plague harried Europeans, and neither ecclesiastical nor secular governments seemed capable of easing the distress. At times the whole structure of European society seemed to be crumbling. Yet the social and political institutions that emerged during this time of troubles were the most powerful in the world, and Europeans soon were engaged in conquering the world. The science and technology, the navies and armies, the governments and business organizations that were to give Europe unquestioned supremacy for 400 years were all taking shape in the fourteenth and fifteenth centuries. The dire stretch of history marked by the Hundred Years' War, the Black Death, and the Great Schism seemed an unlikely seedbed for these great achievements.

TROUBLES OF THE FOURTEENTH CENTURY: ECONOMIC DEPRESSION AND BUBONIC PLAGUE

From the eleventh to the end of the thirteenth centuries, the European economy and population grew steadily. The prosperity of peasant villages increased to the benefit of both villagers and lords. New lands were claimed or brought back into cultivation after centuries of neglect. The pressure for land and the promise of good return from agriculture induced towns and lords to undertake such large-scale projects as the draining of the Roman marshes and the building of dikes in the Netherlands. Much of the land brought into production by these methods was of marginal quality, and the effort was indicative of the needs and opportunities created by growth.

Then, in the last decade of the thirteenth century, a series of bad harvests

Miniature painting of a fourteenth-century pewterer turning a jug on a lathe, from the Guild Book of the Twelve Brothers' Foundation in Nuremberg.

French coin from the reign of Philip the Fair (r. 1285–1314).

declining economic health. During the previous decades, the large landholders had ceased leasing their lands in order to profit from the good markets by farming the lands themselves. As a result, the mid-thirteenth century was a period of avid interest in advanced agricultural techniques and technological innovation, for the great landlords had capital and practiced only market agriculture. Toward the end of the century the Englishman Walter of Henley produced a widely read handbook, *On Husbandry*. But when the harvests failed in the 1290s, the great landowners suffered along with the peasants.

The problems that struck the agricultural system at the end of the century were made worse by inflation. The poor harvests raised prices of food and other farm products, such as wool and flax, and these higher prices in turn drove up the prices of manufactured goods. People on fixed incomes, such as government bureaucrats, struggled to make ends meet, and there was a noticeable rise in the corruption of government. Bribes and gifts became almost a regular part of the income of government officials, and during the fourteenth century there was a steady flow of complaints about the venality of royal and ecclesiastical officials, with the consequence that both secular and Church government lost moral authority.

Then came the plague in 1348. Bubonic plague, spread by fleas that had bitten infected rats, originated in Southeast Asia and was carried over the trade routes to the Middle East. From there it jumped to Constantinople and then to Italy. Soon it spread to the whole of Europe. In two years, about a third of the population of Europe died; in some places there was 80 percent mortality. After the initial onslaught of the disease, it continued to appear here and there until after 1700.

The effect of this disaster was enormous. Villages and farms were abandoned, and the labor force was cut drastically. The labor crisis in rural districts was deepened as surviving peasants migrated to the towns to replace

put an intolerable strain on the overexpanded agricultural system, and widespread famine occurred. By 1300, the population had ceased to grow and, in fact, was beginning to decline. Even worse famines occurred in 1315–17. In good times, the peasants lived not much above the subsistence level, so the famines had a devastating effect. In the early fourteenth century, the population was not only smaller, it was also weaker—more susceptible to disease—than it had been in the mid-thirteenth century.

The poor harvests caused an economic depression that affected every part of the European economy. Agricultural surplus was Europe's primary trade good, and, therefore, the decline of production weakened the economy of the towns. The kings and barons, who depended on agricultural rents for their income, also found themselves in

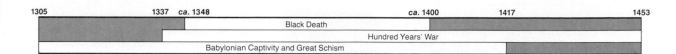

urban workers who had died. However, for a short time the condition of the peasantry actually appeared to have improved. The high wages that peasants could demand for their labor enabled them to purchase the land of those who did not survive the epidemic, and many were able to buy their freedom from feudal obligations. For a few years everyone had more money, although prices also rose rapidly. Then the injury to the system became clear. Prosperity had been based on inflation, not on an expanding market, and soon production was sufficient to meet demand. In this economic environment employers sought to reduce costs, and since the bulk of production costs were in wages, they sought to roll back wages to the level of 1348. The kings tried to help out in this retrenchment. In England, the Statute of Laborers (1351) and later statutes required workers to accept customary wages (those prevailing before the plague) and also fixed the prices of food and other basic necessities at the 1348 level. Other kings and great lords responded to the crisis with similar laws. Although it was very difficult to enforce such legislation, its overall effect was to prevent the peasants from taking full advantage of the labor shortage resulting from the plague.

Nonetheless, rural wages tended to rise, and rural landlords found it advantageous to cling tenaciously to the customary labor services of the peasants; it was too costly to hire workers to exploit the manorial demesne. By the custom of each manor, peasants owed the lord certain labor services, which might include plowing and harvesting his portion of the village fields, mending fences, and providing labor for the construction of buildings. In the economic crisis after the plague, many lords became particular about the performance of these services, which the peasants had always tried to minimize and avoid. However, the process of commutation and leasing the demesne for rent was not arrested entirely. Lords who had already commuted services for a money rent found it no longer profitable to exploit the demesne with hired labor, so they leased their demesne and lived on rents from their whole manors. In either case—whether it was to the lord's advantage to enforce customary services or to convert his whole manor into rent-paying tenancies—the interests of the peasants and their lords clashed. Peasants agitated for commutation of services into cash rents, since they could make more money as wage-earning laborers.

The Black Death in England

Then that most grievous pestilence penetrated the coastal regions by way of Southampton and came to Bristol, and people died as if the whole strength of the city were seized by sudden death. For there were few who lay in their beds more than three days or two and a half days; then that savage death snatched them about the second day. In Leicester, in the little parish of St. Leonard, more than three hundred and eighty died; in the parish of the Holy Cross, more than four hundred, and in the parish of St. Margaret, more than seven hundred. . . .

And the price of everything was cheap, because of the fear of death, there were very few who took any care for their wealth, or for anything else. For a man could buy a horse for half a mark [about 7 shillings] which before was worth forty shillings, a large fat ox for four shillings, a cow for twelve pence, a heifer for sixpence, a large fat sheep for four pence. . . . And the sheep and cattle wandered about through the fields and among the crops, and there was no one to go after them or collect them. They perished in countless numbers everywhere, for lack of watching . . . since there was such a lack of serfs and servants, that no one knew what he should do. For there is no memory of a mortality so severe and so savage. . . . In the following autumn, one could not hire a reaper for less than eight pence [per day] with food, or a mower at less than twelve pence with food.

From Henry Knighton, *Chronicle,* in *The Portable Medieval Reader,* ed. by J. B. Ross and M. M. McLaughlin (New York: Viking, 1949), pp. 218–19.

Manuscript illustration of the crucial point in the meeting of Richard II with the main body of the rebels during the Peasants' Rebellion of 1381. Its leader, Wat Tyler, is being struck down by one of Richard's men.

This agitation grew into a general demand for the abolition of all manorial obligations, as lords tried to compensate for their declining incomes by enforcing their rights over the manorial commons, such as the meadows, fisheries, pastures, and woods, and to enforce the customary payments for use of mills, ovens, and other "appurtenances."

The lot of the urban working class was no better than that of the peasantry. Individual employers, the craft guilds, and town governments all tightened up regulations and laws designed to keep wages low and to protect the static or declining market from outside competition. The Black Death struck impartially at both employer and worker, but after the plague artisans found it more difficult than ever to gain admittance into the craft guilds. The economic and social gulf between masters and workers widened as economic conditions steadily deteriorated. Europe as a whole was confronted with the problem of overproduction. New opportunities to acquire fortunes by taking risks in an expanding market were extremely rare. Under these conditions the efforts of merchants and manufacturers to cut costs sometimes actually depressed the urban working class below the level of subsistence enjoyed by the peasants in the countryside.

The workers and peasants had no legal means for improving their lot. In the countryside, custom and new legislation favored the propertied classes, but at least the customary obligations placed a limit on exploitation of the peasants. In the towns, workers were not protected by such customary rules, and there was great discontent. In the Flemish towns, the merchant guilds and craft guilds struggled for power over the ailing municipal economy. At stake was the power to protect the interests of the various groups through governmental action. The Flemish towns experienced urban rebellions in 1255, 1267, 1275, 1280, and 1302, and throughout the fourteenth century they suffered repeatedly from riots and conflicts. In Florence, the *populo minuto*—the little people—rebelled in 1378 in the so-called Ciompi rising. The countryside was also troubled. In France, the peasants rebelled in 1358, killing hundreds of nobles and their families and burning manors throughout the country. After this great upheaval, there were further, sporadic uprisings. In England, the Peasants' Revolt of 1381 caused widespread damage. The rebellious mobs called for social reforms that would have altered the nature of English society.

These troubles stimulated harsh reactions by the upper classes, and the result of most uprisings was the reassertion of merchant or aristocratic rule in a more tyrannical form than before. The medieval idea that all in the community had both rights and duties was gradually altered to emphasize the duties of all but the upper-class elite, which began to view itself as the sole guarantor of the community's welfare.

The breakdown of order that accompanied the plague and the economic depression affected the mentality of Europeans as well as their social and political life. From the middle of the fourteenth century, there was a rise of millennialism, spiritual movements based on fear that the end of the world was nigh. Even before the plague, in 1327, there had been a scare in France that the Jews and lepers were plotting to overthrow Christendom, and many lost their lives in the riots and trials that were brought about by the rumors. In the later part of the century, groups of penitents wandered the roads preaching the end of the world and beating themselves with whips and ropes. The figure of Death, who spares no one, from king to lowly peasant, became a popular subject of artists commissioned to paint the walls of churches. The ''dance of death'' (a kind of chain dance led by a person dressed as Death) became popular in towns and villages. Many popular preachers said that God was punishing Christendom because the popes resided in Avignon instead of Rome.

THE AVIGNON PAPACY AND THE GREAT SCHISM

The history of the Church before the Reformation of the sixteenth century may be divided into four periods—the Avignon Papacy (1305–78), the Great Schism (1378–1409), the Age of Councils (1409–47), and the period after 1447, when the history of the Church can best be understood in terms of the politics of the various European countries. Here, we deal with the first three periods.

Papal Government at Avignon

The city of Avignon, where Clement V (r. 1305–14), the former archbishop of Bordeaux, settled instead of going to Rome, was French in everything but political allegiance. It was an imperial city—holding a charter from the emperor—situated in a county of Provence that belonged to the papacy. The stay in Avignon might have been temporary, but Clement V filled vacancies in the college of cardinals with Frenchmen, who in 1314 were content to elect another French pope and remain where they were. Until the end of the Avignon papacy, all the popes and most of the cardinals were French.

On the whole, the Avignon popes were able men though not outstanding

religious leaders. Their talents lay in administration, law, and finance, and under them the centralization and bureaucratization of the Church, begun in the eleventh century, reached its culmination. The characteristic feature of this centralization was the system of financial extortion, established principally by John XXII (r. 1316–34), who was almost constantly engaged in political and ecclesiastical struggles. He believed that the Church could not stand up to the secular powers unless the papacy was wealthy enough to be independent of them, and he developed a financial system that drew the resources of the whole Church to the papal curia. The other characteristic of papal government in the Avignon period was the increasing control of all ecclesiastical business by the curia. This feature flowed naturally from the financial system, but it was justified and enhanced by the claim that only if the papacy controlled Church business could it be free of secular interference. The result was the rapid growth of offices and officials, a bureaucratization that made the papal government the largest in Europe.

The papal government at Avignon was divided into four main branches: the chancery, the *camera apostolica* (the apostolic chamber), the Datary, and the hierarchy of judicial tribunals. Of these, the chancery had developed first, as it had in secular governments, and by the fourteenth century the papal chancery had seven offices that dispatched the various kinds of routine administrative correspondence and documents. The chancery also received petitions for papal action, reviewed the qualifications of candidates for offices, and had official custody of the records of curial business.

The *camera apostolica* emerged as a separate financial department in the thirteenth century, and under John XXII and his successors it grew along with the financial system of the papacy. Its administrative head was the treasurer, and its policy-making head was the chamberlain, whose title indicates that he was once a household of-

Death was a favorite subject for illustration in the late Middle Ages. Shown here is the Dance of Death from a manuscript of about 1400. Death, playing a trumpet decked with the papal banner of the keys of St. Peter, summons a pope.

ficer of the popes. Under the Avignon popes, the chamberlain became in essence the prime minister of the papacy, and he always came out of the personal entourage of the pope. The chamberlain handled most instructions to papal legates and ambassadors and nearly all the private and secret correspondence of the popes. He also controlled the papal mint, the tax collectors, and the extensive courier system, was responsible for the receipt and auditing of papal revenues, and supervised a court that heard disputes over papal finances.

The Datary became a separate department only in the first half of the fourteenth century, taking over some of the functions of the chancery. It handled petitions that did not require judicial action. Where there was no dispute and in cases that did not concern matters of conscience, the Datary disposed of appointments to benefices (income-producing properties), dispensations from provisions of the canon law (especially in routine cases of irregularities in marriages), and the granting of papal approval to the disposition of ecclesiastical property or offices among the clergy.

The papal judiciary had developed into an elaborate court system since the papal court had become the busiest in Europe during the twelfth century. The highest court was a full meeting of the pope and cardinals in the Consistory, but most cases were delegated by this court to local judges-delegate or one of the lesser tribunals of the curia. Any number of the cardinals could constitute a court for a particular case, but these courts, too, tended to delegate the hearing of cases to trained auditors. Routine cases were handled by the *Rota*, where litigants could secure final judgments without reference of their cases to the pope or cardinals. The judges of the *Rota* were a panel of auditors from which several were appointed to hear the arguments of each case, but judgment was pronounced by the whole panel after review of the evidence and arguments. At any stage of a proceeding, a case could be referred to a special tribunal, the *Audientia*, which judged technical legal points and investigated the authenticity of documentary evidence. As a result of the interconnection of the tribunals and the participation of the highest officials, litigation in papal courts was complicated and expensive. The judicial machinery was ideal for defendants who sought to delay the due process of law.

The operation of the vast machinery of papal government absorbed most of the time of the popes and cardinals, and the financial needs of the bureaucracy made it rapacious. Critics of clerical wealth and worldliness found in the papacy the worst example of what they denounced. The Avignon papacy suffered a desertion of the intellectuals, led by Petrarch (1304–74) the poet and scholar who coined the term "Babylonian Captivity" to describe the curia at Avignon. Saint Catherine of Siena (1347–80) bombarded the papacy with letters demanding that it return to Rome, and a dispute between John XXII and the emperor Ludwig IV of Bavaria (r. 1314–47) produced bitter denunciations of the papacy as an institution subverted by political ambition and ill-gotten wealth. As time went by, pressure on the popes to return to Rome mounted. Conditions in Rome, long subject to internecine conflict among the noble families and their supporters, improved during the reign of Pope Innocent VI (r. 1352–62), and soon after this the treaty that ended the first phase of the Hundred Years' War released a great many companies of mercenaries that troubled Avignon as well as other French cities. Urban V (r. 1362–70) actually brought the curia back to Rome, but he returned to Avignon after three years of vainly trying to reestablish papal authority in the Holy City. Gregory XI (r. 1370–78) returned once more to Rome, but he too failed to establish himself and planned to return to Avignon. Unfortunately, he died before he could carry out this plan, and the cardinals in Rome held an election under the threat of violence by the Roman mob demanding that they elect an Italian. After electing the archbishop of Bari, many of the cardinals fled back to Avignon, and when the archbishop, as Pope Urban VI (r. 1378–89), turned out to be a reformer determined to root out the corrupt practices of the curia, the Avignon contingent elected another pope, Clement VII (r. 1378–94), claiming that the first election was invalid because it had been held under the coercion of the mob. Thus began the Great Schism, which brought an end to the medieval papacy.

The Great Schism

There were now two popes, since the Italian Urban V, refused to give in, and there was no easy way to tell who was the true pope. The machinery of papal government, already a great burden on the Church and society, was doubled by the schism, as were all its abuses. To the criticism that had been leveled against the Avignon popes was now added the charge of scandal, as each pope hurled anathema at the other. The secular rulers of Europe lined up with one or the other depending on their own political interests. The French and their allies—Scotland, Navarre, Castile, Aragon, and various German princes under French influence—fell into line in support of the Avignon pope. The enemies of France—England, Flanders, Portugal, the emperor, most of the German princes, Bohemia, and Hungary—recognized the Roman line. The Italian city-states were divided and fickle.

Meanwhile, many in the Church tried to find a solution. It was proposed that both popes resign and that the combined colleges of cardinals, since both popes created full colleges with appointees favorable to themselves, elect a new pope. But the two sides did not trust one another, and the popes refused to take the step. Others, led by the theological faculty at the University of Paris, called for a general council to decide the issue.

This solution was attractive, but it was not clear that the canon law permitted a council to depose a pope. For hundreds of years, since the eleventh-century reform movement at least (see pp. 281–85), Church law and practice had emphasized the supremacy of the pope in ecclesiastical affairs. The pope was the supreme judge; he "judges all and is judged by no one." He was the supreme legislator; no ecclesiastical law was valid without his approval. He summoned and presided over councils. Yet, the twelfth-century canonists had wrestled with some difficult constitutional issues raised by this hierarchical view of the Church. They had wondered what would happen if the pope, who was a man like other men, committed crimes or fell into theological error. How could the Church deal with such a crisis? By the beginning of the thirteenth century, the canonists had worked out a theory according to which the promise of Christ that the "gates of Hell shall not prevail" against

The Great Schism   1378–1417

Land giving allegiance to Rome
Land giving allegiance to Avignon
Shifting and divided

the Church (Matt. 16:18) applied not to the pope, but to the Church as a whole. In Matthew's account of the promise, it was part of a speech Jesus made to Peter, from whom the popes claimed to derive their authority. If the promise applied to the Church as a whole, then a general council, representing the Church, was superior to the pope and could deal with an errant pope.

The late-fourteenth-century conciliarists revived these ideas. Their theory of conciliar authority was also based on the idea that Christ made his promise of inerrancy to the Church and that a general council represented the unerring Church. The problem was how to call the council. Some argued that the emperor could summon it, citing, among others, the example of Constantine I who had summoned the Council of Nicea (325). Others thought that the college of cardinals, as the body responsible for electing the pope, might do it. Many thought that only the pope could summon a council, which the rival popes were refusing to do. Even after most people had come to agree that a council was superior to the pope, the practical problem of legitimately summoning it permitted the schism to drag on. When Urban and Clement died, in 1389 and 1394 respectively, each of the rival colleges of cardinals elected a successor to its pope, and the independent lines continued until 1414, when the conciliarists finally got their way.

The conciliar movement took its first practical step in 1409, when the cardinals on both sides agreed to cooperate in a council held at Pisa. Five hundred prelates met in the city and deposed the two popes, Benedict XIII (r. 1394–1423) of Avignon and Gregory XII (r. 1406–15) of Rome as "schismatics and notorious heretics." Then, the council authorized the assembled cardinals to elect a new pope, Alexander V (r. 1409–10). Benedict and Gregory promptly denounced the council and its pope and were able to maintain themselves with the support of their secular allies. There was now a triple schism, which was not resolved when Alexander died because the cardinals at Pisa immediately elected a successor, John XXIII (r. 1410–15). John soon turned on the council, asserting his higher authority as pope, and the churchmen left Pisa without having accomplished anything.

There were immediate calls for a new council, and finally, in 1414, John XXIII was forced by political circumstances to summon a general council. The council met at Constance and soon moved to depose all three popes. Gregory XII of Rome anticipated the action by calling the council, on the grounds that only he as the true pope could do so, and then abdicating (1415). While bowing to reality, these actions preserved the fiction of papal superiority

A manuscript illumination showing an antipope receiving his crown from the Devil and in turn crowning an emperor as a pledge of mutual support against the true head of the Church.

to a council and asserted the legitimacy of the Roman line. John XXIII was forced to abdicate in the same year,* but Benedict XIII, then already 87 years old, refused to step down and retreated to his castle in Spain where he died in 1423 still maintaining the legitimacy of his papacy. In 1417, the council elected a new pope, Martin V (r. 1417–31), to reestablish the true line of papal succession. The council also tried to reform the Church and among its legislation was a decree that the council should meet periodically to supervise the reform.

Martin V and his successors sought to reestablish the power of the papacy over the councils, and although councils did meet after Constance, the popes succeeded in making them ineffective. Yet, the schism and conciliar movement had destroyed the medieval papacy. The popes no longer commanded the extraordinary prestige and power they had had since the eleventh century, and, increasingly, the papacy became an Italian principality.

ENGLAND

The expansionist policies of Edward I (see p. 352) had severely strained England's resources, and it was predictable that a reaction would set in after his death. It was made more acute by the character of Edward II (r. 1307–27), who was weak-willed and frivolous, idle and incompetent. It was the medieval king's business to govern, but this king left government to civil servants and a series of personal favorites. The resulting conflict between the king and the nobility led a group of barons, calling themselves the Lords Ordainers, to impose the Ordinances of 1311 on the king. These statutes curtailed the governmental authority of the royal household and required the approval of the magnates in Parliament

* John was not considered a true pope, so that when, in 1958, a new pope took the name John, he was designated the twenty-third of that name, John XXIII (r. 1958–63).

for appointment of the principal officers of state and for important policy decisions. The defeat of Edward's armies by the Scots at Bannockburn in 1314 further discredited him, and the barons dominated the government. But they too were incompetent and selfish, and in 1322 a moderate royalist party reestablished Edward's power. He immediately moved to nullify the Ordinances, but he did recognize that important legislation should be enacted by the king in Parliament with the consent of those summoned and present. After this royalist restoration, the king again fell under the influence of favorites, and the tragicomedy of his reign climaxed when Queen Isabelle ran off with her lover Mortimer with whom she led a successful rebellion against her husband. Edward was imprisoned and killed in 1327.

Edward III (r. 1327–77) succeeded as a minor, while Isabelle and Mortimer controlled the royal government for their advantage. In 1330 the young king was able to overthrow the regency in a *coup d'état* that cost Mortimer his life and Isabelle her freedom. The king was then able to revive the royal household as the center of government while appeasing the barons with minor concessions. In 1333 he defeated the Scots at Halidon Hill, and although the battle had no lasting effect, it showed Edward that foreign wars could distract the barons from the domestic grievances that had troubled his father's reign. He found his foreign adventure in war with France.

The Hundred Years' War: The First Phase

Warfare between England and France had begun under Edward I and Philip the Fair, but neither monarch had been in a position to carry through a major campaign. Philip had been occupied with Flanders and with strengthening his power over the great feudatories, and Edward had been intent on the conquest of Scotland. Edward III began a war with France in the 1340s, by which time there were many underlying causes of conflict—competition over trade in Flanders (which depended on English wool), French support of Scotland, the old claims of the English king to Normandy and other territories. But the immediate cause of the war was Edward's claim to the French crown through his mother. Edward's contemporary, Philip VI (r. 1328–50) descended from Philip III (r. 1270–85) through Charles of Anjou, Philip the Fair's brother. Edward was Philip the Fair's grandson. No matter how the lawyers figured these relationships, Edward III was one degree closer to the throne than Philip VI, but

Edward's claim had two flaws: first, it descended through a female, and the French lawyers argued that one who could not inherit the crown could not transmit it. Second, the French royal council would not accept Edward, France's hereditary enemy, as king.

In the first phase of the war, the English won an amazing string of victories. Edward won a naval battle at Sluys (1340), which gave him control of the English Channel. His army then nearly annihilated the French army at Crécy (1346) and went on to capture Calais, which remained an English port for two centuries. Ten years later, his son Edward, who was called the Black Prince, defeated the French again at Poitiers and captured King John of France. This battle ended the first phase of the war. In the treaty that followed, the French agreed to pay a huge ransom for the release of their king and to cede about two-fifths of their country to the English. Edward had reconquered most of the territories lost in 1204 by his ancestor King John.

The few decisive battles marked stages in the war but did not account for the main military action. The English carried on the war in campaigns of systematic destruction. A nineteenth-century historian published a list of destroyed structures (counting only the substantial buildings) in two large volumes. Moreover, the battles themselves were not models of feudal warfare. Under Edward I, the English had developed a new type of fighting force made up of men wielding the longbow. This weapon propelled an arrow with great power, had a long range, and could be shot and reloaded rapidly. The longbow could even penetrate chain mail. At Crécy, 15,000 English bowmen nearly wiped out 60,000 mounted French knights.

After the treaty of 1356, France suffered from economic hardship and disorder. The burden of the ransom, together with the effects of the Black Death, ruined peasants and merchants alike and led to the great uprising of 1358, which was put down with much

The Hundred Years' War   1337–1453

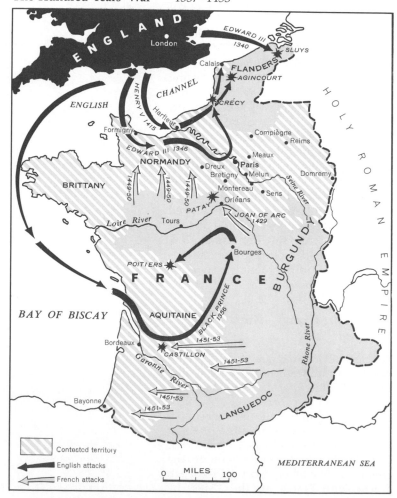

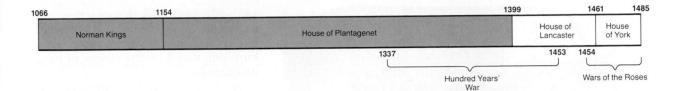

1066	1154		1399	1461	1485
Norman Kings	House of Plantagenet		House of Lancaster	House of York	

1337 — 1453 1454 — 1485

Hundred Years' War

Wars of the Roses

bloodshed. The end of the war also released many mercenary units, which now had to find ways to support themselves. The way they chose most often was banditry, which plagued commerce and towns throughout the country. The wealthy papal court at Avignon was threatened by robber bands several times.

The war started up again in the early fifteenth century. In England, Edward III had been succeeded by his grandson Richard II (r. 1377–99). Richard was a boy when he became king, and the government was in the hands of his elder relatives and of the barons. The great peasant rebellion of 1381 showed the ineffectiveness of their government, and after Richard came of age in 1386 he tried to increase royal power and concentrate authority in his own hands.

But there were serious obstacles to the success of this policy. Most of the armed forces in the country were private companies paid by the king but recruited and commanded by the barons. This system had developed during the early years of the Hundred Years' War when it had seemed easier to allow members of the aristocracy to raise troops than for the government to deal with the tedious problem of recruiting. Any lord with a taste for war could maintain his own little army at government expense, a situation that encouraged disorder and rebellion. Further, Richard had tried to gain control of the government by exiling leading opponents and confiscating their lands. But the barons viewed an attack on some as dangerous to all, so the king's policy actually weakened his government. In 1399, the baronial opposition to Richard came to the point of rebellion under the king's cousin

Henry of Lancaster, who had been deprived of his lands and exiled a few years earlier. At a great parliament, Henry had Richard deposed and then mounted the throne himself as Henry IV (r. 1399–1413). Richard died in prison.

The Hundred Years' War: The Second Phase

The Lancastrian kings, who ruled from 1399 to 1461, never quite lived down the violence through which they had seized the crown. Henry IV had to put down two dangerous rebellions, and his son Henry V (r. 1413–22) tried to unify the kingdom by reviving the war with France. He was a brilliant commander, and in 1415, at Agincourt in Normandy, his small army of bowmen destroyed the cream of the French army of mounted knights. He was also the first in Europe to use siege artillery against walled cities (on the gunpowder revolution, see p. 410).

After the successes of 1415, Henry was able to make an alliance with the Duke of Burgundy—the most powerful lord in France aside from the king himself—so the French king Charles VI (r. 1380–1422) had to accept a treaty in 1421. In the treaty Charles disinherited his own son, married his daughter to Henry V, and recognized that any son born of this union was to be king of France. When both Charles and Henry V died the next year, their thrones were inherited by the nine-month-old Henry VI.

In England, the coronation of baby Henry led to a bitter struggle among the uncles and cousins of the king over who would actually govern in the name of the king. Nonetheless, the English were able to maintain pressure

The battle of Formigny, which was fought at the end of the Hundred Years' War. Notice that the English (right) are on foot and are flanked by bowmen, while the French are delivering a cavalry charge. Usually the English won in such circumstances, but this time they were defeated.

on Charles VII, the disinherited son of Charles VI, who, understandably, renounced the treaty of 1421. Charles was forced to flee south of the Loire, and it looked as if the English would be able to achieve the goals of the treaty, when the tide was turned by the appearance of a young woman, Joan of Arc.

Joan viewed herself as sent by God to save Charles VII and the French kingdom. She succeeded in overcoming the skepticism of the French court and led a force to victory at Patay near Orléans in 1429. Soon afterward, the English captured her and burned her as a witch—the judgment was reversed and she was canonized as a saint in 1929—but the French continued to make progress. The alliance between England and Burgundy broke down, and the French waged a successful war of attrition against the English. By 1453, only the port city of Calais remained in English hands, and the war came to an end.

For both sides, the second phase of the war had long-term effects. In France, the old aristocracy had been decimated by the English victories, and Charles VII was able to install many men of bourgeois origins as counselors and royal servants. His son Louis XI (r.

1461–83) continued this practice, and in his able hands France became a strong bureaucratic state ruled by a king unfettered by the claims of baronial families.

In England, royal authority was weakened at the beginning of Henry VI's reign by the competition for control of the regency government, and this weakness was prolonged when Henry slipped into insanity. Throughout his adulthood, the king alternated between sanity and insanity, and this prevented the establishment of a stable, consistent government. In addition, the defeats in France created dissension among the English leaders.

The Wars of the Roses

The competition for power in England was principally between the Lancastrians and their relatives led by the Duke of York, who represented the oldest line of descent from Edward III. After the Lancastrian Henry VI died in 1461, the Yorkists tried to install their leader as king, and civil war broke out. The Wars of the Roses—so named because people later thought, mistakenly, that the symbol of the House of Lancaster was a red rose, while that of York a white rose—lasted until 1485 and had a devastating effect on the baronial families. The war was the last uprising of the barons, the last attempt of a small clique to take over the central government and use it for its own purposes. But this time the wars destroyed everyone who took part in them—the House of Lancaster, the House of York, and many of the great baronial families. When Henry Tudor—an indirect, illegitimate, and half-Welsh descendant of John of Gaunt (Edward III's son) seized the throne as Henry VII in 1485, he was therefore in a position to build a new monarchy, relatively unchallenged by baronial factions.

Henry VII (r. 1485–1509) was an excellent politician and administrator. He continued the best policies of his predecessors, encouraging commerce and industry and running an economical and effective government. All the kings since Edward III had recognized that so long as England produced only raw materials—such as wool for the Flemish textile industry—it would never grow very rich, so they encouraged the migration of textile workers to England and protected the growing English textile industry. They also encouraged the development of English shipping. The change in England's fortunes came slowly, for even under Henry VII it was far behind Flanders in textiles and Italy in shipping, but a good start had been made, and he furthered the cause. In the 24 years of his reign, Henry established the Tudors as the ruling dynasty and created the basis for a century of peace and prosperity in England.

The Development of Governmental Institutions

There were two important institutional developments in England during the fourteenth and fifteenth centuries: the rise of the justices of the peace and the continuing development of Parliament. Edward III created the justices of the peace to take over some of the work of local law enforcement that had formerly been the duty of the sheriffs and feudal lords. The justices were men of position and leisure, not great lords but well-to-do local landholders of the class that had long carried the heavy responsibilities of local government. This was the class represented in Parliament as the knights of the shires. Like the sheriffs and tax collectors, they served without pay; their reward was leadership of their communities. By the middle of the fifteenth century their powers had grown to the point that they controlled local government. They arrested criminals and tried minor offenses. (Major cases were reserved for the circuit judges sent out from the king's court.) They were responsible for enforcing economic regulations and orders of the central government. They collected information for the King's Council and were supposed to inform

---

Lawlessness in Fifteenth-Century England

John Paston was the son of a royal judge and well-to-do land-owner in Norfolk. His father had bought the manor of Gresham, but in 1448 Lord Molyns claimed it, though he had no right to it. John Paston tried to settle the claim peacefully, but Molyns' men seized the manor house and Paston moved to another "mansion." While he was seeking help from his friends, Paston's wife was left to defend their home. She wrote her husband this letter late in 1448.

Right worshipful husband, I recommend me to you and pray you to get some cross-bows and windlasses to wind them with and arrows, for your house here is so low that no one could shoot out of it with a long-bow, even if we had great need. I suppose you could get these things from Sir John Falstoff [a friend of the Pastons]. And also I would like you to get two or three short pole-axes to guard the doors and as many jacks [padded leather jackets] as you can.

Partridge [leader of Molyns' men] and his fellows are sore afraid that you will attack them again, and they have made great preparations, as I am told. They have made bars to bar the doors crosswise, and they have made loop-holes on every side of the house to shoot out of both with bows and with hand-guns. The holes made for hand-guns are scarcely knee-high from the floor and no one can shoot out of them with a hand bow.

[Margaret Paston apparently took all this as a matter of course; she then turned to an ordinary shopping list.] I pray you to buy me a pound of almonds and a pound of sugar and some cloth to make clothes for your children and a yard of black broad-cloth for a hood for me.

The Trinity have you in His keeping and send you Godspeed in all your affairs.

Put into modern English from Norman Davis, ed., *Paston Letters* (Oxford: Clarendon Press, 1958), pp. 9–10.

---

it of plots against the government. In practice, the justices of the peace were often the creatures of the most powerful baron of their district. But when the Tudors reestablished royal authority, the justices of the peace, with their wide local knowledge and influence, became the chief agents of the crown in the counties.

An English court in the later Middle Ages. This miniature is from a law treatise of the reign of Henry IV (early fifteenth century). At the top are the five judges of the Court of King's Bench; below them are the king's coroner and attorney. On the left is the jury, and in front, in the dock, is a prisoner in fetters, flanked by lawyers. In the foregound more prisoners in chains wait their turn. On the center table stand the ushers, one of whom seems to be swearing in the jury.

knights of the shires, representing the counties, and the burgesses, representing the towns, joined to form the House of Commons. Previously, they had acted separately in presenting petitions to the king and approving taxes. Now, Parliament was organized into two houses (Lords and Commons), and unlike the assemblies of other countries, the Commons included nobles as well as true commoners. The knights of the shires were landlords, like the barons; they could intermarry with the baronial families; and some of them became barons themselves. Their presence gave the House of Commons much more influence than a mere assembly of burgesses (such as the French Third Estate) could have. Through the leadership of the knights, cooperation with the lords could be assured, which gave Parliament great power. For when both houses attacked a minister of the king they could usually force the minister out of office.

By the fifteenth century, Parliament had become an integral part of the machinery of government, and no important act was valid until it had received parliamentary approval. So well established had Parliament become that it survived even the period of strong kingship that began under the Tudors in 1485. But Parliament only gave legal validity to acts of government; it did not make policy, which was the province of the king and his ministers. For example, Edward II and Richard II were not deposed by the initiative or act of Parliament; Parliament was merely asked to ratify the results of revolutions engineered by a few great barons. Not until the seventeenth century did Parliament itself begin to formulate policy.

Meanwhile, the weakness and wartime needs of rulers from Edward II to Henry VI had given Parliament a chance to make itself an indispensable part of the government. Weak kings and usurpers alike sought the support of Parliament, which was the best representative of the country. Thus, Edward III and Henry IV both asked Parliament to ratify the depositions of Edward II and Richard II respectively, which made it appear that Parliament's assent was necessary for major changes in the government. Further, all taxes and most legislative acts were submitted to Parliament for approval.

The strengthening of Parliament also resulted from change in its institutional structure. About 1340 the

FRANCE

The monarchy of France also had its troubles during the fourteenth and fifteenth centuries. The sons of Philip the Fair died in rapid succession, leaving only daughters to succeed them. It was

987		1328	1589
	House of Capet	House of Valois	

this circumstance that created the claim of Edward III to the French throne, but the rule invented to prevent the succession by or through a woman was not only designed to bar Edward. It also prevented any of the French barons from gaining control by marrying a reigning queen. In 1328, the barons placed Philip of Valois, a cousin of the last king and a nephew of Philip the Fair, on the throne. But since Philip owed his position to the barons, he had to spend most of his reign bestowing favors on his supporters and keeping peace among factions of nobles. The broad-based loyalty to the king that had developed during the thirteenth century eroded, and rebellions and acts of treason plagued the country. These internal disorders help to account for the French defeats during the first phase of the Hundred Years' War.

Philip's son John (r. 1350–64) had no better fortune. He was a courtly man whose capture by the English at Poitiers, with the subsequent loss of territory and the heavy taxes needed to pay his ransom, caused widespread dissatisfaction. In 1358 the peasants rose in a bloody and destructive rebellion the *jacquerie* (the nobles called peasants Jacques, as if none had his own name). In the same year, the Estates General, led by the Paris bourgeoisie, tried to take over the government. The attempt failed because the Estates had had little experience in government and because their leaders received no support from the great magnates. John's son Charles V (r. 1364–80) regained much of the lost authority by suppressing his opponents at home and driving the English from one stronghold after another. If his successor had been a more capable ruler, the French might have reestablished their kingdom and brought a successful conclusion to the war with England.

Unfortunately, most of the brains and determination in the French royal family went to uncles and cousins of the new king rather than to the king himself. Charles VI (r. 1380–1422) was never strong in either mind or character, and after 1390 he suffered intermittent spells of insanity. The government was conducted largely by princes of the royal family who quarreled bitterly among themselves over offices, pensions, and gifts of land. When the Duke of Burgundy, the king's cousin, was assassinated in 1419 by followers of the Duke of Orléans, the king's brother, the quarrels turned into a civil war, and the new Duke of Burgundy allied himself with the English. Be-

Charles V, king of France.

The only known contemporary portrait of Joan of Arc.

Road building in rural France (*ca.* 1448).

cause, in addition to Burgundy the Duke had acquired Flanders and other provinces of the Low Countries, he was the most powerful prince in France, and his defection proved disastrous. It was during this period of civil war that Henry V of England made his rapid conquests and forced Charles VI to recognize Henry's son as heir of the French crown.

The Defeat of England

Charles VII (r. 1422–61) faced an almost hopeless situation when his father died. He had been officially disinherited, and the English and their Burgundian allies held the largest and richest part of France. Charles had very little military strength, and he was not using what he did have very effectively. It was at this moment, in 1429, that the peasant girl from the eastern frontier, Joan of Arc, appeared at court and announced that heavenly voices had ordered her to drive the English out of the country. Joan succeeded in shaking Charles out of his lethargy and in talking him into the counteroffensive that turned the tide of the war. Her capture and execution by the English scarcely checked the resurgence of the king, for Charles soon had another stroke of good fortune. England under Henry VI was as torn by factional strife as France had been under Charles VI, and in the

competition for control of the royal government the leader of one faction offended the Duke of Burgundy. The duke returned to the French cause in 1435, greatly weakening the English and facilitating Charles's recovery of northern France.

Joan of Arc rekindled the ancient view that the French kingdom was holy and deserved unswerving support from the people despite the generations of misgovernment. She proclaimed that "to make war on the holy kingdom of France was to make war on the Lord Jesus," and this belief was shared by people of all classes. Thus, in spite of the civil war, the treason, and the treachery, there was at least the beginning of national feeling among the French people. In all the confusion and disorder of the early fifteenth century the French clung to two basic beliefs: faith in the French monarchy and faith in the Christian religion. When the two beliefs were united as they were in Joan of Arc, they were irresistible. Joan foreshadowed that union of religion and monarchy on which the absolutist states of the early modern period were to be built.

The Restoration of Royal Power

France suffered more severely than England during the Hundred Years' War, since all the fighting took place on French soil. Wide areas were devastated by raiding armies, whose campaigns were purposely destructive. During periods of peace, troops of unemployed mercenaries terrorized the country, plundering to keep up the support they had earlier gotten from their employers. But precisely because the French suffered so much more than the English, royal power was restored more rapidly and more completely in France than in England. A king who showed any promise of putting an end to disorder could override most limitations on his power to levy taxes. Charles V began the work of freeing the monarchy from these restraints, and Charles VII finished the job. As

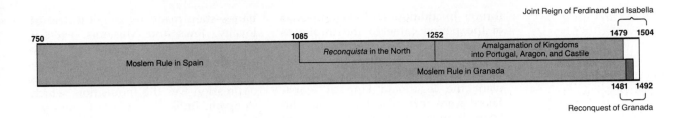

soon as he had the English on the run he began to levy taxes at will, without asking consent from the Estates. His task was made easier by the fact that provincial feeling was so strong in France that a central parliamentary assembly was seldom called, and when it was called it had little authority. The real power lay with the provincial and regional assemblies, with the local Estates of Normandy or of Languedoc rather than with the Estates General. And it was relatively easy for Charles to overcome the fragmented opposition of these local assemblies.

The same overwhelming interest in provincial affairs kept the great French nobles from entrenching themselves in the central government, which remained the preserve of the king and his bureaucrats. Thus, in the long run the Hundred Years' War reinforced tendencies that had been apparent in France prior to the end of the thirteenth century—tendencies toward a bureaucratic state in which the king was strong and all other political forces were weak and divided. This French pattern became the model for the rest of Europe during the early modern period.

SPAIN

Spain was not unified under a single monarchy until the late Middle Ages. Starting in the eleventh century, the kingdoms of Aragon, Leon, and Castile had reconquered the peninsula from the Moors, whose caliphate, centered on Cordoba, had broken into several independent states. By the fifteenth century, Moorish power had been reduced to the little kingdom of Granada, and most military action in Spain was between Spaniards.

Like the rest of western Europe, Spain was racked by civil wars in the late Middle Ages. The competition between the principal kingdoms, Castile and Aragon, was exacerbated by the lack of any fixed rule of succession in either kingdom, so there was often a claim made by internal and external opponents of whoever sat on the

The Reconquest of Spain

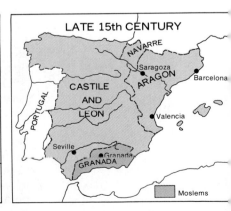

throne. In addition, far too many kings of the period came to the throne as minors, which led to quarrels over the regency at best and attempts by other members of the royal family to supplant the legitimate king at worst. There were few peaceful reigns, and Spanish kings had almost no opportunities to play a role in European politics. At the lowest point, Castile became a pawn in the Anglo-French conflict. Pedro I (r. 1350–69) was opposed by his illegitimate half-brother, Henry of Trastamara. The English supported Pedro, while the French supported Henry, and when the French won a battle in 1366, Henry mounted the throne. Then the tide of war between France and England shifted again and in 1367, Pedro was back in power. He and his English allies were defeated again in 1369, and he was killed in battle. Henry ruled until his death in 1379, but he was constantly challenged by the kings of Aragon, Navarre, Portugal, and Granada, which, although Moslem, played an active role in the politics of the peninsula.

Aragon had a little less trouble because it had created a small empire that provided for the younger sons of the royal house. They could be given the kingdom of Majorca (the Balearic Islands) or Sicily (and eventually Naples) in Italy. Nevertheless, the disorder in Spain continued until John II of Aragon married his son Ferdinand (r. 1479–1516) to Isabella, the heiress of Castile (r. 1474–1504). The union of the two crowns (1479) did not mean that the institutions of the kingdoms were merged, but it did bring a large increase in security for the people of Spain.

On the whole, the Catholic Kings (as Ferdinand and Isabella were called) followed the French model; each province was allowed to keep its old customs, but was administered by officials of the central government. Moreover, the Catholic Kings did not bear that name in vain; in a society of mixed ethnic population—Moors, Jews, and Chris-

tians—they made religion the test of loyalty. Jews and Moslems, even if converted, were suspected of secretly adhering to their old faiths and driven into exile. The instrument of religious oppression was the Inquisition, which in Spain, unlike elsewhere in Europe, was a tool of the monarchy. Hence, the Spanish Inquisition earned a reputation for harsh methods and penalties and for using the charge of heresy or backsliding to achieve the political aims of its masters. Ferdinand and Isabella's religious policy led to the expulsion of the Jews from Spain in 1492, the same year that they finally conquered the kingdom of Granada and forced its population to convert.

In the long run, the kings' religious-political program was harmful, for the Jews and Moslems represented a large segment of skilled labor and they dominated trade, but the loss was not immediately apparent. By 1500 Spain was the strongest kingdom in Europe. It could support the exploration and conquest of the New World, under the aegis of Isabella and the Castilians, while Ferdinand acted as the arbiter of European politics. Even faroff England found it advisable to ally itself with Ferdinand.

GERMANY

The political history of the rest of western Europe during the later Middle Ages resembled that of France and England. Everywhere there were rebellions, civil wars, and attempts to conquer neighboring territories. But all this furor produced surprisingly little change. The political map of Europe in 1450 looked very like the map of 1300, and the basic characteristics of most of the governments were similarly unchanged.

In Germany, however, there were some developments that deserve attention. First, during the fifteenth century the dukes of Burgundy gradually gained control over all the provinces of the Low Countries, roughly the equiv-

Germany in the Fourteenth Century

alent of modern Belgium and the Netherlands. This was one of the most urbanized and richest parts of Europe, and the union of the Low Countries with the house of Burgundy separated their fate from that of the rest of Germany. Gradually, they achieved an independent national identity. At the same time the wealth of the region made it the object of a long series of wars that began in the fifteenth century and continued almost to our own day.

Second, during the fourteenth century the peasants and townsmen of Switzerland gradually gained their in-

dependence from the Habsburg family that had ruled this part of Germany, with Austria, for many generations. In organizing themselves to defeat the Habsburgs, the Swiss, like the English earlier, developed a well-disciplined infantry that could stand against the cavalry troops that were the elite of the medieval army. The Swiss infantry formations were armed with long pikes that could beat off a cavalry charge. By the fifteenth century companies of Swiss infantry were being hired by French kings and Italian princes, including the pope. The Swiss were also

A fifteenth-century Swiss halberd.

demonstrating the possibility of republican government to a Europe that had had little confidence in this system. Up to then, the principal examples of republics had been the faction-ridden Italian cities, which were then losing their independence to tyrants, and the German towns, which had been unable to form a permanent confederation and remained weak and isolated, although for a while the Hanseatic League (a union of North German towns) controlled trade in the Baltic. But the Swiss Confederation, loosely knit though it was, endured. Each district, or canton, had its own institutions, and no canton was under a feudal lord. The towns were ruled by the wealthier burgesses, but the peasant cantons, where the movement for independence had begun, were almost pure democracies.

The third important development in Germany was the rise of a new power center on the middle Danube as a result of the peculiar electoral habits of the German princes. By the fourteenth century the number of princes taking part in imperial elections had been reduced to seven. These great men feared giving the title to any powerful prince, so for some time they regularly chose as Holy Roman emperors counts with small holdings. Though the title gave no real power, it did confer enough social prestige to enable these men to marry well-endowed heiresses. Thus the Habsburgs, petty princes in West Germany who had served briefly as emperors around 1300, managed to acquire the duchy of Austria and nearby counties. A little later, the Count of Luxembourg, an equally undistinguished prince, became emperor and arranged a marriage through which his son received the kingdom of Bohemia. Later Luxembourg emperors acquired Silesia and eventually Hungary. When the last male of the Luxembourg line died in 1438, his nearest heir was the Habsburg Duke of Austria. The union of the two holdings marked the beginning of the vast Habsburg empire, for five centuries one of the great powers of Europe.

ART, LITERATURE, AND SCIENCE

During the late Middle Ages, art, literature, science, and technology experienced the same uneven development as political institutions. In all the arts and intellectual fields, there was a contradictory production of masses of imitative and second-rate work and of some brilliant and historically important works. Overall, the period is exceptionally important in the history of the arts and literature, so long as one does not weigh the good against the bad.

Art

After the thirteenth century, gothic architecture became imitative and overly ornate, and very few churches of the fourteenth and fifteenth centuries command our respect as works of art. One late medieval style is for good reason called Flamboyant, its examples covered with ornate decoration. But in England architects developed a perpendicular gothic style that emphasized height and soaring lines in the structure and windows. The chapel of King's College, Cambridge, is an excellent example of such buildings.

In contrast to the uneven quality of architecture, manuscript illumination reached new heights during the fifteenth century. The rich court of Burgundy supported supremely talented artists who executed elaborate programs of book illumination that are among the most ambitious and beautiful ever accomplished. Many of these manuscripts were books of hours, extremely popular collections of readings from the official service-books of the Church that were used as personal prayer books by the laity. In the wealthy noble households, artists created gems of calligraphy and art, and many of the books, treasured heirlooms, have survived in whole or part. The artists of these books introduced a new realism that played an important role in the history of painting. They produced detailed and realistic renderings of everyday life that for historians remain an important source of information.

The Black Death had a profound effect on painting and sculpture as artists produced renderings of macabre scenes associated with the plague. Skeletons and corpses were accurately depicted on funeral monuments and in representations of the Dance of Death, a favorite subject. The artists of the fourteenth century also produced the first real portraits painted in western Europe and the first attempts to give landscapes more than a conventional shape. As with the book illuminators, the best group of artists were supported by the dukes of Burgundy. The Flemish school of painting, which developed in the late fourteenth and early fifteenth centuries, was a worthy rival of the Italians of the early Renaissance. The artists of the Flemish school did the first painting in oils, the medium that has dominated painting right up to the present day. The best-known Flemish painters, such as the van Eyck brothers, van der Weyden, and Memling, combined meticulous attention to detail with genuine religious feeling. And there is nothing in Italy that quite equals the Flemish portraits of this period, such as Jan van Eyck's picture of the Arnolfinis, or his *Leal Souvenir*.

Literature

In literature there were the same contradictions as in the visual arts. Narrative poems, the old genre derived from the romances of the twelfth century, became fantastic stories (such as those parodied by Cervantes in *Don Quixote*), and the lyrics became society verse. Yet, there were significant advances—deeper psychological insights in describing human behavior and a notable improvement in the writing of prose. It is much harder to write acceptable prose (especially on technical subjects) than passable poetry, and it was only in the later Middle Ages that European

Jan van Eyck, *Giovanni Arnolfini and His Bride* (1434).

writers reached a high literary level in prose. For example, when Nicolas Oresme, a French scholar and bishop, translated Aristotle's *Politics*, he had to invent or redefine many words, and in doing so he greatly enriched the French language. However, many scholars of the period produced overrefined arguments that only interested a few narrow specialists.

The medieval authors most read today all wrote in the fourteenth and fifteenth centuries. The best-known example is Geoffrey Chaucer (*ca.* 1340–1400), who began as a translator and adapter of French works and developed into one of England's greatest poets. His most famous work, the Prologue to the *Canterbury Tales*, reveals his skill in describing individual characters and his wit in depicting human foibles. His people range from the "perfect, gentle Knight" and the poor parson, who taught Christ's lore, "but first he followed it himself," through the earthy Wife of Bath, who had buried five husbands, to scoundrels like the Miller and the Summoner. Perhaps he had met such characters while working in the royal customs service in the port of London, but it was his genius that translated such experience

A fifteenth-century representation of Chaucer from the Ellesmere manuscript of the *Canterbury Tales*.

into literary masterpieces like the *Tales* and *Troilus and Criseyde*. Chaucer saw through pretense and sham, but he maintained an affection for the world and its human characters, and he rose quickly in society under the patronage of John of Gaunt, uncle of King Richard II.

François Villon (1431–?1463) was less fortunate. He confessed himself a friend of the thieves and prostitutes of Paris and was convicted of crime himself. In his poetry he showed how close French society was to breaking down under the strains of war in the first half of the fifteenth century. His poems are in the old forms, but they do not describe courtly society. Rather, they depict life in the taverns and thieves' dens. Yet, Villon also expressed bitterness over his wasted life and portrayed the hopes and fears of the poor and the outcast—the simple piety of an old woman, the last thoughts of men condemned to hang. The tendency toward realism—a literature that presented the real world rather than a world of fantasy—already evident in Chaucer, became still stronger in Villon.

As the Church lost its almost exclusive hold over religious life, laymen sought ways to supplement the conventional observances of the liturgy. After 1300, numerous devotional works were written for laymen. Writers produced innumerable meditations, visions, and moral tracts; the books of hours mentioned earlier were part of this outpouring. Some of the finest religious writings of any period were composed at this time, especially the *Imitation of Christ*, ascribed to Thomas à Kempis. In England, there was *The Vision of Piers Plowman* by William Langland, one of the first important works written in English after the long eclipse following the Norman Conquest. Little is known of Langland, except that he lived in the middle of the fourteenth century and came from peasant stock. The English of *Piers Plowman* is archaic, but it is English, not, as Anglo-Saxon was, an early German language.

Piers Plowman illustrates the widespread desire to transform religion into a strong social force. The poet criticizes every class for its worldliness and selfishness; only by a return to the pure principles of the Gospel can the world be saved. There was nothing anti-Catholic in Langland's work, but it did bear testimony to the continuing inability of the ecclesiastical authorities to satisfy adequately the aspirations of ordinary laymen.

Science

The scientific scholarship of the fourteenth and fifteenth centuries is little known, and historians have usually disparaged it as unoriginal and unimportant. Nonetheless, there were writers of originality, and not all that was written was useless. Columbus based most of his ideas about geography on books written in the fourteenth and early fifteenth centuries. In philosophy, there was a sharp attack on the system of Thomas Aquinas that freed scholars, to some extent, from their adherence to the Aristotelian ideas that had been incorporated into Thomas's theology. This new-found freedom from Aristotle permitted wider speculation on scientific questions, particularly on explanations of motion. The questions through which Galileo revolutionized the science of physics in the sixteenth century had already been raised by fourteenth-century scholars. For example, mathematicians at Oxford came very close to a correct solution of the problem of acceleration; and the French scholar Nicolas Oresme, so important in the development of the French language, was also interested in physics. He was willing to discuss the possibility that the earth rotated.

More important than any specific achievement was the very fact that interest in scientific problems persisted throughout the period. Up to the end of the Middle Ages, western scholars, relying largely on the work of the Greeks and Moslems, had made no outstanding contributions to scientific knowledge. But they were remarkably persistent and eventually began to strike out on their own. From the twelfth century, there were always some scholars in the West who were interested in science, just when the Moslem world, under the influence of al-Ghazzali (see p. 228), was abandoning scientific work. The consistent interest of the westerners led eventually to the great discoveries of the early modern period. Early modern astronomers like Copernicus and Galileo were trained in universities that used the methods and books of the later Middle Ages.

No one has given a completely satisfactory explanation of this continuity of interest in science. However, some possibilities can be put forth. Western civilization was the product of an amalgam of Roman, Judeo-Christian, Celtic, Germanic, and other elements, and no unified principle or idea of authority ever formed in it. Thus, a philosopher of Thomas Aquinas's stature might have become an unchallenged authority in China, but in the West, his system was subjected to critical appraisal almost immediately. Western society recognized different points of view, and its literature as well as its politics showed that. In literature, the great works turned on conflicts of values and ways of life. For example, Wolfram von Eschenbach's *Parzival* (early thirteenth century) contrasted the courtly with the divine and the Christian with the pagan, managing to put non-Christian values in a good light even while showing the superiority of Christian ones. Likewise, in politics, the perennial struggle between ecclesiastical and secular authority divided the European consciousness and permitted Europeans to think of political order from more than one point of view. Such mentalities were essential for scientific research, which rests on the willingness to think about the world in new and unorthodox ways. Comfortable with oppositions, Europeans nonetheless worked hard to resolve them by focusing their attention on the details.

The problems of constitutional law they discovered while seeking an answer to the Great Schism were eventually resolved by small changes in the way they viewed the relationship between pope and council, and the problems they saw in science received similar treatment. Medieval scientific thinkers worked on the details, the observations and explanations of small things, with a faith that such investigations eventually would produce results. In the end, they did, in the hands of Copernicus, Galileo, Kepler, and their successors.

Technology

The question about why the West persisted in the study of science can also be asked about technological development. Why did Europe become the center of technological innovation,

Women preparing pasta in the fourteenth century. The making of noodles was brought to the West from China.

An early gun, lighter and more portable than the first cannon. The gun was placed on a forked stand and was braced against the ground by its long tail (illustration from a German manuscript, *ca.* 1405).

introduction of guns helped to centralize power in the royal governments and a few great lords, such as the Duke of Burgundy.

The development of firearms caused a rapid growth in other branches of technology. Early gun barrels were extremely unreliable, but steel makers were soon producing improved versions based on new metallurgical techniques. To produce truly round barrels that could deliver the full effect of the charge on target, makers had to develop better tools and more precise measuring instruments. The increased demand for metals led to an expansion of mining and smelting, with consequent technological development in those fields. In the early Middle Ages, most ores were taken from surface deposits, but the growth of demand in the later Middle Ages led to the opening of deeper mines that required new techniques. The miners of Germany, Bohemia, and Austria learned to sink their shafts deeper and to pump ground water out of their mines. The increased use of metals and improvements in mining transformed European industry. Inventions like the cylinder pump, developed to drain mines, could be used in other industries and led to related inventions for other functions. The cylinder pump stood near the beginning of the technological development that led eventually to the steam engine.

The invention of printing in the fifteenth century (see p. 458) also owed much to developments in metallurgy. The essential element in printing was the use of movable type, and good type in turn depended on the availability of a metal that would take the exact shape of the mold into which it was poured. Thanks to their knowledge of metallurgy, the Germans succeeded in creating an alloy that expanded as it cooled, so that it fitted the mold exactly. Type faces molded from this alloy produced sharp, clear impressions.

Another technical advance of western Europe in the later Middle Ages was in oceanic shipping. Here develop-

while other civilizations did not pursue and develop what they discovered? The Europeans were consistently innovative in technology, seizing on inventions such as the stirrup, the horseshoe, and paper that came from the East and adding such implements as the horse collar and mechanical clock. Here again the contrast with China is instructive. For example, the Chinese were probably the first to develop gunpowder, and they had cannon about as early as the Europeans. But Chinese guns were never very efficient, and the Chinese never created an army based on firearms. Europeans carried experiments on cannon much further than the Chinese did and, although the first European guns were not very good— as apt to kill the men who fired them as those at whom they were aimed—they had become fairly reliable by the end of the fifteenth century.

The introduction of firearms had a significant effect on the European political order. Cannon made castles untenable—the Turks took Constantinople, formerly impregnable, by using European cannon against it—and reduced the power of the nobility, which had relied on the castle as the basis of its military power. Further, firearms were expensive, and only kings could afford to equip troops with them. Thus, the

ment came as the result of patient experimentation rather than sudden discovery. By the end of the thirteenth century the sailors of western countries had ships that could tack against the wind and were seaworthy enough to survive the storms of the Atlantic. The navigators of the period could find their latitude, though not their longitude, by star and sun sights; they knew that the earth was round and that the distance to the rich countries of the East was not impossibly great. Very little more was needed for the great voyages of discovery except practice, and during the fourteenth and fifteenth centuries daring men were mastering the art of oceanic navigation. French and Spanish seamen had reached the Canary Islands at least by the early fourteenth century, and by 1400 the Portuguese had pushed down to the bend in the African coast, claiming Madeira and the Cape Verde Islands for the king of Portugal.

These voyages illustrate the point that was made earlier: Europeans were no more skillful or intelligent than other peoples; they were simply more persistent and aggressive. During the same period in which the Europeans were venturing out into the Atlantic, the Chinese were sending expeditions into the Indian Ocean. There they found rich countries and profitable sources of trade. In contrast, the Europeans discovered only barren islands and the fever-stricken coast of Africa. Yet the Chinese abandoned their explorations because they, or at least their rulers, were satisfied with what they had at home. The Europeans persisted, though it was almost two centuries before they reached the thriving trading centers of the Orient or the treasures of the New World.

Not as impressive as the early voyages, but almost as significant, was the invention of the mechanical clock. The first clocks, developed in the fourteenth century, were not very accurate, but they were soon improved by the discovery of the principle of escapement—the system by which the train

Early mechanical clockworks (*ca.* 1500). The first clocks had only one movable hand.

of gears moves only a precise distance before it is checked and then released to move the same distance again. In the long run, these crude devices modified the whole outlook of the western peoples. Precise measurement became a central concern of Europeans, and for centuries it was this that most differentiated them from others. Western civilization has come to be dominated by the clock and the timetable, and westerners have had little sympathy with people who have managed to escape this domination. The peculiarly western concern for precise measurement was a sign of westerners' uniquely rational attitude toward nature and social life. The technological and scientific advances of the late Middle Ages stemmed from a desire to master, rather than merely accommodate to, nature, and the mechanization of the world picture, as one historian has called it, affected westerners' approach to political and social institutions as well as to the explanation of natural phenomena.

Suggestions for Further Reading

Economy and Society

On the economic depression of the fourteenth century, see the works cited in Chapters 10 and 12, particularly, the *Cambridge Economic History*. See also M. M. Postan, *The Medieval Economy and Society* (1972), on the economic condition of peasants before the plague. On the bubonic plague, see P. Ziegler, *The Black Death* (1969), and R. S. Gottfried, *The Black Death* (1983). *The Black Death: A Chronicle of the Plague*, ed. J. Nohl, trans. C. H. Clarke (1924), contains a collection of contemporary sources. C. Cipolla, *Cristofano and the Plague* (1973), gives a graphic picture of a community's response to the plague, although he is studying a later epidemic. For a study of the effects of the plague, see *The Black Death: The Impact of the Fourteenth-Century Plague* (1983), which contains the papers given at a conference at SUNY Binghamton; B. H. Putnam, *The Enforcement of the Statutes of Labourers during the First Decade after the Black Death 1349–1359* (1908); and on the effects in one locale, J. A. Raftis, "Changes in an English Village after the Black Death," *Mediaeval Studies* 29 (1967). For a sampling of the views on the effects of the plague, see W. Bowsky, ed., *The Black Death* (1971). For a general interpretation of the social unrest in the late Middle Ages, see R. H. Hilton, *Bondmen Made Free* (1973). *Social Unrest in the Late Middle Ages*, ed. F. X. Newman (1986), and *The English Rising of 1381*, ed. R. H. Hilton and T. H. Aston (1984), contain essays on the popular movements.

The Avignon Papacy

See the work of A. C. Flick cited in Chapter 12. On the Avignon period, see G. Mollat, *The Avignon Papacy* (1963), and Y. Renouard, *the Avignon Papacy* (1970). On the Great Schism and the conciliar movement, see W. Ullmann, *Origins of the Great Schism* (1948); B. Tierney, *Foundations of the Conciliar Theory* (1955); E. F. Jacob, *Essays in the Conciliar Epoch*, 3rd ed. (1963).

England

For late medieval England, see M. McKisack, *The Fourteenth Century* (1959), and E. F. Jacob, *The Fifteenth Century* (1961). There are excellent histories of individual reigns: J. L. Kirby, *Henry IV of England* (1970); R. A. Griffiths, *The Reign of Henry VI* (1981); and S. B. Chrimes, *Henry VII* (1972). On the history of Parliament, see P. Spufford, *Origins of the English Parliament* (1967), and R. G. Davies and J. H. Denton, eds., *The English Parliament in the Middle Ages* (1981). On justices of the peace, see B. H. Putnam, *Proceedings before Justices of the Peace* (1938).

France

On later medieval France, see P. S. Lewis, *Later Medieval France: The Polity* (1967). R. Vaughan, *Philip the Bold* (1962), *John the Fearless* (1966), *Philip the Good* (1970), and *Charles the Bold* (1973), give a history of the rise of Burgundian power. On Burgundy at its height, see J. F. Kirk, *Charles the Bold, Duke of Burgundy*, 3 vols. (1864–68), which treats the man in relation to his times. On the culture of the Burgundian court, see O. Cartellieri, *The Court of Burgundy* (1929), and P. Calmette, *The Golden Age of Burgundy* (1962).

The Hundred Years' War

E. Perroy, *The Hundred Years' War* (1951), is the best short history. H. Lucas, *The Low Countries and the Hundred Years' War (1929)*; K. Fowler, ed., *The Hundred Years' War* (1971); H. J. Hewitt, *The Organization of War under Edward III* (1966); and J. B. Henneman, *Royal Taxation in Fourteenth Century France, 1322–1356* (1971). J. Keegan, *The Face of Battle* (1976), provides a brilliant description of the battle of Agincourt (1415). On Joan of Arc, see L. Fabre, *Joan of Arc*, trans. G. Hopkins (1954), which is a fine biography that presents a fascinating picture of France in the later period of the Hundred Years' War. See also the documents of the trial of Joan translated in *Jeanne d'Arc*, ed. T. D. Murray (1920). G. Pernoud, *Joan of Arc by Herself and Her Witnesses*, trans. E. Hyams (1966), presents a broad picture of Joan's mission and effect.

Spain and Germany

On late medieval Spain, see R. Altimira, *A History of Spain* (1949), and H. J. Chaytor, *A History of Aragon* (1933). R. I. Burns has studied the process of reconquest in *The Crusader Kingdom of Valencia: Reconstruction on a Thirteenth-Century Frontier* (1967), *Islam under the Crusaders: Colonial Survival in the Thirteenth-Century Kingdom of Valencia* (1973), and *Medieval Colonialism: Postcrusade Exploitation of Islamic Valencia* (1975). On late medieval Germany, see G. Barraclough, *The Origins of Modern Germany* (1947), J. Lenschner, *Germany in the Later Middle Ages* (1980); and C. Bayley, *The Formation of the German College of Electors* (1949).

Art, Literature, and Science

On late medieval art, see J. Evans, *English Art 1307–1461* (1949); E. Panofsky, *Early Netherlandish Painting* (1953); L. Baldass, *Jan van Eyck* (1952); M. Meiss, *French Painting in the Time of Jean de Berry*, 2 vols. (1967–68), *Painting in Florence and Siena after the Black Death* (1951), and *The Limbourgs and their Contemporaries* (1974). J. Harthan, *The Book of Hours* (1977), is a history and commentary on the art of the books and contains many color plates. For a history of vernacular culture, see A. W. Ward and A. R. Waller, *The Cambridge History of English Literature*, Vol. 1 (1907). On Chaucer, see D. W. Robertson, *A Preface to Chaucer: Studies in Medieval Perspective* (1962). See also the works cited in Chapter 11. On late medieval science, see the works cited in Chapter 11. On the clock and other mechanical devices, see J. Gimpel, *The Medieval Machine* (1976). For the technology of firearms and sailing, see C. Cipolla, *Guns, Sails and Empires* (1965).

15
South and East Asia, ca. A.D. 600–1600

*D*uring the millenium considered in this chapter, the civilizations of South and East Asia continued to develop in their own distinctive ways. Even the two momentous events that transformed much of Eurasia during this period, the spread of Islam and the creation of the world's largest empire by the Mongols, affected India and China very differently. Meanwhile, the history of Southeast Asia continued to reflect—but not to mirror—that of India while in Northeast Asia Japan fashioned its own culture and institutions under the stimulus of Chinese civilization.

INDIA

After the Guptas, India was divided into a number of states of varying duration and geographical extent. In studying this complex period, it is useful to distinguish North India from South India, even though some states for a time bridged this gap and even though major differences existed *within* each area.

In South India power tended to be focused in two major centers. One was the Western Deccan where the rugged terrain of Maharashtra produced tough fighters. There the Chalyukas of

Opposite: Colossal statue of the Trimurti (Brahma, Vishnu, and Shiva) from a cave temple in western India (eighth century).

414

Shiva as Lord of the Dance (Chola period, twelfth or thirteenth century).

Temple pavillion at Ellora, hewn from natural rock (eighth century).

Badani (their capital), beginning with Pulakeshin I (r. 535–66), developed an empire which reached its largest extent under Pulakeshin II (610–42). After this emperor was killed in battle, the Chalyukas were overthrown by the Rashatrakutas who seized Badani in 752. Their empire was even larger than that of the Chalyukas, but their most permanent monument is to be found at their capital of Ellora where they sponsored one of the world's greatest temples.

The second southern power center was in the Tamil-speaking area of the Coromandel Coast region. Here first the Pallavas (roughly 250–910, with their highpoint around 600) and then their Chola successors (844–1279, highpoint eleventh century) built their states. One reason for taking special note of these two states is their influential role in Southeast Asian history. The Tamil area over which they ruled was a major source for the diffusion of Indian culture to the region. The Cholas, moreover, were able to launch several naval expeditions to Sri Lanka (Ceylon), and in 1020 they even concluded a successful maritime campaign against the Sumatran-Malay state of Shrivijaya.

The southern states, particularly that of the Cholas, were among the most extensive and long lasting of the Indian states during this period. Although they differed in structure, they were similar in being centered on the sacral authority of the king who was identified with Indra and other deities. Consecrated in most solemn enthronement ceremonies, the king commanded the reverent submission due

to the protector of the world. One Cholas institution that provided an important ritual and ideological link between the center and outlying regions was special villages on the plains governed by *brahman* assemblies but also including residents of other castes. The *brahman* priests were linked to the center of authority by their religion while at the same time they provided religious services to the peasant castes with whom they formed close ties.

This relationship between the *brahman* and the peasantry was facilitated by the growth of devotionalism that had already appeared earlier in Hinduism. This movement, particularly in the South but by no means limited to that region, incorporated local deities into the Hindu pantheon and formed a religion basically congenial to settled cultivators. This faith inspired fervent hymns dedicated to Shiva and Vishnu performed in song and dance in Tamil temples. Their main themes were love for God and the personal inadequacy of the devotee. These hymns helped to fire the vitality of Hinduism and to undermine the appeal of Buddhism and other rival faiths.

Hinduism was also strengthened on the philosophical level, most notably by Shankara (*ca.* 788–820), India's most famous philosopher whose basic teaching was an absolute monism. Although a Southerner, Shankara wrote in Sanskrit and traveled widely in India, including the North, debating challengers, founding schools and generally spreading his ideas.

Political fragmentation was characteristic of the North as well as the South. Here too, particularly from the eleventh century, a king exercized only a general overlordship over local warriors outside the area controlled directly by the throne. In a system somewhat similar to Western feudalism, the obligations of these warriors included financial payments, the use of the king's currency, military service, and attendance at the king's court as well as recognition of the king's sacral authority. A local warrior might also be obliged to offer his daughter to the king in marriage. Among the most notable northern rulers were the Rajputs ("Sons of Kings") probably at least partly of central Asian descent but fiercely dedicated to the values associated with India's warrior (*kshatriya*) tradition. The Rajputs were able to stem the tide of Arab Islamic expansion in the eighth century. They and other Hindu rulers in North India maintained their independence until the establishment of the Delhi Sultanate.

The Moslem Invasions and the Delhi Sultanate

The first substantial and lasting Moslem presence in India came early in the eighth century when Arabs annexed Sind, the Indus delta region separated from the rest of India by desert. They incorporated their conquests into the Umayyad Empire and soon recognized Hindus as *dhimmis* (protected people, second-class subjects liable for special taxes, see p. 422). The Arabs were prevented from further expansion primar-

The Rajput Code

A widow speaks to the page who witnessed her husband's death.

"Boy, tell me, ere I go, how bore himself my lord?"

"As a reaper of the harvest of battle. I followed his steps as a humble gleaner of his sword. On the bed of honor he spread a carpet of the slain, whereon, a barbarian his pillow, he sleeps ringed by his foes."

"Yet once again, boy, tell me how my lord bore himself?"

"Oh mother, who can tell his deeds? He left no foe to dread or to admire him."

She smiled farewell to the boy, and adding, "My lord will chide my delay," sprang into the flames.

As quoted in H. G. Rawlinson, *India: A Short Cultural History* (New York: Appleton-Century, 1938), p. 202.

The Moslem Conquest of India   1192–1320

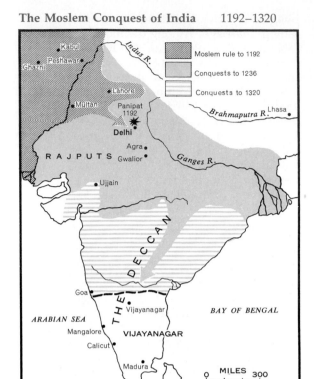

sisted of an essentially egalitarian community of believers. The interaction between Islam and Hinduism, often marred by misunderstandings, tension, and conflict, was to become a major theme in the history of the subcontinent.

By the eleventh century the region to India's northwest was under the control of warlike Turkic peoples who penetrated deeply into India on their raids from their base in modern Afghanistan. The most bloody and destructive of the raiding expeditions were those repeatedly conducted by Mahmud of Ghazni (971–1030) who used the wealth looted from India to turn his own capital in eastern Afghanistan into a major center of Islamic culture.

For several centuries Turko-Afghan invaders were content to return to their home territory beyond the passes carrying their loot with them. But in the last quarter of the twelfth century a new group of Turko-Afghans appeared and in 1206 founded the Delhi Sultanate, which was to last for 320 years. The victory of Islam was accompanied by the wholesale destruction of Buddhist temples and centers of learning. Moslems had long resented Buddhism, which, like Islam, was a proseletyzing religion. Buddhism had already suffered a severe blow in 751 when Islamic forces inflicted a severe defeat on a Chinese army on the Talas River near Samarkand, thereby hastening the end of the period when Buddhism flourished along the central Asia trade routes. Now the Turko-Afghans effectively destroyed a Buddhism already weakened by Hindu opposition and competition. The result was that the faith virtually disappeared in India until 1956 when a substantial number of Untouchables converted to Buddhism.

The Delhi Sultanate was founded by a Turkish slave-general, a Mamluk of the type prominent also in Egypt during this same period. The Mamluk dynasty (1206–90) was the first of five dynasties to rule in Delhi during the

ily by the Gujara-Pariharas (*ca.* 750–1027) who created an empire rivalling that of the Rashatrakutas in the south. However, Arab expansionism was only a minor episode in the broad sweep of Indian history. As ever the main threat came from the northwest.

As we have seen, tough Hunna invaders from central Asia put an end to the Gupta Empire. Such incursions of warlike people from the northwest remained a major theme in Indian history, but with the coming of Islam a new element was added. Now the warrior peoples were imbued with a fierce sense of holy mission; they brought into India a world view which in many essential respects clashed with the native Hindu tradition. The Moslem faith in one God, one prophet, and one book contrasted with the complexity and tolerance of Hinduism, and there was a wide gulf between the hierarchical Hindu view of society and the Islamic belief that the ideal social order con-

ca. 711	1206	1625	1857
Moslem Incursions and Indian Division	Delhi Sultanate	Mughal Empire	

Sultanate. At this time, Turks, many of them slaves, and other foreigners filled key positions in the military and political establishments. In 1221, Chengis (Genghis) Khan, the great conqueror, led a Mongol expedition to the banks of the Indus but then withdrew from India. However, the Sultanate maintained a large army ready in case the Mongols returned. Military leaders were compensated for their service by grants of income from tax-exempt lands.

The Sultanate's decision to maintain a large army was only one of the ways the Mongols influenced the history of the subcontinent. Another was that, being cut off from central Asia, the rulers in Delhi necessarily concentrated their energies on India. A different effect of the Mongol conquests was that the destruction of urban centers in central Asia and Iran brought to India numerous refugee scholars, artists, and religious teachers who carried with them much of the high culture of their homelands. Notably, this included Persian as the prime literary language, which became the language of India's Moslem elite. But Persian influence was not confined to literature; it was apparent in architecture, textile design, and generally in court life and ceremonial.

After the Mongol threat receded, the Sultanate's armies were occupied first in plundering expeditions and then in subduing much of the rest of India. The regime reached the height of its power under the second and third dynasties, the Khajli (1290–1320) and the Tughluq (1320–1414) achieving its greatest territorial extent under the second Tughluq sultan, Muhammad (r. 1325–51) when most of India (except for Kashmir, the lower Indus Valley, and parts of the Rajput area) temporarily accepted Delhi's overlordship.

Tree of Life and Knowledge (southern India, Vijyanagar period, 1336–1546).

However, the Sultanate had overextended itself and lacked the means to consolidate its conquests into a functioning empire. Nor did it have the power to compel the allegiance of distant tribute-paying vassals. Thus in 1336 the Hindu kingdom of Vijyanagar was founded, a state which remained the major southern power for two centuries. Elsewhere, Moslem leaders also declared their independence. One of these proclaimed himself Sultan of the Deccan (South India) in 1347 and founded the Bahmini Dynasty, Vijyanagar's rival. It should be noted, however, that even though Vijyanagar appealed to Hinduism for its ideology, it regularly employed Moslems in its armies just as Moslem states did not hesitate to employ Hindus.

A low point in the Sultanate's fortunes came in 1398 when Timur (Tamerlane) invaded India and sacked Delhi—the same Timur who checked the advance of the Ottoman Turks in the West. Under the fourth dynasty, the Sayyid (1414–51), Delhi remained weak, unable to prevent various regional rulers from establishing their own sultanates even in North India. The Sayyid dynasty was replaced by the Afghan Lodi (1451–1526), but it remained for a new group of foreign conquerors to match and surpass the earlier achievements of the Sultanate.

During the Sultanate period, Islam was firmly established in the Indian subcontinent although the majority of Indians remained Hindu. The main agency for the spread of Islam was not the sultanate and its military and civilian organs; nor was it the *ulama*, that is, "the class of state-supported judges, theologians, and preachers who were collectively responsible for upholding Islamic orthodoxy" in India as elsewhere in the Moslem world. Instead, the prime spreaders of Islam were Sufis, mystics not employed by the state. These men of religion belonged to various orders and varied widely in their methods and personalities: "Some of them wielded swords, others the pen, others a royal land grant, and still others a begging bowl. Some were introverted to the point of reclusive withdrawal, others extroverted to the point of militancy. Some were orthodox to the point of zealous puritanism, others unorthodox to the point of heresy"[*] This quotation, taken from a study of the Sufis in a single Indian state, suggests the adaptability and variety of Islam's holy men but also the dangers of overgeneralization.

Many people came to Islam through peaceful conversion, not holy war; naturally many of the converts came from among those lowest in the Hindu social hierarchy. There was also a trend for Hindu devotionalism and Islamic mysticism to converge, as in the teachings of Kabir (1440–1518), a Moslem weaver, who asked, "If God be within the mosque, then to whom does this world belong?" He won many followers; his verses, written in the vernacular, drew on both Persian and Sanskrit vocabulary to express themes derived from both traditions. Another syncretist was Nanak (1469–1538), the founder of Sikhism, who was born a Hindu but rejected caste and taught devotion to God. Under a succession of gurus (teachers) the Sikhs, spurred on by Mughal intolerance, later developed into a militant community in Nanak's home area, the Punjab (in the northern Indus Valley).

The Mughals

The Mughal empire was founded by Babur (1483–1530), but it was his grandson Akbar (1657–1707) who secured its future and constructed its institutional foundations. Babur and Akbar were Iranicized Turko-Mongols and as such continued certain policies of the Delhi Sultanate including the furtherance of Persian culture. Akbar

---

Moslem and Hindu in the Fourteenth Century

Ala-ud-Din [sultan of Delhi, 1296–1316] was a king who had no acquaintance with learning and never associated with the learned. He considered that policy and government were one thing and law another. "I am an unlettered man," he said, "but I have seen a great deal. Be assured that the Hindus will never become submissive and obedient until they are reduced to poverty. I have therefore given orders that just enough shall be left them of grain, milk, and curds from year to year, but that they must not accumulate hoards and property."

From the Moslem historian Barani, as quoted in H. G. Rawlinson, *India: A Short Cultural History* (New York: Appleton-Century, 1938), p. 228.

---

[*]Richard M. Eaton, *Sufis of Bijapur 1300–1700* (Princeton: Princeton Univ. Press, 1978), p. 283.

was unusual in marrying Rajput princesses—most of the Mughal emperors had Iranian consorts, including the lady buried in the world's most beautiful and perhaps most lavish mausoleum, the Taj Mahal. (Although designed by two Persian architects, this mid-seventeenth century building represents a blend of Persian and Indian elements.) Akbar's marriage policy was just one example of his general inclination toward religious tolerance and toward seeking to reconcile those he could not subdue by military force. The orthodoxy of his religious views has long been argued back and forth, but his sense of divine mission is apparent in his characterization of a king as "a light emanating from God, a ray from the world-illuminating sun." His good will toward Hindus was expressed not only in his own religious attitude but more concretely in his abolition of the tax levied on non-Moslems, and he further placated Hindus by forbidding the slaughter of cows.

Akbar divided the empire into provinces, and his government was conducted by *mansabdars*. These officials were holders of a *mansab*, a military rank defined in terms of the number of troops its holder was obliged to supply. The *mansabdars* were supported by *jagirs*, assignments to collect revenue for the government as well as their salaries and expenses from designated lands. These lands were frequently scattered, subject to reassignment, and not hereditary. One reason for the Mughal success was that the emperors granted *jagirs* to, and thereby made allies of, a diverse elite including Rajputs and Afghans, Turkish and Iranian immigrants, South Indian Moslems, and prominent Hindus as well as Moslems from conquered regional states. The system was designed to prevent *mansabdars* from turning into local power-holders, but it was hard on the people who actually worked the land because the holder of a *jagir* had no incentive to further develop land he would soon lose. His interest was not in the well-being of the peasantry but

The Mughal Empire 1605

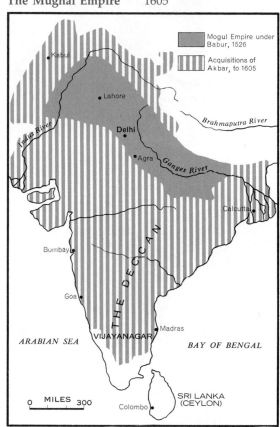

A Portrait of Akbar by His Son

My father always associated with the learned of every creed and religion: especially the Pundits and the learned of India, and, although he was illiterate, so much became clear to him through constant intercourse with them, that no one knew him to be illiterate. . . . In his august personal appearance he was of middle height, but inclining to be tall; he was of the hue of wheat; his eyes and eyebrows were black and his complexion rather dark than fair; he was lion-bodied with a broad chest, and his hands and arms long. On the left side of his nose he had a fleshy mold, very agreeable in appearance, of the size of half a pea. . . .His august voice was very loud and in speaking and explaining had a peculiar richness.

Memoirs of Jahangir, trans. Rogers and Beveridge (London, 1909–14), pp. 33–34 as quoted in H. G. Rawlinson, *India: A Short Cultural History* (London: The Cresset Press, revised ed. 1952), pp. 317–18.

Akbar inspecting building
operations of Fathpur Sikri
(illumination from the Akbar-
nama manuscript, *ca.* 1590).

autonomy. For example, when the Portuguese became the dominant sea-power along India's western coast, the merchants of Gujarat in northwest India dealt with the Europeans quite independently of their sultan who remained unconcerned as long as his own prerogatives were not involved.

The Mughal empire reached its greatest geographical extent under Aurangzeb (1657–1707), a controversial ruler known for his strict adherence to Islam. His reimposition of the tax on nonbelievers was just one of the measures resented by Hindus. However, more serious than religious resentments was the developing crisis in the state's political economy. Most damaging was a growth in the number of *mansabdars* far in excess of the availability of *jagirs* with which to reward them. Pressures on the peasantry increased and there was rural unrest, but the discontent of the elite proved most dangerous to the regime. The succession after Aurangzeb of weak, uninspiring men to the throne and a general decline in administrative efficiency also placed strains on the loyalty of the empire's servants, undermining Mughal military power at a time when it was increasingly challenged by Marathas from India's west and by Afghans and Iranians from beyond the passes. In 1739 Nadir Shah (r. 1736–47), who ruled Iran, became the last foreign conquerer to enter India, devastate the North, and sack Delhi. Although after that, a titular emperor remained in Delhi, actual power was in the hands of local potentates.

In 1765 one of these local rulers granted the British East Indian Company the right to collect revenue in his domains, and eventually the British became the heirs to the Mughal empire. Up to this time, Europeans accepted and worked within the Mughal system. Although they had earlier gained control of the seas and thereby influenced India's trade and economy and although individual Europeans helped to introduce new methods of warfare into India, they had remained

in garnering the maximum revenue in the shortest possible time.

A substantial minority of townspeople were Moslem, but the great majority of peasants were Hindus as were the revenue collectors. Aside from paying their taxes, the villagers had little contact with the state; kinship and village groups remained dominant in their lives. Even in the cities the state rarely interfered directly in people's lives, and various communities and groups enjoyed a substantial degree of

The Taj Mahal (seventeenth century).

largely peripheral to the mainstream of the subcontinent's history.

SOUTHEAST ASIA

Much of the diffusion of Indian culture described earlier (see Chapter 6) took place during the period we are concerned with in this chapter. Other major events, such as the decline of Kampuchea and changes affecting the states of interior Java, were largely determined by internal developments. But Southeast Asia was also affected by Mongol expansionism and by the spread of Islam.

Although Mongol ambitions extended to Southeast Asia and Khublai Khan attempted to force Southeast Asian states into submission, the Mongols did not establish themselves in the area. The giant armada which Khublai sent against Java where his troops landed in 1293 and the armies which he dispatched into what is modern Vietnam, where Hanoi was occupied three times, affected the local balance of power but do not appear to have drastically altered the course of history. Further west, the Mongols, after mastering the techniques of elephant warfare, defeated and conquered Pagan (1287). Yet their efforts to control Burma failed, and old patterns of mutual dependence as well as conflict between the Burmese monarchs and the Buddhist monastic community contin-

Europeans Arrive in Malacca

After a while there came a ship of the Franks from Goa trading to Malaka; and the Franks perceived how prosperous and well populated the port was. The people of Malaka for their part came crowding to see what the Franks looked like; and they were all astonished and said, "These are white Bengalis!" Around each Frank there would be a crowd of Malays, some of them twisting his beard, some of them fingering his head, some taking off his hat, some grasping his hand. . . .

From *Sejarah Melayu or Malay Annuals*, trans. by C.C. Brown (New York: Oxford Univ. Press, 1970), p. 151.

Seated court lady, sculpture of the Tang period (618–906).

ued to dominate Burmese history. The more immediate aftermath of the Mongol irruption was to leave Burma divided. This along with the collapse of Angkor, the other great mainland empire, opened the way for the creation of numerous small states and the emergence to new prominence of Thai rulers, although their states remained fragile since they were held together only by the personal relationship between king and elite.

In contrast to the fleeting impact of the Mongols, Islam became a permanent force in the Malay Peninsula and maritime Southeast Asia. The first Moslems in the area were doubtlessly traders, and the religion generally spread along the trade routes. Its fortunes were greatly increased by the growth of Malacca whose ruler is said to have been converted to Islam in 1414. Malacca, which commands the straits of the same name, became a great center of trade linking Sumatra, Java, and most of the other islands of modern Indonesia to far off China, India, and ports of the Red Sea. The city participated in a giant international commercial network whose other major center was Gujarat, birthplace of many of the Moslem missionaries who came to Southeast Asia. Islam served as a link between Malacca and small states along the coasts of Sumatra and Java as well as ports in India and points

west. It is worth noting that legends from Java, unlike those from Malaya, suggest a gradual process of conversion to Islam. Generally the diffusion of Islam was a gradual, uneven process which continued for many centuries and still continues today.

In this connection it is well to bear in mind the great vitality and powers of expansion exhibited by Islam during the fifteenth century which saw the fall of Constantinople, at the other end of Asia, in 1453. The rise of Europe to global supremacy came later. But the vanguard of European expansionism, the Portuguese, did arrive in Southeast Asia at the beginning of the sixteenth century. They seized Malacca in 1511 but were unable to maintain its commercial prominence. Instead the trade was dispersed to the benefit of, among others, the sultanates of Johor at the tip of the Malay Peninsula and of Aceh on Sumatra. The first Dutch expedition reached the East Indies in 1596; a precursor to a much more ambitious effort than that mounted by the Portuguese, it initiated a new age in the history of the islands which became modern Indonesia.

THE COSMOPOLITAN CIVILIZATION OF CHINA

The Tang Dynasty (618–907)

China was reunified in 589 by the Sui dynasty which laid the foundations on which the Tang (T'ang) built one of China's most illustrious dynasties. Under the Tang, Chinese power once again extended to the Pamirs, and the influence of Chinese culture profoundly affected distant Japan. Within China, the South was more fully integrated into the society because the rich ricelands of the lower Yangzte River were now linked to the capital in the North by the Grand Canal built by the Sui.

The central government was organized into six ministries: Personnel, Revenue, Rites, War, Justice, and Public Works. These ministries reflected

Stone relief of a horse and groom from the tomb of a Tang emperor.

the range of government concerns and were to be retained by subsequent regimes into the twentieth century. Staffing the government were officials of aristocratic background, for most officials entered the civil service through family connections even though a government examination system was initiated by the Sui and continued by the Tang. Indeed, the Tang was the last great age for the hereditary high aristocracy.

The magnificence of the Tang was well expressed in its capital, Changan (Ch'ang-an, modern Xian or Sian). Encompassing about 30 square miles, it was the largest planned city ever built anywhere. Its roughly one million inhabitants also made it the most populous city in the world in its day; another million people lived in the area

outside its walls. In accord with tradition, Changan was oriented so that both the city and the imperial palace faced south. Leading up to the palace and the government complex was an avenue 500 feet wide, well designed to impress envoys from lesser lands with the might and grandeur of the Chinese empire. The people of the city lived in rectangular wards, each a self-contained unit surrounded by walls, with entry provided through a gate that was closed each night.

Tang culture was doubly cosmopolitan: first, in the sense that China was open to cultural influences from India and the distant west; second, in the sense that China itself was the cultural model for the other settled societies of East Asia. Both aspects were reflected in the numerous foreigners to be found

Tang guardian lion of marble and polychrome (*ca.* 618–906).

in Changan. Some were students, including some 8,000 Koreans said to have been in Changan in 640. Other foreigners were engaged in commerce, coming from such distant lands as India, Iran, Syria, and Arabia. At Changan's West Market exotic foods and beverages were on sale, and one could watch performances of foreign acrobats, magicians, and actors. Stylish Tang ladies sported foreign coiffures, while painters and potters had a good time rendering the outlandish features of the "barbarians" from distant lands.

An example of Chinese calligraphy. This stone rubbing was made from an inscription in the Regular Style by Ouyang Xun, a scholar and calligrapher of the Tang period.

樂佳動氣侍流
涼徐淒微嶸
嶸尤
體有金蒸景至
安風無爵炎之

It was characteristic of the robust and cosmopolitan spirit of the age that one of the favorite pastimes of its aristocratic ladies and gentlemen was polo, a game that originated in Persia. The participation of women in such athletic activities is worth emphasis in light of the very different ethos that was to prevail later.

Changan was a religious as well as political center. Manichean, Nestorian, and Zoroastrian temples testified to Tang tolerance, but their congregations were largely foreign. The opposite was true of the many Daoist and even more numerous Buddhist establishments. This was the golden age of Buddhism in China. Just as its pagodas dominated the capital's skyline, the Buddhist faith predominated on the intellectual and spiritual horizon.

In the countryside Buddhist temples performed important economic functions by operating mills and oil presses, maintaining vaults for safe-deposits, and performing other banking services including pawnbroking. The temples also held much land, and they profited from their connections with wealthy patrons who sought to evade taxation by registering land under a temple name. Some temples provided medical care; others entertainment. Architecture flourished, and Chinese Buddhist sculpture reached a classical highpoint. At their very best, Tang sculptures blend Indian delight in the corporality of mass with a Chinese sense of essentially linear rhythm.

The Tang was also the classic age of Chinese poetry, producing a number of excellent poets including the two who came to be admired as China's very best, Li Bo (Li Po, 701–63) and Du Fu (Tu Fu, 712–70). Li Bo was a free spirit who preferred to compose verse in a free style of his own rhythmic and verbal patterns. One of his favorite themes was wine, and there is even a story, most likely spurious, that on a nocturnal drinking expedition on a lake he fell into the water while trying to fish out the moon and died by drowning. Du Fu, in contrast, was particularly effec-

tive in a style of verse governed by elaborate rules of tone and rhythm as well as verbal parallelism. He wrote on many themes but is most admired for his social conscience and compassion. Some of his most moving poems describe the suffering and hardships of ordinary people. He could be biting in his political and social commentary:

> Inside the red gates wine and meat
>   go bad;
> On the roads are bones of men who
>   died of cold.*

These lines are from a long poem Du Fu wrote shortly before the dynasty was shaken and almost destroyed by the rebellion of An Lushan, a general stationed in the Northeast. The rebellion began in 755, only four years after the defeat of a Tang army on the banks of the Talas River opened Central Asia to Islam, and it lasted until 763. Although the dynasty rallied after the defeat of An Lushan and made some important reforms, the general tendency was for regional military governors to assert their independence. Secular culture continued to flourish, but Emperor Wuzong,(Wu-tsung 840–46), beset by financial problems, was unable to resist the temptation posed by the wealth of the Buddhist establishment. In the resulting persecution, monastic lands and wealth were confiscated, monks and nuns returned to lay life, and Buddhist economic power was broken. The government did not concern itself with questions of belief, and the anti-Buddhist policy was promptly reversed by Wuzong's successor, but great damage had been done.

During its last 50 years the dynasty was beset by factionalism and the

*Quoted in A. R. Davis, *Tu Fu* (New York: Twain, 1971), p. 46.

growth of eunuch power at court, mistrust between officials in the capital and those in the field, mismanagement, corruption, and incompetence. Bandit gangs, refuges of the desperately poor and dislocated, increased in number, size, and ambition. Forming themselves into confederations, they progressed from raiding to rebellion. Power, whether bandit or "legitimate," went to the strong and ruthless. Even though the dynasty made occasional gains, each rally was followed by further decline. In the end, Changan was ruined. The city, which the first Han emperor had made his capital over a thousand years earlier, was never again to be China's seat of power.

The Song Dynasty (960–1279)

China was reunited by the Song (Sung). This dynasty did not match the Tang in military power or geographic extent. Indeed, after 1127 North China

The Song and Jin Empires   Twelfth Century

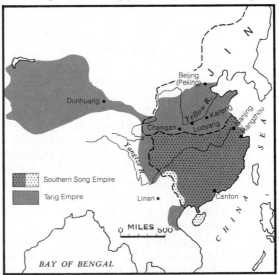

Detail from *Clearing Autumn Skies over Mountains and Valleys*, Song landscape scroll attributed to Guo Xi (Kuo Hsi, *ca.* 1020–90).

was lost to the alien Jurchen Jin (Chin) state but continued in the south as the Southern Song. However, what makes the Song of crucial importance is the emergence of some of the basic features of late imperial China. Major developments included the formation of new elites in place of the old hereditary aristocracy, dramatic economic growth, and the creation of a new intellectual synthesis.

The turbulence that accompanied the decline and fall of the Tang destroyed the old aristocratic families and opened the way for new men who based their prestige on literary learning, their power and status on office holding, and their wealth on land ownership. Although these attributes did not necessarily overlap, when all three were present they reinforced each other: wealth enabled a family to educate one or more sons; education was the key to office; and office provided opportunities for the acquisition and retention of wealth.

After the loss of the North in the twelfth century, the tendency was for elite families to concentrate on strengthening their local roots by assuming leadership in local matters and forming marriage ties with similar fam-

ilies. These families then served as intermediaries between their communities and the state. To distinguish the new elite from the old, scholars have termed them the "gentry" and further distinguished between the local gentry and the office-holding upper gentry.

The preferred path to office was through the civil service examinations. These were open to all men, excluding only a small minority such as the sons of criminals and the like, but, even though printing reduced the price of books, most candidates came from families of some means or status. Structurally the system provided for an orderly progression through a series of written tests (three in the Song, more later). These began at the local level, included an examination in the capital, and culminated in a palace examination held under the emperor's personal auspices. The government went to great lengths to secure impartiality; papers were identified by number and copied by clerks before being submitted to the readers who were thereby prevented from recognizing the author of a paper through his calligraphy. For centuries the battle of wits between would-be cheaters and the authorities was pursued with great ingenuity on both

sides. Despite occasional scandals, the system enjoyed a deserved reputation for honesty.

In the absence of the old aristocratic counterweight, the throne gained in power, but Song officials were by no means faceless bureaucrats. They had their own moral code and political views. Bureaucratic politics, however, tended toward factionalism. Factions could consist of men who agreed on policy matters, but they were likely to be formed around personal relationships and temporary alliances. The ultimate power of decision rested with the emperors who usually ruled by manipulating rather than intimidating their officials. The most outstanding political figure of the Song was not an emperor, but Wang Anshi (Wang An-shih, 1021–86), an official whose vision of integrating state and society remains controversial. Many of his measures dealt with fiscal and economic matters. He intended to help the small farmer, for instance, by establishing a program of state farm loans. Other reforms dealt with military and personnel problems.

Detail of a handscroll showing scenes of daily life in the Southern Song dynasty (thirteenth century).

Porcelain winepot of the Song dynasty.

fited the South. Yields were increased by the use of improved tools, advances in water control, wider application of fertilizers, and the introduction of new strains of rice, most notably an early ripening variety native to central Vietnam. In the southeast it became common for a rice paddy to produce two crops a year, either two harvests of rice or one of rice followed by a crop of wheat or beans.

With increased production commerce flourished. Large ocean-going ships were built to carry several hundred passengers. They navigated with the aid of the compass, were steered by an axial rudder, protected by watertight bulkheads, and armed with small rockets. After the loss of the North, the government derived considerable revenue from foreign trade encouraged by maintaining harbors and canals, building breakwaters, erecting beacons, operating warehouses, and even setting up hotels. One item of export encouraged by the government was ceramics, and the discovery of Song shards not only throughout South and Southeast Asia but also in the Middle East and along the east coast of Africa attests to the wide popularity of the Song product.

Cities flourished; foremost among them was Hangzhou (Hangchow), the capital after the fall of the North. Its merchants, organized in guilds, offered their customers all kinds of products ranging from the staples of life to exotic perfumes and fine jewelry. Like the earlier Song capital in the North and unlike Changan of the Tang, Hangzhou grew haphazardly and featured all the attractions of a lively and thriving center of culture and entertainment, as well as the grimmer aspects of urban life—fire and crime. Hangzhou seems to have merited the praise it received from the cosmopolitan Venetian Marco Polo. Even though he saw the city late in the thirteenth century when it was no longer the capital, he described it as, "without doubt the finest and most splendid city in the world."

Some of his measures involved an increased use of money and thus represented a response to broader economic trends. However, his program ran into strong opposition, and Wang lost office seven years after he had initiated the reforms.

The increased use of money, including the first appearance of paper money, was but one aspect of impressive economic growth. This included progress in paper making, book production, ceramics, tea processing, shipbuilding, and a spectacular advance in the production of coal and iron. Coal and iron were mined in North China in an arc from southern Hebei (Hopei) to northern Jiangsu (Kiangsu). Iron was also carbonized to make steel for weapons, drilling bits for digging wells, and chains for supporting suspension bridges.

Because coal and iron were found in the north, production declined drastically when North China was lost to the Jin, but advances in agriculture bene-

581	618		906		1127	1234	1368		1644

Sui Dynasty | Tang Dynasty | Disunity | Song Dynasty | Jin Empire | Mongol Empire | Ming Dynasty

960   1279

Song intellectual and artistic life was varied and lively. This was, for instance, the classic age of landscape painting. Most influential was a revival of Confucianism that took many forms. It inspired reformers like Wang Anshi, led to a revival of classical scholarship, and stimulated new achievements in historical studies and philosophical thought. The new Confucianism was at once a creed that gave meaning to the life of the individual, an ideology supporting state and society, and a philosophy that provided a convincing framework for understanding the world. This constellation of values and ideas, called Neo-Confucianism in the West, was an organic system in which each aspect reinforced the others. It is called Neo-Confucianism to distinguish it from earlier forms of Confucianism, but its formulators and practitioners thought of themselves simply as Confucians. More than that, they believed that they had retrieved the true meaning of the tradition, lost since Mencius. The most influential Neo-Confucian was Zhu Xi (Chu Hsi, 1130–1200) and his most influential writings were his commentaries on the *Four Books: The Analects, The Mencius* plus *The Great Learning* and *The Doctrine of the Mean*, two chapters of the *Record of Rites* singled out by Zhu Xi.

Although influenced by Daoism and Buddhism, the Neo-Confucians rejected the two rival doctrines as fundamentally anti-social and immoral in

First portion of the oldest printed book, *The Diamond Sutra* (868). It was printed on a scroll from wooden blocks. This page shows Buddha teaching.

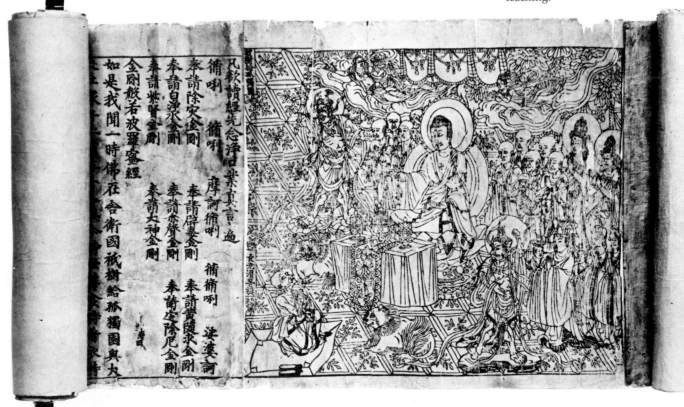

The Neo-Confucian Creed

Heaven is my father and Earth is my mother, and even such a small creature as I find an intimate place in their midst.

Therefore that which fills the universe I regard as my body and that which directs the universe I consider as my nature.

All people are my brothers and sisters, and all things are my companions.

Opening lines of "The Western Inscription" by Zhang Zsai (1020–77) from *A Source Book in Chinese Philosophy*, trans. and compiled by Wing-tsit Chan (Princeton, N.J.: Princeton Univ. Press, 1963), p. 497.

advocating withdrawal from society and seeking purely personal (and therefore selfish) salvation. To Confucians social values were real and compelling. Associated with Song Neo-Confucians was an emphasis on moral seriousness and a moralism that made heavy demands on men and women. At the same time, the old concept of *ren (jen,* humaneness) received new emphasis.

The tone of Song civilization was profoundly civilian, but for many years it sustained itself against external threats by maintaining a large well-equipped, if not always effective, army. The Song also entered into treaties with neighboring states that sometimes entailed payments and furthered its own interests by playing these states off against each other. After it lost the North, it survived in the South protected in part by its naval supremacy and the difficulty northern cavalry had in operating in the south with its paddies and waterways. Even after the Mongols conquered North China in 1234, the Song held out another 45 years before succumbing to the formidable world conquerors.

The Mongol Yuan Dynasty (1279–1368)

Even before Khublai Khan (r. 1260–94) completed the conquest of China, he

transferred his capital from Mongolia to Beijing (Peking), adopted the Chinese name "Yuan" for his state, and also instituted Chinese court ceremonial. Thus he was careful to give at least an appearance of ruling in the Chinese manner. But his ambitions were not limited to China; we already noted his expeditions to Southeast Asia and to these must be added naval expeditions to Japan. To the west, he maintained control of Mongolia but was forced to give up any ambition to control central Asia. As a result, the Yuan was essentially a Mongol regime in China, not the Chinese part of a wider Mongol empire.

To prevent dependence on Chinese officials, the Mongols made a point of employing foreigners, mostly central Asians although the most famous is Marco Polo. The Mongols accorded highest status to Mongols. Next came Mongol allies including central Asians and men from Southwest Asia, such as Turks, Persians, and Syrians. The third status group included inhabitants of North China, the native Chinese or descendants of other groups such as the Jurchen. At the bottom were the southerners who had resisted the Mongols longest and continued to be regarded with suspicion. This fourfold division of society was expressed in the recruitment and appointment of officials, in the conduct of legal cases, and in taxation.

The Yuan generally accorded military officials preference over civilians, and the provinces had a great deal of autonomy. Since the Mongols were slow to reinstitute the examination system and to patronize scholarly learning, men who in other periods would have become scholars turned to other occupations such as medicine, fortune-telling, and the theater. It is no accident that this was the classic age of Chinese drama. Painting also flourished; the idea that a painting reveals the character of the man who created it was already found in the Song, but it was prevalent under the Yuan and inspired work in a great variety of styles. It is worth noting that even though

China was once again open to foreign influences and hospitable to travelers from afar, this had no appreciable impact on the world of the scholar-painter nor was there any awareness, let alone appreciation, of the art of the Chinese literati to be found in the writings of Marco Polo and his successors. Although there was a Catholic archbishop in Beijing and relations across the great Eurasian land mass were often cordial, these relations had a low priority on both sides of the world, for the distances were enormous and both Europe and China faced more immediate challenges and opportunities closer to home.

The Ming Dynasty (1368–1644)

The declining years of the Yuan saw the emergence of regional power centers and popular rebellion. One leader of rebellion, Zhu Yuanzhang (Chu Yuan-chang, r. 1368–98), emerged victorious and founded the Ming dynasty. He was a harsh and vigorous autocrat who personally decided all significant matters and even some not so significant. During the later days of the Ming, too, the effectiveness as well as tone of government was to a large degree determined by the character of the emperors and their devotion to the work of government. Ming government thus ranged from the energetic efficiency of the first two emperors to the laxity of some of the Late Ming rulers, one of whom did not hold an audience for over 25 years.

Meanwhile the local gentry presided over local society that continued to move to its own rhythms. Prominent gentry lineages maintained cohesion by compiling lineage geneologies, maintaining ancestral halls and graveyards, conducting ceremonial sacrifices to lineage ancestors, and maintaining general guides for the conduct of lineage members as well as formal lineage rules. A penalty for severe infractions of these rules was expulsion.

The Ming was generally a period of economic growth and considerable prosperity. It was also capable of

The Complaints of the Ming Founding Emperor

In the morning I punish a few; by evening others commit the same crimes. I punish these in the evening and by the next morning again there are violations. Although the corpses of the first have not been removed, already others follow in their path. The harsher the punishment, the more the violations. Day and night I cannot rest. This is a situation which cannot be helped. If I enact lenient punishments, these persons will engage in still more evil practices. Then how could the people outside the government lead peaceful lives?

What a difficult situation this is! If I punish these persons, I am regarded as a tyrant. If I am lenient toward them, the law becomes ineffective, order deteriorates, and people deem me an incapable ruler. All these opinions can be discerned in the various records and memorials. To be a ruler is indeed difficult.

Proclamation of the Hong Wu Emperor from Patricia B. Ebery, *Chinese Civilization and Society: A Sourcebook* (New York: The Free Press, 1981), p. 125.

strong military assertiveness; from 1405 to 1433 seven great maritime expeditions, commanded by a Moslem eunuch, were launched to Southeast Asia but also reached the Indian Ocean, Arabia, and the east coast of Africa.

The Ming Empire   Fourteenth to Seventeenth Centuries

These expeditions illustrate Chinese strength in the fifteenth century, but, an economic drain, they were discontinued leaving it to the Europeans to take the lead in world navigation and discovery.

Printing, which had been invented in the Late Tang and spread during the Song, continued to expand in the Ming and with it there was an increase in literacy. Bookshops did a brisk business; among their best sellers were collections of model examination papers used by candidates to cram for their

Porcelain jar of the Ming period showing ladies playing a game of *weiqi* (*go* in Japanese).

tests. But they also sold encyclopedias, colored prints, novels, and collections of short stories. There were also guides explaining the classics in simple language and books of moral instruction. Most prized by those who love Chinese literature are the Ming novels. Despite their literary excellence, they did not win respectability until the twentieth century. In traditional China reading a novel was a surreptitious pleasure, something students did when their teacher was not looking—or vice versa.

This period also made notable contributions to drama, painting, and ceramics, and Neo-Confucian thought also flourished. Wang Yangming (1472–1529) stands second only to Zhu Xi in influence and importance. He insisted on the importance of inwardness and is also famed for his doctrine of the unity of knowledge and action. For Wang, knowing and acting are not only inseparable, they are two dimensions of a single process.

The Late Ming was an exciting time intellectually and artistically, but it was also a period of political decay that took a heavy toll in government efficiency and finally led to its collapse. It was brought down by popular uprisings, but the real heirs of the dynasty were not Chinese rebels but Manchu leaders in the area northeast of China who were in the process of constructing a state in the Chinese manner. They established China's last dynasty, the Qing (Ch'ing, 1644–1911) which sought and won legitimization by ruling in a Chinese manner and continuing many Ming institutions while preserving special privileges for the Manchu elite.

Both the Ming and the Qing were much more concerned with China's Inner Asian frontiers, home of the Mongol and other nomadic invaders, than they were with European maritime expansionism. Indeed, it was under the Qing that China reached its greatest territorial extent. As elsewhere, the first Europeans to arrive in Chinese waters were the Portuguese whom the Chinese kept at arms length since they could not drive them off. In 1557 they were allowed to use Macao in return for an annual payment. Of more interest to the Chinese court and officials were Jesuit missionaries who brought with them European science and technology as well as religion. By demonstrating the superiority of their astronomical predictions, they managed to displace Moslem and Chinese experts and established themselves in the Bureau of Astronomy, an important and prestigious office. The Jesuits even made some notable converts and were not seriously affected by the change of dynasties. However, they were there on Chinese terms, and the mission petered out in the middle of the eighteenth century when an impasse developed between the Qing emperor and the pope.

JAPAN

A major theme in Japanese history is the interplay between native and imported elements. In Japan's early history, culminating in the Nara Period (710–84) Chinese influence was enormous. Nara itself, Japan's first capital, was a miniature Changan; the court and political structure were modeled on those of China; writing, Buddhism, and Confucian moral values were among the Chinese imports. Yet Japan never became just a smaller China. Here geography helped, for, while close enough to the continent to receive its influences, Japan was far enough away not to be dominated by it. Other factors, too, made for the integrity of Japanese culture including a language completely different from and unrelated to Chinese, a strong native animistic religion (Shinto), and a very special aesthetic tradition. Furthermore, even during the Nara period, the Japanese state and society had their own character.

One difference between Japan and China was the role of the emperor. The Japanese emperor, unlike his Chinese counterpart, had an irrevocable sacred mandate based on divine descent. Thus, the Mencian idea that the mandate could be lost was disregarded. Political change in Japan took the form, not of deposing the emperor, but of controlling him; after the Nara period the emperor retained his religious aura and his powers of legitimization without any real political authority. In somewhat similar fashion, descent remained a major source of status in Japan.

The Nara period was followed by the Heian period (794–1185) when the capital was established in Kyoto and many Chinese imports were modified or discarded. Now, although Chinese remained the official written language, Japanese was written without depending solely on Chinese characters to render Japanese sounds. Instead, linguistic elements without Chinese equivalents were written in a syllabary (*kana*) with Chinese characters retained for nouns and the stems of words and adjectives to avoid confusion between homonyms. Art and architecture also departed from the international Tang style of the Nara period and became more Japanese in their concern with the texture of natural materials, especially wood, and a general penchant for asymmetry. There was also a certain asymmetry in the political system as, behind the facade of imperial institutions, power came to rest in the hands of those (primarily the Fujiwara family) who held extensive rights in private, tax-exempt estates free from government interference.

This period was famed for its aristocratic culture when noble gentlemen and ladies devoted their lives to beauty and love. One product of this culture was the world's first major psychological novel, *The Tale of Genji*, written by Lady Murasaki. Prince Genji had perfect taste, wrote a beautiful hand, was exquisitely graceful, and ever sensitive to the beauty and sadness of nature's changing moods as he was responsive to the delicate emotions of his many ladies. What he lacked were the martial virtues of the warrior.

The Silver Pavillion at Kyoto combining both Japanese and Chinese elements.

The Kamakura (1185–1333) and Ashikaga (1336–1573) Shogunates

During the Kamakura period the warrior class emerged and gradually occupied center stage. While there had earlier been a provincial warrior aristocracy, these men had been willing to serve civilian masters until the Heian system broke down and warriors were called in to the capital to help settle a political dispute. After some years of turmoil, there emerged a peculiarly Japanese institution: the shogunate. The shogun derived his military power from the loyalty of vassals in an essentially feudal system but received his title and legitimacy from the emperor. In theory he was the emperor's supreme military commander, but in practice he controlled the emperor.

The first shogunate got its name from Kamakura, a village in eastern Japan far away from the imperial court in Kyoto. The choice to keep warriors away from the charms of the imperial capital was a deliberate attempt to preserve the values of the warrior: valor, manly pride, vigor, and undying loyalty. Yet such loyalty had to be rewarded. This was easily accomplished when the shogunate was fighting recalcitrant Japanese, but there were no spoils when Mongol attacks were defeated in 1271 and 1284 and this was followed by the need to maintain a force for many years in anticipation of a third Mongol attack which never came.

The Kamakura shogunate was followed by that of the Ashikaga family who established themselves in Kyoto. In many respects but particularly in culture the ensuing period represented a fusion of aristocratic and samurai traditions. There was a great cultural flowering, for this was the age of the Nō drama, of tea masters and Zen aesthetics, of excellent pottery, of the classic Japanese garden, and of fine architecture drawing on Song as well as on native Japanese forms. However, politically the Ashikaga period degenerated into a century of warfare (1467–1573) followed by a shorter period (1573–1600) of unification and ended with the establishment of the last and strongest shogunate.

The Tokugawa Shogunate (1600–1868)

Under the Tokugawa the shogunate was once more separated from the imperial court in Kyoto. The shogun's capital was Edo, modern Tokyo. There the shogunate's officials kept a close watch over regional lords who were burdened with new obligations—including an obligation to spend alternate years in Edo and leave wives and children behind as hostages when they did go back to their domains. Yet within these domains the local lords were free to pursue their own administrative and economic policies.

A number of Tokugawa policies were meant to ensure a stable future. Thus there was a freezing of class lines

with a clear line drawn between samurai and commoners. The most visible sign of samurai privilege was the exclusive right to wear a sword, yet in a time of peace his duties were largely civilian. Accordingly, the samurai were sent to school to attain at least a degree of Chinese learning, and the shogunate patronized Neo-Confucianism as a philosophy appropriate for the new age.

Intent on stability, the Tokugawa shogunate was not about to tolerate interference from abroad. Originally Portuguese ships and Jesuit missionaries had been warmly received in Japan, but this changed as Japanese leaders became aware not only of the dangers of European expansionism as exemplified by the Spanish seizure of the Philippines but also of the subversive potential of foreign influence. In 1606 Christianity was declared illegal, and in 1614 there was a serious campaign to expel missionaries. Many of the 300,000 Japanese Christians suffered grievously under Tokugawa persecution. In 1637–38 a rebellion in Shimabara, near Nagasaki, was fought under Christian slogans against a lord who combined merciless taxation with cruel religious suppression. Furthermore, trade as well as Christianity was seen as potentially subversive since it would benefit the coastal lords. Consequently, the Tokugawa prohibited not only the foreign religion but expelled all foreigners from the country and only allowed the Dutch to send an annual vessel to a tiny artificial island in Nagasaki harbor. Moreover, Japanese were prohibited from traveling abroad.

In the very long run, of course, the Tokugawa shogunate did not achieve the stability envisioned by its architects. They, no more than anyone else, could stop change. Indeed, their very success in ensuring peace and tranquility led to unprecedented economic growth. Cities such as Edo and Osaka grew and developed their own distinct urban culture. An increased use of money and a new economy baffled the samurai and undermined the social and political order. By the middle of

Interior of a house in Yoshiwara during the Tokugawa period (eighteenth-century woodcut print).

nineteenth century, many felt that Japan was ripe for a change.

However, in the seventeenth century it would have taken superhuman clairvoyance for a statesman in Japan, China, or India to realize that European civilization represented anything but a minor problem. In all three countries, leaders could look back on traditions that had withstood the test of time and contemplate the future with confidence. Little could they know that the future was to bring radically new challenges.

Suggestions for Further Reading

General

For a comparative perspective see E. L. Farmer et al., *Comparative History of Civilizations in Asia*, 2 vols. (1977), also W. H. McNeill, *The Rise of the West* (1963). Also see the general works suggested for Chapter 6.

India

A major advanced analytical study is B. Stein, *Peasant, State, and Society in Medieval South India* (1980). Two highly regarded books deal with Islam in India: Aziz Ahmad, *Studies in Islamic Culture in the Indian Environment* (1964), and Sheikh Mohamad Ikram, *Muslim Civilization in India* (1964). A more specialized study is R. M. Eaton, *Sufis of Bijapur 1300–1700: Social Roles of Sufis in Medieval India* (1978). P. Spear, "The Mughul Mansabdari System," in E. Leach and S. N. Mukherjee, *Elites in South Asia* (1970), is a concise account of that complicated system. M. N. Pearson, *Merchants and Rulers in Gujarat: The Response to the Portuguese in the Sixteenth Century* (1976), offers important insights into India under the Mughuls.

Southeast Asia

D. G. E. Hall, *A History of South-East Asia* (4th ed. 1981), is authoritative. C. Geertz, *Negara: The Theatre State in Nineteenth Century Bali* (1980), is helpful in thinking about earlier Indianized states of Southeast Asia. R. Winstedt, *The Malays: A Cultural History* (1950), is a standard treatment. *Sejarah Melayu 'Malay Annals'* (1970), trans. C. C. Brown is sometimes tedi-ous but also includes passages of great charm. D. K. Wyatt, *Thailand: A Short History* (1984), is definitive and M. Aung-Thwin, *Pagan: The Origins of Modern Burma* (1985), is "must" reading for students of mainland Southeast Asia. M. C. Ricklefs, *A History of Modern Indonesia c. 1300 to the Present* (1981), is a solid account.

China

The Cambridge History of China, Vol. 3, *Sui and T'ang China, 589–906* (1979), ed. Denis Twitchett, is a major work. Also recommended are A. F. Wright, *The Sui Dynasty* (1978); Wright and Twitchett, *Perspectives on the T'ang* (1973); E. O. Reischauer, *Ennin's Travels in T'ang China* (1955); and A. Cooper, *Li Po and Tu Fu* (1973). Good books on the Song include James T. C. Liu, *Reform in Sung China: Wang An-shih (1021–1086) and His New Policies* (1959); J. W. Chaffee, *The Thorny Gates of Learning in Sung China* (1985); R. P. Hymes, *Statesmen and Gentlemen: The Elite of Fu-chou, Chiang-hsi in Southern Sung* (1986); and P. B. Ebrey, *Family and Property in Sung China: Yüan Ts'ai's Precepts for Social Life* (1984). For the Yuan see M. Rossabi, *Khubilai Khan: His Life and Times* (1987); J. W. Dardess, *Conquerors and Confucians: Aspects of Political Change in Late Yüan China* (1973); and J. D. Langlois, ed., *China under Mongol Rule* (1981). Also see R. E. Latham, trans., *The Travels of Marco Polo* (1958). A succinct and definite account is C. O. Hucker, *The Traditional Chinese State in Ming Times* (1961). Hucker is also the editor of *Chinese Government in Ming Times: Seven Studies* (1969). For a fascinating account of a major Qing emperor see J. Spence, *Emperor of China: Self-Portrait of K'ang-Hsi* (1974). There is a growing literature in English on Neo-Confucianism. A good place to begin is W. T. de Bary, *Neo-Confucian Orthodoxy and the Learning of the Mind-and-Heart* (1981), or Wing-tsit Chan, trans. *Neo-Confucian Terms Explained (The Pei-hsi tzu-i) by Ch'en Ch'un, 1159–1223* (1986). An important institution is treated in *China's Examination Hell: The Civil Service Examinations of Imperial China* (1976), by I. Miyazaki, trans. C. Schirokauer.

Japan

The Kodansha *Encyclopedia of Japan* (1983), is a major resource. A general history particularly good on institutions is J. W. Hall, *Japan from Prehistory to Modern Times* (1970). This can be used in conjunction with H. P. Varley, *Japanese Culture: A Short History* (1973). A fascinating evocation of the life of the Heian aristocracy is provided by I. Morris, *The World of the Shining Prince* (1964). For the Ashikaga period see J. W. Hall and Toyoda Takeshi, eds. *Japan in the Muromachi Age* (1977), and G. Ellison and B. L. Smith, eds., *Warlords, Artists, & Commoners: Japan in the Sixteenth Century* (1981). R. Tsunoda et al., *Sources of Japanese Tradition* (1958), is a valuable anthology. For Tokugawa politics see H. Bolitho, *Treasures Among Men: The Fudai Daimyo in Tokugawa Japan* (1974), and C. Totman, *Politics in the Tokugawa Bakufu, 1600–1843* (1967). An important study of social history is *Education in Tokugawa Japan* (1965) by R. P. Dore.

Contacts with Europe

C. R. Boxer, *The Christian Century in Japan* (1951), is well written and informative. Also see G. Elison, *Deus Destroyed: the Image of Christianity in Early Modern Japan* (1973). Recommended for China is J. Gernet, *China and the Christian Impact: A Conflict of Cultures* (1985).

16
The Revival of Europe

The fourteenth century was a disastrous period for medieval European institutions. The Church lost a great deal of prestige during the Avignon papacy (1305–78)—the "Babylonian Captivity," as Petrarch called the papal sojourn in France. The Great Schism (1378–1417) further undermined the reputation of the ecclesiastical hierarchy, while weakening the effective governmental institutions that the Avignon popes had built. Monarchs also lost power and authority during the fourteenth century. The Hundred Years' War weakened both the English and French kings by putting them in debt and making them dependent on the wealthier segments of society. In Germany, the decline of the imperial authority after the death of Frederick II in 1250 continued into the fourteenth century, and by the end of the century the German Holy Roman emperor was no more than a figurehead. In Spain, the reconquest came to a standstill in the fourteenth century, and the development of royal power also stalled because of the competition and conflict between the two main Spanish kingdoms, Castile and Aragon.

However, fourteenth-century writers and scholars rediscovered classical Roman literature and became aware, for the first time, of the cultural separation of the Roman world from their own. This awareness constituted a new historical consciousness that made it possible to speak of historical epochs and civilizations in a new way. While the scholars who revived study of the classics recognized the newness of their own historical consciousness, they could not assess the importance of their work in the history of western civ-

ilization. In fact, the full assessment of their achievement was only made in the mid-nineteenth century, when the Swiss scholar Jakob Burckhardt wrote *The Civilization of the Renaissance in Italy* (1860). Burckhardt posited that the changes in attitude represented in the writings and art of fifteenth- and sixteenth-century Italy constituted a new historical epoch, the Renaissance, and this idea has affected the way subsequent historians have treated the era.

But, recently, historians studying the society, economy, and political fabric of the Renaissance have raised a question about the appropriateness of Burckhardt's conception. While it is clear that there was a sharp break with the medieval philosophical tradition and with medieval artistic style and principles—a renaissance of classical learning and art—in other spheres there was continuity with the later Middle Ages. The changes in the Euro-

Donatello, equestrian statue of the Venetian *condottiere* Erasmo di Nardi, who was called Gattamelata, in the Piazza del Santo, Padua, (*ca.* 1445–50).

pean economy and political institutions during the fifteenth and sixteenth centuries had nothing to do with the new ideas in scholarship and the arts. They were the consequence of changes that had begun before the Black Death. They were the products of the natural evolution of the late medieval society, economy, and polity. In modern historical scholarship, the Renaissance of the fifteenth and sixteenth centuries is placed in its context and is no longer seen to have had the epochal significance that Burckhardt and his followers attributed to it. Nonetheless, there was a revolution in intellectual life and the arts, and its effects are still with us.

THE BACKGROUND OF THE RENAISSANCE

The background against which this new epoch in intellectual life and the arts began was economic depression, social unrest, and malaise in religious life. The society and economy of Europe were severely shaken during the fourteenth century. The droughts and famines of the last decade of the thirteenth century had started a decline in the population, which continued during the first half of the fourteenth century. Because of malnourishment, the European population was in a weakened condition when the bubonic plague hit in 1348–49, beginning a period of epidemics that killed a third to a half of the population in Europe. During the half century after the plague first appeared, the European labor force declined in size and became disorganized as traditional society was disrupted. These economic changes undermined the structure of European society and government, and the upper classes, led by the kings, tried to preserve their privileges and economic well-being by instituting drastic control of prices and wages. By 1400, the European society, economy, and political institutions were in poor condition.

Many of the changes that might have been expected to take place in these circumstances were forestalled by a revival of political and social stability during the fifteenth century. The papacy regained control over its destiny when it defeated the conciliar movement. The monarchies of England and Spain began again the process of centralizing their kingdoms. By the end of the century, the French monarchy also recovered its balance and began to follow the lead of its competitors. The economy and population of Europe began to grow again, the Europeans became world leaders in the development and use of technological inventions. They created mechanical clocks, instruments of navigation, sophisticated milling machines, and cranes. Inventors constantly dreamed up new ways to accomplish industrial and military tasks. The Europeans also became adventurous and, by the end of the century, had discovered the route both around Africa to the East Indies and to the Americas.

The seeds of this recovery were planted in Italy during the most difficult years of the late fourteenth century. In the two centuries between the death of Dante (1321) and the sack of Rome by mutinous imperial troops (1527), Italy exerted increasing influence over the rest of Europe. Italians set the style in architecture, sculpture, and painting; they dictated the literary taste and educational philosophy that Europeans would follow for centuries. Northern Europeans flocked to Italy to learn the arts of civilization— engineering, art, politics, and business—and Italians appeared in every northern court, even in remote Moscow. Italian sailors were among the leaders of the late-fifteenth-century explorations.

There were several reasons why Italy led Europe out of the Middle Ages into a new era. First, cities had begun to flourish there from as early as the tenth century, when the rest of Europe was being feudalized. Feudalism was a form of social, economic, and political organization that gave rural lords power over the northern European cities, which hindered urban development. Largely because of the early revival of cities, feudalism had never been very strong in Italy, and by the early fourteenth century feudal institutions existed in no more than name there. Second, the conflict between the papacy and the Holy Roman Empire had prevented the creation of a unified monarchy in Italy. Consequently, many characteristically medieval institutions did not develop very much in Italy. Third, in intellectual life, scholasticism—which was so strong in the northern universities and schools—never dominated Italian thinking, and in artistic life, Gothic architecture and sculpture did not have much influence in Italy. Thus, the intellectual and artistic traditions of Italians remained free to create and respond to new ideas and styles. Finally, Italian cities, though affected by the famines and plagues of the fourteenth century, had large enough populations, great enough wealth, and enough geographical and political independence to recover quickly from the disasters. The people of other regions looked to Italy for leadership out of economic and cultural stagnation to a new era of creativity in every field of human endeavor.

THE CITY-STATES OF NORTHERN ITALY

The dominant activity in the northern Italian cities was international trade. A third of the population of Florence was engaged in the importation of wool, the making of finished cloth, and the selling of it in foreign markets. Nearly the whole of the populations of Venice and Genoa depended for their livelihoods directly or indirectly on trade with the Levant and with northern Europe. As one would expect, therefore, the dominant persons in the Italian towns were the bankers, the export merchants, and the large-scale manufacturers of textiles.

Although cities in northern Europe controlled the territory immediately around them, the political power of the Italian cities extended much further beyond their walls, and this control of substantial territories made them urban principalities or city-states. The reason for this development in Italy was that the towns had grown powerful so early that a true feudal hierarchy never developed. In fact, the feudal lords were absorbed into the ruling classes of the towns. Without independent and powerful lords to protect them, the small market towns and villages of the Italian countryside (called the *contado*) were annexed by the large cities, creating city-states with domains embracing several hundreds of square miles.

By the late twelfth century, the urban population was divided into classes, which were defined partly by social and partly by economic criteria. The merchant-bankers, some from the old feudal families that were also powerful in the *contado*, formed the ruling class, called the *populo grasso* or "fat people." The largest class was made up of the craftsmen, shopkeepers, and other elements of the lesser bourgeoisie—the *populo minuto* or "little people."

In the eleventh century, the people of many Italian towns had formed political parties called the *patarini*, which fought against the bishops for control of the towns. In that period, the bishops, who were appointed by the emperor, were the dominant powers in the cities, so the *patarini* usually allied themselves with the papacy. By the middle of the twelfth century, the urban populations had succeeded in establishing the independence of their cities and had developed political institutions, dominated by a council, to carry out self-government.

Unlike the classes in the northern European cities, the socioeconomic classes in the Italian cities were not cohesive political entities, and the politics of the Italian cities were rarely affected by class conflict. The cause of this difference was the continual struggle for control of Italy between the German emperors and the papacy. In vir-

A Renaissance prince and his wife: Giovanni Bentivoglio, lord of Bologna, and Ginevra Bentivoglio (details from paintings by Ercole Roberti, *ca.* 1480).

tually every Italian city, political parties that cut across class lines were formed to support one or the other of these external powers.

The supporters of the Hohenstaufen emperors were called the Ghibellines, while the supporters of the papacy were called the Guelfs. The Italian name Ghibelline came from that of Waiblingen, a castle of the Hohenstaufens; the Guelfs took their name from the Welfs, the family of the Bavarian dukes, which was the traditional rival of the Hohenstaufens. By the thirteenth century, the parties had become independent of papal-imperial relations, and the old names—which continued in use—no longer indicated the political aims or allegiances of the parties.

The parties were led by competing families of the elite classes. The leading families appealed to elements of the lower classes by addressing their complaints against the existing political leadership by proclaiming programs of reform, but most often the cry of the opposition party amounted to little more than "Throw the rascals out!" Nonetheless, occasionally, as in Florence in 1378, a transfer of political power was actually accompanied by some of the social and economic reforms demanded by the lower classes. These and other reforms that were made during changes in power usually remained in effect for only a short time, because during the fourteenth century few Italian towns went as long as 30 years without a *coup d'état.*

The constant turmoil drove many leading citizens—such as Dante—from their cities, and, whenever an able man gained power and established a dictatorship that succeeded in suppressing political turbulence, he usually won widespread support from the population. Despots, as the new leaders were called, gained control over many Italian towns in the later fourteenth and fifteenth centuries, and although they exiled, imprisoned, and executed their opponents, they were usually careful to satisfy the majority of the population. The despot commonly improved his city's public works, strengthened its defenses, devised efficient systems of taxation that did not hamper business, and tightened internal security. Many of them tried to impress their peoples by patronizing artists and architects on magnificent public buildings. It was also common for despots to try to gain the support of their citizens by waging wars with neighboring cities.

This last ploy was difficult to carry off, because while the commercial classes wanted to expand the territories and the markets of their cities, merchants and shopkeepers did not want to serve in the armies. The despots also came to recognize that arming their citizens would create potential dangers for themselves. Therefore, they replaced the citizen militias with mercenary troops called *condottieri*. These troops were led by independent captains and were well-trained and fairly reliable—when they were paid on time. However, in a pinch the troops were loyal to their captains rather than to their employers, and the captains were occasionally able to seize power for themselves.

War and Diplomacy

The northern Italian cities were entirely independent, and this circumstance, combined with the despots' incentives to wage wars, produced an endless series of wars and alliances. By the early fifteenth century, Italian city-states had begun to maintain ambassadors at the courts of foreign states to keep rulers in constant touch with governments that were potential allies or enemies. This practice was the beginning of modern diplomacy.

In the second half of the century, the five leading states in the peninsula—Venice, Milan, Florence, the Papal States, and the Kingdom of Naples—had established a kind of "balance of power." The system worked by an

The Italian City-States   1454

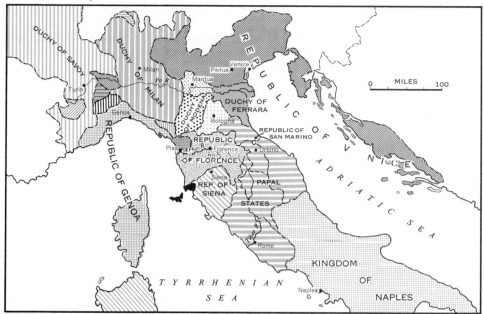

unwritten understanding that no one of the five must be allowed to gain enough power to threaten the others. Both the machinery of diplomacy and the idea of balancing power among a group of sovereign states spread to the rest of Europe, when France and Spain intervened in Italy in the late fifteenth century. By the mid-sixteenth century, resident ambassadors were common throughout central and western Europe, and a rough balance of power had been established between the two most powerful states, France and Spain.

Milan, Venice, and Florence

Although the city-states had much in common with one another, there were striking and important differences among them. Milan was the largest city of the Po Valley and Lombard plain, and historians consider it to be a prime example of the classic Italian city-state. About 1400, it was ruled by a strongman, Gian Galeazzo Visconti, who made Milan one of the leading manu-facturing and trading cities of the peninsula, while encouraging improvements in agriculture. He also came close to uniting all of northern Italy under his power.

Venice was the greatest commercial power of the peninsula. It had risen to prominence as a Byzantine protectorate in the ninth century and had widespread interests in the eastern Mediterranean, controlling trade with Constantinople and Fatimid Egypt. Venice had the oldest republican constitution, and its government was the most stable one in Italy. It had no despot, but was ruled by a small council of commercial leaders—the Council of Ten. The head of state, the doge, was a figurehead, who carried out the policy of the Council. The entire energy of the state and population of Venice was devoted to commerce, and there were no revolutions and few conspiracies in Venetian history. It proclaimed itself "the most serene republic," and the title described it aptly. Until it began to acquire territory on the mainland in the fifteenth century, Venice was relatively isolated from Italian politics.

The rise of the Medici: Cosimo de' Medici has the look of the wily businessman, while his grandson Lorenzo appears every inch the prince. Above: Cosimo, detail from a fresco by Gozzoli. Below: Lorenzo, by an unknown artist.

Florence emerged during the eleventh century as the leading city of Tuscany. Its principal rivals were Pisa and Siena. Florence, like Venice, was a republic, and its citizens maintained their political identity through the centuries by reminding themselves of the difference between their constitution and those of the despotisms against which they struggled. Florentines were particularly proud of having stood against Gian Galeazzo Visconti at the beginning of the fifteenth century.

Florentine society and politics were dominated by the wealthy merchant-bankers and textile manufacturers. Florentine bankers were the most astute in Europe, and the finest textiles were to be found in Florentine shops. But, unlike its sister republic Venice, Florence was constantly troubled by political intrigues and conspiracies. Victorious parties repeatedly tampered with the constitution in an effort to perpetuate their power, until finally, in 1434, an oligarchic party led by the banker Cosimo de' Medici gained power. Cosimo was a political boss, and he preferred to work through others. Although he tinkered with the republican constitution, he maintained power principally by using money and threats to ensure that his supporters won election to the offices of state. This system continued under his son Piero and his grandson Lorenzo the Magnificent (1449–92), so that Florence had 60 years of stability.

Although they were not despots, the Medici devoted much energy to the traditional concerns of despots. They built up the defenses of the city and beautified it by patronizing the best artists and architects of the age. Under the first three Medici, Florence became the center of the Italian Renaissance, and their descendants, who ruled or were prominent in Florence until the eighteenth century, were among the most important patrons of the arts in European history. They allied their family with the leading families in Europe; two Medici became queens of France.

ITALIAN URBAN CIVILIZATION

The new ideals of the urban civilization of Renaissance Italy combined the old feudal-chivalric values and the new urban values. A famous sixteenth-century book by Baldassare Castiglione, *The Courtier,* summed up the ideal of the Renaissance aristocracy—the cultivated gentleman. According to Castiglione, the courtier possessed all the chivalric virtues—physical dexterity and strength, courage, skill in combat, courtesy—and all the new urbane virtues—knowledge of the classics, appreciation of art and literature, eloquence, and good taste. Above all, he had grace; he excelled in every activity without visible effort.

During the Middle Ages, courtliness was considered a result of high birth, but the Renaissance ideal of the courtier admitted the self-made man. Renaissance society permitted considerable mobility to the talented and ambitious, and these men also captured the imagination of contemporaries. There was the *condottieri* captain Francesco Sforza (1401–66), who overthrew the Visconti to become Duke of Milan and founded a dynasty that ruled for a century. There was the genius Leonardo da Vinci and the scholars Lorenzo Valla and Aeneas Silvius Piccolomini (who became Pope Pius II). These men were said to have *virtù*, which meant more than "virtue" in the modern sense; it also meant "virtuosity," that combination of genius and determination that made for greatness in statesmanship, artistic creation, or literature. Eventually, *virtù* came to mean the quality that makes for success in the world.

Individualism

The honor that Italian Renaissance society gave to the individual person amounted to the creation of a new ideology: individualism. It was a society in which the feudal bonds—which in the Middle Ages had held people in their places—had not fully developed. Moreover, the commercial economy of Italy gave people liquid wealth, which permitted them to move from place to place more easily than if their wealth had been in landed estates. The talented person who found the politics or social circumstances in one city to be uncongenial could move to another city.

This social mobility solved some problems, but created others. Many painters and sculptors were members of guilds, but their mobility and the number of their patrons made it impossible for the guilds to regulate their work. Scholars also found patronage in the households of aristocratic or newly rich families—as secretaries and schoolmasters to the children of the household—so they could carry on their work without university appointments. Consequently, the intellectual conservatism of the universities had little effect on the scholarship of the Italian humanists who could pursue their individual interests unfettered. The eagerness of leading families to support artists and writers increased the ability of these people to develop their own styles and interests by drawing subsidies from many patrons. They were not subject to the tastes and interests of any one of their supporters.

In general, the decentralization of patronage and the weakening of such institutions as the Church and the universities created an atmosphere in which individualism flourished. An extreme case was that of Benvenuto Cellini (1500–71), a sculptor and goldsmith who described his violent and colorful career in a famous *Autobiography*. Cellini assumed that autobiography, which had been very rare in the Middle Ages, was a natural form of expression, which would find many eager readers. He began his book, "All men of whatsoever quality they be, who have done anything of excellence, . . . ought to describe their life with their own hand." He also set forth a doctrine that the ordinary laws of mo-

rality were made for ordinary people; they did not apply to geniuses like himself. He claimed to have been absolved of murdering a man because the pope held that Cellini stood above the law.

Secularism

The second mark of the new urban civilization in Italy was its predominantly secular tone. It was not pagan or anti-Christian, but it was concerned with the things of this world—business, the quality and design of houses and clothes, food and drink, and the enjoyment of leisure. The heroes and heroines of Boccaccio's *Decameron* (*ca.* 1350) are not irreligious or critical of Christian ideals, but they despise the hypocrisy of priests and monks; they rejoice in the triumph of clever people over clerical busybodies; and they pay atten-

Minters making silver thalers (from which comes our word *dollar*). A heated metal disk has been placed on top of the die, another die has been placed on top of the disk, and the minter is striking the top die with an iron mallet (detail from the Miners' Altar by Hans Hesse, Church of St. Anne, Annaberg, Saxony).

A Man of Virtù

Benvenuto Cellini, a Florentine goldsmith and sculptor, had struck medals and coins for Pope Clement VII (1523–34). He claimed that he had been insulted by a jeweler named Pompeo (who also worked for the pope), and after several quarrels, Cellini, stabbed Pompeo to death in a street brawl. Clement VII had just died; Cardinal Farnese was elected pope on October 13, 1534, and took the name of Paul III.

After he had put affairs of greater consequence in order, the new Pope sent for me, saying that he did not wish any one else to strike his coins. To these words of his Holiness one of his gentlemen named Latino Juvinale [a Humanist] answered that I [Cellini] was in hiding for the murder of Pompeo of Milan, and set forth what could be argued for my justification in the most favorable terms. The Pope replied: "I know nothing of Pompeo's death but plenty of Benvenuto's provocation, so let a safe-conduct be at once made out for him." A great friend of Pompeo's was there; he was a Milanese called Ambrogio [Ambrogio Recalcati, a papal secretary]. This man said: "In the first days of your papacy it is not well to grant pardons of this kind." The Pope answered: "You know less about such matters than I do. Know then that men like Benvenuto, unique in their profession, stand above the law."

From Benvenuto Cellini, *The Life of Benvenuto Cellini*, trans. by John Addington Symonds (New York: Scribner's, 1926), p. 144.

tion to the affairs of this world, seeming to assert that this is proper for people who live in it.

The secularism of Italian Renaissance society thus consisted of two components—a preoccupation with worldly affairs and a contempt for false spirituality and asceticism. Like their medieval predecessors, Renaissance writers recognized the primacy of man's spiritual goals, but they held those who chose the religious life to an extremely high standard of devotion and honest asceticism. At the same time, these writers were convinced of the propriety of attending to business and pleasure. The coexistence of these two convictions created a tension in Renaissance literature and the impression that Renaissance values were irreligious.

Humanism

The third mark of Italian urban society was its enthusiasm for classical antiquity. Knowledge of the classics was a mark of true gentility in a nobleman, and those who devoted themselves entirely to the study of classical literature—the humanists—were held in high honor. Medieval intellectuals also had an enthusiasm for ancient Latin literature, but they looked on study of classical works as the basis for understanding the Scriptures and the writings of the Church fathers. Renaissance humanists, following Francesco Petrarca or Petrarch (1304–74), extolled the classics for their own sake. Humanist scholars searched the ancient monastic libraries for copies of classical literary texts and found the clear and beautiful books of the Carolingian age. They took these books to be genuine, ancient copies and revived the script in which they were written.

The Renaissance humanists held positions as secretaries in the courts of Europe and as teachers of the children of the ruling classes. Generally, they were laymen who made a living by their learning, rather than clerics or monks who devoted spare time from their regular duties to intellectual work. They were self-made men selling their scholarship in a good market. Enthusiasm for the classics increased after 1395, when the advance of the Ottoman Turks in Asia Minor scared scholars in Constantinople into fleeing to the West. In Italy, these men found willing students of Greek language and literature, and Lorenzo the Magnificent founded a Platonic Academy in Florence, where leading humanists studied and taught Greek philosophy. By the end of the fifteenth century a few Italians were even studying Hebrew and Arabic.

The humanists initiated a revolution in educational theory and practice. The main educational tradition of the Middle Ages had been dedicated to the training of clerics and monks. The intellectual standards of these clerical professions were high, but of course the range of subjects studied by such students were of a limited and specifically ecclesiastical nature. All studies were subordinate to the study of theology. Throughout the Middle Ages, urban schools—which were the descendants of the ancient Roman schools—had continued to exist in Italy, but they were basically elementary schools for the training of future businessmen. They taught reading, writing, and arithmetic, not the seven liberal arts that had constituted the basic curriculum of the medieval ecclesiastical schools since the Carolingian period.

The humanists of the fifteenth century rediscovered what Greco-Roman writers had meant by "liberal arts": the liberating effect on the mind and imagination of the study of great literature and philosophy. To this program of study, they added training in courteous behavior and athletic skill, thereby recovering the ancient idea of *mens sana in corpore sano* ("a sound mind in a sound body"). One humanist educator

Petrarch on the Classics and Christianity

You are well aware that from early boyhood of all the writers of all ages and races the one whom I most admire and love is Cicero. You agree with me in this respect as well as in so many others. I am not afraid of being considered a poor Christian by declaring myself so much a Ciceronian. [This is an allusion to a famous vision of St. Jerome in which God told him: "You are a Ciceronian and therefore not a Christian."] To my knowledge, Cicero never wrote one word that would conflict with the principles proclaimed by Christ. If, perchance, his works contained anything contrary to Christ's doctrine, that one fact would be sufficient to destroy my belief in Cicero and in Aristotle and in Plato. . . .

Christ is my God; Cicero is the prince of the language I use. I grant you that these ideas are widely separated, but I deny that they are in conflict with each other. Christ is the Word, and the Virtue and the Wisdom of God the Father. Cicero has written much on the speech of men, on the virtues of men, and on the wisdom of men—statements that are true and therefore surely acceptable to the God of Truth.

From a letter to Neri Morando, 1358, in *Petrarch's Letters to Classical Authors*, trans. by M. E. Cosenza (Chicago: University of Chicago Press, 1910), pp. 18–19.

Young student reading Cicero (detail from a painting by Vincenzo Foppa).

wrote, "We call those studies liberal which are worthy of a free man . . . that education which calls forth, trains, and develops those highest gifts of body and of mind which ennoble men." To our own day, educators still aim at these goals.

Historical Consciousness

Finally, the fourth mark of the Italian Renaissance civilization was its historical self-consciousness. Medieval historians and their readers viewed history as a continuum divided into epochs by significant events in the relationship between God and man. The Flood, the giving of the Ten Commandments, and the incarnation and resurrection of Christ marked periods in the history of the human race. Medieval people were conscious of the passage of time, but they assumed that their civilization derived without discontinuity from that of the past. In medieval paintings, Julius Caesar (first century B.C.) and Charlemagne (eighth century) wore the same type of costume, and Frederick Barbarossa (twelfth century) did not hesitate to insert his own edicts into the *Corpus Iuris Civilis* of Justinian (sixth century).

Petrarch and his humanist successors in the fifteenth century recognized that the Roman culture they loved was essentially alien from their own, and this recognition revolutionized the Eu-

ropeans' conception of the past. They were able to talk of the "fall of Rome" and of the "dark age" that separated themselves from the glorious time of Cicero. Above all, they saw their own scholarly activities as a revival or rebirth of classical civilization and were highly conscious of their position in history and of their historical mission.

Women and the Family

The ideals of Renaissance family life were those of upper-class urban families—the families of bankers and merchants. The *populo minuto* imitated these ideals to the extent that their finances permitted.

Italian men married rather late, and their wives were usually much younger than they. Hence, widows were almost as common as widowers. Ideally, a widow did not remarry, and a man was advised to discourage his wife from remarrying by leaving his property to her "if she remains a widow and lives with her children." Nonetheless, many women did remarry, and Renaissance families were often very large. Households could contain the children of several marriages.

Young wives had, therefore, to cope with difficult circumstances. Often, their husband's older children were nearly as old as they, and relations between the different sibling groups were strained. The wife was in the middle of

The Adimari Wedding, by an anonymous painter (*ca.* 1450). The painting shows the parade of guests at the wedding reception, held under a canopy outside a church in Florence. Such paintings often adorned the bride's *cassone,* a wedding chest designed to hold her trousseau.

the strife. She also had to take in her husband's illegitimate children and sometimes those of his or her own brothers and sisters. Besides blood and marriage relatives, the households contained servants and slaves, and even their children. It was common for women to be the effective heads of their households, either as widows or because their husbands were on business trips. Such trips could last more than a year, and the wife was expected to raise the children, run the house, and keep the family together and at peace.

Children went through many dislocations and traumas. Infants were normally put out to wet-nurses—usually peasants in the *contado*—with whom they stayed for two years. When they returned to the household in the city, they had to be integrated into the family and to get to know many siblings and even their own parents. Many diaries from the period attest to the feelings of alienation and fear that accompanied this reentry into the home.

From two to seven years old, children were almost exclusively under their mother's care. The father remained rather distant—he was usually rather old—except in times of crisis like a serious illness either of a child or the mother. Nonetheless, the father was responsible for discipline and the early education of the children, and he arranged for their formal education, which usually began at the age of seven.

For boys, formal education meant being sent to a boarding school. They spent three or four years in a grammar school, learning to read and write both in Latin and the vernacular. Then they spent another year or so at a second school studying accounting and business procedures. Finally, they were placed as apprentices with a merchant or banker.

For girls, education meant study at home, not only in the household arts, but also in reading and writing. Women were not as well educated as

How Children Should Be Raised

The Dominican Friar Giovanni Dominici (*ca.* 1356–*ca.* 1420) wrote a treatise on childrearing.

Children should be accustomed to eat coarse food, to wear cheap and common clothes. . . . They should also learn to wait on themselves, and to use as little as possible the services of maid and servant, setting and clearing the table, dressing and undressing themselves, putting on their own shoes and clothes and so forth.

After a boy reaches three years of age, he should know no distinction between male and female other than dress and hair. From then on let him be a stranger to being petted, embraced and kissed by you [the mother] until after the twenty-fifth year. Granted that there will not take place any thought or natural movement before the age of five . . . do not be less solicitous that he be chaste and modest always and, in every place, covered as modestly as if he were a girl.

Quoted by James Bruce Ross, "The Middle-Class Child in Urban Italy, Fourteenth to Early Sixteenth Century," *The History of Childhood,* ed. by L. deMause (New York: Psychoanalytic Press, 1974).

men, but they needed to be literate to run the affairs of their households during the frequent absences of their husbands.

Women were expected to come to their marriages with dowries, and, in Florence and many other cities, parents could invest in dowry banks. These institutions worked like a modern plan for building college funds: the parents made a deposit when their daughter was very young, and the fund grew through the accrual of interest until it was redeemed. From time to time, the dowry bank failed, and girls lost their dowries and their chances for a good marriage.

Women of the middle classes—made up of small merchants, shopkeepers, and craftsmen—probably shared the burdens of their husbands' affairs more than women of the highest class. From the little evidence we have, we can conclude that middle-class families emulated their betters by putting out their children to wet-nurses and educating them. The men of this class did not travel so much as the great merchants, so their wives were not left alone very often, but they did marry late, and widowhood was common here, too.

All in all, the life of a woman in Renaissance society was difficult. She had many advantages—such as economic security and the protection of her husband—but she was likely to be saddled with difficult family relations as a young woman and to be head of a large household by middle age. While her husband lived, he dominated her, and after his death, his will might restrict her options. The law gave her few independent rights.

A late sixteenth-century portrait of Niccolò Machiavelli by Santi di Tito. The artist has tried to suggest both the intellectual brilliance and the shrewdness of the man.

THE RENAISSANCE

Literature, Philosophy, and Scholarship

The earliest humanists—the immediate successors of Petrarch—displayed their enthusiasm for classical literature by imitating its genres and styles. They wrote letters, orations, moral essays, and poetry in the Roman style. Much of early Renaissance literature was imitative, but some writers created new forms such as the sonnet and, later, the essay.

While Renaissance literature rested on Roman foundations, Renaissance philosophy sought its inspiration in the work of Plato. When the Byzantine refugee scholars, who came to the West in the 1390s, had taught a sufficient number of Italians to read Greek, the work of the ancient Greek philosophers became very popular. The Medici fostered an informal group of scholars who became known as the Platonic Academy. Its leading members, Marsilio Ficino (1433–99) and Pico della Mirandola (1463–94), tried to reconcile Plato and Christianity in the same way that Thomas Aquinas had tried to reconcile Aristotle and Christianity. It is fair to say that Plato dominated the imagination of the Renaissance as Aristotle had earlier dominated the thought of medieval scholars.

Renaissance scholars created the basis of modern critical scholarship, which rests on careful linguistic and historical analysis of the literary remains of the past. Lorenzo Valla (ca. 1405–57) showed by such analysis that the Donation of Constantine, on which papal claims to temporal authority over Christendom and the Papal States had rested, was a crude forgery of the early Middle Ages. He also compared several Greek manuscripts of the New Testament with the vulgate translation of Jerome (late fourth century) and showed that the translation was full of errors and distortions. His critical spirit and scholarly technique influenced later scholars, such as Erasmus (see pp. 475–76), who produced the first critical edition of the Greek New Testament.

Social and Political Thought

Most of the social and political thinkers of the Renaissance simply paraphrased the Greek and Roman classics on these subjects, but a few writers advanced significantly beyond classical thought. Leon Battista Alberti (1404–72) wrote a work, *On the Family*, in which he described the interests and ideals of Florentine families he knew. He says that they prized prudence, thrift, foresight, and comfort; had a strong family feeling and little interest in the affairs of the society as a whole; and wanted to own a house in the city and an estate in the country to produce all the family's food. Alberti's account is one of the earliest idealized portraits of what later came to be called the bourgeois virtues. He describes the aspirations and style of families that created the models for all of European society in the early modern period.

Baldassare Castiglione's work *The Courtier* (written 1513–18, published 1528)—already mentioned—described the ideals of the highest social stratum. It was based on Castiglione's experiences at the court of the Duke of Urbino, and it reformulated the ideal of "the gentleman." This ideal owed much to the chivalric tradition of the Middle Ages, but it included typically Renaissance attributes like a liberal education and an idea that nobility described the character rather than the birth of a person.

Perhaps the greatest political theorist of the Renaissance was Nicolò Machiavelli (1469–1527). He combined a wide reading in the classics, particularly history, with extensive experience in political life. He served Florence as an ambassador and as secretary of the state during a period in the early sixteenth century when the Medici were out of power. When the Medici re-

---

Machiavelli on Cruelty and Clemency

Is it better to be loved than feared or feared than loved? It may be answered that one should wish to be both, but it is much safer to be feared than loved when one of the two must be chosen. Men on the whole are ungrateful, fickle, false, cowards, covetous. As long as you succeed, they are yours entirely. They will offer you their blood, property, life, and children when the need is distant, but when it approaches they turn against you. And a prince who, relying entirely on their promises, has neglected other precautions, is ruined. . . . Men have fewer scruples in offending one who is beloved than one who is feared, for love is preserved by the link of obligation which, owing to the baseness of men, is broken at every opportunity for their advantage, but fear preserves you by a dread of punishment which never fails.

Nevertheless, a prince should inspire fear in such a way that if he does not win love, he avoids hatred; because he can endure very well being feared while he is not hated, and this will be true as long as he abstains from taking the property of his subjects or their women. But when it is necessary for him to take the life of someone, he must do it with proper justification and for manifest cause, and above everything he must keep his hands off the property of others, because men more quickly forget the death of their father than the loss of their heritage.

From Niccolò Machiavelli, *The Prince*, trans. by W. K. Marriott (London: Dent, n.d.), pp. 134–35.

---

gained control of the city's government in 1512, Machiavelli was exiled to his country estate. In retirement, he read widely on political history and reflected on the causes of political breakdown, how political leaders obtain and hold power, and what can be learned from history.

Machiavelli's work produced two books—the long, rambling *Discourses on Livy* and the brief and more famous essay, *The Prince*. In these works, Machiavelli undertook to describe political life as it was, rather than as it should be. He analyzed the strengths and weaknesses of various types of constitutions, and his *Discourses* show him to have been in favor of the republican form of government, which he

Aerial view of St. Peter's in Rome. In 1505 Pope Julius II commissioned Bramante to construct a church that would mirror the classical-Christian aspirations of the sixteenth century. The plans were changed several times, and the building was not completed until 1626. Michelangelo designed the dome; the colonnades were designed by Bernini in the 1600s.

Michelangelo's *David* (1501–04). Instead of representing David after his victory over Goliath, as Donatello had done, Michelangelo chose to represent him as watchful of the approaching foe, with muscles tensed in gathering strength.

had served in Florence. *The Prince* focused on the kinds of rulers or heads of state. Here, Machiavelli analyzed the ways men gain power and various techniques for holding on to it. He ended the book with a plea that Italians unify, throw out the foreign invaders, and recreate the glory of ancient Rome. This book became a grammar of political and diplomatic practice and was translated into many languages. Its author's hardheaded account of how things really are in political life and international relations earned him a reputation as the evil genius behind dictators. Yet, while Machiavelli certainly believed that a strong and centralized state was usually the most successful form of government, he did not favor dictatorship. Rather, he believed that a constitution must suit the character of the people it served and thought that an educated and sensible populace could achieve the ideal of strength and unity under a republican constitution.

The Arts

Very soon after the humanists rediscovered Roman literature, the architects rediscovered Roman styles of building. Italy was full of Roman buildings, or their ruins, and architects could see the principles and design characteristics favored by the Romans. Brunelleschi (1377?–1446) was the greatest of the early Renaissance architects, and from about 1420 he was designing new churches in the semiclassical style. His successors continued to base their buildings on the classical tradition, giving their churches great symmetry and clean, stately facades. The greatest example of Renaissance architecture was the new church of St. Peter in Rome, which replaced the fourth-century basilica built by Emperor Constantine I. This church was the largest in Europe and was built by many architects—including Donato Bramante, Michelangelo, and Bernini—over the period from 1506 to 1615.

Renaissance painting was based on a tradition that went back to Giotto (1276–1337), but the essential values of the new style were not fully developed until Masaccio (1401–?28). During the century before Masaccio, Italian painters had learned realism from the Flemish painters patronized by the Burgundian court, and Masaccio raised this realism to a new level. His paintings created a style that united a sense of volume with an organic unity of scene. He suppressed small details to bring out the inner emotion of a scene. After him, Renaissance painting developed rapidly.

The first characteristic that strikes the historian is that Renaissance painting and sculpture were practiced separately from architecture. In the Middle Ages, all the plastic arts had been united in the building of churches and a few other types of public structure. Now, painting and sculpture were no longer subordinate to architecture. Italian painters adorned the walls of existing churches and monasteries with frescoes—a technique of painting on fresh plaster—and they developed easel painting, which was meant to be hung in a house or palace and to be enjoyed for its own sake. Although religious themes remained dominant, painters increasingly portrayed scenes from classical myth and literature, showing the same influences as contemporary humanists.

The classical influence also affected sculpture. Donatello (1368–1466) was the first sculptor since Roman times to model a free-standing nude figure. His *David* was the beginning of a series of great works that led to the masterpieces of Michelangelo (1475–1564). These works revived the Greco-Roman ideal of the human form and brought back the classical ideal of beauty, which is still dominant in western society.

A second striking characteristic of Renaissance artistic life was the heightened individuality and social prestige of the artist. Cellini's *Autobiography*—already mentioned—asserts the self-image of the Renaissance artist as a man of genius who stood outside normal human society. Although some patrons treated artists as common servants, many of the leading artists were able to make a very good living from the commissions of many patrons and, therefore, could establish themselves as independent and honored members of society. By and large, Italy's Golden Age was the golden age of the artist and scholar.

In seeking a higher realism, Italian painters studied the laws of spatial perspective and human anatomy. Their notebooks and sketches show studies of proportion and space as well as of the parts of the human body. Just as the humanists were concerned with the nature of man, so the painters studied human psychology in order to capture the true emotions and understand the significant moments of the scenes they painted. The best example of the painter who was a student of nature and human nature was the lonely scientific and artistic genius Leonardo da Vinci (1452–1519). In his notebooks, he drew designs for mechanical devices that were far ahead of his age: a helicopter, automobile (that is, a self-propelled vehicle), and other machines. He also did studies of perspective, light, and optics, both because of his scientific curiosity and for his painting. In his painting *The Last Supper*, he went against tradition and chose to depict not the moment when Christ told the apostles, ''This is my body . . . ,'' but the much more dramatic one when he announces, ''One of you will betray me.'' The psychological state of each apostle is carefully

Donatello's *David* (ca. 1430–32). Compare this statue with the *David* by Michelangelo on the opposite page.

portrayed, giving the painting tremendous dramatic power.

This tendency to choose the psychologically charged moment was characteristic of Renaissance painting. When Michelangelo painted the *Creation* on the ceiling of the Sistine Chapel in the Vatican, he made the animation of Adam the climactic and central scene. Likewise, when he sculpted Moses, Michelangelo chose to portray him at the moment when he caught sight of the people's idolatrous Golden Calf. His Moses sits tense, looking out fiercely, trying to control his temper.

These examples typify the Renaissance point of view. The central concern was man as he lives here in this world—troubled, striving, with unknown, but great possibilities. In fact, the most important question was "what is to become of man?", for as Pico della Mirandola said in a famous oration on man's dignity (1486), God gave man something he had given to no other creature—freedom. Every other creature had its pattern and limits, but man's nature and destiny, said Pico, were in his own hands. The thinkers and artists of the Renaissance had not lost belief in God, but they gave a new meaning to the Judeo-Christian idea that man was made in God's image: like God, man is a creator, and his principal creations are his own character and accomplishments.

It was not only art and literature that made Italians famous during the Renaissance. The many urban courts employed hundreds of musicians, craftsmen, mechanics, and engineers, and it was to Italy that all Europe looked for the best work in these fields. In fact, working together in the small courts, the specialists in the various fields often cooperated and contributed to one another's endeavors. Artists and physicians advanced knowledge of human anatomy beyond what the Greeks and Arabs, whose works were still read, had known. Painters worked out the mathematical principles of rep-

Michelangelo, *Creation of Adam* (fresco from the ceiling of the Sistine Chapel of the Vatican, 1508–12).

resenting bodies in space and, therefore, contributed to the study of mathematics, which was centered in the University of Padua. Physicians studied astronomy because there was a strong tradition of astrology in medieval medicine—the stars were thought to affect the condition of individuals. Many of the instruments used to observe the stars accurately were designed by physicians. This was a society that appreciated the value of all approaches to knowledge and representation of the world. Its intellectuals, artists, and craftsmen created the basis of many modern fields.

ECONOMIC GROWTH IN NORTHERN EUROPE

The wealth of Italy was based on trade and industry as, for centuries, the urban communities of the peninsula provided the commercial link between the rich eastern Mediterranean civilizations and western Europe. The wealth of the north was based on agriculture and mineral wealth. To be sure, northerners engaged in commerce and industry, also. Western European cities had substantial communities of merchants; Flanders, for example, produced excellent cloth for which there was a strong demand. But the wealth of the region was based primarily on a rich agriculture, for northern Europe is one of the premier agricultural regions on the earth, and the multitude of rivers make it possible to move the crops to the markets cheaply.

While Italian rulers were building city-states based on the wealth derived from their monopoly of Mediterranean trade, northern and western European rulers were building nation-states based on new industries and new trade routes. During the fifteenth century, the accumulation of technological advances—which produced mechanical devices like clocks, mills, and cranes and improved the performance and capacity of ships—formed the basis of

Raphael, detail from *Madonna with the Goldfinch* (1505–06).

Leonardo da Vinci, *Ginevra de' Benci* (*ca.* 1481).

An early printing press, as shown in an early sixteenth-century French print.

town and country and created an increasingly large and mobile labor force that was subject to the vagaries of an international economy over which neither the industrialists nor the workers had any control. The society of free labor was, consequently, both wealthier and more unstable than the medieval society based on agricultural and craft work. The new laborers were alternately richer and poorer than their ancestors.

Progressive landlords tried to introduce the new capitalistic system in agriculture. From the late fifteenth century, a steadily increasing number of those who controlled large estates tried to concentrate on producing the most profitable crops and animal products. Particularly in England—where wool production was well established—landlords fenced, or "enclosed," fields formerly reserved for the common use of villagers and even converted cultivated land to enclosed pastures for huge flocks of sheep. Thomas More—the famous chancellor of England—complained about this movement at the beginning of the sixteenth century, because he thought that it ruined small farmers and was responsible for the creation of a class of "sturdy beggars" or "vagabonds," who were a constant problem for sixteenth-century town governments. In fact, the vagabond problem was created by the growth of population, for the commercial agriculture practiced by the enclosers actually increased the need for labor. Population growth just outpaced the creation of jobs. In the sixteenth century, town governments built prisons and workhouses to lodge the tramps.

Wealth derived from the new industries and commerce tended to concentrate in a few hands in a few places. For a brief period the most powerful banking house in northern Europe, if not on the whole Continent, was that of the Fuggers of Augsburg in southern Germany. Jakob Fugger (1459–1525), as banker for the Habsburgs of Austria—the imperial family—and for the popes, could invest in Austrian mines

a new burst of activity in the transalpine economy.

New industries such as cannon founding and printing required large initial investments in plant and machinery. From the start, these industries were organized as capitalistic enterprises—that is, enterprises in which accumulated wealth was deliberately used to create new wealth. Although medieval merchants had used their profits to buy the goods they traded, most wealth—such as that produced by great agricultural estates—was used to buy "consumer" goods. Now, accumulated wealth was being invested to produce more wealth, which is the essence of capitalism.

The new industries also needed and attracted free laborers who could be employed for a wage and dismissed when business slacked off. Capitalistic enterprises drew their workers from

and Spanish colonies and carry on dealings with every part of the Continent. Nonetheless, the center of European finance from about 1476 to 1576 was Antwerp, with Lyons not far behind. Then, for a century after 1576, Amsterdam took over the role of Europe's Wall Street. Thus, by the later sixteenth century, financial power was shifting from Italy to the north.

POLITICAL CONSOLIDATION AND CENTRALIZATION

In the later fifteenth century, the European monarchies began to recover from the disastrous effects of war and plague. The Wars of the Roses (1455–85) ended with the establishment of a strong new dynasty in England, and the French kings rebuilt their monarchy after the end of the Hundred Years' War in 1453. In Germany, the Holy Roman emperor continued to be weak, but the imperial family enhanced its position by marriage alliances that gave it European-wide power. Spain rose to prominence on the basis of its new colonies. During the fifteenth and sixteenth centuries, the kings moved toward the establishment of the absolute power that had eluded their medieval predecessors.

France

Although France recovered its territory from England under Charles VII (r. 1422–61), Charles was not a great king. However, he was particularly good at choosing able men to work for him (he was known in his time as Charles the Well-served), and these men began to build a strong monarchy around him. In 1438, Charles asserted authority over the French church by the Pragmatic Sanction of Bourges (see p. 471). In the 1440s, he solved the financial problems of the crown by obtaining consent from the Estates to a broad-based tax on land called the *taille*, which he continued to collect on his own authority thereafter. He organized

The Financial Empire of Jakob Fugger   1485–1525

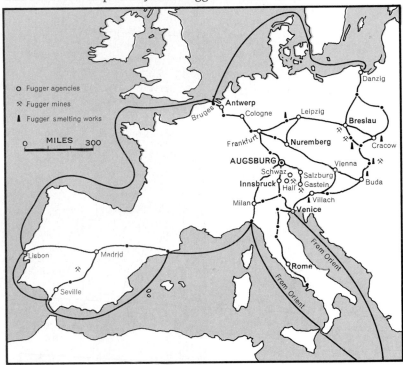

Jakob Fugger with his bookkeeper. The cabinet in the rear lists the names of cities where Fugger had branch offices—Innsbruck, Nuremberg, and Lisbon, among others (detail from a painting by Matthaus Schwartz, 1516).

The Habsburgs: Emperor Maximilian and his family.

a small, but strong, standing army (not more than 25,000 men) and gained the support of the merchant class, from which he took some of his best royal officials.

Charles's son Louis XI (r. 1461–83) left the monarchy stronger than it had been since the early fourteenth century. Louis was a master at diplomacy—he was called "the Spider" because he so often trapped his enemies in a web of intrigue—and won the admiration of Machiavelli. Louis's greatest enemy was Charles the Bold, Duke of Burgundy (r. 1467–77), who successfully outmaneuvered the king while helping him to rid France of the English. Louis

finally succeeded in stirring up Charles's eastern neighbors, and the duke died in a battle against the Swiss pikemen.

The richest part of Charles the Bold's inheritance, the Netherlands, was inherited by the Habsburg emperor Maximilian (r. 1493–1519) through his wife Mary, daughter of the fallen duke. But the strategically located Duchy of Burgundy went to Louis of France. Louis's son, Charles VIII (r. 1483–98), married the heiress of Brittany, thus bringing the last feudal duchy into the control of the French monarchy. Charles also continued his father's policy of encouraging trade, relying on the merchant class, and keeping firm control of the aristocracy and French church.

Once France was fully under control, Charles VIII felt ready to renew ancient claims of the French monarchy. In 1494, he invaded Italy to assert claims to the kingdom of Naples as the heir of Charles of Anjou (see p. 350). The Spanish monarchy also had claims to Italy and reacted quickly to the French invasion. For the next half-century, foreign armies fought over the peninsula, with the result that the city-states lost their prosperity and independence. Eventually, Spain gained the dominant position in Italy and was able to dictate to the city-states of the north. The kingdom of Naples became a dependency of the Spanish crown, while the French king, although he had suffered financial losses, remained one of the most influential powers in Europe.

Spain

The reconquest of the Iberian peninsula had been carried out by several political powers, led by the kings of Aragon and Castile. By the end of the thirteenth century, only the kingdom of Granada remained in Moslem hands, but the reconquest came to a standstill. During the fourteenth and early fifteenth centuries, the peninsula was torn by war and anarchy as the Christian powers struggled for control of the peninsula. Then, in 1469, a momentous marriage was arranged between Ferdinand of Aragon (r. 1479–1516) and Isabella of Castile (r. 1474–1504). The union did not bring about an organic fusion of the two kingdoms, but husband and wife carried out a common foreign policy and their heir would truly be king of "Spain."

In the late fifteenth century, a second marriage greatly affected the position of Spain in European politics. The emperor Maximilian and Mary of Burgundy had a son, Philip, who was heir to Austria through his Habsburg father and to the Netherlands through his mother. Philip married Joanna, the daughter of Ferdinand and Isabella, and their son, Charles, eventually became king of Spain (r. 1516–56) and ruler of the Netherlands, Austria, Milan, Naples, and the Spanish possessions in America. In 1519, the German princes elected him Holy Roman emperor as Charles V.

In the fifteenth century, Spain was neither a wealthy nor a fully amalgamated country. Its old kingdoms held on to their institutions, and even their dialects and languages, under the

Illumination of Ferdinand and Isabella of Spain—known as the "Catholic Kings"—with their daughter Joanna.

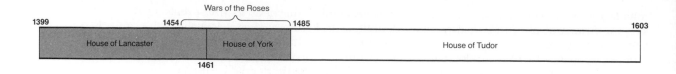

Wars of the Roses

| 1399 | 1454 | 1485 | 1603 |

House of Lancaster | House of York | House of Tudor

1461

united monarchy, but Spanish armies were nonetheless among the best in Europe and were successful north of the Pyrenees. Moreover, Columbus's discoveries in the New World brought in a steady stream of gold and silver, which surpassed all previous dreams of wealth. As a result, Spain became the leading power in sixteenth-century Europe.

England

The man who ended the Wars of the Roses, Henry Tudor (Henry VII, r. 1485–1509), was able to reestablish peace and proved himself to be one of the ablest kings in English history. The aristocracy had been critically weakened by the wars, and Henry was able to fill it with men loyal to his monarchy. He also kept England out of foreign wars, encouraged trade, restored the sources of royal revenue, and eliminated all pretenders to the throne.

Henry's son, Henry VIII (r. 1509–47) inherited a full treasury, a united nation, and a relatively efficient administration. Henry introduced humanist learning to England and began the English Renaissance. He also renovated the Common Law, which had survived intact through all the wars. With the advice of his ruthless chief minister, Cardinal Wolsey, Henry issued numerous statutes to reform the law and correct abuses, and his reign is one of the most innovative periods in the history of the English law.

Henry married Catherine of Aragon and thereby joined the great alliance of families connected with the royal house of Spain, but he and Catherine had only one daughter—son after son was born dead—and he foresaw a dynastic crisis. When he sought to rid

himself of his wife, the church would not grant a divorce. The crisis that this conflict caused ended when the king proclaimed the Act of Supremacy in 1534, declaring himself to be the head of an English church free from the authority of the pope. Chancellor Thomas More, the humanist scholar and brilliant lawyer who succeeded Cardinal Wolsey in 1529, refused to accede to the king's assertion of authority and retired from his office in 1532. When he continued his opposition to the king's remarriage and the Act of Supremacy, he was convicted of treason and beheaded in 1535.

The Consolidation of Monarchical Power

The European monarchs overcame several obstacles in building their power during the sixteenth century—the nobility, the representative assemblies, and the Church. They defeated the nobility either because it had been weakened by wars, as in England, or because it could not afford the new military technology and had to subordinate itself to the king, which happened virtually everywhere. In most nations, the kings also created bureaucracies made up of educated and loyal men of the merchant class. These new bureaucrats balanced the power of the old aristocracy, while simultaneously improving royal finances through innovative taxes and financial management.

The monarchs also overcame the obstacle of the representative assemblies: the Estates General in France, the Cortes in the Spanish kingdoms, and Parliament in England. These assemblies had achieved great power and influence in the fourteenth century, when the kings were in need of assistance because of the constant wars and the effects of the plague. In the fifteenth century, they declined everywhere but in England. In most cases, the assemblies were to blame for their own decline. So long as the king was not asking for financial aid, the regional interests of the delegates became dominant, and the unity and effectiveness of the assemblies were destroyed. As the kings became increasingly strong during the fifteenth century, they manipulated the assemblies by playing classes and regional delegations off against one another, and people lost interest in attending the meetings. The Estates General and Cortes met less and less frequently after the end of the fifteenth century.

In England, Henry VII used Parliament to establish his power, but he seldom summoned it after he gained control of the kingdom. Nonetheless, because the English Parliament could speak for all of the privileged classes of the realm and for all sections of the country, it was more difficult to ignore than the ineffective and disunited assemblies of other countries. Moreover, the Parliament was an excellent source of support for the king who used it wisely. When Henry VIII was in conflict with the pope over his marriage, he summoned Parliament to give him support. By 1600, thanks to the frequent use Henry VIII and his successors made of it, Parliament had become more important in English government than ever before. By that time the representative assemblies on the Continent had become hollow institutions controlled by absolute monarchs.

Finally, the monarchs gained control over the churches in their realms. Principally, this meant that they had control over the appointment of prelates and could tax the churches without the permission of the pope. They also gained control of the appeal of cases to Rome. The kings of England and France had established their right to tax the clergy by 1300. The French king

asserted the right to control appointments in 1438, and in the Concordat of Bologna (1516) the pope granted Francis I (r. 1515–47) the right to nominate the higher clergy and to settle the bulk of ecclesiastical disputes in France. Even Ferdinand and Isabella, the "Catholic Kings," asserted and maintained their right to appoint, tax, and reform the clergy within their kingdoms. Henry VIII's Act of Supremacy (1534) gave him complete power over the English Church in one stroke.

The consolidation and centralization of power that was evident in the kingdoms of western Europe also proceeded in other European kingdoms. The kings of Norway and Sweden consolidated their control over their territories in the fifteenth and sixteenth centuries. In Russia, Ivan the Terrible (r. 1533–84) ruthlessly broke the power of the Russian nobility. But the process did not take place everywhere. In Italy, there was no central government—to the dismay of contemporaries like Machiavelli—and in Germany, the emperor was no more than a figurehead of the Holy Roman Empire. When Charles V became emperor in 1519, his real strength lay in his position as duke of Austria, lord of the Netherlands, and king of Spain. Becoming emperor added something to his prestige, much to his responsibilities, but little to his power. Consequently, there was no power in Germany to resist the exactions of the papacy, which naturally increased as the popes found themselves successfully challenged elsewhere.

This lack of central authority in Germany was crucial in the sixteenth century. It contributed to the success of the Protestant Reformation, which became mixed up in the political competition of the German princes. It also forced the emperor to rely only on his own hereditary domains in meeting the threat of a new power from Asia Minor. The Ottoman Turks had advanced steadily after the fall of Constantinople in 1453. The greatest of their sultans, Suleiman the Magnificent (r. 1520–66), captured Belgrade, won most of Hungary in the battle of Mohacs (1526), and almost took Vienna in 1529. To meet this threat, the Habsburg emperor had to build a new state in his hereditary territory of Austria.

Suggestions For Further Reading

General

The classic work on the Renaissance is J. Burckhardt, *The Civilization of the Renaissance in Italy* (1860). For a recent survey, see D. Hay, *The Italian Renaissance* (1977). W. K. Ferguson, *Europe in Transition: 1300–1520* (1963), emphasizes social and economic history. For a revolutionary view of the economic background of the Renaissance, see R. S. Lopez and H. A. Miskimin, "The Economic Depression of the Renaissance," *Eco-nomic History Review* 14 (1962), and the response by C. Cipolla, "Economic Depression of the Renais-sance?" *Economic History Review* 16 (1963–64). For an overview, see A. Molho, *Social and Economic Founda-tions of the Italian Renaissance* (1969), and G. Huppert, *After the Black Death: A Social History of Early Modern Europe* (1986).

Italian Politics and Society

Recently, historians have written a series of works on individual Italian cities. See G. Brucker, *Renaissance Florence* (1969); D. Herlihy, *Pisa in the Early Renaissance* (1958); and W. M. Bowsky, *The Finances of the Commune of Siena* (1970); D. S. Chambers, *The Imperial Age of Ven-ice: 1380–1580* (1970); and C. M. Ady, *Milan under the Sforza* (1907). See also, R. de Roover, *The Rise and Fall of the Medici Bank* (1963). For a general view, see D. Waley, *The Italian City Republics* (1969).

The classic work on the origins of modern diplomacy is G. Mattingly, *Renaissance Diplomacy* (1955). For back-ground, see D. E. Queller, *The Office of Ambassador in the Middle Ages* (1967). On Renaissance warfare, see C. Oman, *History of the Art of War in the Sixteenth Cen-tury* (1937), and M. Mallett, *Mercenaries and their Mas-ters* (1974).

On the Renaissance family, see L. deMause, ed., *The History of Childhood* (1974); J. Gage, *Life in Italy at the Time of the Medici* (1968); C. L. Lee, Jr., *Daily Life in Renaissance Italy* (1975); G. Brucker, *Giovanni and Lusanna: Love and Marriage in Renaissance Florence* (1986); and P. Aries, *Centuries of Childhood* (1962), a revolution-ary work that uses art to show how views of children changed over time. *The Portable Renaissance Reader*, ed. J. B. Ross and M. McLaughlin (1953), contains a selec-tion from Alberti's *On the Family*, as well as other works.

Humanism

On the origins of Renaissance humanism, see C. Trinkhouse, *The Poet as Philosopher: Petrarch and the Formation of the Renaissance Consciousness* (1979). On the humanist movement, see P. Kristeller, *Renaissance Thought*, 2 vols. (1961, 1965), and C. Trinkhaus, *The Scope of Renaissance Humanism* (1983). H. Baron, *The Cri-sis of the Early Italian Renaissance*, 2 vols. (1966), is an important treatment of the relationship between hu-manist thought and Florentine history in the early fif-teenth century. On Renaissance political thought, see J. W. Allen, *Political Thought in the Sixteenth Century* (1928), and F. Chabod, *Machiavelli and the Renaissance* (1958).

Art and Architecture

There are many histories of Renaissance art and archi-tecture. See P. Murray and L. Murray, *The Art of the Renaissance* (1963); P. Murray, *Architecture of the Italian Renaissance* (1963); and E. H. Gombrich, *The Story of Art* (1953). See also, Gombrich's article on the Medici as patrons of art in E. F. Jacob. ed., *Italian Renaissance*

Studies (1960). B. Berenson, *The Italian Painters of the Renaissance*, rev. ed. (1930), is a classic work. Berenson developed a method of attributing and dating works of art based primarily on stylistic analysis. See also, M. Baxendall, *Painting and Experience in Fifteenth-* *Century Italy* (1972). On the background of Renaissance art, see E. Panofsky, *Early Netherlandish Painting* (1953), and M. Meiss, *Painting in Florence and Siena after the Black Death* (1951).

Economic Growth

For a general history of the European economy, see the *Cambridge Economic History of Europe*, 3 vols. (1952–66). Volume 1 deals with agriculture; Volume 2 with commerce and industry; and Volume 3 with economic organization and policy. H. A. Miskimin, *The Economy of Early Renaissance Europe* (1969), is a good short survey. R. Ehrenberg, *Capital and Finance in the Age of the Renaissance* (1928), is the standard study of the Fuggers. See also, E. Power and M. M. Postan, eds., *Studies in English Trade in the Fifteenth Century* (1953), and A. R. Bridbury, *Economic Growth: England in the Later Middle Ages* (1962). On the low countries, see H. Van Der Wee, *The Growth of the Antwerp Market and the European Economy* (1963). E. Eisenstein, *The Printing Press as an Agent of Change* (1979), is a good account of the invention and its effects.

France, England, and Spain

On late medieval France, see the works cited in Chapter 14. See also, P. M. Kendall, *Louis the Eleventh* (1971); F. Pegues, *Lawyers of the Last Capetians* (1962); and J. H. Shennan, *The Parlement of Paris* (1968). On Spain and England, see the works cited in Chapter 14.

17
Religious Reform and Revolution in Western Christendom

*D*uring the Middle Ages, the Church had become increasingly centralized, and the popes had found ways to control its affairs and to reduce the power of bishops. In the fourteenth century, the papal government at Avignon was the largest and wealthiest in Europe, with an immense bureaucracy and an efficient system for taxing churches and monasteries throughout Christendom. But by the early sixteenth century, the success of the secular rulers in gaining control over the churches in their realms had put the papacy in a difficult position. The popes lost much of the revenue they had enjoyed in the Avignon period, and, after the Great Schism (1378–1417), they were embroiled in Italian politics. By degrees the pope was reduced to the status of an Italian despot.

By the beginning of the sixteenth century, suspicion of the Church's policy and contempt for its leadership had become widespread in Europe. People of every class were so annoyed or out-raged by the persistent financial demands of the Church that attendance fell substantially. However, this did not mean that interest in religion had declined. Evangelical preachers abounded in Europe, and people responded enthusiastically to their sermons. These preachers often aimed criticism at the established ecclesiastical hierarchy, which many viewed not only as worldly and corrupt but also as an unsympathetic landlord.

The Church was also in conflict with the new class of capitalistic merchants and industrialists. It had never been able to incorporate business ethics into its system of values: it inherited both an ancient Roman attitude that business was necessarily corrupting and morally suspect and the Judaic prohibition of usury (the practice of charging interest for loans). Throughout the Middle Ages, merchants had frequently borrowed money to finance their business, but, because of the Church's attitude toward the paying of

Lucas Cranach the Younger,
*Martin Luther and the
Wittenberg Reformers* (*ca.*
1543).

interest, they had had to create ruses to escape the charge of usury. The rise of capitalistic business increased the tension between the commercial classes and the Church because capitalism was based on the idea that money invested in an enterprise ought to produce a return for the investor. Like others in their society, businessmen were frustrated and angered by a Church that did not practice what it preached. Ecclesiastical officials were often among the greediest and shadiest characters in the late medieval economic system. In the schools, one of the questions put to students for debating practice was "Can an archdeacon be saved?" The archdeacon was the principal administrative officer of a bishopric.

THE NEED FOR REFORM OF THE CHURCH

The End of the Medieval Church

The state of the Church during the Avignon "captivity" and the Great Schism (see pp. 391–95) seemed so hopeless that many laymen began to seek salvation through their own efforts. The mildest and probably the most numerous reformers did not break openly with the Church; they simply ceased to rely on it. They formed little associa-

tions, such as the Brethren of the Common Life in the low countries and Rhineland, to encourage one another to lead a devout Christian life and to seek direct contact with God through mystical experiences. The Brethren produced some remarkable works of devotion, such as the *Theologica Germanica*, which influenced later reformers. They also founded schools that were to play a great role in the educational revival of the fifteenth and sixteenth centuries; Erasmus (see pp. 475–76) was educated in a Brethren school. Conservative churchmen looked on these groups of reformers with suspicion, but most of the groups managed to remain within the bounds of orthodoxy.

A more radical element was not content simply to withdraw into devout piety. These men wanted a thoroughgoing reform of the Church, and many of them felt that only laymen could do the job. An early example of this attitude can be seen in the *Defensor pacis*, written about 1324 by Marsilius of Padua. He believed that the state should control the Church just as it controlled other organizations. If the state could regulate the behavior of doctors, it could also regulate the behavior of priests. The Church condemned Marsilius's book, but his ideas inspired further criticism throughout the fourteenth and fifteenth centuries.

Another dangerous critic of the Church was the Oxford professor John Wiclif (*ca.* 1320–84). At first concerned mainly with the problem of private property, including the property of the Church, Wiclif decided that the Church was being corrupted by wealth and that it would be best if kings and nobles took over its property. The leaders of secular society were naturally pleased by this idea, and they protected Wiclif from the wrath of the clergy. Wiclif went on to cast doubt on the orthodox doctrine that the bread and wine in the communion service are transformed into the body and blood of Christ. He ended up by attacking the whole administrative structure of the

A pair of woodcuts by Lucas Cranach the Elder contrasting Jesus and the pope. On the left, Jesus is driving the moneychangers from the temple; on the right, the pope is taking money for indulgences.

Church as corrupt and largely unauthorized by the Bible. He also encouraged his followers to translate the Bible, so ordinary men could understand it when read and could appreciate its message without the mediation of the clergy.

Wiclif had no intention of launching a popular movement, but his ideas spread rapidly beyond the scholarly circles for which he wrote. Wandering preachers used the English Bible in their work and took advantage of social discontent after the Black Death by emphasizing Wiclif's most radical ideas. Many of them became social as well as religious reformers and gained a considerable following among the lower and middle classes in England. Their preaching contributed to the radicalism of the great Peasants' Rebellion of 1381, and the nobles helped the king suppress the religious radicals—called the Lollards—along with the rebellion. But the suppression was not wholly successful. The Lollards went underground, and their religious doctrines and the Wiclifite translation of the Bible survived until the English Reformation in the sixteenth century.

These regional movements for reform were strengthened by the Great Schism, during which the Church nearly dissolved into independent national churches. In 1395 the French became so exasperated with their pope, Benedict XIII of Avignon, that the French clergy, under pressure from the government, withdrew their obedience from him for five years. This was the first appearance of a policy that was to have a fateful future: secession from papal jurisdiction by the clergy of a large nation under the pressure of a secular government.

John Hus

The problem of heresy and radical reform continued into the conciliar epoch, and the councils were much concerned about it. At the beginning of the Council of Constance (1414–18), the danger spot was Bohemia. Here during the preceding century the em-

In the first of this pair of woodcuts, Cranach shows Jesus kissing the feet of his disciples as he washes them. The other woodcut shows the pope offering his foot to be kissed by kings and nobles.

peror Charles IV (who was also king of Bohemia) had helped to foster a cultural awakening among the Czechs. But Czech scholars ran into two obstacles: a corrupt and leaderless Church and a steady influx of Germans into the cities and into the newly founded University of Prague (1348), the first German university. Since the Czechs tended to be reformers, while the Germans generally supported the status quo, the gifted group of Czech preachers and teachers who attacked ecclesiastical abuses soon found themselves leading a movement that was as much patriotic as it was religious. In 1402 a brilliant young leader named John Hus (ca. 1369–1415) emerged. The content of his preaching was that faith must be based on the Bible as the only source of authority; that Christ, not the pope, was the true head of the Church; and that a man is saved by God through Christ, not by trusting in ceremonies and in a mediating priesthood that was thoroughly corrupt. Hus knew and used the ideas of Wiclif, whose books had been brought to Bohemia by Czech students returning from England. But Hus had developed his basic notions independently. By 1414 he had been excommunicated by the Roman pope, but he was at liberty, and his ideas were accepted by a majority of the Czech people.

In 1414, Hus was invited under an imperial guarantee of safe-conduct to defend his ideas at the Council of Constance (called to resolve the Great Schism), and he eagerly accepted. When he arrived, he was almost immediately imprisoned for heresy, the emperor's guarantee notwithstanding. The emperor withdrew his protection as soon as the charge of heresy was leveled at Hus. The conciliar leaders wanted Hus to make a public recantation of his views, but he stood firm. In the dramatic trial that followed, the essential issue was whether the Bible and a man's conscience are the ultimate religious authority as Hus argued or whether the Catholic Church represented by the clerical hierarchy is the sole authority as the council declared. Hus was condemned and burned at the stake outside the walls of Constance in May 1415. One of his followers, Jerome of Prague, was burned on the same spot the next spring.

Before the council disbanded in 1418, civil and religious warfare had broken out in Bohemia. It lasted for almost 20 years, until 1436 when the more conservative Hussites and the Church reached an agreement. The agreement recognized a national church in Bohemia with local control over ecclesiastical appointments and with its own liturgical practices, notably the right to offer the cup as well as the bread to the laity when giving communion. For the first time the Church had made an agreement on equal terms with condemned heretics after having excommunicated them and solemnly preached a crusade against them. Wiclif's Lollards had been driven underground in England, but the Hussite heresy had simply been walled off in Bohemia.

The Papacy's Triumph over the Conciliar Movement

Pope Martin V (r. 1417–31), elected at the Council of Constance, soon commanded the allegiance of all western Christendom except Aragon, which continued to support its native son Pope Benedict XIII, who had defied the law of averages as well as the council by living into his nineties. Successful as it was in ending the schism, the council was unable to institute reform. The English and German delegates worked in vain to have reform considered before the election of a new pope; the Latin nations were more anxious to heal the schism first and let reform come later. Once Martin V was elected, interest flagged in even the mild report of a committee to study abuses, and the council dispersed without ever really facing the evil practices in the hierarchy.

The council fathers at Constance had decreed that the general councils must be summoned every ten years. But the superior diplomacy and the more efficient administrative machinery of the Roman papacy soon made this provision a dead letter. The temper of the time was changing; people now thought the idea that a ruler should be controlled by an assembly led only to confusion. Just as most European kings weakened their parliaments and humbled their nobles, so the popes stopped holding councils at regular intervals and humbled the princes of the Church, the cardinals. By the time Nicholas V (r. 1447–55) became pope, the threat that the Church might be transformed into a limited monarchy was past. Since that time there has not been a general council that the pope could not control.

The popes' triumph over the councils left the papacy stronger in some respects, but weaker in others. No one within the Church could challenge papal power, but, in opposing the reforming element in the councils, the popes had isolated themselves from clerical and lay leaders of opinion, particularly in northern Europe. As a result, the popes depended on the support of the lay rulers and could not resist their efforts to control the clergy within their realms. In 1438 the king of France, Charles VII, summoned an assembly of the French clergy and issued

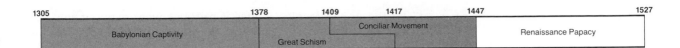

1305		1378	1409	1417	1447	1527

Babylonian Captivity

Great Schism

Conciliar Movement

Renaissance Papacy

a solemn decree known as the Pragmatic Sanction of Bourges. This decree strictly limited the pope's power to appoint and tax the clergy in France and in effect set up a national, or "Gallican," church. In later years the popes were able to persuade the French monarchs to modify this one-sided action by "concordats," or treaties, between the papacy and the French crown, but in these agreements the French kings always retained their rights in the appointment of high clergy. During the fourteenth and fifteenth centuries, the kings of England and Spain established similar limitations of papal authority. In Germany, where there was no central government strong enough to stand up to the pope, papal rights of appointment, taxation, and jurisdiction remained. But elsewhere the popes had eliminated the clerical rivals to their power only to be faced by the much more greedy and formidable lay monarchs.

The period of 80 years between the accession of Nicholas V to the papacy (1447) and the sack of Rome by imperial Spanish troops (1527) is often called the age of the Renaissance papacy. It was a period in which many popes were highly educated patrons of humanists and artists, while other popes were nepotistic despots. Nicholas V founded the Vatican library, one of the premier repositories of books and manuscripts in the world. Pius II (r. 1458–64) was a celebrated Sienese humanist, the former Aeneas Sylvius Piccolomini. Julius II (r. 1503–13) began the rebuilding of St. Peter's. Two popes were particularly renowned for their wars: Sixtus IV (r. 1471–84), who was said to have died of rage at the conclusion of a peace settlement; and Julius II, who was known to his generation as "the Warrior Pope." Alexander VI (r. 1492–1503), Rodrigo Borgia, tried to carve a principality out of the Papal

States for his illegitimate son, Cesare Borgia; Machiavelli focused attention on the Borgias in his work, *The Prince.*

The medieval papacy had often been embroiled in politics, but it had been international politics, and grand principles of political authority were usually at stake. In contrast, the Renaissance popes were embroiled in Italian politics, and only dynastic interests were at stake. In time, the papacy became thoroughly Italianized. (In fact, since the end of the Great Schism in 1417, only two non-Italians have been elected pope, in 1522 and 1979.)

The Renaissance Church had problems elsewhere besides in the openly corrupt papal curia. Bishops and archbishops throughout Europe were generally of noble birth, and many of them had been nominated by monarchs or by the pope as a reward for loyal service rather than for piety or administrative ability. In most cases, the new bishop paid a substantial part of his first year's income to the power that appointed him, which not only was contrary to canon law, but also made the bishops eager to make the most of the potential income of their dioceses. Moreover, many bishops and archbishops held more than one bishopric— also contrary to the law. When a diocese had an absentee bishop, the episcopal income was drained from the local economy, while the church remained leaderless and at the mercy of the greedy priests and secular lords of the district. The absenteeism could be extreme: one bishop visited his bishopric only once, when he was buried there.

Even conscientious bishops found that their power to appoint competent clergy and to reform abuses within their dioceses was very limited. Many rights and powers that formerly belonged to the bishops had either fallen into the hands of local laymen or had

Cesare Borgia, anonymous copy of an authentic portrait.

been "reserved" by the pope. People came to expect their parish clergy to be ignorant and immoral. Furthermore, the parish priests also had to pay taxes to their bishops and to local laymen, which made the priests almost as rapacious as their superiors. The normal income of the churches was composed of tithes (that is, a tenth of the income of parishioners), first fruits (a small payment from the beginning of the harvest), and oblations (gifts offered by parishioners). By the sixteenth century priests added substantially to this income by levying fees for baptisms, marriages, and burials.

During the Middle Ages, monastic orders had provided religious services for the people when parish priests either were unable to—because their flocks had grown too large, as in some rapidly expanding cities—or were incompetent. By the late fifteenth century, the religious orders no longer attracted the pious, and monks had the reputation of living rich and secular lives. The orders no longer had much influence on laymen and had to recruit actively to keep their monasteries populated.

The most common complaints against the Church concerned practices that could be interpreted as the selling of spiritual benefits. The Church was land rich, but cash poor, and its ministers had to find ways to support their institutions. But the methods they used to raise money and the purposes for which they used it—wars, rich living, and the like—outraged many faithful. Clergy at all levels of the hierarchy were criticized, but the papacy was considered the worst offender.

Indulgences

Although it was not the most important source of papal income, the sale of indulgences was the practice that people found most illegitimate and abusive. An indulgence was a remission of the temporal penalty for sin imposed by a priest in the sacrament of penance. Christians were required to confess their sins and receive a penitential penalty, or penance, at least once a year. Penances ranged from saying prayers to going on a crusade or pilgrimage; it depended on the seriousness of the sin and the condition of the sinner.

During the Middle Ages, it became common for people to commute their penances with a money payment, and in the fourteenth century the popes developed the doctrine that Christ and the saints had accumulated a "treasury of merits" from which Christ's vicars—the popes—could dispense benefits to the faithful through indulgences. In the sixteenth century, Sixtus IV expanded this doctrine by claiming the power to release the souls of the dead from the penances they were undergoing in Purgatory—the state in which the soul purged its sins before being admitted to Paradise. This claim transformed the traffic in indulgences into a booming trade and a real money-maker. It was hard for people to resist an offer to ease the suffering of the soul of a dead parent. Yet, when it was clear that the contributions made for the indulgences went not to pious purposes, but to war and ostentatious living, many laymen concluded that the Church was selling salvation as a money-making device.

Criticism and Reform of the Church in the Fifteenth Century

The late fifteenth-century Church was liable to a great deal of criticism, and conscientious and pious ecclesiastical leaders found it difficult to answer it. Their difficulty stemmed not only from the undeniable abuses in the Church's operations, but also from changes in society and social attitudes that reduced the status of churchmen. The European world of 1500 was more secular in its interests and ideals than the world of 1400 had been. Imbued with the new ideals of the Renaissance, many people considered careers in business, politics, and the arts to be as valuable as the clerical professions and hardly less likely than they to lead to salvation.

At the same time, the fifteenth century was a period of heightened religious sensitivity and piety among the lower and middle classes. Late medieval popular piety had spawned a luxuriant growth of religious practices that often verged on superstition and idolatry. The cult of the saints and the veneration of relics became a kind of obsession. In what one historian has called the "supersaturated" religious atmosphere of the fifteenth century, the most observant Church leaders became worried. They recognized that the Church was vulnerable to radicals who could ask: What is the core of Christianity? Is it the ritual and elaborate institutional structure of the Church? Is it the veneration of relics or pilgrimage? Or is it to love one's neighbor and to live simply, as Christ lived?

The new power of the secular rulers to appoint bishops, tax the clergy, and regulate relations between the churches in their realms and the pope also posed a serious threat because the kings could now call for religious reform for their own political purposes. Yet, reform by royal command was sometimes well motivated and had good results: in Spain, Cardinal Jiménez de Cisneros, strongly backed by Ferdinand and Isabella, carried out many reforms of the Spanish clergy at the beginning of the sixteenth century. But there was always the danger that reform imposed by a secular ruler, no matter what its motivation, might result in the state gaining control of the churches and their property.

During the fifteenth century there were several reform movements in the Church, but they were singularly ineffective. In the Netherlands and the Rhineland, the Brethren of the Common Life emphasized direct, intimate communion with God. Even though their emphasis on direct communion with God implied a rejection of the traditional role of the Church as the necessary intermediary between men and God, the ecclesiastical authorities permitted the Brethren to continue their quiet way of life. The movement founded very influential schools to educate a new Christian elite, but it had little effect on the Church in general.

In Florence between 1494 and 1498, one of the most remarkable preachers of the age, the Dominican Savonarola, tried to reform the society of one of Europe's richest and most secular cities. He preached repentance and piety and attacked the leaders of society and the Church. Like the Brethren, Savonarola held to the medieval conception of reform. According to that conception, the Church itself was divinely constituted and could not be "reformed," but the individuals who composed it could be corrupted and, when that happened, they should be reformed.

This old idea of reform had already begun to give way to another. In the early fourteenth century, the leaders of the councils of Constance (1414–18) and Basel (1431–37) intended to reform the institution of the Church by giving substantial power to the council and making the pope a limited monarch. Even more radical, John Hus preached a reform both of the individual and of the institution. Both Hus and Savonarola were burned as heretics.

Despite their initial fervor and popularity, all these movements lost their impetus before the end of the fifteenth century. The strength of vested interests in the Church was so great that it appeared the Church would never be roused from its complacency; the dead weight of ecclesiastical authority appeared to be immovable.

Christian Humanism

The humanistic movement, which was based on an appreciation for the eloquence and literary power of the ancient authors and which sought to reproduce that eloquence in modern writers, spread north of the Alps during the fifteenth century and was well established there by the early sixteenth century. Northern Europeans came to Italy to study with humanists, books were shipped north from Italian centers (some of the most important early presses were in northern Italy), and Italian humanists kept up a lively correspondence with sympathetic northerners. The northern European humanistic movement created by these activities is often called Christian humanism to distinguish it from its Italian parent, but the name is a bit misleading. Even though the Italian humanists were secular in their interests, concentrating their attention on the pre-Christian classical authors, they were Christians and never denied the Christian faith. If there was a difference between northern and Italian humanism, it was that the northern humanists focused more on Christian authors and writings. Therefore, their movement has the appearance of having been Christian in essence.

The basic program of the northern European humanists was not different from that of the Italians. They, too, were primarily concerned with the eloquence and literary character of the ancient writings. In their studies of the New Testament, they sought to expose the faith of the apostles as revealed in the literary language of the biblical documents. This concern led them to concentrate on the letters of St. Paul, in which the faith of a single man was represented in a substantial body of literature. They also studied the Church fathers, in whom they found an explication of the faith of the New Testament unencumbered by the elaborate and abstruse theological constructions of the medieval commentators and scholastic theologians. Not surprisingly, the humanists held St. Jerome in the highest esteem because his Latin was closest to that of Cicero and he was the greatest literary scholar among the fathers.

The principal goal of Christian humanism was to return to the original text of Christianity. Medieval intellectuals did not read the Bible without the aid of commentaries, as they did not read legal, medical, or philosophical texts without an accompanying gloss. During the Middle Ages, the major works in every field received a standard commentary, often called the *glossa ordinaria*, that became, in effect, part of the works themselves. The humanists derided the medieval commentators for their bad writing, which was often ungrammatical and, even when competent, was dense and filled with jargon. The humanists sought to reveal the eloquence of the early Christians. For them, the person who wanted to know what Christianity was

Sir Thomas More, after Hans Holbein (1527).

should go directly to its first writing to hear its original voice.

This program was fundamentally conservative—designed to save the Church from itself—but it had a radical element in that it had confidence in the independent spiritual capacity of educated laymen. Although they were loyal to Rome and the Church, Christian humanists called for vernacular translations of the Bible, so that the laity could participate in the new Christian education and could understand the need for reform. In Spain, Cardinal Jiménez set scholars to producing a monumental edition of the Bible that presented the original Hebrew and Greek texts in parallel columns with the Latin. In Germany, Johann Reuchlin defended the study of Hebrew literature as a means of understanding the Old Testament, while a group of German Dominicans—who saw such study as a threat to the exclusive authority of the Church's hierarchy—sought to destroy all Hebrew books. In France, Lefèvre d'Etaples studied the Epistles of Paul and translated the New Testament into French (1523) in an effort to enlighten his contemporaries and further the cause of reform. In England, Thomas More—the humanist lawyer who became the royal chancellor in 1529 and was executed in 1535 for his loyalty to the Roman Catholic Church—linked education and reform in his literary work. In a famous book, *Utopia*, More revealed the ironies and hypocrisies of contemporary society, politics, and religion and called for the spread of true, simple, Christianity through education and scholarship.

Erasmus

The acknowledged leader of the Christian humanists was Erasmus of Rotterdam (*ca.* 1469–1536). Erasmus was deeply influenced by the schools of the Brethren of the Common Life, which emphasized the study of early Christian writers, and had absorbed the ideals—though not the secular interests—of the Italian humanists. He de-

A Catholic, Sir Thomas More, on the Church

The true Church of Christ is the common known church of all Christian people not gone out nor cast out. This whole body both of good and bad is the Catholic Church of Christ, which is in this world very sickly, and hath many sore members, as hath sometime the natural body of a man. . . . The Church was gathered, and the faith believed, before any part of the New Testament was put in writing. And which was or is the true scripture, neither Luther nor Tyndale [translator of the New Testament into English] knoweth but by the credence that they give to the Church. . . . The Church was before the gospel was written; and the faith was taught, and men were baptized and masses said, and the other sacraments ministered among Christian people, before any part of the New Testament was put in writing. . . . As the sea shall never surround and overwhelm the land, and yet it hath eaten many places in, and swallowed whole countries up, and made places now sea that sometime were well-inhabited lands, and hath lost part of his own possession in other parts again; so though the faith of Christ shall never be overflown with heresies, nor the gates of hell prevail against Christ's Church, yet in some places it winneth in a new people, so may there in some places by negligence be lost the old.

From *The Workes of Sir Thomas More,* (London: Scholar Press, 1978) pp. 527, 852, 853, 921.

voted his life to scholarship in the conviction that sound learning would help save the Church.

As a scholar, Erasmus produced the first critical edition of the Greek text of the New Testament (1516), which was based on the humanist method of comparing ancient manuscripts to produce an accurate text. His preface to the edition urged that the work be used as the basis of new translations into the vernacular languages. In a classic statement of the Christian humanist ideal, he said, "I utterly dissent from those who are unwilling that the sacred Scriptures should be read by the unlearned translated into their vulgar tongue, as though Christ had taught such subtleties that they can scarcely be understood even by a few theologians, or, as though the strength of the Christian religion consisted in men's igno-

Erasmus' Preface to His Edition of the New Testament

I utterly dissent from those who are unwilling that the sacred Scriptures should be read by the unlearned translated into their vulgar tongue, as though Christ had taught such subtleties that they can scarcely be understood even by a few theologians, or, as though the strength of the Christian religion consisted in men's ignorance of it. The mysteries of kings it may be safer to conceal, but Christ wished his mysteries to be published as openly as possible. I wish that even the weakest woman should read the Gospel—should read the epistles of Paul. And I wish these were translated into all languages, so that they might be read and understood, not only by Scots and Irishmen, but also by Turks and Saracens. To make them understood is surely the first step. It may be that they might be ridiculed by many, but some would take them to heart. I long that the husbandman should sing portions of them to himself as he follows the plough, that the weaver should hum them to the tune of his shuttle, that the traveller should beguile with their stories the tedium of his journey.

From Erasmus, "Paraclesis," *Novum Instrumentum*, trans. by Frederic Seebohm, in *The Oxford Reformers* (New York: Dutton, 1914), p. 203.

rance of it." In hundreds of letters and books, Erasmus proclaimed a "philosophy of Christ"—the love of God and neighbor that he considered to be the essence of Christianity.

Erasmus combined great intellect, learning, literary power, and a lively sense of humor in his work, which had enormous influence among his contemporaries. He absorbed the Renaissance interest in life in this world by insisting that the love that was the essence of Christianity be expressed through an active life of good works. He ridiculed monks and priests who thought that withdrawal from the world was the best form of the Christian life. Christ himself came to the world; he did not withdraw from it. Erasmus also rejected the ceremonies and fasts of traditional medieval Christianity. Such acts would not, he said, lead to heaven—or to reform— for Christ said, in effect, "I promised the inheritance of my Father, not to

cowls, prayers, or fasts, but to works of charity." This literary device of imagining how Christ himself would judge the world of the early sixteenth century was characteristic of Christian humanism.

Christian humanism had a lasting influence on European ideas of education and the power of education to effect moral and spiritual reform, but it was a movement based on an ideal of universal intellectual achievement that was bound to fail. It never had much appeal for the mass of the population, for it was too aristocratic and too intellectual.

LUTHER'S REVOLT FROM ROME

On October 31, 1517, an Augustinian friar serving as professor of the Bible in the little University of Wittenberg in Saxony prepared 95 theses—or propositions—for academic debate on the subject of indulgences. The author, Martin Luther (1483–1546), was outraged by the unscrupulous salesmanship of a Dominican friar named Tetzel, who had been hawking indulgences in Magdeburg. Tetzel's sales pitch was effective with simple people, but infuriating to the sophisticated: "So soon as coin in coffer rings, the soul into Heaven springs." The proceeds of this particular sale of indulgences were supposed to go toward the building of the new church of St. Peter in Rome, but half of the money actually ended up in the pockets of the archbishop of Mainz and of the Fugger banking firm.

Luther's theses were immediately printed and debated, not only in Wittenberg, but throughout Germany, and they caused a sensation. His points struck a note of resentment against papal and ecclesiastical exactions and practices that was ready to be sounded in Germany. His main propositions were these:

There is no divine authority for preaching that the soul flies out of

Erasmus, by Holbein.

purgatory immediately the money clinks in the bottom of the chest. . . . It is certainly possible that when the money clinks in the bottom of the chest, avarice and greed increase. . . . All those who believe themselves certain of their own salvation by means of letters of indulgence will be eternally damned, together with their teachers. . . . Any Christian whatsoever, who is truly repentant, enjoys plenary remission from penalty and guilt, and this is given him without letters of indulgence.

At the time he wrote this fiery document, Luther was a brilliant, high-strung man of 34. He was the son of a prosperous peasant turned miner—from a family that had benefited from the economic changes during the fifteenth century—who had been able to give his son a university education. Brilliant and sensitive, the young Luther suffered several emotional crises, which eventually led him to become a friar. In an age of humanism and new learning, Luther followed the old, medieval path toward scholastic learning—which still dominated the university curriculum—and the religious life.

Luther was as intense about his religious life as he was about his studies, but he found no spiritual solace in the prayers, confessions, and penances of

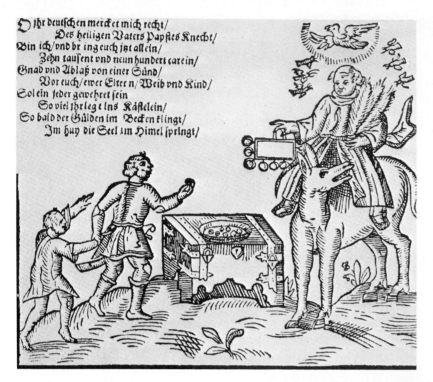

O ihr deutschen merckt mich recht/
Des heiligen Vaters Papstes Knecht/
Bin ich/vnd br ing euch ist allein/
Zehn tausent vnd neun hundert car ein/
Gnad vnd Ablaß von einer Sünd/
Vor euch/ewer Eltern/Weib vnd Kind/
Sol ein seder gewehret sein
So viel ihr legt ins Kästelein/
So bald der Gülden im Becken klingt/
Im huy die Seel in Himel springt/

Contemporary caricature of Johann Tetzel hawking indulgences. The last line of the jingle is: "So soon as coin in coffer rings, the soul into Heaven springs."

the monastic community. He sought certainty that God forgave his sins, but the performance of ceremonial acts of worship and penance gave him no assurance of God's forgiveness. Instead, he became increasingly guilt-ridden and doubtful about the possibility of saving himself by some act of his own.

He found a way out of his spiritual crisis when he suddenly came to an understanding of what St. Paul had meant when he said that a man is saved not by doing the works of the Jewish law, but by his faith in Christ alone. With this new understanding, Luther looked on the ceremonies and religious practices of the medieval Church as a new Jewish law. He recognized that he had been trying to satisfy God by satisfying the demands of Church ritual, and he now saw this ritual as no less demanding or more effective than the Jewish system against which Paul had preached. It became unthinkable for him that human beings, corrupted by sin, could buy God's favor by performing some good deed or sacramental act. He came to believe

that God alone saves men's souls, that men can do nothing but have faith in God's forgiveness.

It took Luther some time to work out the revolutionary implications of his new understanding. He slowly came to view ceremonies and sacraments, pilgrimages and indulgences—everything the medieval Church called "good works"—as irrelevant at best and dangerous at worst. Indulgences were the first "good works" that Luther rejected, and after his attack on them sales dropped off sharply in Germany. When the Dominicans, the chief dealers in indulgences, persuaded Pope Leo X (r. 1513–21) to condemn his theses, Luther was gradually driven into denying the authority of the pope. He also came to believe that John Hus had been right on certain points, despite his condemnation by the Council of Constance, and this belief led him to deny the authority of councils as well.

The development of Luther's thought and the support he gained for his protests against the ecclesiastical authorities brought him before Em-

Portrait of Martin Luther by Lucas Cranach (1533).

peror Charles V (r. 1519–56) at an imperial diet held at Worms in April 1521. Luther was given a safe-conduct—as was John Hus a century earlier—to appear before the diet to defend his propositions. He told the emperor and assembled magnates and prelates of Germany that he was bound by the authority of the Scriptures and his own conscience rather than by that of either the pope or council. Luther could not recant any of his writings, he said, because his conscience was "captive of the Word of God" and because it was "neither safe nor right to go against conscience." The Bible and individual conscience were to become the two principal pillars of Protestant Christianity.

The emperor and his council honored the safe-conduct they had granted to Luther, and he was permitted to return to the protection of his ruler, Frederick, the Elector of Saxony. For 25 years, till his death in 1546, Luther taught, preached, and wrote at Wittenberg. In his new view of Christianity, the active life of the merchant or housewife was as spiritually valuable as the life of a monk or nun, and he himself married a former nun, by whom he had six children. Meanwhile, the revolt against the papacy that he had started gathered momentum and spread over northern Europe. By the late sixteenth century, the unity of western Christendom was permanently destroyed.

Lutheran Principles

There were three main principles in Luther's religious thought: salvation by faith, not by works; the ultimate authority of the Bible; and the priesthood of all believers. The three were closely related. Luther came to his belief in salvation by faith through his reading of the Bible, and he always appealed to the Bible against the authority of tradition or the papacy.

Luther wrote hundreds of letters and tracts proclaiming and defending his ideas, but his greatest literary work was a German translation of the Bible

---

Luther on Justification by Faith

For the word of God cannot be received and honored by any works, but by faith alone. Hence it is clear that, as the soul needs the word alone for life and justification, so it is justified by faith alone and not by any works. For if it could be justified by any other means, it would have no need of the word, nor consequently of faith. . . .

It is evident that by no outward work or labor can the inward man be at all justified, made free and saved, and that no works whatever have any relation to him. And so, on the other hand, it is solely by impiety and incredulity of heart that he becomes guilty and a slave of sin, deserving condemnation; not by any outward sin or work.

Therefore the first care of every Christian ought to be to lay aside all reliance on works, and strengthen his faith alone more and more, and by it grow in the knowledge, not of works, but of Christ Jesus, who has suffered and risen again for him.

From Martin Luther, *On Christian Liberty*, trans. by H. Wace and C. A. Buchheim, in *First Principles of the Reformation* (London: Murray, 1883), pp. 107–08.

(completed in 1534). He wanted to put the text of the Bible into the hands of every German who could read, for he claimed that there was no essential difference between a priest and a layman. A dedicated layman reverently reading the Scripture was closer to the divine truth than a worldly pope proclaiming the dogma of the Church. Thus, a pious layman could serve God as well as a priest or monk. Luther's Bible achieved its purpose, and its literary quality was so original and excellent that it is considered the foundation stone of the modern high German language.

Luther's original protest had been purely religious in character, but by 1520 he was appealing to the cultural nationalism of Germans. "What has brought us Germans to such a pass that we have to suffer this robbery and this destruction of our property by the Pope?" he asked. His message attracted support from princes eager to

Title page of the first German translation of the Bible, by Martin Luther, printed in 1534 with the approval of the Elector of Saxony.

Luther on the Church

Thus it may come to pass that the Pope and his followers are wicked and not true Christians, and not being taught by God, have no true understanding, whereas a common man may have true understanding. Why should we then not follow him? Has not the Pope often erred? Who could help Christianity, in case the Pope errs, if we do not rather believe another who has the Scriptures for him? Therefore it is a wickedly devised fable—and they cannot quote a single letter to confirm it—that it is for the Pope alone to interpret the Scriptures or to confirm the interpretation of them. They have assumed the authority of their own selves. And though they say that this authority was given to St. Peter when the keys were given to him, it is plain enough that the keys were not given to St. Peter alone, but to the whole community. . . . Moreover, if the article of our faith is right, "I believe in the holy Christian Church," the Pope cannot alone be right; else we must say, "I believe in the Pope of Rome," and reduce the Christian Church to one man, which is a devilish and damnable heresy. Besides that, we are all priests, as I have said, and have all one faith, one Gospel, one Sacrament; how then should we not have the power of discerning and judging what is right or wrong in matters of faith?

From Martin Luther, "Address to the Christian Nobility of the German Nation," in *Luther's Primary Works*, ed. by H. Wace and C. A. Buchheim (London: Hodder and Stoughton, 1896), pp.170–71.

confiscate Church property, businessmen unhappy about papal finance and at odds with traditional restrictive ecclesiastical rules governing business practices, and devout laymen and conscientious priests shocked by the corruption of the Church. His religious thought permitted people to reconcile an honest life in the world with the highest spiritual aspirations. Of course, some people also seized on his rebellion for achieving their own selfish purposes.

Luther had no intention of breaking away from the Church or of establishing a competing ecclesiastical organization. But after 1520 he was convinced that the Church founded by Christ had wandered from the true path during the Middle Ages—after the conversion of Constantine, when the Church became entangled in worldly affairs—

and that the bishop of Rome was not the true vicar of Christ, but the Antichrist. He wanted the Church to return to the pure faith and simple religion of the apostles. In the purified church there would be only two sacraments—baptism and communion—in place of the seven of the Catholic Church, a simplified ritual in German rather than in Latin, and more emphasis on the congregation's participation in the service. Luther wrote many hymns for the churches that followed his ideas, and these are still sung today. But while he was proposing radical reforms, he did not want to found a new church. The definitive split between the "Lutheran" and "Catholic" churches occurred gradually and without Luther's explicit approval. The conflict over the nature of the true church merely continued unresolved until there were two human communities set against each other and eager to define their beliefs in opposition to one another.

The Spread of Lutheranism

Against the background of the failed reforms of the fifteenth century, it is striking that Lutheranism—which was one of the most radical movements in Christian history—thrived and spread. One of the great historical questions is why it succeeded. Certainly, one reason was that Luther and his supporters were able to take advantage of the printing press. They wrote hundreds of tracts and used the new technology to distribute their ideas. The nineteenth-century historian Leopold von Ranke calculated that in 1523 Luther and his supporters published nearly 400 books and pamphlets, while pro-Catholics issued only about 20. The rise of printing had the secondary effect of encouraging the spread of literacy, and Luther's confidence in the spiritual instincts of educated laymen created a great affinity between these new readers and his ideas.

Furthermore, Luther received substantial early support from humanists, the intellectual leaders of European society. The humanists were themselves reformers, and they saw in Luther's program many of the same principles they espoused. Like them, Luther attacked the medieval commentators and theologians and sought to return to the unadorned authority of the Bible. Like him, they valued the Church fathers and attacked the financial abuses of the Church. But while the humanists attacked the medieval writers for their lack of eloquence—through which, they thought, the medieval commentators had obscured the pure text of the Bible—Luther attacked them for their theological opinions. While the humanists viewed the fathers as authentic sources, along with the New Testament, of knowledge of the faith of the early Christians, Luther and his supporters viewed them as explicators of the Bible. The commentaries of the fathers were acceptable, where the medieval commentaries were not, because the fathers wrote simply and directly about the meaning of the text. But, for Luther, the sole source of authority for a Christian's faith was the Bible, particularly the New Testament.

The essential difference between the reform ideology of the humanists and Protestantism was that while the former was a reform of the method by which the Christian message was to be understood, the latter was a reform of the content or doctrine of Christianity. Further, the humanists wanted to reform the practices of the Church, while Luther and his followers came to view the Church itself as illegitimate. The difference is well illustrated by the contrast between the view, put forth by such writers as Erasmus and Cardinal Jiménez, that the biblical text had to be raised from the mire of medieval commentaries and the claim of the Protestants that only Scripture was the basis of faith in and understanding of Christ.

The difference is also illustrated by a comparison between a reform document prepared by the cardinals and presented to Pope Paul III (r. 1534–49) in 1538 and Luther's *Address to the Nobility of the German Nation* (1520). The cardinals urged the reform of the parish churches, the ending of the appointment of nonresident bishops, the restriction of the sale of indulgences to once per year, and the reform of the judicial system. They affirmed the authority of the Church. Luther complained about the same abuses, in much harsher language, but he sought to root out the problems once and for all. For example, to combat clerical marriage, the cardinals urged that the rule of celibacy be enforced; Luther argued that clerics be permitted to marry. Again, the Christian humanists and their ecclesiastical supporters wanted to replace the current theology with an older one; Luther wanted to do away with the whole medieval tradition of theology, while denying the authority of the Church it served.

Notwithstanding the profound differences between the humanists and Luther, many of the leading humanists, including Erasmus and Thomas More, at first supported Luther. Erasmus finally broke with him in 1524. More had already broken with him in 1523, when he wrote a *Letter against Luther*.

Luther also received the support of many priests and monks, especially in the German cities. The cities gave Luther his first solid support. Town governments had many grievances

Contemporary engraving depicting a noble lady and her son kneeling before peasant rebels to plead for their lives during the Peasants' Rebellion (1524–25).

against the Church: it controlled prime real estate in towns and wealthy clergy were exempt from local taxes. At the same time, the financial demands of the Church bore most heavily on the urban populations. In town after town, with little violence or disturbance, the conservative clergy were replaced by followers of Luther. Because so many of the cities were politically free (as holders of imperial charters), the reformed churches were, in effect, state churches. These new institutions predated by a decade or more the establishment of Lutheranism as a state religion by some of the German princes.

The peasants were also excited by Luther's message at first, but they lost interest in it after the Peasant's Rebellion of 1524–25. This was the greatest of the late medieval peasant uprisings. Its aim was basically social reform—the abolition of serfdom and of the burdens of the manorial system—but the rebels found religious support for their program in Luther's doctrine. "Therefore do we find in the Scripture that we are free," they argued, "and we will be free." Luther rejected this interpretation of his message—the freedom of which he spoke was spiritual, not social freedom—and he wrote a bitter condemnation of the rebels and their aims. The peasants felt that he had betrayed them, but the middle and ruling classes welcomed his social conservatism. From this period on, Luther and his supporters found themselves between the reactionary Roman Catholic Church and the radical lower classes, fighting against both.

Finally, Lutheranism spread because there was no centralized government in Germany to resist it. The emperor Charles V never wavered from his orthodoxy, but he was preoccupied with holding his vast dominions together and with military threats on every side. From 1522 to 1559, Charles and his son Philip were entangled in a series of conflicts with France that absorbed much of their energy, while Charles and his brother Ferdinand, duke of Austria, were trying to stem the tide of the Turkish advance in the Mediterranean and up the Danube Valley. In 1529, the Turks almost took Vienna.

The emperor had little time to devote to the religious controversy in Germany. Only in 1547—the year·after Luther's death—did Charles have an opportunity to combat Lutheranism, which by then had been accepted by about half the German principalities. A confused religious war dragged on in the country until 1555, when Charles permitted his brother Ferdinand to conclude the Religious Peace of Augsburg. The peace allowed the free cities and principalities in the Holy Roman Empire to choose between Lutheranism and Catholicism and bound them to respect each other's rights. Essentially, religion had become the prerogative of the ruler of each territory; those who disagreed with their ruler could migrate to another state.

The Peace of Augsburg did not solve all aspects of the dispute between Lutherans and Catholics, but it constituted the first official recognition that western Christendom was in a state of disunity and would remain so. In the end, northern Germany became mostly "Protestant" (as Lutherans had been called since 1529, when they presented a "protest" at an imperial diet); southern Germany remained "Catholic." The division remains today about as it was in 1560. Outside Germany, Lutheranism spread widely, but took root only in Scandinavia, where Denmark, Norway, and Sweden became Lutheran by mid-century. The essential Germanness of Lutheranism limited its appeal abroad, where another form of Protestantism, founded by John Calvin, became more successful.

OTHER PROTESTANT MOVEMENTS

Wittenberg was not the only center of reform. Other important centers were Zurich, Basel, Strasbourg, and especially Geneva. In each of these places a type of Protestantism developed that was significantly different in emphasis from Lutheranism. These churches—called "Reformed"—relied on a highly developed system of theology and church organization and put greater stress on the moral conduct and political action of their members than did the Lutheran churches.

Bucer and Zwingli

Among the early reformers were the humanists Martin Bucer of Strasbourg (1491–1551) and Ulrich Zwingli (1484–1531). Bucer began as a Dominican friar influenced by the humanism of Erasmus, but, when Luther's views reached him, he left the order, married a nun, and was excommunicated in 1523. From 1524 to 1548, he led the reform in Strasbourg, introducing liturgical changes as a follower of Luther. During the same period, he participated in colloquies held in Worms, Regensburg, and Hagenau aimed at reconciling Catholicism and Protestantism. He was also active in trying to reconcile Lutheranism and opposing Protestant confessions, particularly that of Zwingli.

Zwingli was born in a rural village in the eastern region of the Swiss Alps and studied classics in Basel. He also fell under Erasmus's influence and was especially attached to the Erasmian idea of a renascent Christianity based on the Scriptures. Zwingli became a priest, beginning as a village parson in 1506. But he continued his scholarly work and rose to become the people's priest in Zurich (1518). This was a prestigious position in a small, but prosperous city, and it put him in contact with the ideas of the day. In Zurich, Zwingli fell under the influence of Luther. Although he always claimed that he had arrived at the basic ideas of reform before he read Luther's work, one of the unanswered questions about Zwingli is how important to the formation of his own thought Luther's ideas actually were.

As in many other cities, the reform proceeded by stages in Zurich. In 1522, some citizens, under the influence of Luther, broke the dietary regulations for Lent, and the city council appointed a commission to investigate. The bishop of Constance, who had jurisdiction over Zurich, asserted his exclusive right to judge matters of religious discipline, but the commission, on which Zwingli sat, proceeded anyway. The report of the commission was equivocal, but a little after the affair Zwingli published a sermon in which he argued that Christians were free from the law, as St. Paul said, so that they did not have to obey it. A person's Christianity consisted in his or her internal beliefs and motivations, not in the external actions prescribed by the Church. Luther had developed the same point.

In 1523, the city council of Zurich, again under the protest of the bishop, held a disputation over questions of religion because there was much confusion and some unrest among the population of the city. In preparation for the debate, Zwingli drew up a list of 67 conclusions on questions of doctrine, morals, and Church discipline. The main ideas in his conclusions were that the Scriptures alone were the basis of true religion and that Christ was the center of Christianity. After this, Protestantism had virtually won out in Zurich, and subsequent disputes focused on how far it should go. One issue was whether the images—paintings, stained-glass windows, and sculptures—should be removed from the churches of the city. Zwingli took the position that when the members of the congregation had become true Christians through interior reform, they would no longer need the outward signs of faith, and the images would be removed. He envisaged a gradual process. However, the people were not so patient, and during 1524 they cleansed the churches of their ornate interiors—whitewashing the walls, pulling down the crucifixes, and destroying the stained-glass windows and sculptures. Finally, in 1525, the reformers, again

Sketch of John Calvin drawn by a student, perhaps during a lecture.

led by Zwingli, replaced the Mass with the simple service in commemoration of the Last Supper. Here again, the city council played a main role, issuing a regulation that did away with the Mass.

Calvinism

The most influential of the new reformers was John Calvin (1509–64). He was born in Noyon, France, and as a young man was sent to study law. However, he was more interested in humanism than in law and soon dropped out of legal studies to concentrate on Greek and Latin. In 1532, he published a commentary on Seneca's treatise *Concerning Clemency* (of the ruler). Around this time, Calvin had what he later called a conversion to Protestantism, and in 1534 he moved to Basel, where Protes-

tants were active. There, he worked on a theological treatise, the *Institutes of the Christian Religion,* which he intended to be a comprehensive presentation of the Protestant position. The first edition of this work, six chapters long, was published in 1536. Thereafter, Calvin worked on it constantly, enlarging and revising it until 1559, when the fourth edition appeared. It contained 80 chapters. The *Institutes* were the first systematic presentation of Protestant theology and have remained important to this day.

Calvin visited Geneva in 1536 with no intention of staying, but Guillaume Farel, a leading Protestant, persuaded him to become his assistant. Farel had introduced Protestantism to the city two months earlier. Together, Farel and Calvin pursued a vigorous program of reform, raising opposition by their strictness and impatience. In 1538, new elections returned a majority of Catholics to the city council, and the two reformers were driven from the city. Farel went to Neuchâtel, where he remained the rest of his life. Calvin went to Strasbourg, where he came under the influence of the moderate reformer Martin Bucer.

However, Protestantism had been established in Geneva, and in 1541 the city council asked Calvin to come back. He seems to have done so reluctantly, but as it turned out he remained there until he died in 1564. For 23 years, Calvin worked for reform, gradually asserting a power over the city council as well as in the church. By the late 1550s, Geneva had become a virtual theocracy.

Calvin's thought derived from Luther's central doctrine of salvation by faith alone. From this foundation, he built a system that emphasized the sovereignty of God and the radical depravity of man. The characteristic doctrine of his system was predestination: no acts of sinful man can earn him salvation; God, through his inscrutable will, has destined some men to be saved and others to be damned. Therefore, the idea that "good works" could affect God's judgment is absurd, but Calvin

The Spread of Protestantism   Sixteenth Century

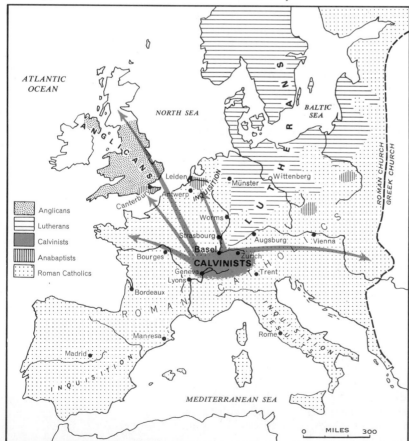

held that a person's behavior did give a sign of his or her status before God. The first sign of being among the elect of God was a true and fervent faith in Christ and the Scriptures. Good works, as commonly understood, were signs of that faith and of divine election.

In 1559, Calvin established an academy in Geneva comprising schools of arts, law, medicine, and theology. Perhaps because of his own fame, based on the *Institutes* and numerous other works, he was able to attract an excellent faculty, and within a few years the academy was flourishing, with more than 1,500 students from all over Europe. Through the fame of its leader, its academy, and its way of life, the community at Geneva became a model for Presbyterian or Reformed churches in France, England, Scotland, the Netherlands, the Rhineland, Bohemia, and Hungary. It later affected the religious life of North America and Dutch South Africa. Calvin's lasting influence was based in part on the ecclesiastical system he created. He advocated that each local church should have a ruling body composed of ministers and elders (or presbyters). These officials were to

Calvin on Predestination

Predestination we call the eternal decree of God, by which he has determined in himself, what he would have to become of every individual of mankind. For they are not all created with a similar destiny; but eternal life is foreordained for some, and eternal damnation for others. . . .

In conformity, therefore, to the clear doctrine of the Scripture, we assert, that by an eternal and immutable counsel, God has once for all determined, both whom he would admit to salvation, and whom he would condemn to destruction. We affirm that this counsel, as far as concerns the elect, is founded on his gratuitous mercy, totally irrespective of human merit; but that to those whom he devotes to condemnation, the gate of life is closed by a just and irreprehensible, but incomprehensible, judgment. . . .

How exceedingly presumptuous it is only to inquire into the causes of the Divine will; which is in fact, and is justly entitled to be, the cause of everything that exists. . . . For the will of God is the highest rule of justice; so that what he wills must be considered just, for this very reason, because he wills it.

From John Calvin, *Institutes of the Christian Religion*, trans. by John Allen (Philadelphia: Westminster Press, 1930), Book III, Ch. 21, pars. 5, 7; Ch. 23, par. 2.

The more rigid Protestants objected to all religious paintings and sculpture as leading to idolatry. In this engraving of 1579, Calvinists are pulling down statues of saints and destroying stained-glass windows.

meet in synods that linked up the Reformed churches in each district. This system was both a tough and a flexible form of church government, and it was particularly resistant to secular control. Therefore, Calvinism never became "nationalized," as had Lutheranism, and it could be easily adapted to local conditions. In Calvin's works, it also possessed a systematic theology that gave it identity and made it attractive to new reformers everywhere.

Calvinists were widely spread by the 1550s, but they were a majority only in Geneva and in Scotland. Elsewhere, they formed a tough, well-organized minority that left a deep impression on their societies. Calvinism was the basis for Puritanism in England, the Huguenots in France, the Dutch Reformed Church, and other groups. It became the militant, international form of Protestantism.

THE RADICALS

Luther, Bucer, Zwingli, and Calvin were relatively conservative reformers. There were others who pushed for radical reform that combined social and religious rebellion against the established churches. These movements stemmed from the social unrest of the period. In Germany particularly—where capitalistic enterprise developed rapidly—workers and peasants were hard hit by economic changes. Among groups of uneducated men and women, old ideas of social and religious reform resurfaced in radical Protestant movements. During the 1520s in Switzerland and in the upper Rhine Valley, little groups of such people proclaimed that a true church of Christianity was a voluntary association of converted believers, not an established or official institution like the churches of the Lutherans or Catholics.

Most of these groups held that baptism, being a sign of belief, could only be effective if the one who offered himself for the sacrament were an adult, capable of conscious belief. This idea had been put forth by certain heretical groups as far back as the twelfth century. In the sixteenth century—as in the twelfth—the idea was attacked, and the opponents of the radical groups called them Anabaptists, or rebaptizers. The liturgy of these communities was simple, and they generally took the Bible literally. Most of them would not take an oath—in court or elsewhere—or accept public office or serve in the military. Some groups

---

Radical Protestantism: The Teaching Of Menno Simons

Menno Simons (1496–1561) was one of the ablest leaders of the radical wing of the Reformation. Simons' followers formed the Mennonite Church, which still exists. His ideas also contributed to the development of the Baptist Church. He never summed up his doctrine in a single document; it has to be put together from scattered pamphlets.

We do not find in Scripture a single word by which Christ has ordained the baptism of infants, or that his apostles taught and practiced it. We say that infant baptism is but a human invention. . . . To baptize before that which is required for baptism, namely faith, is to place the cart before the horse.

Never should any commandment be observed which is not contained in God's holy Word, either in letter or in spirit.

The regenerated do not go to war nor fight. . . . How can a Christian, according to Scripture, consistently retaliate, rebel, make war, murder, slay, torture, steal, rob, and burn cities and conquer countries?

Where have you read in the Scriptures, that Christ or the Apostles called upon the power of the magistracy against those who would not hear their doctrine or obey their words? . . . Faith is a gift of God, therefore it cannot be forced on anyone by worldly authorities or by the sword.

We must be born from above, must be changed and renewed in our hearts and thus be transplanted from the unrighteous and evil nature of Adam into the righteous and good nature of Christ, or we cannot be helped in eternity by any means, divine or human.

From "Selections from the Writings of Menno Simons," in *The Medieval World and Its Transformations,* ed. by G. M. Straka (New York: McGraw-Hill, 1967), Vol. II, pp. 463, 466, 467, 468, 470.

practiced a communism of goods as described in the second chapter of Acts.

The Anabaptists were persecuted by everyone—Catholics and Protestants. After the 1530s they were driven from southern Germany and were to be found mainly in the Netherlands, Bohemia, Poland, and England. But it was in England in the seventeenth century and in the English colonies in America that the ideas of the Anabaptists were fully realized in large and successful religious communities. Modern Baptists (who believe in adult baptism only), Congregationalists (who emphasize the autonomy of local congregations of Christians), and Quakers (who rely on an "inner light" and tend toward pacifism) all trace their origins to the sixteenth-century radicals. American Protestant conceptions of the place of the church in society derive more from the Anabaptists than from either Luther or Calvin.

ANGLICANISM

Although several kings gained effective control over their national churches in the later Middle Ages, they did not do so in order to institute reforms. In England the jurisdictional breach with Rome—which was completed by Henry VIII's Act of Supremacy of 1534—was followed by a decisive religious change. Yet, Henry VIII did not intend to break with orthodox Catholic belief and practice. He made it clear that he would continue to suppress heresy, whether Lutheran or Anabaptist. Nonetheless, he could not seal off England from Protestant ideas, and he could not achieve his break with Rome without the support of Protestant sympathizers. His compromise with these elements was indicated by his approval of the distribution of an English translation of the Bible.

By the time of Henry's death in 1547, a Protestant clergy had developed within the English Church and had found a leader in the ecclesiastical head of the church, Thomas Cranmer,

Title page of Daniel Featley's *Description* of 1645, known also as "The Dippers Dipt," a satirical view of the Anabaptists.

Henry VIII, after Hans Holbein. (*ca.* 1540).

archbishop of Canterbury. Under Henry's son, Edward VI (r. 1547–53), Cranmer worked to transform the English Church into a Protestant church. He gathered together the best parts of the ancient liturgy of the Catholic Church and translated them into English in the majestic Book of Common Prayer (1549). Cranmer tried in this work to accommodate the religious ideas of both Catholics and Protestants, and he satisfied neither. He issued a revised and fully Protestant version in 1552, and this prayer book eventually became a literary symbol of Anglicanism, as Luther's Bible and Calvin's *Institutes* became rallying points for Lutheranism and Calvinism.

Further support of Protestantism in England stemmed from Henry VIII's dissolution of the monasteries. The monasteries represented international orders, often directly dependent on the papacy, and, therefore, they were a countervailing force to the new national church headed by the king. Furthermore, they were vulnerable because monasticism had lost much of its appeal, and many houses were not living up to the rules of their orders. Beginning in 1536, Henry confiscated the properties of the monastic communities and incorporated them into the crown lands. By 1539, the confiscation of the lands and dissolution of the monastic houses was completed. The confiscations virtually doubled the royal income, but the new income could not support the king's wars. As a result, Henry and his successors gradually sold the old monastic properties to aristocratic families, which gave the aristocracy an economic interest in preserving the breach with Rome.

The Protestant reformation in England came to a halt in 1553, when Henry's oldest child, Mary, daughter of Catherine of Aragon, came to the throne. Mary wanted to vindicate her mother, and, therefore, she tried to reunite the English Church with Rome. She abolished all antipapal legislation, deposed Cranmer, and purged the church of his supporters. Cranmer and

about 300 other Protestants were burned as heretics during a period of three years. Mary's religious program may have won some support among conservative Englishmen, but her reign of terror (she is called "Bloody Mary" in English history) and her marriage to Philip II of Spain, son and presumptive heir of Charles V, offended her people's humanity and patriotism. As a result, patriotism and Protestantism became identified in the public mind.

When Mary died in 1558, Elizabeth, the daughter of Henry VIII and his second wife, Anne Boleyn, succeeded to the throne. Just as Mary had had a personal interest in returning to Catholicism, so Elizabeth's legitimacy depended on the validity of Henry's divorce and on the Act of Supremacy. But Elizabeth I (r. 1558–1603) was an educated and intelligent ruler, and she understood that she would have to be tolerant and patient. She had the Book of Common Prayer revised again, to make it acceptable to Catholics and Protestants alike. She refused "to make windows into men's souls," as she put it—that is, she persecuted only those who openly and persistently opposed her policies. Even after the pope excommunicated her in 1570, she tolerated unpolitical Catholics, while treating those who denied her right to rule as traitors.

These cautious and moderate policies did not satisfy everyone. Radical Protestants continued to agitate for a purification of the English Church of Catholic traditions; these were the "Puritans." They were strong in Parliament, and the queen occasionally had to deal harshly with them, but they helped to establish the idea that patriotism required independence from Rome. In the end, England was the largest single state to secede permanently from Roman obedience.

The Protestant church that developed under Elizabeth was very conservative. The Anglican Church looked on Presbyterianism—which had become dominant in Scotland and had spread somewhat in England—with suspicion, and it was contemptuous of the Baptists. During the seventeenth century, there were religious disputes among these groups, and the established church became even more conservative than it had been under Elizabeth. Today many Anglicans would follow Henry VIII in insisting that their church is not "Protestant" at all. According to this view, it was the Catholic Church that strayed from the true path, while Henry VIII and Cranmer restored the true continuity between the church of the fathers and the church of the sixteenth century.

THE CATHOLIC REFORMATION AND THE COUNTER REFORMATION

The great Protestant leaders thought of themselves as reformers of the Church, and to this day the movement they began is generally called the Protestant Reformation. Obviously, the Catholics viewed the reformers as rebels and their reformation as a revolt. For them, a true reformation could only take place within the Church, and churchmen and pious laymen had repeatedly called for reform since the fourteenth century. However, the challenge of the Protestants increased the pressure for reform, which led to a great new movement in the middle of the sixteenth century. Historians call this movement the Catholic Reformation or, sometimes, the Counter Reformation. But properly speaking these two movements were different. The Catholic Reformation was a reform of the Church, while the Counter Reformation was the response of the Catholics to the Protestants. This response was vigorous; the Church used torture and imprisonment as well as gentler means of persuasion to bring people back to its orthodoxy.

The pressure for a Catholic reformation had produced action even before Luther began his protest. In the late fifteenth century, the Oratory of Divine Love was founded in Genoa as a lay brotherhood similar to the Brethren of the Common Life in the north. The Oratory sought to establish a simple Christian life and to reform the clergy. Clergy were gradually admitted to it, and it spread to other Italian cities. By the second quarter of the sixteenth century, it had become the principal source of reform ideas and activities within the Church.

The rise of an internal reform coincided with the decline of the political power of the papacy. The last of the politician popes of the Renaissance was Clement VII (r. 1523–34), who rejected calls for reform while pursuing the old politics of an Italian despot. To counter the power of the Holy Roman Emperor Charles V, Clement allied himself with Francis I of France (r. 1515–47). But the sack of Rome in 1527 by undisciplined imperial Spanish troops effectively ended the political aspirations of the papacy. Italy was now controlled by the imperial power. The next pope, Paul III (r. 1534–49) turned his attention to reform and renewal in the Church. He introduced reformers into the cardinalate and eventually called a great council to the city of Trent—

Engraving showing the third session of the Council of Trent (1562–63). An amphitheater was set up in the church of St. Maria Maggio.

which was under German control—to carry out the reform.

The Council of Trent met in three sessions—1545–48, 1551–52, and 1562–63. Toward the end of the first session, Emperor Charles V made an effort to get the council to deal directly with the Protestants, but the pope moved the meeting to Bologna, and the Protestants would not go to a city controlled by the pope. The second and third sessions returned to Trent and continued the work of reform. In the third session, the council issued a series of reform decrees that clarified Catholic doctrine in response to the Protestants and reformed a great many aspects of Church practice.

The council declared that salvation was indeed granted by God alone and resulted from faith, but that good works demonstrated faith and confirmed the working of God's mercy in the doer. It also asserted that the final religious authority was the Bible *and* tradition, as interpreted by the Roman Catholic Church. The council urged the establishment of seminaries to train priests, and these schools became the basis of a gradual reform of the priesthood. It reaffirmed that clerics could not hold multiple ecclesiastical offices and the absolute supremacy of the pope over the clerical hierarchy.

The later sessions of the council were dominated by the power of Charles V's son, Philip II of Spain (r. 1556–98), who was determined that Spain would stand against the Protestant threat. Spaniards played the largest role in a revived and militant Church throughout Europe. The most powerful agency of the Counter Reformation also stemmed from Spain. It was a new order founded by Ignatius of Loyola (1491–1556), a Spaniard of Basque descent. During the wars between the Habsburgs and the French, Ignatius suffered a severe wound and spent months in recuperation. He devoured books on the lives of the saints, which were the only reading material at hand, and decided to become a kind of Christian knight in the service of the

Virgin Mary. During the lengthy period of his conversion to the new life, he went through a series of "spiritual exercises" that he later passed on to his followers. The exercises consisted in the concentration of one's imagination on the most vivid details of hell and of the life and death of Christ in order to strengthen the will toward salvation. While Ignatius studied at the University of Paris (he was a contemporary there of John Calvin), he enlisted nine friends, who became the nucleus of the new order, the Society of Jesus. Pope Paul III approved the order in 1540, and its members became known as Jesuits.

The Jesuits wore no distinctive habit; they dressed as their job might require. They swore an oath of allegiance to the pope and were carefully selected and trained for the most dangerous and difficult jobs in the Counter Reformation and in later missionary activities in unknown lands. Jesuits preached and carried out secret missions in Protestant regions, exposing themselves to execution if they were caught. They strengthened the pope's control over the Church; they ran the best schools in Europe; and, during the late sixteenth century, they won back most of Bohemia, Poland, Hungary, and southern Germany from Protestantism.

The reformation of the Church was also carried out through revived inquisitions. A new, royal Inquisition had been established in Spain in 1480. It was copied by the Habsburgs in the Netherlands in 1523 and by the Spanish powers in Italy in 1542. A little later, the papacy instituted a system of censorship of printed books, which had been so effective in spreading Protestant ideas. This system was the Index, instituted in 1559 by the pope and approved, with some additions, by the Council of Trent in 1563. The faithful were forbidden to read any book on the Index.

The Catholic Reformation gave new religious vitality to the Church and enabled it to close ranks against the

Protestants. By the second half of the sixteenth century a strong, relatively monolithic Catholic Church, reorganized and backed by Spanish power, faced a Protestant movement that had already begun to break up into warring factions.

THE SIGNIFICANCE OF THE REFORMATIONS

It is not easy to assess the significance of the Protestant and Catholic reformations. They were religious movements rooted in the religious experience of medieval Christianity as it was represented in men like Luther and Loyola. The result was a religious fragmentation that has lasted to the present day. But Luther's protest would not have had this tremendous result if political, economic, and social conditions in Germany and Europe had not been just right. The growth of capitalism and other economic changes had caused serious dislocations that affected the traditional society of the Middle Ages. The growth of monarchical power, nationalism, and secularism also contributed to the success of the religious rebellion. Overall, it is difficult to distinguish cause and effect. Protestants used political events and conditions—such as the political divisions in Germany or King Henry VIII's desire for a divorce—to further their cause. Secular rulers used the religious movement to justify the seizure of church property and to establish state churches.

One thing is clear. The era of reform and revolution in the Church temporarily halted the trend toward secularism that had been evident in late medieval and Renaissance thought and institutions. After Luther, all issues were religious issues. For the next century, the most serious disputes in Europe were religious disputes; the wars were complicated by religious feelings; and most leading figures were either men of religion or men deeply affected by religion. Until the eighteenth century one of the certainties of life in Europe was that religious conflict led to civil war and the collapse of civil society. The idea of religious toleration, which rests on a moderation of religious feeling, arose because of the terrible experience Europeans had during the wars of religion. The medieval Church had advocated toleration to a large degree, but the reformations and counter reformation of the sixteenth century buried that venerable tradition under a thick layer of religious fanaticism.

Modern historians have vigorously debated the political, economic, and

Luther tweaks the beard of Calvin as both of them pull the hair of the pope. This satirical engraving presents a Catholic view of the Reformation controversy.

CALVIN   LE PAPE   LUTHER

cultural effects of the Protestant Reformation. They have both affirmed and denied that Protestantism—which recognized the possibility of serving God in one's secular calling and appreciated bourgeois virtues of honesty, thrift, and self-discipline—provided the necessary religious sanction for the development of capitalism. Lutheranism has been blamed for the growth of absolute monarchy; Calvinism has been credited with giving impetus to constitutionalism; Anabaptism has been considered one of the sources of modern socialist thought; and all of these propositions have also been denied. Protestants cleansed the ornate churches that they seized from the Catholics, and some historians have therefore blamed them for stopping the development of art, which had had a predominantly religious character during the Middle Ages. Other historians have denied that they are responsible for the early modern changes in western art. The good and bad in modern capitalism, modern nationalism, and modern secularism have all been attributed to Protestantism by one historian or another.

The historical record will not support dogmatic judgments of such issues. The permanent schism of western Christendom and the intensification of religious motives in European affairs can be attributed to the Protestant movement. Beyond this, all that can be said with certainty is that Protestantism allied itself with developments in the society and the economy that had their origins long before the Reformation. The Protestants sometimes accelerated and sometimes hindered these developments, but they did not cause them. Capitalism, nationalism, absolute monarchy, democracy, and secularism appeared in Catholic as well as Protestant regions, and none of these phenomena can be explained by a simple chain of causes leading back to Luther and his break with Rome.

Suggestions for Further Reading

Background of the Reformation

Several works put the Reformation in a historical context, see S. Ozmont, *The Reformation in Medieval Perspective* (1971); G. Strauss, *Pre-Reformation Germany* (1972); and J. Bossy, *Christianity in the West, 1400–1700* (1985). On the background of Protestantism, see H. Oberman, *The Harvest of Medieval Theology* (1963); and A. McGrath, *The Intellectual Origins of the European Reformation* (1987). J. Huizinga's *The Waning of the Middle Ages* (1924), is the classic work on the cultural changes during the fourteenth and fifteenth centuries.

The Religious Upheaval

On the Hussite movement, see M. Spinka, *John Hus and the Czech Revolution* (1941); F. G. Heymann, *John Zizka and the Hussite Revolution* (1955); and H. Kaminsky, *A History of the Hussite Revolution* (1967). On the spread of humanism, see P. O. Kristeller, "The European Diffusion of Italian Humanism," *Renaissance Thought* II (1965), and L. Spitz, *The Religious Renaissance of the German Humanists* (1963). On Erasmus, see J. Huizinga, *Erasmus* (1952), and R. H. Bainton, *Erasmus of Christendom* (1969). For a specialized study of Erasmus's reform views, see J. B. Payne, *Erasmus: His Theology of the Sacraments* (1970). Erasmus's writings are widely available; see, for example, J. P. Dolan, ed., *The Essential Erasmus* (1964).

There are many histories of the Protestant Reformation. H. Holborn, *A History of Modern Germany: The Reformation* (1959), is excellent on Germany. See also B. Moeller, *Imperial Cities and the Reformation* (1972), and G. Strauss, *Luther's House of Learning* (1978). L. W. Spitz, *The Renaissance and Reformation Movements*, Vol. 2 (1971), is an excellent brief history. J. Lortz, *The Reformation in Germany*, 2 vols. (1969), gives a fair statement of the Catholic view. A. G. Dickens, *The German Nation* and *Martin Luther* (1972), emphasizes the urban nature of the Reformation. H. J. Hillerbrand, *The Protestant Reformation: A Narrative History* (1964), contains a good anthology of contemporary writings.

On the spread of Protestantism, see S. Ozment, *The Reformation of the Cities* (1975). On Zwingli, see W. P. Stephens, *The Theology of Huldrych Zwingli* (1986). On the iconoclasm of the Protestant movement, see C. M. N. Eire, *War Against the Idols* (1986), and C. Christensen, *Art and the Reformation in Germany* (1980). W. J. Bouwsma, *John Calvin* (1988), is a fine biography and introduction. F. Wendel, *Calvin, The Origin and Development of his Religious Thought* (1963), is an excellent introduction. On the radicals, see G. H. Williams, *The Radi-cal Reformation* (1962); F. H. Littell, *The Free Church* (1958); R. H. Bainton, *The Travail of Religious Liberty* (1951); and C. L. Clausen, *Anabaptism: A Social History* (1972). The best work on England is A. G. Dickens, *The English Reformation* (1964). J. J. Scarisbrick, *Henry VIII* (1968), is a brilliant work. For the Puritans, see P. Collinson, *The Elizabethan Puritan Movement* (1967).

An excellent discussion of the Catholic Reformation is H. Daniel-Rops, *The Catholic Reformation*, 2 vols. (1961). See also, A. G. Dickens, *The Counter Reformation* (1969). For the Council of Trent, the definitive work is H. Jedin, *History of the Council of Trent*, of which the first two volumes appeared in English translation in 1957.

Results of the Reformation

On the economic, political, and cultural consequences of the Reformation there are wide differences of opinion. The starting point of modern debate was an "essay" by M. Weber, *The Protestant Ethic and the Spirit of Capitalism* (1905). *Protestantism and Capitalism: The Weber Thesis and Its Critics*, ed. by R. W. Green (1973), is a convenient collection of selections from the literature. See also, L. W. Spitz, *The Reformation: Basic Interpretations* (1972), and R. Kingdon and R. Linder, *Calvin and Calvinism: Sources of Democracy* (1972). For a readable and perceptive survey of the period, see A. G. Dickens, *Reformation and Society in Sixteenth-Century Europe* (1966).

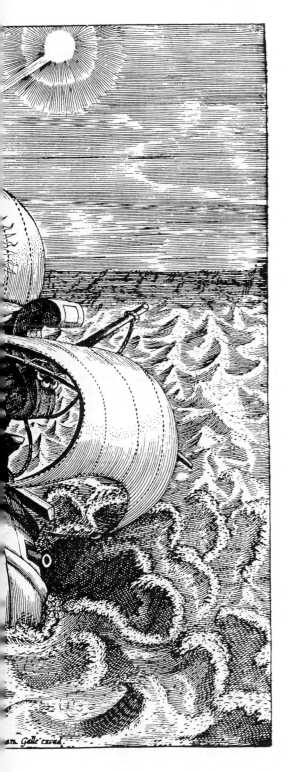

an Galle excud.

18
The Age of Discovery and the Greatness of Spain

*T*he Protestant Reformation was only one of three revolutions that gave birth to a new epoch in European history around the turn of the sixteenth century. Humanist thought and the Renaissance in the arts had already begun the second of the revolutions— the creation of a new historical consciousness that made Europeans aware of the rise and fall of civilizations. The third great revolution was caused by the discovery of the sea route around Africa to India and the Orient and the discovery of the New World.

For Europeans, the fifteenth and sixteenth centuries were the age of discovery without parallel. Although the expansion of European knowledge and experience of the world had roots in medieval civilization, the new explorations had a revolutionary effect on Europeans' consciousness because the voyages put them for the first time in direct contact with all the inhabited continents on the globe and with all the civilized peoples who inhabited them. By the time the Peace of Augsburg (1555) set the foundation for the settlement of religious strife in Germany, the contact with the non-European world

Opposite: A sixteenth-century sailing ship, with its navigator (left, center) sighting the sun to determine his latitude. The foremast (right) is square-rigged for running with the wind. The mainmast and the mizzenmast astern (left) are lateen-rigged for better tacking against the wind.

had begun to have a profound effect on the economy, politics, and intellectual life of Europe.

The contact with alien civilizations forced Europeans to reconsider the ideas they had about their relationships with non-Europeans. Their traditional ideas had been formed in centuries of conflict with the Moslems and interaction with Jews. But these peoples were part of the family of civilizations of the Mediterranean Basin and the conflicts among them were in the nature of family feuds. Now, Europeans faced the challenge of completely unknown and different peoples, and thinkers—particularly Spanish thinkers—tried to develop ethical and legal principles that could guide their compatriots in dealings with those who had built civilizations without the benefit of Christianity.

THE DEVELOPMENT OF OCEANIC COMMERCE

In 1400 Europeans knew scarcely more about the earth than the Romans had, for during the Middle Ages Europe itself had been the goal rather than the source of explorations and migrations. Only a few Europeans had ventured beyond the Mediterranean Basin. During the eleventh century—at the beginning of the crusading movement—western Europeans became directly acquainted with the whole Mediterranean world, but this first expansion of Europe only reestablished the boundaries of ancient civilization. The crusaders and those who followed them were setting foot in lands already described in their old books.

In Scandinavia there was a true expansion beyond the old world. The sagas recorded traditions of the voyages of Lief Ericson and other Viking seamen to North America. During the eleventh century, the Icelanders had established settlements on Greenland and around Hudson Bay, and they apparently had coasted down the eastern seashore of North America, but these expeditions left little evidence behind to mark their occurrence. The Hudson Bay communities apparently lasted only a short time, but the Greenland settlements throve until the middle of the thirteenth century. At that time, there was a cooling trend—which might also have been responsible for the climatic troubles in European agriculture later in the century—that forced the abandonment of the Greenland communities in 1258, although there is evidence that English sailors visited them up to the end of the century.

As Greenland was being abandoned, Italians were opening up an overland trade route to China. Franciscan friars and the Polo family of Venice showed that China could be reached by land across the steppes of Central Asia. Marco Polo (*ca.* 1254–1324) went east with his father and uncle in 1271 and remained in China, at the court of the Mongol emperor, for over 15 years. He returned in 1295 and wrote an account of the journey. The book was widely read in Europe and contributed greatly both to the Europeans' geographical knowledge of the East and to their interest in Chinese civilization. But after the collapse of the Mongol Empire in the fourteenth century the routes across the steppes were no longer safe for missionaries and merchants. The new enthusiasm for Chinese and other eastern goods was now satisfied by Arab sailors who operated in the Indian Ocean. They brought spices and textiles to Alexandria and Beirut, from which the Venetians distributed them to European markets.

By the end of the sixteenth century, these indirect contacts with the Orient had been replaced by a worldwide trade controlled by the Europeans. The ocean had become the world's highway, and Europeans were in a position to dominate the world by controlling the sea. The Mongol Empire—the largest in geographical extent ever known up to that time—had rested on mastery of the steppes. The empires of the future would rest on mastery of the seas.

When the first ship to circumnavigate the globe completed its journey in 1522, Europe had begun to cast a web of communication and influence around the earth. During the next four centuries that web was to draw all the civilizations of the world under the influence of Europe.

Conditions for Maritime Discovery

The age of exploration could not have occurred without significant advances in both the design of ships and knowledge of navigation. The Vikings had made relatively short voyages across the North Atlantic—Greenland was twelve days' journey from Norway—but in their small, open boats, even these trips were daring. What made the western explorations possible at all was a rare climatic condition of the North that occasionally gave Scandinavian boatmen a hazy glimpse of a land beyond the horizon; men in boats off the western coast of Iceland could "see" Greenland. The phenomenon is a reverse of the one familiar to almost everyone—the mirage. In hot, dry weather one sees water at a distance, even though one knows the ground is dry. This mirage is caused by a reflection of the sky on the ground, which results from the great difference in temperature between the hot ground and the cool air. In the northern seas, this extreme temperature difference occasionally occurs in reverse, when the water is colder than the air in winter, and the reverse mirroring effect can occur. Land that is far out beyond the horizon—over the curvature of the earth—is reflected in the sky. These occurrences provided would-be explorers with a direction and a confidence that land would be reached just beyond the usual range of sight.

On their way to Greenland, Scandinavian sailors could stop off in Iceland and the Faroe Islands. Therefore, their small boats and their lack of navigational skills did not prevent them from making their wonderful discoveries. But the Northmen's boats were too

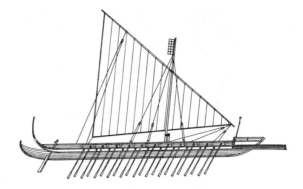

small and too unseaworthy for maintaining regular contact, a true oceanic commerce, with North American colonies, so the small communities that they established in Greenland and in the Hudson Bay region of North America had a precarious, largely independent existence in a difficult climate. Before Europeans could make a sustained drive to push out across the great Atlantic distances in the temperate zones and before they could estab-

Top: Mediterranean war galley with lateen sail (*ca.* twelfth century); middle: lateen-rigged vessel, much like Columbus' *Niña* (early fifteenth century); bottom: Spanish galleon of sixteenth century, the typical long-distance ship for Spanish commerce.

lish thriving colonies that were commercially linked with the mother countries, they had to develop better ships, more reliable aids to navigation, and stronger motivation than their Norse predecessors.

The development of oceangoing ships took a long time. Ships of the Mediterranean were oar-propelled galleys that were effective in the coastal waters in which they most often operated. Sailors rarely struck out across the Mediterranean and did so only in those places where it was relatively narrow—as between Sicily and North Africa. By the thirteenth century, Genoese and Venetian galleys were venturing out into the Atlantic to Morocco and Flanders, but they did so by keeping close to the coast. On the open seas, where the distances were vast, mariners needed sails rather than oars and broad, round hulls rather than long, narrow ones such as the galleys had. These needs stemmed from the equation of manpower and provisions that were required for a long journey on the sea. The galleys had 50 or more rowers who expended an enormous

number of calories each day and consequently required vast amounts of provisions. But these ships, which were built for a coasting trade or for the brief encounters of war, could not carry such stores. The new sailing ships could operate with small crews whose bodies did not burn up provisions in strenuous physical labor. Only such ships, which balanced the needs of their crews with their capacity to carry provisions, could make the months-long journeys across the Atlantic in the temperate zones.

The Portuguese, who faced the Atlantic directly, were the ones who finally developed a truly oceangoing vessel. By the fifteenth century they had built the squat, three-masted caravel, which combined the shipbuilding techniques of the Europeans and Moslems. The caravel had two masts with square sails in the European mode and one with a triangular lateen sail favored by the Moslems. The square rigs were best for running before the wind, while the lateen rig was better for sailing close to the wind. The new ship was slower and less maneuverable than the galley, but it had more space for cargo and provisions for long voyages.

But before mariners could venture out on the vast open waters of the western ocean, shipmasters had to have some way of determining their direction and position. The compass (used in Europe by the thirteenth century) gave them a sense of direction in cloudy weather when they could not see the sun or stars; the astrolabe (used by the eleventh century, but perhaps as early as the third century B.C.) enabled them to determine their latitude by measuring the elevation of the sun and stars; and the portulan charts (first developed for the Mediterranean) gave them confidence that they could recognize the approaches to most European ports. (No precise way to determine longitude was discovered until the eighteenth century, when Edmund Halley—for whom the comet is named—developed a reasonably accurate method.)

An illustration from a sailing book, *Art de Naviguer* (1583), demonstrating how to determine latitude by observing the sun's height.

Besides technological advances, the exploration of the oceans required political and economic development. City-states were the original bases for long-range shipping. The ancient Phoenicians sent out expeditions to the western Mediterranean—at least as far as Sicily and Sardinia—and the Greeks discovered the Black Sea to the east and also traveled west. The Venetian and Genoese merchants linked the Black Sea and eastern Mediterranean with England and Flanders, and the merchants of the Hanseatic League (a confederation of north German cities) traded from Russian Novgorod to French Bordeaux. But transoceanic exploration, trade, and colonization required resources far beyond the capacities of city-states. It was only after the western European monarchies had consolidated their power and unified their countries that there existed enough concentration of wealth to man and equip fleets of oceangoing vessels. Thus, after 1400 the western monarchies gradually replaced the cities as the major centers of commercial enterprise.

It is not easy to determine why, among the seafaring peoples of the world, the Europeans desired so strongly to discover the unknown world. This question is related to the problem of why the Europeans were so inquisitive about nature and so eager to develop new technological devices, while the Moslems and Chinese, who had some instruments for industry and science much earlier than the Europeans, never fully exploited them. Moslem traders had been venturing across the Indian Ocean for centuries, but they never went beyond the familiar coastal routes into the Pacific or around Africa. The Chinese had also regularly sailed into the Indian Ocean and up and down the coast of East Asia, but they too did not venture into the unknown. Perhaps the perennial conflict of the different civilizations in the Mediterranean prevented Europeans from developing a complacency about their civilization and its circumscribed world

Toynbee on the Age of Discovery

Since A.D. 1500 the map of the civilized world has indeed been transformed out of all recognition. Down to that date it was composed of a belt of civilizations girdling the Old World from the Japanese Isles on the north-east to the British Isles on the north-west. . . . The main line of communication was provided by the chain of steppes and deserts that cut across the belt of civilizations from the Sahara to Mongolia. For human purposes, the Steppe was an inland sea. . . . This waterless sea had its dry-shod ships and its quayless ports. The steppe-galleons were camels, the steppe-galleys horses, and the steppe-ports "caravan cities." . . . The great revolution was a technological revolution by which the West made its fortune, got the better of all the other living civilizations, and forcibly united them into a single society of literally world-wide range. The revolutionary Western invention was the substitution of the Ocean for the Steppe as the principal medium of world-communication. This use of the Ocean, first by sailing ships and then by steamships, enabled the West to unify the whole inhabited and habitable world.

From Arnold J. Toynbee, *Civilization on Trial* (New York: Oxford University Press, 1948), pp. 67–70.

and produced a missionary spirit in them—first mobilized in the crusades—that impelled them to convert all peoples to their religion. Perhaps the universalism of Christianity and the belief that the longed-for end of the world would not take place until all were converted to Christianity made Europeans willing to risk their lives in oceanic adventures. The reasons the Europeans were so extraordinarily venturesome are not clear, but it is clear that religious and worldly motives were inextricably combined in the exploration movement.

One worldly motive for exploration was the need to find new, direct trade routes to East Asia. In an age without refrigeration, the spices that helped preserve meats and make them palatable—pepper from India, cinnamon from Sri Lanka (Celyon), ginger from China, nutmeg and cloves from the East Indies—were luxuries that were almost necessities. The Arab-Venetian trade monopoly made these goods—

and others such as cotton and silk textiles—extremely expensive, and the
newly powerful monarchs of western
Europe, particularly those in the Iberian peninsula, were eager to find an
independent route for the trade.

A second, and probably the principal, motivation for exploration was the
need to find precious metals. The Europeans had a serious trade imbalance
with Asia because the Asians did not
need the products of the European
economy. Furthermore, since most of
those products were bulky—such as
wood and iron—or both bulky and
perishable—such as foodstuffs—they
were not suitable for the long-distance
trade. Before a credit system became
widely used in the seventeenth and
eighteenth centuries, the only practical
way to provide money for the imports—
and for other projects such as industry—
was to increase the supply of bullion.
European gold and silver mines had
never been especially productive and

were nearly exhausted by 1400. Moreover, there was a steady flow of gold
and silver out of Europe to East Asia.
European monarchs were therefore
acutely aware of their need for new
sources of gold.

By the late fifteenth century a restless, energetic, and bold seafaring population was scattered along Europe's
Atlantic coastline. They had strong religious motivations and ships and navigational instruments good enough to
allow them to overcome their fear of
the open, unknown sea. They also had
enough mistaken information to make
success appear almost probable. Europeans' knowledge of the earth's size
rested on the theory of the second-
century Greek writer Ptolemy, who
had underestimated it. As a result, fifteenth-century geographers were convinced that Japan and China lay only a
few thousand miles west of Europe.
The size of Africa had also been underestimated, so an eastern route around

The World of the Voyagers   1415–1550

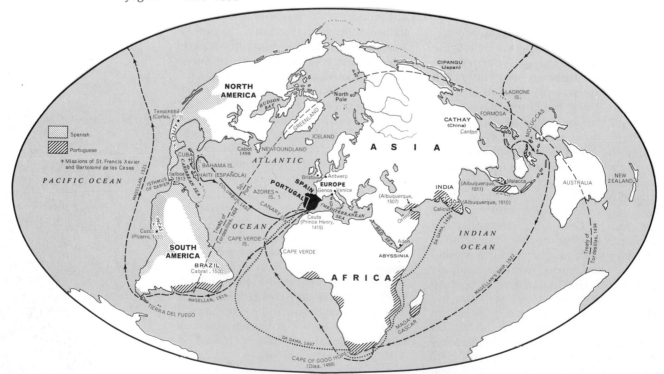

it seemed relatively easy. Therefore, both an eastern and a western route seemed possible, and the European monarchs had both the motivation and resources to make the exploration worth the risk.

Portuguese Exploration

At the beginning of the age of exploration stands one of its most interesting figures—Prince Henry the Navigator (1394–1460), the younger son of King John I of Portugal. At a remarkable observatory at Sagres on Cape St. Vincent, on the southwestern tip of Portugal, Henry assembled the scientific and seafaring knowledge of his day. He devoted his life to organizing, equipping, and sending out fleets to explore the coast of Africa, with which he was virtually obsessed. He had vague notions of outflanking Islam by reaching lands that the Moslems had never touched, but his main goal was to find gold. When his fleets reached the Gold Coast of Africa in the 1450s, he achieved this objective.

After Henry's death, the Portuguese exploration lost its impetus for a time. His countrymen did discover and settle clusters of small islands in the Atlantic—the Madeiras and the Azores—but the islands were not very profitable. The discovery was only of importance because it showed that there was land 800 miles out in the Atlantic, which encouraged further exploration.

The interest in the voyages was taken up again by Henry's grand-nephew, King John II (r. 1481–95), who encouraged the effort to find an all-water route to India that would destroy the Arab-Venetian monopoly. By 1488 Bartholomeu Dias had discovered the Cape of Good Hope, and in 1497 Vasco da Gama rounded the cape with four ships. Da Gama reached Calicut on the Malabar Coast of India in 1498 and was back in Lisbon with two of his ships in 1499. In 1500 Pedro Álvares Cabral led a large fleet to Brazil and then on to India.

Vasco da Gama.

The Portuguese as others saw them: African bronze sculpture of a Portuguese man.

Cabral established the first Portuguese trading stations in India, and his work, following da Gama's, had a lasting importance. At first, however, the Portuguese did not find a particularly warm welcome from either the Hindus or the Moslems in India. Da Gama found Indian civilization unimpressive and apparently said so. Cabral had to defend himself against hostile Moslems who killed many of his men. But during the sixteenth century the Portuguese strove to build a commercial empire in the Indian Ocean. The architect of this new empire was Alfonso de Albuquerque, the governor of Portuguese India from 1509 to 1515.

Already before his appointment to the governorship, Albuquerque had been active in the Indian Ocean. He had conquered Goa, which later became his capital, and had established strategic fortresses in eastern Africa to disrupt Arab trade with India. As governor, he seized Malacca on the Strait of Malacca to control the trade between the Spice Islands and the Indian Ocean, and Ormuz—an island in the Persian Gulf—from which he could raid the coasts of the region and disrupt Arab shipping. He tried but failed to take Aden, which would have given him control of the Red Sea, through which the Arab-Venetian trade passed. At his death, Portugal controlled a large portion of the spice trade and had strategic bases all the way from Africa to the East Indies.

Portugal's success was short-lived. Although the early voyages earned large profits, the country was small and relatively poor and did not have the resources to establish colonies in India or to maintain the navy required to protect its commerce. Italian, German, and Flemish bankers soon dominated the Portuguese trade, and the spices that arrived at Lisbon were sent on directly to Antwerp, which proved to be a better point from which to distribute them to Europe. The burden of empire was already extremely heavy when Portugal fell into the grip of Spain in 1580.

Columbus and Spanish Exploration

In 1484, before the Portuguese had reached the Cape of Good Hope, a Genoese sailor named Christopher Columbus had tried in vain to persuade King John II to back him in a voyage of exploration to the west. Based on the earlier experience of Portuguese sailors and on the geographical knowledge derived from Ptolemy, Columbus was convinced that it would be relatively easy to reach Cipangu (Japan) by sailing due west. But for a long time he could not persuade any monarch to back him. Then in January 1492, the combined Spanish monarchies under Ferdinand and Isabella finally conquered the Kingdom of Granada, the last Moorish stronghold on the Iberian peninsula, and the kings were free to turn their attention and

resources to other projects. Isabella of Castile agreed to equip Columbus for his famous voyage. It took the Portuguese almost a century of patient effort to develop the eastward route to the Old World; the Spanish reached the New World westward in one brilliant voyage.

Columbus touched land in the Bahamas on October 12, 1492, thinking he had struck some small islands in the Japanese archipelago. Throughout four voyages and until his death in 1506, he remained convinced, even after touching the mainland, that he had reached the Old World of Japan and China. It was Columbus who named the natives he found in the newly discovered lands "Indians."

The man who recognized that what had been discovered was a new world was Columbus's fellow Italian, Amerigo Vespucci, who was head of the Medici branch bank in Seville, Spain's principal port. Vespucci sailed on both Spanish and Portuguese voyages and

Christopher Columbus, the Genoese sailor who sailed west in search of Japan and found the New World. This portrait of Columbus is thought to be the closest existing likeness of him. It is a copy, made in about 1525, of an earlier painting that has been lost.

described what he saw in letters that were published and read throughout Europe. In one he referred to the great southern continent in the west as *Mundus novus*, the New World. Later map makers labeled the two new continents "America," after the man who had first recognized their significance in the earth's geography. Vespucci's letters inspired Thomas More to write his *Utopia* (see p. 462).

The Treaty of Tordesillas, 1494

From the beginning of Spanish exploration, Spain and Portugal knew that they were in direct competition for the newly discovered lands. The two countries turned to the pope, Alexander VI (r. 1492–1503), to draw a line of demarcation between their respective areas of potential empire. Alexander was a Spaniard and his line—100 leagues west of the Cape Verde Islands (off the coast of Mauritania in western Africa)— favored the Spanish. In 1494, the Portuguese persuaded the Spanish to negotiate the bilateral Treaty of Tordesillas, which made a division that both could be reasonably happy with and that would avoid unwanted war. This treaty also used the Cape Verde Islands as the point of reference, but it drew a line from pole to pole 370 leagues west of the islands.

However, misunderstanding remained. The Portuguese assumed that the line applied only to the Atlantic (it gave them Brazil, though they did not know this in 1494), while the Spanish thought the line went clear around the earth. By this interpretation the Spanish could claim the Moluccas, which were the heart of the Spice Islands, and in fact it would also have given them part of what is now Indonesia. But the trouble that these conflicting interpretations of the treaty might have caused did not occur, because Spain became so occupied with its new possessions in the Americas that in 1527 it sold its claims in the East to Portugal.

By 1512 Albuquerque had established the Portuguese in the Moluccas, and a year later the Spaniard Balboa sighted the Pacific Ocean from the Isthmus of Darien (south of Panama) in Central America. The first of these achievements increased the need of the Spaniards to find a route westward to the Spice Islands, and the second made it seem that it would be possible to find a passage through the New World. In 1519, the Portuguese navigator Magellan—with Spanish backing, since his success would benefit Spain under the treaty of 1494—undertook the third of the great voyages, along with those of Columbus and da Gama. Magellan negotiated the treacherous straits at the southern tip of South America and made it across the Pacific despite incredible hardships, only to be killed by natives in the Philippines. His navigator, Sebastian del Cano, brought one of the five original ships back to Lisbon by way of the Cape of Good Hope in 1522— the first ship to circumnavigate the world.

THE SPANISH EMPIRE IN THE AMERICAS

About the time Magellan sailed, the Spanish began to carve out an empire in the New World. From 1520 to 1550, Spanish conquistadors conquered wealthy civilizations in Mexico and Peru. The most notable of the conquistadors were Hernando Cortés and Francisco Pizarro. From 1519 to 1521 Cortés conquered the formidable Aztec Empire in Mexico with 600 men, 16 horses, and a few cannon, and from 1533 to 1534 Pizarro conquered the Inca Empire in the Andes of Peru with even fewer men.

The American civilizations were wealthy and sophisticated, but they did not have a military technology to match that of the Spaniards. In addition, the few Spanish troops were well disciplined and daring and took advantage of every opportunity. Their initial successes were easy to consolidate later for two basic reasons: first, the political power of both the Aztecs and the Incas

Magellan plotting his position (detail from an allegorical portrait by De Bry).

ycpolinhq̃ mexııca

Cortés accepting the surrender of Quauhtemoc, last king of the Aztecs. The artist was a Spanish-trained native from Tlaxcala, who chronicled Cortés' conquest of Mexico. Notice the mixture of European and Indian styles.

1550 to 1620, the number of goats and sheep rose from about half a million to 8 million, while the cattle herds increased from about 10,000 to 100,000. The Indian peasant farmers had been replaced by great herds and flocks of range animals. Further, the goats and sheep were extremely destructive because they uproot the plants they eat leaving a desert behind.

The new empire raised conflicts within Spain, because different groups wanted to accomplish different ends in the new lands. There were three competing elements—the settlers who went out to the New World, the government in Madrid, and the Franciscan friars. The settlers sent to the new colonies wanted to exploit the land by setting up a manorial system based on the old European model and by using the forced labor of the natives. The colonists also did not want to take orders from or to serve the interests of the Spanish government. The government naturally wanted to centralize all power over the colonies in its own hands, and its principal goal was to find and exploit sources of precious metals. Since the Aztecs and Incas used an enormous amount of gold for ornamentation, the government had great confidence that this policy could be successful. The friars wanted to convert the new populations.

The discovery of civilized heathens raised theological and moral questions about how such people ought to be treated. Spanish scholars dredged up the works of medieval thinkers who had speculated about whether the biblical texts according to which rulers receive their authority from God (such as Romans 13) applied to those who did not accept or did not know the sacred text. There were also questions about the marriages of the new converts. Were the "marriages" of heathens valid? The Church considered marriage to be a sacrament—God joined husband and wife—and medieval thinkers developed a theory that the marriages of such people were valid, but not licit. According to this conception, God cre-

had been highly centralized, so after the collapse of the central authorities there were no local leaders who could continue to resist. Second, the Europeans brought diseases (especially smallpox) against which the native populations had no natural defenses, and within a short time the natives were so reduced in numbers that rebellion was impossible.

The demographic and ecological effects of the conquests are illustrated by what happened in Mexico. While it is difficult to estimate the size of the Indian population before the conquest, it appears to have been at least 25 million. Beginning in 1519, it dropped precipitously to about 6 million by 1540, 4 million in 1563, and 2.5 million in 1600. It reached its nadir about 1650, when it was 1.5 million. Thereafter, it climbed gradually until it reached a little more than 3.5 million in 1793. By contrast, the population of goats, sheep, and cattle, introduced to Mexico by the Europeans, rose dramatically in the second half of the sixteenth century. From

ated the union in such marriages—which made them valid—but the Church had not recognized them—which made them illicit or outside the law. The distinction here was basically the one between acts performed in accordance with natural law (which stems from God directly) and human law (which stems from God indirectly, through the medium of human institutions), and sixteenth-century thought about the status and condition of the Indians made much of this basic distinction. The Indians lived not according to canon law, but by natural law alone; they were God's people who lived without the benefit of the Church. The man who worked out this theory most fully was the Dominican Bartolomé de Las Casas (1474–1566).

Las Casas went to the New World in 1502 to convert the Indians, and he soon was engaged in a struggle to get better treatment for them. He and his fellow missionaries wanted to treat the converts as fellow Christians, and he made several trips back to Spain to plead for support in reaching this goal. In the early 1520s, he was involved in a project to found free cities of Christianized Indians, but this failed, and Las Casas returned to Spain and retired into the religious life. In retirement, he wrote many learned works defending his position and completed a great *History of the Indians,* based on what he had learned while in America.

The policy of the Spanish Empire was a compromise among the three interests represented by the settlers, the government, and the friars. The settlers were permitted to command the forced labor of the subject Indians, but they were regulated by public authority, which ameliorated some of the worst abuses. Meanwhile the friars were given a wide latitude to evangelize the native population and to bring them into the fold of European civilization, and this process also balanced the tendency of the settlers to exploit and mistreat the Indians. By contemporary standards, Spanish imperial policy was quite humane, and the Spanish came

Las Casas on the American Indians in the Sixteenth Century

It has been written that these peoples of the Indies, lacking human governance and ordered nations, did not have the power of reason to govern themselves—which was inferred only from their having been found to be gentle, patient and humble. It has been implied that God became careless in creating so immense a number of rational souls and let human nature, which He so largely determined and provided for, go astray in the almost infinitesimal part of the human lineage which they comprise. From this it follows that they have all proven themselves unsocial and therefore monstrous, contrary to the natural bent of all peoples of the world.

. . . Not only have [the Indians] shown themselves to be very wise peoples and possessed of lively and marked understanding, prudently governing and providing for their nations (as much as they can be nations, without faith in or knowledge of the true God) and making them prosper in justice; but they have equalled many diverse nations of the world, past and present, that have been praised for their governance, politics and customs, and exceed by no small measure the wisest of all these, such as the Greeks and Romans, in adherence to the rules of natural reason.

From Bartolomé de las Casas, *Apologética historia de las Indias,* in *Introduction to Contemporary Civilization in the West,* 3rd ed. (New York: Columbia University Press, 1960), Vol. 1, p. 539.

close to accomplishing what the Portuguese failed to accomplish in the East and what the English never attempted in North America: the Christianization and Europeanization of a whole native population.

Nonetheless, the primary purpose of the Empire was economic exploitation. After the discovery of enormously rich silver mines in Mexico in 1545, the extraction and shipment of silver became the main business of the Empire as a whole. Every spring after 1564 the plate fleet of 20 to 60 ships gathered at Havana harbor to be convoyed by warships to Seville. And every year the Spanish government waited anxiously until the bullion, which everyone agreed was the key to national strength, was safely in harbor.

The Spanish Empire in America   Sixteenth Century

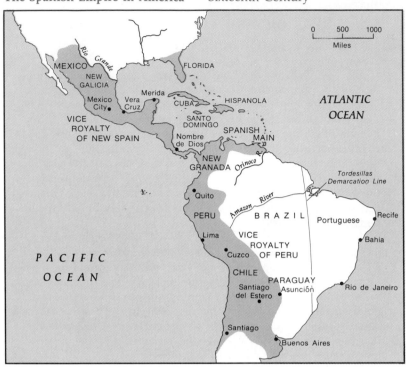

Philip II of Spain, by Titian.

ther, Maximilian, and the Netherlands through his mother, Mary of Burgundy, and was elected Holy Roman emperor in 1519. He effectively used Spanish money and troops to counter the Protestant heretics, to protect Austria from the Turks, and to conquer the New World. These far-flung actions stretched Spanish resources to the maximum, but under Charles and his son King Philip II (r. 1556–98), the newly powerful nation was almost equal to the task. The sixteenth and early seventeenth centuries were the golden age of Spain.

Philip II did not inherit the whole of his father's holdings. In 1555–56 Charles V divided the family territories between his brother Ferdinand and his son. To Ferdinand went the Habsburg possessions in central Europe—those in Austria, Bohemia, and Hungary— and the imperial crown (still elective in theory, but by now always bestowed on a Habsburg). To Philip went the western European holdings—the crowns of Castile and Aragon, with Castile's possessions in the New World, the Kingdom of Naples and the Duchy of Milan (which meant control of Italy), and the Netherlands. Thus for a century and a half after 1556 there were "Austrian Habsburgs" and "Spanish Habsburgs," separate ruling houses but houses that cooperated closely in matters of dynastic policy. Except for the Netherlands, which might have gone to Ferdinand because of their close cultural, geographical, and economic ties with the Holy Roman Empire, the possessions of Philip II formed a more tight-knit and centralized state than his father's holdings.

Although he was the scion of a "European" family, Philip was thoroughly Spanish in speech, thought, and character. After 1559, when the Habsburgs concluded peace with France, he spent the remaining 40 years of his life in Spain. He was a conscientious king, but he was also distrustful of his advisers, unable to delegate even in minor matters, and strongly Catholic in reli-

The land had agricultural wealth as well, particularly in the wet lowlands of the Caribbean. When sugar became an important crop in these places, the Spanish settlers found that the Indian workers died in droves from disease, and they began to import Negro slaves from Africa. While the Spanish and Indian populations tended to intermarry, so that the mestizos—offspring of mixed marriages—eventually outnumbered the pure-bred of either race, the Negroes remained outside the society, enslaved.

IMPERIAL SPAIN: THE REIGN OF PHILIP II

The wealth produced by the colonies made Spain the most powerful nation in Europe at the same time that the accession of the Habsburg Emperor Charles V (r. 1516–56) gave Spain a new role in European affairs. Charles had inherited Austria through his fa-

Europe about 1560

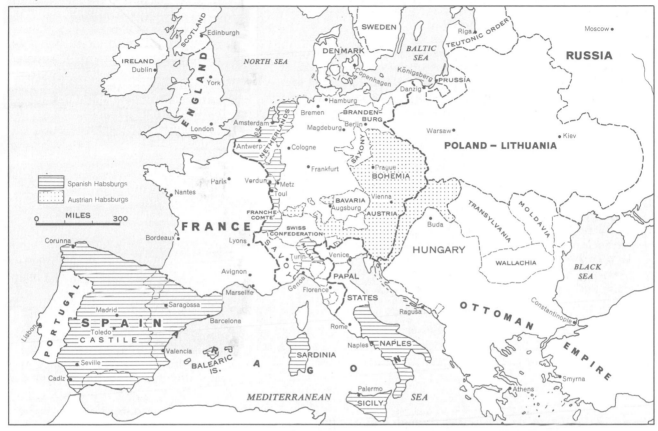

gion (his enemies would have said "bigoted"). He devoted himself to restoring the unity of the Christian world, with the Spanish monarchy as its temporal leader.

Economic Policy

Early in the sixteenth century the bullion imported from the New World in steadily increasing amounts had been mostly gold, but after 1545, it was mostly silver. The value of the treasure rose dramatically during the century. In the early years it amounted to something under $300,000; by about 1550 the value had increased 15 times; and by 1600 it was about $12,000,000. Then a steady decline set in, until about 1660 the average value was down to $1,200,000. The Spanish crown received about one-quarter of the total as its share.

The influx of bullion, together with internal financial problems, contributed to a steep rise of prices. By the middle of the sixteenth century, the inflation was rampant and had spread from Spain to the rest of Europe. It has been estimated that prices quadrupled in Spain in the course of the century.

The rise in prices outstripped the rise in tax revenues, and Philip II was forced to repudiate his government's debts three times—in 1557, 1575, and 1596. (His successors had to do the same in 1607, 1627, and 1647.) In effect, these repudiations were declarations of bankruptcy in which the king announced that he could not repay his debts and would not do so. As might be expected, such events sent shock

On Philip II of Spain

The pallor of his complexion was remarked on by all observers, and most of them drew the proper conclusion, namely, that it indicated a weak stomach and lack of exercise. Reddened eyes were a penalty of his excessive devotion to the written word both day and night. . . . Reading and writing occupied the major portion of Philip's day. . . . He had taken deeply to heart his father's injunction to direct everything himself, and never to give his full confidence even to the most faithful of his ministers, and the natural result was that his time was completely occupied with receiving and answering reports and letters. . . . Reports, reports, and even more reports; Philip was literally submerged with them in his later years, and moreover he did not stop at reading them; he annotated them, as he went along, with comments on matters as absurdly trifling as the spelling and style of the men who had written them—all in that strange, sprawling hand of his, one of the most illegible hands of an age more than usually replete with chirographical difficulties.

From R. B. Merriman, *The Rise of the Spanish Empire in the Old World and in the New* (New York: Macmillan, 1934), Vol. IV, pp. 21–24.

of a desert than of a land of heretics. His grandparents, Ferdinand and Isabella, had already forced the Moors and Jews to convert and had set the Spanish Inquisition to watching that they remained Christian. Nonetheless, it was widely believed that the Moriscos (former Moors) continued to practice their original religion in private, and Philip moved to eradicate such practices. In 1566, he ordered the Moriscos to stop using the Arabic language, to give up their traditional dress, and to stop taking hot baths, as was their custom. Three years later the Moriscos rebelled against this suppression of their cultural heritage, and Philip savagely put down the rebellion and drove them out of Andalusia, the southern region where they chiefly lived. Many left Spain for North Africa, depriving Spain of an important segment of its population, since the Moriscos were among the leaders of Spanish agriculture and industry.

This internal religious policy was coupled with a foreign policy aimed at waves through Europe's financial institutions, but besides damaging Spain's credit, the inflation ruined its industry, which had looked promising at the beginning of the century. Because prices rose first and fastest in Spain, its producers were at a disadvantage in the international markets, and there was a perennial trade imbalance against Spain. As imports increasingly outstripped exports, Spanish industry withered, and Spanish bullion flowed out of the country. When the sources of bullion in America began to dry up in the mid-seventeenth century, Spanish industry and agriculture were ruined, and the nation quickly declined into a second-rate power.

Religious Policy

Philip II's religious policy was the most narrowly intolerant of his time. He once said that he would rather be king

Contemporary map showing Spain as the head and crown of sixteenth-century Europe.

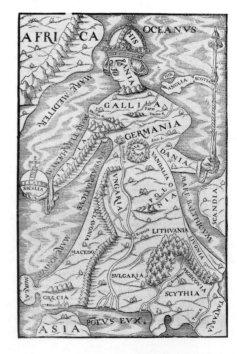

controlling the Turks in the eastern Mediterranean. In 1570 the Turks took Cyprus from the Venetians, and the next year a combined Spanish and Venetian fleet defeated the Turks at Lepanto in the Gulf of Corinth. The victory was hailed throughout Europe, but it had little effect because the Christian forces were unable to take advantage of it.

Immediately after Lepanto, Philip was at the height of his power and prestige. But the moment of greatness was brief. During the last quarter of the sixteenth century, his dream of a revived Catholic Europe under his authority was shattered by the revolt of the Netherlands, the rise of English sea power, and the accession of a former Protestant to the throne of France.

THE REVOLT OF THE NETHERLANDS

The 3 million people in the 17 provinces of the Netherlands constituted one of the most prosperous populations in Europe. The comfortable houses of Bruges, Ghent, Antwerp, and Amsterdam were built with the profits of a flourishing textile industry and a widespread commercial network. During the fifteenth century, the provinces had been united in a personal union by the dukes of Burgundy, but there was little national consciousness until the reign of Charles V. Charles was the closest thing to a native ruler the united Netherlands had ever had, but he regularly sacrificed the interests of the cities to his imperial aims. This treatment created the first stirring of nationalism in the provinces.

Under Philip II, religious conflict added to the Netherlanders' sense of alienation from Habsburg rule. The Netherlands were a crossroads of ideas as well as of commerce, and the teachings of Luther and Calvin had taken root there early. By the 1550s, tight-knit Calvinist minorities existed in most of the cities of the 17 provinces.

Philip's religious policies were bound to alienate most of his Dutch and Flemish subjects. The urban-commercial culture of the region had already been out of tune with the Catholic Church because of its restrictive attitude toward business practices, and the northern urban populations had evolved a tradition of moderation in religious matters—which had permitted the rise of such groups as the Brethren of the Common Life—that was to-

The baptism of Moslem women, from a Spanish relief (1520).

ca. 1400		1519	1581		1648
	Low Countries United under Dukes of Burgundy	Spanish Rule		Dutch Wars of Independence	

tally at odds with the king's religious fanaticism. But Philip increased his problems in the Netherlands by overstepping the traditional limits of his authority. The cities had won substantial liberties from earlier dukes, but in his effort to stamp out heresy Philip ignored the traditional restraints on his authority as duke of the provinces.

In reaction, Calvinist mobs began to break images of the saints and smash

William the Silent, by Anthony Moro.

stained-glass windows in Catholic churches throughout the Netherlands in 1566. Philip sent the Duke of Alva with about 10,000 Spanish regulars to suppress the iconoclasts. Alva set up what came to be called the "Council of Blood" and boasted (with some exaggeration) that in his six year's residence in the Netherlands (1567–73), he executed 18,000 people. His government also confiscated enormous tracts of land and imposed a 10 percent sales tax that seriously injured commerce.

These measures solidified resistance, and by 1572 the Dutch had found a leader in William the Silent, Prince of Orange, the wealthiest landowner in the provinces. William lost almost every battle he fought against the Spanish, but he had political wisdom, integrity, and patience. He also had a deep hatred of religious fanaticism and was thus a foil for Philip II. Dutch nationalism increased under his leadership, helped by the actions of the Spanish themselves. In 1576, the Spanish responded to Calvinist excesses by a frightful sack of Antwerp, which became known as the "Spanish Fury." Frightened by this event, the 17 provinces rushed into an agreement to present a united front against Philip—the so-called Pacification of Ghent.

The union did not last long. The religious fanatics on both sides—Calvinist and Catholic—went out of control, and the moderates of both parties lost influence. The almost universal opposition to Alva and his successors gradually gave way to a savage civil war in which the Calvinists—the best organized minority—gained the upper hand. The result was that the Catholics fled south to the ten Walloon provinces that were under the protection of the Spanish troops, while the Calvinists migrated north to the Dutch regions. In 1579 the Dutch provinces formed the Union of Utrecht, which ultimately became the

The Division of the Netherlands 1581

foundation of the United Provinces or Dutch Netherlands. These provinces declared their independence from Philip II in 1581. The southern provinces remained under Habsburg rule and eventually (in 1830) became the kingdom of Belgium.

The Rise of the United Netherlands

After the declaration of independence in 1581, the Dutch had to fight for two generations to achieve actual independence. William the Silent was assassinated in 1584, but his descendants carried on his tradition of able and disinterested leadership. The "United Provinces" was never more than the loosest of confederations, but the Dutch fought with a fierce stubbornness whenever they had to.

Philip II had countered the union by sending the Duke of Parma—one of the age's best military leaders—in 1578, but Parma was hampered by his inability to control the sea. The Dutch privateers—called "Sea Beggars"—controlled the English Channel and prevented the resupply of the Spanish troops by sea. The naval problems in

the campaign against the Netherlands brought Spain into conflict with England—of which Philip had once been the royal consort as husband of Queen Mary—and in trying to deal with the English, the Spanish sent a great flotilla to clear the English Channel. The defeat of this armada—which will be treated later—ended any chance of a reconquest of the Dutch provinces. Finally, in 1648, the king of Spain formally recognized the independence of the Dutch.

The Dutch emerged from this war as the most powerful commercial nation in Europe. By the early seventeenth century, they were building more and better ships than all other nations combined—it was said that they built 2,000 per year—and they were capturing more and more of the carrying trade not only of Europe but of the whole world. After the Dutch closed off Antwerp, which was in the region controlled by Spain, Amsterdam became the commercial and financial capital of Europe.

The geographical extent of Dutch shipping and commercial operations was remarkable. The Dutch handled much of the grain trade of the Baltic and a large part of the carrying trade of England, France, Italy, and Portugal. When Philip II closed Lisbon to the Dutch—after he seized the crown of Portugal in 1580—the Dutch merely went directly to the source of spices in

Example of a propaganda badge worn by Dutch "Sea Beggars." The insurgents' hatred of Catholicism is expressed in the inscription: "Better the Turks than the pope."

Amsterdam harbor, center of
a worldwide trade (detail
from an engraving by Pieter
Bast, 1597).

World. When the French and English
began to develop overseas empires in
the seventeenth century, they found
the Dutch ahead of them all over the
world.

ELIZABETHAN ENGLAND

For a few years in the middle of the sixteenth century (1554–58), England was
brought within the orbit of Habsburg
power when Queen Mary of England
(r. 1553–58) was married to Philip II of
Spain. But the accession of Elizabeth I
(r. 1558–1603) after Mary's death
changed everything. Elizabeth was the
greatest Tudor monarch of England—
the last of the direct descendants of
Henry VII Tudor. She was a cautious
and moderate ruler, whose instinct was
to temporize and compromise. Although she could never allow England
to submit to papal authority—which
had declared the marriage of her
mother, Ann Boleyn, to Henry VIII
invalid—she followed a moderate religious policy and was herself conservative in theological and liturgical
matters.

She compromised and temporized
in foreign policy also. She tried to
avoid committing herself, kept a dozen
intrigues afoot at all times to give herself an avenue of escape, and seems to
have aimed at avoiding war at any cost.
The chief foreign danger to the realm
when Elizabeth came to the throne was
from French influence in Scotland.
Elizabeth's cousin, Mary Stuart, Queen
of Scots, was married in 1558 to the
heir of the French crown, and the alliance between the French and Scots
looked as if it would become truly formidable.

But in 1559 the Scot John Knox returned from Geneva and began preaching Calvinism, and his success undermined the influence of Catholicism and
the French. In this instance Elizabeth
made a rapid decision. She allied herself with the Calvinist party in Scotland
and tried to keep the French out. By
1560, Knox, the Kirk (Scottish Church),

the Moluccas. In 1602 the Dutch East
India Company was formed and soon
established its headquarters at Batavia
on the island of Java. By the middle of
the seventeenth century, the Dutch
were in control of the richest part of the
Portuguese empire in the East, and in
1652 they established a colony at the
Cape of Good Hope as a way station on
the route to the East. A few decades
earlier, they had almost ousted the Portuguese from Brazil and had founded a
colony, called New Amsterdam, on
Manhattan Island in the Hudson River
(1624), which became the center for a
large Dutch carrying trade in the New

1485	1509	1547	1553	1558	1603
Henry VII	Henry VIII	Edward VI	Mary	Elizabeth I	

and the pro-English party were in control, and the French had lost all influence in Scotland.

While these things were happening, Mary had been in France. She returned to Scotland in 1561, after the death of her husband, and hoped to reestablish Catholicism along with her own authority. But she faced unbending opposition from Knox and the Kirk, and after a second marriage that turned out badly, she was forced to abdicate in 1567. A year later Mary fled to England, where Elizabeth received her coolly, but permitted her to stay. Mary soon became the center of every French and Spanish plot against Elizabeth, who kept a watch on her, but refused to imprison or execute her. Then in 1587 Elizabeth's ministers presented incontrovertible evidence of Mary's complicity in an assassination plot, and the queen reluctantly consented to her execution.

The Anglo-Spanish Conflict

Although there were many causes of conflict, Philip II of Spain and Elizabeth I of England remained on good terms for over 20 years. The quarter century of peace gave English industry and commerce a chance to expand considerably, and when the Spanish were unable to produce sufficient goods for their colonies—for reasons that have already been noted—the English were ready to supply the deficiency. In 1562 an aggressive merchant named Sir John Hawkins was the first Englishman to carry both goods and slaves directly to the Spanish settlements in the New World. The Spanish sought to prevent such direct trade, which drew profit from their colonies without giving the mother country its due, and in 1569 Sir John and his cousin Sir Francis Drake were almost wiped out by a Spanish

fleet. In revenge, Drake seized the silver shipment from Peru. From 1577 to 1580, he followed Magellan's route around the world and demonstrated the vulnerability of the Spanish Empire. Meanwhile other English sailors were probing the coasts of North America in search of a Northwest Passage that would outflank the Portuguese route to the East Indies. By that time, the English were contesting the Spanish-Portuguese monopoly of overseas trade.

However, it was the revolt of the Netherlands that finally broke the peace between Spain and England. For centuries the English had had close commercial ties with the Low Countries; Flanders had been the first and remained the best customer for English wool and other goods. Furthermore, Englishmen sympathized with their fellow Protestants in the United Provinces, and English privateers—the Sea Dogs—cooperated with their Dutch counterparts—the Sea Beggars—against Spanish shipping and communications. For their part, Philip II's ambassadors in England were deeply involved in successive plots against Elizabeth's life, one of which led to the execution of Mary Stuart.

Then in 1588 Philip decided to make a bold attempt on England. He assembled an enormous fleet, the Invincible Armada, and sent it north to clear the English Channel and prepare the way for an invasion of England by the Duke of Parma. The English met the Armada with smaller, faster ships that could fire at longer range than the Spanish boats, and, when the Armada anchored off Calais to await Parma, the English sent fire ships among the Spanish ships and caused panic. The fleet fled north, where the English attacked them off Gravelines. The stormy weather of the North Sea completed what the English

Elizabeth I of England, and her signature. The silver medal commemorates the defeat of the Spanish Armada (1588).

Mary Stuart, Queen of Scots, and her signature. Lead medal by Jacopo Primavera (*ca.* 1572).

The British fleet attack the Spanish Armada.

sailors had started, and fewer than half of the Armada's ships struggled home by going north and west around the British Isles.

The victory gave a lift to the morale of Englishmen and Protestants everywhere. It ended all further threat of a Spanish conquest of England and also made it impossible for them to reconquer the United Provinces in the Netherlands. When a peace was finally signed in 1604, the English—with the Dutch—were nearly the equals of the Spaniards on the sea.

THE FRENCH WARS OF RELIGION

The rise of Spain and the relative peace in which England lived during Elizabeth's reign certainly resulted in part from the weakness of France, which was the most populous and largest nation in Europe. The later sixteenth century was a period of civil and religious strife in France. From 1562 to 1593 the French fought furiously with one another while the monarchy was helpless to restore order and unity.

Although France was the largest nation in Europe under a single monarchy, it was really not as unified as England or Spain. The aristocracy was still powerful and turbulent, and the provinces had held on to their local customs and privileges. These problems contributed to the divisions that resulted when Calvinism began to spread. Calvin had published a French version of his *Institutes*, and the work appealed to many Frenchmen. On the

The Armada

When the Spanish Armada challenged the ancient lords of the English on their own grounds, the impending conflict took on the aspect of a judicial duel in which as was expected in such duels, God would defend the right. . . . So when the two fleets approached their appointed battleground, all Europe watched. For the spectators of both parties, the outcome, reinforced, as everyone believed, by an extraordinary tempest, was indeed decisive. The Protestants of France and the Netherlands, Germany and Scandinavia saw with relief that God was, in truth, as they had always supposed, on their side. The Catholics of France and Italy and Germany saw with almost equal relief that Spain was not, after all, God's chosen champion. From that time forward, though Spain's preponderance was to last for more than another generation, the peak of her prestige had passed. . . . So, in spite of the long, indecisive war which followed, the defeat of the Spanish Armada really was decisive. It decided that religious unity was not to be reimposed by force on the heirs of medieval Christendom, and if, in doing so, it only validated what was already by far the most probable outcome, why, perhaps that is all that any of the battles we call decisive has ever done.

From Garrett Mattingly, *The Armada* (Boston: Houghton Mifflin, 1959), pp. 400–01.

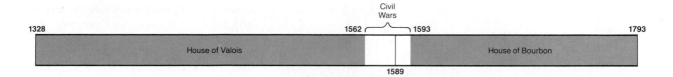

Civil
Wars

1328 — House of Valois — 1562 — 1593 — House of Bourbon — 1793

1589

eve of the civil wars the French Calvinists—nicknamed the Huguenots—had about 2,500 churches, and, as elsewhere, they formed a small, but well-organized and aggressive minority. They also had support from people in the highest levels of French society. Arrayed against the Huguenots were strongly Catholic noble families, and, more important, the University of Paris and the *parlement* (high court) of Paris. Moreover, the French monarchy had no interest in religious change, because the Concordat of Bologna (1516) had given it control over the appointment of clergy.

The wars of religion broke out after the death of King Henry II, the husband of Mary Stuart of Scotland, in 1559. Royal authority fell into the hands of the Queen Mother, Catherine de' Medici, who controlled the government during the reigns of Henry's three weak brothers—Francis II (r. 1559–60), Charles IX (r. 1560–74), and Henry III (r. 1574–89). Catherine was an astute ruler, but she lacked formal authority and could not prevent the religious fanatics on both sides from warring. Calvinists sided with discontented nobles and provinces eager to affirm local autonomy. The government and conservative nobility were on the Catholic side. Fanatics on both sides appealed for foreign support— the Huguenots to the English and Dutch, and the Catholics to Spain. England and Spain actually sent troops, mostly at the beginning and end of the wars.

The fighting was savage—as civil wars often are—and devastated large areas of the country. The Catholics won most of the battles, but they could not wipe out the Huguenots. In 1572 Catholic fanatics convinced Catherine that one sharp blow would destroy the Protestants and end the strife. At two o'clock in the morning of St. Bartholomew's Day (August 23), armed bands of Catholics attacked Huguenot leaders who were in Paris for the wedding of the Huguenot Prince Henry of Navarre to the king's sister. The St. Bartholomew's Day Massacre touched off a wave of violence against Protestants that soon spread to other cities. Between late August and October, over 10,000 Protestants—3,000 in Paris alone—were murdered. The event hardened the religious hatred in France and in Europe generally. Pope Gregory XIII and Philip II of Spain hailed the massacre as progress in the fight against Protestantism. Protestants throughout Europe were horrified.

The wars dragged on for 20 years, becoming more and more confused and purposeless, until the Huguenot Henry of Navarre came to the throne as Henry IV (r. 1589–1610). Henry was the nearest male heir to the crown, but his relationship to the previous king was nonetheless quite distant, and he found it difficult to make good his claim. He faced a Catholic League that held Paris and troops of Philip II that intervened from the Netherlands under Parma. After four years of struggle, Henry decided that the only way to consolidate his control over the monarchy would be to renounce his Protestantism and become a Catholic, which he did in 1593. However, he did not turn against his former coreligionists, and five years later he issued the Edict of Nantes (1598), which granted freedom of conscience, freedom of worship in specified places, equal civil rights, and control of some 200 fortified towns to the Huguenots. The Edict constituted the first official French recognition that two religions could coexist without destroying the state.

Catherine de' Medici in 1561, by an unknown artist.

Massacre of St.
Bartholomew's Day, 1572
(detail from a painting by an
eyewitness, François Dubois).

THE EFFECTS OF RELIGIOUS CONFLICT

The world of Philip II and Elizabeth I was one in which religion strongly affected political and social conflicts. The conflicts themselves stemmed from economic and political changes that predated the Protestant Reformation, but the religious schism embittered every issue and drove out moderation. Some monarchies that had been progressing toward consolidation of their power—like France and Germany—were weakened by the religious strife, while others—like Spain and England—were strengthened. In Spain, embattled Catholicism rallied around Charles V and Philip II. In England, patriotism and Protestantism became associated after Mary tried to reverse the reformation begun by her father, Henry VIII.

Just as the troubles of the Great Schism in the Roman Catholic Church (1378–1417) had stimulated thinkers to create a new constitutional theory of the Church—conciliarism—so the wars of religion inspired important new works on political theory. French theorists first created a doctrine of political obligation that justified rebellion against constituted authority on certain grounds. Protestants in Germany, the Netherlands, and France relied on such theories in arguing that they were justified in rebelling against monarchies that sought to impose a false religion on them. After a generation of religious civil war, French writers like Jean Bodin (1530–96) created a new secular theory of political sovereignty that could justify obedience to properly constituted authority without appeal to religious doctrine. This theory became one of the bases of modern political thought.

The religious passion of the age also spawned a terrifying witch-craze in Europe. The craze began in the mid-sixteenth century and lasted about a century. Before it ended, thousands of persons—mostly women—had been burned or hanged as witches. The horror seems to have begun when the religious passions created by the Protestant and Counter Reformations mixed with the ancient—pre-Christian—superstitious beliefs and practices that had survived the Middle Ages. Almost every community had its wizard and cunning woman, to whom neighbors turned when the ministrations of priests or physician did not avail. From time to time during the Middle Ages, people like these had been convicted of malevolent witchcraft—that is, of attempting to use occult means to inflict death or disease on others.

During the sixteenth century the number of people accused of witchcraft increased dramatically. In communities throughout Europe accusations of witchcraft triggered chain reactions of arrests. The accused were tortured into confessing the most fantastical acts—of participating in obscene "witches' sabbaths" and of diabolical schemes to harm their neighbors. They were also forced to name their accomplices in these pacts with the Devil, and so one arrest led to others. Often, dozens, even hundreds, in a single community were led to the stake.

By 1660 the witch-panics were subsiding and by 1700 they had all but disappeared. It is hard to say why they ended. Religious warfare ended in the mid-seventeenth century and passions cooled as religious toleration became the normal public policy in Europe. Perhaps more important, the development of a modern scientific outlook—which, among other ways, manifested itself in a dispute over the credibility of miracles—reduced belief in invisible spirits and occult forces among the educated leadership of society. Without the support of these elite elements, the hunt for witches gradually ended. The century-long witch-craze was one of the most tragic episodes in the history of European civilization.

THE EUROPEAN WORLD IN THE LATER SIXTEENTH CENTURY

The Status and Economic Condition of Peasants

Although much of the last two chapters has concentrated on cities and urban life, the overwhelming majority of the sixteenth-century population was rural. By the late sixteenth century there had been significant changes in the economic and social conditions of the peasants, but the changes were immensely different from one country to the next. In France and western Germany, the position of the peasants improved. In Spain, eastern Germany, and the eastern European countries, it deteriorated.

In most of western Europe the disastrous plagues of the fourteenth century undermined the old feudal system that had held the peasants in service to the lords. Rural communities and agriculture broke down, and, when they began to recover in the fifteenth century, the lords granted favorable terms to the peasants in order to induce them to cultivate their lands. Some lords had been so seriously damaged by the disasters that they had to sell their lands, and their own peasants were often among the buyers. By the later six-

---

Religion and Patriotism

A Spanish ambassador reporting the words of a French Catholic in 1565:

Nowadays Catholic princes must not proceed as they once did. At one time friends and enemies were distinguished by the frontiers of provinces and kingdoms, and were called Italians, Germans, Frenchmen, Spaniards, Englishmen, and the like. Now we must say Catholics and heretics, and a Catholic prince must consider all Catholics of all countries as his friends, just as the heretics consider all heretics as friends and subjects whether they are their own vassals or not.

■ ■ ■

An English Protestant writing in 1589:

All dutiful subjects in this land desire with all their hearts the continuance of God's religion; the preservation of Queen Elizabeth; and the good success of the English navy. These particulars, I grant, are not expressed in flat in the Lord's Prayer; but they are contained within the compass of, and may be deduced from the petitions of that excellent prayer. Whosoever doubteth of this is void of learning.

As quoted in Erich Marks, *Die Zusammenkunft von Bayonne* (Strasburg: K. J. Trübner, 1889), p. 14; as quoted in Benjamin Hanbury, *Historical Memorials Relating to the Independents* (London: Congregational Union of England and Wales, 1839–44), Vol. I, p. 71.

---

teenth century, about 5 percent of the peasants in France and western Germany owned their own land, and about an equal percentage remained bound in serfdom. The great majority of peasants rented their land, but the law increasingly recognized the right of these leaseholders to sell or grant their properties.

In 1480, the king of Castile released all peasants from serfdom and gave them proprietary rights in their land. But the Castilian peasants were not able to take advantage of their new position because the same government that had granted them freedom followed economic policies that undercut them. Within a couple of generations of the act of emancipation the royal gov-

Summer, by Peiter Brueghel, showing peasants at work in the fields.

ernment was encouraging the importation of cheap grain, and the peasants could not meet the foreign competition. The peasants of Aragon suffered doubly, since they had not been released from serfdom. By the late sixteenth century, the rural populations were suffering a serious economic depression, and agriculture was one of the weakest elements in Philip II's Spain.

Finally, while the economic and social position of western European peasants generally improved, that of their eastern counterparts worsened. The northeastern parts of Germany, which had been conquered from the Slavs in the later Middle Ages, were regions of large estates that could use the superb river systems to get their crops to the growing urban markets of northern Europe. Consequently, in the later sixteenth century the lords imposed a full serfdom on their peasants in order to exploit their labor. In Russia, Tsar Ivan the Terrible (r. 1533–84) helped his nobility engage in a similar oppression. He rewarded service to the state by granting large estates with the right to force the peasants into serfdom. Fur-

thermore, the Russian lords had a legal right to punish serfs for wrongdoing.

Urban Life

One of the unusual features of sixteenth-century political and economic life was that the cities functioned almost as independent states. Starting in the twelfth century, the cities had achieved a virtual independence by winning charters from the kings and emperors. The charters freed them from the power of local feudal lords and gave them the right to govern themselves. By the sixteenth century, cities were independent actors in the political and economic spheres. Although they did not have the resources to support the exploration and settlement of the Orient and the New World, their influence and power was seen everywhere in Europe and along the trade routes opened up by the explorers.

The sixteenth-century city was a remarkable organism. One historian has likened citizenship in the early modern city to enrollment in a club. Every aspect of life was regulated by a system of associations under the ultimate control of the city council. The craft guilds closely regulated their trades. They set the conditions for apprenticeships, regulated wages for journeymen, and provided their members with a substantial amount of social security. Masters were almost invariably married men because they had to provide a family setting for apprentices and needed the support of a wife in their businesses. Usually, men waited to get married until they were ready to become masters and open their own shops, and they tended to marry young women. The wedding was almost as much an affair of the guild as it was the start of a new family. As a social community, the guild was an association of families.

The guilds had officers, and a young master could expect to be elected to a lower office about six years after becoming a full member. It usually took another eight years for the master to be elected to higher office. The guilds themselves occupied specific positions in the socioeconomic structure of the city, and the principal officers of the leading guilds could move on to city offices. High office in the guild of merchants almost assured an important role in the town government, which usually consisted of a large and a small council.

In addition to the guilds, most towns had religious confraternities or brotherhoods that cut across guild and social structures. The brotherhoods were responsible for organizing the important citywide festivals, in which the guilds also had their particular places, and the participation in them of men from all walks of life tended to reduce the potential tension among the guilds. Holding office in a brotherhood was another avenue to power in the city government.

The system of wards was also separate from the guilds. The wards were geographic areas of the city, neighborhoods through which the city government organized the watch, taxation, and the militia. Each ward had to provide for the security of its area and to provide a set number of men for the town militia. The wards also provided men for the night watch on the walls and at the gates. While some wards were dominated by one or another of the guilds, because some crafts were consciously located in certain areas (for example, butchers and tanners were typically settled along the river), in most neighborhoods the population was quite mixed. The sixteenth-century city did not have high-rent and low-rent districts; the rich lived cheek-by-jowl with the poor. Further, the ward associations, responsible for so many of the formal activities of the city, earned the very strong allegiance of their members.

This tight organization by the guilds, wards, and city government reached into every aspect of the citizens' life. The day and week were fully organized. The gates opened at 4:00

A.M. and closed at 8:00 P.M., about an hour after the workday ended. After the gates closed, the town authorities imposed a curfew to control crime and keep the peace. Payday was Saturday, when workers got off early, and Sunday was a day of rest. One imagines such days to be like "Childrens' Games" painted by Pieter Brueghel the Elder (*ca.* 1525–69), the Flemish artist famous for his paintings of peasant life.

Of course, there were problems in this well-organized frame of life. About a fifth of the population, more in large cities, lived outside the guild structure. This was the class of day laborers and other poor. Although not members of a guild, such people were within the social and political orbit of the ward system, and, therefore, they, too, had their particular place in the city. Widows, of which there were many because men married late and tended to take young wives, were a special problem. Some towns required widows to live in groups in houses set aside for them, at least until they were past 50 years old. An old woman could live by herself. The purpose of such regulations was to protect the women and make it easier for the town authorities to give them support.

Relations between men and women were difficult in many respects. Because men had to establish themselves before marrying, there was a large population of sexually frustrated young men in most towns. These men constituted a constant threat to unprotected women—rape, including group rape, was a common event—and the authorities, representing the established and married men of the city, were always on the watch against such outrages. One outlet provided by the city fathers was the public brothel, where the women were licensed. Even prostitutes who worked the streets were licensed and wore badges to denote the fact. The town bathhouse, also fully licensed, was another place where men, at least upper-class men, could find prostitutes. Young men's associations were a different kind of outlet. These were sanctioned organizations patterned on the religious brotherhoods, but their purpose was anything but religious. The members were dedicated to rowdy fun at the expense of the "establishment," and their officers bore titles like Prince of Youth and Abbot of Fools. They organized satirical presentations at festivals and weddings. Their special target was the elderly widower who married a young woman, thereby reducing the population of eligible women for whom the young men hankered. The story of the old man with or seeking a young wife and challenged by a young man became one of the enduring themes in European comedy.

Women played an important role in the life of the sixteenth-century city, not only as wives, but also as craftspeople and merchants. Of couse, the principal role of women was as wife and mother, but in the household of a craftsman, that role was of central economic importance. A craftsman could not function—in some guilds he was not permitted to function—without a wife, who provided support for the apprentices and often ran the shop where the master's product was sold. Guilds protected the secrets of their trades carefully, but they permitted members to impart them to their wives as well as to their apprentices. The craftsman's wife was his partner in business as well as in life.

Beyond this, many women were independent participants in the commercial life of the cities. Women practiced crafts such as silk weaving, retailing, and brewing, and they often functioned as agents for foreign merchants doing business in their towns. However, wherever the business touched communal interests, women tended to be excluded. They were limited to crafts and businesses that had a household character; once a business became a matter of public importance, it was taken over by men. Thus, urban women, who had increasingly become literate and who played a major role in the Reformation as early adherents of the Protestants (who advocated a direct relationship between God and the individual, the priesthood of all believers), remained subordinate within their community. The woman's place was in the home, as wife, mother, and businesswoman; she could not participate in the guild, the brotherhood, or the city government.

ART, LITERATURE, AND SCIENCE IN THE SIXTEENTH CENTURY

Art

Against the backdrop of religious fanaticism and strife, the sixteenth century was a golden age of art and literature. Renaissance art reached its zenith in the first two decades of the century, when Leonardo da Vinci (1452–1519), Raphael (1483–1520), Albrecht Dürer (1471–1528), and Michelangelo (1475–1564) were active. Their work realized the classical aesthetic of the Renaissance style in works of lasting beauty and importance in art history. After the 1520s, influenced by Luther, Dürer, who thought that the Renaissance style and subject matter were too pagan, simplified his work and concentrated on biblical scenes. Another German painter influenced by Luther, Hans Holbein the Younger (1497–1543), devoted himself to portraits, traveling to Switzerland and England in search of commissions. He settled in England as a court painter and is famous for his portraits of King Henry VIII, Thomas More, and other figures at the English court.

Michelangelo also abandoned the high Renaissance style after 1520, developing a new style that broke the serene lines of his early work. For example, his ceiling frescoes in the Sistine Chapel, painted around 1510, are organized in well-ordered panels with figures reminiscent of the classical sculpture that inspired the Renaissance. The action of the Genesis story is represented in static images of the crucial moments. By contrast, his wall fresco of the Last Judgment in the same chapel, painted during the 1530s, is a crowded scene of twisted bodies in which the action of condemnation and salvation of souls is captured in a dynamic composition. The same trend can be observed in Michelangelo's sculpture. His early work realized the classical ideals of the Renaissance, while his later work rebelled against proportion and graceful line, producing tortured shapes of great emotional power.

While some artists, like the Venetian painter Titian (*ca.* 1477–1576), continued to work in the Renaissance style and subject matter, many others followed Michelangelo into a new style. These artists are called Mannerists because they painted in the manner of Michelangelo, and few of them produced work of lasting value. However, two stand out: Tintoretto (1518–94) and El Greco (*ca.* 1548–1614). Tintoretto was a Venetian who consciously tried to combine the styles of Titian and the late Michelangelo. He painted scenes of saints and miracles and, in imitation of Michelangelo, executed some very large wall paintings. His works project a sense of movement and action, much like his mentor's Last Judgment. El Greco (Domenikos Theotocopoulos, born on the island of Crete) studied in Venice and Rome, but eventually settled in Spain, where he hoped to become a court painter, as Holbein had done in England. But King Philip II was enamored of the work of second-rate Spanish mannerists, and El Greco, as the Spaniards called him, never found favor in Madrid, Philip's new capital. He was an original artist, whose paintings exude a strong mystical aura. His sparse, elongated figures project great tension and strength.

The Flemish school of painting underwent similar changes. Hieronymus Bosch (*ca.* 1450–1516) painted works that showed in exaggerated form the physicality of human life. His works concentrated on religious themes and are dark and foreboding. Modern scholars have discovered in them a complex symbolic visual language that expresses his mystical view of the world. The Brueghels, Pieter the Elder (*ca.* 1525–69), Pieter the Younger (1564–1637), and Jan (1568–1625), avoided the religious subjects of Bosch and earlier painters and painted scenes from everyday life. Pieter the Elder became famous as a painter of rural scenes, particularly a series of works on the

Virgin with Sts. Ines and Tecla, by El Greco.

months that showed the various agricultural labors appropriate to each period of the year. His few religious paintings, such as the "Slaughter of the Innocents," broke new ground by depicting not the scene itself, but the moment before it, so that viewers are caught up in the suspense of knowing what is about to happen. His son Pieter became known for works that depicted Hell, though he also painted scenes of peasant life like his father, and Jan was famous for landscapes and still lifes. The Brueghel dynasty of painters lasted into the eighteenth century.

Literature

In literature, the sixteenth century was the great age of drama. Medieval drama had developed as part of the urban tradition of celebrating religious festivals. During the festivals, the guilds would put on traditional plays about saints' lives and miracles. The universities provided another tradition of drama. Students had put on plays since the thirteenth century. The earlier dramas had been based on the stories of biblical figures, such as Daniel and Herod, but in the fifteenth and early sixteenth centuries, the students were creating secular dramas based on Roman models. Being within the university world, these plays were meant for an elite, educated audience. The great age of theatre began in the 1570s when in England and Spain actors and playwrights created new professional companies that played to the general public.

In London, there were several companies founded in the 1570s, and two playwrights gained a great following, Thomas Kyd (1558–94) and Christopher Marlowe (1564–93). Kyd's *Spanish Tragedy* and Marlowe's *Tamburlaine* were the first great popular successes of the English stage. Both works are action-packed, and Kyd's play, about a father's revenge of his son's death, established the theme of revenge as a commonplace of English tragedy. Marlowe's heroes were powerful, romantic figures who dominated all the other

characters, and he was the first to use blank verse in dramatic writing. But it was Marlowe's contemporary, William Shakespeare (1564–1616), who rose out of the crowd to become the greatest English poet and dramatist.

Shakespeare made a good enough living on the stage as a playwright, actor, and producer to retire to his native town of Stratford (not far from Oxford) in 1613. He founded a company of actors, the Lord Chamberlain's Company (later called the King's Company), that remained intact for more than two decades, and he wrote his plays for the 20 or so actors of this company. The life of the stage was a hectic one. Companies presented plays six afternoons a week throughout the year and had to keep about 50 plays in their repertory. Shakespeare must have written a large number of plays, but he considered them the property of his company and did not publish them. However, many of them were so successful that 18 were published in illegal editions during his lifetime. After his death, Shakespeare's friends gathered the surviving manuscripts and published them in a folio volume in 1623, following the example of Ben Jonson (1573–1637) who had shown the way by publishing his own plays in 1616. The first edition of Shakespeare's work contained 36 plays; since then scholars have added one, *Pericles*, which probably had scenes written by the master. The plays can be divided into three groups, tragedies (such as *Hamlet* and *King Lear*), comedies (such as *Taming of the Shrew* and *As you Like It*), and histories (such as *Richard III* and *Henry V*). Shakespeare borrowed his themes from classical and English history and from the Italian literary tradition, which had become popular in England early in the sixteenth century.

The theaters of Shakespeare's London were of two types—large open buildings and small enclosed halls. Shakespeare's Globe Theater was of the first type. It was a round building without a roof that could hold up to 3,000 people. The audience could stand in the pit below the stage or in boxes

The portrait of William Shakespeare from the title page of the first published collection of his plays (1623).

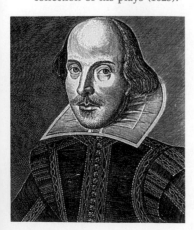

along the walls. Entrance to the pit cost a penny or two, making theater one of the least expensive pastimes in the city. The boxes cost much more. Thus, the plays had to appeal to the widest conceivable spectrum of the city's populace. The small theaters, such as Blackfriars, where Shakespeare's company also performed, were rectangular buildings that could hold a few hundred people. Entry to these halls was more expensive than to open theaters, and the plays written for them could appeal to a more sophisticated audience representing a narrower slice of London society. Given the boom in theater during the period 1580–1640, it is estimated that playwrights wrote over 6,000 plays in the period. About 2,000 of them survive.

In Spain, the theater became popular soon after the middle of the century, but, as in England, it experienced an explosion of popularity in the 1570s. Spanish plays combined dramatic scenes with interludes of dance and musical entertainment, and unlike their English counterparts, Spanish companies employed women as entertainers and actresses. The Spanish "Shakespeare" was Lope de Vega (1562–1632), who wrote about 1,500 *comedias*, as the Spanish called the plays. About 500 of his works survive. As might be expected, Lope de Vega's stupendous production of work used only a few plot lines, but he achieved spectacular fame and earned a good living. By contrast, the greatest literary figure of sixteenth-century Spain, Miguel de Cervantes (1547–1616), suffered through a life of trials and penury. He began writing dramas in the early 1560s, but he seems to have gotten in trouble with the law and went to Rome. From there, he enlisted in the naval force being prepared by the Philip II to fight the Turks, and he distinguished himself at the Battle of Lepanto (1571). In 1575, while on his way back to Spain to seek an officer's commission, he was captured and enslaved by the Turks of Algiers, and for the next five years he repeatedly tried to escape while his family tried to raise

a ransom. After he was freed by his family's efforts, he returned to Spain and became a royal bureaucrat in Seville, but accounting was not his strong suit, and he continually found himself in trouble with his superiors. He left the royal service in 1600.

While still serving in Seville, Cervantes again began to write for the stage, and he won a first prize for poetry in a contest held in Zaragoza in 1595. After he left government service, he spent three years in obscurity writing a great work satirizing the chivalric romances that had become phenomenally popular in Spain. This work, *Don Quixote*, is considered the first novel, a prose work concerned with the character and adventures of a knight and his man, and it became immediately popular. Philip III (r. 1598–1621 is said to have remarked, when he observed a young man in stitches over a book, that he was either crazy or reading *Don Quixote*. The work has been translated into more languages than any other book except the Bible. It was first translated into English in 1612. Toward the end of his life, Cervantes published the first short stories in Spanish in a work entitled *Twelve Exemplary Novelas* (1613).

Theater did not become popular in France until the seventeenth century, but French writers of the sixteenth century also contributed to the literary revolution that created the foundations of modern literature. The French nobleman Michel Montaigne (1533–92) created the genre of the essay after he had retired from the royal court in disgust over the fanaticism engendered by the conflict between the Huguenots and the Catholics. Educated as a humanist, Montaigne explored human nature in his *Essays* by focusing on himself, the person he knew best. His essays are witty and wise, and they are still treasured for their author's insights into the human condition.

Science

Finally, during the sixteenth century, a few great scholars laid the foundations

Miguel de Cervantes, portrait by Juan de Juaregui (1600).

of modern science. The story of the scientific revolution will be examined in Chapter 21, but it rests on the work of Nicholas Copernicus (1473–1543), Tycho Brahe (1546–1601), Johannes Kepler (1571–1630), and Galileo Galilei (1564–1642). These men combined theoretical work with experiment and observation to transform the medieval world view. Copernicus, working in a monastic house located in Prussia, far from the centers of intellectual and cultural life, tried to resolve the discrepancy between the observed movement of the planets and the Ptolomaic view that they and the sun orbited around the earth. Eventually, in a work published the year of his death, he proposed that the planetary movements could best be explained if one supposed that the earth and planets circled the sun. This heliocentric theory did not gain wide acceptance until late in the century. By that time, Brahe's careful observations of the motion of heavenly bodies, which he intended to demonstrate the validity of the Ptolemaic paradigm, had shown that Copernicus was correct. The discrepancy between the observed movements and the Ptolomaic explanation was even greater than Copernicus had known. Brahe's assistant, Kepler, then showed that the motion of the planets was consistent with a modified Copernican thesis. The planets did travel around the sun, but not in the perfect circles that Copernicus had thought. Rather, they followed elliptical orbits, for which Kepler provided a mathematical explanation.

Galileo confirmed Copernicus's theory by using a telescope, which he built after hearing about a Dutch inventor's spyglass. The telescope, which magnified objects 30 times, permitted him to make numerous discoveries. He was the first to see mountains on the moon, the rings of Saturn, and the composition of the Milky Way. He also did a great deal of work on mechanics, providing mathematical explanations for the way objects move and describing the use of the pendulum in clocks. His most famous experiment was the one in which he dropped objects of different weights from the leaning tower of Pisa. The test showed that all the objects fell at the same rate of acceleration. Galileo then proposed a mathematical formula to describe the universal rate of acceleration of falling objects. His work did more than anyone's to establish the principle that mathematics truly describes the world. As he said, "The book of nature . . . is written in mathematical characters."

These men demonstrated the power of experimentation and observation to bring about an advance in scientific knowledge and established the connection between mathematics and reality. The foundations of modern science rest on those two principles.

Suggestions for Further Reading

Geographical Discovery

For a detailed account of the geographical discoveries of the fifteenth and sixteenth centuries, see J. H. Parry, *The Age of Reconnaisance* (1963). For the technological basis of the explorations, see C. Cipolla, *Guns and Sails in the Early Phase of the European Expansion* (1966). For the Mediterranean background of oceanic navigation, see M. E. Mallet, *Florentine Galleys of the Fifteenth Century* (1967), and F. C. Lane, *Venetian Ships and Shipbuilders of the Renaissance* (1934).

Effects on Europe

On the effect of the discoveries on Europe, see J. H. Elliott, *The Old World and the New* (1970). H. H. Hart, *The Road to the Indies* (1950), describes the Portuguese expeditions, J. B. Brebner, *The Explorers of North America, 1492–1806* (1933), and A. P. Newton, *The European Nations in the West Indies, 1493–1688* (1933), treat exploration in particular areas. The best account of Columbus is S. E. Morrison, *Admiral of the Ocean Sea*, 2 vols. (1942). For an overall view, see Morrison's *The European Discovery of America* (1971). For good, unpreju-

diced histories of the early Spanish colonies, see C. H. Haring, *The Spanish Empire in America* (1947); L. Hanke, *The Spanish Struggle for Justice in the Conquest of America* (1949); and R. Cameron, *Viceroyalties of the West* (1968).

Spain

On Spain in the sixteenth century, J. H. Elliott, *Imperial Spain, 1469–1716* (1964), is excellent. R. T. Davies, *The Golden Century of Spain, 1501–1621* (1937), and *Spain in Decline, 1621–1700* (1956), are sometimes controversial, but good accounts. For the effect of imperialism on Spanish government, see J. H. Parry, *The Spanish Theory of Empire in the Sixteenth Century* (1940). E. J. Hamilton, *American Treasure and the Price Revolution, 1501–*

1650 (1934), is the starting point for studies of the economic effects of empire. See also C. Cipolla, *Money, Prices and Civilization in the Mediterranean World* (1967). The classic work on the Armada is G. Mattingly, *The Spanish Armada* (1959). F. Braudel, *The Mediterranean and the Mediterranean World in the Age of Philip II*, 2 vols. (1972–73), is a masterpiece.

The Netherlands

The best history of the Dutch rebellion is P. Geyl, *The Revolt of the Netherlands, 1555–1609* (1932), and *The Netherlands Divided, 1609–1648* (1936). For a well-written biography of William the Silent, see C. V. Wedge-

wood, *William the Silent* (1944), and on the English involvement in the rebellion, see C. Wilson, *Queen Elizabeth and the Revolt of the Netherlands* (1970).

Elizabethan England

There is a wealth of good scholarly books on Elizabethan England. See J. Neale, *Queen Elizabeth I* (1952). C. Read's thorough biographies, *Mr. Secretary Walsingham*, 3 vols. (1925) and *Mr. Secretary Cecil* (Lord Burghley), 2 vols. (1955, 1960), provide detailed infor-

mation about the politics of the period. For a social history, see A. L. Rowse, *The England of Elizabeth* (1950) and *The Expansion of Elizabethan England* (1955). On the English entry in the explorations, see J. A. Williamson, *The Age of Drake*, 3rd ed. (1952).

France

There is not much work in English on sixteenth-century France. J. W. Salmon, *Society in Crisis: France in the Sixteenth Century* (1975), is the best general treatment. J. E. Neale, *The Age of Catherine de' Medici* (1943), and H. Pearson, *Henry of Navarre* (1963), are useful. On the government, see N. M. Sutherland, *The French Secretaries of State in the Age of Catherine de Medici* (1962).

J. W. Thompson, *The Wars of Religion in France, 1559–1576* (1909), is still useful. For brief scholarly accounts, see F. C. Palm, *Calvinism and the Religious Wars* (1932), and A. J. Grant, *The Huguenots* (1934). On the development of French political thought during the civil wars, see W. F. Church, *Constitutional Thought in Sixteenth Century France* (1941).

Social History

On rural life in the sixteenth century, see E. Le Roy Ladurie, *The Peasants of Languedoc* (1974), and M. R. Weisser, *The Peasants of the Montes* (1976). N. Z. Davis covers various aspects of French social history in a series of essays in *Society and Culture in Early Modern France* (1975). See also L. Febvre, *Life in Renaissance France* (1979). G. Huppert, *After the Black Death: A Social History of Early Modern Europe* (1986), concentrates on

urban society. There are several excellent studies of individual cities. See G. Strauss, *Nuremburg in the Sixteenth Century* (1976); C. R. Friedrichs, *Urban Society in an Age of War: Nördlingen, 1580–1720* (1979); and C. Pythian-Adams, *Desolation of a City* (1979), concerning Coventry, England. On urban women, see M. C. Howell, *Women, Production, and Patriarchy in Late Medieval Cities* (1986).

Art and Literature

On the art of the sixteenth century, see W. Friedländer, *Mannerism and Anti-Mannerism in Italian Painting* (1957). The works of Marlowe, Shakespeare, Lope

de Vega, Cervantes, and Montaigne are available in numerous modern editions.

19
Political and Economic Crises: The Seventeenth Century

*T*he seventeenth century was the century in which modern European civilization took on recognizable form. Political, social, and economic upheavals almost as dangerous as those that had shaken medieval civilization in the fourteenth century convulsed Europe. In the 1640s, as challenges to the growing power of the state arose, great rebellions weakened England, France, and Spain, the three most powerful European monarchies. The last wars of religion merged with wars to expand commerce or to overthrow or preserve the balance of power. Weather, famine, and plague compounded the ravages of war. The slow rise in population that followed the Black Death halted. The Thirty Years' War (1618–48) and plague epidemics actually forced the populations of Germany and Spain downward. Prolonged economic depression marked the middle decades of the century. Harvests repeatedly failed. The flow of silver from the New World that had stimulated the European economy dropped off sharply. Handicraft production in Europe increased only slightly if at all. Growth turned upward

Opposite: Rembrandt van Rijn, *Syndics of the Cloth Guild* (1662).

527

again only gradually after 1670. Poverty sharpened social unrest and inadequate revenues limited state power.

That unpromising environment nevertheless gave birth to a new Europe that was richer, controlled more of the world's commerce, and had more effective government in 1700 than in 1600. The troubles of the fourteenth century and the religious conflicts of the sixteenth century had in general slowed the process of building the sovereign territorial state begun in the thirteenth century. But it now proceeded rapidly. In the realm of theory, the process required defining the concept of sovereignty. In the realm of practice, it meant concentrating supreme power in some organ of the state, either in the monarchy as in France and most other states, or in a representative assembly, as ultimately happened in England. And Europe simultaneously underwent an intellectual revolution, a sharp change in conceptions about humanity and the universe far deeper and broader in its consequences than the Italian Renaissance (see pp. 446–52).

FRANCE'S SEARCH FOR ORDER AND AUTHORITY, 1598–1661

The anarchy and religious violence that lasted from 1562 to the Edict of Nantes in 1598 deeply marked seventeenth-century France. Three feeble kings had allowed the unruly great nobles to raise arms against the monarchy. The wars had torn the fabric of trade that linked the merchants and manufacturers of the towns. The wanderings of ragged, undisciplined armies had savaged the peasantry. The population longed for security despite a continuing suspicion of any authority that might violate local privileges or increase taxes.

The lawyer Jean Bodin (1530?–96), the most penetrating political thinker of the tragic years of the Wars of Religion, offered a theory that spoke to the universal yearning for order. Bodin's *The Republic* (1576) argued that a well-ordered state must lodge supreme power—sovereignty—clearly in some organ of the state, preferably the monarchy. Bodin defined sovereignty as the essential characteristic of the state: the power of "giving laws to the people as a whole without their consent."

Bodin did not consider that supreme power to be arbitrary or capricious. The laws of God and nature still bound Bodin's sovereign. But Bodin insisted that no human agency must limit the sovereign. Power must be "absolute," not divided, to be effective. Neither *parlements* (the highest French law courts) nor Estates General should veto or modify decisions of the sovereign. Bodin defined sovereignty far more clearly than previous theorists. He persuasively presented it as the only alternative to insecurity and civil war. The French absolute monarchy of the seventeenth century appeared to fulfill Bodin's prescription, and became the model and envy of many of Europe's rulers.

Henry IV and Sully

Henry IV (r. 1589–1610) began the process of restoring royal power and French prosperity. Victorious founder of the Bourbon dynasty, he was a popular king—courageous, vigorous, humorous, tolerant, and sound in his judgment of subordinates. But he spent much time in pursuit of game and women and happily left the routine business of government to his chief minister, Maximilien de Sully, an austere and parsimonious ex-Huguenot artillery officer. Sully restored the monarchy's solvency by canceling some debts, avoiding expensive foreign wars, and patching up the inefficient, corrupt, and inequitable tax system.

The monarchy, like most early modern governments, "farmed" its taxes; that is, it granted the right to collect taxes to private entrepreneurs who paid the government a fixed sum and then extracted all they could from the population. The burden fell most heavily on the peasants because nobles and the upper strata in the towns were ex-

Jean Bodin on Sovereignty

Political thinkers had recognized the *fact* of sovereignty for some time, but Bodin was the first to express the *idea* in clear and uncompromising terms.

Sovereignty is supreme power over citizens and subjects unrestrained by laws. . . . A prince is bound by no law of his predecessor, and much less by his own laws. . . . He may repeal, modify, or replace a law made by himself and without the consent of his subjects. . . . The opinion of those who have written that the king is bound by the popular will must be disregarded; such doctrine furnishes seditious men with material for revolutionary plots. No reasonable ground can be found to claim that subjects should control princes or that power should be attributed to popular assemblies. . . . The highest privilege of sovereignty consists in giving laws to the people as a whole without their consent. . . . Under this supreme power of making and repealing laws it is clear that all other functions of sovereignty are included.

From Jean Bodin, *Six Books Concerning the Republic,* from the Latin version of 1586, trans. by F. W. Coker, in *Readings in Political Philosophy* (New York: Macmillan, 1938), pp. 374, 375, 376, 377, 380.

Triumphal Entry of Henry IV into Paris, a large sketch by Peter Paul Rubens (*ca.* 1630).

empt from major taxes. The nobility would not tolerate attempts to redistribute the tax burden, and helped to bring down the French monarchy in 1788–89 over that precise issue (see pp. 648–49). What Sully could and did do was to improve the system he inherited, by attacking the crooked and inefficient tax farmers who as a rule pocketed as much as half the taxes collected in France before they reached the treasury. The reestablishment of internal order allowed agriculture and commerce to recover and increased the government's revenues, especially from customs duties. By the time a Catholic fanatic assassinated Henry IV in 1610, France's treasury contained a sizable surplus.

Decline and Resurgence of the Monarchy, 1610–42

A few years of weakness at the center reduced the work of Henry IV and Sully to ruins. The regency of Henry's widow, Marie de' Medici, allowed rapacious courtiers the run of the treasury and permitted Spain to intervene once more in French affairs, sometimes in bizarre alliance with the Huguenots. Incompetence soon dissipated the financial surplus Sully had left and led in 1614 to a summoning of the Estates General of France to one of its rare meetings. But the deliberations of the Estates General soon produced deadlock over taxation and religious issues between the First and Second Estates (the clergy and the nobility) and the Third Estate (the middle classes of the towns, represented largely by provincial royal officers). The Estates General dissolved inconclusively after issuing a declaration that "the king is sovereign in France, and holds his crown from God only." They did not meet again until 1789, on the eve of the French Revolution.

Fortunately for the monarchy, a minister far more powerful than Sully soon emerged. Henry IV's son, Louis XIII (r. 1614–43), superseded his mother's regency when he reached the age of 13. In 1624 he appointed a brilliant young cardinal, Armand Jean du Plessis de Richelieu (1585–1642), as chief of the king's council. From then until his

Three views of Cardinal Richelieu, by Philippe de Champaigne.

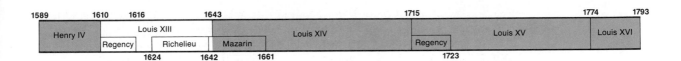

1589	1610	1616	1643		1715		1774	1793

death Richelieu was the real ruler of France. The great Cardinal, rather than any member of the Bourbon dynasty, founded the French absolute monarchy.

Richelieu had the clearest and most penetrating mind of any statesman of his generation as well as a largely deserved reputation for diabolical cleverness. He sought to establish the power and prestige of the French monarchy beyond any possibility of challenge. He came to his task with a startling grasp of political and diplomatic possibilities, an infallible memory, and an inflexible will unconstrained by moral scruple. Richelieu admired Machiavelli, and the heart of the Cardinal's political creed was *raison d'état*, "reason of state": the good of the state was the supreme good. That good justified the use of any means whatsoever—a stern creed the great Cardinal neatly reconciled with his own religious conscience. Richelieu deemed it "essential to banish pity" when judging "crimes against the state," for mercy in the present only led to greater bloodshed in the future. He coolly sent innocent men to their deaths to enhance royal authority and terrify troublemakers. When Louis XIII expressed moral qualms, Richelieu beat the king's objections down with brutal frankness: "Man is immortal; his salvation is hereafter; the state has no immortality, its salvation is now or never."

Richelieu pursued simultaneously four concrete objectives. He sought to destroy the power of the Huguenots, crush the great nobles, exclude the Habsburgs from French domestic politics, and decide in France's favor the Bourbon–Habsburg rivalry that dated from the sixteenth century. The Edict of Nantes, the compromise of 1598 that ended the religious civil wars, had allowed the Huguenots to garrison about 200 towns. Richelieu persuaded Louis XIII that he would never be master in his own house until he had wiped out this "state within a state." A monopoly of force within its borders, then as now, was the essential characteristic of statehood.

Rumors that the government had decided to attack provoked the Huguenots to rebel, and Richelieu proceeded to besiege and capture their chief stronghold at La Rochelle on the Atlantic coast. Unexpectedly generous, despite contempt for what he described as the "pretended Reformed religion," he allowed the Huguenots to worship as they pleased once he had eliminated their political and military autonomy. He sought to conciliate Protestants abroad who might help him in war with Spain and Austria and he hoped to make dependable and useful citizens of the Huguenots. In that, he was successful. The Huguenots served the crown in the war of 1635–59 against the Habsburgs and remained loyal in the great domestic crisis of the Fronde that followed Richelieu's death.

Richelieu's attack on the nobility was less successful. Aristocratic intrigues threatened him until the very end of his career. In response to that threat, he developed a network of spies, created a special tribunal to try noble lawbreakers, and sternly forbade duelling, a privilege that symbolized the nobility's freedom from ordinary restraints. He gradually weakened the power of the great nobles who were provincial governors and gave more and more local administrative responsibility to direct representatives of the crown, the *intendants*. These temporary appointees came not from the old "nobility of the sword" but from the commons or the *noblesse de robe*, ennobled judicial officeholders of middle-class ancestry who had purchased their offices as part of yet another bizarre old regime financial expedient. The economic and social privileges of the nobility survived Richelieu, but he curtailed its political power.

Richelieu was no financier and had no more interest in bettering the condition of the common people than had the rulers of other early modern states. He spent large sums to rebuild the armed forces and even more in wars against the Habsburgs. He left the state's finances and the peasantry which supported those finances in worse condition than he had found them. But his subtle diplomacy and well-timed intervention in the Thirty Years' War (see pp. 544–45) made France instead of Spain the leading European power.

Mazarin, the Fronde, and the Advent of Louis XIV

Richelieu's death in 1642 and that of Louis XIII in 1643 put the great Cardinal's work to a severe test. Louis XIV was a child of 5 when his father died, and his mother, Anne of Austria, became regent. She left the business of government to the man whom Richelieu had trained as his successor, Italian Cardinal Giulio Mazzarini (1602–61), known in France as Mazarin.

Richelieu's successor had some of the subtlety of his master but lacked his relentless will and self-confidence. He sought to continue the war against Spain until the defeat of the Habsburgs and to maintain the prestige of the monarchy that Richelieu had restored. But the nobility despised Mazarin as a foreign upstart and the urban middle classes hated him for the high taxes that war demanded. The result was a complicated and uncoordinated movement of resistance known as the Fronde, the most serious rebellion against the monarchy before the Revolution of 1789.

The word *Fronde* referred to a game of the unruly children of Paris, who threw clods at passing coaches. The rebellion coincided with a period of severe harvest failures and lasted from 1648 to 1652. Like the game, it was annoying, but it ultimately failed to deflect the monarchy from its path. The Fronde's leaders were the judges of the *Parlements* or High Courts, the chief financial officers who owned their offices and were thus hereditary bureaucrats, and the nobility under the guidance of princes of the royal family. Each group hoped merely to increase its own influence, not destroy the French monarchy or upset the established social order.

They also failed to agree on a joint program beyond the purely negative policy of exiling Mazarin. The *parlements*, which began the struggle, stood for the privileges of the corporations of bureaucrats who controlled the courts and the ramshackle tax machinery. They wanted the king to rule with their advice rather than through councilors whom he could make or break at his pleasure. They insisted especially that he impose no tax without their consent. The nobles, who joined the rebellion later, had no intention of letting the *parlements* become dominant in government. They instead sought to abolish the *intendants* and regain their old powers as provincial governors.

The result might have been different had any group dared to mobilize fully the deep-seated resentment of the lower classes—a resentment expressed throughout the century in numerous urban riots and peasant rebellions against taxation and the intrusion of government. A few theorists, especially Huguenots, had argued that subjects possessed a "right of resistance" to unjust authority. But unlike the contemporary English rebellion, which took up radical doctrines and defeated the king, the groups that led the Fronde were unwilling to unleash forces from below that might prove uncontrollable. That innate conservatism, combined with the disunity of the rebels, eventually led to the Fronde's collapse.

Mazarin fled the country in 1651 and again in 1652–53, but returned to the

Cardinal Mazarin.

Fighting in Paris during the Fronde, 1648.

saddle without difficulty, thanks to the support of Anne of Austria. By 1659, Mazarin had achieved victory over Spain. France gained two counties in the Pyrenees and Maria Theresa, daughter of Philip IV of Spain, as a bride for the young Louis XIV. That outcome symbolized the humiliation of Spain and the triumph of France as the leading power in Europe. The young king profited both from widespread revulsion against the disorders of the Fronde and from the prestige that foreign victory brought. The morning after Mazarin died in March 1661, Louis XIV announced to his ministers that he would henceforth be his own first minister. Richelieu had triumphed at last. The French monarchy had outlasted Huguenots and Fronde at home and Habsburgs abroad. Louis XIV henceforth ruled as an absolute monarch, endowed with a fuller sover-

eignty than any yet seen in western Europe.

ENGLAND: IN SEARCH OF CIVIL AND RELIGIOUS LIBERTY, 1603–60

While Richelieu and Mazarin laid the foundations of absolute monarchy by divine right in France, England slowly developed a constitutional, parliamentary system. The English groped toward a conception of sovereignty rooted in law rather than in personal authority and lodged in the hands of an assembly that represented the community—or at least its more wealthy and influential members. England was not alone in its resistance to absolute monarchy, but the result elsewhere tended to be anarchy and confusion as in Poland or the victory of the crown as in France.

The Tudors: Crown and Parliament

England, on the periphery of European civilization, had always been peculiar. The strong monarchy of the Tudors (1485–1603) was part of a general European trend, but the survival and strengthening of Parliament under such a monarchy had no parallel elsewhere. While rulers on the Continent felt that representative assemblies diminished the crown's power and therefore sought to abolish them, the Tudors grudingly used Parliament to legitimate legislation and the raising of taxes. In the delicate area of religion, the Tudors found Parliament indispensable. Henry VIII had aspired to rule as an autocrat but had needed Parliament to break with Rome. Mary had asked Parliament to restore England to the Roman Church by statute. Elizabeth I had by statute once more broken with the Pope.

Elizabeth quarreled with her Parliaments, but the threat from Spain and the political good sense of both the queen and the parliamentary leaders had prevented a break. Both parties tacitly recognized that only Parliament could make a law or impose a tax. Parliament in turn recognized that making policy, especially foreign policy, lay within the sphere of "royal prerogative." Elizabeth's Parliaments tried more than once to reform the Anglican Church in a Puritan direction or nudge the queen on foreign policy—presumptuous acts for which Elizabeth scolded them sharply. But she was too popular for Parliament to challenge her directly and too astute to demand a clear definition of her prerogative.

Under the Tudors, Parliament acquired a corporate feeling and a sense of being an integral part of government. The absence of provincial estates or privileges like those in France further increased its power. By the sixteenth century the lower house, called the House of Commons (see p. 400), represented both the landed gentry of the countryside and the richer mercantile elements of the towns. The gentry had been increasing in numbers, wealth, and political influence since Henry VIII had dissolved the monasteries. They governed England at the local level as justices of the peace, for the English monarchy failed to develop paid bureaucrats like the French *intendants*. The gentry dominated the House of Commons by sitting as representatives not only of the counties but of many urban boroughs as well.

England was peculiar socially as well as politically. Custom and wealth largely determined social status, for the rigid boundaries between social "orders" defined by law on the continent were largely absent. Unlike France, England's titled nobility defined by law was minuscule in numbers—a mere 121 English peers in 1641. Below that line came the gentry—baronets, knights, esquires, and simple "gentle-

A formal meeting of Parliament in 1625. The Lords are seated; the Commons stand outside the bar.

men." Custom rather than law defined gentry status; in law the gentry were commoners. Their numbers included the younger sons of the nobility, who received neither land nor title thanks to the system of primogeniture that preserved noble estates by passing them in their entirety to the eldest son. Noble younger sons thus linked nobility and gentry; many pursued middle-class careers in the law or even commerce. Simultaneously, English merchants continually moved upward into the gentry by buying land. English society was hierarchical, but less so than the societies of the continental monarchies. That relative openness and the cohesion of England's governing elite—the nobility and gentry—was one source of the fateful clash between Crown and Parliament.

James I: Crown against Parliament

The Tudors had long ago ended the threat of violence by the high nobility. Peace with Spain in 1604 and Europe's growing absorption in the Thirty Years' War after 1618 removed the danger of foreign invasion. Under Elizabeth I, foreign and domestic perils had rallied the Commons to the monarchy, but the absence of threats thereafter lessened the authority of the Stuart family, which succeeded the childless queen in 1603.

James I (King of Scotland and of England, r. 1603–25) was the son of Mary, Queen of Scots. Well-meaning but pedantic, he failed to understand the social structure or the political realities of the kingdom he had inherited from Elizabeth. The regents who ran Scotland after his mother's exile had raised him as a Protestant, but he had not relished that grimly Presbyterian upbringing. His aims were entirely reasonable; he sought peace with Spain, toleration of England's Catholic minority, the union of England and Scotland, and a strong but benevolent monarchy.

But James, afflicted with a tendency to drool, preferred hunting, banqueting, and dalliance with male favorites

to the sustained effort needed to govern. He failed to inspire confidence. And unlike Elizabeth, who often concealed her imperious will in ambiguous language, James liked things dangerously clear. In a famous speech to the House of Commons in 1610, he proclaimed that "The state of monarchy is the supremist thing on earth; for kings are not only God's lieutenants upon earth, and sit upon God's throne, but even by God himself they are called gods." That impolitic belief, his disorderly style of life, and the conspicuous financial corruption and bumbling foreign policy of the chief royal favorite, the Duke of Buckingham, offended many of the groups represented in Parliament.

The indolent James I.

The House of Commons began to attack the royal prerogative with arguments based on innovative readings of England's common law. The king in return denounced the parliamentary opposition. The "country"—the nobility and gentry who ruled England at the local level and represented it in Parliament—attacked the "court party" of the increasingly friendless king. "Country" spokesmen denounced the court as crypto-Catholic, influenced culturally by Spain and France, and financially and morally corrupt. The delicate Tudor balance collapsed.

Crown and Parliament clashed over three related issues: religion, money, and foreign policy. The Puritans and their sympathizers in the House of Commons wished to "purify" the Anglican Church of everything that savored of Catholicism, from "Popish" ritual to the authority of bishops. James for his part knew from his youth in Scotland the Presbyterian system of church government that the Puritans sought. He was convinced that it would remove the church from royal control and threaten the monarchy itself. "No bishop, no king," he shouted in a moment of frustration.

Parliament increasingly decried the extravagance of the court and soon denied James the money needed to meet Elizabeth I's war debts and the

1485		1603	1642	1660		1714
House of Tudor		House of Stuart	Civil War and Republican Experiments	House of Stuart		

rising cost of government in an age of inflation. James then raised money without parliamentary approval by such steps as increasing customs duties. Parliament contested his right to do so, but the courts ruled in the king's favor—appropriately, since his foreign policy prerogatives extended to foreign trade. The seeming subservience of the courts to the royal will further exercised Parliament.

James I's foreign policy likewise exasperated his critics. He was too friendly with Catholic Spain for Puritan tastes, he did little to defend Protestants abroad against the militant Counter-Reformation, and he tried in vain to marry his son Charles to the Spanish Infanta. When James chided the House of Commons in 1621 for even discussing his foreign policy, the House bristled. It passed a unanimous Protestation defending its right to discuss "the arduous and urgent affairs concerning the King, State, and defence of the realm, and of the Church of England." That was revolutionary talk. James tore the resolution from the Commons' *Journal* with his own hand, but he could not undo what the Commons had done. An aggressive and influential element among James I's subjects increasingly demanded rights and powers that he was utterly unwilling to grant.

Charles I: The English Revolution

This crisis rapidly worsened after Charles I (r. 1625–49), second of the Stuarts, came to the throne. Charles tried to placate Parliament by attacking Catholic states. But Buckingham, the foppish favorite inherited from his father, failed to capture Cadiz in Spain or to save the French Huguenots besieged at La Rochelle. Parliament had urged war but had failed to grant sufficient

The autocratic Charles I.

taxes. Charles therefore levied a forced loan and imprisoned those who objected. In 1628 Parliament drew up a formal protest, the "Petition of Right," and compelled Charles to approve it. The Petition established that the king should henceforth levy neither taxes nor loans "without common consent by Act of Parliament" and that the government should imprison no one without showing cause. The king's subjects had begun to claim ever-broader rights against the state. Unlike the subjects of the continental monarchies of the seventeenth century, they ultimately proved able to sustain their claims by force.

In 1629 Charles again roused the House of Commons to fury by asserting his full control of Church and state. The Commons in reply declared that whoever introduced practices savoring of Catholicism into the Anglican Church was "a capital enemy to this kingdom and commonwealth," and that anyone who advised or submitted to taxation without parliamentary consent was "a betrayer of the liberties of England." The Commons thus raised the issue of the power to make law. Where did it lie—in the king or in Parliament? The old answer, that it lay in the "king-in-Parliament," was no longer convincing. James I and Charles I between them had brought into the open the latent conflict between royal prerogative and the traditional "liberties of England" that ultimately descended from the *Magna Carta* of the barons (see pp. 338–39).

Charles, more stubborn than his father, then defied the opposition and ruled without Parliament from 1629 to 1640. In an attempt to duplicate Richelieu's absolutism, he chose advisers whose slogan was "thorough," such as Thomas Wentworth, Earl of Strafford, for political matters, and William Laud, Archbishop of Canterbury, for ecclesiastical affairs. Charles and his advisers devised new methods of taxation that did not require Parliament's approval and provided money enough to run the government if it stayed out of war. Laud challenged the Calvinist doctrine of predestination and sought to reestablish the authority of the bishops and reintroduce ritual into the Anglican service; the Puritans denounced him as a disguised Catholic. Influential gentry and even peers opposed Laud, and many deserted the Anglican Church. Up to 20,000 religious dissenters emigrated to the Netherlands or to bleak and distant Massachusetts. And Charles was unable to raise enough money to create the twin pillars of French-style absolutism—a royal administrative machine and a royal standing army.

Charles I nevertheless prevailed until 1637–38. Then Laud tried to force the Anglican Book of Common Prayer on fiercely Presbyterian Scotland while Charles, with amazingly poor timing, alienated the Scottish nobility by seeking to reclaim from them the Church lands they had acquired under Henry VIII. A fierce and well-led Scottish army was soon encamped in northern England. Charles and Strafford, unable to raise an army willing to fight the Scots, had to summon Parliament to vote money to buy them off. The "Long Parliament" met in November 1640 and lasted until 1653. It became a workshop of revolution. It sent Strafford and eventually Laud to the execution block. It dictated that the king must summon Parliament at least every three years. It outlawed all nonparliamentary taxation. It abolished the special royal law courts, the Court of Star Chamber and the Court of High Commission, the chief instruments of Charles I's "Eleven Years' Tyranny." In less than a year (1640–41) Parliament destroyed absolute monarchy in England.

Charles I secretly vowed revenge, but acquiesced. He had no choice, for his government had alienated virtually all of the traditionally loyal groups whose cooperation he needed to rule England. Then the Catholics of Ireland decisively altered the situation. They imitated the Scottish revolt, and slaughtered Protestant settlers that Elizabeth I and James I had planted in Ireland. Suppressing the Irish required raising an army once more—and Parliament distrusted the vengeful king too much to allow him to control that army. Simultaneously, the radical Puritans in Parliament abolished bishops in the Anglican Church. The inescapable issue of whether king or Parliament was to control army and Church thereupon split England's ruling nobility and gentry. The growing political and religious radicalism of the House of Commons gave Charles what he had until then lacked—a royalist party that

The English Revolution   1642–49

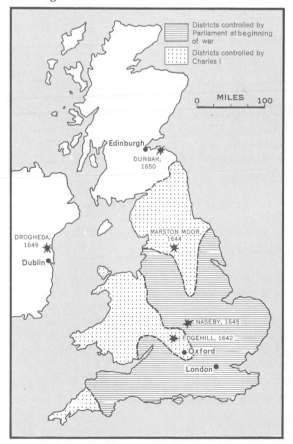

would fight to reassert his prerogatives. Thus encouraged, Charles attempted to arrest his parliamentary
opponents in January 1642. By summer, England was at war.

That civil war, a confused struggle
between factions of nobility and gentry, became the English Revolution.
Both Parliamentarians and Royalists
claimed to support traditional English
political and religious freedoms. London, most towns, the middle classes,
and the economically advanced south-

east of England generally supported
Parliament, although large segments of
the population sought to remain neutral. Many rural areas and the backward northwest supported Charles.
But the divisions between the parties
did not correspond closely to England's
economic, social, or regional cleavages.
Nobility, gentry, and artisans from all
over England fought on both sides. The
fierce religious and ideological issues at
stake split many families, both noble
and gentry.

Unlike the Fronde, in which narrow
interest groups failed to proclaim programs with broad appeal, the English
Revolution offered dramatic alternatives to the established order—parliamentary monarchy instead of royal absolutism and a Presbyterian Church
with elected "presbyters," or elders,
instead of an Anglican Church under
crown-appointed bishops. Unlike the
Fronde, the English revolutionary Civil
War produced radical movements that
sought to abolish the monarchy, the
established Church, and the landlords.
"Levellers," "Diggers," and millenar-
ian sects such as the "Fifth Monarchy
Men" sought to inaugurate a new age
of radical egalitarianism or rule by
"saints."

Parliament based itself on London,
Europe's largest city, and proved more
successful than the king at raising
money and armies. Oliver Cromwell, a
brilliant and ruthless cavalry officer,
pressed successfully for the creation of
a "New Model Army" drawn largely
from his fellow Independents, strict
Bible-reading Puritans who believed in
democratically organized independent
congregations with little or no church
structure.

Cromwell and Parliament's numerically superior and ideologically motivated army ("Truly, I think he that
prays best will fight best") defeated the
king's forces decisively in June–July
1645. The king surrendered a year
later. Then the army fell out with the
Presbyterians, who had dominated
Parliament since the Anglicans had
withdrawn in 1642 to join Charles I.

Democratic Radicalism in the English Revolution   1647

With victory assured, Cromwell's army turned to politics. In 1647
a Council of the Army debated constitutional issues at Putney,
outside London. Radicals and representatives of the common soldiers, influenced by the Levellers, pressed for political rights for
all men. Gentry figures such as General Ireton, Cromwell's forceful son-in-law, countered with the claim that only ownership of
land conferred the right to representation.

MAJOR RAINBOROUGH: I think that the poorest he that is in England
hath a life to live, as the greatest he, and therefore truly, sir, I
think it's clear, that every man that is to live under a government
ought first by his own consent to put himself under that government, and I do think that the poorest man in England is not at all
bound in a strict sense to that government that he hath not had a
voice to put himself under.

GENERAL IRETON: Government is to preserve property. . . . The
objection does not lie in the making of the representation more
equal but in the introducing of men . . . in this government who
have no property in this kingdom. . . .

SEXBY [a representative of the troops]: I see that though liberty
were our end, there is a degeneration from it. We have ventured
our lives to recover our birthrights and privileges as Englishmen, and by the arguments urged there is none. There are many
thousands of us soldiers that have ventured our lives; we have
had little property . . . yet we have had a birthright. But it seems
now, except a man hath a fixed estate in this kingdom, he hath
no right in this kingdom. I wonder we were so much deceived.

From *Puritanism and Liberty*, ed. by A. S. P. Woodhouse (Chicago: University of Chicago Press, 1951), pp. 53, 62, 69.

Groups in Parliament and army with views ranging from relative social and religious moderation to extreme radicalism quarreled over the constitutional and religious settlement. The king sought to exploit the divisions of his opponents by duplicitous negotiations. In November 1647 he escaped to launch a brief second round of civil war.

The Independents in the army were now determined to root out all opposition. They "purged" Parliament of their Presbyterian rivals, defeated the king, and called the untrustworthy "Charles Stuart, that man of blood, to an account for the blood that he had shed." Cromwell, after initial hesitation, had Charles I executed in 1649, abolished the monarchy and House of Lords, and set up a republic or "Commonwealth" with the "rump" of the Long Parliament as its government and himself as its unchallenged leader. Parliament had tried a king ordained by divine right for treason against his own subjects, had cut off his head, and had abolished the very institution of kingship. England had set an example that was long remembered.

Cromwell: The Lord Protector

Unlike later continental figures who seized command of a state through revolution, England's new dictator was a deeply religious man who did not initially seek supreme power. Yet power, and inevitable opposition to his will, brought out Cromwell's ruthlessness. He suppressed with fire and massacre the Irish rebellion that in 1641–42 had helped trigger the Civil War. He drubbed the Scots in two great battles when they intervened in favor of the son of Charles I. He presided over a commercial war with the Dutch from 1652 to 1654. He wrathfully dissolved the rump of the Long Parliament in 1653, saying "You are no Parliament, I say you are no Parliament; I will put an end to your sitting." But he failed in his efforts to guarantee religious toleration to all Protestants except determined

Anglicans and to find a satisfactory constitutional basis for government.

Cromwell attempted to rule with the assent of Parliament and through a written constitution, the "Instrument of Government"—the first such document in the history of a major state. He took the title of Lord Protector instead of king, but quarreled with Parliament as bitterly as had the Stuarts. In 1655 he installed an open military dictatorship to keep Parliament from disbanding his army and persecuting his coreligionists. Most Englishmen still rejected religious toleration, especially toleration of the religious and political radicals who made up a large part of Cromwell's army. And it became increasingly evident that England—like other states in the following centuries—could not break utterly with history and set up a new regime simply by drafting a constitution. An unwritten "constitution" already existed, deeply ingrained in English political traditions.

Cromwell's death in 1658 made General George Monck, his most important military subordinate, the most powerful figure in England. Monck recognized that Parliament was the only alternative to military dictatorship and that restoring Parliament also required recreating the monarchy. In 1660, a "Convention Parliament" under his protection invited the son of Charles I to return from France and take up the crown.

The Legacy of Revolution

The Civil War had made clear that England would not tolerate an absolute monarchy. Strafford and Laud had tried to do for Charles I what Richelieu and Mazarin had done for Louis XIV. But while the Frenchmen had died in their beds, the Englishmen had lost their heads on the block. The new Parliament confirmed many of the severe limitations upon royal power that the Long Parliament had instituted before the outbreak of the Civil War. The turmoil of the first half of the century left most Englishmen with half-expressed

A Dutch view of Cromwell (1653).

Oliver Cromwell, by Samuel Cooper (1609–72).

The restoration of King Charles II: the coronation in Westminster Abbey (from a contemporary print).

convictions that had lasting effects—a fear of too great a concentration of power, a deepened respect for government by law rather than by royal command, a reverence for Parliament as the defender of individual rights against royal despotism, and a fervent distaste for standing armies.

The early seventeenth century was a brilliant age in the history of English literature and thought. It included Shakespeare's mature work and the early years of the great poet John Milton. In 1611 the Authorized, or King James, Version of the Bible first emerged from the presses. Its sonorous cadences have influenced the writing of English to the present day. States-

men and pamphleteers arguing for royalist, parliamentary, or radical principles likewise made this a formative period of modern political thought.

Thomas Hobbes's *Leviathan* (1651) was the foremost product of the political insights and fears of the years of civil war. Under the influence of Thucydides's great history of the Peloponnesian War (see p. 50), of which Hobbes wrote the first English translation, Hobbes saw in humanity "a perpetual and restless desire of power after power." Without some authority to enforce law, no society or order could exist, but only "a war of every man against every man." Life without government was "solitary, poor, nasty, brutish, and short." Hobbes, following thinkers that included Huguenots seeking to justify revolt against France's Catholic monarchy, postulated that humans had set up a sovereign power by agreement or contract.

But Hobbes drew from this "contract theory" of government conclusions opposite to those of the Huguenots, and of Cromwell and his army, who had declared "the king is king by contract" and had severed Charles I's head for violating that contract. For Hobbes, all had agreed to obey the sovereign because he alone could maintain order. To ensure the maintenance of order, the sovereign's powers had to be absolute. Hobbes's contract entailed no right of resistance to unjust authority. He claimed that it bound the subjects, not the ruler: "There can happen no breach of the Covenant on the part of the Sovereign; and consequently none of his Subjects . . . can be freed from his subjection."

Hobbes thus took contract theory and subtly transformed it into a justification of unfettered and arbitrary power. Any sovereign, whether king or parliament, could claim Hobbes's sovereign as its model and rule without restraint. English political theorists during the remainder of the seventeenth century devoted much effort to finding some way to refute Hobbes—to subject political power to the restraint of law and to the consent of the governed.

GERMANY: DISINTEGRATION AND DISASTER, 1618–48

While France built the mightiest monarchy in Europe and England underwent a crisis from which it emerged with new strength, the German-speaking peoples suffered the Thirty Years' War. It was in reality four successive wars that began in 1618 in Bohemia, spread to the rest of the Holy Roman Empire, and before its end in 1648 involved most major continental powers.

It was a savage and demoralizing conflict that left "Germany" poorer and weaker than the states to its west for the next 150 years.

The Causes of the Thirty Years' War

The war sprang from a complicated mixture of religious and political quarrels. Lutherans and Catholics had remained at peace since the Peace of Augsburg (1555). But in spite of the provisions of the peace, most Catholic bishoprics in north Germany had fallen into Lutheran or secular hands, caus-

The title page of Thomas Hobbes's *Leviathan*, one of the fundamental works of Western political theory. Hobbes described the sovereign power of the state as "that great Leviathan, or rather (to speak more reverently) that mortal God, to which we owe under the Immortal God, our peace and defence."

ing discontent in the Catholic camp. The Jesuits and the German Catholic princes, particularly Maximilian, Duke of Bavaria, began to create an ultra-Catholic movement. The spread of Calvinism introduced a new source of friction, for the peace of Augsburg had not accorded that sect a recognized status.

In 1608 Maximilian of Bavaria roughly disciplined the Protestant town of Donauwörth. Frederick V, the Calvinist ruler of the Palatinate, a small state on the middle Rhine, thereupon formed a Protestant Union of the German princes and cities. In reply, Maximilian organized a Catholic League. By 1609 two religious-military alliances thus faced one other within the Holy Roman Empire. Each was determined to prevent its rival from making further gains.

Revolt in Bohemia

These signs of anarchy and religious division within the Holy Roman Empire prompted the Habsburgs, who held the imperial title, to attempt to rebuild their authority. They began by seeking to consolidate their hold over their long-time family domains of Austria, Bohemia, and Hungary. The aging emperor Matthias secured the election of his heir-apparent, Ferdinand of Styria, as king of Bohemia in 1617.

Bohemia was a flourishing territory in which two chief nationalities (Germans and Czechs) and a variety of religions (Catholicism, Lutheranism, Calvinism, and remnants of the Hussite movement of the fifteenth century) lived in relative peace under Habsburg promises of toleration. But Ferdinand was a zealous Counter-Reformation Catholic. He had ruthlessly re-Catholicized Styria, and the Protestant majority in the Bohemian Estates rightly feared that he planned the same for Bohemia. In May 1618 the Bohemians therefore threw their imperial governors from the windows of Prague castle (an incident thereafter known as the "defenestration of Prague"). The Estates raised an army, deposed Ferdi-

nand, and offered the crown of Bohemia to Frederick V of the Palatinate. Frederick's unwise acceptance extended the war from Bohemia to the Empire as a whole. Frederick's Protestant Union took the side of the Bohemian Estates, while Maximilian of Bavaria swung the Catholic League behind Ferdinand, who had been elected Emperor.

The Bohemian phase of the war ended swiftly. In November 1620, at the battle of the White Mountain near Prague, the Imperial forces crushed the Bohemian rebels. Frederick V fled, and Emperor Ferdinand proceeded to make Bohemia over at the cost of wrecking its economy and society. War and plague cut the population almost in half. The Czech nobility lost everything. Half the land in Bohemia changed hands through confiscation, and Ferdinand created a new nobility of adventurers from as far away as Ireland. The Jesuits, with Ferdinand's full backing, set out to reconvert the country to Catholicism by force. Within ten years they had stamped Protestantism out or driven it underground. The Czechs became a people without a ruling class and without a claim to an independent historical existence for two centuries. The Habsburgs and their Catholic allies had decisively won the first round of the great war.

Danish Intervention and Catholic Triumph

The fall of Bohemia terrified the German Protestants and elated the Catholics. The Spanish Habsburgs had also intervened against the Protestant states of north Germany, and the armies of the Catholic League were everywhere triumphant. But common danger failed to unite the Protestants. The Lutherans feared a Calvinist victory in Bohemia more than an Imperial triumph. The Lutheran Kingdom of Saxony had actually helped Ferdinand put the Czechs down. And although Frederick V was the son-in-law of James I, Protestant England gave no help; James I and his successor Charles I were locked in their struggle with Parliament.

The Protestant King of Denmark joined his fellow Protestants in 1625, but his principal motive was greed for territory in north Germany. Within a year, the Catholics had beaten him back. Albrecht von Wallenstein, a brilliant military entrepreneur who had offered the emperor his services, crushed the Danes with a large and expert mercenary army that at its height mobilized 125,000 men. Wallenstein's long-term aim was probably to secure central Europe for himself. His immediate goal was to build an Imperial Habsburg military machine that could eliminate the Protestants without the help of other forces in the Empire, or the Catholic League. By 1628 Wallenstein and the League were as much at odds on the Catholic side as Calvinists and Lutherans were on the Protestant. Religion slowly receded in significance as the war became a struggle between armies and states alone, a struggle for mastery in Europe.

The Habsburg and Catholic cause reached its high-water mark in 1629. Denmark withdrew, leaving Wallenstein's army supreme. The Catholic League and Jesuit advisers persuaded Ferdinand to issue an Edict of Restitution that restored to Catholic hands all ecclesiastical lands lost to Protestantism since 1552. Carrying out the edict meant yet more bloodshed to restore the dispossessed Catholic bishops of Protestant north Germany. That would also destroy utterly both the rough religious balance between Catholicism and Protestantism in Germany and the power balance between the north German states on the one hand and Austria and Bavaria on the other. That threat finally roused Lutherans inside and outside Germany to action.

The "Lion of the North": Gustavus Adolphus

In 1630 Sweden, a country until now on the periphery of the European state system, intervened to check the

The siege of Magdeburg in 1631 by Habsburg and Catholic forces, which ended with one of the bloodiest massacres of the war.

Habsburgs. Its masterful king, Gustav II Adolf or Gustavus Adolphus, was the ablest ruler of his generation. Sweden had roughly 1.25 million people, perhaps a fifteenth of the population of France. But Gustavus had cultivated rich copper and timber exports, a sophisticated iron and armament industry, and the most advanced army of the day. That army was not large, but it was the first in Europe recruited by universal conscription and it possessed a high morale born of fierce patriotism. It also had the first uniforms, the first artillery light enough for battlefield maneuver, improved muskets, regular pay, and discipline, a rarity indeed in the Thirty Years' War. Its victories over Russia, Denmark, and Poland between 1611 and 1629 made the Baltic almost a Swedish lake.

The Sack of Magdeburg   1631

For a generation after the destruction of this German city, the phrase "Magdeburg quarter" meant "no quarter."

Then was there naught but beating and burning, plundering, torture, and murder. Most especially was every one of the enemy bent on securing much booty. When a marauding party entered a house, if its master had anything to give he might thereby purchase respite and protection for himself and his family till the next man, who also wanted something, should come along. It was only when everything had been brought forth and there was nothing left to give that the real trouble commenced. Then, what with blows and threats of shooting, stabbing, and hanging, the poor people were so terrified that if they had had anything left they would have brought it forth if it had been buried in the earth or hidden away in a thousand castles. In this frenzied rage, the great and splendid city that had stood like a fair princess in the land was now, in its hour of direst need and unutterable distress and woe, given over to the flames, and thousands of innocent men, women, and children, in the midst of a horrible din of heartrending shrieks and cries, were tortured and put to death in so cruel and shameful a manner that no words would suffice to describe, nor no tears to bewail it.

From Otto von Guericke, in *Readings in European History*, ed. by James Harvey Robinson (Boston: Ginn, 1906), Vol. II, pp. 211–12.

Gustavus stepped into the great war in Germany to defend Sweden's Baltic interests, which Wallenstein's operations in north Germany appeared to threaten. But as the war continued, Gustavus began to toy with a broader aim—the creation of a federation of German Protestant states under Swedish leadership. He arrived too late to save the great city of Magdeburg from sack, massacre, and destruction by the Imperial forces in May 1631, an event that for generations symbolized the all-devouring brutality of this war. But in the fall of 1631 Gustavus shattered the Imperial armies at Breitenfeld in Saxony, and marched triumphantly to the Rhine.

That emergency compelled the Emperor to recall Wallenstein, whom he had dismissed at the insistence of the Catholic League. Gustavus defeated Wallenstein decisively at Lützen in 1632, but paid for victory with his own life. Without Gustavus's leadership the outnumbered Swedes could not maintain their dominance in Germany. Swedish weakness in turn freed the Emperor from dependence on his over-mighty subject, Wallenstein, who perished by assassination at Ferdinand's orders. In the fall of 1634 the Imperial armies checked the Swedes at the battle of Nördlingen. Gustavus Adolphus had saved German Protestantism but had failed to decide the war.

Richelieu Intervenes

The most powerful state of all now acted, and ushered in the fourth and final phase of the war. Since his appointment as chief minister in 1624, Richelieu had followed the war closely through his ever-present ambassadors and agents. His aim was to crush both Austrian and Spanish Habsburgs. Under his leadership, Catholic France accepted as allies all opponents of the Habsburgs regardless of religion. His first allies were the Protestant Dutch, who in 1621 had again gone to war with their ancestral enemy, Spain.

Then Richelieu subsidized Sweden, until the Imperial defeat of the Swedes in 1634 forced him to choose between direct French intervention and Habsburg domination of Europe. In May 1635 he chose intervention; France declared war on Spain and allied itself with Sweden in Germany.

The Thirty Years' War had by then lasted for 17 years. It continued drearily for a further 13 years, although the man who had done most to launch it, Emperor Ferdinand, had died in 1637. French, Swedish, and Dutch armies slogged across central Europe pursuing or pursued by the Habsburg forces. The rebellions of Portugal and of the rich province of Catalonia in 1640 weakened Spain. In 1643, on the battle-field of Rocroi in the Netherlands, the French finally crushed the Spanish *tercios* and their legend of invincibility. Habsburg allies, drawing conclusions from that defeat, deserted the Empire. Soon the Swedes besieged Prague and menaced Vienna. The Habsburg attempt to roll back the Reformation in Germany and establish mastery over central Europe had failed utterly.

Peace of Exhaustion: Westphalia, 1648

Habsburg defeat opened the way to the peace negotiated between 1644 and 1648 at the Congress of Westphalia. The gathering was Europe's first great peace conference and the first inter-state meeting of importance since the Council of Constance of 1414–18. But unlike Constance, the atmosphere and the business of the Congress that met at Münster in western Germany were now entirely secular. The Congress was a meeting of sovereign states that recognized no earthly superior and only the most shadowy common interests. "Christendom" had dissolved, but its purely secular replacement, the word *civilization*, did not come into general use until the following century.

The Congress confirmed the importance of the sovereign state and set a framework for central European poli-

tics that endured until 1801–06. In recognizing the German principalities' right to make alliances and to declare war, the Congress accepted the disintegration of the Empire into over 300 separate sovereignties. Switzerland and the Dutch Netherlands finally achieved recognized status as independent sovereign states. While France acquired ambiguous rights to Alsace, Sweden gained strips of German territory along the Baltic and the North seas. The two German states of Brandenburg and Bavaria increased their territory and prestige.

As for religion, the Congress reaffirmed the principle of *cuius regio, eius religio* originally established in the Peace of Augsburg of 1555, and at last added Calvinism to Catholicism and Lutheranism as one of the recognized faiths. To prevent further dispute the Congress froze the ownership of church lands as of 1624. North Germany remained Protestant and south Germany Catholic. Only France and Spain failed to reach agreement. Their war continued until Spain conceded to Mazarin, in the Peace of the Pyrenees of 1659, the victory the great Richelieu had sought.

The Consequences of the War

The Thirty Years' War was one of the most destructive wars in recorded history. In Europe no later conflict matched it in ruthless devastation until the new "thirty years' war" of 1914–45. Armies living off the land pillaged, raped, and murdered their way across central Europe. The soldiery wiped towns from the map and reduced cities to a small fraction of their original populations. Cultivated land reverted to waste. Destruction of livestock even more than of crops crippled a primitive and mostly agrarian economy, for plough and dairy animals were difficult to replace. Starvation and the massive plague epidemics that marched with the lice-ridden armies killed more than the sword.

Europe in 1648

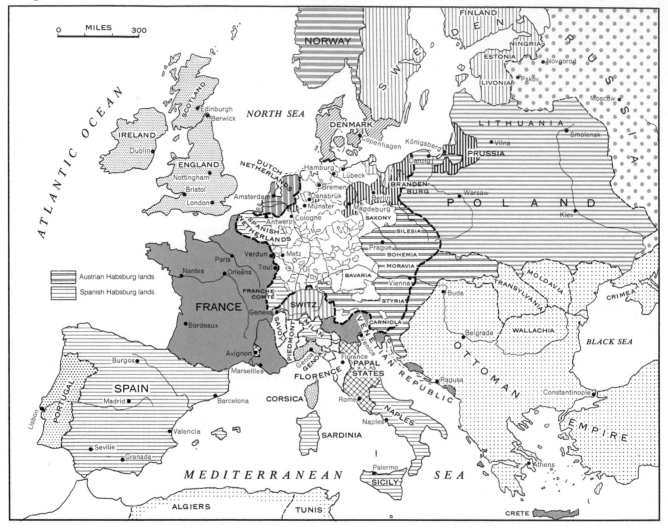

The absence of census figures makes it difficult to establish conclusively the extent and distribution of the losses, but the Holy Roman Empire (including Bohemia) apparently lost 4 million out of roughly 21 million inhabitants. A few areas, such as Mecklenburg, lost up to 80 percent of their populations. The war also had deep psychological, social, political, and economic effects. Generations grew up accepting large-scale violence as normal, and were happy to acknowledge any authority however brutal if it promised peace. The fragmentation of the Holy Roman Empire into small states quirkily di-

vided by customs barriers hampered economic recovery. The war helped delay until the nineteenth century the emergence of a state called "Germany" and helped make its emergence an event from which Europe has yet to recover.

DUTCH UNREST AND SPANISH DECLINE

The political upheavals of the early seventeenth century touched many areas of Europe other than France, England, and central Europe. Even distant Russia underwent an anarchic "Time of Troubles" before settling down uneasily under the rule of the first Romanov Tsar in 1613. In the west, violent convulsion shook the Netherlands and Spain.

By 1609 the northern areas of the Netherlands had achieved effective independence from Spain and enormous economic success. Yet intertwined political and religious conflicts still tore the United Provinces. One aggressively Calvinist party pressed for renewed war against Spain in the southern Netherlands. Its leader was Maurice of Nassau, son of William the Silent, chief of the House of Orange and commander of the highly competent Dutch army. A second party, that of the mercantile class, enjoyed the support of the religiously tolerant Arminians (those unwilling to accept Calvin's stern doctrine of predestination). It hoped to reestablish peaceful trade with Spain.

In 1619 Maurice of Nassau overthrew this "peace party" and had its leader executed after a political trial. The war with Spain resumed in 1621 and continued inconclusively until the Peace of Westphalia. Tensions between the House of Orange and the mercantile "regent class" continued throughout the century. For two decades after 1650 the "regents" dominated Dutch affairs. But when invasion—from France rather than Spain—came again in 1672 the old conflicts reopened. A mob in The Hague tore the leading regent, Johan de Witt, limb from limb and publicly sold his remains. The Dutch summoned the head of the House of Orange, the young Prince William, to lead them victoriously against overwhelming odds.

In Spain, religious-ethnic persecution marked the beginning of irreversible decline. In 1609 the monarchy and the Inquisition launched a campaign similar to the expulsion of Spain's 150,000 Jews after 1492 (see p. 508). In fanatical pursuit of religious uniformity and "purity of blood" (*limpieza de sangre*), the authorities deported to north Africa in 1609–14 as many as 275,000

"*moriscos*," the insufficiently converted descendants of the Moors who had given the Iberian peninsula much of its civilization. That savage persecution deprived Spain of a creative minority that it sorely needed. Plague and economic collapse made this a period of dramatic population drop, from perhaps 8.5 million in 1600 to 7.5 million in 1650.

War, both foreign and domestic, likewise contributed to Spain's shrinkage as a power. The leading minister from 1621 to 1643, the proud Count-Duke of Olivares, committed Spain to war in Germany in 1620 and against the Netherlands in 1621. War with France capped those wars in 1635 and placed intolerable fiscal burdens on the Spanish monarchy's patchwork of disparate provinces, jealous of their traditional rights and liberties. Olivares struggled gloomily to establish a centralized administration with an effective system of tax collection. But as so often happened in early modern Europe, centralization—the creation of a modern state machine—provoked bitter revolt. In 1640 Portugal, forcibly united with Spain since 1580, rose and made good its independence. The rich towns of the province of Catalonia likewise revolted, attracted French support, and defied the monarchy until 1652. Spain's Italian possessions likewise revolted.

Spain, overcommitted on many fronts, ultimately yielded to France the position of leading power in Europe in 1659. Spain's political and military decline was in part a consequence of the overreaching of Olivares. But its deeper causes were economic and internal. Of all the powers, Spain suffered most from the crises of the European and world economy of the seventeenth century.

EUROPE'S POPULATION AND ECONOMY IN CRISIS

The tyranny of the seasons still ruled the societies of early modern Europe. Despite the gradually gathering force of commerce and industry, the economy was still overwhelmingly agricultural. And the 150 years from the 1590s to the 1740s was a "little ice age." Rivers such as the Thames, normally ice-free, repeatedly froze over in winter; spring and summer turned rainy and cold. Even in the relatively warm fifteenth and sixteenth centuries, England had suffered one poor harvest in four, and one disastrous harvest in six. Between 1594 and 1597 rain and cold wrecked four harvests in succession from Ireland to east central Europe; the result was widespread famine. The harvests from 1647 to 1652–53 were similarly catastrophic, above all in France and Spain. The 1690s were the coldest decade in 700 years; in 1696–97 about a quarter of the population of Finland perished by famine. The "great cold" of 1709–10 produced a general crop failure in France, and paupers froze to death in the streets of Paris.

Human and animal epidemics inevitably accompanied famine, as malnutrition reduced resistance to disease. Spain lost perhaps a half million dead from bubonic plague between 1647 and 1652, and outbreaks were widespread until the early eighteenth century. The population of Europe west of the Urals, after growing from an estimated 60 million in 1400 to 100 million in 1600, probably dropped slightly after 1620. It stood at only 105 million in 1650, before rising to an estimated 120 million by 1700 (see Figure 19-1). France, Europe's most populous nation, gained relatively little, from perhaps 16 million in 1600 to 20 million in 1700; population may actually have dropped from the 1690s to 1710. Only after 1750 did a mellower climate, crop rotation techniques pioneered in the Low Countries, New World crops such as the potato and maize, and dramatic improvements in transport allow a new and sustained increase in Europe's population.

A second powerful force intensified the effects of the seventeenth century climate on Europe's fragile economy and population—the movement of prices. In the sixteenth century two trends had united to produce a "price revolution": the sudden and massive influx of New World silver and gold, and the rapidly increasing sophistication of Europe's merchants and bankers, who had multiplied the effective volume of money by speeding its circu-

FIGURE 19-1   The Population of Europe, 1000–1700 (including Russia west of the Urals)

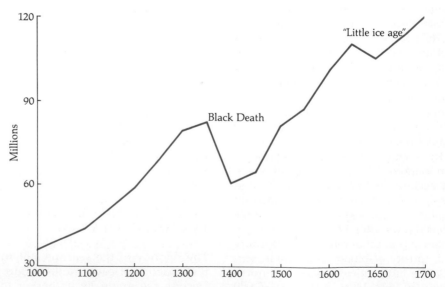

lation and by using credit far more extensively than in previous centuries. In consequence, by 1600 prices had reached levels four to five times above those of 1500. That inflation, although modest by twentieth-century standards, had deeply unsettling effects upon societies that still adhered to the Medieval myth of a "just" price. The penetration of the money economy ever deeper into the countryside brought with it price fluctuations that intensified the distress of the peasantry and ruined aristocrats who failed to adapt to the hard new age of profit and loss.

After about 1620 the influx of New World silver slowed as the mines of Mexico and Peru reached the point of diminishing returns. Loss of revenue crippled the ambitious policies of Olivares. Throughout Europe price inflation gave way to deflation and hectic growth to relative stagnation. The wars and troubles after 1620, from the Thirty Years' War to the English Civil War to the Fronde, further intensified the downward pressure. Only after 1670 did some northern areas of Europe, most notably England and the Dutch United Provinces, begin to enjoy once more a steady prosperity. In Spain, the pressure of taxes to finance Olivares's wars and the dead hand of his bureaucracy crushed what little independence and enterprise the middle classes of Castile had possessed; in the countryside, as in the Spanish New World, sheep replaced peasants. In France, the pressure of the monarchy's taxation, further intensified in the wars of Louis XIV after 1667 (see pp. 564–68), caused repeated revolts in the provinces.

Yet despite the "little ice age," deflation, and war, the seventeenth century was a period of rapid economic change. In industry—the production of goods for market using specialized labor and equipment—new techniques rapidly gained ground. In the 1580s, the Dutch introduced power saws worked by windmills. Water-driven power hammers for forging became common. Coal, at least in England, became the cheapest source of energy. Coal fuelled London's growth from 200,000 inhabitants in 1600 to over 550,000—Europe's largest city—by 1700. Coal permitted the creation in England of the most modern glass industry in Europe, and shops with glass window-panes at which visitors marveled.

All over Europe, commerce and industry began to break out from the medieval framework of town and guild monopolies. A new form of craft organization that bypassed the guilds, the "putting-out system," spread from the Low Countries. Traveling merchants supplied rural home workers with raw materials, then returned later to collect the finished product for sale. "Putting-out" was particularly effective in the greatest industry of early modern Europe, textiles. It was also well suited to an age in which techniques were simple, and hand or animal power drove most industrial equipment. It allowed the rapid expansion, or contraction, of production depending on demand, and minimized the overhead of the entrepreneur. To the peasant family, it provided income that in years of crop failure might mean the difference between life and death. Putting-out slowly eroded guild restrictions, channeled money into the countryside, and dissolved the old peasant barter economy. It was a major stimulant to Europe's economic growth.

In trade and finance, the century was one of continued rapid change. The use of credit intensified, as an ever-widening banking network spread across Europe from Seville facing the New World to the Baltic grain and timber ports. A new institution apparently invented in Italy, the joint-stock company, made possible a far more widespread mobilization of capital than traditional family firms or partnerships. Individuals who were not necessarily traders could buy "shares" in great commercial enterprises such as the Muscovy Company (1553), the English East India Company (1600), and the Dutch East India Company (1602). The company directors then

Page from a promotional pamphlet issued in 1609 by the London Company to attract investors to its enterprise in Virginia.

used the resulting capital for their operations. Soon a vast market developed in the "shares" themselves, the ancestor of the modern stock exchange.

A further source of change was geographic. By the middle of the seventeenth century the westward and northward shift in Europe's economic center of gravity that began in 1492 was complete. The Mediterranean and central Europe became backwaters. Venice, victorious over the Turks at sea, suffered disastrous shrinkage both in its industries and in its trade with the eastern Mediterranean. The westward shift of trade to the New World and around the Cape of Good Hope helped destroy German banking dynasties such as the Fuggers of Augsburg, while the Thirty Years' War completed Germany's economic ruin.

But even economies open to the ocean failed. Spain, thanks to religious persecution, rigid government controls, and the pressure of taxation, soon yielded the control of much of its New World trade to Genoese and Dutch merchants. Antwerp, the great trading and banking center of northern Europe until the mid-sixteenth century, failed to assert its political independence. It lost its economic position as well to its Dutch neighbors to the north. The founding of the Bank of Amsterdam in 1609—the same year as the truce by which Spain recognized Dutch independence—symbolized the supremacy of Amsterdam as the center of Europe's economy, a supremacy that lasted throughout the seventeenth century. But the Dutch Republic, with a tiny territory and a population that reached 2 million in 1650 but then remained essentially static until 1800, was little more than a glorified city-state.

The future belonged to those powerful engines of growth, the consolidated "national markets" within the large territorial states, France and England. France seemed by far the richest, for it possessed the largest territory of any

The world's first stock exchange, at Amsterdam, in the mid-seventeenth century.

state west of Russia and a population greater than any other. But its agriculture suffered badly in the "little ice age," and savagely braked both population and economic growth. France's sheer size, the absence of good roads or navigable waterways, and the innumerable customs barriers both between provinces and between towns and countryside likewise stunted growth. The centralized war-making state crushed the peasants under a taxation that, along with dues to landlords and Church, deprived them of roughly half their income.

Nor did the efforts of France's government to promote economic growth help. The great finance minister of Louis XIV, Jean-Baptiste Colbert (see p. 561) made an almost despairing attempt to promote the development of industry and commerce in the face of the economic depression that lasted through the 1680s. He founded in the 1670s a series of enterprises from textile firms staffed with Dutch experts to cannon foundries, strengthened the guilds as a means of ensuring the quality and uniformity needed to promote exports, and attempted to crush the Dutch with tariffs and with his master's wars. Colbert was the most consistent adherent of a series of loosely linked notions, characteristic of a world of warring states, usually known as "mercantilism"—state intervention to promote industry and maximize exports, protective tariffs to minimize imports, and strenuous attempts to create a trade surplus that would suck in gold and silver from one's competitors. Such methods long outlived the seventeenth century, but they did not help France. Most of Colbert's industries proved ruinously unprofitable, and his reinforcement of the guilds was an unmitigated disaster for French industry. His tariffs damaged France more than the Dutch. France's commercial economy developed, but largely despite Colbert.

England was different. It too employed "mercantilist" practices, such as the Navigation Acts that after 1651 restricted all trade with England and its colonies to English shipping, and channeled the most important colonial products through English ports. England, too, fought commercial wars with the Dutch, in 1652–54, 1665–67, and 1672–74. But internally, England was already a large unified market; its guilds were decayed relics; its textile, coal, and iron industries were gradually expanding. By 1700 its economy, the least "mercantilist" and state-controlled in Europe, owed a third of its national product to commerce and industry, while the proportion in France was a fifth or less. Such an economy could not fail to have an impact on the world beyond Europe.

THE EUROPEAN EMPIRES

Europe's overseas expansion slowed briefly in the seventeenth century. Spain required time to digest the conquered Aztec and Inca empires. In India, China, and Japan the Europeans faced ancient civilizations that still had the power to hold Europe at arm's length. Developing the North American wilderness required settlers in numbers as yet unavailable. And the extension to the outside world of the warlike competition between European states slowed Europe's economic penetration of the non-European world.

Trade and plunder had lured the Europeans overseas. Portugal persisted in that pattern, and its "colonies," with the exception of its early settlements on Madeira or its great land empire in Brazil, remained fortified trading posts that dealt in spices or slaves through native middlemen. The Dutch sought to follow the Portuguese example after 1600, when they seized from Portugal the mastery of the Indian Ocean and China Sea. But in their Spice Islands south of the Philippines the Dutch soon found that maintaining the flow of commodities required more than trading posts. As the Spaniards discovered during their feverish search for gold and silver in the Americas, trade and plunder led to rule and settlement.

The new model colonies of the seventeenth century were thus settlement colonies. The pattern dated from Portugal's settlement in the 1420s of the uninhabited Atlantic island of Madeira, and Spain had followed it in the Americas after the 1520s. The function of the settlement colonies was to complement the trading economy of the mother country by producing essential raw materials. That purpose required the export of European institutions, technology, plants, and animals in order to set up overseas societies on the European model. In Africa, malaria and yellow fever killed the vast majority of Europeans who attempted to penetrate inland, and Europe's military technology did not yet provide effortless superiority over the natives on their own ground. Native middlemen and rulers continued to provide apparently inexhaustible supplies of slaves; the trading post system persisted.

But in the New World above all, settlement was possible. And settlement meant production of the commodity most prized after gold and silver—sugar. Cultivating that addictive substance, first brought to Europe by the Crusaders, required back-breaking labor. As the Portuguese had demonstrated on Madeira, enslaved natives from the Canary Islands or from Africa most conveniently supplied that labor. Tobacco, coffee, and in East Asia tea and spices created similar patterns of cultivation and settlement. The riches these products generated proved an irresistible source of conflict.

The Struggle for Mastery in the East

East of Africa and south of China the Portuguese soon lost the trading empire they had acquired after the voyages of Vasco da Gama. Dutch, English, and French interlopers appeared. Portuguese sea-power failed to keep pace with that of nimbler rivals. Portugal was too economically and demographically weak and too technologically backward to hold empires both in the New World and in the East simulta-

Miniature by an Indian artist of a Western merchant (*ca.* 1600).

neously, and its subordination to Spain from 1580 to 1640 exposed it to Dutch attack. Portugal's rivals founded powerful East India Companies: the English in 1600, the Dutch in 1602, the French in 1664. The Dutch proved the most ruthless, well-organized, and successful. Their seizure of the Cape of Good Hope in 1652 created the largest white community in Africa as a way-station for their shipping. Their massacre of English merchants on Amboina in 1623 and their command of Batavia on Java from 1619 and of the strategic Malacca strait after 1641 persuaded the English to concentrate on India. There England and France set up trading posts on the Portuguese model at Bombay, Madras, and Calcutta for England and at Pondicherry for France. The power of the Mughal empire that dominated south Asia barred the way inland. Only its collapse after 1707 drew the Europeans into the struggles of the native successor kingdoms, and ultimately replaced Mughal hegemony with that of Britain (see pp. 759–60).

The Caribbean

In the Caribbean, the Dutch, English, and French competed for crumbs from Spain's overfilled table. After war between the Dutch and Spain resumed in 1621, the Dutch sought to damage Spain by seizing sugar-rich Brazil from Spain's dependency, Portugal. The Dutch failed, but they did take the Caribbean island of Curaçao as a base for raids on Spanish commerce. England settled Barbados in 1624 and acquired Jamaica in 1655, while the French took Guadeloupe and Martinique. They had come for plunder in the Dutch manner, but they stayed to grow sugar. And sugar plantations required a ready supply of labor—unfree labor. The Caribbean Indians were in the process of extinction, thanks to small-pox, massacres, and slave labor exacted by Spain. The interloping powers therefore brought their own labor with them. On Barbados, white small farmers who cultivated tobacco gave way in

A tropical Amsterdam, complete with canals: the great Dutch port of Batavia, on Java (1682).

the 1640s and 1650s to large economically efficient plantations grouped around great sugar mills. At first white contract labor worked the plantations. These "indentured servants" undertook to work off the price of their passage to the New World by years of servitude. But white labor could not compete with black slaves from Africa. Slaves were virtually unlimited in supply and cost less than whites—slavery was for life, not three, five, or seven years.

African rulers, Arabs, and Portuguese had pioneered the slave trade long before the discovery of the New World. The Portuguese had experimented with slave cultivation of sugar on Madeira. The extension of that savage system to the New World required the transportation across the Atlantic of almost a million Africans in the course of the seventeenth century. Death rates ran as high as 20 percent during transport inside Africa and another 20 percent on the Atlantic crossing. Disease and ill-treatment prevented the slave populations in the New World from reproducing enough to increase their numbers. The expansion of the sugar economy thus required the import of ever-greater numbers of slaves. A triangular trade pattern developed— Europeans took goods such as weapons, rum, or tobacco to Africa, bartered them for slaves that the kings of west Africa had seized from neighboring African tribes and kingdoms, and exchanged those slaves in the West Indies for tropical commodities that included molasses from which to make more rum. As the Portuguese slowly lost control of the west coast of Africa, the Dutch, English, and French stepped in to supply slaves both to their own sugar islands and—through smuggling—to the plantations of Spain. Slavery as yet attracted little attention as an institution of peculiar cruelty. The Europeans of the seventeenth century, like the Africans and the inhabitants of the Islamic world, looked upon it as part of the natural order of things.

North America: The Dutch, the French, and the English

North of the sugar islands lay an immense waste of swamp and woodland: North America. Its only known resources were the codfish off New-

The Indian village of Pomeiock, in what is now North Carolina, by John White, who participated in Raleigh's attempt to establish a colony at Roanoke, Virginia, in 1685.

foundland and the furs and timber of its great forests. But three powers nevertheless attempted settlements there in the hope of turning Spain's flank and breaking its near monopoly of the New World. The failure of Sir Walter Raleigh to found a colony in Virginia during the 1580s revealed some of the difficulties. Cold winters and poor soil made the creation of a tropical plantation economy difficult, while hostile natives were still relatively strong. Planting a permanent colony in North America required the transport of a large labor force and its support over many years until the settlement achieved self-sufficiency. That demanded capital, numerous emigrants, and unshakable determination.

The Dutch and French failed both demographically and economically. The Dutch explored the Hudson River in 1609 and had settled New Amsterdam on Manhattan Island by 1624. But their colony of "New Netherland" never became more than a center for maritime trade and fur exports. The English seized it in 1664, immediately before the second of their wars with the Dutch (see p. 569).

The French excelled in the backwoods. Jacques Cartier discovered the St. Lawrence River in 1535 and Robert de La Salle coursed the Mississippi in 1682. France's explorers and fur-trading *"coureurs de bois"* ("wood runners") were more adventurous and France's Jesuit missionaries more determined than the New World representatives of any other European state except perhaps the Portuguese of Brazil. By 1605 French settlers had planted villages in Acadia, and in 1608 Samuel de Champlain founded Québec. By 1640 perhaps 3,000 French inhabited Canada, but the population reached only 10,000 by 1700.

Growth was slow because the French government succeeded too well in imposing French absolutism and social patterns on its colonies. It regulated, and stultified, economic life while granting land in large blocks or *seigneuries* to a few proprietors under semifeudal conditions. Except under Colbert in the 1660s and 1670s, it gave French peasants little inducement to emigrate. For religious reasons it strictly barred from Canada all Huguenots, who took their economic talents to the English colonies instead. A cluster of French settlements spread across the St. Lawrence Valley, but the English settlers to the south far outnumbered the "New France" of *seigneurs* and peasants.

The constitutional and religious struggles of the seventeenth century spurred emigration from England. English governments, whether Stuart or Cromwell, encouraged colonizing projects but left great latitude to the individuals or joint stock companies they chartered to found colonies. Above all, English governments allowed religious minorities that wished to emigrate to settle in English colonies. That speeded mightily the growth of an enterprising, independent, and rapidly multiplying population.

The Virginia Company planted England's first successful colony at Jamestown in 1607. It almost failed, but then the settlers discovered that the rage in Europe for a native weed, tobacco, provided them with a cash crop that paid for the manufactured goods they needed from England—and ultimately for African slaves to cultivate the tobacco. The small band of religious dissenters who landed at Plymouth in 1620 lost half their number during the first winter. But the Massachusetts Bay Company, which founded Boston, was able to profit by the Pilgrims' experience. In 1630 it transported 900 settlers across the ocean in a large and well-planned operation. Within ten years— thanks in part to Laud's persecution of dissenters at home—the population of Massachusetts had swelled to about 14,000, and by 1650 the population of "New England" was about 20,000. The settlers developed a surplus of food for export, and shipped fur, fish, and timber to England.

By 1700 the English colonies held almost 200,000 settlers, and dominated the continent. Twelve colonies existed, offshoots of the original settlements or created by royal grants to "proprietors"; Georgia, the thirteenth, was founded in 1732. And unlike New France, which suffered under a royal central administration at Québec, the English colonies were in effect self-governing. Each colony acquired an elected representative assembly that controlled its legislation and taxation. A royal governor appointed by London provided an executive that in theory was not responsible to the assembly. But because the governor generally depended on the assembly for his salary, his executive power and London's reach was effectively limited. In the 1660s Parliament did its best to impose mercantilist practices by requiring the export of certain "enumerated" colonial goods directly to England in English or colonial ships. Those restrictions caused much complaint and smuggling; after the Glorious Revolution of 1688 (see p. 571) London gradually became less insistent on asserting its authority. The colonists accepted regulation of their trade so long as London did not enforce that regulation too strictly.

Unlike the colonial subjects of all other powers, the inhabitants of British North America thus became increasingly accustomed to self-government. Without conscious design, England had fashioned a new kind of empire. Armed trade had been the foundation of the Portuguese and Dutch empires. The empire of Spain placed a ruling class of soldiers, planters, and missionaries in command of large native populations. But the Protestant English felt none of the responsibility for the Indians that weighed upon the missionaries of Spain, nor could the English exploit the labor of the thinly settled populations of North American Indians. Instead, the English settlers and the Dutch of New Holland simply displaced the natives. England transferred an entire European population to a new environment and allowed it to blend the institutions brought from home with the innovations that new surroundings demanded. The result was a unique experiment, largely unanticipated and unsought by London, in economic, political, and religious freedom.

Russia Reaches the Pacific

While France and Britain pushed westward across North America, the Muscovite state was pressing eastward from the Ural Mountains across Siberia toward the Pacific. Muscovy reached the Pacific first; no ocean separated its new dominions from the center of its power around Moscow. In 1581 groups of Cossacks—the "pioneers" or "frontiersmen" who had earlier pushed back Tartars and Turks and had settled the lower valleys of the Dnieper, Don, and Volga rivers—struck eastward from the Urals. Their fierce leader, Yermak, enjoyed the patronage of Tsar Ivan IV, the Terrible. Like the French in Canada, the Cossacks sought furs, particularly the incomparable sable. They therefore followed the pine forests and the northern tundra rather than the open steppes to the south. The innumerable rivers and lakes of Siberia allowed the Cossacks, like the French *coureurs de bois*, to flow swiftly eastward, occasionally halting to found fortified outposts.

The Cossacks reached the Pacific in the early 1640s, three generations and 3,000 miles after their eastward movement began. Unlike America, no great mountain chains barred the way. Resistance from the small Tartar states and the numerically weak tribal peoples of Siberia was slight. The advanced civilization of China ultimately checked Muscovite expansion in the Amur River valley. In 1689, Russia and China concluded their first treaty at Nerchinsk, and Russia withdrew from the Amur basin for almost 200 years.

Like the English, the Cossacks sought freedom as well as furs. Their early communities in Siberia were as wild and lawless as the later towns of the American West. But like the French administration in North America, the despotism of the tsars soon reached out across the vast distances to clamp its administration and its taxes on the lucrative fur trade. By 1700 several hundred thousand Russians had settled Siberia. By the end of the century, Russian traders had ventured across the Bering Strait to Alaska and down the North American coastline in search of seals. Long before the English in America reached the Pacific, the Russians had through individual daring and government backing staked a claim to the northern half of Asia and had reached out toward the Western Hemisphere.

The first half of the seventeenth century was thus a period of fierce turmoil both within Europe and in Europe's relations with the wider world. The French monarchy consolidated itself but remained vulnerable to its turbulent nobles. The English monarchy for a time collapsed. From 1618 to 1648 the states of central Europe—and outside powers from France to Sweden—

fought the last and bloodiest of the wars of religion. European economic and demographic growth faltered under the battering of wars, epidemics, and adverse climatic and economic trends. Yet Europe's expansion into the outer world continued ceaselessly, if less rapidly than in the sixteenth century. The rise of Europe's new territorial states continued. And after 1660, one state rose so high that it threatened the very fabric of the emerging European state system.

Suggestions for Further Reading

General

D. Ogg, *Europe in the Seventeenth Century* (1925, 1960), and G. N. Clark, *The Seventeenth Century* (1931), offer useful surveys. G. Parker, *Europe in Crisis* (1979), reflects recent work in the field. For a model comparative analysis of the upheavals that convulsed most early modern states, see P. Zagorin, *Rebels and Rulers, 1500–1660* (1982).

France, England, and Germany

For events in France, see the detailed survey of R. R. Treasure, *Seventeenth Century France* (1966). C. V. Wedgwood, *Richelieu and the French Monarchy* (1962), and C. J. Burckhardt, *Richelieu: His Rise to Power* (1964), are informative. P. Goubert, *The Ancien Regime: French Society, 1600–1750* (1973), is excellent on French social structure. On England, see especially C. Hill, *The Century of Revolution, 1603–1714* (1961); L. Stone, *The Causes of the English Revolution, 1529–1642* (1972); and C. V. Wedgwood, *The King's Peace, 1637–1641* (1955) and *The King's War 1641–1647* (1958). M. Ashley, *The Greatness of Oliver Cromwell* (1966), and C. Hill, *God's Englishman* (1970), deal in lively fashion with a central figure. P. Laslett, *The World We Have Lost* 2nd ed. (1971), gives an enthusiastic introduction to England's seventeenth-century social history. On events in central Europe, see especially R. W. J. Evans, *The Making of the Habsburg Monarchy* (1979); C. V. Wedgwood, *The Thirty Years War* (1938); and G. Parker et al., *The Thirty Years' War* (1974).

The European and World Economies

On Europe's economic crises, see especially C. M. Cipolla, *Before the Industrial Revolution* (1976); F. Braudel, *Civilization and Capitalism, 15th–18th Centuries* (1982); and *The Cambridge Economic History of Europe*, Vol. 4 (1967). C. McEvedy and F. Jones, *Atlas of World Population History* (1978), provides the best set of—admittedly speculative—population figures. For relations between Europe and the world, see particularly J. H. Parry, *The Age of Reconnaissance* (1964), and J. H. Elliott, *The Old World and the New* (1970). A. W. Crosby, *The Columbian Exchange* (1972), and *Biological Imperialism: The Biological Expansion of Europe, 900–1900* (1986), provide elegant treatments of neglected but decisively important events.

20

Absolutism and Constitutionalism, 1660–1715

*T*he last half of the seventeenth century was the age of France. Its population of roughly 18 million in 1650 dwarfed the 7.5 million of Spain and the roughly 5 million of England. Its economy and its bureaucratic-military machine were the largest in Europe, and much of Europe imitated its culture.

But French power had limits. Internally, high taxation, government regulation of the economy, religious persecution, and oppressive censorship stunted economic growth. Externally, Louis XIV's attempts to dominate western Europe welded together a series of coalitions against France. In the two great worldwide conflicts of 1689–97 and 1701–14, England, the Dutch United Provinces, and Habsburg Austria compelled even the magnificent "Sun King" of France to recognize the law of relations between states: the law of the balance of power.

Other powers declined with giddying rapidity, or stagnated. Sweden, outclassed militarily and demographically, ceased to be a great power. The Ottoman Turk state mounted its last great threat to western Europe, and then began the decline that by the late eighteenth century made it the "sick man" of the state system. The internal anarchy and external decline of Poland that led to its disappearance from the map between 1772 and 1795 became visible. Spain declined further. The Dutch reached their economic and demographic limits, and settled down to enjoy their riches.

Winners also emerged. The Habsburgs at last defeated the Turks for good, and consolidated their own hereditary possessions into a state more centralized than anything before it in south-central Europe. England took from the Dutch the mastery of the outer seas, as the Dutch had taken it from Portugal. Russia, a backward power until now outside the European system, suffered the first of the barbaric "revolutions from above" that ultimately made it a military giant. And the uncouth electorate of Brandenburg, a poor and obscure state on the eastern fringes of Germany, began its momentous rise to great power status.

Opposite: Louis XIV, by Hyacinthe Rigaud (1701).

THE FRANCE OF LOUIS XIV

Louis XIV, the "Sun King" (r. 1643–1715), was the living symbol of French military, political, and cultural domination. He was born in 1638 and took power decisively into his own hands the day after Mazarin's death in 1661. He died at the age of 77 and left the throne to his great-grandson. By temperament and training he incarnated divine-right monarchy—the notion that hereditary monarchy was the only divinely approved form of government, that kings answered to God alone for their conduct, and that subjects owed absolute obedience to their king as the direct representative of God on earth. His education was sketchy, and he had little imagination and no sense of humor. But he possessed the qualities indispensable for personal rule—willingness to work relentlessly, a commanding presence, and an imperious will.

Louis may not have said the famous words often ascribed to him—"I am the state." But he practiced them. He sought to personify the concept of sovereignty. He took a deep interest in the elaborate etiquette and ceremonial of his court, for it dramatized his supremacy over the nobility. He also conducted the business of the state in per-

The Sun King's emblem.

Bishop Bossuet on Absolutism

Jacques Bénigne Bossuet was tutor to Louis XIV's son in the 1670s, and the most zealous and prominent theorist of the king's absolutism.

The royal power is absolute. With the aim of making this truth hateful and insufferable, many writers have tried to confound absolute government and arbitrary government. But no two things could be more unlike. . . . The Prince need render an account of his acts to no one. . . . Without this absolute authority the king could neither do good nor repress evil. . . . God is infinite, God is all. The prince, as prince, is not regarded as a private person: he is a public personage, all the state is in him; the will of all the people is included in his. As all perfection and all strength are united in God, so all the power of individuals is united in the person of the prince. What grandeur that a single man should embody so much! . . .

From Jacques Bénigne Bossuet, "Politics Drawn from the Very Words of Scripture," in *Readings in European History*, ed. by James Harvey Robinson (Boston: Ginn, 1906), Vol. II, pp. 275–76.

son, as his own "first minister," from Mazarin's death in 1661 to his own in 1715. That required a dedication uncommon in monarchs, but Louis XIV set his preferred pastimes of hunting and womanizing aside when the state demanded it. "If you let yourself be carried away by your passions," he once remarked, "don't do it in business hours."

The administrative machine that served Louis XIV culminated in a three to five member "High Council" (*Conseil d'en Haut*) of great ministers that met almost daily under the king. Professional "secretaries" at the head of bureaucracies then executed the decisions taken in council. In the provinces, the *intendants* received ever more power as the direct representatives of the central government for justice, finance, and general administration.

Three great ministers of middle class origin, Jean-Baptiste Colbert, Michel Le Tellier, and his son, the Marquis de Louvois, directed this machine under the king's close supervision. Colbert, cold, gloomy, and fanatically precise, served as Controller General of Finance. He reduced waste, attempted to streamline the tax system, and gave France its first serious attempt at an annual budget of income and expenditure. He sought to force France's economic growth by punitive tariffs against the Dutch, state-supported industrial projects, and colonial enterprises. He doubled the king's net income between 1661 and 1671. Le Tellier and Louvois, as ministers of war, then spent the proceeds.

The old French monarchy had imposed its authority through its law courts. It had also frequently consulted provincial assemblies or the Estates General of France. The new monarchy that Richelieu had founded and Louis XIV perfected imposed its authority and its taxes by decree. Louis XIV checked the pretensions of the *parlements*, deliberately neglected to summon the Estates General, and crushed with military force and mass hangings the many attempts at tax rebellion in

Louis XIV on the Duties of a King

In the 1660s and 1670s, Louis XIV and his staff prepared notes to instruct his son in the art of ruling.

I have often wondered how it could be that love for work being a quality so necessary to sovereigns should yet be one that is so rarely found in them. Most princes, because they have a great many servants and subjects, do not feel obligated to go to any trouble and do not consider that if they have an infinite number of people working under their orders, there are infinitely more who rely on their conduct and that it takes a great deal of watching and a great deal of work merely to insure that those who act do only what they should and that those who rely tolerate only what they must. The deference and the respect that we receive from our subjects are not a free gift from them but payment for the justice and the protection that they expect to receive from us. Just as they must honor us, we must protect and defend them, and our debts toward them are even more binding than theirs to us, for indeed, if one of them lacks the skill or the willingness to execute our orders, a thousand others come in a crowd to fill his post, whereas the position of a sovereign can be properly filled only by the sovereign himself.

. . . of all the functions of sovereignty, the one that a prince must guard most jealously is the handling of finances. It is the most delicate of all because it is the one that is most capable of seducing the one who performs it, and which makes it easiest for him to spread corruption. The prince alone should have sovereign direction over it because he alone has no fortune to establish but that of the state.

From Louis XIV, *Memoirs for the Instruction of the Dauphin*, ed. by Paul Sonnino (New York: Free Press, 1970), pp. 63–64.

The medal on the left (1661) celebrates the young Louis' purported accessibility to his subjects. The one on the right (1685) extols the new discipline and professionalism of his armies.

the provinces. Above all, the king completed Richelieu's work of destroying the political power of the French nobility.

The Domestication of the Nobility

The Fronde had forced Louis XIV to flee Paris three times, and had left him fiercely determined, above all else, to break the turbulent nobility to the monarchy's service. His principal weapons were three. First, he denied the nobility its traditional share in the power of the state, while sharply curtailing independent noble power in the provinces. He chose his ministers almost exclusively from commoners, rotated provincial governors to prevent collusion with the local nobility, and treated *parlements* and provincial assemblies with contempt. Second, he cheapened the status of the nobility by deliberately increasing its numbers; the title of Marquis soon became almost a joke. Finally, he required the high nobility, upon pain of harassment, to serve him at court.

That service was bound up with Louis XIV's deliberate display of himself as the symbol of the state. In 1683 he moved court and government from the Louvre in central Paris to Versailles, 15 miles away. There he made his home in the formal gardens and ornate chateau that he had built on marshland, at great cost in lives and treasure. There he also felt safe; Versailles was the first French royal residence completely without fortifications.

Louis moved with impassive dignity through the innumerable court gatherings in the mirrored halls of Versailles. Years of self-conscious practice in kingship gave him a public façade—cool, courteous, impersonal, imperturbable—that fitted perfectly the artificiality of the small world of the court, as far removed from reality as Versailles itself was physically removed from the bustle of Paris. In that atmosphere, a ball seemed as important as a battle, and holding the basin for the king's morning ablutions became a task as coveted as the command of armies. Instead of competing in the provinces for political power against the monarchy, nobles squandered their fortunes and exhausted their energies in jockeying for social prestige under the king's vigilant eye.

He left the nobility one additional outlet—war. Military service harnessed the nobility's inborn aggressiveness to the purposes of the state. But that service also had a political cost. It created a noble "war party" at court that encouraged the king's own megalomania.

The Destruction of the Huguenots

Beside the nobility, only religious forces and groups stood as potential challenges to Louis XIV's absolutism. The king clashed with several popes who challenged his "Gallican" claim to control the Church in France. But those quarrels never led to a break with Rome, for in doctrine Louis XIV was strictly orthodox. And after 1680 he became increasingly concerned about the fate of his own soul. When his queen, Maria Theresa, died in 1683, he gave up all mistresses except the pious Madame de Maintenon, whom he secretly married. The king's growing piety naturally expressed itself politically. The wars of religion were over, but in the late seventeenth century religion and affairs of state remained tightly intertwined.

Louis XIV enthusiastically persecuted the Jansenists, an austere group of Catholic "puritans" who emphasized the teachings of St. Augustine on original sin, the depravity of man, and the need for divine grace. Louis, whose confessors were Jesuits, thought the Jansenists impertinent in their disapproval of his numerous mistresses, and subversive, for the pope had condemned them. In 1710–12 Louis razed their principal monastic center to the ground.

But it was the Huguenots, one of the most loyal and industrious groups in France, who felt the full force of Louis XIV's religious enthusiasm. Two religions under one prince was indeed, by seventeenth-century standards, a strange anomaly. And the French clergy had long insisted that the continued existence of Protestantism in France was an insult to the king's dignity and authority. After 1679 Louis apparently embraced the idea of atoning for his own numerous sins of the flesh—and his tacit alliance with the Ottoman Turks against Catholic Habsburg Austria—by crushing heresy in France.

He began by gradually tightening his interpretation of the Edict of Nantes, by which Henry IV had granted toleration to the Huguenots and ended France's religious civil wars in 1598. Louis proceeded by forced conversions of Protestants, the destruction of Protestant chapels, and the quartering of royal troops on Protestant families. In 1685 he took the final step. At the urging of his Jesuit advisers, he announced that since all heretics had reconverted to Catholicism, the Edict of Nantes no longer served any purpose and was therefore revoked. The state closed all remaining Protestant churches and schools, and the Church baptized all Protestant children as Catholics. Louis enforced the Revocation with imprisonment, torture, and condemnation to the galleys. Many Huguenots continued to practice their faith in secret. Perhaps 200,000, over a fifth of the Protestant population of France, fled to England, the Dutch Netherlands, Brandenburg, and the New World. Their industry and skill

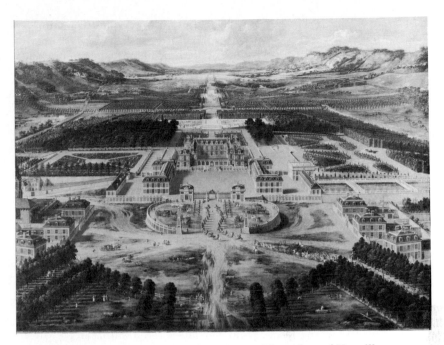

The palace of Versailles (1686), with the king arriving by carriage.

contributed mightily to the rapid economic growth of their new homes.

The Revocation of the Edict of Nantes was an act of religious intolerance that rivalled the Spanish expulsion of the *moriscos* in 1609–14, the Habsburg ravaging of Bohemia after the battle of the White Mountain in 1620, or the systematic impoverishment and degradation of the Catholics of Ireland by English conquerors from

Cartoon of 1686 showing a royal dragoon, as "missionary," forcibly converting a Huguenot "heretic" to Catholicism.

Elizabeth I to Cromwell and his successors. But in those cases, unlike that of France, ethnic hatred had compounded religious savagery. The revocation of the Edict of Nantes was unique in the seventeenth century—a large-scale act of barbarism that was *purely* religious in origin. It was the last such act in western Europe until Germany's attempt to exterminate the European Jews between 1941 and 1944.

Literature and Fashion: The Primacy of France

To dramatize his conception of kingship, Louis chose as his emblem the sun god, Apollo. The symbol of the sun, on whose rays all earthly life depends, became the theme of the architecture and sculpture of the new palace at Versailles. The "Sun King" patronized and presided over an "Augustan Age" of French culture. As befitted such a patron, the prevailing taste was classical. It emphasized form, order, balance, and proportion—the presumed ideals of reasonable individuals throughout history.

Pierre Corneille (1606–84) was the father of French classical tragedy. In 1636 he wrote *Le Cid*, the first of a series of powerful dramas that glorified willpower and the quest for perfection. Corneille was still active when Louis began his personal rule, but the dramatist's brilliant younger contemporary, Jean Racine (1639–99) soon eclipsed him. Racine wrote more realistically than Corneille about human beings in the grip of violent and sometimes coarse passions. He brought French tragedy to its highest point of perfection between 1667 and 1677. Then he underwent a religious conversion that caused him to renounce drama as immoral.

Some of the audience for the tragedies of Corneille and Racine had little respect for the comic playwright Molière (1622–73), but his biting satirical dramas became an unsurpassable model for future French dramatists. From 1659 to his death in 1673 he was the idol of aristocratic audiences at Versailles. All three playwrights concentrated on portraying types, not individuals—the hero, the man of honor violently in love, the miser, the hypocrite—embodiments of human passions and foibles that belonged to all times and places. Partly as a result, French classical drama of the age of Louis XIV was easily exportable. French literary standards influenced cultivated Europeans everywhere, although French literary creativity flagged in the later years of Louis XIV's reign, as religious persecution, religious and political censorship, and economic exhaustion intensified.

In the other arts, and in social conventions, France likewise swayed the rest of Europe, although Louis XIV's growing religious intolerance and military aggressiveness prompted resistance to French culture, especially in Protestant republics such as the Dutch United Provinces, where middle-class art and manners flourished. French fashions in dress nevertheless spread across Spain, Italy, and much of Germany. The masters of the ponderous French baroque style, which ruled the design and decoration of Versailles, replaced the Italians as the arbiters of European architecture. The French language became the language of diplomacy and polite conversation, and the French court became the model for countless smaller courts throughout Catholic Europe. As Florence had been the center of the Italian Renaissance, and Spain of the Counter-Reformation, so France in the late seventeenth century was the center of European politics, diplomacy, and culture.

France's Bid for European Domination

Richelieu and Mazarin had begun the process of creating a large and dependable standing army to replace the disorderly semi-mercenary, semi-feudal military system of the previous century. Louis and his formidable ministers of war, Le Tellier and Louvois, completed

Caricature of Molière as an actor.

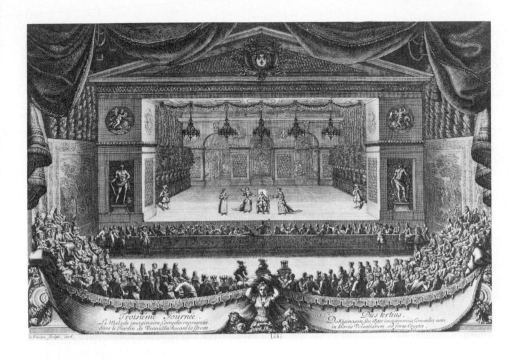

Engraving of a performance of Molière's last play, *Le Malade imaginaire* (1673). Molière died on stage on the fourth night of the performance.

that task. The ministers subordinated the aristocratic officer corps and the provincial private armies to royal authority, developed a supply system that functioned, standardized the organization of infantry and artillery, and followed the example of Gustavus Adolphus in giving the troops uniforms. The Seigneur de Vauban, the father of modern military engineering, invented the first effective bayonet and perfected the science of building—and smashing—fortifications in the age of gunpowder. Above all, Le Tellier and Louvois provided their master with numbers. By the 1660s Louis possessed by far the largest and best-equipped army in Europe: 100,000 men in peace and up to 400,000 in war, numbers not seen in the West since the fall of Rome.

This unprecedented power inevitably brought the temptation to use it. War aroused the enthusiasm of the nobility and kept it occupied in ways that did not threaten the state. War exercised and justified the enormous and costly standing army. Above all, successful war enhanced the glory of the monarch, a glory that was Louis XIV's constant concern. War might per-

The Conquests of Louis XIV   1661–1715

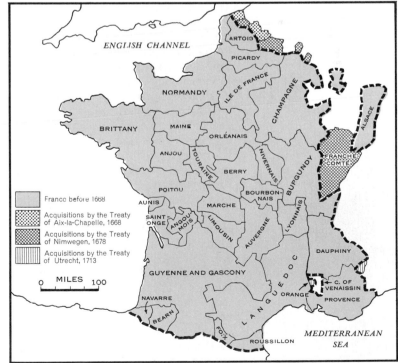

France before 1668

Acquisitions by the Treaty of Aix-la-Chapelle, 1668

Acquisitions by the Treaty of Nimwegen, 1678

Acquisitions by the Treaty of Utrecht, 1713

Louis XIV entering Strasbourg, September 1681. Note the fortifications in the style of Vauban.

Officer and musketeer of the French Guard (late seventeenth century).

haps make him the arbiter not only of France but of Europe as well.

Louis XIV's first two wars (1667–68, 1672–79) were relatively limited in aim. The decline of Spain and the collapse of the Holy Roman Empire left a power vacuum on France's eastern borders; Louis therefore sought to annex the Spanish Netherlands (later Belgium), Franche-Comté, and parts of western Germany and to reduce the Dutch to commercial and territorial vassalage. In each of the two wars, alliances that at different times included the United Provinces, Sweden, and the Habsburg monarchy checked him after initial French victories. The Dutch held off his first onslaught in 1672 by opening their dikes and flooding their countryside. England simultaneously attacked the Dutch by sea, but withdrew from the war in 1674. By 1678 Louis had gained only Franche-Comté and a few border fortresses in Flanders.

Thereafter, Louis briefly chose legal chicanery over musketry. He established French courts called Chambers of Reunion to "reunite" to France all lands on France's borders that had in

the past been dependencies of French territories. That gave Louis control of the independent Protestant republic of Strasbourg in 1681, much to the indignation of the inhabitants and of Protestants throughout Europe. The Revocation of the Edict of Nantes in 1685 provided further evidence of the Sun King's arrogance.

In 1686 the Habsburg Emperor, Spain, Sweden, and several German states formed the defensive League of Augsburg. Habsburg victories in Hungary over the Turks, who were allied with Louis, shifted the balance in the West against France. Louis replied with the most senseless atrocity since the Thirty Years' War—his armies systematically devastated the Palatinate in 1688 simply to cow his enemies. That act instead helped weld his opponents together. And French distraction in Germany allowed William of Orange, ruler of the Dutch Netherlands and Louis XIV's most implacable enemy, to claim the English throne in 1688–89. England and the Dutch, the two greatest economic powers of the age, then joined the League of Augsburg and closed the circle around over-mighty France.

The participants' newly acquired worldwide interests made this war the first world war, waged in India, the Caribbean, and North America as well as in Europe. After ten years of fighting, France agreed to the Peace of Ryswick in 1697. Louis retained the gains made before 1678, but had to renounce nearly all conquests after that date except Strasbourg. England emerged from the war stronger than it had been in 1689, and France weaker.

The War of the Spanish Succession, 1701–14

The Peace of Ryswick brought only four years' respite. Louis had made peace in the hope of gaining a greater prize than any for which he had yet contended—the Spanish Empire. Charles II of Spain, bizarre end-product of generations of syphilitic degeneration and Habsburg inbreeding, and last of the Spanish Habsburg line that had ruled since 1516, was losing a 30-year struggle against numerous diseases. By 1697 he was close to death and had no direct heir. That raised an issue of vital importance to all Europe: would the Spanish Empire fall to Emperor Leopold I of the Austrian Habsburg line, pass to the French Bourbon dynasty (for Louis XIV was both the son and the widower of Spanish Habsburg princesses), or suffer dismemberment among its rivals?

England and the Dutch had obvious economic and strategic interests in preventing France from grasping Spain's colonial trade or the Spanish Netherlands. Louis seemed willing to compromise and twice concluded secret treaties that partitioned the Spanish dominions with the English and Dutch. But when news of the second treaty reached Madrid, the dying Charles II lost his temper. He refused to see parts of his Catholic empire pass to Protestant powers; instead, he made a will that left all his dominions to a grandson of Louis XIV. After the death of Charles II in 1699, Spain proclaimed that grandson King Philip V of Spain.

Louis XIV tore up the secret partition treaties, recognized the will of Charles II, and sent French troops to claim the Spanish Netherlands. In 1701 William of Orange formed yet another coalition against France, the Grand Alliance of the Hague. England, Holland, and Emperor Leopold I of Austria bound themselves to fight until they had ended the threat of Bourbon control of Spain and of the Spanish colonies. Louis had made his last and most far-reaching bid for the domination of Europe. But this time his enemies were as unyielding and powerful as he was, and they forced him to fight for France's life.

Warfare had by now become thoroughly professional. In the long wars since 1618, innovators such as Gustavus Adolphus, Maurice of Orange, Le Tellier, and Louvois had replaced noble amateurism and independent military entrepreneurship with professional officers corps that bore the "king's commission." Ragged bands of freebooters yielded to disciplined ranks, rigidly drilled in the new fire tactics. The combination of musket and bayonet united fire and shock in one weapon, and drove out the clumsy combinations of pikemen and musketeers that had ruled the battlefield since the Spanish victory at Pavia in 1525. Commanders learned to coordinate infantry, the new mobile artillery, and cavalry. Sieges, thanks to Vauban, became a scientific exercise; the precise orchestration of artillery fire and trench digging permitted the battering of breaches in the strongest fortifications and their seizure by infantry assault.

In the new world war of 1701–14, the French soon found themselves outdone. Two commanders of genius led the Allied armies—England's John Churchill, first Duke of Marlborough, and the great Habsburg general and scourge of the Turks, Prince Eugene of Savoy. Marlborough's diplomacy held the ramshackle coalition together while his generalship smashed the great armies of Louis XIV in four battles of unprecedented slaughter that cost France up to 80,000 casualties—Blenheim (1704), Ramillies (1706), Oudenarde (1708), and Malplaquet (1709). England trounced the French at sea and seized Gibraltar, from which it thereafter dominated the western Mediterranean. An allied army even invaded Spain and several times took Madrid.

Louis XIV, with France exhausted militarily and in the grip of famine, sued for peace in 1709–10 on almost any terms. The Allies thereupon demanded that he send French troops to help expel his own grandson from Madrid. That was too great a humiliation; Louis XIV refused, and appealed with success to his subjects. Famine and economic crisis filled the French armies with new recruits, who preferred the risks of the battlefield to the certainty of starvation. A xenophobic reaction in Spain, and French generalship, helped drive the English and

Austrian invaders out. In 1710 the English war party, the Whigs, gave way to the Tories, and a war-weary England recalled Marlborough. In 1712, at Denain, the French severed Prince Eugene of Savoy's communications and forced him to retreat. It was the Allies' turn to seek peace.

The Peace of Utrecht, 1713–14

In theory, the Peace of Utrecht of 1713 and other treaties of 1714 that ended the war of the Spanish Succession gave France the prize that Louis had sought since 1701. Louis's grandson remained on the throne of Spain as Philip V—but only on condition that no subsequent Bourbon should unite the crowns of Spain and France. And Louis gave up all conquests east of the Rhine and his bid for the Spanish Netherlands and for Spain's colonial trade. France survived as the greatest single power, but the war had drained it of money and blood, and had made Louis XIV's government bankrupt and hated. When the great king died at last in 1715, France's common people reputedly "openly returned thanks to God."

England was the chief victor. It emerged from the war with the dominance of the seas that it held until the twentieth century. From France it took Newfoundland, Acadia (modern New Brunswick and Nova Scotia), and the Hudson's Bay Territory. It kept Gibraltar and Minorca, seized from Spain, and received the *Asiento*—the lucrative privilege of supplying African slaves to the Spanish colonies that provided an opening for large-scale smuggling of other goods.

The Austrian Habsburgs gained the Spanish Netherlands (which now became the Austrian Netherlands), and replaced Spain as the dominant power in Italy through the acquisition of Milan, Naples, and Sicily. Two new smaller powers, Brandenburg-Prussia and the Duchy of Savoy, increased their territories and prestige; they had chosen the winning side. The Dutch achieved their minimum war aim—

they kept the Scheldt River closed, thus blocking the trade of Antwerp, the chief port of the Austrian Netherlands. But the long strain of fighting France for almost half a century had demoralized them. They could no longer compete at sea with England and soon slipped from the ranks of the great powers.

The Peace of Utrecht ended the first bid for European hegemony since the days of Philip II of Spain. Louis XIV's attempt to gain for France the domination of western Europe and the wider world had summoned up, through the workings of the balance of power, the coalition that had checked France. War had prevented the universal domination of one power. The European state system had survived a challenge to its very existence.

ENGLAND: THE EMERGENCE OF PARLIAMENTARY MONARCHY

While Louis XIV consolidated absolute monarchy in France, the English created a constitutional monarchy controlled by Parliament. The restoration of king, Parliament, and Anglican Church in 1660 had established an equilibrium between Crown and Parliament. But that balance had remained unstable. Who was to exercise sovereignty, the king or the gentry and merchants of Parliament? What was the religious settlement to be, and who was to make it? Who was to control foreign policy? These three questions had dominated the preceding 40 years of turmoil and civil war. They still awaited answers.

Charles II and the "Cavalier Parliament"

Charles II (r. 1660–85), utterly unlike his too stubborn father, was witty, attractive, worldly, a king of hearty sexual appetites and shrewd political sense. He had lived long in exile in France, and took his cousin Louis XIV

The House of Commons, on the Great Seal of England (1651).

as his model. Charles was resolved not to risk exile or execution in the manner of his father. He instead hoped to restore England to Catholicism and to establish a French-style absolute monarchy through dissimulation, manipulation, and compromise. That ambition Charles II pursued through 25 years of court intrigue, party politics, and secret diplomacy that kept both Parliaments and ministers guessing about the king's intentions.

The "Cavalier Parliament" of 1661–79 held a commanding position at the beginning of the reign. It was the preserve of the gentry and of the aristocracy, now partly restored to its ancient influence in both local and national government. Both groups were for the moment strongly royalist and determined to stamp out all remaining political and religious radicalism. But they also had no intention of allowing the Crown to be financially independent of Parliament.

In place of the old idea that "the king should live of his own," Parliament now granted Charles a regular income from customs and excise duties. But it was not enough to meet even the ordinary expenses of government, let alone the expenses of Charles's wild doings at court or of his numerous mistresses and illegitimate children. And foreign war was unthinkable unless Parliament approved the objectives and voted money. Charles therefore allowed Parliament, under the leadership of his father's adviser, Edward Hyde, Earl of Clarendon, to have its way for a time.

Parliament thus dictated the religious settlement. The Cavalier Parliament was as strongly pro-Anglican as it was pro-royalist. Between 1661 and 1665 it passed statutes known inaccurately as the "Clarendon Code"—Clarendon himself favored toleration—that excluded from local government Puritans who "dissented" from the established Church and purged Puritan ministers from the Anglican clergy. Later legislation barred dissenters from Parliament, from service in the army or

navy, and from the universities at Oxford or Cambridge.

Puritanism and social radicalism appeared to be intertwined. The Cavalier Parliament was therefore determined to stamp out the first and discourage the second. But while the Clarendon Code lowered the social status of dissenters and narrowed their opportunities, it did not greatly decrease their number. Presbyterians, Congregationalists, Baptists, and Quakers formed persistent and numerous religious minorities that bitterly opposed both Anglicanism and Catholicism. Charles himself sought toleration as a first step to restoring Catholicism. In 1672 he issued a "Declaration of Indulgence" that suspended the operation of the Code against both Puritans and Catholics, and appeared to assert—in the manner of Charles I—that royal prerogative could thwart acts of Parliament. Parliament forced him to withdraw the Declaration, and imposed on him a Test Act that excluded non-Anglicans from civil and military office. To the Anglican gentry of Parliament, Puritans remained radicals and Catholics traitors.

Foreign Policy: The French Alliance

Two natural calamities, a fierce outbreak of bubonic plague that killed 60,000 of the 450,000 inhabitants of London in 1665 and a fire that destroyed much of the city in 1666, contributed to widespread unrest. Public opinion blamed the fire on an alleged Catholic plot. Uneasiness increased as king and Parliament drifted apart over foreign policy. In 1665 Parliament forced Charles into a commercial war with the Dutch, but denied him the money needed to win. When swift victories did not follow, Parliament unfairly held Clarendon responsible, and exiled him.

After Louis XIV began his attack on the Spanish Netherlands in 1667, English opinion began to see the military power of Catholic France as more threatening than the commercial ri-

Charles II, the "Merry Monarch."

London's catastrophic great
fire of 1666.

valry of the Protestant Dutch. But
Charles held to his connection with
Louis, and in 1670 Charles allied England with France against the Dutch
through the notorious secret Treaty of
Dover. In the Treaty, Louis XIV offered
money and French troops if Charles
were to declare himself a Catholic and
reconvert England to Catholicism.

Charles was probably unsure of how
far down that road he meant to travel.
He did acquire both a pro-French foreign policy and a French mistress who
reported to Louis XIV's ambassador.
English forces also attacked the Dutch
along with the French in 1672. Between
1675 and 1681 he concluded with Louis
four additional secret agreements in
which he undertook to thwart Parliament's anti-French moves in return for
more French money. The existence of
this close understanding with Louis
inevitably leaked out and created fear
of French domination and a return to
Catholicism. The landed classes represented in Parliament were increasingly
suspicious of Charles II and prone to
panic.

Whigs and Tories:
The Origins of Party Politics

In 1678 these accumulated fears exploded in the lurid "Popish Plot." A
disreputable former Anglican clergy-

man named Titus Oates concocted a
story about a Jesuit plot to kill the king,
to place his Catholic brother James,
Duke of York, on the throne with
French help, and to massacre England's Protestants. Parliament described it as "a damnable and hellish
plot, for assassinating and murdering
the king and rooting out and destroying the Protestant religion." A new
civil war seemed about to break out.

The Earl of Shaftesbury, a great
landowner who had fought for Parliament in the Civil War, rallied a "Country Party" that campaigned fiercely to
exclude James from the succession to
the throne. In response, an Anglican
and royalist "Court Party" assembled,
although at first without much enthusiasm, to support Charles II and his
brother. The Court party denigrated
the Shaftesbury group as "Whigs," a
name hitherto applied to Scottish Presbyterian rebels. The Whigs in turn baptized their antagonists "Tories," a kind
of Irish Catholic brigand.

The Whigs controlled the three brief
Parliaments that followed the dissolution of the Cavalier Parliament in 1679.
Shaftesbury and his associates merrily
pressed the execution of some 35 Catholics for alleged complicity in the imaginary "Popish Plot." But the Whig
leaders overplayed their hand. Opinion swung back toward the king, and it
was soon the turn of the Whigs to suffer. By 1681 Shaftesbury had fled
abroad, the inventors of the Popish
Plot were disgraced or executed, and
Charles II was stronger than any monarch since the early days of James I.
Until his death in 1685 Charles ruled
without Parliament, with his brother
James by his side and with the subsidies of Louis XIV filling his coffers.

These difficult years were nevertheless momentous for the West's tradition of political liberty. This struggle
between the king and factions of the
gentry in Parliament created the ancestors of modern political parties—
groups organized for the purpose of
electioneering and of controlling government through a representative as-

sembly. Whigs and Tories were in part the descendants of the Parliamentarians and Royalists of the 1640s. But the great crisis of the 1680s, instead of civil war, produced the system of Parliamentary rule that England later passed on to its colonies and indirectly to the West as a whole.

The "Glorious Revolution" of 1688

James, Duke of York, succeeded his brother Charles II in 1685 as James II (r. 1685–88). He was a bigoted convert to Catholicism who lacked Charles's shrewdness and flexibility. Within three years he had infuriated almost every political and religious group of importance in England, and had provoked the revolution that Charles II had succeeded in avoiding.

Early successes made him overconfident. He introduced Catholics into the high command of both army and navy, and camped a standing army a few miles from London. He surrounded himself with Catholic advisers and attacked Anglican control of the universities. He claimed the power to suspend or dispense with acts of Parliament. In a vain attempt to win the support of Puritans as well as Catholics, he issued a Declaration of Indulgence along the lines of his brother's—thus further alienating the Anglican establishment. By revoking borough charters and browbeating sheriffs, he tried to ensure the election of a Parliament favorable to his policies. These measures, along with the example of Louis XIV's revocation of the Edict of Nantes in 1685, terrified England's Protestants.

The event that triggered James II's downfall was a happy one—the unexpected birth in June 1688 of a son to his Catholic queen. Until then, Protestants had consoled themselves with the thought that James II's two elder daughters by another marriage, Mary and Anne, were Protestants, and would succeed James. Now the existence of a Catholic male heir prolonged the Catholic threat indefinitely into the future. But unlike the events of 1641,

the intense political tension of 1688 did not produce civil war. This time the king had no "king's party." He had alienated Anglicans and dissenters, Tories and Whigs, aristocracy and commoners. The result was instead a bloodless "revolution," a rapid and fundamental political change that established the limited or parliamentary monarchy that has persisted to the present.

The agent of James II's downfall was William of Orange, *stadholder* and hero of the Dutch Republic, the man who had opened the dikes to halt the French invasion in 1672. In 1677, in pursuit of allies against France, he had married James II's eldest daughter, Mary, and had thus acquired a claim to the English throne. In June 1688 a group of prominent Englishmen, both Whigs and Tories, invited William to cross the English Channel and save the Protestant cause in England. That November William landed a Dutch army on the southern coast and marched slowly toward London. The countryside rose against James II, and William tactfully allowed the friendless king to flee to France. An improvised Parliament declared that James had abdicated the throne by flight and invited William and Mary to become joint sovereigns on condition that they accept a "Bill of Rights" that severely limited royal power.

This bloodless "Glorious Revolution" established at last the sovereignty of Parliament, which had made a king and could regulate the succession to the throne. William was strong-willed, but his priorities were continental and Dutch—the forging of an ever more powerful coalition against Louis XIV. He therefore grudgingly accepted Parliament's conditions. The "Jacobite" supporters of James II and his son invaded Ireland in 1690 and staged two bloody rebellions in the Scottish Highlands in 1715 and 1745, but all such attempts at a second Restoration failed. Parliament had won.

The Bill of Rights emphatically barred the king from suspending acts

James II, who swiftly alienated even traditional supporters of the monarchy (engraved after a painting by Kneller, 1688).

The speaker of the House of Lords offers William and Mary the English crown (from a contemporary engraving).

John Locke (1632–1704), champion of "natural rights" and government by consent.

of Parliament or interfering with the courts. It furnished a base for the steady expansion of civil liberties in the generation after 1688. Parliament established religious toleration and freedom from arbitrary arrest. Censorship of the press quietly withered. The king had to summon Parliament annually, for he could neither pay nor control his armed forces without parliamentary consent. Regular meetings of Parliament in turn strengthened the parties and made the king dependent on their support. The monarch vetoed a parliamentary bill for the last time in 1707.

Hobbes Answered: John Locke and the Theory of Limited Government

The English Civil War and Glorious Revolution followed the Dutch revolt against Spain as the second of the Western revolutions that ended absolute monarchy and ultimately led to democratic representative government. The weight of tradition demanded that English leaders in 1641–49 and 1688–89 deny that their acts were revolutionary. Parliament chopped off the head of one

king and replaced another in the name of the *traditional* "liberties of England." But that half-fiction was unsatisfactory.

John Locke (1632–1704), a friend of the Earl of Shaftesbury who had founded the Whig party, provided a theoretical foundation for what Parliament had done and for the subsequent evolution of representative government. Locke probably wrote most of *Of Civil Government: Two Treatises* while in political exile in Holland in 1683–89, but it emerged from the presses in 1690 as a belated rationale for the acts of Parliament during the Glorious Revolution. In it he at last answered Thomas Hobbes's justification of absolute sovereignty with a convincing theory of limited government.

Locke attacked the divine-right theory of monarchy and challenged Hobbes's claim that the only alternative to anarchy was absolute authority. Locke's first principle was that all individuals possess a natural right to "life, liberty, and property." That notion was revolutionary in his age of entrenched privilege. It remains revolutionary in our own, in which dictatorships rule most of humanity. From this premise of "natural rights," and from a more optimistic view of human nature than that of Hobbes, Locke derived the rest of his system. Like Hobbes and many predecessors and contemporaries, Locke argued that government was a contract in which humanity exchanged the anarchy of the "state of nature" for the security that government provided. But Locke's insistence that rights were "natural" and prior to all government allowed him—unlike Hobbes—to limit the authority of government. The source of sovereignty, thanks to the natural rights of the governed, was the governed themselves: "The people alone can appoint the form of the commonwealth." It therefore followed, for Locke, that a government acting without the consent of the governed thereby dissolved the contract and gave the subject a right to resistance or revolution.

Locke also provided a principle for the ordering of government. Fearing the concentration of power, he proposed a strict separation of powers that would allow the elected representatives of the people to check a tyrannical executive. Above all, he relentlessly emphasized property as the foundation of all freedom and the purpose of government itself: "The great and chief end. . . . of men's uniting into commonwealths and putting themselves under government is the preservation of their property." Some twentieth-century commentators have denigrated what they describe as Locke's doctrine of "possessive individualism," his equation of property and liberty—but have failed to offer concrete examples of societies that enjoy liberty without property.

In the eighteenth century, Locke's ideas were a powerful rationale for a society based on wealth rather than inherited privilege and for a new kind of government, limited in its powers. Inalienable natural rights, government by consent, right of revolution, and the sanctity of property seemed increasingly "self-evident" to Englishmen

after 1688, and ultimately to the American colonists in 1776.

The Emergence of the Cabinet System

At the level of practice rather than that of theory, factional struggles in Parliament replaced struggles between king and Parliament after 1688. The Glorious Revolution made gentry and merchants the real masters of both central and local government in England. Generally speaking, aristocratic landowners, bankers, merchants, and most dissenters were Whigs, while the smaller gentry, the Anglican parish clergy, and some great lords were Tories. But parties were still loosely organized, and small cliques often held the balance of power.

Given the fluidity of parliamentary alignments and the monarchy's residual powers, it took over a century for a smoothly operating system of constitu-

---

Locke on Government by Consent   1690

Compare with "Bishop Bossuet on Absolutism," page 560.

Men being, as has been said, by nature all free, equal, and independent, no one can be put out of this estate and subjected to the political power of another without his own consent, which is done by agreeing with other men, to join and unite into a community for their comfortable, safe, and peaceful living, one amongst another, in a secure enjoyment of their properties, and a greater security against any that are not of it. . . . When any number of men have so consented to make one community or government, they are thereby presently incorporated, and make one body politic, wherein the majority have the right to act and conclude the rest. . . . Absolute, arbitrary power, or governing without settled standing laws, can neither of them consist with the ends of society and government, which men would not quit the freedom of the state of Nature for, and tie themselves up under, were it not to preserve their lives, liberties, and fortunes, and by stated rules of right and property to secure their peace and quiet.

From John Locke, *Of Civil Government: Two Treatises* (New York: Everyman's Library, 1924), pp. 164–65, 186.

Medal of Queen Anne (1702–14).

Anti-Catholic woodcuts showing the "prodigious cruelties" of religious warfare in Ireland (1689).

tional government to emerge by the slow accretion of precedent. The ultimate answer was the "cabinet system"—government by a committee of leaders of the majority party in Parliament, acting under the leadership of a "prime minister" and acknowledging primary responsibility to Parliament rather than to the crown for their actions.

During the reigns of William and Mary (1689–1702) and of Mary's sister, Queen Anne (1702–14), the foundations of that system emerged, although parliamentary leaders had as yet no sense of their goal and monarchs still considered ministers responsible to themselves rather than to Parliament. The old privy council had long been too unwieldy for effective action. Instead, a "cabinet council" or inner circle of important ministers had developed under Charles II. The members of this "cabinet" slowly discovered that efficiency demanded that they settle major issues among themselves and then present a united front to the monarch. And within the cabinet a leader, the "prime minister," inevitably emerged.

In order to gain Parliament's indispensable support in war or peace, both William and Anne occasionally found it advisable to choose their ministers from the majority party. By Queen Anne's death in 1714 it had become evident that the real government of England was slowly falling into the hands of a cabinet of ministers who controlled a parliamentary majority, often by bribery, but felt themselves ultimately responsible to the political interests of that landed and moneyed majority.

The Religious Settlement

The Glorious Revolution also produced an unprecedented measure of religious toleration. The fanaticism unleashed in the Civil War had given religious intolerance a bad name, and both Anglicans and Puritans were now more afraid of Catholic France than of one another.

Puritans had supported Anglicans against the Catholic, James II, but King William, thanks to the Dutch Republic's unique tradition of toleration, now insisted on a religious truce. The result was the "Toleration Act" of 1689, which allowed dissenters to worship as they pleased and to educate their clergy and laity in schools of their own. Most of the existing anti-Catholic statutes, along with the acts excluding dissenters from civil and military offices remained in effect, but after 1689 their enforcement lacked rigor.

The Act of Settlement of 1701 provided that the sovereign should always be an Anglican Protestant and finally quieted fear that a Catholic might succeed to the throne. The act also settled the succession, in case James II's two daughters should die without children, on the descendants of that daughter of James I who had married the ill-fated Frederick V of the Palatinate before the Thirty Years' War. That succession brought the Elector of Hanover to the throne in 1714, when Queen Anne died without direct heirs, and the Stuart dynasty ended.

Ireland and Scotland: Repression and Union

Civil War and Glorious Revolution also indirectly furthered the unification of the British Isles. England, Ireland, and Scotland all had the same king from James I's succession in 1603, but union went no further than the common crown. The two smaller kingdoms, especially Ireland, suffered greatly during the seventeenth century from involvement in England's religious and political struggles.

The native Irish were Catholic; Protestant England therefore despised them and feared them as potential allies of Catholic Spain and France. To cope with that strategic threat, James I had settled Protestant colonists in the northeastern province of Ulster. But the Ulster Protestants were Presbyterians and soon became anti-Stuart, while the Catholic Irish were generally loyal to the Stuart dynasty. In 1641 the Catholics had revolted. Cromwell crushed them with fire and terror in 1649, and massacred the Catholic garrisons at Drogheda and Wexford (". . . being in the heat of action, I forbade them to spare any that were in arms in the town."). In 1690, James II landed in Ireland with French troops and Catholic support, but William of Orange routed him at the Battle of the Boyne. The much-celebrated anniversary of that Protestant victory remains to the present day a source of sectarian bloodshed in Ulster. After the Boyne, English and Irish Protestant landlords systematically persecuted the Catholic Irish and their religion, while reserving both economic and political power for themselves.

The Scots, who had given England a king in 1603, had somewhat better fortune. Scotland had a sixth of England's population, but its Protestantism, its long tradition of parliamentarism, its military power, and its poverty—which made it unrewarding as prey—allowed it to make a satisfactory bargain. Scottish resistance to the imposition of Anglicanism had triggered the crisis that ultimately led to Civil War in 1642. Nevertheless, much of Scotland, especially the Highlands inhabited by the turbulent and ruthless Catholic clansmen, remained strongly attached to the native Stuart dynasty. From 1650 to 1745, the clans provided a base for risings in support of the Stuarts. The Scots parliament accepted the Revolution of 1688, but refused the Act of Settlement of 1701. It threatened to choose a separate king of its own—possibly the exiled pretender James II—if James II's last daughter, Anne, died without producing an heir.

That frightened London into serious negotiation. In 1707 the Whig government and the Scots agreed to an Act of Union that eliminated the risk that Scotland might choose a separate monarch, and created the kingdom of "Great Britain." Scotland retained its own laws and its Presbyterian state religion, but surrendered its separate parliament in return for representation in London and full participation in the dynamic English economy. The loss of political independence and the coming of a money economy even to the wild Highlands caused disgruntlement, especially among the clans. But the Act of Union was successful, unlike England's difficult relationships with Ireland or with the colonies in America. Scottish merchants and administrators helped build the British empire. Scottish philosophers, economists, and historians contributed mightily to the widening of human knowledge in the eighteenth century known as the Enlightenment (see pp. 601–11).

The Growth of British Power

A final consequence of the Revolution, after parliamentary government, religious toleration, and the settlement with Scotland, was to unite crown and Parliament on foreign policy and to turn the energies of the next generations from domestic conflict to foreign war. Given England's fear of Catholicism, William of Orange had no difficulty bringing his new kingdom into the Grand Alliance against Louis XIV, who had given refuge to James II. Parliamentary monarchy soon demonstrated that it was more deadly to its enemies than Stuart absolutism. The government of William and his successors was able to raise money, the sinew of war, in ways that only the Dutch could match.

In 1694 William's Whig ministers created a Bank of England to mobilize England's growing commercial and financial power against France. Within a few days of its founding, the Bank had raised over a million pounds of investors' money, and it promptly lent the money to the government at 8 percent interest. The resulting permanent national debt was a revolutionary instrument. It financed the defeat of Louis XIV and provided the foundation for the subsequent commercial and maritime supremacy of Britain. Throughout the next century British wealth, trans-

The Economic and Social Division of Europe

muted into ships of the line, gave the island kingdom a striking power out of all proportion to its size and population. The Peace of Utrecht of 1713 gave British sea power, the guarantor of British trade, a position without serious rivals. That heralded the elimination of France as a colonial competitor and Britain's domination of the world outside Europe.

CENTRAL AND EASTERN EUROPE, 1648–1721

An imaginary line running north from the Adriatic Sea to the Elbe River that flows into the North Sea divided the economy of early modern Europe into two sharply defined halves. West of that line, the towns and their trade were increasingly dominant. The majority of the population still lived on the land, but most peasants were free workers and many of them small landowners. Most serfs had become agricultural wage laborers in and after the crisis of the Black Death. Most nobles had become landlords who hired labor for wages, or simply lived on rents from tenants. Though still a minority, the urban middle classes were increasingly influential.

East of the line, in Hungary, Bohemia, Poland, Prussia, and Russia lay a land of lord and peasant. Towns were small, poor, and weak. Landed estates were larger and the landed nobility far more powerful politically than in western Europe. And in the sixteenth and seventeenth centuries, noble power was still growing. Grain prices rose with the price revolution of the sixteenth century, while the growth of the trading networks centered on Antwerp and Amsterdam offered export markets. That situation provided an economic rationale for the imposition of a "second serfdom" in eastern Europe. The nobles, now enmeshed in a money economy, sought to lower labor costs by binding their peasants to the land and imposing on them two to five days a week of compulsory labor. The profits earned on exports in turn further increased the nobles' power. And in the political sphere, the states of eastern Europe encouraged and promoted noble domination. Either the state was the nobility, as in Hungary or Poland, or it made a tacit bargain that delivered the peasants to the nobility in return for noble service to the state, as in Brandenburg-Prussia and Russia.

As in western Europe, states were machines for power. They had to be, for the flat plains of central and eastern Europe offered no "natural frontiers" to check the invader. A state could only remain a state so long as it had an army. But the revolution in military technique since gunpowder had become widespread in the fifteenth century had so raised the costs of armies that only stongly centralized states with relentless tax systems could afford them. Few such states existed in central and eastern Europe in the seventeenth century. Most eastern rulers faced the same obstacles to centralized government that western rulers had faced two centuries or more before—a powerful landed nobility, a church that owned large portions of the land, a middle class too small to bear the weight of heavy taxation, a desperately poor agrarian economy, a limited commerce,

The crown of the Holy Roman Empire of the German Nation, used from 961 to 1792.

infant industries, and a peasantry tied to the land and thus incapable of meeting the need of new industries for labor.

The Holy Roman Empire

The one large political organization that bridged eastern and western Europe was the Holy Roman Empire. But the Thirty Years' War had left it a political fiction. A Habsburg remained emperor and a Diet or deliberative assembly met "perpetually" at Regensburg after 1663, but the Empire had no common army, administration, taxes, laws, calendar, or tariffs. It included perhaps 1,800 political units and petty rulers, including free cities, free imperial knights, ecclesiastical principalities, counties, margravates, duchies, and the kingdom of Bohemia. The Peace of Westphalia had recognized the full sovereignty of the 300 or so larger units within the Empire and had accorded France and Sweden the right to take part in the Diet's deliberations. This Empire, as Voltaire (see p. 603) remarked in the mid-eighteenth century, was "neither Holy, nor Roman, nor an Empire."

The ruling families of a few large states—Bavaria, Saxony, Hanover, Brandenburg, and Austria—sought to expand their territories and prestige by war or marriage. Augustus the Strong of Saxony, in addition to fathering according to legend more than 300 children, secured election in 1696 as king of Poland. In 1701 the Elector of Brandenburg obtained the emperor's consent to style himself "king in Prussia." And in 1714 the Elector of Hanover became king of Britain. But only two great powers emerged from the wreck of the Holy Roman Empire—Austria and Brandenburg-Prussia.

The Habsburgs: Europe and Austria Defended

The attempt of Emperor Ferdinand II (r. 1619–37) to revive and strengthen the Empire under Habsburg control collapsed in the Thirty Years' War. The Habsburgs of Vienna thereafter turned to a policy that Ferdinand had also fostered. The Habsburgs sought to consolidate and expand their hereditary lands in Austria and the Danube Valley into a centralized monarchy that could hold its own against the states of western Europe. The chief architect of that policy was Emperor Leopold I (r. 1658–1705), with the help and occasional prodding of some capable civil servants and one remarkable general, Prince Eugene of Savoy.

Achieving the Habsburg objective required the reduction of Austria, Bohemia, and Hungary to a semblance of uniformity and obedience. In the Duchy of Austria and neighboring Tyrol, Leopold's lawyers established his ascendancy over the nobility. Bohemia was even less of an impediment. The Emperor Ferdinand II had smashed its native Czech nobility after the Battle of the White Mountain in 1620, and in 1627 had made the previously elective crown of Bohemia a hereditary possession of the Habsburg family. Hungary, on the fiercely contested border between the West and Islam, was different. Although the Habsburgs had usually been the elected monarchs there since early in the sixteenth century, the Ottoman Turks directly or indirectly ruled almost two thirds of the kingdom. The Hungarian nobility was turbulent, and the Hungarian Protestants were numerous and inclined to fear the Turks less than the Catholic Habsburgs.

But the Ottoman Empire was no longer the power that had taken Constantinople in 1453, smashed the Hungarians at Mohács in 1526, and sought Mediterranean mastery at Lepanto in 1571. The Ottomans failed to keep pace with the West in technology, above all in the technology of war. Their metallurgy, their cannon and handguns, remained those of the sixteenth century. Ottoman logistics and tactics likewise failed to match the growing professionalization that overtook war in the West during and after the Thirty

Emperor Leopold I (above) and Prince Eugene of Savoy (below), who ended the Ottoman Turk threat to central Europe.

Years' War. But Ottoman troops nevertheless remained fearsome in the attack and tenacious in defense. And after 1656, the Ottoman central government briefly revived under a vigorous line of grand viziers (first ministers to the Sultan), the Köprülü family. In the 1660s the Ottomans began a new thrust up the Danube Valley against their Habsburg antagonists. Louis XIV, intent on tipping the European balance in France's favor, allied himself with the Turks and with Hungarian rebels against Leopold I.

But Austria prevailed and acquired a prestige and a sense of mission that long endured. From July to September 1683 a Turkish army of more than 100,000 besieged Vienna after laying waste to everything in its path. Volunteers rushed to Austria's aid from all across the Continent. The greatest pope of the century, Innocent XI, proclaimed Europe's last crusade against Islam. A coalition army under the leadership of King John Sobieski of Poland descended from the heights outside Vienna upon the Turks and routed them. For the next 16 years, Austria and its allies fought their way laboriously back down the Danube Valley. In 1697, Prince Eugene of Savoy at last broke the Turkish army at the battle of Zenta, near the present Yugoslav-Hungarian border. Turkey ceased to be a threat and soon became a victim.

The resulting Peace of Carlowitz in 1699 gave the Habsburgs all of Hungary. The Emperor crushed the Hungarian Protestants and executed many of them for treason. The Hungarian nobility retained its serfs and many of its old privileges in return for recognizing the ultimate sovereignty of Vienna. But the Habsburgs imprudently left local administration to the nobility, and failed to create a uniform, centralized system of administration for all their possessions. Eugene's victories nevertheless established a strong state in the Danube Valley where none had existed before. The Treaties of Ryswick in 1697 and Carlowitz in 1699 thus marked the emergence of the two new great powers that had risen to check the overbearing ambition of Louis XIV—Britain and Austria. And by the end of the century, two further contenders for great power status had begun their ascent—Brandenburg-Prussia and Russia.

The Curious Rise of Brandenburg-Prussia

Prussia, the power that emerged from the obscure Electorate of Brandenburg, was the most improbable of all seventeenth- and eighteenth-century claimants to great power status. The Habsburgs and even the primitive Grand Duchy of Muscovy had extensive territorial bases. The Hohenzollern dynasty that created Prussia had been mere margraves—counts of a "mark," or frontier province—in Brandenburg since 1417. The one distinction of the small, sandy, and barren principality around Berlin was that after about 1230 it was one of the seven "electorates" of the Holy Roman Empire, states whose rulers—at least in theory—voted to elect the emperor.

In the early seventeenth century, by the accidents of dynastic inheritance, the Hohenzollern family acquired two further territories of importance—the Duchy of Cleves and some neighboring lands on the Rhine in 1614, and the Duchy of Prussia on the Baltic coast to the northeast in 1618. The total population of all Hohenzollern possessions was perhaps 1.5 million. The provinces lacked defensible boundaries, standing military forces, and a central administration other than the household of the Elector. Each of the provincial estates jealously guarded their inherited privileges. Nothing suggested that this chance agglomeration of provinces was capable of becoming a powerful state, especially since the Thirty Years' War had devastated Brandenburg. Berlin lost over half its population, and the Hohenzollern dominions as a whole probably lost almost one-third of their people, a loss that took 40 years to make up.

One man changed this situation. Frederick William of Hohenzollern, the Great Elector (r. 1640–88), was the first of the line of remarkable rulers that made Prussia. Born in 1620, he succeeded to power in 1640 after an education in Holland that had emphasized the latest in statecraft and technology. A devout Calvinist, he had learned toleration from the Dutch, and, in an age of fanaticism he respected the Lutheranism of his subjects. Above all, he learned from the helplessness of Brandenburg during the war. "A ruler is treated with no consideration if he does not have troops and means of his own," he advised his son in 1667. "It is these, Thank God! which have made me considerable since the time that I began to have them."

He inherited in 1640 a poorly equipped and mutinous army of 2,500 men. Before the end of the Thirty Years' War in 1648 his ceaseless efforts had increased it to 8,000 disciplined troops; by his death in 1688 he had a peacetime force of 30,000 which could expand to 40,000 in time of war. In the 48 years of his reign, the Great Elector built upon Brandenburg-Prussia's meager population the strongest military power in Germany, except for Austria's.

To accomplish that end, he needed money. Raising it required administrative centralization and the crushing of the provincial estates that largely controlled taxation. In Brandenburg he struck a bargain with the Estates in 1653 that provided him with a lump sum that he used to raise further troops. That force in turn allowed him to collect taxes without further votes by the Estates, which—like Louis XIV—he never summoned again. In Prussia, far to the east, the townsmen were more stubborn than in Brandenburg, and the hard-bitten nobility, the *Junkers* (from *Jungherr*, "young lord"), proved exceedingly unruly. The provincial opposition turned to Poland for support, but Frederick eventually crushed the resistance and executed its leaders. After campaigns against both Poland and Sweden, he also secured clear title to Prussia, which he had originally held as a fief from the King of Poland. Only Cleves and the western principalities defied Frederick with some success. There he was unable to introduce his most hated tax, the excise, despite nine separate attempts.

Despite some setbacks, Frederick set up a tax system under civil servants of his own choosing that extended to all his territories. He deprived the nobility of the power it had exercised through the Estates and pressed it into state service as officers in the new standing army. In return, he confirmed and strengthened Junker control over the serfs. Power, not the betterment of the lowly, was the Great Elector's objective.

But against the background of the Thirty Years' War, the creation of the standing army and the order it brought was nevertheless a contribution to the welfare of the population. Devastation by foreign armies was even worse than Junker oppression. With the relative peace that Frederick William brought, the population could tolerate heavier taxation and centralization. Frederick William's foreign policy was cautious. He sold his support to a succession of temporary allies in return for subsidies that helped pay for his army, while avoiding heavy fighting. The Swedes came close to Berlin in 1675, but he drove them off at the battle of Fehrbellin, a sign of Brandenburg-Prussia's rise and of Sweden's decline.

Frederick William likewise tailored economic and religious policy to the needs of the state. He helped revive and improve agriculture after 1648 and encouraged industry and commerce. He made Brandenburg a haven for religious refugees—Lutherans, Calvinists, and large numbers of Huguenots after Louis XIV revoked the Edict of Nantes in 1685. These immigrants, together with Dutch, Swiss, and other newcomers, brought new skills in agriculture and industry, helped increase the population, and added considerably to the strength of the state. He welcomed

Frederick William, the Great Elector, painted by his contemporary, Mathias Czwiczeic.

even the more radical Protestant sects and the Jews but drew the line at the Jesuits, whom he considered too intolerant.

The recognition in 1701 of the Great Elector's son as Frederick I, "King in Prussia" (that is, in the province of Prussia, outside the boundary of the Empire) symbolized the appearance of a new power in Europe. In 1720, at the end of the Great Northern War that paralleled in eastern Europe the War of the Spanish Succession, the Hohenzollerns gained Pomerania and the vital port of Stettin from Sweden.

Prussia, as the Hohenzollern lands became known, had in 80 years transformed itself from a chance agglomeration of feeble provinces into a state on the threshold of great power status. The coincidental weakness of its neighbors, rivals, or overlords—Sweden, Poland, Russia, and the Empire—gave it the opportunity. But this "Sparta of the North" rose primarily through its own efforts, through its army. All states in the fiercely competitive European system were machines for war, but Prussia devoted to its military relatively more of its population, resources, and energies than any other state. The army was the first institution common to all the Great Elector's lands, and its supporting bureaucracy was the model for Prussia's later organs of civil government. The nobility served the state in the army and bureaucracy, and came to identify itself with state and army to an extent without parallel elsewhere. That army, the army that conquered true great power status for Prussia in the coming wars of the mid-eighteenth century, *was* the Prussian state.

Russia: Revolution from Above

To the east of Prussia, Sweden, Poland, and the Ottoman Empire, no great power existed in the seventeenth century. The only contender was Muscovy, a state closer in constitution to the Ottoman Empire than to anything in Europe. As in the Ottoman Empire, in India, and in China, the Muscovite tsar "owned" his territory and his subjects, who enjoyed no rights against the state. That was no accident. Muscovy acquired its statecraft from Byzantium, and above all from the Mongols, its overlords from around 1240 until 1480 (see pp. 377–79).

The rulers of Muscovy were fully conscious of their uniqueness. They derided the "limited" monarchs to the west as "men under contract" to their subjects. In a letter addressed to Queen Elizabeth I of England in 1570, Tsar Ivan the Terrible had mocked her as no true sovereign, but one who had "men who rule beside you, and not only men, but trading boors." In Russia, even nobles lacked rights—even property rights—against the state; Ivan broke the hereditary nobility or *boyars* by torture, massacre, and wholesale confiscation of land in the 1560s and 1570s. He largely replaced them with a new "service nobility" that owed abject obedience to the autocrat. Scornful xenophobia characterized Muscovy's external relations. The alternation of despotism and anarchy marked its internal politics.

Anarchy at first seemed Muscovy's lot after the unlamented death of Ivan the Terrible in 1584. The customary succession disputes, the "Time of Troubles," lasted until the accession in 1613 of the Romanov dynasty, which ruled Russia until 1917. Thereafter, religious strife compounded the weakness of the state. A reforming leader of the Orthodox Church, Patriarch Nikon, provoked a devastating schism in the 1660s by revising ritual and liturgy to bring them closer to the original Greek text of the Bible. That exasperated the traditionalist masses, to whom the Old Slavonic texts were sacrosanct. The Church split into a shallowly based state institution and fiercely independent sects of "Old Believers" who braved executions and exile for their faith. As many as 20,000 may have burned themselves to death in the belief that the end of the world was at hand.

ypcpolínhq mexuca

Cortés accepting the surrender of Quauhtemoc, last king of the Aztecs. The artist was a Spanish-trained native from Tlaxcala, who chronicled Cortés' conquest of Mexico. Notice the mixture of European and Indian styles.

had been highly centralized, so after the collapse of the central authorities there were no local leaders who could continue to resist. Second, the Europeans brought diseases (especially smallpox) against which the native populations had no natural defenses, and within a short time the natives were so reduced in numbers that rebellion was impossible.

The demographic and ecological effects of the conquests are illustrated by what happened in Mexico. While it is difficult to estimate the size of the Indian population before the conquest, it appears to have been at least 25 million. Beginning in 1519, it dropped precipitously to about 6 million by 1540, 4 million in 1563, and 2.5 million in 1600. It reached its nadir about 1650, when it was 1.5 million. Thereafter, it climbed gradually until it reached a little more than 3.5 million in 1793. By contrast, the population of goats, sheep, and cattle, introduced to Mexico by the Europeans, rose dramatically in the second half of the sixteenth century. From

1550 to 1620, the number of goats and sheep rose from about half a million to 8 million, while the cattle herds increased from about 10,000 to 100,000. The Indian peasant farmers had been replaced by great herds and flocks of range animals. Further, the goats and sheep were extremely destructive because they uproot the plants they eat leaving a desert behind.

The new empire raised conflicts within Spain, because different groups wanted to accomplish different ends in the new lands. There were three competing elements—the settlers who went out to the New World, the government in Madrid, and the Franciscan friars. The settlers sent to the new colonies wanted to exploit the land by setting up a manorial system based on the old European model and by using the forced labor of the natives. The colonists also did not want to take orders from or to serve the interests of the Spanish government. The government naturally wanted to centralize all power over the colonies in its own hands, and its principal goal was to find and exploit sources of precious metals. Since the Aztecs and Incas used an enormous amount of gold for ornamentation, the government had great confidence that this policy could be successful. The friars wanted to convert the new populations.

The discovery of civilized heathens raised theological and moral questions about how such people ought to be treated. Spanish scholars dredged up the works of medieval thinkers who had speculated about whether the biblical texts according to which rulers receive their authority from God (such as Romans 13) applied to those who did not accept or did not know the sacred text. There were also questions about the marriages of the new converts. Were the "marriages" of heathens valid? The Church considered marriage to be a sacrament—God joined husband and wife—and medieval thinkers developed a theory that the marriages of such people were valid, but not licit. According to this conception, God cre-

described what he saw in letters that were published and read throughout Europe. In one he referred to the great southern continent in the west as *Mundus novus*, the New World. Later map makers labeled the two new continents "America," after the man who had first recognized their significance in the earth's geography. Vespucci's letters inspired Thomas More to write his *Utopia* (see p. 462).

The Treaty of Tordesillas, 1494

From the beginning of Spanish exploration, Spain and Portugal knew that they were in direct competition for the newly discovered lands. The two countries turned to the pope, Alexander VI (r. 1492–1503), to draw a line of demarcation between their respective areas of potential empire. Alexander was a Spaniard and his line—100 leagues west of the Cape Verde Islands (off the coast of Mauritania in western Africa)— favored the Spanish. In 1494, the Portuguese persuaded the Spanish to negotiate the bilateral Treaty of Tordesillas, which made a division that both could be reasonably happy with and that would avoid unwanted war. This treaty also used the Cape Verde Islands as the point of reference, but it drew a line from pole to pole 370 leagues west of the islands.

However, misunderstanding remained. The Portuguese assumed that the line applied only to the Atlantic (it gave them Brazil, though they did not know this in 1494), while the Spanish thought the line went clear around the earth. By this interpretation the Spanish could claim the Moluccas, which were the heart of the Spice Islands, and in fact it would also have given them part of what is now Indonesia. But the trouble that these conflicting interpretations of the treaty might have caused did not occur, because Spain became so occupied with its new possessions in the Americas that in 1527 it sold its claims in the East to Portugal.

By 1512 Albuquerque had established the Portuguese in the Moluccas, and a year later the Spaniard Balboa sighted the Pacific Ocean from the Isthmus of Darien (south of Panama) in Central America. The first of these achievements increased the need of the Spaniards to find a route westward to the Spice Islands, and the second made it seem that it would be possible to find a passage through the New World. In 1519, the Portuguese navigator Magellan—with Spanish backing, since his success would benefit Spain under the treaty of 1494—undertook the third of the great voyages, along with those of Columbus and da Gama. Magellan negotiated the treacherous straits at the southern tip of South America and made it across the Pacific despite incredible hardships, only to be killed by natives in the Philippines. His navigator, Sebastian del Cano, brought one of the five original ships back to Lisbon by way of the Cape of Good Hope in 1522— the first ship to circumnavigate the world.

THE SPANISH EMPIRE IN THE AMERICAS

About the time Magellan sailed, the Spanish began to carve out an empire in the New World. From 1520 to 1550, Spanish conquistadors conquered wealthy civilizations in Mexico and Peru. The most notable of the conquistadors were Hernando Cortés and Francisco Pizarro. From 1519 to 1521 Cortés conquered the formidable Aztec Empire in Mexico with 600 men, 16 horses, and a few cannon, and from 1533 to 1534 Pizarro conquered the Inca Empire in the Andes of Peru with even fewer men.

The American civilizations were wealthy and sophisticated, but they did not have a military technology to match that of the Spaniards. In addition, the few Spanish troops were well disciplined and daring and took advantage of every opportunity. Their initial successes were easy to consolidate later for two basic reasons: first, the political power of both the Aztecs and the Incas

Magellan plotting his position (detail from an allegorical portrait by De Bry).

Abroad, Russia fared poorly against Swedes, Poles, and Turks, and remained cut off from access to either Baltic or Black sea. English merchants made contact with Moscow in the 1550s by the icy route around Norway to the bleak port of Archangel on the White Sea, and German merchants were also active in the capital. But Russia's chief import, then and later, was the West's technology, especially its military technology. The Renaissance and Reformation reached only as far as Catholic Poland.

In 1689, a new monarch, Peter I (r. 1682–1725), seized power at the age of 17 in a palace coup. He was nearly seven feet tall, with inexhaustible energy and appetites, and a ferocious will. His insatiable curiosity led him to spend much time with the Dutch and Germans who lived in the "German Quarter" of Moscow. There he probably conceived the ambition of making Russia a great power by rapidly adopting western technology, civil and military institutions, and customs. The partial realization of that ambition ultimately earned for him the title of Peter the Great.

Peter at first allowed others to rule for him, but in 1695 he ventured a first campaign against the Turkish fortress of Azov, where the Don River enters the Black Sea. The attack failed, but in 1696, with the help of Swiss, Dutch and Habsburg experts, he built a fleet on the Don River, cut the fortress off from supplies and reinforcements, and stormed it. The lesson Peter I drew was that he needed additional western expertise to create a navy and to modernize his archaic army.

In 1696–97, thinly disguised as a private citizen, Peter visited Holland, England, Germany, and Austria. There he learned how societies centuries ahead of Russia built ships, made munitions, and conducted government and diplomacy. He worked in the shipyards, eagerly questioned everyone he met about western naval and military technology, and drank steadily through the night with his Russian companions. When he returned to Russia he brought with him over a thousand Western experts—seaman, gunners, shipwrights, engineers, mathematicians, surgeons.

An outburst of xenophobia at home cut short his European tour. The *strel'tsy*, a barbarous and undisciplined palace guard that he had thwarted in his seizure of power in 1689, remained a threat. In 1696, in league with the "Old Believers" and distrustful of Peter's increasingly obvious intention of introducing Western innovations, the *strel'tsy* marched on the Kremlin. Peter hastened back to Moscow to find that trusted aides had suppressed the revolt. He then made an example of the rebels that would long haunt even the memories of his countrymen, long accustomed to indiscriminate bloodshed. The tsar executed over a thousand *strel'tsy* to the accompaniment of torture on a scale not seen since Ivan the Terrible.

He also determined to use his autocratic sovereign power to "westernize" his subjects externally, by force if need be. In 1699–1700 he forbade the traditional long robes and the beards that his subjects wore in the belief that God was bearded and man was made in his image. The tsar himself took a hand in the shaving of his courtiers. He fought the resulting xenophobic and Orthodox reaction with brutal repression. He also ended the seclusion of women and instituted western-style social gatherings of both sexes at which polite conversation and ballroom dancing rather than strong drink were the chief entertainments. His will to transform Russia brooked no opposition; when his son and heir Alexis showed himself a slothful devotee of tradition, Peter I had him arrested, tortured, and put to death in 1618.

But Peter I's priorities were above all military. He sought first to imitate Western power, not Western civilization. Beginning in 1699, he set up a new army using German and other foreign experts as officers. An overwhelming defeat by the Swedes at

Contemporary cartoon of Peter cutting the beard of a Russian noble. Those who kept their beards had to pay a tax and carry a license (below).

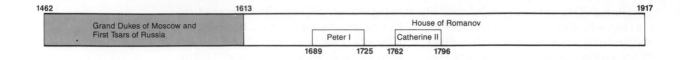

1462		1613				1917
Grand Dukes of Moscow and First Tsars of Russia		House of Romanov				
			Peter I	Catherine II		
		1689	1725	1762	1796	

Narva in 1700 only spurred him on; Russia had to either modernize its army, or perish. The tsar encouraged the vital iron industry of the Urals, set up cannon foundries, and created schools for gunnery, navigation, engineering, and officer training. By 1709, the year of his great victory over Charles XII of Sweden at Poltava, Russia had a modern army of over 100,000. By the end of Peter's reign in 1725 that army had swelled to 210,000 regulars and 100,000 auxiliaries that included the dreaded Cossack cavalry. The navy had grown from nothing to 24 ships of the line. Those were powerful forces indeed for a state with a population of only 8 million.

The army, the largest in eastern Europe, had the chance to achieve results, for Russia was at peace only one year in all of Peter's long reign. In the south it failed to hold Azov. Peter had to leave the Turks to his successors. But in the Great Northern War, the tsar seized

Peter the Great.

from Sweden the vital coastline on the Gulf of Finland. That gave him the "window on the sea," the direct contact with western Europe through the ice-free southern Baltic that was his primary geopolitical goal.

Peter's subjects, who bore the weight of his gigantic social engineering project, bought these military accomplishments dearly. The net effect of Peter's sometimes haphazard social and fiscal legislation was to divide a relatively complex society with a variety of subtle status gradations into two great classes—the "service nobility," and the more or less enserfed peasantry. A century after Peter I, a Russian intellectual could still quip bitterly that Russian society was divided into "slaves of the sovereign [the nobles], and slaves of the landlord [the serfs]; the former are called free only with regard to the latter."

Peter systematized the service nobility system he had inherited. All land-owners owed service, and he decreed in 1714 the hated innovation of primogeniture, which forced noble younger sons off the land and into the army and navy. By instituting a fourteen-step "Table of Ranks" of 1722, Peter defined nobility in terms of one criterion alone, service. He made explicit what Louis XIV and the Great Elector could only implicitly practice—that service to the state, not birth, determined rank. In Russia, a lieutenant's commission now automatically brought noble status. That provided a career leading to ennoblement for the ambitious sons of commoners and helped divert them into state service and away from commerce and industry.

But it was the peasantry, not the nobility, that paid most for Peter's innovations. In return for its service, the nobility gained a freer hand than ever before in dealing with serfs. A new tax census classified all doubtful cases as servile, thus increasing the number of serfs. And the state demanded from the peasantry forced labor, military service, and taxes on an unprecedented scale. Supporting the new army required conscription, on the model of Sweden. After 1705 each 20 households had to furnish one recruit every year. The state provided the new military industries with serfs and convicts as labor, while a new head tax ("soul tax") tripled both state income and the tax burden. Forced labor and taxation, by one estimate, extorted from each household the equivalent of 125 to 187 days of labor each year. The ultimate result was depopulation, as peasants died of their privations or fled to the Don Cossacks to the southeast.

After 1709 Peter moved the seat of government from Moscow to a new city built on conquered territory on the Gulf of Finland: St. Petersburg, named for his patron saint. That change was the symbol of the tsar's aim of rivaling the West. The new city faced west, and its nearby naval base, Kronstadt ("royal city" *in German*) claimed the mastery of the Baltic. The methods that created the new capital, and its price, were also characteristic both of Peter's work and of that of later autocrats who sought to imitate him both in Russia and in other backward states. St. Petersburg rose in an unhealthy marshland at the mouth of the Neva River and was a deliberate break with the Moscow-centered past. Peter compelled nobles and merchants to settle and build there. Construction proceeded rapidly through annual forced labor drafts of 20,000 peasants. Many perished from disease and exposure.

This new capital, founded upon the bones of dead peasants, became the center of a new bureaucratic structure that the tsar built haphazardly over the primitive central administration he had inherited. The western conception of "the state," as distinct from the private staff of the sovereign, now made its entry into Russian history. Peter set up provincial administrations, supervisory boards to coordinate the bureaucracy, and a "senate," or central administrative body tasked with interpreting his orders. He also created an organ, the *Preobrazhenskii Prikaz*, to ferret out "political crime," from tax evasion, to criticism of the tsar, to coup attempts. The deliberate vagueness of its charter, its sweeping authority, and its ruthless suppression of individuals for their political opinions rather than their deeds made it the ancestor of the modern police state.

The new Russian state that Peter created thus dominated its society in a way unknown even in Brandenburg-Prussia, much less in western Europe. The state mastered the Orthodox Church, already weakened by the great schism. After 1700 Peter neglected to appoint a patriarch and made the Church a mere department of his bureaucracy. The state defined the nobil-

Peter the Great: The Bronze Horseman

The first and greatest modern Russian poet, Aleksandr Sergeyevich Pushkin (1799–1837), summed up Peter's place in Russian history in "The Bronze Horseman" (1833), named for the tsar's statue at St. Petersburg.

That square, the lions, and him—the one
Who, bronzen countenance upslanted
Into the dusk aloft, sat still,
The one by whose portentous will
The city by the sea was planted . . .
How awesome in the gloom he rides!
What thought upon his brow resides!
His charger with what fiery mettle,
His form with what dark strength endowed!
Where will you gallop, charger proud,
Where next your plunging hoofbeats settle?
Oh, Destiny's great potentate!
Was it not thus, a towering idol
Hard by the chasm, with iron bridle
You reared up Russia to her fate?

From Alexander Pushkin, *Collected Narrative and Lyrical Poetry*, trans. by Walter Arndt (Ann Arbor: Ardis Publishers, 1984), p. 437.

ity by its service, and by demanding residence at St. Petersburg reinforced an already existing pattern of absentee landlordism that weakened the grip of the nobility on rural society. The state stunted the towns, and ensured that the small and timorous middle classes that eventually emerged would be dependent on state employment and state contracts.

The state then ordered its subjects to develop a consciousness, a public opinion. Peter was the first Russian sovereign to speak of "the common good." He founded Russia's first newspaper. He recognized that rivalling the West ultimately required the voluntary collaboration of his subjects and the development of economic and intellectual initiative *from below*. But as his successors discovered, initiative from below was a deadly threat to the autocracy's own power. That tension, the result of the grafting of Western technology and military institutions onto non-Western social and political structures, was a pattern much seen later. Its consequence was a cycle of repression, "thaw," and further repression that has continued—despite the leap from tsarist to Communist autocracy in 1917—to the present.

But that ultimate consequence of Peter's work was far in the future when he died in 1725. What he left was a Russian great power, a military giant, irrevocably part of the European state system. And his example created a tradition of dynamic autocracy, of brutal revolutions from above carried through by pitiless force, that later Russian rulers sought to emulate or surpass.

The Losers: Sweden and Poland

While Prussia grew and Russia transformed itself, their Swedish and Polish neighbors declined. Sweden had burst on Europe as a military power of first rank when Gustavus Adolphus had swept into Germany in 1630–31. The Baltic virtually became a Swedish lake, with Swedish imperial outposts that stretched from the Gulf of Finland to the North Sea. Copper, iron, and agriculture were Sweden's chief resources; superior cannon and muskets its chief military advantage. But Swedish power rested on shaky foundations. The country had a population of less than 2 million—not much larger than Brandenburg-Prussia or the Dutch Republic. The empire that Gustavus Adolphus had acquired was overextended; its enemies, from Russia and Poland to Prussia and Denmark, were hungry for revenge.

When young Charles XII (r. 1697–1718) came to the throne, a coalition of Russia, Poland, and Denmark pounced on his Baltic territories. But Charles proved a greater commander even than Gustavus Adolphus. He crushed the coalition's forces in a series of lightning campaigns. Then success intoxicated him. In 1708–09 he launched Sweden into a foolhardy attempt to smash Russia, and met devastating defeat at Poltava in the Ukraine. He subsequently escaped to Turkey, spent some years at the Ottoman court seeking allies, and died in the siege of an obscure Norwegian fortress in 1718. His meteoric career exhausted Sweden. In the peace settlements of 1719 to 1721 that ended this "Great Northern War," Hanover, Denmark, Prussia, and Russia divided Sweden's Baltic empire. Sweden retired for good into the ranks of the second-class powers.

Poland, an elective monarchy originally formed in 1386 through the union of the crowns of Poland and Lithuania, suffered a similar fate. Polish prosperity and culture had reached their peak in the sixteenth century. Roman Catholicism had linked Poland to western Europe and had conveyed the influence of the Renaissance, the Protestant revolt, and the Counter-Reformation. But by the beginning of the seventeenth century Poland's economic and political decline had begun.

In France, Prussia, and Russia the state tamed the nobility. In Poland the nobility gradually became the state, thanks to the elective character of the monarchy. Until the 1570s the Polish

The Baltic: A Swedish Lake   1621–1721

Swedish territory, 1621-1721

Swedish gains and losses, 1621-1721

nobility had usually elected the legal heirs of their monarchs, but thereafter they chose candidates that appeared to favor their own interests. By 1700 the nobility had deprived the monarchy of most of its powers, although petty German princes still sought election to gain the prestige of a royal title.

Noble power had consequences. It sunk the peasants more deeply in serfdom than anywhere else in Europe. It checked the small and weak towns, prevented the rise of urban middle classes, and froze the Polish economy in rural backwardness. Above all, it concentrated political power in the Polish Diet, which now represented only the nobility, since representatives of the towns no longer dared attend.

The Diet's procedure, tailor-made to preserve noble domination, was notorious—one negative vote, the *"liberum veto,"* could block any action. Moreover, the *liberum veto* allowed any member to "explode" a Diet session—to dissolve it and wipe out all legislation it had passed up to that moment. Of 57 Diets held in the century after 1652, all but nine "exploded," and in one case a member cast a veto simply to see what would happen. And if by some accident legislation did emerge from the Diet, no machinery existed to enforce it against the provincial assem-

Medals celebrating an abortive "Treaty of Eternal Peace" between Russia and Poland (1686). Left: King John Sobieski, Poland's last great king. Right: personifications of Poland and Russia.

blies of lesser nobles or the private estate jurisdictions of the landed magnates. John Sobieski (1674–96), a native Pole of high integrity, was the last great king. He saved Vienna from the Turks but failed to save Poland from its nobility. After him Poland declined into incoherence, and extinction at the hands of Austria, Russia, and Prussia between 1772 and 1795.

ABSOLUTISM, CONSTITUTIONALISM, AND THE BALANCE OF POWER

The half century from 1660 to 1715 was thus a period of dramatic change. Internally, absolute divine-right monarchy reached its height in the France of Louis XIV. Powers from Madrid to St. Petersburg attempted to imitate the French model. Nevertheless, a few smaller peoples such as the Swiss had rejected monarchy in favor of republican government. The Dutch "sea beggars" had even shown that a republic could compete in the great power

arena. But it took England's Glorious Revolution and Marlborough's victories to demonstrate to Europe that even the very greatest powers could choose alternatives to absolute monarchy.

Externally, relations between states and the workings of the balance of power almost completely superseded the religious-ideological conflicts that had rent Europe before 1648. France's bid for mastery after 1672 provoked the rise of England and Austria as great powers. Two great empires of the sixteenth century, Spain and the Ottoman Turks, continued their decline. Two peoples of limited resources and numbers, the Dutch and the Swedes, briefly claimed great power status in the mid-seventeenth century, but lacked staying power. Two new powers appeared in eastern Europe to join the balance—military Prussia and semi-barbaric Russia. The rivalries of these states—Britain against France, France against Austria, Austria against Prussia, Austria and Russia against the Ottoman Empire—were the forces that moved European war and diplomacy after 1715.

Suggestions for Further Reading

Western Europe

J. Stoye, *Europe Unfolding, 1648–1688* (1969), and J. B. Wolf, *The Emergence of the Great Powers, 1685–1715* (1951), provide useful introductions, but see also W. Doyle, *The Old European Order, 1660–1800* (1978).

C. J. Friedrich and C. Blitzer, *The Age of Power* (1957), covers the general theme of this chapter. R. Hatton, *Europe in the Age of Louis XIV* (1969), is excellent on social history. P. Goubert, *Louis XIV and Twenty Million*

Frenchmen (1970), wittily relates the career of the king to the social history of France. See also J. B. Wolf, *Louis XIV* (1968), and W. H. Lewis, *The Splendid Century* (1954), an elegant account of the reign. On England, see especially C. Hill, *The Century of Revolution, 1603–* 1714 (1961). G. N. Clark, *The Later Stuarts, 1660–1714* (1934), is a fine synthesis. C. H. Wilson, *England's Apprenticeship, 1603–1763* (1965), covers England's emergence as a great power.

Eastern Europe

For the lands east of the Elbe, see especially S. H. Cross, *Slavic Civilization Through the Ages* (1948), and O. Halecki, *Borderlands of Western Civilization* (1952). On Germany, see H. Holborn, *A History of Modern Germany, 1648–1840* (1964). R. W. J. Evans, *The Making of the Habsburg Monarchy* (1979), and H. G. Koenigsberger, *The Habsburgs and Europe* (1971), are useful surveys. On Prussia, S. B. Fay and K. Epstein, *The Rise of* *Brandenburg-Prussia to 1786* (1937, 1964), is concise. See also F. Carsten, *The Origins of Prussia* (1954). B. H. Sumner, *Peter the Great and the Emergence of Russia* (1950), is a useful short account. For analysis, see especially R. Pipes, *Russia under the Old Regime* (1974), and J. Blum, *Lord and Peasant in Russia from the Ninth to the Nineteenth Century* (1961).

21
The Scientific Revolution and the Enlightenment

*U*ntil the seventeenth century the growth of knowledge about nature had been slow, fumbling, and discontinuous. Scholars had observed natural phenomena, had in many cases recorded them, and had sometimes derived useful generalizations from those observations. But "experiments" in the modern sense had been largely absent, and scientific inquiry was scarcely distinguishable from theological speculation.

That changed. By the eighteenth century, the age of rapidly broadening and deepening knowledge that became known as the Enlightenment, the West had accumulated a large body of empirically verifiable principles that allowed the prediction and manipulation of nature. That type of knowledge has continued to accumulate, with revolutionary effect. The ever-accelerating understanding of and mastery over nature, for good or ill, was the achievement of the West, the first civilization in history to make a clear distinction between science on the one hand and religion or magic on the other.

THE SCIENTIFIC REVOLUTION

A new method of inquiry, later called the "scientific method," emerged from the universities of Western Europe in the late thirteenth and fourteenth centuries, and achieved wide currency in western Europe after 1600. The new method was essentially a combination of two elements: careful observation and controlled experiment, and rational interpretation of the results of observation and experimentation, preferably using mathematics. That was the origin of modern science, an endeavor that a great twentieth-century mathematician-philosopher described as the "vehement and passionate interest in the relation of general principles to irreducible and stubborn facts."

The Medieval Universe

Precisely *why* the West took the lead in scientific speculation over the other great civilizations, China, Islam, and

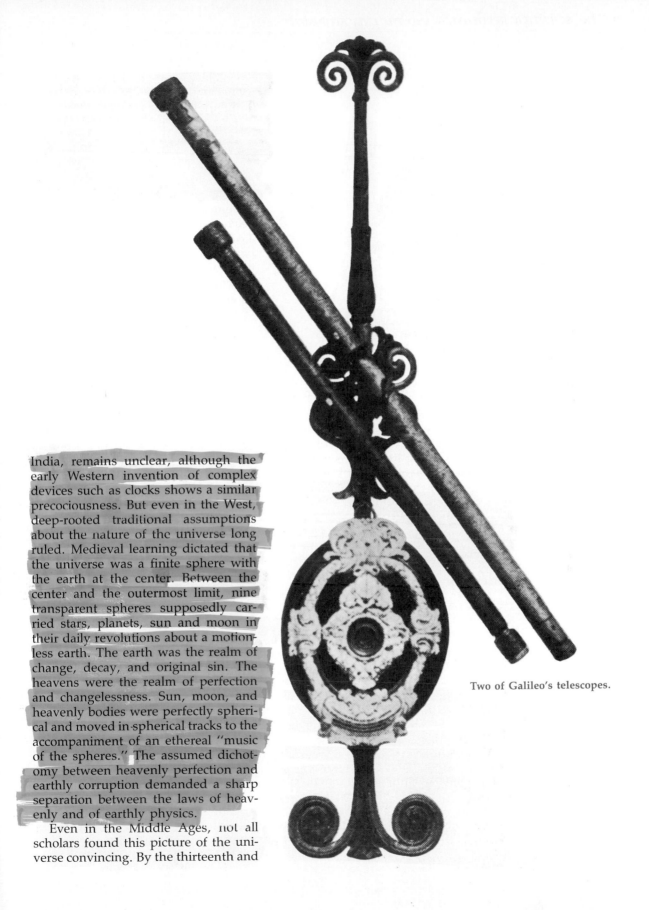

Two of Galileo's telescopes.

India, remains unclear, although the early Western invention of complex devices such as clocks shows a similar precociousness. But even in the West, deep-rooted traditional assumptions about the nature of the universe long ruled. Medieval learning dictated that the universe was a finite sphere with the earth at the center. Between the center and the outermost limit, nine transparent spheres supposedly carried stars, planets, sun and moon in their daily revolutions about a motionless earth. The earth was the realm of change, decay, and original sin. The heavens were the realm of perfection and changelessness. Sun, moon, and heavenly bodies were perfectly spherical and moved in spherical tracks to the accompaniment of an ethereal "music of the spheres." The assumed dichotomy between heavenly perfection and earthly corruption demanded a sharp separation between the laws of heavenly and of earthly physics.

Even in the Middle Ages, not all scholars found this picture of the universe convincing. By the thirteenth and

The observatory of the Danish astronomer Tycho Brahe was the finest of the sixteenth century. Note the domes protecting the instruments.

fourteenth centuries a small but increasing number had begun to question it, including Franciscans, perhaps inspired by their founder's sensitive feeling for nature. The study of the Greco-Arabic scientific texts that had reached the West stimulated a group of scholars at Oxford and Paris to apply mathematical reasoning to problems of physics and astronomy, such as accelerated motion. Professors at the University of Padua continued these speculations in the fifteen and sixteenth centuries. At Padua, a center of medical training for three centuries, scholars vigorously debated the proper method of studying nature in the course of arguments about Aristotle. Medieval universities such as Oxford, Paris, and Padua kept interest in science alive and nurtured the first faint beginnings of the scientific revolution.

Most Europeans of 1500, however, did not question the Greek authorities, who had decreed that the normal state of everything in the universe was a state of rest. Aristotle had said that bodies moved only if a mover pushed or pulled them. Galen of Pergamum, in the second century A.D., had described

the anatomy of the human body so convincingly that doctors still saw it through his eyes. In that same century, the Greco-Egyptian astonomer Ptolemy had systematized a mathematical description of the observed irregularities of the movements of the planets so ingenious that European authorities saw no need to discard it until after 1500. Ptolemy assumed that all motion in the heavens was circular and proceeded at a constant rate. But since the observed pattern of actual planetary motion in the heavens was not precisely circular, Ptolemy had invented the "epicycle," an additional small circle in which the planet moved while traveling around the circumference of its larger "sphere" around the earth. He and his successors needed 80 epicycles to force the observed motion of the planets to fit the theory, but in the end Ptolemy's system explained what astronomers saw. Even more important, it permitted the prediction of lunar and planetary motion with some precision. At the close of the Middle Ages, few scholars saw much need to improve upon the observations and theories of the ancients.

The Background of Change

Nevertheless, forces in European society in the fourteenth, fifteenth, and sixteenth centuries prepared the way for a challenge to this orthodoxy. Artisans and craftsmen gradually adopted techniques more advanced than those of their medieval predecessors. The development of the glass industry and the invention of the lens at some point before 1300, to take but one example, gave the promise of vastly extending humanity's ability to observe natural processes. Breakthroughs in shipbuilding and navigation (see p. 497) permitted the voyages of discovery, which in turn stimulated interest in nature generally.

The Renaissance, with its emphasis on literature and art and its veneration for the wisdom of the ancients, was in some respects antiscientific. But the

Humanists were interested in Greek scientific texts as well as in Greek literature, and Renaissance patrons of the arts were also patrons of inventors and technicians. Humanistic study revealed that ancient scientific authorities had differed among themselves on key issues, just at the moment when the authority of Galen and Ptolemy was becoming shaky for other reasons. Anatomical studies by the great Renaissance artists and the increasing practice of dissection suggested that Galen had made mistakes. Growing skill in mathematics exposed the clumsiness of Ptolemy's explanations. By the opening years of the sixteenth century, conditions were ripe for a dramatic shift in the West's underlying assumptions about the universe.

1543: *Vesalius and Copernicus*

In 1543 two notable scientific works heralded the end of Medieval science. Andreas Vesalius, a Flemish anatomist at the University of Padua, published *On the Structure of the Human Body,* a marvelously careful description of human anatomy based on direct observation during dissection, and illustrated with graphic and accurate plates. Vesalius did not free himself completely from the authority of Galen, nor did his book offer much theoretical insight. But it was an influential example of the power of observation.

Even more powerful in its ultimate effect was the work of a Polish scholar, Mikolaj Kopérnik, better known as Copernicus. *On the Revolutions of the Heavenly Bodies* was a brilliant mathematical treatise that showed how to reduce Ptolemy's 80 epicycles to 34 by assuming that the earth turned on its axis once a day and moved around the sun once a year. Unlike Vesalius, Copernicus was not primarily an observer. During study at Padua in the early years of the century he had learned that some ancient authorities had held that the earth moved. That assumption made the motions of the moon and planets far simpler to explain mathematically than the accepted earth-centered theory. Copernicus, following the Medieval notion that "nature always acts in the simplest ways," eventually discarded Ptolemy on grounds of logic, rather than from observation. His ideas gradually spread.

In 1600, the Inquisition tried a former monk named Giordano Bruno as a heretic and burned him at the stake in Rome. He had published works arguing that the universe was not finite but infinite in extent, that numberless suns and planets like our own filled it, and that God was equally present in every planet or atom in the cosmos. He also maintained that the existence of the infinite made it impossible to arrive at absolute truth, or find limits to the extent of knowledge. Co-

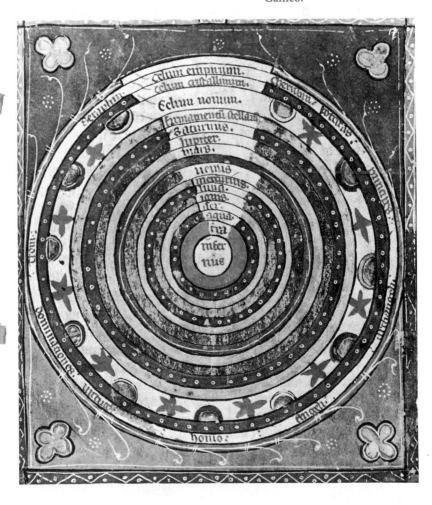

Ptolemy's earth-centered and finite cosmos fit both available astronomical evidence and prevailing theological dogmas well enough to endure from the second century A.D. until the discoveries of Copernicus and Galileo.

Scientific revolutionaries of the seventeenth century: Francis Bacon (above) and René Descartes.

pernicus had inspired him, although Copernicus himself believed in the finite sphere of the fixed stars and the uniqueness of the earth. Despite the fires of the Inquisition, Bruno's intuition of the infinity of the universe ultimately prevailed. It was the beginning of modern cosmology.

The Purposes and Method of Science: Bacon and Descartes

Two major prophets of the early Scientific Revolution, Francis Bacon (1561–1626) and René Descartes (1596–1650) followed precursors such as Copernicus. Bacon, an English lawyer, statesman, and essayist, waged a vigorous scholarly battle against the deductive method of Medieval scholasticism, which began with premises usually taken on authority and deduced from them their logical consequences. That might help to organize truths already known, argued Bacon, but it could never discover new truths. Only inductive reasoning, starting from the direct observation of phenomena and developing from them principles that explained those observations, could produce new truths.

Bacon set a practical goal for science, the "domination" of humanity over nature. He pictured an imaginary future society of scientists whose end was to benefit mankind by conducting hundreds of experiments that discovered useful facts. Bacon failed to appreciate the importance of mathematical models in theoretical analysis, and he found Copernicus unconvincing. Although he praised experimentation, he performed almost no experiments and collected his data in the traditional way, from books. His writings nevertheless dramatized the importance of empirical research. The founding in 1662 of the Royal Society of London, the first scientific society in England, owed much to Bacon's inspiration. He was the remote ancestor of the great laboratories and team research projects of the twentieth century. His goal, the

mastery of nature through rational analysis, has—despite continuing criticism of its alleged arrogance—marked the West off from the other historic civilizations.

Descartes, a French mathematician and philosopher, was an even more important figure than Bacon, but he lacked Bacon's intuitive understanding of the need for observation. To Descartes, the excitement of science lay in mathematical analysis and theory. In a famous autobiographical account, he told how the literature and philosophy that he had studied as a youth had left him unsatisfied because he reached no *certain* conclusions. By contrast, the precision and certainty of mathematics aroused his enthusiasm. He set out to discover a mathematical "method of rightly conducting the reason and discovering truth in the sciences."

In November 1619, in a moment of intuition, he saw the exact correspondence between geometry and algebra—the truth that equations and curves on graphs were interchangeable. That intoxicating vision suggested to him a new way of grasping ultimate truth. If humanity systematically doubted all notions based on authority or custom and started with clear and precise ideas known to be true, it might deduce systematically the entire universe from a few simple principles, just as he had derived curves from equations.

Descartes was one of the first to believe that science could save humanity. His enthusiasm was infectious, and outran the knowledge available in the seventeenth century. He reduced the universe, including the human body, to a mathematically intelligible machine. Only the human intellect, he believed, resisted mathematical description. He therefore defined it as being outside the world of matter: mind comprehended the world but did not exist in it. His generalizations in astronomy, physics, and anatomy were often premature, and his passion for system building went far beyond his capacity to confirm generalizations by experiment. He did important work in optics, but that in no way confirmed his far-ranging theories.

Nevertheless, Descartes' enthusiasm for scientific "method," his belief that mathematics could describe all phenomena, and his insistence on systematic doubt of all earlier theorizing left a profound mark on the scientific thinking of three centuries that followed. Descartes made it easier for his successors to reject old ideas, and they gradually came to accept his belief that mathematics must be the language of science.

Experiment and Mathematics

Bacon and Descartes were too optimistic. Bacon thought that a generation of determined experimentation would establish a solid structure of knowledge about the universe. Descartes expected that a few basic mathematical axioms would soon lead, by deduction, to a universal science. He also believed in a universe far simpler than it now appears. One of Descartes' pupils even described the world as a gigantic piece of clockwork.

Meanwhile, experimentation and mathematics were developing steadily in the hands of a growing host of scientists. William Gilbert (1544–1603), court physician to Elizabeth I, coined the word "electricity" and deduced that the earth itself was a huge magnet. His *De magnete* (1600) remained the foremost work on magnetism until the early nineteenth century. William Harvey (1578–1627), who had studied at Padua, argued in a work published in 1628 that the blood must circulate from arteries to veins to heart, thence to the lungs, back to the heart and on once more to the arteries. He did this by estimating the amount of blood the heart pumped in a minute and arguing that it must go somewhere. Later in the century the new microscope revealed the tiny capillaries that actually connect arteries to veins.

Harvey Discovers the Circulation of the Blood

Since calculations and visual demonstrations have confirmed all my suppositions, to wit, that the blood is passed through the lungs and the heart by the pulsation of the ventricles, is forcibly ejected to all parts of the body, therein steals into the veins . . . flows back everywhere . . . from small veins into larger ones, and thence comes at last into the vena cava and to the auricle of the heart; all this too in such amounts that it cannot be supplied from the ingesta [food] and is also in greater bulk than would suffice for nutrition.

I am obliged to conclude that in all animals the blood is driven around a circuit with an unceasing, circular sort of motion, that this is an activity of the heart which it carries out by virtue of its pulsation, and that in sum it constitutes the sole cause for the heart's pulsatile movement.

From C. C. Gillispie, *The Edge of Objectivity* (Princeton, N.J.: Princeton University Press, 1960), p. 71.

Evangelista Torricelli (1608–47), Blaise Pascal, and others investigated the ancient proposition, long believed by most scholars, that "nature abhors a vacuum." They created vacuums in test tubes, invented the barometer, and discovered that the pressure of the atmosphere varies between sea level and mountain top. They proved inherited wisdom false, and their work showed a growing precision in observation and an increasing sophistication in controlling experiments and in quantifying their results.

Mathematics likewise rapidly advanced. The invention of decimals and of logarithms early in the century facilitated calculation. Pascal inaugurated the study of probability. At the end of the century Sir Isaac Newton and Baron Gottfried Wilhelm von Leibniz (1646–1716) crowned the work of many others by simultaneously but separately inventing the calculus, which provided the first mathematical method for describing accelerating or decelerating motion.

Kepler: The Foundations of Celestial Mechanics

It was in astronomy and physics that observational techniques and mathematical methods first united—producing results of a beauty and explanatory power that shattered for good all traditional notions of the place of science in human knowledge and of humanity in the universe.

The German astronomer Johannes Kepler (1571–1630) found discrepancies in Copernicus's theory troubling, although he nevertheless believed in it. He worked from the observations of his master, the Danish astronomer Tycho Brahe (1546–1601), which were far more accurate than those available to Copernicus. Brahe's data ultimately caused Kepler to discard reluctantly the universal belief, which Copernicus had not challenged, that heavenly bodies moved in circles.

Kepler concluded that the ellipse, whose properties geometricians had studied since the time of the Greeks, fitted Brahe's observations of Mars, the planet whose motion most contradicted the Ptolemaic and Copernican systems. The orbits of the planets, Kepler suggested, were elliptical, with the sun at one of the two foci of the ellipse. Further, he demonstrated that a line from the sun to a planet swept out equal areas of the ellipse in equal times and that the cube of the distance of each planet from the sun was proportional to the square of the time of its revolution. That was astounding proof of the intuition of Descartes and others that nature was in some mysterious sense mathematical. A geometrical figure, studied for centuries as an abstract form, "fit" the facts of nature. By implication, nature was perhaps itself a machine, intelligible to the careful observer equipped with mathematics.

The New Universe: Galileo

Kepler's work describing many of his findings appeared in 1609. During that same year a professor at Padua and Pisa, Galileo Galilei (1564–1642), turned on the heavens a newly invented instrument, the telescope. He soon published an account of what he saw. The changeless perfection and perfect sphericity of the heavenly bodies had dissolved before his gaze. He saw that the moon had craters and mountains, that spots moved on the sun, that rings encircled Saturn, and that Jupiter had four moons of its own. A bright new star—a supernova—had already appeared in 1572, and Brahe had noted it. In 1577 a new comet had cut a path through what should have been unchanging crystalline spheres. Now Galileo's telescope shattered forever the immutable, finite, spherical universe of the Middle Ages. Thoughtful scholars suspected that Bruno had been right. Humanity was looking out into infinite space, at a sparse population of stars like the sun that might themselves have solar systems.

The Medieval distinction between terrestrial and celestial physics was apparently dissolving. The moon and sun were not perfect globes and the stars were not changeless. Nor was the earth any longer the motionless center of the universe. The earth, like Mars and Jupiter, was a planet circling the sun against a backdrop of silent, infinite space. Perhaps the same forces and laws operated both on earth and in the heavens.

Such views soon attracted the wrath of the Church of the Counter-Reformation, which had denounced the Copernican theory in 1616. The Roman Inquisition condemned Galileo himself in 1632, threatened him with torture, and forced him to recant. The legend soon arose that after retracting his "heretical" view that the earth moved around the sun, he nevertheless muttered stubbornly under his breath *"Eppur si muove"*—"It *does* move." Nor could the Inquisition suppress Galileo's brilliantly written dialogues, which contributed mightily to the overthrow not only of Ptolemy in favor of Copernicus, but also of Aristotle in favor of a new physics.

The speculations of the fourteenth-century Franciscans inspired Galileo's physics, but he was far more thorough and accurate than they in developing mathematical formulas to describe motion. He worked out by experiment the law of falling bodies—the distance fallen increases as the square of the time fallen. He saw that projectiles followed parabolic paths that were the resultant of the two forces acting upon the projectile—the initial impetus that launched it and the downward pull of the earth. That insight was the beginning of modern ballistics, the scientific foundation of the new warfare.

Galileo also came close to formulating the key concept of modern mechanics, the law of inertia: that bodies tend to remain at rest or to continue in motion in straight lines unless outside forces act upon them. That deceptively simple proposition—so fundamentally different from Aristotle's conception of motion as the result of some mover's action—was the source of the law of gravitation. Galileo prepared the way, but it was a man born in the year Galileo died that made that decisive breakthrough.

The Synthesis of Celestial and Terrestrial Mechanics: Newton

Sir Isaac Newton (1642–1727), the greatest figure of the Scientific Revolution, was the man who married Kepler's astronomy to Galileo's mechanics, broke down all distinctions between celestial and terrestrial physics, and accomplished at least part of Descartes' dream of establishing a "universal science." A fundamental intuition came to Newton while he was still a student in his twenties at Cambridge University: the force that bends the moon into its orbit about the earth must be the same force that pulls an apple from its branch to the ground. A reciprocal force of attraction between every body in the universe must exist, and that force—although as yet inexplicable—must be calculable.

Newton's earliest calculations came close enough to mathematical proof to persuade him that the same force indeed operated on the moon and on the apple, and that this force varied "directly as the product of the masses" involved and "inversely as the square of the distance" separating those masses. For some time after formulating this "law" of gravitation in 1664–66 he seems to have lost interest. But twenty years later a friend, the astronomer Edmund Halley (who calculated the orbit of the famous comet) persuaded Newton to publish. Newton developed the necessary mathematics—the calculus—to prove his theory to his own satisfaction. He published his conclusions in 1687 in his *Philosophiae naturalis principia mathematica*, the "mathematical principles of natural philosophy." It was one of the most influential books in the history of human thought.

To scientists Newton's law of gravitation provided a simple and elegant explanation of a growing mass of data in astronomy and physics, and laid the foundations of future research in both sciences. Further, Newton improved on Bacon and Descartes by giving the scientific method its classic formulation in his fourth "Rule of Reasoning":

> In experimental philosophy [science] we are to look upon propositions collected by general induction from phenomena as accurately or very nearly true, notwithstanding any contrary hypotheses [theories] that may be imagined, till such time as other phenomena occur, by which they may either be made more accurate or liable to exceptions.

Newton's support of the experimental or inductive approach was aimed against the premature generalizing, the theoretical "system[s] . . . little better than a Romance," of Descartes and his followers. But Newton, unlike Bacon, was fully convinced of the necessity of mathematical theory. Newton combined at last both celestial and terres-

The greatest scientific revolutionary of all: Sir Isaac Newton, painted by Kneller.

Newton invented and built this first reflecting telescope.

trial physics on the one hand, and empirical observation and mathematical interpretation on the other.

The Newtonian Universe

News of Newton's work spread rapidly among laymen, thanks to popular scientific works that soon began pouring from the presses of London and Amsterdam. The new universe that Newton disclosed was far different from the comforting finite universe of the Middle Ages. Bodies moved through infinite space in response to predictable, universally operating forces. Mass, force, and motion were the key concepts, and mathematics made them intelligible.

The question "Why?" had obsessed the scholars of the Middle Ages, who had felt they understood a natural phenomenon once they had discovered its end or purpose. Seventeenth-century scientists limited themselves to asking "How?" The discovery of regular patterns in natural processes satisfied most of them. The world of Kepler, Galileo, and Newton was a vast machine, working according to laws expressible in mathematics, laws intelligible to anyone who followed the proper experimental and mathematical methods. The telescope continued to reveal an ever-larger portion of an apparently infinite cosmos. The new astronomy, after displacing the earth as the center of the universe, displaced the sun as well. The microscope, after the 1660s, began to reveal the wonders of the infinitely small foundations of life—bacteria, spermatozoa, cells, capillaries.

The question "Why?" nevertheless remained unanswered. What was the place of God and of humanity in this universe? That question did not become acute until the eighteenth century. No prominent seventeenth-century scientist thought that he was reading God out of the universe. Descartes considered himself a good Catholic and apparently did not see the theological dangers inherent in his sharp separation of the world of matter from the world of mind. Newton spent many of his later years absorbed in theological speculation and alchemy. The border between science and religion or magic was still fluid, and contradictions between faith and science were not clearly evident to most seventeenth-century scientists, or to their audience.

The French philosopher-scientist Blaise Pascal (1623–62), inventor of probability theory and of the first calculating machine, and contributor to fields as diverse as the calculus and the dynamics of gases and fluids, indeed attempted a synthesis between faith and the new sciences that were now revealing the infinitely great and the infinitesimally small. For Pascal, "the whole visible world [was] only an imperceptible atom in the ample bosom of nature," and the universe "an infinite sphere, the center of which is everywhere, the circumference nowhere." "The eternal silence of these infinite spaces frightens me," he confessed. Yet to examine a mite, "with its minute body and parts incomparably more minute, limbs with their joints, veins in the limbs, blood in the veins, humors in the blood, drops in the humors, vapors in the drops," was equally astonishing. "What is man in nature? A Nothing in comparison with the Infinite, an All in comparison with the Nothing, a mean between nothing and everything." Pascal related the new universe explicitly to Christianity, to Christ's sacrifice on the cross which made humanity, despite its apparent insignificance, the greatest presence in the universe beside God. Others soon saw less need to invoke Christianity.

By the later seventeenth century the hold of religious orthodoxy on Europe's intellectual elite was beginning to weaken. Religious authorities could no longer simply forbid scientific speculation or experiment. The burning or torture of "heretics" such as Giordano Bruno slowly went out of fashion, except in Spain. And scientists themselves began to demarcate their activities sharply from questions of faith. The charters of the many scientific societies and academies that sprang up throughout Europe during the century usually contained clauses forbidding purely theological or political discussion and establishing that the group would not investigate "ultimate" or "final" causes.

The earliest history of the Royal Society of London, published in 1667, suggests that scientific discussions offered a peculiar attraction to thoughtful individuals during and after a fanatically bitter religious and civil war such as the English Revolution. Science, which by definition dealt with the empirically verifiable, might thereby become politically and theologically neutral and benefit humanity in practical ways. Scientific truth gradually emerged as an alternative to theological truth. It was not entirely accidental that modern science arose as religious warfare went out of fashion, amid general revulsion at the devastation that fanaticism had wrought.

Nevertheless, Newton's new "world picture" did not explicitly contradict religious feeling. Some indeed found in the mechanistic universe a source of religious awe. Baruch or Benedict Spinoza (1632–77), an Amsterdam lens grinder and philosopher descended from the Jewish communities that Spain had expelled, concluded that the new universe of mass, force, and motion, operating in strict obedience to inexorable laws, *was* God. Spinoza saw no need to consider God as above, behind, or beyond nature, as a "free cause" apart from natural law. God was not "Creator" or "Redeemer," but a "God *or* Nature" that included all being and incarnated natural law: "God never can decree, nor ever would have decreed, anything but what is; God did not exist before his decrees, and would not exist without them." Humanity, like all else, was part of the natural order and thus of God, and wisdom consisted of contemplating that order with serenity and delight.

Both Jewish and Christian contemporaries considered Spinoza a dangerous atheistic radical, although he was the mildest, kindliest, and most optimistic of men. Most of his works emerged in print only after his death. Contemporaries pointed out that to claim that humanity was part of God made it difficult to explain evil. Later critics discerned in "Whatever is, is in God" a dangerous fatalism. But his notion of religion was destined to have great influence in the eighteenth century.

THE CULTURE OF THE BAROQUE

The age of the scientific revolution was also, especially in the Catholic areas of the Continent, the age of the "baroque" style in the visual arts. The baroque sprang up in the later sixteenth century, reached its climax about the middle of the seventeenth, and came to its end around the middle of the eighteenth. Eighteenth-century critics invented the term *baroque* (French for "odd" or "irregular"), after tastes had again changed, to stigmatize seventeenth-century art as a grotesque corruption of Renaissance styles. But by the late nineteenth century critics had come to consider the baroque a great achievement. More than most styles, it is difficult to define because it reflected the contrasts and contradictions of seventeenth-century culture as a whole—religious ecstasy and worldly sensuality, credulity and rationalism, violence and respect for order.

Baroque painters and sculptors portrayed voluptuous women in repose, heroes in battle, and saints in ecstasy with equal skill and zest. In general, the dominant notes of the baroque were tension and conflict, and a penchant for the grandiose and dramatic. Renaissance painters and writers had been interested in humanity itself. Ba-

The German high baroque: Vierzehnheiligen Church in Weiss, Bavaria.

trayed figures in a space bathed in and suffused with light. The greatest of Dutch painters, Rembrandt van Rijn (1606–69), spotlighted figures in the midst of darkened space, while others pictured them floating through apparently infinite voids. To baroque artists the supernatural was natural. The scientists' concern with mass, force, and motion paralleled the painters' and poets' concern with individuals caught in the tension between elemental forces. The typical hero of baroque literature, critics have suggested, is Satan in John Milton's *Paradise Lost* (1667), the only great epic poem in English. Swayed by colossal passions, Satan moves through vast three-dimensional spaces, and bends the forces of the universe to serve his implacable will to domination: "To reign is worth ambition though in hell:/Better to reign in hell than serve in heav'n." But God nevertheless frustrates Satan's designs in the end.

The most typical, although not usually the most beautiful products of baroque architecture were the great palaces: Versailles and the remodeled Louvre in France, Schönbrunn in Austria, or Blenheim, the regal residence in England that Marlborough received for his victories. The style of these buildings was fundamentally Renaissance-classical, but grander, more ornate, and above all larger, often to the point of excess. As with the many descendants of Versailles, the neo-classical official buildings of later centuries, excess served a political purpose. Sheer mass emphasized the power of the state. In this, as in much else, Louis XIV led the way. Even some baroque religious architecture, such as the massive elliptical colonnades that the great Giovanni Lorenzo Bernini (1598–1680) erected to frame St. Peter's in Rome, conveyed the majesty of God rather than his mercy.

The most original creation of the baroque were the operas that originated in Italy early in the seventeenth century. Drama set to music had existed in the West since the twelfth cen-

roque artists depicted the conflicts of humanity against the universe, of man against man, and of man within himself on a tragic and heroic scale.

Instructive parallels exist between the thought-worlds of the baroque artists and those of the seventeenth-century scientists. Galileo and Newton studied bodies or masses moving through space under the influence of conflicting forces such as gravitation and centrifugal force. To the great French dramatists of the age—Corneille, Racine, and Molière—the objects of study were typical human beings torn between conflicting passions, such as love and duty. Space intrigued baroque painters. The Dutch master Jan Vermeer (1632–75) por-

tury. But the music had been essentially choral and polyphonic until around 1600, when a group of Florentine composers devised a *"dramma per musica"* (drama through music) in which the characters sang their parts as simple melodies without choral accompaniment. Opera immediately became, and has remained, a vast popular success. The grandiose and palatial stage settings, the dramatic conflicts of the action, and the emotional power of the music exactly suited the taste of the period. Italian composers led the way until the end of the seventeenth century—Claudio Monteverdi (1567–1643), Girolamo Frescobaldi (1583–1643), Alessandro Scarlatti (1660–1725), and the greatest master of Italian Baroque music, Antonio Vivaldi (1675–1741). But it was an Englishman, Henry Purcell (1658?–95), who wrote the most moving opera of the century, *Dido and Aeneas* (1687).

SEVENTEENTH-CENTURY THOUGHT ABOUT HUMANITY

While the outlook of the vast majority of the population of western Europe remained Medieval, the most adventurous minds of the seventeenth century developed notions about humanity that rested on Renaissance views but pressed beyond them. Their conceptions fall conveniently into three categories: individualism, relativism, and a rationalism tempered with empiricism.

Individualism

Radical thinkers of the seventeenth century took an increasingly individualist view of man in society. The most intense Christian piety of the period—whether it was the Catholic devotion preached by St. François de Sales, the stern conscience of the Puritans and Jansenists, or the warm inner conviction of the German Pietists—was highly individualistic. That trend was equally evident in political theory. The fashion was to start with the individual and then seek explanations of and justifications for the existence of societies and states.

Supporters of the divine-right theory of kingship remained numerous, but by mid-century the notion of an explicit or implicit "contract" between people and ruler was widespread. Hobbes and a few others that included Spinoza argued that this contract, once made, was irrevocable, and bound the ruled but not the ruler. Others, like the Parliamentarians in the English Civil War and John Locke in political philosophy, argued for a right of rebellion against rulers who broke the terms of the contract by acting against the general welfare.

The idea of a "social contract" soon took its place by the side of that of a "political contract." Society, according to social contract theorists, was itself the result of a voluntary agreement among individuals who had been absolutely independent in their original "state of nature." The two ideas mixed, somewhat confusedly, in Locke and later political philosophers. In both contracts, the individual with his rights and his "natural" independence logically came first; then came society or the state. The more radical thinkers of the seventeenth century thus came to think of society as an artificial organization of independent individuals that rested on the consent of those individuals. That was a radical break with the

Opera singers of the Baroque. Detail from an opera setting drawn by Ludovico Burnacinia, Vienna (1674).

Medieval conception of society as an organism or a "body" of which individuals were mere "members," each with an assigned place.

Relativism

The greatest thinkers of the Middle Ages were confident that the peoples of Christendom were God's chosen people, and that divine revelation gave humanity all necessary truths. But that self-assurance weakened during the sixteenth and seventeenth centuries, thanks to Humanism, to the voyages of discovery, and to the development of science.

Humanism had begun to reveal Greco-Roman civilization in historical perspective. Ancient literature, art, and historical writing brought alive a long dead society that offered numerous alternatives to the Medieval Christian system of belief. The Renaissance had first created the modern disciplines of history, archaeology, and philology. Seventeenth-century scholars broadened and deepened them. That steady development slowly impressed on thoughtful Europeans that other societies had existed in other times with values, beliefs, and institutions quite different from their own. That recognition was the origin of the concept of historical relativism, of the notion that value systems—including those of Christian Europe—were historical phenomena subject to change.

The age of discovery added to historical relativism a geographical counterpart. The discovery in America and Asia of other societies shattered European provincialism. The tribal hunter-gatherers of America and Africa, the urban civilizations of Aztecs and Incas, and the great empires of Asia with their advanced arts and amenities inspired study and reflection. Perhaps the "noble savages" of the New World were happier than the more cultured but "corrupted" Christians of Europe. Perhaps Persian sages and Chinese philosophers had something to teach Christians. Each society had different standards—was any value system grounded on anything more solid than custom? Doubts on these points affected increasing numbers of European thinkers in the seventeenth and eighteenth centuries. And scientific discovery likewise widened their vision of humanity's place in nature. European Christianity was not alone in time and space, and humanity itself might not be alone in the universe.

The work of Pierre Bayle (1647–1706), the great scholarly skeptic of the later seventeenth century, exemplifies the results of historical study, geographical exploration, and scientific discovery. Bayle was born a Huguenot, briefly converted to Catholicism, and then renounced all orthodox belief when his brother died in a French dungeon during an attempt at forced conversion. Bayle took up residence in the relatively tolerant Dutch Netherlands and devoted the latter part of his life to a crusade against superstition, religious intolerance, and dogma of all kinds. In 1697 he published a huge rambling book, the *Historical and Critical Dictionary*, which had enormous influence on eighteenth-century thought. Into the book he poured a relativism and skepticism acquired through extensive historical study, an amateur knowledge of science, and experience.

He defied convention by insisting that religion and political stability were not inseparable—atheists could be good citizens. He denounced religious conversions by force. He ridiculed astrology, a form of superstition even more current then than now. He derided tales of miracles. He distrusted all historical authorities, including the writers of the Old Testament, unless their account of events was inherently credible. An admirer of Descartes, his test of truth was "reason", and many scriptural accounts failed that rigorous test. Bayle was the most destructive critic of his generation. His war against traditional religion replaced, and in part derived from, the scarcely ended wars of religion.

Rationalism and Empiricism

The leading thinkers of the seventeenth century began a process that reached completion only in the eighteenth century by replacing the lost certainties of religious belief with a new object of worship—reason. It was the faculty that in theory distinguished humanity from the animal world. It was trustworthy; the triumphs of seventeenth-century science had proved that. An increasingly optimistic age concluded that reason gave humanity the *certain knowledge* of the world that religion no longer appeared to offer.

And reason provided a law, "natural law," to replace the foundation that religious belief now failed to provide for human knowledge. The idea of a law of nature that served as a standard of behavior for all humans at all times was not new. Greek philosophers such as Aristotle had enunciated a version of it, the Stoics had pressed it further, and Cicero had given the idea classic formulation: "There is in fact a true law—namely, right reason—which is in accordance with nature, applies to all men, and is unchangeable and eternal. By its commands this law summons men to the performance of their duties; by its prohibitions it restrains them from doing wrong."

St. Augustine had then Christianized that law by identifying it with the law of God. The Medieval scholastics had enthusiastically explicated it in the greatest detail as the basis of earthly law and morality. During the Renaissance and the Reformation, the rediscovery of Stoic texts and the work of Protestant scholars such as the father of modern international law, the Dutch jurist and diplomat Hugo Grotius (1583–1645), had secularized natural law once more, as a "law" inherent in the nature of humanity. Grotius, in *On the Law of War and Peace* (1625), attempted to find in natural law some basis for a "law of nations" that would transcend and moderate the religious fanaticisms of the Thirty Years' War. And the discovery of scientific "laws of nature" such as Kepler's laws of planetary motion further reinforced the belief that natural laws of human behavior must also exist. Success in proving mathematical and scientific laws inspired faith that reason could discern "natural law" in human affairs.

The most influential example of that faith was John Locke's claim that every individual in the "state of nature," before the existence of organized societies, possessed certain "natural rights," most notably life, liberty, and property. From that premise it followed, as proof followed axiom, that humanity had formed societies and set up governments mainly to preserve these rights. While Descartes had hoped to deduce the universe from a few central mathematical principles, Locke in his *Second Treatise of Government* (1690) assumed that he could deduce society and government from a few simple axioms about humanity and natural law.

An undercurrent of empiricism, of respect for the experience of the senses, nevertheless qualified that enthusiastic rationalism. Here as well, Locke led the way in his *Essay Concerning Human Understanding* (1690), which many readers hailed as the counterpart in the study of humanity to Newton's work on the forces of nature. Locke argued that all human ideas came from the experience of the senses. The mind at birth was a *tabula rasa*, a clean slate, on which experience gained through the senses gradually imprinted conceptions. No "innate ideas" exist, and contrary to Descartes, no axioms were self-evident. Outside forces, acting upon the mind, explained all human ideas.

That was the purest empiricism. Locke hoped that it would provide a weapon for destroying the superstitions and prejudices of the past. It proved destructive of much else, including some of Locke's own doctrines. Locke's theory of the mind did away with original sin, for experience might mold the *tabula rasa* of the mind to do good rather than evil. It did away equally with the revelation on which Christianity rested and with mathe-

The title page of John Locke's *Essay Concerning Human Understanding* (1690).

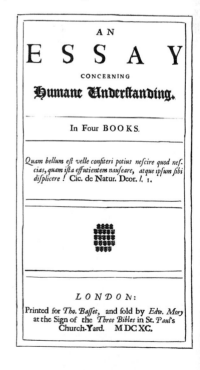

AN

ESSAY

CONCERNING

Humane Underſtanding.

In Four BOOKS.

Quam bellum eſt velle confiteri potius neſcire quod neſcias, quam iſta effutientem nauſeare, atque ipſum ſibi diſplicere! Cic. de Natur. Deor. *l.* 1.

LONDON:

Printed for *Tho. Baſſet*, and ſold by *Edw. Mory* at the Sign of the *Three Bibles* in St. *Paul's* Church-Yard. M DC XC.

matical axioms, for neither derived from the senses. Above all, it undermined Locke's own conception of "natural rights" that were innate and not based on experience.

The rationalism of Locke's natural-law theory of society clashed both with the empiricism of his theory of the mind and with the relativism in time and space that the Humanists and the great navigators had disclosed. The eighteenth century, the age known as the "Enlightenment," inherited this agonizing contradiction between rationalist faith in natural law and empiricist trust in sense-experience and in the evidence of comparative history.

THE ENLIGHTENMENT

The task that the leading thinkers of the eighteenth century set themselves was to popularize the methods and principles of seventeenth-century natural science and to apply these methods and principles to God, humanity, and society. Scientific discovery continued, but the most brilliant writers of the age concentrated their effort on applying the new scientific method to long-festering human ills—economic, social, political, and ecclesiastical. Their concern was less to discover new truth about nature than to apply the methods of natural science to the transformation of society.

The eighteenth century's own name for this movement was "the Enlightenment"—*les lumières* in French. The term suggested the dawn of a new age of reason and knowledge after a long dark night of ignorance, superstition, intolerance, and despotism of kings and priests. That new light was the light of science, as the great English poet Alexander Pope (1688–1744) elegantly proclaimed:

Nature and nature's law lay hid in
   night;
God said, "Let Newton be, " and all
was light.

Correspondence, exchange of publications, and travel linked together a cultural movement that transcended state and religious boundaries. "Enlightened" writers and readers spanned Europe, from Russia to Spain, from Edinburgh to Naples, from the Philadelphia of Benjamin Franklin to the Virginia of Thomas Jefferson. But the center of the movement was indisputably Paris.

That was no accident. Most other countries were either too small or too backward to become major centers of "Enlightenment" thought and agitation. The major exception, England, had already fought its battles for religious toleration and political freedom. It had established after 1688 a freedom of thought and publication unprecedented elsewhere, even in the Dutch Netherlands. It had already had an Enlightenment or "pre-Enlightenment" through Hobbes, Locke, and many others. By 1715, the England of gentry and merchants was too successful, both internally and externally, to provide much nourishment for intellectual movements that fed on dissatisfaction with the existing order. Only the Scots, who delighted in stirring up their richer and duller neighbors to the south, were an exception. The philosopher and historian David Hume (1711–76) and the economist Adam Smith (1723–90) were major Enlightenment figures, and Edinburgh in the eighteenth century was one of the great European intellectual centers.

Three tendencies in French society united to make France the center of the Enlightenment. First, French government after the death of Louis XIV in 1715 became steadily more inept and ineffectual, both internally and in its wars and diplomacy (see pp. 624–25). Irresolution at home and defeat abroad sapped the prestige of the existing order and of the Church that upheld it. Second, the aristocracy began to take its revenge on the monarchy that had reduced it to the role of courtly lapdog. In the realm of ideas, that revenge consisted of the articulation and eager propagation of advanced and potentially subversive ideas. Finally, the gradually increasing wealth that commerce and industry produced inspired in the growing urban middle classes an increasing consciousness of their own worth and importance. That led to rising social tension between the privileged and the less privileged. That tension helped encourage an increasing body of literature that attacked the existing order at its weakest points: the obscurantism of the Church, the bureaucratic ineptitude of the noble-dominated royal administration, and the irresponsibility and arrogance of the nobility itself.

The weapons of the French Enlightenment writers were clarity, wit, and a deliberate ambiguity designed to ward off the wrath of officialdom. Government censors were often too slow-witted to catch hidden barbs aimed at Church or state, and after mid-century they often secretly agreed with the critics. Censorship stopped only the most blatantly subversive or obviously blasphemous attacks on the existing order, and after the 1750s it was almost powerless against the flood of social criticism and satire that poured from the presses. The source of that flood was Paris, the center of the intellectual life of continental Europe in the eighteenth century. There the greatest intellectual figures of the age met and conversed in the *salons* or weekly gatherings that intellectual women of the aristocracy had begun to organize. The inhabitants of this world of ideas, whether commoner or noble, shared a common feeling that they were leading a revolution of ideas without precedent in European history, a crusade to end the absurdities and barbarities of the old order.

The "Philosophes": Voltaire, Montesquieu, Diderot

London initially helped inspire Paris. The conventional date for the beginning of the Enlightenment as a movement was the visit to England in 1726–29 of a certain François Marie Arouet (1694–1778), better known by his pen-name, Voltaire. The French government had twice imprisoned Voltaire in the Bastille fortress in Paris for alleged or actual witticisms made at the expense of royal or noble personages; on the second occasion he had only achieved freedom by promising to leave for London. The man who came to personify the Enlightenment thus had good reason to hate the old regime.

In England he read Newton and Locke, and relished the relative freedom of English society in comparison with his own. After returning to France he published *Philosophical Letters on the English* (1733), which passed on to his readers in nonmathematical form Newton's main principles and popularized Locke's theories of human nature and limited government. Voltaire skillfully contrasted the rationality of Newton's method and the tolerant reasonableness of the English way of life with the arbitrary and capricious realities of Church, state, and society in France.

Voltaire's English letters set the tone of "enlightenment" propaganda in France for the next half-century. They were "philosophical" in the broad sense because they reflected on the

A gathering of *philosophes,* including Voltaire (center, with arm raised), Diderot (on Voltaire's left), and Condorcet (between them), from a contemporary engraving by Jean Huber.

facts of human existence and attempted to discover their meaning, and they searched for general principles useful to humanity as a whole. But the *philosophes*, as Voltaire and kindred spirits became known, had little use for metaphysics. They were less philosophers than popularizers, crusaders for the application of the best intellectual tools of the century to social problems. Voltaire was the greatest of them—the most prolific, the wittiest, the most readable, and perhaps the angriest. His preferred targets were bigotry, superstition, and despotism.

"*Écrasez l'infâme*," cried Voltaire in his innumerable letters, pamphlets, stories, and satires: crush that "infamous thing," the Church. In the famous entry on "Religion" in his *Philosophical Dictionary* (1764), he described a vision he claimed to have had of a desert filled with piles of bones of "Christians with their throats slit by one another in metaphysical disputes." He went on to report a "philosophical" conversation with the shades of Socrates and Jesus, who both deplored the spectacle he had just seen. And he attacked the religious intolerance of con-

temporary France as vigorously as the barbarism of the past. When he died in 1778, Voltaire was the most widely read author in Europe, the first writer to have made a fortune from the sale of his own writings. Paris buried him with a ceremony worthy of a king.

A second leading Enlightenment figure was the Baron Charles Louis de Secondat de Montesquieu (1689–1755), sometime president of the *parlement* of Bordeaux. Montesquieu attempted to create a "social science" by applying the methods of the natural sciences to the study of society. In his most famous work, *The Spirit of the Laws* (1748), he suggested that climate and other environmental factors helped determine forms of government, and he tried to discover what form of government best fitted a given set of environmental conditions. *The Spirit of the Laws* was not "scientific" by later standards, but it was the first serious attempt since the Greeks at tracing relationships between systems of government and the environment. In his popular *History of Civilization* (1756), Voltaire took over and elaborated Montesquieu's concepts.

Montesquieu, like Voltaire, found Locke's theory of limited government persuasive. As a French noble he wished to limit the perceived excesses of royal absolutism. He followed Locke in concluding that the ideal political form involved the separation and balancing of powers within government. That conclusion later had great influence on the authors of the American Constitution (see p. 644).

A third major figure of the French Enlightenment was Denis Diderot (1713–84), co-editor of the famous *Encyclopédie*, an immense encyclopedia designed to sum up the totality of human knowledge. Despite Jesuit protests and cuts by timorous printers, it appeared in 35 volumes between 1752 and 1780. Diderot was an enthusiast for science and saw the relationship between science and technology more clearly than most *philosophes*. The most remarkable feature of the *Encyclopédie* was the plates that show machinery

---

Voltaire on Superstition   1776

Almost everything that goes beyond the adoration of a Supreme Being and submission of the heart to his orders is superstition. One of the most dangerous is to believe that certain ceremonies entail the forgiveness of crimes. Do you believe that God will forget a murder you have committed if you bathe in a certain river, sacrifice a black sheep, or if someone says certain words over you? . . . Do better, miserable humans; have neither murders nor sacrifices of black sheep. . . .

Notice that the most superstitious ages have always been those of the most horrible crimes. . . . The superstitious man is ruled by fanatics and he becomes one himself. On the whole, the less superstition, the less fanaticism, and the less fanaticism, the fewer miseries.

From Voltaire, *Dictionnaire philosophique* (Paris: Editions de Cluny, n.d.; reproduction of the edition of 1776), Vol. III, pp. 218–25.

and industrial processes. But Diderot was no mere compiler; he was a confident prophet of the Enlightenment's this-worldly religion of humanity. The entries and content of the *Encyclopédie* reflected the interests and enthusiasms of Diderot and his fellow *philosophes*, and contained many of their most trenchant writings. The work was an immense success, and became the bible of the "enlightened" everywhere. Through it ran faith in humanity's reason, pride in its accomplishments, and sublime confidence in its future.

The Enlightenment Faith

No intellectual movement is successful unless it has followers as well as leaders. The Enlightenment, like the Renaissance, produced its full quota of earnest hacks and disreputable scribblers. It also enjoyed a public, vast by previous standards, of silent supporters. Twentieth-century scholarship has shown that the *Encyclopédie* enjoyed astonishing sales in tiny provincial towns. Periodicals, libraries, book societies, and literary and scientific discussion groups spread knowledge, social criticism, and scandalous gossip. The main ideas of the Enlightenment struck root all over Europe, and a new generation absorbed from them entirely new conceptions of human nature, society, and religion. Five words, each of which bore a heavy freight of meaning in the eighteenth century, sum up these ruling ideas: reason, nature, happiness, progress, and liberty.

The eighteenth century believed as passionately in reason as the seventeenth, but with a difference. The "reason" of Voltaire relied more upon experience and less on mathematics than that of Descartes. It was a weapon of skeptical inquiry based on observed facts—or on what Voltaire thought were facts—rather than a method of deduction from axioms. To the thinkers of the Enlightenment, reason was the alternative to superstition and prejudice. It was the only sure guide to the principles that governed humanity and

---

Historical Relativism in Montesquieu: The Effects of Climate and Geography

In Asia they have always had great empires; in Europe these could never exist. Asia has larger plains; it is cut out into much larger divisions by mountains and seas . . . and the rivers being not so large form more contrasted boundaries. Power in Asia, then, should be always despotic; for if their subjugation be not severe they would soon make a division inconsistent with the nature of the country.

In Europe natural divisions form many nations of moderate extent, in which ruling by laws is not incompatible with the maintenance of the state: on the contrary, it is so favorable to it that without this the state would fall into decay. It is this that has formed a genius for liberty that renders each part extremely difficult to be subdued and subjected to a foreign power. . . . Africa is in a climate like that of the south of Asia and is in the same servitude. . . .

Monarchy is more frequently found in fertile countries and a republican government in those which are not so, and this is sometimes a sufficient compensation for the inconveniences they suffer by the sterility of the land. Thus the barrenness of the soil of Attica established a democracy there.

From Charles de Secondat de Montesquieu, *The Spirit of the Laws* (Bohn Standard Library edition), Vol. I, Book XVII, Chs. 6, 7; Book XVIII, Ch. 1, pp. 289–91.

---

nature. Reason could discover the fundamental rationality of the universe, and it could also make human societies more rational. The *philosophes* were less interested in "pure" science than in applied science, less concerned with intellectual system-building than with specific reforms. They regarded "reason" as a pragmatic instrument, applicable equally to agriculture, government, social relations, astronomy, and physics.

Nature was a second favorite word of the Enlightenment. The precise meaning the *philosophes* attached to "nature" was not always clear, but to nearly all of them "nature" or "the natural" were the proper standards for measuring God and humanity. A thing "according to nature" was reasonable and therefore good. Voltaire and his contemporaries brought the idea of natural law to the peak of its prestige. One of them devised the following definition of natural law:

> The regular and constant order of facts by which God rules the universe; the order which his wisdom presents to the sense and reason of men, to serve them as an equal and common rule of conduct, and to guide them, without distinction of race or sect, towards perfection and happiness.

Order and law, then, ruled throughout the universe of the *philosophes*—laws of economics, of politics, and of morality as well as of physics and astronomy. Reason permitted the discovery of those laws. Humans might ignore or defy them, but did so at their peril. To the "enlightened," the road to happiness lay in conforming to nature and nature's laws. The enlightened elite of the eighteenth century looked on those who "broke" nature's laws in the same spirit as the clergy of the Middle Ages had regarded heretics who broke God's laws: they were rebels against the order of the universe.

Happiness in this world, not salvation and eternal rejoicing in the next, was the end the *philosophes* had in view. The Enlightenment, like the Scientific Revolution, was a secular movement. When Thomas Jefferson (see p. 642) cited "the pursuit of happiness" along with life and liberty as inalienable human rights, he was expressing a general sentiment of the age. Medieval Christianity's toleration of misery in this life in the expectation of compensation in the next angered the *philosophes*. They demanded the realization of Christian ideals here and now. They abominated cruelty, judicial torture, slavery, and the callous treatment of the insane. An enlightened Italian civil servant of the Habsburgs, Cesare Beccaria (1738–94), was the first to suggest that savage penalties do not necessarily prevent crime and to propose a theory of penology. And the

philosophes were also cosmopolitan and even pacifist in temper. Voltaire penned some of the bitterest passages ever written about the "insanity" of war and the absurdity of blind patriotism.

Progress was an even more central constituent of the Enlightenment faith than happiness. The *philosophes* took the Christian idea of the spiritual progression of humanity from the Creation through the Incarnation to the Last Judgment, and secularized it. The progress of civilization, they believed, was now out of God's hands and in those of humanity, thanks to the discovery and use of nature's laws in government, economics, and technology. The *philosophes* were in general confident that both humanity and society were perfectible through human effort.

This was a major revolution in western thought. The Middle Ages could not have conceived of a progress that was purely secular and unrelated to God. Renaissance thinkers still felt themselves inferior to the heroic Greeks and Romans. But even before a symbolic literary battle between "ancients" and "moderns" that began in 1687, some thinkers had suggested that the "moderns" were as good as, and probably better than, the "ancients." By 1750 a French *philosophe*, economist, and civil servant, Anne-Robert-Jacques Turgot, could suggest that the essential element in history was humanity's slow struggle upward towards the crucial discovery of the scientific method. In 1794 the Marquis de Condorcet, a mathematician and aristocratic reformer under sentence of death during the French Revolution, wrote a *Sketch for a Historical Picture of the Progress of the Human Mind* that summed up all the optimism of his century. He saw "the strongest reasons for believing that nature has set no limit to the realization of our hopes" and foresaw "the abolition of inequality between nations, the progress of equality within nations, and the true perfection of humanity."

Progress, Condorcet concluded, was now "independent of any power that might wish to halt it" and "will never be reversed." The scientific method was irrevocably fixed in the human mind, and scientific knowledge of natural laws would continue to accumulate. Progress was thus accelerating and irreversible. The coming "perfection of mankind" was an intoxicating vision, a vision the majority of the enlightened shared, despite the abundance of historical evidence suggesting that civilizations declined as well as rose. How Condorcet reconciled his vision of progress with his own status as fugitive from the guillotine of the Revolution of "Liberty, Equality, Fraternity" is unclear.

Liberty, indeed, was yet another favorite word of the *philosophes*. They were acutely aware of the prevalence in France of arbitrary arrest and restrictions on speech, religion, trade, and employment. Looking at England through lightly rose-tinted glasses, they envied Englishmen their economic, political, and religious liberties. Their concern for liberty was potentially the most explosive tenet of their faith, but few considered that violence was necessary to secure it. Liberty, for the *philosophes*, was inseparable from reason. Reason would soon reveal the true natural laws governing all things, from trade, to government, to religion. The artificiality and corruption of the present would become evident to all. A "benevolent despotism," an enlightened philosopher-king, would lead humanity into a new golden age—or so Voltaire and many other *Encyclopédie* authors hoped. But what if despotism was by its very nature not benevolent?

The Enlightenment and Religion

The new ideas inevitably had religious consequences. To the "enlightened," religious fervor savored of the fanaticism of the wars of religion. The Enlightenment only prized enthusiasm for its new religion of reason, progress, and the "perfection of humanity." The fashionable form of belief common among the eighteenth century's educated elite came to be Deism, the belief in a God who is Creator but not Redeemer. The God of the Deists was a celestial watchmaker who had created the universe, wound it up, and then stepped aside to let it run according to natural law that he had laid down. God did not concern himself with humanity, or act in or through human history.

The essence of religion, for the Deist, was thus awe and reverence before the rationality and perfection of the universe—a feeling reflected in the beautiful hymns of Isaac Watts still heard in many Protestant churches. To a Deist such as Voltaire, talk of revelation, miracles, or the special intervention of God in the natural order was false. Dogma and ritual were "superstition", for humanity needed only reason to see God. The heart of natural religion was a morality common to all mankind. "Light is uniform for the star Sirius," Voltaire wrote, "and for us moral philosophy must be uniform."

Deism obviously tended to undermine orthodox Christianity and to substitute for it a rationalist belief in God as First Cause and in "natural law" as humanity's moral guide. A few *philosophes* such as Diderot went further and dared the censors by pushing beyond Deism to atheism. Baron Paul Henri d'Holbach (1723–89) was the complete "materialist," an ancestor of much nineteenth-century thought. His universe contained nothing but matter, humanity itself was a conglomeration of atoms, and natural law was the sole determinant of all events.

In the end, many Protestants found a compromise between Christian faith and the Enlightenment's rationalism, humanitarianism, and tolerance. The result was the nineteenth-century development of a liberal Protestantism. Others took the road of more intense piety. The cold rationality of Deism held no appeal for emotional natures, and only the educated could understand it. Hence the wide popularity of two warmly emotional Protestant movements, Pietism in Germany and Methodism in England and America.

Both emphasized the importance of the inner religious experience of individual "conversion." Pietism was a second and milder Protestant Reformation that challenged not the Pope, but the twin extremes of dogmatic orthodoxy and Deism that verged on unbelief. Individualist, tolerant, and indifferent to ceremonies, Pietism attracted followers among both Catholics and Protestants.

John Wesley (1703–91) was the leader of a somewhat parallel revival of a warm and personal Christian piety in England in the years following his conversion in 1738. When the Anglican clergy resisted his efforts, he took his message directly to the people. He addressed huge outdoor congregations and prayer meetings in remote chapels, taught his followers to sing their way to heaven with the hymns of his

brother Charles, and deluged the congregations he had established with streams of pamphlets from his printing presses. In the end, Anglican opposition forced Wesley to leave the established church and create a new denomination, Methodism, which took its name from the "methodical" piety of Wesley's followers that the orthodox had originally mocked. Methodism touched many thousands of Englishmen at home and in the colonies who found repellent the arid intellectualism that characterized much eighteenth-century Anglicanism. Methodism's wide following, its emphasis on other-worldly concerns, and its conspicuous loyalty to temporal authority in this world made it a more effective buttress of the social order than Anglicanism.

Economics, Society, and Politics

The *philosophes* were interested in social and political issues, but they were reformers, not revolutionaries. Their formula for reform was simply to discover by reason and experience the natural laws that should operate in any given situation and to clear away all supposedly artificial obstacles to their operation. The result, "reason" indicated, would be "progress" toward happiness and freedom.

That outlook encouraged the beginnings of the modern discipline of economics. In 1758 François Quesnay published his *Economic Survey*, which proposed the existence of natural economic "laws" and urged the end to all restrictions, such as government control of grain supplies and prices, that prevented those laws from operating. But Quesnay and French economists of his school were too much the products of France's predominantly agricultural society. They saw in agriculture the source of all wealth, and damned industry as "sterile" and commerce as parasitic. Adam Smith of Edinburgh saw more clearly. In *An Inquiry into the Nature and Causes of the Wealth of Nations* (1776), the first classic of modern economics, Smith extended the concept of

John Wesley preaching.

"natural liberty" to commerce and industry.

He denounced all "mercantilist" practices, although he admitted that an age of warring states might make measures such as the Navigation Acts necessary for a time. In general, however, Smith maintained that state intervention interfered with the workings of the natural law of supply and demand and thus decreased rather than increased national wealth. The "invisible hand" of natural law, Smith argued, was a self-regulating mechanism that automatically maximized the wealth and freedom of any society that respected it. To tamper with it was both dangerous and self-defeating.

In political theory, similar lines of reasoning led to three distinct schools of thought. The first rested on the notion of "enlightened absolutism." The *philosophes*, children of their age, were no democrats. Voltaire thought government should be for the people, but by kings: "The people, stupid and barbarous, needs a yoke, a cattle prod, and hay." Most *philosophes* hoped for a mellowing of divine-right monarchy into a benevolent "enlightened" philosopher-kingship that would govern—perhaps with well-rewarded *philosophe* advice—according to natural law rather than royal caprice. A second, minority school believed that "reason" pointed in the direction of an English-style constitutional monarchy based on natural rights and on an explicit contract that bound the sovereign to respect his subjects' liberties. And a very few advanced a third theory, still too radical to be of much immediate influence: the theory of democratic government. That school's foremost prophet was the eccentric Jean-Jacques Rousseau (1712–78), author of *The Social Contract* (1762).

Rousseau: Prophet of Democracy and Despotism

Rousseau, a native of Geneva, appeared in Paris in 1742 after a wandering youth, came to know Diderot and other *philosophes* and for a time attempted to join them. But he was never easy in their company. He trusted reason, but relied even more on emotion. He trusted nature, but to him nature was the unspoiled simplicity of precivilized humanity, the "noble savage." After a sudden illumination experienced in 1749, he became convinced that humanity had lost more than it had gained by cultivating the arts and sciences. He lost all faith in progress. The seeming artificiality of Paris society increasingly irritated him, and he broke with his former friends. Voltaire thought him insane, and in his miserable later years Rousseau indeed suffered from delusions of persecution.

Rousseau was the greatest social critic of the Enlightenment. By temperament he was a shy and sensitive misfit who desperately wanted to belong. He knew himself to be "good," on the model of the "noble savage." He therefore blamed his unhappiness, his failure to fit in, on the alleged artificiality of existing society. That society of kings, aristocrats, and priests—he felt—had "corrupted" and humiliated him. Consequently he imagined an alternative, not as a program for revolution—although many readers took it as one—but as a critique of existing societies. In Rousseau's utopia, described in *The Social Contract*, free citizens associated by choice in a community of equals to govern themselves. By agreeing to form a community, they gave up all individual rights to the group. From their deliberations, a "general will" would inevitably emerge. Rousseau's belief in humanity's essential goodness precluded conflict or dissent within his ideal community. And once the "general will" emerged, all owed it absolute obedience.

Rousseau's ideal democracy was "direct democracy", the self-rule of a tightly knit community of active male citizens—for like most men of the Enlightenment, Rousseau considered it part of "the order of nature that woman obeys man." Perhaps Rousseau had in mind an idealized image of Ge-

The misfit as social critic: Jean-Jacques Rousseau.

neva as he wrote *The Social Contract*. In that city-state, citizens knew and trusted one another, and the minority normally accepted the majority's view with good grace, out of loyalty to the community. But it was Sparta, that least individualist and most austerely military of the Greek city-states, that recurred frequently in Rousseau's pages. It was his favorite model.

Perhaps Rousseau's knowledge of Sparta—of its relentless regimentation, its murderous *krypteia* or secret police, its ruthless enslavement of all surrounding cities—was imperfect. Perhaps, as modern scholarship has tended to assert, his proposals for a "progressive" education that would bring out the child's "natural" goodness and intellectual curiosity make Rousseau a prophet of individual freedom rather than Spartan uniformity. Perhaps his hostility to kings and aristocrats, indeed his temperamental aversion to all forms of authority, absolve him of responsibility for excesses committed after 1789 in the name of the "general will." But his theory of democracy was nevertheless a momentous illustration of the consequences—even the unintended consequences—of ideas.

Locke and Montesquieu had argued that the guarantee of political liberty was the separation of executive and legislative powers, since concentration of power threatened freedom. Their theory derived from an essential pessimism about human behavior, a long experience of human ambition and fallibility gained in the world of politics. Their theory of liberty was "negative"—liberty arose when institutional and legal checks limited the powers of government. That negative theory of liberty, of individual rights *against* government, was the foundation of modern representative democracies such as Britain and the United States.

Rousseau, an intellectual without worldly experience, took an entirely different view. For him humanity was "good" with the goodness of the noble savage. That goodness would express itself naturally in politics once the artificial restraints and corrupting influences of the old society fell away. Checks and balances, the separation of powers, the protection of specific rights would serve no purpose if "the people" governed itself. The "general will," by definition, could not will harm to itself! Rousseau's theory of liberty was "positive"—his liberty was the willing obedience to laws and decisions that the individual himself had helped to make. Rousseau's theory of liberty thus set no limit at all on what government could do if it expressed— *or claimed to express*—the general will. In a justly famous passage in *The Social Contract*, Rousseau even asserted that the community could force individuals to be free. That hard phrase was the precursor of an even harder reality after 1789.

Utopian visions like those of Rousseau, it later became clear, often originated among and appealed to intellectuals alienated from societies that in their view did not sufficiently appreci-

Rousseau: The Despotism of the General Will

The problem is to find a form of association . . . in which each, while uniting himself with all, may still obey himself alone, and remain as free as before. This is the fundamental problem of which the Social Contract provides the solution: . . . the total alienation of each associate, together with all his rights, to the whole community. . . . Each man, in giving himself to all, gives himself to nobody. . . . Each of us puts his person and all his power in common under the supreme direction of the general will, and, in our corporate capacity, we receive each member as an indivisible part of the whole. . . . In order that the social compact may not be an empty formula, it tacitly includes the undertaking, which alone can give force to the rest, that whoever refuses to obey the general will shall be compelled to do so by the whole body. This means nothing less than that he will be forced to be free.

From Jean Jacques Rousseau, *The Social Contract* (New York and London: Everyman's Library, 1913), Book I, Chs. 6 and 7, pp. 14–18.

ate them. Utopianism flourished best under autocracies—like that of the successors of Louis XIV—that pursued policies sufficiently repressive to generate hostility, but not repressive enough to crush it. And the utopian search for a society without conflict, of which Rousseau was the greatest forerunner and prophet, could even lead to an attack on representative democracies whose "negative freedoms" appeared to foster doubt, dissatisfaction, and disunity. Rousseau died in 1778, but only chronology bound him to the Enlightenment. His true home was the post-1789 world of revolution, nationalism, and Romanticism that he helped to shape.

ARTS AND LETTERS IN THE EIGHTEENTH CENTURY

The art and literature of the later seventeenth and early eighteenth centuries reflected the pervasive belief of Enlightenment scientists and philosophers in the rationality, intelligibility, and order of the universe. Rationalism blended easily with classicism. The regularity and harmony of Newton's universe seemed to accord both with the balance, proportion, rationality, and restraint for which classical Greek architecture and Greek and Roman writers had striven. The dictators of literary and artistic taste at the close of the seventeenth century were classicists. When *philosophes* such as Voltaire wrote dramas, they accepted classical standards as unquestioningly as had Corneille and Racine. The architects of the "Georgian" buildings of England and the beautifully proportioned Place de la Concorde in Paris accepted classical rules of balance and unity with equal zeal. Enthusiasm for classical antiquity reached its post-Renaissance climax after 1748, when Europe discovered the remains of the Roman city of Pompeii in startlingly well-preserved condition under the ashes and cinders from Mt. Vesuvius that had covered it in A.D. 79.

Jonathan Swift: social commentary through satire (portrait by Charles Jervas)

An Age of Prose

The "age of reason" was an age of prose. Essays, satirical tales, novels, letters, and histories were the characteristic literary forms of the eighteenth century. Authors bent their energies to description and narrative rather than to suggestion and imagination. The essays of Joseph Addison and Richard Steele, which began to appear in 1709, sketched a delightful picture of English rural society. Jonathan Swift's *Gulliver's Travels* (1726) and Voltaire's *Candide* (1759) offered biting social and philosophical commentary. As the century progressed, the novel emerged as the favorite form of literary expression; the most enjoyable example was perhaps Henry Fielding's *Tom Jones* (1749). Alongside fiction, philosophy, economics, and history prospered. The eighteenth century's greatest monument of historical scholarship was Edward Gibbon's history of *The Decline and Fall of the Roman Empire* (1776–88), which in a luminous style that will forever delight its readers, sardonically described the "triumph of barbarism and religion" over the greatest empire of the ancient world.

Painting, especially the portraits that now became exceedingly fashionable, well disclosed the elegant aristocratic flavor of eighteenth-century society. The delicate-featured and exquisitely groomed women who look coolly down on the observer, and the worldly, sometimes arrogant, faces of their husbands under their powdered wigs suggest the artificiality of aristocratic society, and sometimes the hardness of character of those who inhabited it. Opulent furniture and tableware, and the great town and country houses of nobles and wealthy merchants reflect the same aristocratic elegance.

But not all books and art served the enjoyment of the aristocracy. The first newspapers written for a wide audience of educated readers emerged in the eighteenth century. William Hogarth (1697–1764) made engravings of his satirical sketches of English society, and sold them by the thousands. Above all, novelists, dramatists, and musicians in London and Paris began to appeal to a middle-class audience. The Paris stage, with productions such as *The Barber of Seville* (1775) and *The Marriage of Figaro* (1784) of Pierre de Beaumarchais, turned a keen satirical edge against the aristocracy. The heroes and heroines of novels tended in-

Eighteenth-century art for the aristocracy: detail of a painting by Thomas Gainsborough (*ca.* 1748)

creasingly to imitate the middle-class origins of their audiences.

An Age of Music

But the greatest cultural achievement of the age was its music—above all German music. Two great Germans dominated the musical world of the early eighteenth century: Johann Sebastian Bach (1685–1750) and George Frederick Handel (1685–1759). Handel in his oratorios for chorus and instruments and Bach in his richly varied works for keyboard instruments, chamber groups, orchestras, and choruses, realized all the dramatic and emotive possibilities of the baroque style. As the century drew on, the orchestra, which had originated in the seventeenth century, expanded and took in new instruments, the pianoforte replaced the harpsichord, and music began to move from the aristocratic salon into the public hall.

Franz Joseph Haydn (1732–1809), who wrote both for chamber groups and for orchestras, developed the musical forms known as sonatas and symphonies. The other outstanding musical personality of the latter half of the century was Wolfgang Amadeus Mozart (1756–91), who was probably the most gifted musician in history. Born in Salzburg in Austria, he began his career as a child prodigy, lived only 35 years, and died in poverty. But within that short span he produced over 600 compositions that included unequalled masterpieces of invention and form—string quartets, sonatas, concertos, masses, symphonies, and operas such as *Le Nozze di Figaro* (The Marriage of Figaro, 1786), *Don Giovanni* (1787), and *Die Zauberflöte* (The Magic Flute, 1791).

THE LIMITS OF THE ENLIGHTENMENT

The Enlightenment was the creation of a small elite, although many of its essential ideas circulated widely and penetrated far down the social scale. It was largely confined to western Europe and the English-speaking world. And counter-currents soon arose to challenge the supremacy of reason in philosophy and of rational structure and classical balance in art.

Pietism, Methodism, and Rousseau's preference for emotion over reason were evidence of these currents. Even philosophers saw reason's limits. David Hume, who was along with Adam Smith the greatest figure of the Scottish Enlightenment, started from a close study of the great French skeptic Bayle. Hume ended by denying the possibility of certainty. Only the experience of the senses, unverifiable by any independent means, kept the mind informed about external reality. And for Hume, sense-experience was a sequence of disjointed impressions, upon which the mind—and the mind alone—imposed regularities, patterns, connections.

Hume's position, which has remained logically unassailable, cut at the root of the Enlightenment faith in the capacity of reason to discover laws in nature and human behavior. Hume did not doubt the validity of Newton's laws as a rule of thumb. What he denied was that anyone would ever be in a position to claim with certainty that Newton's laws applied to *all* times and in *all* places throughout the universe. Even observations that seemed to confirm those laws might not do so, for the evidence of the senses might be a snare. The sun *might* rise tomorrow; but then again it might not.

Hume was happy to concede that some kinds of knowledge were more certain than others. But he was the first philosopher to see the full depths of the predicament into which the collapse of the Medieval religious certainties had plunged humanity. In the philosopher's study, if not in practical affairs, certainty was unattainable. That was "the whimsical condition of mankind." The observer's point of view helped determine what the observer saw. Knowledge, like the human value-systems that varied

Wolfgang Amadeus Mozart

through historical time and geographic space, was relative.

Hume's skepticism did not yet shake an optimistic age that sought to replace God with Newton's clockwork universe. But a few farseeing individuals nevertheless understood what he had done. The greatest philosopher of the century, Immanuel Kant (1724–1804), took up Hume's challenge, although Kant never traveled more than a few miles from his native city of Königsberg in East Prussia. In his *Critique of Pure Reason* (1781), the most opaquely written of all the great works of Western thought, Kant saved scientific reason, at least in his own judgment, by limiting its domain to appearances, to the data of sense-experience.

The mechanical world of physics, Kant argued, *was* knowable with certainty, although only knowable to an observer equipped with concepts inherent to the mind, such as space and time. What was not knowable with certainty, for Kant, were the *true* natures of the "things-in-themselves" that humans perceived through their senses. Nor could reason deal with the domain of metaphysics and religion, the realm of things that transcended experience. Many thinkers saw in Kant's refutation of Hume a mere confirmation of the Scot's skepticism. Others reacted by taking Kant, who himself argued for the necessity of belief in God as one foundation of morality, as a point of departure for a renewed "leap into faith" in religion.

In literature, the slowly gathering revolt against the Enlightenment took the form of a celebration of emotion that defied classical notions of rationality and balance. French and English novelists cultivated extremes of sentimentality. Heroines suffered heart-rending misfortune and mistreatment, while the author sought at every turn to arouse the reader's anger, pity, love,

or terror. The most influential example was Samuel Richardson's 2,000-page tear-jerker, *Clarissa* (1748), which influenced Rousseau's *Nouvelle Héloise* (1761). The bizarre, grotesque, and fantastic returned to fashion. In both architecture and literature, critics began to revive the Gothic, despised since the Renaissance.

In Germany, which had never fallen totally under the sway of the French Enlightenment, a "Storm and Stress" (*Sturm und Drang*) movement in literature emphasized the great elemental emotions and denied the supremacy of reason. Johann Gottfried von Herder (1744–1803) conceived a philosophy of history that emphasized the uniqueness of each nation or race, the individuality of its genius, and the falsity of any view that denied that uniqueness in the name of universal reason. Johann Wolfgang von Goethe (1749–1832) published at the start of his long literary career *The Sorrows of Young Werther* (1774), a morbidly sentimental tale ending in suicide. The "Age of Reason" thus summoned up its opposite and successor—the age of Romanticism. The new age prized fierce emotion over harmony and equilibrium, and celebrated individual and national peculiarity over a cosmopolitan reason that embraced all humanity.

The Scientific Revolution and the Enlightenment were the most decisive break in the history of Western thought. The world picture of fifth-century Greece and of the Old and New Testaments, preserved through the Middle Ages and Renaissance, now gave way to a distinctively "modern" cast of mind. The world of Luther and Loyola, of Charles V and Philip II, was still organically related to the Middle Ages. The world of Newton and Locke, of Voltaire and Rousseau, was unmistakably our own.

Suggestions for Further Reading

The Scientific Revolution

M. Ashley, *The Golden Century* (1968), offers a fine survey of seventeenth-century social and cultural history. A. R. Hall, *The Scientific Revolution 1500–1800* (1966), is the best recent account. H. Butterfield, *The Origins of Modern Science 1300–1800* (1949), is highly readable, but C. Brinton, *The Shaping of the Modern Mind* (1953), covers a longer period. T. S. Kuhn, *The Copernican Revolution* (1957), describes the transformation of astronomical thought and offers an influential interpretation of how science advances. On the social background of scientific development, see D. Stimson, *Scientists and Amateurs: A History of the Royal Society* (1948). G. de Santillana, *The Crime of Galileo* (1955), elucidates the most famous case in the history of freedom of thought.

The Enlightenment

P. Hazard, *The European Mind: The Critical Years, 1680–1715* (1935, 1952), offers a still useful study of the transition from Scientific Revolution to Enlightenment. The most searching interpretation of the Enlightenment as a whole is E. Cassirer, *The Philosophy of the Enlightenment* (1932, 1951). C. Becker, *The Heavenly City of the Eighteenth Century Philosophers* (1932), attacks the *Philosophes* as doctrinaires, while P. Gay, *The Enlightenment: An Interpretation*, 2 vols. (1966–69), defends them. N. Hampson, *A Cultural History of the Enlightenment* (1969), is a useful introduction. C. R. Cragg, *Reason and Authority in the Eighteenth Century* (1964), and D. Mornet, *French Thought in the Eighteenth Century* (1929), deal with England and France respectively. R. S. Westfall, *Never at Rest: A Biography of Isaac Newton* (1981), discusses some of the leading intellectuals of the period, but see also T. Bestermann, *Voltaire* (1969), and J. N. Shklar, *Men and Citizens: A Study of Rousseau's Social Theory* (1969). L. Krieger, *Kings and Philosophers, 1689–1789* (1970), relates thought to politics. On specific topics, see M. F. Bukofzer, *Music in the Baroque Era* (1947); F. Fosca, *The Eighteenth Century* (1953) on painting; B. Semmel, *The Methodist Revolution* (1973); G. R. Craig, *The Church in the Age of Reason* (1961); and E. Fox-Genovese, "Women and the Enlightenment," in R. Bridenthal et al., *Becoming Visible: Women in European History* (1987).

22
The Twilight of the Old Regime, 1715–1789

The 75 years between the death of Louis XIV in 1715 and the outbreak of the French Revolution in 1789 were a period of relative stability, without religious wars or great rebellions, except for a desperate serf rising in distant Russia and the revolt of Britain's North American colonies in 1776. Monarchy remained the prevalent form of government, but divine-right monarchy evolved into "enlightened absolutism."

And monarchy, as in the seventeenth century, nevertheless rested on a compromise with the aristocracy. Even the republican or constitutional governments of the eighteenth century were aristocratic in tone. Whig aristocrats and merchants dominated the English Parliament. After the death of Louis XIV, French nobles of the sword and the robe prevailed in the royal councils, and reestablished the powers of the *parlement* law courts. Junkers commanded the armies of Prussia. Polish nobles made the Polish Diet a farce. The "service nobility" of Russia gradually emancipated itself from its duties to the state after the death of Peter the Great. And small oligarchies based on wealth ruled the Dutch Republic and the German "free cities" of the Holy Roman Empire.

Throughout Europe, the aristocracies of birth, office, and wealth reclaimed powers, rights, and privileges lost to the centralizing absolute monarchies of the seventeenth century. Only monarchs or chief ministers of unusual ability succeeded in bending the revival of aristocratic influence to the purposes of the state. The undeclared war between monarch and aristocrat normally led to tacit compromise, an uneasy balance between centralization and decentralization, between absolute monarchy and aristocratic privilege. That balance was perhaps lacking in clarity and logic, but all remembered how fanatical adherence to principle had given birth to the bloody religious and civil wars of the previous two centuries. Elites that had the luxury of choice were therefore usually glad to accept the structure of society and government as they found it after 1715.

Abject poverty, injustice, and brutality remained widespread, but to the elite, the brilliant "civilization"—a word that first appeared in the 1750s—of the Paris salons or the London coffeehouses appeared to outweigh the tribulations of the poor. To those who looked back upon the devastation of the Thirty Years' War or the fanaticism of the "saints" of the English Revolution, social stability and political equilibrium were worth a high price in injustice. That eighteenth century equilibrium later seemed a lost golden age to the generation of aristocrats that witnessed 1789. A French noble spoke for his caste when he remarked that those who had not lived before the Revolution lacked all conception of the sweetness of life.

Opposite: Jeanne Antoinette Poisson, a witty and well-read daughter of a banker, received the title of Marquise de Pompadour after becoming mistress to Louis XV. She helped to ward off government and Church attempts to suppress or censor the *Encyclopédie*.

Frederick the Great of Prussia
inspects his troops (1778).

THE STATE SYSTEM

Equilibrium was likewise the rule in relations between states. The defeat of Louis XIV's bid for mastery had cost much blood and treasure. The great powers after 1715—France, Britain, Austria, Prussia, and Russia—agreed on few things, but they remained determined to prevent the dominance of a single state. Tacit "rules of the game" therefore evolved, for only issues of power divided these states. Unlike the two centuries that preceded it or the two that followed, no religious, national, or ideological quarrels rent the European state system in the eighteenth century. Chief of the "rules"

was "compensation"—the principle that if one state were fortunate or daring enough to acquire new territory, the other powers would receive compensating advantages, in order to preserve the power balance. "Compensation" often meant that small states suffered mutilation or suppression at the hands of the great. But the practice of compensation helped preserve the balance and sometimes preserved the peace.

Wars remained frequent, but were uniquely "limited" in both means and ends—although that happy situation was not always apparent to the relatively small numbers of professionals who fought, suffered, and died in them. Eighteenth-century war affected the civilian population far less than did war before 1715 and after 1789. Armies avoided pillaging, even on enemy territory. To allow the troops to forage gave them a chance to desert, and the devastation of territory that the state might later annex was bad business. Conscription fell out of fashion except in Russia, where most troops were serfs, and to a limited extent in Prussia. The troops, in the words of a British commander of a slightly later period, tended to be "the scum of the earth, enlisted for drink," or foreign mercenaries. Only esprit de corps, constant drill that made obedience in battle automatic, and a discipline based on flogging and hanging welded these forces together. The aim, in the view of Prussia's greatest king, was to make the troops more terrified of their own officers than of the enemy.

Warfare itself consisted of elaborate maneuver. Commanders normally avoided pitched battles, for trained troops were a precious investment. The 43,000 casualties at Malplaquet (1709) had shown all too well the vast slaughter that ensued when armies equipped with muskets blasted one another at ranges of 50 paces or less. Armies also moved slowly, for the axle-deep mud of Europe's roads did not allow swift movement of the artillery or of the thousands of wagons needed to transport food. In winter, war normally ceased. Campaigns usually centered around a single province or fortified strongpoint and ended indecisively. The ruling system of naval tactics had similar results. Fleets sailing in rigid battle lines blasted at one another from a distance. Engagements were rarely decisive, for commanders feared losing control of their fleets and shunned the bloody and confused close-range ship-to-ship duels that alone ensured annihilation of the enemy.

Limited objectives corresponded to these limitations of methods. The enemy of today might be the ally of tomorrow. Defeating any power too thoroughly might disturb the power balance and summon up unforeseeable complications. In these "cabinet wars"—decided in and directed from the royal cabinet or secretariat—statesmen and generals normally sought concrete political and economic objectives, not unconditional surrender or total destruction. Once a power attained its objectives or became convinced that they were unattainable, it concluded a truce or a peace. In spite of relentless competition—over prestige, land, population, colonies, and trade—the monarchs, bureaucrats, and aristocrats of the eighteenth century felt themselves part of a common civilization. The secret of the eighteenth-century equilibrium was the absence of the twin forces that drive inter-state conflicts to extremes—religious or ideological strife, and bids for universal domination by a single power.

Eighteenth-century statesmen were not unaware of the similarities between their system and Newton's picture of the universe—a stable order of perfectly balanced gravitational attraction and centrifugal repulsion in which every mass moved along predictable lines of force. Ministers took pride in their mastery of "political algebra," the exact calculation of the forces acting on state policy. Soldiers of a literary bent created elaborate geometrical systems to describe, on the model of siege warfare, the century's art of war. Only after mid-century did French theorists, such as Pierre de Bourcet and François de Guibert, begin the creation of a new strategy, operations, and tactics of movement, flexibility, surprise, and annihilation—the methods of the new revolutionary armies after 1792.

The eighteenth-century equilibrium remained precarious, a balance between dynamic forces. Wealth and trade increased steadily, for revolutions both in agriculture and industry were slowly beginning. Europe's economy and diplomacy were becoming global rather than continental; the struggle for empire reached toward the farthest corners of the earth. For the first time, battles fought in America,

The French nobility lampooned: *The Baron* (1785).

Europe in 1715

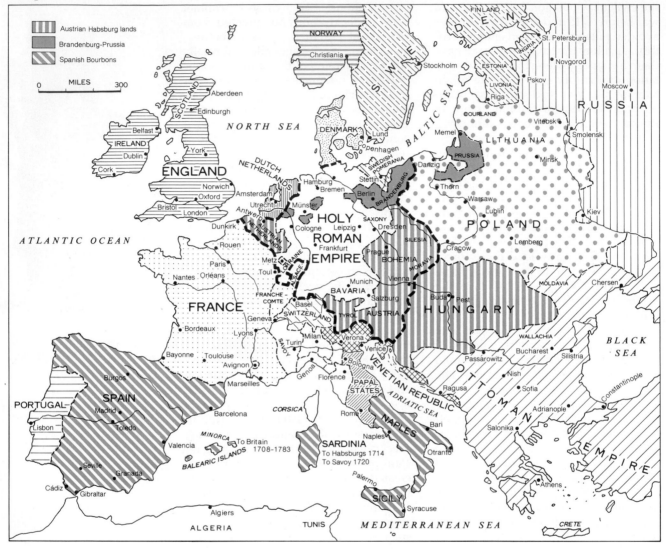

Africa, and Asia affected the balance of power in Europe. And in trying to maintain its position, each country accentuated its own particular sources of strength. Britain relied increasingly on naval power and commerce. Prussia depended on its army and bureaucracy. Russia intensified its reliance on serfdom. Austria compensated for weakness in Germany by increasing its power in southeastern Europe. France, the one power that refused to specialize, condemned itself to naval weakness, while its intellectual and cultural leadership masked, but did not remedy, its failure to overhaul its British rival in commerce and industry. Inept generalship and financial weakness even prevented France from profiting from its greatest strength before 1715 and after 1789, its land power.

Despite the appearance of equilibrium, powers still rose and fell, sometimes swiftly and decisively, as in the case of Poland. Intellectual and political change intersected with social and economic rivalries that culminated in the great upheavals after 1789. The years between 1715 and 1789, the twilight of the "old regime," fall conveniently into three periods of roughly a quarter-century each: (1) a generation of peace and relative prosperity from 1715 to 1740; (2) a period of worldwide warfare from 1740 to 1763; and (3) an interval of enlightened absolutism, aristocratic resurgence, and domestic unrest from 1763 to 1789.

PEACE AND PROSPERITY, 1715–40

Governments and peoples were thoroughly weary of war by the time the treaties of 1713–14 and 1719–21 restored peace to both western and eastern Europe. The age that followed was unheroic and happily corrupt, as postwar periods often are. But peace allowed the restoration of order and of law, and stimulated an enormous expansion of trade, particularly in western Europe.

Commerce and Industry

Seaborne commerce was the most conspicuous source of Europe's wealth during the eighteenth century. Thanks to the enterprise of their merchants and the technical skill of their mariners, the volume of foreign trade in Britain and France multiplied itself by five during the century. In the British case, colonial trade led the increase. Britain therefore needed and acquired a larger merchant marine than its rivals and the strongest navy in the world. In the French case, trade with other European states was the greatest source of increase. In both cases the accumulation of wealth in the hands of the upper classes was spectacular. For the first time the total wealth of Europe began to eclipse that of Asia. The two preceding centuries of exploration, conquest, and establishment of overseas trading networks now paid off handsomely. Sugar from the West Indies, wine from Portugal, and tobacco from Virginia might grace the tables of Liverpool merchants. Their wives might wear printed calico from

India in summer and furs from Canada in winter. Their daughters might marry the heirs of aristocrats whose elegant and capacious Georgian houses were the visible evidence of the combined profits of land and mercantile investment.

The labor of slaves or serfs produced many of the commodities in which Europe's thriving trade dealt. The plantations of the West Indies serviced Europe's ever-increasing craving for sugar. That demand in turn created an almost insatiable demand for African slaves. Liverpool and London slave traders largely met that demand. The serfs who toiled without recompense for their landlords in the grain-producing regions of eastern Europe played a similar role in the economic order as the slaves of the West Indies. Some of the European economy still rested, as had the economy of the ancient world, on servile labor.

Despite the immense increase in overseas trade, the vast bulk of European commerce was within the European states themselves. And in all states except the Dutch Netherlands and perhaps Britain, agriculture still furnished most of the national product. Even Britain's vast foreign trade in the last third of the century only amounted to perhaps 10 percent of the growing British economy. And it was in Britain that the beginnings of revolutionary changes in industry became visible after mid-century (see pp. 681–87).

Boom and Bust: The Mississippi and South Sea Bubbles

European commercial capitalism, which had created the first joint-stock companies, stock exchanges, and state banks, continued to expand. The coming of peace in 1713–14 encouraged both financial speculation and wildcat commercial ventures. Those ventures in turn led in 1719 and 1720 to the first large-scale example of a typically modern phenomenon, a stock crash— or, as contemporaries described it, a "bubble."

1. Moulin.   2. Fourneaux   3. Förmes.   4. Vinaigrerie.   5. Cannes   SVCRERIE.   6. Gros   7. Latanir.   8. Pajbmirioba   9. Choux   10. Cafes   11. Figuir . 138.
   et Chaudieres.   de Sucre   Cocos, p 155. p. iti.   p. 92.   Caraibes.   de Negres .

The sugar economy: a white overseer directs the slaves at a seventeenth-century West Indian sugar mill.

The wars of Louis XIV burdened both French and British governments with debt. In the French case only bankruptcy appeared to promise relief. That plight offered opportunities to plausible figures such as the Scottish promoter John Law, who appeared at the French court after the death of Louis XIV and offered to solve the monarchy's financial woes. After his commercial bank in Paris prospered, he received in 1717–20 control of French taxes, the right to issue paper money, a virtual monopoly on foreign trade, and the office of Controller General of Finances. His Mississippi Company, chartered to trade with France's colony in Louisiana, soon mutated into a "Company of the Indies" and assumed France's state debt, which it paid off by promoting a boom in its own stock. Law's "system"—his reforms of government finances, his paper money, and his expansion of the credit avail-

able to merchants—stimulated the French economy. But when the price of his company's stock reached 36 times its original value, investors began to sell in order to protect their paper profits. The market collapsed and Law fled.

A parallel episode occurred in London. Promoters organized a South Sea Company to exploit the trade with the Spanish colonies provided for in the Peace of Utrecht. It likewise took over much of the government's debt, and it too deliberately promoted a boom in its own stock. In 1720, a few months after Law's failure had shown the precariousness of stock booms, the South Sea Bubble burst.

These twin financial catastrophes slowed the development of joint-stock companies, and ruined many individual investors. But despite their speculative excesses, the bold experimenters in London and Paris had nevertheless shown new ways to mobilize capital for

1660	1689	1714		1917	
Restored House of Stuart	Wm. & Mary, Anne		House of Hanover		(House of Windsor)

commerce and industry and to support the public debt from hitherto untapped sources. After reorganization, both companies made money for their investors for many years. However, the French government, by partially repudiating its debt in the wake of the crash, lost the confidence of investors. The French acquired a fierce distrust of credit, an attitude that thenceforth constricted their economic growth. London did not make that mistake. The British government never again permitted private interests to assume responsibility for the state debt. Britain thus assured itself the credit that meant the difference between victory and defeat in a world of warring states.

The England of Walpole

The generation of external peace after the death of Louis XIV allowed England to consolidate its internal peace. Under the Act of Settlement of 1701, the Elector of Hanover succeeded Anne as ruler of England in 1714. The first two Hanoverian monarchs, George I (r. 1714–27) and George II (r. 1727–60), were dull-witted and spoke little English. Their only claim to distinction was their patronage of the great composer Handel, whom they induced to settle permanently in England. In politics, their chief contribution was petty interference in minor details of government; the "inner cabinet" of ministers therefore became increasingly responsible for framing policy. Although the king in theory remained free to choose his own ministers, Parliament's control over finances meant that he had to select men who could influence elections and command a majority. These leading ministers inevitably met frequently and developed a series of tacit rules of the game. Ministers usually accepted the leadership of the ablest or most

powerful minister, who presented their policy to the king. Those who disagreed with the group's majority lost their offices. These informal practices foreshadowed the nineteenth century "prime minister" and "cabinet system" that later became almost universal in the representative democracies of western Europe and of the English-speaking world.

Robert Walpole, a country squire with family connections to both the landed gentry and commercial interests, was the first prime minister, although he did not accept that title. For some 20 years, from 1721 to 1742, he managed the Whig party in Parliament and led the government. The first two Hanoverians by necessity chose their ministers from the Whigs who dominated the House of Commons, for affection for the Stuarts tainted the Tories after the abortive Scottish Jacobite rising in 1715.

Walpole was a consummate manipulator who held his parliamentary majority together by tact, persuasion, patronage, and bribery. He maintained George I's favor by passing generous budgets for the king's household through Parliament, and by an occasional donation to the royal mistress. His enjoyment of drink and off-color tales—as well as a steely ambition—helped him to manage the Whig merchants and landed gentry who controlled Parliament and ran local government as justices of the peace. But his principal appeal was that he offered to England a political stability unknown since Elizabeth I.

"Let sleeping dogs lie" was Walpole's motto. He sought to defuse religious conflict. He maintained the Test Act to reassure the Anglicans, but conciliated dissenters by annual parliamentary votes that in effect suspended the Test Act temporarily and allowed

The first two Hanoverians: medal and signature of George I of England, and a caricature of George II drawn by a British officer (below).

Robert Walpole (left) dominating the House of Commons (engraving after a painting by Hogarth)

shoes") from the parliamentary opposition.

Under Walpole's ministry, Britain and its colonies prospered; the credit of the government remained high; the ruling aristocracy of landed and commercial wealth governed in its own interests, but far less repressively than did other European ruling classes. Voltaire, after his visit to England between 1726 and 1729, somewhat idealized English society and government. He neglected to mention to his French readers the ferocity of eighteenth-century English law toward crimes against property. In theory it imposed death by hanging for over 200 offenses, including on occasion the theft of items worth as little as 5 shillings. In practice, "transportation" to the colonies usually took the place of hanging, and English laws guaranteed equality and individual freedom to an extent unknown on the continent except perhaps in the Dutch Netherlands and Switzerland. But Walpole's golden age of the gentry did not last. In 1739 the London merchants and their spokesmen in Parliament forced him into a commercial war with Spain. Within three years his majority collapsed and he left office.

France: Louis XV and Cardinal Fleury

The peace that brought strength to Britain brought weakness to France. Louis XIV's great-grandson, Louis XV (r. 1715–74), became king at the age of five. The Duke of Orléans, the nephew of Louis XIV who governed as Regent during the new king's minority, secured his own power by concessions to the powerful elements in French society that the Sun King had kept leashed. Nobles reappeared as royal ministers. The *Parlement* of Paris boldly reasserted its ancient claim to register and enforce royal legislation—or not—as it saw fit. The French monarchy remained as absolute as ever in theory, but after Louis XIV it lacked the ruthless will needed to translate theory into practice. The

dissenters to hold public office. His policy of "salutary neglect" left the colonies to grow in population and wealth by their own efforts. Above all, he did his best to avoid war; he maintained until the 1730s the alliance with France that his predecessors had concluded in 1716–17 in order to safeguard Hanoverian possessions in Germany. Walpole's principal failure was domestic. He failed in 1733 to reform taxation by replacing customs duties, which encouraged smuggling, with excise taxes on tobacco and wines. The issue provoked a storm of irrational abuse ("No excise, no popery, no wooden

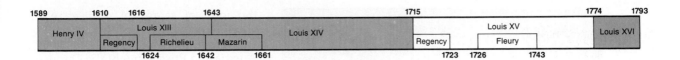

1589	1610	1616	1643		1715		1774	1793
Henry IV	Louis XIII		Louis XIV			Louis XV	Louis XVI	
	Regency	Richelieu	Mazarin		Regency	Fleury		
		1624	1642	1661	1723	1726	1743	

consequent reinforcement of the privileges of the aristocracy exasperated the middle classes and in the long run condemned the royal government to financial ruin.

Cardinal Fleury, the leading minister from 1726 to 1743, arrested the decline for a time. But Fleury was no Richelieu. He came to power at the age of 73, and his policy, much like Walpole's, sought to avoid expensive wars and to conciliate rather than confront powerful domestic interests. Fleury dissociated himself from the courageous attempt of another minister to tax the nobility. He nevertheless stabilized the currency, encouraged trade, and had considerable success in damping down the continuing religious struggle between Jansenists and Jesuits. In foreign policy his overriding goal was to prevent the renewal of the coalitions against France that Louis XIV had inspired. Fleury therefore sought to cooperate with Walpole in making the Anglo-French alliance work.

When Fleury died in 1743 at the age of 90, Louis XV took Louis XIV as his model. Henceforth he sought to govern personally, without a first minister. But although Louis XV had inherited many of his great-grandfather's tastes—women and the hunt above all—he lacked the Sun King's relentless capacity for sustained work. The court frivolity with which Louis XIV had sought to corrupt the aristocracy had also corrupted the great king's successor. The consequence of the indolence of Louis XV, given the centralized administrative machine that the Sun King had left behind, was a fatal lack of coordination between the various branches of the bureaucracy and frequent paralysis. Louis XV did not govern himself, and from 1743 until his death in 1774 he largely prevented others from governing for him.

The aristocracy and the royal mistresses, of which the Marquise de Pompadour (1745–51) and Countess du Barry (1768–74) were the most conspicuous, inevitably filled the resulting power vacuum. Louis XV was not unaware of the declining health of the state: "After me, the deluge" was his most famous—and justly remembered—remark. But France, thanks to its size, its population, and a growth rate in trade and industry as rapid as Britain's, nevertheless remained potentially the most powerful nation in Europe.

Declining or Stagnant Powers

Elsewhere in Europe, with few exceptions, monarchical institutions likewise declined. In Spain a remarkable woman ruled: Elizabeth Farnese, the strong-willed Italian queen of that Philip V of Bourbon (r. 1700–46) whom Louis XIV had established on the throne. With the help of her husband's chief ministers, Elizabeth Farnese beat back the claims of the nobility, encouraged trade and industry, and reestablished Spain's diplomatic status as a great power. But Spanish society and government failed to respond to treatment. Centralization that robbed subjects of all initiative, a taxation more crushing than anything west of Russia, absurd guild regulations, a pitilessly intolerant Church that was the single largest social institution, an indolent nobility that amounted to 5 percent of the population, and a culturally rooted distaste for commerce and industry had bitten too deep. Spain failed to recover from depopulation, deforestation, and lethargy. Its economy, colonies, army, and navy stagnated, while other powers pressed onward.

Austria remained an imperfectly united empire that linked the three kingdoms of Austria, Bohemia, and

Habsburg domestic life, painted by Meytens: Empress Maria Theresa of Austria with her husband, Emperor Francis I, and their eleven children. The future Emperor Joseph II stands at right center.

the form of scraps of territory elsewhere; Spain received Naples and Sicily from Austria. Simultaneously, Austria and Russia fought the Ottoman Turks, whose decline accelerated as Europe's technological lead continued to grow.

Russia after Peter I failed to make its full weight felt for a generation. His succession law, enacted after his mortal quarrel with his son Alexei, gave the autocrat power to choose his own successor. That in effect made Russia until after 1800 an elective monarchy—and the Guards regiments and court nobles did the electing, with bayonets. Between 1725 and 1741, palace coups gave the crown successively to women or children who reigned but did not rule. From 1741 to 1762 Elizabeth, a daughter of Peter I, ruled firmly after seizing power with the help of the Guards and eliminating her opponents in the customary fashion—by torture, execution, deportation, and confiscation of land.

German and particularly Prussian influence predominated at court. As in France, the nobility freed itself from many of the restrictions that a great monarch had placed upon it. The Russian nobility extended the power over the serfs that Peter I had given it, while gradually escaping its corresponding obligation to serve the state. In Russia, as in Hungary and Prussia during the eighteenth century, the peasant thus sank ever deeper into serfdom, while the government made repeated concessions to the nobility. Until the accession of Elizabeth, and especially of Catherine the Great in 1762, Russia lacked strong rulers. But the feebleness of Peter I's immediate successors showed the full extent of his greatness. Despite weakness at the center, Russia retained the great power status the great tsar had won for it.

Prussia: Sergeant King, Undisciplined Son

Prussia, as usual, was an exception to a general trend, for its monarchy became more rather than less absolute. King

Hungary with two dependencies of entirely different cultures and traditions, northern Italy and the southern Netherlands. And the dynastic ties that bound together this bizarre assortment of territories were themselves open to challenge. The Habsburg Emperor Charles VI (r. 1711–40) had no son. He therefore spent almost 30 years in persuading both his provinces and the powers to accept a "Pragmatic Sanction" that established his daughter Maria Theresa as heir to his scattered lands. By his death in 1740 he had secured the agreement on paper of all concerned. But in the absence of a strong Habsburg army and central bureaucracy, treaties were a fragile defense against the greed of neighboring monarchs and the restlessness of the Hungarian nobility.

Farther to the east, the Polish and Ottoman empires continued their decline. France and Spain fought a desultory and trivial war against Austria and Russia over the succession to the Polish crown between 1733 and 1738. The Russian candidate for the throne won. The losers received "compensation" in

Frederick William I of Brandenburg-Prussia (r. 1713–40) was the most successful ruler of his generation. This strange, uncouth, and furious man, who smoked tobacco and drank beer in Gargantuan quantities, was the second of the three great Hohenzollerns that made the poor and backward territories of Brandenburg-Prussia into a great power.

Frederick William followed in the footsteps of the Great Elector, centralizing his administration in a board known as the General Directory, paring civil expenditures to the bone, and working his subordinates remorselessly. The purpose of this drill-sergeant king was to build the most formidable army in Europe. He echoed Richelieu in demanding absolute obedience to the state: "Salvation is from the Lord, but everything else is my business." After 1733, he militarized the peasantry by imposing a form of conscription, the "Canton System." Peasants in the ranks served Junker officers who were the brothers or cousins of the Junker landlords they labored for in civilian life. Frederick William doubled Prussia's peacetime standing army to 80,000, nearly equal to Austria's theoretical total of 100,000 men. But he was careful not to use his blue-coated and precisely drilled army, for he loved his "blue boys" too much to expend them in war.

His son Frederick II (r. 1740–86)—the third great Hohenzollern—thus inherited a treasury surplus, a ruthlessly efficient civil bureaucracy, and an army that was the fourth largest force on the continent and the most relentlessly trained. Frederick had initially impressed his father as a pathetic figure, unmilitary in habits and possessed of decadent tastes such as reading Voltaire and playing the flute. The irate father burned books, smashed flutes, and had Frederick beaten. When Frederick attempted to flee the country with a friend in 1730, the king had the friend beheaded before Frederick's eyes, threatened Frederick himself with death for "desertion," and set him to work in the provincial bureaucracy.

The experience rendered Frederick cold, dissimulating, and supremely cynical. But he also acquired a passion for administration and war, and a burning ambition to acquire glory and "establish his sovereignty like a rock of bronze." His opportunity came in 1740, the year in which his hated father and Charles VI of Habsburg both died.

THE WORLD WARS OF MID-CENTURY, 1740–63

Two great wars, the War of the Austrian Succession (1740–48) and the Seven Years' War (1756–63) punctuated the middle of the century. The wars were linked, and derived from two irreconcilable rivalries—Hohenzollern against Habsburg in central Europe, and Britain against France in North America, the West Indies, Africa, and India. Twice these separate conflicts became entangled, although the powers exchanged partners between the two wars. In the end, as established in the Peace of Paris of 1763, Britain and Prussia defeated France and Austria.

Father and son: Frederick William I in a characteristic pose, and the young Frederick II (below).

British Navy, Prussian Army

These wars demonstrated the superiority of the two greatest military institutions of the eighteenth century, the British navy and the Prussian army. Superiority in both cases rested on the unrivaled excellence of the officer corps. But behind the "wooden walls" of Britain's fleets or the ruler-straight ranks of Prussia's blue-coats stood two sharply different societies and political systems, each well adapted to the competitive environment they faced.

British sea power enjoyed many advantages. Britain was an island, safe from invasion by land and therefore able to pour into ships the men and money that continental rivals such as the Dutch or the French had to devote to armies. Maritime enterprise was both profitable and patriotic. Seafaring careers attracted enterprising younger sons of the nobility and gentry as well as yeomen and artisans. Britain's reservoir of experienced sailors was larger than that of France, its nearest rival, because the British by mid-century had the largest merchant marine in the world. Finally, the government and the groups represented in Parliament recognized the paramount importance of trade and sea power. Despite occasional periods of neglect, Parliament supported naval construction and encouraged British shipping.

Britain's rival France had corresponding advantages—experienced sailors, a large merchant marine, warships superior in design even to the British, and colonial bases overseas. But France lacked secure access to the "strategic raw materials" of the day, the immense mast timbers and the turpentine and pine-tar of the Baltic. Above all, France had long land frontiers and a tradition of pushing those frontiers eastward. France inevitably gave its army priority, and exposed its navy to defeat. Like later continental challengers to the English-speaking sea powers, it lacked the resources to be *both* the greatest land power and the greatest sea power.

Nor did France prosper on land, for it ultimately faced a far more efficient power machine than itself: Prussia. The Prussian bureaucracy and fiscal system had emerged from institutions devised to support the army. The Junkers had

Maritime supremacy: the British Channel Fleet (1790).

acknowledged that their calling was to serve the king, in the army by preference, in the bureaucracy if necessary. Enterprising members of the small middle class established state-supported war industries or enlisted in the civil service. Serfs did labor service as civilians and military service as conscripts. The example of this army, with its harsh *"Kadavergehorsam"*—"corpse-obedience," the obedience that supposedly made the dead snap to attention—permeated Prussian society. In Britain, central government by Parliament, local government by amateurs, and freedom of opinion and commerce proved a formula for sea power. In Prussia, absolute monarchy, centralized professional administration, a disciplined aristocracy, state regulation of the economy, and automaton-like obedience produced the most effective land power for its size since Sparta.

The War of the Austrian Succession, 1740–48

In 1740 Maria Theresa (r. 1740–80), a beautiful, strong-willed, courageous, but inexperienced woman of 23, succeeded her father Charles VI in the Habsburg dominions, as established by the Pragmatic Sanction. That gave Frederick II of Prussia his opportunity. He had published an anonymous pamphlet against the supposed immorality of Machiavelli's political precepts, but he had learned the great Florentine's lessons well. In December 1740 he seized Silesia, Austria's rich province to the northeast of Bohemia. Possession of Silesia, with its million inhabitants, its linen industry, and its iron ore, would finally make Brandenburg-Prussia a great power.

Frederick's thrust caught Maria Theresa off guard, and the success of Frederick's shameless aggression encouraged Bavaria, Spain, and finally France to join in the attack, in violation of their Pragmatic Sanction pledges. But Hungary, which resented Habsburg rule, ironically proved Maria Theresa's salvation. When she traveled to Budapest with her infant son and made an emotional appeal to the Hungarian Parliament, her bravery and tact inspired the Hungarian nobility to rise tumultuously to her support. An able minister, Count Haugwitz, centralized the Habsburg administration and reorganized the army during the wars that followed. Austria, a helpless victim in 1740, revived and become a formidable antagonist. But Frederick's armies fought brilliantly, and at Hohenfriedberg in 1745 he achieved Prussia's first great victory due above all to his own generalship. The combined pressure of France, Bavaria, and Prussia—shaky though their alliance was—proved too much for Maria Theresa. In 1748, at Aix-la-Chapelle, she consented to a peace treaty that left Silesia in Frederick's hands.

The Anglo-French overseas rivalry intersected with continental war. Britain went to war with Spain in 1739 over Spanish maltreatment of English merchants smuggling goods to the Spanish empire. That "war of Jenkins' Ear" (named after an unfortunate English trader), and French intervention in Germany in support of a Bavarian claimant to the office of Holy Roman Emperor, made conflict between France and Britain almost inevitable. France and Spain, thanks to their Bourbon family ties, normally cooperated closely after 1700, and France had developed a large economic stake in the Spanish colonies, which it supplied with most of their manufactured goods.

British and French interests also clashed in North America and India. The French military hold on Canada and Louisiana appeared to threaten the British colonies that stretched from Boston to Savannah. The fantastic rates of population growth of the British colonies on the eastern seaboard prompted a northward and westward expansion that appeared to threaten the French. In the West Indies both sides glowered at one another from their sugar-island strongholds. In India, where the Mughal empire had fallen into near-anarchy after the death in 1707 of the merciless Aurangzeb, its last strong ruler, the French and British East India companies sought to fill a power vacuum. From their respective bases at Pondicherry and Madras, each European power mobilized native rulers against the other. From Canada to the Carnatic Coast of India, France and Britain prepared for war, and British and French troops clashed in Germany as early as 1743.

In 1744 France declared war on Great Britain, and merged the continental and overseas wars. In 1745 a force of American colonial militia with British naval support boldly seized the key to Canada, the great fortress of Louisbourg on Cape Breton Island in the St. Lawrence estuary. In 1746 the French seized Madras. But the overseas conflict was indecisive because Britain failed to set clear objectives and establish priorities. The "Patriot" partisans of overseas war in Parliament denounced the continental commitment as "Hanoverianism," a pandering to the interests of George II, who led the British army in Germany to defend his possessions as Elector of Hanover against France. The French defeated the British in a hard-fought battle at Fontenoy in the Austrian Netherlands in 1745, while in 1747 the British navy twice annihilated French fleets escorting West Indies convoys. George II's son, "Butcher" Cumberland, savaged the Highland clans after his victory over the last pro-Stuart rising, which had broken out with French encouragement in 1745.

Neither side pressed its successes far, except in Scotland. The War of the Austrian Succession was a typical "limited" war. The Anglo-French duel ended in stalemate. The French surrendered Madras and the British government, much to the disgust of the American colonists, gave back Louisbourg. The French emerged from the war with increased prestige, an enlarged debt, and no concrete gains over either Britain or Austria. The British emerged with a clear sense of how to fight their next war with France.

The Overseas "War Before the War," 1749–55

The peace of Aix-la-Chapelle did not end the overseas conflict between Britain and France. Joseph Dupleix, France's greatest colonial adventurer, sought after 1748 to make the French East India Company a political as well as a commercial power in India. By securing allies among the warring native states that contended within the hollow shell of the Mughal empire, he hoped to increase his company's revenue and ultimately drive the British from India. The English East India Company reinforced its outposts. Clashes ensued in which the British largely prevailed, thanks to command of the sea and the brilliant leadership of Dupleix's great adversary, the legendary Robert Clive. In 1754 the company directors, fearing that Dupleix had overreached himself, recalled him to France. The ensuing truce merely postponed the struggle for mastery in south Asia that Dupleix had begun.

In America, open warfare did not break out until 1752. The French in Canada used the interval of peace to build a chain of forts from the St. Lawrence down the Ohio to the Mississippi to block the westward thrust of Britain's American colonists. London countered, reinforcing the colonies with ships and troops. Britain held the advantage; 1.2 million British subjects, including slaves, faced roughly 60,000 French. The French sought to even the odds by an alliance with Indian tribes whose interest in preventing British westward penetration ran parallel to that of France. French raids in turn provoked in 1754 an unsuccessful attempt, under the leadership of Lieutenant Colonel George Washington of the Virginia militia, to capture the vital French base at Fort Duquesne, on the site of modern Pittsburgh. In 1755, near the same spot, General George Braddock and a force of British regulars discovered that rigid European tactics were ill-suited to war in the woods. The "French and Indian War," the final round of the Anglo-French struggle for North America, had begun.

1701	1714		1740	1748	1756	1763		1789	1815
War of Spanish Succession	Walpole, Fleury, and Frederick William I		War of Austrian Succession	Diplomatic Revolution	Seven Years' War		Last Years of the Old Regime	Revolutionary Era	

The Climax of Old Regime Statecraft: The "Diplomatic Revolution" of 1756

Overseas struggle was merely one prelude to a second round of war in Europe. The other prelude was a "diplomatic revolution" by which the chief antagonists of the first general war of mid-century changed partners in preparation for the second. Britain had fought the War of the Austrian Succession in loose agreement with Austria, its traditional ally from the wars of 1689–97 and 1701–13. But London saw no British interest served in fighting simply to restore Silesia to Maria Theresa. Bourbon France had fought against its traditional Habsburg enemy in a still looser alliance with Prussia; Frederick distrusted Paris and twice deserted it to make truces with Austria. By 1748, all four major powers were disenchanted with their traditional allies.

The chief instigator of the ensuing "revolution" was Maria Theresa's chancellor, the wily Prince Wenzel Anton von Kaunitz. He began from the premise that the reconquest of Silesia—and the annihilation of Prussia—was the prerequisite for Austria's resurgence as a great power. That aim prompted Kaunitz to think the hitherto unthinkable. He sought to replace the ancient antagonism between Bourbon and Habsburg with a Franco-Austrian alliance, possibly with Russian support, against Prussia. Even the battlefield genius of Frederick II, Kaunitz was confident, would be helpless against the three strongest land powers in Europe.

Kaunitz sought with success to win over the Marquise de Pompadour, the current mistress of Louis XV. But the king remained reluctant—until Britain and Prussia unintentionally convinced him. London had long feared that its Austrian ally lacked the will and ability to help Britain defend Hanover against France, and the outbreak of Anglo-French hostilities overseas increased British anxieties. In 1755 London therefore sought Russian help in the usual British way; a subsidy treaty that exchanged British gold for allied troops. That treaty alarmed Frederick II, for it raised the specter of a large Russian army encamped on his eastern border. He therefore approached London, and in effect outbid Russia. By the treaty of Westminster of January 1756, Prussia itself agreed to defend Hanover, naturally in exchange for a British subsidy.

The spectacle of Prussia, France's ally, contracting a quasi-alliance with Britain, a power already in conflict with France from the Ohio to the Carnatic, finally aroused the wrath of Louis XV. Bourbon France made a defensive alliance with Habsburg Austria. Kaunitz also enlisted Russia, and planned war for 1757. Frederick II judged that his only chance was to strike first. The Austrians had hoped for such a blow, to weld Kaunitz's grand coalition together. Unfortunately for Kaunitz, Frederick II struck in August 1756, a year earlier than Vienna had anticipated. Unfortunately for Frederick, his aggression indeed did Kaunitz's work. It brought into play Austria's French alliance and created a grand coalition that almost destroyed Prussia.

The Seven Years' War, 1756–63

In the new war, the greatest worldwide conflict of the old regime, Britain thus fought for empire and Prussia for its life. After an inauspicious beginning, William Pitt became virtual prime minister of Britain. Pitt possessed a Roman nose, a talent for commanding oratory, and a clear sense of Britain's global objectives. Convinced of his own indispensability ("I am sure I can save this country, and nobody else can") he pushed his way into the cabinet in spite of the disfavor of George II. From 1757 to 1760, he tirelessly directed Brit-

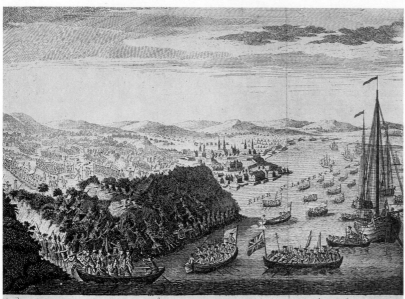

View of the Taking of QUEBECK by the English Forces Commanded by Gen.ᵃˡ Wolfe Sep: 13.ᵗʰ 1759.

Britain's command of the sea in action: Wolfe takes Québec, 1759.

ain's war and drove his subordinates to unprecedented exertions. In 1757, at Plassey near Calcutta, Robert Clive destroyed France's principal client, the Nawab of Bengal, and seized his rich province for Britain. That broke French power in India. Britain conquered France's chief slaving station at Gorée in Senegal and cut France's West Indian sugar islands off from their supplies of slaves and manufactured goods.

In the "year of miracles" of 1759, Pitt conquered for Britain the domination of the outer seas that it held with only brief interruptions until 1941. A brilliant young general, James Wolfe, led an amphibious expedition up the St. Lawrence River. Outside the walls of Québec city he defeated France at the cost of his own life, and ended the French empire in North America. British fleets captured the rich West Indies sugar island of Guadeloupe and drove the French fleet in a gale onto the lee shore of Quiberon Bay in western France. Command of the sea was the decisive ingredient in Britain's triumphs.

On the continent, Prussia survived only thanks to Frederick II and to his long-suffering troops, whom he drove toward the enemy with sarcastic wit: "You dogs, do you want to live for ever?" Prussia's "year of miracles" was 1757. At Rossbach in Saxony, Frederick with 21,000 troops decisively defeated a French army of 64,000 by attacking them in the flank. Having thus checked one of his three enemies, he hastened back to defend Silesia from Austrian invasion. A bare month after Rossbach he smashed an Austrian army of 80,000 at Leuthen with a mere 36,000 Prussian troops. A Prussian feint lured the Austrians into weakening their left, which Frederick then rolled up.

But these great victories produced no decisive strategic result. Frederick was the supreme artist of eighteenth-century warfare, but his instrument did not permit battles of annihilation. Pursuit, necessary to prevent a beaten enemy from reforming to fight again, was impossible with troops that deserted once out of sight of their officers. And Prussia's desperate position, exposed to the French from the west, the Austrians from the south, and the Russians from the east, prevented the great king from finishing off any one of his adversaries. The war dragged on; Russia made its weight felt, and in 1759 an Austro-Russian army heavily defeated Frederick at Kunersdorf in Silesia.

Frederick thought despairingly of abdication. But the divisions of his enemies saved him and Prussia. Kaunitz had not promised to France and Russia enough of the expected spoils to stimulate them to all-out effort. Austria understandably feared that Russian troops, once invited into central Europe, would not leave. France's naval and overseas campaigns had exhausted its treasury, and the disgrace of Rossbach had shattered the monarchy's already low reputation at home. Pitt's lavish subsidies to the armies of German princelings, along with token British forces, pinned the French down in bloody fighting in western Germany.

In 1760 Frederick temporarily lost Berlin and by the end of 1761 he appeared close to total defeat, as 300,000 allied troops penned him into a fortified camp in Silesia. His British ally abandoned him. George III (r. 1760–1820), who had succeeded his grandfather, wished to prove himself thoroughly English, unlike the first two Georges. He therefore withdrew from all involvement in German affairs and drove Pitt to resignation in October 1761. Lord Bute, George III's Scottish favorite, became chief minister and sought peace with France at almost any price, including the sacrifice of Prussia.

Then, on January 5, 1762, Elizabeth of Russia died. Her successor was the weak and eccentric Tsar Peter III, a German by birth and a fond admirer of Frederick the Great. He immediately withdrew Russia from the coalition. Only a crippled and sulking France now supported Vienna, and Maria Theresa and Kaunitz grudgingly abandoned their hopes of crushing the Prussian upstart. In February 1763, by the treaty of Hubertusburg, Austria and Prussia restored the boundaries of 1756. Prussia had successfully sustained its claim to Silesia and to great power status.

The Peace of Paris, 1763

The peace that emerged in January 1763 from the Anglo-French negotiations at Paris was overwhelmingly favorable to Great Britain. But contrary to Pitt's wishes it did not entirely eliminate France as an overseas rival. France received back most of the economic outposts it had lost—trading stations in India, Gorée in West Africa, rich sugar islands in the West Indies, the fishing rights off Canada, along with two tiny islands off Newfoundland, St. Pierre and Miquelon.

But in the long run only the continents counted. Trading posts could only flourish if they controlled a large hinterland. Sugar islands produced great wealth in a few square miles, but were incapable of defending themselves against a power, such as Britain, that controlled the sea. Failure at sea and the collapse of French land power in India and North America broke the

first French colonial empire for good. France agreed to maintain no further troops in India and to recognize Britain's native client rulers. France ceded to Britain all of Canada and of Louisiana east of the Mississippi, and Louisiana west of the Mississippi passed to Spain. Henceforth the British had no serious rivals in North America except the colonists they had planted there.

ENLIGHTENED ABSOLUTISM, 1763–89

In the quarter century that followed the Peace of Paris, the ancient institution of monarchy briefly seemed to take on new life. The major ideas of the Enlightenment—reason, natural law, happiness, progress, liberty—filtered through to the rulers. Some monarchs accepted the criticisms that *philosophes* had leveled at aristocratic and ecclesiastical privilege, unequal taxation, and the degraded condition of the peasantry and the urban lower classes. In addition, the great wars of mid-century strained the social fabric of most European states. The resurgence of the aristocracy forced monarchs to look to the middle classes for support. Only reform could restore order, revive trade, refill the treasuries of Europe's monarchs, and check the pretensions of the nobility. The fusion of new ideas and practical needs produced the phenomenon that contemporaries described as "enlightened absolutism."

The enlightened absolutist was naturally an ideal type that fitted few rulers of the later eighteenth century. George III of England made no pretense to "enlightenment," nor would his subjects have applauded if he had, for English loyalty to the post-1688 status quo ran deep. In his last years, Louis XV of France showed unexpected resolution and zeal, but during most of his reign he was enlightened in few senses of the word. A few minor monarchs such as Gustavus III of Sweden (r. 1771–92) and Charles III of Spain (r. 1759–88) had some claims to the title. But the three rulers that *philosophes* cited most often as enlightened absolutists were Catherine the Great of Russia, Frederick the Great of Prussia, and Joseph II of Austria.

The attack of the enlightened absolutists on irrational customs and vested interests, on aristocratic and Church power, on town and provincial privileges was not new. It was in most respects a continuation of the centralizing drive of the seventeenth-century monarchies. What had changed was the climate of opinion in which monarchs acted. The ideas of the Enlightenment, the practical example of Britain, and the victorious struggle for self-government of the British colonies in North America after 1776 stripped the doctrine of divine right of kings of its persuasiveness. Monarchs therefore had to appeal to their increasingly literate subjects with talk of following reason and of serving the public good. Frederick the Great described himself as "merely the first servant of the state." That state was not the people; their duty also was to serve the state—which the monarch personified. Monarchs might be "enlightened," but they sought to remain absolute. That monarchy felt compelled to justify itself by reference to the good of society was nevertheless a sign of fatal weakness.

Russia: Catherine the Great

Catherine II (r. 1762–96), the most remarkable woman ruler of the century, was no Russian. Princess of the German line of Anhalt-Zerbst, she married the eccentric crown prince Peter in 1745. A woman of high intelligence, masterful cunning, implacable will, and a warm heart, she maintained a succession of lovers with lavish gifts of lands and serfs; as the poet Pushkin later remarked, "many were called, and many chosen." In her youth, Catherine survived the snake-pit of the St. Petersburg court by making pretense of frivolity, while finding allies and a lover among the officers of the crucial Guards regiments. Her husband Peter,

after his accession as Peter III in 1762, alienated those same regiments by proposing to reform them along Prussian lines. He also appalled the pious by confiscating church lands. Six months after Peter's accession, Catherine seized power with the help of the Guards. Peter perished while under arrest, apparently at the hands of a relative of Grigori Orlov, Catherine's lover.

Catherine came to power with a genuine desire to improve the lot of her subjects. She read the works of *philosophes* such as Montesquieu and advanced thinkers such as Beccaria. She corresponded with Voltaire, persuaded Diderot to visit her court, and proclaimed publicly her adherence to the Enlightenment. But as autocrat she could not afford too much enlightenment. Survival required escape from the grip of the faction that had brought her to power and the elimination of all potential rivals for the throne. She therefore sought to widen her political base by conciliating the nobility as a whole. She confirmed the most important act of her husband's brief reign, his release of the nobility from any obligation to serve the state. She gave the nobility a monopoly on land ownership. She made promotion in the bureaucracy automatic, by seniority, a step that gravely weakened the effective power of her successors. In 1785 she granted the nobility a charter that conceded at last some rights against the state, some exemption from arbitrary arrest and the barbaric punishments customary in Muscovite law and practice. But since the autocrat could still revoke noble status at any moment, the rights Catherine's charter granted were as much a matter of form as of substance.

In 1767–68 she even summoned a Legislative Commission to codify Russia's laws. Every social group except serfs sent representatives, who assembled armed with statements of grievances. That was the autocracy's first open appeal to its subjects, its first at-

Determination: Catherine the Great, on a medal struck to commemorate her accession as empress of Russia.

tempt to give them a voice in government. It was also the last before the twentieth century, when the last tsar conceded under duress a sham parliament. Catherine dissolved the Commission before it could suggest laws; its passing marked the waning of her "enlightened" phase.

She nevertheless drew from it a sense of what her subjects, especially the nobility, wanted. What they wanted and Catherine conceded was the strengthening of serfdom. As early as 1765 she gave landlords the power to condemn serfs to forced labor without legal formalities. In 1767 she forbade serf complaints against landlords upon pain of penal servitude for life and flogging with the dreaded Russian whip—the knout. The knout, now that the nobility was no longer obliged to do state service that justified their holding of serfs, was soon needed, for the freeing of the nobility in turn raised expectations among the serfs. When Catherine disappointed those expectations, the greatest of all Russian peasant revolts convulsed the Volga region from 1773 to 1775 under the leadership of the Cossack Emelyan Pugachev, who claimed to be Peter III. The army ultimately massacred the insurgents and brought Pugachev in an iron cage to Moscow. There, in time-honored fashion, Catherine had him broken on the wheel, beheaded, dismembered, and burnt.

In the following years she sought to reorganize and strengthen local government to prevent further revolts, while extending the institution of serfdom to newly conquered provinces and to hitherto free categories of peasants. By the end of her reign, by one estimate, 34 million of the 36 million subjects of the Russian monarchy were serfs. By her encouragement of the nobility she furthered a process that never reached completion, the transformation of the service nobility into a Western-style aristocracy with rights against the state. In Russia, unlike western Europe, that process rested

upon the further enslavement of the peasantry, and left a dangerous legacy.

Conquest, not reform, made Catherine II "the Great" in her own lifetime. Peter the Great had broken a window to the west by driving the Swedes from the Baltic coast. Catherine pushed Russia's borders southward and westward against Poland and the Ottoman Empire. Poland was her first victim, for its borders at her accession were a mere 200 miles from Moscow. In 1763 Catherine secured the election to the Polish throne of a former lover, Stanislaus Poniatowski. Thereafter, Catherine and Frederick II of Prussia worked to block constitutional reforms that might revive the fortunes of the Polish state. In 1772 the two monarchs combined to carry out a First Partition of Poland. Frederick took West Prussia, and thus

Russia's Expansion in Europe   1462–1796

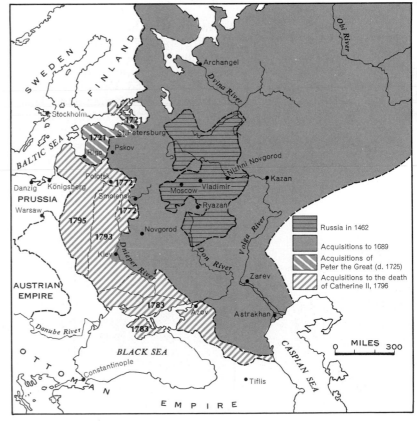

Russia in 1462

Acquisitions to 1689

Acquisitions of Peter the Great (d. 1725)

Acquisitions to the death of Catherine II, 1796

son of state triumphed over personal morality.

The first partition shocked the Poles into a patriotic revival that swept up even Poniatowski, who forgot that he owed his throne to Catherine. In 1791, after the outbreak of the French Revolution, Poland enacted a remarkable reform constitution that abolished the *liberum veto* and established a strong monarchy. Catherine gave a swift and ruthless answer. Early in 1792 she ceased a promising war against the Turks, rushed an army to Poland, and restored the old anarchy. In 1793, in partnership with Prussia alone, she carried out a Second Partition that reduced Poland to a narrow strip, wedged between Prussia, Russia, and Austria. The inhabitants of this rump-Poland, under the leadership of Thaddeus Kosciuszko, who had fought conspicuously in the American Revolution, rose against the partitioning powers. But Catherine's armies tracked down Kosciuszko and forced Poniatowski to abdicate. A third partition in 1795 wiped rump-Poland from the map by dividing it between Russia, Prussia, and Austria. In the three partitions, Catherine secured almost two-thirds of Poland's original territory. A Polish state did not reemerge until the simultaneous ruin of the three partitioning powers in 1917–18.

Catherine's successes against the crumbling Ottoman Empire were al-

secured a land bridge between Brandenburg and the province of Prussia. Catherine took a generous slice of northeastern Poland, with the pretext that Russian and Orthodox populations there were suffering under Polish rule. To preserve the balance of power the two monarchs thought it wise to offer the province of Galicia, northeast of Hungary, to Maria Theresa. That gift distressed the pious empress, but rea-

The Partitions of Poland

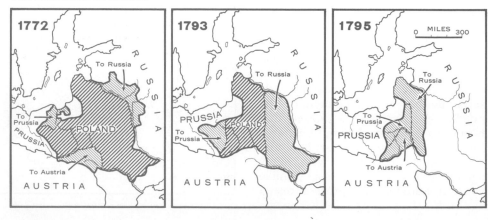

most as decisive. In wars in 1768–74 and 1787–92, Catherine secured most of the northern shore of the Black Sea. By the Treaty of Kütchük Kainardji that ended the first war in 1774, Russia also received a vague right to protect Orthodox Christians in the Ottoman Empire, a right that later served as a perennial pretext for Russian intervention at Constantinople. Kütchük Kainardji marked the opening of the "Eastern Question"—the decay and partition of the Ottoman Empire—that bedeviled European diplomacy until its resolution by force in 1914–18. For the moment, the Ottoman Empire escaped the fate of Poland because of its size, its remoteness, and the mutual jealousies of its two European adversaries, Austria and Prussia. But at Catherine's death in 1796, little seemed to stand between Russian power and Constantinople, the gate to the Mediterranean.

Prussia: Frederick the Great

Frederick II of Prussia, who ruled until 1786, had better claims than Catherine to the title of "enlightened absolutist." The state he inherited, despite its military narrowness, was unlike the "half-German, half-Tartar" autocracy that fell to Catherine II. Prussia's enserfed peasants suffered under the Junkers but had far more rights than the serfs of Russia. Prussia possessed a middle class and was a recognizably Western society capable of accepting gradual reform.

Frederick burnished his reputation for enlightenment by inviting Voltaire to Potsdam. They eventually quarreled over the merits of Frederick's rather awful poetry, but agreed that the king's duty was to combat ignorance and superstition, to enhance the welfare of his subjects, and to promote religious toleration. The king welcomed all religious exiles, even Jesuits; only Jews remained hedged about with vexatious regulations. As a religious skeptic, Frederick found toleration easy.

In economic policy, he was the most determined "mercantilist" since Colbert. His state-directed enterprises sought to give Prussia self-sufficiency,

The Rise of Brandenburg-Prussia   1640–1795

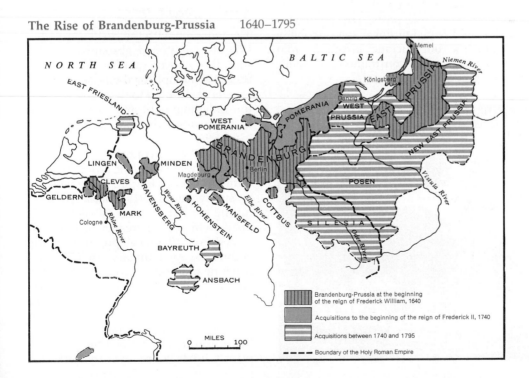

Brandenburg-Prussia at the beginning of the reign of Frederick William, 1640

Acquisitions to the beginning of the reign of Frederick II, 1740

Acquisitions between 1740 and 1795

- - - - Boundary of the Holy Roman Empire

above all in military supplies and equipment. He encouraged the new scientific agriculture that was slowly spreading from Holland. His policies induced 300,000 immigrants, including many skilled agricultural and industrial workers, to settle in Prussia. He also introduced Europe's first scheme for universal primary education, and thus founded a tradition that Prussia built on in the next century with startling effect. Finally, Frederick implemented a typical objective of enlightened absolutism by rationalizing Prussia's laws and court procedures.

Yet in many respects Frederick was less than "enlightened." He believed firmly in birth and privilege. The Junkers served him well as officers in the most important organ of the state, the army. In return for that service he trusted the nobility far more than had his father or the Great Elector. Frederick improved the lot of serfs on his own estates, but had little enthusiasm for emancipation. During his reign, noble estates expanded and the condition of the serfs worsened. His conception of society was static: nobles, townspeople, and peasants should remain at their respective posts. His preference for rigid caste lines over social mobility and for bureaucratic direction from above over unconstrained economic

initiative from below ultimately proved self-defeating.

Despite Frederick's enlightened pose, the discipline, efficiency, and ruthless centralization of the Prussian monarchy ultimately derived from a long Hohenzollern tradition entirely unrelated to the Enlightenment. The state that Frederick erected in wars between 1740 and 1763 and consolidated in peace from 1763 to 1786 was the most striking political achievement of his time. But without him, without a genius at the helm, it was doomed to stagnation thanks to his economic and social policies. Prussia's shattering military successes and the great king's monopoly of diplomacy, strategy, and tactics put the officer corps to sleep. The coming storms of the revolutionary era almost destroyed Prussia. It survived only thanks to the emergence of a "bureaucratic absolutism" in which the bureaucracy and army ran the state themselves, without much need of a monarch. That was Prussia's dangerous legacy to the German state that it ultimately created.

Austria: Joseph II

The monarch with the best claim to the title of enlightened absolutist was Joseph II of Austria (r. 1780–90). He professed contempt for the *philosophes* but was more devoted to the main tenets of the Enlightenment and to the welfare of his peoples than any of his fellow monarchs.

Frederick II's conquest of Silesia in 1740 prompted a drastic reorganization of the Habsburg Empire that enabled it to survive until 1918. Maria Theresa, during her long reign (1740–80), developed an imperial bureaucracy that controlled from Vienna all provinces of the empire except Hungary. In 1775 that machine imposed a tariff union on the empire, except for Hungary. It compelled the nobles to assume some of the burden of taxation. It limited the amount of labor they could extort from the peasantry and curbed the power of private noble courts over the serfs, for

Joseph II urging agricultural improvement on his peasants.

whom Maria Theresa did more than any other ruler of her time.

Her son Joseph, who became emperor and co-regent after the death of her husband in 1765, took an increasingly energetic part in her efforts at reform. But Joseph sought to move farther and faster than his mother. Until her death in 1780 he chafed under Maria Theresa's compromises, particularly over religion. During the ten years that Joseph II ruled, thousands of decrees poured from the imperial chancellery in Vienna. He proclaimed religious toleration for all Christians and Jews. He dissolved monasteries devoted solely to religious contemplation and gave their revenues to the hospitals that in the next century made Vienna the medical center of Europe. He applied to everyone in the Habsburg dominions, regardless of rank or nationality, a system of equal taxation in proportion to income. He imposed one language for official business, German, on all parts of the empire, including Belgium, Italy, and Hungary. Above all, Joseph II abolished serfdom. Early in his reign he issued a number of decrees that gave all serfs in the Habsburg dominions personal freedom—freedom to leave the land, to marry as they pleased, to choose whatever job they liked. That act of Joseph II was permanent, even though his successors repealed other decrees by which he sought to make those peasants who remained on the land into property owners, free of all forced labor obligations.

Through his policies of centralization and drastic reform, Joseph naturally made mortal enemies of the clergy, the landed nobility, non-German nationalities such as the Hungarians, and even peasants who failed to understand his intentions. In 1789, when revolution broke out in France, peasants in the Austrian Empire began to plunder and to murder landlords to gain the rights Joseph had held out to them. By 1790 both Belgium and Hungary were in revolt against his rule, and the Church was bitterly hostile.

Joseph II, the Enlightened Despot   1783

The following extracts illustrate the paradox of enlightened absolutism; only autocratic methods made reform conceivable.

I have not confined myself simply to issuing orders; I have expounded and explained them. With enlightenment I have sought to weaken and with arguments I have sought to overcome the abuses which had arisen out of prejudice and deeply rooted customs. I have sought to imbue every official of the state with the love I myself feel for the wellbeing of the whole. . . .

The good of the state can be understood only in general terms, only in terms of the greatest number. Similarly, all the provinces of the monarchy constitute one whole and therefore can have only one aim. It is necessary therefore that there should be an end to all the prejudices and all the jealousies between provinces [and] all races which have caused so much fruitless bickering. [Circular letter of Joseph II, 1783.]

But given Austria's structure and traditions, only the monarch could dictate unity and the end of "prejudices." The state needed a common language; Joseph II determined what it should be.

The German language is the universal tongue of my empire. I am the emperor of Germany. The states which I possess are provinces that form only one body—the state of which I am the head. If the kingdom of Hungary were the most important of my possessions, I would not hesitate to impose its language on the other countries. [Letter to a Hungarian noble, 1783.]

From T. C. W. Blanning, *Joseph II and Enlightened Despotism* (London: Longman Group, 1970), pp. 131–32, and Louis Léger, *Histoire de l'Autriche Hongrie* (Paris, 1879), p. 373.

Joseph lamented to his brother and successor Leopold that "I am the only one holding to the true course, and I am left to labor alone. . . . I am without any assistance whatsoever." Worn out, he died in 1790 after choosing a rueful epitaph: "Here lies Joseph II, who was unfortunate in everything that he undertook."

Joseph II, the "revolutionary Emperor," built a structure stronger than he knew. It survived both the revolutionary era and the coming nineteenth century. The crippling limitations under which Joseph labored stemmed above all from his position as a revolutionary without a party. His only supports were an unimaginative bureaucracy, a secret police that he had set up to combat opposition, and the Habsburg army. His brand of enlightened absolutism might have formed a bridge between divine-right monarchy and democratic politics. But his fate suggested that radical changes, at least on the Continent, demanded a broader base of popular support than he had been able to command.

BRITAIN, FRANCE, AND THE AMERICAN REVOLUTION, 1763–89

In France and British North America, revolution from below took the place of reform from above. Louis XV made a belated but vigorous attempt to quell internal opposition between 1770 and 1774. Thereafter the French monarchy drifted until its collapse after 1789 in the greatest of modern European revolutions. Overseas, the American colonists claimed their independence in the name of reason and natural rights. When Britain resisted, the colonists broke away by force.

France: Abortive Revolution from Above, 1770–74

The Seven Years' War severely strained both British and French government finances. Louis XV proposed to cope by making permanent a temporary war tax that fell on nobles and commoners alike and by levying a new tax on those who had bought judicial and administrative offices from the monarchy. Such measures, necessary if the monarchy hoped to avoid bankruptcy, raised a storm of opposition from nobility and middle classes alike. The *parlements*, narrow oligarchies of officeholders who had bought their positions, rationalized their privileges by borrowing from Locke. Any attack on their own tax exemption, they impudently proclaimed, violated the "fundamental laws" of the kingdom and the "natural rights" of Frenchmen.

In 1770–71 Louis XV finally acted. His forceful ministers, the lawyer René de Maupeou for political affairs and the Abbé Joseph Marie Terray for finances, closed the *parlements*, exiled their most fractious members to distant villages, and reassessed taxes. Public opinion—except, significantly, for Voltaire—rose in outrage. But the king held fast and won. A new system of royal law courts replaced the *parlements*. Maupeou prepared to rationalize at last France's administration and finances. Then, in 1774, Louis XV caught smallpox and died. His son, Louis XVI (r. 1774–92), well-meaning and lamentably weak, was the monarchy's downfall. He dismissed Maupeou, acquiesced in the restoration of the *parlements*, and presided first over bankruptcy, then over revolution.

The Revolt of Britain's American Colonies

France's revolution did not begin until 1788–89, but events overseas furnished a powerful example. Britain's "salutary neglect" of its North American colonies did not survive the Seven Years' War. As in France, the financial strain of that conflict prompted a search for new revenues. Parliament in London naturally looked to its colonists. The colonies had in the past paid no taxes to Britain, but only customs duties that Parliament had imposed—but only loosely enforced—to channel colonial trade to Britain. The colonists' tax burden was thus a mere 4 percent of the average Englishman's. And while the colonists had done little fighting, London had paid dearly to defend them against the French, against France's Indian allies, and against the 1763 uprising of the Ottawa chief Pontiac. But unfortunately for the British government, its entirely reasonable efforts to raise revenue coincided with the elimination of French power in North America, which freed the colonists of their dependence on Britain. The result, thanks to the traditions of government that the colonies had acquired from England itself, was an explosion that shattered the British Empire.

"Salutary neglect" had permitted a political experiment possible in no other European colonial empire. The thirteen colonies, from quasi-theocratic Massachusetts, to anarchic Rhode Island, to Catholic Maryland, to Anglican Virginia, were in effect self-governing. The ministry in London appointed royal governors, but under the charters granted the colonies, the colonial legislatures, not Parliament, paid the governors' salaries and voted—or refused to vote—the revenues needed to carry on government. Elections to those legislatures were far more democratic than those for Parliament or for other European representative bodies. And the colonists took seriously John Locke's theory of limited government and the practice of England's "Glorious Revolution" of 1688. For them, the British Empire was a quasi-federal structure that rested on consent.

Parliament took a different view. In March 1765, it imposed a stamp tax on printed papers, including legal documents, commercial agreements, and newspapers. That tax, all too familiar to Europeans, aroused furious opposition in America among the most articulate and disputatious groups—lawyers, newspaper editors, and merchants. A congress of delegates from nine of the colonies urged "that no taxes be imposed on them but with their own consent." They claimed further that distance made it impossible in practical terms for Parliament to secure American "consent" to taxation. Parliament retreated. It repealed the Stamp Act in 1766 but at the same time declared that crown and Parliament had the right to tax the colonies if they so wished. In 1767 Parliament returned to the attack with an act that imposed duties on imports into the colonies of tea, paper, paint, lead, and glass. Unlike previous duties, its purpose was to raise revenue, not to regulate trade. The colonists replied with boycotts, and in 1770

Parliament withdrew all duties except those on tea.

Up to that point the colonists had shown little understanding of Britain's financial and military plight, and Parliament had shown little appreciation of the tradition that made the colonists doubt or fear its authority. But despite the death in 1770 of five Boston demonstrators at the hands of British troops (the so-called "Boston massacre"), the quarrel had not led to an irrevocable break. That changed after 1773, when Parliament replaced the East India Company's rule in India with a royal governor general. To compensate the Company for its lost independence, Parliament authorized it to sell its surplus tea directly to American retailers. That would presumably lower prices, increase sales, and thus increase British revenue from the tea duty.

A radical Massachusetts minority—not unconnected to the smuggling trade injured by the East India Company's tea imports—thereupon took action. A party of Bostonians thinly disguised as American Indians boarded three East Indiamen in Boston harbor in December 1773 and dumped thousands of pounds' worth of tea into the murky water. Parliament reacted to this "Boston Tea Party" with fury. In 1774 it closed the port of Boston, deprived the Massachusetts legislature of much of its power, and ordered the deportation of offenders for trial in England. That drove the other twelve colonies to rally behind Massachusetts out of fear that Parliament would likewise revoke or amend their charters.

Worse still, Parliament passed an otherwise statesmanlike measure, the Quebec Act of 1774, at a moment when it appeared to be a further attack on the English-speaking colonies. The act guaranteed the preservation of the French language and the Catholic religion in Canada, and defined Canada to include all territory north of the Ohio River and west of the Allegheny Mountains. It forbade American settlement beyond the mountains. That—and the Act's toleration for "Popery"—

Third of the Hanoverians: the unfortunate George III.

In April 1775, the British garrison at Boston sought to seize arms and gunpowder that the colonists had assembled at Concord. The Massachusetts militia met the redcoats on Lexington green and fired the shots "heard 'round the world." Although the redcoats reached their objective at Concord, American fire from behind houses and stone walls mercilessly harried them back to Boston. A Continental Congress assembled at Philadelphia and formally declared the colonies independent of king and Parliament on July 4, 1776. Its ringing words were Lockean to the very marrow:

> We hold these truths to be self-evident, that all Men are created equal, that they are endowed by their Creator with certain unalienable Rights, that among these are Life, Liberty and the Pursuit of Happiness. That to secure these rights, Governments are instituted among Men, deriving their just Powers from the Consent of the Governed. That whenever any Form of Government becomes destructive to those ends, it is the Right of the People to alter or to abolish it, and to institute new Government. . . .

That was a call to revolution in the Old World as well as in the New.

annoyed both rich and poor, land speculators and pioneers, in the English-speaking colonies.

The Quebec Act and the so-called "Intolerable Acts" against Massachusetts between them marked the point of no return. To George III and to a large majority of his English subjects, the American colonists had proved themselves childish and irresponsible rebels. To a majority of the colonials, Parliament was seeking to impose an unbearable tyranny, the kind of tyranny that they now argued it had been their main purpose to escape when they had originally emigrated. The government of George III succeeded in driving toward rebellion even sober, propertied men who feared unrestrained democracy as "the madness of the multitude." The colonists began to arm.

The American War of Independence

The ensuing War of Independence was a civil war in both colonies and mother country. The colonists had sympathizers in both England and Ireland. A Whig faction that included the founder of modern conservatism, Edmund Burke, in vain urged conciliation on George III and his inept prime minister, Lord North (1770–82). A group of "radicals," under the inspiration of a boisterous and debauched demagogue, John Wilkes, attacked the king's influence in Parliament, urged the publication of Parliamentary debates, and agitated for a democratization of parliamentary elections. Wilkes eventually made his peace with the king, and the English radicals were too small a minority to carry much weight. But they nevertheless proclaimed the political faith of the Declaration of Independence, that government must rest on consent. Conversely, numerous "Tories" in the colonies, from Boston to the backwoods of North Carolina and Georgia, sympathized with or fought for the king. In the course of the war and its aftermath, some 80,000 fled or were driven out to Canada, and their lands confiscated.

The war itself pitted the disorganized colonial militias and the small Continental Army under George Washington against a succession of seaborne British task forces. The Americans' strengths were Washington's unique combination of daring and caution, the sluggish generalship of his British opponents, the smuggled muskets and powder that France supplied after 1776, and widespread popular support for the cause of independence. The British and their Hessian mercenary troops rarely commanded more than the ground under their own feet. Britain's assets were the battlefield professionalism of its troops and its command of the sea.

In October 1777, American forces cornered at Saratoga some 5,000 British troops that had descended from Canada. That victory, although it immediately followed Washington's loss of Philadelphia, ultimately decided the war. It induced Louis XVI and his ambitious foreign minister, the Comte de Vergennes, to intervene actively. French enthusiasts for American independence such as the Marquis de Lafayette had joined Washington well before France acted, but Vergennes, less idealistic than they, sought the humiliation of Britain. The French navy, improved since 1759, fought the British to a standstill in 1778 off Ushant, at the mouth of the Channel. Across the Atlantic it deprived Britain's forces of supplies and seaborne mobility until French defeat at the Battle of the Saintes (West Indies) in April 1782 restored Britain's naval supremacy.

That victory came too late for Britain in North America. At Yorktown in Virginia, a British force of 7,000, penned between the newly hostile sea and American and French troops, had surrendered on October 19, 1781. London, although it still occupied New York with 30,000 troops, recognized the futility of seeking to hold the colonists down by force. In the Treaty of Versailles of 1783, Britain conceded to the thirteen colonies their independence and all land east of the Mississippi, north of Florida, and south of the Great Lakes. France gained revenge for the loss of Canada, some colonial outposts, and immense new debts.

George Washington, victorious at the battle of Princeton (1777), by Charles Wilson Peale.

Yet independence did not settle the form of the new American state. During the war most colonies had summoned conventions and drafted written constitutions with bills of rights. Between 1777 and 1781 the Continental Congress had united the ex-colonies in a loose federal union under the Articles of Confederation. In July 1787 Congress enacted the Northwest Ordinance, a momentous document that extended the principles for which the colonists had fought to the still unsettled western territories. When these territories became populated, they would become not colonies or dependencies but "states," equal in status to the thirteen original members of the union.

But by 1787 it was clear that the Articles of Confederation failed to provide the necessary machinery for a common economic or foreign policy. The result was the summoning of a Constitutional Convention that hammered out, in secret proceedings at Philadelphia between May and September 1787, a new federal Constitution. That document, which began with a characteristic flourish ("We, the People of the United States . . ."), has endured. The Constitution and the Revolution that created it founded the longest continuous tradition of democratic politics in history.

The American Revolution in History

The American Revolution had profound effects on Europe and eventually on the world. America was not the first "new nation"; the Dutch United provinces that had defeated Spain had that honor. But it was the only "new nation" of the Enlightenment. Its revolution was entirely secular and its principles claimed universal applicability. It had proclaimed and acted on Locke's theories of natural equality, unalienable natural rights, government by consent, and the right to revolution. Its state and federal constitutions demonstrated Montesquieu's theory of the separation of powers. Its constitutional conventions showed that a people could create a new government in an orderly fashion by formal contract, and that liberty need not mean anarchy. Its example showed that small political units could federate into a larger union without recourse to centralized despotism. The American Revolution dramatized and propagated two of the West's principal political ideas—limited constitutional government and popular sovereignty or democracy. The latter, but not the former, was destined to play a decisive role in the coming revolution in France.

As the century that had opened with the wars of Louis XIV began to ebb, the movement of ideas and of politics was running strongly against the old regime. Aristocracy and enlightened absolutism were ceasing to command loyalty or even respect. The desire for equilibrium, whether social, international, or intellectual, no longer inspired the educated. Balance and order in both art and politics was giving way to the cultivation of emotion and the thirst for change. The American Revolution accelerated that movement. After 1789, the greatest of European revolutions provided emotion, change, and violence enough for all.

Suggestions for Further Reading

General

For overviews, see especially M. S. Anderson, *Europe in the Eighteenth Century* (1961); G. Rudé, *Europe in the Eighteenth Century* (1972); L. Krieger, *Kings and Philoso-* *phers, 1689–1789* (1970); and W. Doyle, *The Old European Order, 1660–1800* (1978). The relevant volumes of the *Rise of Modern Europe* series remain useful: P. Roberts, *The Quest for Security, 1715–1740* (1947); W. L. Dorn, *Competition for Empire, 1740–1763* (1940); and L. Gershoy, *From Despotism to Revolution, 1763–1789* (1944). O. H. Hufton, *The Poor of Eighteenth-Century France, 1750–1789* (1975), and L. Stone, *The Family, Sex and Marriage in England 1500–1800* (1977), are pioneering studies; A. Macfarlane, *Marriage and Love in England: Modes of Reproduction, 1300–1840* (1986), reaches conclusions radically different from those of Stone.

J. H. Parry, *Trade and Dominion: The European Overseas Empires in the Eighteenth Century* (1971); C. G. Robertson, *Chatham and the British Empire* (1948); and L. B. Wright, *The Atlantic Frontier: Colonial American Civilization, 1607–1763* (1947), provide useful discussions of overseas expansion. On economic and social change, see above all F. Braudel, *Civilization and Capitalism, 15th–18th Centuries* (1982).

The Major States

For discussions of developments within the major states, see especially J. Lough, *Introduction to Eighteenth-Century France* (1960); J. H. Plumb, *England in the Eighteenth Century* (1951); W. H. Bruford, *Germany in the Eighteenth Century* (1952); and H. Rosenberg, *Bureaucracy, Aristocracy, and Autocracy, the Prussian Experience, 1660–1815* (1958). For biographies of leading figures, see J. H. Plumb, *The First Four Georges* (1957); G. Ritter, *Frederick the Great* (trans. 1968); C. L. Morris, *Maria Theresa: The Last Conservative* (1937); and G. S. Thomson, *Catherine the Great and the Expansion of Russia* (1950). On the American Revolution see especially E. S. Morgan, *The Birth of the Republic, 1763–1789* (1956); R. M. Calhoon, *Revolutionary America: An Interpretive Overview* (1976); and R. W. Tucker and D. C. Hendrickson, *The Fall of the First British Empire: Origins of the War of American Independence* (1982).

23

The French Revolution and Europe, 1789–1815

*T*he French Revolution, along with the industrial revolution that was simultaneously gathering force in Britain, changed the face of Europe and ultimately of the world. The Revolution was both political and social. Politically, it was a violent attack on the old order first in France and then in much of western Europe. The French monarchy, which traced its traditions to Charlemagne, collapsed. The French Republic's victorious wars with the monarchies of Europe created a belt of satellite republics from Holland to Italy. Socially, the Revolution swept away the clearly defined ranks of the old order. A new hierarchy, based in theory on wealth and talent rather than birth, took the place of the old regime's three-part division between nobles, clergy, and common people.

Above all, the Revolution changed the ways in which the peoples of western Europe looked at themselves. It created new words for new things. "Citizen," "revolutionary," "counter-revolutionary," "reaction," "guillotine," and the political concept of the nation-state joined the West's political vocabulary. The Revolution gave birth to nationalism and mass politics. It opened the modern age of mass-based democracy and mass-based despotism in which we still live.

UNDERLYING PRECONDITIONS FOR REVOLUTION

The collapse of the monarchy in 1788–89 came suddenly. Long-term forces in French society nevertheless prepared it—population growth, the expansion of the middle classes, and the rise of an informed public opinion equipped with

advanced notions that were subversive of established authority. The eighteenth century had been one of dramatic rise in France's population, which increased by 40 percent, from 20 to 26 million, between 1700 and 1789. *La grande nation,* as the French called themselves, had a larger population than any other European state.

Rapid growth in numbers, then as now, meant youth. In 1789, 36 percent of France's population was under 20 years of age. That growth was precarious, for it rested on improvements in transport and distribution of food, not on major increases in agricultural productivity. A young and active population remained at the mercy of nature. Drought, storm, or grain blight produced serious shortages in 1770, 1774, 1778, 1782, 1784, and 1786. The years after 1770 were ones of increasingly violent fluctuations in agricultural out-put and prices, while population increase depressed wages.

Expansion and diffusion of wealth nevertheless paralleled expansion of numbers. The size of the middle classes rose from perhaps 700,000 to 800,000 in 1700 to 2.3 million, or between 8 and 9 percent of the total population in 1789. The nobility at the apex of the pre-1789 society of orders remained essentially static over the century at between .5 and 1.5 percent of the population. Increasing numbers of wealthy commoners might hope to rise into the nobility, but only slowly, over several generations. Land ownership remained the chief source of wealth and badge of status, although nobles increasingly took an interest in trade and industry and the lines between noble and commoner were gradually blurring.

With the spread of wealth down the social ladder came the growth of a phe-

The Tennis Court Oath, by Jacques-Louis David, official painter to the Constituent Assembly and later to Napoleon. David did not complete this immense canvas, for most of those shown in it fell under suspicion during the Terror.

nomenon new in France, although already visible in England from the Civil War in the 1640s: literate public opinion. By 1789 perhaps 37 percent of France's people could read and write. The press grew from three semiofficial newspapers in 1700 to several hundred weeklies and dailies by 1789. Libraries and reading rooms sprang up even in the provinces. Nobles and commoners alike collaborated in spreading the ideas of the Enlightenment. The condemnation of ignorance, prejudice, and superstition by Voltaire and Diderot and the egalitarian creed of Rousseau reached a widening audience. The example of the American Revolution, carried back to France after 1783 by officers such as Lafayette, suggested that enlightened humanity could remodel institutions and society at will.

The new ideas divided nobility and middle classes alike. Only a small minority of either renounced loyalty to monarchy and Church in favor of Deism and a "republic of virtue." But the new ideas had consequences. They offered new myths, the perfectibility of man and of society and the primacy of the "general will," in place of the old certainties—original sin, redemption, and obedience to priests, nobles, and a God-ordained King.

FINANCIAL CRISIS AND NOBLE REVOLT

These long-term forces would have brought change. That they brought an explosion was the result of the coincidence of two short-term factors. The unusual incompetence of the royal government destroyed its authority just as the last and worst of a series of poor harvests encouraged peasants and urban crowds to revolt.

The crisis began as a financial and administrative one. War, sport of kings and aristocrats and vehicle for the aggrandizement of the state, had always imposed crushing burdens. Prosperity

after 1715 had freed France only gradually from the immense war debts that Louis XIV had left. The Seven Years' War of 1756–63 again brought heavy deficits. Then intervention in the American Revolution once more reduced France's finances to near-collapse.

Louis XVI, unlike his two immediate predecessors, kept no mistresses and lived a modest life, for a monarch. But he had neither the brains nor the ruthlessness needed to master events. Under his loose supervision, three ministers struggled against the approach of bankruptcy. Jacques Necker, a ponderous and supremely vain Swiss banker, coped during the American war by borrowing at ever higher rates while assuring King and public that the budget balanced.

With the end of war in 1783 came a reckoning. Louis XVI replaced Necker with Charles Alexandre de Calonne, whose ingenuity matched his poor judgment. By 1786 Calonne could borrow no more. He concluded that the only solution to the financial crisis was radical reform of what he described as "a Kingdom made up of lands with estates, lands without, lands with provincial assemblies, lands of mixed administration, a Kingdom where provinces are foreign one to another, where multifarious internal barriers separate and divide the subjects of the same sovereign, where certain areas are totally freed from burdens of which the others bear the full weight, where the richest class contributes least, where it is impossible to have either a constant rule or a common will . . . ."

Calonne proposed rationalization of France's ramshackle structure and the imposition of a single uniform land tax. It would strike the previously tax-exempt nobility and clergy that held between a third and a quarter of France's major source of wealth, the land. Since by custom the monarch needed some sort of approval for new taxes, Calonne in 1787 put the reforms to a hand-picked assembly of the very orders he proposed to tax.

When this Assembly of Notables predictably balked, Louis dismissed Calonne and replaced him with one of his fiercest critics, Loménie de Brienne, archbishop of Toulouse. Brienne in office attempted to cajole the Notables into accepting the reforms that he had himself denounced while in opposition. They refused. They demanded the convening of the Estates General of France, which had not met since 1614. Only that body, they now claimed, could approve new taxes. The nobility had opened the attack on the monarchy in the name of its own "historic privileges." It was the first of many groups to fish in troubled waters and be swept away.

Louis XVI sent the Notables home, and told the *parlement* of Paris, the judicial organ of the crown whose traditional task it was to register new laws, that the taxes were legal "because I wish it." Brienne's energetic minister of justice closed the *parlements*. Despite a petition from the dukes and peers of France, and riots in the provinces under the leadership of nobles and *parlement* lawyers, the King held firm. It looked briefly as if the government had won.

Then the bankers, friends of the still-ambitious Necker, refused to lend the money needed to operate. That blow brought the royal government to its knees. In August 1788 Louis XVI called the Estates General to meet in May 1789 and allowed Brienne to resign. The King then reappointed Necker, who brought with him fresh credit but no policy. The government had confessed incompetence and bankruptcy, and had appealed to its subjects for help. The Revolution had begun.

THE "THIRD ESTATE" AND THE MASSES

What sort of Revolution it would be was as yet undecided. The nobles and clergy who had defied their royal master expected to dominate the Estates

Caricature of the French peasant supporting the clergy and nobility, while doves and rabbits, protected by law for the sport of the nobility, eat the peasant's grain.

General. But the aristocratic agitation of spring and summer 1788, and still more the approach of the Estates General, drew into politics groups that had until now played no role.

The first of these was the middle classes. The reinstated *parlement* of Paris had decreed in September that voting in the Estates General be by order, following the 1614 precedent. That arrangement would place the commons, or Third Estate, who represented 98 percent of the population of France, in a permanent minority. Political clubs, in many cases led by nobles of advanced views, urged the "doubling" of the Third Estate, giving it twice its traditional number of representatives in order to equal the other two orders combined. The Abbé Emmanuel Sieyès, chief theorist of this movement, published in January 1789 the most famous pamphlet of the Revo-

Emmanuel Joseph Sieyes.

Theorist of the "Third Estate": the Abbé Sieyès.

lution: *What Is the Third Estate?* It began with three questions: "What is the Third Estate?—*everything*. What has it been until now in the political order?—*nothing*. What does it seek? *To be something*." Sieyès went on to demand the drafting of a constitution "which the nation alone has the right to do." That appeal to the *nation*, to popular sovereignty, meant the end of divine-right monarchy and ultimately of peace in Europe.

Initially the King encouraged the commons. At the end of December 1788 Necker proposed to checkmate

the nobles by agreeing to double the Third Estate. The King concurred. Louis XVI's appeal to the privileged orders had begun the Revolution; his appeal to the Third Estate led to its breakthrough. But as the Estates General assembled at Versailles in May 1789, forces far more menacing to the established order than the lawyers, professional men, and bureaucrats of the Third Estate appeared on the scene—the peasantry and the urban lower classes. Their intervention converted a political struggle between elites, a conflict between the privileged and the merely rich or educated, into an upheaval that terrified nobles and Third Estate alike.

The motive force behind that upheaval was the traditional source of disorder in agricultural societies: hunger. The harvest of 1788, for the first time since the famine year of 1709, had been poor to disastrous throughout all of France. In Paris, the price of bread, the staple food of the population, rose by 60 percent between August 1788 and February 1789. Widespread distress in the countryside also decreased demand for manufactured goods. Production of textiles, France's major industry, dropped perhaps 50 percent. Urban workers lost their jobs just as food prices escalated.

The consequence was a rapid breakdown of order in the spring and summer of 1789, before the new harvest arrived. In the past, the government had coped with similar crises with price controls, emergency grain shipments, and judicious use of police and army. But now the royal administration was in a shambles and the example of the revolt of nobles and *parlements* emboldened the crowds.

In the cities, bread riots and other disturbances broke out with increasing frequency. In the countryside, the peasants ceased to pay taxes. They also ceased to pay the curious assortment of medieval obligations owed to landlords, local nobles, and the Church—money dues on land, the duty to use the nobles' flour mills, bakeries, wine presses or law courts, and tithes. These "seignorial dues," which a legal treatise of the day described as a "bizarre form of property," had been the chief grievance of the peasants against what now, at a stroke, became the "old regime."

The peasants burned tax records and registers of dues. Where they did not find the registers, they burned the castles of the nobles to make sure. In late July 1789 rumors swept the countryside that "the brigands," the "English gang" (shades of the Hundred Years' War), or "the aristocrats" were approaching to slaughter and pillage. This "Great Fear," symptom of social breakdown, was both cause and consequence of peasant violence against the privileged orders.

FROM ESTATES GENERAL TO OCTOBER DAYS

When the Estates General met on May 23, 1789, the royal government, ever indecisive, went back on the implicit alliance with the Third Estate it had sought in December 1788. The King refused to allow the commons to sit with the other two orders, and denied voting by head, which would have given the Third Estate a majority.

Under the leadership of Sieyès, the Third Estate therefore voted on June 17 to constitute itself as the "National Assembly"—a new authority, independent of the monarchy and implicitly claiming sovereignty. Liberal clergy and nobles joined the Third Estate. And when the King ordered the Assembly's meeting-hall closed on June 20, it met at a nearby indoor tennis court. In the first of many scenes of dramatic oratory that punctuated the Revolution, the representatives solemnly swore the "tennis court oath": not to disperse before they had given France a constitution.

The King, briefly resolute, replied on June 23 with a defense of "his" nobility and clergy and veiled threats to dissolve the Estates General. After he had left the hall, the leaders of the Third Estate exploded: "The nation in assembly does not take orders. . . . We will not move from our seats unless forced by bayonets." The resistance of the privileged orders crumbled. More and more joined the Assembly. It now officially took the title of Constituent Assembly and empowered a committee to write a constitution.

Paris Speaks: The Fall of the Bastille

Louis XVI, after wavering, swung again toward resistance. Royal troops, many of them Swiss and German regiments, concentrated around Paris. The King dismissed Necker. Counter-revolution seemed imminent. Then the removal of Necker set off an explosion in Paris that put the Constituent Assembly firmly in power. This city of 600,000, which dwarfed even the largest French provincial towns, was hungry. The urban crowds of shop owners, artisans, and housewives, with the backing of a rapidly growing ward organization independent of the royal authorities, attacked jails and barracks, seeking weapons. The police, a mere 2,000 backed by 3,500 troops, were powerless.

On July 14, 1789—coincidentally or not the day of the highest Paris bread prices in the entire eighteenth century—the crowd attacked the royal fortress at the center of Paris, the Bastille. With the assistance of royal troops who had mutinied, the crowd took the fortress and butchered its commander. With royal authority utterly destroyed and Paris in the hands of the insurgents, Louis XVI temporarily resigned himself to being a constitutional monarch.

The Fourth of August and the "Rights of Man"

The Constituent Assembly soon faced an emergency more serious than the menace of royal counter-revolution. By the end of July the revolt of the peasants, threatened not only noble prop-

The Bastille surrenders, July 14, 1789.

14 Juillet 1789.
Prise de la Bastille.

The Declaration of the Rights of Man and the Citizen   August 27, 1789

The representatives of the French people, constituted as a National Assembly, and considering that ignorance, forgetfulness, or contempt for the rights of man are the sole causes of public misfortunes and the degeneration of governments, have resolved to set forth in a solemn declaration the natural, inalienable, and sacred rights of man so that this declaration, constantly kept in mind by all members of society, may unceasingly recall to them their rights and duties. . . .

1. Men are born, and remain, free and equal in rights. Social distinctions can only be founded on usefulness to society.
2. The aim of every political bond is the preservation of the natural and inalienable rights of man. Those rights are liberty, property, security, and resistance to oppression.
3. The source of all sovereignty is in essence the nation. No body or individual can exercise authority that does not derive expressly from it. . . .
6. Law is the expression of the general will. All citizens have the right to contribute, personally or through their representatives, to its creation. It must be the same, whether it protects or punishes, for all. . . .

From *Archives parlementaires de 1787 à 1860*, première série, (Paris: Librairie Administrative de Paul Dupont, 1877), Vol. 9, p. 236 (translation by M. Knox).

rights of their towns and provinces. On sober second thought the Assembly decreed in the following days that some dues be paid off in installments. That hardly impressed the peasants, and seignorial dues were dead even before their final abolition without compensation in 1793. The old order, in law as well as fact, was gone. The Assembly achieved its object, and disorder in the countryside subsided for the moment.

At the end of August, in its second major act, the Constituent Assembly adopted a preamble to the new constitution—the "Declaration of the Rights of Man and the Citizen." The document owed something to the American Declaration of Independence, Constitution, and Bill of Rights. It proclaimed liberty, and equality of rights, in stark contrast to the legal and social distinctions between orders current across the continent. It led in 1791 to the emancipation of the Jews from the legal disabilities fastened upon them in the Middle Ages. Even women, whom most revolutionaries, with Rousseau, sought to confine to the role of wife and mother, began to demand equality through its principles. Olympe de Gouges, a woman writer in Paris, published in summer 1791 a widely discussed "Declaration of the Rights of Women."

But the Declaration's fundamental ideas were not those of Locke nor of the tradition of English common law that had molded the American Revolution. The Americans sought above all to prevent the executive or the national legislature, even if elected by the majority of the nation, from trampling upon individuals or upon local and state governments. The French, however, blithely assumed that the nation, once freed of "ignorance, forgetfulness, or contempt for the rights of man," would spontaneously express a General Will. That Will would in turn produce laws. Will and laws would by definition be incapable of oppression, except the presumably justified oppression of those whose actions or

erty, but all forms of property in the countryside. Some members of the Assembly responded with calls for the restoration of order by force. Other more radical elements had begun to meet in a political club that later become known as the Jacobins. On the night of August 4, 1789, they took the Assembly by surprise. They induced the liberal—and landless—Vicomte de Noailles to propose the voluntary renunciation of noble and Church privileges.

In a frenzied meeting that lasted until two the next morning, the delegates renounced tithes, dues, the privileges of their orders, and the traditional

opinions violated their "duties" as citizens.

To these potentially dangerous notions the 1789 Declaration of the Rights of Man added an even more explosive element—the concept of the sovereign nation. In America, and even in a Britain that included Welsh and Scots, popular sovereignty meant little more than rule by elected representatives. In continental Europe, following the French example, it soon came to mean rule by one's own national or ethnic group. The political definition of the nation enshrined in the 1789 Declaration superseded the vague cultural notions of nationhood that had spread in the course of the eighteenth century with the increase in literacy.

This invention of 1789 later became known as national "self-determination" or "nationalism." It ultimately meant war of all against all, and war of unprecedented intensity. Monarchies might occasionally bow to custom, religion, or law, but the new nation-state recognized no law other than reason—its own reason. When its reason conflicted with that of others, force was the final arbiter. And the concept of nation made possible, for the first time in Europe, near-total mobilization. What other cultures had achieved with slave labor the French revolutionaries and their successors across Europe accomplished with the enthusiasm of free citizens.

The October Days

All this was still in the future in the late summer of 1789. The Constituent Assembly had partially pacified the peasantry, but it still faced revolutionary Paris. Its chief support was a middle-class militia, the National Guard, born in the disorders of July. The Guard, under the leadership of the "Hero of Two Worlds," the Marquis de Lafayette, was small guarantee against the increasingly politicized Paris crowd.

The grain harvest of 1789 was good, but had not yet reached the market. Supplies from the poor harvest of 1788

had run out. By late September Paris rang with cries of "When shall we have bread?" (as a pamphlet title put it). In this atmosphere, the arrival of a fresh regiment of royal troops at Versailles, greeted conspicuously by the unpopular queen, Marie Antoinette of Austria, set off a new explosion.

An armed crowd with 6,000 militant Paris housewives at its head marched on Versailles. They overwhelmed the royal guards and triumphantly brought king, queen, and crown prince ("the baker, the baker's wife, and the little baker's boy") back to Paris. Alongside the royal coach the crowd carried on pikes the heads of the guards killed defending their king. That was an inauspicious beginning for constitutional monarchy.

THE CONSTITUENT AND LEGISLATIVE ASSEMBLIES, 1789–91

With the royal family virtual prisoners in the Tuileries palace in Paris and the Constituent Assembly in undisputed control of government, the Revolution seemed to have won. What remained was to recast France's society and administration. A new hierarchy based on property replaced the old regime's decaying society of orders. The Constituent Assembly wiped from the map the old regime's quaint provincial and regional distinctions, and substituted 87 "departments" of roughly uniform size. Elected assemblies received control of local government, a brief reversal of the old regime's drive toward centralization. France's first constitution, adopted in September 1791, set up a single-chamber Legislative Assembly elected only by men wealthy enough to pay the equivalent of three days' wages in taxes. That was perhaps 15 percent of the total population. A further, steeper property qualification restricted eligibility for membership in the Legislative Assembly.

The new regime faced three problems to which it had no answer—the

Revolutionary propaganda: "Frenchwomen become free."

Playing cards of the Revolution: "Equality" and "Freedom of Religion" have taken the place of kings and queens.

financial crisis that had felled the old regime, the continuing agitation in Paris, and above all the refusal of the king to play the part assigned him. For the financial crisis, the nimble Marquis Charles Maurice de Talleyrand, bishop of Autun, found an expedient. The state would dissolve monasteries and nunneries, seize and sell off the Church lands, and in return give the parish clergy and bishops guaranteed salaries. The land expropriation went smoothly, but the July 1790 "Civil Constitution of the Clergy" aroused widespread resistance. Priests all over France refused to swear the required oath of loyalty to the state, and Rome soon backed them. The Revolution had gained a new and formidable adversary, and had opened a quarrel with the Church that divided France until the twentieth century.

Nor did the seizure of Church lands solve the financial crisis. The *assignats*, the new currency issued with land sale proceeds as backing, fuelled an inflation that guaranteed further urban unrest even when harvests were good. The lands themselves, sold off at scandalously low prices, enriched only their

middle-class and peasant buyers. The main benefit to the revolutionary state of this massive transfer of property was indirect. Along with the sale after 1792 of the property of nobles who had fled abroad, it tied powerful middle-class and peasant groups to the Revolution.

The Constituent and Legislative Assemblies also failed to master Paris. The middle- and lower-middle classes there had by 1790–91 achieved a degree of politicization unthinkable under the old regime. The revolutionary ward organizations or *sections*, made up of fiercely radical butchers, bakers, innkeepers, and artisans, met frequently. The Paris municipal government, or *Commune*, was likewise soon in the hands of extremists. Around these organizations and around the frequent "Jacobin Club" meetings at the former Jacobin monastery there arose a unique revolutionary subculture. The *sans-culottes*, literally those "without knee breeches," self-consciously repudiated the dress code of the old regime. Wearing trousers and red caps, carrying pikes and muskets, they addressed one another as "citizen" and demanded equality of wealth as well as of political rights. In this atmosphere, professional agitators and extremist journalists—Jacques Hébert, Georges Danton, Jean Paul Marat, and Camille Desmoulins—rubbed shoulders with international hangers-on of revolution such as the Prussian ex-baron and "orator of the human race," Anacharsis Clootz. With such leaders to spur it, revolutionary Paris was ready enough to turn its pikes and cannon even on the representatives of the nation, should it suspect them of betraying the Revolution.

Those representatives gave Paris occasion soon enough, for the conduct of the king soon rendered their moderation suspect. Louis XVI maintained secret contacts with monarchical elements in the Constituent Assembly, his many relatives who had fled abroad, and with Austria. In June 1791 he dashed for the nearest friendly border, Austrian Belgium. Hostile town authorities blocked the royal family's escape at Varennes, just short of safety. Once more France's king, queen, and crown prince returned to the Tuileries in humiliation.

The new constitution was thus practically useless even before its formal adoption in September 1791. The Constituent Assembly found itself with a monarch who had publicly demonstrated his disloyalty to revolutionary France. The king continued to appoint ministers and sanction legislation. But neither his throne nor his head were safe. Nor was the new Legislative Assembly, which replaced the Constituent Assembly in October 1791, well-suited to giving France stable government. Thanks to a proposal of Maximilien de Robespierre, the Jacobin provincial lawyer who had emerged as the most vocally high-principled of revolutionaries, the Constituent Assembly had voted to bar its members from running for the new Legislative Assembly. The measure did not encourage the self-denial and republican "virtue" it symbolized. Its main effect was to eliminate the modest store of parliamentary experience and political sense acquired since 1789.

Robespierre, "the Incorruptible."

WAR AND TERROR, 1792–94

Rather than govern, the Legislative Assembly went to war with all Europe. The dominant force in the new chamber proved to be a Jacobin group loosely associated with the commercial center of western France, Bordeaux. Collectively known as the "Gironde" after the name of Bordeaux's estuary, their leaders—Pierre Victurnien Vergniaud, Maximin Isnard, and Jacques Pierre Brissot—were above all brilliant orators. The Girondin recipe for leadership was simple—war.

In August 1791, after the king's flight to Varennes, the emperor of Austria and King of Prussia had proclaimed the intention of restoring Louis XVI to his rightful place in full control of France. This "Declaration of Pillnitz" was a deliberately empty threat, for emperor and king had made action dependent on cooperation from the rest of Europe. But along with the assembling of vengeful aristocratic

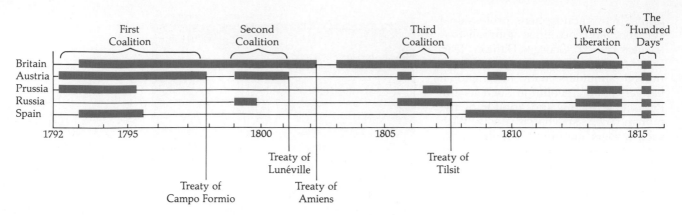

FIGURE 23-1   France at War with Europe, 1792–1815

émigrés in the German states along the Rhine, Austrian and Prussian hostility gave the French war party its opening. War, in Isnard's fervent words to the Assembly, was "indispensable for completing the revolution." At home it would consolidate Girondin power. Abroad, this "crusade for universal liberty," this war "of peoples against kings," would smash the old order in Europe as the Revolution had done in France.

Robespierre, almost alone, made a stand against war. The enemies of the Revolution, he insisted in debate with Brissot at the Jacobin Club, were within. King, court, and aristocrats wanted war to ensure French defeat. But Brissot's talk of easy victory over an immense conspiracy of "kings against peoples" carried the excitable Legislative Assembly. In April 1792 France declared on Austria a war that soon expanded to embrace all Europe. Except for a brief interval in 1802–03, war was to last until France's final defeat in 1814–15 (see Figure 23-1).

The Fall of the Monarchy: August–September 1792

The Gironde did not survive that long. The first act of the war galvanized Paris, and Paris destroyed the monarchy and ultimately the Gironde as well. The 1792 campaign began badly. Revolutionary indiscipline, lack of supplies, and the emigration of aristocratic officers crippled the army. The Prus-sian and Austrian armies advanced ponderously into eastern France. On July 25 the Prussian commander, the Duke of Brunswick, publicly proclaimed the intention of "delivering the King, the Queen, and the royal family from their captivity." That well-intentioned announcement seemed to revolutionary extremists the definitive proof that Louis XVI and his Austrian queen were conspiring with the enemy. The result was the "second revolution," the Paris insurrection of August 10, 1792.

That day far surpassed Bastille Day in violence. The king fled the Tuileries before the attacking crowd and revolutionary troops closed in. While his Swiss guards died at their posts, he placed himself and his family under the protection of the Legislative Assembly. That body, itself facing the pikes and cannon of the Paris wards, voted to "suspend" the king. A temporary executive council took charge until the election of a new legislature by universal male suffrage. The equality of "one man, one vote" thus came to France, and to Europe, for the first time. With it came equality of another kind. The guillotine, set up in a Paris square for the first time on August 13, extended the nobility's former privilege of decapitation to all.

The fall of the monarchy induced Lafayette, the commander of the army in Belgium, to defect to the Austrians; the Revolution had no more room for moderates. The Austro-Prussians

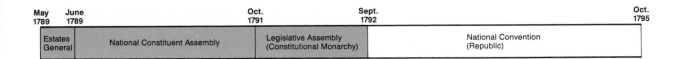

May 1789	June 1789		Oct. 1791	Sept. 1792	Oct. 1795
Estates General	National Constituent Assembly		Legislative Assembly (Constitutional Monarchy)	National Convention (Republic)	

seized the key border fortress of Verdun. In Paris, the fiery orator Danton urged the nation to rise: "Gentlemen, we need boldness [*de l'audace*], boldness, always boldness, and France is saved." On September 20, 1792, at the battle of Valmy, the revolutionary armies held, to the cry of *"Vive la Nation!"* The old regime's artillery, the best in Europe, persuaded the Prussians to withdraw.

Revolutionary Paris, without help from either Brissot or Robespierre, had again imposed its will on August 10. But it was not yet finished. Two hours after Danton's impassioned plea for boldness, the Paris *Commune* summoned its crowds to arm against Prussians and counter-revolutionaries. In this heated atmosphere, rumors flew of a supposed plot to let loose imprisoned aristocrats to slaughter the wives and children of patriots. Crowds attacked the Paris prisons. Brutal, sometimes drunken massacres disposed of between 1,100 and 1,400 aristocrats of all ages and both sexes, along with priests and other prisoners. Robespierre immediately justified these "September Massacres": "Do you want a Revolution without revolution?" He and his Jacobin associates now sought to turn the wrath of Paris against their Girondin rivals.

The Convention Executes the King

The new republic appeared to be the culmination of the Revolution. Within a year its partisans had remade even the calendar, making September 22, 1793, the first day of Year I and abolishing Sundays. The red, white, and blue tricolor of France replaced the Bourbon family's white with lilies. The *Marseillaise*, rousing and bloodthirsty marching song of a Marseilles battalion called to Paris during the August 10 rising, became the "national hymn."

The new assembly, the National Convention, was the most radical of the many legislative bodies of revolutionary France. For good reason. Public voting under the scrutiny of the revolutionary activists, not secret ballot, had been the preferred method of election. Only 10 percent of France's eligible population was brave enough or friendly enough to the Revolution to vote. Brissot and his Girondin companions returned, reelected in the provinces, and outnumbering Robespierre and his partisans.

But Robespierre took the initiative at home while the French armies, buoyed up by a fierce national pride, invaded Belgium and crossed the Rhine. In late November the revolutionaries discovered in the Tuileries a safe containing Louis XVI's secret correspondence with the émigrés. Robespierre and his terrifying young associate, Louis Antoine Saint-Just, demanded execution without trial: the king was guilty not merely of treason, but of being a king. The Convention nevertheless decided on a trial.

The affair desperately embarrassed the Gironde, which despite its hostility to the monarchy shrank from committing itself irrevocably by killing the king. The "mountain," Robespierre and the Jacobin extremists in the highest seats at the back of the Convention, carried the rest of the assembly with them. Louis XVI died by guillotine on January 21, 1793. Revolutionary France had executed a king who had ruled by divine right. It had eliminated what little chance still existed of internal and external peace. A week later, the Republic declared war on Great Britain and its ally Holland.

The Committee of Public Safety

Internal crisis and external defeat again combined to drive the Revolution to

Louis XVI in prison after the August 1792 insurrection, by Joseph Ducreux.

Queen Marie Antoinette resolutely faces the guillotine (sketched from life by David).

Portrait de Marie Antoinette

extremes. Paris food riots in February and March 1793 maintained pressure on the Convention. In March the imposition of conscription provoked the Catholic peasants of the Vendée, in the traditionalist far west of France, to revolt under royalist leadership. That guerrilla war dragged on for years and cost the young Republic dearly. The commander of the army in the low countries, Charles Dumouriez, lost decisively to the Austrians at Neerwinden, then defected. The supposedly oppressed peoples on France's borders proved remarkably reluctant to join the "crusade for universal liberty." The second city of France, Lyons, rose in May. In June and July much of the south, including Marseilles, followed. Royalists handed over to a British fleet the great Mediterranean naval base of Toulon.

The Convention proved equal to these challenges. In March it established a revolutionary court and "surveillance committees" to deal with dissent and counter-revolution. In April it created an executive, the Committee of Public Safety. To pacify Paris it temporarily imposed price controls (the "maximum") on grain and flour, and sent rapacious foraging parties into the countryside. Danton and Robespierre attacked the Gironde for alleged complicity with Dumouriez. The Convention, surrounded by the armed crowds of the Paris wards with 150 cannon, decreed the arrest of the Gironde for treason on June 2, 1793. In July, Robespierre and Saint-Just joined the Committee of Public Safety. France, for the first time since Louis XIV, had a government determined to rule.

The Committee included Lazare Carnot, the "organizer of victory" (for the army), Robert Lindet (for food supplies), Bertrand Barère de Vieuzac (for relations with the Convention), and the men of blood, Jean Nicolas Billaud-Varenne and Jean-Marie Collot d'Herbois (for repression). Ideological leadership rested with "the incorruptible" Robespierre and with Saint-Just. Responsible in theory to the Convention, in practice the great Committee ruled France alone for the next year. Its rule, which the revolutionary martyr Marat hailed as the "despotism of liberty," was more absolute than the old regime, and infinitely more effective.

Against the external enemy, the Committee ordered in August 1793 the mobilization of the entire population by the famed *levée en masse*. By 1794 850,000 men were under arms, far outnumbering the armies of the kings that France faced. Against the peasant guerrillas of the Vendée, the Committee sent General François Kellermann, victor over the Prussians at Valmy, with orders to deport noncombatants and seize crops and livestock. After the army retook Lyons, Collot d'Herbois and Fouché, emissaries of the Committee, killed thousands in reprisal for the revolt. The Convention changed the very name of France's second city to "Freed-City" (*Ville-Affranchie*). At Toulon an artillery major of Corsican extraction, Napoleon Bonaparte, found the key to driving the British fleet from the harbor, and retaking the town. His reward was promotion to brigadier general at age 23, for the Revolution

---

The Modern State Mobilizes its Citizens: The Levée en Masse

Barère to the Convention, August 23, 1793:

From this moment, until our enemies have been driven from the territory of the Republic, the entire French nation is permanently called to the colors. The young men will go into battle; married men will forge weapons and transport supplies; women will make tents and uniforms, and serve in the hospitals; children will make old cloth into bandages; old men will have themselves carried to the public squares to rouse the courage of the warriors and preach hatred of kings, and the unity of the Republic.

From *Archives parlementaires de 1787 à 1860,* première série (Paris: Librairie Administrative de Paul Dupont, 1907), Vol. 72, p. 674 (translation by M. Knox).

could not afford to neglect talent. By the end of 1793 the emergency in the south was over.

The Great Terror

Internally, the Committee and its lesser fellow, the Committee of General Security, moved to institutionalize terror. That instrument was too important to leave to the Paris agitators and crowds to which Convention and Committees owed their power. Committee and Convention damped down the activities of the Paris ward meetings, muzzled the press, and arrested some leading extremists in September 1793.

But the Committee's chief business was with those not extreme enough. "The gods," wrote the Robespierrist journalist Desmoulins, "are thirsty." Marie Antoinette, accused of treason and trumped-up charges of immorality, died bravely in October. The Gironde met the guillotine in November. Aristocrats, monarchist politicians, unsuccessful generals ("to encourage the others") followed. In the provinces, the traveling representatives of the Committees dispensed death to priests, aristocrats, and moderates by portable guillotine, firing squad, grapeshot, and "vertical deportation" (drowning). Perhaps 20,000 men and women perished in the Great Terror of 1793–94. Although that was a small number by the standards twentieth-century revolutions have set, the Terror left memories in France that long endured.

Elimination of the Gironde did not give Robespierre rest. The theories of the Enlightenment decreed that society, freed of the shackles of the old regime, would spontaneously express a General Will. Yet Robespierre recognized bitterly that revolutionary politics had failed to produce "one will, *one*." The fault therefore had to be that of surviving evil men—plotters, traitors, Parisian ward extremists, lukewarm Jacobins, and counter-revolutionaries. It was not simply war and internal threat that drove the revolu-

> ## The Spirit of the Terror: Sayings of Saint-Just
>
> **This man [Louis XVI] must reign or die. . . . All kings are rebels and usurpers.**
> > —*To the Convention, November 1792.*
>
> **The French people votes the liberty of the world.**
> > —*Draft constitution, April 1793.*
>
> **The people and its enemies have nothing more in common except the sword. . . . *We must oppress tyrants.***
> > —*To the Convention, October 1793.*
>
> **Spare the aristocracy, and you will give yourselves fifty years of troubles. *Dare!* That one word summarizes the entire politics of our Revolution.**
> > —*To the Convention, February 1794.*
>
> **There is something terrifying in the sacred love of one's country. It is so all-exclusive that it sacrifices everything, without pity, without fear, without regard for humanity, to the public interest. . . . You cannot make a republic with compromises, but only with ruthless severity, inflexible severity, toward those who have betrayed.**
> > —*To the Convention, for the Committee of Public Safety, demanding the heads of Danton and others, March 1794.*
>
> From Louis-Antoine de Saint-Just, *Pages Choisies* (Paris: Éditions du Point du Jour, 1947), pp. 121, 123, 162, 199, 206, 223; and Denis Roche, ed., *La liberté ou la mort* (Paris: Tchou, 1969), p. 49 (translation by M. Knox).

tionaries to shed ever more blood. It was their faith in the perfectibility of humanity and their claim to incarnate the General Will.

The leaders of the Paris crowd, Hébert and the *Enragés* or "wild men," were more radical socially than the Committee. They continued to agitate and tried to raise Paris in late March 1794. They failed and perished under the blade. Those more moderate than Robespierre—Danton, Desmoulins, and their allies in the center of the Convention—helped him against the Paris extremists. Then the moderate Jacobins began to plead for a relaxation of the Terror, for freedom of the press, and even for peace, for the spring of 1794 was a spring of French victories.

Here Lies All of France: cartoon of
Robespierre executing the last Frenchman—
the executioner.

Within a week of the decapitation of
Hébert, the Committee arrested Danton and his group. Saint-Just, in the
name of the Committees, accused them
of treason before the Convention. They
too died.

By these blows against Hébertists
and Dantonists, the Committee created
a wasteland around itself. The execution of the "wild men" destroyed its
ties to the Paris wards. That of the Dantonists weakened the Committee's
hold on the center of the Convention,
the moderates from the provinces who
held the parliamentary balance. The
Committee now ruled by terror alone.
The pace of arrests and executions increased rapidly. More than 1,400 perished in Paris alone in June and July
1794.

Thermidor

Victory sealed the fate of Robespierre,
as defeat had that of the Gironde.

French troops, ever more experienced
and more numerous, flooded once
more across Belgium. The military
emergency that had justified terror was
over. Robespierre's associates began to
think of their own survival. The relatively moderate Carnot and Barère
joined with jealous members of the
Committee of General Security. The
bloodiest-handed of all, Collot d'Herbois and Billaud-Varenne, hoped the
elimination of Robespierre would
prove their ticket to respectability. The
center of the Convention secretly offered support.

A Robespierre speech denouncing
unspecified enemies induced the plotters to act before it was too late. On
July 27, 1794—9 Thermidor by the revolutionary calendar—the plotters bodily prevented Robespierre from speaking to the Convention. Then, in command of the rostrum, they rushed
through a decree for the arrest of the
Robespierrists. The Paris wards, summoned to the rescue, understandably
responded poorly; they too had suffered under the Committee's dictatorship. The next day, 10 Thermidor,
Robespierre, Saint-Just, and company
met the guillotine to which they had
sent so many others. The Revolution
had "iced over," Saint-Just wrote
shortly before his arrest. The
Robespierrists themselves, by their
elimination of Hébert and the Paris
ward agitators, had halted the seemingly unstoppable movement toward
ever greater extremism. The Revolution was over, except for the endless
war it had launched.

FROM CONVENTION TO DIRECTORY, 1794–99

The "reaction" of Thermidor, as it soon
became known, produced a widespread sense of relief. French society,
no longer cowed by terror and censorship, reasserted itself. The urban middle classes that had profited from the
Revolution now sought to enjoy those
profits in a frenetic round of banquets
and dances. The *salons*, which educa-

ted women of the middle classes now led, reappeared. There ex-terrorists drank champagne with ex-aristocrats and with the new rich, land speculators and army contractors. The "gilded youth" of the better-off quarters of Paris equipped themselves with clubs and hunted Jacobins. In the provinces, a royalist "white terror" against republicans repeated the horrors of the terror of the Committees.

The relaxation of the price controls that the Robespierrists had imposed brought new Paris food riots in April and May 1795. But the Convention suppressed them and likewise crushed a revolt of royalist "gilded youth" in October. In the last case, young General Bonaparte mowed down the crowd with field artillery. Grapeshot, scientifically employed by loyal troops, made 1789-style urban insurrection obsolete.

What Thermidor failed to provide was a stable government responsive to the new society, ordered by wealth rather than rank, that emerged from the Revolution. The end of dictatorship by the executive meant increased danger of a restoration of the monarchy. The Convention nevertheless decreed a revolving membership for the Committee of Public Safety, and a reduction of its powers. In 1795, the Convention drafted and adopted yet another constitution, which remained in effect until the end of 1799. It divided power between a Directorate of five members and a legislature, the Five Hundred. Wealth once more became a prerequisite for voting.

The directors included Carnot, the Vicomte de Barras, and Jean-François Reubell, an Alsatian for whom France's "natural frontier" lay on the Rhine. Two thirds of the Five Hundred came by law from the outgoing Convention—the so-called "perpetuals." The Convention intended this measure as a guarantee against royalist agitation in the provinces. It helped achieve that object at the price of discrediting the new regime's claims to represent the nation.

The residual threat from Paris soon subsided. A poor harvest and an un-precedentedly severe winter in 1795–96 reduced the poor to near-starvation. Survival, not revolt, became the chief concern of the remaining *sans-culottes.* The last major attempt to mobilize Paris was the so-called "Conspiracy of the Equals" in spring 1796. The "Equals," especially Gracchus Babeuf and the Italian revolutionary Filippo Buonarroti, confusedly advocated extreme egalitarianism and a primitive agrarian communism. Their plot failed utterly, but left an ideological legacy for the future.

It was the royalists who threatened the middle-class republic of 1795–99. But fortunately for the Directory, the young son of Louis XVI had died in prison in June 1795. His uncle, in exile, took the title of Louis XVIII and announced his intention of restoring the old regime in its entirety. That program inevitably alienated both the constitutional monarchists and the powerful middle-class and peasant groups that had profited from the Revolution. A royalist uprising in the west of France inadequately coordinated with a British and émigré landing at Quiberon ended in failure and massacre in 1795. Royalist deputies nevertheless did well enough in elections in 1797 and 1798 to force the Directors into a series of coups d'état and purges to maintain control of the Five Hundred.

Stability and representative government had been impossible under the Convention because of the strength of disloyal opposition and the exaggerated expectations of unity of ideologues such as Robespierre. It was likewise impossible under the Directory. By the end, in December 1799, the regime rested only on the army.

SON OF THE REVOLUTION: BONAPARTE

That army had in the hard years since 1792 acquired matchless military experience and prestige. The old regime had bequeathed it the most mobile and powerful artillery in Europe and the innovative tactical and strategic theories of Guibert and Bourcet. The war "of peoples against kings" unleashed the energies and loyalties needed to use those theories to the fullest. The result was a new kind of warfare.

Under the old regime, the eagerness of troops to desert and the inadequacy of the supply services had restricted the size and mobility of armies. No commander could easily control, feed, and move more than 70,000 men. But the new French armies, filled with nationalist fervor, deserted less and showed a fierce initiative on the battlefield. Their leaders could trust them to fight as skirmishers, tormenting with fire the rigid ranks of the old regime armies as the American revolutionaries had tormented the redcoats. The new

The Man of destiny: the young Napoleon, by David.

armies could march dispersed, in self-contained "divisions" of 8,000 to 10,000 infantry equipped with their own artillery for support. This style of movement helped prevent bottlenecks and allowed armies to feed themselves by looting the countryside through which they passed. The divisions, and still more the next largest units, the *army corps* of perhaps 30,000 men, offered unparalleled offensive and defensive power. Corps could and did hold against an entire enemy army—until other French corps arrived with crushing effect on the flank or rear of the enemy. Concentration of forces on the move, on the field of battle itself, replaced the old regime's rigid and time-consuming deployments. The new system of warfare, the ruthlessness of the French revolutionary commanders, and the numbers, fervor, and readiness for sacrifice of the French troops themselves overwhelmed their traditionalist opponents.

The supreme master of the new techniques, and ultimate beneficiary of the army's role as the Directory's sole support, was the young General Bonaparte. He rehabilitated himself from suspicions of terrorist and Jacobin sympathies by crushing the Paris crowd in October 1795. After a love match with the ex-mistress of the Director Barras, the fascinating Joséphine de Beauharnais, Bonaparte received command of the Army of Italy in the spring of 1796. He was 27 years old.

The Directory's chief war aim was to secure the west bank of the Rhine; Italy was a sideshow. Bonaparte made it the main theater. He began the fateful extension of French conquest far beyond the geographic "natural frontiers" supposedly sought by Louis XIV. In the brilliant campaign of 1796–97 he first crushed the Piedmontese allies of the Austrians, then the Austrians themselves. Increasingly independent of the Directory, he ruled and looted north Italy as he pleased. In 1797 the Austrians sued for peace. By the Treaty of Campo Formio they relinquished their claims to Belgium and to the north Italian plain. In compensation they received from Bonaparte and the Directory the cynical gift of the once-proud republic of Venice.

By late 1797 France dominated Europe from Holland to north Italy. Prussia, preoccupied with seizing its share of the third and final partition of Poland in 1794–95, made a separate peace with France in 1795. Only Britain, surrounded by its seas and fleet, now stood against revolutionary France. The First Coalition of the powers of Europe against Revolutionary France had collapsed.

The Revolution and Europe

For Bonaparte, the Revolution was "an idea that has found bayonets." France's ever-broadening rule indeed meant more than the rights of man. Intellectuals in lands as different as Britain and Germany initially greeted the revolution with delight. "Bliss was it in that dawn to be alive / And to be young was very heaven," the English poet William Wordsworth wrote of 1789. Others were less optimistic. As early as 1790 the passionate Anglo-Irish parliamentarian and political philosopher Edmund Burke prophesied, in his *Reflections on the Revolution in France*, that the uprooting of historic institutions would lead to the rule of "some popular general."

The common people on France's borders soon found that occupation by the republic's undisciplined armed hordes brought pillage and rape, the systematic exactions of French officialdom, and attacks on the Church. Even the "rights of man" offended against deeply held popular prejudices such as those against the Jews. The association of liberty and equality with French domination was ominous, because the counter-nationalisms that French ideas and French bayonets summoned up might eventually oppose democracy at home. For the moment, sporadic urban revolts and guerrilla struggles did no more than annoy the victorious Republic.

CANONNIER

"Great battles are won by artillery," wrote Napoleon of his favorite weapon, pictured above.

A New French Empire in the Middle East?

Fearing both inactivity and premature involvement in the intrigues around the Directory, Bonaparte sought the leadership of a French expedition to Egypt in 1798. That dependency of the Ottoman Empire, the Directory thought, had potential as a French colony, as compensation for the lost empire of 1763. It might also threaten Britain's road to India.

These ambitions did not survive the destruction of the French fleet at the battle of the Nile in August 1798. Horatio Nelson, Britain's greatest naval leader, cut Bonaparte's naval communications and marooned him and his 40,000 troops. After a year of unre-

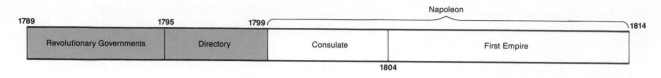

warding campaigning against Egyptians, Turks, and British, Bonaparte slipped stealthily back to France in a frigate, and his discarded army ultimately surrendered to the British.

Strategically, that outcome was no surprise. French domination, then and later, ended at the high-tide mark. Culturally, however, the Egyptian expedition gave an immense impulse to Western historical and linguistic studies. Bonaparte, man of the Enlightenment, had taken with him to Egypt teams of experts to study the monuments and loot the artifacts of one of the oldest civilizations in continuous existence. In the booty the French swept up and the British later captured was a stone slab, found at Rosetta in the Nile delta and now in the British Museum in London. On it are three inscriptions of the same text: one in ancient Greek, one in phonetic Egyptian script, and one in hieroglyphics. The "Rosetta stone" provided the key with which a brilliant young scholar, Jean-François Champollion, deciphered hieroglyphics in 1821–22. That achievement opened the road to the reconstruction of three millennia of Egyptian history. The Egyptian expedition was not only symbolic of European colonial greed. It also demonstrated the West's voracious curiosity, which in the coming century blossomed into a series of new disciplines aimed at understanding other cultures—comparative history, philology and linguistics, anthropology, and sociology.

FROM FIRST CONSUL TO EMPEROR, 1799–1804

Bonaparte timed perfectly his arrival in France in October 1799. A Second Coalition against France had replaced the first. The Egyptian expedition had drawn Russia into the war, for Tsar Paul resented non-Russian attempts to bully the Turks. The Austrians also resumed fighting. A short but nasty Russian incursion into Switzerland and north Italy thoroughly alarmed French opinion. The Directory, internally split, was utterly discredited, and restoration of the monarchy threatened once more.

Sieyès, the propagandist of the Third Estate who had helped launch the Revolution, had only survived the Terror by being discreet. In May 1799 he reemerged to join the Directory. He sought now to stabilize the rule of the beneficiaries of the Revolution, the Third Estate, through one last coup d'état. For that he needed "a saber," a docile general. Bonaparte, whom Sieyès approached, was willing to consider the role with one difference: he would make this coup for himself.

And so, on November 9 and 10, 1799—18 Brumaire of the soon discarded revolutionary calendar— Bonaparte acted. With the help of his politician brother Lucien, of Sieyès, and of the bayonets of the army, he cowed the legislature and assumed power as "First Consul." Sieyès found himself shunted off into gilded retirement. Much of French opinion had hoped for and expected a monarch. Instead, France received a dictator.

To consolidate his rule, Bonaparte fell back on the technique of which he was the unparalleled master, battle. In the spring of 1800 he led a French army once more across the Alps and fell upon the Austrian rear. Close and bloody victory at Marengo, and General Jean-Victor Moreau's triumph at Hohenlinden on the German front compelled Austria to negotiate. The Second Coalition, as disunited as its predecessor, collapsed. By the Treaty of Lunéville (February 9, 1801), Austria conceded to France the Rhine frontier and dominance in Italy. Russia, following the dictates of the mad Tsar Paul, had already withdrawn from the war. Even Britain now consented to negotiate a grudging peace, the March 1802 Treaty of Amiens. Britain's mercantile elite was willing to attempt coexistence with the "Corsican tyrant," although continuing French control of Holland and Belgium was a threat to British security far greater than any conquest of Louis XIV.

Victory and peace allowed Napoleon, as he now began to style himself, to consolidate his hold on France. In the summer of 1802 he had himself proclaimed "First Consul for Life," and in December 1804, "Emperor of the French." The pope, with whom Napoleon had signed in 1801 a Concordat partly bridging the gap between France and the Church, officiated at the imperial coronation. But in an act contrary to custom that symbolized his will to power, Napoleon crowned himself.

Napoleon's rule meant more for France than the imposition of a new monarchy and a new aristocracy of generals and Bonaparte relatives. It completed the old regime's drive toward centralization, toward enlightened absolutism. The departments now received permanent administrators sent from Paris. These "prefects," almost all-powerful representatives of the central will in the provinces, long outlasted Napoleon. They still exist, although with recently diminished powers. This pattern of the modern, centralized, bureaucratic state was the most powerful legacy of the Revolution. It found ready imitators throughout continental Europe and, much later, in the "Third World."

Along with centralization came legal uniformity. Napoleon's second major internal innovation was his law code, eventually known as the Code Napoléon. It replaced the old regime's patchwork of customary and Roman law with a single national code. It proclaimed equality before the law, reverence for property, and the authority of the male head of the family. The Code, like the prefects, was a pattern much imitated. French bayonets imposed it in the ever larger areas annexed to France. Its example impelled satellites and even opponents to legal reforms. Eventually only England, with its constitution formed through the slow accretion of custom and precedent, remained unmoved.

THE CONQUEST OF EUROPE, 1803–07

Works of peace, although not uncongenial to Napoleon, did not for long contain his ambition. From late 1802 on he dispatched agents to the Middle East and prepared to stir up trouble for Britain in India. In Germany, after Lunéville, Napoleon acted as arbiter of a "princes' revolution" by which the larger territorial states gobbled up the ecclesiastical rulers. That display of French power offended Austria, which still held nominal overlordship over the now crippled Holy Roman Empire.

Britain, confident that a new coalition would soon form, resumed war in May 1803. Initially, London stood alone, and Napoleon concentrated 400,000 men of his newly reorganized *Grande Armée* on the Channel coasts. Southern England was virtually defenseless, at least by land. "If we can be the masters of the narrows for six hours, we shall be masters of the world," Napoleon wrote to one of his admirals. Neither six hours, nor the week actually needed were forthcoming. Napoleon had starved his navy of money, supplies, and equipment. Many of the technically skilled officers had emigrated, and revolutionary enthusiasm was little help at sea. The British blockade had prevented the French navy from acquiring the sea experience needed to mount an effective challenge. Napoleon waited with increasing impatience on winds, tides, and his ever-delaying admirals.

In the event, the campaign of 1805 was on land, in Germany. There Napoleon could bring his skill and France's

Napoleon'a claim to universal domination: the Emperor on his throne, by Ingres (1806).

power to bear. His coronation as emperor, with its overtones of a claim to the legacy of Charlemagne, had alarmed the Austrians. His crowning in May 1805 as "emperor" of the satellite kingdom of north Italy—where Charlemagne had also ruled—proved the final step that brought a new coalition into being. Austria and Russia now joined England. Irresolute Prussia, intent on absorbing the fat English-ruled German state of Hanover, remained neutral.

Napoleon broke camp at Boulogne and flung the *Grande Armée* into south Germany before Austrians and Russians could join forces. One Austrian army, under the inept General Karl Mack, found itself enveloped and forced to surrender at Ulm on October 20. But in the distant seas off Spain, the British navy the next day reversed Napoleon's run of luck. At Cape Trafalgar Nelson captured or sank over half the combined French-Spanish fleet. He paid for victory with his life, but ensured that Napoleon could never repeat the invasion threat of 1804. Trafalgar and the arrival of Russian armies in central Europe impelled Prussia slowly toward the coalition.

To extricate himself from an increasingly threatening situation, Napoleon characteristically chose battle. He lured the combined Austro-Prussian forces to attack him prematurely. On December 2, at Austerlitz north of Vienna, he faced 90,000 Austrians and Russians with 70,000 French. An Austro-Russian drive at Napoleon's flank led to weakness in their center. Napoleon saw his chance and sent a corps forward to break through and roll up the enemy line. The Austro-Russians lost 27,000 dead and prisoners to Napoleon's 8,000 casualties. Austria left the war. It was Napoleon's most brilliant victory.

The collapse of Austria left Napoleon master of the German states, which he had already helped restructure after Lunéville. Now, in July 1806, Napoleon imposed a second round of revolution from above. The Holy Roman Empire, now a decrepit relic,

died unlamented. Napoleon replaced it with a league of satellites, the Confederation of the Rhine. The remaining small states fell prey to their more powerful neighbors. The Germany of 1801 had had over 1,800 separate political units. By the end of 1806 fewer than 40 remained. Centralization was convenient for Napoleon's tax collectors, and for the Bonaparte relatives who received German states as gifts. But it also proved a mighty step toward the German nation-state that within a century came to dwarf and humiliate France.

Only Prussia, afraid that Napoleon would make peace with London and force it to disgorge Hanover, remained aloof from Napoleon's new German system. In October 1806, alone except for distant reassurances from St. Petersburg, Prussia went to war. Within a week Napoleon had launched the *Grande Armée* around the flank of the rigidly old-regime Prussian army. On October 14, 1806, converging French corps annihilated the Prussians at the twin battles of Jena and Auerstädt.

Within weeks Napoleon was in Potsdam, paying homage with his marshals at the tomb of Frederick the Great: "Hats off, gentlemen; if *he* were still alive, we would not be here." But unlike Austria the year before, Prussia did not quit at once. Europe's resistance to Napoleon's ever more explicit claim to universal domination was gradually stiffening. In cooperation with their Russian allies, the Prussians fought on in Poland. There, unlike the green lands of western Europe, the French found little to eat. The few roads were ice-covered bogs. The Russians appeared in force, and in the great slaughter at Eylau in February 1807 proved dogged if unimaginative opponents. The coming of summer helped the French maneuver. At Friedland in June Napoleon finally crushed the Russians with a victory he proclaimed "as decisive as Austerlitz, Marengo, and Jena."

Tsar Alexander, erratic grandson of the great Catherine and son of the

The imperial seal of Napoleon, "Emperor of the French, King of Italy, Protector of the Confederation of the Rhine."

madman Paul, whose removal by palace coup he had connived at in 1801, offered negotiations. The tsar met Napoleon on a raft moored in the river Niemen at Tilsit, and totally reversed Russian policy. Russia agreed to divide Europe—not for the last time—into western and eastern spheres of influence. Napoleon kept Germany, including Alexander's Prussian ally. To Russia fell Finland, Sweden, and Turkey. Alexander in return promised secretly to declare war on England and to cooperate with French efforts to close the continent to British trade.

Such a boycott, after the loss of much of the French navy at Trafalgar, was Napoleon's only weapon against Britain. In the "Berlin Decree," issued in November 1806, he had declared a "blockade" against British exports to the Continent. Bankruptcy, and revolts by factory workers thrown suddenly out of work, would in theory compel London to make peace. But this "Continental System" had leaks. Along the coastline that stretched from Spain to Russia, smugglers plied a roaring trade, with the connivance of corrupt French officials. And the British were lucky or skilled enough to avoid a total closing of their other markets. Until 1812 they avoided war with their most powerful seagoing neutral trading partner, the United States, despite bitter conflict over British searches and seizures of U.S. vessels. And in 1812–15, when the United States did go to war with Britain, Napoleon's break with Alexander once again opened Scandinavia and Russia to British exports.

FRANCE AND EUROPE, 1808–12

The manifest failure of the Continental System was only one sign that Napoleon's power had begun to wane after

Napoleonic Europe   1812

A Goya sketch of "The Disasters of War": a French dragoon contemplates Spaniards he has hanged.

Tilsit. More serious was growing resistance on the Continent. Revolutionary France had invented modern nationalism and through it had tapped unprecedented military power. Now others, in Prussia and even in Austria, began to follow its example. But the first check to Napoleon's power came from a country scarcely touched by the Enlightenment—Spain.

There, in 1808, a savage guerrilla war broke out against the French troops sent to impose Napoleon's brother Joseph on the throne of the Spanish Bourbons. In scenes fixed forever in historical memory by the genius of the Spanish painter Francisco Goya, the French shot, hanged and impaled the guerrillas, who in return hacked at the French with improvised weapons. Nobles, priests, and brigands led the masses, for the revolt was as much a reaction against the ideas the French brought as against the French themselves. Unaided, it might have petered out.

But Britain soon sent armies to Spain and Portugal. On the far periphery of Europe, sea communications were more efficient than the appalling Spanish roads that linked the French to Paris. At Lisbon the Duke of Wellington, a skillful commander already proven in India, found a secure base. The "Spanish ulcer" resisted treatment by Napoleon in person in late 1808. Henceforth he left the matter to less competent subordinates, whom Wellington gradually wore down.

In Germany, the Tilsit settlement failed to extinguish the embers of a modern nationalism that eventually proved itself more terrifying than that of the French. Germany's sense of nationhood was at least as old as Luther's German Bible. The cultural revival of the late eighteenth century had given Germans a justified pride in their literature, which by the 1790s had begun to rival that of France. But it was French conquest that made German nationalism political. That origin gave it a peculiarly militant cast. And the imposition from without of the "rights of man and the citizen" and of the *Code Napoléon* helped make German nationalism potentially antidemocratic. In France, nationalism was subversive of the old regime. In Germany and further east it might serve to reinforce it.

That was certainly the lesson that Prussian soldiers and bureaucrats derived from defeat in 1806–07. King Frederick William III, his dominions halved after Tilsit, was even willing to appeal to his people in order to survive. He gave power to a cadre of unconventional civil servants and generals: Karl vom und zum Stein, Karl August von Hardenberg, August von Gneisenau, Gerhard von Scharnhorst. To defeat the French, Prussia needed what Hardenberg described as a "revolution in the good sense," an authoritarian "revolution from above." The reformers abolished serfdom, although dogged noble resistance prevented full implementation. They gave towns and cities limited self-government in order to engage the population in politics in support of the state. They abolished most of Frederick the Great's restrictions on freedom of commerce and industry and opened land ownership to non-nobles. Above all, they laid the basis for the imposition in 1814 of universal military service and the recruitment of non-noble officers. Their military-bureaucratic revolution from above sought to shore up enlightened absolutism with popular support. Its ultimate consequence was "bureaucratic absolutism," a power-state that bureaucrats and officers ruled under a thin veneer of royal authority.

For the moment the Prussian reformers could only hope that Napoleon would eventually falter. Austria, in April 1809, took Napoleon's Spanish defeats as a signal to renew the war. The Habsburgs incited the Tyrolese, whom Napoleon had detached from Austria, to a desperate guerrilla revolt. Dynastic Vienna appealed publicly to "the German nation." The old regime was learning new tricks. The Habsburg Archduke Charles, one of the most talented of Napoleon's opponents, fought him to a standstill at Aspern, near Vienna. Then Napoleon triumphed in a

Prussia Responds: Revolution from Above

Baron von Hardenberg to King Frederick William III, "On the Reorganization of the Prussian State," September 12, 1807:

The French Revolution, of which the present wars are the continuation, has given the French amid bloodshed and upheaval entirely new energies . . . . Neighbors and conquered have been carried away by the flood. All barriers created to dam it up have proved feeble. . . .

The illusion that we could withstand the Revolution most effectively by holding fast to the old . . . has itself resulted in the promotion and ever greater extension of the Revolution. The power of its principles is so great, they are so generally recognized and widely spread, that the state that fails to take them up voluntarily will either suffer destruction or be compelled from outside to accept them. . . .

Therefore, our goal, our guiding principle, is a revolution in the good sense, leading straight to the great purpose of the ennoblement of humanity through the wisdom of those in authority, rather than through a violent upheaval from below or without. Democratic principles in a monarchical government: that seems to me the form appropriate to the current spirit of the age. . . .

In other, but similar circumstances, although under an entirely different spirit of the age, Elector Frederick William the Great revolutionized . . . his state and laid the foundations for its later greatness.

From Georg Winter, ed., *Die Reorganisation des Preussischen Staates unter Stein und Hardenberg* (Leipzig: S. Hirzel, 1931), Vol. I, pp. 305–306 (translation by M. Knox).

gruelling two-day struggle at Wagram on July 5–6, 1809. Victory was becoming more difficult, as the rest of Europe began to imitate the revolution.

Austria, in the absence of Russian or Prussian support, eventually resolved on peace. Its new foreign minister, the devious Clemens von Metternich, bought Napoleon's good graces with the marriage offer of a Habsburg archduchess, Marie-Louise. Napoleon was happy to discard Joséphine and accept. Marriage alliance with the oldest major

The *Grande Armée's* flight across the icy Beresina River (late November 1812).

ruling house of Europe offered the Bonaparte dynasty much-needed legitimacy.

FROM MOSCOW TO SAINT HELENA, 1812–15

Napoleon's power still rested ultimately on force. With defeat in Russia in 1812, that force melted away. Until the end of 1811 Napoleon had expected that threats would hold Tsar Alexander to the Tilsit bargain. But Russian cooperation with the Continental System against Britain had always been weak, and Alexander had secretly approached Prussia and Austria with proposals for a new coalition. In the spring of 1812 Napoleon broke relations and launched what he himself described as "the most difficult enterprise I have ever attempted": the invasion of Russia.

The vanguard of the largest field army yet seen, over half a million men of whom 250,000 were French, crossed the Niemen in June 1812. The immense distances, the absence of roads, and

shortage of food and fodder devoured the *Grande Armée*. Russian resistance, compounded of equal parts courage, stubbornness, and vodka, stunned the French with its bitterness. As in Spain, guerrillas attacked French communications. Napoleon failed to bring the ever-retreating Russian armies to decisive battle. The immense slaughter at Borodino (almost 70,000 casualties) and the capture of Moscow in September 1812 were not victories. The Russian governor put the capital to the torch. Tsar Alexander, perhaps fearful of being deposed and strangled like his father should he show weakness, adamantly refused negotiation. After a month of indecision, Napoleon resolved upon a withdrawal for which he had made no preparations. The Russian winter and the pursuing Cossack cavalry did the rest. Perhaps 10,000 men out of the entire *Grande Armée* recrossed the Niemen in any condition to fight.

As Napoleon sprinted by coach for Paris to raise a new army, Germany turned against the French. Princes, literati, and middle classes united in an outpouring of national feeling. A mutinous Prussian general joined the advancing Russians with his army corps on New Years' Day 1813. The Prussian state soon followed. Austria too joined the new coalition after Metternich had in vain pressed Napoleon to settle for an empire confined to France and a European balance of power. Napoleon had replied that any such settlement would deprive him of the prestige needed to rule France itself. It was that iron law, and his own immense ambitions, that had impelled him toward universal empire.

Napoleon's utter refusal to compromise thus created the coalition that finally brought France down. By August 1813 the alliance was complete. Its forces caught and destroyed Napoleon's new and inexperienced army at Leipzig in October. The Allies had discovered how to defeat Napoleon by coordinating their movements, giving battle only when united, and defeating Napoleon's less talented subordinates separately before closing in on the Emperor himself.

With Germany gone and with Wellington advancing across the Pyrenees from Spain, Napoleon fought a desperately imaginative spring 1814 campaign north and east of Paris. He himself now suffered from a variety of ailments, his troops were green, his marshals weary, and his subjects desperate from never-ending war. But the Emperor proved as dangerous as ever on the battlefield.

The last coalition nevertheless held. Viscount Castlereagh, the British Foreign Secretary, welded the disparate allies—Britain, Austria, Russia, Prussia—together with the Treaty of Chaumont (March 9, 1814). That Quadruple Alliance pledged to fight on, to restore the balance of power, to confine France to its traditional boundaries, and to remain united for 20 years after war's end. The Allies drove toward Paris and ignored Napoleon's last bold attempt to cut their communications. Military defeat, the plotting of his ex-foreign minister, Talleyrand, and the

defection of key military figures finally brought Napoleon down. In early April 1814, he abdicated and received from the Allies the Tuscan island of Elba for his retirement.

Louis XVIII, his relatives, and their court returned to France in the baggage trains of the victorious allied armies. The restored Bourbons rapidly made themselves unloved. When Napoleon escaped from Elba and landed in southern France in March 1815, the army rallied to him. Joyous crowds carried the returned Emperor up the steps of the Tuileries.

The Allies were less delighted. Wellington and the Prussian commander, Blücher, rapidly concentrated in Belgium. Napoleon, intent on one last throw of the dice, advanced to meet them. After drubbing the Prussians at Ligny he attempted on June 18 to overwhelm Wellington at Waterloo before Blücher could join him. Wellington, as he freely if ungrammatically admitted, had been "never so near to being

Napoleon I: The Myth   1817

In spite of all the libels, I have no fear whatever about my fame. Posterity will do me justice. The truth will be known; and the good I have done will be compared with the faults I have committed. I am not uneasy as to the result. Had I succeeded, I would have died with the reputation of the greatest man that ever existed. As it is, although I have failed, I shall be considered as an extraordinary man: my elevation was unparalleled, because unaccompanied by crime. I have fought fifty pitched battles, almost all of which I have won. I have framed and carried into effect a code of laws that will bear my name to the most distant posterity. I raised myself from nothing to be the most powerful monarch in the world. Europe was at my feet. I have always been of opinion that the sovereignty lay in the people. In fact, the imperial government was a kind of republic. Called to the head of it by the voice of the nation, my maxim was, *la carrière est ouverte aux talents* [careers are open to talent] without distinction of birth or fortune. . . .

From *The Corsican*, ed. by R. M. Johnston (Boston: Houghton Mifflin, 1910), p. 492.

beat." Then the Imperial Guard recoiled from the thin red line of British infantry and the Prussians attacked Napoleon's flank. Napoleon's last "Hundred Days" in power and revolutionary France's career of conquest were over.

The Bourbons once more returned. Napoleon surrendered to the British, who shipped him to the desolate South Atlantic island of St. Helena. There he occupied himself until his death in 1821 with the construction of the Napoleonic myth: his empire built on force had been "a kind of republic," and he himself had been the champion of the national principle for other nations besides France.

The wars of the Republic and Empire had cost the *Grande Nation* perhaps 1.8 million lives. The rapid population growth of the eighteenth century subsided as the peasantry concentrated on enjoying and conserving. France henceforth lacked the will for a serious bid to overturn the balance of power. But war and Revolution had set loose and Napoleon had spread ideas and forces that victorious armies could not still. It had unleashed through the concept of the nation-state new energies within and new conflicts without. It had demonstrated to Europe that a society could discard its rulers and freely adopt new myths and institutions. It had established the pattern of the modern bureaucratic state. And it had shown that popular sovereignty unlimited by law might produce a "despotism of liberty" instead of democracy. These were powerful lessons for the future.

Suggestions for Further Reading

The French Revolution

The most balanced recent general history of the Revolution is F. Furet and D. Richet, *The French Revolution* (1970); for the "classic" French Marxist view, see G. Lefebvre, *The French Revolution* (1962–64), and A. Soboul, *The French Revolution: 1787–1799* (1971). C. Brinton, *A Decade of Revolution, 1789–1799* (1934), and A. Cobban, *A History of Modern France, Vol. I, 1715–1799* (1957), are fine introductory summaries. R. R. Palmer, *The World of the French Revolution* (1971), places the Revolution in its broader European context; E. J. Hobsbawm, *The Age of Revolution, 1789–1848* (1962), does the same, brilliantly, from a Marxist viewpoint. T. C. Blanning, *The Origins of the French Revolutionary Wars* (1986), is excellent on the Revolution's early foreign relations.

A good introduction to the fierce debate over whether the Revolution was a "class struggle" is the anthology of N. Hampson, *The Social History of the French Revolution* (1962). A. Cobban, *The Social Interpretation of the French Revolution* (1964), wittily attacks Lefebvre and Soboul. J. Talmon, *The Origins of Totalitarian Democracy* (1952), and F. Furet, *Interpreting the French Revolution* (trans. 1981), stress ideology rather than class as the Revolution's driving force. For the masses, see G. Rudé, *The Crowd in the French Revolution* (1959), and R. Cobb, *The Police and the People* (1970). On various phases of the Revolution, the following stand out: W. Doyle, *The Origin of the French Revolution* (1980); J. M. Thompson, *Robespierre and the French Revolution* (1953); R. R. Palmer, *Twelve Who Ruled* (1941); A. Soboul, *The Parisian Sans-Culottes and the French Revolution* (1964); C. Tilly, *The Vendée* (1964); M. Lyons, *France under the Directory* (1975); and A. Forrest, *The French Revolution and the Poor* (1981).

Napoleon

On Napoleon, G. Bruun, *Europe and the French Imperium, 1799–1814* (1938), is still serviceable. G. Lefebvre's two-volume *Napoléon* (trans. 1969), is masterful and comprehensive. P. Geyl, *Napoleon: For and Against* (1949), remains useful as a guide to early historical debate about the period. On Napoleon's domestic policy, see R. Holtman, *The Napoleonic Revolution* (1967); on foreign policy, S. T. Ross, *European Diplomatic History 1789–1815: France Against Europe* (1969). For Napoleon's relations with the two peripheral great powers that brought him down, see C. Oman, *Britain Against Napoleon* (1944), and A. Palmer, *Napoleon in Russia* (1967). D. Chandler, *The Campaigns of Napoleon* (1966), is a thorough recent treatment of Napoleon's wars, with good maps; for a contemporary's reflections on what those wars meant, see Carl von Clausewitz, *On War* (1976), ed. M. Howard and P. Paret.

24
The Demographic and Industrial Revolutions, 1750–1900

While the French Revolution convulsed Europe, other even more revolutionary forces had begun to transform the world. The coming of the machine, the substitution of mechanical precision and power for human skill and human or animal strength, was the greatest single change in humanity's existence since the agricultural revolution of the New Stone Age. In the late eighteenth century, one economy began for the first time in human history to generate an appreciable and ever-increasing surplus of food and goods. That economy was Britain's. Western Europe, the United States, and one non-European power, Japan, were soon to follow that lead.

Opposite: Iron and glass: the revolutionary Crystal Palace, site of Britain's Great Exhibition of 1851.

Steel for a new age: the Bessemer process.

This Western invention, the invention of widespread affluence and of sustained and self-sustaining economic growth, in turn made possible the continuation of an unprecedented growth of population that had begun before the coming of the machine—the demographic revolution. These two revolutions together provide the physical foundations of the societies in which we now live, societies orders of magnitude larger, richer, and more powerful than any before the nineteenth century. These twin revolutions provided both impetus and opportunity for the culmination of the Europeanization or "westernization" of the world begun in 1492. And the industrial revolution, the revolution of technology and science, shows signs of continued acceleration.

THE BIOLOGICAL AND ECONOMIC "OLD REGIME"

Before considering the origins of the demographic and industrial revolutions, it is worth describing the human and economic landscape they revolutionized. Before the eighteenth century, the lives of all except kings, large landowners, upper clergy, and small merchant and professional elites tended to be "nasty, brutish, and short." In most of western Europe agricultural technique was primitive and had changed relatively little from the

eleventh to the seventeenth centuries. Nobility, clergy, and warring states tended to eat up the small surpluses these economies generated after their inhabitants were fed. A precarious existence depended above all on two factors: favorable weather and the absence of disease. Drought or downpour, hail or frost—any vagary of the climate might spell famine and death. Plant or animal diseases might cause crop failures in isolated areas, or across the continent. By one count France had 13 general famines in the sixteenth century, 17 in the seventeenth, and 16 in the eighteenth century.

Human epidemics were even less forgiving than those of the plant and animal world. The Black Death of the fourteenth century remained a serious threat as late as the early 1700s. It struck Amsterdam each year between 1622 and 1628, killing perhaps 35,000. It struck Paris six times between 1612 and 1668, and London five times between 1593 and 1664–65. In greater London in 1664–65 it killed perhaps 60,000 out of a population of roughly 450,000. Columbus's discovery of America also contributed by introducing smallpox to the Indians and syphilis to the Europeans. The latter spread with fierce virulence from Spain across the Continent after 1493. A new form of tuberculosis, more dangerous than its predecessors, arrived in Europe from India in the eighteenth century. As late as 1831–32 the arrival of cholera from India produced a terrifying epidemic. And along with the great diseases came the lesser endemic ones. Smallpox infected perhaps 95 percent of the inhabitants of early modern Europe—and perhaps one in seven of those infected died. Malaria lessened life expectancy by perhaps a third. Before the eighteenth century it was endemic in marsh areas as far north as England. Typhus, typhoid fever, and a variety of no-longer identifiable but often fatal diseases were likewise widespread.

Death was thus ever-present under the "biological old regime." The death rate exceeded the birth rate—

population actually decreased—during famines and epidemics. Rapid temporary rises of the birth rate marked the recoveries from successive disasters, but infant mortality struck even more heavily than in the contemporary "Third World." In one prosperous French province in the seventeenth century infant deaths ran between 25 and 33 percent of all newborns in their first year. Only half of all newborns lived to the age of 20.

Accompanying the ever-presence of death was an overwhelming dreariness of life. Since the industrial revolution it has been fashionable to lament, on well-filled stomachs in the comfort of our well-heated houses, the purity and authenticity of "the world we have lost." But the inhabitants of pre-industrial Europe did not live in picturesque rural bliss. They fought a grim and often losing struggle for survival amid a squalid poverty without contemporary equivalent except in the "Third World."

The vast majority of Europe's inhabitants lived for and through backbreaking toil in fields and cottage workshops. Children worked with and for their parents from the moment they were capable. Those who did not work starved, and often enough those who did work starved. Agricultural work followed the tyranny of the seasons. There was too little work in winter, and too much and all at once at ploughing or harvest time, lest the crops spoil. Food had a desperate sameness. In the aftermath of the Black Death, population shortage and high wages had made meat a frequent food of the common people. But by the seventeenth century the population was again pressing against the limits of subsistence, and the vast majority of Europeans ate little but cereal. Wheat was the staple food, at least in Western Europe. Rye, barley, or oats—"in England a food for horses, in Scotland for men"— prevailed in outlying areas of the east and north. Rice was an exotic eastern import until the creation of broad malarial rice-fields in northern Italy after the fifteenth century. In the seventeenth and eighteenth centuries the New World crops, maize (corn) and potatoes, began to spread slowly but without changing the underlying pattern. The population ate peasant bread baked a few times a year and stored like bricks. Ergot fungus, which causes hallucinations and convulsions, often contaminated rye. Too exclusive a diet of corn meal mush (the Italian *polenta*) caused pellagra, a vitamin deficiency disease. Only the rich, and the small populations in the mountains and wastelands given over to sheep and cattle, ate much meat. As for shelter, the common people, until very late, lived in thatched hovels with dirt floors and one or two articles of furniture. In many cases the peasants shared the roof with their animals, as well as with bedbugs, fleas, and lice. Clothing was scarce, expensive, and rarely washed.

The monotony of isolation added to that of work, food, and lodging. Most peasants did not move beyond their native valleys. Peasant villages and even small towns were tight little societies riven with small hatreds and fiercely antagonistic toward outsiders. Only the rare journeys to local market towns or fairs, or the brief village religious festivals with their ritualized overeating and drunkenness, punctuated a bleak existence. Small wonder that the peasants of the French Alps summarized the height of happiness in such macabre terms as "happy as a dead'un." Misery seemed tolerable because it was familiar; no alternative had ever existed except for the small percentage of the population living above subsistence level.

The demographic and economic "old regime" began to give way to the new age in the course of the eighteenth century. The population of Europe had increased before, from 1100 to 1350. Then the Black Death had cut population by up to a third. Growth had resumed from 1450 to 1630, until the stagnation of the "seventeenth century crisis." Now, after 1750, Europe's population began to increase with an un-

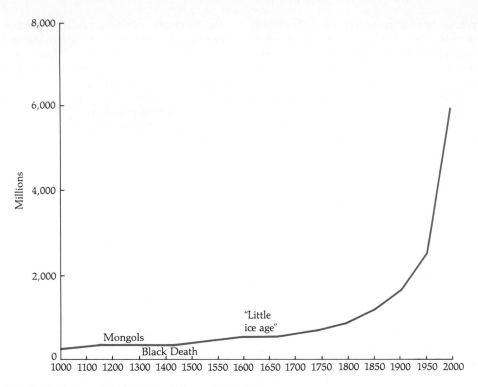

FIGURE 24-1   World Population, 1000–2000

precedented and apparently uncheckable rapidity. The pattern was not unique. The populations of China and India, although statistics are sketchy, apparently grew at a similar rhythm, which clearly had a general cause (see Figure 24-1). The most likely source of the general upturn after 1750 is a change in weather patterns. After the "little ice age" in seventeenth and early eighteenth century, world climate appears to have warmed significantly. Agricultural production and thus nutrition improved. The death rate slowly declined and the birth rate rose. Population growth resumed at a rapid rate.

Two things that had little or no effect on the initial upturn of the population curve, despite the contrary impressions of contemporaries and historians, were modern medicine and sanitation and industrialization itself. Medicine and sanitation, with the possible exception of vaccination for smallpox, introduced in 1796, played little role before the 1850s, and then primarily in England,

the most advanced nation. The widespread draining of marshes, the removal of rotting refuse from villages and towns, the spread of soap and bathing, and the increasing commonness of cotton (and hence washable) underclothes probably cut the insect population of Europe. Malaria, transmitted by mosquitoes, and flea- and louse-borne plague and typhus did decrease. But the purpose of draining the marshes was to reclaim land for farming, and the other changes served comfort, not medicine. Conscious efforts against disease had to await the identification of causes and carriers of disease in the early and mid-nineteenth century.

As for industrialization, it affected Britain first, and primarily after 1760. The 1780s was the decisive decade in which British economic growth turned sharply upward. Industry, in other words, did not itself cause the demographic revolution. Nor does industry's existence or absence correlate neatly with population growth. Western Europe, which industrialized, grew 280 percent between 1680 and 1900 (71.9 million to 201.4 million), whereas China, which did not, grew at a roughly similar rate (150 million to 450 million). The peak growth rates of industrializing regions within Europe did outstrip most other areas. The presence of work encouraged both migration and earlier marriages that produced more children. England's population grew by a staggering 133 percent (from 4.93 million to 11.5 million) between 1680 and 1820, and 86 percent of that increase took place after 1760. But population also grew rapidly in nonindustrial areas. The population of England and Wales grew 48 percent between 1751 and 1801; that of Ireland, 75 percent.

Whatever its sources, the consequences of growth were startling. The total population of Europe to the Ural Mountains grew from perhaps 140 million in 1750 to 390 million in 1900. England and Russia, at opposite ends of the Continent and of the scale of social and economic development, led the way (see Figure 24-2). In Central Europe the populations of Germany and Austria-Hungary approximately doubled. Italy, thanks to massive emigration to the New World in the last quarter of the century, grew only 87 percent. France, whose career as *la grande nation* was over demographically as well as militarily, increased only 65 percent. And Ireland, the classic European example of the consequences of unchecked population growth unaccompanied by industrialization, suffered catastrophe. Population doubled in the seventeenth century, then more than doubled in the eighteenth century at the steepest rate in all Europe. That rise continued, from 5.25 million in 1800 to 8.5 million in 1845—of whom perhaps a quarter were unemployed. Then a potato blight and catastrophic famine in 1845–48 killed perhaps a million Irish, and flight to the New World cut population to around 4.5 million, where it thereafter remained.

What prevented further demographic catastrophes of the kind that afflicted Ireland, or China in the 1850s and 1860s, when perhaps 20 million

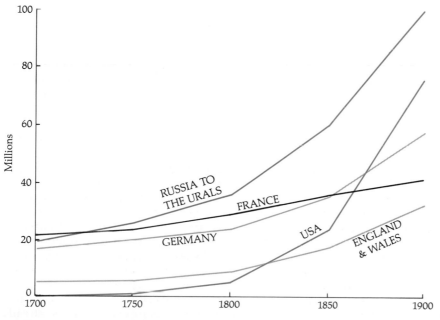

FIGURE 24-2   Population Increase by Country, 1700–1900

died in famines? As in Ireland and China, Europe's death rates gradually declined in the course of the century. Although birth rates also dropped, the spread between death and birth rate curves rapidly opened, and the population leapt upward. But unlike the outcome in Ireland and China, industrialization and medicine sustained Europe's increase. Only after the turn of the century did most of Europe pass through a "demographic transition" to a new pattern of lower birth rates. That transition was one symptom of the maturing of Europe's new industrial societies.

THE INDUSTRIAL REVOLUTION: CAUSES

The World Primacy of the West

Why did it happen? One way of addressing the question is to ask why it happened where it happened. First of all, why did it happen in the West? Second, why in Britain? Elimination offers a partial answer to the first question. Two other contenders, the Islamic World and China, might have led the way. They did not, although as we have seen, Islam had in the early Middle Ages provided the relatively backward West with lost Greek texts and irreplaceable concepts such as decimal numbers and algebra. In 1078 China briefly achieved a level of coal-smelted iron production (125,000 tons) that Britain did not match until 1796.

But the Islamic World and China shared negative characteristics. The savage waves of nomads from Central Asia hit them harder than Europe. The Jurchen nomads conquered China's major iron-producing provinces. The Mongols sacked Baghdad and ruled China as the Yuan dynasty. The Ottoman Turks overran and held the core lands of Islamic civilization. In China a second "conquest dynasty," the Manchus, had effects as disruptive as the Mongols.

Even more serious than invasion and foreign rule was a loss of impetus,

an intellectual turning inwards in those civilizations themselves. In the Islamic World, the phenomenon perhaps had doctrinal roots. "Islam" means "submission"—to the will of God. From the beginning, the religion's thrust toward a life totally devoted to God entailed potential hostility to nonreligious knowledge. In the tenth century, the "gates of independent judgment" about the Koran began to close. Futher speculation, either about theology or about the physical world became increasingly suspect, and slowed dramatically (see pp. 233–34). As for China, the Ming dynasty's great trading and war fleets of 1405–33 dominated the South China Sea and Indian Ocean, and were technologically superior to the Portuguese who followed less than 70 years later. But China's supremely confident ethnocentrism and the nomad land threat to its northern border turned it inwards for good.

Political disabilities multiplied the disadvantages of circumstances and culture. The Islamic World and China shared a similar form of government—centralized despotism. Caliphs, Ottoman sultans, and emperors of China in theory *owned* their territories and the inhabitants of those territories. Human inefficiency, frequent succession struggles, and the inevitable need to rely on elites, such as China's scholar-gentry, that might in time take on independent life, often tempered that absolute power in practice. But the claim to power remained total. All property in theory belonged to the ruler. He merely lent it to his subjects and could tax or reclaim it when he chose.

Europe—except for the Russian state (see pp. 580–84)—was different. After the assimilation or defeat of the Viking and Magyar raiders in the tenth century Europe suffered relatively little from outside invasion. Mongols and Turks only devastated fringe areas such as Muscovy, Hungary, and the Balkans. And far from relapsing into self-satisfaction, Europe developed that uniquely inquiring cast of mind already described in discussing the Renaissance and the seventeenth century scientific revolution. Theological speculation separated from inquiry about the physical world. Slowly and haltingly the West crossed the divide between magic and science. And after 1100 Europe's science and technology slowly overtook and surpassed those even of China. The Western obsession with clocks, with the mechanical measurement of time, was symbolic of far more—the application of rationality, calculation, and step-by-step empirical problem solving to broader and broader areas of human existence.

Politics also helped. Despite the efforts of popes and emperors, Europe remained divided into warring states and principalities. Charlemagne, Gregory VII, Charles V, Philip II, Louis XIV, and Napoleon all failed to establish universal empires. Europe also lacked the identification of government and religion seen in both Islam and China. The Investiture Conflict and the Protestant Reformation guaranteed that Caesar and God would remain distinct. That left space, however small at first, for freedom.

Finally, political diversity from very early allowed subordinate groups and small polities to claim *rights*, even against their rulers—a concept almost unimaginable elsewhere. From the security of their fortified walls, medieval towns could and did defy their overlords. The barons extorted the Great Charter from the English monarchy. The right of resistance to oppression became a stable principle of European political thought, and of no other. Relative freedom under laws, however limited in practice, persisted and widened over the centuries.

And its close connection to the free enjoyment of property allowed unprecedented latitude and security for economic activity. In western Europe, and in western Europe alone, great bankers such as the Medici or Fuggers could deal almost as equals with crowned heads. The straightjacket of the European mercantilist state was a small impediment to growth compared to the punitive taxation or confiscation that awaited Moslem or Chinese magnates whose economic success made them too conspicuous. Relative freedom from nomad devastation, the preeminence of curiosity and rationality, political pluralism and division between religious and secular power, and the concept of rights against the ruler were decisive in propelling Europe past its rivals.

The Primacy of Britain in Europe

Within Europe, Britain led the way after the seventeenth century. Even more than the rest of Europe, it enjoyed relative freedom from external threat. The last successful invasion had been that of 1066. Internal turmoil, from the Wars of the Roses to the Civil War of the 1640s and the anarchic Highland clan risings of 1715 and 1745, was superficial and short-lived compared to the great wars that rent the continent. And an inquiring cast of mind had long distinguished England, the land that had contributed more than any other to the scientific revolution. The Reformation and the ensuing breaking of the religious monopoly of the established church in the Civil War meant that religious restraints on freedom of speculation and the free flow of knowledge were conspicuous by their relative absence.

Finally, the nature of English politics and society made for English primacy over rivals such as France, just as the nature of European politics and society gave Europe the lead it had acquired by 1700. The remnants of English feudal institutions and land tenure had disappeared by the sixteenth century. England had ceased to have serfs or even a hereditary peasantry. After the mid-sixteenth century even mining rights, except in gold and silver, belonged to the landowner and not the monarch—a situation unique in Europe. When the Civil War of 1641–48 had pitted the crown against England's landowners organized in Parliament, the landowners had won, and had completed the process begun with the *Magna Carta*. Rights of property became absolute, conditional neither on service nor on claims of overlords, tenants, or Church. The purpose of government itself, as Locke had spelled it out in 1690, was simple: "The great and chief end . . . of men's uniting into commonwealths and putting themselves under government is the preservation of their property." That conception of property was far more absolute than that prevailing even in old-regime France, much less in lands east and south of France.

The consequence of England's history, by the eighteenth century, was thus a society with rights but without legally defined orders, a society enjoying social mobility undreamed of on the Continent. "All are accounted gentlemen in England who maintain themselves without manual labor," remarked a well-known eighteenth-century traveler's handbook. In this relatively "open aristocracy," wealth bought status with a speed and directness not visible in France. That was an immeasurable encouragement to the getting of wealth, and unlike its continental counterparts the British elite was relatively unembarrassed about how it acquired that wealth. In eighteenth-century Britain the barriers against nobles engaging in trade and industry that had begun to break down in old-regime France scarcely existed. At lower social levels, guild restrictions that still lived on the continent, especially in Germany, had likewise long crumbled.

British family structure and inheritance customs also fostered mobility and growth. Unlike France, where all children of the nobility inherited their parents' status, the younger sons of the great English families inherited neither land nor title. On the Continent, caste-bound younger sons had to make do with careers in church or army. In Britain younger sons went out into the world to earn money. These features made England into Europe's most dynamic society. It industrialized first because it alone was ready.

If the nature of English society explains why it industrialized, other factors help explain why it industrialized when it did. First among them was the gradual but impressive growth of English agriculture, which between 1700 and 1800 increased its output per acre by 44 percent. New timetables for ploughing, new methods of field rotation with crops such as clover or turnips that returned nitrogen to the soil and supplied fodder, larger numbers of sheep and cattle eating that fodder and manuring the fields, selective breeding of livestock—all contributed to growth. The absence of a hereditary peasantry made it possible for landowners, whether "gentlemen" or merely prosperous farmers, to consolidate the medieval village common lands into "enclosed" fields, either by agreement with the villagers or by act of Parliament. Consolidation of holdings was virtually complete by the first decades of the nineteenth century. It made England a land of economically efficient large and medium farms, far different from the patchwork of open-field strips and peasant small-holdings still found in much of the Continent.

This "agricultural revolution" had three major consequences for British industrialization. Contrary to widespread opinion, enclosure apparently did not contribute by driving laborers off the land and into the new industrial labor force. The enclosed fields with their livestock and multiple crops required more rather than less labor than the old system. It was rural population increase, not enclosure, that filled the new industrial cities. But agriculture did help to keep that urban population fed, while enclosure freed land for industrial or mining development, and agricultural prosperity increased the market for industrial products.

But agriculture only provided a foundation for growth. Upon it and alongside it a rich commercial and industrial economy had arisen that already supplied a third of England's national product as early as 1700; by comparison, commerce and industry in France was at that date perhaps a fifth or less of the French economy. And England's commerce, unlike that of France, had already by 1700 created a

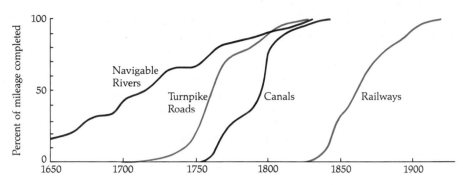

FIGURE 24-3   The Transport Revolution in Britain
From Eric Pawson, *The Early Industrial Revolution* (New York: Harper and Row, 1979), p. 153.

national market that matched goods with buyers. A cash economy centered on London reached to the far corners of the island, while barter, still prevalent in backward areas of France, was relatively rare. The internal customs barriers that bedeviled French merchants and the inter-state ones that cut eighteenth-century Germany into incoherent dwarf economies did not exist in England.

Even geography had favored the creation of a national market, for no part of Britain is more than 70 miles from the sea. Navigable rivers—the Thames, Severn, Tyne, Humber—improved with man-made banks and locks, made possible the economical transport of bulk cargoes such as coal, of which London already consumed 100,000 tons a year by the early seventeenth century. Beginning on a large scale in the 1760s, entrepreneurs promoted a massive expansion of canals and linked the major rivers into a national transport network. Similar private companies made British roads the best in Europe by the end of the eighteenth century (see Figure 24-3). Nor did the British market end with Britain itself. England's export trade, which grew sixfold during the eighteenth century, offered a further incentive for firms to expand production relentlessly.

England was thus already rich, and its people, along with those of Holland and the United States, enjoyed the world's highest standard of living in the late eighteenth century. That wealth, and the extent of England's national market, made it the only country in Europe that possessed the beginnings of a true mass market, a public capable of buying large quantities of inexpensive goods. The pull of that market at last brought into its own the West's love of gadgets and its willingness to search for practical results by trial and error. The pull of that market prompted the emergence of a cluster of technological innovations, swiftly spreading and mutually reinforcing, that propelled Britain into spectacular growth. For the first time in history, an economy expanded not primarily by increasing the input of labor but by replacing labor with machinery.

THE FIRST INDUSTRIAL REVOLUTION

The innovations of this "first industrial revolution" affected above all three key industries: cotton, coal, and iron. Cotton, the miracle fiber from India, the Middle East, and the slave economies of the Caribbean and American South, led the way. It was durable, lighter than linen, and easily washed, dyed, printed, or worked by machine. It also faced insatiable demand: As a London magazine put it in 1783, "every servant girl has her cotton gown and her cotton stockings."

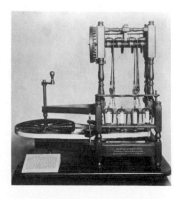

A replica of Arkwright's water frame, patented in 1769.

In the 1730s the first of the major innovations, John Kay's flying shuttle, dramatically speeded up the weaving of cotton cloth. That created a bottleneck at the intermediate step of spinning the raw fibers into thread. By the 1750s the flying shuttle was in general use, and tinkerers and entrepreneurs bent to the task of mechanizing spinning. James Hargreaves's "spinning jenny" of 1765, Richard Arkwright's larger and more powerful "water frame," and Samuel Crompton's "mule," a hybrid with features from its two predecessors, filled the gap.

The new devices produced cotton thread in unprecedented quantities, and of a strength and fineness unattainable by hand spinning. A twelvefold leap upwards in cotton production and consumption between 1770 and 1800 in turn created further imbalances. The embryonic chemical industry found itself pressed for unprecedented quantities of soaps and bleaches to process textiles. And the flying shuttle of the home weavers could no longer keep up with the output of thread. The answer was Arkwright's power-loom, invented in 1787. By 1833 one man with a 12-year-old boy as helper could produce as much as 20 hand-weavers. Annual production of cotton cloth skyrocketed from perhaps a million pounds a year in 1730 to 100 million in 1815.

That expansion created an entirely new institution, the factory. The grouping together of workers in large workshops was not new. It had existed in the ancient world and in Europe before the Industrial Revolution. But in all except the heaviest metal industries, such workshops had little or no competitive advantage over dispersed production. In 1770, the date of Arkwright's first large factory, the vast bulk of production still took place in home workshops under the "putting-out" system. The entrepreneur provided raw material to home workers (his subcontractors) and sold the finished product. Then the advent of power-driven machinery that was swifter, more efficient, and larger and more expensive than anything possible in the home or in small workshops compelled a concentration of industry into ever-larger units, into factories built around their machines and power sources. The "factory system" was an organizational and logistical leap comparable in magnitude to the technological advances that made it both necessary and possible.

The take-off of the cotton industry, with its pattern of new machines perpetually challenging entrepreneurs to further mechanize the slower phases of the production cycle, encouraged other industries as well. Coal and iron, the other two sectors of this first industrial revolution, felt the stimulus. Water power, which drove the early factories, was proving inadequate by the 1790s. Its force varied with the seasons and it compelled entrepreneurs to locate their factories only on suitable streams, often far from markets or sources of raw materials. The answer to that bottleneck was to tap an inanimate source

The Coming of Steam: A View from the Bottom   1818

When the spinning of cotton was in its infancy, and before those terrible machines for superseding the necessity of human labour, called steam engines came into use, there were a great number of what were then called *little masters;* men who with a small capital, could procure a few machines, and employ a few machines, and employ a few hands men and boys (say to twenty or thirty). . . . A few years however changed the face of things. Steam engines came into use, to purchase which, and to erect buildings sufficient to contain them and six or seven hundred hands, required a great capital. The engine power produced a more marketable (though not a better) article than the little masters could at the same price. The consequence was their ruin in a short time; and the overgrown capitalists triumphed in their fall.

Black Dwarf, September 30, 1818, pp. 623–24, quoted in Theodore Hamerow, *The Birth of a New Europe* (Chapel Hill: University of North Carolina Press, 1983), p. 13.

of power whose supply seemed almost infinite, coal.

The machine that turned the energy of coal into rotary motion to drive the new textile machines was the steam engine, the very symbol of the Industrial Revolution. Playthings such as the rotating kettle powered by a steam jet had existed since antiquity. But the first practical steam engine did not emerge until Thomas Savery's "fire engine" or steam-powered pump of 1698. Seven years later Thomas Newcomen, a blacksmith of Dartmouth in southern England, built the first true steam engine. It operated a crossbeam connected to a pump cylinder. Less than 1 percent of the energy released from its fuel did useful work, but that was enough. The machine was tireless and could be almost any size required. Its immediate use was to pump out and ventilate coal mines. It permitted a rapid expansion of coal production from ever-deeper seams, although its inefficiency prevented its use any distance from cheap coal.

Then, in the 1770s, James Watt invented an improved engine four times as efficient. This breakthrough created the "age of steam." The effectively unlimited coal deposits of northern England could henceforth power ever larger spinning and weaving machines. Watt's partner was appropriately immodest about their achievement: "I sell, Sir, what all the world desires to have—power."

Steam for pumping had permitted further expansion of coal production. Steam for industry in turn increased demand for coal. Steam power, coal, and the demands of war after 1793 between them revolutionized the iron industry. The English by 1740 had already consumed 10 or 11 pounds of iron per capita each year, far more than the French (although as late as the 1780s France's iron production was in absolute terms larger than Britain's). But English metallurgy soon came up against a seemingly unbreakable bottleneck in the need for fuel. The supply of wood to make charcoal for smelting

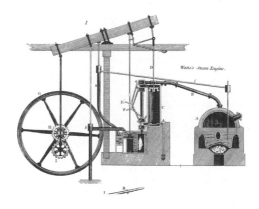

Watt's design drawing for his steam engine (1769).

iron ore into pig iron was limited. Coal, in its charred form, coke, normally contaminated the iron with impurities that rendered the finished product unusable.

After long experiment, Abraham Darby successfully smelted iron ore with coke (as the Chinese had before him) in 1709. But not until the 1750s did the technique become widespread. The triumph of coke metallurgy and further innovations such as the steam-powered forced-blast furnace and the preheated air blast drove British production of pig iron upward from 17,350 tons in 1740 to 2.7 million tons in 1852. That vast increase called forth further innovations elsewhere in the production cycle. The decisive breakthrough

The world's first cast-iron bridge, built in 1779 over the Severn River in England.

Iron ships: the huge *Great Eastern* (1858), built by Isambard Kingdom Brunel (1806–59), one of Britain's greatest engineers.

The opening of the world's first freight and passenger railway, the Stockton-Darlington Railway, on September 27, 1825.

As iron became ever cheaper, new sources of demand appeared. Weapons had traditionally been the largest single use of iron, and they remained so until after 1800. Royal Navy orders made the success of the Carron Company, Scotland's first major ironworks (1759), whose "carronade" or short naval cannon became synonymous with execution at short range. A new precision process for boring cannon from solid castings speeded production and made weapons more accurate. The steam engine's leaky cylinders also benefited from the new boring techniques. Iron beams began to appear in buildings and bridges in the 1770s, and the first practical fully iron-hulled ship emerged in 1815. Iron frames, rollers, gears, and pushrods replaced wood in the new generation of steam-powered textile machines, cutting vibration and permitting ever-higher operating speeds.

in the processing of pig iron (from 2.5 to 5 percent carbon) into wrought iron (less than .1 percent carbon) came in the 1780s with Henry Cort's "puddling" and steam-powered rolling process. Crude standardized shapes such as iron beams, bars, and rails became possible for the first time. Britain's iron industry left France's in the dust.

The culmination of the age of steam was of course the application of coal power to transport—the railroad and steamship, the first self-moving vehi-

cles in world history. The first practical steamships were the creation of a French marquis, Claude Jouffroy d'Abbans, in the late 1770s and early 1780s. Americans and British developed the innovation further, and the first partially steam-powered Atlantic crossing came in 1819. The railroad was a combination of the steam engine with the rail-borne wagons used since the late sixteenth century in mines and quarries. In the late 1750s iron rails had begun to replace wood. Then, after 1800, a series of inventors sought to power a vehicle to run on those rails. In 1801–04 Richard Trevithick, developer of a high-pressure engine more efficient than Watt's, succeeded. After the mid-1820s the first railways began to spread across Britain and the United States.

Railroad and steamship drove forward the transport revolution begun with roads and canals. Railways immeasurably expanded the internal market, while the steamship widened the international one. Railway and steamship together provided the iron industry with demand that stretched it, as the consumer market had stretched the cotton industry. Each mile of railway track required three hundred tons of iron. By 1851, the year of the Great Exhibition at London that measured Britain's achievements against those of its European rivals, Britain had over 9,000 miles of track. Rails covered Britain like a web, linking mines, factories, ports, and cities of unprecedented size. The railroad was the last of the cluster of technologies of that first industrial revolution that made Britain the "workshop of the world."

THE SECOND INDUSTRIAL REVOLUTION: THE "FOLLOWERS"

By the time of the Great Exhibition, England had a commanding lead over its rivals. Its share of world industrial production had nevertheless already begun to drop, as others caught up (see Figure 24-4). In the next five decades

The factory: steam power and long rows of iron-framed machines. An English cotton mill in the early 1820s.

they closed the gap. New rivals beyond the seas, in America and ultimately in Japan (see pp. 778–80), rose to challenge both Britain and Europe.

These "followers" suffered from one major disadvantage. Their infant industries, especially in textiles, faced the competition of low-cost mass-produced British goods. But the followers were also the beneficiaries of Britain's pioneering. After Britain, industrialization would never again be an unforeseen and totally unplanned process. The followers had a model, and could study and seek to avoid some of that model's shortcomings. Second, followers could adopt technology already pioneered in Britain and save development costs. Finally, the industrialization of the followers roughly coincided with a new wave of innovations, the "second industrial revolution," that appeared between 1850 and 1880. The followers could enter the new industries of this second wave without the encumbrance of investment or labor force tied up in mature industries. In the new industries the followers could in some cases compete on even terms.

The new technologies were the four that propelled the industrial world into and through much of the twentieth century: steel, chemicals, electricity, and the internal combustion engine.

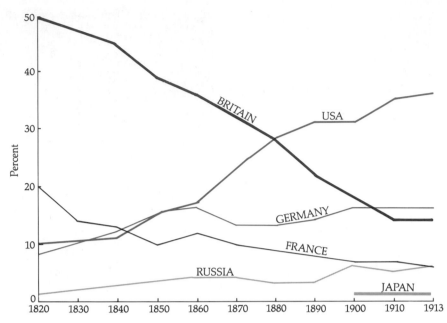

FIGURE 24-4   Leader and Followers: Relative Shares of World Industrial Production

Steel was initially the most important. An alloy of iron known since antiquity, steel contains between .1 and 2 percent carbon. It combines strength, hardness, and elasticity in unique proportions. It holds under stresses that snap brittle pig or cast iron (2.5 to 5 percent

The new metallurgy: smelting iron with coke in Upper Silesia, 1841.

carbon) and spread wrought iron (less than .1 percent carbon) like butter.

Until the 1850s no process existed for making steel cheaply and in quantity. The oldest technique involved baking wrought iron bars at high temperature in a bed of carbon to diffuse it into the iron. Then a blacksmith laboriously reheated, folded, and hammered the iron bars into themselves by hand to distribute the carbon throughout the iron evenly. In the 1740s, along with the other metallurgical discoveries of the early Industrial Revolution, came a process, long known in China and South Asia, for making steel in small melting pots, or crucibles. After baking the wrought iron bars in carbon, the foundry masters melted them in crucibles, skimmed off impurities, and poured. The crucible process was small-scale and expensive, but it produced the hardest and most uniform steel yet made in appreciable quantities. And it made possible for the first time the casting of large steel objects such as drive shafts, railroad wheels or axles, and immense shell-firing cannon.

Then came two breakthroughs. In the 1850s Henry Bessemer, an armament designer, discovered that blowing air through a crucible filled with molten pig iron burned off the excess carbon rapidly and in the process generated the heat needed to keep the iron molten. The Bessemer converter eliminated the laborious intermediate steps required in earlier processes. Amid spectacular showers of sparks, it accomplished in ten or twenty minutes what had taken 24 hours and immense quantities of coal. The slightly later Siemens-Martin open-hearth furnace, which recirculated superheated combustion gases to create ever-higher temperatures, similarly made steel that was as cheap as wrought iron. That revolution made the age of steel, an age only now ending (see Figure 24-5).

In chemicals, another series of breakthroughs created entirely new industries. Until the mid-nineteenth century chemical production had mostly catered to the expanding textile industry's appetite for soaps and bleaches. Then, thanks to British and French laboratory work on organic chemicals derived from coal, came the synthetic dyes. There followed mineral oils, mineral oil derivatives, the anesthetic chloroform, nitrated high explosives and fertilizers, celluloid, cellulose fiber textiles such as rayon, and the first primitive plastics. Alfred Nobel, Swedish inventor of stabilized nitroglycerine, felt such remorse at the military uses of his product and the wealth he gained from it that he established the prizes—ironically including one for peace—that bear his name.

Electricity, the third key technology, came into its own in the 1800s. Its first practical use, the telegraph, dated from 1837–38. Undersea telegraph cable linked Britain and France by 1851 and spanned the Atlantic by 1866. The telegraph, Alexander Graham Bell's telephone (1876), and Guglielmo Marconi's radio (1897–1901) revolutionized communications. But electricity's most important use was as a source of power, after a series of inventions—

Rolling steel in a mill.

generators, alternators, transformers—from the 1860s to the 1880s. Electricity not only lighted the new industrial cities, replacing the coal gas lighting pioneered in Britain around 1800. Electricity also provided cheap, portable power in the factory, ultimately replac-

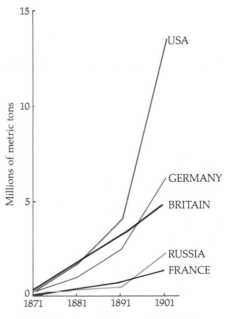

FIGURE 24-5   The Age of Steel

ing dangerous and breakdown-prone webs of transmission belts with compact, powerful electric motors.

Last came the internal combustion engine. By the mid-nineteenth century the limitations of steam were apparent. Steam engines were heavy. Their usual fuel, coal, was equally so, and required handling by legions of sweating stokers. Those characteristics made steam unsuitable for powering small vehicles. A German, Nicolaus Otto, provided the answer in 1876 with the first really practical internal combustion engine, which ran on coal gas. When converted to gasoline, it provided the motive power for the first automobiles in the 1890s, and for powered flight in 1903.

The technologies of the second industrial revolution encouraged changes in the techniques and organization of production. Cheap steel and the machine tool industry it greatly encouraged allowed the production for the first time of machines with interchangeable parts that required a minimum of filing and hand fitting during assembly. That innovation, despite the claims of Samuel Colt for his revolvers, remained more aspiration than reality until the 1870s. But after that, high-speed cutting steels, precision gauges, and a drive toward discipline and standardization in contentious matters such as screw threads made possible the mass production of ever more intricate machines.

Small arms were naturally the first application of interchangeable parts. By the 1850s a revolution in weaponry was underway. The flintlock musket, unreliable in rain and accurate to a mere hundred yards, had ruled the battlefield from the late seventeenth century to Waterloo. By 1850 the musket had given way to the Minié rifle with the all-weather mercury fulminate percussion cap. The new rifles fired heavy cylindrical bullets with hollow bases that expanded under pressure of the explosion to take the grooves of the rifle barrel. The resulting spin stabilized the bullet and made it lethal to a thousand yards.

Breech-loading arms, and weapons that did not have to be reloaded after each shot soon followed. Prussia's Dreyse and France's Chassepot breech-loading rifles offered a rate of fire five times higher than the muzzle-loading Minié. The first effective repeater was the revolver of the American, Samuel Colt. Brass cartridges replaced paper, making ammunition durable, waterproof, and quicker to load. Finally, in the 1880s came nitrated smokeless powder, the bolt-action magazine rifle, and the machine gun—a machine tool for killing. The latter was the creation of yet another American, Hiram Maxim, who succeeded in making a weapon that was truly automatic. The recoil from each shot reloaded and cocked the weapon, which was far lighter and more rapid-firing than its hand-cranked predecessors, the clumsy Gatling gun of the U.S. Civil War and the French *mitrailleuse* of 1870. Britain found the Maxim gun supremely useful in Africa, and made its inventor Sir Hiram Maxim.

The new techniques of mass production with interchangeable parts also found early application in the sewing machine. The American firm of Isaac Singer marketed this first domestic appliance on a worldwide scale after the 1850s. The same techniques, further rationalized, made possible in the twentieth century the production of automobiles on assembly lines. Mass production, in the proud words of the pioneer Henry Ford, was "the focusing upon a manufacturing system of the principle of power, accuracy, system, continuity, and speed."

The technology and organization of the second industrial revolution was different from that of the first. First, the new technologies required far greater amounts of capital than early textile innovators or even the eighteenth-century ironmasters had required. Until the coming of the railroads, entrepreneurs had tended to form closed partnerships that expanded primarily by ploughing back profits into the enterprise. The scale of the new industries placed family firms and partnerships at a disadvantage, except for a few giants such as the firm of Friedrich and Alfred Krupp, the "cannon kings" of the Ruhr. The solutions to this financial bottleneck, especially after mid-century, were the joint-stock company and large-scale bank loans to industry. Giant enterprises, bank financing, and close connections to the state became and remained conspicuous characteristics of German industry, and of those of many other followers. Britain, by contrast, resisted concentration and thus increasingly missed out on the economies of scale from which giant enterprises usually profit.

The second characteristic of the new technologies that aided the followers was a close connection to science. The inspired tinkerers that led the first industrial revolution shared the analytical, problem-solving, empirical cast of mind that had made the scientific revolution. But their discoveries had originated in workshop and forge, not in the laboratory. And their achievements were those of individual brilliance, not of teamwork. The new metallurgical, chemical, and electrical industries were different. From the beginning, the contribution of scientific theory to practice was great and ever-growing. Science-intensive industries in turn required ever larger numbers of scientists and trained technicians. The sheer size of the new enterprises required a group effort of management, scientists, and technicians.

In France, state institutions such as the *École Polytechnique* and lesser provincial institutes filled the gap in knowledge. But it was the reforming bureaucrats of Germany that triumphed in the new world of applied science and teamwork. Universal primary education and a widespread network of technical schools in many German states from the 1820s had no parallel on the continent, or anywhere else except perhaps the United States after mid-century. Britain, where primary education did not become compulsory until 1880 and where the elite studied Latin and Greek but not chemistry, suffered accordingly. By 1872 the University of Munich alone had more graduate research chemists than all English universities combined. And German and American management proved remarkably skilled at the large-scale organization of research, development, and production.

The followers inevitably developed at different rates and achieved widely varying results. Belgium and France started first, in the 1820s. Belgium probably became the first society after Britain whose industry produced more by value than its agriculture. But it lacked the population and resources to be more than a minor industrial power. France was a potential rival to Britain, but it suffered from major constraints. Until the railway boom of the 1850s its communications were poor. Its large peasant sector acted as a drag on the rest of the economy, lessening demand. Above all, old habits of mind died hard. The French entrepreneur, with some exceptions, bowed to the social pressures of a society that despite Revolution and Terror remained less competitive and more hierarchical than Britain's. The French and even the Germans tended until quite late to see business as a zero-sum game in which victory came only at the expense of others—who also had their right to a "fair" living. Robber-baron success appeared antisocial. The French economy grew steadily, but industry's share of the national product did not surpass that of agriculture until 1909.

Germany and the United States took up the British challenge most fully. By the end of the century, thanks to the coal and iron of the Ruhr and to economic unity bloodily achieved in 1866–71 (see pp. 744–51), Germany had surpassed Britain. Pig iron output increased 20-fold between 1850 and 1870. Giants such as Krupps or the Borsig engineering works in Berlin dominated the production of locomotives, machinery, and engines of destruction. In chemicals, great firms such as AGFA, Höchst, and BASF captured 90 percent of the world market for synthetic dyes by 1900. AEG and Siemens, the electric giants, achieved positions in the world market that only their counterparts in the United States rivalled.

The economic development of the United States was if anything even more spectacular than Germany's. Growth rested on several factors. Land, once violently cleared of Indians, was "free." Vast mineral resources, from Appalachian coal to the Mesabi iron range to the gold of California, fuelled development. The highest birth rate in the West and the immigration of 30 million people between 1845 and 1914 provided enough labor to meet needs, but not so much to depress wages or to discourage the introduction of labor-saving machinery. Relatively high wages in turn promoted consumer demand.

Mechanization began in textile production, as in Britain, in the 1770s in the water-powered mills of New England. Eli Whitney's cotton gin (1793), which separated fibers from seeds quickly and cheaply, helped create a boom in the slave South. Cotton shipments to the mills of Massachusetts and Lancashire leapt upwards. By 1840 the United States had already passed Britain in steam engine horsepower. The Erie Canal, opened in 1825, cut across the Appalachians and connected the industry of the East with the grain of the Midwest. After 1830 railroads opened up sources of coal and iron and fed ever larger cities. Large farms and a relative shortage of labor encouraged a mechanization of agriculture on a scale undreamed of elsewhere. Cyrus McCormick's reaper (1831), the railroad, and the steamship allowed grain from the Great Plains to undersell European grain in European markets by the 1870s. Refrigeration, invented in the 1830s, made possible by the 1880s the mass distribution and export of meat. And in heavy industry, the United States created a Ruhr that stretched from Pittsburgh to Chicago

and outclassed all rivals. By 1914 the industrial output of the United States was almost 80 percent that of all Western Europe.

Last of the early followers came Italy, Russia, and Japan. Italy broke into rapid growth in the first decade of the new century, but its depressed agriculture and shortage of energy resources held it back until after 1945. Russia and Japan were the first cases of a phenomenon increasingly familiar later in the new century—the industrialization of societies that were either partially (Russia) or wholly (Japan) non-Western in politics and culture. Economic growth in both cases was spectacular. But political and cultural traditions did not always encourage the sober use of the unprecedented power that industrialization brought.

The second industrial revolution and the industrialization of the followers made a true world market. Before the French revolutionary wars Europe's mercantile world economy had shown some signs of the now familiar boom and bust pattern of the business cycle. The depression that followed the wars of the French Revolution had been unusually severe and widespread. By mid-century, transport and communications had begun to weld the world together. The California gold strike and an outbreak of railway fever fuelled an American, European, and world boom that broke in the first true world depression, the panic of 1857. Further growth culminated in a second collapse in 1873. That crash inaugurated a 20-year period of falling prices known misleadingly as the nineteenth century "great depression." The term is a misnomer because this was a period of unparalleled growth in output for the followers, especially Germany and the United States. Falling prices caused dislocation, especially in European agriculture. But they were a sign of health, a sign of the abundance that the mechanization of industry, agriculture, and transport made possible. And after

1896 a new boom lifted the world economy, with a brief interruption in 1907, until 1913.

THE INDUSTRIAL REVOLUTION: HUMAN AND SOCIAL CONSEQUENCES

The Industrial Revolution inevitably transformed or helped transform underlying features of all societies it touched—standard of living and life expectancy, the location and occupations of the population, the structure of the social hierarchy, and the character of the basic human unit, the family.

The Rise in Living Standards and Life Expectancy

England, along with Holland and the infant United States, had enjoyed the highest living standard before indus-

trialization. It preserved that lead throughout the nineteenth century except against the United States. Advance was nevertheless far from smooth; Britain, in particular, paid the price of pioneering. From the 1790s to the 1840s English real wages (wages adjusted for the cost of living) appear to have stagnated. The peak of the birth rate coincided with the triumph of the factories over domestic handicrafts. In addition, after the 1790s women and children made up an increasing proportion of the work force in factories and mines. Entrepreneurs could pay them less and dominate them more effectively than they could men. Factory work and the filth of the improvised industrial cities dragged life expectancy down below that of most rural areas.

In the realm of intangibles, the workers of the early Industrial Revolution also suffered. They exchanged the familiar if want-racked countryside or

The new industrial city, crowded and sooty. London by Gustav Doré.

small-town workshop for filthy slum streets and "dark satanic mills" enveloped in clouds of coal soot. The "Black Country" around Birmingham came by its name honestly. The workers exchanged the tyranny of the seasons and of crop blights for that of the tireless machine. Breaking the new industrial labor force to the discipline of the clock was one of the major challenges facing the early entrepreneurs. Workers long resisted the habit of regularity, of arriving for work on Mondays or arriving sober on Tuesdays. And the tyranny of the business cycle replaced that of nature. Overproduction or disruption of normal trade patterns could spell unemployment and massive distress for entire regions. The "cotton famine" that resulted from the U.S. Civil War (1861–65) caused near starvation in industrial Lancashire. In the new cities, overcrowding, poverty, and the sudden release from the traditional religious and social restraints of the tight rural community led to widespread illegitimacy, alcoholism, and prostitution.

But after 1840 conditions slowly improved. Between 1851 and 1878, British per capita real income increased by a startling 30 percent. Until 1900 it continued to rise at the unprecedented rate of between 17 and 25 percent per decade. And workers worked less; the average (estimated) workweek in British industry declined from almost 60 hours in the 1860s to around 53 hours in 1900. In Europe as a whole the estimated average workweek dropped from an appalling 84 hours in 1850 to 60 hours in 1910.

A dramatic increase in life expectancy reflected and paralleled the rise in real income. The crucial factor was a decline in infant mortality. The death rate of infants aged under one year dropped in England from 36 percent in 1751–60 to 11.7 percent in 1906–10. France's infant mortality after the turn of the twentieth century was slightly higher than Britain's, and Sweden's somewhat lower. Russia's remained at 25 percent as late as 1900–09. Adults

also lived longer. The drop in infant mortality and greater longevity together raised life expectancy in western Europe from below 40 years in 1840 to the mid-50s by 1900. That rapid change was unparalleled in human history.

What did this mean for the bulk of the population? For the first time, appreciable numbers of people began living significantly above subsistence level and consuming an ever-increasing variety of goods. Already in the 1780s English workers had come to expect tea, coffee, sugar, and inexpensive cottons. After 1850 workers paid an ever-decreasing proportion of their wages for food and lodging. They began to have money and time to spend on leisure and entertainment.

Industrialization naturally did not distribute its benefits equally. The elites had always lived better and longer than those at the bottom of the social pyramid. And industrialization opened the *relative* gap between rich and poor: the rich grew richer faster than the poor. The concentration of wealth therefore increased. The immense fortunes of the entrepreneurs generated envy in the increasingly politically conscious workers and fear in the landowning elites which had until now dominated society. That trend had political consequences.

Urbanization and Emigration

The new age also brought migrations unprecedented since the fall of the Roman Empire. Population growth dictated movement. The agricultural countryside simply could not support the increase in numbers after 1750. The growth of industry encouraged movement by providing jobs. After 1850 the revolution in transportation, the railroad and the steamship, made movement on an unprecedented scale possible. The result was urbanization and emigration.

Urbanization, the concentration of the population in cities, was most conspicuous in Britain, where the monster city, London, had long been the largest in western Europe. In 1800 it contained about 12 percent of Britain's total population (see Figure 24-6). By 1890 over 60 percent of the British lived in cities of over 10,000. German and Belgian figures were in the 30 percent range, and France's only 25 percent. Where sheep had grazed a generation or two before stood the largely unplanned cities of Manchester and Birmingham and the mine tailings and slag heaps of the Ruhr and the Pas-de-Calais. Not until after mid-century did the new cities gradually receive sewage systems, relatively clean water supplies, and housing that even remotely approximated the population's needs.

Emigration was the alternative to the cities. It tended to affect all countries with high rates of population increase, whether they led or followed industrially. Britain grew from 8.9 million in 1801 to 32.5 million in 1901, but nevertheless gave up millions of emigrants. Germany, between the "hungry forties" and the maturing of its industrial economy by 1900, gave up perhaps 5 million emigrants. France, with its stable peasant economy, low birth rate, and slow industrialization, showed a unique pattern of low emigration.

Predominantly agricultural countries also participated in this continent-wide migration. Ireland, after the famine, gave up roughly 3 million emigrants up to 1900. Scandinavian emigration peaked in the 1880s. Emigration from relatively backward areas such as Russia, Spain, and Italy continued to increase until World War I cut it short in 1914. Italy, with its overpopulated South and late industrialization, gave up an unprecedented 880,000 emigrants in 1913. The recipient of most of this great migration was the United States, which took 82 percent of all transatlantic emigration in 1866–70 and was still taking 61 percent in 1896–1900.

The combined effect of urbanization and emigration was to open up the old rural societies, as well as creating new social relations in the new cities and

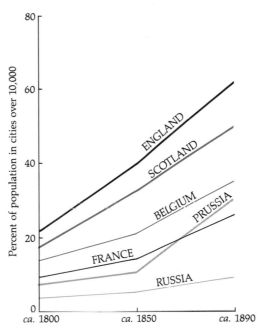

FIGURE 24-6 The Urbanization of Europe

the new lands across the oceans. Returnees from the cities and even from the New World (10 million people went back to Europe between 1886 and 1915) brought new ideas into the narrow agricultural communities from which they had escaped. Compulsory military service, which became almost universal after 1870, had similarly broadening effects. The knowledge that better or at least profoundly different patterns of life existed elsewhere was itself a powerful solvent of what remained of the old order.

Social Structure

The continent-wide transformation weakened old social groups and created new ones. The rapid rise of a new business elite undermined the social power of the nobility far more than the events of 1789 had done. In Britain the aristocracy controlled perhaps 20 percent of the national product in 1820. By 1850 that proportion had sunk to 10 percent. A decline in the role of agriculture paralleled that of the nobility, the elite that defined itself by ownership of

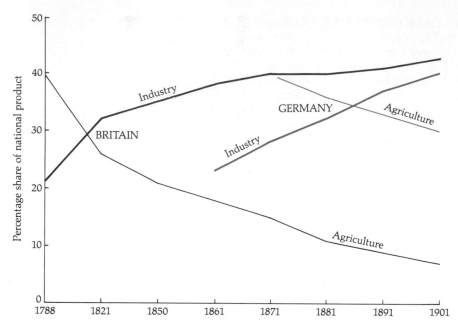

FIGURE 24-7   The Triumph of Industry over Agriculture: Germany and Britain

land. In the extreme case of Britain, decline was so precipitous that by 1901 less than 5 percent of the population actually worked in agriculture or fishing. France, as usual, resisted the trend. Simultaneously, the industrial population and the proportion of the national wealth that industry produced swiftly increased (see Figure 24-7). Industry's proportion of the national product passed agriculture before 1820 in Britain, around 1890 in Germany, and in the first decade of the new century in France.

In the new cities, the middle classes expanded rapidly. By the end of the century they made up a far larger proportion of the total population than ever before—from perhaps 20 percent in northwestern Europe to 5 percent in the south and east. The middle classes consisted first of all of the entrepreneurs, the driving force and chief beneficiaries of the new age of cotton, coal, and steam. Then came the professional middle classes, the ever-growing ranks of lawyers, doctors, higher bureaucrats, professors, and professional intellectuals. They lived not from entre-

preneurship but from intellectual work. The nineteenth century was theirs as no other century has been, for the nobility had lost its monopoly of power and the masses were as yet hesitant in pressing their claims.

Below the entrepreneurial and professional middle classes, new groups proliferated. Increasing specialization of work paralleled and influenced the increasing number of subtle gradations in the social hierarchy. The artisans and home handicraft workers, victims of the machine, dwindled. Only the continued existence of trades difficult to mechanize fully, such as clothing manufacture, guaranteed their continued existence. Alongside this "old lower middle class" of distressed artisans, there grew a "new lower middle class" of white collar workers in government or business bureaucracies. This group was as characteristic of the new age as the industrial workers below it.

The lower classes divided into numerous subcategories. Peasants and landless rural laborers stood at the bottom of the hierarchy in the country-

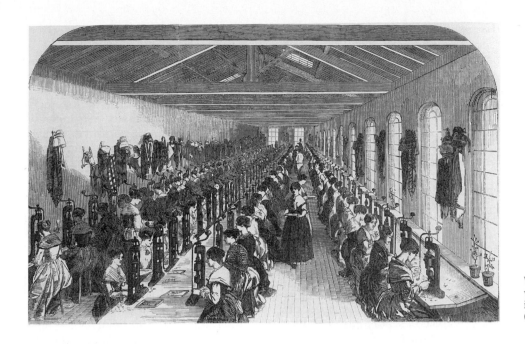

Women in the industrial work force: slitting pen nibs in a Birmingham factory (1851).

side. A large class of domestic servants made possible the leisured existence of the new middle classes. The industrial workers themselves were anything but uniform. They ranged from the "labor aristocracy," skilled iron and steel workers, machinists, and foremen, to unskilled or semiskilled workers at starvation wages. Below the working classes was an underclass of pickpockets, prostitutes, and beggars, sometimes organized into elaborate hierarchies, but often anarchic and always violent.

The lines between groups remained far more fluid than under the old society of orders on the Continent. Becoming an entrepreneur was relatively easy at first, at least in Britain, but class lines hardened as the century wore on. The amount of capital needed to enter industry increased dramatically with the advent of the steam engine and still more with the second industrial revolution. The new cities, unlike the old, were segregated by class. Workers had lived in attics and cellars, above and below the rich. In Manchester and Birmingham, the new rich instead retreated to villas in the countryside,

leaving the pestilential city centers to the poor. And the growth of an independent working-class culture and ideologies in response to the Industrial Revolution (see pp. 719–21) acted as a barrier to mobility. Those who did rise socially risked ostracism for "betraying their class."

From Traditional to Nuclear Family

Finally, the processes of industrialization and urbanization affected the very structure of the family and the role of women. Even before industrialization, the early modern family, with its extended kin networks and family ties based on subordination and respect, had begun to give way to the nuclear family of parents and children. The new nuclear family of parents and children, based at least in theory on love, may have existed in England since the late Middle Ages. It had in any case conquered the English middle classes by 1800. Family and workplace separated. The family became a private realm. The increasing fashion for romantic love as the chief rationale for marriage undermined the old role of the father as a monarch in miniature. Once children chose their own mates, patriarchal authority was under attack.

Similar developments, with a considerable lag, penetrated the urban areas of the Continent as well. First the upper middle classes adopted the new style, then the nobility. Finally it trickled down the social scale as the nineteenth century drew on. Increasing affluence, literacy, and longer lives encouraged the transition. Unlike the biological old regime, when plague or famine might at any moment strike down a spouse or child, affection was now a sounder emotional investment.

The new family structure hardly liberated women, but it did improve their status. The social conventions of romantic love ultimately sapped the Code Napoléon's attempts to bolster the power of the father, and eroded the all-dominance of the bewhiskered patriarchs of nineteenth-century Britain or Germany. A man could only with difficulty combine the roles of master, companion, and lover. And the separation of work from the home and the profusion of domestic servants meant that middle-class women had more lei-

sure than before industrialization. A British male commentator noted in the 1850s that "the day is thrown idle on woman's hand. The thousand exciting events and under-takings that . . . stretch the faculties of man, are reckoned beyond her sphere." That leisure gave more and more educated women opportunity to reflect on their condition, and eventually to revolt against it.

By 1900, most of western Europe had passed through the fires of industrialization. Britain, Germany, and France had become industrial great powers. The United States had outstripped all rivals. Russia and Japan were beginning to overhaul Western Europe. Industrialization had transformed the ways of life of the peoples and classes it had touched. Some groups had lost; many more, despite the bitterness of the struggle, had won. And industrialization, along with that other revolution in France, had also helped transform the ideas and categories through which the West understood the world, and sought to change it.

Suggestions for Further Reading

The Pre-industrial World

On the world before industrialization, see the analysis of C. Cipolla, *Before the Industrial Revolution* (1975); for England, P. Laslett offers a quasi-nostalgic view in *The World We Have Lost* (1971). For the adventurous, F. Braudel, *Civilization and Capitalism, 15th–18th Centuries* (1982), provides an unparalleled guided tour of the pre-industrial world economy. C. McEvedy and F. Jones, *Atlas of World Population History* (1978), is first-rate.

Why the West, and Why Britain?

On the West's primacy and its causes, see especially D. Landes, *The Unbound Prometheus* (1972); E. L. Jones, *The European Miracle* (1981); W. O'Neill, *The Pursuit of Power* (1982); and N. Rosenberg and L. Birdzell, *How the West Grew Rich* (1986). For England's peculiarities, see the contrasting accounts of A. Macfarlane, *Marriage and Love in England* (1986), and L. Stone, *The Family, Sex, and Marriage in England 1500–1800* (1977), and the summary of recent demographic research in E. A. Wrigley, "The Growth of Population in Eighteenth-Century England," *Past and Present* (February, 1983), pp. 121–50. H. Perkin, *The Origins of Modern English Society 1780–1880* (1969), offers an excellent synthesis of the social causes of British industrialization.

The Industrial Revolution

On the interrelationship of technological change and economic growth, see above all D. Landes, *The Unbound Prometheus*. P. Deane, *The First Industrial Revolution* (1965), and E. Pawson, *The Early Industrial Revolution* (1979), are useful on Britain, as is T. S. Ashton, *The Industrial Revolution* (1970). On the industrialization of the followers, see T. Kemp, *Industrialization in Nineteenth-Century Europe* (1969), and C. Trebilcock, *The Industrialization of Continental Europe* (1981). B. Mitchell, *European Historical Statistics* (1981), is a useful source, and Paul Bairoch, "International Industrialization Levels from 1750 to 1980," *Journal of European Economic History* 2, no. 2, provides indispensable data on shifts in the economic balance of power. T. Hamerow, *The Birth of a New Europe* (1983), is a fine recent survey of the social and political consequences of industrialization.

25

The New Age: Theory and Practice

*T*he twin revolutions in France and in the mills and iron foundries of Britain inevitably generated new ideas and profoundly modified old ones. The old certainties of religion, whether Catholic or Protestant, retained their validity for the great mass of the population of Europe throughout the nineteenth century. But religion gradually became central to fewer lives. Science appeared to undermine it. Urbanization and the decay of the traditional village community lessened its grip. In the realm of culture, a new movement, romanticism, fiercely attacked both the ideas and the style of the Enlightenment. In philosophy, two generations of Germans laid the foundations for much of nineteenth-century political thought. In politics, a "counter-Enlightenment" in some ways parallel to romanticism developed—conservatism, the ideology of opposition to revolutionary France and to all revolution. The antagonist of conservatism was the ill-assorted conglomerate of economic and political doctrines that goes by the name of liberalism. And beyond liberalism but related to it and locked in struggle with it came socialism, a ready-made political faith for the new industrial workers. Last of all, the French revolution's most powerful progeny, nationalism, spread eastward across Europe.

In the realm of practice, as opposed to theory, a variety of forces and tendencies modified European intellectual and social life. Literacy and increasing wealth brought into existence the phenomenon known as public opinion. Submerged social groups and categories, women and workers, began for the first time to make themselves heard.

THE FORCE OF IDEAS

Science and Scholarship

The nineteenth century opened new and unsuspected vistas. Mathematics, that abstruse discipline seemingly so remote from experience, equipped itself with the tools needed to inspire

700

Charles Darwin, father of modern biology and greatest scientific mind of the nineteenth century.

and describe the physical discoveries of the twentieth century. The creation of the first non-Euclidian geometry by a Russian, Nikolai Ivanovitch Lobachevsky (1793–1856) led to the invention of topology by Georg Friedrich Riemann (1826–66) of Göttingen. That, and the tensor calculus of Gregorio Ricci (1853–1925), in turn made possible the twentieth-century mathematics of space-time and gravity.

In physics, electricity and heat were the phenomena that nineteenth-century science explored most successfully. The discovery of electric current in 1786 led to Alessandro Volta's battery in 1799, to Hans Christian Oersted's discovery of a connection between magnetism and electricity of 1819, and to Michael Faraday's theory of electromagnetic induction of 1831. Ultimately James Clerk Maxwell, in his *Electricity and Magnetism* (1873) provided a mathematical synthesis suggesting that light was also an electromagnetic phenomenon. With electricity, advances in the laboratory created later technologies. The reverse occurred with the steam engine. It inspired Sadi Carnot, son of the Carnot of the Committee of Public Safety, to formulate in the 1820s generalizations that later physicists codified as the first and second laws of thermodynamics.

Chemistry's advance was even more spectacular than that of physics. John Dalton's sketch of an atomic theory in the first decade of the century opened the way for the study of chemical compounds and structures. The synthesis in 1828 of a compound found in nature, urea, opened the study of organic chemistry, the chemistry of carbon. By the 1860s, chemists had begun to explore the molecular structure of simple compounds such as benzene. In 1869 Dimitri Ivanovitch Mendeleev formulated a periodic law and table of elements that for the first time gave scientists a sketchy notion of some of the basic building blocks of the universe. It predicted the existence of elements as yet unknown; researchers using Mendeleev's theory isolated gallium (1871),

scandium (1879), germanium (1886), and helium (1895).

But it was not until the end of the century that a series of breakthroughs on the boundary of chemistry and physics revolutionized science's picture of the world and placed the old Newtonian certainties in question. Wilhelm Roentgen's discovery of X rays (1895) soon led to the unearthing of radioactive elements that apparently emitted particles smaller than the atom. By the turn of the century the theoreticians Max Planck and Albert Einstein had begun to lay the foundations for a non-Newtonian physics that unified the universe of subatomic particles with that of space-time, and predicted the convertibility of matter into energy.

Biology, basically a creation of the nineteenth century, developed immediate practical uses after mid-century. The explorations of the world of bacteria by Louis Pasteur (1822–95) and Robert Koch (1843–1910) opened the door to an understanding of many diseases and aided Joseph Lister (1827–92) in the development of sterile surgical procedures.

But the greatest biological questions were theoretical. What caused the unparalleled diversity of life forms that eighteenth- and early nineteenth-century naturalists had classified? How had humanity originated? Studies in embryology in the 1820s implied that embryos, during their growth, might be recapitulating their species history, for bird embryos developed gill-slits. The study of fossils, still in its infancy, suggested change and development over immense periods of time. The discovery in 1856 of an apelike but large-brained skull at Neanderthal near the Ruhr implied that humanity might have nonhuman ancestors.

Geology, an entirely new science, appeared to offer corroboration. Charles Lyell's *Principles of Geology* (1830–33) provided the first satisfactory explanation of the Earth's physical features and their evolution. A variety of speculative thinkers suggested that life—and thus humanity as well—might also be the result of evolutionary processes. But the mechanism by which that evolution occurred was as yet a mystery. Jean Baptiste Lamarck, who invented the term "biology," proposed in 1809 that creatures acquired characteristics in response to changes in their environment and subsequently passed those characteristics to their offspring. That would account for diversity and change—if it were true.

It was Charles Darwin (1809–82) who most cogently suggested, after long investigations on the isolated Galápagos islands off Ecuador and elsewhere, that species evolved through a savage "struggle for life." Darwin announced that conclusion in 1858, after a fellow biologist, Alfred Russel Wallace (1823–1913), had sketched out a similar theory. The following year, Darwin published his path-breaking synthesis, *The Origin of Species by Means of Natural Selection, or the Preservation of Favored Races in the Struggle for Life*. Darwin argued, with a crushing weight of examples drawn from field research, that scarcity of food produced a fierce competition that killed off "unfit" variants of a given species before they could reproduce. "Sexual selection," or the triumph of the "fittest" males in competition for females further reinforced that mechanism. "Natural selection," working over immense spans of time, had produced the rich diversity visible in nature.

Darwin, although he recoiled from inevitable controversy with the religious establishment, ultimately extended his logic explicitly to humanity itself in *The Descent of Man* (1871): "Thus from the wars of nature, from famine and death, the most exalted object which we are capable of conceiving, namely the production of higher animals, directly follows." That claim, popularized in innumerable works by other "Darwinists," accomplished the most far-reaching revolution in the West's conception of itself since Copernicus had suggested that the Earth was not the motionless center of the universe. Darwin's explanation of humanity's place in the new world that science was uncovering made him the most widely influential scientific thinker of the century.

His theories also made him the father of modern biology. With a single powerful generalization he accounted for all the diversity of life. But Darwin's theory of evolution nevertheless had a major weakness: it accounted only for the change of *entire* species over time. Darwin could not provide a convincing physical cause for the all-important variations between *individuals* that drove those species changes. He fell back in part on Lamarck's untenable theory of the inheritance of acquired characteristics. Not until later did the long-neglected work of the Bohemian monk Gregor Mendel (1822–84), the father of genetics, provide the answer. In 1901 Hugo De Vries drew on Mendel's work to formulate a theory of genetic mutation by sudden random leaps. Subsequent experiments using the fast-multiplying fruit fly laid the groundwork of modern genetics, which explained individual variation and provided Darwin's basic insights with powerful support.

In the social sciences, the nineteenth century likewise opened a new age. The eccentric Auguste Comte (1798–1857) invented the word sociology, if not the discipline it describes. A revolution in sources, methods, and subjects transformed history—for better or worse—from a literary pastime into a scholarly profession. The German scholar Leopold von Ranke (1795–1886) laid down the doctrine that historians must first of all investigate and cross-check primary source materials, the evidence the historical actors themselves had left. Ranke's notion that the historian's duty was to reconstruct events "as they actually happened" was not new. Thucydides the Athenian had suggested something of the sort in his fifth-century B.C. history of the Peloponnesian War. But now, in the early nineteenth century, it was at last possible to attempt to translate that precept systematically into practice. In England, France, and Germany governments and private groups founded institutions such as London's Public Record Office for the collection and eventual publication of historical sources.

Vast multivolume national histories began to appear, monuments to the industry and learning of their authors, though, alas, not always readable. The Prussian professor of jurisprudence, Karl von Savigny (1779–1861) founded a historical school dedicated to explaining the evolution of law. He proclaimed the superiority of law grown by the slow accretion of precedent over the artificial law codes of the French.

Historical investigation even touched scripture. David Friedrich Strauss's *Life of Jesus* (1835) examined the Gospels as historical documents and expressed skepticism about their subject's divinity—and existence. The French intellectual Ernest Renan provoked outrage in the 1860s by describing Christ as "an incomparable man"; his biography of Christ was a popular success.

Finally, historians and philologists also began investigating the diversity of human languages and deriving general laws. A British scholar, Sir Henry Rawlinson, followed up Champollion's 1822 decipherment of hieroglyphics by reading Persian cuneiform inscriptions in 1835. German philologists studied shifts of consonants in numerous languages over many centuries, and deduced laws governing the evolution of languages. They demonstrated that the Indian language Sanskrit and most European languages shared a common Indo-European origin. That discovery helped open up the study of the prehistory of Europe and of South and Central Asia (see pp. 6–8).

Religion

Religious skepticism, as described in Chapter 21, had become commonplace among the educated in the course of the eighteenth century. The novelty of the nineteenth century was that detachment from religion began to spread among the masses. That was partly a consequence of politics. The American and French Revolutions, unlike the English Revolution of the 1640s, had been secular upheavals, and many French revolutionaries had been overtly anticlerical. Urbanization and its consequent social dislocation likewise sapped religion. In the improvised city of Birmingham in 1851 the churches could hold less than a third of the population. And many of the new industrial workers resented the churches' defense of the social status quo. Finally, the retreat from religion was in part a consequence of the same process of scientific advance that had inspired the deists and skeptics of the Enlightenment.

But the science of the nineteenth century appeared far more powerful, and less compatible with traditional religion, than that of the eighteenth century. Lyell's geology and Darwin's evolution placed in question the biblical account of creation. That above all affected Protestants (and to a lesser extent Jews), given the central place of the biblical texts in their beliefs. Darwin's work provoked a veritable "warfare of science and theology." The Archbishop of Canterbury, in a furious debate in 1860, sarcastically asked "Darwin's Bulldog," the biologist Thomas H. Huxley, which side of his family descended from apes. A minority of "fundamentalist" Protestants, especially strong in the United States, continued to assert the literal truth of the biblical account of creation. The majority, thanks to Protestantism's emphasis on the individual's freedom and direct relationship with God, made a variety of compromises between faith and reason.

Strong forces nevertheless counteracted the decline of religion. Women of the lower classes, submerged by custom and enforced illiteracy, tended to traditional piety. The rural masses held to their faith whether they remained at home or emigrated, as did so many Irish and Italians. Governments, whether of kings or liberals, continued to prize religion as a foundation for social order. Religion itself showed continued vitality and expansive force.

In England and the United States the nineteenth century was a time of intense religious ferment. The impetus of German Pietism and of its derivative, John Wesley's Methodism, were far from spent. Other Protestant sects expanded with equal rapidity. Waves of religious enthusiasm swept over South Wales, for instance, in 1807–09, 1828–30, 1839–48, 1854, and 1859. In America after 1800 a "Great Revival" moved westward with the frontier.

The politics of Wesley, the Pietists, and their offshoots tended to bolster the social order. In the words of the *Statutes of the Wesleyan Body* (1792), "the oracles of God" commanded obedience to the secular power. That attitude permeated English and American popular religion. Along with the early spread of democratic politics in those societies, it limited the appeal of the radical panaceas for the ills of *this* world so popular in continental Europe. And the spread of democracy helped the churches by providing a widely popular and easily defensible status quo.

European Catholicism was even more closely intertwined with the existing order than Protestantism, and after 1789 that order was under attack. Some advanced Catholic thinkers foresaw the need for the Church to distance itself from monarchy, lest the Church perish in monarchy's ruin. Félicité de Lamennais, a formerly ultra-conservative French cleric, published *Words of a Believer* after the 1830 Paris revolution (see p. 730). It appealed for equality and democracy, and denounced "the passion to acquire and to possess." Rome damned Lamennais in two thundering encyclicals.

Pope Pius IX (r. 1846–78) appeared briefly as a champion of change. Then the revolutions of 1848 (see pp. 732–38) dissuaded him. His encyclical *Quanta cura* of 1864, with its appended *Syllabus*

errorum or "listing of errors," denounced the notion that "the Roman Pontiff can and ought to reconcile himself to and agree with progress, liberalism, and modern civilization." The reforming Pope Leo XIII (r. 1878–1903) reversed that uncompromising stance in a path-breaking encyclical of 1891 entitled *Rerum novarum* ("Of New Things"). The gradual de-christianization of the urban masses and the challenge of socialism had induced a rethinking. *Rerum novarum* was the charter of a new social and reforming Catholicism that condemned both capitalist greed and socialist denial of God. Leo XIII's successor, Pius X (r. 1903–14), reverted to rigid defense of received doctrine and purged the Church of "modernists" who sought to reconcile science with theology. But in the end it was Leo XIII's policy of adaptation to the new age that triumphed.

Romanticism

The notion of a new style, opposed to the rationalism and classicism of the Enlightenment (see pp. 612–13), emerged toward the end of the eighteenth century. The stormy young German writers of the *"Sturm und Drang"* movement of the 1780s, in particular, had defied convention and celebrated emotion. By 1800 German critics had coined the distinction between "classical" and "romantic." The term "romantic" has nevertheless escaped definition.

Some romantics, such as the great English poet George Gordon, Lord Byron (1788–1824), thought of themselves as revolutionaries: "I have simplified my politics into a detestation of all existing governments." The French poet, dramatist, and novelist Victor Hugo (1802–85) could write that "romanticism is liberalism in literature." Byron's friend Percy Bysshe Shelley (1792–1822) proclaimed that "poets are the unacknowledged legislators of the world." Heinrich Heine (1797–1856), the last major German romantic poet and the greatest German lyric poet of the century, was a life-long radical democrat. The French painter Eugène Delacroix (1798–1863) could paint, in *Liberty Leading the People* (1834), the quintessential romantic vision of the triumph of revolution (see p. 724).

Still other romantics, such as the English lyric poets William Blake (1757–1827) and William Wordsworth (1770–1850), outdid one another in their rejection of the "dark satanic mills" of the new age. In politics, Wordsworth's original enthusiam for the French Revolution gave way to bitter opposition even to modest Parliamentary reforms in England. Especially in Germany, romanticism turned increasingly into celebration of the Middle Ages, supposedly more authentic than the classical age, the Renaissance, or the alleged artificiality and frenchified rationalism of the detested eighteenth century. The eerie landscapes of Caspar David Friedrich (1774–1840), painted from imagination rather than life, well illustrate that preoccupation. In England, the medievalizing novels of Sir Walter Scott, the paintings of John Constable

and Joseph Turner, and the revival of Gothic as an architectural style embodied similar tendencies.

What the romantics, however diverse their politics and aesthetics, tended to share were four things. First, they rejected the eighteenth century's "classical" limitations on form and structure in art. In music, romantics from the unparalleled master of the symphony, Ludwig van Beethoven (1770–1827) to the dogmatic theorist and practitioner of "total opera," Richard Wagner (1813–83), gleefully disregarded inherited conventions of form, and of orchestra size and composition. Poets such as Wordsworth deliberately chose a poetic vocabulary closer to spoken English than to the measured couplets of predecessors such as Alexander Pope. Even continental drama discarded for good the restrictions on subject, time, and place that Aristotle's aesthetic theories had imposed.

Second, the romantics prized emotion, the stronger the better. That preoccupation led even former fellow travelers such as the great German poet

Cloister Graveyard in the Snow (1810), by Caspar David Friedrich.

Johann Wolfgang von Goethe (1749–1832) to conclude that "classic is that which is healthy, romantic that which is sick." The line between emotion and morbid self-preoccupation was narrow. But the romantic emphasis on the creative power of the individual's imagination was a liberating force. In combination with craftsmanship and self-discipline it could produce masterpieces.

Third, the romantics tended to celebrate nature. Their nature was not the manicured eighteenth-century ornamental garden, but the craggy uplands of Wordsworth's imagination:

> Once again
> Do I behold these steep and lofty cliffs
> That on a wild secluded scene impress
> Thoughts of more deep seclusion;
>   and connect
> The landscape with the quiet of the sky.

Rousseau, with his mystical *Reveries of a Solitary Wanderer* (1776–78) had shown the way. Nature, the "nature or God" of Spinoza, brought humanity—or at least skeptical intellectuals—closer to an otherwise unknowable God. The popularization of this "natural supernaturalism," as the English philosopher-historian Thomas Carlyle (1795–1881) called it, was one of the major legacies of romanticism.

Finally, the romantics both celebrated and embodied the cult of the solitary, youthful, misunderstood genius. The genius defied convention and perhaps suffered persecution for political radicalism, or like Byron, for sexual peccadillos. Like Shelley, the genius might be dead by 30; tuberculosis was as much the romantic disease as morbid introspection. The cult of the artist as misfit was in part an extension of romantic emphasis on imagination, on the creative powers of the individual. The collapse of aristocratic art patronage after 1789 may also have contributed, for the middle classes were not yet rich enough to step in. Age, respectability, and middle-class patrons nevertheless tamed those roman-

tics who survived. The movement did not outlast mid-century, but it broke Enlightenment formalism for good. Art was henceforth what the artist, the individual as towering genius, decreed it to be.

The Revolution in German Philosophy

Parallel to romanticism and not unrelated to it came an explosion of creativity in German philosophy. Misty speculation, including opposition to Newton's mathematically precise account of matter and motion, had long been a German specialty. Immanuel Kant (see p. 613) had sought to rescue reason from the skepticism of Enlightenment philosophers such as David Hume, who refused to accept as certain the evidence of the senses. Kant saved reason by limiting its domain. He postulated that the human mind was capable of limited knowledge of the world around it, but only on the basis of categories such as space and time, categories already built into the structure of the mind itself. Humanity could not perceive "things in themselves," things as they really were, except through those categories.

Kant's second main contribution was related to his theory of knowledge. Moral judgment was akin to the mind's inborn mechanism of perception, Kant argued. Morality was the result of a universal law found within ourselves. And for Kant, freedom was obedience to that law. The poet Heine rightly remarked that as a revolutionary, Kant put Robespierre in the shade. Kant's notion of morality, in particular, opened the way for individuals to discover moral standards for themselves. Kant was a loyal supporter of the Prussian state, but his doctrine struck at the root of any claim to authority that individuals chose not to accept.

Kant's theory of knowledge provoked his successors, especially Johann Gottlieb Fichte (1762–1814) and Georg Friedrich Wilhelm Hegel (1770–1831) to a decisive step. Fichte saw the implau-

Johann Wolfgang von Goethe, greatest of German poets, from a medal of 1829.

sibility of saying that things-in-themselves existed but that the mind could not know them. If the mind knew about them, they must exist. Rather than falling back into Enlightenment rationalism, Fichte and Hegel took a leap of faith even greater than Kant's. Both things-in-themselves and the mind must be part of a larger whole, a universal consciousness, an all-encompassing "world spirit" that was a descendant of Spinoza's "nature or God."

Hegel, the most influential philosopher of the century, proclaimed that history was the process of the self-realization of that world spirit. History thus had a goal. It also had a mechanism, the "dialectic," a step-by-step progress through a series of reversals or negations. It had already passed through three stages: the oriental, in which the despot alone was free; the ancient world, in which a few men in Greece and Rome had been free; and the Christian-Germanic civilization of northern Europe, which had at last recognized that humanity itself was or could be free.

In this process, this ever-upward striving toward the self-realization of the world spirit, the role of the individual was clear. Kant's self-determining individual must will an ever-closer identification with the world spirit. Hegel, as befitted a professor of philosophy at the University of Berlin, came to identify the world spirit with the Prussian power-state: "The State is the divine Idea as it exists on earth." Others took Kant's notion of self-determination and Hegel's goal-oriented theory of history, and put them to uses which their originators could hardly have foreseen.

Conservatism

Although Hegel inclined toward defense of the status quo, the doctrines that have acquired the name of conservatism had entirely different sources. First and most important was the Anglo-Irish Tory, Edmund Burke (1729–97). His inspired diatribe of 1790, *Reflections on the Revolution in France,* was uncannily prophetic. It still reads as if written in 1793–94, against the background of war and Terror. Burke denounced the doctrinaire logic of the French revolutionaries, whose "rage and frenzy will pull down more in half an hour than prudence, deliberation, and foresight can build in a hundred years." His model was the English constitution, that agglomeration of custom and precedent which over many centuries had created what freedom existed in Britain. Organic growth, not radical panaceas, was the only sound basis for a polity. Change was admissible, although "when I changed it should be to preserve." Even revolution, as in 1688 and 1776, might be permissible if it reasserted a historic tradition. But plans for change should not assume human perfectibility. They should postulate, on the basis of long sad experience, the "ignorance and fallibility of mankind."

Burke's commitment to individual liberty, which had led him to sympathize with the complaints of the American colonists, did not survive his translation into French and German. Burke militant, the Burke who wrote in 1796 that "it is with an *armed doctrine* that we are at war," was the Burke who inspired continental conservatives to create their own armed doctrines of counterrevolution. Joseph de Maistre (1754–1821), the most lively of the French conservative theorists, acknowledged Burke's influence. But his doctrine had little place for freedom: "All power, all discipline, are based on the executioner. He is at once the horror of human society and the tie that binds it together. . . . " In Germany, admirers of Burke invoked his name to support notions of a return to divine-right monarchy and medieval Christianity. That was not conservatism, but "reaction," an attempt to erase everything after 1789.

Liberalism

Conservatism or reaction was the faith of what became, from its place in the seating arrangements of the post-1815 French assemblies, the "Right." Liberalism was the creed of the "Left." Like most "isms," the term is exceedingly vague. It has so broadened in the twentieth century that it now conveys a mood rather than a body of ideas.

Nineteenth-century liberalism was narrower. It meant, first of all, a body of economic thought that preached *laissez-faire*, the removal of all artificial constraints on the market. In politics, nineteenth-century liberalism stood, more or less squarely, for individual freedom and for equality of opportunity if not of outcome. Political liberalism—like Locke, its founding father—identified liberty with property; that was the link between political and economic liberalism. Liberalism was an optimistic creed, uniting capitalism and individualism under the banner of "progress," that faith of the Enlightenment. Liberalism was the creed of the middle classes, to whom the explosive growth of industry and trade gave increasing self-confidence.

The "classical economists," of whom the three most conspicuous were Adam Smith (1723–90), Thomas Robert Malthus (1766–1834), and David Ricardo (1772–1823), asked many of the questions that still preoccupy economists. Smith and Ricardo in particular argued that the market alone could efficiently allocate resources. The "hidden hand" of supply and demand, by a self-operating law, would maximize the increase in wealth.

In his *Essay on the Principle of Population* (1798, revised 1803), Malthus explored the relationship between population and food. He concluded gloomily that "population, when unchecked, increases in a geometrical ratio. Subsistence only increases in an arithmetical ratio." Malthus's generalization that population—"when unchecked"—tends to outrun food made

nineteenth-century economics the "dismal science." It also provided Darwin with his principle of the "struggle for survival" in the face of inevitable scarcity.

But Malthus qualified his theory in an important way that escaped many later critics. A "preventive check" on population increase existed: the tendency in Europe and especially in Britain for men and women to marry late, and hence have fewer children than the biological maximum. Malthus theorized that "moral restraint" or a growing taste for consumer luxuries might induce individuals to procreate less. Eventually, such tendencies could lead to a shortage of labor, and "in the natural course of things" to a rise in wages. Malthus was a prophet of affluence as well as of doom.

His contemporary Ricardo had less foresight. In his *Principles of Political Economy and Taxation* (1817), the last great work of classical economics, Ricardo proclaimed what soon became known as the "iron law of wages." Since labor supply supposedly increased geometrically, wages would always remain just above starvation level. Raising wages above that level would merely encourage procreation. That would in turn increase the supply of labor until wages once more dropped. Generosity toward the workers was thus futile, even pernicious. Ricardo's misunderstanding of Malthus was highly convenient to the mill owners, hard men reared in a hard school. They enthusiastically embraced his doctrine. Economic science had shown conclusively, Ricardo's popularizers trumpeted, that poverty was inevitable and that efforts to avert it would produce ever more poverty.

Ricardo's other major contribution was to systematize a concept found in Adam Smith's work that had profound political implications. That was the "labor theory of value," the notion that the "value" of a manufactured article was proportional to the amount of labor required to make it. Ricardo used

Portrait medal of Adam Smith (1797).

Thomas Robert Malthus, pioneer of the study of population growth.

Jeremy Bentham contemplating "the greatest happiness of the greatest number."

John Stuart Mill, the conscience of nineteenth-century liberalism.

the theory to explain where profits came from. For him they were the difference between the cost of labor per article to the industrialist and the selling price of the article, after the deduction of the industrialist's overhead costs. Ricardo applauded profit; others could and did use his work to argue that profits were "surplus value" stolen from the workers.

The political ideas of nineteenth-century liberalism in part contradicted the "dismal science." The English philosopher and reformer Jeremy Bentham (1748–1832), the key figure in the transition from Enlightenment to nineteenth-century liberal thought, rejected the Lockean tradition of "natural rights." Instead, as befitted an age of machinery, Bentham postulated that "utility" must guide humanity. Bentham's utility dictated the search for "the greatest happiness of the greatest number," and he defined happiness merely as "pleasurable feelings and . . . freedom from pain." Translated into politics, that meant that the best government delivered the most pleasure and the least pain to the most people. "Utilitarianism" or "philosophic radicalism" legitimized democracy through utility rather than through natural rights. It also legitimized social engineering. "Utility," for Bentham, dictated the regimentation of the poor by their intellectual betters.

Bentham's most influential successor, John Stuart Mill (1806–73), drove Benthamite liberalism to one possible logical conclusion, and inevitably made himself unpopular. As a child prodigy, he had begun learning Greek at three under the supervision of his father James Mill, disciple of Bentham and a historian of India. As an adult, John Stuart Mill ran the examinations for the elite Indian Civil Service. His *On Liberty* (1859) proclaimed utility as "the ultimate appeal in all ethical questions." Government was suspect: "That government is best that governs least." Mill asserted that "the only purpose for which power can rightfully be exer-

cised over any member of a civilized community, against his will, is to prevent harm to others."

Mill, like Bentham, deduced that utility demanded democratic government. But what if that government, faced with the horrors of the contemporary factory system and with the plight of the poor, demanded limits on the economic freedom of the entrepreneur? Mill ultimately came to the conclusion that the state must intervene to protect children and improve living and working conditions. He also took up the domination of men over women. After raising the issue of votes for women in Parliament in 1867, he published *The Subjection of Women* (1869). The work largely derived from ideas that his wife, Harriet Taylor Mill, had already put forward. It scandalized middle-class opinion by insisting that women, too, should enjoy liberty. That demand followed from Mill's premises and from those of nineteenth-century liberalism generally. But few accepted that in the 1860s.

On the Continent, liberalism was more cautious than in Britain, as befitted the relative weakness of the middle classes until industrialization was well under way. In politics, constitutionalism before liberty was the preference of Benjamin Constant (1767–1830), France's answer to Bentham. Constant proclaimed liberty as "the object of all human association" but resisted extension of France's limited franchise. German liberals (see p. 739) tended to confuse national self-assertion with liberty. And in the realm of economics, French and German thinkers resisted the full force of *laissez-faire,* with its potential for dissolving all traditional social ties. Some German economists challenged liberal orthodoxy frontally. The influential Friedrich List (1789–1846) argued that industrialization in the face of British competition required a neo-mercantilist planned economy, protective tariffs, and state-supported railway construction.

Socialism

Despite its internal contradictions, economic and political liberalism was a thumping success as a secular religion of progress for the middle classes. Inevitably, it summoned up a counter-ideology, "socialism." The term, almost as indefinable as liberalism, implies concern for the good of society as a whole, in opposition to liberalism's focus on individual liberty, property, and profit. Socialism and its overlapping but more extreme companion, "communism," had a pedigree going back at least to the abortive Paris rising of Gracchus Babeuf and the "Equals" in 1796. But after 1815, as industrialization gathered force, it acquired new meaning.

Middle-class thinkers began to postulate an irrepressible enmity between workers and industrialists. Ricardo's economics, with its emphasis on inher-

ent conflicts of interest between labor, capital, and landed wealth, provided tools for a radical attack on existing society. In England, a successful entrepreneur, Robert Owen (1771–1858), presented an alternative vision. Abolition of the profit motive and its replacement by "cooperation" would remake humanity, which in predictable Enlightenment fashion Owen saw as a product of its environment. Across the Channel, Charles Fourier (1772–1837) pressed similar notions, which included the foundation of "phalanxes," or self-sufficient model agrarian communities. Owen demonstrated the fallacy of Ricardo's "iron law" by raising wages and providing housing for the workers in his model factories at New Lanark, Scotland, while simultaneously increasing output and profits. His later attempt to found a utopia at New Harmony, Indiana, was less successful.

Robert Owen's vision of New Harmony, his utopian community in the Indiana wilderness.

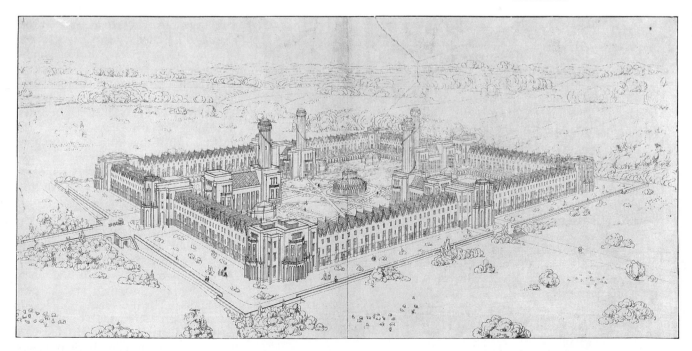

Karl Marx, the bourgeois patriarch (right), with his wife, two daughters, and Friedrich Engels in the 1860s.

Marx the Determinist Philosopher of History

In the social production of their existence, men enter into definite, predetermined relationships that are independent of their will. Those relations of production correspond to a given stage of the development of material productive forces. The totality of those relations of production forms the economic structure of the society, the real base, upon which a juridical and political superstructure rises, and to which given forms of social consciousness correspond. The mode of production of material life conditions the social, political, and intellectual life process itself. It is not the consciousness of men that determines their existence, but rather the reverse: their social existence determines their consciousness.

From Karl Marx, preface to *A Contribution to the Critique of Political Economy* (1859), (translation by M. Knox).

A sterner prophet than Owen or Fourier was the French Count Henri de Saint-Simon (1760–1825). Although frequently classed with the "utopian" socialists Owen and Fourier, Saint-Simon was no enthusiast for model communities. He was the first to conceive of socialism as the outcome of an inexorable historical process affecting the whole of society. He prophesied that in the new society "rule over men" would give way to "the administration of things." His brave new world would be an earthly paradise in which *École Polytechnique* technocrats tamed nature for good with immense engineering projects. He was thus not only a father of socialism, but also the inspiration of the heroic age of French engineering that produced the Suez Canal (1869) and the first railroad tunnels through the Alps.

The theory that came to dominate European socialism, although it owed something to Saint-Simon, derived above all from a strange marriage between the misty realms of Hegelian philosophy and the apparent rigor of classical economics. Karl Marx (1818–83), a German Jew from the Prussian Rhineland, and Friedrich Engels, the scholarly son of a prosperous Rhineland industrialist, were its fathers. Marx became interested in philosophy while studying law at the University of Berlin, and gravitated to the "Left Hegelians." These followers of the recently dead Hegel had discovered that his dialectic, that process by which the world spirit constantly struggled for greater self-realization through successive negations, provided a basis for attacks on all existing ideas and institutions.

Following the example of Kant and Hegel, Marx set out to create a system. By 1844–46, he had arrived with Engels's help at a preliminary synthesis. Marx retained Hegel's dialectical mechanism and goal-oriented stage theory of history. But he replaced Hegel's mystical world spirit with humanity as a species. From another Left-Hegelian, the rigorous materialist Ludwig Feuerbach ("Man is what he eats"), Marx took the notion that humanity's essence was work. Human nature was to be a "free producer." But under capitalism, as Ricardo had seemingly demonstrated, humanity lost the product of its labor through the capitalist's appropriation of "surplus value." Under capitalism, Marx added, private property and specialization of work ("division of labor") had "alienated" humanity from its true nature as "free producer." Marx's theory was a sophisticated Hegelian version of the romantic and utopian socialist rejection of existing industrial society.

But for Marx, unlike his "utopian" predecessors, history would inexorably remedy the ills of past and present. Marx translated Hegel's dialectic of world spirit, of humanity's self-realization, into economics. Marx joked that he had stood Hegel "right side up," and discovered the "rational kernel within the mystical shell." Work, not the world spirit, powered history. Successive "modes of production," succeeding one another dialectically, created new modes of consciousness, new stages in the upward progress of the spirit. And instead of Hegel's oriental, ancient, and Germanic-Christian stages of history, Marx discerned a progression from ancient slave society, through "feudalism," to industrial capitalism, to communism.

For the dialectic expressed itself politically as the struggle between economic classes: "The history of all existing society is the history of class struggle." That struggle now pitted the new working class, the "proletariat" born of the industrial revolution, against the capitalist "bourgeoisie." That struggle, Marx confidently predicted, would end with "the victory of the proletariat," since capitalist industrialization created ever-larger numbers of ever more impoverished proletarians. And the proletariat's victory would bring the end of history—or rather of what Marx called "the prehistory of human society." For the proletariat, the class supposedly more alienated than any other in history from humanity's essence as "free producer," had a historical mission. Victorious revolution would turn philosophy into reality: "The government of persons is replaced by the administration of things, and by the conduct of the processes of production. The state is not 'abolished.' *It withers away.*"

Marx had elaborated the main lines of his vision even before writing the fa-

Marx the Revolutionary Prophet

The history of all hitherto existing society is the history of class struggles.

Freeman and slave, patrician and plebeian, lord and serf, guild-master and journeyman, in a word, oppressor and oppressed, stood in constant opposition to one another, carried on an uninterrupted, now hidden, now open fight, a fight that each time ended, either in a revolutionary re-constitution of society at large, or in the common ruin of the contending classes. . . .

The modern bourgeois society that has sprouted from the ruins of feudal society has not done away with class antagonisms. It has but established new classes, new conditions of oppression, new forms of struggle in place of the old ones.

Our epoch, the epoch of the bourgeoisie, possesses, however, this distinctive feature: it has simplified the class antagonisms: Society as a whole is more and more splitting up into two great hostile camps, into two great classes directly facing each other: Bourgeoisie and Proletariat. . . .

All previous historical movements were movements of minorities, or in the interests of minorities. The proletarian movement is the self-conscious, independent movement of the immense majority, in the interests of the immense majority. . . .

The advance of industry, whose involuntary promoter is the bourgeoisie, replaces the isolation of the laborers, due to competition, by their revolutionary combination, due to association. The development of Modern Industry, therefore, cuts from under its feet the very foundation on which the bourgeoisie produces and appropriates products. What the bourgeoisie, therefore, produces, above all, is its own grave-diggers. Its fall and the victory of the proletariat are equally inevitable.

From Karl Marx and Friedrich Engels, *The Communist Manifesto* (1848).

mous *Communist Manifesto* with which he and Engels sought unsuccessfully to influence the 1848 revolutions (see pp. 732–38). Marx spent the next 35 years as an exile in the center of world capitalism, London. There, drawing on the immense resources of the hospitable British Museum library, Marx fitted out his Hegelian framework with economic evidence that he believed proved its validity.

In *Capital*, the great unfinished work that began to appear in 1867 and set forth his system in its most elaborate form, Marx analyzed and damned the "capitalist mode of production." Its essence was greed: the capitalist was " . . . capital personified. His soul is the soul of capital." Capital was "dead labor, which, vampire-like, lives only by sucking living labor, and lives the more, the more labor it sucks." This demonic vision of capitalism had much in common with Marx's views on Judaism, as set forth in his notorious *On the Jewish Question* (1843). There, in pathological language, he had proclaimed that "money is the jealous God of Israel," and demanded an end to "the *empirical* essence of Judaism—huckstering."

Marx's system was at least four things: a philosophy of history, an economic theory, an analysis of society, and a call to revolution. The philosophy of history foundered on both logical and empirical grounds. Logically, no system can describe the "meaning" of history, as Marx or Hegel claimed to do. Neither the whole past nor the future is knowable. Statements about the meaning and destination of something in part unknowable are either guesses or professions of faith.

Empirically, most of Marx's professions of faith have fared badly, although he and Engels described them as "scientific." Capitalist industrialization has not produced societies polarized into ever-larger masses of ever more degraded proletarians and ever-smaller groups of ever-richer capitalists. Revolution has *not* come to the most advanced capitalist countries.

Capitalism has not collapsed. Instead, capitalist industrialization has led to relative affluence and to an ever-broadening number of social sub-categories (see pp. 695–97). In the most advanced countries it is the industrial proletariat, not the state, that has withered.

In addition, Marx's apparent assertion that economics determines all else has caused perplexity. If on the one hand the economic "base" strictly and directly determines the political-ideological "superstructure," much of recorded history is puzzling. Why did the "slave society" of antiquity produce such a startling variety of "superstructures," from the monarchies, aristocracies, tyrannies, oligarchies, and democracies of the Greeks to the Roman imperial order? How did the Catholic Church survive and why did its "superstructure" change so little from the "slave society" of Rome to the "late-capitalism" of the twentieth century? And if on the other hand, as Engels suggested in a famous escape clause, the "base" determines "the superstructure" only "in the last resort," what remains of Marx's grandiose system except the truism that economics interacts with other spheres of human activity?

Marx's economics have likewise proved an embarrassment. His prediction of an ever-falling rate of profit under capitalism ignored the "dialectical" driving force of science and technology. New technologies create industries that are vastly profitable until they grow to saturate their markets; then still newer technologies supersede them. Nor has Marx's labor theory of value, on which his critique of capitalist "exploitation" rests, aged well. It was as arbitrary and metaphysical as anything in Hegel. Marx was unable to measure "value" empirically, although he thought he could. Only prices are measurable, and they depend partly on factors—such as supply and demand—that have nothing to do with labor costs.

Marx's analysis of societies in terms of economic classes, although not original to him, has fared better. It filled a need for a short-hand to describe the distinctions between aristocrats, middle classes, and workers or peasants that actually existed in the European societies of his day. But despite Marx's claims to scientific rigor, he never defined class. The last chapter of volume III of *Capital*, where he attempted that task, breaks off unfinished. Marxist social analysis has thus suffered from a lack of clearly defined tools. Marx's prediction of increasing polarization between "proletariat" and "bourgeoisie," and the rigidity of his categories, have also made it difficult for later Marxists to classify white-collar workers, professionals, and their own class, the intellectuals.

Marx's call to revolution has proved to be the most powerful and durable part of his work. From the 1860s it made him the unchallenged intellectual leader of European and world socialism. But Marx's call to revolution has also labored under irreconcilable contradictions. His philosophy of history appeared to predict the almost automatic extinction of capitalism once economic conditions had ripened. That comforting thought might lead socialists to await the great day passively, a conclusion Marx and many later Marxists rejected. Marx left unresolved that tension between determinism and voluntarism, between the temptation to await the foreordained and the urge to force the pace of history.

Marx's occasional endorsement of revolutionary terror and of "dictatorship of the proletariat" also implicitly threatened his proclaimed goal of freedom. Marx celebrated Jacobin-style violence as midwife of history: under some circumstances there was "only one means to *curtail*, simplify and localize the bloody agony of the old society and the bloody birth-pangs of the new, only one means—the revolutionary terror." But he also recognized that humanity made its history not "as it please[d] . . . but under circumstances directly found, given, and transmitted from the past." Revolutionary terror

would constitute part of the new society's "past," and might influence its future in directions other than liberation.

And what if the "dictatorship of the proletariat" refused to wither away? Marx doggedly refused to take that question seriously, even when his rival in the international socialist movement, the eccentric Russian aristocrat Mikhail Bakunin (1814–76), attacked him publicly. Bakunin's anarchist answer to oppression was improbable: smashing the state would return society to a state of nature in which humanity's essential goodness would at last prevail. But on the likely consequences of a transitional revolutionary dictatorship, Marx was the utopian and Bakunin the realist: "No dictatorship can have any other aim than to perpetuate itself."

Marx's vision conflicted in other ways with his goal of liberation. His claim to possess the truth about history encouraged a dangerous intolerance. If Marx, in Engels's famous words, was the Darwin of human society, if he had "discovered the fundamental law that determines the course and development of human history," then those who stood against Marx stood against history. Marx was not slow to point that out.

And as later critics have suggested, Marx's ideas contained implications for revolutionary regimes that went far beyond his advocacy of terror and temporary dictatorship. Since for Marx social antagonisms stemmed from class conflict, conflicts after the revolution were of necessity rooted in resistance by the old ruling classes. Anyone who disagreed with the new regime might thus become a legitimate target for further liberating violence. And if freedom meant social unity, as Marx—following thinkers as disparate as Rousseau and Hegel—assumed, then the more unity the more freedom. That notion could likewise easily lead to the elimination of all who failed to fit in. And if, as Marx argued, communism would enable humanity to control the conditions

Mikhail Bakunin, aristocrat and professional revolutionary.

Bakunin the Anarchist Foresees a Dictatorship over the Proletariat

In 1874–75 Marx copied into his notebooks long passages from *Statehood and Anarchy*, a work of his anarchist rival Mikhail Bakunin, and adorned them with furious comments (printed in brackets).

(Bakunin) . . . the so-called people's state will be nothing other than the quite despotic administration of the masses of the people by a new and very non-numerous aristocracy of real and supposed learned ones. The people is not learned, so it will be entirely freed from the cares of governing, wholly incorporated into the governed herd. A fine liberation! The Marxists sense this [!] contradiction and, realizing that the regime of the learned [*quelle reverie!*], the hardest, most offensive, and most contemptuous in the world will in fact be a dictatorship in spite of all the democratic forms, console themselves with the thought that the dictatorship will be temporary and short-lived.

(Marx commentary) [*Non, mon cher!* The *class domination* of the workers over the resisting strata of the old world must last until the economic foundations of the existence of classes are destroyed.]

(Bakunin). . . . They say that such a state yoke, a dictatorship, is a necessary transitional means for attaining the most complete popular liberation. So, to liberate the masses of the people they first have to be enslaved. Our polemic rests and is founded on this contradiction. They maintain that only a dictatorship, their own naturally, can create the people's will; we answer: no dictatorship can have any other aim than to perpetuate itself. . . .

From Robert C. Tucker, ed. *The Marx-Engels Reader*, 2nd ed. (New York: W. W. Norton, 1978), pp. 546–47.

---

of its existence, then a regime that described itself as communist could do *anything it liked*. Nothing, no law either economic or moral need constrain it.

Marx's legacy was thus profoundly ambiguous. He made economics part of history. Economic forces, "modes of production," and social classes were henceforth objects of historical study alongside kings and battles. He offered a scathing critique of capitalism, although the credibility of that critique diminished as the brutal conditions of early British industrialization gave way to rising real wages. Above all, Marx created a messianic faith in revolution. That faith arrived on the scene too late in the nineteenth century to preside over a genuine revolution. The twentieth century offered new opportunities.

Nationalism

From the beginning, socialism found itself in competition with an even more powerful ideological force: nationalism. The political notion of the nation-state, born in the French Revolution and spread in its wars, sowed deeper divisions than any between labor and capital. Nationalism, as it developed in nineteenth-century Europe, had four major components.

First was the political theory of the social contract and general will that the French Revolution had attempted to translate into political reality. When the nation of king and nobles gave way to the nation of freely associating citizens, nothing except the "general will" limited that nation's actions. Second came Kant's doctrine of the moral autonomy of the individual. When extended to nations, that autonomy, that "self-determination," likewise meant that nations need acknowledge no law they did not themselves choose. Third came Hegel's notion of the state as the moral force in a history that was proceeding through struggle toward a goal. Hegel was no German nationalist; he had hailed Napoleon as a historic individual whose conquests advanced the self-realization of the world spirit. But Hegel's deification of the Prussian state had nationalist uses.

The fourth and final component of European nationalism was the ethnic concept of the nation. That too was a German contribution. Johann Gottfried von Herder (1744–1803), a prominent exponent of *Sturm und Drang*, had worked out in the 1770s and 1780s a philosophy of history that provided a rationale for German resistance to the cultural domination of France. For

Herder each nation, each *"Volk,"* was equally close to God. Each therefore had the duty to cultivate its own peculiarities: "Spew out the ugly slime of the Seine / Speak German, O you German!" Herder rejoiced in human diversity; like Hegel, he was no nationalist. But once again, his ideas had nationalist uses.

Successors such as Fichte were soon proclaiming the superiority of German. The French, Fichte wrote after French conquest in 1806, were Teutons who had frivolously abandoned their native tongue for a language derived from Latin. That had infected them with a "lack of seriousness." Herder and Fichte between them established language as a new test for nationhood. Language thus became a criterion for drawing or redrawing boundaries. It became what it had rarely been before: a matter of life and death.

In the decades after 1815, the French revolutionary conception of the general will, the notion of self-determination, the concept of the state as the moral force in history, and the ethnic-linguistic conception of the nation fused. The result was a unique invention, *a secular religion of the nation-state.* For the nationalist, individual freedom and self-fulfillment lay only in service to such a state. That peculiar belief distinguishes nationalism from patriotism, the instinctive loyalty to homeland, or from xenophobia, the traditional and unthinking hatred and contempt for foreigners. Patriotism and xenophobia have existed throughout history, but nationalism was an invention of the decades after 1789.

It soon spread eastward. Herder had provided a rationale for the study and cultivation of the language and culture of one's own *Volk.* In Germany the brothers Jakob and Wilhelm Grimm collected folk tales and Teutonic mythology, and explored the roots of the national language. Poles, Czechs, and Balkan nationalities followed their lead. Dictionaries and editions of medieval epic poems appeared, monuments to the peculiarities of each nation's his-

tory. Poets such as Sándor Petöfi (1822–49) in Hungary and Giacomo Leopardi (1798–1837) in Italy wrote verse celebrating the national spirit and demanding national liberation.

Politics followed poetry. Napoleon had attempted to mobilize Italians (1796), Hungarians (1809), and Poles (1812) in his wars against Austria and Russia. His defeat did not remove nationalism from politics. Italy, which remained under Austrian domination, gave the example. The conspiratorial sect of the *carbonari* ("charcoal burners") had originated in south Italy as a protest against French rule. After 1815, although lacking a discernible program, it served as a magnet both for police spies and for youth disaffected with the status quo. One such youth was Giuseppe Mazzini (1805–72), the greatest prophet of nineteenth-century nationalism.

Mazzini joined the *carbonari* in 1827 in his home town of Genoa and spent time in jail in 1830 for subversive activity. In exile in 1831 he founded a new type of conspiratorial organization: *Giovine Italia* or "young Italy." The movement had little practical success but its romantic emphasis on youthful fanaticism set a powerful example. Mazzini proclaimed liberty, but his liberty was the liberty of the individual to serve the national idea. Nationalist politics was a *"fede,"* a faith, a political religion.

Mazzini proclaimed the equality of all nationalities and their inevitable harmony once Europe became a "Europe of the Peoples." But he also insisted it was Italy's mission to provide "a new and more powerful Unity to all the nations of Europe." Italy had given Europe unity under Rome and under the Papacy. Now the "Third Rome," the "Rome of the Italian people," would fulfill that same universal mission. It would create a "third and still vaster Unity." That was no small claim, and it helped set a widely imitated pattern of nationalist megalomania. Nor did Mazzini address the decisive question. When the claims and "rights" of

The invention of national traditions: German peasant costume, as imagined by Ludwig Emil Grimm (1828).

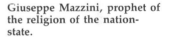

Giuseppe Mazzini, prophet of the religion of the nation-state.

nationalities conflicted, who or what would decide?

FROM THEORY TO PRACTICE

Without a public capable of receiving them, ideas have little practical effect. In nineteenth-century Europe the gradual widening of literacy and of leisure created that public. States began systematically to take responsibility for their subjects' welfare and education. And submerged groups such as workers and women reacted to the new age with broadening demands for social and political rights.

The Role of the State

States traditionally have been machines for power, not welfare. Yet in the seventeenth and eighteenth centuries, the states of western Europe began to recognize that the prosperity and education of their inhabitants might increase that power (see pp. 633–40). Bureaucrats and enlightened absolutists began an expansion of the role of the state that ultimately created immense organizations supervising the education, health, and wealth of the citizenry. Power, necessary for survival, remained the state's ultimate purpose, but alongside it there gradually emerged the modern bureaucratic "welfare state."

The states of the nineteenth century, as befitted the age of *laissez-faire*, removed economic restraints that appeared to impede the creation of wealth. By the 1860s, the centralizing bureaucracies of the German states had overcome the fearful rear-guard action of small-town Germany, with its xenophobic guilds and restrictions on free competition. In Britain, a militant middle-class movement institutionalized *laissez-faire*. In 1846 Parliament abolished the grain tariffs or "Corn Laws" that the landed interests had imposed in the post-1815 slump. That step marked the political triumph of Britain's all-conquering industries over agriculture.

The state also intervened in the economy. Especially on the Continent, it took the lead in the creation of national markets and industrial economies. The obvious abuses of the factory system and the disastrous sanitary conditions in the new industrial cities also provoked outcry and government action. In Britain, legislation as early as 1802 had attempted to regulate working hours for apprentices. In 1819 Parliament passed the first of a series of Factory Acts, forbidding the work of children under nine and limiting the work of children over nine to twelve hours a day. An act of 1831 forbade night work by individuals under 21; an act restricting the work day to ten and a half hours passed in 1850. The first Factory Acts applied only to cotton mills but by the 1860s legislation covered most industries. Acts in 1841 and 1855 forbade the employment of women and children in mining. Parliament also sought to regulate city sanitation and standards for wholesome food and drink, beginning with the Public Health Act of 1848. France and Prussia passed similar laws. Despite a long record of poor enforcement and of collusion between factory inspectors and manufacturers, working and living conditions gradually improved.

In the face of British industrial competition, the continental states adopted various forms of protective tariffs. Prussia, in particular, made tariff policy an instrument of state power. Beginning in 1818, reforming Prussian bureaucrats aggressively pressed customs unions upon their smaller neighbors. In 1833, Prussia succeeded in creating a *Zollverein* or customs union that eventually covered all important German states except Austria. Prussia's bureaucracy and military also took the lead in the expansion of the railroad network. After mid-century, the army began gearing the railroads to its ever-faster mobilization system. Only the Russian state, in the period of its industrial "take-off" after 1880, surpassed the role of the Prussian state in economic development.

Prussia led in a second, absolutely decisive area: its school system pioneered mass literacy. That was a daring step. The value of widespread literacy in the eighteenth century was far from obvious, at least to the European upper classes. Catherine the Great neatly summarized their attitude in a letter reputedly sent to a subordinate: "We must not in any way provide instruction for the lower class of people. If they knew as much as you or I . . . they would no longer want to obey us. . . . " Even after 1800 members of the British Parliament could rail against the democratization of knowledge; it might render the lower orders "insolent to their superiors."

The Prussian bureaucracy, ruling over what a French intellectual in the 1830s described as the "classic country of barracks and schools," had no such qualms. Prussia, after 1819, became the first state in history to proclaim and begin to enforce universal school attendance. A literate subject was a more productive subject and a better soldier. France followed in 1833 by requiring villages and towns to maintain schools. The Habsburg monarchy followed in the 1860s. Britain, in the spirit of *laissez-faire*, neglected the issue, and paid dearly. It only established the principle of universal primary schooling in 1870 and only made it compulsory in 1880.

The coming of literacy worked yet another revolution. For most of human history, only very small elites had been able to read or write. At the beginning of the nineteenth century slightly over half of all adult males in England and France and perhaps one in three or four women could write their own names. A century later, literacy in the developed countries of western Europe was well over 95 percent of both men and women (see Figure 25-1). The industrial revolution made mass literacy possible, but it was the state that turned that potential into reality.

The inadequacies of the English school, 1856.

Workers

Mass literacy, among its many side effects, made the claims of the outsiders increasingly difficult to ignore. In politics, both workers and women participated in the revolutionary ferment that culminated in Europe-wide uprisings in 1848. In the workplace, workers by that point had long since begun to organize against the oppression they perceived. The introduction of machinery led to widespread artisan protest and machine breaking both in England and on the Continent. From 1811 to 1816 English rioters rose repeatedly to smash knitting machines and power looms in the name of a mythical "King Ludd." Agricultural workers imitated the "Luddites" in 1830–32 by smashing threshing machines and burning barns.

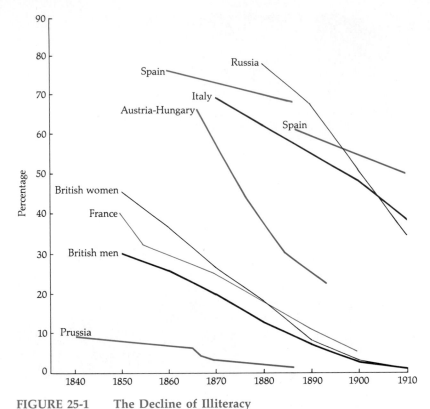

FIGURE 25-1   The Decline of Illiteracy

From Theodore S. Hamerow, *The Birth of a New Europe* (Chapel Hill: University of North Carolina Press, 1983), p. 169.

But incoherent protest and anarchic violence had little chance even against the decentralized British state. Workers explored other paths, beginning in the 1820s. With the Combination Acts of 1799 and 1800 Parliament had ended early attempts to organize rudimentary labor unions under the inspiration of the French Revolution. In 1824–25 Parliament relented and weakened the Acts, thanks to continued unrest and to the pleas of middle-class reformers for toleration of working-class "co-operation." Strikes remained illegal but unions could now organize with relative freedom. In 1829 Robert Owen presided over the founding of a "Society for Promoting Co-operative Knowledge" that in 1831 became the "National Union of the Working Classes," the first true British trade union.

The system of a national "general union" soon showed its limitations;

regional and craft loyalties were stronger than working-class solidarity. Nevertheless, the recurrent economic crises and the pressure of population growth meant continued unrest. In 1838 a leading workers' group, the London Working Men's Association, initiated a nationwide campaign of agitation for adoption by Parliament of universal male suffrage and other reforms embodied in a "People's Charter." Chartist agitation, under the leadership of the fiery journalist and speaker Feargus O'Connor, continued sporadically for the next ten years but failed to move Parliament.

Chartism's internal rivalries and political failure did not inhibit other working-class efforts. A National "Association for the Protection of Labour" emerged in 1845 and by 1859 was able to persuade Parliament to authorize peaceful picketing. In 1868 a Trades Union Congress that represented over 100,000 workers met at Manchester. By 1875 British trade unions had won the right to strike and picket.

On the Continent working-class organization inevitably lagged, given the gap in development between Britain and its followers and the relative unfamiliarity of the notion of individual rights. Belgium prohibited labor unions until 1868. Revolutionary France had forbidden unions and strikes, and Napoleon's code had confirmed that ban in 1803. Socialist underground secret societies such as those of the agitator Auguste Blanqui and uprisings such as those of the impoverished silk workers of Lyon in 1831 and 1834 merely provoked savage repression. Not until after 1871 did the French working classes organize effectively. In Germany, revolutionary sects such as the tailor Wilhelm Weitling's "League of the Just" emerged a generation before the creation of an organized German labor movement in the 1860s.

Despite rivalries between regions and crafts, home artisans and factory workers, skilled "labor aristocrats" and simple laborers, the European working classes were by the 1870s nevertheless well on their way to creating stable organizations through which to press their interests. In England the ideological glue that held them together was frequently the piety of the Protestant sects. On the Continent, most adopted orthodox Marxism under the guidance or inspiration of the "First International," the "International Working Men's Organization" that Marx and Engels helped found in 1864. Workers' organizations soon made increasingly effective demands for change, and gave birth to the first workers' political parties.

Women

The French and industrial revolutions made relative freedom for women possible, but did not produce it. As with workers, only struggle could do that. Olympe de Gouges had pointed out the inconsistency of proclaiming the Rights of Man while denying those rights to women. In her path-breaking *Vindication of the Rights of Women* (1792), the English writer Mary Wollstonecraft demanded equality, and freedom for women to best employ their talents. The romantic poet Shelley, son-in-law of Mary Wollstonecraft, put it succinctly in 1817: "Can man be free if woman be a slave?"

That question passed through three overlapping phases in the course of the nineteenth century: literary self-assertion, theoretical elaboration, and political action. First came literary self-assertion. Women intellectuals began to write with a frequency and eloquence that eventually won them grudging respect. Germaine de Staël, daughter of the banker Necker and France's leading woman writer until her death in 1817, took on Napoleon in print and had to take refuge in exile. Her novels *Corinne* (1804) and *Delphine* (1807) attacked conventional views of marriage and of woman's education. She also played a decisive role in explaining German romanticism to the rest of Europe. Napoleon had the first edition of her *De l'Allemagne* (1811) burned as "un-French."

The French romantic novelist and social critic George Sand (Amantine-Lucile-Aurore, Baroness Dudevant, 1804–76) was an adherent of Fourierist utopianism who scandalized French polite society by wearing men's suits and smoking in public. Fleeing a provincial marriage of convenience, Sand went to Paris and wrote some 80 popular novels. She supported herself and her two children on the proceeds, a virtually unprecedented achievement. She also advocated and practiced "free love," by which she and other Fourierists and Saint-Simonians meant cohabitation or marriage based on equality between the sexes and on sexual or emotional inclination rather than social convention. Sand, despite her deliberate unconventionality, was one of the prototypes of a phenomenon more common later in the century—the successful professional woman.

By mid-century, women authors were emerging whose achievements were unrivalled. Charlotte Brontë, in her novels *Jane Eyre* (1847) and *Shirley* (1849), presented strong women heroines in quest both of love and independence. Her sister Emily, before her death of tuberculosis, produced the violent and terrifying *Wuthering Heights* (1847), one of the greatest of English nineteenth-century novels.

By that point a growing theoretical literature by both men and women had begun to explore the question of woman's role. Their views fall into three rough categories: those who reaffirmed woman's traditional subordination to man, those who argued that women were equal but different, and those who insisted on an absolute legal and political equality that would allow women to be like men if they so chose.

The overwhelming mass of male opinion inevitably argued for woman's subordination. Many women still agreed. Woman's role was to obey, help, and comfort man the breadwinner, to bear and raise his children, and to preside over the home, a warm sanctuary in a cold and increasingly competitive new industrial world. That was the prescription of Sarah Stickney Ellis, an English writer of women's handbooks from the late 1830s on, and of numerous continental theorists from reactionaries such as De Maistre to liberals of all stripes.

The "equal but different" tradition was most prominent on the Continent. The title of a French tract of the 1830s sums up its message: *The Education of Mothers; or the Civilization of Mankind by Women.* Woman's first role was as mother. The mother's calling was to be the educator, the bearer of culture, the civilizer of the drunken, destructive, childlike male. As Jeanne Deroin (1805–94), the foremost French woman's advocate of mid-century, put it in the newspaper she published during the 1848 revolution, woman's "sublime humanitarian maternity" had the duty to "teach everyone how fraternity should be practiced." The world of politics and of relations between states should conform to the standards of the well-ordered home.

Nor should women seek to imitate men, insisted Louise Otto (1819–95), Deroin's foremost German counterpart. "True womanliness" was the goal. "Georgesandism" outraged Otto as much as it did any defender of the old order. Emancipation must not "[devalue] woman to become a caricature of a man." This tradition had appeal not only in Germany and France, but even in England and the United States. There it contributed not only to the assertion of women's rights but also to the temperance movement that gathered force as the nineteenth century drew on. And the notion of the mother as educator appealed to female eastern European nationalist theorists. It gave woman a decisive role in the national struggle. Man's vocation was to fight; woman's to transmit the *Volk* language and nationalize the minds of the young.

The third tradition that emerged in the course of the nineteenth century drew its ultimate inspiration from Locke. Men enjoyed autonomy and self-determination by natural right. To deny that same right to women was neither just nor civilized. Women must receive the same autonomy and education as men, even if that meant painful social readjustment. Wollstonecraft gave first expression to such views. John Stuart and Harriet Taylor Mill's *The Subjection of Women* (1869) provided the tradition's basic text. Its ideas were particularly influential in Britain and the United States, where they meshed with the Lockean political culture from which they derived.

Theorists of the "equal but different" tradition—and male supremacists—inevitably derided Mill for inciting women to what they described as antisocial self-indulgence. Ruthless individualism, the critics claimed, was no answer to the biological and social imperatives that governed women's conduct. Emancipation could not and must not mean emancipation from children, or from marriage, the fundamental building block of society. Women's biological role demanded special legal protection for the family, not the cold comfort of strict equality with men.

The issues at stake were so intractable and emotion-laden that the argument between the two schools has continued to the present. But regardless of theoretical differences, by the 1860s and 1870s a broadly based movement of women, primarily of the middle classes, had arisen both in Europe and in the United States. It increasingly turned to political action to secure women's rights (see pp. 800–801).

The new age of ideas after 1789 was thus both a continuation and a repudiation of the Enlightenment. Faith in "progress" and in the perfectibility of humanity swelled with the advance of science, the coming of steam-powered industry, and the spread of liberalism and socialism. Hitherto submerged groups found voices; states began to act as machines for welfare as well as for power. Yet strong countercurrents persisted. Conservatism or "reaction" inspired both nobles and intellectuals; the peasantry and many in the middle classes still held to traditional community and dynastic loyalties. Romanticism damned the new industrial age but also undermined the remains of the old order through its stormy cult of the individual. And nationalism, which many conservatives mistook for liberalism, soon revealed itself as the overriding political faith of the nineteenth and twentieth centuries, the force that transmuted "geographical expressions" into nation-states.

Suggestions for Further Reading

Science, Religion, and Culture

For overviews that place nineteenth-century thought in its political and social setting, see E. J. Hobsbawm, *The Age of Revolution, 1789–1848* (1962), and *The Age of Capital, 1848–1875* (1975). F. L. Baumer, *Modern European Thought: Continuity and Change in Ideas, 1600–1950* (1977), offers a useful general survey of the movement of ideas. For the fate of religion, see O. Chadwick, *The Secularization of the European Mind in the Nineteenth Century* (1975). On the impact of Darwin and geology, see especially W. Irvine, *Angels, Apes, and Victorians* (1955); J. C. Greene, *The Death of Adam* (1959); and C. C. Gillispie, *Genesis and Geology* (1951). For romanticism, see especially J. Barzun, *Classic, Romantic, and Modern* (1961); J. B. Halstead, ed., *Romanticism* (1965); J. Clay, *Romanticism* (1981); and M. le Bris, *Romantics and Romanticism* (1981). On German philosophy, see R. N. Stromberg, *European Intellectual History After 1789* (1981); R. Scruton, *From Descartes to Wittgenstein* (1981); K. Löwith, *From Hegel to Nietzsche* (1964); and G. D. O'Brien, *Hegel on Reason and History* (1975).

Social, Economic, and Political Thought

The best introduction to convervatism is still E. Burke, *Reflections on the Revolution in France*; K. Epstein, *The Genesis of German Conservatism* (1966), describes some of conservatism's continental ramifications. For liberalism, both economic and political, the classic texts are A. Smith, *The Wealth of Nations*; T. R. Malthus, *An Essay on Population*; and J. S. Mill, *Autobiography* and *On Liberty*. On Mill and his fellows, see especially J. Hamburger, *Intellectuals in Politics: John Stuart Mill and the Philosophic Radicals* (1965). G. Lichtheim, *The Origins of Socialism* (1969), and P. Singer, *Marx* (1980), offer concise introductions to socialism. K. Marx and F. Engels, *The Communist Manifesto*, and R. Tucker, ed. *The Marx-Engels Reader* (1972), provide a selection of the essential texts. L. Kolakovski, *Main Currents of Marxism*, Vol. 1 (1978), lucidly analyzes the intellectual development of Marx and Engels, explains their debts to earlier thinkers, dissects the weaknesses of their system, and suggests some of the potential consequences of their ideas—but see also D. Conway, *A Farewell to Marx* (1987). E. Kedourie, *Nationalism* (1966), is exemplary: one of the few intelligent books on a subject of overriding importance.

Consequences of the Industrial Revolution

For the intellectual and social impact of the industrial revolution, see especially the broadly conceived work of T. S. Hamerow, *The Birth of a New Europe* (1983). A. Briggs, *The Age of Improvement, 1783–1867* (1959), and E. P. Thompson, *The Making of the English Working Class* (1963), offer differing perspectives on English workers; L. Chevalier, *Working Classes and Dangerous Classes in Paris During the Nineteenth Century* (1971), and B. Moss, *The Origins of the French Labor Movement* (1976), cover France. R. Bridenthal et al., *Becoming Visible. Women in European History* (1987), offers a useful introduction to the changing status and aspirations of nineteenth-century women.

26
The Breakthrough of the Nation-State, 1815–1871

The defeat of revolutionary France ushered in a century of relative peace between European states. Four general wars and innumerable minor conflicts had punctuated the eighteenth century. Prussia and Russia had become great powers. Sweden had ceased to be one. Poland had ceased to be. But from 1815 to 1914 only three major conflicts—the Crimean War (1854–56) and the wars of Italian (1859–60) and German "unification" (1864, 1866, 1870–71)—affected even parts of Europe. And the nineteenth-century conflicts, unlike the world wars of 1701–14, 1740–48, 1756–63, and 1792–1815, were short and involved only some of the great powers.

The secret of this relative peace and stability was both ideological and structural. Fear of "the Revolution" had at last welded together the final coalition that brought Napoleon down. That fear inspired a settlement in 1814–15 that bound the powers together in a network of treaties and mutual obligations. Treaties, custom, and the consolidation of neutral buffer states separating the great powers made it harder than before for one power to challenge the rest. And fear of revolution, a fear that the three waves of unrest that convulsed Europe in 1820, 1830, and 1848 repeatedly reinforced, did not abate until after mid-century.

Then the collapse of the revolutionary myth in the failures of 1848 ushered in a brief era of almost unrestrained pursuit of state interest. And states pursued that interest under the banner of nationalism. The consequence was the breakthrough of the nation-state in central Europe: the creation of Italy in 1859–60 and of Prussia-Germany in 1866–71. Those "revolutions from above," especially the German one, destroyed the small and intermediate buffer states that had been a key restraining element in the 1814–15 settlement. Nevertheless, thanks to the weakness of the new Italian state and the temporary self-restraint of the German one, the main lines of the 1814–15 settlement survived the wars of mid-century. Only the rise after 1890 of a new challenge to the balance of power ended the "long peace" and inaugurated a new century of world wars.

UNDER THE SHADOW OF REVOLUTION: THE CONGRESS OF VIENNA AND AFTER

The victors over Napoleon faced two intertwined tasks—the restoration of a balance of power internationally and of internal stability to the wide areas of Europe that French arms had revolutionized. As Britain's foreign secretary, Castlereagh, put it, the victors needed to return Europe to "peaceful habits."

Opposite: The romantic vision of the 1830 Revolution: *Liberty Leading the People,* by Eugène Delacroix.

725

The Congress of Vienna: the official view, by Isabey.

The diplomats redrew the map of Europe in 1814–15 in ways that bore little relationship to the wishes of the populations concerned. Internally, the "reaction" that followed the restoration of many of Europe's ruling houses was undeniably oppressive. But by the standards set in later peace settlements, that of 1814–15 was both humane and durable.

Architects of the Vienna settlement: Castlereagh (left) and Metternich (right).

"Europe"—or rather the five great powers—met at Vienna in September 1814 to draw up the settlement. The four decisive figures in this first general European settlement since the Peace of Westphalia in 1648 were the neurotic Tsar Alexander of Russia, the wittily devious Talleyrand for Bourbon France, the bold and determined Castlereagh for Britain, and the self-infatuated host, Chancellor Prince Metternich for Austria. The indecisive Frederick William III of Prussia and his ministers cut lesser figures. Around the principals danced the nobility of Europe and its innumerable hangers-on, while Metternich's secret police rifled wastebaskets and boudoir drawers in search of diplomatic correspondence.

The two overriding issues were the settlement with France and the division of the spoils in central and eastern Europe. The allies initially tried to exclude Talleyrand from their deliberations. But the unpredictable tsar soon provoked a crisis that reversed the powers' roles. If France was the threat of yesterday, Alexander, with his insistence on entering Paris as a conqueror, might be that of tomorrow. His demand that the Congress confirm his control of most of Poland provoked alarm, since a Russia that close to central Europe would be an over-mighty neighbor. Even Alexander's promise to equip his Polish possessions with a constitution seemed a fig-leaf for the voracious expansionism of the Russian state. It was also ideologically unpleasing to Metternich, no lover of constitutions.

The tsar's ally Prussia acted in a manner only slightly less ominous for the future. The Prussian military reformers, intoxicated with their victory over Napoleon, now demanded the annexation of Saxony, whose king had changed sides too late in 1813. (In revolutionary times, as that expert at well-timed changes of allegiance, Talleyrand, remarked, treason was "a question of dates.") The upshot was deadlock. Prussia and Russia faced England and Austria, while the Prussian generals muttered of war. To redress the balance, Castlereagh and Metternich brought a willing Talleyrand into play. A brief triple alliance of the old enemies, France, Britain, and Austria, persuaded the Prussians and the tsar to back down.

France received back its historic borders and even pocketed some minor territorial gains. Russia gave up some Polish territory. Prussia kept some of Poland and secured only half of Saxony. It gained in compensation the ex-Napoleonic territories in northwestern Germany. Castlereagh placed a re-

luctant Prussia on the Rhine, in the front lines against a possible renewal of the French threat to the balance. England and Austria thus also unwittingly gave Prussia the immense coal and iron deposits of the Ruhr valley, with economic and political consequences immeasurably important for the future of Prussia, Germany, and Europe. The separation of the new Prussia into eastern and western halves generated additional pressure, if the Prussian power-state needed such pressure, for further expansion.

Europe in 1815

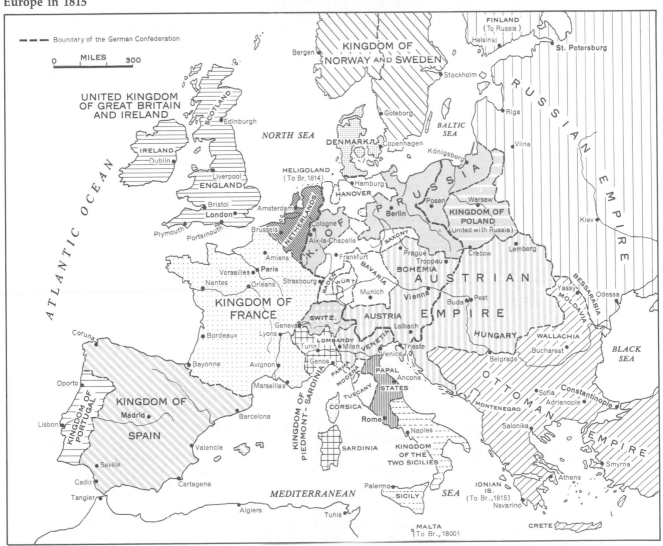

The Bourbons restored: Louis XVIII of France.

Lesser issues at Vienna generated less tension than the Poland-Saxony deadlock. In principle—as proclaimed by Talleyrand and Metternich—"legitimacy" was to guide the settlement. That slogan was convenient for Bourbon France and Habsburg Austria. But it explains the actual shape of the settlement less than the need for stability and balance that all concerned deeply felt after almost 25 years of revolution and war.

The Bourbons indeed returned to France, Spain, and eventually to Naples. The Pope reclaimed the Papal States, stretching across central Italy. Switzerland, released from its status as satellite of revolutionary France, received a guarantee of perpetual independence and neutrality. But at British insistence Holland received the ex-Austrian territory of Belgium to strengthen it as a barrier against France. Piedmont-Sardinia likewise and for the same reason received the former republic of Genoa. Austria itself kept Venetia and Lombardy.

In Germany expediency and the quest for stability triumphed. The surviving princes, beneficiaries of the princes' revolution of 1801–03 and of

Napoleon's redrawing of the map in 1806 and after, were poor examples of "legitimacy." What emerged from the deliberations of the German states at the Congress was a loose league, a German "united nations" of 39 states and mini-states, with an assembly sitting at Frankfurt. Austria held the presidency of this German Confederation with Prussia as its sometimes reluctant second. The Confederation's two-fold function was to give the awakening German nation a political home now that the Holy Roman Empire no longer existed, and to serve as a defensive barrier against a resurgent France or an over-mighty Russia. The Confederation's principal weaknesses were its built-in split between Austria and Prussia and the egotism of the lesser princes. Both conspired against the greater unity that German nationalists were already demanding.

The inconsiderate return of Napoleon in 1815 emphasized further the need for continuing great power solidarity. France escaped after Waterloo with the loss of some further small border territories and a cash indemnity. The allies renewed the Quadruple Alliance for 20 years, thus confirming the principle established at Vienna: the great powers in concert would decide all major international questions.

But reaffirmation of the balance of power against France was the extent of great-power agreement. The second decisive issue that the powers faced in recasting Europe, that of the nature of the internal regimes of Europe's states, brought the parting of the ways. The symbol of the latent divergence between Britain and the three eastern monarchies was Tsar Alexander's treaty of the "Holy Alliance" of September 1815. This "piece of sublime mysticism and nonsense," in Castlereagh's scathing phrase, pledged Russia, Austria, and Prussia to conduct their policies in accordance with the principles of the Christian religion. Those principles, as interpreted by the eastern monarchies, apparently included the suppression of liberalism and revolution everywhere. The accession of most European states to the "Holy Alliance" diluted its already vague content and ensured that it had little practical effect, but the treaty gave its name to an era of obscurantism, arbitrary imprisonment, and muzzling of the press.

In Spain and Naples the restored Bourbons abolished the constitutions they had granted in 1812. Pope Pius VII reestablished his authority in the Papal States by again confining the Jews to ghettos, by reviving the Inquisition, and by abolishing the reforming law codes the French had brought. In Germany, Metternich struck effectively at freedom of expression. In 1819 a compliant Prussia and German Confederation adopted Metternich's repressive "Carlsbad Decrees," and suppressed liberal and nationalist agitation in Germany for a decade.

Even England passed through a brief but symptomatic repressive phase. The inevitable crisis of readjustment to a peacetime economy in 1815, combined with population growth, brought widespread poverty and unemployment. Unlike their counterparts on the Continent, middle-class radicals called not for revolution but for reform of the corrupt parliamentary voting system. The Tory (Conservative) government nevertheless replied with ill-considered force in 1819. Manchester constables routed a peaceful crowd of demonstrators with considerable loss of life in the so-called "Peterloo Massacre." Parliament passed the notorious "Six Acts" that made the expression of advanced opinions a crime. But neither Britain nor the continental monarchies had the bureaucratic machinery or propaganda techniques needed to remold their subjects' thought; that was reserved for the despotisms of the next century.

As for the "concert of Europe," for which the Quadruple Alliance had prescribed regular meetings, it soon broke up. At the conference of Aix-la-Chapelle (Aachen) in 1818 the great powers again welcomed France to their midst.

Cavalry disperses the crowd at the "Peterloo Massacre" (1819).

Then, in 1820, the first of a series of disturbances in southern Europe posed the question of intervention by the powers. A constitutionalist revolt against the Spanish Bourbons triggered disturbances in Naples, Piedmont, and Portugal. Castlereagh refused to attend the Congress of Troppau (1820) at which the three eastern monarchies declared their readiness to act. The ensuing congress of Laibach (1821), over British protests, authorized Austrian military intervention to restore the Bourbons in Naples and Sicily. Metternich dealt similarly with Piedmont. In October 1822, at Verona in north Italy, the last congress met to discuss intervention in Spain. Britain refused its consent, and withdrew: "Every nation for itself and God for us all," quipped George Canning, Castlereagh's successor.

British disapproval did not prevent a French army from crossing the Pyrenees to restore the Spanish Bourbons. Unlike 1808, no guerrilla resistance resulted. France was intervening for rather than against the Bourbons, the Church, and the landowning nobles. And the three eastern powers declined to follow Canning's dictum; the custom of consultation between great powers established at Vienna continued, though less formally than in the congress period.

If Britain's departure from Verona marked the effective end of the Quadruple Alliance, the Greek war of Independence (1821–29) soon crippled the "Holy Alliance" as well. The war was a major step in a process soon drearily familiar to European statesmen: the "Eastern Question," the breakup of the Ottoman Turk empire under the pressure of hostile great powers without and of nationalism within. Russia had humiliated the Turks in Catherine the Great's wars. The Serbs, under their chieftain "Black George," had set the example of national—or tribal—revolt against Constantinople in 1804. By 1817 the embryo of a Serb state had emerged, although under Turkish overlordship. The Greeks followed in 1821, by massacring all Turks in the Peloponnese—a massacre the Turks repaid with interest.

The Greek cause attracted support among western admirers of ancient Greece. Flamboyant figures such as the brilliant and dissolute English romantic poet Lord Byron flocked to Greece. Russia, always hostile to Turkey and now solicitous of its Slav "little brothers" under Turkish rule, broke with Metternich and lent aid to "the Revolution." A bizarre alignment of Britain and France with the Russia of Alexander's successor, the reactionary Tsar Nicholas I, annihilated the Turkish fleet at Navarino in 1827. In 1832 independent Greece received from Europe the quaint gift of a Bavarian prince as a ruler.

From 1830 Revolutions to 1840 Crisis

The second wave of revolutions, in 1830–32, was a more serious affair than the first. The breakdown of the "Holy Alliance" over Greece, the fading of the memory of revolutionary turmoil—but not of revolutionary achievements—contributed to its force. And far more than in 1820–21, nationalism drove events. Finally, as in 1789, Paris set the example that had been missing in 1820. Louis XVIII, who had acquiesced to a degree of constitutionalism after 1814, died in 1824. His successor, Charles X, considered himself king by divine right. He muzzled the press and defied the liberal majority in his Chamber of Deputies. The appointment of an ultra-monarchist ministry in 1829 brought deadlock in the middle of a series of poor harvests.

When Charles X attempted in July 1830 to dissolve the Chamber and reduce the already small electorate to a mere 25,000 wealthy men, Paris responded with the well-tried methods of July 1789. Charles, amazingly unprepared to crush the revolt he had provoked, abdicated. Moderate liberals, with the help of that hardy perennial of Paris revolutions, the Marquis de Lafayette, took control. Their candidate, Louis Philippe of Orléans, son of a renegade cousin of Louis XVI who had helped unleash the revolution of 1789 and had taken the name "Philippe-Egalité," ascended the throne as first and last of the Orléans dynasty. The new "July monarchy" promised France an end to experiments in absolutism.

News of the Paris revolution swept across Europe and ignited further outbreaks. But these, with the exception of stirrings in Britain and the overthrow of a number of unpopular German princelings, were of a different pattern than events in France. In Belgium, north-central Italy, and above all in Poland, the 1830 revolutions were nationalist revolts against foreign domination. The Catholic and French- or Flemish-speaking Belgians assigned to Holland after 1815 increasingly chafed under Protestant Dutch rule. Their revolution succeeded because Britain, France, and Prussia restrained the Dutch from attempting reconquest. In 1839, the five great powers guaranteed Belgium the same perpetual independence and neutrality accorded Switzerland in 1815. In Italy, revolutionaries seeking a unified Italian state, and cooperating more effectively than in 1820–21, took over Modena, Parma, and much of the Papal States. Then Metternich's armies marched south once more and restored the "legitimate" rulers.

The most tragic of the events of 1830 occurred in Poland. There intellectuals and patriots rose against the relatively mild form of Russian rule experienced under Tsar Alexander's 1815 constitution. The Russian authorities initially showed the same unpreparedness and irresolution as Charles X and the Dutch, but they soon corrected their mistake. The Russian reconquest, aided by internal dissension among the Poles, brought mass executions and imprisonment, Russian military rule, and brutal though unsuccessful attempts to Russify the population. A generation of Polish intellectuals died or emigrated.

In Germany, minor disturbances led to the granting of constitutions in Saxony, Hanover, Brunswick, and

King Louis Philippe courts the public, in a contemporary cartoon.

Hesse-Kassel. In 1832, a nationalist mass movement staged a *Nationalfest* at Hambach near Frankfurt. A crowd of 30,000 heard speakers demand wider voting rights and a national state. Metternich replied with new Carlsbad-style decrees. Silence again descended in Germany.

Finally, the July Revolution of 1830 had repercussions even in Britain. The Conservative regime of the "Peterloo Massacre" had slowly mellowed. In 1829 the Duke of Wellington's cabinet tolerated Parliament's removal of long-standing discriminatory laws against Catholics. But the scandal of the parliamentary electoral system persisted. The absence of a mechanism for redistricting meant that the new industrial cities such as Birmingham and Manchester had no representation, while "pocket boroughs" and sleepy villages under the domination of one or two great landowners had seats in Parliament.

When the Conservatives balked at reform, elections in 1831 gave a majority to the opposition Whigs, or liberals. In 1832, after the House of Lords had tried and failed to block reform, the Reform Bill became law. It eliminated the worst abuses and extended the suf-

THE REFORM BILL.

The Reform Bill of 1832, dramatized in a contemporary cartoon. Pocket boroughs go into the "Reform Mill" and a triumphant Britannia emerges.

frage to one adult male in five, compared to one in twenty in Louis Philippe's France. Gradual reform, although fitful and grudgingly granted, helped Britain escape the continental cycle of bloody repression and bloodier revolution.

Internationally, the 1830 outbreaks restored the solidarity of the three eastern monarchies that the Greek war had broken. All three ruled Poles. Austria, Prussia, and Russia therefore met in 1833 at Münchengrätz in Bohemia. Under Metternich's guidance they arrived at agreements in the spirit of the "Holy Alliance" that lasted until 1848 and after. Russia and Austria pledged to resist jointly any threat to their Polish lands. They also bound themselves to oppose further changes in the status quo in Turkey and to act together if a change seemed unavoidable. This last agreement was a symptom of the continuing importance of the "Eastern Question," which was to drive Austria and Russia apart repeatedly until the final crisis of 1914.

After the close of the Greek affair, Russia had moved to assume the position of "protector" to and eventual heir of the ever-declining Ottoman Empire. A few months before Münchengrätz, Russia had landed troops at Constantinople to protect the Sultan from attack through Syria by his rebellious Egyptian vassal, the former Albanian bandit chieftain Mehemet Ali. Russian protectorate of Turkey inevitably aroused Britain, whose strategic interest in maintaining its Mediterranean route to India dictated keeping Russia locked in the Black Sea.

But not until Mehemet Ali's second war with Turkey in 1839–40 did the British have an opportunity to act. The boisterous Lord Palmerston, a fit successor to Castlereagh and Canning as foreign secretary, made full use of British power, now reaching its zenith relative to continental rivals. When Mehemet Ali's forces drove into Lebanon on their way to Constantinople, Palmerston orchestrated diplomatic cooperation between Britain, Austria

and Russia. At the scene, the Royal Navy bombarded Beirut and a landing force cut the Egyptians to shreds. Mehemet Ali subsided; the Turkish empire for the moment survived.

The only opposition came from Louis Philippe's France. Nostalgic for the Egyptian colony that Napoleon had failed to bequeath, France broke with its "liberal" partner, Britain, and in 1840 briefly challenged all of Europe. British naval supremacy and a sudden blaze of hostility to France across the Rhine brought Louis Philippe's ministers to their senses. As the crisis subsided, Britain took Russia's place as chief "protector" of Turkey. The Turkish Straits, by 1841 treaty between the great powers, were now closed to warships in time of peace: thus Russia was caged. If war came, Palmerston was confident Russia would remain so, for Turkey and Britain would be allies and Russia's Black Sea coasts would lie open to bombardment by the Royal Navy.

In Europe itself, the chief importance of the 1839–40 crisis was as warning for the future. The Germanies had reacted in kind to French bellicosity. Nationalist sentiment reached heights not touched at Hambach in 1832. "The Watch on the Rhine," a catchy anti-French tune, enjoyed fierce popularity. The marvelous Habsburg anthem of the great composer Haydn received new German-national words: "Germany, Germany, before everything, before everything in the world." The lack of moderation of *Deutschland über Alles* was symptomatic. Also symptomatic was Prussia's role in the crisis. As Germany's bulwark against France, the Prussian power-state gained a new German-national prestige.

THE END OF REVOLUTION, 1848–50

Fear of revolution, the chief inhibition of the status quo powers, still held German nationalism in check. Before the way was clear for the subversion of the international status quo, Europe had to pass in 1848–49 through a third and culminating round of the revolutions that had shaken it since 1815. The new upheavals combined features of 1789, 1820, and 1830.

The underlying structural preconditions for revolution in 1848 were similar to those of 1789 and 1830. Predominantly agrarian societies with rapidly expanding populations and relatively slow increases in productivity faced a food crisis. The population of most European states had increased by 30 to 40 percent in the 30 years from 1815 to 1845. Urban workers spent between 60 and 70 percent of their wages on food. And in the previous 50 years the working classes had come to depend disproportionately on one crop, an innovation from the Americas—the potato.

When a fungus rotted potato crops from 1845 to 1847 and grain blights also struck most of Europe, the result was unrest from Ireland to Poland. Agricultural collapse, as in 1788–89, also gen-erated a downturn in commerce and industry; food prices and unemployment rose simultaneously in the cities, with grim consequences. Grain prices peaked in early 1847 and declined thereafter, but the business slump, and unemployment, continued (see Figure 26-1). And this temporary crisis sharpened the impact of a deeper structural change: the creeping introduction of machinery had begun by 1848 to impoverish or drive from business many of the artisans who formed the majority of the urban population. These conditions, in combination with the political myth of the Great Revolution of 1789, produced a chain reaction in the spring of 1848: western and central Europe's last revolutions from below.

But 1848 was also not 1789. The essential differences that made the transnational movement of 1848–49 far wider but immeasurably shallower than 1789 were four. First, the example of the Terror of 1792–94 deterred the

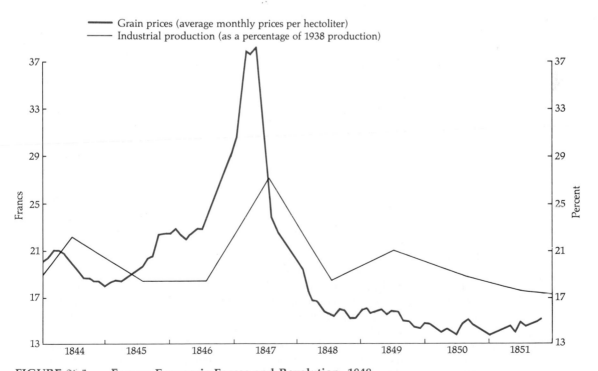

FIGURE 26-1   France: Economic Forces and Revolution, 1848
From Maurice Agulhon, *1848 ou l'apprentissage de la République* (Paris: Éditions du Seuil, 1973), pp. 100–01.

moderate liberals who led most of the revolutions from pushing too hard against the old order. One seasoned observer and participant in the events (Alexis de Tocqueville, whose *Democracy in America* is among the two or three greatest nineteenth-century works on politics) put it well: "We sought . . . to warm ourselves with the passions of our fathers, without quite managing it; we imitated their gestures and poses as we had seen them on the stage, since we could not imitate their enthusiasm or feel their rage."

Second, this absence of fanatical leadership from above found a counterpart below, at least in the countryside. The peasants of central Europe sacked a few manor houses and attacked Jewish moneylenders. But the old order in the countryside did not totally break down, as it had in the Great Fear of 1789. The ingredient that had helped convert noble and urban revolt into the destruction of the old order was largely absent in 1848.

In France the peasants had profited from 1789 and were now indifferent or hostile to Parisian radicalism. In Germany and Austria both monarchical bureaucrats and liberals moved swiftly to bribe the peasants into passivity. Officials and parliamentarians rather than revolutionaries abolished most remaining vestiges of service obligations to landowners. In Austrian Poland, in one of the earliest incidents in the wave of unrest that preceded 1848, the authorities had even crushed a nationalist rising by inciting non-Polish peasants to massacre their Polish landlords.

The revolutions of 1848 were thus essentially urban, except where, as in Hungary, the rural upper classes helped lead a national insurrection. And the revolutions came above all from two groups: the intellectuals and the aritsans. The former generally hated the old regime for its failure, as they saw it, to recognize their talents. Hunger or fear of hunger moved the artisans. The intellectuals demanded political or national rights; the artisans

economic ones. The intellectuals for the most part called for free competition, for industry, for "progress." The artisans aspired to return to the cozy world of guild restrictions, or, as a minimum, to a job guaranteed by the state. The intellectuals feared "the mob." The artisans in turn soon recognized how little the intellectuals offered them. This mutual hostility of the two principal revolutionary forces (forces briefly allied in 1793–94 under Robespierre) was the third major reason for the collapse of the 1848 revolutions.

The fourth and most important difference between 1848–49 and 1789–94 was the absence of war, which had spread the revolution of 1789 across Europe while necessitating and justifying radicalization at home. In 1848 the moderate liberals riding the wave of Parisian radicalism soon showed unexpected caution. The new French foreign minister, the poet Alphonse de Lamartine, took a sober line in the face of radical demands for yet another crusade of peoples against kings: "We love Poland, we love Italy, we love all oppressed peoples, but we love France above all else. . . ." Middle classes and peasantry, beneficiaries of 1789, had lost all desire to export revolution. France once again became a republic, but remained a status quo power. Further east, German radicals and even moderate liberals yearned for a great war—but the Prussian monarchy refused to oblige. And without a great revolutionary war to throw central and eastern Europe into the melting pot, the old order was bound to recover.

1848–49: From Outbreak to Collapse

The year of revolutions opened with a Sicilian uprising against the Bourbons of Naples: an antitax revolt, mixed with brigandage and Sicilian particularism. It was the overthrow of the king of the French, Louis Philippe of Orléans, on February 22–24, 1848, that roused Europe. The opposition to Louis Philippe staged banquets featuring speeches in favor of wider voting rights. When the government banned further banquets, the result was the now-customary explosion of violence. After fighting that produced fewer than 400 dead, Louis Philippe fled for London. Lamartine and other moderate republicans proclaimed the second French republic.

News traveled rapidly. On March 13, crowd violence in Vienna led to panic at the Habsburg court, which dismissed Metternich. The symbol of the reactionary Holy Alliance departed ignominiously for exile—in liberal London. Metternich's replacement with a cabinet of indecisive bureaucrats was the signal for further revolutionary outbreaks. The city of Milan, in an action justly famous as the first mass example of Italian nationalism, revolted against Austria. In five days of bitter fighting in March, the Milanese, armed with a few muskets and with pikes from La Scala opera house, harried the Austrian garrison. Field Marshal Joseph Radetzky, veteran of the wars against Napoleon, withdrew in defeat. The Hungarians, the principal subject nation of the Habsburgs after the Germans, demanded and received the right to domestic self-government. To the north, news of Metternich's fall unleashed street demonstrations in Berlin and other German cities. In Berlin, after his troops fired on the crowd on March 18, the eccentric King Frederick William IV panicked and virtually surrendered. Military Prussia received a ministry of moderate liberals and a constitution.

The revolution seemed to have swept all before it. Only the two great powers at the opposite ends of Europe and of the scale of political, social, and economic development were exempt: Britain and Russia. In Russia only the nobility was as yet politically conscious. In Britain the Chartist League's agitation for universal manhood suffrage never passed beyond the stage of decorous mass meetings.

But even in Paris, Vienna, and Berlin appearances were deceptive, for the armies remained intact. France unex-

The Vienna crowd mounts the barricades, March 1848.

pectedly took the lead in reining in the revolution. In April 1848 the new republic held the first free elections under universal manhood suffrage of any major European power. The results were a stinging repudiation of revolutionary Paris. Peasants and provincial middle classes voted for moderates and monarchists.

The new national assembly, faithfully representing the views of the majority of the electorate, soon began to dismantle the most striking gain the Paris crowd had achieved in the February revolution: the "national workshops" that gave the unemployed work at government expense. The unemployed and the revolutionary artisans of Paris understandably reacted. Without political leadership, without coordination, but with the tenacity of despair, they rose on June 22. The army and the paramilitary National Guard, under Eugène Cavaignac, a

The adventurer: Napoleon III.

republican general who had learned his trade in colonial Algeria, fought back pitilessly. Perhaps 5,000 died in the "June Days"; at least 3,000 were insurgents shot after resistance had ceased.

The republic, with its moderate-monarchist chamber, then faced the future without a monarch. Bourbons and Orléans had in turn proved themselves unsuitable. As in 1799, a Bonaparte stepped in to fill the vacuum. In December 1848 the votes of moderates and peasantry bore the dissolute and eccentric nephew of the great Napoleon, Louis Napoleon Bonaparte, into office as president of the republic. Revolutionary universal suffrage had proved remarkably conservative in practice.

The example France had given in the June days found a parallel in central Europe. Prince Alfred Windischgrätz, commander of the Habsburg forces in the Czech lands, crushed a quasi-insurrection in Prague in mid-June and dispersed the Slav Congress that had met to call for Czech rights. A man "equally devoid of fear or pity," he hit upon the simple expedient of withdrawing his troops from the rebellious city and bombarding it into submission with artillery.

In Italy, the Habsburgs also recovered rapidly. Charles Albert of Piedmont-Sardinia followed up the victorious insurrection of the Milanese by declaring war on Austria. Italy, he proclaimed grandly, would "do it itself": Piedmont alone would defeat Austria and seize north Italy. But his poorly led army ran afoul of the canny Radetzky at the battle of Custoza in July. Charles Albert's attempt to reverse that verdict the next spring led to a second defeat at Novara and his own abdication; his principal legacy was the constitution he had grudgingly granted in March 1848. Further south, the visionary Mazzini and the greatest soldier of Italy's wars of independence, Giuseppe Garibaldi, led an epic defense of the Roman republic that radical democrats had proclaimed in February 1849. French troops that Louis Napoleon sent—in a

bid for French Catholic support—ultimately prevailed.

Victory at Prague and Custoza emboldened the Habsburg court. The addled young emperor Ferdinand ultimately abdicated in favor of his military-minded nephew Francis Joseph. Revolutionary Vienna received the Windischgrätz treatment. By late fall 1848 only Hungary, against which the Habsburgs had mobilized smaller nationalities such as the Croats, still asserted autonomy. In April 1849, after victories over invading Habsburg armies, Hungary's most radical leader, the fiery Lajos Kossuth, proclaimed Hungarian independence within "historic" borders that included large numbers of Slavs and Rumanians. Revolutionary greater Hungary proved more than a match for the Habsburgs and their Croat and Rumanian allies. But Russia, fearing that Austria's collapse would mean revolution throughout central Europe and confident by now that France would not launch a war over Poland, intervened massively. By August 1849 Russian arms had bloodily restored Hungary to Habsburg control.

Far to the north, in Germany, the revolution fared no better. In the spring of 1848 leading liberals such as Max von Gagern of Hesse-Darmstadt urged on Frederick William IV of Prussia a revolutionary German-national war against Russia. Restoring Poland was to be the pretext, German unity and German domination of central Europe the real goal. But Frederick William, irresolute in many things, was firm on monarchical solidarity. He angrily rejected German liberalism's war: "By God, I shall not draw the sword against Russia."

The movement of German intellectuals that culminated in an all-German Parliament at Frankfurt in May 1848 therefore faced an insoluble dilemma. The war that nationalists yearned for to achieve unity required the cooperation of the very dynasties and princely armies that stood in the way of unity. The Frankfurt Parliament of lawyers and professors did succeed in launch-

Nationalities of the Habsburg Empire

ing a brief war against Denmark in April 1848, after the disputed but overwhelmingly German-speaking border duchies of Schleswig and Holstein had revolted from Denmark. But the Prussian troops who did most of the fighting stopped on Frederick William IV's orders when the king found he faced British, French, and above all Russian disapproval. A brief renewal of the war in 1849 ended similarly.

In Prussia itself the army and bureaucracy took heart after Windischgrätz's reduction of Vienna. Frederick William appointed a general as prime minister in November 1848. Then the king closed parliament and imposed a conservative constitution to match the new face of his government. In spring 1849 Prussian troops moved south to crush short-lived democratic republics in Saxony, the Bavarian Palatinate, and Baden. The revolutionaries who had overthrown the grand duke of Baden fought with particular tenacity against a Prussian army under Frederick William IV's brother and eventual successor William. William in turn had a number of captured revolutionary leaders shot.

The end of revolution did not restore stability immediately to Germany. Frederick William had refused the crown of a united Germany that the moribund Frankfurt Parliament had offered him in April 1849. But his disdain for this "crown smelling of the gutter" did not prevent him from aspiring to a similar offer from his fellow-princes. Embarrassment in Hungary might yet induce Vienna to accept Prussian domination of Germany. By summer 1849 Frederick William had recruited most German princes for his "Prussian Union." Then Austria moved to reconstitute the German Confederation of 1815. Both powers appealed to Russia. In November 1850 a standoff nearly led to war when Austria and the Confederation challenged Prussia's control of the vital military roads across Hesse that linked the Prussian Rhineland to Berlin. Austrian and Prussian patrols traded shots for the first time since 1778. Prussia mobilized. Russia, seeking to restore the pre-1848 status quo and unenthusiastic about the emergence of a powerful united Germany, backed Austria. Some Prussian generals were confident of victory but Frederick William was no more willing to fight Russia than he had been in 1848. By the treaty of Ol-mütz (November 29, 1850) Prussia agreed to dismantle the Prussian Union and to demobilize. After long negotiation, Berlin also consented to restore the German Confederation of 1815. That agreement, which Prussian chauvinists denounced as the "humiliation of Olmütz," put off the struggle for mastery in central Europe for a generation.

From Revolution to Nationalism

The failure of revolution in 1848 meant the end of an era dominated by the example of 1789. The old pattern of periodic agricultural crises, urban and rural revolt, middle-class radical leadership, and government irresolution and ineptitude had shown its limitation—at least in the absence of a continent-wide war. Railroads henceforth brought cheap food to urban markets and industrialization supplied work for impoverished and displaced ex-artisans. Middle-class intellectuals feared the masses they claimed to lead more than the old order they aspired to overthrow. And after the first shocks of March 1848, governments had swiftly recovered their resolve. The brilliant generalship of Radetzky and the successful brutality of Cavaignac, Windischgrätz, and Prince William of Prussia showed that the triumph of "the Revolution" was far from inevitable. Governments even began to imitate Britain in co-opting the lower orders.

The freedom from fear of revolution that Europe's statesmen now enjoyed liberated them from some pre-1848 restraints on vigorous pursuit of state power interests. The year 1848 also changed the definition of those interests by revealing the full power of the revolution's child, nationalism. From the Turkish Balkans to Schleswig-Holstein, awakened nationalities clamored for self-determination. History

The balance of power, by the French artist and caricaturist Honoré Daumier.

and reason, their nationalist intellectuals claimed, gave them "historic rights."

Under the old dynastic order, nationality and language had only sometimes been a matter of life or death. Now they became the single most powerful source of bloodshed. For each nationality defined "history" and "reason" according to its own convenience, and the mixed settlement pattern of central Europe ensured that right conflicted with right. The only remedy, as Kossuth had explained to the Serbs in 1849, was naked force: "The sword shall decide between us." That sword, the sword of nationalism, was to cleave first Europe and then the world.

In 1848—and this too was a portent for the future—the most powerful of European nationalisms showed its hand. The Frankfurt Parliament was short on deeds and long on deliberation, but it had one indisputable merit. Its discussions registered faithfully in cold print the aims of the German national movement. The Parliament debated the claims of the Poles in Posen, the activities of the Slav Congress in Prague, the rights of the Danes of Schleswig. Voices of moderation stood little chance in the face of calls for "healthy national egotism," of exhortations to resist "the attempts of the puny little nationalities to set up housekeeping in our midst, and like parasites to destroy our own existence," and of proclamations that Germany's final mission was to wrest world mastery from Britain. The unanswered long-term question was whether Europe could tolerate such a Germany.

THE MAKING OF ITALY AND GERMANY

In the aftermath of the year of revolutions, the "Holy Alliance" alignment that had maintained stability since 1815 appeared restored. Russia had underwritten Austria's survival and had shepherded Frederick William IV back

---

German Nationalism Speaks: Voices from the Frankfurt Parliament

To want to resurrect Poland merely because its downfall fills with justified regret, I call moronic sentimentality. . . . Our right is none other than the right of the stronger, the right of conquest. . . . The German conquests in Poland were a necessity of nature. The law of history is not the same as that in the law books. History knows only the laws of nature, one of which tells us that a people does not gain the right to political independence through mere existence, but only through having the power to assert itself as a state among other states.

—*Wilhelm Jordan (Berlin), a member of the center-left, in the debate on Posen, July 25, 1848.*

. . . but it is our aim to found a giant empire [*Reich*] of 70 million, and if possible of 80 or 100 million, and plant the standard of Arminius [a famous Germanic chieftain who had smashed three Roman legions in A.D. 9] in that *Reich,* to stand there armed against east and west, against the Slavic and Latin peoples, to wrest mastery of the seas from the English, and to become the most powerful nation [*Volk*] on this earth—*that* is Germany's future! With that prospect in view, petty debates over the drafting of our constitution, all petty debates, [must] retreat into the background. . . .

—*Count Friedrich Deym, a liberal Austrian noble, in the debate of October 27, 1848.*

Stenographischer Bericht über die Verhandlungen der deutschen constituirenden Nationalversammlung zu Frankfurt am Main (Leipzig: Teubner, 1848–49), Vol. 2, pp. 1144–46; Vol. 4, p. 2882 (translation by M. Knox).

---

into the conservative fold. But restoration swiftly proved an illusion.

Napoleon Tilts the Balance, 1852–56

The chief agent of upheaval, for the last time in Europe's modern history, was France—or rather a Bonaparte. Louis Napoleon, political speculator and gang leader of the conspirators who had helped him to power, had none of the attributes of his great uncle. What he did have was a messianic belief, derived from a naive reading of his uncle's cynical propaganda, in the virtues of national self-determination. Even before taking power, he had conceived vague schemes for the reorganization

A CONSULTATION ABOUT THE STATE OF TURKEY.

A Consultation about the State of Turkey, a mid-nineteenth-century cartoon. The "Sick Man of Europe" (Turkey) is threatened by Death (Russia), while the physicians (France and England) hold their consultation.

Nicholas miscalculated both London's willingness to see Turkey bullied and the influence of a new factor in international politics, British public opinion. The Turks, confident of French and British support, refused Russia's demands.

Russia thereupon occupied the Turkish principalities at the mouth of the Danube, threatening Austria as well as Turkey. Britain and France ordered their fleets to Constantinople to overawe the tsar. That move encouraged the Ottoman Sultan, in October 1853, to declare war on Russia. In November, Russia's annihilation of the Turkish fleet at Sinope in the Black Sea (the "Sinope Massacre") galvanized the British public, which abhorred Russia after its intervention in Hungary.

When Russia refused to evacuate the Danubian principalities, Britain and France declared war. Britain fought to humble Russia and keep it from further encroachments on Turkey that would threaten British communications to India. Napoleon III fought to stir up trouble in Europe. Neither ran serious risks, for neither shared a border with Russia. For Austria it was otherwise; geography dictated that if it fought Russia it would fight for life itself. Austria therefore remained on the fence. It mobilized to urge Russia out of the principalities, but made no move. That fact, and the neutrality of Prussia and the lesser German states, prevented general war.

Instead, once the Russians evacuated the principalities in August 1854, Britain and France no longer had an objective. Russian "aggression" against Turkey had ceased. But bloodless victory did not lead to peace. The ebullient Palmerston spurred the cabinet and an inflamed British public demanded action. The allies pressed on in an attempt to destroy Russian power to threaten Turkey in the future. An allied amphibious expedition landed in the Crimea to attack Russia's principal Black Sea naval base, Sebastopol.

Predictably, given bitter Russian resistance and the immense logistical ef-

of Europe along lines far different than those of 1815. After the inevitable coup d'état in December 1851, he proclaimed himself Napoleon III, Emperor of the French, and began searching for a way to throw Europe's borders into the melting pot.

Given the newly restored stability in central Europe and Russian backing for Austria in Italy, the "Eastern Question" seemed to offer the best opportunities. Napoleon III might there acquire the Napoleonic prestige needed to consolidate his rule at home, and compel Russia to give up its role as guarantor of Austria. In 1851–52 Napoleon III challenged Russian claims to a protectorate over the Christian holy sites in the Ottoman Empire, which included Palestine. French battleship diplomacy at Constantinople provoked Tsar Nicholas to send an uncouth representative of his own to bully the Sultan. But

fort of maintaining large forces by sea, the expedition was a fiasco. It required 18 months of bloody fighting to take Sebastopol. The new industrial firepower was already beginning to make movement on the battlefield difficult. The Crimean War cost at least three quarters of a million dead, of which 80 percent died of cholera, dysentery, or typhus.

The war's main consequence was the disruption of the European state system, a disruption that ultimately permitted the wars that created Italian and German nation-states in 1859–60 and 1866–71. Russia indeed suffered a decisive check. It lost the right to have a Black Sea fleet, as Britain desired. But the war had other consequences London had neither bargained on nor greatly welcomed. Under Nicholas I's successor, Tsar Alexander II, Russia turned inward for a generation. Russian power no longer threatened Turkey. It also no longer upheld Austria. Indeed, Russia now sought revenge for the Austrian "ingratitude" that had repaid Russia's aid in Hungary in 1849 with a tilt toward the western powers in 1853–56.

France was the chief beneficiary of this breakdown of the conservative alignment. Napoleon III presided imperially over the 1856 Paris peace conference. Much to the disgust of the British, he was soon intriguing for a bargain with Russia that would help him to redraw the map of Europe. In this new situation, other statesmen also stirred.

The Making of Italy, 1858–60

In the last stages of the Crimean War, the "Italian Question" had reemerged from the limbo into which Radetzky's victories had thrust it in 1848–49. Piedmont had sent 15,000 troops to the Crimea to gain favor with Britain and France. Charles Albert's successor, the erratic Victor Emmanuel II, had wanted to fight at all costs to restore the prestige tarnished at Custoza and Novara. His liberal prime minister, Count

Britain in the Crimea: bewhiskered officers of the 8th Hussars.

Camillo di Cavour, had imposed war on his cabinet colleagues rather than risk a royal coup against the constitution and war under a ministry of conservatives. Cavour thus gained access to the Paris conference, at which he proceeded to embarrass the Austrians by criticizing their support of corrupt regimes in the Papal States and Bourbon Naples.

Dictatorial in temper but an admirer of the British parliament, Cavour was an unparalleled master of political improvisation, a "Piedmontese Machiavelli." His chief weakness was his tendency, striking even in the age of the duplicitous and vacillating Napoleon III, to flagrant untruths that diminished his credibility: "If we did for ourselves what we are doing for Italy, we should be real scoundrels." His goal was to expand Piedmont, not to create an Italian nation-state. He also labored under severe constraints. National revolution, if encouraged too much, might yet turn into barbaric peasant revolt. And only north Italy appeared suitable for annexation to Piedmont. The South

The makers of Italy: Count Camillo di Cavour (left) and Giuseppe Garibaldi (right).

was a world centuries behind Lombardy and Piedmont; great landowners and gangs—*mafia, n'drangheta*, and *camorra*—dominated a downtrodden peasantry under the theoretical sovereignty of pope and Bourbons. Above all, Cavour faced the unbroken power of Austria. The lesson of 1848–49 was that Italy could *not* do it itself.

Not all Italians agreed. Mazzini held to his vision of an Italy created through spontaneous uprising from below by the—nonexistent—nationalist masses. An Italian National Society came into being in 1857 with a more practical goal: support for a renewed Piedmontese bid for expansion. Garibaldi, revealed in 1848–49 as a great military talent, awaited his chance. The creation of an Italian state was ultimately the product both of a "royal war" of Cavour, king, and Napoleon III, and of pressure from below from Mazzini's ideas and Garibaldi's freebooters.

Initially everything depended on Napoleon III. In January 1858 the explosion of an Italian revolutionary's bomb outside the Paris Opera reminded Napoleon that he had yet to do "something for Italy." He soon approached Cavour. The two met in secret at Plombières near the Piedmontese border in July 1858 and agreed

on a program. A French-Piedmontese war against Austria would seize Lombardy, Venetia, Parma, and Modena for Piedmont. In return for committing 200,000 troops, Napoleon would receive Savoy, an Italian satellite state, and the domestic prestige of a Napoleonic Italian campaign. The Pope would lose territory but become head of an Italian confederation of states. To Cavour, Napoleon III allotted the task of provoking Austria into war without himself appearing the aggressor, and of providing 100,000 troops.

To present this Franco-Piedmontese war of conquest to international opinion as justified self-defense required all of Cavour's ingenuity. At the end, in April 1859, Austrian recklessness saved him. Vienna's bullying ultimatum demanding that Piedmont demobilize destroyed what little was left of Austria's international backing. England, despite misgivings about Napoleon III, stood aside; the aftermath of the 1857 Indian mutiny (see pp. 759–60) had absorbed most of Britain's limited land power. Russia watched Austria's humiliation with satisfaction. Only Prussia, Austria's other rival, offered aid. But its price was the reversal of Olmütz: Prussian supremacy in north Germany.

The Making of Italy   1859–70

The war itself was swift, for Napoleon III and Cavour had isolated their opponent. The Piedmontese army only scraped together 50,000 men instead of the 100,000 Cavour had blithely promised, but this time it faced no Radetzky. Piedmont fought a creditable holding action until the French arrived, partly by rail. In two bloody battles of June 1859 at Magenta and Solferino the French drove the Austrians back with furious charges against Minié rifle fire. Fortunately for the French, the Austrians were remarkably poor shots.

Then Napoleon III, appalled at a carnage for which he lacked his uncle's strong stomach, incensed at the meagerness of his allies' contribution, disquieted by signs that Cavour coveted central as well as north Italy, and unnerved at a Prussian threat on the Rhine, called a halt. By the July armistice of Villafranca with Emperor Francis Joseph, Napoleon III abandoned Cavour to his own devices. Piedmont would receive only Lombardy. Cavour, when he heard that Victor Emmanuel II had agreed without consulting him,

resigned in chagrin. He seemed to have lost.

But Cavour had proved his indispensability, and Victor Emmanuel II recalled him in January 1860. Cavour soon engineered the annexation of Tuscany, Romagna, Parma, and Modena to enlarged Piedmont. Rigged plebiscites, a favorite Napoleonic device, seemingly confirmed the unanimity of national sentiment. Napoleon III, outwitted in his attempt to confine Piedmont to the north Italian plain, now demanded his price: Savoy, which was French-speaking, and the city of Nice, which was not. Cavour acquiesced, to the fury of Piedmontese public opinion. Garibaldi bitterly resented the cession of Nice, his home town, but he soon had his revenge. Despite Cavour's half-hearted attempts to stop them, Garibaldi and a volunteer "thousand" left Genoa for Sicily in early May 1860. Against Cavour's expectations and hopes, Garibaldi's ill-equipped troops routed the Bourbon army, raised the Sicilian peasantry, crossed to the mainland, and took Naples.

The epic campaign of "the Thousand" made Italy. To derail the social revolutionary elements of Garibaldi's program and to rescue the prestige of Piedmont, Cavour and Victor Emmanuel II had to act. The Piedmontese army invaded the Papal States and moved on Naples. Garibaldi, a monarchist at heart unlike the fiercely republican Mazzini, yielded his conquests to the new Kingdom of Italy. He received scant thanks from Cavour or from the Piedmontese army.

Italy was complete except for Venetia, which the new state received in 1866, Rome, which it took in 1870, and Trento and Trieste, which it did not conquer until 1918. As a colleague and rival of Cavour put it, the process of "making Italians" remained. Cavour's representatives in the South soon made themselves more hated than the Bourbons. The brutal imposition of Piedmont's French-style prefects, military conscription, and high taxes on the southerners triggered a guerrilla war that lasted over five years and cost more dead than the wars of 1848–49 and 1859–60. Italy's *Risorgimento*, its political unification, had come so swiftly and had joined areas so different in culture and traditions that "making Italians" required generations. Cavour, perhaps fortunately for his reputation, died of malaria and inept doctors in mid-1861. Time alone would tell if the foundations of the Italy that he and Garibaldi had created were sound.

The Struggle for Mastery in Germany, 1862–66

Austria's isolation had made a united Italy possible. That same isolation was the precondition for a far greater revolution in the state system than the birth of Italy, "least of the great powers." That revolution was the creation of a Prusso-German nation-state.

The Prussian military monarchy at first seemed an unlikely ally for the German nationalism it had spurned in 1848. But German unity, if it came at all, clearly had to come through one of the two German great powers, Prussia and Austria. And by the early 1860s Prussia possessed advantages Austria could not match. First, except for its Polish provinces, it was wholly German. Second, its Ruhr Valley coal and iron and its leadership since the 1830s of a German Customs Union, the *Zollverein*, had already made it the economic nucleus of any conceivable German nation-state. Third, its role as military bulwark against France and if need be Russia gave even its dynastic military establishment a certain national aura. Fourth, that military establishment soon proved that it had learned from Jena and Auerstädt. In its technique if not in its politics, the Prussian army was by 1860 the most innovative armed force in the world. Finally, after September 1862 Prussia had a leader as indispensable as Cavour—Otto von Bismarck.

Bismarck was a Pomeranian Junker by birth ("I am a Junker and I mean to profit by it") but his deep understanding of historical forces and political tactics far surpassed the blinkered outlook of his caste. He combined apparently genuine Pietist religious convictions with a total absence of political scruple. But like Cavour and unlike their successors in both countries, Bismarck recognized limits. Politics was "the art of the possible." Statesmen could exploit great historical forces but not stand against them: "the stream carries you, but cannot be ruled" ran his favorite Latin tag. Bismarck's political technique—like that of the great Napoleon in warfare—was to aim at a range of alternative goals and to be prepared to achieve them by a variety of means, always leaving for himself a fall-back position in the event of failure. When Bismarck gambled on war it was only after exploring and ruling out less risky alternatives and after reducing incalculable dangers as far as possible. And once war had achieved his ends, he became as fierce a defender of the new status quo as he had been an opponent of the old.

"Mad Junker" and maker of Prussia-Germany: Otto von Bismarck.

Bismarck, like Cavour, did not set out to found a nation-state. His early career as fiery opponent of liberalism and nationalism in the Prussian Chamber in 1848 had branded him, in words that Frederick William IV had perhaps meant as a compliment, as a "red reactionary, smells of blood." But Bismarck's appointment as Prussian ambassador to the German Confederation in 1851 led to a slow change in his outlook. He came to recognize two things—that Austria's claim to leadership of the Confederation was incompatible with Prussia's dignity and security, and that Prussia's natural ally in the struggle for mastery in Germany was German nationalism. Monarchical solidarity abroad and unbending conservatism at home were contrary to Prussia's interests as a state: "Prussia's mission is to extend itself." Prussia must not tie its trim frigate to the "moth-eaten Austrian galleon." In 1859 he had urged Berlin to "let Austria get thoroughly bogged down in its war with France and then break out southwards with our entire army, taking our border posts in our knapsacks and planting them either on [the Swiss border] or wherever the Protestant religion ceases to predominate. . . ."

Berlin ignored that shocking advice. What catapulted Bismarck into power as prime minister and foreign minister in September 1862 was not his ruthlessly unconventional approach to foreign affairs. It was rather the ever-deepening deadlock between the Prussian Chamber and the new king, William I, who had succeeded his incapacitated brother Frederick William IV as regent in 1858 and as king in 1861. The military-minded new king sought to more than double the strength of the army's line units to half a million men and to reduce correspondingly the role of the reserves, which had middle-class officers. The reorganization and the accompanying increase of compulsory military service from two years to three would drastically increase the weight of the army within Prussian society. It would also dramatically increase Prus-

---

Bismarck Takes Office: "Iron and Blood"

1862

Germany looks not to Prussia's liberalism, but to its power; Bavaria, Württemberg, Baden may indulge in liberalism, but Prussia's role is not for them. Prussia must concentrate its power and hold it concentrated for the favorable moment that we have already several times missed. Prussia's borders as drawn in the Vienna treaties do not favor a healthy state existence; the great questions of our time are not decided through speeches and majority votes—that was the great error of 1848 and 1849—but through iron and blood.

—*Bismarck, to the Prussian Chamber's budget committee, September 27, 1862.*

From *Bismarck: Die gesammelten Werke* (Berlin: Otto Stollberg Verlag, 1928), Vol. 10, p. 140 (translation by M. Knox).

---

sia's external striking power. But the liberal majority in the Prussian Chamber repeatedly blocked funding of these plans. William, determined to have his way on grounds both of military efficiency and of monarchical authority, morosely contemplated the English precedent, the struggle between crown and parliament in the 1640s. In this impasse the king turned to Bismarck as the one man steadfast enough to dominate the Chamber and see the king's will done.

Bismarck immediately sought to defuse the constitutional conflict by playing the card of German nationalism. In a speech that was half challenge and half enticement, he announced that "iron and blood" would settle the German question. The liberals professed to be shocked. Bismarck's first bid for liberal cooperation had failed, although some of them had long called for "a great genius or mighty tyrant . . . capable of decisive action."

The "iron and blood" speech also appalled the king. But Bismarck put the issue to him in military terms: he could fight for his throne or tamely surrender. The fight involved muzzling the press, disciplining liberal sympathizers in the bureaucracy, and spending money that the Chamber had not appropriated on an army reorganization that it opposed. To the Chamber Bismarck impudently proclaimed his "loophole theory" of the constitution: when king and parliament disagreed, the king's latent powers entitled him to act for the general welfare. The conflict deepened. New elections returned the latest in a series of ever larger liberal majorities. Thanks to the "three-class" Prussian election law, which weighted votes by wealth, those majorities represented only middle-class opinion. But Bismarck's fellow Junkers would not yet let him play the masses against the liberals.

Foreign policy ultimately offered a way around the impasse, as Bismarck had hoped. A new Polish revolt, even more tragic than that of 1830, convulsed Russian Poland in 1863. Russian repression of the Poles alienated Napoleon III, whose alignment with Russia had underwritten the Italian war. Now each of the European great powers were isolated from one another—except Prussia, which maintained its "line to St. Petersburg." In this open situation, Bismarck soon found a cause that would allow him to undermine the status quo while professing conservative intentions acceptable to Russia and Austria. In 1863 the Danish monarchy moved to incorporate Schleswig, with its minority of Danes and majority of Germans, into Denmark. That step was a flagrant breach of the 1852 Treaty of London that had ended the first two rounds of German-Danish fighting in 1848–49 and had confirmed the continued membership of the Duchies of Schleswig and Holstein in the German Confederation. In January 1864 Bismarck therefore secured an alliance with Vienna to restore the status quo, if need be by force. He himself secretly aspired to annex the Duchies to Prussia as the first step toward Prussia's long-sought hegemony in north Germany.

The Danish war of 1864 was swift and decisive, and British protests to Berlin and Vienna were half-hearted.

Britain had tilted too close to the Confederacy in the U.S. Civil War, and found itself by 1864 facing the eventual prospect of a million battle-hardened Union Veterans on Canada's indefensible borders. It had no troops to spare to rescue Denmark. When the Danes foolishly rejected Bismarck's offer of a compromise, the Prussians stormed the key Danish position at Düppel in April 1864. In August, in the face of a Prussian amphibious threat to Copenhagen, the Danes ceded both Schleswig and Holstein unconditionally to Prussia and Austria.

That triumph demonstrated the power of the newly reorganized Prussian army, and lessened domestic pressure on Bismarck. Influential liberal publications soon came around to the view that Prussian state interest and German nationalism ran parallel: Prussia should annex the Duchies. Bismarck himself settled for a policy of gradual encroachment upon his Austrian partner. He would "try all roads, the most dangerous road, last." If Austria would concede Prussia the Duchies and the mastery of north Germany, Prussia would perhaps underwrite Austria's survival. If Austria proved obstinate, force would decide.

The Austrians professed themselves shocked at Bismarck's suggestions of virtual Prussian annexation of their joint property, the Duchies. Vienna had joined Bismarck's Danish war in hopes of a conservative partnership to cement the status quo in central Europe. Too late it discovered that its partner had other ideas. But Bismarck was not ready for war in 1865, although the newly victorious chief of the general staff, Helmuth von Moltke, was confident. Prussian and Austrian leaders met at Bad Gastein in August and "papered over the cracks." Prussia would administer Schleswig, Austria Holstein, and the partners would reject the claims of the German-national candidate to rule the Duchies, the Duke of Augustenburg.

The Gastein agreement lasted only a few months. Vienna was dimly aware

The new model Prussian army, 1861.

that it could only preserve its position in the German Confederation with the support of the lesser states. It therefore broke the Gastein agreement and courted Augustenburg, the candidate of those states and of non-Prussian liberal opinion. Bismarck, on holiday at Biarritz, sounded out Napoleon III in October 1865; the Emperor did not object to Prussian expansion. He presumably expected a long and indecisive Austro-Prussian war that would give France numerous opportunities to intervene and demand its price. By February 1866 Bismarck was sure of his course. He put Austria's violations of the Gastein agreement to a Prussian crown council. William I, convinced of Austrian disloyalty, agreed that Prussia must prepare for war. The issue was simple: who was to be master in Germany.

Yet Bismarck still had to secure allies, and overcome William I's lingering scruples. Italy was happy to sign a three-month offensive alliance in April, thus performing the essential function of tying down large Austrian forces in Venetia. Bismarck, the conservative statesman, also conspired with Hungarian revolutionaries, justifying himself with a favorite quotation from Vergil: "If I cannot prevail on heaven, I shall mobilize hell." And he again appealed to German nationalism. Prussia promised to Germany after victory a parliament elected under universal manhood suffrage.

Securing allies was easy compared to the frustrations of managing the king's conscience: "I have brought the horse to the ditch; he must jump!" Then, as in 1859, Austria rescued its enemies with an ill-timed gesture that appeared provocative. Vienna's slow and cumbersome mobilization system meant that it could not wait if hostilities seemed inevitable. And Austrian mobilization, along with warnings from conservative aides against a "second Olmütz," finally induced William I to jump. On June 7, 1866, Prussian troops attacked the Austrians in Holstein and began to concentrate on the

---

Bismarck Demands War   February 1866

The Minister President spoke . . . [to the Prussian crown council] in the following terms: Prussia is the only workable political unit that has emerged from the ruins of the old German *Reich* [the Holy Roman Empire], and that is why Prussia had been called to lead Germany. Austria in its envy has always resisted the natural and entirely justified efforts of Prussia toward that goal; it has refused to concede to Prussia the leadership of Germany that it is incapable of exercising itself. . . . Austria has granted Prussia neither the influence due it in Germany, nor the secure position in the [Schleswig-Holstein] duchies necessary to both Prussia and Germany, nor the fruits of [Prussia's] victories. . . . It would be a humiliation, if Prussia now withdrew. Any such humiliation must be avoided at all costs. But in that case a break with Austria is probable. We must therefore discuss and decide the question of whether Prussia should pull back in fright from this obstacle—a break and possible war with Austria. . . . The whole historic development of German affairs and the hostile attitude of Austria drive us toward war. It would be an error to seek to avoid it now. . . .

From the Prussian crown council minutes, February 28, 1866, in *Die auswärtige Politik Preussens 1858–1871* (Berlin: G. Stalling, 1939), Vol. 6, pp. 611ff (translation by M. Knox).

---

borders of Bohemia.

The "Seven Weeks' War" was a startling demonstration of Prussia's efficiency and might. Moltke used telegraph and railroad, proven in the U.S. Civil War (see pp. 770–74), effectively for the first time in a European war. Three Prussian armies detrained on the Bohemian border and converged with unexpected speed on the Austrian forces east of Prague. On July 3, 1866, two of the Prussian armies attacked the Austrian positions at Königgrätz (Sadowa). The firepower of the Dreyse breechloading rifle shocked the Austrians: it fired five rounds a minute to the Austrian Miníe's one and a half. And unlike troops using muzzle-loaders, the Prussians could reload and fire while lying down. The Austrians held with counterattacks and heavy artillery fire. Then, in mid-afternoon, the third Prussian army under Crown Prince Frederick arrived on the Austrian

The Making of Germany   1866–71

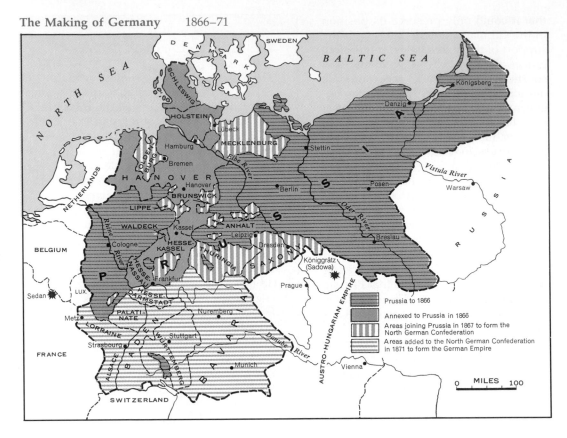

flank, and decided the fate of Germany. The Austrians lost 25,000 dead and wounded and 20,000 prisoners.

Bismarck stepped in to check the enthusiasm of king and generals for a push on Vienna. Further fighting would only provoke French intervention, without serving any useful purpose. Bismarck insisted that Protestant Prussia could not successfully absorb the Catholic German populations that the total destruction of the Habsburg Empire would deliver to it. The king and Moltke yielded grudgingly. By the treaties of Nikolsburg and Prague (July–August 1866) Austria renounced any role in north Germany, acquiesced in Prussia's absorption of Schleswig-Holstein, Hanover, Hesse-Cassel, and Frankfurt, and agreed to the dissolution of the German Confederation of 1815 and the creation in its place of a North German Confederation under Prussia. To avoid French intervention Bismarck left nominal independence to defeated Baden, Württemberg,

and Bavaria. But he fastened upon them military alliances that in wartime made their armies mere appendages of Prussia's.

Domestically, the war of 1866 ended the Prussian constitutional conflict. Elections, held on the day of Königgrätz, returned a conservative majority. Victory intoxicated the remaining liberals, who gladly accepted Bismarck's promises that he would in future respect the Chamber's budget rights. With the liberals as allies, Bismarck now molded the North German Confederation, the pattern for the German nation-state. He personally supervised the drafting of the new constitution. It played off a universal male suffrage *Reichstag* or lower house against representatives of the princes in the upper house. Bismarck, as Prussian prime minister and foreign minister and as chancellor of the new Confederation, held the balance. Prussia had conquered Germany, and Bismarck Prussia.

The Struggle for Mastery in Europe, 1867–71

Yet the North German Confederation was not the Germany of the dreams of the German national movement. Bismarck himself, while no nationalist, aspired from the beginning to draw the south German states into his greater Prussia. Unfortunately the economic attraction of the Prussian *Zollverein*, of a unified national market with uniform tariffs, weights, measures, and law codes, was not enough to overcome south German particularism. "Württemberg wants to remain Württemberg as long as it has the power," said that state's chief minister—a sentiment heartily echoed in Bavaria and even Baden.

Bismarck therefore once more fell back on foreign policy to drive domestic affairs. Napoleon III offered the occasion. Disgruntled at his 1866 miscalculation, smarting over the 1867 defeat of his hare-brained scheme for an empire in Mexico (see p. 764), and under increasing pressure from a liberal public opinion he had helped create by loosening his control of press and politics in the early 1860s, Napoleon III too sought a foreign victory. An initial public clash in early 1867 over a French plan to buy Luxemburg from its ruler, the king of Holland, ended in humiliation for Napoleon. Both France and Prussia came to consider war inevitable as soon as frantic French military reforms were complete.

War came in 1870. The candidacy of a junior member of the Prussian royal house for the vacant throne of Spain offered the occasion. Bismarck had pressed the plan in secret, as one more small diplomatic blow against France, but he could not have known from the beginning that it would lead to war. When the candidacy prematurely became public, the French ambassador visited William I at the summer watering place of Ems, and impertinently demanded that Prussia renounce the candidacy "forever." William I, miffed, cut the interview short. When Bismarck received the foreign office tele-

gram describing the interview, he asked Moltke if the army was ready. The chief of the general staff replied that the sooner war came, the greater Prussia's relative strength. Bismarck then edited the "Ems telegram" for release to the press. The edited version implied that William I had curtly refused the French demand and had ruled out further negotiation, thus handing France a major diplomatic humiliation.

In Paris, Napoleon III's ministers and supporters reacted as Bismarck had expected. Hysterical at the visible loss since 1866 of France's leading role in Europe, they clamored "To Berlin!" France declared war on July 19, 1870, without allies. Austria had no stomach for a rematch. Italy wisely chose to remain neutral, despite the childlike enthusiasm of Victor Emmanuel II for war, any war. Russia's only thought was to free itself of the degrading Black Sea naval disarmament imposed after the Crimean War. Britain watched impotently.

Moltke's mobilization timetables once again delivered three superlatively equipped Prussian and south German armies, now totalling 380,000 men, to their railheads. The French muddled about in tragic disorder. They now had a better breechloading rifle than the Germans, the Chassepot, and a secret weapon, the *mitrailleuse*, a primitive machine gun. But the cast-steel artillery of Krupp outclassed anything the French could field, and French logistics were chaotic.

The Germans drove across the border and pushed the French back in a series of punishing battles. At Gravelotte-St. Privat, on August 18, the elite Prussian Guard corps attacked uphill across open ground. The Chassepots of the French killed or wounded 8,000 Prussians, mostly in the space of 20 minutes. Fortunately for the Germans, the ineptly led French then fell back on the fortified city of Metz. Leaving a force to screen the city, the German armies pressed on to squash Napoleon III's reserve army against the Belgian border. Desperate breakout attempts by French cavalry failed in a hail of Prussian rifle fire. The French charges were magnificent, but no longer war; the armies of Europe were beginning to discover that firepower killed. On September 2, 1870, Napoleon III surrendered his army at Sedan.

Unlike Königgrätz in 1866, Sedan did not end the war. This last of Bismarck's wars was no "cabinet war" but rather the first of three Franco-German national wars that tore Europe apart and destroyed its world position. Paris, besieged, resisted under increasingly radical leadership. A French republic based on Tours and then on Bordeaux raised new armies in the style of 1793. Guerrillas, including the intrepid Garibaldi, harried Prussian patrols and rail lines. The Prussians replied by summarily executing civilians and burning farms and villages. Those brutal measures the normally humane Bismarck, after the third bottle of looted champagne, heartily approved.

Finally, after much death, destruction, and bitterness, the French agreed to an armistice in January and signed a peace treaty at Frankfurt on May 10, 1871. The war had cost perhaps 190,000 lives. Bismarck exacted an indemnity equivalent to a billion dollars, and annexed Alsace-Lorraine, whose inhabitants mostly spoke indeterminate dialects but considered themselves French. That least moderate of his peace settlements was the consequence of the nationalist furor Bismarck had helped stir up—to compel the south German states to put their weight behind the war effort and to acquiesce in greater unity. And Bismarck achieved that last objective even before the end of war with France. With bribes from the funds of the dispossessed house of Hanover, Bismarck overcame the scruples of the king of Bavaria, the last and most powerful holdout. On January 18, 1871, in Louis XIV's Hall of Mirrors in the Versailles palace, Bismarck had William I proclaimed German Emperor, or *Kaiser*.

Bismarck had said in 1866 that "If there is to be revolution, we would rather make it than suffer it." He had made it. His "revolution from above" had produced a German national state that dwarfed its neighbors militarily

Europe in 1871

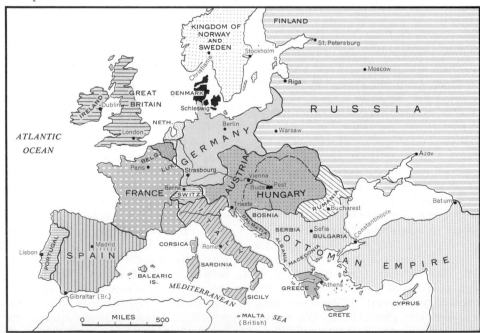

and was soon to do so economically. Internally, Bismarck had struck a compromise with middle class national liberalism, a compromise that preserved Junker power far into the twentieth century. What he deliberately did not do was to fulfill all aims of the German national movement.

Except for the annexation of Alsace-Lorraine, Bismarck had struck compromises with the defeated. He had accepted limits. He had left the Catholic Austrian Germans outside his Protestant-dominated "lesser Germany." The unsatiated aspiration of many German nationalists for a "greater Germany" spanning the continent from Schleswig to Trieste and from Strasbourg to Riga might yet undo Bismarck's work.

Western and central Europe had traveled a long road since 1815. Revolution, the legacy of 1789, was played out. A final despairing outbreak, the "Paris Commune" of March–May 1871, succumbed to the troops of the French republic soon after France's peace with Germany. The republic shot 20,000 insurgents and deported another 10,000 to a tropical death in French Guyana. The myths and realities of the new nation-state— flag-bedecked ceremonies, conscription, elections, compulsory schooling, bureaucracies, and railroads—filled the place of revolution. The power of the nation-state held great potential for good, for the prosperity and freedom of its populations, but also for evil.

Suggestions for Further Reading

General

A brilliant introducton to the period up to 1848 is E. J. Hobsbawm, *The Age of Revolution, 1789–1848* (1962). For more detail, see F. A. Artz, *Reaction and Revolution, 1814–1832* (1934); W. L. Langer, *Political and Social Upheaval, 1832–1852* (1969); and J. Droz, *Europe between Revolutions, 1815–1848* (1968). For the various powers, see especially A. Briggs, *The Making of Modern England* (1959); A. Cobban, *A History of Modern France*, Vol. II (1957); T. S. Hamerow, *Restoration, Revolution, Reaction: Economics and Politics in Germany, 1815–1871* (1958); A. J. P. Taylor, *The Habsburg Monarchy, 1809–1918* (1948); and the sardonic and brilliant R. Pipes, *Russia under the Old Regime* (1975).

Europe to 1848

On international politics before 1848, H. Nicolson, *The Congress of Vienna: A study in Allied Unity, 1812–1822* (1946), and H. G. Schenk, *The Aftermath of the Napoleonic Wars* (1947), remain serviceable. The most successful overviews of 1848–49 are P. Robertson, *Revolutions of 1848: A Social History* (1952), and P. Stearns, *1848: The Revolutionary Tide in Europe* (1974). T. S. Hamerow, *Restoration, Revolution, Reaction* (1958), is outstanding on Germany. L. Namier, *1848: The Revolution of the Intellectuals* (1964), stresses the emergence of savagely competing nationalisms; see also, in general, E. Kedourie, *Nationalism* (1960).

Europe after 1848

The best survey of the post-1848 period is again E. J. Hobsbawm, *The Age of Capital, 1848–1875* (1975). A. J. P. Taylor's brilliant *The Struggle for Mastery in Europe, 1848–1918* (1954), is still the best synthesis of nineteenth-century international politics. M. S. Anderson, *The Eastern Question* (1966), expertly chronicles the decay of the Ottoman Empire and its consequences. On the Crimean War and after, see both W. E. Mosse, *The Rise and Fall of the Crimean System, 1855–1871* (1967), and P. W. Schroeder, *Austria, Great Britain, and the Crimean War* (1979). For France after 1848, see J. M. Thompson, *Louis Napoleon and the Second Empire* (1955). D. Mack Smith, *Cavour and Garibaldi, 1860: A Study in Political Conflict* (1954), *Victor Emmanuel, Cavour, and the Risorgimento* (1971), and *Cavour* (1985), are excellent on the creation of the Italian state. On Bismarck's revolution from above, see especially O. Pflanze, *Bismarck and the Development of Germany: The Period of Unification 1815–1871* (1963), and L. Gall, *Bismarck* (1986); T. S. Hamerow, *The Social Foundations of German Unification, 1858–1871* (1969), supplies the domestic background. On the military events, D. E. Showalter, *Railroads and Rifles: Soldiers, Technology, and the Unification of Germany* (1975); G. Craig, *The Battle of Königgrätz* (1965); and M. Howard, *The Franco-Prussian War* (1961), are excellent. H. Strachan, *European Armies and the Conduct of War* (1983), provides a useful overview.

27

Europe and the World in the Nineteenth Century

*I*n the wider world, the nineteenth century was the century of Britain. Its unchallengeable superiority at sea after Trafalgar (1805) ensured that the peace outside Europe would be a *pax Britannica*. Its growing industrial might and demographic prowess led to an expansion, virtually constant throughout the century, of the area under the British flag. By 1900 the British Empire ruled 23 percent of the world's land surface and 20 percent of its population. It was Britain that for the first time in history united most of humanity in a world market that pulsed with the erratic rhythms of the business cycle. The force of that market, more than anything else, drove to its culmination the Western conquest of the world begun in 1492.

But Britain's effortless superiority in the first decades after 1815 did not last. Its economic lead slackened as the "followers" industrialized, with political consequences in the wider world. By the 1840s and 1850s American power was beginning to make its weight felt in North America and the Caribbean. As early as the 1850s America's maritime reach touched Japan. Northern victory in the U.S. Civil War meant that Britain faced an industrial giant which it could not match in the long run. And by the 1880s European rivals were appearing in strength in Africa and East Asia: France in West Africa, Indochina and China; Germany in Africa; and Russia in north China. By the end of the century a non-European power, Japan, had risen to dominate northeast Asia. That force was a sign of the impermanence of the garish empires British and Europeans had patched together. For along with the world

The impact of Western technology on the wider world. The East India Company's steamer *Nemesis* annihilates a Chinese fleet, 1841.

market, along with gunboats, Maxim guns, rum, and Bibles, the Europeans brought nationalism to the wider world.

THE BRITISH WORLD EMPIRE

The 1815 Settlement outside Europe

Britain had consolidated its first empire in the Seven Years' War. The loss of the American Colonies and the inconclusive war of 1812, embarrassing to both parties, had given the British "official mind" a sharp lesson in the limitations of British power in North America. But elsewhere Britain was unchallenged. Wars in India after 1798 confirmed the verdict of Plassey (1757): Britain was paramount on the subcontinent.

That immense land empire in South Asia provided both the troops and the commercial and strategic motives for further British acquisitions throughout the century. By 1815 the requirements of Imperial communications with India appeared secure. Britain held or had recently acquired title to a chain of bases controlling the decisive routes to India: Gibraltar and Malta, Ascension and St. Helena in the distant South Atlantic, and the Cape of Good Hope, Mauritius, and Ceylon seized from French and Dutch. Singapore, commanding the straits between the Indian Ocean and the China Seas, followed in 1819.

British naval supremacy had far-reaching effects. It largely ended piracy, from the Caribbean to the seas off Borneo. It also gradually curtailed the African slave trade. Britain had con-

The British Empire in the Nineteenth Century

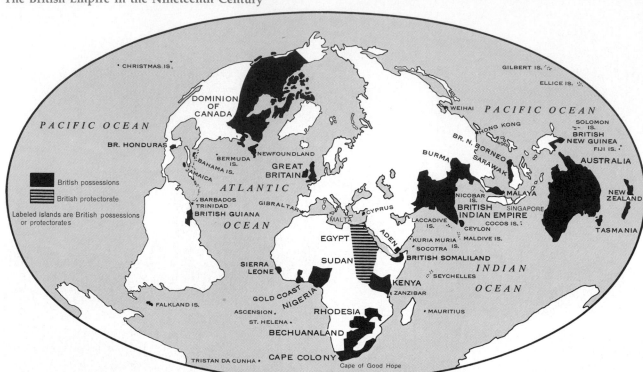

trolled half of that trade by 1800, but had outlawed it by act of Parliament in 1807, thanks to the pressure of crusaders such as the redoubtable William Wilberforce (1759–1833). The United States, despite vociferous objections from its slave states, had followed suit the next year. Castlereagh had secured from the assembled powers at Vienna a declaration condemning the trade. In the ensuing decades, British diplomacy secured the agreement of holdouts such as France, Spain, and Portugal (1820). The frigates of the Royal Navy enforced the ban with increasing success. That did not end the vast forced migration to the new world of perhaps 11.7 million Africans, of whom 1.9 million died on the crossing; only the closing of the slave markets in New Orleans, Havana, and Brazil could do that. But it was a start. And Britain was the first major power in human history to abolish the institution of slavery it-

self, in 1833. For the moment, most others declined to imitate that example.

The Dynamics of British Expansion

Britain soon pressed on beyond the acquisitions of 1815. The forces behind that expansion came not from the corridors of power in London but from the mills and foundries of the Midlands and North, the slums of Birmingham and Liverpool, and the crumbling peasant societies of Scotland and Ireland. Britain imported raw materials and food, especially after the repeal of the Corn Laws in 1846, from the corners of the globe. It exported both goods and people. First came the adventurers, in search of booty or high-profit trade, and the missionaries, intent on imposing Christianity and "progress" on "the heathen." Then came the trading companies with systematic plans for development. To

Singapore, one of Britain's far-flung outposts, in 1830.

states that were capable of aspiring to follow the West's lead—the Ottoman Empire, Egypt, and some societies in Latin America—bankers happily extended credit. Finally, in areas where "white" settlement appeared promising, increasing numbers of emigrants set up societies that replicated the British and North American pattern.

The motive forces behind imperial expansion, economics and demography, remained virtually constant over the century except for a gradual decline in the rates of population increase and of economic growth. What changed, and what accounts for the changes in the forms that expansion took, was the available means. Western expansion had always faced constraints of distance and natural obstacles, disease, the resistance of native societies, and the unwillingness of European governments and peoples to make major sacrifices for empire. These constraints had not prevented the conquest of most of the new world. But between them they had limited European penetration before 1815 to the maritime fringes of Asia and Africa. On the Asian mainland only India had succumbed, after drawing the British in

through its constant internecine strife and rich commerce.

After 1815 the means available to the Europeans and particularly to the British changed dramatically, thanks to the Industrial Revolution. First came steam. From the mid-sixteenth century, European sailing ships with their heavy weight of cannon had outmaneuvered and outfought Arab dhows and Chinese junks on the high seas. But inshore, square-riggers were clumsy and vulnerable to grounding or shifting winds. They could not move up narrow winding rivers against the current, and towing by human strength in the form of ships's boats was pathetically inefficient. European naval power thus ended at the high water mark except where the prize ashore was worth landing a substantial ground force.

Steam opened up the Asian and African coastal waters, and at last allowed European trade and power to penetrate the interior with little effort. The British East India Company gave the first demonstration of the potential of a steam-powered "river war" in its 1824–26 conflict with India's eastern neighbor, the kingdom of Burma. The Com-

Sir William Wilberforce, whose crusade against slavery led to its abolition throughout the British Empire in 1833.

pany's three shallow-draft steam craft carried the war as far as 500 miles up the Irrawaddy River, towing sailing ships, bombarding forts, destroying or capturing Burmese war boats. The British acquired large areas of the Burmese borderlands in the first of three wars that ultimately ended in 1885 with the total conquest of Burma.

Iron-hulled steam vessels were the next step. They demonstrated their worth in the 1839–42 "First Opium War" between Britain and China. River steamers such as the *Nemesis*, built for the East India Company in 1839, forced their way past the antiquated Chinese forts barring the way to Canton. Chinese defenses and war-junks had been adequate against wooden-hulled sailing ships that were unable to maneuver on rivers. Against iron-hulled steamboats they were powerless. The war ended when British steamers penetrated the Yangtze River and cut the Grand Canal, which supplied Beijing (Peking) with rice. Steam played a decisive role, albeit without open conflict, in Commodore Matthew Perry's opening of Japan in 1853–54. And in Indochina the French likewise made good use of river steamers in their conquests in the 1870s and 1880s.

The second of the major innovations that made British and European expansion possible was quinine. Of all the major tropical diseases—dysentery, yellow fever, dengue, and the numerous nameless fevers—the African falciparum strain of malaria is the most consistently lethal. A few lucky and intrepid individuals, such as the Scottish East India surgeon Mungo Park, who explored the river Niger in the 1790s, managed to survive it. But the first attempt to navigate the Niger by steam, in 1832, ended with the death of 40 of 49 whites on the expedition. British garrisons on the Gold Coast between 1817 and 1836 lost 66 percent of their strength each year.

The antimalarial properties of the bark of a South American tree, the chinchona, had long been known or suspected. But not until 1820 did two French chemists isolate the alkaloid, quinine, that produced the effect. By the 1830s production of quinine in quantity had begun; experience soon suggested that it served best when taken regularly as a preventive. In 1854 a Niger expedition returned without casualties. The way for trade far in the interior and ultimately for the extension of European power into all of sub-Saharan Africa lay open.

The final change that permitted the British and European conquest of the world was the revolution in weaponry. The percussion cap in the 1820s and the revolver in the 1840s gave Europeans advantages over Indians or Chinese armed with flintlocks or matchlocks. But the chief advantage of the Europeans, as it had been for 200 years, was their logistical organization, trained leadership, and cohesion under fire. The bayonet remained as important as fire from the one-round-per-minute musket. Skilled enemies with European muskets, such as the Algerians or Afghans who resisted the French and British in the 1830s and 1840s, could turn colonial conquest into an expensive, long-drawn-out, and exceedingly grim business—or block it altogether. The greatest European advantage in weaponry was artillery, which was hard to transport except by river and small help against guerrillas.

Then came the Minié ball, which made the percussion cap rifle a deadly long-range weapon, and breechloaders such as the Sharps, Dreyse, and Chasse-

"Whatever happens we have got / The Maxim Gun, and they have not," wrote the British satirist Hilaire Belloc (1870–1953) of this essential tool of empire.

pot. By the 1880s the box-magazine breech-loading rifle and the Maxim gun gave even small European forces, unless led with gross ineptitude, the ability to destroy native armies many times their size. In the climactic 1898 battle against the forces of the *Mahdi*, the Islamic prophet who had raised the Sudan against the unbeliever, the British lost 48 men. The *Mahdi*'s armies lost 11,000. The Maxim gun made possible a brief age of military tourism.

Demographic and economic forces drove expansion, and the revolutions in transport, tropical medicine, and weaponry made it far easier and cheaper than before. And British expansion was anything but a carefully planned process, obedient to the dictates of London. The government from the beginning held to the utilitarian principle that the best government governed least. Until the 1860s those who made British policy were supremely confident in the benefits of free trade to the world as well as to Britain. Palmerston had summed up that credo in a parliamentary speech in 1842, the year of the British victory that opened China. Commerce would lead "civilization with the one hand and peace with the other"; it would render mankind "happier, wiser, better." Free trade, one of its spokesmen announced in 1846, would make "foreign nations . . . valuable Colonies to us, without imposing on us the responsibility of governing them." The British formula, as two later historians have described it, was "informal empire"—"trade with informal control if possible; trade with rule when necessary."

Increasingly as the century drew on, trade with rule seemed more and more necessary, despite the laments of a central bureaucracy bent on sparing the taxpayers. Trade might make humanity "better"—more like the British—but not in the short term. Trade, and the inevitable missionaries and settlers (where appropriate), invariably required the protection of the flag. Trade required enforceable contracts and security for money and goods. Trade frequently conflicted with the customs, laws, or policies of those upon which it impinged, from the tribal empires of Africa to the long-established states of China and Japan. Trade and the loans that came with it in Latin America, the Ottoman Empire, and Egypt in many cases destroyed the authority of those who accepted it.

Trade, loans, missionaries, and settlers thus generated a variety of unstable mixtures of resistance and collaboration in the native societies affected. The interaction between the outward thrust of Britain and its imitators and the resistance or lack of it in non-Western societies was the mechanism that created the British Empire and completed the Western domination of the world.

Resistance took many forms. Tribes from the Afghans northwest of India to the Kaffirs and Zulus of Africa raided British possessions on the innumerable turbulent frontiers of empire. Religious or proto-nationalist groups—the Mahdists of the Sudan, the Egyptian army, and the Boer farmers of South Africa—rose against the British or against rulers who collaborated with them. And states such as China and Japan adamantly refused to open their markets or provide security for the persons and property of British merchants. Resistance or defiance normally called forth a British response. Typically, London or its agents on the spot intervened militarily to protect what they perceived as existing British interests. The security of India's borders, of the China trade, of the Suez Canal or Cape of Good Hope demanded increasingly strenuous action. That mechanism explains the patchwork character of expansion. Britain did not obey a grand design; it responded when action appeared unavoidable.

Collaboration, the converse of resistance, also helped govern the timing, extent, and ultimate demise of British and Western dominance. One corollary to London's belief in free trade and an absolute minimum of government intervention was the imperative need for willing native auxiliaries. Princes and tribal rulers, native troops, and Western-educated natives might all serve as more or less willing collaborators with Britain's informal empire. The collaborators found themselves caught between two worlds: the British world market and their own societies. If the market pressed too rapidly and disruptively against the native economy, institutions, or religious and cultural traditions, collaborators might fumble and collapse in the face of antiforeign revolt. That presented Britain with unenviable choices: to get out, or to go in at great and continuing expense and rule directly. And the establishment and maintenance of direct rule itself required continuing collaboration from the conquered. When that collaboration faltered or ceased, the European empires ultimately deflated like pricked balloons.

The "White" Colonies

The ideal collaborators were of course the colonists of Canada, Australia, New Zealand, and South Africa. The societies they created, with the exception of those of the French Canadians and Dutch-descended Boer farmers that London acquired in 1763 and 1814, were replicas of Britain. Britain's demographic expansion drove them. The satellite economies of Australia, New Zealand, and eventually Canada in turn contributed wool, grain, meat, and markets to British economic expansion. Along with the United States and Argentina, they also took the majority of Britain's immense overseas investments.

London, after its sad experience with the thirteen American colonies, did its best to defuse discontent by conceding self-government as soon as possible. Canada, the most populous and turbulent, came first. Conquest in the Seven Years' War and the subsequent immigration of large numbers of American loyalists after 1775–83 had disquieted the deeply rooted Catholic society of Norman peasants that France had planted in Québec. An effort, in the Constitutional Act of 1791, to give each of the two nationalities its own province failed to quiet unrest.

In 1837 the suppression of a Québecquois rising and a revolt in the English-speaking province of Upper Canada (now Ontario) required British troops. In the aftermath, the Earl of Durham, one of the authors of Britain's 1832 Reform Bill, became governor-general of the colonies. He recommended representative self-government of a unified province in which English-speakers would swamp the French. London adopted his recommendations in the 1840s, but the French-English conflict inevitably persisted. By the time of the U.S. Civil War, the need of a strong central government to promote internal cohesion, defense, and railway development was obvious. In 1867, after long negotiation between Canadian leaders, Parliament in London passed the British North America Act. Québec once again received its own administration, within the "Dominion of Canada," a federation that included the maritime provinces. Britain happily conceded to the colonials the management of their own affairs, including defense against rebellion and Indian raids.

The invention of the status of self-governing "Dominion" was decisive for Australia and New Zealand. The various territories of Australia, which had served from 1788 as a dumping ground for English convicts, received representative self-government in 1851–55. By then free immigrants far outnumbered the descendants of those deported to Botany Bay. In 1901 London was happy to concede Dominion status to the Commonwealth of Australia, a continent spanned by railroads and rich in wool, grain, and gold. The independence of New Zealand was a slower process, largely because of a series of exceedingly unpleasant land wars with the native Maoris, a fierce and tenacious Polynesian warrior people. The land-hungry settlers refused to dispense with London's protection before British troops broke Maori resistance. Self-government nevertheless

		Great Mutiny 1857	Indian Independence 1947
1756 1763			
Seven Years' War	British East India Company Control (Mughals keep imperial title)	Direct Rule by British Government	

came in 1876 and Commonwealth status in 1907.

The Indian Empire

In India the British, alone of the colonial powers, took steps in the nineteenth century to prepare the way for the ultimate independence of the non-European peoples they had conquered. The process was neither swift nor peaceful. To protect and extend its trade the East India Company had succeeded the Mughal emperors as paramount power on the subcontinent. That thrust culminated in the Third Mahratta War of 1817–18; the Company broke for good the power of the warrior Hindu states, the Mahratta confederacy. By that point the Company itself had ceased to be a private entity with a monopoly on India's trade. As early as 1773 the crown had taken for itself the power to appoint a governor-general. In 1784 London had asserted control of the Company's political activities. In 1833 the Company lost its trading function entirely; henceforth its only mission was to govern India through the elite Indian Civil Service.

The end of the Company trade monopoly and the extension of British direct rule intensified pressure on the native societies of the subcontinent. The Company had been content to leave Indian social and religious custom undistrubed except for ill-considered attempts to rationalize the tax structure and introduce Western notions of property law in place of the old relationships between peasant community and overlord. Once the Company lost its monopoly, the way was open for the ever-intensifying penetration of independent British merchants and missionaries. Pressure in Parliament and in the British press for the reform of Indian society mounted.

By the 1830s the reformers had won. A sense of mission impelled these disciples of Bentham: India was theirs in trust, to Westernize and prepare for self-government at some point in the far distant future. The great British historian Thomas Babington Macaulay, one of the reformers, spelled out the goal: to create "a class of persons Indian in colour and blood, but English in tastes, opinions, and intellects." And Karl Marx, from the depths of the British Museum library, celebrated in 1853 newspaper articles the creation in India of "a fresh class . . . endowed with the requirements for government and imbued with European science." Britain's mission, he triumphantly announced, was "the annihilation of the old Asiatic society, and the laying of the material foundations of Western society in Asia." Old Company hands had misgivings about this revolution from above and about the blind self-confidence that drove it. "Englishmen are as great fanatics in politics as Mohommedans in religion. They suppose that no country can be saved without English institutions," fumed a former governor of Madras.

The reform effort culminated with the 1848–56 administration of governor-general Lord Dalhousie, the very personification of utilitarian enterprise and "progress." Dalhousie introduced the telegraph, built the famous Grand Trunk Road across northern India, and planned the railways that by 1905 were the longest and best in Asia, with 33,000 miles of track. His irrigation canals made vast areas of northern India fertile.

In politics, a field less tractable than engineering, Dalhousie's messianic faith in the benefits of Western civilization made him an annexationist. He completed the conquest of the Sikhs of the Punjab, seized Sind in the west and lower Burma in the east, and gradually

A scene from the Great Mutiny, 1857: British firepower and discipline defeats the sepoys at Cawnpore.

annexed those Indian states under Company protection whose thrones fell vacant. British rule now brought ever-increasing missionary activity, equality before the law that disrupted these societies of rigidly demarcated castes, and interference with Hindu religious customs such as *sati*, the ritual burning of widows on their husbands' funeral pyres.

By 1857, the strain upon native society had grown intolerable. Over wide areas of northern India the population, from lord to peasant, had become convinced that Britain's ultimate purpose was to abolish Indian society and religion, whether Hindu or Moslem. The occasion but not the cause of the ensuing explosion was the foolish introduction into the Company's Indian army of Minié rifles that took paper cartridges waterproofed with tallow. Loading required biting the cartridge open. And when rumors, later confirmed, flew that the manufacturers had used tallow made from a blend of pig and cow fat, the *sepoys* or native soldiers faced an appalling dilemma. The cow was sacred to Hinduism, the pig forbidden to Moslems. The troops could bite the cartridge and suffer loss of caste if Hindu or defilement if Moslem. Or they could betray their deeply felt oath to the army.

Many chose mutiny, and rose against the British with the support of much of the population of the dusty plains around Delhi. Native leaders harked back to the proud days of Mahrattas and Mughals, and sought to drive the British from India. The *sepoys* committed numerous atrocities against British prisoners, women, and children. The British, isolated and fearful amid an immense and largely hostile population, fought a pitiless race war. They celebrated the reconquest of Delhi by lashing *sepoy* prisoners across gun barrels and blasting them to shreds. London dissolved the Company, drastically reorganized its Indian army, made India a possession of the crown, and publicly disclaimed any intention of tampering with its subjects' religions.

The Great Mutiny of 1857–58 was a shock not only to the British rulers of India, but to British imperial self-confidence. It drove home the obvious: non-Western societies did not automatically take to Western values. It revealed that the reformers' "fresh class" of English-educated collaborators lacked roots in the Indian population. The English henceforth proceeded with greater caution and infinitely lower expectations. Stability not social revolution became their goal. Creeping annexation ceased. The Indian subject princes, who for the most part had remained loyal, preserved their possessions into the twentieth century. Britain henceforth confined its activities primarily to administration, engineering, and the defense of India's borders.

Nevertheless, the reformers succeeded in the long term. The Great Mutiny was the last sizable traditional Indian revolt. English-educated Indians took an increasing role in the junior ranks of the administration, in the new English-speaking law courts, and in the creation of textile, coal, and steel industries. By the 1880s a modern Indian public opinion, both Hindu and Moslem, had come into being. The foundation, with help from British liberals, of the Indian Congress party in 1885 marked the birth of the force that ultimately succeeded the British. The Indians that Britain had educated in turn invented Indian nationalism.

Britain in Africa

Except for the Cape Colony and a few fever-ridden trading stations on the west coast, Britain in 1815 had little use for Africa. That changed. The penetration of British palm-oil traders, missionaries, and antislavery reformers, especially after mid-century, brought increasing clashes with indigenous forces. In West Africa, the warlike Ashanti kingdom in the hinterland of the Gold Coast was the main barrier. A punitive expedition in 1874 checked its power, but final annexation did not ensue until 1896. In East Africa, British attempts to put down the slave trade destroyed the authority of Britain's client, the Sultan of Zanzibar. That drew London ever deeper into the affairs of East Africa.

But the extension of British rule to much of Africa followed from two great crises in the 1880s and 1890s, both connected with the security of the routes to India. In North Africa the stake was the great canal across the Suez isthmus that the Saint-Simonian engineer and promoter, Ferdinand de Lesseps, had completed in 1869. In 1876 the Khedivate, the regime of the successors of Mohammed Ali, collapsed in bankruptcy; it had attempted to modernize Egypt on European credit. The French and British governments took command of Egyptian finances and taxation to see their bondholders paid.

That intrusion was the latest of the series of defeats and exactions at the hands of unbelievers since Bonaparte. It generated a radical response; unlike the Indian Mutiny, that response was recognizably modern. In 1882 a movement in the partially Westernized Egyptian army overthrew its own government and defied the West to which that government appeared too subservient. The movement's ideological basis was a modernizing current of Islam; its program, Egypt for the Egyptians; its leader, the charismatic Colonel Ahmed Arabi Pasha.

That situation, now all too familiar, took Britain and France aback. A joint naval demonstration of the traditional sort merely provoked a massacre of for-

The strategic Suez Canal, in the 1890s.

eigners at Alexandria. The British responded with cannon fire. That was the point of no return: British prestige was committed, the prestige required to hold India. The pacific Liberal cabinet of William Ewart Gladstone (see p. 784) unhappily landed an army to restore a suitably cooperative Egyptian government. The French chamber and cabinet had no need of a route to India, and refused to follow.

The British convincingly crushed Arabi's army, and found themselves ruling Egypt. To Gladstone's dismay, the old techniques of informal empire no longer served. British interests appeared too great, Egyptian resistance too fanatical. If Britain withdrew, its discredited clients would again collapse, leaving Canal and debt at the mercy of anti-Western forces. Britain therefore stayed, despite the increasing hostility of the French, who illogically concluded that the British had slyly usurped the Egyptian empire that Bonaparte had failed to bequeath to France.

Worse, Egypt was not self-contained: the mighty river Nile upon which its agriculture depended rose in the Sudan, far to the south. That province was in theory Egypt's, held through isolated garrisons. But in 1881 an Islamic figure even more charismatic than Arabi had arisen there and had begun to weld the Dervish religious orders into an army and a state. The *Mahdi*, Mohammed Ahmad, swept the Egyptian garrisons out of the Sudan in 1883. In 1885 he destroyed at Khartoum

Nationalism against the West: Ahmed Arabi Pasha of Egypt (1839–1911).

The Scramble for Africa   1884/1914

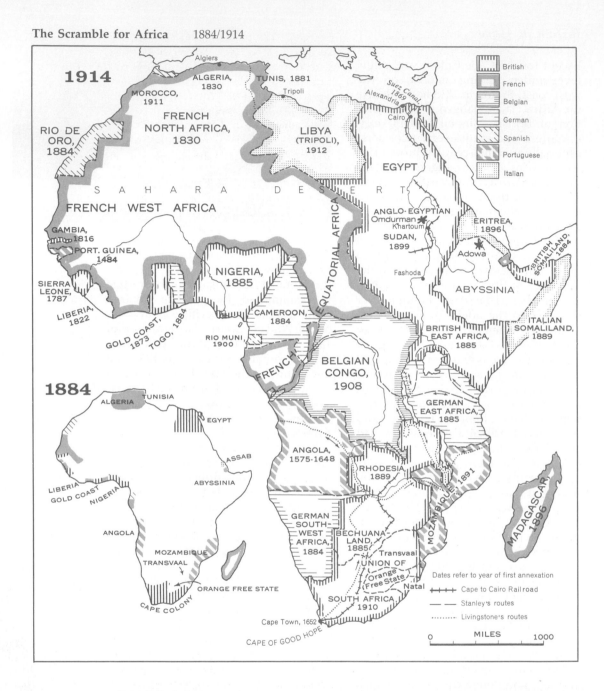

a British-led force under an eccentric soldier of fortune, General "Chinese" Gordon.

Gladstone, lamenting his "Egyptian bondage," left the *Mahdi* for later British governments to deal with. But British occupation of Egypt had unleashed French acquisitiveness in West Africa. Other powers also took a hand. The resulting "scramble" for protectorates and annexations divided the African continent, at least on paper, in the 20 years after 1882. In West Africa Britain left much to the French but kept Nigeria and a number of smaller river colonies. In East Africa the British were less generous to their rivals. Proximity to India impelled them to keep most of the coast, except for areas conceded, graciously or not, to Italians and Germans.

And a second great crisis far to the south drove Britain to extend its control still further. Britain's principal stake at the Cape of Good Hope was also in origin strategic. The Cape was an indispensable base, "the true centre of the Empire . . . clear of the Suez complications, almost equally distant from Australia, China, India, Gibraltar, the West Indies, and the Falklands," as a Colonial Office official put it in the 1870s. Unfortunately, the Cape had a land frontier. It also had non-British white inhabitants: the Dutch settlers that the Dutch East India Company had planted in 1652 to provide supplies for its shipping.

British relations with the Cape Dutch after annexation were amicable; the colony received representative self-government in 1872. Dealings with the Boer ("peasant") farmers of the inland frontier were less satisfactory; British humanitarians frowned on the Boer habit of enslaving the Africans. Between 1835 and 1844, hungry for land and determined to preserve a white supremacy they considered God had ordained, the Boers streamed north across the Vaal River and out of British control. The climax of that "Great Trek" came at the battle of Blood River in 1838. A Boer wagon train defeated the onslaught of the Zulu king Dingaan, heir of the great Shaka, who had created the mightiest army south of the Sahara. To the "*Trekboers*," reared in the stern Old Testament faith of the Dutch Reformed Church, victory proved that God had chosen them.

The twin Boer republics of the Orange Free State and Transvaal were thus in their very origins a reaction to British penetration, a reaction almost tribal in character and intensity. London hoped to pressure the Boer republics into a Cape federation that would eventually become a Dominion. Britain proclaimed the annexation of the Transvaal in 1877 and defended it against a new assault of the Zulu regi-

ments in 1879. The Zulus lost, but in the process crushed a British force at Isandhlwana; the Boers bid for independence once the British had quelled the Zulu threat. At Majuba Hill in 1881, Transvaal Boer rifles picked off an isolated and ill-led British detachment. Gladstone conceded independence to the Transvaal while retaining only a vague right of veto over Boer relations with foreign powers. Unlike Egypt, the stakes were not high enough to warrant a major British commitment, and Boer nationalism was clearly too tough to take on lightly.

Gladstone's retreat postponed the struggle for mastery in South Africa. That development, like the climax of the British-French struggle for the Nile and the crises in East Asia around the turn of the century, is best left for discussion in its international context (see pp. 821–23). But even before the second round against the Boers, and despite doubts and hesitations in London, Britain had annexed most of a new empire in Africa. Egyptian revolt, the fanaticism of the *Mahdi*, and Boer proto-nationalism had marked the limits of informal influence. Africa's resistance drove Britain to defend by ever broader acquisitions what Britain already held. And the growing rivalry from the other European powers increasingly confirmed the British on the path they had chosen.

BRITAIN'S EUROPEAN RIVALS

The other European powers inevitably sought to imitate Britain. But each power did so in its own way. And they ultimately did so at Britain's pleasure, for neither separately nor in concert could they challenge British naval supremacy.

French imperialism, which created the second largest of the nineteenth-century European empires, was primarily military in inspiration. It began in 1830 with an attack on the pirate kingdom of Algiers. The moribund

Colonial troops: An Algerian officer in the French army of the 1880s.

Bourbon dynasty sought the prestige of conquest; Louis Philippe inherited some coastal outposts and a hinterland that resisted fiercely. The French army, in almost 20 years of bloody campaigns and hair-raising atrocities, prevailed by 1847 against the canny resistance leader Abd-el-Kader.

The Algerian outpost provided security for French Mediterranean shipping. Its conquest both demanded and gave a home to that quintessential French colonial force, the Foreign Legion. It offered a training ground for generations of colonial officers. And thanks to French and European immigration and agricultural settlement, Algeria almost began to pay for itself after the suppression of a further Moslem uprising in 1870.

But Algeria was no product of trade and industry, the power behind British expansion. And even if the French had aspired to an informal commercial empire in North Africa, Moslem intransigence would have thwarted them. The French empire did have economic functions. But its reason for existence lay above all in the belief of successive French governments before 1870 that France's claim to European primacy required colonial perquisites. And the loss of that primacy in 1870 made colonial self-assertion a welcome compensation for European humiliation.

Under Napoleon III, General Louis Faidherbe applied proven Algerian methods to make Senegal, France's most important West African outpost, a major source of native troops. In 1858–59 Napoleon made good longstanding French influence in Vietnam by seizing Saigon and Da Nang in reprisal for native killings of French missionaries. In the 1860s France annexed the southern areas of Vietnam. Napoleon III exploited the U.S. Civil War to impose with Foreign Legion bayonets an Austrian Archduke as Emperor of Mexico. Union victory and Mexican resistance brought French withdrawal and the Archduke's death by firing squad in 1867.

The Franco-Prussian war inevitably imposed a pause. But by the early 1880s France had again begun to expand. It forced a protectorate on Tunis, Algeria's difficult neighbor, in 1881. After the humiliation unintentionally inflicted on France in the Egyptian crisis, French consuls and officers on the West African rivers began feverishly staking claims that Paris until then had been unwilling to back. Collision with a series of unbending Moslem theocracies in the interior compelled the French to make good with Maxim guns their paper pretensions. The colonial army and France's formidable naval infantry happily bent to that task. By 1902 France had extended its control from Algeria to the Gulf of Guinea, and had annexed Madagascar on the Indian Ocean flank of the Cape of Good Hope.

The German and Italian empires had even less economic function than the French; as latecomers Germany and Italy could only aspire to territories so worthless that Britain and France had passed them by. Bismarck had utter contempt for the German colonial enthusiasts who had inevitably emerged after 1871. He nevertheless unleashed them in 1884–85 to claim Togo, Cameroons, South-West Africa, and German East Africa while he created artificial friction with London. At the 1884–85 Berlin colonial conference he also helped give the brutal King Leopold II of Belgium control of the Congo basin; British-French rivalry benefited other powers besides Berlin.

Bismarck's purposes in picking a quarrel with Britain were diplomatic and domestic, not colonial: rapprochement with France, a thumping nationalist vote in the 1884 elections, and reinsurance against dismissal by the mildly liberal and pro-British Crown Prince Frederick when William I ultimately died. Those passing needs saddled Germany with expensive and useless African territories and an assortment of Pacific islands. Bismarck's successors acquired a Chinese port. That unsatisfactory empire did not disillusion German opinion; it whetted its appetite for larger things.

Italy, as the least of the great powers, found even slimmer pickings than Germany. It acquired the Red Sea port of Assab in 1882 and asserted a protectorate over the Coptic Christian kingdom of Ethiopia in 1889. The Amhara rulers of Ethiopia appeared to acquiesce, then resisted further Italian encroachment. Menelik, the emperor, acquired large stores of European rifles and the assistance of French experts. On March 1, 1896, at Adowa he dealt the Italians the worst defeat inflicted upon a would-be European colonizer in the nineteenth century. In the face of an enemy that outnumbered them by five to one, the Italians had divided their forces and had struck out on divergent routes across unmapped mountains. They lost 6,000 dead and 4,000 wounded or captured; political chaos at home precluded any renewal of the war. Italy contented itself for a generation with the coastal enclaves of Eritrea and Somalia.

Finally, Russia rounded out an empire in central and east Asia in the course of the nineteenth century. That process was like French expansion in that it was military, and like that of the United States in that it pursued geopolitical "manifest destiny." The Crimean War checked Russia in Europe but sharpened its appetites elsewhere. In 1853–54 it annexed large areas around the Aral Sea. In the next 20 years it methodically crushed the central Asian nomad peoples and the surviving Tartar Khanates of Bukhara, Khiva, and Kokand. By 1884 Russia had reached the Afghan border. Further east, it pressed into Mongolia. And in 1858 and 1860, by the army's bayonets and the treaties of Aigun and Beijing (Peking), it seized from the Chinese the Amur and maritime provinces opposite Japan. At the southern tip of the maritime province it founded a naval base with a name that was a program: Vladivostok, "Ruler of the East." And from 1891 Russia began pushing a railroad

---

Tocqueville Foresees the World Domination of Russia and America 1835

There are at the present time two great nations in the world, which started from different points, but seem to tend towards the same end. I allude to the Russians and the Americans. . . . All other nations seem to have nearly reached their natural limits, and they have only to maintain their power; but these are still in the act of growth. . . . These alone are proceeding with ease and celerity along a path to which no limit can be perceived. The American struggles against the obstacles that nature opposes to him; the adversaries of the Russian are men. The former combats the wilderness and savage life; the latter, civilization with all its arms. The conquests of the American are therefore gained by the plowshare; those of the Russian by the sword. The Anglo-American relies upon personal interest to accomplish his ends and gives free scope to the unguided strength and common sense of the people; the Russian centers all the authority of society in a single arm. The principal instrument of the former is freedom; of the latter, servitude. Their starting-point is different and their courses are not the same; yet each of them seems marked by the will of Heaven to sway the destinies of half the globe.

From Alexis de Tocqueville, *Democracy in America* (New York: Vintage Books, 1953), Vol. I, p. 434.

---

across Siberia toward Vladivostok, to make that program reality.

A SECOND EUROPE: THE UNITED STATES

The Young Republic

By that point an entirely different sort of state had reached the New World's Pacific shores. The United States that emerged from the Revolutionary War of 1775–83 and the Constitutional Convention of 1787 was a unique experiment. It was a new state, not founded through the slow processes of dynastic accretion and military-bureaucratic consolidation that had made the states of Europe. Its sovereign people—"We the people of the United States"—did not claim to be a "nation," a political unit preordained by language, culture, and territory. America's language and culture were initially British and its territorial boundaries lost in the endless forests of the Appalachians and the swamps of southern Georgia. The foundation of the new state was principles: "We hold these truths to be self-evident, that all Men are created equal, that they are endowed by their Creator with certain unalienable rights, that among these are Life, Liberty, and the Pursuit of Happiness. . . . " The securing of those natural rights was the purpose of American government, the unity of the thirteen colonies was the means.

To their purpose the framers of the Constitution brought an understanding of human nature and of political practice laboriously acquired in town and county meetings, state assemblies, and the Revolutionary War. More experienced than the French revolutionaries who followed, the framers took a pessimistic view of humanity. James Madison of Virginia, one of the Constitution's principal architects, put it well: "If men were angels, no government would be necessary." Majority will unchecked by law meant tyranny over both individuals and states. Madison and others therefore built into the Constitution what a great American historian has described as a "harmonious system of mutual frustration": the separation of powers.

Legislature, executive, and judiciary checked and balanced one another, as did the new federal government and the thirteen states. Within Congress, the indirectly elected Senate moderated the potentially impetuous House of Representatives. Neither majority whim in Congress, nor the authority of that elected monarch, the president, nor any caprice of the Supreme Court's judges could prevail for long without cooperation of the other branches. That system, so seemingly cumbersome in theory, in practice usually forced the deliberate creation of the compromise and consensus without which democratic polities fall into incoherence or despotism. The Constitution's paragraphs did not guarantee the success of the American experiment: that depended above all on the common sense, civic spirit, and political experience of the citizenry. But it did provide a framework that used those qualities to advantage.

The Constitution was above all a democratic document, although its framers were men of property and social distinction, and it made allowances for the South's "peculiar institution," slavery. In order to secure the assent of the southern states, the framers counted each slave, for purposes of apportioning representation, as three-fifth of a white. Despite that concession to inequality, the Constitution swiftly developed in the direction of yet greater democracy. To overcome opposition to its adoption, Madison and others put forward a further series of guarantees that the new federal government would not replicate the "tyranny" of George III. The first ten amendments or Bill of Rights, adopted in 1789–91, placed the rights of the individual against the state at the center of the new political system. Those rights gradually grew as the country expanded and the political weight of the socially stratified east coast states decreased. Most states that had restricted voting through religious tests or property qualifications enacted universal male suffrage by the 1820s.

The founders gradually passed from the scene, leaving a vacuum that political parties ultimately filled. The first alignment of importance was the "Federalists," whose advocacy of a strong central government helped push the Constitution through. Their leading light was Alexander Hamilton, first Secretary of the Treasury and prophet of the economic development of the United States. Their program implied the supremacy of industry and commerce over agriculture and of the cultivated elite over the masses. Thomas Jefferson and Madison of Virginia formed a "Democratic-Republican" party that opposed Hamilton with a vision of an egalitarian farmers' republic; great cities, Jefferson wrote, were "pestilential to the morals, the health, and the liberties of man."

That conflict of ideologies and interests persisted throughout the century and beyond. It soon became at least in part a sectional division. The egalitarian frontier triumphed in the 1828 election, the first fought by recognizable national parties. Andrew Jackson, "the People's Choice" against the Eastern elites, was ironically a Kentucky magnate. But his overwhelming popular vote victory at the head of the Democratic party was a mighty step toward the emergence of the system of two national parties, powerful engines of consensus, that still exists.

By 1828 the United States was well on its way to territorial consolidation. Jefferson, as president in 1803, had bought from Napoleon the Louisiana territory that commanded the mouth of the Mississippi and stretched west to the Rocky Mountains and north to the still unmarked Canadian border. In the aftermath of the war of 1812, Britain and the United States agreed to demilitarize the Great Lakes and establish the 49th parallel as their mutual border as far as the Rockies. In 1819 Spain sold Florida to the United States. By 1837 the original thirteen states had doubled in number. Jackson encouraged and speeded the "removal" by force of most of the remaining Indian tribes east of the Mississippi. Only Mexico to the south was now a potential rival.

Unassailable continentally, the United States even began to interest itself in Latin American affairs. Napoleon, by deposing the Bourbons in 1808, had cut the Spanish Empire in Latin America adrift. The ensuing revolts against Spain had produced by the early 1820s a collection of weak and internally divided states. After France's 1823 invasion of Spain to restore the Bourbons, French backing for Spanish efforts at reconquest appeared to threaten what Britain considered a promising market. Castlereagh's suc-

cessor as British Foreign Secretary, George Canning, suggested a joint British-United States declaration to ward off European intervention.

But President James Monroe preferred to act unilaterally, with a characteristically American statement of republican principles. He announced to Congress in December 1823 that the United States would regard attempts to establish or reestablish European control in the western hemisphere as signs of "an unfriendly disposition towards the United States." Canning could boast to Parliament that he had "called the New World into existence to redress the balance of the Old." But it was the Royal Navy, not the still minuscule seapower of the United States, that initially backed the Doctrine with force. Until the very end of the century the Royal Navy, in Britain's own interest, served as ultimate guarantor of the maritime security of the United States.

"Old Hickory": Andrew Jackson (1767–1845)

Expansion and Disunion

Economic and territorial expansion soon strained both the principles and

---

The Monroe Doctrine   1823

The political system of the allied [European] powers is essentially different . . . from that of America. . . . We owe it, therefore, to candor and to the amicable relations existing between the United States and those powers to declare that we should consider any attempt on their part to extend their system to any portion of this hemisphere as dangerous to our peace and safety. With the existing colonies or dependencies of any European power we have not interfered and shall not interfere. But with the [Latin American] governments who have declared their independence and maintained it, and whose independence we have, on great consideration and on just principles, acknowledged, we could not view any interposition for the purpose of oppressing them, or controlling in any other manner their destiny, by any European power in any other light than as the manifestation of an unfriendly disposition toward the United States.

From the message to Congress of President James Monroe, December 2, 1823.

The mechanization of the slave economy: Eli Whitney's cotton gin.

John C. Calhoun (1782–1850), the voice of the South.

the political fabric of the Republic. The trading Northeast, which acquired a merchant marine second only to Britain's, rapidly industrialized (see pp. 691–92). The Erie Canal and the railroad opened the Midwest to settlers, and gave those settlers new markets in the East for their grain.

The South, despite the qualms of figures such as Jefferson ("Indeed I tremble for my country, when I reflect that God is just"), further refined the slave economy established in the seventeenth century. Tobacco was less and less profitable, but after 1793 the cotton gin of the Yankee Eli Whitney made the short-fiber cotton that grew easily in the South into a fabulously profitable plantation crop. The slave economy spread rapidly westward, creating a "Cotton Kingdom" from Savannah to Mobile and New Orleans. By the 1820s the South was shipping 60 million pounds of raw cotton annually to the mills of Europe.

Old divisions between states blurred. Fissures between Puritan trading New England, the religiously and socially varied central Atlantic states, and the Anglican slave South had been less important than the fundamental divide between the settled and relatively hierarchical societies of the coastal plains and the egalitarian frontiersmen of the Appalachians and beyond. Now canal, railroad, and river steamer riveted North and South firmly to their respective hinterlands. Free

labor spread across the northern back-country, slave across the South.

Economic and territorial expansion brought to a head the fundamental conflict of principles: could a system founded on individual freedom ultimately tolerate slavery? By the 1830s stern New England voices had begun to attack the Cotton Kingdom at its most vulnerable point—its principles. Agitators such as William Lloyd Garrison and Wendell Phillips ceaselessly pounded at the irreconcilability of black slavery and white freedom. Garrison denounced the Constitution itself as "a covenant with death and an agreement with hell," for it permitted slavery. The Southern response was increasingly implausible and hysterical. John C. Calhoun, the South's greatest national political figure, told the Senate in 1837 that slavery was no evil, "but a good, sir, a positive good." The Abolitionists were and remained a tiny though noisy minority, but they inspired a persecution mania in the South that in the end drove it to revolt and ruin.

Economic issues also helped strain relations between the two sections. The South, as befitted a satellite economy of Britain, demanded free trade; the industrializing North with its Midwestern markets sought protective tariffs. In 1832 that conflict led to a great crisis. The "sovereign state" of South Carolina, under Calhoun's leadership, "nullified" a protective tariff that Congress had passed. President Jackson prepared to use force: "The laws of the United States must be executed." Since the issue was not slavery itself, the other Southern states were not prepared to back South Carolina. A compromise deferred until later the issue of "states' rights": the rebellious state withdrew "nullification" and Congress agreed to reduce tariffs. Nor did economics always pull the sections apart. Northern industry's dependence on Southern cotton led the South to bet heavily though in vain upon the existence of an implicit alliance between plantation chattel slavery and factory "wage slavery," between the "lords of the lash and the lords of the loom."

Territorial expansion, by constantly raising the stakes in the competition between two irreconcilable systems, ultimately brought the parting of the ways. Admitting new states created a series of ever greater crises. Missouri's admission as a slave state was only possible as part of an 1820 compromise that established latitude 36° 30', Missouri's southern border, as the future boundary between slave and free territories.

Then, in the 1820s and 1830s, settlers that included planters and their slaves flocked into the Mexican territories west of Louisiana, ironically at the invitation of the Mexican government. Attempts to reassert Mexican control led to settler revolt in 1835–36 and the proclamation of a "Republic of Texas." Eight years later the Democratic party under James K. Polk carried the presidential election on a platform of the annexation of Texas, which had asked to join the Union. Mexico's warnings that it would fight what it regarded as aggression, and clashes with Mexican patrols on the Rio Grande, brought war in 1846–48. The minuscule U.S. Army outclassed its adversary. It captured Mexico City and seized by force the entire Southwest from Texas westward to California.

The extension of U.S. power, and Polk's compromise with the British to extend the 49th parallel border with Canada westward to the Pacific across the Oregon territory, created a far greater crisis than had Missouri. Polk had promised the northern states an Oregon-Canada border ("Fifty-four forty or fight!") far to the north of the one he ultimately secured. Northern leaders retaliated by demanding that Congress exclude slavery from the territories wrested from Mexico. The South, which had contributed disproportionately to victory, replied with threats of secession from the Union.

The Compromise of 1850 failed to paper over the cracks. It admitted Cali-

fornia as a free state but left the status of the lands between California and Texas to the choice of their eventual inhabitants. It also pledged the North to return fugitive slaves, thus forcing northern authorities to choose between conscience and federal law. And Harriet Beecher Stowe's popular novel, *Uncle Tom's Cabin* (1852), dramatized the nature and consequences of slavery for the Northern public. The conflict deepened.

Congress and the Southern-dominated Supreme Court tore up the Missouri Compromise in the Kansas-Nebraska act of 1854 and the Dred Scott decision of 1857. All territories, even those previously covered by the Missouri Compromise, could now choose to be free or slave. The consequence was a savage guerrilla struggle, punctuated with mob violence, in "bleeding Kansas," west of Missouri but north of the Missouri Compromise line.

Quasi-war over Kansas opened the door to the men of blood on both sides. There an Abolitionist extremist, John Brown, made a name for himself by a series of unsavory killings. In October 1859, impelled by visions of arming the slaves and provoking an immense revolt, he and a band of followers seized the federal arsenal at Harpers Ferry, Virginia. Colonel Robert E. Lee, U.S. Army, swiftly turned him out. Virginia as swiftly hanged him. Brown provided Abolition with a martyr and convinced the increasingly deluded South that it stood alone, for "states' rights" and slavery, against the rest of the Union.

The election of 1860 showed that political polarization was complete. Abraham Lincoln of Illinois ran for the new Republican party ("free soil, free men") that represented North and Northwest. He carried 17 of the 18 free states. The 15 slave states overwhelmingly opposed him. Lincoln sought to preserve the Union with conciliatory gestures. He abhorred slavery but was a practical politician, not a zealot. The

Slave States and Free States   1861

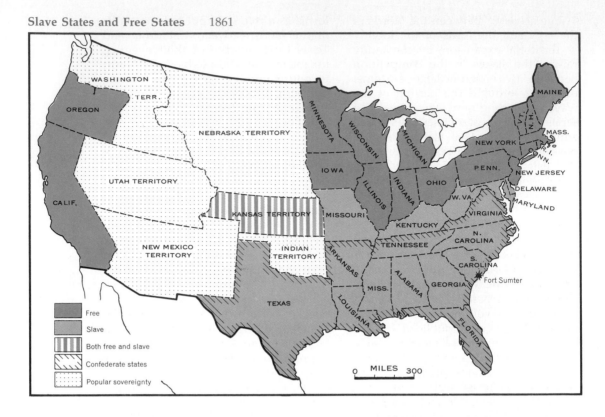

fire-eaters of the South, trusting in the economic power of "King Cotton" over both New England and Lancashire, and in their military spirit and talent as a planter aristocracy, determined on secession. Beginning on April 12, 1861, South Carolina bombarded and took Fort Sumter, the federal outpost in Charleston harbor. The "irrepressible conflict" had begun.

The Second American Revolution, 1861–65

The slave South's appeal to arms unleashed the world's first industrialized war, a war that ultimately became a second American revolution. The Crimean War had come too early and Bismarck's wars were too short to show what happened when industrialized powers collided. The U.S. Civil War was different. It was the first conflict between Western powers unlimited in aims since the Wars of Religion. To the South's limited war to assert the "right" of states to preserve slavery, the North replied. Reestablishment of the Union required *unconditional surrender*—a war aim the French revolutionaries had hinted at but which even Napoleon had hesitated to pursue. Reestablishment of the Union ultimately demanded the total destruction of the South's military power, the elimination of slavery, and the remaking of Southern society.

Neither side possessed at the outset a military establishment serious by European standards. The 16,367 officers and men of the peacetime U.S. Army split. A quarter of the 1,066 regular officers went South, including Colonel Lee, who stood with Virginia when it seceded to join the Confederate States of America. The Confederacy used these defectors wisely, to train and lead the state militias that became its army. The Union inherited the regular army, and kept its officers with regular army units. The Northern militias, sketchily trained and led by political appointees and elected officers, paid in blood for that mistake. Not until 1863–64 did Union battlefield effectiveness begin to rival that of the "rebels."

The Confederacy faced a daunting but by no means impossible task. It initially produced 26,000 tons of mostly charcoal-smelted pig iron annually, to the Union's 160,000 tons made with coke. The Union had 22,000 miles of railroads to the Confederacy's 9,000. The Union included a population of 22 million; the Confederacy's whites were 6 million, with 3.5 million slaves. Weight of numbers and an almost infinitely expandable productive capacity were thus the Union's greatest assets. The Confederacy nevertheless coped in the short term. It improvised military-run war industries virtually overnight, in Birmingham, Selma, Atlanta, Richmond. And the new fire-power of the Minié rifle, deadly to a thousand yards, favored the tactical defensive.

Union morale was also anything but firm; the Confederacy's will to resist, at least in the early years, was unconditional. "Peace Democrats"—"Copperheads" to the supporters of the Union cause—sought with considerable success to undermine Lincoln. In the border states partisans of the Confederacy intrigued, plotted, and spied. The 1863 introduction of a draft in the North caused an insurrection in New York City; mobs burned government offices and killed blacks as scapegoats for the war. Putting these "draft riots" down required a Union army corps. To cope with Confederate sympathizers Lincoln took the drastic step of partially suspending the Bill of Rights and trying civilians in military courts. The Confederacy's purely negative war aim gave it a further advantage. A few striking victories might win the war. Northern opinion might desert Lincoln; Britain and France might recognize the Confederacy.

Lincoln had no military experience. Like so many of his troops and generals, he learned on the job and he learned well. He swiftly adopted the key elements of the "Anaconda plan" that the aged generalissimo of the Mexican war, Winfield Scott, had proposed. The Union navy would blockade the Confederacy's coasts and dominate the Mississippi. But Lincoln could not afford to wait for strangulation to do its work; Union opinion demanded action. He also soon concluded that strangulation alone could not produce unconditional surrender. Union armies had to penetrate the heart of the Confederacy and destroy it.

The Confederate armies in northern Virginia dominated the first phase of the war, which lasted until mid-1863. They threw back repeated but inept Union attempts to seize Richmond. The terrain was a hundred-mile stretch of wooded rolling hills between Chesapeake Bay and the Blue Ridge; numerous rivers flowing west to east favored the defenders. Lee nevertheless failed to exploit the inexperience of the Union armies to deliver the crushing counteroffensive blow needed to unseat Lincoln.

The Confederacy's two major attempts to invade the North ended in disaster. The first, in September 1862, led to the appalling bloody draw at Antietam Creek in Maryland. The Union won a strategic victory, for Lee had to retreat. That gave Lincoln the platform to launch a political offensive of momentous consequences. On September 23, 1862, he announced that after January 1863 all slaves in states still in rebellion would be free. And on New Year's Day he promulgated the Emancipation Proclamation. It made the war a crusade to end slavery. It captured for the Union the support of European liberal opinion. It threatened the cohesion of the Confederacy's home front. It gave the Union armies, by the end of the war, almost 180,000 black soldiers, an eighth of their strength.

Lee's second invasion of the North, in June–July 1863, ended at Gettysburg, the largest battle so far fought in North America. Lee's instinct for the Napoleonic tactical offensive betrayed

The strain of war: Abraham Lincoln, April 1865.

him. The artillery and rifle fire of the new industrial age shredded the ten brigades he launched at the Union center. His army, less over 20,000 dead, wounded, or missing, retreated through rain and mud to defend Virginia.

The Union had not merely checked Lee's last offensive. In the hitherto neglected western theater Lincoln had found a winning strategy and two generals equal to any who fought for the Confederacy. Ulysses S. Grant, a whisky-sodden failure in peace, had revealed himself in 1861–62 as a brilliant strategist and dogged tactician. On July 4, 1863, the day after Gettysburg, the Confederate citadel at Vicksburg in Mississippi fell after a long amphibious campaign to Grant and his subordinate William Tecumseh Sherman. The greatest river of the continent belonged to the Union from Ohio to New Orleans; the Confederacy was cut in two. After Grant and Sherman took Chattanooga at the end of 1863, the way was open for a Union drive through the Appalachians to cut the South in three and tear out its heart.

That task fell to Sherman, who practiced to the fullest his insight that "War is hell." He marched on Atlanta, the hinge in the rail system that linked the arsenals of Alabama with the Richmond front. He took and burned Atlanta and its factories. Then he discarded his precarious rail links and marched to meet the Union navy at Savannah, cutting a 50-mile-wide swath of scorched earth across Georgia's richest plantations. Sherman's victories gave Lincoln the decisive edge against Democrats and Copperheads in the hotly contested 1864 election.

To the north, Grant had become commander-in-chief under Lincoln. He methodically ground Lee's forces down in a year of staggeringly bloody battles of attrition around Richmond. To deprive Lee of the often-used Shenandoah Valley route outflanking Washington, Grant sent Philip Sheridan with instructions to so waste the Valley that crows crossing it would need to carry rations. Lincoln had at last found the method appropriate to the Union's unlimited war aim. As Sheridan remarked to the Prussians while observing their 1870–71 campaign, the object was to leave enemy civilians with "nothing but their eyes to weep with over the war."

Industrial firepower: "The Dictator," a Union 13" mortar.

The ruins of Richmond, 1865.

The end came in March–April 1865. While Sherman savaged the Carolinas on his way north toward Lee's rear, the Confederate armies began to melt. Sherman's destruction of farms and livestock created an irresistible urge to desert. And the inexorable pressure of Grant's will and of the Union's immense manpower on the Confederate trenches at Petersburg near Richmond ultimately forced Lee out. Cornered in the open at Appomattox Court House, he surrendered to Grant on April 9, 1865. Five days later, a Confederate sympathizer assassinated Lincoln.

Reconstruction, the process of reintegrating the South into the Union, would have to go forward without the political genius of this greatest of presidents. The North faced a choice: it could simply concede amnesty, and return the South to the rule of the unrepentant planters in return for promises not to repeal the experiment of secession. Or it could attempt to reconstruct the South on a Northern pattern, ensuring that the newly freed slaves would receive the equality that blacks and many Northern whites had fought to achieve.

The first path was that of Lincoln's successor Andrew Johnson; it led to his impeachment at the hands of the Republican majority in Congress, which imposed the second alternative, "radical reconstruction." But martial law and federal aid for the ex-slaves were not enough to break the united resistance of planters and poor whites. The South's commitment to victory was as fierce after 1865 as before, and the North's staying power was limited.

Within twelve years, Ku Klux Klan terrorism and the more subtle opposition of the South's political class had won. To carry the disputed election of 1876 the Republicans in Congress agreed to end Reconstruction. Henceforth the white South, in return for being left alone, gave the Democratic party a bloc of safe congressional seats. Blacks in effect lost the guarantees of life, liberty, property, and the vote given them in the thirteenth through fifteenth amendments of 1865–70. Compulsory labor, sharecropping, and debt bondage to the landlord replaced the old slave order, and guaranteed a future of poverty. Sharecroppers and their masters do not innovate, nor do they give industry the markets needed to support growth. And in the course of the war Egyptian and Indian cotton had conquered the South's export markets; low cotton prices further slowed recovery from the devastation of war.

Despite its immense cost—roughly 359,000 Union and 258,000 Confederate dead—and a legacy of stagnation and resentment in the South, the Civil War had decided issues as vital as the Revolutionary War. The United States would remain united, rather than splitting into rival assortments of squabbling states; Napoleon III had to end his Mexican escapade. Slavery was dead; the United States would be a predominantly industrial society of free men and women. And Reconstruction was a battle better fought and lost than not fought at all.

Toward an Industrial Society

In the North and West, the years after the war were ones of unprecedented expansion and change. William H. Seward, secretary of state to Lincoln and Johnson, bought Alaska from Russia in 1867 for 7.2 million dollars. He also annexed the island of Midway, halfway across the Pacific. The completion of the first transcontinental railroad in 1869 welded California to the East. The Great Plains fell under the new steel plows or suffered division by barbed wire. By 1890 the frontier was passing.

The new age brought to the North and West the usual conflicts of industrialization. The towns and cities, in which over a third of the North's population already lived in 1860, asserted their power over the countryside. Railroads and banks dominated the farmers of the plains, setting freight rates and conceding credit on whatever terms they pleased. "Trusts," vertically integrated monopolies such as John D. Rockefeller's Standard Oil, and giant corporations, such as Andrew Carnegie's U.S. Steel, replaced old-style family firms. Wall Street buccaneers such as Jay Gould and Jim Fisk left behind them trails of looted companies.

Industry demanded and received from the most uproariously corrupt Congresses of U.S. history the highest protective tariffs in the world. But a reaction against monopolies eventually set in. The Interstate Commerce Act of 1887 sought to regulate the railroads in the interests of the farmers. The Sherman Antitrust Act of 1890 made a gesture toward controlling the trusts. And in national politics, farmers organized. From the National Grange of 1867 through the Farmers' Alliance of the

1880s to the People's party or Populists of 1891, they sought to defend the Jeffersonian vision of an agrarian republic. They stood against banks, cities, and the ever-growing masses of immigrants. The "prolific womb of governmental injustice," the Populists thundered, was breeding "two great classes—tramps and millionaires."

In the 1896 election the Populists coalesced with the Democratic party under the leadership of William Jennings Bryan, later famous as an opponent of the teaching of Darwinism. His florid oratory ("You shall not crucify mankind upon a cross of gold") failed to carry the Northeast and Midwest against the Republican and industrial candidate, William McKinley. Industry, which had already passed agriculture's share of the national product in the 1860s, had defeated agriculture for good.

In the cities the Populists so abhorred, new forms of organization were emerging. The Knights of Labor, formed in 1869, had over 700,000 members at its height. An 1886 episode of European-style anarchist bomb violence at the Haymarket in Chicago helped discredit the Knights, although they were not involved. The American Federation of Labor (AFL), an organization of skilled craft unions under the decidedly reformist Samuel Gompers, replaced them. The first major union actions inevitably brought defeat. The Pinkerton guards of Andrew Carnegie and his partner Henry C. Frick crushed their AFL opponents in the great 1892 Homestead steel strike in Pittsburg. Eugene Debs's American Railway Union likewise failed in its bitter confrontation with the Pullman Company in 1894. But the unions survived.

In politics, the industrial cities of the Northeast and Midwest were the scene of a vast social experiment—the creation of Americans out of speakers of languages other than English. This was relatively new, for until the 1870s the only non-English-speakers to arrive in large numbers had been Germans. The waves from eastern and southern Europe after 1870 soon learned; their children grew up as Americans, thanks to compulsory elementary schooling. Their political participation, with the hearty encouragement of the big city machines ("Vote early and often"), gave new meaning to the liberties proclaimed in the Constitution. A country as empty and short of labor as America, a country founded on principles rather than on notions of ethnic identity, lay open to anyone willing to subscribe to those principles—except for the Chinese and Japanese, excluded by racist public opinion in 1882 and 1907 respectively. Industry and immigrants together transformed the United States from farmers' republic into cosmopolitan industrial empire, another Europe in size, ethnic variety, and power.

RESISTANCE AND EMULATION, FAILURE AND SUCCESS

Others were less fortunate. The major non-European states that faced the Western challenge in the nineteenth century responded in a variety of ways. Some vegetated. Some collapsed. Some attempted to adapt Western technology while rejecting the ideas that had created that technology. And one, the empire of Japan, carried out a revolution from above that in 40 years, from 1854 to 1894, transformed it from victim into conqueror.

Latin America: Anarchy and Dictatorship

The states that emerged from the collapse of Spain's New World empire between 1808 and 1824 suffered from serious disabilities. Spain had created societies stratified by blood. First came the Spanish administrators, then the Creoles—native-born of Spanish blood—then the *mestizos*—those of mixed Indian and Spanish descent. At the bottom were the Indians and the black slaves or ex-slaves of the Caribbean and Brazil. These societies had no

tradition of self-rule; the jealous centralization of Spain, which distrusted the Creoles, had seen to that. And racial stratification meant weak states in which the masters had more in common with their counterparts in neighboring states than with their own peasants.

Repeated Creole revolts against Spain produced an unstable collection of 15 states. Only Brazil, which achieved independence under the heir to the Portuguese throne, escaped a major upheaval. The new states oscillated between anarchy and the rule of narrow landowner oligarchies or despotic *caudillos*. Simón Bolívar (1783–1830), liberator of half the continent, despaired: " . . . America is ungovernable." By 1826 he already foresaw the future: "Many tyrants will rise upon my tomb."

The inland state of Paraguay provided the most spectacular example of those tyrants. Three men ruled it mercilessly between 1811 and 1870: José Gaspar Rodríguez de Francia (1811–40), Carlos Antonio López (1840–62), and his son, Francisco Solano López (1862–70). Francia created a police state cut off from the outside world and an army that under his successors became the most powerful in Latin America. In 1864 López junior took that army to war against all three of Paraguay's neighbors: Brazil, Argentina, and Uruguay. By the end, in 1870, the population of Paraguay had fallen from over half a million to less than a quarter; almost all adult males were dead.

A few states, especially after midcentury, began to develop economically, as part of the British informal empire—Argentina, Brazil, Chile. Increased European immigration, especially to Argentina, speeded the pace of change. Elsewhere, savage struggles between peasants, rancher oligarchs, and the immensely powerful landowning Church produced repeated civil wars. Mexico changed chief executives 46 times in its first 30 years. It suffered a massive civil war and French intervention in mid-century, and the quasi-

Hero of the independence struggle against Spain: Simón Bolívar, el Libertador.

dictatorship of Porfirio Díaz from 1877 to 1911. Much of Latin America ended the century further behind the West in economic and social terms than it had been in 1800.

Egypt and the Ottoman Empire: Collapse and Survival

Closer to Europe, the Islamic world faced the full force of Western power. Algeria, Tunisia, and Morocco (in 1911) succumbed to French military colonialism. Persia and the weak states of the Persian Gulf fell under the protectorate of Britain's Indian Empire. Only Egypt and Turkey were strong enough to have a chance at survival.

Egypt failed. The cotton boom of the 1860s encouraged the successors of Mehemet Ali to launch ambitious public works such as the reconstruction of Cairo in the image of Napoleon III's Paris. By the 1870s the Khedive Ismail was spending annually twice Egypt's revenue and plugging his deficit with European loans. Bankruptcy and the fierce reaction of Egypt's partially Westernized elites to the Khedive's subservience to Britain and France produced the explosion that led an unhappy Gladstone to occupy Egypt. The country's vital strategic importance to Britain, its easily mastered terrain, and its still largely peasant society doomed it.

The Ottoman Empire was both more fortunate and less digestible than its sometime vassal Egypt. It faced stirrings of nationalism, reinforced by religion, among its Balkan peoples. Russia, despite defeat in the Crimea, remained a major threat. Bankruptcy and foreign financial controls, as in Egypt, followed upon incautious borrowing and frivolous expenditure in the 1870s. But the empire's international function and military tradition saved it from dismemberment in the nineteenth century. Britain propped it up to keep Russia from the Middle East. Austria supported it lest the demise of the Ottoman multinational empire free Balkan nationalities to turn against the

multinational Habsburg empire. Germany supported it to stabilize Austria and as a field for German "informal empire." France supported it because France held much of the Ottoman debt. The powers would not tolerate one of their number monopolizing the empire, nor could they agree on how to divide it. Its poor but warlike peoples and its mountainous terrain made it an unpromising conquest.

Under the stubborn and wily Abd al-Hamid II ("the damned"), who ruled from 1876 to 1908–09, the empire survived war with Russia in 1877–78 (see p. 816). It acquired military equipment and training from Prussia-Germany. In 1908–09 a group of Westernized "Young Turk" officers on the pattern of Arabi made the Sultan a figurehead. In the following years they proved that the Ottoman warrior tradition could inspire a twentieth-century fighting force. That force ultimately upheld Turkish independence.

China: Resistance and Decline

The China that faced the Europeans in the middle decades of the nineteenth century was the most populous state on earth, with a tradition that stretched back three millennia. To the Manchu aristocrats of the Qing (Ch'ing) dynasty (1644–1911) and the Confucian scholar-gentry who ruled China, the "Middle Kingdom" was the center of the universe. The overseas "barbarians" who had first appeared around China's coasts in the sixteenth century seemed no different than the nomads of central Asia or the tributary kingdoms of Vietnam, Korea, and Tibet. Barbarians could only enter into relations with China by bringing tribute and prostrating themselves before the emperor. The dynasty kept them in their proper place in the eighteenth century by restricting them to the single trading port of Canton.

But China proved less and less capable of imposing Chinese norms on the seaborne barbarians or on the Russian land power to the north. Externally,

Sultan Abd al-Hamid II, known for his cunning and cruelty.

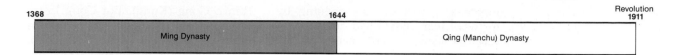

1368		1644	Revolution 1911
	Ming Dynasty	Qing (Manchu) Dynasty	

the barbarian technological lead lengthened decisively with the coming of steam and shell-firing cannon. Internally, the Qing dynasty appeared to be following the law of cyclical rise, crisis, and decay that had long shaped Chinese thought about history and politics. By 1800 the dynasty had passed its peak and was descending, amid secret society agitation, peasant rebellions, massive overpopulation, and immense natural catastrophes that took millions of lives. The sheer size of the empire, along with administrative inefficiency, corruption, and the inherent conflict between Manchu and Chinese, crippled efforts at reform.

The end of the East India Company's monopoly of the China trade in 1833 led to a rush by private British

China in the Nineteenth Century

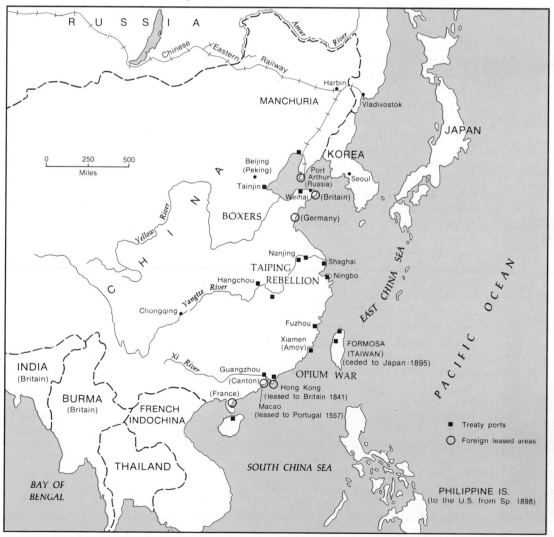

merchants, and China's opening by force. British traders had developed a lucrative Chinese black market for the Indian-grown opium that paid for the West's imports of tea, silk, and the gleaming ceramics that had inspired envy and imitation in eighteenth-century Europe. To a desperate attempt of the Beijing (Peking) government to close down the opium trade for both fiscal and health reasons, the British replied with gunboats. The first and second Opium Wars of 1839–42 and 1856–60 flattened the dynasty's armed forces, opened numerous ports to European trade, delivered Hong Kong to Britain and vast northern territories to Russia, and gave foreigners immunity from Chinese law, with its custom of judicial torture. Traders, missionaries, and diplomats flocked in, rousing xenophobia. Killings of foreigners and frequent gunboat reprisals were the predictable result.

Internally, defeat in the First Opium War and the strains of dynastic decline unleashed an immense civil war. Hong Xiuquan (Hung Hsiu-ch'üan), the principal leader of the "Taiping Rebellion" that conquered south-central China in the 1850s, believed that he was the younger brother of Jesus and that his mission was to exterminate the Manchus. Hong's unstable blend of Western religious ideas and Chinese peasant millenarianism attracted a wide and fanatical following. But its foreign elements made it suspect to the Confucian provincial gentry. Eventually the dynasty rallied, thanks to armies the gentry raised and led. With help from foreign military experts such as "Chinese" Gordon, they crushed the Taipings by 1864. The European powers, in the end, preferred the Qing to chaos. Twenty million peasants perished in the war and its accompanying famines.

Qing survival now required drastic measures—not merely the adoption of Western techniques, but of the concepts on which they rested. The dynasty made a start in the late 1860s under the leadership of the Manchu

The Empress Dowager Ci Xi (T'zu Hsi) (r. 1861–1908), whose fierce resistance to change helped doom the Qing dynasty.

Prince Gong (Kung). But Gong lost a series of palace struggles to the pitiless Empress Dowager Ci Xi (Tz'u Hsi), who henceforth dominated court and central administration until her death in 1908. Her hostility to anything she did not control paralyzed the regime. And to a true Confucian, the West's material and military success was irrelevant; tradition and virtue were their own reward. China's "self-strengthening" program grudgingly acquired armament plants, railways, and a military academy, but it lacked conviction. Neither dynasty nor scholar-gentry created the leadership and institutions required to save China from further dismemberment at the hands of Europeans and Japanese.

Japan: The Meiji Restoration

Japan, until the arrival of Perry in 1853–54, was even more closed than China. The great lord Tokugawa Ieyasu (1542–1616) had unified it in a series of wars that lasted until 1600. He and his successors imposed peace, exterminated or forced underground the Christian communities the Jesuits had founded, and recognized only the Dutch—limited to one port and one ship a year—as trading partners. The Tokugawa discouraged and occasionally persecuted Japanese who pursued "Dutch learning," the new European knowledge.

The Japanese system was nevertheless very different from anything in China. Both Western scholars and their twentieth-century Japanese counterparts have frequently described it as "feudal," for its basis was some 250 domains, or *han*, whose lords were dependents or vassals of the Tokugawa. But a key element in European feudal institutions, the rights of the vassal against the lord, was largely lacking, and the system was infinitely more centralized than anything resembling it in Europe. Most of Japan's hereditary warrior caste, the samurai, did not even own land, but received stipends in rice from their *han*. Their ethos stressed above all service to their lord.

Japanese politics were thus far different from those of China. The Tokugawa ruled, at least in theory, as deputies (*Shōgun*) of the imperial house, which had reigned although rarely ruled from time immemorial. The emperor was both a figurehead for the Tokugawa and the most powerful symbol of Japanese unity. He might become a figurehead for others, legitimizing revolutionary transformation. And the division of Japan into domains offered regional bases for any movement to overthrow the Tokugawa.

Culturally, Japan had a tradition of borrowing. It acquired Confucianism and Buddhism from China and sixteenth-century guns from the Portuguese. The curiosity of Japanese scholars about the outside world had no parallel in China. And the practical warrior ethos of the samurai took precedence over Confucianism. On the bat-

tlefield virtue was irrelevant; the issue was victory or defeat. A leader in ''Dutch learning,'' Sakuma Shōzan (1811–64), compiler of foreign language dictionaries and cannon-foundry master, put it caustically: China had lost the First Opium War ''because foreign learning is rational and Chinese learning is not.''

Structurally, Japan was small and ethnically homogeneous, with a fierce sense of distinctness. During the long Tokugawa peace, it had developed a flourishing agricultural economy and a large and growing merchant class. The Tokugawa, although still in control in 1854, were losing their grip upon an increasingly rich and diverse society. Like eighteenth-century Britain, Japan had the cultural and social potential for a vast leap in productivity.

Finally, Japan's economy, although dynamic, was—unlike China's—not conspicuously rich enough to attract Western greed from the beginning of the century. The opening of Japan was

A Japanese view: Commodore Matthew C. Perry, charged by President Millard Fillmore with opening Japan to Western trade, parades through the streets of Yokohama (1854).

1598		1868	1912
Tokugawa Shogunate		Meiji Era	

an afterthought; that was why Perry got there first. And the Japanese, in framing their response to Perry's peremptory demands, had the advantage of knowing what had happened to China. Collaboration, not resistance, was clearly wisest until Japan was stronger.

Perry's arrival created a revolutionary situation. The Tokugawa Shogunate grudgingly opened Japanese ports and conceded extraterritorial jurisdiction in "unequal treaties." Xenophobic "men of spirit" among the lower samurai replied by assassinating foreigners and the Tokugawa officials who collaborated with them. In 1863 Britain bombarded the city of Kagoshima in reprisal. The Shogunate's impotent collaboration with the West, like that of the Khedivate in Egypt, deprived it of the legitimacy needed to rule.

But Japan took a different path than Egypt or China. The Shogunate avoided open war with the West. And in the outer *han* of Satsuma, Chōshu, Tosa, and Hizen, middle and lower samurai with some notions of the outer world offered an alternative to supine acquiescence or self-destructive fanaticism. In 1868 they induced their lords to revolt in the name both of tradition and modernity; the Tokugawa Shogunate fell after a brief but bloody civil war.

The insurgents "restored" the emperor, who took the reign-title of Meiji. The new leaders were ruthless and clear-sighted—Ōkubo Toshimichi, Yamagata Aritomo, Kido Kōin, Ōkuma Shigenobu, and Itō Hirobumi. Backed by imperial authority and the newly invented tradition of the Shintō state religion, they swiftly swept away all perceived obstacles to a "rich country, strong army." Loyalty previously given to "feudal" superiors proved readily transferable to emperor and nation.

The Meiji oligarchs pensioned off the domain lords in 1871. In 1873 Yamagata began the creation of a Prussian-style conscript army, breaking the "feudal" samurai monopoly of arms. The oligarchs abolished their own caste, the samurai, to mobilize all energies in a race against time to ensure Japan's independence. In 1877 their new army pitilessly crushed a last great rising of dissident samurai under a former comrade, Saigō Takamori. The oligarchs created state enterprises with Western machinery, and sold them off to a merchant class that rose eagerly to the challenge of creating an industrial economy. The oligarchs imposed Western-style code law, and compulsory education to reinforce powerfully Japan's existing traditions of learning, hard work, and deference to authority. They secured French, Prussian, and British advisers for army and navy. They created a military-bureaucratic absolutism with a Bismarckian constitution (1889) as fig-leaf. And in foreign affairs, they succeeded in appearing meek until Japan was strong enough to face the West on equal terms. The Meiji oligarchs created a mighty modern state, a powerful engine of change and conquest. Its chief lack, it later emerged, was brakes.

Japan was an exception. It avoided Western domination in the nineteenth century and soon acquired the strength to create an empire of its own. The United States, thanks to mighty demographic and economic growth and Northern victory in the Civil War, likewise escaped the hegemony of Britain. Other states, from Latin America, to Egypt, Burma, and China, failed to rise to the challenge, and suffered colonial occupation or "informal" domination through gunboats and treaties. When

Britain's "followers" sought to rival it in the wider world, Africa too went under the knife, divided by diplomacy and Maxim gun in less than 20 years. But the world hegemony of Britain and of Europe was precarious, for it rested on narrow demographic foundations and on the long but increasingly fragile peace in Europe itself.

Suggestions for Further Reading

British and European Expansion

For much of the conceptual framework of this chapter, see the essays of J. Gallagher and R. Robinson in W. R. Louis, ed., *Imperialism* (1976), and D. Headrick, *Tools of Empire: Technology and European Imperialism in the Nineteenth Century* (1981). B. Porter, *The Lion's Share: A Short History of British Imperialism, 1850–1983* (1984), is useful on Britain. D. K. Fieldhouse, *The Colonial Empires* (1966), and *Colonialism, 1870–1945* (1981), offers a comparative perspective, as do S. K. Betts, *Europe Overseas* (1968), the sardonic V. Kiernan, *From Conquest to Collapse: European Empires from 1815 to 1960* (1982), and W.

Baumgart, *Imperialism: The Idea and Reality of British and French Colonial Expansion, 1880–1914* (1982). For Britain's "white" colonies, see D. G. Creighton, *Canada's First Century* (1970); E. McInnis, *Canada: A Political and Social History* (1947); and C. H. Grattan, *The Southwest Pacific to 1900* (1963). On India, see J. M. Brown, *Modern India: The Origins of an Asian Democracy* (1985), and S. Wolpert, *A New History of India* (1982). R. Robinson, J. Gallagher, and A. Denny, *Africa and the Victorians: The Climax of Imperialism* (1968), is delightfully provocative on the "scramble for Africa."

The United States

The literature on the United States is distressingly vast; J. M. Blum et al., *The National Experience: A History of the United States*, 7th ed. (1989), is an excellent introductory survey with detailed bibliographies. On the pre-Jacksonian period, see G. Dangerfield, *The Awakening of American Nationalism* (1965); J. C. Curtis, *Andrew Jackson and the Search for Vindication* (1976), covers the "Age of Jackson." For the road west, see R. A. Billington,

Westward Expansion (1967). On slavery, see especially E. D. Genovese, *Roll, Jordan, Roll: The World the Slaves Made* (1974). J. M. McPherson, *Battle Cry of Freedom: The Civil War Era* (1988), describes the greatest crisis in America's history; C. V. Woodward, *Origins of the New South, 1877–1913* (1951), deals with its long-term impact.

Latin America, the Islamic World, and East Asia

For general surveys of Latin America, see J. F. Rippy, *Latin America: A Modern History* (1958, 1968), and T. H. Skidmore and P. H. Smith, *Modern Latin America* (1984); J. Lynch, *The Latin American Revolutions, 1810–1826* (1973), describes the initial upheaval that brought independence. For the fates of Ottoman Turkey and Egypt, see respectively B. Lewis, *The Emergence of Mod-*

ern Turkey (1968), and J. C. B. Richmond, *Egypt, 1798–1952* (1977). On China and Japan see C. Schirokauer, *A Brief History of Chinese and Japanese Civilizations*; 2nd ed. (1989); J. K. Fairbank, *The Great Chinese Revolution, 1800–1985* (1986), *The Cambridge History of China*, Vols. 10 and 11 (1978, 1980); and W. G. Beasley, *The Modern History of Japan* (1981), and *The Meiji Restoration* (1972).

28

Europe in the Long Peace, 1871–1914

*T*he years between 1871 and 1914 were the longest period of uninterrupted peace in Europe since the "five good emperors" of the first and second centuries A.D. Only minor Balkan conflicts disturbed the peace. The workings of the balance of power and above all the self-restraint of the new Germany prevented war between great powers. Only after 1890 did the German bid for continental hegemony and world power status (see pp. 831–43) lead to a new age of world wars.

Internally, monarchy and its attendant aristocracy remained the preeminent form of government. Landed wealth still dominated state administrations, diplomatic services, and standing armies. Revolution was no longer practical politics, although faith in it persisted and even broadened. The demands of the working classes had little political weight until after 1900. The welfare state, with its bureaucracies, regulations, and taxes was still in its infancy. These conditions along with the immense strides of industry and commerce made these de-

Opposite: The golden age of the middle classes: a holiday in the park, late 1870s.

783

cades the golden age of the middle classes. Money, although it still sought to climb through marriage into families of noble birth, had become the foremost source of social status. The middle-class citizen of Europe, thanks to steam, electricity, and the absence of government restrictions on movement, could travel as never before or after. Letters of credit and British banknotes took the place of passports.

This golden age was short. Both liberal principles and the preservation of political stability after the coming of mass education and the second industrial revolution seemed to demand an ever-wider expansion of the franchise. Universal male suffrage in turn created the first workers' parties and encouraged women to demand the vote. In the realm of ideology and culture, a confident middle-class materialism compounded of Darwin, steel, and electricity provoked a response: outright hostility to the gospel of science and "progress." The rapidity of change itself created immense tensions, psychological as much as political and intellectual. Those tensions ultimately discharged in spontaneous rejoicing

among the urban masses at the coming of war in August 1914.

EUROPEAN POLITICS AND SOCIETY

England: The Limits of Gradualism

By the 1860s Britain's spurt of dramatic economic growth was ending. From the 1870s its rivals began pressing ever more insistently at its heels. Yet as late as 1914 London remained the center of the world economy. Britain's money market was the largest, although upstart New York increasingly rivalled it. Britain dominated insurance and other services reserved for mature economies. Britain controlled the world's largest merchant marine. Britain's overseas investments rose from 1 billion to 2.5 billion pounds between 1870 and 1900; in 1914 they still dwarfed those of other powers, and underwrote economic growth on every continent. Britain's export of know-how and import of interest and insurance premiums increasingly rivalled its trade in goods. But financial dominance proved to be a poor substitute for the mastery of world manufacturing that was passing to others (see Figure 24-4, p. 688).

Politically, the Britain of Queen Victoria (r. 1837–1901) was a time of gradual adjustments to the demands of the new age. The irascible Palmerston had dominated a period of shifting factional alignments until his death in 1865. Parties remained incoherent collections of notables, without central machinery or discipline. The Queen, in this situation, was able to assert considerable powers as constitutional monarch. But under Palmerston's two great successors, Benjamin Disraeli and William Ewart Gladstone, Liberals and Tories (Conservatives) took on their modern shape, following a pattern also visible in the United States. The monarchy's influence receded as that of the mass electorate advanced.

The parties alternated in power, spurring one another in succession to

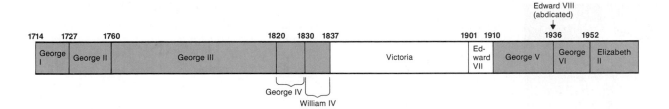

1714	1727	1760		1820	1830	1837		1901	1910	1936	1952
George I	George II	George III				Victoria		Edward VII	George V	George VI	Elizabeth II

Edward VIII (abdicated)

George IV
William IV

enlarge the franchise and appeal to the new electorate. Gladstone, "the People's William," took the initiative on the franchise in 1866. But it was Disraeli, son of a converted Jew, author of novels about the social question, and radical Tory, who preempted his rival with the Second Reform Bill of 1867 that almost doubled the electorate. Gladstone, during his governments of 1868–74 and 1880–85, then introduced the secret ballot in 1872 and a Third Reform Bill in 1884 that gave most adult males the vote.

The consequences of the coming of democracy were at least three. First, it created the modern machinery of mass parties. Disraeli pioneered a network of constituency organizations coordinated from the center in the 1874 election. Gladstone replied in 1880, damning Disraeli's foreign policy in Britain's first populist stump speeches by a major political leader. Such tactics, along with Gladstone's persistent inability to distinguish morality from foreign policy, had prompted Disraeli earlier to describe his rival as an "unprincipled maniac, and with one commanding characteristic—whether preaching, praying, speechifying or scribbling— never a gentlemen." The day of the gentleman in politics was indeed passing. The Liberal party machine, under "Radical Joe" Chamberlain, self-made businessman and reforming mayor of Birmingham, improved on Disraeli's 1874 example and converted Gladstone's "speechifying" into victory. Appeals to and organization of the new mass electorate replaced social standing as the key determinants of political success.

The second major consequence of democracy was to raise the problem of Ireland, Britain's earliest colony. Elizabeth I, James I, and Cromwell had imposed Protestant landlords on Ireland's Catholic peasants. An Irish nationalist revolt in the 1790s had failed. The famine of the 1840s had cut the population by a third, but the problem of peasant land tenure remained. A "Fenian Brotherhood" founded in 1858 in New York pressed the Irish cause with intermittent terrorism. And the Second Reform Bill and secret ballot between them brought over 50 Irish nationalist members to Parliament. There they obstructed proceedings with long speeches demanding rights for the peasantry, and autonomy within the British empire—"home rule"—for Ireland.

Gladstone's first administration (1868–74) made an inadequate start on the peasant question; his second (1880–85) settled it with the Land Act of 1881. But he was already too late. Exorbitant rents, arbitrary evictions, peasant boycotts, violence against landlords, and Irish nationalist assassinations of high British officials had created an atmosphere in which extremism on both sides prospered. Gladstone's conversion to Irish home rule and his attempts to implement it in 1886 and during his tragic last government in 1892–94 were in vain. Home rule meant placing Protestant landlords and the Presbyterian Scottish settlers of Ulster under the "Rome rule" of the Catholic majority.

To the delight of the Tories, who thereby gained uninterrupted power from 1895 to 1905, home rule split Gladstone's party. "Radical Joe" Chamberlain and his followers joined the Tories; Chamberlain became a spokesman for British supremacy in

The great antagonists: Disraeli and Gladstone (below).

David Lloyd George (1863–1945), the last of the great Liberal reformers and war prime minister, 1916–22.

South Africa. The Irish question, which had now become a religious-national conflict between Protestant Ulster and the Catholic south and west, festered. On the eve of World War I the Liberals made a final attempt to impose home rule. Ulster, armed to the teeth, defied London. The army officer corps, as closely connected to Ulster as its Prusso-German counterpart was to Prussia's Polish borderlands, resisted government policy in a fashion unprecedented since Cromwell. Then war in Europe postponed civil war in Ireland.

The ballot had brought the Irish question, which arguably had no peaceful solution, to a head. Ballot and Irish question together introduced the third major consequence of democracy, the rise of a worker's party. Until the 1890s the working-class movement had confined itself to trade unionism. Craft unions had organized the Trades Union Congress in 1868; unskilled workers won their first major victory in the great London dock strike of 1889. But Gladstone and Liberals to his left on social issues, such as Chamberlain, held the working man's vote—until the party split over home rule.

Chamberlain's defection to the Tories created the political space for a working-class party. Keir Hardie, Scottish leader of the miners, organized the Independent Labor Party (ILP) in 1893. In 1900 the ILP, the gradualist middle-class "Fabian Socialists" of Sidney and Beatrice Webb, and a variety of other groups coalesced to form what became the Labour Party. In the 1906 election it won 29 seats. Although the Liberals carried the election of 1906, they henceforth had to reckon with an increasingly formidable force to their left. That strengthened Liberal resolve in pressing expensive social reforms such as old age pensions (1908) and unemployment and health insurance (1911) under the leadership of the "Welsh magician," David Lloyd George.

When the unrepresentative Tory majority in the House of Lords balked at Lloyd George's "People's Budget," the Liberals rammed through a Parlia-

ment Act in 1911 that stripped the Lords of their veto over money bills. But the Liberals did not recapture Labour. Indeed, a wave of strikes after 1911 culminated in the ominous 1914 "Triple Alliance" of railwaymen, transport workers, and miners. Here also the coming of war rescued the Liberals from grave crisis—but that rescue proved only temporary.

France: The Third Republic Beleaguered

France entered the long peace with a difficult legacy. Since 1789 three constitutional monarchies (1789–92, 1815–30, 1830–48), two republics (1792–99, 1848–51), and two Bonaparte dictatorships (1799–1815, 1851–70) had attempted to rule it. All had collapsed within 20 years. Savage disputes divided Bourbon Legitimists, Orleanists, and Bonapartists, moderate "opportunists" and radical republicans, clericals and anticlericals. War, defeat, and the crushing of the Paris Commune in 1871 had created lasting bitterness. Yet by 1879 France had established a regime that weathered one world war and only succumbed after crushing defeat in a second.

The Third Republic would have gladdened the heart of Edmund Burke. It institutionalized the triumph of the provinces over radical Paris. Thanks to its middle-class leadership and its peasant voters, it proved remarkably conservative. And unlike its two predecessors it had no prefabricated constitution.

Its origin was Bismarck's demand for a French regime with a popular mandate to make peace. The universal male suffrage elections of February 1871 returned a chamber of monarchists because the republicans had discredited themselves by preaching war to the bitter end. But the monarchists failed to restore the monarchy. The Legitimist claimant, the childless Count of Chambord, refused to abandon the white flag with lilies of his royal forefathers. The country would

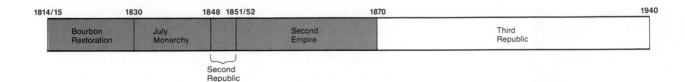

| 1814/15 | 1830 | 1848 1851/52 | 1870 | 1940 |

Bourbon Restoration — July Monarchy — Second Empire — Third Republic

Second Republic

not give up the Revolutionary and Napoleonic tricolor. Nor while Chambord lived would the Legitimists support the more flexible Orleanist claimant, the Count of Paris.

The monarchy's moment soon passed. The monarchists had brought peace, but the peasantry feared that if left too long in office they might attempt to restore the old regime. Elections between 1871 and 1874 gradually tipped the balance in favor of the republicans. In 1873 the monarchist majority removed from power the grand old man who had made peace with Bismarck, Adolphe Thiers. In his place it installed Marshal MacMahon, who had become an Orleanist after an astounding demonstration of battlefield incompetence in 1870. MacMahon was to serve as provisional executive until Chambord died or otherwise resolved the monarchist deadlock.

But the republicans forestalled MacMahon. In 1875 they pushed through by one vote a motion establishing a procedure for choosing MacMahon's successor as president. That was the Third Republic's basic law; it made the provisional permanent. And when MacMahon dissolved the Chamber in May 1877 in order to seek a monarchist majority, the republicans won. When they captured the Senate in 1879, MacMahon resigned. France received, in Jules Grévy, its first republican president.

The republican president, however, was not to be the Third Republic's executive. A strong presidency might fall to another Louis Napoleon or MacMahon. Henceforth prime minister and cabinet, ever-changing according to the Chamber's whims, ruled France. The Third Republic so diffused power that paralysis sometimes resulted.

Yet it was capable of decisive action. Under the stern leadership of Jules Ferry, minister of education from 1879 to 1881 and prime minister in 1880–81 and 1883–85, the Republic created a national educational system independent of the implacably hostile Church. The mission of France's new school teachers was to nationalize and republicanize the rural masses, and to make France competitive with Prussia-Germany. In the villages, the "schoolmaster's party" now faced the "priest's party." Railways, another priority of Ferry and of his colleague Charles de Freycinet, likewise opened up the countryside to new ideas. The Republic finished the rail net that Napoleon III had begun, and at last consolidated France as a national market.

Its successes did not save the Republic from two major internal crises before the turn of the century. Despite the collapse of the royalists and the extinction of Bonapartist hopes with the death of Napoleon III's son in the Zulu War of 1879, the Right remained unreconciled. The agricultural downturn of the 1880s, the phylloxera vine blight that almost destroyed France's historic wine industry, and a slow-down in industrial growth sapped the regime's popularity. After 1885 the moderate "opportunist" republicans who had presided over the establishment of the Republic no longer had a majority. Three groupings of roughly equal size, the Right, the Opportunists, and the radical republicans, faced one another.

In this tense situation the chief figure among the Radicals, Georges Clemenceau, imposed his protégé, General Georges Boulanger, on the cabinet as minister of war. Boulanger, an impressive figure on horseback, cultivated popularity with the troops and

Statesmen of the Third Republic: Jules Grévy, president, 1879–87, and (below) Jules Ferry, prime minister, 1880–81, 1883–85.

The young Georges Clemenceau, "Tiger" of the Radicals and war prime minister, 1917–20.

made imprudent remarks about Germany, remarks Bismarck gleefully exploited. When the government fell in 1887, Boulanger intrigued with both Catholic Right and extreme Left. In his support the ferocious anti-Semite Edouard Drumont joined the demagogue Paul Déroulède, one of the first of those nationalist extremists, common in the twentieth century, whose politics failed to fit the classic nineteenth-century Left-Right distinction. Boulanger began posing as a potential Bonaparte—until a resolute Opportunist government frightened him into exile in 1889. There he committed suicide upon the grave of his mistress.

The Republic survived, despite continuing depression and a series of scandals that included revelations that de Lesseps's Panama Canal company, which had failed to repeat his triumph at Suez, had paid off numerous deputies. The Republic's second major crisis came from a different direction. In 1894 army intelligence recovered from a wastebasket at the German embassy a document suggesting that a member of the French general staff was selling war plans to Germany. The army immediately fixed upon a culprit, Captain Alfred Dreyfus, the only Jew on the staff. It court-martialled him without a shred of evidence, stripped him of his rank, and condemned him to imprisonment on Devil's Island off French Guyana. His family protested but failed to gain a hearing until evidence emerged that the leaks to Germany were continuing.

In 1898 the flamboyant novelist Émile Zola wrote an open letter to the president of the Republic entitled "J'accuse!" He accused the army of unjustly condemning an innocent man and of covering the real traitor. He challenged the authorities to sue him for libel. The "Affaire Dreyfus," or simply "the Affair," split France into warring camps. The clericals, who had in 1892 refused a pressing invitation from the reforming Pope Leo XIII to "rally" to the Republic, stood with officer corps, monarchists, anti-Semites, and the radical Right of the streets. For

them, Dreyfus was guilty; he must be guilty—for his innocence meant the guilt of army, aristocracy, and Church. The Left stood in general for Dreyfus, although nationalism impelled many Opportunists and Radicals to support the army.

The government, which had incautiously claimed in 1897 that "there is no *Affaire Dreyfus*," collapsed. The suicide of the officer who had forged the cover-up evidence and the flight of the real traitor, a Lieutenant Esterhazy, led to a succession of new trials and Dreyfus's eventual rehabilitation. A Déroulède coup attempt in 1899 failed. Anticlerical Radical governments dissolved religious orders that had attacked the Republic, took the Church off the state payroll, and purged the army. The Republic won its confrontation with the Right and carried to completion the process of secularization begun with the Civil Constitution of the Clergy of 1790.

Finally, the Republic even deflected or absorbed the rise of the workers' movement. The elections of 1893 brought almost 50 socialists into the Chamber. The economic upturn after 1896 eased France's domestic distress and encouraged socialist and trade-union struggles. France acquired, in the CGT or General Confederation of Labor and in a unified Socialist party after 1905, a workers' movement second only to that of Germany. Marxism, which the austere Jules Guesde had introduced into the French labor movement in the late 1870s, prospered. Yet the greatest of all French Socialists was only a Marxist by courtesy. Jean Jaurès, the man who unified the movement's quarreling sects, had concluded that capitalism did not necessarily lead to revolution. By temperament he preferred conciliation to violence. And in advocacy of violence the Marxists had a powerful rival—the anarchist myth of the revolutionary general strike, creation of the eccentric Georges Sorel, author of *Reflexions on Violence* (1908). Militants influenced by Sorel captured the CGT amid violent strikes in 1905–06.

Clemenceau and Aristide Briand, prime ministers in 1906–10, ruthlessly suppressed them and broke Sorel's myth. But the Republic demonstrated great powers of absorption as well as of repression. To the left of the now-respectable Radicals an exotic new hybrid, the "Radical-Socialists," sprang up. A genuine though non-Marxist Socialist joined a government for the first time in 1899. Others eventually followed.

The Republic, to the surprise of all, far outlasted it predecessors. It proved strong enough to face war squarely in 1914. As international tension mounted after 1911 the Chamber swallowed its qualms about leadership. It appointed as president Georges Poincaré, a dour, forceful, and logically uncompromising Alsatian. It increased compulsory military service from two years to three to compensate partially for Germany's population advantage. When war came, even the Socialists marched.

Germany: Bismarck and After

The new Reich was a hybrid—partly centralized and partly federal, part military dictatorship and part constitutional monarchy. The King of Prussia and German Emperor (Kaiser), as "All-Highest War-Lord," personally controlled the German army. The Emperor appointed and dismissed the Reich chancellor without reference to the Reich's legislature. Prussia, which made up over three-fifths of the Reich, dominated the upper house of that legislature, the representatives of the German princes. The lower house or *Reichstag*, elected under universal male suffrage, had the indispensable right of approving or disapproving the budget; that much the Prussian Liberals had won in the constitutional conflict of 1862–66. Nor could the Reich government levy direct taxes. The states retained that right, and made occasional contributions to Reich finances at their pleasure. Finally, the constitutions of the states, especially the inequitable "three-class" franchise law of Prussia,

---

Zola Accuses
January 1898

I accuse Lieutenant Colonel Du Paty de Clam [the investigating officer] of having been the diabolical author of the [original] judicial error—unknowingly, I may hope—and of thereafter defending his evil work, for the last three years, by the most bizarre and reprehensible machinations.

I accuse General Mercier [the former Minister of War] of having become the accomplice, at best through weakness of intellect, of one of the greatest iniquities of the century.

I accuse General Billot [the present Minister of War] of having had in his hands the indisputable proofs of the innocence of Dreyfus, and of having suppressed them. . . .

I accuse General de Boisdeffre and General Gonse [chief and deputy chief of staff of the army] of having become accomplices in that same crime. . . . .

I accuse the first court martial [of Dreyfus] of having violated the law by condemning the accused on secret evidence, and I accuse the second court martial of having covered up that illegality, on orders from above. . . .

In making these accusations, I am not unaware that I am placing myself in jeopardy under articles 30 and 31 of the press law of July 29, 1889, which punishes the crime of defamation of character. I do so voluntarily. . . .

I have only one passion, that of enlightenment, in the name of humanity, which has suffered much and has a right to happiness. . . . Therefore let them dare to take me to court, and may the investigation take place in the light of day!

I am waiting.

From Émile Zola, *Oeuvres Complètes* (Paris: Cercle du Livre Précieux, 1969), Vol. 14, pp. 930–31 (translation by M. Knox).

---

balanced the universal suffrage of the *Reichstag*.

This was a system of checks that only Bismarck could balance. Its complexity was in part a result of his desire to make himself indispensable, and in part a reflection of the strength of the various mutually antagonistic forces with which he had to deal. The "National" Liberals who had chosen to

The French army, determined to brand Dreyfus as a traitor, provides him with a "guard of dishonor" whose backs are turned (1899).

cooperate with Bismarck after 1866 initially controlled the *Reichstag*. The Conservatives, thanks to the weighting of votes by income in the Prussian elections, held Prussia. The states retained the power to paralyze Reich finances.

All three forces were losers in the long term. The National Liberals failed to make the leap from mid-nineteenth-century party of notables to mass party that British Liberals and Tories had made between 1868 and 1880. That failure doomed the German liberals to long-term electoral decline. The Conservatives, despite an increasingly populist style from the 1890s on, only survived thanks to the three-class franchise and the votes of the landless peasants of the great estates. Conservatism lost whatever Pietist ethical content it may have had, and became the party of Junker "agribusiness." And the states lost vitality as national integration proceeded. That left a vacuum into which other forces gradually moved.

First of those forces were the German Catholics, who made up over 30 percent of the Reich's population. They responded to Bismarck's Protestant "Greater Prussia" with a national Catholic political party, the Center. When Bismarck and the National Liberals attacked them in the early 1870s as "ene-

mies of the Reich" who took their orders from Rome, Catholics rallied to Church and Center party. This "*Kulturkampf*" or "cultural struggle" between the Prusso-German state and the Catholic Church consolidated German political Catholicism as a party that held as much as a quarter of the popular vote. That electorate, precisely because its bond was religion, came from all classes, although it concentrated regionally in the Catholic south and west.

The second German mass party was that of the workers. Various workers' parties had emerged in the course of the 1860s, and in 1875 they coalesced to form the Social Democratic Party of Germany (SPD). Like the Center, the SPD suffered a Bismarckian preemptive attack. In 1878–79, in the course of a major policy change that involved alliance with Vienna, heavy protective tariffs, and the deliberate splitting of his National Liberal allies, Bismarck induced the *Reichstag* to outlaw SPD propaganda and mass meetings. He and his successors attempted to wean the workers away from the SPD with factory legislation and with the world's first state sickness and accident insurance (1883–84) and old age and disability pensions (1889). Neither stick nor carrot checked the SPD's growth. The masses flooding into the new industrial cities voted, and voted Socialist.

By 1891, affiliated with highly disciplined trade unions and equipped with a Marxist program, the SPD was poised for expansion. By the Reich's last election in 1912, it had conquered 29 percent of the vote, the largest of any single party—and the largest vote for any workers' party in the world. This massive bureaucratic organization, with its women's and youth affiliates, its social clubs and workers' libraries, its newspapers and periodicals, was the mainstay of the international working-class movement, the "Second International" that emerged in 1889 after the collapse of Marx's "First International."

Despite its verbal commitment to revolution, its "proletarian internation-

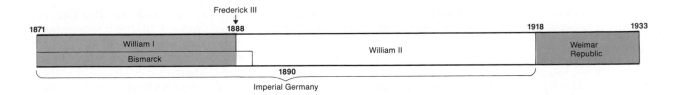

Frederick III
↓
1888

1871

William I

Bismarck

1918 1933

William II

Weimar Republic

1890

Imperial Germany

alism," and its hostility to "militarism," the SPD was and remained a working-class copy of the organization, sobriety, and discipline of the Prussian army. But it was not monolithic. The "revisionists" of its center and right, under the leadership of Edouard Bernstein, proposed to "revise" Marx. Like Jaurès in France, Bernstein believed that revolution was neither inevitable nor necessary, for the standard of living of the workers was rising. Social reform could and should come through ballot box and trade union. The SPD left, whose leading theoretician was the formidable Rosa Luxemburg, replied with vituperation. Reform was a "bourgeois swindle" and the revolutionary general strike was the just and necessary weapon of the "proletariat." That split increasingly threatened to crack the party open.

Failure to strangle the SPD at birth was the greatest of Bismarck's domestic defeats, but not the only one. His turn to protection in 1878–79 missed its two main goals. It did not provide the Reich with an adequate source of revenue independent of the states. Nor did it give the government a stable *Reichstag* majority. The often stormy alliance between right National Liberals and Conservatives, industry and agriculture, "iron and rye" that Bismarck created around protective tariffs only gained an absolute majority once, in the 1887 elections. Without a Boulanger, without an emergency real or imagined with which to rouse the electorate with cries of "the Fatherland in danger," neither Bismarck nor his successors were able to dominate the universal suffrage *Reichstag* he had created.

Ultimately he was also unable to dominate the Kaiser. The dependable William I died in 1888 at age 91. His successor, the reputedly liberal Frederick III, died of throat cancer shortly after ascending the throne, and had no time to remove Bismarck. Instead, William I's brilliant and unstable grandson became Kaiser William II. His education, received from a dour Calvinist pastor and the Prussian Guards officers' mess, was poorly calculated to induce moderation. His mother, Queen Victoria's daughter, voiced forebodings: "My son will be the ruin of Germany."

William II did not merely lead the new German industrial military monarchy forward, as he put it, "toward glorious times." He personified its blend of manic self-confidence and inward self-doubt, of fear and aggression. He soon fell out with Bismarck. The old man, to render himself indispensable, even wrecked the *Reichstag* coalition of 1887; he also proposed to suppress the SPD with Maxim guns. In March 1890, after an exchange of insults, the Kaiser sent Bismarck into vengeful retirement.

Henceforth William II planned to rule personally. But he failed to fill Bismarck's heroic role, and he and his subjects increasingly lacked Bismarck's sense of limits. The Kaiser's frequent "oratorical derailments" created chaos in both foreign and domestic affairs. By 1897 he did acquire a team capable of translating his enthusiasms into coherent policy: the 78-year-old Prince Chlodwig von Hohenlohe-Schillingsfürst as figurehead chancellor, the slippery Bernhard von Bülow as foreign secretary, and the supremely devious Admiral Alfred von Tirpitz as chief of the navy that was to make the new Germany a world power (see pp. 829–30). But William's short attention span and inability to resist the influences of

William II, king of Prussia and emperor of Germany, 1888–1918, in a favorite uniform—that of the Death's Head Hussars.

the fire-eating young Guards officers of his entourage guaranteed further crises.

In 1908, after a series of scandals at court had sapped the monarchy's reputation, William gave an interview to the British *Daily Telegraph* in which he unwittingly offended British and German public opinion simultaneously. The ensuing outcry included criticism of the All-Highest in the *Reichstag,* and gave him a nervous breakdown. Henceforth his interventions were less frequent, although his fear of being thought weak played a fateful role in 1914.

The force that increasingly took the monarchy's place and filled the political vacuum that the failure of the National Liberals had left was German nationalism. The Liberals had themselves promoted the growing Bismarck cult to combat regional particularism. On the far right a variety of groups emerged with more extreme visions. The Farmers' League, a rabble-rousing spin-off of the Conservatives, began in the 1890s to mobilize the rural masses with anti-Semitism. Jews, money, machinery, cities, the SPD, modernity—all were allegedly ruining the world of authentic German values and destroying the *Volk* community.

This sort of racist "cultural pessimism" was not unique to Germany. French racist fanatics such as Count Arthur de Gobineau (*On the Inequality of Human Races,* 1859) and Drumont had thought up or propagated many of the notions that became current in Germany in the 1880s and 1890s. But France was industrializing less rapidly than Germany and was thus under less intense social strain. Above all, its political tradition since 1789 had stressed equality and rights. In Germany, once religious anti-Semitism met Darwin's ambiguous legacy in the 1880s, restraints collapsed. The Conservatives made anti-Semitism socially respectable, part of the ideological armory of the new nationalism.

Other groups, such as the Navy League to which Tirpitz played sorcer-er's apprentice and the Pan-German League founded in 1890, increasingly put forward megalomaniacal foreign policy programs with domestic implications. Their more extreme members created a grass-roots right-wing politics of a new kind, independent of the parties and the government. This loose movement was increasingly divorced from the monarchy and from the nobility, whom the new nationalists saw as castebound and inadequate. Erich Ludendorff, non-noble general staff officer, anti-Semite, and personification of the new outlook, put it well after 1914. Asked for his views on the monarchy, Ludendorff replied "I prefer to call it Fatherland." All that such people lacked was a vehicle and an occasion for mobilizing the masses. The coming great war gave them that and much else.

Russia: Despotism and Revolution

"Russian government is an absolute monarchy tempered by assassination," wrote a French observer in the 1830s. Despite Catherine the Great's concessions to the nobility, the tsar, thanks to the Tartar autocratic tradition of the Muscovite state, remained a ruler more absolute than any eighteenth-century Western enlightened absolutist. Preserving autocracy as the nineteenth century drew on required ever-sterner measures.

Nicholas I succeeded the neurotic Alexander I in December 1825. Confusion over the succession prompted dissident noble officers under the influence of half-understood French liberalism to attempt a palace coup. After its failure, Nicholas had personally interrogated the surviving "Decembrist" leaders and had vowed to prevent a recurrence. His remedy was an ever more extensive and powerful secret police and laws against what the next century came to call "thought-crime." The tsarist criminal code of 1845 was unique in Europe. It devoted 54 pages to "crimes against the state" and decreed savage penalties for merely raising "doubts" about the authority of the tsar.

The autocracy nevertheless faced a fundamental contradiction. The preservation of its power rested on external success. Yet the bayonets of conscripted serfs were no longer enough; defeat in the Crimea in 1854–56 had proved that. The continuance of success, and thus autocracy, in the machine age required a society capable of economic growth. But growth in turn created demands for political participation that threatened autocracy.

The successor of Nicholas, Tsar Alexander II (r. 1855–81) chose development, but with what he hoped were safeguards. In 1861, following the example of Peter the Great, he imposed on Russia a revolution from above: the emancipation of the serfs. The end of bondage would permit universal military service, raise agricultural productivity, free labor for industrialization, and galvanize society into a prosperity that would restore Russia's threatened power position. Alexander's great Emancipation Edict of 1861 freed from the rule of their landlords the 22.5 million serfs that made up almost 38 percent of the Russian empire's population. What it did not do was free them from the land. To aid tax collection and to retain control of the peasantry, the autocracy kept the peasants bound to their village community, the *mir*. The landowners retained two thirds of the land and the former serfs received only a third, for which they had to pay through installments that extended over the following 49 years.

Land redemption debt, the stifling effects of the *mir* on enterprise among its members, and massive population growth ensured that emancipation merely turned a serf problem into a peasant problem. The rural population leapt upward from 50 million in the early 1860s to 82 million in 1897. Competition from newly created industries in the cities lessened peasant income from traditional village handicrafts. Peasants who stayed on rather than migrating to mines and cities waited expectantly for a final redivision of the land that would wipe the landlords out.

More immediately damaging to the autocracy than this growing potential for rural revolt was a loss of control over educated society. Russia had few cities and no middle class of any size in 1800. It developed them hesitantly, with the support of the autocratic state's efforts at industrialization. What it above all developed was an intelligentsia, a minority defined first by its education and then by its opposition to the autocracy. That minority produced some of the nineteenth century's greatest literature in any language, from the poetry of Pushkin to the novels of Turgenev, Tolstoy, and Dostoyevsky. But thanks to the autocracy that prevented it from acquiring political experience, it also developed, like the thinkers of Enlightenment France, a variety of dangerous utopias.

The generation that followed the Decembrists took their inspiration from Hegel rather than liberalism. They asked how Russia might contribute to the self-realization of the world spirit. In the 1840s and 1850s their dominant school, the "Slavophiles," argued that Russia's very differences from the West were Russia's strength. The Westernizing experiment of Peter the Great, they insisted, had been a disastrous mistake that had fortunately failed. Thanks to Orthodox Church and *mir*, Russia had not succumbed to rationalism, individualism, alienation. Russia's mission, they proclaimed, was therefore to give humanity back its soul. A variety of critics, often called "Westerners," pointed out that the *mir* was above all an invention of the autocracy's tax collectors, and suggested that talk of Russia's soul was utopian glorification of backwardness. But Slavophilism persisted, and furnished much of the substance of Muscovite "Great Russian" nationalism.

The generation that followed emancipation argued more about politics than about Russia's soul. By the 1860s non-nobles had reached the universi-

Alexander II, "tsar Liberator" of the serfs.

ties in numbers. The learned professions were beginning to proliferate, providing political radicalism with a social base. A Left emerged that derided the reforms of the 1860s as insufficient and dedicated itself to the autocracy's overthrow. In 1874 several thousand students went "to the people" to create a peasant revolutionary movement. Peasants reacted to these "populists" with suspicion and revealed a deep interest in private property that shocked students brought up on Slavophile visions of peasant communism.

Defeat in the countryside and mass arrests impelled some radicals toward terrorism. A tiny conspiratorial group, with the presumption characteristic of those who believe they possess the absolute truth, named itself "The People's Will" (*Narodnaya Volya*). It hunted the tsar himself and killed him in March 1881. The new tsar, Alexander III (r. 1881–94), crushed *Narodnaya Volya* and created the dreaded *Okhrana*, a secret police even more powerful than its predecessors. Repression froze what little political life Russia pos-

sessed. An anti-Semitic radical Right grew, with government support, to oppose the revolutionary intelligentsia. Slavophilism mutated into Russian nationalism and Pan-Slavism, the claim that the Russian state was the patron of Slavs everywhere. Right-wing opinion, as in Imperial Germany, began to place limits on the autocracy's flexibility in foreign affairs.

At home, after the defeat of *Narodnaya Volya*, the radicals turned increasingly to the "scientific" certainties of Marxism. But Marxism was a theory of revolution for advanced countries. That posed a dilemma in Russia, which still awaited both a "bourgeoisie" and a "bourgeois revolution." Vladimir Ilyitch Ulyanov, brother of a hanged member of *Narodnaya Volya* and son of an imperial bureaucrat, found the answer. Under the alias of V. I. Lenin, he embraced the voluntarism that was one part of Marx's legacy. It was the task of Russian Social Democracy, Lenin announced, to force the pace of history. It must take command of Russia's small but growing industrial working class and itself overthrow the autocracy.

The professional revolutionary: Vladimir Ilyitch Lenin (center) with associates (1895).

For that task, Lenin created a new kind of organization, the embryo of the twentieth-century one-party state. The history of Europe after 1848, Lenin saw, demonstrated that Marx had been wrong. The proletariat under capitalism was not spontaneously revolutionary. "The working class, exclusively by its own effort, is able to develop only trade-union consciousness," he wrote with contempt. Logically enough, Lenin recognized that the vehicle of socialist revolution was not the working class, but the "bourgeois intelligentsia: contemporary socialism was born in the heads of individual members of that class." Only the mobilization of that "class" could bring revolution. In 1902 he spelled out what was needed in a famous tract, *What Is to Be Done?* An organized minority of "professional revolutionaries" must serve as vanguard to the childlike masses. "Give us an organization of revolutionaries," wrote Lenin, "and we will overturn Russia!" That organization arose from Lenin's splitting of the Russian Social Democratic party at its conference in London in 1903. His faction henceforth claimed for themselves the title of "men of the majority," or *Bolsheviki,* and imposed on their irresolute opponents the demeaning title of *Mensheviki,* or "men of the minority." Lenin's narrow sect ("better fewer, but better") slowly grew.

Imperial Russia's first revolution owed nothing to the Bolsheviks. The autocracy sought reinforcement by courting "a victorious little war" against Japan in 1904 (see pp. 829–31). Defeat instead led to urban and rural revolt. Russia after 1890 had begun to industrialize at a startling rate under the impulse of French loans and of bureaucrats such as Sergei Witte, creator of the Trans-Siberian Railway. The opening up of the coal and iron of the Donetz basin and the oil of the Caucasus made Russia an industrial world power. In the cities of northern Russia, textile and mechanical industries grew feverishly. And an industrial work force torn from its villages and as yet

---

Lenin Invents the Dictatorship of the Vanguard Party   1902

I assert:

(1) that no revolutionary movement can endure without a stable organization of leaders maintaining continuity;

(2) that the broader the popular mass drawn spontaneously into the struggle, which forms the basis of the movement and participates in it, the more urgent the need for such an organization, and the more solid this organization must be (for it is much easier for all sorts of demagogues to side-track the more backward sections of the masses);

(3) that such an organization must consist chiefly of people professionally engaged in revolutionary activity;

(4) that in an autocratic state, the more we *confine* the membership of such an organization to people who are professionally trained in the art of combating the political police, the more difficult it will be to unearth the organization.

From Vladimir Ilyitch Lenin, *What Is to Be Done? Burning Questions of Our Movement* (New York: International Publishers, 1969), p. 121.

---

largely unprotected by factory legislation proved far more radical than Lenin had suspected.

The shooting in front of the Winter Palace of an unarmed crowd petitioning the tsar on January 22, 1905, "Bloody Sunday," touched off a widespread anarchic revolt in the cities. But that spontaneous popular insurrection failed to find leaders. The Mensheviks lacked the will; they expected that in the fullness of time a "bourgeois revolution" would pave the way for their own socialist one. The Socialist Revolutionaries, heirs to the Populists, expected peasant uprisings and were unprepared to lead the workers. The Bolsheviks were too few, and naturally distrusted this spontaneous expression of the popular will. The last tsar, the fatuous Nicholas II (r. 1894–1917), was thus able to end the Revolution of 1905. He conceded his subjects a legislature or *Duma,* while loyal troops, bureau-

Bloody Sunday, January 22, 1905. Tsarist troops fire on a procession of workers, killing 70 and wounding 240.

crats, and police gradually suppressed the revolutionary workers' councils or Soviets that had given the revolution what little organization it possessed. The far Right, organized with official approval in the "League of the Russian People" or Black Hundreds, massacred Jews and opponents of the autocracy.

Constitutional experimentation soon ended. Two successive *Dumas* defied the government with demands for civil rights and reforms. Nicholas refused to surrender his autocratic power. Restriction of the franchise produced a Third *Duma* (1907–12) of "masters, priests, and lackeys" that proved more pliable. Under its last strong minister, Peter Stolypin, the autocracy attempted belatedly to finish the emancipation of the peasants from the *mir*, while suppressing all opposition. Stolypin died by assassination in 1911. More despotism bred further extremism and pushed Russia's few Liberals to believe naively that the far Left was preferable to the autocracy. As a new war approached in 1914, waves of massive strikes convulsed urban Russia.

Tsarism desperately needed victory, but victory might not suffice to save it.

Austria-Hungary: Dynastic Empire in an Age of National States

For Austria, 1866 was not merely a military defeat, but a portent. The breakthrough of the national state in central Europe threatened the break-up of the empire itself. Austria survived because Bismarck needed it. "If you ask me what we have promised Austria in return for her friendship, I should answer 'life,'" remarked Prussia's ambassador in Vienna to his Russian colleague in the fall of 1870. Austrian collapse would saddle Protestant Prussia with the Catholic Austrian Germans and with Austria's Balkan quarrels with Russia.

But German goodwill alone could not ensure Austria's long-term survival. That required an ideology, an "Austrian Idea," to counter the nationalism of the subject peoples. Preserving the economic integration of the Danube basin, the ties of agrarian Hungary to industrial Vienna and Bohemia, was not sufficiently inspiring. Good government from the most efficient bureaucracy of east central Europe was likewise no answer to the increasing clamor of the nationalities for rule—or misrule—by their own. And Austria's substitute for colonial expansion, its "civilizing mission" in the Balkans, encouraged the same sort of nationalist reaction that bedeviled the European powers in Asia and Africa.

Emperor Francis Joseph (r. 1848–1916) and his ministers faced a central paradox. Preserving Habsburg freedom of action, as always, required playing off the empire's provinces and nationalities against one another. But in the age of nationalism, that strategy could only encourage the nationalities to greater and greater mutual intolerance, and tear the monarchy apart. And if, by some miracle, the monarchy should successfully promote compromise between the nationalities, they would then be free to combine against the monarchy itself.

The dynasty therefore played for time. In 1866–67 Francis Joseph grudgingly struck a bargain with Hungary to prepare the way for a war of revenge against Prussia. That *"Ausgleich"* or compromise of 1867 gave the Hungarians what their moderates had sought in 1848: full control of affairs within the far-flung borders of a "greater Hungary" that included millions of Rumanians, Serbs, and Croats. The only institutions of importance that Hungary thereafter shared with the rest of the monarchy were the emperor and the ministries of foreign affairs and war. And Hungary received, in effect, a veto over Habsburg foreign and military policy.

When Austrian revenge on Prussia seemed possible in alliance with France in 1870, the Hungarians exercised that veto. Prussia had made the *Ausgleich* possible; a Habsburg reversal of the verdict of 1866 would automatically place Hungary's hard-won autonomy in question. The revolutionary alliance with Hungary against Vienna that Bismarck had toyed with in 1866 thereby became a tacit German-Magyar agreement to preserve the new status quo. Thus the provisional became permanent. The *Ausgleich* made Austria the "Dual Monarchy" of Austria-Hungary until 1918. In Hungary, the gentry ruthlessly Magyarized the subject nationalities and dominated the voteless and voiceless Hungarian peasantry. In the remainder of the empire, the German "ruling *Volk*" fought a losing battle against the rise of the Czechs.

After a series of unsatisfactory German liberal ministries, Francis Joseph turned in 1879 to an aristocrat of Irish extraction, Count Eduard Taafe. Taafe's formula was simple and for a time effective. In the *Reichsrat*, the legislature of the non-Hungarian parts of the empire, he created a government bloc of loyal Poles, clericals, and Czechs, the so-called "iron ring." With that support, and with the aim of keeping "all the nationalities of the empire in a balanced state of mild dissatisfaction," he kept the peace until his fall in 1893.

The German-Czech conflict over rich and rapidly industrializing Bohemia burst Taafe's framework. Since 1848 the Czechs had developed a high culture, complete with composers such as Bedřich Smetana and Antonín Dvořák, that put to shame German claims of cultural superiority. The Czechs had nationalized their masses with schooling in Czech and with a university at Prague. They were developing an industrial middle class. And their most advanced politicians, the "young Czechs" (shades of Mazzini) refused to subscribe to Taafe's proposed arrangement for sharing power with the Germans in Bohemia.

The Germans were equally obdurate. In Vienna, that cosmopolitan city of art and vice, a variety of anti-Slav and anti-Semitic demagogues arose. The fanatical Georg von Schönerer preached that "religion is irrelevant, *race* is the source of the swinishness" that he ascribed to the Jews. The mayor of Vienna, Karl Lueger, organized a "Christian Social" party that mixed populist clericalism with an anti-Semitism more decorous than that of Schönerer; its descendants still give Austrian politics their peculiar tone. Even Austrian social democracy divided into German and Czech national socialisms. Language and culture proved, there and elsewhere, more powerful than class.

In 1897 the dynasty tilted decisively toward the Czechs. It pushed through a decree requiring that state officials in Bohemia be bilingual in Czech and German. Since no German would deign to learn Czech, that excluded the Germans from state employment and from power. The Germans rioted. Schönerer thundered at the dynasty's betrayal of Germandom. He and other lesser fanatics looked to Prussia-Germany against a Habsburg state which they accused of submerging the Austrian Germans in Slavs and Jews.

In the short term the Germans won. The monarchy dismissed Count Casimir Badeni, responsible for the language decree, and rescinded the decree itself in 1899. Naturally the Czechs rioted in response. Slovenes and Italians fought in Trieste. Some Croats began to feel the pull of the notion of a "South Slav" (Yugoslav) state of Croats, Slovenes, and Serbs. The "South Slav" idea had little basis in history, culture, or religion, for Slovenes and Croats were Catholic and Western in orientation, Serbs Orthodox and Balkan. But it gradually spread; fear that independent Serbia might prove the "Piedmont of the South Slavs" provoked hysteria in Vienna.

In 1906–07 the dynasty at last fell back on universal suffrage, hoping to submerge the competing nationalisms in a flood of loyal clerical peasant votes. But universal schooling had made the peasants into Germans, Czechs, Croats, and Slovenes. After 1909 Francis Joseph and his ministers therefore ignored the *Reichsrat* and ruled by decree. Reformers floated a variety of federal or "trialist" plans to give Slavs equality with Germans and Magyars. But Germans and Magyars preferred to wreck the monarchy rather than suffer diminution of their "historic rights." In the face of ever-intensifying internal conflict, Austria-Hungary's "idea" remained Church, dynasty, bureaucracy, and army. By 1914 those institutions were strong but wasting assets.

Italy: Least of the Great Powers

The weight of Italy's historic greatness almost crushed the new Italian national state. Ideologues from the radical Mazzini rightwards insisted that the new Italy must be and act as a great power. The legacy of the Roman empire and of Italy's economic and cultural primacy in the Renaissance demanded no less.

Italian reality was ill-equipped to live up to such expectations. The South, where landlords' horses lived better than peasants, was two centuries or more behind the North. At unification in 1861, illiteracy ranged from 54 percent of the population over six years of age in the North to 89 percent in the South and the islands. Even the relatively prosperous North lacked an industrial base, for Italy had little iron and almost no coal.

The new state also had a narrow political base. In part this was deliberate. Cavour and his heirs feared the masses with their potential for anarchic radicalism or Bourbon-clerical revolt. Until 1882 the electoral law gave 2 percent or less of the population the vote; after that date 7 to 9.4 percent could vote. In part, narrowness was unavoidable. The illiterate, until they encountered conscription, had little idea that they even belonged to a national state. And after 1870, furious at his loss of Rome, Pope Pius IX had locked himself in the Vatican and ordered a Catholic boycott of Italian politics. That was no small loss for a state with a population that was nominally 99 percent Catholic.

Finally, the later stages of unification were demoralizing. War in 1866 brought Venetia into the state, but only because Prussia won at Königgrätz; Italy itself suffered humiliating defeats by land and sea. The taking of Rome from the Pope in 1870 was inglorious. The petty spectacle of parliamentary politics provoked the scorn of the aged Mazzini and of nationalists such as the poet Giosuè Carducci: "Oh for the days of sun, of liberty and glory in 1860. . . . Oh for the struggles of titans between Cavour and Garibaldi in 1861!" "What have we become?" asked Carducci despairingly.

What Italy had become was a moderately successful parliamentary regime under a series of centrist coalitions resembling those of France's Third Republic. Defeat in 1866 at least banished the specter of a revival of royal absolutism. Victor Emmanuel II and his army henceforth lacked the prestige for Bismarckian solutions. Under Cavour's heirs, the moderate liberal *Destra* or Right, Italy paid the immense debts of the wars of unification and balanced the budget. The money came mostly from the hard-pressed peasantry, but at least Italy did not follow Egypt and Turkey into debt bondage. The *Destra* reformed the army, although that institution still lacked the prestige needed to attract first-rate officer material. Finally, the *Destra* gave Italy some small voice in the councils of the great powers.

In 1876 a motley coalition of northern left-liberals and southern landowners, henceforth known as the *Sinistra* or Left, ousted the *Destra*. The *Sinistra* extended the franchise and made elementary education free and compulsory in law if not yet in fact. It also created a parliamentary tradition that outlasted the century, for the southern landlords, in return for patronage jobs and public works, gave the government of the day their votes. That bargain, rather like the tacit agreement that ended Reconstruction in the United States, helped stabilize parliament at the price of social and political stagnation in the South.

By the 1890s a variety of forces pressed against the system. The steamship brought in cheap grain and ruined southern agriculture, then bore away the resulting emigrants. Peasant unrest in Sicily unnerved the governments of the early 1890s. A socialist movement, Bakuninite in the 1870s and Marxist by the 1890s, gained ground. And unlike their counterparts elsewhere, the Italian socialists successfully organized parts of the countryside. By the first decade of the new century the unions of landless agricultural laborers of the rich Po Valley in north Italy were strong enough to stage bitter province-wide strikes.

Even Catholicism began to stir politically. Leo XIII (r. 1878–1903) weakened his predecessor's prohibitions of Catholic political participation in Italy, just as he had urged Catholics to "rally" to the Third Republic in France. Then his successor Pius X (r. 1903–14) revived some of Pius IX's denunciations of modernity. The entry of organized Catholicism into Italian politics

was thus slow. But by the 1913 election it was an accomplished fact.

The *Sinistra* had its last incarnation under the charismatic Sicilian and ex-Mazzinian, Francesco Crispi (prime minister, 1887–91, 1893–96). It fell resoundingly after catastrophe at Adowa ended Crispi's bid for a vast East African empire. Riots against the African war and hard times at home inaugurated a period of bayonets in the streets and right-wing governments. The king, Victor Emmanuel's son Umberto I, imposed a general as prime minister before his own assassination by an anarchist in 1900. Parliament fought back, and won decisively.

With the new century came economic takeoff and political stability under the greatest of Cavour's successors, Giovanni Giolitti (prime minister 1903–05, 1906–09, 1911–14). Giolitti despised rhetoric; that won him respect but no fanatical followers. He knew well that Italy's uneven economic and social development had produced bizarre political effects—including his own need to pay southern deputies for their support. If you cut a suit for a hunchback, he once remarked, you get a hunchbacked suit.

What he attempted was gradual reforms that would integrate the new mass forces, the Socialists and Catholics, into the Liberal parliamentary system without destroying it. He refused to persecute the Socialists. To the horror of Italy's industrialists, he did his best to keep the state neutral in labor disputes. His greatest monument was the enactment in 1912 of virtual universal male suffrage, which expanded the electorate from 3.3 million to 8.6 million. It was also his downfall.

The Catholics proved difficult and demanding allies. On the Left, extremists that included a certain Benito Mussolini (see pp. 914–919) captured the socialist party leadership and closed off any chance of cooperation with Giolitti. The prime minister's own supporters in parliament resented concessions he had made to the Catholics, and overthrew him in March 1914. "Red Week,"

Francesco Crispi, Mazzinian revolutionary and colonial enthusiast.

Facts, not rhetoric: Giovanni Giolitti (1842–1928), five times prime minister of Italy.

an immense wave of Anarchist and left-Socialist-led riots that swept north Italy in June 1914, soon made Giolitti's sober common sense and conciliation look outdated and naive.

Intellectuals of all stripes had long railed against his lack of charisma. The young literary firebrands of the Italian Nationalist Association lamented that Italy "had been too much made with diplomatic intrigues and foreign arms." They and others forcefully revived a myth widespread since the anticlimax of the *Risorgimento.* "Making Italians," the completion of national integration, required a great war. Giolitti's right-Liberal successor Antonio Salandra was soon to find that war, and with it destroy Liberal Italy.

BATTLES FOR WOMEN'S RIGHTS

The coming of mass politics for men inevitably raised the question of the rights of women. It opened an arena in which large numbers of women could for the first time press their case not merely for the vote but for equality between the sexes. That was a question that went far beyond politics.

Male domination of women has taken many forms. Its foremost mid-

Crusader for hospital reform: Florence Nightingale (1820–1910).

nineteenth-century incarnation was middle-class woman's role as pedestal-mounted "angel in the house." That notion was in part a consequence of the separation of life into work and home, male and female domains, that came with industrialization. But it also had pseudo-scientific underpinnings. Learned doctors discoursed on women's presumed lack of sexual passion and on the alleged "gigantic power and influence of the ovaries" over woman's whole being. For such pundits, women's position was biologically determined: "What was decided among the prehistoric Protozoa, cannot be annulled by Act of Parliament." What passed for science thus dispensed even liberals from giving women the same rights as men. Religion contributed as well to the myth of woman's domestic nature. In the 1820s the churches took to insisting that women, who were proving more resistant than men to the temptations of religious skepticism, were also "purer" than men. Preservation of that purity required their continued confinement to the home.

By the 1860s, especially in Britain, these notions were under attack. Women had penetrated previously male citadels such as hospitals and schools. Florence Nightingale made nursing a profession for women by her crusade against the British army's grotesque mismanagement of medical services in the Crimea. Soon a broad women's movement pressed for higher education and careers for single middle-class women. In the 1870s Girton and Newnham Colleges at Cambridge began giving women degrees. Pioneers opened up medicine and the law. Agitation led to reforms in the 1870s and 1880s of Britain's crude laws governing marriage, divorce, and the age of consent. Women's bodies and property ceased to belong to their husbands in a literal, legal sense.

The British "feminists"—the French word became current in the 1890s—also attacked the legal double standard in a more spectacular way. They crusaded successfully against the Contagious Diseases Acts (repealed 1886) that mandated venereal disease examinations and quarantine for prostitutes— but not soldiers—in garrison towns. The acts, they insisted, were government endorsement of the creation of "a *slave* class of women to minister to lust." The crusaders sought to do more than raise the status of women. They proposed to reform men and revolutionize the relationship between the sexes.

When the Liberals came to power in the 1906 election, the women's movement attempted to hold them to liberal principles. But the evasive Herbert Asquith (prime minister, 1908–16) and the even more slippery Lloyd George torpedoed women's suffrage legislation in 1910. The Women's Social and Political Union (WSPU), under the leadership of Emmeline Pankhurst and her daughter Christabel ("Votes for Women, and Chastity for Men"), thereupon declared war on government, Parliament, and men. "Suffragette" activists attempted to force police cordons in Parliament Square; the police and male bystanders replied with violence and sexual abuse. Christabel Pankhurst orchestrated a campaign of window-smashing, burning of country houses, attacks on art galleries, and bombs in Westminster Abbey. To trial and imprisonment, the WSPU replied with hunger strikes. The government countered with forced feeding. Opinion, including opinion among women, was overwhelmingly against WSPU defiance of the law. But WSPU tactics provoked the government to acts that weakened its position.

Finally, in June 1914, Asquith consented to receive a delegation of working women under the leadership of Sylvia Pankhurst, Christabel's sister and a labor activist. The specter of a potential mobilization of working-class women into a genuine mass movement apparently made Asquith quail. He lost all stomach for further warfare between the sexes, and undertook to support a women's suffrage bill. The war delayed it until 1918, but eased its passage. The

A policeman carries Mrs. Emmeline Pankhurst bodily off to jail during a 1911 suffrage demonstration.

contribution of women to the war effort made it impossible to deny them the vote.

Continental feminists faced societies far less tolerant than Britain (or than the United States, where suffrage agitation developed intertwined with evangelical religion and the temperance movement). And as with continental liberalism, continental feminism tended to be far less radical than its British counterpart. In France and Germany, middle-class feminists inclined toward the "equal but different" school. Woman's role as mother and her right to control reproduction was the focus of the work of widely influential figures such as Ellen Key (1849–1926) of Sweden or Nelly Roussel (1878–1922) of France. The most radical continental women tended to gravitate to the women's affiliates of the socialist parties, which took more interest in woman's presumed oppression by capitalism than her domination by man. Nevertheless, the socialist parties of the Second International were the first continental political parties to endorse women's suffrage. By the end of the great war that began in 1914 much of western Europe was ready to follow them.

RISE AND FALL OF THE CULT OF SCIENCE

The waning of traditional forms of religious belief helped open space for a variety of other faiths. Nationalism and socialism provided their adherents with many of the consolations that earlier generations had gained from religion. After mid-century a misunderstood science provided a third secular religion: the "cult of science."

The furious attacks of religious figures on Darwin and Lyell were misplaced; the rise of science did not challenge religion in any direct, logical sense. God is not subject to empirical proof or disproof. But the new science did provide a semblance of empirical underpinning for statements of faith—in science. The source of the cult was the Enlightenment vision of a machine-like universe in which everything was in principle knowable. The cult's nineteenth-century founder, Auguste Comte (1798–1857), attempted from the 1820s to the 1850s to systematize all of human knowledge. He postulated—like Hegel and Marx—a series of stages. For Comte, humanity's road led from theology to metaphysics and from metaphysics to science, which was the domain of what Comte called "positive" or empirically verifiable knowledge. The "Positivism" of Comte and successors enshrined science as the new diety. Comte was confident that even the messy affairs of humanity would eventually yield scientific general laws in the form of a discipline of "sociology."

That discipline has still to yield general laws. That did not stop Comte's most conspicuous successor, the indefatigable Herbert Spencer (1820–1903) from following in his footsteps. Spencer's *Synthetic Philosophy* (1862–96) attempted in ten volumes what Comte had attempted in six, the compression of all of human knowledge into a positivist framework. And Darwin was the centerpiece of Spencer's work, but a Darwin misapplied to social phenomena. Darwin himself was in part responsible for this misunderstanding. In *The Descent of Man* he incautiously speculated that "the wonderful progress of the United States, as well of that character of its people, are the results of natural selection; the more energetic, courageous, and restless men from all parts of Europe having emigrated during the last ten or twelve generations to that great country. . . . "

Alongside Spencer a wide variety of "social Darwinists" proliferated. Most argued (in the words of Walter Bagehot, high priest of the English constitution) that "the majority of the groups which win and conquer are better than that majority which fail and perish." That was a wonderfully convenient rationalization for "might makes right" among nations, social groups, and individuals. The oil king John D. Rockefeller trumpeted that business was "merely the survival of the fittest . . . the working out of a law of nature and a law of God."

In Germany the task of propagating and popularizing Darwinian biology fell to Ernst Haeckel (1834–1919). He followed in the footsteps of Feuerbach (whose materialism had influenced Marx) and of the best-selling crank Ludwig Büchner (1824–99). Büchner's *Force and Matter* (1852) confidently asserted that since matter and energy were eternal, it was "impossible that the world can have been created. How could anything have been created that cannot be annihilated?"

Haeckel, simultaneously Darwinist and social Darwinist, defied 25 centuries of Western thought by abolishing any distinction between humanity and nature; he called the cult he founded and led "Monism." In his international best-seller of 1899, *The Riddle of the Universe*, he mocked theological and metaphysical speculation. Questions not susceptible to empirical answers were not questions. And "Monism" meant that upon pain of degeneration humanity must live in harmony with "the laws of nature." Chief of those laws was natural selection. When Haeckel's notion of nature as legislator for man

The Thinker: Friedrich Nietzsche, the last great German philosopher.

met the ideas of racist cranks such as Gobineau, the results were intellectual high explosive. Marx had abolished all theoretical restraints on revolutionary dictatorship and on the elimination of the "class enemy." Haeckel, Gobineau, and Kaiser William II's friend, the racist-social Darwinist Houston Stuart Chamberlain (*The Foundations of the Nineteenth Century,* 1899) similarly abolished intellectual and moral restrictions on the liquidation of the "racial enemy."

The Revolt against Positivism

The domination of the positivist cult of science was shortlived, although its influence persists to our own day. In the realm of philosophy, a commanding figure soon emerged who denounced almost every aspect of the present, science and its idolaters included. Friedrich Nietzsche (1844–1900), son of a Protestant pastor, was the last great German philosopher of the nineteenth century. He was the antithesis of his system-building predecessors, whose work he ridiculed. From 1872 until his final collapse into syphilitic dementia in 1889 he bombarded a growing public with at least one work each year. One of the greatest masters of the German language, he leapt from one striking aphorism to the next. He frequently contradicted himself, and always contradicted others. He damned the smugness of the age.

Nietzsche's message was at bottom consistent. Contradiction was life. Philosophy was not systemic, but perpetual question and experiment. Morality— for Nietzsche in his eccentric way was the last great moralist—took precedence over knowledge. Scientific truth was valuable only insofar as it contributed to "life." And to Nietzsche the law of the modern world was not the survival of the fittest but that of ever-growing mediocrity. Darwin had it backwards. In reality "happy accidents are eliminated, the more highly evolved types lead nowhere, it is the average and below average types

---

Nietzsche Speaks

Truths are illusions that one has forgotten *are* illusions.

Nothing is true, everything is permitted.

Why morality, when life, nature, and history are "unmoral"?

The common man alone has the prospect of carrying on, of propagating himself—he is the man of the future, the only survivor; "Be like him! Become mediocre!" is now the only morality that still has a meaning or an audience. But it is hard to preach, this morality of mediocrity.

Objection, evasion, gleeful mistrust and irony are signs of health. Everything absolute belongs to pathology.

In individuals, insanity is rare, but in groups, parties, nations and epochs, it is the rule.

The thought of suicide is a powerful consolation; with it one can get through many a bad night.

Man must be trained for war and woman for the recreation of the warrior: anything else is silliness.

I have only rarely the courage of what I know.

Dear Professor, in the end I would have much preferred being a Basel professor to being God. But I did not dare carry my private egotism so far as to omit—for its sake—the creation of the world. . . . [Nietzsche's last letter, to the Basel historian Jacob Burckhardt, January 1889]

From *Friedrich Nietzsche, Werke in Drei Bänden,* ed. by Karl Schlechta (Munich: Karl Hanser Verlag, 1954–56), 3:314, 2:889, 2:645, 2:737, 2:637, 2:328, 3:1272, 3:1351 (translation by M. Knox).

---

which ineluctably ascend to power." Women's emancipation was "one of the worst developments of the general *uglification* of Europe." Nationalism was unbearably crass: the new Reich of 1871, bristling "hedgehog-fashion" with arms was "the most stupid, the most depraved, the most mendacious form of 'the German spirit' that ever was." Nietzsche likewise denounced anti-Semitism and the Germanic tribal cult of the composer Richard Wagner, whom he had originally admired.

Christianity, for Nietzsche, was worst of all. It stifled "life" and dragged down the exceptional individual with its "slave morality" of meekness and compassion. Nietzsche consoled himself by contemplating what he described as "the greatest event of recent times—that 'God is dead,' that the belief in the Christian God is no longer tenable." Nietzsche's morality was that of the isolated exception, the aristocratic *Übermensch* or "superman" living "beyond good and evil" and outside society and politics. "Life," the "will to power," was supreme over all else.

That proved a dangerous legacy. In the short term Nietzsche appealed to socialists, anarchists, and outsiders. His denunciations of German nationalism infuriated the pan-Germans. But Nietzsche's popularization, which ironically accelerated immediately after his descent into madness, ultimately made "the will to power" and the "superman" into myths of the new populist Right. "Everything is permitted" became a credo for political "supermen" riding the coming wave of war and revolution.

Other late nineteenth- and early twentieth-century philosophers, especially the Frenchman Henri Bergson (1859–1941), shared Nietzsche's abhorrence of rationalist system-building. But it was the world of medicine and scholarship that offered the most decisive rejection of positivism. In the mid-1890s a Vienna medical figure, Sigmund Freud (1856–1939) began publishing a series of works that offered the first serious attempt to understand the human mind. To the horror of a prudish age, Freud argued that sex was the root of human motivation. He pioneered the exploration of unconscious layers and processes in the mind, thus exploding the assumption of positivists and rationalists that "mind" meant the conscious mind. He tapped the unconscious with novel techniques: hypnosis, dream interpretation, and free association. What Marx did for economics as a historical force, Freud did for the unconscious.

Unfortunately for the further development of his new discipline of psychoanalysis, it soon emerged that Freud's elaborate theoretical structure was metaphor rather than a verifiable scientific theory. Freud warred with prominent disciples such as Carl Gustav Jung (1875–1961) and Alfred Adler (1870–1937) over key points of interpretation. Even more than Marxism, Freudianism and the larger psychoanalytic movement that it created has relished the hunt for error and deviation. That has placed in question its claim to be science; for good or ill science is about empirical proof. And Freud's attitude towards women, whom his odd theory of "penis-envy" consigned anew to biological inferiority, has not gone unchallenged. But Freud was in some ways a good prophet of the coming century, thanks to his experience of Austria-Hungary's vicious ethnic quarrels and to his membership in Vienna's most conspicuously persecuted minority, the Jews. Humanity, Freud asserted, was irremediably predatory.

A final challenge to positivism emerged in the social sciences. The man who actually founded the "sociology" that Comte had named was Max Weber (1864–1920), Prussian reserve lieutenant and professor. Weber, the "bourgeois Marx," was a realist: "All ideas aimed at abolishing the dominance of men over men are 'Utopian.'" He began by asking a question that Marx had neglected: how did "capitalism" originate? Weber hit upon religion as the key variable that distinguished societies that had industrialized from those that lagged. And within Western society he found a close historical association between the "Protestant ethic," especially that of Calvinism, and the joyless drive to accumulate ever-greater masses of capital. This "Weber thesis" has proved a fruitful source of argument from his day to the present, although critics have pointed out that the earliest European capitalism—in the Italian city-states—was Catholic.

Weber's other major contribution was his attempt, in a massive and often obscure unfinished work entitled *Econ-*

Sigmund Freud, explorer of the unconscious mind.

omy and Society, to make sense of the relationships between economics and social and political forms. But unlike many later sociologists, Weber rejected the Comtean notion that the social sciences, like the natural sciences, must formulate general laws. In the human sciences, Weber pointed out, verification through controlled experiment was unfeasible. The researcher's own value system inevitably intruded on the results. Truth was only possible within narrow limits. Weber's work on method demolished the positivist approach to society and history. Humanity would have to make do with lawlike hypotheses such as the "Protestant ethic."

Finally, Weber was in his way a prophet, although a self-limiting and modest one. Like Marx but without Marx's dogmatism, he saw goal-oriented movement in history: the "disenchantment of the world," the decay of traditional religious and social certainties in the face of ever-increasing rationalization and bureaucratization. Weber feared that in the new century that process would end with humanity bound in a static "iron cage of serfdom" under immense self-perpetuating state and capitalist institutions. His prophecy ignored both the growing freedoms of the West's democratic societies—of which Weber the Prussian lieutenant had little understanding—and the dynamism of technological change. But Weber's "iron cage" metaphor proved far less off-center than the prophecies of Marx.

ART IN AN AGE OF SCIENCE

In the realm of culture, the last half of the nineteenth century was a period of crisis. Romanticism had broken all restraints on form or content. Everything was permitted. A bewildering proliferation of styles and radical disagreement about the purposes of "art" was the ultimate result. That proliferation destroyed the dominant idea of Western art since Plato and Aristotle, the notion that art should imitate reality or nature.

Architecture and design were the principal exceptions to this growing stylistic confusion. The fragmentation of architecture had begun well before that of literature and the visual arts. In the late eighteenth century, a profusion of "revivals" had succeeded the dying Baroque. As the nineteenth century drew on, Greek temples mutated into churches, museums, and banks; Gothic cathedrals provided models for hideous town halls in grimy industrial cities; Romanesque arches adorned the massive temples of science at the universities. Furniture became ever heavier, ever more overstuffed and hideously carved. But by the end of the century a reaction had set in.

In design, the opening of Japan in 1854 was as important to the nineteenth century as the influence of Chinese art had been to the eighteenth. The geometric shapes and absence of ornament of Japanese interiors were a revelation to European designers and architects. Simultaneously, the machine stimulated new thought. Some, such as England's William Morris (1834–96), revolted against mass production. Morris's politics were a romantic socialism, his taste an attempt to relive a lost golden age of craftsmanship now submerged in shoddy machine-made furniture. His "Arts and Crafts Movement" created a spare geometric style that was the beginning of modern home furnishing. German designers in the *Werkbund* or Craft League that flourished from 1907 to 1914 pioneered a style that in some ways resembled Morris's—but they did not share his irrational hostility to the machine.

Architecture developed in a like manner. Steel and glass were its materials. The Crystal Palace of the 1851 Great Exhibition, the immense canopy of St. Pancras station in London (1863–65), and the Eiffel Tower (1889) pioneered their use. But it was America, thanks to sheer technological exuberance and to the high property costs in its new city centers, that invented the steel-framed skyscraper in the 1880s. The Americans Louis Sullivan (1856–1924) and his pupil Frank Lloyd Wright (1869–1959) gave the new architecture its slogan: "form follows function." Sullivan did not disdain ornament, although he aspired to buildings that would be "comely in the nude." After 1890, his buildings took on a geometric grid-like pattern. German architects associated with the *Werkbund*, especially Walter Gropius (1883–1969) and Bruno Taut (1880–1938), had also begun before 1914 to design functional steel and glass buildings. The "international style" of the twentieth century, the first unified style in Western architecture since the Baroque, had arrived.

The fate of literature and the visual arts was entirely different. Old conventions of form and substance collapsed, but fragmentation instead of unity was the consequence. The novel, the nineteenth century's foremost art form, passed from the psychological "realism" of Gustave Flaubert (1821–80) to the pseudo-positivist "naturalism" of Émile Zola (1840–1902). Flaubert, in his great *Madame Bovary* (1856), dissected the consciousness of a small-town doctor's wife whose dreamy reading of romantic novels leads her to adultery and destruction. Both subject and technique scandalized contemporaries. The far less talented but infinitely more prolific Zola churned out a sequence of 20 novels between 1871 and 1893 that traced "the social and natural history of a family" during the Second Empire. Zola kept careful track of his "facts," and propounded laws of human nature. But his sometimes lurid style suggested the opposite of scientific detachment. His Naturalism was above all social criticism; his intervention in the Dreyfus case and brief exile to escape prison was the high point of his career.

The work of the great Russians, Count Leo Tolstoy (1828–1910) and Feodor Mikhailovitch Dostoyevsky (1821–81) showed a similar tension between psychological observation and social and political commitment. Tolstoy eventually repudiated his greatest works, *War and Peace* (1869) and *Anna Karenina* (1871), and turned his back on Russian society in favor of a mystical New Testament asceticism and pacifist "non-resistance to evil." Dostoyevsky migrated from advanced revolutionary beliefs to a mystic Slavophilism. In *The Possessed* (1871–72) he drew on his youthful experiences and his deep psychological insight to suggest the demonic nature of revolutionary messianism—just as much of the Russian *intelligentsia* embraced that messianism.

One conspicuous exception to this pattern of ideological commitment was the great American expatriate, Henry James (1843–1916). His many novels, novellas, and short stories combined Flaubert-like psychological observation with penetrating commentary on the contrast between European and American manners and morals. James's European-style novels earned him an international reputation; his most conspicuous American contemporaries, Herman Melville (1819–91) and Mark Twain (1835–1910), remained curiosities to Europeans. Melville's great symbolic epic of whaling and the struggle between evil and good, *Moby Dick* (1851), derived from the Protestant biblical tradition, not the European novel. Twain achieved the impossible. In *The Adventures of Huckleberry Finn* (1884) he rendered backwoods dialect—or rather a carefully contrived illusion of dialect—into art, in a comic yet often grim tale of life on the Mississippi against the ominous background of the slave South. Twain was deliberately and aggressively provincial; he frequently spoofed European social and linguistic snobbishness.

While Flaubert, James, and the Russians between them seemingly exhausted most of the novel's possibilities, the Norwegian Henrik Ibsen (1828–1906), the Swede Johan August Strindberg (1849–1912), and the Russian Anton Pavlovitch Chekhov (1860–1904) did the same for drama. Ibsen mercilessly attacked social pretension and the oppression of women. He depicted the quest of the modern individual for self-understanding. The truth, he suggested, could destroy as well as free. But humanity was not irredeemable; love was still conceivable. Not so for Strindberg, who created increasingly dreamlike plays in which unlovely characters, "bound together by guilt and crime," inexorably destroyed one another. Chekhov, who depicted symbolically the dissolution of Russian aristocratic society, pioneered a drama that turned its back on conventional notions of plot. He gave artistic form to the anarchy of life. Chekhov's characters speak in seemingly disconnected remarks, dramatic development occurs within the characters themselves, and action is inconclusive.

It was in poetry, music, and painting that the breakthrough to the artistic fragmentation of the twentieth century was most dramatic. In poetry, late Romantic lyricism dissolved into Symbolism. Intended for a few initiates rather than for a mass audience, Symbolism was in part a reaction to the dreary Naturalist notion that art should serve social and political betterment. Symbolism's predecessor was the dissipated "accursed poet," Charles Baudelaire (1821–67), and its banner "art for art's sake." The Symbolists, above all the schoolboy prodigy Arthur Rimbaud (1854–91), Stéphane Mallarmé (1842–98) and Paul Verlaine (1844–96), wrote a poetry of deliberate obscurity and musical effects. Their style influenced the two greatest German poets of the new century, Rainer Maria Rilke (1875–1926) and Stefan George (1868–1933). It furnished the basis for much twentieth-century poetry.

In music, Richard Wagner's "total work of art," his four evening long *Ring of the Nibelungen* opera cycle (1853–74), was the end of romantic music as well as one starting point of the new German *Reich's* political mythology. Gustav Mahler (1860–1911) and others continued Wagner's tradition of orchestral excess and startling effects, but with less conviction. In France, Claude

Debussy (1862–1918) and Maurice Ravel (1875–1937) pioneered a new style that deliberately paralleled Symbolist poetry. The irregular rhythms and harsh dissonances of Igor Fëdorovitch Stravinsky's *Rite of Spring* caused a riot at its Paris première in 1913. Arnold Schönberg (1874–1951) and his pupils attempted to create a new "atonal" music that defied traditional notions of melody.

In painting, an entire epoch in Western art ended with the school known as the Impressionists. Claude Monet (1840–1926) and Auguste Renoir (1841–1919) were its originators and greatest masters. They discarded the age-old attempt to render reality on canvas literally. Photography, invented in the 1820s, had by the 1860s rendered "realism" seemingly superfluous. Instead, the Impressionists sought to use the play of light, represented with dabs of color, to show scenes as they appeared to the mind's eye. Their paintings shocked contemporaries accustomed to increasingly sterile imitations of ancient or Renaissance models. But the Impressionists were not revolutionaries; they were the brilliant end of a long tradition.

After them came Paul Cézanne (1839–1906), proclaiming both in words and on canvas that "all of nature is formed by the cylinder, the sphere, and the cone." Vincent Van Gogh (1853–90) reproduced a tortured life in violent colors and swirling shapes. Georges Seurat (1859–91) composed

From realism to impressionism and beyond: *The Shepherdess* by Jules Dupré (1880).

A pioneering landscape, *Montagne Sainte-Victoire* (*ca.* 1885–90) by Paul Cézanne.

The "Yellow Press": A Novelist's View

In *New Grub Street* (1891), the English novelist George Gissing presented through the mouth of his fictional editor, Whelpdale, a view of the mass media's conception of its audience that is still surprisingly up-to-date.

No article in the paper is to measure more than two inches in length, and every inch must be broken into at least two paragraphs. . . . Let me explain my principle. I would have the paper address itself to the quarter-educated; . . . the young men and women who can just read, but are incapable of sustained attention. People of this kind want something to occupy them in trains, and on buses and trams. . . . What they want is the lightest and frothiest of chit-chatty information—bits of stories, bits of description, bits of scandal, bits of jokes, bits of statistics, bits of foolery. Am I not right? Everything must be very short, two inches at the utmost; their attention can't sustain itself beyond two inches.

From George Gissing, *New Grub Street* (London: Eveleigh Nash & Grayson, 1927), p. 419.

chine-driven rotary press permitted the first truly cheap newspapers, the first modern "mass media" based on advertising. Great press barons arose, profiteers of ignorance with a secret contempt for their public. Alfred Harmsworth (later Lord Northcliffe) of the London *Daily Mail* first achieved a daily circulation of over a million, with a paper that combined gossip and crude xenophobia in equal proportions. Publishers churned out vapid "best-sellers" by the hundreds of thousands. The mass press was not responsible for its readers' lack of sophistication, but it worked hard to perpetuate it. That narrowed the market for genuine art, and gave it a snobbish exclusiveness that further deepened the gap between high and low culture characteristic of the new century.

Like the aristocrats who after 1789 lamented a lost golden age, the middle classes of Europe were soon to mourn the long peace. The years from 1871 to 1914 were the peak of Europe's power and wealth relative to the other continents. The cultural brilliance of Europe's capitals, above all Paris and Vienna, made the last decades of peace a *"belle époque,"* a delectable era. But powerful forces were working against equilibrium and tolerance. Those forces, above all the impetus of nationalism and the growing economic power of the new Germany, slowly undermined the stability of the European state system. That shift, invisible to peoples engrossed in their everyday lives, in the end proved a matter of life and death for millions of Europeans.

stiff, flat figures out of thousands of tiny colored dots. And after 1900 Pablo Picasso (1881–1973), Wassily Kandinsky (1866–1944), the "Cubists," and Italy's fiercely irreverent "Futurists" began to cut painting's links with visual reality. The art of the twentieth century was to be an art of increasing abstraction and of ever-proliferating schools and slogans.

It was also increasingly an art for the few rather than the many. Until the nineteenth century Western art had always spoken to a unified audience, a cultivated and largely aristocratic elite. Mass literacy and mass market ended that. Wood-pulp paper and the ma-

Suggestions for Further Reading

General

E. J. Hobsbawm, *The Age of Capital, 1848–1875* (1975), and *The Age of Empire, 1875–1914* (1987), are outstanding works of synthesis. Readable surveys include N. Rich, *The Age of Nationalism and Reform, 1850–1890* (1977), C. J. H. Hayes, *A Generation of Materialism, 1871–1900* (1941), and O. J. Hale, *The Great Illusion, 1900–1914* (1971).

Domestic Affairs

On Britain, see above all A. Wood, *Nineteenth Century Britain* (1960), G. Dangerfield, *The Strange Death of Liberal England, 1910–1914* (1935), and F. Bédarida, *A Social History of England, 1851–1975* (1979). The most accessible discussions of France are A. Cobban, *A History of Modern France*, Vol. 2 (1957), and R. D. Anderson *France, 1870–1914: Politics and Society* (1977); E. Weber, *Peasants into Frenchmen: The Modernization of Rural France* (1976), is full of wonderful material. For Germany, H. U. Wehler, *The German Empire, 1871–1918* (1985), is short and provocative, but the relevant portions of G. Craig, *Germany, 1866–1945* (1978), are a better guide to what actually happened. For Russia see R. Pipes, *Russia under the Old Regime* (1974); H. Seton-Watson, *The Russian Empire, 1807–1917* (1967);

A. Ulam, *Lenin and the Bolsheviks* (1966); and the intelligent popular account of E. Crankshaw, *The Shadow of the Winter Palace: Russia's Drift to Revolution, 1825–1917* (1976). On Austria-Hungary, C. A. Macartney, *The Habsburg Empire* (1969), is lucid and balanced; A. J. P. Taylor, *The Habsburg Monarchy, 1809–1918* (1948), is one-sided and entertaining. On Italy, the best treatment is C. Seton-Watson, *Italy from Liberalism to Fascism, 1870–1925* (1967), but see also the pertinent portions of D. Mack Smith, *Italy, a Modern History* (1959–), and M. Clark, *Modern Italy, 1870–1982* (1984). J. A. Thayer, *Italy and the Great War: Politics and Culture, 1890–1914* (1964), describes the fatal fascination that a last great war to achieve national integration exercised over Italy's elites.

Society and Culture

On the rise of feminism, see especially R. Bridenthal et al, *Becoming Visible: Women in European History* (1987), and S. K. Kent, *Women and Suffrage in Britain, 1860–1914* (1987). The best introductions to Nietzsche are J. P. Stern, *Nietzsche* (1978); W. Kaufmann, *Nietzsche: Philosopher, Psychologist, Antichrist* (1956); and R. Heyman, *Nietzsche: A Critical Life* (1980). On Freud and his legacy, see especially R. Wollheim, *Sigmund Freud* (1971), and the critical treatment of H. J. Eysenck, *The Decline and Fall of the Freudian Empire* (1984). On Freud's environment, see above all

C. Schorske, *Fin-de-Siècle Vienna: Politics and Culture* (1980). W. J. Mommsen, *The Age of Bureaucracy* (1974), offers an excellent short introduction to Max Weber and his ideas. E. Wilson, *Axel's Castle: A Study in the Imaginative Literature of 1870–1930* (1931–), is still the best introduction to literature from the Symbolists onward. R. Raynal, *The Nineteenth Century: New Sources of Emotion from Goya to Gauguin* (1951), with fine illustrations, and F. Mathey, *The World of the Impressionists* (1961), remain excellent introductions to the new painting.

29

From Balance to Breakdown, 1871–1914

In international politics, neither fear of revolution nor "concert of Europe" secured the long peace. Princes and standing armies had crushed the myth of revolution in 1848–49, and the concert of Europe had died in the Crimea. Europe, Bismarck scoffed, was a mere "geographic expression": "I only hear a statesman use the word 'Europe' when he wants something for himself." The long peace from 1871 to 1914 was rather the classic age of the balance of power, a mechanism as ostensibly self-operating as the free market. Excesses by one power led to the automatic combination of others against it, and its enforced retreat.

But the balance was above all a balance in Europe alone, and by the 1890s the European system ceased to be self-contained. The rise of two great powers outside Europe, the United States and Japan, created for the first time a world balance. At the same time it undermined the European equilibrium. Developments within Europe worked in the same direction. The new Germany's explosive economic growth surpassed Britain's between 1900 and 1913. And Prussia-Germany, already the greatest land power, challenged Britain after 1897 for world mastery at sea. New technologies of war and transport privileged the great continental powers and increasingly threatened Britain's ability to bring its seapower to bear. The tilt of the balance in Germany's favor and Germany's imprudent attempt to exploit that shift eventually drove Britain to ally with Germany's neighbors, France and Russia. Germany answered with war.

THE FORCES BEHIND DIPLOMACY

The economic development and gradual democratization of Europe also meant the mechanization and democratization of war and foreign policy. Generals, admirals, and diplomats resisted but could not reverse those forces. The war of 1866 was the last "cabinet war." Thereafter victory required and nationalism inspired the participation of the masses. The expansion of literacy and extension of the franchise meant that the masses began to intrude on foreign policy as well.

Toward Mass Armies and Industrial War

Until 1871 only Prussia possessed a genuine mass army based on the concept of universal military service. The French, despite or because of the revolutionary effects of the *levée en masse* of 1793, preferred long-service professional forces after 1815. Long-service troops were more effective than conscripts on the battlefield, and infinitely more trustworthy in suppressing domestic disturbances. The other European powers had in general imitated *la grande nation*.

Then the Prussian mass army, created in 1814 and doubled in size in William I's military reforms in the 1860s, crushed the French. That compelled others to follow Prussia if they hoped to remain or become great powers. Austria-Hungary, thanks to its lesson in 1866, introduced universal service in 1868; France, Italy, Russia, and Japan

Opposite: Sarajevo, June 28, 1914: Archduke Francis Ferdinand and his wife walking to the automobile in which they were to die.

811

followed in the 1870s. Only Britain and the United States, which faced no major land threats, basked in the luxury of volunteer services. Britain's medium-sized army was an imperial police force; the U.S. Army, a dwarf service tailored to fighting Indians.

Military power thus rested more than ever on demographic strength. That weakened the position of France even more than had defeat in 1870, for France's population growth slowed after 1800, while Germany's rapid increase continued (see p. 679). By 1911 France needed 83 percent of its available manpower to produce the same sized army that Germany achieved by conscripting only 53 percent. Only Russia and the remote and self-absorbed United States surpassed Germany in total population. And Russia's economic weakness and political decrepitude rendered numbers its only great asset.

A revolution in destructiveness paralleled the revolution in numbers. Alfred Nobel's nitrated powder gave higher pressures than the old unsatisfactory mixture of charcoal, saltpeter, and sulfur that had propelled musket and cannon balls since the fourteenth century. The result was unheard-of muzzle velocities, lightweight small-caliber bullets, and trajectories virtually flat for 300 to 400 yards. With the new

The French 75mm field gun.

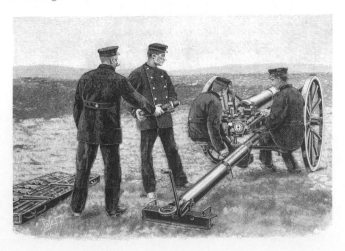

powder, unlike classic gunpowder, combustion was virtually complete. Nitrated powder neither gummed weapons with soot, nor gave away the rifleman's position, nor fogged the battlefield with smoke. Combined with the bolt-action rifle and Maxim's machine gun, smokeless powder created the modern battlefield, astoundingly empty because all visible movement draws fire.

Artillery changed more slowly than small-arms, but as dramatically. Nitrated powders flattened trajectories and multiplied range. Nitrated explosives made possible shells of unprecedented destructive power. The recoil-absorbing gun carriage, first employed effectively on the legendary 75mm French field gun of 1897, speeded fire dramatically by making it unnecessary to resight the gun after each shot. The *soixante-quinze* or "French 75" had a peak rate of fire of 20 rounds per minute.

Leveling devices, telescopic sights, surveying techniques, and the field telephone, which allowed forward observers to "walk" shells from distant hidden guns onto a target, made possible unprecedented accuracy and timeliness of fire. By the end of the century European armies had heavy guns with an effective range of 6 miles—compared to half a mile for the cannon of the Napoleonic wars. And by 1914 the first precariously droning aircraft could conduct reconnaissance or direct artillery fire. Cannon and small-arms between them reversed the advantage the offensive had enjoyed in the days of the great Napoleon. Attackers could now prevail only with crushing superiority of fire and numbers. Success might extend only so far as the next belt of enemy positions.

By 1900 the railroad had also worked a revolution. It had vastly increased the potential strategic mobility of land powers. In the Napoleonic wars, Wellington's sea communications proved better than the road links of his French adversaries. The railroad changed that; land powers could now rapidly meet amphibious threats with overwhelming force. And the new mass armies could mobilize with unprecedented rapidity. Mobilization and concentration for battle became a single continuous operation. Speed, as the Prussians had demonstrated in 1866 and 1870, was all-important. The power that mobilized first and fastest, the general staffs of Europe concluded, would win.

What the staffs ignored was that industrialization and the new firepower it had created made swift decision increasingly unlikely. Prussia's victory in 1870 had been a fluke, a consequence of France's disorganized mobilization and its ineptitude in the first battles. War between industrial powers, as the U.S. Civil War had demonstrated, tended inexorably toward immense struggles of attrition. The outcome of such protracted wars turned not on rifle strength in the first battles, but on industrial might and financial stamina. And in total industrial potential, by 1913, one power had surpassed all others except the United States: the Germany of William II. That was a momentous shift in the balance of power (see Figure 29-1).

Technology also revolutionized war at sea and threatened Britain's position. Napoleon III had embarrassed his British allies and rivals in 1859 by introducing the world's first armored warship, the frigate *Gloire*. Armor and shell-firing cannon made the wooden ships that had won at Trafalgar obsolete. The 1862 success of the Confederate ironclad *Merrimac* in smashing Union wooden ships drove the point home. The Union answer, the *Monitor*, with its all-iron construction and revolving turret, was the ancestor of all subsequent armored warships. In the 1870s and 1880s the European navies, with Britain in the lead, dropped auxiliary sails and adopted steel cannon and armor.

Numbers counted alongside quality. The Eastern crisis of 1885–87 (see p. 818) prompted scrutiny of Britain's neglected navy. The result was the Naval Defense Act of 1889, which mandated the construction of ten capital ships over three years. Britain adopted a permanent yardstick of naval strength: the Two-Power Standard. British strength had to equal that of the two next-ranked naval powers. Neither

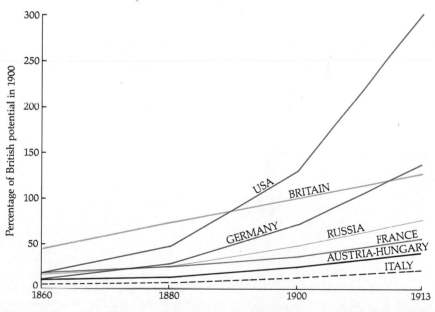

FIGURE 29-1   The Balance Shifts: Total Industrial Potential of the Great Powers

The first duel between armored warships: the *Monitor* against the *Merrimac* (renamed *Virginia*) at Hampton Roads, March 1862.

the protests of Gladstone at a further "monstrous scheme of the admirals" nor his resignation in 1894 checked the Royal Navy's expansion. Britain laid down an average of seven battleships a year throughout the following decade. And by 1900 those battleships each mounted four 12-inch guns, displaced 14,000 tons, and were capable of 18 knots. Then the British, to outpace all rivals, introduced in 1904–05 the first all-big-gun ship, H.M.S. *Dreadnought*.

With its ten 12-inch guns and 21-knot speed, it could stand off at long range and batter any earlier battleship into flaming scrap.

But Britain's rivals followed: by 1912 every great power had Dreadnoughts. And other weapons challenged the supremacy of the battleship and thus of Britain. An Englishman, Arthur Whitehead, invented a self-moving steam torpedo in the 1860s; the Russians first used it effectively in the Russo-Turkish

The ten 12-inch guns of the H.M.S. *Dreadnought* (launched 1906), outclassed all previous warships.

war of 1877–78. Torpedo boats posed an increasing threat to battleships close to shore. Mines, an unglamorous but highly effective weapon proven in the U.S. Civil War and thereafter also a Russian specialty, were even more menacing. Finally, the French, always on the lookout for technological shortcuts that might embarrass their British rivals, drew on U.S. Civil War precedents. By 1899 France had developed the first practical torpedo-firing submarine, the *Gustave Zédé*. Torpedoes, mines, submarines, and eventually aircraft evened the contest between Britain and its rivals, between the greatest sea power and the land powers.

Technology also inevitably raised the cost of warfare and of preparation for war. Britain's defense expenditure more than doubled between 1890 and 1914. Germany's almost quadrupled. But since their economies were also expanding, the burden of military expenditure as a percentage of gross national product did not increase as sharply as did the absolute amounts spent. What many contemporaries perceived as an uncontrolled upward-spiralling "arms race"—to use a metaphor that became current in the decade before 1914—was in reality a slow climb. Nevertheless, the weaker or slower-growing powers, Italy, Austria-Hungary, Russia, and France, found it harder to become or remain great powers than did the economic giants. In a long war, those that had difficulty keeping up before 1914 might well go to the wall.

Public Opinion and Foreign Policy

Educated opinion naturally first began to affect foreign policy in Britain and the United States. Opinion made the Crimean War and unmade the cabinet that bungled it. Opinion was decisive in making and—under Lincoln's inspired leadership—in deciding the U.S. Civil War. Gladstone mobilized opinion against Disraeli's foreign policy in the 1880 election; his command of Parliament began to crumble when

the public discovered how his muddling had sent Gordon to his death at Khartoum.

As public opinion broadened, it began to affect policy in a variety of ways. First, its frequent ambiguity increasingly provoked—or excused—the indecision of policymakers. As Gladstone's Conservative successor Lord Salisbury lamented in 1895, "when the great oracle speaks, we are never quite certain what the great oracle said." Democratic opinion often appeared to want no foreign policy at all.

Second, reversals of opinion made continuity of policy increasingly difficult. Democracy, as Tocqueville pointed out in the 1830s, "can only with great difficulty regulate the details of an important undertaking, persevere in a fixed design, and work out its execution in spite of serious obstacles. It cannot combine its measures with secrecy or await their consequences with patience." The British foreign office made the fickleness of Parliament a virtue, a ready excuse when other powers inconveniently pressed for British commitments. The French Chamber destroyed its government for attempting to cooperate with Britain in Egypt in 1882, then paradoxically held a grudge against the British for going ahead alone. In 1885 the Chamber suddenly overthrew Ferry after a minor defeat in Tonkin; colonial entanglements momentarily appeared a betrayal of France's "lost provinces" of Alsace-Lorraine. Italian governments fell for "losing" Tunisia to France in 1881 and for losing at Adowa in 1896. Lack of continuity and of patience was no argument against democracy, but it did place increasing constraints upon makers of foreign policy.

Third, Liberal opinion in Britain and Socialist opinion on the continent tended to confuse morality with policy, to the dismay of self-proclaimed realists such as Disraeli and Bismarck. State interests often appeared to require actions, such as the threat of war, or clients, such as the Turks, that were distasteful to an electorate under the influence of Gladstonian moralizing. Extreme moralists rejected the rules of the international game altogether. Richard Cobden and John Bright, middle-class crusaders against Britain's Corn Law tariffs, denounced the Crimean War and lost their seats in Parliament. They shared a faith that free trade would act "on the moral world as the principle of gravitation in the universe—drawing men together, thrusting aside the antagonism of race, and creed, and language, and uniting us in the bonds of eternal peace." Free trade triumphed, but eternal peace did not appear. Cobden and Bright blamed that "foul idol," the balance of power, and the aristocracy, a historical fossil for which the diplomatic service allegedly served as a gigantic welfare system.

Socialist utopianism saw a different villain. Capitalism, the root of all evil, must also be the cause of war, not its cure (as Cobden and Bright had claimed). "For this system, not a man or a penny," ran the slogan of Germany's Social Democrats. Rosa Luxemburg and Lenin clashed over whether the party's leadership or the spontaneity of the masses were the key to revolutionary struggle, but they fervently agreed that imperialism and war were fruits of capitalism. They and others in the revolutionary wing of the Second International proclaimed that capitalist-imperialist war would and must lead to socialist revolution. Less dogmatic continental thinkers merely deplored expenditure on armaments. Countess Bertha von Suttner, an Austrian writer, gained wide success with her pacifist novel, *Lay Down Your Arms* (1889), and helped inspire the guilt-ridden Alfred Nobel to establish the prizes that bear his name. In 1905 she was the first woman to receive a Nobel peace prize.

Even states played to pacifist opinion. Nicholas II of Russia, fearing that his ramshackle finances would not support re-equipping his army with the French 75 or its equivalent, proposed a ten-year "holiday" on armaments in 1898. But the 1899 disarmament conference at The Hague in Holland failed. That meeting, and a second in 1907, merely produced a World Court charged with deciding minor disputes involving "neither honour nor vital interests," a series of agreements on treatment of neutrals, prisoners, wounded, and non-combatants, and the stipulation that small-arms bullets must have full metal jackets rather than the more lethal expanding lead tip. Most rulers and military figures were secretly grateful to William II for sabotaging the conferences. The Kaiser scoffed rudely in private, and proclaimed his reliance "on God and on my sharp sword." Sir John ("Jacky") Fisher, the reforming admiral responsible for the *Dreadnought*, was equally forthright: "The essence of war is violence. Moderation in war is imbecility." What counted was winning, and winning required the swift application of overwhelming force without regard for niceties.

William II and Fisher need not have worried. In the age of nationalism, the more democracy, the more nationalism. That was the fourth major consequence of the growth of the power of public opinion. Pacifist sentiment remained confined to powerless minorities. The principal prewar leader of the SPD, August Bebel, admitted in 1892 that even his own party was "a sort of preparatory school for militarism." In Britain and France, "jingoism" (see p. 818) and Boulangism testified that even the public opinion of universal male suffrage was not necessarily pacific.

And even authoritarian regimes had to consider the views of their publics and officer corps. Nationalist opinion had driven Napoleon III, against his better judgment, to war and his doom in 1870. Nationalist opinion, originally unleashed with government support, helped drive Imperial Germany after 1905 to make good its bid for the mastery of Europe. By the 1870s, Slavophilism had mutated into Russian nationalism and had taken the cloak of

Bertha von Suttner (1843–1914), recipient of the 1905 Nobel Peace Prize.

"pan-Slavism." Russia was the patron and protector of its Slav "little brothers" everywhere—a sacred duty that extended the Russian state's potential claims far into central Europe and the Balkans. Journalists such as Nikolai Katkov of the *Moscow Gazette* preached that duty and those claims in a manner the tsars, given Russia's tradition of assassination, found increasingly difficult to ignore. Even in Japan, the oligarchs and their successors were responsive to opinion, especially military opinion. Assassination sometimes struck down those who appeared insufficiently resolute in defending Japan's security and rights.

BISMARCK THE CONSERVATIVE, 1871–90

German victory in 1870–71 dismayed Disraeli: "The balance of power has been entirely destroyed. . . ." The prophecy was 30 years too soon. Bismarck had harnessed German nationalism to Prussian state purposes. He was not about to loose that nationalism after 1871. The new Germany, he explicitly declared, was a "satiated" power. Bismarck henceforth sought to preserve the quasi-hegemonic position in Europe that he and Moltke had won.

That meant keeping the peace. In a future great war the powers whose mutual antagonisms had neutralized them in 1866 and 1870 might yet combine against Germany. France, unreconciled to the loss of Alsace-Lorraine, was the chief threat. If France found allies, Germany would face a dangerous coalition. And if Russia's Balkan friction with Austria-Hungary led to open conflict in eastern Europe, Germany might have to support Vienna, while St. Petersburg would bid for French support. The annexation of Alsace-Lorraine meant that an Austro-Russian conflict might well become a general European war in which Germany would have to fight on two fronts.

Bismarck the conservative.

Bismarck therefore sought, as Lord Salisbury uncharitably remarked, to use "his neighbors to pull out each other's teeth." He encouraged the powers' mutual tension to keep them dependent on Berlin. He diverted conflict to Europe's periphery, away from Alsace-Lorraine. Bismarck's policy, as much as the new Germany's strength, made Berlin the center of European diplomacy for a generation.

To freeze the status quo, Bismarck attempted above all to restore the unity between Vienna, St. Petersburg, and Berlin that had guaranteed stability before the Crimean War. His two "Three Emperors' Leagues" of 1872–73 and 1881 were above all devices to prevent Austria-Hungary and Russia from clashing in the Balkans. Bismarck was less successful than Metternich; neither league held for long.

In early 1875 Bismarck also attempted to bully a fast-reviving France with press warnings ("Is War in Sight?") and private threats of war. That provoked a crack in the first Three Emperors' League: Russia, for the first time since its resistance to Prussia's thrusts against Denmark in 1848–50, joined Britain. The tsar and Disraeli jointly warned Berlin that they would not allow Germany to crush France. Bismarck retreated. Unlike Moltke, he was not an apostle of the Prussian doctrine of "preventive" war, which went far beyond the preemption of *impending* enemy attack, and sanctioned wars to strike down *potential* future enemies before they became too strong. The balance of power, the mechanism that 30 years later was to bring Britain, Russia, and France together once more, had shown Bismarck his limits—limits he had himself established in 1871.

The Great Eastern Crisis and the Congress of Berlin, 1875–78

The "war-in-sight crisis" was transitory, despite its ominous undertone for Germany. It was the Balkans that wrecked both Three Emperors' Leagues. And the great Balkan crises of 1875–78 and 1885–87 were entirely different than their predecessor, the Crimean War. Not the great powers but the subject nationalities now threatened the Ottoman Empire. Balkan nationalism had come of age.

The Christian Slavs of Bosnia triggered the first and greatest crisis by rising in revolt against the Ottomans in July 1875. The revolt spread to the province of Bulgaria and the Turks replied with massacres. Tsar Alexander II, under pressure from pan-Slav opinion, prepared to rescue Russia's Balkan "little brothers"—and secure Constantinople. Unlike the clash in 1854, France abstained. Britain was paralyzed: Gladstone, in opposition, used the "Bulgarian horrors" to undermine Disraeli and Britain's traditional policy of supporting Turkey to keep Russia from the Dardanelles. Austria-Hungary likewise stood aside. Vienna feared that the triumph of Balkan nationalism over Turkey would make Austria-Hungary itself the next "Sick Man" of Europe. But in the absence of British support, Vienna made the best bargain it could. The Russians offered

Austria-Hungary territorial compensation in the western Balkans, and promised not to create a "large compact Slav state" that would threaten Vienna.

To everyone's surprise, the Turks held when Russia went to war in April 1877. At the entrenched camp of Plevna that blocked the main pass leading to Constantinople, their British magazine rifles stalled the ill-equipped Russians until December. Osman Pasha, the Turkish commander, gave the Ottoman Empire another 40 years of life. The Russians reached the outskirts of Constantinople exhausted. Britain's fickle opinion swung decisively: the Turks were no longer butchers of Christian Slavs but plucky defenders of Plevna. That freed Disraeli to send the British fleet to face Russia at the Straits, and gave the world a new word for populist bellicosity, "jingoism":

> We don't want to fight,
> But by Jingo, if we do,
> We've got the ships,
> We've got the men,
> We've got the money too.

Russia was now in no condition to fight Britain, but the tsar's peace treaty of San Stefano with Turkey (March 1878) nevertheless overreached. It created a great Bulgaria covering the entire eastern Balkans. That "large compact Slav state" and Russia's failure to offer the promised compensation induced Vienna to join Disraeli. Then Bismarck stepped in as "honest broker," and convened an international "Congress of Berlin" in June–July 1878. Its location symbolized the new Germany's decisive voice.

Disraeli returned from Berlin triumphant, with Turkish Cyprus as a sort of payment for saving Constantinople. Russia grudgingly divided the great Bulgaria of San Stefano into three: Bulgaria, an "Eastern Roumelia" technically under Turkish suzerainty, and a "Macedonia" that returned to Turkey. Austria-Hungary received its compensation—the Serb-inhabited provinces of Bosnia and Herzegovina to administer as a sort of trust. Serbia officially became independent of Turkey, although in 1881 Austria-Hungary made it a client state for a generation. The Congress of Berlin patched up a map of the Balkans that endured with minor modifications until 1912. Russia turned to expansion in Central Asia.

Bismarck's Alliances

In the aftermath, Bismarck accepted the logic of his policy of giving Austria-Hungary life. He took the very step for which he had reproached the Prussian governments of the 1850s: he tied the trim Prussian frigate to the "moth-eaten Austrian galleon." In September 1879 he signed at Vienna a defensive military alliance against Russia that endured until 1918.

This first peacetime alliance between great powers since the eighteenth century served several purposes. Bismarck hoped to reassure Vienna about its security and thus in theory make it more conciliatory to Russia. Since the alliance was defensive, Bismarck could always imply that he would leave Austria-Hungary to its fate if it actively provoked Russia. Domestically, the Dual Alliance gave German nationalism a surrogate for the "greater Germany" that Bismarck's creation of a greater Prussia had blocked. The existence of the alliance was immediately publicized, although its terms were secret until Bismarck published them in 1888.

Bismarck's solution held great dangers. Assurance of German backing if its survival was at stake increased rather than decreased Vienna's aggressiveness. And Bismarck's coupling of alliance politics with nationalist public opinion made it less and less possible for him to threaten Vienna with abandonment. Bismarck's successors considered themselves bound to Vienna by German nationalist *"Nibelung* loyalty"— a doom-laden Wagnerian motif that presided over the destruction of both empires in 1914–18. Finally, the alliance irrevocably tied Alsace-Lorraine

The Treaty of San Stefano   1878

The Congress of Berlin   1878

and the "Eastern Question" together, if doubt still existed about their connection. Germany, bound to Austria-Hungary by alliance and divided from France by an insoluble quarrel, was the link between east and west. Germany and Austria-Hungary would face France and Russia no matter how the war started.

To put off that day, Bismarck followed the Dual Alliance in 1881 with his second Three Emperors' League. Russia agreed not to join France in a Franco-German war and the three powers agreed to tolerate no Balkan changes except by mutual consent. The League rested on even weaker foundations than its predecessor. Tsar Alexander III, in power thanks to his father's assassination, was a narrow autocrat of nationalist bent. Monarchical solidarity meant little to him and still less to Vienna, which Bismarck had to pressure into signing.

To compensate Vienna for this enforced cohabitation with Russia, Bismarck made yet another treaty. In 1882 he roped the Italians into a Berlin-Vienna-Rome triangle, the Triple Alliance. Rome, humiliated over French seizure of Tunisia in 1881, was delighted at recognition of Italy's importance, however insincere. Vienna received an unconvincing Italian promise not to seek Trento and Trieste if Russia attacked Austria-Hungary. Bismarck paid the bill by guaranteeing Italy against French attack, a contingency he thought unlikely to arise.

In 1883 Bismarck added Rumania to his increasingly bizarre structure. That for the first time directly contravened his assurances to Russia that he was merely underwriting Austria-Hungary's existence, not its Balkan interests. The Rumanian treaties blocked Russia's land route to Constantinople. The Balkans, as Bismarck had told the *Reichstag* in 1876, contained no German interests worth the "bones of a Pomeranian musketeer." Yet Bismarck had now committed Germany to their defense against Russia.

Eastern Crisis and Reinsurance Treaty, 1885–87

Bismarck's diplomacy increasingly resembled an elaborate conjuring trick. The second of the great Balkan crises of these years, which opened in 1885, tested his ingenuity to the fullest. The issue, fortunately, was less explosive than in 1877–78. Russia's fundamental goal was now mere security against British naval attack in the Black Sea and free passage through the Dardanelles for its growing grain exports from the Ukraine.

Nevertheless, Russia found occasion to quarrel with Britain in 1885–87, first by encroaching on Afghanistan, India's vital buffer, then by pressing Bulgaria, the gateway to the Straits. The first crisis blew over after the powers unanimously warned Gladstone against attempting to imitate Palmerston and Disraeli by threatening Russia in the Black Sea. The second crisis lasted longer. Russia sought to dominate Bulgaria with threats and military advisers. When it found it could not, it attempted to block the efforts of the Eastern Rumelians to join Bulgaria—ironically reaffirming the partition of the "great Bulgaria" of San Stefano that the powers had originally forced on Russia in 1878. In late 1887, Russia appeared poised for intervention in Bulgaria; then it accepted a face-saving solution. East Asia beckoned.

The crisis drove Britain, under Gladstone's Conservative successor, Lord Salisbury, towards the Triple Alliance. In two "Mediterranean Agreements" of 1887, Salisbury joined Italy and Austria-Hungary in guaranteeing—against Russia and France—the territorial status quo in the Mediterranean and Black Sea. That blocked Russia at Constantinople, with Bismarck's blessing. Bismarck added the final touch to this eccentric combination by negotiating a secret agreement with the Russians to replace the collapsed Three Emperors' League. The three-year "Reinsurance Treaty" of June 1887 pledged support for an eventual Russian drive on Constantinople. The parties also promised benevolent neutrality should war come, except if Germany attacked France or Russia attacked Austria-Hungary.

That assurance contradicted the spirit if not the letter of the Dual Alliance linking Berlin and Vienna. And by promising Russia the Straits, the Reinsurance Treaty contradicted the second Mediterranean Agreement between Bismarck's allies. Bismarck had created a system of mutually contradictory commitments that froze the Austro-Russian quarrel while keeping Germany's "line to St. Petersburg" open. If treaties could not keep the Balkans quiet, he would have to choose. His choice could only be Austria-Hungary, and a German clash with Russia.

The Collapse of Bismarck's System

Running a system of such complexity taxed even Bismarck. It also had unforeseen effects. France, weary of isolation, reluctantly drew closer to Russia. Tsarist Russia, annoyed at Bismarck's renewed backing of Austria-Hungary and at his closing of the Berlin loan market during the Bulgarian crisis, swallowed its qualms about the French Republic's money. The Russians secured their first sizable French loan in October 1888. In January 1889 they ordered a large quantity of French rifles after promising not to use them against France.

In Berlin, Bismarck was no longer sufficiently in control to counter this threat. The new Kaiser, William II, was under the influence of Moltke's successor, the warlike Count von Waldersee, who consistently counseled "preventive" war against Russia before it became too strong. In fall 1889 William II assured Vienna, without Bismarck's approval, that German mobilization would immediately follow that of Austria-Hungary, whatever the source of the quarrel. He also visited Sultan Abd al-Hamid II at Constantinople, a gesture implicitly hostile to Russia. Germany was abandoning its Russian connection.

Then Bismarck and the young emperor quarreled over domestic policy in March 1890. When the Russians anxiously proposed renewal of the Reinsurance Treaty, the man who had made it was gone. Bismarck's successor was a conscientious but limited general, Count Leo von Caprivi. He found

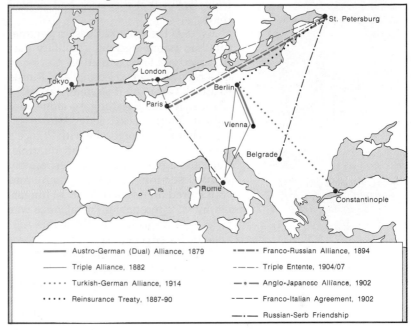

Alliances and Alignments before 1914

——— Austro-German (Dual) Alliance, 1879	═══ Franco-Russian Alliance, 1894
——— Triple Alliance, 1882	---- Triple Entente, 1904/07
····· Turkish-German Alliance, 1914	—•— Anglo-Japanese Alliance, 1902
····· Reinsurance Treaty, 1887-90	--- Franco-Italian Agreement, 1902
	—•— Russian-Serb Friendship

Bismarck's foreign policy too complex and self-contradictory. He feared that St. Petersburg might leak word of Germany's promise to support Russia at the Straits. That would irreparably damage German ties with Russia's adversary Britain. Nor would German opinion or the Vienna government take kindly to Germany's sins against the "*Nibelung* loyalty" supposedly enshrined in the Reinsurance Treaty.

Germany therefore declined the Russian offer and drew closer to Britain with an 1890 colonial agreement that traded nebulous German claims to Zanzibar for the British-controlled North Sea island of Helgoland. The end of the Reinsurance Treaty and Germany's wooing of Britain accelerated Russia's move toward France. In July 1891 a surly Tsar Alexander III stood at attention for the playing of the *Marseillaise*, hymn of revolution, during a visit of the French fleet. Bismarck had deliberately isolated France; William II and Caprivi had left Russia isolated. In August of 1891 France and Russia agreed to coordinate their foreign poli-

Tsar Alexander III, the French Republic's grudging alliance partner.

cies. Both sought the independence from Berlin that Bismarck had denied them.

By 1892 French and Russian negotiators had hammered out a military pact that pledged France to attack Germany if Germany attacked Russia, and Russia to attack Germany if Germany attacked France. If Austria-Hungary alone mobilized, France also pledged to mobilize. That provision broke with France's previous reticence in Balkan quarrels, but Paris agreed because it desperately wanted security against Germany and considered an isolated Austro-Hungarian move improbable. The alliance was to last almost as long as the Triple Alliance of its adversaries.

The ratification of this Franco-Russian Alliance in December–January 1893–94 did not, as often suggested, make a general war inevitable. The annexation of Alsace-Lorraine and Bismarck's Dual Alliance had already done that. The effect of the Franco-Russian alliance was rather to end the German political hegemony in Europe that Bismarck had established. The young Kaiser might as late as 1892 confide to associates his vision of erecting "a sort of Napoleonic supremacy" in Europe "in the peaceful sense." But after the Franco-Russian alliance, a German "Napoleonic supremacy" could come only through war.

THE BREAKTHROUGH TO WORLD POLITICS, 1890–1905

Europe nevertheless continued to enjoy unprecedented peace. The Franco-Russian alliance made both parties feel relatively secure in Europe. A new Near Eastern crisis in 1895 over Turkish massacres of Armenians failed to embroil Russia with Austria-Hungary. Indeed, in 1897 the two powers agreed to put the Balkans "on ice." For a generation Europe turned to Africa and east Asia. And for the first time non-European great powers, Japan and the United States, made their presence felt. That made the Eu-

ropean balance a world balance. Such a system, commentators discerned, suddenly made dwarves of powers such as France that were merely European in scale.

Theories of World Politics

Theorists such as Sir Charles Dilke and Sir John Seeley had begun to notice that even the British Empire lacked the vast territorial and demographic base of continent-spanning powers such as the United States and Russia. Britain could only compete, argued Seeley in the 1880s, if it welded the often wayward white colonies and Britain into a world-spanning trans-national federation, a "Greater Britain." That remedy appeared less and less plausible, for the white colonies were developing away from Britain, not toward it. Particularly after 1900, informed British opinion inclined toward anxiety about preserving the Empire from disintegration.

In Germany, the professorial elite provided a conceptual framework suitable for a "rising" power. From the summit of the German historical profession, the liberal Johann Gustav Droysen and the far less liberal Heinrich von Treitschke declared that unity under Prussia was the culmination of all previous German history. Droysen's fourteen-volume *History of Prussian Policy* (1853–86) and Treitschke's five-volume *History of Germany in the Nineteenth Century* (1879–94) portrayed the past, in good Hegelian fashion, as the upward struggle of a Prussian state embodying the world spirit. They also looked forward to higher things: Germany's mission in the world paralleled Prussia's pre-1871 mission in Germany. An entire generation absorbed their outlook.

Max Weber, in a famous 1895 speech, suggested that German unity had been a waste of time unless it served as prelude to a "German world power policy." The founder of the odd quasi-discipline of geopolitics, Friedrich Ratzel, suggested in his *Political*

Geography (1897) that state boundaries were fluid and ephemeral. Organization and numbers were the key elements in an eternal struggle for "space." A variety of theorists proclaimed that Britain's decline was Germany's opportunity to break through into the charmed circle of true world powers, alongside Russia and the United States. The Kaiser himself remarked hopefully in 1899 that "old empires are fading away and new ones are about to be formed."

In Russia, figures such as Katkov temporarily set aside pan-Slav fantasies for a Russian nationalist "manifest destiny" in East Asia. Russia in Asia, Katkov argued, was "as much at home as in Moscow." The Russians were not "foreign intruders from afar, as England is in India." As the Trans-Siberian Railroad crept eastward, the tsar and his subordinates began to look to control of northeast Asia as the foundation of Russia's world power status.

In the United States, pundits urged a search for new frontiers beyond the seas to replace the land frontier that was passing. "Manifest destiny," a phrase that a Southern journalist had coined in 1850, appeared to extend beyond the Pacific shores to "universal empire." But America's most influential prophet of empire was more modest. When Captain Alfred Thayer Mahan of the U.S. Naval War College published *The Influence of Seapower Upon History, 1660–1783* in 1889, it enjoyed instant success. Mahan derived two laws from the age of British naval supremacy. One he merely implied: seapower, from Roman empire to British empire, made for supremacy. The second he stated baldly: seapower meant a battle fleet, not commerce raiders. The France of Louis XIV and successors had sinned against both precepts with its "false policy of continental extension" and its preference for privateering over fleet actions. Both notions made Mahan's book the bible of the U.S. Navy and of its great-power counterparts. The Kaiser "devoured" it, and decreed that every German ship re-

ceive a translation. Mahan offered a recipe for success in the new age of world politics: build battle fleets and seize overseas bases and colonies to protect and foster an ever-expanding commerce. Mahan, ironically, achieved prominence just as railroad, torpedo, mine, and submarine were evening the contest between land and sea power, and non-European nationalism was making colonies an increasingly doubtful investment.

The Struggle for Mastery in Africa

The new age of world politics after 1890 involved two principal theaters of action. Britain and France confronted one another in the culmination of the "scramble for Africa" begun with the British occupation of Egypt in 1882. In East Asia, China's failure to keep pace with Japan or with the European powers led to a decade of bitter conflict.

In Africa, France's refusal to accept British control of Egypt led it into dangerous paths. In 1897 Paris sent a small expedition under Captain Jean-Baptiste

Kitchener, victor over the Dervishes—and the French.

Marchand of the French naval infantry to stake a diplomatic claim on the upper Nile, the key to Egypt's water supply. But London, after Salisbury and the Conservatives returned to power in 1895, had decided to avenge the Mahdi's 1885 defeat of Gordon at Khartoum. Egypt's security demanded command of the Sudan.

A British army under Sir Herbert Kitchener ascended the Nile by steamer to face the Dervishes of the Mahdi. That made the issue between Britain and France one of power alone. At Omdurman, in September 1898, Kitchener crushed the Dervishes. Three weeks later, Kitchener found Marchand and his small force at Fashoda on the upper Nile. To make good its claim, France would now have to go to war. Salisbury refused to negotiate: "We claim the Sudan by right of conquest . . . ." The Dreyfus affair crippled Paris politically, and France remained mindful that Britain still held that control of the Mediterranean won in 1798 at the battle of the Nile. Marchand received orders to withdraw.

Fashoda was not the end of London's African woes. The great conflict between Britain and the Boers, which Gladstone had postponed by retreating in 1881, finally erupted. The discovery of gold on the Rand in 1886 made the Boer Transvaal republic the greatest power in southern Africa. British entrepreneurs rushed in to exploit the mines—but every ounce of gold they extracted strengthened the Boers. After

Architects of empire, and of the Boer War: Joseph Chamberlain (above) and Cecil Rhodes (relaxing in the bush during the Matabele war, 1896).

1894 the Transvaal secured an independent link to the outside world by a railroad to Delagoa Bay in Portuguese East Africa. German political and economic influence flowed in, to the alarm of the British.

Most alarmed was Cecil Rhodes, the great robber baron of the Kimberley diamond mines and Rand gold fields. In a departure from custom, London had allowed Rhodes to become prime minister of the Cape Colony and had thus put British policy in the service of Rhodes's investments. Rhodes of course saw it differently: his failed efforts to outflank the Transvaal and lessen its economic preponderance by finding gold in "Rhodesia," to the north, were service to the empire.

In 1895 Rhodes at last decided to destroy the Transvaal before its growing strength imperiled Britain's control of the Cape and Rhodes's own interests. With the connivance of the ex-Liberal Joseph Chamberlain, now Salisbury's secretary for colonies, Rhodes prepared a raiding force. Under the leadership of a Dr. Jameson, the raiders were to attack the Transvaal in support of a planned uprising of British settlers and miners inside the Transvaal itself. But the "Uitlanders," as the Boers called them, failed to rise. Boer mounted infantry efficiently rounded up Jameson and his raiders in January 1896.

The Jameson Raid fiasco sent Rhodes into eclipse, but Chamberlain persisted. The mercurial Kaiser had sent the president of the Transvaal, the bearded patriarch Oom Paul Kruger, a telegram of congratulations that seemed to presage German meddling in southern Africa. Chamberlain began preparing British opinion for war. Chamberlain's new deputy at the Cape, Sir Alfred Milner, sought and prepared for war itself. The Cape Dutch, he feared, would in the long run desert Britain for the Transvaal. Economic and political trends were running strongly in favor of the Boers. Britain must fight before it was too late. Salisbury was unhappy: "I see before us the necessity for considerable military effort, and all for people whom we despise and for territory which will bring no power and profit for England." Chamberlain and Milner had their way. In October 1899 Milner succeeded in provoking the Boers into a declaration of war.

Contrary to Milner's expectation, the war was no walkover. Britain commanded the seas; despite European disapproval and violent pro-Boer agitation in Germany, Britain's European rivals were powerless. Not so the Boers. Unlike Dervishes or Zulus they did not obligingly charge into British Maxim guns. The Boers instead allowed the British to attack, and sent them reeling with Mauser rifles and Krupp field guns. Boer knowledge of the country and mounted mobility gave them operational as well as tactical superiority in the early engagements. Not until June 1900 did a huge and clumsy British army conquer the Boer capital, Pretoria. Britain, to defeat a few backwoods farmers, had found it necessary to commit a grand total of 450,000 men.

Milner was now master of Pretoria and the Rand, but not of southern Africa. The Boers persisted in a bitter guerrilla struggle. Boer commandos of 50 or 100 mounted raiders smashed British outposts and railroad lines. The British replied with African and Boer defector scouts, irregular cavalry given to savage reprisals, and "concentration camps": barbed-wire open-air prisons for the Boer civilian population and their black dependents, to cut off supplies to the commandos. Roughly 20,000 Boers and 12,000 blacks died behind the wire from typhoid, measles, dysentery, and British mismanagement. The Liberal opposition damned the government for defending civilization with the "methods of barbarism." Soon all except the most determined "jingoes" were heartily tired of the brutality and sacrifices that empire entailed.

In the end, attrition and Britain's increasing use of Boer turncoats and

Three generations of defiant Boers, with their Mauser rifles.

native auxiliaries induced the commandos to give up in May 1902, and acknowledge British sovereignty. The greatest colonial war of the century was over. But the fierceness of Boer resistance compelled London to conciliate its new subjects. In 1910, Britain conceded Dominion status to a Boer-dominated Union of South Africa. The Boers had won in all but name.

The final British advance toward Johannesburg (1900).

Asia in 1880

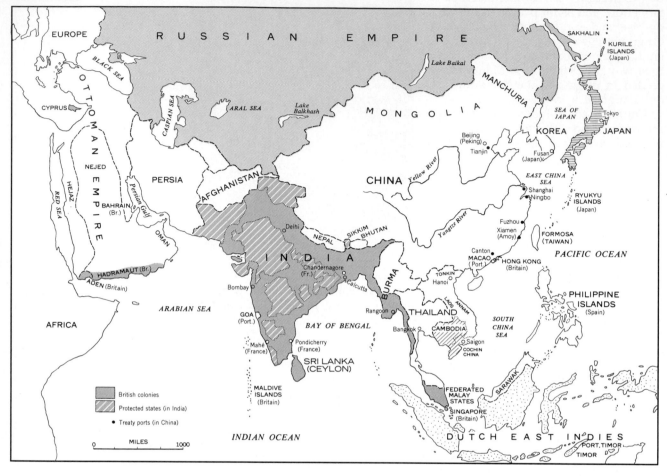

The Struggle for Mastery in East Asia, 1894–98

African struggles were still largely part of the inherited framework of European and colonial rivalries. East Asia was different. There a new power, Japan, burst upon the scene by attacking China in September 1894. In the 1870s the Meiji oligarchs had restrained Japan's extremists, who had urged a war with China's dependent kingdom, Korea. Japan had been as yet too weak for conquest; it had settled for "opening" Korea, Perry-fashion, to Japanese trade in 1876. It had smoothed over a crisis with China over Korea in the mid-1880s. Now it was ready, and friction over Korea provided the occasion.

Japan's new army threw the Chinese out of Korea and invaded Manchuria. Japan's new navy battered the poorly trained Chinese fleet off the mouth of the Yalu River; the Empress Dowager had spent much of China's naval budget to build the Summer Palace in Beijing (Peking). Japan seized the vital base of Port Arthur on the Liaodong Peninsula. By the Treaty of Shimonoseki of April 1895, Japan imposed on China the cession to Japan of Port Arthur and recognition of Korea's independence—from China, not from Japan.

Then disaster struck. Russia and its French ally took the occasion to pose as China's protectors. Their adversary in Europe, Germany, joined them in

Asia in 1914

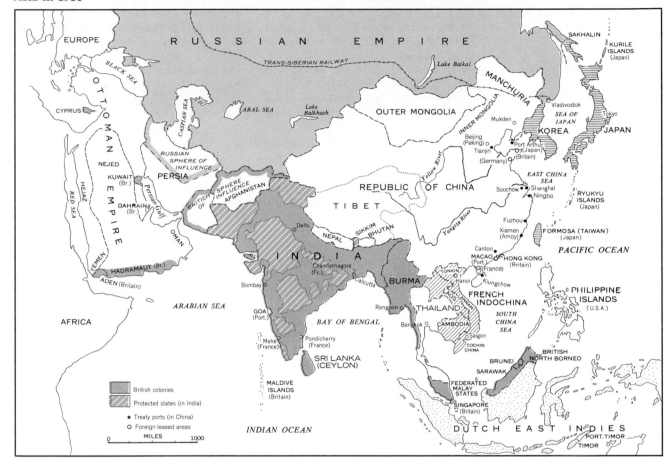

hopes of currying favor with the Russia it had estranged in 1890. The three powers "advised" Japan against keeping Port Arthur and the Liaodong Peninsula. The resentful Japanese disgorged; their one major prize was Taiwan, which they henceforth ruled as a colony.

Japan's victory over China opened a new scramble for concessions and ports that seemed to presage the final collapse of the ramshackle Chinese empire. Russia made its own bid for control of northern China and Korea. Count Witte, architect of the Trans-Siberian Railway, plied the Chinese with loans. Russian emissaries negotiated the right to build a railway spur directly across Manchuria to Vladivostok. In December 1897 Russia seized

and "leased" the prize the Japanese had sought, the ice-free naval base of Port Arthur, and secured the right to connect it to the new railroad. In 1897–98 Germany and Britain acquired ports on the Shandong Peninsula, opposite Port Arthur. Italy demanded a port, but China had learned enough about Europe to know that it could safely refuse. The powers divided China into spheres of influence: Manchuria to Russia, southwest China to France, the Yangtze Valley to Britain, and the Shandong area to Germany.

The United States as a World Power

While the powers stripped China to the bone, a power potentially greater than any of them began to acquire a foreign policy. That was a novelty, and not always a welcome one, for the United States. Thanks to its ocean boundaries and the indirect protection of the British fleet, the United States had largely ignored the European balance throughout the century. But a new assertiveness emerged in the 1890s, as industrial America reached maturity. In 1895 President Grover Cleveland's secretary of state intervened in a boundary dispute between Britain and Venezuela with the uncivil but accurate claim that "the United States is practically sovereign on this continent, and its fiat is law . . . ."

In 1898 the second of two Cuban revolts against Spain tempted the United States to make good that assertion of hegemony. The battleship *Maine*, anchored in Havana harbor, exploded and sank in February 1898—the new nitrated powders tended to instability in hot climates. The jingoist press of William Randolph Hearst claimed a Spanish plot: "Remember the *Maine*!" That agitation and the coming election pressed the invertebrate President William McKinley to act.

The shining new U.S. Navy, built up on Mahanian lines since the early 1890s, swept the decrepit fleets of Spain from the seas. A hastily improvised U.S. expeditionary force landed on Cuba and eventually prevailed, despite inadequate training and logistical chaos. Theodore Roosevelt, soon to succeed McKinley, made a name leading the dashing "Rough Riders." The navy reached out across the Pacific toward China, following Mahan's precepts. Commodore George Dewey crushed the Spanish fleet in the Philippines at the battle of Manila Bay. He then challenged a German squadron that was loitering nearby in hopes of snapping up a coaling station. The Germans wisely declined.

The Filipinos proved more difficult than Spain or the Germans. Already in revolt against Spain, they failed to see the charm of United States domination, enlightened though it might be. It re-

quired up to 70,000 troops, three years, and all the U.S. Army's Indian-fighting expertise to defeat the insurgency of Emilio Aguinaldo. Anti-imperialists at home fervently denounced the war. Ultimately the United States mastered its empire in the Philippines and in nominally independent Cuba by political solutions. In return for the loyalty of the planter oligarchy Spain had created, the United States promised order. That guaranteed stability, but offered no long-term release from the fierce conflicts inherent in such sharply stratified societies.

The United States thus acquired an overseas empire, rounded out with the annexation of Guam, Puerto Rico, and Hawaii. It also intervened diplomatically—with a pronouncement mixing moralism and American interests in the style of the Monroe Doctrine—in faraway China. In 1899 McKinley's secretary of state, John Hay, asserted the "Open Door" to trade, and China's territorial integrity, against the projects of the powers for exclusive spheres. The powers humored the newcomer and agreed. Paper promises were cheap, and easy to disavow later.

Closer to home, the United States also made good the claim to an exclusive sphere in Latin America first asserted in the Monroe Doctrine. Britain tacitly conceded United States hegemony in the Caribbean in the Hay-Pauncefote treaty of 1901. Under Roosevelt and his successors William Howard Taft (1909–13) and Woodrow Wilson (1913–21), the United States engineered the secession of "Panama" from Colombia, and between 1904 and 1914 carried through the Panama Canal project that had defeated de Lesseps. U.S. Marines brought imperial order to Central America and the Caribbean while diplomats sought, in Wilson's words, to teach the inhabitants "to elect good men." A navy of Dreadnoughts, with bases stretching from Manila Bay to Norfolk, assured the security of the new empire and of America's growing trade. And America's immense and still-growing share of the world's industrial production buoyed up its power claims.

The Struggle for Mastery in East Asia and the European Balance, 1899–1905

Meanwhile, the unprecedented scale of Western intrusion into China after 1897 triggered the greatest spontaneous anti-Western rising since the Indian Mutiny of 1857–58. The "Righteous and Harmonious Fists" or "Boxers" originated as an antidynastic secret society. It claimed Daoist magic powers that made its adherents impervious to Western bullets. In 1898–99 it spread across northern China as a mass movement to "expel the foreign bandits and kill the Christian converts." The Dowager Empress and her conservative advisers tacitly encouraged the Boxers, who obligingly ceased opposition to the Qing dynasty.

International intervention to protect the missionaries triggered a Boxer-led rising that bottled up the Westerners in Beijing in the embassy quarter. Boxers assassinated the German minister. The Qing declared war on the powers. Boxers sought to exterminate all Westerners they could catch. As an Italian nationalist cynically remarked a year or two later, only an invasion from Mars could unite humanity. China briefly fulfilled the same function: Europe, Japan, and the United States momentarily forgot their quarrels. William II dispatched Field-Marshal Waldersee to lead the conquest of northern China. The Kaiser sent the troops off with an impromptu speech that exhorted them to take no prisoners, and to rival the fearsome reputation of Attila and his Huns. That phrase Germany's enemies long remembered.

Even before Waldersee's arrival, Daoist magic had succumbed to Maxim guns. The victorious powers exacted a stiff settlement, but preserved the Qing by endorsing the fiction that the Boxers had been an anti-Manchu rebellion. The dynasty staggered on; the death of the Empress Dowager in 1908 and a

The Western powers line up for their slices of China (from a German cartoon, 1900).

revolution of provincial armies and westernized intellectuals in 1911 ultimately destroyed it.

In the short term, Russia remained in possession of Manchuria and for a while of Beijing itself. That disquieted Britain. London now felt little need of allies in Europe, for in the mid-1890s Salisbury had at last felt strong enough to weaken Britain's commitment to defend the Turkish Straits. Revived British naval power and the possession of Egypt had made "splendid isolation" practical. But to resist Russia in China, Britain needed a land ally. Between 1899 and 1901 Chamberlain therefore sought agreement with Germany. The Germans proved slippery, for good reason. British goodwill and Germany's small stake in China were no recompense for risking Russia's enmity. Germany shared European borders with Russia and with Russia's French ally; Britain did not.

In January 1902 Britain found a different partner, that other "island empire," Japan. The parties pledged to fight only if their ally faced *two* great powers in East Asia. That meant Britain and Japan would fight side by side only if France intervened alongside its Russian ally. Britain's role was to hold the ring while Japan, if necessary, stood up to Russia. And the Russians soon made war inevitable. In March 1903 the first train across the Trans-Siberian Railway reached Port Arthur. The tsar dismissed Witte, and appointed a dangerous fanatic for Asian expansion, A. M. Bezobrazov, to office. A member of Bezobrazov's circle, Vice-Admiral E. I.

Alekseev, became viceroy of Russia's Asian possessions. Alekseev pressed forward: Bezobrazov had established Korea as Russia's ultimate objective. But Korea, as a Prussian general staff adviser had taught his Japanese pupils, was of supreme geopolitical importance. It was "a dagger pointed at the heart of Japan." Yamagata Aritomo, founder of Japan's modern army and most Prussian of the surviving oligarchs, pressed for war.

St. Petersburg rejected Japan's offer that Russia recognize Japanese preponderance in Korea in return for a more qualified Japanese acknowlegment of Russia's position in Manchuria. In reply, Japanese torpedo boats attacked and crippled the Russian fleet at Port Arthur on February 8, 1904. Japan thus secured command of the sea. In May 1904 a Japanese army invaded Manchuria from Korea while Japanese forces laid seige to Port Arthur. Russian machine-gun fire piled thousands of dead Japanese attackers on the new barbed wire obstacles. The Japanese persisted, and took Port Arthur in January 1905. By March they had worn the Russians down in immense battles of attrition in Manchuria. The Trans-Siberian Railway was as yet single-tracked, and Russian supplies and reinforcements were precarious. The Russians retreated northwards from Mukden.

And at the end of May 1905 the Russian Baltic fleet, dispatched half way around the world to rescue Port Arthur, met the Japanese off the island of Tsushima, south of Korea. Admiral Togo Heihachiro "crossed the T" of the advancing Russian fleet, sweeping the leading Russian ships with the long-range broadsides of his entire force. The annihilation of that last Russian fleet and the revolution that broke out in European Russia in January 1905 (see pages 795–96) forced Russia to cease fighting. "Teddy" Roosevelt, trying out America's new status as Pacific great power, stepped in to mediate and to preserve a balance that would keep China alive. The Treaty of Portsmouth (New Hampshire) of September 1905 recognized Japan's "paramount interests" in Korea, forced Russia to return Manchuria to China, and presented Japan with Port Arthur, its railway, and the southern half of the island of Sakhalin. Within five years Japan had annexed Korea. A non-European power had for the first time defeated a European great power.

The Russo-Japanese war decisively altered the European scene. The approach of war caused the French deep anxiety: would Russia's conflict with a British ally drag France into hostilities with Britain? Theophile Delcassé, France's canny foreign minister, turned in the course of 1902–03 toward Britain. The British, for similar reasons, turned toward France. Queen Victoria's successor, the high-living Edward VII, wooed French opinion with a state visit in 1903 and with less official gastronomic and amorous cross-Channel excursions. By April 1904 the parties had arrived at a settlement of the colonial disputes that had divided them since the occupation of Egypt in 1882. France traded its existing interests in Egypt for a British promise to support its eventual annexation of Algeria's western

A Japanese view of the sinking of the Russian flagship *Petropavlovsk* at Port Arthur, 1904.

neighbor, the decrepit Sultanate of Morocco. This Anglo-French *"Entente Cordiale"* was thus East Asian in origin and colonial in nature. But it soon became an alliance in all but name, facing the greatest European power, Germany.

That fateful development was a consequence of a second major repercussion of the Russo-Japanese war: the disruption of the European naval and military balance thanks to Russia's defeat. Until Russia recovered, Germany was supreme on the continent. Its naval buildup soon outpaced the Franco-Russian alliance and threatened to outpace Britain. Its land forces, freed temporarily from the two-front threat, held France hostage. And its consequent efforts to reduce France to vassalage impelled Britain, for the first time since Waterloo, to contemplate committing British forces to a great land war in western Europe.

GERMANY ON THE LOOSE, 1905–14

The German Challenge at Sea

The restless Kaiser spent much of the 1890s seeking a means to achieve the "Napoleonic supremacy" to which he aspired. The Franco-Russian alliance barred the way on the continent. Germany's future, the Kaiser concluded, lay "on the waters." Personal rivalry with his English naval cousins, identification with the world-spanning goals of German middle-class nationalism, and a dilettantish interest in naval technology made him from early 1890s the chief advocate of enlarging Germany's coastal defense navy into something larger and more impressive. The Kaiser read Mahan in 1894 and became a convert to the gospel of the battle fleet. But not until 1897 did he find the team capable of translating his wishes into budgets and battleships: Bernhard von Bülow at the foreign office and Admiral Alfred von Tirpitz at the Reich naval office.

Bülow provided the foreign-policy cover for the fleet effort. Germany was to preserve a "free hand" and avoid entanglement with either of the two great antagonists, England and Russia, while creating a fleet that would alter the world balance of power. It was the task of Tirpitz, who possessed an impressive bifurcated beard and the wiliest political mind of William II's Germany, to provide that fleet. The admiral's opponents did not call him "the Father of the Lie" for nothing.

To convince the *Reichstag* of the need for a battleship navy, he mounted Germany's first modern advertising campaign. Charts showing Germany's comparative naval strength appeared in dentists' waiting rooms all over Germany. School children chipped in pennies for the fleet. Professors and industrialists spoke and wrote fervently of Germany's "sea interests" and world mission. In 1898 the *Reichstag* passed a first naval law providing 19 battleships, and in 1900 accepted a second that doubled the fleet to 38 battleships and stepped up the building tempo to three ships each year.

To justify to the *Reichstag* both the enormous expense and a program of advance appropriations stretching over decades, Tirpitz claimed that Germany's increasing foreign trade and colonial empire required a fleet for its security. Only a fleet capable of placing "the greatest naval power" at serious risk would provide that security. Tirpitz's so-called "risk theory" thus appeared on the surface to be defensive, a strategy of deterrence. But no power threatened Germany's commerce or its largely useless colonial empire. Nor was deterrence Tirpitz's aim. In his internal memoranda for the Kaiser and others, he preached decisive battle "between Helgoland and the Thames." For the "greatest naval power," the opponent Tirpitz had chosen, was Britain.

Victory over Britain, Tirpitz calculated, depended on four conditions. Rivalry with France and Russia would continue to bind the British navy in

Admiral von Tirpitz, who built the fleet against Britain.

China and the Mediterranean, leaving Britain weak in the North Sea. The effete British would neither pay for nor be able to man—with expensive volunteers—the additional ships needed to keep pace. Technology, Tirpitz assumed, would remain static; German battleships built in 1900 would be roughly equivalent to later British and German ships. Finally, in the event of war the British fleet would charge into the mine- and submarine-infested German waters and mount the traditional close inshore blockade of enemy ports. That would give the Germans their opportunity to fight on advantageous terms.

The Kaiser was enthusiastic. The fleet would assure him his place in Prusso-German history. Just as his grandfather William I—thanks to Bismarck—had used the Prussian army to give the new Germany a semi-hegemonic position in Europe, so he would use the navy to break through into the circle of true world powers. And just as William I and Bismarck had mastered Prussian Liberalism by victory abroad, so he and his "second Bismarck," Bülow, would master Social Democracy. And his fleet, thanks to provisions in the naval laws that automatically replaced over-age ships, would ultimately be independent of the hated *Reichstag*. William II would become a naval "People's Kaiser" ruling a "German world empire."

The British were not amused. Britain by 1900 had progressed farther than Germany along the road to becoming an industrial society; over half of Britain's food was imported, and those imports inevitably came by sea. Naval supremacy was for Britain not a luxury but a matter of survival. The British navy scrapped its Chinese river gunboats and its Caribbean squadron to free manpower for the North Sea. After 1903 it created new naval bases facing Germany at Rosyth in Scotland and at Scapa Flow in the Orkneys. Admiral "Jacky" Fisher, reforming Admiralty chief after 1904, supervised Britain's technological leap to the all-big-gun

ship, the *Dreadnought*—and urged destruction of the German fleet in harbor, before it was strong enough to challenge Britain. The British foreign office sought closer ties with France and eventually with Russia. By 1905, the principal assumptions of Tirpitz's plan were thus proving false. Germany had summoned up a naval competition that its British opponent dared not lose and had isolated itself diplomatically except for alliance to an increasingly ramshackle and dependent Austria-Hungary.

The First Morocco Crisis, 1905–06

Germany might have sought to loosen by good behavior the "encirclement"—as the Germans now began to call it—that Germany had itself summoned up. Britain, France, and Russia were an odd assortment: two parliamentary regimes, one brutal autocracy. Britain and Russia might still clash anywhere from China to Persia, if Germany lay low. But Bülow and the chief brain at the German foreign office, the secretive Friedrich von Holstein, chose to break "encirclement" with threats. Russia's defeat at the hands of Japan removed France's continental backing. Bülow and Holstein sought to exploit that weakness by picking a quarrel with France and reducing it to vassalage by proving that it could not rely on Britain.

They chose French encroachment on derelict Morocco as a pretext. The "First Morocco Crisis" was in reality not colonial, but a crisis of the European balance. In March 1905, with Russia in chaos, Bülow and Holstein diverted the Kaiser's habitual Mediterranean cruise to Tangier. The "All-Highest" landed reluctantly, and asserted Germany's non-existent "great and growing interests in Morocco." Tension mounted as summer, the season for war, drew near. In June the French cabinet cracked, and dismissed Delcassé as foreign minister.

Germany appeared to have won; William II made Bülow a prince. And in July William II succeeded during a yachting encounter off the Finnish island of Björkö in persuading his cousin "Nicky"—Tsar Nicholas II—to sign an alliance with Germany. Nicholas agreed in the hope that German backing would help him get better peace terms from Japan. Germany had apparently broken the Franco-Russian alliance, and achieved supremacy on the Continent.

But Russia in defeat and revolution needed French money more than ever before. France's price was naturally Russian repudiation of Björkö, which the Russians in any event found less necessary after making peace with Japan in September 1905. The Germans also made a fatal error. Instead of pressing for a bilateral Moroccan bargain with France that would recognize their victory, they sought an international conference.

At Algeciras, opposite Gibraltar, the representatives of the powers met in January 1906. Germany found itself isolated except for Austria-Hungary. Even its Triple Alliance partner Italy stood with France. In 1900 Italy had secretly secured French acquiescence to Italian designs on Libya in return for Italian support in Morocco. In 1902 Rome had even sinned against the Triple Alliance with a secret promise of neutrality in the event Germany "provoked" France to a declaration of war.

The Algeciras conference therefore handed Germany a major diplomatic defeat. And Britain had already taken secret steps to bolster the French. When the Liberals took office in December 1905, talks were already underway between the British and French army staffs about committing a British army on the left wing of the French, if Germany attacked. The crisis Germany had launched had mightily reinforced the "ring" forming around Germany. Bülow and Holstein had converted an Anglo-French colonial entente into a quasi-alliance against Germany to preserve the European balance of power. And on August 31, 1907, Russia and Britain, the two most persistent antag-

onists of the nineteenth century, signed a colonial entente settling their long-standing disputes in Tibet, Afghanistan, and Persia. The "Triple Entente" of Britain, France, and Russia now faced the Triple Alliance of Germany, Austria-Hungary, and Italy.

The German Challenge: The View from London

On January 1, 1907, Sir Eyre Crowe, the best brain in the British foreign office, dissected Imperial Germany's motives and policies in a long and prescient memorandum for his superiors. His analysis was potentially applicable to the armament programs and foreign policies of later expansionist powers.

Either Germany is definitely aiming at a general political hegemony and maritime ascendancy, threatening the independence of her neighbors and ultimately the existence of England; Or Germany, free from any such clear-cut ambition, . . . is seeking to promote her foreign commerce, spread the benefits of German culture, extend the scope of her national energies, and create fresh German interests all over the world wherever and whenever a peaceful opportunity offers, leaving it to an uncertain future to decide whether the occurrence of great changes in the world may not some day assign to Germany a larger share of direct political action over regions not now a part of her dominions . . . .

In either case Germany would clearly be wise to build as powerful a navy as she can afford. The above alternatives seem to exhaust the possibilities of explaining the given facts. The choice offered is a narrow one, nor easy to make with any close approach to certainty. It will, however, be seen, on reflection, that there is no actual necessity for a British Government to determine definitely which of the two theories of German policy it will accept. For it is clear that the second scheme (of semi-independent evolution, not entirely unaided by statecraft) may at any stage merge into the first, or conscious-design scheme. Moreover, if ever the evolution scheme should come to be realized, the position thereby accruing to Germany would obviously constitute as formidable a menace to the rest of the world as would be presented by any deliberate conquest of a similar position by "malice aforethought."

From *British Documents on the Origins of the War, 1898–1914,* (London: His Majesty's Stationary Office, 1928), Vol. III, p. 417.

Naval Race and Bosnian Crisis, 1907–09

The Germans learned little from the first Morocco crisis. The noisy diplomacy of Bülow and Holstein had contradicted Tirpitz's need for quiet in which to build a fleet against Britain. Now Tirpitz's fleet cut across Germany's far greater need to lie low. By 1908 Tirpitz faced the possibility that he might fail. The Liberals in Britain, despite their detestation of "great armaments" and their desire to increase social spending, would not give up Britain's lead over the German fleet. Tirpitz, amid clamorous anti-British propaganda from the German Navy League, therefore pushed a third naval law through the *Reichstag*. The German building tempo rose to four Dreadnoughts per year.

Britain replied with a proposal for a one-year "naval holiday." Berlin rejected it. Except for the pacifist Cobdenite wing of the Liberals, British opinion was now unanimous. Britain must keep its lead whatever the cost. "We want eight [Dreadnoughts] and we won't wait!" clamored the popular press. In 1909–10 Britain laid down ten battleships and battle cruisers. When the time came to pay the bill, the Liberals raised the income tax, instituted inheritance taxes, and overrode the protests of the House of Lords. In Germany, Bülow's attempt to raise taxes to cover the vast increases in fleet costs led to the defection of the Junker Conservatives and the collapse of the government's *Reichstag* majority. The Reich's antiquated fiscal structure proved unequal to the strain, while the knowledge that naval superiority was a matter of life and death strengthened British resolve.

As Anglo-German tension mounted, Germany's ally Austria-Hungary made its own contribution to the growing European crisis. For a decade it had held to its 1897 agreement with Russia to keep the Balkans quiet. But in 1903 a group of fanatical Serb officers slaughtered Vienna's clients, King Alexander and Queen Draga Obrenovitch of Serbia. Austria-Hungary's relations with Serbia deteriorated. French capital fortified Serbia against an Austro-Hungarian tariff war. By 1908 the Austro-Hungarian foreign minister, Count Aehrenthal, had concluded that Vienna's prestige was at stake.

As a blow against Serbia he sought Russia's acquiescence to the annexation of Bosnia and Herzegovina, the largely Serb-inhabited provinces bordering Serbia that the Congress of Berlin had allowed Austria-Hungary to occupy in 1878. Aehrenthal's Russian counterpart, Count Isvolsky, agreed, on condition that Austria-Hungary help secure a long-standing Russian goal, the opening of the Turkish Straits to Russian warships.

Aehrenthal was too clever. He announced the annexation of the provinces in October 1908, before the Russians had time to secure the agreement of other powers to the opening of the Straits. The other powers, in any event, did not agree. Aehrenthal pocketed Bosnia and Herzegovina, while Isvolsky grumbled and threatened, and the Serbs agitated against Austria. Eventually William II appeared, as he himself put it, "in shining armor" alongside Austria-Hungary. Berlin cabled St. Petersburg to accept the annexation, or else: "We would have to consider an evasive, conditional, or ambiguous reply as a refusal." The Russians accepted; they had not yet recovered from war with Japan. What from Berlin appeared a triumphant reassertion of German and Austro-Hungarian prestige seemed to the other powers dramatic evidence of German aggressiveness. Bülow, leaving office after a personal clash with William II, claimed to have given this sound advice: "Do not repeat the Bosnian Crisis."

The Second Morocco Crisis, 1911

Bülow's successors, Chancellor Theobald von Bethmann Hollweg and foreign secretary Alfred von Kiderlen-Wächter, did not act on it. Instead, Kiderlen again attempted to use Morocco as a pretext to bully France, in the hope of breaking the Entente and riding nationalist enthusiasm to victory in the 1912 German elections. In May 1911 the French occupied Fez, the capital of Morocco, after the usual disorders threatening European businessmen. Kiderlen met with the pan-Germans and enlisted them as propagandists for his policy. He then dispatched a gunboat, the *Panther*, to the Moroccan Atlantic port of Agadir on the pretext of protecting German lives, which were not threatened. The German nationalist press was ecstatic: "Finally, a Deed!"

Kiderlen, a jovial Swabian given to canary-yellow vests, conducted a policy so secretive that the austere and bureaucratic Bethmann Hollweg had to ply him with drink to find out what he had told the French. Kiderlen had threatened war while offering to settle for the entire French Congo in compensation for France's seizure of Morocco and as symbol of France's dependence on Germany. But the French and Russian armies were stronger than in 1905. Britain, through the mouth of Lloyd George, whom the Germans had thought was a pacifist Liberal, stiffened the French with Jingo oratory.

Although Bethmann Hollweg shared what his private secretary described as "the authentic and fitting German idealist conviction that the *Volk* needs a war," the Kaiser was less enthusiastic. Kiderlen had to settle for several strips of French Congo swamp. France retained its independence. The pan-Germans vented their fury on the Reich government for this "new Olmütz." And the crisis brought Britain to make further secret commitments to France. London reaffirmed its plans to send a British Expeditionary Force (B.E.F.) in the event of German attack. Sir Edward Grey, the foreign secretary, authorized increasingly binding military discussions with the French while keeping the Cobdenites in the cabinet

in the dark. And Sir Winston Churchill, civilian chief of the navy after 1911 and a distant descendant of the great Duke of Marlborough, called the Mediterranean fleet home to face the Germans in the North Sea. The French took over Britain's Mediterranean duties in return for a secret British undertaking to protect the coasts of northern France against the German fleet. That was Britain's most far-reaching commitment against Germany to date.

Germany Prepares, 1912–13

The German response to defeat in the Second Morocco Crisis was retrenchment—of a sort. Tirpitz lost the unchallenged right to funding which his navy had enjoyed. In 1913 and 1914 the German building tempo fell to two ships a year. Berlin at last recognized that it must secure its continental base before defeating Britain. The Kaiser and Bethmann Hollweg now gave the army priority. Radicals on the general staff such as Erich Ludendorff broke down aristocratic inhibitions against expanding the army with non-noble officers. In 1912 and 1913 two army bills added 165,000 first-line troops. The *Reichstag* at last passed an inheritance tax over Conservative objections. Tirpitz's only consolation was the Kaiser's rejection of yet another British "naval holiday" proposal.

The army increase was necessary, if Germany were to implement its chosen strategy in war. Waldersee's successor as Chief of the Great General Staff, Count Alfred von Schlieffen (1891–1905), faced the same nightmare of a two-front war as his predecessors. But his answer was different. Instead of attacking in Russia and defending in fortified Alsace-Lorraine, as both Moltke and Waldersee had proposed, Schlieffen planned to strike France first. France, he reasoned, was vulnerable to a swift decisive blow, whereas the Russians could always retreat into their limitless spaces as they had in 1812.

Schlieffen's Plan

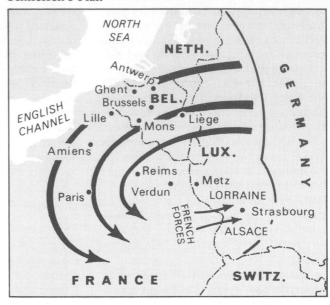

Schlieffen had studied military history, classifying battles as a bug-hunter does insects. Decisive battles, he concluded, were all envelopments. The most perfect was Hannibal's crushing double envelopment of the Romans in 216 B.C. at Cannae in southern Italy. But mountains, French fortifications, and the absence of space for Germany's million-man army did not permit a double envelopment on the Franco-German border. Instead, Schlieffen planned a holding action there to distract the French. Meanwhile an immense right wing, three-quarters of the entire German army, would swing down through neutral Belgium upon the unfortified and undefended French rear.

Timing was everything. If Germany did not mobilize in time, or failed to knock France out immediately, the "Russian Steamroller" would crush Germany's skeleton force in East Prussia, and drive on Berlin. And Schlieffen, in his admiration of Hannibal, had forgotten one vital fact: Rome had ultimately defeated Hannibal. It had destroyed Carthage through attrition and through command of the sea.

Schlieffen's plan dictated that any German war, even one stemming from a Balkan quarrel, would begin with an attack on France that staked Germany's future on a single card. And the violation of Belgium, whose neutrality the powers had guaranteed in 1839, virtually ensured that Britain would join

"War the sooner the better": Helmuth von Moltke the younger, Prussia-Germany's chief of staff, 1906–14.

Germany's enemies. To Schlieffen that seemed unimportant. Britain had no mass army, and the war would be over—*must* be over—before it had time to raise one. Those were dangerous misapprehensions.

Schlieffen retired in 1905, leaving his plan to Helmuth von Moltke the younger, high-strung and indecisive nephew of the great Moltke. The new chief of staff had doubts about Schlieffen's "infallible recipe for victory" but kept them to himself. He added additional troops to both wings of the German deployment; later charges that he "watered down" Schlieffen's plan were unjust.

And at the end of 1912 the German leadership apparently decided to act. A British warning that Britain would stand by France in the event of war enraged the Kaiser. On December 8, 1912, he presided over a conference of his military advisers at Potsdam. Moltke, according to the diary of the Kaiser's chief naval aide, counseled a Prussian-style preventive war "the sooner the better" to crush Germany's

adversaries while Germany could still do so. New Russian railways in Poland and rearmament of the Russian army with modern weapons would make the Schlieffen plan impractical by 1917. Tirpitz advised restraint—for the moment. His navy was not ready. Only in June 1914 would the vital canal across Jutland between the Baltic and the North Sea be widened for Dreadnoughts, and the submarine pens on Helgoland be ready. The conference, without consulting Bethmann Hollweg, decided to mobilize the press to prepare the German public for war. With government encouragement, stories increasingly hostile to Russia began appearing.

And at the general staff, Moltke and his assistant Ludendorff made two fateful changes in 1913. First, they discarded Germany's one remaining alternate plan, which had provided for an offensive deployment against Russia and defense against France. Second, Ludendorff added to the Schlieffen plan the requirement that German troops must move immediately upon

The Dissolution of the Ottoman Empire   to 1914

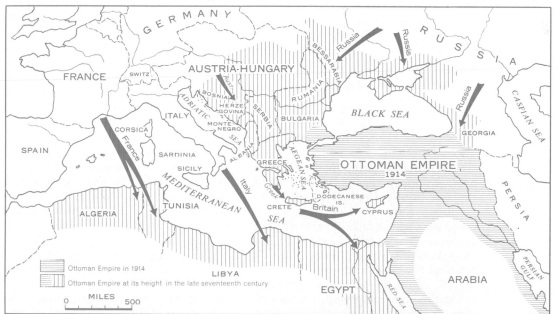

The Balkan Wars: Turkish infantry moves up.

mobilization into neutral Luxembourg and Belgium to seize the key rail junction of Liège. If the war for which Moltke was pressing came, Germany would violate Belgium upon mobilization and attack France regardless of the war's origin.

The Balkan Wars, 1912–13

While the Germans prepared, the great powers lost control of the Balkans. France's absorption of Morocco produced a chain reaction. Giovanni Giolitti of Italy, fearing that the French now no longer needed to honor their promise to support Italy's acquisition of Libya, acted. No Italian government could survive if it failed to assert Italy's great-power status. In September 1911 Italy declared war on Turkey, Libya's nominal overlord, and sent its fleet to Tripoli. A hastily improvised landing failed to subdue the warlike Arabs or their Turkish advisers. Italy therefore seized Turkish islands in the Aegean

and attacked the Dardanelles. Not until October 1912 did the Turks cede a still unpacified Libya to Italy.

The Italian example emboldened the Balkan states. Serbia and Bulgaria, with Russia as godfather, signed an alliance in March 1912. Greece and Montenegro joined. The Russians thought of the new alliance as defensive; the Balkan states had other ideas. In September the Balkan League attacked Turkey and swiftly partitioned Turkey's territory in Europe. Then the victors fell out over the division of the spoils. Bulgaria attacked Serbia in the hope of seizing the province of Macedonia, of which it claimed the powers had defrauded it in 1878. Serbia, Greece, Montenegro, Rumania, and Turkey smashed the Bulgarians.

The Serbs gained most from the wars, although Austria-Hungary fiercely barred them from the Adriatic in Albania. The powers, under the leadership of Sir Edward Grey of Britain, cooperated in holding Serbia back and in creating an independent Albania. The victory of Balkan nationalism had ended the multinational Turkish empire in Europe. That made the new "Sick Man" of Europe, Austria-Hungary, increasingly desperate to reassert its shrinking prestige against Serbia, the "Piedmont of the South Slavs." The Balkan Wars were clearly not the last Balkan crisis.

"EVEN IF WE END IN RUIN"— JULY 1914

On June 28, 1914, at Sarajevo in Bosnia, a Bosnian-Serb terrorist assassinated Archduke Francis Ferdinand, heir to the throne of Austria-Hungary. The terrorists, following a pattern common later in the century, were connected with a secret society—the "Black Hand"—under the sponsorship of Serbia's military intelligence department. Vienna did not know that, but it reacted with predictable fury. The chief of staff, the bloody-minded Conrad von Hötzendorff, looked for a war to restore Habsburg prestige and crush Serbia for good. Austria-Hungary's foreign minister, the frivolous Count Leopold von Berchtold, concurred. Only the Hungarians, appalled by the thought of annexing yet more Slavs, opposed action.

Berlin broke the deadlock. When Berchtold's envoy called upon the Kaiser on July 5, William II counseled immediate war against Serbia, regardless of Russia's reaction. He repeatedly assured a confidant, Krupp von Bohlen, that "this time I will not chicken out [*Diesmal falle ich nicht um*]." Bethmann Hollweg told his closest confidant on July 8 that Germany would probably win a general war. If Russia pulled back, Germany would nevertheless split the Entente, and achieve a decisive diplomatic and strategic victory. In Vienna, Berchtold used Berlin's so-called "blank check"—in reality a virtual order to act—to break Hungarian opposition. Since 1866–67 Greater Hungary had owed its independence

Sarajevo, June 28, 1914: The arrest of the assassin, Gavrilo Princip.

The Kaiser Spurs Vienna On   July 5, 1914

The Kaiser's message, as reported by Austria-Hungary's ambassador, Count Ladislaus Szögyény, was no simple "blank check" or assurance of support. It was an incitement to war.

After lunch, when I once again underscored with the greatest emphasis the seriousness of the situation, His Majesty [Kaiser William II] authorized me to report to our most gracious Majesty [Emperor Francis Joseph] that in this case as in others we could count on Germany's full support. . . . He (Kaiser William) was of the opinion that this action must not be delayed. Russia's attitude will in any event be hostile, but he had been prepared for that for years, and should it come to a war between Austria-Hungary and Russia, we could be assured that Germany would stand by our side with its usual faithfulness to its alliances. . . . He understands full well that His royal and imperial Apostolic Majesty [Emperor Francis Joseph] would be reluctant, given his well-known love of peace, to march into Serbia. But if we had really become convinced of the necessity of military action against Serbia, he (Kaiser William) would regret it if we allowed the present highly favorable moment to pass unused.

From Immanuel Geiss, ed., *Julikrise und Kriegsausbruch 1914* (Hannover: Verlag für Literatur und Zeitgeschehen GmbH, 1963), pp. 83–84 (translation by M. Knox).

Conrad von Hötzendorff, Austria-Hungary's chief of staff, contemplates war on three fronts (1914).

to Berlin; it could not refuse Berlin's order.

But partly out of Viennese languor and partly out of calculation, Berchtold delayed issuing the ultimatum to Serbia until July 23. That gave Austria-Hungary's action an appearance of cold premeditation that weakened Vienna's moral position. And the 48-hour ultimatum itself appeared a deliberate provocation. One German ambassador could not believe that Vienna had drafted the document; its brutal tone was "Prussian to the very bones." Berchtold made the deliberately humiliating demand that Austro-Hungarian police enter Serbia to join the hunt for the terrorists and their accomplices. Vienna also announced that it would treat refusal of any single condition as a total rejection. The Serbs made a conciliatory answer. But perhaps thanks to Russian reassurances, they refused to accept Austro-Hungarian intervention inside Serbia itself.

That was enough for Vienna, and for Berlin, where official circles, in the words of a participant, "worried only that the Serbs might swallow the note." Bethmann Hollweg sabotaged efforts by Grey to arrange a conference of the kind that had prevented the Balkan Wars from growing into great power conflict. On July 28, with strong German encouragement, Austria-Hungary declared war on Serbia. Austro-Hungarian mobilization was too slow to permit an invasion for several weeks, but Vienna and Berlin were determined to present the powers with a violent *fait accompli*. Austria-Hungary therefore shelled Belgrade, the Serb capital.

Russia now had to respond or suffer a humiliation far worse than the Bosnian crisis. Nicholas II and his Foreign minister, Sergei Dimitrievich Sazonov, reluctantly attempted to deter Vienna. On July 28 they fatalistically ordered mobilization of the four Russian military districts opposite Austria-Hungary. Then the generals reported that Russia's cumbersome mobilization system permitted only a general mobilization. On July 31 Russia published the order for general mobilization. That proved the point of no return, although the Russian purpose was deterrence, not war.

In Berlin, the news was welcome indeed. The Kaiser had begun to waver, while Moltke pressed Bethmann Hollweg with increasing vehemence to mobilize before Russia. Bethmann Hollweg himself feared the domestic consequences of mobilizing first; it was his task to keep the German Social Democrats loyal to the coming war effort. Russia's mobilization appeared heaven-sent. "The mood is brilliant," wrote the Kaiser's naval aide in his diary on August 1, "The government has succeeded very well in making us appear as the attacked." Germany dispatched an ultimatum to Russia summoning it to demobilize. Russia refused.

On August 1 Germany declared war on Russia and mobilized. France responded to its alliance obligations to Russia by mobilizing. A German ultimatum to Paris demanding French neutrality followed. The ultimatum was for show only; German strategy dictated war on two fronts. If France dared to upset the Schlieffen plan by abandoning its Russian ally and remaining neutral, the German ambassador in Paris was to ask provocatively for the surrender of French border fortifications. That would force France to fight. In the event, France did not accept the ultimatum. On August 2 Germany invaded Luxembourg and summoned Belgium to give free passage to German troops. Belgium refused. On August 3 Germany declared war on France. On the morning of August 4 German troops entered Belgium—and pushed the indecisive British cabinet into war. The violation of Belgium allowed the Liberals to feel moral about a war to defend British security and the balance of power; the Cobdenite pacifist Liberals resigned. At midnight on August 4 London's ultimatum to Berlin expired. As the Kaiser addressed the *Reichstag* amid stormy applause, the war minister, Erich von Falkenhayn, was overcome by emotion: "Even if we end in ruin, it was beautiful." That was a fitting epitaph for Imperial Germany and for the long peace.

"War Guilt"

Later, after 1918, it became fashionable to dispute Germany's preeminent responsibility for the war of 1914–18. German scholars rallied around their foreign office, and accused Russia or Britain. Anglo-Saxon "revisionists" did their best to charge Vienna, St. Petersburg, Paris, and even London with "war guilt." Guilt is a notion best left to psychoanalysts and theologians—but causation and responsibility are of interest to the historian.

Nor, for all the oceans of ink spilled over the origins of this conflict, is apportioning responsibility difficult. The long-term causes of the war were two: Austria-Hungary's decline and Germany's rise. Balkan nationalism threatened an Austria-Hungary embroiled in perennial struggle with Russia. German nationalism, after 1890, proved not at all "satiated." Bismarck, with the dual alliance of 1879, had inextricably tied together these two principal sources of European conflict. After

---

Bethmann Hollweg's Calculations
July 1914

Kurt Riezler, Bethmann Hollweg's private secretary and author of a work on politics with the symptomatic title of *The Necessity of the Impossible* (1913), recorded in his diary his July 1914 conversations with the Chancellor. They leave little doubt about the extent of Bethmann Hollweg's, and Germany's, responsibility for the outcome.

July 7, 1914. . . . **In the evening a long talk about the situation . . . [Bethmann sees] Russia's military power swiftly growing; once [the] strategic buildup in Poland [is] complete, [our] situation untenable. Austria ever weaker and less dynamic. . . . I was appalled; I did not see things that darkly. . . . [Bethmann:] The future belongs to Russia, which grows and grows. . . .**

July 8, 1914. . . . **The Chancellor thinks the old Kaiser [Francis Joseph of Austria] may not decide to go ahead. If war comes from the East, so that we have to go to war for Austria-Hungary rather than Austria-Hungary for us, we have the prospect of winning. If war does not come, if the Tsar doesn't want it or France, appalled, counsels peace, then we nevertheless still [doch noch] have the prospect of maneuvering the Entente apart through this action.**

July 14, 1914. . . . **For him [Bethmann Hollweg] action is a leap in the dark, and a heavy duty. Kiderlen always said we would have to fight. Berchtold is considering the timing [of the ultimatum], whether before or after the visit of Poincaré [the French president] to St. Petersburg. Better before, for then the chance is greater that France, panicked by the sudden appearance of the specter of war, will warn Russia to keep the peace.**

From Kurt Riezler, *Tagebücher, Aufsätze, Dokumente* [Göttingen: Vandenhoeck & Rupprecht, 1972], pp. 182–84 (translation by M. Knox).

1905 they interacted explosively. Balkan nationalism sapped Austria-Hungary just as the German threat drove the Entente powers to coalesce against Germany.

In the final crisis, responsibility was unevenly divided. Britain merely intervened once the Germans invaded Belgium. Contrary to later German accusations, Grey scarcely hid the likelihood that Britain would act if Germany sought to crush France—but fear of Britain did not deter Berlin. France merely accepted a war that Germany forced on it. The Serb government did not seek war, although it nurtured the terrorists. St. Petersburg encouraged Serb expansion in 1912 and after, and possibly nerved Belgrade to refuse Austria-Hungary's most humiliating demands. Russia also mobilized first, although its intention was not war, but getting Vienna's attention.

Austria-Hungary's responsibilities were more serious. It sought war with Serbia, made sure that its ultimatum meant war, and shelled Belgrade. But it was Berlin that took the key decisions: without German pressure, Austria-Hungary would never have acted. Since late 1912 Germany's leaders had inclined toward a general war, given a suitable occasion. Moltke actively sought war "the sooner the better." His purpose was to strike down Germany's *potential* enemies before they became too strong—a goal little different from outright aggression. Bethmann Hollweg, obsessed with the specter of the ever-growing—though hollow—Russian colossus, and inclined to optimism about German military prospects if general war came soon, was more than willing to risk it. All trusted in a "fresh and joyous war" (in the phrase of the Kaiser's obstreperous son, Crown Prince William), short and victorious in the style of 1870.

Germany's minimum goal was a small Balkan war to bolster a flagging Austria-Hungary and split the Triple Entente. Its maximum goal was the domination of Europe. And the Schlieffen plan—after 1913 Germany's *only* war plan—ensured that war against Russia would begin with an attack on France through Belgium. That guaranteed British intervention. Germany made a Balkan war, then turned it into a world war.

Suggestions for Further Reading

Europe in the Age of Bismarck

The relevant chapters of L. C. B. Seaman, *From Vienna to Versailles* (1955), offer a good brief guide to international politics after 1871. A. J. P. Taylor's indispensable *The Struggle for Mastery in Europe* (1954), gives a detailed and brilliantly sardonic account, but see also P. Kennedy, *The Rise and Fall of the Great Powers* (1987), for the underlying trends. W. L. Langer, *European Alliances and Alignments, 1871–1890* (1950), is still useful on the diplomacy of Bismarck's conservative phase. M. Hurst, ed., *Key Treaties for the Great Powers*, vol. 2, *(1871–1914)* (1972), gives English texts of agreements such as the Triple Alliance. Among the many accounts of the policies of the different powers, see especially G. Bourne, *The Foreign Policy of Victorian England* (1970); B. Porter, *The Lion's Share* (1984); and D. Geyer, *Russian Imperialism* (1987). On military affairs, see the relevant chapter in H. Strachan, *European Armies and the Conduct of War* (1983); G. Ritter, *The Schlieffen Plan* (1958); and P. Kennedy, ed., *The War Plans of the Great Powers, 1880–1914* (1979).

World Politics

For the rise of "world politics," see especially the chapter on international affairs in G. Barraclough, *An Introduction to Contemporary History* (1964). W. L. Langer, *The Diplomacy of Imperialism* (1950), covers the 1890–1902 period in informative detail. H. W. Morgan, *America's Road to Empire* (1965), provides a convenient summary of America's entry into world politics; see also C. S. Campbell, *The Transformation of American Foreign Relations, 1865–1900* (1976), and H. K. Beale, *Theodore Roosevelt and the Rise of America to World Power* (1956). R. Van Alstyne, *The Rising American Empire* (1960), offers a jaundiced view of U.S. motives. T. Pakenham, *The Boer War* (1978), and I. Nish, *The Anglo-Japanese Alliance* (1966), are excellent.

The Road to World War I

The best single work on the origins of the First World War remains L. Albertini, *The Origins of the War of 1914* (1952). P. Kennedy, *The Origins of the Anglo-German Antagonism, 1860–1914* (1980), is a model of analysis. V. Berghahn, *Germany and the Approach of War in 1914* (1973), and Z. Steiner, *Britain and the Origins of the First World War* (1977), offer parallel accounts that emphasize German responsibility. On France, Russia, Austria-Hungary, and Italy see J. Keiger, *France and the Origins of the First World War* (1983); D. Lieven, *Russia and the Origins of the First World War* (1983); F. R. Bridge, *From Sadowa to Sarajevo: The Foreign Policy of Austria-Hungary, 1866–1914* (1972); and R. Bosworth, *Italy and the Approach of the First World War* (1983). V. Dedijer, *The Road to Sarajevo* (1967), throws some light on Serb machinations. For the final crisis, I. Geiss, ed., *July 1914* (1967), is indispensable. F. Fischer, *Germany's Aims in the First World War* (1967), and *War of Illusions* (1975), makes a strong case for a premeditated German war of aggression.

30
War and Revolution, 1914–1929

*T*he war that began in August 1914 irrevocably changed Europe and the world. Contrary to almost unanimous expectation, neither Jena-Auerstädt nor Sedan repeated themselves. Instead, as in the U.S. Civil War, industrialized states mobilized their full reserves of human and machine power, and battered one another into collapse. In the process, Europe forfeited a world economic leadership that the growth of the United States already threatened. The nationalism of the colonial peoples received powerful reinforcement. The four great empires of Europe and the Middle East perished. One of them, Russia, suffered a revolution of utopian claims and unparalleled ferocity, the first Marxist revolution. The European balance of power broke down: victory over Russia potentially gave Germany the mastery of Europe. Only the intervention of a power from outside Europe, the United States, brought Germany's final defeat. And swift U.S. withdrawal after 1919 left the exhausted victors, Britain and France, face-to-face with a vengeful Germany that did not acknowledge defeat. Those conditions made the war of 1914–18 merely the *First* World War.

THE WAR OF MOVEMENT, 1914

The dead Schlieffen's stupendous gamble failed. The initial coup at Liège went well. The great German right wing, a million men in four armies, began to swing. The French, fervent for the offensive, obligingly attacked the German fortifications in Lorraine and thus plunged deeper into the German trap. There, France lost 300,000 dead, wounded, and missing, a loss never made good.

But Schlieffen and his successor, Moltke the younger, had allowed neither for enemy reaction nor for "friction," that force of chance and circumstance that makes even the simplest plans in war excruciatingly difficult to execute. The Belgians wrecked their railroads. Belgian civilians, despite German massacres in reprisal, fired on German columns. German transport beyond the railheads was increasingly inadequate. The immense march distances exhausted the reservists, who were of necessity not in peak condition. By September, wrote an officer of the German army with the farthest to travel, "the men stagger forward, their

Machine warfare: a British
tank moves up, 1917.

faces coated with dust, their uniforms in rags, looking like living scarecrows. They march with their eyes closed, singing in chorus so as not to fall asleep. . . . It is only the delirium of victory that sustains our men."

Delirium was not enough. As the Germans neared the Franco-Belgian border, they encountered both the French and the 120,000 professionals of the British Expeditionary Force (B.E.F.). The Kaiser exhorted his commanders to "exterminate the treacherous English" and walk over their "contemptible little army." The B.E.F. replied with rifle fire so rapid and accurate that the Germans thought they faced a new form of machine gun. German numbers eventually flanked British and French, and forced withdrawal southwards. But the price of German victory was high. It increased further as the French commander in chief, the imperturbable "Papa" Joseph Joffre, gave up the Lorraine offensive and switched forces by rail to face the German right wing. Schlieffen had simply assumed the French would be too paralyzed to outflank the German right wing; the French decided otherwise.

The Germans, footsore in the August heat, found by the end of the month that they lacked the troops to envelop Paris as Schlieffen had originally hoped. The Russian threat in East Prussia had forced diversion of two corps to the eastern front; even had they stayed, they would have been too few to cover the front and flanks of a drive around Paris from the west. And as the outermost German army swung inside Paris, it exposed its flank and rear to French forces in the city. Joseph Galliéni, conqueror of Tonkin and Madagascar, threw his troops onto the German weak point and mobilized the taxis of Paris to bring up reserves. Alexander von Kluck, the German army commander, frantically turned his five corps back to the northwest to counter Galliéni; that opened a fatal gap between Kluck's army and its neighbor to the east. On September 8–9, thanks to the persistence of Joffre ("the honor of England is at stake"), the battered B.E.F. staggered forward into that gap and threatened to roll up von Kluck. On September 9 the outflanked and exhausted German armies withdrew northward toward the river Aisne. Moltke, who had urged war for so long, suffered a nervous breakdown. France's defensive victory on the Marne meant that Europe faced a long war.

Moltke's replacement as Germany's chief of staff, the moody Erich von Falkenhayn, might yet have flanked the British and French north and west of Paris and have seized much of France's Channel coast. But he refused to withdraw further than the Aisne, and thus lacked the mass of troops needed for a concentrated drive. Instead, he dissipated German reserves in a series of piecemeal attacks north of Paris. The B.E.F. and the French held with difficulty, but they held.

This "race to the sea" ended in October–November 1914 with a huge slaughter in Flanders. At Langemarck, near Ypres, Falkenhayn committed scarcely trained volunteers, fresh from school or university, against the remains of the B.E.F. It was a "massacre of the innocents." Little remained of the volunteers, of whom Germany had much need later, or of the B.E.F., the main repository of experienced leaders for Britain's coming mass armies. In mid-November Falkenhayn admitted to Bethmann Hollweg that the Imperial German Army was "a broken instrument," incapable of forcing a decision. By year's end Germany had lost almost a million dead and wounded, and France at least 900,000. Trenches and barbed wire stretched from the Channel to Switzerland. Until early 1918 the lines scarcely moved, despite unparalleled carnage.

In eastern Europe the Germans had better fortune. The "Russian Steamroller" rolled into East Prussia and broke down. When the outnumbered German defenders gave way, Moltke dragged a senior general, Paul von Hindenburg, out of retirement and

The First World War   1914–18

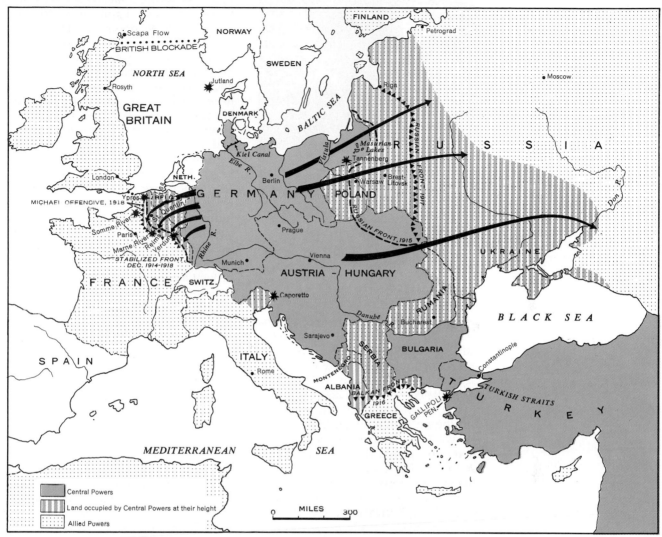

gave him Ludendorff as chief of staff. Ludendorff, with the help of intercepted Russian radio communications, concentrated all German forces against one of the two Russian armies and crushed it at Tannenberg by August 29. Russia lost 92,000 men and 400 guns. Then Ludendorff turned on the other Russian army and drove it back in disorder. That made Hindenburg and Ludendorff much-needed symbols of German invincibility, compensation for defeat on the Marne.

Germany's ally fared less well. Austria-Hungary's first invasion of Serbia was a fiasco and the main Russian attack in Galicia drove Conrad von Hötzendorff's armies back to the Carpathian mountains in confusion. But by the end of the year German troops had retrieved the situation. In the vast spaces of eastern Europe, movement was still possible, although here too siege warfare around key fortresses and rail junctions dominated.

To the south, one member of the Triple Alliance did not go to war in August 1914: Italy. Its grounds were eminently reasonable, for the alliance did not require it to share a war of aggres-

Victors on the eastern front: Hindenburg (left) and Ludendorff.

sion about which Berlin and Vienna had failed to consult it in advance. But Italian neutrality did not prevent the spread of the war beyond Europe. A German Mediterranean detachment, the battle cruiser *Goeben* and the cruiser *Breslau*, evaded an inept British pursuit and sought refuge at Constantinople in August 1914. The Turkish government thereupon gambled on the victory of Germany, its longtime patron, over Russia, its perpetual enemy. When *Goeben* and *Breslau* bombarded Odessa in October, Russia declared war and attacked Turkey in the distant Caucasus. The entry of Turkey extended the war to the entire Middle East, from the Caucasus to Suez to the Persian Gulf.

Farther afield, British seapower was supreme. Britain swept the seas of German surface raiders by the end of 1914. And the Grand Fleet did not charge into the mines and submarine ambushes off the German fleet base of Wilhelmshaven, as Tirpitz had expected. Instead, it established blockade lines at the Channel and from Scotland to Norway, a "distant blockade" outside the effective reach of the fleet that Tirpitz had built. Britain, thanks to its geographic position, could cut Germany off from the outer world without

fighting the fleet action on German terms for which Tirpitz had planned.

Thanks to seapower, the Dominions were free to join Britain and the German colonies were easy prey. Even the Boer leaders cooperated with London, and themselves suppressed a short-lived backwoods anti-British revolt. French and British seized Togo, Cameroons, and South-West Africa. Only in and around German East Africa (now Tanzania) did the Germans hold out for long. There, until 1918, Paul von Lettow-Vorbeck and his native *askaris* repeatedly made fools of their British, Indian, British-African, and Boer pursuers. The "war of the white tribes" of Europe and the sight of Lettow-Vorbeck's *askaris* defeating whites proved a major stimulus to African nationalism.

And in Asia the war was Japan's opportunity to reverse the verdict of 1895, when the powers had forced it to relinquish its gains in China. Tokyo enthusiastically offered Britain its support in August 1914. It gobbled up the German outpost in Shandong, and the German island possessions in the Pacific that did not fall to Australia. In January–May 1915 it imposed on derelict China the famous "twenty-one demands" that consolidated Japanese control of the Shandong Peninsula and claimed southern Manchuria, Inner Mongolia, and an industrial region in central China. British persuasion secured the "postponement" of the most extreme claims, such as a right to impose advisers on China's central government. But protests could not remove Japan's continuing threat to China, and to Europe's domination of Asia and the Pacific.

THE INDUSTRIAL AND GEOGRAPHIC BALANCE

The sources of the stalemate that begun in 1914 are clearer in retrospect than they were to contemporaries. Railways allowed the mobilization and movement to battle of immense armies. The size of those armies allowed the occupation of ever-wider defensive frontages. Finding an enemy flank upon which to launch a decisive attack, as the "race to the sea" demonstrated, was now almost impossible. And on the battlefield itself, the storm of steel and lead, the ever-thicker coils of barbed wire, and the absence of transport for troops, ammunition, and food, immobilized the mass armies. Cars, trucks, and motorcycles were neither bulletproof nor available initially in adequate numbers. Reserves, thanks to railroad, telephone, and radio, could always reach a threatened point faster than attackers could break through on foot. Air reconnaissance and air photography allowed defenders to detect offensive preparations, and made surprise difficult. Strategic mobility checkmated tactical decision, firepower crushed movement, communications and air reconnaissance removed surprise.

Two other factors made the war of 1914–18 an unprecedented struggle of attrition. First, although the staffs of Europe had largely ignored it, the U.S. Civil War had demonstrated that industrial powers fought long wars even when one contender was far stronger industrially than the other. In the absence of striking military ineptitude of the sort the French had displayed in 1870, only attrition could decide the outcome. And the coalition nature of the 1914–18 war likewise prolonged the struggle. As in the world wars of the eighteenth century but unlike 1859, 1866, and 1870–71, the belligerents of 1914–18 had great-power allies. When the weak faltered, their allies usually sustained them. And although Russia indeed collapsed in 1917, the United States simultaneously intervened to shore up a flagging France and Britain with money, food, munitions, and troops.

The keys to victory in this world struggle were industrial might, geographic position, and access to raw materials. The three Allied powers, Britain, France, and Russia, had in 1913 a total industrial potential a third greater than that of the Central Powers, Germany and Austria-Hungary. But the Central Powers were superior to France and Russia alone and after 1914 probably also to Britain and France combined. The Schlieffen Plan had accomplished one major if unsought objective: it deprived France of a fifth of its wheat, half of its coal, and two-thirds of its iron production. Only U.S. intervention in 1917 gave the Allies the better than two-to-one margin in total industrial power that brought victory.

In geographic position, the Central Powers enjoyed one decided advantage and one serious but not insuperable drawback. The advantage was the obverse of Germany's two-front predicament; German possession of "interior lines" allowed swift transfer of forces from west to east to meet successive threats. Given the stalemate at the tactical level, that was no small advantage. The Allies, conversely, were unable to link their major source of manpower, Russia, with the weapons and ammunition produced in the West.

But "encirclement" also had a major disadvantage for the Central Powers: it cut them off from the world market. Shortages of vital materials such as nitrates, rubber, and copper developed immediately. The Germans at first coped. Holland and Scandinavia served as transshipment points for German imports and exports. A German Jewish research chemist, Fritz Haber, broke the nitrate bottleneck with his nitrogen fixation process, perfected in 1913: the inexhaustible nitrogen of the atmosphere gave Germany the explosives it needed to continue the war.

In the long run, Germany suffered. Command of the sea allowed Britain and France to draw on munitions made in the United States and on loans with which to pay for those munitions. The United States, at least at first, would have gladly done business with the Germans as well. But German shipping remained locked in the Baltic and North Sea. And Britain slowly overcame U.S. resistance to "rationing" neutrals near Germany to their pre-war levels of imports. The loss of overseas food and fertilizer imports, the forced slaughter of livestock to save fodder, and farm labor shortages crippled German agriculture. First potatoes and then turnips became the staple of the German diet. The blockade failed to paralyze German industrial production, but it did slowly sap civilian morale through hunger.

On balance, the Germans had the advantage until 1918. German possession of northern France deprived the Allies of key assets and forced them to take the offensive. Under prevailing tactical conditions and given the dogged ineptitude of most Allied generals, that meant immense slaughter for no gain. Geography isolated Russia and political and industrial weakness made it increasingly vulnerable. Finally, the quality of German leadership at the tactical and operational levels compensated for the Central Powers' two-to-three disadvantage in total potential against the Triple Entente. Germany, by 1917, had virtually won the war it had started. It went under only because it started another war with another continent, the United States.

POLITICS, SOCIETY, AND THE "HOME FRONT"

All powers, except perhaps Italy or Rumania, entered the war with the certainty—in some cases spurious—that they were victims of unprovoked aggression. That conviction—and the sense of sudden release from the cares, frustrations, and social tensions of Europe's rapidly changing yet narrowly class-bound societies—brought widespread rejoicing. Everywhere, especially in the cities, reservists marched to the stations through crowds waving flags and pelting them with flowers. As the trains rolled, the troops chalked "To Paris!" or "To Berlin!" on the boxcars. They expected to be home before the autumn leaves fell.

Those who lived through the August days never forgot the spontaneous outpouring of a national enthusiasm that momentarily abolished social distinctions. Bethmann Hollweg's assistant, Riezler, noted with wonder on August 14: "War, war, the *Volk* has risen! . . . All deeply joyful, to live, for once, caught up in a great cause." And a recent immigrant to Munich from Austria-Hungary, a certain Adolf Hitler, later wrote in his memoirs that "overpowered by stormy enthusiasm, I fell down on my knees and thanked Heaven from an overflowing heart for granting me the good fortune of being permitted to live at this time." Then as later, he expressed a widespread emotion.

That emotion everywhere guaranteed national cohesion across class and party lines. The socialist Second International collapsed amid the mutual recriminations of its members. In Germany, the government declared a political truce, the *Burgfrieden* ("peace inside the fortress"). Even revolutionary Social Democrats, at the request of the SPD leadership, voted for the first war appropriations. Good Marxists could not refuse a seemingly defensive war against tsarist Russia, the European state Marx had hated above all others. But Germany's unity was short-lived.

For the Reich, despite its public protestations, fought to create an immense central European empire as the basis for German world mastery. In September, as the German armies began their retreat from the Marne, Bethmann Hollweg drafted a confidential memorandum setting forth Germany's aims: annexations in France and Belgium that would reduce them to vassalage, the absorption of Luxembourg, and the creation of a central European customs union that would guarantee Germany's economic as well as military supremacy on the continent. German war aims in eastern Europe did not take concrete shape until 1915, but they were even more voracious. And the leaders of the Reich looked beyond Europe to vast African annexations and to a victory that would give Britain's world position to Germany. The war, as Riezler noted in his diary in mid-1916, was in part a "struggle with England for world mastery."

Public discussion of Germany's aims, despite the attempts of Bethmann Hollweg to still it, increasingly broke into the open. By 1915 politicians, business figures, and pan-Germans were vying with one another to claim ever-larger areas of Europe and ever-tighter control over the small states, Germany's vassals-to-be. Racist pan-Germans urged the removal of inconvenient Poles from the annexed lands. Much of the Left soon concluded that the war was a war of conquest. The Right coupled demands for total victory and immense annexations with total refusal to reform the unequal Prussian franchise. Germany's lack of cohesion at home was its weak point. But only military defeat could transmute weakness into collapse.

In France, all political forces joined a *Union Sacrée* against the German invader. In Britain, German aggression against Belgium utterly discredited the Cobdenite pacifist Liberals. Volunteers swamped the British army. In Austria-Hungary, quarreling nationalities loyally answered the call to the Habsburg colors. Even the Russian autocracy gained a brief reprieve: the pre-war strike wave subsided and the peasant reservists marched. Only Italy, which chose intervention in 1915 without disguising it as national defense, faced from the beginning an internal struggle against those who failed to see the necessity of war.

Parliamentary regimes showed greater staying power than their autocratic counterparts. Warfare in the age of the masses required popular support and only political participation reliably guaranteed that support. That was one secret of France's survival, despite the death or wounding of 60 percent of all Frenchmen who reported for duty between 1914 and 1918. Britain, with amazing unanimity, abolished cherished traditions of *laissez-faire*. When

volunteers began to fall short in 1916, the British cabinet took the radical step of conscription. Conversely, once the war turned sour in 1915–16, internal social and national tensions placed Austria-Hungary, Russia, Italy, and even Germany at risk.

Parliamentary regimes also proved surprisingly successful at directing their war efforts. At first the soldiers dominated in Britain, France, and Italy, thanks to their allegedly esoteric professional wisdom. But much of that wisdom proved wrong. When the generals failed to force a decision, the civilians took a hand. In December 1916 the feeble—or too humane—Asquith gave way to a Liberal-Conservative-Labour coalition under Lloyd George, a man known to have "fire in his belly." Lloyd George reasserted, not always successfully, London's control over Britain's intractable commander on the western front, Sir Douglas Haig. The French Chamber made Joffre a figurehead in December 1916. The national emergency of 1917 made the cynical and iron-willed Clemenceau, "the Tiger" of the Radicals, prime minister and virtual dictator by consent of the Chamber and the nation. Vittorio Emanuele Orlando, a less compelling figure, assumed some of the

Britain recruits a mass army, 1915: the appeal, and the result (below).

same powers in Italy's dark winter of 1917–18.

The autocracies took two paths. In Russia and Austria-Hungary, the monarchies held jealously to power, while inefficiency and defeat sapped their store of prestige and public trust. The essential question on the eastern front until 1917 was which of the two great empires would win the race to military collapse and political disintegration. Germany traveled another road. The Kaiser's blood-curdling asides and blustering orders of the day imperfectly concealed his indecision and proneness to nervous collapse. By 1916 he had become a figurehead. In his place Germany received a military rather than a parliamentary dictatorship.

Socially, the war marked the real beginning of the "century of the common man." Until 1914 aristocrats and landowners had dominated the bureaucracies, diplomatic services, and officer corps of Europe. The war did not end that domination everywhere, but it made a mighty start. The military aristocracies paid in blood for their privileges. Pomeranian Junkers, Ulster landowners, Russian nobles, Hungarian gentry, and the impoverished aristocracy of France led their peasant soldiers from in front, and suffered accordingly. Noble families that lacked daughters died out, their sons fallen on the Marne, in Galicia, or in the great 1915–16 battles of attrition in the West. By 1916 the professional officers of 1914 were mostly dead. Those who survived graduated gratefully to staff jobs and higher commands.

The middle classes took their place as company and battalion officers. The lower middle classes, which in peacetime had rarely aspired to ranks higher than sergeant, suddenly became lieutenants. These "temporary gentlemen" suffered the sneers of the officers' mess at their accents and demeanor. The Germans created a special indeterminate rank of "officer substitute" to avoid giving deserving sergeants commissions. But the new men proved themselves in battle. The Great War,

along with death and bereavement, brought social promotion to an entire class. That sudden increase in social mobility, along with the classless society of shared danger at the front, was the origin of powerful myths. Finally, the war integrated the peasantry into the nations of the middle and upper classes far more than universal schooling or even peacetime military service had done. Enforced travel, mixing with men from different regions and backgrounds, and above all the experience of fighting together for the national cause made Pomeranian, Swabian, or Bavarian peasants into Germans and made Bretons, Normans, or Gascons into Frenchmen.

At home, industrial mass warfare dictated a new sort of labor force. With men at the front, women and unskilled adolescents joined the work force in numbers not seen since the early industrial revolution in Britain. Almost a quarter of the workers in France's war industries were women, as were 60 percent of the workers in Britain's munitions plants. British craft unions fought jealously against this "dilution" of the work force, but lost. War work expanded women's horizons and gave them a new sense of confidence and competence.

Industrial mass warfare also dictated an unprecedented intensity and extent of state action. The autocracies already had strong traditions of "state capitalism." The democracies mobilized their economies with similar and often more drastic methods: a bewildering variety of war-production and raw-materials allocation boards and bureaucracies, and close coordination between the state, the labor unions, and the military. The wartime industrial state incarnated Weber's "iron cage" of bureaucracy and furnished the model for the welfare state of the later twentieth century.

Finally, mass warfare dictated the mobilization of mass opinion. German propaganda damned the barbaric British "hunger blockade" and stressed the German world cultural mission that overrode the rights of "parasitic" small nations such as Belgium. British, French, and (after 1917) U.S. propaganda dwelt on "Hun" barbarism: poison gas and Zeppelin or submarine warfare against noncombatants and neutrals. Opinion was as powerful as high explosive, and both sides sought to exploit it to the full.

ATTRITION, 1915–16

In 1915 the belligerents made a series of confused attempts to break the unexpected deadlock. The Germans were most successful. In the West Falkenhayn stood on the defensive. He remained so until 1916, except for a brief experiment of Fritz Haber's with chlorine gas near Ypres in April 1915. The German command failed to mass reserves to exploit the unexpected gap the gas opened in the Franco-British lines. Introduction of this new and apparently barbaric weapon profited the Germans nothing and mightily helped the Allies in the battle for neutral opinion.

For most of the year, Britain and France attacked. Their strategic goal was to drive Germany out of France and win the war; that dictated the offensive. But their generals had no better method for restoring movement to the battlefield than ever heavier weights of high explosive shell to blast the German wire flat and silence the machine guns. At Neuve Chappelle, and Loos, and in the repeated French "pushes" in Artois and Champagne, the Allies suffered repeated bloody reverses and gained virtually no ground. The Germans became ever cannier at sheltering their troops in dugouts and in positioning reserves and artillery in depth. In 1915 the French lost 1,500,000 dead and wounded, Britain 300,000, and the German defenders perhaps 875,000.

In eastern Europe, Generals August von Mackensen and Hans von Seeckt broke through the Russian front in Galicia. By September 1915 they had sent the tsar's armies reeling back 300 miles with a loss of 1.7 million dead, wounded, and captured. Yet Falkenhayn did not believe that the eastern front offered a chance of decisive victory. He declined to press on, although the immense defeat of 1915 had opened wide the political fractures within Russia that the German declaration of war had temporarily closed in 1914. The Germans, totally discarding what little remained of European traditions of monarchical and elite solidarity, attempted to widen those fractures by covert action. SPD leaders with ties to their Russian counterparts funneled large sums into Russia to foment disorder. And in the Middle East, German agents based in Turkey sought with some success to raise Islam against the Allies.

Far to the southeast, new fronts opened. Britain, thanks to the impulsive genius for war of the young Winston Churchill at the Admiralty, attempted to seize Constantinople and open a year-round warm-water supply route to Russia. The muddled British high command proved unequal to the task of coordinating a simultaneous land and sea assault. The British navy, using expendable pre-Dreadnought battleships, failed to force the shore batteries and mines defending the Dardanelles in February–March 1915. The

Gas! British troops blinded by mustard gas (1918).

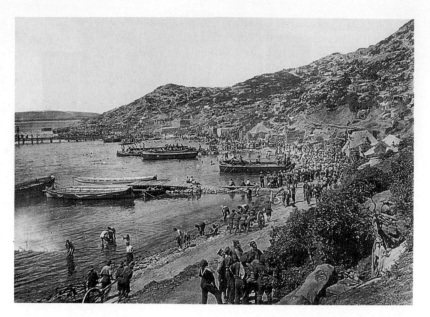

Between the Turks and the sea: Gallipoli, 1915.

war against the will of parliament. Italy's armies crossed the Austro-Hungarian border and ran headlong into long-prepared defenses on the Isonzo River. There the Italians stalled, despite repeated bloody offensives.

And in fall and winter 1915 the Germans confirmed the verdict of Gallipoli. Bulgaria joined the central powers after an auction similar to that in Rome. German, Austro-Hungarian, and Bulgarian armies attacked Serbia from three sides. By enticing Bulgaria into the war and by smashing Serbia, Germany had secured its communications through the Balkans to Turkey. Russia would receive no Allied aid through the Straits. Only the icy sea route to Murmansk and Archangel and the single track of the Trans-Siberian Railway linked Russia to the West.

Yet by December 1915 Falkenhayn was understandably not satisfied. Germany's immense losses had brought it no closer to its goal: a strategic decision over one of its three adversaries. In his 1915 "Christmas Memorandum," Falkenhayn concluded that Britain was the keystone of the enemy alliance. To strike it required the intensification of submarine warfare against merchant shipping, which the Germans had introduced in February 1915, and of terror attacks on British civilian targets with Zeppelin airships.

Falkenhayn identified French morale as Germany's second, and most promising, objective. Its collapse would "strike England's best sword from her hand." The method he chose was attrition, and he sought an objective "for the retention of which the French leadership will commit their last man. If they do this, France's strength will be bled white, since once committed to such a course there is no alternative for them, whether we reach the objective itself or not." Limited German infantry attacks would pin the French defenders under a giant mincing machine: the German artillery. Falkenhayn baptized his brainchild Operation GERICHT—"execution place."

Turks ran out of ammunition just as the admiral in charge pulled back. Then it was the turn of the army. British and Australian landings on the Gallipoli Peninsula in April soon bogged down; the Turks proved unexpectedly dogged and skillful. The only British success was the brilliantly planned and coordinated evacuation of the failed beachheads by January 1916; France and Britain retained a toe-hold at Salonika in Greece.

The Gallipoli landings, before British bungling became apparent, impelled the least of the great powers to take a hand. In October 1914 Salandra, Italy's prime minister, had incautiously announced that henceforth "holy national egoism"—*sacro egoismo*—would guide Italy's course. In winter–spring 1914–15 he proved as good as his word. Salandra and his foreign minister, Sidney Sonnino, secretly auctioned Italy to the two groups of powers. The Allied bid was inevitably higher: Trento, Trieste, and Dalmatia (where Italian-speakers were a tiny minority) from Austria-Hungary, a piece of Turkey, and unspecified colonial gains. On May 24, 1915, Salandra, Sonnino, and King Victor Emmanuel III took Italy to

1916: *Verdun and the Somme*

On February 21, 1916, the army of the German Crown Prince attacked the objective Falkenhayn had selected, the fortified city of Verdun at the hinge of the French line. German guns that eventually numbered over 2,200 tore the French to pieces with the heaviest artillery fire so far seen. As the French cracked, Joffre appointed Henri Pétain, a master of the defensive, to command Verdun. "Courage! We'll get them!" was his watchword. In the course of the next eight months, over three quarters of the French army passed down the muddy truck route to Verdun and emerged shattered.

Yet France held. By May 1916, despite German innovations such as flamethrowers, phosgene gas shells, and masses of fighter aircraft, Falkenhayn was caught fast in the snare he had rigged for the French. The Germans had themselves invested so much prestige, morale, and blood at Verdun that they had to take the city. The French fought them to a standstill by July, then counterattacked in October, November, and December to regain the lost ground. Verdun cost the French 377,000 dead, wounded, and missing and the Germans at least 337,000. Neither army, but especially that of France, was ever the same again.

The agony of France had repercussions. As in 1914, Russia sought to help its ally. Russia's most noteworthy commander, Alexei Brusilov, launched a major offensive in the Ukraine in June. Shortage of ammunition dictated a short bombardment, and Brusilov spread his preparations over a broad front to preserve surprise. Austria-Hungary's eastern armies collapsed; the Russians took 200,000 prisoners. Conrad von Hötzendorff had to break off a promising "punitive expedition" against his favored victim, Italy. Falkenhayn loosened his grip at Verdun and sent divisions eastward to prop up Austria-Hungary.

Then, on July 1, 1916, Sir Douglas Haig attacked on either side of the Somme River. On a day of "intense blue summer beauty," after a seven-day bombardment of unprecedented weight, the infantrymen of Britain's volunteer "New Armies" climbed from their trenches. Loaded with a minimum of 66 pounds of gear per man, aligned in rigid formations, they walked toward the German wire, which in most areas the British artillery had failed to cut. As the British bombardment lifted, German machine-gunners scrambled unhurt from their deep concrete-lined dugouts and massacred the British infantry. German artillery observers had never before seen such tempting targets. The French, further south, advanced in small groups,

Pétain of Verdun.

Verdun 1916: The Return from the Front

I have never seen anything more heart-rending than the passage of the two regiments of the brigade that flowed past me on that road [from Verdun] the whole day long. . . .

First came skeletons of companies, sometimes with a surviving officer in front, propping himself up with a cane; all walked or rather moved with short steps, bent knees forward, folded into themselves, staggering as if gripped by drink. Then came groups that were perhaps squads, or even platoons; there was no telling. They advanced, head down, staring blankly, crushed under their rucksacks, holding by the slings rifles red with mud. The color of their faces scarcely differed from that of their overcoats. Mud had covered everything and dried, then more mud had covered them once more. . . . Cars thundered past in close-packed columns, scattering this pitiable flotsam, survivors of the great slaughter. But [the troops] said nothing, made no sound. They had lost even the strength to complain. . . .

Some reservists, from the roadside, looked on somberly. . . . I heard one saying: "It's not an army; it's corpses!". . . . Two of the reservists cried silently, like women.

From Georges Gaudy, *Les trous d'obus de Verdun (février-août 1916)* (Paris: Plon, 1922), pp. 233–34 (translation by M. Knox).

taking cover wherever possible. They did rather better.

Haig's army lost 57,470 dead and wounded—nearly half the men engaged—on the first day. But Haig, "brilliant to the top of his army boots" (as Lloyd George later put it) remained convinced that German losses were so severe that the enemy was bound to crack. Using the same unimaginative tactics, he persevered until the battlefield became a sea of icy mud in November. The maximum British penetration was less than 6 miles. British losses were 419,000, those of the French, over 200,000. The German defenders lost over half a million.

As Brusilov's push petered out and the British pressed on the Somme, a sudden emergency provoked Falkenhayn's downfall. Rumania, like Italy, had been associated with the Triple Alliance; it had likewise chosen neutrality in 1914. Now, in August 1916, Brusilov's success inspired the Rumanians to join the Allies. Their timing was remarkably poor. The Kaiser dismissed Falkenhayn as chief of staff but gave

British troops fix bayonets before going "over the top" on the Somme, 1916.

him Rumania as consolation prize. Falkenhayn, Mackensen, and Seeckt rolled up the inept Rumanians within four months.

At German supreme army headquarters, a new team took control—Hindenburg and Ludendorff. Hindenburg, the "wooden Titan," was content to be a symbol of national resistance. Ludendorff, the dominant partner, brought a new ethos to the supreme command, the ethos of the pan-German "right opposition." He despised the Kaiser as a weakling. His devious aide, Colonel Max Bauer, cultivated pan-Germans and right radicals. Domestically, Ludendorff and Bauer soon erected a virtual dictatorship over the war economy and increasingly over the civilian political leaders. The Kaiser feared his nominal subordinates; Hindenburg and Ludendorff alone commanded the confidence of the masses. Once he had appointed them, the Kaiser could only remove them at the risk of his throne.

The new team had two principal recipes for victory. First, total war demanded total mobilization. Under the "Hindenburg Program," Germany planned to double its production of shells and treble that of artillery and machine guns. The army, with the assistance of the SPD unions and of the industrialists, applied compulsory service to the work force. Substitute—*ersatz*—materials would make up for shortages. Germany, by a supreme effort of will, would submerge its opponents in fire and steel. The new team's second major innovation was to stake Germany's future on one card, in the manner of Schlieffen. The card they chose was the submarine.

THE WAR IN THE BALANCE, 1917

Germany Challenges America

The U-boat question had been long in ripening. Tirpitz soon realized that the distant blockade had neutralized his battle fleet. He therefore pressed for the use of submarines, which he had scandalously neglected before 1914, against British merchant shipping. But submarines were only effective if used from ambush. Attempts to board and search merchant ships before sinking them, as international law required, might expose the surfaced submarine to deadly fire from camouflaged guns on the merchant ship. The Germans therefore adopted in February 1915 a policy of "sink on sight" around the British isles. On May 7, 1915, Germany's U-20 sank the British liner *Lusitania* off the southern tip of Ireland and killed 1,198 people, of whom 128 were U.S. civilians. The Germans struck a medal to commemorate their feat of arms.

President Woodrow Wilson, a dour ex-academic of messianic bent, had no intention of leading the United States into war. Unlike his rival, "Teddy" Roosevelt of the Rough Riders, Wilson took pride in being "too proud to fight." He was soon to run for reelection in 1916 on the slogan "He kept us out of the war." But the *Lusitania* outrage prompted even Wilson to bombard Berlin with stern summonses to obey international law.

U.S. opinion had long been suspicious of Imperial Germany. Germany's treatment of Belgium and first use of poison gas had appalled it. The *Lusitania* sinking swung it heavily against the Central Powers. Bethmann Hollweg persuaded the Kaiser and the navy to retreat and postpone confrontation. Then Falkenhayn, in his "Christmas Memorandum," urged the renewal of unrestricted U-boat warfare. In February 1916, the Germans synchronized "intensified" submarine warfare around Britain with their attack at Verdun. The inevitable sinking involving U.S. citizens followed in March, and Wilson's typewriter clattered threateningly once more. The Germans again retreated. Bethmann Hollweg, at least, was now aware that further sinkings might goad Wilson into "a sort of crusade against Germany."

The German navy tried to make do with surface action. On May 31, 1916, Admiral Reinhard Scheer took the German High Seas Fleet out. But the British had intercepted Scheer's radio messages, and Admiral John Jellicoe's Grand Fleet was waiting off Jutland. Tirpitz's Dreadnoughts and their British rivals faced one another for less than 30 minutes, until the outnumbered Scheer frantically turned away into clouds and smoke and ran for Wilhelmshaven. The Germans lost fewer ships, and claimed victory. But the British were the strategic victors, for they still controlled the exits from the North Sea. And the Germans concluded from their narrow escape that surface action offered no means of breaking the blockade.

Thus when Hindenburg and Ludendorff arrived on the scene in August 1916, they found the navy once more pressing for a decision to unleash the submarines. Tirpitz had resigned over the issue in March and had raised a fanatical public outcry for U-boat war. To buy time and to preempt a mediation attempt by Wilson, Bethmann Hollweg launched a Central Powers "peace offer" in mid-December 1916. The offer failed to mention the restoration of Belgium, and was thus unacceptable to the Allies. Its inevitable re-

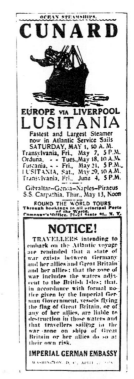

U-boat warfare: Germany warns neutral travelers that it will sink the *Lusitania* if it can. U-boats at sea in the Mediterranean (below).

jection, Bethmann Hollweg apparently hoped, might turn Wilson's wrath on Paris and London, and give Germany a convincing pretext for launching unrestricted submarine warfare.

At the Castle of Pless in Silesia, on January 9, 1917, the Germans took the decision that doomed them. The navy sang its usual tune: U-boats would bring Britain "to its knees" in a few months. Hindenburg and Ludendorff argued fiercely for action, regardless of consequences. They made the same error with the United States that Moltke had made with Britain in 1914. Because their prospective enemy had no mass army, they assumed that it was safe to defy it. Germany's U-boats received orders to sink all shipping around Britain after midnight on January 31, 1917. Wilson broke relations with Germany but still hoped to keep the United States neutral in order to mediate a "peace without victory."

But by 1917 the powers had invested too much blood and money to settle for peace short of victory or defeat. Nor, thanks to the Germans, did U.S. neutrality remain tenable. The Reich foreign secretary, Arthur Zimmermann, soon proved that the stresses of total war had caused Berlin to take leave of its senses. Using the telegraph channel that Wilson had thoughtfully provided the Germans for possible peace negotiations, he cabled the German ambassador in Mexico City. The ciphered message offered the Mexicans a war alliance and the recovery of Texas and the Southwest. The British intercepted it, deciphered it, and delivered it to Wilson along with proofs of its authenticity. It arrived at the end of February, along with news that a U-boat had sunk the British liner *Laconia* with the death of three Americans, two of them women.

Wilson gave the Zimmermann telegram to the press on March 1. Zimmermann compounded his amazing blunder by admitting that the telegram was genuine. Even voices of the isolationist Midwest such as the Chicago *Tribune* and the Cleveland *Plain Dealer* accepted war. A Germany that incited Mexico to attack the United States was intolerable. On April 2, Wilson, to repeated applause, addressed Congress: "The world must be made safe for democracy." The United States declared war on Imperial Germany. The New World was coming, somewhat belatedly, to restore the balance of the old.

The Zimmermann Telegram   January 19, 1917

[To German Ambassador, Mexico City]
Top Secret—Decipher Personally

We intend on 1 February to begin unrestricted U-boat warfare. We shall nevertheless attempt to keep America neutral. Should that not succeed, we propose to Mexico an alliance on the following basis. Joint conduct of the war. Joint peace settlement. Lavish financial support and agreement on our part that Mexico should reconquer its lost territories in Texas, New Mexico, and Arizona. We leave settlement of the details to your Excellency.

Your Excellency should disclose the above offer in the greatest secrecy to the President [of Mexico, Don Venustiano Carranza] as soon as outbreak of war with the United States seems certain, and add the suggestion that he should on his own initiative invite Japan to join the alliance, and [that he should] simultaneously mediate between Japan and ourselves.

Please call to the President's attention the fact that merciless use of our U-boats now offers the prospect of forcing England to make peace within a few months.

Acknowledge receipt.

Zimmermann

From Herbert Michaelis, Ernst Schraepler, eds., *Ursachen und Folgen vom deutschen Zusammenbruch 1918 und 1945* (Berlin: Dokumenten-Verlag Dr. Herbert Wendler, 1958), Vol. 1, pp. 151–52 (translation by M. Knox).

The Russian Revolutions: February and October

While Wilson debated his course, events in eastern Europe disclosed the full magnitude of Germany's blunder in provoking the United States. Russia ceased to count as a belligerent, and Germany faced only a weakening

France and Britain. In 1916 munitions strikes paralyzed industry in Moscow and Petrograd (the new, non-German name given to St. Petersburg in 1914). Russia's railroads broke down. Refugees and wounded swamped tsarism's decrepit administrative machinery. Food ran short in the cities; conscription and government purchases of food at artificially low fixed prices alienated the peasantry. The ultimate failure of the Brusilov offensive and the antics of the tsarina's favorite, the faith-healing charlatan Grigorii Rasputin, lost the autocracy what little public support it still possessed. Strikes and food riots by workers and housewives in Petrograd challenged the autocracy in early March 1917 (February by the "old style" Julian calendar that symbolized Russia's apartness from Europe). The peasant soldiers deserted the autocracy on March 12; it fell without a struggle.

A provisional government of liberals, Mensheviks, and Socialist Revolutionaries born from the last *Duma* attempted to fill the vacuum the "February Revolution" had left. But in Petrograd the Soviets, or councils of workers, soldiers, and sailors, now controlled the streets. On March 14, 1917, the central Petrograd Soviet addressed to the war-weary world a proclamation that blamed "monarchs, landholders, and bankers" for the war, and demanded an immediate end to the "horrible slaughter." Similar appeals in 1915 and 1916 from the wrangling representatives of the parties of the Second International had lacked resonance. The call of the Petrograd Soviet was different: it came from a body with power. And its claim to world ideological leadership conflicted with the call for "war to end war" that Wilson was soon to issue from Washington.

Soon after the Petrograd Soviet's peace message, the Germans made a further contribution to the disruption of Russia. They shipped Lenin and a few chosen Bolsheviks home to Russia from their place of exile in neutral Switzerland in a sealed boxcar ("like a plague bacillus," as Winston Churchill

later observed). Lenin arrived at Petrograd's Finland Station on April 16, 1917, and dictated to his small and hitherto confused party a few simple policies: support of the Soviets, implacable hostility to the provisional government, and an immediate end to the war.

In June 1917, Lenin launched a slogan of vast appeal to the peasantry that made up 80 percent of Russia's population and to the overwhelming majority of Russia's 7 million troops: "Bread, Peace, Land." His aim was as simple as his slogan. He proposed to seize power and hurl backward Russia directly into socialism. Revolutionary breakthrough in Russia would then trigger the revolution in western Europe without which a socialist Russia, isolated, would inevitably perish.

The provisional government was divided and inexperienced, thanks to the stifling effect the autocracy had had on Russian political life. The new government shared power uneasily with the Petrograd Soviet while seeking to continue the war against Germany. The government's most conspicuous personality, the Socialist Revolutionary Alexander Kerensky, identified himself with a final bungled offensive in July 1917. Bolshevik appeals spread through the army and undermined what little discipline remained. Peasants, weary of war and obsessed with the notion that revolution meant the long-awaited final redivision of the *mir* land (see p. 793), "voted with their feet." Many went home; those that stayed demanded an end to the fighting.

A spontaneous Petrograd quasi-insurrection against the provisional government in July showed that the Bolsheviks were gaining ground. In their unyielding utopian radicalism they proved better attuned to the mood in the cities than their more responsible or faint-hearted opponents. Kerensky arrested some Bolsheviks but lacked the ruthlessness or perhaps the power to suppress them outright. Then, in August, General Lavr Kornilov, Keren-

"The Russian Ruling House": a contemporary cartoon of Rasputin manipulating Tsar Nicholas II and Tsarina Alexandra.

The new master: Lenin in Moscow, 1917.

sky's commander in chief, marched on Petrograd to restore order. Workers and mutinous troops from the capital persuaded Kornilov's forces to defect.

Kornilov's failed coup from the Right further weakened Kerensky and his allies. Mensheviks and Socialist Revolutionaries, by their association with the Provisional Government and the continuing war, forfeited much of the popular support they had enjoyed in Petrograd in the spring. The Bolsheviks painted the distintegrating provisional government and its parties as Kornilov's accomplices; Bolshevik numbers swelled.

On November 6–7 (October 24–25 by the Russian calendar), Lenin and his dashing ex-Menshevik associate, Leon Trotsky, launched their own coup from the Left. The Military Revolutionary Committee of the Petrograd Soviet, of which Trotsky had gained control, seized key points with picked troops. On the evening of November 7 (October 25), the provisional government's last stronghold, the tsar's Winter Palace, fell. Kerensky fled. The Bolsheviks had acted in the name of the Soviets against the provisional government. The Bolsheviks soon infiltrated or cowed the Soviets while taking for themselves the mantle of legitimacy that the Soviets provided. And in January 1918 Bolshevik bayonets dispersed Russia's first and last democratically elected parliament, the Constituent Assembly.

The Bolsheviks had won less than 25 percent of the seats in the Constituent Assembly. But they had guns and organization, and they briefly commanded a popular majority in Petrograd and Moscow. Above all, they moved swiftly to institutionalize terror. In December 1917 Lenin's security officer, the fanatical Pole Feliks Dzerzhinsky, became chief of a new organization, the "All-Russian Extraordinary Commission for the Struggle Against Counterrevolution and Sabotage," known by its acronym of CHEKA. Its task was to exterminate the enemies of the revolution; their place, in Lenin's words, was "against the wall."

In January 1918 the Socialist Revolutionaries, whose peasant loyalists had given them more votes than any other party, fought back against the dissolution of the Constituent Assembly. They rose against Bolshevik dictatorship— and Lenin and Dzerzhinsky massacred them. In July 1918 the Bolsheviks likewise shot the ex-Tsar Nicholas II and his entire family. By that point Lenin and his CHEKA had discarded the concept of individual responsibility for actions, the basis of Western and even tsarist law. The CHEKA defined its enemies by class, and killed them not as individuals but as members of a category. The bourgeoisie was "objectively"—by its very existence—guilty of counterrevolution. That was a logic not seen in action in the West since the September massacres of 1792 and the Jacobin Terror of 1793–94. It was the logic of genocide.

Terror worked well internally. Externally, Lenin faced an immediate crisis. The German masses did not overthrow their rulers in response to the "Decree on Peace" that Lenin and Trotsky published immediately after the October Revolution. Instead, Russia's peasant armies continued to melt, while the

The Logic of the Red Terror   1918

M. Y. Latsis, the terrifying Latvian who was Dzerzhinsky's chief subordinate at the CHEKA, spelled out in a 1918 newspaper article the logic under which his organization acted.

We are not carrying out war against individuals. We are exterminating the bourgeoisie as a class. We aren't looking for evidence or witnesses to reveal deeds or words against the Soviet power. The first question which we ask is—to what class does he belong, what are his origins, upbringing, education, or profession? These questions define the fate of the accused. This is the essence of Red Terror.

Quoted in Harrison Salisbury, *Black Night, White Snow: Russia's Revolutions, 1905–1917* (Garden City: Doubleday, 1978), p. 565.

Germans advanced toward Petrograd. Lenin therefore sought a breathing-space for the Revolution, to give time for the western European and world revolution he unrealistically expected; he had predicted in September 1917, before taking power, that "to secure an armistice means *to conquer the world.*"

He secured that armistice from the Germans in December, and began negotiation at Brest-Litovsk in Poland for a Russo-German peace. But the Bolshevik negotiators soon found that "self-determination," as the Germans interpreted it, meant stripping away the conquests of all tsars since the seventeenth century. The border peoples, from Finland through the Ukraine to the Caucasus, were to become independent under German "protection." When the Bolsheviks balked, the Germans resumed their effortless advance on Petrograd. Lenin then dragooned his wavering comrades into signing; the Revolution had to swallow the German terms if it hoped to survive. On March 3, 1918, the Bolsheviks signed. The treaty of Brest-Litovsk deprived Russia of a quarter of its European territory, a third of its population, over half of its coal and iron, and a third of its industry. But it left the Bolsheviks in power.

The Crisis of the Allies

The collapse of Russia came close to wrecking the Allies. The October Revolution, which took Russia definitively out of the war, followed an unmitigated series of catastrophes. Germany's submarines almost throttled Britain's Atlantic supply line between March and August 1917. Sinkings peaked in April at 881,000 tons. British food stocks, despite rationing, fell to a mere two months' worth. But the German navy soon found that it was unable to sink ships faster than the United States could construct them. Lloyd George stormed into the Admiralty and compelled it to institute convoys, which it had originally despised as a "defensive" and therefore inferior

form of war. Mine barriers partially closed the exits from the North Sea even to U-boats. The U.S. Navy, with its eight Dreadnoughts and its indispensable escort craft, reinforced the British.

As the U-boats battered Britain, France faltered. Joffre's replacement, Robert Nivelle, was convinced that he had found the secret of victory: surprise. The discovery was not original. And Ludendorff dislocated Nivelle's offensive of April 1917. In Operation ALBERICH, named after the malevolent dwarf in Wagner's *Ring of the Nibelungen,* Ludendorff withdrew to a new line 12 to 25 miles behind the original front. And the Germans had a further surprise for the French: flexible defensive tactics far superior to the thin and brittle trench lines of 1914–16. The German "defense in depth"—deep belts of strongpoints interlocked by fire, coordinated artillery barrages, and swift and terrifying counterattacks—broke Nivelle's offensive and inflicted 200,000 casualties. The French army had believed in Nivelle; now its morale cracked. From the end of April until June 1917, units mutinied. Some waved red flags; the example of the Petrograd Soviet, with its call for immediate and unconditional peace, was contagious.

Fortunately, German intelligence was characteristically poor. Had Ludendorff known of the mutinies, he could and doubtless would have driven France from the war. Instead, Pétain, who had saved France at Verdun, now had time to save it once more. He suppressed the mutinies with a judicious combination of firing squad and conciliation. He listened to the troops and gave them what they wanted: leaves, better food, and no more offensives. The French army would do its part in defense, but others would have to break Germany.

The mutinies gave Haig what he thought was his opportunity. In the third battle of Ypres, from July to December 1917, Haig threw his troops again and again at the German lines as

Before and after:
Passchendaele, 1917.

heavy artillery and rain churned the soil of Flanders into "a porridge of mud." As in 1916, Haig suffered from the delusion that the Germans were about to crack. The maximum British and Canadian penetration was about 5 miles around the village of Passchendaele; the cost, perhaps 400,000 dead and wounded. By the end of the year British morale was scarcely higher than that of the French.

Finally, far to the south, the Germans showed that they were developing a tactical answer to the riddle of the trenches. On October 24, 1917, after a brief surprise bombardment, an Austro-German army crashed through the Italian defenses on the Isonzo around the village of Caporetto. The Germans moved in small, stealthy groups equipped with light machine guns. Instead of advancing on a broad front and slowing to tidy their flanks, they pushed rapidly through weak points and on into the Italian rear, sowing alarm and despondency. Positions too difficult to take they simply bypassed.

The Italian army crumbled and withdrew almost to Venice. Then, to the surprise of Germans and Austrians, it held on the Piave River even before British and French troops arrived to prop up Italy. Caporetto and the resulting loss of most of Italy east of Venice at last made the unpopular war a war of national defense.

On the home front, 1917 was equally disastrous for the Allies. Commodity shortages and the indiscriminate printing of money to finance the immense war expenditures drove prices steadily upward. Inflation and scarcity gener-

ated popular discontent (although troops on leave found civilian complaints about rationing increasingly tiresome—the civilians were safe from shell fire.) The extreme left of the European socialist parties took up with enthusiasm the slogans of the Petrograd Soviet and of the Bolsheviks. Shortly before Caporetto, a socialist-led revolt convulsed one of Italy's principal industrial centers, Turin. Civilian disturbances and demonstrations accompanied the French mutinies. Agitators at the Paris railway stations incited the troops to desert. Even Britain experienced unrest.

Nevertheless, the outlook was not totally bleak either on the western front, in the Middle East, or in central Europe. In November 1917, at Cambrai, Haig for the first time committed en masse that bizarre British invention, the tank. The British high command had failed to find a tactical answer to the trench deadlock, but a few innovators, among them Winston Churchill, had found a technological one. The combination of the internal combustion engine, caterpillar track, armor, and machine guns or cannon might yet restore mobility to the battlefield. Unfortunately, Haig had squandered surprise by using a few isolated tanks on the Somme in 1916. At Cambrai, the 400 tanks that Haig committed overwhelmed the terrified Germans. But the characteristic British failure to coordinate infantry, artillery, and reserves left the tanks exposed to a German counterattack that regained most of the ground lost.

In the Middle East, Turkey was beginning to crack, despite its victory at

Gallipoli and an appalling series of British blunders in Mesopotamia in 1914–16. Sir Edmund Allenby, perhaps the most imaginative British commander of the war, took Jerusalem in November 1917 after a push northwards from Egypt into Ottoman Palestine. Simultaneously, Britain issued the Balfour Declaration, which appeared to promise "the establishment in Palestine of a national home for the Jewish people." London sought to mobilize Zionist—Jewish nationalist—support in Europe and to create a buffer between the Suez Canal and the postwar sphere allotted to the French in Syria. With the aid of Arab irregulars led by the eccentric T. E. Lawrence (later "Lawrence of Arabia"), Allenby pressed on for Damascus and Constantinople.

Finally, Austria-Hungary too was beginning to crumble. Allied statesmen had already reluctantly dabbled in the subversion of Austria-Hungary as early as 1916. The "old Kaiser," Francis Joseph, who had reigned since 1848 and had become the symbol of the Dual Monarchy, died that November; his death deprived Austria-Hungary of its essential symbol of unity. In 1917 the Petrograd Soviet and the Bolsheviks, among their many slogans, launched that of "self-determination." Wilson took it up, lest the Bolsheviks monopolize it. In his statement of American war aims of January 1918, the famous "Fourteen Points," he demanded "autonomous development" for the peoples of Austria-Hungary and the recreation of the Polish state destroyed in 1795. Self-determination was a powerful political weapon in the hands of the Allies. But it was a weapon of desperation that might well destroy all prospect of postwar order in central and eastern Europe.

As the year 1917 closed, the Allied leaders contemplated their position with alarm. Russia had dissolved. Britain, France, and Italy had each in turn come close to collapse. Germany was victorious in eastern Europe and in Italy. It seemed poised to attack in the West. The home front was wavering. The "Yanks," Allied propaganda insisted, were coming. Would they come in time?

GERMANY'S LAST THROW, 1918

"Michael"

Ludendorff might have played for time and trusted to Germany's defensive expertise to blunt Allied offensives in 1918. But time appeared to be working against Germany. Since the "turnip winter" of 1916 the British blockade had bitten ever-deeper into German civilian morale and health. Austria-Hungary, Bulgaria, and Turkey were on the verge of collapse. Time would allow the Americans to mobilize a mass army and would fortify the Allies with U.S. food and munitions. Ludendorff also rejected a political solution that the war-weary Allies might have had to accept in the dark winter of 1917–18: German withdrawal from Belgium and northern France in return for a peace that conceded to Germany its immense gains in eastern Europe—and thus the mastery of the Continent.

With defense and negotiation ruled out, the remaining solution was attack. Russia's collapse freed enough German forces to ensure a temporary rough equality in France by March 1918—although Ludendorff's megalomania nevertheless kept a million Germans in eastern Europe to bring in the grain of the Ukraine and seize the oil of the Caucasus. Ludendorff proposed to use the reinforcements and the methods proven in Russia and at Caporetto to "hack a hole" in the western front. The rest, Ludendorff insisted, would "take care of itself." The great German offensive, in the words of a member of his staff, "would not be a battering ram, pounding head-on against a wall, but rather like a flood of water, flowing around obstacles, isolating them, and following the path of least resistance

T. E. Lawrence, greatest of English eccentrics, in Bedouin dress.

March 21, 1918: Germany Attacks

Ernst Jünger, winner of Germany's highest decoration, the *Pour le Mérite*, and of its foremost literary award, the Goethe Prize, led a *Stosstrupp* in the 1918 offensives. His vision of war, set forth in post-war memoirs such as *Storm of Steel,* was very different from the laments over war's futility and waste frequently found in British and French war writing. Here he describes Ludendorff's stunning opening bombardment and the initial German assault.

The minute hand moved closer and closer; we counted off the last minutes. Finally it stood at 0505. The hurricane broke loose.

A fiery curtain rose high in the air, supported by sudden, unceasing upwellings. A raging thunder, into which even the heaviest shell-bursts merged, shook the earth. The gigantic eruption of annihilation from the innumerable [German] cannon [firing overhead from] behind us was so frightful, that the greatest of the battles we had passed through before this seemed like children's games. . . . The enemy artillery remained dumb; it was flattened as if by a single blow from a giant's club. . . .

It had become day. Behind us the immense din still grew. Before us rose an unpierceable wall of smoke, dust and gas. Men ran through the trench and yelled joyfully in one another's ears. Infantry and artillery, combat engineers and field telephone linemen, Prussians and Bavarians, officers and men, all were overmastered and gripped with enthusiasm by this elemental outpouring of our power, and were burning for the assault at 0940. . . .

Even the laws of nature seemed to have lost their validity. The air shimmered as on a hot summer day and its varying density [with the shockwaves] made solid objects seem to dance back and forth. The din had become so absolute that we ceased to hear. . . .

The great moment had come. The barrage rolled across our first line. We attacked. . . . The overpowering desire to kill gave my feet wings. Rage squeezed bitter tears from my eyes. The immense desire to destroy and annihilate that hovered over the battlefield thickened our minds and dipped them as if in a red haze. We called to each other stumbling and stammering disjointed phrases, and an outside observer might perhaps have believed that we were overcome by an excess of joy.

From Ernst Jünger, *In Stahlgewittern* (Berlin: E. S. Mittler, 1941 [1st. ed., 1920]), pp. 253–57 (translation by M. Knox).

deep into the enemy's territory." Throughout the winter the German staffs pulled divisions out of the line, formed assault battalions (*Stosstruppen*), trained them in the new "infiltration" tactics, and rested them for a last supreme effort. Ludendorff knew the risks. When a politician asked him what would happen if he failed, he was frank: "Then Germany is finished."

The German leadership's irreducible objective of dominating Europe, the German style of all-or-nothing gambles, and the immense expectations that victory over Russia had aroused in the German public all dictated action. No political check on Ludendorff existed. In January 1917 Bethmann Hollweg had given up his small remaining authority by acquiescing in unrestricted submarine warfare. In July 1917 Hindenburg and Ludendorff forced Bethmann Hollweg's resignation by threatening their own. The intimidated Kaiser appointed an unknown bureaucrat as Chancellor. Tirpitz organized the political underpinnings of the Hindenburg-Ludendorff dictatorship. On Sedan Day, September 2, 1917, a "Fatherland Party" (*Vaterlandspartei*) emerged, proclaiming pitiless war until final victory over both Allies and SPD, and massive annexations in east and west to secure that victory for all time. Germany's mission, Tirpitz announced, was to lead Europe against the "all-devouring tyranny of Anglo-Americanism." The *Vaterlandspartei* soon had more members than the SPD. It was the first—but not the last—fanatical mass party of German nationalism. Its spirit momentarily galvanized the home front in the expectation of final victory.

On March 21, 1918, the first of Ludendorff's offensives, baptized MICHAEL, struck the British line between St. Quentin and La Fère. The British defenders massed in their forward trenches and German high explosive and gas shells massacred them. Haig had failed to learn from the German defense in depth that had cost the Allies so dear in 1917. Then the new German infantry tactics—attack in depth—tore a hole in the British 30 miles deep. It was the greatest gain on the western front by either side since 1914. The French prepared to withdraw to defend Paris.

But the British ultimately held. Ludendorff broke his own rule of always bypassing resistance, and shattered his reserves against the stubborn British defense of Arras. In April a second German offensive in Flanders took back the gains Britain had achieved at heartbreaking cost in the 1917 Passchendaele offensive. A third attack, in May–June 1918, drove the French back to the Marne and came within 40 miles of Paris. Each time, Ludendorff achieved operational freedom but failed to translate it into a strategic victory that would force the Allies to make peace before the Americans came.

The Yanks arrive: General John J. ("Black Jack") Pershing (right) meets Haig.

The Yanks Arrive

And on the Marne, U.S. Army and Marine Corps units joined the French in counterattacks at Belleau Wood and Château-Thierry. The Americans lacked experience. But they were willing to die in a manner not seen since 1914–16, the manner of Langemarck and the Somme. That spirit, and American numbers and weight of artillery terrified the Germans even as they shot the Americans down in droves.

Ludendorff's fourth and fifth offensives failed miserably, at great cost. The American counterattacks helped divert German reserves from the fourth, in early June, and the French dislocated the fifth with a tactical withdrawal of the sort that had crushed Nivelle in 1917. Ludendorff had bled the German army to death. In March his forces in the West had numbered 3,800,000. By July they had suffered 2,000,000 casualties; the cream of the German army was dead or wounded. German troops shipped in from Russia as replacements began to vote with their feet and jump from the slow-moving troop trains before they reached the western front. Yet in the face of hunger, desertion, demoralization, and defeat, Ludendorff still refused to allow negotiations with the Allies.

In July, August, and September, the Allies began to counterattack in a series of carefully limited operations. An inter-Allied high command under the hard-driving Marshal Ferdinand Foch of France at last began to coordinate Allied actions effectively. Allied infantry, often with tank support, would break into the German lines until German reserves arrived and resistance stiffened. Then the Allies would shift the battle to another sector.

These attacks slowly nibbled away the German gains of the spring and further demoralized the Germans. On August 8, the "black day of the German army," German units surrendered whole for the first time to British tanks and infantry. In September, Haig, at last using intelligent tactics, broke through the strongest German defenses in the West, the "Hindenburg Line." By now the U.S. Army in France was 1,500,000 strong and under its own commander, John "Black Jack" Pershing. It pinched out the St. Mihiel salient east of Verdun and prepared for a massive drive into Lorraine to roll up the German front and meet the British in central Belgium.

At the end of September, Ludendorff's fears about Germany's allies at last proved correct. The Franco-British army at Salonika broke the Bulgarians and drove north through the Balkans, threatening Austria-Hungary and Germany's southern border. Ludendorff panicked and demanded the appointment of a German civilian government to take the blame for defeat. He insisted that Germany seek an armistice from Wilson before total collapse ensued. The Fourteen Points, Ludendorff slyly assumed, would allow Germany to keep at least some of its gains. Pershing foresaw that the Germans would deny they had lost, unless the Allies dictated peace at Potsdam. Wilson, less prescient, entered negotiations in October.

Then events took command. Italy attacked on October 24 and reached Trieste by November 3. Austria-Hungary collapsed into a chaotic mass of seething nationalities, each attempting to carve out its own state. The German naval command, knowing the war was lost and hoping to create a suitably Wagnerian legend for the future, attempted to send the High Seas Fleet on a death ride down the English Channel. The sailors understandably mutinied and seized Kiel naval base. Revolution spread to Munich and Berlin. The SPD leaders in Berlin proclaimed a German Republic on November 9; the Kaiser abdicated and fled ignominiously to Holland. And the Allies, under pressure from Wilson and from their own war-weary public opinion, conceded the Germans an armistice while Germany still occupied most of Belgium and some French territory.

On the "eleventh hour of the eleventh day of the eleventh month" of 1918, silence at last descended on the western front. As the armistice terms commanded, the Germans withdrew to the Rhine, demobilized, and sailed their fleet to Scapa Flow. The war had cost at least 20 million lives. Germany suffered 2 million military dead, Russia 1.7 million, France 1.3 million, Austria-Hungary 1.1 million, Britain and its empire 750,000 and 250,000 respectively, Italy about 500,000, Turkey somewhat less, and the United States 114,000. Civilian casualties included 100,000 killed by U-boats and air raids, 30,000 Belgians killed by German forced labor, reprisals, or artillery fire, and at least 1.5 million Armenians whom the Turks had massacred in 1915. A further 20 million died in the great influenza pandemic that struck the world in 1918.

TREATIES WITHOUT PEACE

The first general European peace conference since Vienna in 1814–15 met at Paris in January 1919. It faced a more difficult task than had Metternich and Castlereagh. They had merely attempted to return the world "to peaceful habits" and reestablish a balance of power that France had upset. The peacemakers at Paris in 1919 faced similar requirements, and far more.

Scores of outraged nationalities, mercifully silent at Vienna, now clamored for self-determination and "rights"—including the right to oppress minorities or neighboring nationalities. Public opinion, mobilized to hate for four long years and politically potent thanks to universal suffrage, made moderation difficult. Bolshevism, a revolutionary threat without parallel in 1814–15, appeared to menace central Europe. War and self-determination had disrupted complex industrial economies; the permanence of peace might depend in part on the economic solutions the peacemakers found. And Wilson, who insisted on attending the conference in person, rejected a French proposal for drafting a clear agenda and order of business. The "Big Four," Wilson, Lloyd George, Clemenceau, and Orlando, leapt from issue to issue. Out of confusion, they created chaos.

Germany's fate was the chief issue facing the conference, and its chief failure. In the abstract, two courses were available that might prevent Germany from again attempting the experiment of 1914. The Allies and the United States could conciliate the new German republic by offering a lenient peace. Or they could fasten on Germany a genuinely Carthaginian peace that would undo Bismarck's work and divide Germany into two or three: Prussia, Catholic south Germany, and an independent Rhineland. Clemenceau, who had seen two German invasions of France in his lifetime, naturally preferred the second alternative. But neither Lloyd George nor Wilson were neighbors of Germany. Britain had already interned the German fleet; it could calmly disparage Clemenceau's fears and reject the open-ended military commitment needed to enforce his drastic solution. And Germany was an economic unit essential to European and British prosperity, and the only remaining counterweight to Bolshevik Russia in eastern Europe.

The Big Four therefore compromised. Bismarck's Reich remained in existence, and Britain and the United States calmed France with the offer of an Anglo-American security guarantee, a military alliance against German resurgence. But having decided to preserve Germany, the Allies failed to adopt the corollary of that decision, a peace as lenient as that offered to Bourbon France in 1814–15. Allied public opinion, even in Britain, shouted "Hang the Kaiser!" The disorderly procedure of the Paris conference meant that demands on Germany accumulated piecemeal and found their way into the treaty without any weighing of their cumulative effect. And their own disunity prevented the Big Four, despite initial good intentions, from inviting the Germans to help draft the treaty, as the French had in 1814.

Not that the treaty that the German delegation grudgingly signed in the Hall of Mirrors at Versailles on the fifth anniversary of Sarajevo (June 28, 1919)

The "Big Four" at Paris, 1919: Orlando makes a point to Lloyd George, while Clemenceau (center) and Wilson (far right) look on.

was severe, compared to Brest-Litovsk. Germany lost a mere 13.5 percent of its 1914 territory, mostly areas inhabited by Poles, Danes, and French. The Allies piled on (1) financial "reparations"; (2) disarmament to a force of 100,000 men without heavy equipment, aircraft, or general staff; (3) the end of Tirpitz's navy; (4) temporary Allied occupation and permanent demilitarization of the Rhineland; (5) the loss of the Silesian coal fields; (6) the temporary cession to France of the Saar; (7) the loss of Germany's useless colonies; and (8) a prohibition on union with German-speaking rump Austria. The essentials of Bismarck's Reich nevertheless remained intact.

Yet compared to German expectations, the "Diktat" or dictated peace the Germans received at Versailles was a nightmare. For four years German propaganda had told the German people that a savage ring of aggressors had attacked Germany out of Cossack bloodlust, French thirst for revenge, and British "trade envy." Germany's leaders had assured their public that victorious occupation of Belgium, northern France, and vast stretches of Russia guaranteed Germany a victorious peace. And the Germans had also, quite without justification, expected a

Wilsonian "peace without annexations or indemnities" as their reward for proclaiming a republic. They had evidently not read Wilson's Point 13, which specified the creation of a Poland with access to the sea, inevitably across German territory.

The abrupt transition in 1918 from the expectation of victory to the reality of defeat, of territorial loss and national humiliation, lessened German opinion's already tenuous grip on reality. Germany, its political leaders at its head, denied the obvious. Germany, they claimed, had not provoked the war—although numerous German documents soon emerged indicating precisely the opposite, and few could deny that Germany had attacked Belgium without provocation. The Germans damned as a "war guilt lie" the Allied attempt, in Article 231 of the Versailles Treaty, to establish the financial responsibility of Germany and its allies for "loss and damage" resulting from the war imposed on the Allied Powers "by the aggression of Germany and its allies." The Germans, from the beginning, furiously denied the Treaty's moral validity.

Nor had Germany suffered military defeat, according to most German leaders, including the new SPD president of the republic, Fritz Ebert. Through the mouth of Hindenburg, the Right added the crucial corollary. If the Allies had not defeated Germany, the culprits could only be the "November Criminals" of the SPD, whose Revolution had allegedly stabbed the heroic troops "in the back." The twin legends of Allied victory through trickery and German defeat through a "stab-in-the-back" ensured that Germany would have the will to reverse the verdict of 1914–18.

And the Versailles Treaty's relative lenience ensured that it would have the means. For east-central Europe was now a power vacuum. The collapse of Austria-Hungary brought into being five miniature Austria-Hungaries: rump Austria, a diminished Hungary, Czechoslovakia, Poland, and a Serb-dominated kingdom of Serbs, Croats, and Slovenes that later took the name of Yugoslavia. Rumania, which now absorbed both Transylvania and the Rumanian-inhabited ex-Russian territory of Bessarabia, formed a sixth weak state between Germany and Russia. Italy, by seizing Trento and Trieste, became the seventh "successor state" of the defunct Habsburg empire.

With Russia temporarily in eclipse and German economic and demographic power virtually intact, only the

The Peace Settlements in Europe   1919–20

Territories lost by:

- Germany
- Bulgaria
- Austria-Hungary
- Russia
- Plebiscite areas
- Demilitarized Rhineland zone of Allied occupation

United States could balance Germany once it began to revive. The war, despite Germany's defeat, had paradoxically made Germany potentially stronger *in relative terms* than in 1914. The states of eastern Europe, the Germans correctly judged, were *Saisonstaaten*, "states for a season" destined to wilt in the hot sun of renewed German greatness.

And Wilson soon hastened that sunrise by destroying the prospect of continued U.S. participation in the European power balance. In the course of 1917–18 the notion of a "League of Nations," brainchild of British pacifists such as Lord Robert Cecil, captivated the President. He saw in the League an alternative to the alleged evils of the balance of power and of secret treaties that Cobdenite mythology blamed for the war.

In the Paris negotiations Wilson therefore devoted an increasing portion of his energy writing the League's "Covenant" into the Versailles Treaty, thus confusing further the process of settlement with Germany. The League, Wilson increasingly hoped, would remedy admitted imperfections in the German clauses of the Treaty, bind the potentially isolationist United States to Europe, and ensure the perpetual peace that Wilson had promised would emerge from this war to "make the world safe for democracy."

In pursuing the mirage of the League, Wilson destroyed the prospect that the United States would underwrite European stability by a permanent commitment of its power, the power that had defeated Germany. The Republicans took control of the Senate in the fall 1918 elections. They balked at the open-ended global commitments that League "collective security" entailed. Their leader, Henry Cabot Lodge, was no isolationist; he favored a continued commitment of American power to prevent Germany from renewing its "war of world conquest." But Wilson rejected Lodge's offer to ratify the Treaty with reservations. Wilson—professorially dogmatic about

National Minorities in Central Europe   1919

presidential prerogatives, always rigid of character, and now increasingly ill—defied an essential feature of the Constitution: the requirement that the President lead rather than command the Congress.

Wilson's reward, after he had suffered nervous collapse and an incapacitating stroke while taking his case to the people, was Senate rejection of the Treaty in March 1920. The British economist John Maynard Keynes influenced the Senate with his vitriolic pamphlet against Wilson and the Treaty, *The Economic Consequences of the Peace.* Wilson himself ensured rejection by ordering his loyalists to vote against the amended version the Republicans proposed. And the wreck of Wilson's policy and presidency destroyed any prospect of an Anglo-American security guarantee for France. The Republican presidential candidate, Warren G. Harding, summed up the rising national yearning for a return to the womb with a word of his own invention. America needed "normalcy." Harding carried the 1920 election. The United States retreated into resentful isolation, except for its petulant demands for repayment of Allied war debts.

The Pacific proved the one area in which the United States continued to play a great-power role. Wilson had sought unsuccessfully at Paris to move the Japanese from Shandong and compel them to rescind the "twenty-one demands" they had forced on China in 1915. U.S. opinion also looked unkindly on the Anglo-Japanese alliance, and U.S. admirals saw in it a two-ocean threat that demanded a fleet larger than the navy second to none projected in 1916, after the first submarine outrages. The United States, with the help of Canada, forced Britain to choose between its alliance with Japan and its friendship with the United States. Britain, in no condition to engage in a naval "race" with the United States, acquiesced. Britain had abandoned the "two-power standard" to face the German challenge; now it abandoned its alliance with Japan and accepted formal parity with the greatest naval power, the United States.

At the Washington Conference on arms limitation and Pacific affairs in 1921–22, the powers laid down a new naval and East Asian order. The Washington Naval Treaty of February 1922 apparently froze the world hierarchy of naval power. It decreed a ten-year "holiday" in battleship construction and limited total tonnage of capital ships to 500,000 each for Britain and the United States, 300,000 for Japan, and 175,000 each for France and Italy. The powers relieved China of most Japanese encroachments and reaffirmed the "Open Door." The Anglo-Japanese Alliance dissolved into a meaningless Four-Power Treaty in which Britain, France, Japan, and the United States pledged to preserve the Pacific status quo. Japan acquiesced to the Washington settlement in return for British and American pledges not to build fortified bases north of Singapore and east of Hawaii. Tokyo retained both naval supremacy in northeast Asia and Hong Kong and the Philippines as hostages. The Washington treaties seemed to promise an era of peace. Their real results were a perilous complacency in the democracies and the cutting loose of Japan from the restraining influence of its alliance with Britain.

WARS AFTER THE WAR, 1919–23

Meanwhile, U.S. withdrawal left Europe on its own. Peaceful habits did not return. Social and national struggles convulsed Europe until 1923. The League of Nations generated immense masses of paper and gave small nations a forum for interminable talk. But it proved impotent whenever it faced a great power. Even Italy defied it in 1923 over an incident with Greece.

In Germany and Hungary, short-lived Left-extremist uprisings or regimes perished when faced with ruthless counteraction from the Right. The SPD government of the German republic, unable to impose order with the debris of the Imperial German Army, authorized the recruitment of right-wing freebooters, the *Freikorps.* Such units appealed to Germans of the Ernst Jünger type, who had enjoyed the Great War and were reluctant to give it up, and to nationalist students too

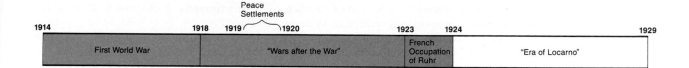

1914	1918	1919	Peace Settlements	1920	1923	1924	1929
First World War			"Wars after the War"		French Occupation of Ruhr	"Era of Locarno"	

young to fight in 1914–18. In January 1919, after an abortive Communist ("Spartacist") coup in Berlin, the *Freikorps* shot Rosa Luxemburg and other leaders of the far Left "while attempting to escape." That was a euphemism much imitated later. A *Putsch* or military coup by *Freikorps* elements and a subsequent Communist uprising in the Ruhr almost destroyed the German republic in 1920.

In Italy, the Liberals failed to master the mass political forces that Giolitti had unleashed by conceding virtual universal male suffrage in 1912–13. The Italian socialists succumbed to the delusion that Italy was Russia. Their verbal threats of revolution and occasional violence against landowners and veterans soon provoked a virtual civil war, which they naturally lost (see pp. 914–17).

Further east, Bolshevik Russia fought for survival. The 1918 Armistice had forced Germany to disgorge the gains of Brest-Litovsk, but the Bolsheviks continued to proclaim the goal of World Revolution, without which they expected a Communist Russia to succumb to "capitalist encirclement." Lenin and associates split the European socialist parties by founding their own Third ("Communist") International in March 1919. They also appealed to the colonial peoples, furthering the disruption of the European empires that the war had begun.

Trotsky raised Bolshevik armies and fought with increasing success against "White Russian" forces under former tsarist generals who sought to restore the old regime. The Allies landed troops in 1918 at Vladivostok and Murmansk to secure the supplies they had sent to the tsar and to support the Whites. Except for the ever-acquisitive Japanese, who remained at Vladivos-

tok until 1922, the Allies soon found their position untenable and withdrew. By 1920 the Red Army had defeated the Whites, but the Poles made the error of attempting to seize the Ukraine. In July 1920 the Red Army drove into Poland with hopes of continuing westward. Then the Poles under Marshal Josef Pilsudski held at Warsaw. Russia's borders stabilized. Finland, Estonia, Latvia, and Lithuania kept their newly acquired independence; Rumania kept Bessarabia. In other respects Bolshevik Russia preserved the inheritance of the tsars.

In the vacuum between Germany and Russia, the successor states quarreled. The diplomats at Paris did their best to draw new borders for Germany's former allies by the treaties of St. Germain (September 1919) for Austria, of Neuilly (November 1919) for Bulgaria, and of Trianon (June 1920) for Hungary. These frontiers, although

Postwar wars: street fighting in Berlin, 1919.

much criticized as a source of conflict, in most cases merely ratified or systematized what the nationalities of eastern Europe had done in pulling Austria-Hungary down. The great powers thereafter showed little ability to moderate the squabbles of the small. Poland and Czechoslovakia disputed the border town of Teschen. Lithuania quarreled over its borders with Poland and Germany. Hungary claimed territory from all three of its neighbors—Rumania, Czechoslovakia, and Yugoslavia. The neighbors sought security through alliances with one another, a combination the Hungarians disparaged as the "Little Entente." France, seeking an eastern ally to replace Russia, itself contracted alliances with Poland and Czechoslovakia, and consultative pacts with Rumania and Yugoslavia.

Germany and Bolshevik Russia, the pariahs of the international scene, sought solace together. In 1922, at Rapallo, they publicly and demonstratively canceled their mutual debt and reparations claims. Secretly, Red Army and German *Reichswehr* contracted a profitable bargain. Germany furnished the Bolsheviks with modern military technology and in return received an opportunity for secret experiment in Russia with weapons such as gas and aircraft, forbidden under the Versailles Treaty.

Far to the south, the Turks reacted to the collapse of their empire by creating a national state, under the leadership of the victor of Gallipoli, Mustafa Kemal Pasha. A foolhardy Greek advance into Turkey in pursuit of the "Great Idea" (*Megali Idea*) of a Greek empire from the Adriatic to the Black Sea led to disaster in 1922. The Turks then massacred or expelled the 1.35 million Greeks of Asia Minor whose ancestors had lived there for three millennia. The Greeks in turn drove almost half a million Turks from Greek Thrace. This "exchange of populations," as League bureaucrats euphemistically described it, still appeared conspicuously barbaric in the 1920s.

Unfortunately it did not appear so for long.

After a confrontation with British troops at Chanak near Constantinople that brought down Lloyd George's government in October 1922, the Turks permitted the Allies to leave them alone. The 1923 Treaty of Lausanne recognized the independent Turkish state. Kemal, who later took the name Atatürk ("father of the Turks"), abolished the Ottoman Sultanate and ruled ruthlessly until his death in 1938. The "Eastern Question" was closed. Its worthy successors were the merciless struggles throughout the Middle East between the Ottoman's Empire's former subjects.

Meanwhile, France and Germany fought a deadly although as yet largely bloodless struggle. The issue was simple: would Germany accept the apparent demotion to second-rate power visited upon it in 1918? Germany refused to acknowledge as final the loss of Posen, West Pussia, and Upper Silesia to Poland. Above all, it refused to pay promptly and fully the reparations that the Allies had fixed in 1921 at a theoretical total of $32 billion dollars.

The French faced immense expenses to repair the devastation that the war and the methodical German wrecking during the 1917 and 1918 retreats had wrought. France also hoped that heavy reparations would make it harder for Germany to rearm. It therefore attempted to hold Germany to its obligations, especially since the $32 billion reparations total set in 1921, by a feat of bureaucratic sleight-of-hand, in actuality amounted to only $12.5 billion, a figure well within German capacity to pay.

When the Germans defaulted massively in late 1922, France and its ally Belgium acted. Poincaré sent French troops into the Ruhr Valley to seize Germany's mines and factories. Mining coal with bayonets was expensive, but the French made a modest profit. The German government of Wilhelm Cuno decreed passive resistance. Cuno began printing marks feverishly, fuelling an inflation already underway thanks to Germany's immense internal war debt. Cuno wrecked Germany's currency to prove that Germany could not pay. What he proved was that Germany would not pay.

In August–September 1923 Cuno and passive resistance collapsed as the mark rose from 4 million to 160 million to the dollar. Gustav Stresemann, a crafty ex-National Liberal with an extreme annexationist past, took power as Chancellor. He mastered internal disorder, which included a radical nationalist uprising in Bavaria under the leadership of a fanatical ex-corporal and winner of the Iron Cross, Adolf Hitler.

Stresemann sought a compromise with France that would give Germany a breathing space. Britain and the United States, concerned at the economic repercussions of chaos in Germany, helped. They threatened economic reprisals if Poincaré did not withdraw from the Ruhr. By spring 1924 Stresemann had stabilized the currency by introducing a new mark. Poincaré gave way to a left-wing coalition in the May 1924 French elections; his successor, Aristide Briand, was a weaker and more conciliatory man. An emissary of the United States, Charles G. Dawes, patched together a temporary reparations settlement, the Dawes Plan. It lowered payments to a level Germany consented to pay and underwrote Germany's solvency with a U.S. loan, the first of many. Henceforth U.S. credit to Germany indirectly furnished the sums Germany paid as reparations. The last French troops left the Ruhr in August 1925. France had lost a great trial of strength.

THE ILLUSIONS OF LOCARNO, 1925–29

Worse, from the French viewpoint, followed. Austen Chamberlain, Britain's foreign secretary, had thought to prevent a repetition of the Ruhr occupation by giving France security against

France occupies the Ruhr, 1923.

Germany in an Anglo-French pact that would replace the failed 1919 Treaty of Guarantee. Stresemann got wind of the project, and slyly preempted it with an offer of a general western security pact that Germany would also sign.

Instead of a revival of the Anglo-French Entente Cordiale, the French received the multilateral Treaty of Locarno (October 16, 1925). France, Germany, and Belgium pledged to respect their mutual borders, as drawn in the Versailles Treaty, and to preserve the demilitarization of the Rhineland. Britain and Italy acted as outside guarantors against "unprovoked attack," a singularly vague and elastic phrase. And France could now only respond militarily to "flagrant violations" of the demilitarization of the Rhineland. That phrase significantly weakened a key provision of Versailles.

Despite Stresemann's professions of conversion to being a "good European," Locarno was an immense German victory. It prevented a repetition of the Ruhr experiment: if France sought to use force to uphold the Ver-

Having restored Germany's international respectability, Stresemann addresses the League of Nations in 1929.

sailles Treaty, Britain might be treaty-bound to fight France! Locarno thus precluded Anglo-French staff talks on the pre-1914 model, much to the relief of the British army and government. And Locarno covered only the West. Germany retained freedom to redraw, by force if necessary, its eastern borders.

A brief Indian summer of illusion, the "era of Locarno," followed the treaty. France and Britain repeatedly ignored massive German violations of the Versailles Treaty's disarmament provisions. They gave up their right of on-site inspection of German violations. Germany entered the League of Nations. In 1929, in a second reparations settlement (the "Young Plan") negotiated under U.S. auspices, Germany agreed to make modest payments until 1988. France in turn undertook to evacuate its Rhineland occupation zone by summer 1930, five years ahead of the Versailles Treaty schedule.

Western public opinion demanded from its political leaders forgetfulness and illusion, and received them. The Great War, Western opinion concluded, had been an exercise in criminal futility that must never be repeated. Alliances and armaments—not German aggression—had caused the war. Therefore alliances and armaments (except semi-clandestine German armaments) were evil. Enlightened international public opinion, working through the League of Nations, would prevent war.

Illusion reached its height with the famous pact "outlawing war" that Aristide Briand and Frank B. Kellogg, the U.S. secretary of state, drafted in 1928. Briand hoped the pact would bind the United States, however tenuously, to Europe. But the Kellogg-Briand Pact, which 62 nations happily signed, contained no enforcement provisions whatsoever. It also included an escape clause wide enough to accommodate entire tank armies: signatories could still fight in self-defense. The pact had all the force of a pious declaration against sin.

Fifteen years of war and revolution had broken for good the "peaceful habits" acquired in the nineteenth century. For four years millions of men had killed one another in mud holes while Europe had transmuted its vast accumulated wealth into steel and high explosives. Those who returned from the front took the language and habit of violence into politics. In the East, a pitiless utopian sect had taken control of a great power of immense economic and military potential. In central Europe, the greatest European power of all had emerged from the war unreconciled to defeat. The victors had checked at heartbreaking cost the German bid for European and world mastery, but had left a Germany capable of repeating that bid. Soon—with the onset of the Great Depression in 1929—the world economy collapsed. That enfeebled the democracies and unleashed voracious "have-not" powers in Asia and Europe. The Great War receded into memory, but others took its place.

Suggestions for Further Reading

General

No adequate one-volume history of the war exists. M. Ferro, *The Great War, 1914–1918* (1973), A. J. P. Taylor, *The First World War* (1972), and G. Hardach, *The First World War, 1914–1918* (1977), offer intelligent surveys. Z. Zeman, *The Gentlemen Negotiators* (1971), covers war diplomacy with style. P. Kennedy, "The First World War and the International Power System," *International Security*, 9 (1984), analyzes the relative strength of the powers. On life in the trenches, see especially the chapter on the Somme in J. Keegan, *The Face of Battle* (1976).

War and Revolution

For Germany's war, see above all F. Fischer, *War of Illusions* (1975), and *Germany's Aims in the First World War* (1967); H. W. Gatzke, *Germany's Drive to the West* (1950); T. Lupfer, *The Dynamics of Doctrine: the Changes in German Tactical Doctrine During the First World War* (1981); and J. Kocka, *Facing Total War: German Society, 1914–1918* (1984). On Britain, see especially E. L. Woodward, *Great Britain and the War of 1914–1918* (1967); also useful are P. Guinn, *British Strategy and Politics, 1914 to 1918* (1965), and A. Marwick, *The Deluge: British Society and the First World War* (1965). For France, see especially P. Bernard and H. Dubief, *The Decline of the Third Republic, 1914–1938* (1985), and A. Horne, *The Price of Glory: Verdun, 1916* (1962). S. Fitzpatrick, *The Russian Revolution, 1917–1932* (1982), offers a useful overview; A. Ulam, *Lenin and the Bolsheviks* (1965), and L. Schapiro, *The Russian Revolutions of 1917* (1984), are more detailed; L. Trotsky, *History of the Russian Revolution* (1936), is an unparalleled history-memoir by a key participant. On U.S. intervention, see especially B. Tuchman, *The Zimmermann Telegram* (1958); E. May, *The World War and American Isolation, 1914–1917* (1959), and D. Smith, *The Great Departure: The United States and World War I* (1965).

Settlement and Aftermath

On the power consequences of the war, see Kennedy, "The First World War" cited above; G. Weinberg, "The Defeat of Germany in 1918 and the European Balance of Power," *Central European History* 2 (1969); and H. Holborn, *The Political Collapse of Europe* (1954). P. Birdsall, *Versailles Twenty Years After* (1941), remains the best treatment of the peace conference, but see also K. Schwabe, *Woodrow Wilson, Revolutionary Germany, and Peacemaking, 1918–1919: Missionary Diplomacy and the Realities of Power* (1985). On the aftermath, S. Marks, *The Illusion of Peace: International Relations in Europe, 1918–1933* (1976), is unsurpassed. C. A. Macartney and A. W. Palmer, *Independent Eastern Europe* (1962), is excellent. S. Marks, "The Myths of Reparations," *Central European History* 11 (1978), demystifies a widely misunderstood issue.

31

The Interwar World, 1919–1939

*T*he virtual withdrawal of the United States and Russia from world politics fostered a moment of illusion. The victorious powers of western Europe, Britain and France, appeared to dominate Europe and the wider world as they had in the early nineteenth century. But France's failure to cow even a disarmed Germany and Britain's economic and imperial troubles soon revealed the hollowness of appearances. Germany enjoyed a brief prosperity after 1924, thanks to U.S. credit. But political stability eluded it. Few of the new states of central and eastern Europe enjoyed either stability or prosperity. The United States enjoyed an unprecedented prosperity—in isolation.

Then came the Great Depression. It extinguished the few surviving parliamentary regimes between Germany and Russia. It virtually destroyed world lending and trade. It mortally wounded the great democracies, confirmed the United States in its isolationism, and freed unsatiated or defeated powers to attack the West both in Europe and Asia. Fascist Italy under Benito Mussolini, a racist Germany under Adolf Hitler, and a militarized Japan destroyed the Versailles-Washington Treaty order while Lenin's implacable successor, Joseph Stalin,

The guardians of the peace:
negotiators at a 1930
reparations conference caught
napping by the mischievous
photographer Erich Salomon.

sought to profit from the resulting
chaos. Britain, France, and the United
States met these global challenges
demoralized and disunited. France
went under; Britain nearly perished;
the United States paid dearly for its irresponsibility after 1919.

THE TWENTIES:
A GOLDEN AGE?

Britain: Stability and Stagnation

War and aftermath broke the Liberals.
In 1916 Asquith gave way to Lloyd
George. In May 1918, Asquith attacked

Lloyd George in the House of Commons and split the Liberal party. In the
"khaki election" of December 1918
Lloyd George led his wartime Liberal-
Conservative coalition to crushing victory over both Asquith and Labour.
That condemned the divided Liberal
party to permanent opposition and
decline.

But the Conservatives soon found
Lloyd George's leadership galling. His
brinkmanship in the Chanak crisis with
Turkey in October 1922 gave the stolid
foot soldiers of the Conservative party
their opportunity. The comfortable,
avuncular, pipe-smoking Stanley Baldwin rose up and denounced Lloyd

George as "a great dynamic force"—"a very terrible thing." By 1923 Baldwin, whose enemies disparaged him as "a man of the utmost insignificance," was prime minister.

He remained so until 1929, except for a brief Labour minority government in 1924. Baldwin was the tweedy personification of a largely defunct rural England. A master of conciliation, of fudging issues, he defused social conflict with the soothing syrup of his "fireside chats" on that new medium, the radio. He found foreign policy boring. The Locarno treaty seemed to make foreign policy superfluous; he did his best to have none.

The mass army that had broken the Hindenburg Line shrank to a numerically insignificant imperial police force. The new Royal Air Force remained a hollow shell. The navy languished. In 1928 Britain adopted as permanent a 1919 budgetary invention of Lloyd George—the "ten year rule." All defense expenditure and planning was to rest on the assumption that Britain would not fight a great power for at least ten years. That assumption proved a rationalization for unilateral disarmament.

At home, Baldwin's government weathered in 1926 the general strike feared since the miners, dockers, and railwaymen had formed a "triple alliance" in 1914. The Polish and German mining industries had recovered from war and disruption, and had forced coal prices down. Britain's miners struck to protest the resulting pay cuts. Transport and other workers joined the miners in sympathy. But the Cabinet did not need the armored cars that Churchill, by then a defector to the Baldwin cabinet from the dying Liberals, gleefully displayed in Hyde Park. Baldwin supervised a conciliatory settlement for the transport workers; the miners, left to their own devices, eventually surrendered.

The General Strike of 1926 left a legacy of bitterness, especially among the miners. But in other industries it brought to the fore conciliatory union leaders. Baldwin's tranquilizing manner preserved Britain's traditions of

The General Strike, 1926: London police protect delivery workers from possible reprisals by strikers.

gradualism and relative social peace, despite the rise of Labour and the strain of a structural unemployment in declining areas and industries that idled over 10 percent of Britain's labor force in every year except 1927. But Baldwin was certainly no "dynamic force." Neither he nor his Labour successor of 1929–31, Ramsay MacDonald, were the men to counter the decay of Britain's heavy industry or arrest Britain's military decline.

France: Instability and Resilience

France, at least superficially, contrasted sharply with Britain's orderly alternation between Conservatives and Labour. France enjoyed the dubious benefits of 17 governments between 1920 and 1929. Once the war emergency was past, the Chamber reasserted its dislike of leaders; it did away with Clemenceau in 1920. The Ruhr crisis with Germany over reparations brought Poincaré to the fore in 1922–24. Then *"Poincaruhr"* departed when the May 1924 victory of the moderate left *Cartel des Gauches* displaced the nationalist chamber elected in the enthusiasm of 1919. The Cartel, in turn, displayed political incoherence; Radical-Socialists and Socialists squabbled. The Communists, who had captured from the Socialists most members of the largest union, the General Confederation of Labor (CGT), gleefully attacked the Cartel from the left. Moscow demanded then and later that all Communist parties concentrate their fire not on the Right but on their Socialist rivals. A "cascade" of short-lived Cartel ministries proved incapable of governing in 1925–26, as the franc declined catastrophically thanks to the repercussions of the Ruhr crisis. Poincaré returned in July 1926; his authority saved the franc. Remarkably, he remained—and retired voluntarily in 1929.

The appearance of chaos, except under Poincaré, was deceptive. The Third Republic succeeded in rebuilding the war-devastated areas by the end of the 1920s. The return of the coal and iron of Lorraine fuelled a sharp rise in steel production. André Citroën pioneered—in Europe—the mass production of automobiles, an innovation the British were slow to follow. Hydroelectric power and bauxite deposits in southern France made it a major producer of that new light metal, aluminum. While unemployment laid waste to Britain's mining and shipbuilding areas, France suffered a labor shortage. Prosperity and the immense wartime losses created openings; 1.5 million immigrants from eastern Europe and the colonies filled them.

But France's position was precarious; it rested above all on German disarmament. For as in 1914, France's industrial economy was about half the size of Germany's, and three Germans of military age still faced every two Frenchmen. After the Ruhr and Locarno, which barred France from invading western Germany, the French sought security in defense, and implicitly abandoned their eastern alliances. In 1929, the government initiated a gigantic engineering project to seal France's eastern borders and protect its vital industries from a repetition of 1914. The Maginot Line, named for the minister of war of the moment, André Maginot, was an immensely strong crust of obstacles and fortresses linked with tunnels and underground rail-

Underground in the Maginot Line.

1871		1918	1933	1945
German Empire ("Second Reich")		Weimar Republic	Hitler ("Third Reich")	

ways. It had one weakness: it did not cover the Belgian border. Belgium was a French ally and had its own fortifications facing Germany. If Belgium ceased to be an ally, both the Maginot Line and France might fall.

Germany: Republic without Republicans

Germany's new democracy showed neither British stability nor French resilience. The SPD, Center, and German Democratic (left Liberal) parties received 70 percent of the vote in the January 1919 elections, thanks to Germany's need to appear democratic for the Paris peace conference. That coalition repaired to the provincial town of Weimar, safe from the Spartacists in Berlin, and drafted the most democratic constitution conceivable. It provided votes for both sexes at age 20 and an extreme form of proportional representation that measured, like a delicate seismograph, every quirk and blip of public opinion. Any party that could collect 60,000 votes in all of Germany

could have a *Reichstag* seat. That was an invitation to political fragmentation; by 1928 Germany had at least 45 parties.

The Weimar constitution contained a further decisive weakness, which in the end proved fatal. Max Weber, who helped draft the constitution, saw in a strong American-style presidency a guarantee of leadership that would ward off what he took to be democracy's tendency toward incoherence. Thanks to Weber and to Germany's monarchical tradition, the Republic received *both* a Chancellor responsible to the legislature *and* a popularly elected Reich President. And the Reich President had something his American counterpart did not have, although Lincoln at war had in practice claimed it: emergency powers to make law by decree.

The Weimar constitution failed to work because its drafters superimposed it upon a state and an electorate that were anything but democratic. The officer corps, core of the old Reich, saved itself in 1918–19 by cooperation with the SPD. Thereafter, under General von Seeckt, it supported the Republic grudgingly so long as the Republic tolerated the army's semi-independent status as a "state within the state." As for the electorate, it voted its convictions in the 1920 election, which placed the founding parties of the Republic in a permanent minority. Democracy had failed as a means of ensuring a lenient peace. Middle-class Germans had no natural love of democracy for its own sake, and therefore deserted the German Democratic party for the Right. Even the SPD and Center parties were scarcely democratic by vocation. The SPD had to retain its Marxist rhetoric to prevent further defections to the increasingly vocal Communists to its left; the Center had a built-in authoritarian bent.

Seeckt, planner of German victories over the Russians and Rumanians in 1915–16, made Germany's post-war 100,000-man force an elite "army of leaders," cadres for a future mass army.

That the Republic survived as long as it did, and that it provided the backing for Stresemann's moderate foreign policy from 1923 to 1929, was almost miraculous. This was a political system unable to reach agreement on the colors of the national flag; a cabinet fell over the issue in 1926. Coalitions, to command a *Reichstag* majority, had to extend so far left or right that they were prone to breakdown at any moment.

Nevertheless, three factors preserved the Republic. No alternative commanded support. The monarchy was politically dead; Communist risings failed in 1919, 1920, and 1923; *Putsches* from the Right collapsed in 1920 and 1923 because Seeckt was neutral or hostile. Second, the Republic acquired an unexpected respectability in 1925. Tirpitz, in his last contribution to German politics, persuaded Field Marshal von Hindenburg to run for Reich President. Hindenburg's triumphant election compelled the traditionalist Right to moderate its hatred for the Republic. Finally, Germany after 1924 began to recover its pre-1914 prosperity, thanks primarily to U.S. short-term loans. But if a political alternative arose, if Hindenburg disappeared, if the army turned against the Republic, or if prosperity ended, Weimar might end as well.

The Successor States: Democracies and Dictatorships

German democracy, however precarious, was an earthly paradise compared to conditions further east. The states of eastern Europe greeted 1919 clothed in Wilsonian democratic garb. Within a decade, the absence of native parliamentary traditions and the pressures of nationalism and peasant-landlord conflict had made most of them dictatorships.

As Austria-Hungary collapsed, its nationalities had erected national states. Inevitably, given central and eastern Europe's mixed pattern of settlement, the new borders included large national minorities. Rumania

The dreariness of Weimar depicted by Georg Grosz, an artist of the Left who bitterly attacked the Republic.

forcibly incorporated the 1.5 million Hungarians of Transylvania, and returned with interest the treatment the Hungarians had meted out to the minorities of pre-1914 greater Hungary. The Poles sometimes dealt arrogantly with their German minority, despite the danger of provoking the German state. Orthodox Serbs lorded it over Catholic Croats and Slovenes, former subjects of Austria-Hungary. Virtually everyone mistreated the Jews. League of Nations safeguards for ethnic minorities proved mere scraps of paper.

Social oppression was almost as pervasive as national oppression. Except in industrial Czechoslovakia and rump Austria (which consisted of Vienna and an assortment of Alps), the chief class was the peasantry. It ranged in size from 80 percent of the population in Bulgaria to 55 percent in Hungary. Controlling it was the chief preoccupation of eastern Europe's landholding ruling classes. In the Baltic states of Estonia, Latvia, and Lithuania the landlords were predominantly Russians, Germans, or Poles; the new nationalist governments happily took their land. Elsewhere, peasant land

"Strong men" of eastern Europe: Horthy of Hungary (above) and Pilsudski of Poland (below).

hunger and landlord resistance contributed mightily to political instability.

By 1930, Hungary, Poland, Lithuania, Yugoslavia, Bulgaria, and Rumania were all essentially dictatorships. Hungary went first. From March to November 1919 it suffered the Bolshevik dictatorship of Béla Kun, Rumanian invasion, and finally a bloody reconquest by the Right under the leadership of Austria-Hungary's greatest naval leader, Admiral Nicholas Horthy. The result was a gentry-controlled sham parliament that cloaked a narrow oligarchy with Horthy at its head. A nationalist dictatorship of the peasant Right emerged in Lithuania in 1926. Poland's parliamentary interlude yielded to a 1926 coup by that ex-socialist "man on horseback," Marshal Joseph Pilsudski. In Yugoslavia, the assassination in parliament of the chief Croat leader in 1928 rendered the country ungovernable. King Alexander imposed a royal dictatorship that rested upon Serb bayonets; some Croats replied with terrorism. And in Bulgaria, a military coup in 1923 displaced the ruthless peasant leader, Alexander Stambolisky, who had ruled since 1919. Stambolisky and some 10,000 of his followers perished in ensuing uprisings and massacres. In 1925 a Communist bomb dropped the roof of Sofia cathedral on the representatives of the Right. Enough survived to massacre the Left and impose a royal and military dictatorship with parliamentary trimmings. In 1930 the dissolute King Carol of Rumania returned from exile and adopted a similar solution.

Two exceptions to this pattern existed. Austria, despite the economic ruin of separation from Hungary and Bohemia and a built-in cleavage between "Red Vienna" and the *Freikorps*-like hearties of its Alpine valleys, managed to last out the decade as a parliamentary regime. Czechoslovakia, although a veritable patchwork of nationalities, was an island of relative freedom and prosperity under the enlightened leadership of its Czech founders, Thomas Masaryck and Eduard Beneš. But no eastern European state was equipped to face the coming storm.

The United States: The "Roaring Twenties"

Unprecedented domestic prosperity appeared to reward the international irresponsibility of the United States. The economy grew steadily after the brief worldwide slump of 1920–1921. By 1929 the real per capita income of the average American had improved by more than a third compared to 1921. The automobile came into its own as the engine of growth and symbol of the "American way of life." By 1926, Henry Ford had sold 16 million Model T's, the first true mass-production automobile. By 1929, the United States had one car for every five people; European automobile production was a mere 13 percent of the U.S. level. The U.S. electrical industry followed suit: radios, refrigerators, and vacuum cleaners deluged a public that displayed an apparently insatiable appetite for consumer goods.

Politically, the 1920s were a placidly Republican decade. President Harding died suddenly in 1923 during the revelation of financial scandals that involved his associates. His Vice President, Calvin ("Silent Cal") Coolidge, then presided in masterful inactivity until 1928. A man of few words but pithy ones, he made no secret of his conviction that "the business of America is business."

The 1920s were also a decade of stern intolerance. As Wilson lay paralyzed, his attorney general, A. Mitchell Palmer, mercilessly hunted foreign-born "Reds." In laws of 1921 and 1924, under the guise of immigration quotas, Congress extended to southern and eastern Europeans the policy of exclusion adopted earlier against Chinese and Japanese. The Ku Klux Klan revived, and lynched blacks and Jews. And after 1917, temperance crusaders

1913		1921	1923		1929	1933		1945
Wilson (D)		Harding (R)	Coolidge (R)		Hoover (R)	FDR (D) and the "New Deal"		

dragooned the state legislatures into ratifying an Eighteenth Amendment that prohibited "the manufacture, sale, and transportation of alcoholic beverages."

Prohibition—not repealed until 1933—was the revenge of rural and Protestant America upon the great cities and their immigrants. But Prohibition also took revenge upon its proponents. The Eighteenth Amendment and the Volstead Act of 1919 that enforced it created an immense illegal beer and liquor industry under the control of the very immigrants whom the temperance movement had sought to discipline. Prohibition made the great "families" of organized crime, and made them a permanent feature of American life.

License accompanied intolerance. War, Prohibition, and prosperity broke down inherited standards. Prohibition, an unenforceable law, led to contempt for all laws; it also increased the attraction of alcohol. Relief from the strain of war, the emancipation of women not merely politically but sexually, and the freedom that affluence and automobiles conferred created a hectic and exhilarating "Jazz Age." But all things end. The 1920s ended in an economic catastrophe that appeared to place capitalism itself in question.

Prohibition in action: Federal agents destroy barrels of liquor (1920s).

THE GREAT DEPRESSION

The collapse of the New York stock market in October 1929 helped trigger a depression that lasted until the next great war, for which it was partially responsible. The Great Depression's ultimate causes, a subject of much dispute, were essentially three.

First, the war distorted the fabric of world trade, and political rigidities thereafter prevented readjustment. Britain and Germany hurled the products of their industries at one another for four years. When they resumed peacetime production the result was worldwide overcapacity, thanks to a vast economic expansion in the United States and Japan that had filled the wartime gap in the world market. The same process operated in agriculture: the United States, Canada, Argentina, Australia, and New Zealand had multiplied their agricultural production after 1914. After 1919, governments dared not permit the market to curtail the resulting surpluses. Industrialists and bankers made their money talk; workers and farmers voted. Instead of allowing production to fall, most states chose price subsidies and tariffs—a choice that simply prolonged overproduction. Despite the best efforts of the bureaucrats, agricultural prices turned irrevocably downward. Cotton peaked in 1923, and grain in 1924–25; by 1927 the slide in prices was general.

Second, the war burned up the capital needed to propel Europe's growth. France lost over half its 1914 foreign investments—a quarter had been in Russia. Britain took on a debt of $1 billion in paying for U.S. supplies. Britain's allies owed it $1.7 billion. The resumption of economic growth depended on renewed U.S. lending.

And the policies of the United States—the third major cause of the Great Depression—were irresponsible and self-contradictory. In the war, America replaced Britain as the world's greatest creditor; U.S. foreign investments rose from $2 billion in 1913 to $15 billion in 1930. But the isolationist United States of the 1920s refused to play the part that its wealth thrust upon it, the part of leader and ultimate guarantor of the stability of the world market. It rejected any thought of cancellation of the crushing burden of war debts, incurred in a common cause, under which its allies labored. Coolidge well expressed the implacable American view of those debts in a famous remark in his Vermont twang: "They hired the money, didn't they? Let them pay it!"

Worse, the United States barricaded itself behind the Fordney-McCumber tariff in 1922. High tariffs were traditional, but now they deprived Europe of a market desperately needed to earn profits from which to pay war debts. The president of the Chase National Bank put it well: "The debts of the outside world to us are ropes about their necks, by means of which we pull them towards us. Our trade restrictions are pitchforks pressed against their bodies, by which we hold them off."

Not that the United States did not have a foreign economic policy of sorts. Well-meaning emissaries such as Dawes and Young attempted to rationalize reparations and stabilize Europe economically. But in the absence of tariff reduction and debt cancellation they merely produced a financial merry-go-round. U.S. short-term loans fuelled the German economic expansion that underwrote reparations to France, which in turn paid war debts to Britain. Both Britain and France then paid war debts to the United States. But what if Europe's economy turned downward or U.S. lending ceased?

Both began to happen in 1927–28. Germany's agricultural prices crumbled and its industrial growth stopped. In the United States the Federal Reserve System, an innovation of Wilson's first administration designed to stabilize the banking system, made existing economic instability worse. Since 1921 it had happily pumped in credit, creating hectic growth. In mid-1927, sensing a possible downturn, the "Fed" pumped harder than before.

Easy credit helped stimulate an already foolhardy stock market to the greatest speculative boom in history. The Dow Jones index doubled in value, from 191 to 381, between early 1928 and September 1929. The Wall Street boom put pressure on Europe by diverting money from foreign lending. It squeezed U.S. banks and industry by sucking funds out of bank savings, industrial investment, and consumer spending.

In spring and summer 1929, U.S. economic activity turned downward. Production outran demand as speculative mania drained cash from the pockets of businesses and consumers. The market continued vertiginously upward. Then the bubble burst. Wall Street slipped on October 3, 1929. By the end of the month, after "Black Thursday" (October 24) and "Black Tuesday" (October 29) the Dow index was falling free. Investors who had bought stocks on credit trampled each other to sell, or leapt from high places into Wall Street. Business activity, commodity prices, foreign trade, and the vital lending to Europe all collapsed.

Congress reacted predictably. In March–June 1930 it passed the notorious Smoot-Hawley Tariff, the highest in U.S. history. Coolidge's successor, the unlucky and unloved Herbert Hoover, signed that tariff into law despite a monster petition from a thousand U.S. economists beseeching him to veto it. The tariff and the cut-off of American short-term credit upon which Europe depended were the principal forces that transmuted the Wall Street crash into the Great Depression.

All nations sought to keep their industries and farmers afloat by excluding imports. In spring and summer of 1931, the year of wrath, the banking system of central Europe collapsed. A subversive German scheme for economic union with Austria—a disguised annexation—provoked French financial retaliation. An already frail Austrian bank, the Credit Anstalt, failed. The resulting sudden flight of U.S. short-term loans from Germany almost

destroyed a banking system that agricultural depression and industrial malaise had already enfeebled. The German economy, the motor of central Europe, stalled; 17,000 industrial enterprises shut down.

Britain, after a last despairing gesture toward Austria—a credit offer of a mere $7 million for a week—itself came under pressure. In September 1931 London suspended payments in gold, which it had discontinued during the war and painfully reestablished in 1925 only thanks to U.S. help. The pound sterling became just another paper currency, rather than the unchanging world standard it had been throughout the nineteenth century. That was the end of Britain's already shattered claim to leadership. Hoover belatedly and half-heartedly laid claim to Britain's role by proposing a one year morato-

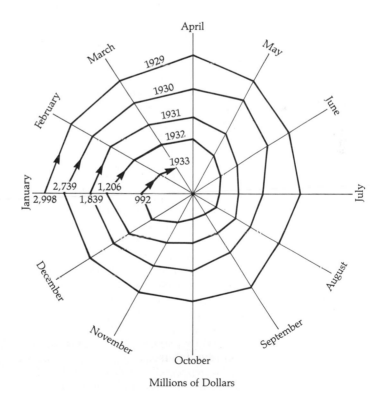

FIGURE 31-1   Down the Drain: The Contracting Spiral of World Trade, 1929–33

From Charles P. Kindleberger, *The World in Depression, 1929–1939* (Berkeley: University of California Press, 1973), p. 172.

rium on reparations and war debt payments in June 1931. Cancellation would have been more appropriate but U.S. opinion would not permit it. Regardless of U.S. wishes, war debt and reparations payments effectively ceased, although negotiations lingered until 1932–33.

Governments sought to promote recovery by drastic expenditure cuts to balance their budgets. That further depressed their economies by lessening demand. All, especially Germany, feared inflation so much that they fought deflation with more deflation. Tariff and currency devaluation wars continued, further deepening and widening the Depression. Britain, formerly the world bastion of free trade, adopted tariffs in 1932. The United States left the gold standard and devalued the dollar in 1933. In Germany and the United States, the worst-hit powers, roughly one worker in four was unemployed by the time the Depression reached bottom in 1932. The Great Depression cut world industrial production by almost a third and world trade by two thirds. The world market almost ceased to exist (see Figure 31-1). Then the precarious peace of 1919 collapsed.

THE WEST AND THE WIDER WORLD, 1919–39

The war discredited empire as well as destroying empires. The victors received German colonies, chunks of the Ottoman empire, or Pacific islands not as outright possessions, but as "mandates" from the League of Nations. In theory the purpose of colonialism was now to prepare the subject peoples for independence. That colonialism now needed fig-leaves was a sign of its impending demise.

And especially in Asia and the Middle East, war and Bolshevism encouraged the ultimate agent of that demise—nationalism. Japan's economic expansion encouraged it to press its claim to hegemony in East Asia. China's reac-

tion and the Great Depression soon impelled Japan to make good that claim by force. That challenge undermined the essential foundation of colonialism everywhere, the prestige won in the nineteenth century through the West's effortless domination of the wider world.

Culmination and Twilight of the Colonial Empires

In 1919, Britain appeared more supreme outside Europe than at any time since the 1870s. Along with its South African and Australian dominions, Britain had taken the lion's share of the colonial booty. It had at last secured the east coast of Africa from the Cape to Cairo. It had triumphantly completed the partition of the Ottoman empire that the Balkan nationalities had begun in 1878. Its major rivals were out of the running. Germany was defeated, Russia was in chaos, and the United States had no desire for further colonial acquisitions; in 1933–34 it pledged to give the Philippines independence by 1945 and renounced unilaterally its treaty right to intervene in Cuba. Britain's only remaining competitors were its allies, France and Japan.

But Britain's position was hollow. By May 1920 the chief of the general staff, Sir Henry Wilson, noted despairingly that "in no single theater are we strong enough—not in Ireland, nor England, not on the Rhine, not in Constantinople, nor Batoum, nor Egypt, nor Palestine, nor Mesopotamia, nor Persia, nor India." Nationalist revolts, Britain's shattered economic position, and the domestic priorities of its mass electorate made it impossible to hold either the immense gains of 1914–18, or Britain's first colony, Ireland.

At Easter 1916 a band of Irish nationalists had risen in Dublin with German promises of support. British troops put the rebels down and tactlessly executed the movement's leaders. That "blood sacrifice" destroyed the position of moderate Irish proponents of home rule, and made the radical nationalist

The Easter Rising, 1916: ruins in central Dublin after British artillery bombardment.

Sinn Fein a mass movement. In 1919 an offshoot of Sinn Fein, the "Irish Republican Army," launched a campaign of assassination and urban guerrilla war. The British responded. The feared "Black and Tans," former western front desperadoes, reinforced the Royal Irish Constabulary. Anonymous gangs caused suspected I.R.A. members and sympathizers to disappear. Even partition in 1921–22 between an Irish Free State in the south and Protestant Ulster in the north did not end "the troubles." I.R.A. diehards refused to accept partition, continued to assassinate British officials, and forced on the Free State itself a civil war more savage than the one the British had waged. A semblance of peace did not return until 1923, and in Ulster sporadic violence has continued to the present.

In Egypt, pivot of the empire, nationalist riots and assassinations in March 1919 likewise showed the limits of British power. Britain gave Egypt nominal independence in 1922 while retaining control of foreign policy, defense, and the all-important Suez Canal. In Iraq the British conceded sham-independence, inexpensively enforced by punitive raids with the fighter-bombers of the infant Royal Air Force.

Palestine was more difficult. The Balfour declaration of 1917 and the war itself speeded Jewish emigration from Europe to Palestine. The ideal of a Jew- ish state was a creation of Theodor Herzl, who in 1897 had founded a Zionist Organization to promote it. Jewish immigation and aspirations to state-

The Balfour Declaration

Foreign Office
November 2nd, 1917

Dear Lord Rothschild,

I have much pleasure in conveying to you, on behalf of His Majesty's Government, the following declaration of sympathy with Jewish Zionist aspirations which has been submitted to, and approved by, the Cabinet.

"His Majesty's Government view with favour the establishment in Palestine of a National Home for the Jewish people, and will use their best endeavors to facilitate the achievement of this object, it being clearly understood that nothing shall be done which may prejudice the civil and religious rights of existing non-Jewish communities in Palestine, or the rights and political status enjoyed by Jews in any other country."

I should be grateful if you would bring this declaration to the knowledge of the Zionist Federation.

Yours sincerely,
(Signed) Arthur James Balfour

Quoted in L. Stein, *Zionism* (London: Ernest Benn, 1925), p. 377.

hood inevitably cut across the claims of Palestine's Arab inhabitants, many of whom, paradoxically, had moved to Palestine to benefit from the economic upsurge the Jews brought. In 1929 Arab-Jewish conflict erupted in the "Wailing Wall" riots in Jerusalem. After 1933, thanks to Adolf Hitler, Jewish immigration to Palestine doubled the Jewish population in three years. After 1936–37, a guerrilla struggle between Arabs and Jews tied down two British divisions sorely needed elsewhere. A British ban on Jewish immigration in 1939 failed to placate the Arabs and aroused the fierce hostility of the Zionists.

Worse still for Britain, India repeatedly erupted. Among the many ambiguous British promises of the dark year of 1917—when a mere 15,000 troops upheld British rule on the subcontinent—was a pledge of "responsible government" as reward for India's notable contribution to the war effort. Postwar British conduct appeared to betray that pledge. In April 1919, after a series of attacks on British civilians at Amritsar in the Punjab, General Reginald Dyer ordered his troops to disperse a crowd with rifle fire. In this "Amritsar Massacre" at least 379 died and over 1,200 suffered wounds. The massacre, and the ensuing celebration of Dyer in British Conservative circles as the man who had prevented a second Indian Mutiny, opened an unbridgeable gulf between Britain and educated Indian opinion.

Amritsar impelled Mohandas K. Gandhi, a Hindu lawyer who had made his name as a leader of the Indian community in South Africa, to launch the Congress party on a campaign of nonviolent civil disobedience. That collapsed in 1922, but British concession of self-government was slow; Gandhi revived his movement in 1930. The imprisonment of 60,000 demonstrators and Gandhi's rejection of British compromise offers again led to the movement's collapse; Gandhi had outrun Indian opinion. Then Britain gave in. The Government of India Act of 1935

conceded a constitution and a firm promise of independence, despite fierce opposition in London from Conservative diehards such as Winston Churchill. The Congress party swept the 1937 elections. But by that point, despite Gandhi's charismatic appeal, Indian nationalism had divided along the Hindu-Moslem line. A Westernized Moslem lawyer-politician, Mohammed Ali Jinnah, created a Moslem League that by 1940 was demanding partition of the subcontinent into Hindu and Moslem states.

Not even the white Dominions showed the unquestioning loyalty for which British imperialists hoped. Their share in Britain's 1914–18 sacrifices and victory gave the Dominions claims on Britain. With Canada and South Africa in the lead, the Dominions sought full sovereignty at the Imperial Conference of 1926. By the Statute of Westminster of 1931 they received it. The British Empire took the ambiguous title of "British Commonwealth of Nations." And in 1932, Eamon De Valera, sole survivor of the leaders of Easter 1916, became prime minister of the Irish Free State. In 1937 he took the Free State out of the Commonwealth in everything but name, and set a powerful example.

France preferred the Foreign Legion bayonet to the subtleties of negotiation. It was little more successful than Britain. Its 1919 acquisitions, Syria and Lebanon, proved combative and unrewarding. The French thought themselves compelled to batter Damascus with artillery as late as 1925. The Berbers of Morocco destroyed a Spanish army in 1921, and attacked the French. It took Pétain, tanks, and four years of fighting to reestablish colonial order. Algeria and Tunisia were intermittently restless.

In Indochina, under a placid surface, nationalist and Communist clandestine organizations spread, with encouragement from China. The Depression brought starvation to the Vietnamese peasantry and offered occasion for the first serious insurrections since French conquest in the nine-

The young Gandhi (1910).

Revolution 1911	1916	1921	1929	First Communist Republic Set Up 1931	1945	Communist Victory 1949
Rule of General Yuan	Chaos	Guomindang Campaigns to Unify China		Guomindang Nominally in Control	Civil War	

teenth century. At Yen Bay, north of Hanoi, nationalists rose in 1930; Communists organized strikes and risings. Ho Chi Minh ("the bringer of enlightenment"), agent of the Communist International for Southeast Asia, founded a Communist party of Indochina. French reprisals were brutal even by French standards. Ho escaped to China and Moscow, and dryly observed that had the nonviolent Gandhi been born in a French colony he "would long since have entered heaven." France's control appeared unshaken. But soon white power everywhere in East Asia was at risk.

The Struggle for Mastery in East Asia Renewed

The Depression unleashed a struggle for supremacy in Asia that pitted Japanese imperial claims against both Chinese nationalism and the remnants of European domination. That struggle was long in the making. The decrepit Qing dynasty had expired in 1911–12 in the face of military revolt in southern and central China. The leading proponent of a Western-style Chinese nationalism, Sun Yat-sen, blessed that outcome—which destroyed what little prospect remained for a Japanese-style revolution from above that harnessed dynastic loyalty to the task of transformation. Sun instead helped found a political party, the Guomindang, and strove to give China constitutional government.

But power in the new China—as in most other societies whose traditional order collapsed under the impact of the West—now came from the barrel of a gun. The end of the dynasty and the crumbling of Confucianism in the face of Western ideas left no other form of

legitimacy. Yuan Shikai, most successful leader of the Western-armed provincial armies, had the most guns. He attempted to make himself emperor. Regional warlords resisted; Yuan fell ill and died in 1916. Thereafter warlord armies fought obscure struggles the length and breadth of China; those around Beijing (Peking) contended for the honor of manipulating a sham parliament. Chinese nationalism, outraged at the persistence of European and Japanese encroachments, sought in vain for a political vehicle.

Two contenders soon arose. Sun discarded parliamentarism for Leninism without Marxism. The Soviet Union, seeking a sphere of influence in China, delightedly offered advisers and arms. With the help of Michael Borodin, the Communist International's man in China, Sun drafted a new statute for the Guomindang that made it a centralized "vanguard party"—but one without a coherent ideology. Sun's military assistant, Chiang Kai-shek, created a party army in southern China with Soviet rifles and advisers, and inherited the Guomindang upon Sun's death in 1925. But the Soviet Union had a second string to its bow: the Chinese Communist Party (CCP) that groups of Beijing and Shanghai intellectuals had founded with Soviet advice in 1920–21. Those groups included the sturdy and pugnacious son of a rich peasant, Mao Zedong (Mao Tse-tung).

In 1927, as Chiang extended Guomindang control to central China, the collaboration that Moscow had imposed between Communists and Guomindang broke down. Chiang crushed the Communists in Shanghai and elsewhere with much slaughter; soon the CCP had forfeited its original base, the embryonic working classes of

Sun Yat-sen, theorist of Chinese nationalism (1923).

Rivals for the mastery of China: Chiang Kai-shek and Mao Zedong (below).

the industrializing coastal cities. Mao escaped to the hills on the Jiangxi-Hunan border, created a Party army of peasants and bandits, and ultimately purged his remaining rivals in the Party leadership. Lenin had adapted Marxism to a largely peasant country but had kept Marx's notion of the industrial proletariat as chosen people. Mao discarded even that; his Marxism for Chinese conditions made it an ideology of peasant revolt *against* the cities.

After temporarily suppressing the Communists, Chiang Kai-shek defeated the northern warlords and seized Beijing in 1928. That nominally unified China. But Chiang's rule was precarious; the Guomindang absorbed a variety of quarrelsome warlord elements as it expanded. The Communists in the hills remained a threat, despite five Guomindang "bandit-extermination campaigns." In 1934–35 Mao's forces escaped from south-central China and in an epic "Long March" of 6,000 miles sought refuge at Yenan in the remote northwest.

By that point, Chiang had another adversary to occupy him. Japan had yielded up most of its claims on China in the Washington treaties of 1922. The Western-style political parties that had arisen under Japan's Bismarckian constitution of 1889 were at the height of their influence in the early and middle 1920s, despite occasional assassinations of politicians by ultra-nationalist sects. But Japan's era of liberalism within and peace without was brief, thanks to both external and internal pressures. At Paris the powers had humiliated Japan by refusing its request to incorporate into the Versailles Treaty a declaration on racial equality. The corollary of that refusal was the banning of Japanese immigration to the United States and to Australia. Simultaneously, U.S. tariffs constricted Japanese exports and U.S. pressure dictated in 1921–22 the end of the alliance with Britain that had tied Japan, how-

ever tenuously, to the international status quo.

Inside Japan itself, by the late 1920s, explosive economic growth, population increase, and radical ideologies pressed against that status quo. Economic growth between 1900 and 1929, at 4.2 percent a year, was faster than that of any other power. Population grew from 43.8 million in 1900 to 71.1 million in 1940. American tariffs and immigration restrictions pushed Japan toward dependence on mainland raw materials and emigration outlets, especially in coal- and iron-rich Manchuria.

Ultra-nationalist sects, a feature of the Japanese scene since the "men of spirit" of the 1850s, proliferated. Ideologues such as Kita Ikki (1883–1939) proposed vague syntheses of Marxism and nationalism, and looked forward to a world-dominating Japan with vast colonial possessions and a population of 250 million. In the military such ideas prospered, especially among middle-level and junior officers with rural backgrounds. Ishiwara Kanji, most formidable of the middle-level officers, foresaw world conquest by stages. Japan would seize Manchuria, then fight Russia, Britain, and the United States in turn. Each victory would bring Japan the resources needed for the next step: "war can maintain war." Ishiwara was no isolated dreamer; he had the ear of the army's chiefs. And the army, like its German counterpart during the Hindenburg-Ludendorff dictatorship, soon became the decisive force in the state, responsible only to a figurehead emperor.

Chiang's conquest of northern China and the Depression almost coincided. Together they triggered this explosive mixture. Chinese nationalist boycotts of Japanese goods, Chinese aspirations to regain full control of Manchuria, and the Depression-borne collapse of Japan's already stagnant peasant economy impelled the Japanese army officer corps to strike, to secure Japan's vital Manchurian hinterland before it was too late. In September 1931, Ishiwara and a group of like-minded officers acting with the connivance of the staff in Tokyo planted explosives on Japan's railway in Manchuria and blamed the Chinese. The army swiftly cleared Manchuria of Chinese forces and created the puppet state of Manchukuo. The navy collided with the Chinese at Shanghai and extricated itself by ruthlessly bombarding the Chinese quarters of the city—in front of Western newsreel cameras. The cabinet in Tokyo, divided and terrified of assassination, acquiesced. When the League of Nations mildly reproved Japan in February 1933, the Japanese delegation stalked out, never to return.

The West failed to do anything effective, despite outrage over Shanghai. Britain now faced the same unpleasant situation that Russian occupation of northern China had created in 1900. London could not realistically fight a great war to preserve distant China; no vital British interest was at stake. In 1901–02 London had therefore taken on Japan as junior partner. But now Japan itself was the threat, and its relative strength was immeasurably greater

Mao Proposes a Peasant Revolution 1927

Mao's "Report on an Investigation of the Agrarian Movement in Hunan" of March 1927 was his earliest attempt to persuade his Party that it must either lead China's peasantry, or succumb to it.

The force of the peasantry is like that of the raging winds and driving rain. It is rapidly increasing in violence. No force can stand in its way. The peasantry will tear apart all nets which bind it, and hasten along the road to liberation. They will bury beneath them all forces of imperialism, militarism, corrupt officialdom, village bosses and evil gentry. Every revolutionary party, every revolutionary comrade will be subjected to their scrutiny and be accepted or rejected by them. Shall we stand in the vanguard and lead them or stand behind them and oppose them? Every Chinese is free to pick his answer. However, destiny will force us to pick an answer soon . . . .

From Benjamin I. Schwartz, *Chinese Communism and the Rise of Mao* (Cambridge: Harvard University Press, 1964), pp. 74–75.

than in 1902. This time Britain's only potential allies were the Soviet Union and the United States. But the Soviets were as great a threat to British interests in China as was Japan. And while Washington sternly refused to recog-

Japanese troops in Shanghai, 1933.

nize Japan's acquisition of Manchuria, it refused with equal sternness to back its moralistic talk with economic reprisals, much less with force. Braving U.S. disapproval, Britain soothed the Japanese and attempted to limit the damage.

Japan made that difficult. Its navy embarked on a new and massive program; in 1934 Japan withdrew from the Washington naval treaty. The elaborate structure of interwar naval disarmament came crashing down. Japanese politicians increasingly deferred to the military. Some who deferred with insufficient speed suffered the fate of prime minister Inukai Tsuyoshi in 1932, assassination. In 1936 junior officers, with the collaboration of Kita Ikki, attempted a coup in Tokyo and slaughtered several ministers. The high command reasserted itself with loyal troops and executions.

That ended the day of junior officers and freelance ideologues. Senior generals such as Tōjō Hideki increasingly directed Japanese policy in rivalry with the admirals. And in July 1937 an accidental brush with Guomindang forces near Beijing swiftly escalated into an open-ended China war. A militarized Japan, fighting under the unintentionally ironic slogan of "Asia for the Asians," sought to make China a Japanese colony. The first of the wars that ultimately converged to make the Second World War had begun.

THE THIRTIES: THE DEMOCRACIES FALTER

The Japanese threat caught the democracies as the Depression and their own demoralization touched bottom. Japan's success soon emboldened others. Fascist Italy, the Germany of Adolf Hitler, and ultimately even the Soviet Union broke the peace (see pp. 917–36). They met little opposition until very late.

Britain: Highmindedness and Decline

The Depression destroyed Ramsay MacDonald's second Labour government, which had taken office in 1929. Labour, trembling at the displeasure of the financial markets and lacking imagination, met the Depression by imposing balanced budgets. That required cuts in unemployment payments and provoked a cabinet and labor-union revolt in the catastrophic month of August 1931. MacDonald stayed on at the head of a "National Coalition" with Liberal and Conservative backing; Labour went into opposition.

As in Lloyd George's coalition, the Conservatives were the dominant partner. Baldwin flattered and mollified parliament and public; Neville Chamberlain provided the efficiency and drive. He was Austen Chamberlain's unlovable and iron-willed younger brother, in Lloyd George's unkind words "a good mayor of Birmingham in an off-year." In 1935 an enfeebled MacDonald retired, and Baldwin led

---

Churchill Warns MacDonald and Baldwin   1932

On November 23, 1932, in the House of Commons, Churchill commented scathingly on MacDonald's continued pursuit of Western disarmament in the face of the growing German threat:

Do not delude yourselves. Do not let His Majesty's Government believe—I am sure they do not believe—that all Germany is asking for is equal status. . . . That is not what Germany is seeking. All these bands of sturdy Teutonic youths, marching through the streets and roads of Germany, with the light of desire in their eyes to suffer for their Fatherland, are not looking for status. They are looking for weapons, and, when they have the weapons, believe me they will then ask for the return of lost territories and lost colonies, and when that demand is made it cannot fail to shake and possibly shatter to their foundations every one of the countries I have mentioned [France, Belgium, Poland, Rumania, Czechoslovakia, Yugoslavia], and some other countries I have not mentioned. . . .

From Martin Gilbert, *Winston S. Churchill*, Vol. V, *1922–1939. The Prophet of Truth* (Boston: Houghton Mifflin, 1977), p. 451.

the Conservatives to victory over La-
bour by shamming action to block
Italy's conquest of Ethiopia (see p. 918).
Then Baldwin bequeathed his iron-clad
House of Commons majority to Cham-
berlain in 1937.

By that point Britain's world position was precarious. Japan's thrust into
Manchuria had prompted the scrap-
ping of the "ten year rule" and the creation of a committee to look into defense needs—but nothing more
concrete. MacDonald, a quasi-pacifist
during the First World War, deferred to
the World Disarmament Conference
that met in 1932–34, just as the revolt
of the discontented powers took shape.
Not until March 1934, after the Conference's inevitable collapse, did the British cabinet begin to debate rearmament. And only Winston Churchill,
ceaselessly harassing the cabinet from
outside, looked on the German threat
with any urgency. Conservative opinion considered him "unsound" since
his association with the Dardanelles
fiasco (which others had mismanaged);
his fierce opposition to the government
over India had not enhanced his reputation. Baldwin's indolence and Chamberlain's niggling defense of financial
orthodoxy triumphed. Large-scale British rearmament did not begin until
1936–37. It proved too little and too
late.

France: Cynicism and Decline

Highminded professions of faith in the
League and in disarmament accompanied the decline of Britain. The French
were more cynical; the only disarmament that interested them was that of
Germany, and that collapsed in 1932–
1933. Yet France failed to react. The
Depression struck France later than
Britain or Germany, thanks to France's
lesser degree of industrialization. But it
hit hard and kept hitting. Industrial
production stagnated at between 80
and 90 percent of its 1928 level from
1931 to mid-1939 (see Figure 31-2). Economic stagnation inevitably worsened
drastically the central vice of French
politics, ideological polarization. The
always disorganized Third Republic
tottered.

The Communists polled a million
votes in 1928 and gained another half
million by 1936. A further sharpening
of Moscow's anti-Socialist line in 1928
produced open war between Communists and Socialists. That stopped the
Socialists from collaborating for long
with the Radical-Socialists to their
right, for fear of losing yet more voters

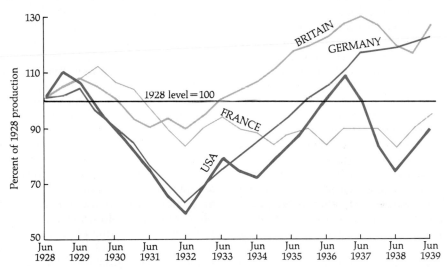

FIGURE 31-2   Depression and Recovery: Failure and Success
(Industrial Production as a Percentage of 1928 Production)

and union members to the Communists. Nor were the deputies of the center numerous enough to command the Chamber. And alongside the old Right of the Dreyfus era and the "two hundred families" that supposedly controlled French industry, a new populist Right emerged. The "Leagues," bands of trench-coated anti-Semitic thugs with lead pipes and revolvers, professed ideologies ranging from monarchism to extreme nationalist authoritarianism.

In January 1934, after two years of weak governments of the Left that rivalled the "cascade" of 1925–26, one of the Republic's characteristic scandals erupted. A shady financier of eastern European extraction, Alexander Stavisky, committed suicide or was murdered after the exposure of frauds apparently committed with the backing of prominent politicians. The Republic seemed even less reputable than usual. On February 6, 1934, the Leagues attacked parliament while Communists rioted in the industrial suburbs of Paris. Police firepower saved the Republic amid tension not seen in Paris since Boulanger and Dreyfus. The *"six février"* served notice that the Republic lived on borrowed time.

A change of line in Moscow gave the Left a second wind. In 1935 the Communist International, faced with the rise of Hitler's Germany, reversed its previous attempt to stamp out its Socialist rivals. In France the result was a "Popular Front" coalition of Radical-Socialists, Socialists, and Communists. Léon Blum, a vacillating Socialist intellectual, led the government that emerged from the Popular Front's election triumph of April–May 1936. Blum suppressed the Leagues. To the accompaniment of sit-in strikes and industrial turmoil he decreed paid vacations, the 40-hour week, and other concessions that French workers considered long overdue. Those restrictions on industry slowed rearmament and caused French investors to move their capital into harder currencies than the franc. That in turn brought Blum down in June

1937. The Left could win elections but could not govern.

Nor did Blum, torn between abhorrence of war and the pressing need for rearmament to face Germany, find a coherent foreign policy. Not that the Right would have necessarily performed better; much of it mouthed the slogan "better Hitler than Blum." Blum's foremost successor, Edouard Daladier, was a Radical of Napoleonic appearance but less than Napoleonic strength. His minister of finance, Paul Reynaud, saved the franc in the manner of Poincaré. But that success proved irrelevant. Under Daladier and Reynaud, France first abandoned its eastern allies, then itself collapsed.

The United States: Political Success and Economic Failure of the New Deal

Hoover appeared helpless as the economic fabric of the United States disintegrated. Stock prices continued to slide, wiping out much of the savings of a generation; U.S. Steel plunged from $262 a share in 1929 to $22 in 1932. U.S. industrial production dropped by 1932 to half of its 1929 level. Only unemployment rose: from 5 million in December 1930 to 13 million in December 1932. The unemployed and their families sought refuge in shantytowns, named with bitter irony "Hoovervilles."

Hoover lost the 1932 election. His threadbare protestations that prosperity was "just around the corner" were unconvincing. His spending on public works, although far greater than that of any previous administration, proved insufficient to spark the economy. His Democratic opponent, the New York grandee Franklin Delano Roosevelt, accepted the nomination with a pledge of a "new deal for the American people." But before Roosevelt could take office the overstrained banking system followed the rest of the economy, as panicked depositors stormed the tellers' windows. On inauguration day, March 4, 1933, Roosevelt shut the re-

The impact of the Depression: a "Hooverville" in Seattle, 1933.

maining banks before they collapsed. Capitalism itself seemed in ruins.

Roosevelt brought a short-term remedy that had eluded Hoover: force of conviction. "So first of all let me assert my firm belief that the only thing we have to fear is fear itself—nameless, unreasoning, unjustified terror . . . ," rang his presidential address. In a mere five days he pushed through Congress a Hoover plan to shore up the banks. In the first of a series of radio "fireside chats" that gave the nation back some of its lost self-confidence, he announced that the banks would reopen. By June 1933 he had averted the threat of total economic collapse. Industrial production briefly equalled the level of 1929.

Roosevelt and his "brain trust" of young intellectuals directed at Congress a torrent of legislation that established public works programs far vaster than those of Hoover, and recruited the unemployed into a quasi-military Civilian Conservation Corps; the first New Deal administration created 6 million

jobs. To raise agricultural prices, government paid farmers not to plant crops. Government extended to farmers and householders some protection from the mortgage foreclosures that meant economic ruin, and gave unemployment benefits to workers. Government ultimately guaranteed the right to organize unions and created the compulsory pension plan known as Social Security. And thanks to the free-trade convictions of Roosevelt's otherwise ineffectual Secretary of State, Cordell Hull, U.S. trade barriers dropped after 1934. That was too late to save the fragmented world market—but better later than not at all.

The New Deal's European-style welfare-state measures seemed revolutionary—and aroused the bitter enmity of business interests. Soon the Republican establishment was denouncing Roosevelt as a "dictator" and traitor to his class. Labor, blacks, and most middle-class Americans took a different view. Roosevelt won his second term in 1936 by an unprecedented margin of 11 million votes; his Republican opponent carried only Maine and Vermont.

But stability and prosperity failed to return. Production briefly surpassed 1928 levels in 1936–37, then dropped again catastrophically (see Figure 31-2 on p. 893). By December 1937, the largest steel industry in the world was operating at 26 percent of capacity. Roosevelt had vastly increased the role of government in the economy—but until 1938 he held to the Hoover orthodoxy of balanced budgets. Unfortunately, unbalanced budgets were precisely what the economy required to stimulate demand. Not until his 1938 recovery plan did Roosevelt halfheartedly opt for deficits. And it was not New Deal economic policies but necessity that generated recovery after 1939. Armament production for global war dragged the United States out of the Depression as the revolt of the discontented powers in Europe and Asia dragged it back again into world affairs.

THE AGE OF UNCERTAINTY

The 20-year truce was not merely a time of demoralization for the democracies or of triumph for savage dictatorships—a theme taken up in the following chapter. It was also an era of disorienting intellectual, social, and cultural change. Science continued its rapid expansion of human knowledge of the cosmos and of the building blocks of matter itself. Technology transformed everyday life. The state took on vast new duties. The war had accelerated the rise of workers' parties and the political, economic, and sexual emancipation of women. It had speeded the breakdown, among much else, of previous notions of what constituted art. A new writing, art, and architecture, reflecting disenchantment with the certainties of the pre-1914 era and rejection of the war, flourished. The mass culture born before the war reached maturity, especially in the United States, to the horror of many

Giant of the new physics: Albert Einstein in Berlin, 1920.

traditionalist intellectuals. And the war acted as catalyst for new and terrifying ideologies.

Science: The End of Certainty

By 1900, and still more by 1919, phenomena had emerged that were puzzling or inexplicable to physicists. Neither electromagnetism nor light conformed precisely to the traditional Newtonian framework. Worse, the theorists soon had to cope with X-rays (1895), radioactivity (1896), and Ernest Rutherford's 1911 discovery that atoms were not solid, as assumed since the first atomic theories had emerged in ancient Greece. Atoms apparently contained electrons, nuclei, and much empty space. Radioactive decay emerged in 1913; uranium and thorium, it appeared, turned into lead. Atomic nuclei might contain further particles.

Matter, considered fixed and untransmutable since the birth of modern chemistry in the eighteenth century, was thus again in flux. In 1919 Rutherford bombarded nitrogen with helium nuclei, and produced oxygen. Researchers discovered neutrons and positrons in 1932 and 1933. The "cyclotron" or racetrack-like particle accelerator first proposed in 1932 allowed, among much else, the laboratory creation of the "transuranic" heavy elements. The first were neptunium and plutonium in 1940.

The theorists soon attempted to explain some of what the researchers were finding. Max Planck of Berlin suggested in 1900 that energy from warm bodies did not radiate at uniform levels across the spectrum, but jumped in steps or *quanta*; the amount of energy released varied with its wavelength. Albert Einstein, at that point an obscure patent examiner in Switzerland, suggested in 1905 that light too was "quantized." Niels Bohr of Denmark applied the quantum concept in 1913 to Rutherford's new atom, and explained both atomic structure and the differing spectra that various elements emitted. In 1927 Werner Heisenberg of Leipzig, in the course of researches on quantum theory, suggested that the very act of measuring the position, velocity, or mass of a particle interacted with the particle, introducing uncertainty into the measurement. Prediction of the action of subatomic particles fell back on mere statistics—a most un-Newtonian and disquieting state of affairs.

By that point Einstein had established the theory of relativity, the foundation, along with quantum theory, of modern physics. In 1905, in a paper that outlined his "Special Theory of Relativity," Einstein asserted that time and space were not absolute entities, as Newtonian physics required, but rather varied relative to the observer's velocity and location. The only absolute in Einstein's new universe was the speed of light—186,300 miles per second—which was the absolute limit of velocity. Mass increased with velocity, and mass, times a constant squared, was equivalent to energy: $E = mc^2$. That fateful notion as yet lacked empirical confirmation.

By 1916 Einstein had incorporated gravitation into his theory, which now became the "General Theory of Relativity." And in 1919 an eclipse permitted the first confirmation of the General Theory. Starlight passing through the sun's gravitational field bent by the amount Einstein's theory predicted. Newton's tidy universe gave way to a four-dimensional and curved "space-time continuum." Attempts to unify the General Theory of Relativity with quantum theory, and to explain everything from gravitation to the birth and death of the cosmos and the ever-expanding world of subatomic particles, proliferated.

It soon emerged that Einstein's insights had dramatic practical application. In January 1939, building on work by Niels Bohr, Enrico Fermi, and others, Otto Hahn and Fritz Strassmann of Berlin announced that they had split the nuclei of uranium atoms by bombarding them with neutrons. The process transmuted the uranium into barium and a small amount of the uranium's original mass into an as-tounding amount of energy, as Einstein's formula suggested. The race to create a self-sustaining atomic chain reaction—and weapons of unprecedented destructive power—began.

Biology and medicine experienced the same accelerated pace of advance that was visible in physics. Even before the First World War, the first crude antibiotics—organic poisons that killed disease organisms but not their human hosts—appeared. Salvarsan, an arsenic compound that revolutionized the treatment of syphilis, became available as early as 1909. The sulfonamides, effective against pneumonia and gangrene, followed in 1935–38. Penicillin emerged in the laboratory in 1929; its first medical use in 1940 proved it startlingly effective against a wide range of diseases and infections.

Advances in immunization had in 1914–18 at least spared western Europe the typhoid epidemics that had accompanied previous great wars. In the interwar period inoculations for diphtheria, yellow fever, typhus, and bubonic plague became available. The discovery of hormones such as insulin (1922) and cortisone (1936) permitted the development of therapies for such previously untreatable conditions as diabetes. The identification and isolation of vitamins helped eradicate deficiency diseases such as pellagra. Thanks to improvements in blood typing, transfusions became normal procedure after 1940. And insecticides, especially DDT (1939) showed promise of eliminating insect carriers of disease. For the Germans, who first developed them, the new insecticides also showed promise of another sort. In 1936 the great German chemical trust, I. G. Farben, began a crash program to develop, from a family of insecticides that killed by disrupting nerve impulses, a weapon for use against humans: the first nerve gas.

Technology: Steel, Oil, and Electricity

The war and the interwar period accelerated dramatic changes in materials and energy sources that were already underway. Steel remained king, thanks to a bewildering variety of new stainless or extremely hard alloys with metals such as chromium, vanadium, tungsten, nickel, and molybdenum. Concrete, reinforced with steel rods, came into its own as a structural material that permitted the most astounding architectural shapes. Aluminum, refined with electric power, became the material of choice for everything from aircraft to cooking pots. Plastics developed rapidly; by 1939 they provided everything from transparent canopies and windows for aircraft to flexible insulation for electrical cables. Synthetic rubber, another German innovation, became vitally important both to Germany and to the United States after 1939. Artificial fibers such as rayon and its numerous derivatives made possible garments even less expensive than cotton. But artificial yarns made from wood or cellulose fibers were only the first step. In the 1930s the first truly synthetic fiber, derived from oil, became available—nylon. Its great strength made it ideal for everything from stockings to parachutes.

In the realm of energy sources, oil and electricity now triumphed, along with their associated technologies. The First World War had made demands for transport that only the internal combustion engine could meet, and had immensely accelerated motorization. Trucks, tanks, and tractors supplemented and in many cases superseded the horse. Oil-fired high-compression steam turbines or diesel engines replaced clumsy coal, which required stokers and prevented refueling at sea. By the mid-1920s aircraft had ceased to be underpowered kite-like objects of wood, cloth, and wire. By the early 1930s the first multiengined all-metal airliners were carrying passengers rich and daring enough to try them. Even humanity's oldest form of combustion-propelled projectile revived. In 1926 the visionary Robert Goddard developed the first practical liquid-fuelled rocket. His work attracted little attention in his native United States, but observers in Russia and Germany found it intriguing.

Electricity revolutionized communications and created new mass media: motion pictures, sound recordings, radio, and television. Motion picture technology originated in the 1890s in the United States and France; by 1914 "movie houses" were common. Record players and radios, thanks to Lee DeForest's triode amplifier tube (1906–07), were widespread by 1928, the year of the first "talkie." Television—images electronically scanned, transmitted by radio, and displayed on a cathode ray tube—emerged in U.S. and British laboratories in the mid-1920s, although it did not begin to reach the public for another two decades.

Electronics had more deadly uses: the detection of submarines by sound ranging (sonar) and above all of aircraft and surface ships by radio ranging (radar). After 1935 Britain and Germany raced one another for mastery over those vital auxiliaries to air and sea warfare. As the unquiet truce ended, science was developing a potential it had not yet possessed in 1914: the potential to decide the outcome of war between great powers.

The State in Crisis

The First World War ended for good the state that governed best by governing least. The state henceforth took responsibility for guaranteeing the survival and welfare of the individual. Prewar measures such as old age pensions and industrial-accident insurance expanded. Unemployment benefits became law. In Germany, workers briefly gained a state-sanctioned voice in management decisions. The United States of Coolidge and Hoover resisted such allegedly socialist measures; then Roosevelt adopted many of them.

The war had also introduced management of currency and foreign exchange, and vast bureaucracies to plan investment and allocate raw materials. Peace had dismantled that planning

The RCA Victor trademark, symbol of the new recorded sound.

"HIS MASTER'S VOICE"
REG. U.S. PAT. OFF.

machinery, but the example of the Hindenburg Program lived on in the Soviet Union (see pp. 911–12). The Depression, a crisis in some ways more severe than the war, gave the state back its wartime role—in "peace." The state grudgingly took responsibility for the fate of the economy.

Most democracies adopted a degree of economic planning. But as Roosevelt's confused experimentation suggests, they lacked a theory. In 1936, John Maynard Keynes at last provided a theory for an era in which laissez-faire appeared to lead ever deeper into the abyss. In his *General Theory of Employment, Interest, and Money,* Keynes argued that government deficit financing—the creation of money by decree—was the obvious antidote to deflation and unemployment. Government spending put people to work; their spending, through the "multiplier effect," put others to work. Ideas require time to penetrate, and Keynes's arrived too late. The old orthodoxy dominated as late as 1937, when a tax increase and a tightening of the money supply produced a renewed economic nosedive in the United States. To recover, Roosevelt adopted by trial and error a mild version of deficit financing. Within a decade, Keynes's theories had become conventional wisdom, the charter for continuous state management of market economies.

Workers: Expectations Disappointed

At the outbreak of war in 1914, Britain's Liberal foreign secretary, Sir Edward Grey, dolefully foretold its political and social consequences: "There will be Labour governments everywhere after this." Britain, France, and Weimar Germany indeed received governments that workers' parties led or dominated. But those governments, and the labor unions that furnished their largest single bloc of support, operated under severe limitations.

First, the workers were themselves divided. Regional and craft lines fractured the unions of Britain and the United States; racial and ethnic lines also divided U.S. workers. On the Continent, Communists sought to destroy Socialists in both the unions and the political arena. In Germany, as described in Chapter 32, the Communist offensive after 1928 helped kill the Weimar Republic; both Socialist and Communist parties perished in a common ruin.

Second, the Depression dramatically lowered morale. Especially in Europe, it weakened the main weapon of industrial workers, the strike. Few strike when one worker in four has no job. Finally, industrial workers, contrary to the predictions of Marx, found themselves in the minority in advanced capitalist societies. Except in egalitarian Scandinavia, political parties claiming to represent workers consistently failed to achieve more than a third of the vote. Insuperable social and ideological barriers prevented further growth—a profoundly demoralizing situation.

If the workers accepted democratic rules, socialism was clearly impossible, for the "bourgeoisie" would hardly vote its own demise. But if the workers chose the path of revolution, the other two-thirds of society, with the help of the state apparatus, would inevitably prevail. These constraints and the moderate instincts of western Europe's social democrats confined unions and workers' parties in the interwar period to a "war of position"—a trench struggle for gradual reform of the economic system rather than for its overthrow. Given their minority status, those workers' parties that did achieve power rarely governed long. In the Depression many even failed to prevent their political adversaries from balancing government budgets by reducing unemployment benefits and state employee salaries.

Women: New Predicaments for Old

Women in Britain, Germany, Scandinavia, and the United States likewise discovered that the vote and the workings of the political system changed their status only slowly. Giving the vote prevented a repetition of the prewar confrontations in Britain. It channeled women's political activities to the existing parties. It helped women's groups to lobby for full equality before the law and for legislation protecting mothers and children. But the onset of the Depression and the coming of a new war soon diverted politically active women from "women's issues" to more general ones.

Many countries, among them France, Italy, Belgium, and Switzerland, did not concede even the vote, thanks to the weight of male opinion and of the Church. And women's economic position between the wars was even more precarious than that of men. Demobilization of the mass armies and conversion to peacetime production led to mass dismissals of women from industry. Structural changes—the continuing decline of peasant agriculture and of "mom and pop" retailing—likewise narrowed women's employment possibilities.

But women were unwilling to give up their new-found economic independence. Many had to earn a living in any case: their husbands were dead. The interwar growth of business bureaucracies and of that temple of consumption, the department store, offered a substitute for industrial employment. Women penetrated the professions at a greater rate than before, especially in the United States, Britain, and Scandinavia. They maintained their positions in fields such as nursing, primary-school teaching, and librarianship. They nevertheless normally received less money than men—for the same work.

In one vital area the interwar period was the scene of truly dramatic change—control of reproduction. During and immediately after the war, pioneers such as the American Margaret Sanger (1883–1966) and the English-woman Marie Stopes (1880–1958) made contraceptive information available to a mass audience for the first time. A Dutch invention, the diaphragm, joined the condom, an eighteenth century device popularized—like cigarettes—in the First World War.

Women thus for the first time acquired efficient means to determine when and by whom they had children. Improved childbirth techniques and nutrition ensured that fewer of the children born subsequently died. Fewer children in turn meant that the average woman now spent four years or less—instead of fifteen or more—pregnant or nursing. That was a historic achievement that allowed some women, for the first time, to aspire to have both a career and a family.

Most men still objected. And the new science of the mind offered small improvement over nineteenth-century medical notions of female inferiority. In Freud's view, woman's unconscious yearning for a penis allegedly led her to seek a penis-substitute: babies. Above all, the course of interwar politics menaced emancipated women; Fascists and Nazis sought to crush all challenges to male supremacy. The mission of the allegedly "inferior sex of the master race" was to breed large broods of heroes. But even those regimes failed to reverse the decline of the birth rate that industrialization had brought and contraception accelerated.

The High Culture of Disenchantment

The war broke down inhibitions in literature and art as well as in life. William II had insisted that "an art that transgresses the laws and barriers recognized by me ceased to be an art." Now he was gone; censorship, both formal and informal, diminished in intensity throughout northern Europe. Avant-garde literary and artistic trends that had originated before 1914 now became dominant, at least in high culture.

The prevailing mood was one of disenchantment. The war was the formative experience of an entire generation. Its apparent futility marked their writing, especially in highminded Britain, where the sordid brutality of war had come as a greater shock than elsewhere. British "war poets" such as

Margaret Sanger, pioneer of birth control for the masses, about to appear in court (1917).

Wilfred Owen, Robert Graves, and Siegfried Sassoon wrote eloquent verse that damned the war and the western front. The peculiar conditions of the war, the stark contrast between apparently futile slaughter at the front and almost complete safety beyond artillery range, engendered a fierce hatred of all symbols of authority. Sassoon, a highly decorated officer, railed with particular bitterness at generals, staffs, politicians, and civilians. French war writing, especially *Under Fire* (1917) by Henri Barbusse, who later became a Communist, reflected France's immense losses. Even German war literature occasionally sounded a despondent note, as in Erich Maria Remarque's *All Quiet on the Western Front* (1929).

But Germany was different from the West. There, heroic nihilists of the Ernst Jünger stamp dominated. Works such as *Battle as an Inner Experience* (1922), *Fire and Blood* (1925), and *Artillery Barrage Around Germany* (1928) convinced the German young that they had missed something. Jünger spoke or claimed to speak for his generation: "War, the father of all things, is also our father; it has hammered, hewn, and tempered us into what we are. And so long as the spinning wheel of life turns within us, this war will be the axis about which it whirls."

In England, the aesthetes of the "Bloomsbury Group" devoted themselves to the destruction of what little remained of Victorian morality in their own private lives. Freud appeared to suggest that conventional morality was an elaborate hypocritical cloak over unconfessable desires. He appeared to legitimate not merely confessing but advertising and even gratifying those desires. And his doctrines were an inexhaustible source of small talk. Freud's works now became a popular success.

Bloomsbury also attacked the symbols of Victorianism. Lytton Strachey's *Eminent Victorians* (1918), with its inaccurate but compelling demolitions of Florence Nightingale, "Chinese" Gordon, and other national totems, was an instantaneous success. Keynes, a Bloomsburyite by adoption, expiated his guilt—in Bloomsbury's eyes—for having worked for the government during the war by savaging his former chief, Lloyd George, in *The Economic Consequences of the Peace* (1919).

In poetry, two transplanted Americans and an Irishman—T. S. Eliot (1888–1965), Ezra Pound (1885–1972), and William Butler Yeats (1865–1939)—gave English poetry a modern shape that ultimately derived from the French Symbolists: loose in structure and playing on layer upon layer of symbolism and allusion to mythology and literature. Eliot's greatest work, a manifesto for the new English poetry, was *The Waste Land* (1922). Its bleak vision of London and modern life as Dante's *Inferno* fitted precisely the post-war mood among intellectuals:

> Unreal City,
> Under the brown fog of a winter dawn,
> A crowd flowed over London Bridge, so many,
> I had not thought death had undone so many.

Pound, more difficult and allusive even than Elliot, eventually succumbed to an obsessive anti-Semitism and took Fascist Italy as his adopted country. Yeats, like the others, wove symbols and bizarre occult or cosmological references into his poems. But he also wrote some of the most lucid and musical English verses of the twentieth century, such as the famous lines of "The Second Coming" (1921) that prophesied the interwar triumph of political barbarism:

> Things fall apart; the centre cannot hold;
> Mere anarchy is loosed upon the world,
> The blood-dimmed tide is loosed, and everywhere
> The ceremony of innocence is drowned;
> The best lack all conviction, while the worst
> Are full of passionate intensity.

In the novel, a new technique, the "stream of consciousness," prevailed briefly. Marcel Proust pioneered it in his monumental *Remembrance of Things Past* (1913–27), in which he abandoned narrative in favor of an apparent reconstruction of the thoughts and memories of the novel's protagonist. Virginia Woolf, the one great literary talent of Bloomsbury, experimented with it. But its greatest master was the Irish expatriate, James Joyce. His *Ulysses* (1921) was a minute reconstruction of a day in the life of a Dublin salesman, Leopold Bloom, organized around themes from Homer's *Odyssey*. Its occasional passages about sex prevented it from appearing in England or the United States, much less in Ireland. Banning, and its spread through copies smuggled from Paris, only enhanced its reputation. It was the most influential English novel of the century. In its sequel, *Finnegan's Wake* (1939), Joyce pushed his language beyond comprehensibility and left his audience behind.

On the Continent, Thomas Mann confirmed his position, acquired before the war, as Germany's greatest living man of letters. His monumental symbolic novel, *The Magic Mountain* (1924), was an ambiguous saga of good and evil that conveyed despair in the power of reason in human affairs. Despair in reason was a step forward for Mann. During the war, he had actively urged the rejection of reason, democratic politics, and the West in a long tract entitled *Reflections of an Unpolitical Man* (1918).

German writers of the "Expressionist" school experimented with a drama of unbridled emotion, Freudian symbolism, and Left politics. Expressionist

sons messily murdered their fathers and the other figures of authority that the lost war had discredited. The greatest talents of the school were Bertolt Brecht (1898–1956), and the novelist and short story writer Franz Kafka (1883–1926). Brecht soon exchanged Expressionism for Leninism. Kafka constructed a symbolic world in which fear, guilt, and the merciless arbitrariness of incomprehensible forces torture the isolated individual. Kafka's novella, "The Metamorphosis" (1915), sums up Kafka's view of humanity's fate in the modern world. His hero, Gregor Samsa, wakes up one morning and discovers that he has inexplicably become a giant cockroach.

In the visual arts and architecture, new schools proliferated. The Great War slaked Italian Futurism's thirst for violence and change; it emerged enfeebled. "Dada," a Parisian fashion of the teens and twenties, poked fun at art itself and celebrated the absurd and unpredictable. Its progeny, "Surrealism," sought to represent inner reality in paintings strewn with half-melted pocket watches and Freudian symbols. The center of excitement in the visual arts moved briefly from Paris to Berlin and Munich, thanks to Expressionist masters such as Paul Klee (1879–1940). And in architecture, Walter Gropius, Mies van der Rohe, Bruno Taut, and others secured the first large-scale commissions for the new functional architecture, the "international style." The architects at least were optimists; they sought to remake humanity by remaking its environment. The last was too ambitious a project—but they did revolutionize architecture and design.

Mass Culture and Its Critics

One source, beside the shock of the great war, of the despondency that afflicted many intellectuals in the 1920s was the appalling discovery that this was indeed the "age of the masses." A variety of German thinkers stigmatized democracy as the "rule of the inferior." Ortega y Gasset, a Spanish philosopher and literary critic, won immediate fame

The Bauhaus school of architecture and design, Dessau, Germany (1926).

with his denunciation of *The Revolt of the Masses* (1929). Ortega complained that unwashed legions, half-educated through universal primary schooling and given power through the vote, were besieging the citadel of Western civilization. The liberal elites born in the nineteenth century had ceased to lead; chaos had resulted.

The reason for that failure of leadership was obscure to Ortega. But it was plain enough. Liberals deplored as an affront to their own cultural standards or to human dignity the methods seemingly needed to exert leadership. Others were less squeamish. Georges Sorel, the pre-1914 French seer of revolution, had developed the concept of "political myths" that mobilized the masses. The French psychologist Gustave Le Bon (1841–1931) had argued that "the crowd" was "feminine" and had claimed that it demanded the domination of a charismatic male. And in the Anglo-Saxon countries, vast engines of publicity sold everything from soap to vacuum cleaners to wartime hatred of "the Hun." The foremost characteristic of the operators of that machinery was their contempt for the public they manipulated.

The "age of the masses" was thus to be an age of emotion, not reason. Advertising used the same techniques to sell a charismatic leader or a Lucky Strike. New media such as film, radio, and illustrated magazines proved especially effective at conveying and appealing to emotion. Politics in Fascist Italy and in Germany after 1933 took on quasi-religious overtones as vast regimented throngs hailed their leaders.

What most critics of interwar mass culture failed to remember was that historically speaking, the alternative to semiliteracy had been no literacy at all. Until the nineteenth century only narrow elites had fully enjoyed the written word. Its extension to the majority of the population inevitably involved a lowering of standards, by the standards of the elite. But that was not the end of the world; one answer to semiliteracy was better mass education. Nor was the thrust of the mass market to-ward the lowest common denominator an all-encompassing and uniform thrust.

The continuing rise in living standards, except during the Depression, did not invariably foster mediocrity and uniformity. It also permitted excellence and diversity. Bauhaus architecture and design was a genuine popular success. In film, German directors before 1933 created popular successes that were also works of art. Even Hollywood, which established an absolute dominance over the world film industry in the 1930s, occasionally made movies that were not totally frivolous. And in politics, as Roosevelt's radio talks demonstrated, genuine democrats could mobilize a mass public as effectively as the new barbarians.

The Revolt against Reason

War and Depression unleashed those barbarians. In Germany above all, defeat and revolution made anti-Semitic conspiracy theories seem plausible to a wide audience. The wartime propaganda of Tirpitz's *Vaterlandspartei* against the West, the Left, and the Jews found its logical continuation in scores of radical nationalist prophets and sects.

An eccentric Munich schoolmaster, Oswald Spengler (1880–1936), provided a pseudo-historical legitimation for the new barbarism of the racists and of the visionaries of "soldierly nationalism" such as Jünger. In the summer of 1918, Spengler published the first volume of a turgid 900-page work entitled *The Collapse of the West*. For Spengler, history was a vast cyclical process in which civilizations, the products of creative minorities of Nietzschean supermen, rose, decayed, and collapsed. The West was nearing the end of its cycle. Amid chaos and the brutal self-assertion of new creative minorities a new civilization might soon be born.

As history, Spengler's grandiose vision was oddly compelling although sometimes laughably distorted. As prophecy it proved almost self-fulfilling. The book's coincidence with Germany's defeat ensured its success. To many Germans, war and an unwanted revolution indeed seemed like the collapse of civilization. And in ensuing years, in works such as *Prussianism and Socialism* (1920) and "The Political Duties of German Youth" (1924), Spengler spelled out in detail the ruthless commitment he thought the new age demanded.

German philosophy added its authority to the chorus of unreason. Nietzsche had denounced Judeo-Christian values as a "slave morality" and had subordinated all morality to "life." His most prominent successor, Martin Heidegger (1889–1976), altogether denied that moral values had a rational basis. In Heidegger's *Being and Time* (1927), the individual was utterly alone, imprisoned in time. The only certainties were *Angst* (usually translated, too strongly, as "dread") and death. Only by living in full awareness of *Angst* and death could a select few define themselves and live "authentically"—a claim that ironically smacked of moral judgment.

This quest for "authenticity"—in a world where values apparently have no foundation or validity outside the individual—had curious consequences. It often led to self-affirmation through radical politics: the more radical, the more self-affirming. Heidegger himself made his choice in 1933. Academic freedom, he announced in his inaugural speech as rector of Freiburg University, was "inauthentic." Like Spengler, he enthusiastically urged German youth to serve German radical nationalism and a leader. Unlike Spengler, Heidegger had a specific leader in mind—Adolf Hitler.

Others chose different leaders. Bertolt Brecht and the literary critic György Lukács (1885–1971) picked Stalin, to whom Lukács made embarrassing obeisance. Lukács's commitment to an irrational political faith did not make him self-conscious; he later wrote an entire volume lovingly demolishing German "irrationalism" from the romantics to Heidegger and Hitler. Brecht, in one of his Depression plays, used his unmatched command of German to celebrate the omniscience and ruthlessness of the Leninist "vanguard of the masses" in verses that the German Communist Party found excessively enthusiastic and frank.

Even in strongholds of middle-class values such as Britain and the United States, the war, the Depression, and the crises of the 1930s prompted intellectuals to irrational enthusiasms. Freud, although he claimed to be a rationalist, undermined reason through his faith in the overwhelming power of the savage forces he saw in the unconscious mind. Those who nevertheless retained a faith in "progress" and reason tended to lean leftward. Lincoln Steffens, a crusading American journalist, returned in 1919 from Russia with a jubilant announcement: "I been over into the future, and it works!" He was the first of many. Widespread loss of faith in the future of Western society engendered an irrational desire to believe in progress *somewhere*. Visiting Western liberals noisily embraced the Soviet Union and resolutely ignored all

Spengler on the Political Duties of German Youth   1924

Whether one is right or wrong—that doesn't amount to much in history. Whether or not he is superior to his adversary in a practical way, that is what decides whether he will be successful. . . . To be honorable and nothing else—that's not enough for our future. . . . To train oneself as material for great leaders, in proud self-denial, prepared for personal sacrifice, that is also a German virtue. And, given the case that, in the hard times ahead, strong men will appear, leaders to whom we must entrust our fate, then they must have something upon which they can rely. They need a generation such as Bismarck did not find, which appreciates their kind of action and does not reject it for romantic reasons, a dedicated band of followers who have, by way of long and serious self-training, come to the point of understanding the necessary and do not—as would doubtless be true today—reject it as un-German.

From Gordon A. Craig, *Germany 1866–1945* (Oxford: Oxford University Press, 1978), p. 491.

evidence that contradicted the facade behind which their jolly Soviet hosts hid a reality of mass executions and starvation. In the mid-1930s American Communism successfully wooed some disenchanted liberals; it claimed to be "twentieth century Americanism."

War and Depression together created a disorienting and demoralizing world. Empires fell. Political and social landmarks crumbled. Religious, moral, political, and even scientific certainties undermined in the nineteenth century now collapsed. An exaggerated faith in the power of reason gave way to the fanatical celebration and cynical manipulation of emotion. The "best," the defenders of Western civilization and of democracy, lacked the conviction to squarely face the "passionate intensity" of their enemies, the nationalist-racist and Marxist-Leninist dictatorships. The 1920s were no golden age, even in western Europe. The 1930s opened with war in East Asia. They closed with the greatest war in history.

Suggestions for Further Reading

Interwar Politics

A good introduction to interwar Europe is R. J. Sontag, *A Broken World, 1919–1939* (1971). S. Marks, *The Illusion of Peace: International Relations in Europe, 1918–1933* (1976), is excellent on relations between states; for eastern Europe see C. A. Macartney and A. W. Palmer, *Independent Eastern Europe* (1962). On Britain, A. J. P. Taylor, *English History, 1914–1945* (1965), is highly readable; see also M. Muggeridge, *The Thirties* (1940), and G. Orwell, *Down and Out in Paris and London* (1933), and *The Road to Wigan Pier* (1937). On France, see especially P. Bernard and H. Dubief, *The Decline of the Third Republic, 1914–1938* (1985), and A. Adamthwaite, *France and the Coming of the Second World War* (1977). On the United States, W. E. Leuchtenburg, *The Perils of Prosperity, 1914–1932* (1958), is still rewarding, but see also E. W. Hawley, *The Great War and the Search for a Modern Order* (1979); for the 1930s, R. S. McElwaine, *The Great Depression: America, 1929–1941* (1984), is excellent. For Germany's brief democratic experiment, see especially A. J. Nicholls, *Weimar and the Rise of Hitler* (1968); E. Eyck, *A History of the Weimar Republic* (1967); and the relevant portion of G. Craig, *Germany, 1866–1945* (1978).

The Great Depression

For the causes and course of the Great Depression, J. K. Galbraith, *The Great Crash, 1929* (1955), and C. Kindleberger, *The World in Depression, 1929–1939* (1973), are useful; D. Landes, *The Unbound Prometheus* (1972), places the event in long-term perspective. For events in the colonial empires, see especially E. Monroe, *Britain's Moment in the Middle East, 1914–1956* (1963); A. Williams, *Britain and France in the Middle East and North Africa, 1914–1967* (1968); B. N. Pandey, *The Break-Up of British India* (1969); and J. M. Brown, *Modern India: the Origins of an Asian Democracy* (1985). On China, see J. K. Fairbank, *The Great Chinese Revolution, 1800–1985* (1986); *The Cambridge History of China*, Vol. 12, Part I (1983); and J. E. Sheridan, *China in Disintegration* (1975). For Japan, see especially W. G. Beasley, *Japanese Imperialism, 1894–1945* (1987), and J. B. Crowley, *Japan's Quest for Autonomy* (1966).

Culture Between Two Wars

On the intellectual impact of the war, the broad survey of R. Wohl, *The Generation of 1914* (1979), and the relevant portions of H. S. Hughes, *Consciousness and Society: The Reorientation of European Social Thought, 1890–1930* (1958), are excellent. For the sharp contrast between Britain and Germany, compare the writers discussed in P. Fussell, *The Great War and Modern Memory* (1975), with the widely shared views expressed in E. Jünger, *The Storm of Steel* (1920). H. S. Hughes, *Oswald Spengler: A Critical Estimate* (1952), is perhaps too kind to Spengler. For Germany's decisive contributions to interwar high culture, see especially P. Gay, *Weimar Culture* (1968); J. Willett, *Art and Politics in the Weimar Period: The New Sobriety, 1917–1933* (1979); and B. M. Lane, *Architecture and Politics in Germany, 1918–1945* (1968). For the many interwar intellectuals who despaired of their own societies and sought solace in Moscow, see P. Hollander, *Political Pilgrims: The Travels of Western Intellectuals to the Soviet Union, China, and Cuba, 1928–1978* (1981).

32
The Totalitarian States

*B*y 1933 the demoralized democracies faced not only a militant Japan, but three great dictatorships: the Soviet Union of Joseph Stalin, the Fascist Italy of Benito Mussolini, and the National Socialist Germany of Adolf Hitler. Dictatorship was not new. Lenin, an expert, defined it as "a power that is not limited by any laws, not bound by any rules, and based directly on force." Despots from the god-emperors of the ancient world to the tsars of Russia had ruled without laws or rules that limited the sovereign. But custom, the merciful inefficiency of their bureaucracies, and the inadequacies of the technologies at their command had limited their power.

Robespierre and the Committee of Public Safety had briefly wielded, in the name of the General Will, power more total than that of any preceding European state. Now, in the twentieth century, war and revolution made possible the perfection of the dictatorship of the General Will sketched out in 1793–94. It soon acquired a name. Giovanni Amendola, an Italian liberal later murdered by the thugs of the Italian dictatorship, coined in 1923–24 the adjective *"totalitario"* to describe Fascist election methods. Mussolini happily

Opposite: Totalitarian mass politics: Hitler (on platform, center) greets his following at a 1936 party rally.

plagiarized it in 1925; he relished its brutal sound.

"Totalitarianism" thus became a generic term for the dictatorship of the age of mass politics, a dictatorship that set itself a limitless goal: *total power over the individual*. That goal distinguished it from earlier despotisms, and from "authoritarian" regimes such as the dictatorships of interwar eastern Europe or Latin America, which sought above all to conserve their power. The totalitarian states sought instead to create a "new man." And their external goals were almost equally limitless, for the example of freedom anywhere was a mortal threat for all such regimes.

Yet distinctions did exist between the three regimes, despite their frequent imitation of one another and their ultimate collaboration in producing the Second World War. Russia, the only Marxist-Leninist state of the three, was also the most economically and socially backward. Russia's middle class was small and the Orthodox Church relatively weak, even before the Bolsheviks decided to exterminate the one and virtually abolish the other. And Bolshevik power came from victory in a merciless civil war; from the beginning it was "based directly on force." Lenin and his successor Stalin thus faced none of the constitutional or social obstacles to total power present in the more developed societies of the West.

Mussolini and Hitler, by contrast, came to power in apparent legality in societies that in theory still had parliamentary regimes. They faced mighty entrenched interests and institutions—armies, industrialists, and churches—whose assistance was necessary for the consolidation and expansion of the regime. In Russia the regime was free from birth to begin the total transformation of Russian society accomplished by the late 1930s. All that it lacked was an implacable will, and that Stalin supplied. In Italy and Germany the despots had to purchase their freedom. The method they chose was war.

RUSSIA: FROM REVOLUTION TO GENOCIDE

From Tsarist to Communist Autocracy

Within five years of the collapse of tsarism in 1917, Russia was once again an autocracy. After October 1917, Lenin systematically crushed all opposition—the short-lived Constitutional Assembly, the other left-wing parties, and the counterrevolutionary "Whites." The workers' Soviets withered away; the secret police (CHEKA) swelled to 30,000 and the Red Army to 5.3 million. Soon all that remained of the workers' Soviets was the name, which the Party appropriated for its new state: the Union of Soviet Socialist Republics.

In 1921, with the civil war against the Whites virtually won, the Bolsheviks faced still graver crises. War, revolution, and civil war had cost Russia over 10 percent of its 1913 population of 159 million. At least 2 million had died in the First World War, a million had emigrated, up to 10 million had died in the civil war and accompanying famines, and as many as 5 million had perished in drought and famine in 1921–22. Between 1917 and 1920, food shortages, the brutalities of Bolshevik mismanagement, and civil-war chaos had cut Russia's "proletariat" in half, from 3 million to 1.5 million. The industrial work force, recently recruited from the peasantry, simply returned to the villages. The peasantry itself fiercely resented the ruthless Bolshevik confiscation of crops to feed the cities. Externally, defeat in Poland in 1920 and the failure of world revolution to materialize meant isolation and peril.

In February 1921 strikes against the self-proclaimed "workers' state" swept Petrograd. In March, sailors at Kronstadt, the nearby naval base that had once furnished fanatical recruits to Bolshevism, rose against Bolshevism on behalf of the half-starved remnant of Russia's workers. Millions of peasants in central Russia were already in armed revolt against the exactions of "war communism," the forced requisition of food. The regime appeared close to collapse.

Lenin and the Party acted. Mass arrests clamped Petrograd down. Trotsky besieged Kronstadt and annihilated the sailors at the cost of 10,000 Red Army casualties. Lenin outlawed internal "factionalism" and reproved those comrades who still took seriously the Party's claim to represent the *existing* Russian proletariat. In the Party's eyes, the workers and Kronstadt sailors who demanded free elections to the Soviets had ceased to be proletarians.

To placate the peasantry, the only great social group the Party was not yet strong enough to crush by force alone, Lenin and his associates retreated from "war communism." The "new economic policy" or NEP of 1921–28 restored a degree of free enterprise to the countryside and even to industry. It was a recognition of reality—external isolation and internal weakness—that ended for the moment Lenin's attempt to force the pace of history and leap directly from tsarism to Communism.

The NEP was an economic success. Agricultural production passed 1913 levels in 1924. Enterprising peasants prospered. By 1926–27 even the cities had begun to revive. But the NEP proved a brief respite. In May 1922, Lenin suffered the first of a series of incapacitating strokes. In January 1924 he died. By that point the struggle for the succession had already begun; Trotsky was the leading candidate. But his Menshevik past, Red Army ties, and lack of modesty alienated a fiercely clannish Party that feared "Bonapartism"—the rule of a successful general. Trotsky's rival was that self-effacing bureaucrat from Georgia in the Caucasus, Joseph Stalin, a former seminary pupil and revolutionary bank robber. Lenin had placed Stalin in charge of the central Party machine, and thus of recruitment. Stalin soon allied himself with Trotsky's rivals on the Party

Trotsky, victorious Commissar for War, reviews his troops (1920).

"Left," Grigorii Zinoviev and Lev Kamenev.

Stalin craftily cloaked his ambition in mock humility, and easily deflected Lenin's dying demand that the Party demote the uncouth Georgian, who was "too rude," a fault "insupportable in a general secretary." Stalin's deluded allies of the "Left" found him less threatening than Trotsky, and the new Party rank and file with whom Stalin was rapidly swamping the "Old Bolsheviks" owed their careers to him alone.

Stalin was careful always to speak in the name of the Party while consolidating his own power. Since Lenin had forbidden "factionalism," opponents of Stalin were automatically opponents of the Party. They thereby forfeited both legitimacy and self-confidence; Stalin used the Party's cult of unity against them to force humiliating recantations and "self-criticisms." The CHEKA, renamed GPU, then OGPU, and finally NKVD, became Stalin's ally and chosen instrument; it soon overshadowed the Party. And Stalin had Lenin embalmed, and placed on exhibit as a holy relic of the new state religion: "Leninism." Petrograd became Leningrad; all across the Soviet Union statues of the prophet arose. The cult of Lenin legitimated Bolshevik power and created the role that Stalin himself was soon to fill.

In 1925 Zinoviev and Kamenev led the pack against Trotsky, and expelled him from his Party and army offices. In 1926 Stalin turned on his allies and demoted them with the help of the Party "Right" formed around the theorist Nikolai Bukharin. Trotsky had urged continued conflict: "permanent revolution" abroad and, at home, increased pressure on the peasants to squeeze from them capital for a crash industrialization program to achieve the Communist utopia. Zinoviev, though personally fiercely hostile to Trotsky, had in essence agreed. Stalin and Bukharin triumphed within the Party by asserting a seemingly moderate course: "socialism in one country" and continuance of the NEP.

Once Trotsky, Zinoviev, and Kamenev were disposed of, Stalin took over their domestic policy. The naive Bukharin suddenly discovered that Stalin was "an unprincipled intriguer who . . . changes his theories depending on whom he wants to get rid of at any particular moment." Terrified, Bukharin belatedly sought alliance with Kamenev and Zinoviev: Stalin was "a new Ghenghis Khan; he will strangle us all." In 1927–28, Stalin began warning that the Soviet Union faced war at the hands of the encircling capitalist powers. A five-year plan of crash industrialization was therefore imperative. But the NEP was already failing to provide enough grain for the towns, as the peasantry resisted Party attempts to keep agricultural prices artificially low. Stalin could therefore argue that the NEP, if it continued, would make it impossible to extract from the peasants the surplus needed to finance industrialization and feed a larger factory work force. Party and OGPU pressure on the most prosperous peasants—the so-called *kulaks* ("fists")—increased.

By early 1929, Stalin had forced Trotsky into exile (and had him murdered in 1940, after expunging his name from the history of the Bolshevik Revolution). Stalin then demoted Bukharin and the "Right" by exposing their attempts to ally with the discredited "Left," and ended the NEP. Lenin's party had erected a new autocracy over Russia. Stalin, whom his press increasingly hailed as the "Great Leader," was now close to erecting an autocracy over the Party. In the absence of laws and rules, Bolshevik dictatorship over the proletariat was swiftly becoming the dictatorship of an individual. And that individual, because he commanded the instrument of terror and embodied the purported will of the proletariat and

Stalin Demands Crash Industrialization

Stalin shrewdly blended Marxism-Leninism and Russian nationalism in his rationale for crash industrialization. He advanced his thesis most forcefully in a speech of early 1931.

To reduce the tempo [of industrialization] would mean to fall behind. And those who fall behind get beaten. But we do not want to be beaten. No, we refuse to be beaten! One feature of the history of old Russia was the continual beating she suffered because of her backwardness. She was beaten by the Mongol Khans. She was beaten by the Turkish beys. She was beaten by the Swedish feudal lords. She was beaten by the Polish and Lithuanian gentry. She was beaten by the British and French capitalists. She was beaten by the Japanese barons. All beat her— because of her backwardness, military backwardness, cultural backwardness, industrial backwardness, and agricultural backwardness. They beat her because to do so was profitable and could be done with impunity. . . . It is the jungle law of capitalism. You are backward, you are weak—therefore you are wrong; hence, you can be beaten and enslaved. You are mighty— therefore you are right. . . . We are fifty or a hundred years behind the advanced countries. We must make good this distance in ten years. Either we do it, or we shall be crushed.

From Basil Dmytryshyn, *USSR: A Concise History* (New York: Charles Scribner's Sons, 1978), p. 158.

the supposed laws of history, could do anything he pleased.

The Great Famine, 1929–34

On December 27, 1929, as the first Five Year Plan went into effect, Stalin informed Russia of its fate: "either we go backward to capitalism or forward to socialism. What does this mean? It means that after a policy that consisted in limiting the exploitative tendencies of the *kulaks*, we have switched to a policy of liquidating the *kulaks* as a class."

Crash industrialization and the consolidation of Soviet power, for Stalin, required the transformation of the landowning peasantry into a rural proletariat—serfs of the Soviet state—working the land with state-owned machinery. The goal of "complete collectivization" that Stalin announced in December 1929 would end forever the mortal internal threat that Lenin had discerned: "Capitalism begins in the village market-place." It would also provide external might, to defend and advance the Revolution. With collectivization, Stalin made good his claim to be Lenin's true heir—despite the doubts Lenin had expressed about Stalin's manners. Stalin proposed to force the pace of history and complete the revolution that Lenin had launched in 1917.

Nor was Stalin's choice of the word *liquidate* an accident. The Party activists, army, and OGPU troops who forced the peasants into state-controlled collective farms received orders to designate fixed quotas of *kulaks* and "*kulak* henchmen." Between 5 and 20 percent of the rural population, depending on the area, suffered deportation to Siberia and Central Asia. Most of those deported died, either on the march or under the care of the OGPU's newly established "Main Administration of Corrective Labor Camps," best known by its sinister acronym, GULAG. The remaining peasants resisted. They slaughtered and ate their livestock rather than deliver it to

---

The "Mutability of the Past"

In his novel *1984*, published in 1949, the British essayist and novelist George Orwell (1903–50) depicted a nightmare totalitarian future that drew on Stalin's attempts to *control the past*.

The mutability of the past is the central tenet of Ingsoc [Orwell's fictional state ideology]. Past events, it is argued, have no objective existence, but survive only in written records and in human memories. The past is whatever the records and the memories agree upon. And since the Party is in full control of all records, and in equally full control of the minds of its members, it follows that the past is whatever the Party chooses to make it. It also follows that though the past is alterable, it never has been altered in any specific instance. For when it has been recreated in whatever shape is needed at the moment, then this new version *is* the past, and no different past can ever have existed. . . . At all times the Party is in possession of the absolute truth, and clearly the absolute can never have been different from what it is now. . . .

From George Orwell, *1984* (New York: Signet, 1961), p. 176.

---

the collective farms. They refused to plant more than a bare minimum of crops. Villages and entire regions defied the regime. Red Army sweeps and mass executions gradually subdued them.

Stalin's war on the Soviet Union's 120 million peasants culminated in a devastating famine in the Ukraine and elsewhere in 1931–32. Stalin barred relief shipments, to bring home to the peasantry the cost of defying him; Soviet food *exports* during the famine exceeded those during the prosperous years of the NEP. With macabre relish Stalin publicly commanded merriment: "Life has become more joyous, comrades; life has become gayer." Privately he remarked much later, to Winston Churchill, that 10 million had suffered death or deportation. Soviet demographers later admitted a population loss of 7.5 million; the true figure may have been as high as 15 million. Not accidentally, figures for livestock deaths—149.4 million head between 1929 and

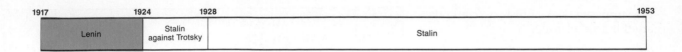

1917		1924	1928		1953
Lenin		Stalin against Trotsky	Stalin		

1934—are more readily available than those for people.

Stalin's war on the peasantry so devastated Soviet agriculture that in per capita terms it produced scarcely more in 1953 than it had in 1913. The catastrophic losses to agriculture probably exceeded the gains of the rapidly expanding industrial sector. Conciliation of the peasantry and continuation of the NEP, as Bukharin had urged, would in all likelihood have led to a higher over-all rate of economic growth than Stalin actually achieved.

But the terror-famine achieved its political purpose. The Party broke the one great social force in Russia. By 1932 the state had seized 88 percent of Russia's farmland; by 1937 collectivization was almost total. And Stalin did extract the labor and some of the needed capital for the Five Year Plan. According to some estimates, "de-kulakized" slave laborers furnished over 5 percent of the Soviet labor force by 1933. Peasants fled the land for the industrial cities and mines of the Don Basin and the Urals. Food extracted from the peasantry at gunpoint helped the regime to more than triple Russia's industrial work force. Terror and propaganda whipped the exhausted workers onward, amid immense waste and confusion. Vast hydroelectric dams and steel mills arose, based on technology bought from the West with exported grain and with gold that camp inmates dug from the arctic tundra. The first Five Year Plan increased Soviet capital-goods production two and a half times. At the "Party Congress of Victors" in January 1934 Stalin savored a success he had bought through the crippling and stunting of his society: "The line of the Party has triumphed."

Joseph Stalin at his desk: "To choose one's victims, to prepare one's plans minutely, to slake an implacable vengeance, and then to go to bed . . . there is nothing sweeter in the world."

The Great Terror, 1934–39

As the crisis of collectivization passed, Stalin nevertheless found himself under attack. In 1932 opponents circulated a long document full of devastating criticism of his wasteful and erratic economic leadership, and of the Party's alienation of the working class it claimed to incarnate. Stalin responded with orders to scrutinize the Party membership and purge those suspected of opposition. But he failed to persuade his colleagues on the Party's ruling committee, the Politburo, to redefine dissent within the Party as "counterrevolutionary activity," which carried the penalty of death.

That impasse ended on December 1, 1934. A dissident Party member, with the apparent complicity of the NKVD, assassinated Sergei Kirov, boss of Leningrad and rising young star of the Party. Much later, after Stalin's death, Soviet leaders hinted broadly that Stalin was behind the murder. It gave him a pretext to clamp down once more. Having enserfed the peasantry, he now set as his goal the destruction of the doubters and of all *potential* sources of future opposition. Hitler had set the example that June with a massacre of associates who had become politically inconvenient (see p. 923).

In the aftermath of Kirov's assassination, the NKVD under Stalin's personal direction received the power to shoot summarily anyone it pleased. It soon discovered a mythical "terrorist center" in Leningrad. In early 1935 it dredged up Zinoviev and Kamenev for the first of a series of show trials, an art form already perfected in trials of Socialist Revolutionaries, Mensheviks, and foreign engineers falsely accused of sabotage. Calls went out to the Party to unmask "Trotskyites" and "Zinovievites." Soviet law, a flexible instrument, soon provided swift death not only for alleged spies and "parasites," but also for those who had knowledge of their activities and failed to denounce them—including children of 12 years or older. The families and children of those arrested became hostages, liable to punishment—a further extension of the genocidal notion of "class justice" that Dzerzhinsky and Latsis of the CHEKA had pioneered. *Pravda* began to carry stories that praised children who had reported their parents to the NKVD.

In August 1936, amid mounting anxiety, Stalin announced a new Soviet constitution that contained lavish guarantees of individual freedoms. But woe to those who failed to exercise those freedoms "in accordance with the interests of the workers and for the purpose of strengthening the socialist system." The same month, Zinoviev and Kamenev obligingly admitted to having planned Stalin's assassination; the court had them shot. Terror became all-pervasive.

But Stalin was not content. He accused the NKVD leadership of footdragging and moved the appointment of a new man, the "bloodthirsty dwarf," Nikolai Yezhov. In January 1937 Yezhov mounted yet another Moscow show trial, of the fancifully named "terrorist counterrevolutionary Trotskyite-Zinovievite bloc." Mass arrests and lesser trials occupied the rest of the year. The NKVD and its informers feverishly invented conspiracies, beat prisoners into confessions that implicated ever more suspects, and shot in the prison cellars those who were no longer of use.

Stalin also turned on the Red Army, which he apparently feared might threaten his power in the event of an ever more probable European war. The generals proved tougher than the Party; they refused to confess to being in league with Germany and Japan.

Stalin had his own high command shot in secret in June and July 1937, and announced the executions after the event.

The last great trial, in March 1938, was that of the so-called "bloc of anti-Soviet rightists and Trotskyites." It included a wide range of victims, from Bukharin to Genrikh Yagoda, the ex-head of the NKVD whom Stalin had replaced in 1936 for insufficient zeal. Old Bolsheviks confessed to sabotaging butter production with ground glass and to conspiring with Trotsky, Germany, Japan, Britain, and Poland. Western observers, including Roosevelt's ambassador and the correspondent of the *New York Times*, swallowed these absurd tales whole. Bukharin was puzzling, however. He confessed to almost everything, then implicitly retracted. Above all, he refused to admit to having plotted Lenin's murder, as Stalin's vindictive prosecutor, Andrei Vishinsky, alleged. The court had Bukharin shot with the rest, but he had marred the illusion of guilt that Stalin sought to create.

The great terror, like the terror-famine that preceded it, accomplished its objective. It remade the Party. Seventy percent of the Central Committee of 1934 perished; Stalin wiped out the leading Old Bolsheviks, and any alternative within the Party to his own domination. Terror remade the armed forces. Half of the officer corps, 35,000 men, fell victim: 3 of 5 marshals of the Soviet Union, 13 of 15 army commanders, 57 of 80 corps commanders, 70 of 190 division commanders, all 11 vice commissars for war, and all 8 admirals. And only 10 percent of those destroyed in the great terror were members of the Party and army. The rest were victims of chance associations, of neighbors' denunciations, of family relationships to suspects, of the envy of subordinates at work, of membership in national minorities. The victims of Stalin's genocide died not because of anything they had done, but because of what they were. They perished *by categories*, from *kulaks* and "*kulak* henchmen," to Ukrainians, to Old Bolsheviks, to suspects of "Trotskyism," to relatives of suspects, to individuals whose only "crime" was that they belonged to a generation that remembered Russia before 1917.

The replacements of those "purged" were younger, with fewer such memories than their predecessors. They were unlikely to question Stalin's leadership. Above all they were bound to Stalin: they owed their rapid promotions to the vacancies that he and his NKVD had created. In many cases they had helped, by opportune words to the NKVD about their superiors—for Stalin was not the sole author of the terror. He had millions of helpers, bound irrevocably to their master by fear, gratitude, and complicity. Stalin had created a new ruling class in his own image.

The cost was high. The secret 1937 census, according to some accounts, showed that the Soviet Union had 21.5 million people less than the second Five Year Plan had forecast. Stalin, furious, had the demographers denounced as a "serpent's nest of traitors" and shot or sent to GULAG for having allegedly "exerted themselves to diminish the numbers of the population of the Soviet Union." Stalin reserved that privilege to himself. By 1939, the GULAG concentration camps held an estimated 10.4 million people—10 percent of the Soviet labor force. The death rate in the camps was as high as 10 percent each year. By 1940, Stalin's genocide had through famine, terror, and slave labor killed between 12.7 and 22.1 million people—on top of the immense losses between 1914 and 1922. He had also signed a pact with Hitler.

ITALY: FROM DICTATORSHIP TO EXPANSION

To achieve total power in a developed Western society was a challenge more difficult than that facing Stalin. But the First World War created conditions that made it thinkable. The war into which Antonio Salandra, Sidney Sonnino, and King Victor Emmanuel III had flung Italy in 1915 caught the country as it made the delicate transition to mass politics after Giolitti had greatly enlarged the suffrage in 1912.

The Crisis of Liberal Italy

War and the example of the Russian revolution mobilized the masses; the 1919 election destroyed the hegemony of the Liberals. Two great mass parties, the Catholic People's Party (*Popolari*) and the Socialists, henceforth commanded between them a majority in parliament. But unlike Weimar Germany, the mass parties refused to coalesce and rule. Socialists embraced the half-understood example of Lenin. The *Popolari*, under Vatican influence, had in part entered politics to counter the Socialist threat. Parliamentary deadlock and a series of weak Liberal cabinets resulted. And for the Right, the Liberal regime had lost its small stock of prestige when the Allies at Paris had "mutilated" Italy's victory by refusing to concede Sonnino's colonial and Balkan claims.

Outside parliament, the Socialists confusedly took the offensive in the "two red years" of 1919–20. Their agricultural unions and political machines organized the landless laborers and soon ruled Italy's richest farming region, the Po Valley. Landowners who refused to hire labor at the rates and in the numbers that the Socialists decreed suffered boycotts, arson, mutilation of livestock, and worse. Factory and transport workers struck repeatedly. But incessant Socialist talk of revolution, violence against landowners, and public abuse of veterans as warmongers and capitalist dupes inevitably backfired.

In October 1914 Benito Mussolini, whom Lenin had seen as the future leader of Italian Socialism, had quarreled with the party over its refusal to support war. Mussolini, the brutal and charismatic son of a village blacksmith, had agitated for war, then served in the infantry until wounded. In March 1919, he founded a movement to carry the war into politics: the *Fasci di Combattimento* ("combat leagues"). Its initial recruits were a curious mixture of former shock troops, wartime junior officers, nationalist students, and ex-socialists who had opted for war in 1914–15. "Fascist" ideology was and remained amorphous, but its principal components were two: fierce hostility to the Left and a resentful expansionist nationalism.

The Socialist offensive in the Po Valley flatlands and agitation by the Slovenes of newly annexed Trieste made the summer of 1920 "the hour of Fascism." Fascist gangs in black shirts or wartime field-gray attacked Socialists and Slavs with clubs, knives, pistols, and hand grenades. Landowners and the occasional industrialist happily contributed funds. Army commands secretly provided trucks and weapons. The numerous landowning peasants, whom the Socialists had alienated with talk of collectivization of the land, joined the Fascist *squadre*. Some Liberals in Rome deplored Fascist violence, but lacked the resolve to restore order. Other Liberals, among them Giovanni Giolitti, saw the Fascists as a healthy patriotic reaction against the excesses of the Socialists and the encroachments of the *Popolari* on the Liberal state.

By the summer of 1921 Fascism had smashed the Socialists in the Po Valley and Tuscany, and had set itself the task of conquering Italy. In Rome, Fascist deputies took the battle into parliament thanks to an electoral alliance that Giolitti offered. In the countryside, "punitive expeditions" of truck-borne blackshirts grew ever larger and more ferociously effective. But mutual hostility between Socialists and *Popolari* still prevented them from joining hands against the Fascist threat.

By October 1922 Liberal Italy was in dissolution. Right Liberals such as Salandra sought to co-opt Mussolini, to tame him by admission to government.

In a two-track maneuver that combined an insurrectionary "March on Rome" with negotiations with Salandra and others, Mussolini demanded the prime ministership. The last Liberal cabinet feebly attempted to persuade the King to command the army to restore order. Victor Emmanuel III consulted his generals, who answered that the army would do its duty, but that it would be better not to put it to the test. King, army, and Right Liberals chose Mussolini over a civil war that they feared would strengthen the Left. They made Mussolini prime minister of Italy on October 31, 1922.

The Fascist State

As Mussolini admitted privately in 1924, the "March on Rome" was no revolution: "The revolution comes later." He initially had no majority in parliament and therefore took fellow-traveling Liberals and *Popolari* into his cabinet. He depended on Italy's industrialists and on foreign bankers to keep the economy from faltering. And to the end his authority ultimately derived from the king who had appointed him. The Fascist regime remained a "dyar-

Mussolini, surrounded by the commanders of the "March on Rome," strikes a pose before assuming power.

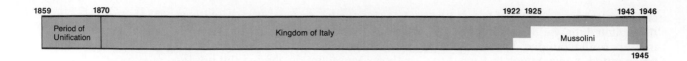

chy,'' a system in which dictator and king shared power. The regime was thus the least "totalitarian" of the three great dictatorships: Mussolini's "NEP" lasted until 1935–36.

But Mussolini nevertheless aspired to total power and moved to achieve it by stages. From the beginning he chipped away both at opponents and at conservative "flankers" who sought to use him merely to tame the Left. Fascist violence continued in the provinces; a new electoral law guaranteed a Fascist majority in the 1924 elections.

That victory led Mussolini to overreach. His most conspicuous opponent, Giacomo Matteotti, rightly claimed to parliament in June 1924 that the Fascist election majority was the product of force and fraud. A few days later, Mussolini's "CHEKA," as he only half-jokingly called his bodyguard of thugs, took Matteotti for a fatal ride in the country. Bystanders noted down the license plate of Matteotti's abductors; the police, not yet fully under Fascist control, traced the vehicle to Mussolini's entourage. The perfect political crime had failed.

Mussolini himself preserved what a later age was to call "plausible deniability." Pressure for his resignation nevertheless mounted among Liberals in the cabinet and in parliament. Mussolini privately railed at the Italian people's "absurd fuss" over the death of one man. Then and later he secretly envied the Bolsheviks, who faced no such constraints.

Socialists, *Popolari*, and Left Liberals, briefly united, seceded from parliament in protest. That was suicidal; it split the opposition between those who seceded and those who stayed. Mussolini bought off with concessions some of the Liberals remaining in parliament. He faced down waverers in the cabinet by threatening to fight rather

than yield power. As in 1922, he offered the Italian establishment a simple choice: him or civil war.

On January 3, 1925, with the King's acquiescence, Mussolini announced that he would remain in power indefinitely. The police closed the opposition press. A succession of botched attempts to assassinate Mussolini soon gave welcome pretexts to rule by decree and outlaw all opposition parties. Within the Fascist party, Mussolini abolished the few shreds of internal democracy that survived from 1919–21: "The Revolution has one Leader." By 1928 he had grafted the party into the state and had given the party's highest organ, the Grand Council of Fascism, power to regulate the succession to the throne. He created a Fascist youth movement to imbue the coming generations with a brutish nationalism and a pagan "sense of virility, of power, of conquest."

Mussolini also secured a prize that had eluded his Liberal predecessors: a settlement of Italy's festering quarrel with the Church. The Lateran Pact of February 1929 created a Vatican City mini-state and gave the Vatican a large sum in Italian state bonds as indemnity for the territory seized in 1870; a Concordat between Church and state made Catholicism the state religion. In return, Pope Pius XI hailed Mussolini as "the man whom Providence has placed in Our path." That blessing and the enthusiastic support of the rural clergy for the regime made Mussolini's position unassailable. A plebiscite and one-party election in March 1929 gave Mussolini an overwhelming and mostly genuine majority, and returned a black-shirted parliament. The dictatorship rested on monarchy, military, and police, but also on the acclamation of the masses and the blessings of the Church.

Mussolini Breaks Through: Ethiopia and After

Yet control of government and the growing cult of the *Duce* was not enough. In 1925 Mussolini had expressed many of his ultimate goals in a speech to the party. Fascism's "fierce totalitarian will" would "'fascistize' the nation, so that tomorrow Italian and Fascist, more or less like Italian and Catholic, will be the same thing." He also discerned a method for achieving that goal. Like the Girondin orator Isnard, who in 1792 had foreseen a war "indispensable for completing the revolution," Mussolini saw a connection between war and revolution. In 1914–15 he had demanded a "revolutionary war." That war had destroyed Liberal Italy and placed him in power. Only more war could make that power total.

And from the extremists of Italy's Nationalist party and from his navy, Mussolini acquired a vision of Italy's goals in that war. "A nation," he informed a group of high officers in 1926–27, "that has no free access to the sea cannot be considered a free nation; a nation that has no free access to the oceans cannot be considered a great power. Italy must become a great power." Britain and France, and Italy's ties to the world market, stood in the way of Mediterranean domination and of what Mussolini later described as Italy's "march to the ocean." By 1923–24, if not before, Mussolini had already foreseen that a vengeful nationalist Germany would be Italy's most promising ally in that march.

Waiting for Germany was tedious. Between 1922 and 1931 Mussolini crushed with massacres and concentration camps the Arabs of Libya, whom the Liberal state had been unable to subdue. He dabbled with plans for attacking Turkey, and sponsored Croat and Macedonian terrorist forays against neighboring Yugoslavia. But British disapproval, Italy's economic and financial weakness, and the Depression forced Mussolini to sham a deep love of peace—but the Depres-

> # Mussolini: War, Revolution, and Empire   1925
>
> At times I look with favor in the idea of [creating] generations in the laboratory, of creating, in other words, the class of the warriors, who are always ready to die, the class of the inventors, who pursue the secrets of the mysteries [of nature]; the class of judges; the class of the great captains of industry; of the great governors. It is through this sort of methodical selection that one creates the great elites that in turn establish empires. . . . War and revolution are two terms that are almost always linked. Either war produces revolution or it is revolution that leads to war. Even the strategy of the two movements is alike: as in war, in revolution you do not always attack. Sometimes you must make more or less strategic retreats. Sometimes you must rest for long periods on positions you have conquered. But the goal is there: empire.
>
> Speech to the Fascist party congress, June 22, 1925, from *Opera Omnia di Benito Mussolini* (Florence: La Fenice, 1956), Vol. 21, pp. 362–63 (translation by M. Knox).

sion also ended the foreign loans that bound Fascist Italy to the status quo.

In early 1933, as Hitler came to power, Mussolini briefly thought he had blackmailed the French into abandoning their support of their Yugoslav ally, a Mussolini target since the 1920s. Then the king and generals vetoed a

Mussolini harangues a Roman crowd, 1931.

Balkan war that would risk French retaliation and "a lesson that would last us for a century." It was nevertheless France, terrified at the rise of Hitler, that finally gave Mussolini the opening he sought. In July 1931 its prime minister, the unscrupulous and gullible Pierre Laval, had suggested to an Italian emissary that Italy might assuage its thirst for expansion in Ethiopia. France would acquiesce, in return for Italy's help in maintaining the status quo in Europe against Germany.

Mussolini at first rejected this offer as a French trick to bog Italy down in Africa just as Germany was opening up possibilities in Europe. Then, in early 1934, he reversed himself. He had quarreled with his would-be ally, Hitler, over Austria. If war in Europe was impossible, war in Africa might yet serve his purpose. The king, the military, and the Italian establishment were lukewarm rather than actively hostile, as they had been over Yugoslavia. They were willing to "avenge Adowa" if Mussolini insisted and no great power objected.

In January 1935, Mussolini and Laval signed the Rome Agreements, which conceded Italy a "free hand" in East Africa in return for the abandonment of Italian colonial claims on France and for Italian backing for France in Europe. The last part of the

Italian troops depart for Ethiopia, 1935.

bargain Mussolini regarded skeptically; to Berlin he confided through intermediaries that "he would exploit the French, if they offered him anything, without becoming dependent upon them."

Large Italian forces, the first of almost half a million troops and laborers, began shipping out for East Africa. Britain feebly objected. War in Africa would make cooperation with Italy against the German threat impossible, and in an election year Baldwin could not abandon the League of Nations, of which Ethiopia was a member. When Mussolini wrecked British efforts at compromise, London reluctantly sent additional battleships to the Mediterranean to deter him. The League, impotent in the Manchurian crisis, rallied behind Britain—and the overwhelming power of the British fleet. But Baldwin's foreign secretary secretly assured Mussolini that Britain did not intend war. That pledge, and intercepted British radio messages suggesting the fleet was short of ammunition, allowed Mussolini to overrule his hesitant military and overawe the King. On October 3, 1935, Italy attacked Ethiopia.

Britain reacted with economic sanctions against Italy organized through the League of Nations. Sanctions proved easy although expensive to evade, and thanks to a British failure of nerve they did not cover the imported oil that fuelled Italy's armed forces. Their main consequence was to cut Italian dependence on British coal—in favor of the coal of the Ruhr. London also pressed on the French and on Mussolini yet another compromise that gave the Duce only parts of Ethiopia. When this "Hoare-Laval Plan" leaked to the press in December 1935, British and French opinion damned it as a sellout of Ethiopia and forced its abandonment. Mussolini was much relieved; his war could proceed.

On the battlefield, the armies of emperor Haile Selassie almost routed the Italians in December–January 1936; then Italy's lavish use of tanks, artillery, aircraft, and mustard gas crushed them. At the beginning of May 1936,

Italian forces entered the Ethiopian capital, Addis Ababa. Mussolini hailed before a delirious crowd the "reapparition of empire, after fifteen centuries, on the fateful hills of Rome." War and the brutal Italian occupation of 1936–41 cost the lives of a million Ethiopians.

War also made Mussolini "founder of the Empire." Ex-Liberal or Nationalist flankers, generals, and king now counted for less. Mussolini listened less and advisers dared offer less and less advice. Sanctions inflamed Italian opinion against the West and made it easier for Mussolini to overawe the industrialists and militarize the Italian economy under the banner of "autarky," the illusory pursuit of self-sufficiency in raw materials. And Italy's quarrel with the League and subsequent intervention in the Spanish Civil War in July–August 1936 gave him the opportunity to move closer to Berlin. In October 1936, he and Hitler inaugurated the "Rome-Berlin Axis." In 1938 he imitated Hitler's anti-Semitic legislation.

In 1940, after long struggle with the generals, king, and moderate opinion, Mussolini led Italy into the Second World War. Only war, he told the crowd on June 10, 1940, would "resolve . . . the problem of our maritime frontiers" and "break the military and territorial chains that suffocate us in our sea, for a people of forty-five million souls is not truly free unless it has free access to the ocean." Victory would give him the prestige needed to smash the monarchy and to break the grip of the Church on Italian society. Defeat instead hurled the regime and Italy itself into the abyss.

GERMANY: FROM WAR TO WAR

Adolf Hitler

The man who opened the road for Mussolini and invited Stalin into central Europe began as modestly as his fellow dictators. Son of an Austro-Hungarian customs official, Adolf Hit-ler imbibed pan-Germanism and anti-Semitism from his surroundings. He failed admission to the Vienna Art Academy in 1907–08—no loss for art, but unfortunate in view of his subsequent career. He drifted to Munich in 1913 rather than serve in the armies of the Habsburg dynasty he despised for its compromises with Slavs and Jews. War in 1914 he regarded as a deliverance (see p. 850). Always a loner, he found in the German army a home and in battle a vocation. From October 1914 to October 1918 he served at the front in the most dangerous job the infantry offered: battalion messenger. He earned two Iron Crosses, decorations rarely given to lance-corporals.

Word of revolution and defeat reached him as he lay in hospital, temporarily blind from British gas; the news roused him to fury. As the army demobilized, he remained in service at Munich for lack of anything better. The army's propaganda branch took him in. There he made a discovery that changed Europe and the world: "I could 'speak.'" And in September 1919 his superiors sent him to listen in at a meeting of a radical rightist sect of Munich railway workers, the German Workers' Party (DAP).

There Hitler immediately attracted attention and an invitation to join. News of his talent for the spoken word spread rapidly in Munich's right radical circles. By July 1921 he had taken the DAP away from its founders, had changed its name to National Socialist German Workers' Party (NSDAP), and had made himself its sole dictatorial leader. By late 1923 his party had 55,000 members and a paramilitary mass army, the brown-shirted SA (*Sturmabteilungen*, "storm troop sections") under the leadership of Ernst Röhm, a fiercely politicized ex-army officer.

The *"Führer,"* as Hitler now became, spoke powerfully to a nation that had become convinced, however perversely, that it had suffered foreign aggression and unmerited demotion to second-class power. Hitler's ideological delusions and those of his ever larger audiences coincided, thanks to Germany's defeat. His starting point was the extremist form of social Darwinism that had long been popular in Germany. Following pseudo-biological prophets such as Ernst Haeckel (see pp. 802–803), Hitler assumed that nature's laws—the "survival of the fittest" or the "free play of forces"—offered the sole "healthy" rule for human conduct. Humanity was one with nature, not apart from it or above it; biology was supreme in all spheres of human activity.

That insight, Hitler insisted, was science. Like his rivals the Marxist-Leninists, Hitler and his followers combined materialist pseudo-positivism with bizarre ideological claims. For Communists, economics was the secret essence of human history, the history of class struggle. For Hitler, biology held the key: race—not class—was "the driving force of world history." History was the history of race struggle. And like the Marxist-Leninists, who saw "the capitalist" as demon, Hitler too saw a historic villain.

For Hitler, the Jewish people were a "race-tuberculosis of nations" who had supposedly lived "parasitically" throughout history from the labors of peoples that had given them shelter—especially the "Aryan" or "Nordic"

peoples of Europe to whom Hitler ascribed biological superiority. Throughout history, the Jews had allegedly sought the "eternal Jewish goal—world domination." They were responsible for Germany's internal weakness and thus for its defeat through the purported stab-in-the-back of 1918. The alleged Jewish threat, Hitler informed his beer-hall audiences, now placed the world before a stark alternative: "either victory of the Aryan side or its annihilation and victory of the Jews." Only Germany could ensure "Aryan" victory; Germany's "historic mission" was to found "an Aryan world order." Hitler's goal was racist world revolution.

More immediately, recovery from the lost war required a new state: "We need a dictator who is a genius, if we want to rise again." But in the age of mass politics, even dictatorship required pseudo-democratic phrases and mass enthusiasm or mass terror to make it workable. Hitler therefore proclaimed that nationalist dictatorship was "Germanic democracy." His mass following, and many in Munich's social elite, appeared to agree.

The Ruhr crisis of 1923 shook Weimar's authority and led Hitler to bid for power before inaction could sap the enthusiasm of his increasingly fanatical following. On the night of November 8–9, 1923, Hitler and the SA seized key points in Munich and sought to launch a "March on Berlin" modelled on Mussolini's October 1922 exploit. But unlike Mussolini, Hitler failed to secure the support of army and police; they soon crushed this "Beer Hall *Putsch.*" Hitler's oratory at his subsequent high treason trial nevertheless turned defeat into victory. His allies, who included Ludendorff, sheepishly evaded their responsibilities. Hitler affirmed his own and appealed to a higher court: Weimar judges might condemn the rebels, but history would triumphantly acquit them. He emerged from the trial as uncontested leader of German radical nationalism.

His short term in prison was a welcome rest, a chance to "confirm his

Hitler and associates in prison after the "Beer Hall *Putsch.*"

ideas by the study of natural history." There he began a memoir and political tract entitled "A Four and One-Half Year Struggle against Lies, Stupidity, and Cowardice." A merciful editor later shortened the title to the catchier *Mein Kampf*—"My Struggle." Its 600 turgid pages included much wisdom about propaganda technique, expressed with a cynical frankness that distinguished Hitler from the theorists of commercial advertising. It also suggested that Hitler saw himself as that rare phenomenon, a combination of prophet and political leader.

Last but not least, *Mein Kampf* offered a foreign policy program. In late 1922, Hitler had already formulated in private how he proposed to go about fulfilling Germany's world mission: "We should attempt the carving up of Russia with English help." In *Mein Kampf* Hitler laid out this program in detail, beginning with a critique of William II's too ambitious foreign policy, which had alienated Britain, France, and Russia all at once. Germany should instead proceed to world domination by stages, smashing one adversary at a time: first the internal enemies, then France, and finally Russia, where Germany would seize the *Lebensraum* or "living space" it required, the vast blockade-proof empire Ludendorff had briefly grasped in 1918. Britain and Italy, both hostile to France during the Ruhr crisis, appeared available as allies; Hitler had inevitably conceived an admiration for Mussolini, who furnished a welcome prototype for nationalist dictatorship. In an unpublished "second book" of 1928 Hitler also discovered Germany's final adversary in the quest for world domination: the United States.

For the moment, such vistas were beside the point. Prosperity and the success of Stresemann's foreign policy lessened the appeal of radical nationalism. The NSDAP, which Hitler had reorganized as a tightly centralized "Führer-party" after his release from prison, received a mere 12 *Reichstag* seats in the 1928 election. But two

---

Hitler, Master of Propaganda   1925

Hitler set forth four mutually reinforcing principles for effective propaganda: it addressed "the most limited intelligence" in its audience, it appealed to emotion rather than intellect, it was relentlessly repetitive, and it displayed and fostered a fanatical one-sidedness.

All propaganda must be popular and its intellectual level must be adjusted to the most limited intelligence among those it is addressed to. . . . The more modest its intellectual ballast, the more exclusively it takes into consideration the emotions of the masses, the more effective it will be. . . . The art of propaganda lies in understanding the emotional ideas of the great masses and finding . . . the way to the attention and thence to the heart of the broad masses. . . .

The receptivity of the great masses is very limited, their intelligence is small, but their power of forgetting is enormous. In consequence . . . all effective propaganda must be limited to a very few points and must harp on these in slogans until the very last member of the public understands what you want him to understand. . . .

What . . . would we say about a poster that was supposed to advertise a new soap and that described other soaps as "good"? We would only shake our heads. Exactly the same applies to political advertising. The function of propaganda is . . . not to make an objective study of the truth . . . ; its task is to serve our own right, always and unflinchingly. . . . It does not have multiple shadings; it has a positive and a negative: love or hate, right or wrong, truth or lie, never half this way and half that way. . . .

From Adolf Hitler, *Mein Kampf*, trans. by Ralph Manheim (Boston: Houghton Mifflin, 1943), pp. 180–83.

---

things suggested that it was ready for further growth: its relentless emphasis on organization and propaganda, and its increasing success with the hard-hit peasantry of north Germany as the agricultural depression deepened after 1927.

The Nazi Revolution

Hitler's breakthrough into national politics came in 1929–30, even before the Depression hit Germany in full force. The press and film magnate Alfred

Hugenberg, an extreme pan-German, had taken over the party of the traditional Junker Right, the German National People's Party (DNVP). Hugenberg, unlike the DNVP's preceding leaders, was fanatically committed to bringing Weimar down. The Young Plan reparations settlement of 1929 offered him an occasion for a massive propaganda campaign against the Republic that had consented to the alleged "enslavement of the German people" through reparations.

Hugenberg enlisted the help of Hitler and the NSDAP—and firmly established Hitler on the national political scene. Then the last Weimar coalition government collapsed; the SPD, like Labour in Britain in 1931, rejected balancing the budget by cutting unemployment benefits. It successor, the government of the authoritarian Center Party leader, Heinrich Brüning, lacked a firm *Reichstag* majority. Brüning therefore committed an act of folly. He called an election for September 1930.

The French had evacuated their last Rhineland occupation zone that June; Germans were now free to vote their views without fear of consequences. Brüning's deflationary measures against the deepening Depression made him unloved. Hugenberg's campaign against the Young Plan had allowed Hitler to create an agitation and propaganda machine that utterly outclassed that of the other parties. The 1930 vote was therefore an electoral earthquake: 107 Nazi *Reichstag* seats, and 6.4 million Nazi votes of 34.9 million votes cast.

The NSDAP was now Germany's second largest party, after the SPD. It tailored its appeals to every conceivable interest group, but its program was above all a name: Adolf Hitler. Hitler offered to fill the role that Bismarck had created and that William II had failed to fill, the role of national *Führer*. He symbolized a radical alternative to Weimar's economic misery, dreary indecisiveness, class and religious division, and national humiliation. The NSDAP, ranted one of Hitler's lieutenants, was

"the opposite of everything that now exists." Increasing numbers of Germans found that deliberately vague appeal compelling.

The principal question in German politics after September 1930 was when, and under what conditions, Hitler would achieve power. In the next two years, as the Depression shrank Brüning's authority, the Junker kitchen cabinet around Reich President Hindenburg became increasingly desperate. They applauded the NSDAP's nationalist fanaticism and sought to use it to buttress their own power, while resisting Hitler's increasingly pressing demands for the chancellorship. But like the similar efforts of Salandra and Giolitti in 1921–25, repeated conservative attempts to domesticate Hitler failed.

In spring 1932, Brüning sponsored Hindenburg's reelection for a second seven-year term, and Hitler unchivalrously ran against the "Old Gentleman." Hindenburg won, but only thanks to the votes of the SPD, which preferred even a Prussian field marshal to Hitler. After the election, Hindenburg dismissed Brüning, who had outlived his usefulness and had provoked Hitler by attempting to abolish the SA. The army, which played an increasing political role, resisted curbs on what it naively perceived as the SA's young "idealists."

A *Reichstag* election in July 1932 gave the NSDAP an unprecedented 230 seats, amid SA violence that left hundreds dead. With the help of the 89 Communists, who opposed democracy as bitterly as the NSDAP, Hitler now had a *Reichstag* majority not merely against any cabinet or chancellor, but against the Weimar Republic itself. NSDAP obstruction and Hitler's demand for the chancellorship produced political paralysis. Hindenburg as yet refused to hand over Germany "like a laboratory rabbit" to the bold experimenters of the NSDAP. But Brüning's two successors as chancellor failed to master the Depression, the *Reichstag*, the continuing violence, and back-biting in the conservative camp. On January 30, 1933, Hindenburg gave in and made Adolf Hitler chancellor of the German Reich in a coalition cabinet with Hugenberg and numerous other conservatives.

Hitler soon disabused his conservative allies of the illusion that they had "hired him" as their front man. He established a direct alliance with the military high command on February 3 with promises to "exterminate Marxism root and branch," reawaken the German people's "will to arms," and create a new armed forces (*Wehrmacht*) once more based on universal military service. He extracted from Hindenburg permission to hold a new election and emergency presidential powers that restricted press and other freedoms. The SA and its elite offshoot, the SS (*Schutzstaffel* or "security echelon"), terrorized political opponents and German Jews with the approval of the Prussian police, which was now under the management of Hitler's close associate Hermann Göring.

On February 27, 1933, the *Reichstag* building in Berlin mysteriously burned; Hitler and his propaganda chief, the malevolent Joseph Goebbels, seized on this as evidence of a "Communist plot" that justified the suppression by presidential decree of all remaining constitutional freedoms. After the election on March 5, 1933, gave the conservative-NSDAP coalition a majority, Hitler bullied the new *Reichstag* into voting an "Enabling Act" that gave the chancellor himself the power to make law by decree. That made him independent of both *Reichstag* and of Hindenburg. By July 1933, Hitler had abolished all parties other than the NSDAP, including the DNVP of his conservative allies. He had purged the civil service of political opponents and Jews—a measure that initiated an intensifying effort to define who was a Jew and to isolate those so defined from the rest of the population.

Hindenburg and the army acquiesced. They approved heartily of Hitler's crushing of Communists and SPD, and swallowed whatever modest qualms they may have had at the anti-Jewish measures, which roused a storm of protest abroad. Hitler also received the blessings of the Vatican, which abandoned the Catholic Center party as it had the Italian Catholic *Popolari* and signed in July 1933 a Concordat with Hitler similar to its 1929 arrangement with Mussolini. In November 1933 a plebiscite and *Reichstag* election gave Hitler a brown-shirted parliament and an 87.8 percent majority. Hitler had achieved in nine months what Mussolini, with far less mass support in 1922 than Hitler had in 1933, had needed seven years to accomplish.

But while Hindenburg lived, Hitler still faced an authority higher than his own. In preparation for the "Old Gentleman's" demise, Hitler consolidated his alliance with the army, that "state within the state" equally indispensable to his domestic power and to his plans for war. When the SA under its chief Ernst Röhm challenged the army for leadership of the rearmament effort, Hitler opted decisively for the army. On June 30, 1934, with trucks and weapons the army provided, Hitler's SS forces rounded up and shot over 200 of the SA leadership, Röhm included. That "night of the long knives" sealed with blood Hitler's alliance with the military leadership. On August 2, after the ailing Hindenburg finally died, the *Wehrmacht* took an oath to Hitler personally. As "*Führer* and Reich Chancellor," a position that united his own prerogatives with those of the Reich President, Hitler now enjoyed powers that far surpassed Mussolini's.

In the ensuing years Hitler consolidated and extended that power. The NSDAP did its best to mobilize the population, including the industrial workers, who received membership in a Nazi "German Labor Front" in place of the smashed SPD trade unions. German youth, by 1936, was subject to compulsory membership in the "Hitler Youth" and "League of German Maidens." And the SS proved a far more formidable rival to the army than had Röhm's SA. Its fanatically loyal and

On Hitler's order, the party organized a boycott of Jewish shops and offices in April 1933. The placard reads: "Germans! Defend yourselves! Don't buy from Jews!"

Heinrich Himmler (left) and Ernst Röhm a few months before Himmler had Röhm shot at Hitler's order.

state bureaucracy and with Hitler's approval gradually usurped its powers. The SS, with Hitler's explicit backing, encroached on both army and judiciary. "Political free enterprise," as one scholar has well described it, was the ruling principle of Hitler's Reich. From his villa in the Bavarian Alps, far above the struggle, Hitler encouraged the rivalries of his subordinates. Internecine struggle strengthened his own power and served as a form of "natural selection" in molding the new National Socialist governing elite. The regime's dynamism was in part a consequence of this system, which contrasted with the more rigid top-down style of Stalin and even Mussolini. Hitler defined the goal of competition—to fulfill the *Führer*'s will—and left it to his subordinates to guess that will and strive frenetically to implement it. That was his most original contribution to the technique of total power.

"Everything for the Wehrmacht!"

Nazi Germany's road to that power led through massive rearmament and conquest. On February 3, 1933, five days after taking office, Hitler addressed a private meeting of his generals and admirals. As well as promising them the elimination of the Left and rearmament, he announced that the power of the new *Wehrmacht* would serve for "the conquest of new *Lebensraum* [living space] in the East and its ruthless Germanization." The generals did not take that statement seriously until much later, but they were delighted that he proposed to give them arms once more.

In the following year the army, Germany's dominant service, accelerated the clandestine rearmament plan upon which it had already embarked under Weimar. When the Disarmament Conference of the League of Nations threatened to get in the way of that plan, Hitler left both Conference and League in October 1933, with the unanimous support of his generals, ex-conservatives, and diplomats. His es-

fastidiously precise leader, Heinrich Himmler, had by 1934 seized control of the Reich police forces, established a network of concentration camps outside the control of the normal judiciary, and set up a small but growing private army that included an SS bodyguard regiment for the *Führer*. By 1936, Himmler was officially "Reich leader of the SS and chief of the German Police," a unique party-state hybrid. And the regime struck once more at Germany's half-million Jews. In September 1935, at the annual Nuremberg party rally, Hitler proclaimed a "Reich citizenship law" that made the German Jews less than full citizens and forbade the intermarriage of "Germans" and "Jews." The definition and increasing segregation of the "racial enemy" proved a mighty step toward extermination.

By 1936–37, within the shell of the Weimar constitution, Hitler had created a system that German jurists described as a "*Führer*-state." Party organizations proliferated alongside the

tablishment "flankers" enabled him to rearm and to launch the war that culminated in their own ruin.

Externally, rearmament inevitably led Germany into a "danger zone" in which it ran the risk of preventive war. Hitler warned his generals in February 1933 that they would soon find out "if France has statesman; if so, it will not give us time but will attack us (presumably with [its] eastern hangers-on)." France had no statesmen, and Hitler neutralized Poland with a surprise non-aggression pact in January 1934. Each time Western outrage at Germany's anti-Jewish measures or its rearmament reached dangerous heights, Hitler soothed foreign opinion with a "peace speech" that played on the credulity and yearning for peace of the democracies.

That tactic served even to cover Germany's March 1935 declaration that it had unilaterally torn up the disarmament provisions of Versailles. Germany, Hitler triumphantly announced, had an air force—the *Luftwaffe*—and would soon have a vast mass army based on universal service. London and Paris made feeble protests; then Britain legalized Germany's violations of the Versailles treaty by conceding to Hitler a fleet a third the size of Britain's in the Anglo-German Naval Agreement of June 1935.

Internally, Hitler broke the opposition to breakneck rearmament that emerged in 1935–36, as the economy achieved virtual full employment. Germany's steel barons, whose excess capacity had almost ruined them in the Depression, balked at investing in new plants. Big business leaders warned that the armament boom was overheating the economy; labor and raw material shortages would soon lead to massive inflation and financial ruin. Hitler treated the doubters with contempt. He was secretly confident that the *Wehrmacht*'s future loot would keep the economy going. He also had the support of the army leaders, who wanted armaments and did not share the industrialists' qualms. Hitler gave Hermann Göring, now chief of the *Luftwaffe* and second man in the Nazi state, full powers over the economy in mid-1936, and simple orders: "Within four years the German *Wehrmacht* must be ready to fight; within four years the German economy must be ready for war."

The rearmament effort itself proceeded rapidly, gobbling up an ever-greater portion of Germany's gross national product (see Figure 32-1). By 1939, despite the belated beginnings of rearmament in the democracies, Germany was out-spending all its Western rivals combined by a factor of almost two to one. Hitler's effort produced results: the most powerful air force and army in the world. All that remained was to use them. As Hitler remarked retrospectively in November 1939, "I did not create the *Wehrmacht* in order not to strike."

Germany's first and last "Minister for Public Enlightenment and Propaganda," Joseph Goebbels.

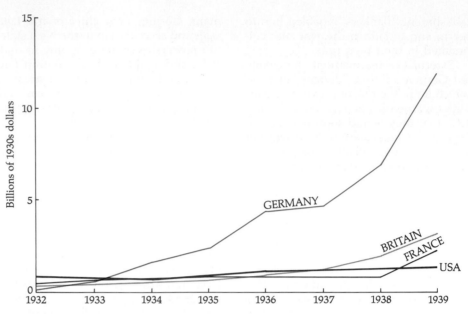

FIGURE 32-1   Hitler Rearms, the Democracies Falter: Military Expenditure, 1932–39

THE ROAD TO WAR

The massive extent of German rearmament soon made it the decisive driving force in world politics. But what did the *Wehrmacht* mean? The powers sought to divine Hitler's intentions but shrank from the obvious answer, that German rearmament served the purpose announced in *Mein Kampf*, the conquest of *Lebensraum*. Recognizing Hitler's warlike intentions required abandonment of the cherished myth that World War I had been so terrible that another great war was inconceivable. Recognizing Hitler's warlike intentions dictated war to stop Hitler before he was too strong. The Western powers shrank from that conclusion. Their reward was war once Hitler was too strong to stop.

Diplomatic Revolution in Europe, 1936

By 1936, Germany's growing might and the Ethiopian quarrel between Italy and the West offered Hitler a unique opportunity. In February 1936 he sounded the Italian attitude toward Locarno; Mussolini made clear that he would not object to a German breach of that treaty, of which Italy was a guarantor. On March 7, 1936, Hitler's forces occupied the Rhineland demilitarized zone without warning. Germany had broken not only the "dictated peace" of Versailles, but Locarno, a treaty Germany had freely signed.

Hitler's action was by far the greatest risk he had yet taken. The German army was in the initial phases of massive expansion and was correspondingly disorganized. The French could have brought overwhelming force to bear. Victory would not have been bloodless; Hitler had given orders to fight, and to hold the line of the Rhine. But Germany was not yet ready to put up lengthy resistance.

It did not have to. Britain, tied up facing Italy, pressed Paris not to take rash action. As *The Times* of London indulgently put it, Hitler's coup was no more than the occupation of "territory indisputably under German sovereignty." The French military made clear to its politicians that it too preferred inaction. The politicians in turn happily seized on Britain's pusillanimity as excuse for their own. Hitler, who launched the crisis despite wavering among his generals, saw the outcome as confirmation of his own superior judgement. He now had the measure both of the West and of his own timid high command.

The remilitarization of the Rhineland was a strategic and diplomatic revolution. Now Hitler could fortify Germany's western border and prevent France from defending its eastern allies

Europe before the Second World War   1930–39

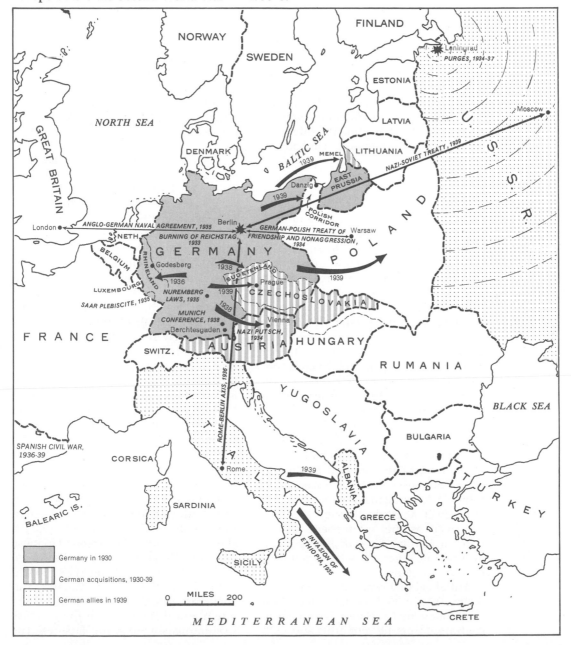

by attacking Germany. The smaller powers rushed to seek favor with the new master. Belgium, convinced of the futility of its French alliance, retreated into neutrality in November 1936. That potentially uncovered France's northeastern border, which the Maginot line did not protect. Austria, which Mussolini had tacitly abandoned to Hitler in January 1936, contracted in July 1936 a treaty that gave Hitler a voice in its foreign and domestic affairs. The Balkan states expanded their already close economic ties with Germany. Stalin, apparently after reading *Mein Kampf*, had in 1934 become a belated convert to the League of Nations and "collective security"—but he now made intensified efforts to tempt Hitler into a mutually profitable arrangement. Hitler saw no need as yet to answer. He had the initiative.

Spain and China, 1936–39

Hitler was not the sole source of conflict, but he found the quarrels of others tactically useful. Mussolini's Ethiopian adventure had distracted attention from German rearmament and offered an opportunity to pocket the Rhineland. New conflicts in Spain and China offered similar advantages.

In July 1936, a group of traditionalist generals rose against the republic that had taken the place of Spain's enfeebled monarchy in 1931. Popular resistance blocked the coup in most of Spain. Generals Francisco Franco and Emilio Mola then appealed to Fascist Italy and Nazi Germany for assistance. They received it. Mussolini had visions of dominating the western Mediterranean and saw conflict in Spain, as in Ethiopia, as a means of increasing Fascist power at home through what he described as the "permanent revolution" of warfare. He sent aircraft and a ground force that ultimately amounted to four divisions.

Hitler simply wanted a conflict in Spain that would prevent the West from following too closely his doings in central Europe; he sent arms and *Luftwaffe* units. Even Stalin, who apparently saw the Spanish Civil War as a vehicle for keeping the "capitalist" powers at one another's throats, intervened on the side of the Republic with arms, advisers, and Communist-organized "International Brigades." Only Britain and France abstained. London viewed both sides with distaste and feared that the Spanish Civil War might lead to general war. Léon Blum's France offered hesitant unofficial assistance to the Republic but shrank from greater risks.

In the ensuing three years, over half a million Spaniards died in massacres of prisoners and civilians, in battles around Madrid in 1936–37, in bloody winter fighting in 1937–38, and in the final campaigns in southeastern Spain that ended with the collapse of the Republic in March–April 1939. The war became a symbol. For Germany and Italy, the battle against the Republic was a struggle against "Bolshevism"— a convenient propaganda theme to cloak the Italian and German threat to the status quo. For the Left of western Europe and the United States, the war was a struggle against "fascism"—a generic concept that the Communist International had popularized to distinguish "capitalist" from Soviet dictatorship. Few recognized that this was above all a *Spanish* civil war, last of a long series of struggles between military-clerical Right and liberal or socialist Left that had convulsed Spain since Napoleon's invasion in 1808. It ended with the victory of the clerical-military dictatorship of Francisco Franco, who cannily outlasted his Nazi and Fascist patrons and died in power, and in bed, in 1976.

Full-scale war in East Asia soon overshadowed in bloodshed and extent the events in Spain. In July 1937, a shooting incident between Japanese and Guomindang troops at the Marco Polo Bridge near Beijing (Peking) led both sides to reinforce. Chiang Kaishek had grudgingly agreed in 1936 to a temporary alliance with the Chinese Communists against the Japanese; he now felt compelled to fight. The Japanese army welcomed the chance to reduce all China to colonial subjection. The Tokyo government, under a prime minister who had made his name as an expansionist ideologue, Prince Konoe Fumimaro, backed the army.

A Japanese landing force took Shanghai with much slaughter. In a series of swift campaigns, the Japanese forced Chiang southward. In December 1937 they seized Chiang's capital at Nanjing and massacred between 100,000 and 300,000 Chinese amid scenes of mass rape and displays of swordsmanship against unarmed prisoners. Almost simultaneously, Japanese aircraft sank the U.S. gunboat *Panay* on the Yangtze River. That was an unambiguous warning to the West. China was Japan's preserve: "Asia for the Asians."

The West showed small resolve. Baldwin's successor, Neville Chamberlain, hoped to avoid provoking Japan until he had conciliated Hitler and Mussolini. American opinion, after abandoning Europe in the 1920s, had justified itself by creating the myth that bankers and armaments barons—rather than Ludendorff and Zimmermann—had forced the United States into war in 1917. Between 1935 and 1937 an isolationist Congress passed three "Neutrality Acts" to prevent U.S. sales of arms and ammunition to belligerents, and thus supposedly avoid another war.

When Roosevelt vaguely urged nations to "quarantine" the aggressors in an October 1937 speech, a fierce isolationist chorus attacked him. His modest rearmament plan of January 1938 provoked a furor in Congress, but eventually passed. Roosevelt did join the British in January 1938 in secret naval talks directed against Japan. He contemplated imposing economic sanctions on Tokyo, and eventually entering hostilities undeclared and, by stages, bypassing the isolationists in Congress—both notions that came into their own in 1941. But Roosevelt was a master of ambiguity, of avoiding commitment until it was inescapable. Chamberlain found no reason to reverse his judgment of late 1937 that it was "always best and safest to count on *nothing* from the Americans except words."

Japan's China war therefore proceeded without Western interference. By 1939 the Guomindang had retreated to Chongqing (Chungking) in Sichuan province in the far southwest. Japan had won the war but could not end it. The "New Order in Asia" that Konoe proclaimed in November 1938 remained an order upheld only by Japanese bayonets. Japan neither subdued China nor secured the resources that its own economy lacked.

Alliances against the West

By late 1937, Hitler had reached a number of conclusions and decisions. He recognized that Britain was willing to acquiesce in the peaceful achievement of German aspirations in Austria, Czechoslovakia, and the Polish Corridor. But it was unlikely to fall in with the far wider program put forward in *Mein Kampf* and to become junior partner in a German quest for *Lebensraum* and world domination. Hitler therefore recognized the need for alliances against Britain, to deter it or distract it militarily.

In the fall of 1936, thanks to Mussolini's parallel search for allies against the West and to Italo-German cooperation in Spain, Hitler and Mussolini contracted a "Rome-Berlin Axis." Mussolini's triumphal visit to Germany in September 1937 confirmed that alignment. Footdragging by Mussolini's conservative flankers and fear of becoming a satellite of the Reich kept him from seeking a formal military alliance until early 1939. But he pledged his good faith to Hitler by ostentatiously adopting German-style laws against Italy's 50,000 Jews in the summer–fall of 1938, over opposition that included powerful elements within the Fascist party. Japan signed on with Hitler in November 1936, in an agreement ostensibly directed against the Communist International. That "Anti-Comintern Pact" in reality involved a secret military commitment against the Soviet Union and an unspoken hostility to Britain. Italy joined the Anti-Comintern Pact in November 1937 when it followed the German and Japanese example, and left the dying League of Nations.

None of these "Hitler coalition" pacts as yet offered firm guarantees that Germany would have allies. But they scared London, which intensified—in the hope of binding Hitler to the status quo—its efforts to "appease" what it regarded as his legitimate claims in central Europe. Hitler inevitably viewed such efforts as signs of British irresolution and as an incitement to further German coups. On November 5, 1937, he informed his high command and his conservative foreign minister that Germany might have the opportunity to seize Austria and/or Czechoslovakia in the near future. War with Britain and France must in any event come before 1943–45. Germany was ready to move from rearmament to war.

His listeners, except Göring of the *Luftwaffe* and Admiral Erich Raeder of the navy, found Hitler's resolve to launch a war of aggression imprudent. They grumbled that Germany's strategic situation was as yet unfavorable. Hitler took note, and in January–February of 1938 he exploited questions about the moral character of his minister of war and army commander-in-chief to dismiss both them and his conservative foreign minister. He himself became minister of war and chose new military subordinates pathetically eager to please their *Führer*. Joachim von Ribbentrop, the former champagne salesman and NSDAP foreign policy pundit who had negotiated the Anglo-German Naval Treaty and Anti-Comintern Pact, became the new foreign minister. Hitler had cleared the way for further expansion by consolidating his control over the German army and foreign office, the last preserves of the conservatives who had brought him to power.

Bloodless Victories: Vienna, Munich, Prague, 1938–39

External opportunity immediately arose. In February 1938 the prime minister of Austria, Kurt von Schuschnigg, visited Hitler to attempt to placate him. Hitler bullied Schuschnigg unmercifully and extorted his agreement to take two Austrian NSDAP leaders into his cabinet as ministers of war and of the interior. Once back in Vienna, Schuschnigg thought better of his promise to thus hand over Austria to Hitler. But British and French support was not forthcoming, and Italy had given up its claim to be Austria's protector in 1936. On March 11–12, 1938 the *Wehrmacht* rolled bloodlessly across the Austrian border.

The Austrians received the *Wehrmacht* and its *Führer* with flowers and delirious applause. Hitler responded by proclaiming the immediate *Anschluss* ("merging") of Austria into Germany. Savage SS persecution of Vienna's Jews began immediately; the Austrian army received new uniforms and Prussian drill instructors. And Austria's northern border allowed the new "Greater Germany" to surround Czechoslovakia on three sides.

Unlike Austria, Czechoslovakia had a military alliance with France, 35 well-equipped divisions, and fortifications that in some areas rivalled the Maginot line. But like Austria, it lacked Western support. The France of Daladier shamefacedly sought a way of avoiding fulfillment of its alliance obligations. A prominent Englishman privately advised a German contact not to shoot Czechoslovakia, but to strangle it.

Strangulation, or what his diplomats jokingly described as an ethnic "chemical solution," was indeed Hitler's first thought. The German minority of 3.25 million in Czechoslovakia's northern border area—the Sudetenland—was his chosen instrument. In April he instructed the political leadership of the Sudeten Germans to press on Prague a series of ever-escalating demands that would lead ultimately to the dissolution of the Czech state. "Autonomy" for the Sudetenland would render Czechoslovakia indefensible by depriving it of its border fortifications and industries.

When the Czechs mobilized their army in May 1938 in response to bogus rumors of an impending German attack, Hitler changed his policy and resolved on force instead of subversion: "It is my unalterable intention to smash Czechoslovakia by military action in the near future." He set a target date of October 1, 1938, and intensified work on Germany's fortified *Westwall*, to keep the French at bay while he crushed Czechoslovakia.

By early September, as Goebbels's propaganda about fictitious Czech atrocities against the Sudeten Germans reached a crescendo, a covert German mobilization had readied the *Wehrmacht* for use. Sudeten Germans rioted on orders from Berlin, and Hitler demanded their "self-determination" at the close of the last Nuremberg party rally on September 12. Mussolini, on a speaking tour of northern Italy, derided the Czechs and pledged his support to Hitler. The Czechs, despite intense pressure from London and Paris, readied themselves to fight for their existence.

This crisis impelled Neville Chamberlain to act, to carry to its logical conclusion the policy of active, preemptive "appeasement" he had followed since becoming prime minister in 1937. He flew to Germany twice and urged the

Hitler receives the applause of the Vienna crowd, March 14, 1938.

dictator to accept the Sudetenland by slices rather than all at once. Hitler naturally responded to Chamberlain's attempts at conciliation with further demands: the entire Sudetenland by October 1. But Chamberlain failed to bend his cabinet colleagues to accept that humiliating ultimatum. Hitler, in a speech at the Berlin Sports Palace on September 26, then raved at the Czechs and offered them a stark choice: "Peace or war!" Chamberlain's reply was a mournful radio address to the British people in which he confessed his dismay over this "quarrel in a far away country between people of whom we know nothing." Chamberlain's cabinet colleagues displayed greater resolve; they ordered the Royal Navy mobilized and the blockade prepared. The French unhappily followed. Hitler's insistence on unilateral violent solutions appeared to have at last summoned up a coalition capable of blocking Germany before it achieved European hegemony.

Then Hitler had second thoughts. German crowds greeted the approach

of war with a sullen silence far different from the delirious enthusiasm of August 1914. Germany could crush the Czechs. But Czech fortifications would exact a stiff price and the army was still far from ready for general war; it was not scheduled to reach its projected full strength until 1940–41. Finally, Germany in 1938 lacked the oil and raw materials that a long war against Britain and France would demand.

When Chamberlain proposed a further compromise through Mussolini, Hitler therefore resentfully acquiesced to a four-power conference at Munich on September 29–30, 1938. There Chamberlain and Daladier pressed on him a phased occupation of the Sudetenland by October 10. Roosevelt, from the background, urged London and Paris to avoid war. To save the West's face, the dictatorships agreed to an unenforceable four-power guarantee of the mutilated and militarily defenseless remainder of Czechoslovakia.

The Munich agreement was an immense moral, political, and strategic defeat for the West, a defeat that made

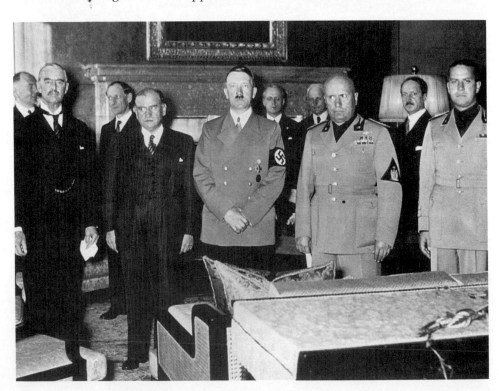

The Munich Conference, September 29–30, 1938. Chamberlain, Daladier, Hitler, Mussolini, and Ciano decide Czechoslovakia's fate.

possible Hitler's destruction of the European and world order in 1940–41. The West abandoned its one industrialized eastern European ally, and Germany's annexations in the Sudetenland included a rich booty: over 70 percent of Czechoslovakia's major industries.

Chamberlain nevertheless returned from Munich bearing what he claimed was "peace with honor," "peace for our time." Churchill and a small band of dissident Conservatives thought otherwise. So did Hitler, who immediately and publicly rejected British attempts to hold him to the Munich agreement: "We will suffer the tutelage of governesses no longer!" He was privately furious that his "entry into Prague had been spoiled." In a secret speech to his press representatives on November 10, he regretted that his peace speeches had misled the German people: "Force of circumstances was the reason I spoke for years only of peace." Now the task was to turn the *Volk* around: it must stand like "formed-up troops" behind his leadership. Doubters in the "intellectual strata" unfortunately still possessed necessary skills: "otherwise one could exterminate them, or whatever." As Hitler spoke, party activists devastated synagogues and Jewish shops all over Germany at his command, in the regime's last public attempt to mobilize the German people against the Jews.

By early 1939, Hitler had begun to see the realization of his program within his grasp. He inaugurated a new naval building plan: by the mid-1940s Germany would have an 800-ship fleet far superior to Britain's and capable of taking on the United States. He accelerated an immense construction plan to remake Germany's city centers within ten years. Huge domes and halls, designed so that their ruins would be impressive thousands of years hence, were to fit Berlin for its new status as capital of the world. To his officer corps, he insisted that Munich was not an end but a beginning; Germany was bound for world domi-

nation. It must move forward as it had since 1933, "without letup, exploiting every opportunity, however small, to move immediately toward a new success." And he publicly warned that "international Jewry" was the source of foreign accusations that he sought war. He promised retribution.

Convinced of the feebleness of Western resistance, Hitler saw no reason to resist the temptation to absorb the remainder of Czechoslovakia. On March 14–15, 1939, he bullied its hapless government into placing itself under German "protection." Hitler and the *Wehrmacht* entered Prague. Germany's overheated war economy received a fresh infusion of booty. But Hitler had at last gone too far. His con-

---

Churchill on Munich   October 5, 1938

To the accompaniment of heckling from Chamberlain loyalists, Churchill sought unsuccessfully to convince the House of Commons that "peace for our time" was defeat without war.

CHURCHILL: . . . I will . . . begin by saying the most unpopular and most unwelcome thing. I will begin by saying what everybody would like to ignore or forget but which must nevertheless be stated, namely, that we have sustained a total and unmitigated defeat, and that France has suffered even more than we have.

VISCOUNTESS ASTOR: Nonsense.

CHURCHILL: When the Noble Lady cries "nonsense," she could not have heard the Chancellor of the Exchequer [Sir John Simon, speaking for the Chamberlain government] admit in his illuminating and comprehensive speech just now that Herr Hitler had gained in this particular leap forward in substance all he set out to gain. The utmost my right hon[orable] Friend the Prime Minister [Chamberlain] has been able to secure by all his immense exertions . . . the utmost he has been able to gain—[*Hon Members*: "Is peace."]. . . . The utmost he has been able to gain . . . has been that the German dictator, instead of snatching his victuals from the table, has been content to have them served to him course by course. . . .

From Martin Gilbert, *Winston S. Churchill*, Vol. V, *1922–1939: The Prophet of Truth* (Boston: Houghton Mifflin, 1977), p. 997.

"Peace for our time"? Chamberlain returns from Munich, 1938.

The morning after *Kristallnacht* ("plate glass night"), the Nazi party attack on synagogues, Jewish businesses, and Jews which Goebbels organized on November 9–10, 1938.

quest of territories inhabited almost entirely by Czechs made a mockery of his claims that he sought only self-determination for Germans. His breach of the Munich agreement and of his September 1938 promise that the Sudetenland was his "last territorial demand in Europe" showed that he was utterly untrustworthy. The Prague coup crystallized opinion in Britain, which had turned increasingly against Germany after Munich and the November 1938 attack on Germany's Jews.

The Totalitarians United, and the Coming of Hitler's War

A storm of public protest enveloped Chamberlain, who had initially sought to avoid a response to the Prague coup. His response, when it came on March 31, 1939, was ill-considered. Britain and subsequently France guaranteed Poland, which appeared to be Hitler's likely next victim, against threats to its independence. They soon extended similar guarantees to Rumania and to Greece, which Mussolini appeared to

menace by his annexation of helpless Albania on April 7. Chamberlain, with Paris in tow, belatedly attempted to create a structure of diplomatic deterrence that would halt Hitler.

But Hitler played by war-fighting rules. Paper guarantees of states that the Western powers could not help in war did not impress him. The Western pledge to Poland simply convinced him that the Poles, who had resisted secret German territorial demands, should definitely be his next target. On April 3 Hitler set September 1, 1939, as the planning date for the attack on Poland.

The Western guarantee to Poland also made Stalin the man of the hour: the "capitalist" powers were now pledged to fight among themselves. All Stalin had to do was to await bids for his support. He had made clear his policy as early as 1925: "We will have to intervene, but we will intervene last [of all the powers], in order to throw a decisive weight onto the scales." But Soviet participation in war might not be necessary; the Soviet Union and Nazi Germany might exercise joint domination of the Eurasian land mass. Stalin's daughter, who later defected to the West, testified to her father's conviction that "together with the Germans, we would have been invincible!"

In May 1939, Stalin removed his foreign minister, Maxim Litvinov, lest his Jewish antecedents complicate negotiations with Berlin. Stalin's creature Vyacheslav Molotov took Litvinov's place and renewed Moscow's long-standing secret proposals for a German-Soviet political agreement. The British and French also explored cooperation with Russia, but sent their negotiators to Leningrad by slow boat. Chamberlain lacked enthusiasm for a Bolshevik alliance, and London, thanks to Stalin's removal of half the Soviet officer corps, doubted the military usefulness of that alliance.

Hitler also moved to secure Italy, which would serve to distract Britain and France in the Mediterranean while he attacked Poland. Thanks to Mussolini's impatience, the Axis powers concluded a war alliance, the so-called "Pact of Steel," on May 22, 1939. It was to operate automatically if either power "became . . . involved in warlike actions," regardless of who had provoked the conflict. Mussolini privately attempted to limit his commitment by pointing out that Italy needed another three years to strengthen its armaments; Hitler was silent.

The day after the signing of the Pact of Steel, Hitler addressed his generals. The German-Polish border dispute over West Prussia and the German-inhabited city of Danzig was merely the occasion for war; the issue was "the enlargement of *Lebensraum* in the East." That was necessary soon; Germany had a choice between continuing rise, or decline. And this action would be different from Czechoslovakia: "There will be fighting." If the West objected, he would fight it as well.

By mid-August, as the Goebbels propaganda machine barraged the Poles, the *Wehrmacht* had again covertly mobilized. Talks in Moscow progressed well: Hitler and Stalin spoke the same language. On August 20 Hitler wrote urging Stalin to receive Ribbentrop to put the finishing touches on a Russo-German "non-aggression" pact. Stalin agreed. The British and French negotiators in essence offered Stalin war with Germany and no gains. Hitler offered him no war and a division of eastern Europe into Nazi and Soviet spheres. Stalin thereby achieved objectives sought since the beginnings of the Soviet state. The foundation of the Non-Aggression Pact, Stalin later informed the British ambassador with amazing openness, was the common Russo-German aim of destroying the "old balance" of power that had existed in Europe.

On the night of August 23–24, in the Kremlin, Ribbentrop and Molotov signed the Nazi-Soviet Non-Aggression Pact in Stalin's presence. Its contents belied its name: it promised benevolent neutrality in the event that either power became involved in war, even a war of aggression. And its se-

---

Hitler "Foresees" the Holocaust   1939

In his *Reichstag* anniversary speech of January 30, 1939, Hitler made clear publicly that he reserved a special fate for Europe's Jews.

I have in my life very often been a prophet, and was generally laughed at. In the period of my struggle for power it was the Jewish people who first of all received my prophecies exclusively with laughter, [when I said] that I would one day take over the leadership of the state and thus of the entire German people, and that I would among many other things also bring to solution the Jewish problem. I believe that the laughter of German Jewry that then resounded has since died in their throats.

I will today once more be a prophet: if international finance Jewry inside and outside Europe succeeds in plunging the nations into a new world war, the outcome will not be the Bolshevization of the earth and thus the victory of Jewry, but the extermination [*Vernichtung*] of the Jewish race in Europe.

From *Hitler: Reden und Proklamationen 1932–1945*, ed. by Max Domarus, (Munich, 1965), Vol. 2:1, p. 1058 (translation by M. Knox).

---

cret protocol drew a line through eastern Europe and Poland that divided the two parties' respective booty in "the event of a territorial-political remodeling of the territories belonging to the Polish state." At the close of the negotiations, Ribbentrop ventured a joke: Berlin humorists were saying Stalin was about to join the Anti-Comintern Pact. Stalin too offered a witticism: "The Germans wanted peace. . . ." And Stalin toasted both Hitler and Heinrich Himmler, that "guarantor of order in Germany."

Even before Ribbentrop had closed with the Russians, Hitler again harangued his generals: "We must act." Now was the point of Germany's greatest relative strength. His own leadership was irreplaceable: "I can at any time be removed by an idiot or criminal." In a few years British and French armaments would begin to catch up, while Germany's war economy would run down for lack of raw materials. Hitler's sole fear, according to one ac-

Stalin and Ribbentrop enjoy a joke at the signing of the Nazi-Soviet Pact, August 23–24, 1939.

count of his remarks, was "that Chamberlain or some other swine [*Saukerl*] might arrive at the last moment" with peace proposals. He ordered the attack on Poland for August 26.

Britain's signing on August 25 of a military alliance confirming the guarantee to Poland and Mussolini's concurrent confession that Italy was too weak to fight led the *Führer* to waver briefly. Then, surrounded by SS advisers, Hitler confirmed his choice for war. Germany's long-term situation was "very difficult, perhaps hopeless." But as he had written in *Mein Kampf*, Germany would "either be a world power, or would cease to be." At 4:45 A.M., German summer time on September 1, 1939, the *Wehrmacht* attacked Poland from north, west, and south.

In the next two days a disconsolate Chamberlain and the fearful French sought to promote, with Italian help, yet another conference. But the House of Commons balked. The Labour opposition and dissident Conservatives combined to "speak for England" and demand that Chamberlain honor Britain's pledge to Poland. The March guarantee had perhaps been a tactical diplomatic error, but it had one great virtue at the end. Hitler, in challenging it, forced Chamberlain to declare war or suffer the certain collapse of his government. The British ultimatum to Germany expired at 11:00 A.M. on September 3. The last European war had begun.

The causes of the war of 1939 have generated less dispute than those of World War I, of which it was a continuation. Britain, France, and the United States made a second war possible by failing either to dismember or conciliate Germany in 1919. Subsequently, their supine inaction and preemptive concessions permitted Hitler to rearm and strike. The Prusso-German conservatives helped Hitler to power and collaborated enthusiastically with him in creating the *Wehrmacht* that destroyed the European and world balance. Stalin sought alliance with Hitler for the overthrow of the European balance and the extension of Soviet power. Stalin gave Hitler the chance to strike when he did. But in the end, it was Hitler's drive toward total power and his vision of racist world revolution that made this greatest of wars: "The decision to strike was always in me."

Suggestions for Further Reading

Totalitarianism

H. Arendt, *Totalitarianism* (1951), remains the classic description of the phenomenon, but is often eccentric. W. Laqueur, *The Fate of the Revolution*, rev. ed. (1987), conveniently summarizes current debate about the concept and about the Soviet regime. G. Orwell, *1984* (1949), and *Animal Farm* (1946), offers biting analysis in fictional form of totalitarianism in general and of Stalin in particular.

Stalin

On the Soviet Union, M. Heller and A. Nekritch, *Utopia in Power* (1982), is a lively introduction; B. Dmytryshyn, *USSR: A Concise History* (1978), provides a brief narrative and key documents. H. Carrère d'Encausse, *Lenin: Revolution and Power* (1981), and *Stalin: Order Through Terror* (1981), offer clearsighted analysis. On Stalin see especially A. Ulam, *Stalin* (1973). On Stalin's consequences see R. Conquest, *The Harvest of Sorrow* (1986); *The Great Terror* (1968); *Kolyma: the Arctic Death Camps* (1978); and A. I. Solzhenitsyn, *The GULAG Archipelago* (1973). The numbers Stalin killed remain a subject of hot debate; the most convincing estimates are S. Rosefielde, "An Assessment of the Sources and Uses of GULAG Forced Labour, 1929–56," "Excess Mortality in the Soviet Union," and "Incriminating Evidence: Excess Deaths and Forced Labour Under Stalin," *Soviet Studies*, 1:1981, 3:1983, 2:1987. On Stalin's foreign policy, see above all A. Ulam, *Expansion and Coexistence* (1968).

Mussolini

The Italian dictatorship is insufficiently studied. C. Seton-Watson, *Italy from Liberalism to Fascism* (1967), offers an excellent introduction to the circumstances that made it possible. A. Lyttelton, *The Seizure of Power* (1973), describes ably its first decade. M. Knox, *Mussolini Unleashed, 1939–1941* (1982), and "Conquest, Foreign and Domestic, in Fascist Italy and Nazi Germany," *Journal of Modern History*, 56:1 (1984), explore where it was going.

Hitler and War

The best introduction to Nazi Germany remains K. D. Bracher, *The German Dictatorship* (1970). K. Hildebrand, *The Third Reich* (1984), and P. Ayçoberry, *The Nazi Question* (1981), are excellent on the interpretive issues. On Hitler himself, see first of all his own words: A. Hitler, *Mein Kampf* (Ralph Manheim translation, 1943), and *Hitler's Second Book* (1961). J. Fest, *Hitler* (1975), is by far the best biography. On the inner workings of the regime, M. Broszat, *The Hitler State* (1981), is outstanding. W. Deist, *The Wehrmacht and German Rearmament* (1981), is the best introduction to Hitler's war preparations. K. Hildebrand, *The Foreign Policy of the Third Reich* (1973), and G. Weinberg, *The Foreign Policy of Hitler's Germany* (1970, 1980), are excellent on foreign policy. W. Murray, *The Change in the European Balance of Power, 1938–39* (1984), provides outstanding analysis of the strategic consequences of Munich and dissects the West's failure to stop Hitler before he became too strong. On Hitler's responsibility for and movement toward genocide, see especially G. Fleming, *Hitler and the Final Solution* (1982), and R. Hilberg's classic, *The Destruction of the European Jews* (1961; revised and expanded, 1985).

Finally, A. J. P. Taylor's *The Origins of the Second World War* (1961), raised a storm by arguing that Hitler had no long-term vision and that war in 1939 was simply a result of opportunism and miscalculation. That view has found few supporters; Hitler's words, both public and private, demonstrate otherwise. C. Thorne, *The Approach of War, 1938–39* (1967), remains the best short narrative; G. Martel, ed., *The Origins of the Second World War Reconsidered* (1986), offers mostly hostile retrospective comment on Taylor.

33
From Second World War to Cold War, 1939–1949

The war that began on September 1, 1939, grew within two and a half years into a global conflict. Hitler destroyed Poland, invaded Scandinavia, and crushed France. That victory permitted Mussolini to overrule his flankers and begin a Mediterranean and Balkan war. It also encouraged Japan to move southward on a collision course with Britain and the United States. And it gave Hitler the strategic and economic base needed to begin "his" war for *Lebensraum* in the East and racist world revolution.

On June 22, 1941, Germany attacked the Soviet Union. That at last brought into existence an "anti-Hitler coalition" powerful enough to bring the Reich down. On December 7, 1941, Imperial Japan completed that coalition by forcing into war a still reluctant United States. Hitler and Japan made the "last European war" of 1939–41 a global struggle; henceforth others beside Europeans would decide Europe's fate.

Only Hitler united his enemies. As the Reich began to fail in its desperate battle against three world powers, those enemies diverged. Stalin sought to expand his power far beyond the eastern European sphere that Hitler had conceded him in 1939. Britain and America hesitantly sought the Soviet despot's cooperation in a postwar system of world order, a successor to the defunct League of Nations. Given that

fundamental divergence, "cold war" predictably succeeded war once Hitler was dead. By 1947–48, what remained of eastern Europe after Hitler's end had suffered yet another revolution from above—Soviet style. But this time, unlike 1919, the United States did not withdraw from Europe. It reluctantly committed forces to hold in "peacetime" against Stalin the positions stormed in war against Hitler. Global war gave way to global confrontation between the new superpowers, under the shadow of weapons of unimaginable power, atomic and then thermonuclear bombs.

THE NEW WARFARE

The internal combustion engine gave the Second World War an entirely different character from its predecessor. When combined with armor, radios, and airpower, it gave back the battlefield mobility that industrial firepower had taken away in 1914–18. The second German war was a war of movement; its pace at times rivalled or exceeded the campaigns of Napoleon. Only in fortified areas and when evenly matched forces met head-on did the fighting congeal for months at a time into something that resembled Verdun.

The tank came into its own. British theorists had suggested in the 1920s

Opposite: The face of a new world war: German mechanized infantry destroys a Russian village, 1941.

that large armored formations might restore movement to the battlefield. But cavalry conservatism, Chamberlain's budget stringency, and his government's resolve before 1939 to never again fight on the Continent killed innovation in Britain. In Germany the tank caught on during the rapid expansion after 1933; in 1935 Germany set up its first *Panzerdivisionen* or armored divisions. By September 1939 it had six of them.

Contrary to myth, Germany's armored forces did not arise in response to a Hitler demand for tools with which to implement a "*Blitzkrieg*" or "lighting war" strategy that would substitute short decisive campaigns for the grinding attrition of World War I. Until 1938, Hitler gave the army its head. He was fortunate and Europe and the world unfortunate that his professionals successfully combined motors, armor, radios, and the German deep penetration tactics of 1917–18 into an instrument capable of smashing the European balance of power.

At sea, oil-fired turbines and diesel engines gave the great fleets far greater range than their coal-fired predecessors. A new capital ship, the aircraft carrier, rivalled and soon replaced the Dreadnought as the backbone of seapower. The fast fleet carriers of the Imperial Japanese and U.S. navies could by 1941 reach out several hundred miles beyond the horizon to rain armor-piercing bombs on the enemy. Refuelling at sea gave the fleets combat ranges of many thousands of miles. And the amphibious techniques that the U.S. Marine Corps pioneered— partly to ward off raids on its budget between the wars—allowed Americans and British to fight their way back after the opening Allied disasters.

In the air, the scene was likewise entirely changed. Airpower was no longer an infant. It proved capable of a multiplicity of missions, from "strategic" bombing of the enemy's homeland, to transport of troops and supplies, dropping of parachute or glider infantry, close support of ground troops, deep photoreconnaissance, attack on opposing fleets, antisubmarine patrol, and air defense. Air superiority was the key to rapid forward move-

Fleet carrier: the USS *Lexington* in 1939.

ment whether by land or sea, and was indispensable for amphibious landings. Only the Germans, in the last phases of the war, proved tough and expert enough to fight successfully for long without air cover.

The greatest novelty of all was the role of science and technology. Fritz Haber's nitrate process had made Germany's survival possible until 1918. But in World War I science had in other respects been a mere auxiliary. By 1939 that was no longer true. Decisive or potentially decisive weapons such as radar, liquid-fuel ballistic missiles, jet aircraft, computers to decipher enemy signals, and the atomic bomb required a high level of scientific skill, technological expertise, and economic power.

The bomb's practical realization was only possible thanks to an unprecedented commitment of scientific talent and resources, a commitment only the United States was equipped to make. The spur for this first example of "command science"—a vast government-directed research project aiming at a goal—was the fear that the Germans would reach that goal first. Fortunately, German physicists advanced slowly and hesitantly, and Hitler gave priority to projects that promised us-

able weapons soon. The American "Manhattan Project" spent a staggering $2 billion and drained away the hydroelectric power of the Tennessee Valley and Pacific Northwest. But by July 1945 it had produced uranium and plutonium bombs usable against Japan. Science made possible and war demanded weapons of mass destruction that were for the first time potentially capable of annihilating humanity.

THE INDUSTRIAL AND GEOGRAPHIC BALANCE

Even more than its predecessor, the war was a struggle between opposing war economies. Germany began at a slight disadvantage in total industrial potential compared to that of Britain and France. But its unassailable geographic position, control of Rumania's oil, and economic aid from Stalin more than compensated. A major proportion of Germany's rubber requirements flowed in through Vladivostok. The oil of Baku fuelled the Reich's U-boats, aircraft, and tanks. Turkey's chrome and Finland's nickel hardened the armor of the *Panzer* divisions. In 1940 Sweden provided almost half of Hitler's iron ore

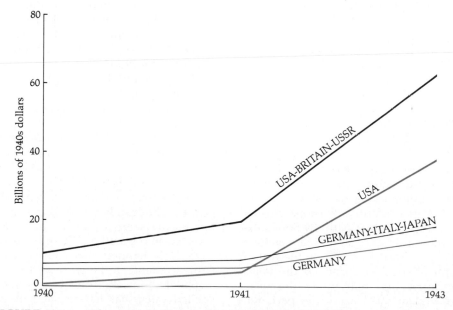

FIGURE 33-1   The Axis Defeated: War Production, 1940–43

through the Baltic and the coastal waters of Norway. This time, the British blockade was ineffective.

The collapse of France brought much booty, and France's industries, which henceforth worked for the Reich rather than against it. But Italy's consequent entry into the war extended Germany's military and economic liabilities without compensation; Britain now had an enemy it could defeat in Africa and the Mediterranean. And by the fall–winter of 1940, the economic power of the United States had begun to swing against Germany.

That threat helped decide Hitler for war against the Soviet Union, which he expected would swiftly crumble. But the Soviets held, although barely; Germany thereafter faced a coalition of world powers with at least three times Germany's industrial potential. The addition of Japan to the Axis powers in December 1941 was small gain; Britain, the United States, and the Soviet Union still had over two and a half times the potential of the "Hitler-coalition" of Germany, Italy, and Japan (see Figure 33-1). The Soviet refusal to collapse and Hitler's rejection of Stalin's secret bids for an armistice left one alternative: the eventual destruction of the Reich under a rain of fire and steel from the east, the west, and the skies.

FROM EUROPEAN TO GLOBAL WAR, 1939–41

Poland: Defeat and Vivisection

Poland fought bravely, but not long. The *Luftwaffe* savagely bombed railroads, roads, refugees, and cities. German armored units stormed forward in north and center, and sliced the Polish forces into pockets. The slower masses of German infantry divisions crushed everything in their path. By September 15 the most serious fighting was over. Stalin attacked the Poles in the rear on September 17 and claimed the Polish territories due him under the secret protocol to the Nazi-Soviet pact. Rib-

bentrop returned to Moscow and ironed out with his hosts, "as if in conversation with old party comrades," the new Russo-German border. The Germans also agreed to take in several hundred thousand ethnic Germans from the Baltic States of Estonia, Latvia, and Lithuania, upon which Stalin now forced a Soviet protectorate.

In Poland, Soviets and Nazis indeed showed a remarkable similarity of method. As Stalin remarked much later to a Yugoslav Communist, "This war is not as in the past; whoever occupies a territory also imposes on it his own social system. . . . It cannot be otherwise." Beginning in September 1939, Stalin deported to the GULAG over a million Polish prisoners of war and civilians. To decapitate any future Polish national resistance, Stalin's secret police (the NKVD) shot roughly 11,000 Polish officers in April 1940; the bodies of many of them turned up in 1943 in a mass grave in the Katyn forest in western Russia. The Baltic States suffered similar deportations and massacres when the Soviet Union swallowed them totally in June–July 1940. And Stalin, who so loved foreign Communists that he had liquidated many of them in the Great Terror, also handed over to the SS hundreds of German and Austrian Communists who had sought refuge in the Soviet Union. Stalin was not joking when he publicly hailed "Russo-German friendship, cemented by blood."

Himmler and his sinister subordinate Reinhard Heydrich lacked Stalin's long experience in truly large-scale killing; they found in Poland a convenient proving ground. With the advancing *Wehrmacht* forces came *Einsatzkommandos* ("task forces") of SS and Police, with the mission of killing both Jews, and Poles with an education, especially priests. Thousands perished in experimental massacres; German army protests led to a brief halt. Then the army sheepishly handed over control of occupied Poland to the party and SS.

Hitler himself, on October 18, spelled out what he expected of the

Poles: "cheap slaves." Himmler concentrated the Jews of Poland in artificially created ghettos as a "first prerequisite" for an as yet unspecified "final goal." He also shipped in Baltic Germans and carpetbaggers from the "Old Reich" to fill areas cleared of Poles and Jews. And war freed Hitler even inside Germany. In October 1939 he ordered, in secret, the killing of mental patients and the handicapped in order to rid the "race" of "worthless life." The totalitarian reshaping of Europe had begun.

Grossdeutschland Triumphant

The West made no attempt to help the Poles, despite repeated pre-war French pledges to attack Germany from the west. The French instead peered fearfully from their casemates and ventured a few inept patrol actions. By the end of September 1939 the Germans were happily redeploying their forces from Poland to the French and Belgian borders.

Hitler immediately demanded of his generals an attack in the west. Time was against Germany. The British were belatedly creating a new mass army; Allied war production was rising; America "was still not dangerous to us because of her neutrality laws," but that might change. Germany must "choose between victory or defeat. I choose victory." The generals grumbled that they needed more time. Some hesitantly plotted against the regime.

Unfortunately for the West, weather forced repeated postponements on Hitler. That unsought breathing space gave the German army time to add additional vehicles, draw lessons from the fighting in Poland, and train relentlessly. Hitler and a brilliant junior general, Erich von Manstein, also had time to replace the army staff's hastily improvised copy of the Schlieffen Plan with an unexpected armored thrust through the hills around Luxembourg.

Distractions in Scandinavia, where the Soviets were active, also dogged Germany throughout the winter. Stalin misjudged the Finns: they did not tamely acquiesce to Soviet demands for military bases and territory as had the defenseless Baltic states. On November 30 Stalin therefore attacked Finland and proclaimed a puppet Finnish Communist government in a captured border town. The League of Nations, in its last memorable act, expelled the Soviet Union. But the Finns and the great powers, not world opinion, determined the outcome. Russian numbers finally wore the Finns down in February–March 1940, but not before Stalin's ineptly led troops had suffered several hundred thousand casualties. Fearing that Soviet occupation of Finland would lead to continued fighting and Allied intervention in Scandinavia, Stalin imposed on the Finns only the small amputations he had demanded at the outset.

War in Scandinavia indeed attracted Allied and German hopes and fears. Paris sought to expand the war on the periphery, away from the plains of northern France. Winston Churchill, whom Chamberlain had found himself compelled to take into the cabinet as chief of the Royal Navy, urged attacks on Germany's vulnerable iron ore supply line to neutral Sweden. The Germans prepared to parry; they in turn coveted for their submarines and commerce raiders a window on the Atlantic in Norway.

The Germans struck first. On April 9, using the *Luftwaffe* to compensate for their naval inferiority, they seized key points in Norway with brilliant amphibious and airborne coups. German ground troops also swiftly bagged Denmark. Britain and France belatedly landed forces in central and northern Norway but German speed, skill, and air superiority drove them out by early June.

Defeat in Scandinavia at last destroyed the doleful Chamberlain as a war leader. On May 10, 1940, Winston Churchill came to power at the head of an all-party coalition. Labour, which had damned Churchill in earlier years for his uncompromising hostility to striking miners, Gandhi, and Hitler,

Victor and vanquished, June 1940: British troops await shipping on the Dunkirk beaches; Hitler tours Paris.

now staunchly refused to serve under Churchill's appeasement-minded conservative rival, Lord Halifax. Churchill, it now appeared, had at least been right about Hitler.

But Churchill arrived almost too late. The day of his appointment, May 10, 1940, was the day of the long-awaited German offensive against France and the Low Countries. The Germans had prepared well. The *Luftwaffe*, despite heavy losses, swept the skies of French aircraft and savagely bombed Rotterdam to cow the Dutch. German infantry swiftly crushed the small and inexperienced armies of Holland and Belgium. Seven *Panzerdivisionen* and three motorized infantry divisions struck through Luxembourg and the Ardennes hills, and reached the Channel on May 20, cutting off 40 of the best-equipped Allied divisions in the Low Countries. Of that huge force, 1.2 million fell prisoner; only 226,000 British and 112,000 French escaped from the beaches of Dunkirk.

On June 17, after the Germans had seized Paris, a new French government under the aged Marshal Pétain sued for armistice. By June 24 France was out of the war; only small "Free French" forces under the command of a charismatic junior general, Charles de Gaulle, fought on overseas with British help. Hitler occupied the north and west of France, and conceded to Pétain only an enclave in the south with a capital at Vichy. Greater Germany—*Grossdeutschland*—now controlled Europe from the North Cape of Norway to the Spanish border. Hitler had apparently succeeded where William II and Ludendorff had failed. In the intoxication of victory and looted champagne, the German generals and Hitler's remaining conservative opponents forgot their earlier doubts. War, as he had hoped, had made Hitler *Führer* indeed.

Britain, America, and the German Strategic Impasse

Victory in France did not end the war. Hitler expected Britain to "see reason" and join the Reich as a junior partner. But Churchill refused to give in: "Nations that went down fighting rose again but those which surrendered tamely were finished." He carried the cabinet against Chamberlain and Halifax, who in the name of "realism" sought negotiations from weakness. Churchill was confident that rising British fighter production would keep the Germans from achieving air superiority and invading Britain.

He also bid ruthlessly for the American support needed to fight on; better Roosevelt as senior partner than Hitler. On May 20 Churchill secretly warned the U.S. president that failure to support Britain might lead to a new British government, committed to negotiations. Such a government might swing the British fleet to the Axis side and mortally threaten the United States in the North Atlantic. And to show Roosevelt and the world that Britain would fight so long as he led it, Churchill on July 3 crippled with coordinated naval attacks the fleet of Britain's ex-ally, France. That blow removed the possibility that the new Pétain regime in

France might swing the Mediterranean and Atlantic naval balance in favor of the Axis.

The fall of France at last galvanized American opinion; Roosevelt belatedly responded both to Churchill's polite blackmail and to his demonstration of resolve. Congress conceded America's first peace-time military draft in August 1940; America's dwarf army of 280,000 thus had the means to once more become a serious force—in a few years. For the present, Roosevelt defied the spirit of a congressional ban on weapons sales. In September 1940 he traded 50 obsolete U.S. destroyers for base rights in Newfoundland, Bermuda, and the Caribbean, and for a pledge that Britain would never turn its fleet over to the Germans. In November 1940 Roosevelt rode triumphantly over his Republican opponent, Wendell Willkie, to an unprecedented third presidential term.

Hitler drew the moral from these events as early as July 31: "England's hope is Russia and America. If hope in Russia falls away, America too falls away, for after elimination of Russia an immense increase in Japan's power in East Asia follows." If Germany destroyed the Soviet Union, Japan would be free of threat on its northern flank and would keep the Americans busy in the Pacific. Hitler thus sought an immediate attack on the Soviet Union. War in the East was not only "his" war, sought since 1922, to secure for Germany a vast blockade-proof eastern empire, a "German India." It was also the answer to the increasing support of the United States for Britain. A German "world *Blitzkrieg*" would make Germany unassailable by conquering the Soviet Union before Roosevelt could bring to bear the immense economic and military potential of the United States.

But Hitler's planners soon told him that weather would not permit an eastern campaign that fall. He therefore fell back on stopgaps. Germany launched a sea and air war against Britain's Atlantic supply lines, but that struggle of at-

Churchill inspects the ruins of the House of Commons after a German attack.

The German navy and Ribbentrop offered other options. The Navy pressed for a Mediterranean campaign that would seize Britain's outpost at Gibraltar with the help of Franco's Spain and would galvanize the Italians to take Suez. Ribbentrop attempted to create a world coalition from Madrid to Tokyo against the Anglo-Saxon powers. On September 27, 1940, Ribbentrop succeeded in enlisting the Japanese and Mussolini in a "Tripartite Pact" that pledged all three powers to come to one another's aid in the event of war with America. But Franco and Mussolini between them wrecked the navy's plan and the European part of Ribbentrop's planned coalition. Franco set his price for intervention higher in supplies and territory than Hitler was willing to pay. That scotched the Gibraltar operation. Mussolini, at the end of October 1940, threw the Mediterranean theater into chaos. He attacked Greece without Hitler's approval; the Greeks hurled the ill-trained Italians back into Albania in confusion. British torpedo bombers subsequently sank three Italian battleships at anchor and British armored forces from Egypt crushed the large but ill-led Italian army in Libya between December 1940 and February 1941.

Italy's disasters compelled Hitler to intervene in the Mediterranean—not to achieve final victory over Britain, but merely to rescue his ally. U-boats, a *Luftwaffe* air corps, and armored units under the brilliant but erratic Erwin Rommel arrived in time to prevent the collapse of Italy's position in northern Africa, and of Mussolini's regime. In spring 1941 Hitler extricated the Italians from Greece by striking south through Rumania and Bulgaria into Greece, and by dismantling with much slaughter a potentially hostile Yugoslavia.

These new victories did not offer Germany a long-term strategic alternative. No defeat in the Mediterranean or Middle East could force Britain to make peace, so long as it held the North Atlantic and the support of the United

trition offered no prospect of immediate results and threatened to speed Roosevelt's drift toward war. A second possibility was operation SEA LION, an invasion of Britain for which the Germans began preparation in July. But in vast battles over southern England that reached their climax on September 15, the Spitfires and Hurricanes of the Royal Air Force (RAF) denied the *Luftwaffe* air superiority. The Germans, in a fury at RAF nuisance raids on Berlin, switched to the night bombing of the winter 1940–41 "Blitz." They razed large areas of London and killed civilians by the thousands but failed to break British morale.

States. And Roosevelt, despite a continuing isolationist opposition that trumpeted that "the British, the Jew[s], and the Roosevelt administration" sought to force America into war, was at last achieving results. In February–March 1941, Anglo-American staff talks secretly established the strategic principle that was to govern the future U.S. war effort—*"Germany first."* If and when the United States entered the war, it would concentrate its power against the West's most dangerous enemy. In March 1941 Congress passed a "Lend-Lease Act" that offered to a financially exhausted Britain, and thereafter to other U.S. allies, an almost unlimited supply of arms on long-term credit. Credits later turned into outright gifts, and ultimately amounted to $43 billion.

Racist War of Annihilation: BARBAROSSA

Even before Lend-Lease offered unambiguous evidence that the United States was moving toward Britain, Hitler had decided on his response: "his" war, the war in the East. Ribbentrop had invited the Soviets to Berlin to explore the possibility of Soviet participation in the Tripartite Pact. The uncouth Molotov's visit, on November 12 and 13, 1940, was decisive. To Ribbentrop's fantasies about a Soviet outlet to the warm seas through Iran and British India, Molotov replied with a long shopping list in Europe. Stalin wanted Soviet bases at the Turkish Straits, the addition of Bulgaria to the Soviet "security zone," the removal of tacit German protection over Finland, and joint Soviet-Danish—but not Soviet-German—control over the exits from the Baltic. Molotov also stressed the Soviet Union's "interest" in Rumania, Hungary, Yugoslavia, Greece, and even the portion of Poland currently assigned to Germany under the Nazi-Soviet Pact. The tactlessness and breadth of Molotov's demands suggested that Stalin expected the Anglo-

Spitfire!

Saxon powers to defeat Germany and was claiming his booty in advance.

Hitler was relieved. Stalin had "let the cat out of the bag." The Russo-German "marriage of convenience" was over. On December 18, Hitler issued a directive for the greatest land war in history, Operation BARBAROSSA: "The German *Wehrmacht* must

St. Paul's Cathedral, London, under *Luftwaffe* bombardment, January 23, 1941.

be prepared to *overthrow Soviet Russia in a swift campaign,* even before the end of the war with England." BARBAROSSA would annihilate all Soviet forces in European Russia and seize a line from Archangel to Astrakhan. Hitler and his planners assumed that stroke would crush the Soviet regime and would ultimately give Germany world mastery.

The generals bent to planning and deployment with a will. They shared Hitler's racist contempt for the Red Army and found the destruction of the Soviet Union an "intriguing" operational problem. But for Hitler it was more than that. "The coming campaign," he told his subordinates on March 3, "is more than a mere armed conflict; it also entails a struggle between two ideologies." And since, by Hitler's racist logic, Bolshevism was an outgrowth of Judaism, the ideological struggle required "racial" measures: "The Jewish-Bolshevik intelligentsia . . . must be removed."

What that meant in practice soon became clear. Hitler's military assistants issued orders empowering Himmler of the SS to accomplish "special tasks" in the coming area of operations. *Einsatzgruppen* ("task groups") of the SS and Police, with army cooperation, would take "executive measures with respect to the civilian population" of Russia. The army itself, under the "Commissar Order" of May–June 1941, became for the first time a direct extension of Hitler's racial goals. That order required the shooting upon capture of all Red Army political officers and Communist party members. The *Wehrmacht* estimated that it would take 3.5 million prisoners of war but allocated rations for only 790,000; the rest would presumably starve. And the experts of Göring's economic planning staff established the principle that the territories to be conquered would have to feed the *Wehrmacht*—leaving no food for the cities of European Russia. "X millions of people will die out," noted the bureaucrats dispassionately. BARBAROSSA was to be a racial and ideological war of extermination, a war that

trampled underfoot all limits on interstate violence established in Europe since the Thirty Years' War. Colonial war had come home to Europe.

On June 22, 1941, the *Wehrmacht* struck the Soviet Union on a front that stretched from the Baltic to the Black Sea. Germany had deployed 3 million troops, 625,000 horses, 600,000 motor vehicles, 3,380 tanks, and 7,184 artillery pieces. Stalin received numerous warnings, but spurned them as "capitalist provocations" designed to involve him in an unwanted and unnecessary war with Hitler. The German deception plan held. Until the last, thanks to numerous rumors that the Germans had planted to make their deployment appear a gigantic attempt to extort more raw materials from the Soviet Union, Stalin expected a German ultimatum.

He instead received an attack. "What shall we do?" he reportedly asked the Politburo before suffering a nervous collapse. Not until July 3 did he belatedly take to the radio and in a broken voice exhort his Soviet "brothers and sisters" to resist to the last. Stalin evidently had difficulty believing that those whom he had terrorized would fight for him. They fought above all for biological survival and Great Russian nationalism. Immense German massacres of prisoners of war and Jews stiffened Soviet resistance. And the Soviet regime now appealed not to "proletarian internationalism" but to something far stronger. It invoked the Russian traditions that Stalin had himself fostered through the historical rehabilitation, in the 1930s, of past rulers whose methods resembled his own: Ivan the Terrible and Peter the Great.

The Germans nevertheless advanced swiftly, thanks to strategic surprise and to their overwhelming advantages in doctrine, experience, and *Luftwaffe* airpower. By the first days of August they had taken Smolensk, halfway to Moscow, and had killed or taken prisoner well over a million Soviets. Hitler looked to the future; he believed he had won. He ordered German armament efforts shifted to air and sea warfare against the Anglo-Americans. Subordinates drafted a directive for German thrusts in "the period after BARBAROSSA" through the Caucasus to the Middle East oilfields. Germany, Hitler privately declared, would raze Moscow and Leningrad to the ground, exterminate much of the population of European Russia, and replace it with German settlers. The term "Greater German World Empire," which Goebbels had banned from his press in 1940 as premature, no longer seemed inappropriate.

July–December 1941: The Culmination of the War

Others saw different vistas. Churchill and Roosevelt immediately offered aid to a surprised Stalin. The despot accepted it in the spirit in which it was offered; as he once remarked, "In war I would deal with the Devil and his mother." But the Western powers nevertheless assumed that the Germans would destroy Russia. Roosevelt and Churchill met on shipboard near Newfoundland in mid-August 1941, and produced an "Atlantic Charter," a declaration of war aims in the style of Woodrow Wilson.

The Charter implied that the United States would eventually enter the war. It proclaimed that Britain or America sought "no aggrandizement, territorial or other" and desired "no territorial changes that [did] not accord with the freely expressed wishes of the people concerned." It announced that both powers would seek free markets, freedom of the seas, and "freedom from fear and want" for all humanity. The Western powers made no reference to the third member of the new "Grand Alliance," or to that power's entirely different principles and methods. Roosevelt and Churchill evidently expected that they alone would dictate the outcome of the new world war. The United States prepared to do its part by planning an army that would surpass

the *Wehrmacht:* 215 divisions of which 61 would be armored.

The Newfoundland meeting was the outward and political expression of a halting change in Roosevelt's policy. In the conviction that the aid "short of war" promised with Lend-Lease was not enough to defeat Hitler, he began to take steps toward war itself. Without the formal approval of Congress, Roosevelt embarked between July and September on an undeclared naval conflict in the North Atlantic. U.S. forces relieved the British troops occupying Iceland, an outpost Hitler coveted, and Roosevelt agreed to convoy British shipping from Canada to Iceland. In September, after the inevitable naval incident, he gave the U.S. Navy orders to "shoot on sight" at U-boats.

Immediately before sailing to meet Churchill, Roosevelt also moved against Japan. Hitler's May–June 1940 victory in Europe had encouraged Tokyo to turn southward toward the vital oil of the Dutch East Indies. That thrust, and gestures such as the Berlin-Rome-Tokyo Tripartite Pact alliance of September 1940, had freed Roosevelt to react. Then a Soviet-Japanese nonaggression pact of April 1941 and Hitler's attack on the Soviet Union in June ended Tokyo's latent fear of a Soviet threat on its northern flank in Manchuria. In July 1941, Japan occupied bases in the southern part of French Indochina and prepared for further moves toward the oil of the Dutch East Indies. Roosevelt in reply ordered all Japanese assets in the United States frozen, and restricted the U.S. oil exports upon which Japan depended. The Dutch took similar measures. Japan in the space of a week lost 90 percent of its oil supplies. Roosevelt himself seems to have intended only to throttle back those supplies as a warning; zealous subordinates were responsible for the total cutoff.

Tokyo responded with an offer to moderate its activities in China and Indochina. Roosevelt and his advisers judged Japan insincere and its offer impossible of fulfillment given the Jap-

Before the rains came: the German drive on Moscow, October 1941.

Pearl Harbor, December 7, 1941.

anese army's long record of dominating governments in Tokyo. The Japanese army privately concurred; it refused to give up its Chinese colony. Tokyo decided in September to go to war with the United States while its navy still had oil stocks and before U.S. naval rearmament was complete, unless a breakthrough occurred in negoti-

ations. None did. In mid-October the military rulers of Japan dropped their facade; Prince Konoye's civilian cabinet gave way to the government of General Tōjō Hideki. On November 26, as Roosevelt again insisted on Japanese withdrawal from China, Japan's fast carrier forces secretly sailed.

In Russia, the Germans belatedly closed on Moscow. Hitler had in July and August diverted armored forces south to the Ukraine, where they took another 650,000 prisoners in a great encirclement at Kiev. The Ukraine operation, troop exhaustion, and logistical difficulties delayed the final drive on Moscow until early October. But once lauched, operation TYPHOON made dramatic progress. The Germans demolished yet another Soviet army group and seized a further 600,000 prisoners in the great battles of Vyazma and Bryansk.

In the Soviet capital, the NKVD disappeared from the street-corners. Bonfires in the ministry courtyards consumed mountains of files. Bureaucrats fled for Kuibyshev on the Volga River, designated as alternate capital. The announcement that Stalin remained in the Kremlin and a few exemplary shootings stabilized the situation briefly—but the Soviet regime appeared close to collapse. Then the fall rains bogged the *Panzerdivisionen* and their supply echelons in Russian mud. The ensuing freeze briefly speeded the advance again, although Soviet resistance stiffened. German reconnaissance units reached the outskirts of Moscow; they could see the flashes of the anti-aircraft guns on the Kremlin roof. But the Germans were desperate. By early December, only a quarter of their original tank force could move and 23 of every 100 German soliders who had invaded the Soviet Union were dead, missing, or wounded. On December 5 Hitler consented to halt. The next morning fresh Soviet troops counterattacked and threw the Germans into confusion. Hitler had failed to destroy the Soviet Union.

The following day, December 7, 1941, came news that the Japanese naval air arm had struck the U.S. base at Pearl Harbor and had crippled the battleship force of the Pacific fleet. The military logic of the Japanese attack was as impeccable as its execution was flawless—except that it missed the fleet carriers, which were at sea. The U.S. Navy was the main obstacle to a Japanese southward advance to the oil of the Dutch East Indies. A preemptive strike to eliminate it had therefore appeared necessary. But the Japanese in their desperation had given small thought to Pearl Harbor's political and strategic consequences. It freed Roosevelt of the delicate task of persuading Congress to declare war in defense of British and Dutch colonies, and produced instantaneous unanimity in the United States. Isolationists, many of whom regarded themselves as defenders of American ethnic purity against contamination from the outside world, took up with a fierce racism the cause of crushing Japan. Nor had Tokyo, thanks to its own racist disdain for outsiders and its consequent underestimation of American resolve, given much thought to methods of ending the war it had begun, a war that it entered at an economic disadvantage of at least six to one.

Hitler closed the circle on December 11, 1941; he declared war on the United States. He apparently hoped that a simultaneous two-ocean war would prevent America from concentrating its power decisively in either theater. His decision, like that of the Japanese, handed Roosevelt an immense political-strategic victory. The president now had no need to persuade Congress to declare the war on Germany that he needed to implement America's long-decided strategy of "Germany first." Hitler's declaration of war compelled an American effort in Europe and guaranteed that it would be wholehearted. Hitler and Tokyo between them ensured the defeat of the Axis and the end of Europe's independence.

THE "FINAL SOLUTION"

The realization that Germany might lose spurred Hitler to greater military efforts. It also led him to make sure of one thing: the accomplishment of the "historic mission" he had defined for Germany, the elimination of the alleged threat of "Jewish world domination." The "executive measures" of the SS against the civilian population of Russia that Hitler ordered in March–April 1941 took effect during the head-

---

Hitler Gloats Openly over the Extermination of the Jews 1942

Few Germans later admitted to having known about it, but Hitler publicly boasted in scarcely veiled language about the "Final Solution" on four occasions in 1942 (January 30, February 24, September 30, and November 8):

I told the *Reichstag* session [January 30, 1939; see p. 935] two things:
First, that once they had forced the war upon us, neither armed force nor passage of time would bring us down, and second, that if Jewry were to unleash an international world war for the purpose of exterminating the Aryan peoples of Europe, then it would not be the Aryan peoples that would be exterminated, but Jewry. . . . The Jews in Germany once upon a time laughed at my prophesying. I do not know if they still laugh, or whether their laughter has already ceased. I can however now assure you that they will never laugh again [*es wird ihnen das Lachen überall vergehen*]. And *that* prophecy of mine will also be confirmed.

You will still remember the Reichstag session in which I declared:
If Jewry thinks it can produce an international world war to exterminate the European races, then the consequence will not be the extermination of the European races, but rather the extermination [*Ausrottung*] of Jewry in Europe. People have always laughed at my prophecies. Of those who laughed, innumerable ones no longer laugh, and those who still laugh will perhaps in a little while also no longer laugh.

Hitler speeches at Berlin and Munich, September 30 and November 8, 1942, in *Hitler: Reden und Proklamationen 1932–1945*, ed. by Max Domarus, (Munich, 1965), Vol. II:2, pp. 1920, 1937 (translation by M. Knox).

long *Wehrmacht* advance from June to December. SS and Police *Einsatzgruppen* rounded up and shot as many of European Russia's 4.7 million Jews as they could catch.

The *Wehrmacht* protested far less now than it had over the 1939 killings in Poland. Hitler's victories had immeasurably reinforced his authority and that of his ideology, and the army too had its *Freikorps* tradition, the shooting of Bolsheviks "while attempting to escape." Until the war turned in December 1941, high German commanders such as Manstein or Walther von Reichenau had no qualms about ordering subordinates to shoot Soviet prisoners and Jews: "The [German] soldier must be fully convinced of the necessity of harsh, but just expiation by the Jewish-Bolshevik subhumans."

But the Jews of Russia were only part of the target. At the height of his victories in July 1941, Hitler remarked of the Jews of Europe that "if any [European] state . . . permits a Jewish family to remain, that [family] will become the bacteria-breeding-ground for a new infection." On July 31, 1941, Himmler's subordinate Heydrich received orders to organize, "with the

The "Final Solution": Jewish deportees arrive at Auschwitz.

participation of all necessary German central bureaucracies, all preparations for a general solution of the Jewish Question in Europe."

Hitler himself was apparently careful not to sign a document authorizing what soon became known in the SS and the German ministries as the "Final Solution of the Jewish Question." But both his public remarks and private actions leave little doubt that he was the driving force behind it. He repeatedly demanded reports of the progress of the killings, and in November 1941 promised the Grand Mufti of Jerusalem, leader of the Palestinian Arabs, that when Germany conquered the Middle East he would "annihilate" the Jews there as well.

In September–October 1941 the SS began deporting the Jews of Germany and Austria to Poland and occupied Russia. The SS shot many in mass executions. But that method soon proved cumbersome given the immense numbers of Jews anticipated. In the fall, winter, and spring of 1941–42, Himmler and his subordinates therefore set up camps in occupied Poland designed as factories of death, with gas chambers and crematoria: Auschwitz-Birkenau, Treblinka, Lublin, Sobibor, Belzec, Chelmno. In January 1942, at a conference in the flossy Berlin suburb of Wannsee, Heydrich asked the major Reich ministries to assist him in deporting the Jews—men, women, and children—to the death camps: "Europe will be combed through from west to east."

The "Final Solution" did not end until November 1944, when Himmler, on his own initiative, suspended it as the Reich neared collapse. Its consequence was the murder of over 6 million Jews including a quarter of a million from Germany, well over a million from Russia, 3 million from Poland, 200,000 from western Europe, and at least 750,000 from eastern Europe.

But the Jews were only the victims with the highest priority. The Gypsies of Europe also suffered deportation to the death camps on "racial" grounds;

hundreds of thousands perished. German experts tested killing factory techniques on German mental patients and handicapped as well as on Jews. Between 1941 and 1945 the SS and *Wehrmacht* between them killed the staggering total of 3.3 million Red Army prisoners from shooting or maltreatment. The Poles suffered over 2 million dead during German conquest and occupation. And Hitler's intention in the event of military victory was to remove most of the population of eastern Europe and European Russia. Hitler's genocide was not simply a Holocaust of the Jewish people. It was part of a pseudo-biological attempt to remodel humanity—a racist world revolution.

It also went unchallenged, except on distant battlefields and in a doomed 1943 uprising in the Warsaw ghetto. French police and Dutch SS helped round up Jews for deportation. Slovaks, Greeks, and Hungarians cooperated with greater or lesser enthusiasm. Rumanians and Croats organized their own massacres of Jews; Latvians, Lithuanians, and Ukrainians provided the SS with valuable auxiliaries. The major exceptions were Denmark, Norway, Bulgaria, and even Fascist Italy; those governments and peoples faced the Germans with bureaucratic roadblocks and passive resistance, and saved many of their Jews.

The churches and the Allies did little. Protestants were generally silent except in Scandinavia. Pope Pius XII, despite excellent information about the death camps, offered only generic condemnations of the killing of civilians. Even the October 1943 deportation to Auschwitz of the Jews of Rome— "from under his windows," as the German ambassador put it—did not move Pius XII to public protest, although the Church did help to hide Jews. Stalin was himself a longstanding and virulent anti-Semite. Many high British and American bureaucrats harbored a poorly concealed distaste for Jewish refugees.

The Allies initially disbelieved the reports of the killing; deliberate, mech-

The "Final Solution"

The first train arrived . . . 45 freight cars with 6,700 people, of which 1,450 were already dead on arrival. . . . A large loudspeaker blares instructions: undress completely, take off artificial limbs, glasses, etc. Hand in all valuables. Shoes to be tied together (for the clothing collection). . . . Women and girls to the barber, who cuts off their hair in two or three strokes and stuffs it into potato sacks.

Then the line starts moving. . . . At the corner a strapping SS-man announces in a pastoral voice: Nothing will happen to you! Just breathe deeply inside the chambers, that stretches the lungs; this inhalation is necessary against the illnesses and epidemics. When asked what would happen to them, he replies: Well, of course the men will have to work, build houses and roads, but the women won't have to work. If they want to they can help in the household or the kitchen. For a few of these unfortunates a small glimmer of hope which suffices to have them take the few steps to the chambers without resistance—the majority knows what is ahead, the stench tells their fate. . . .

The wooden doors are opened. . . . Inside the chambers, the dead are closely pressed together, like pillars of stone. . . . Even in death one recognizes the families. They still hold hands, so they have to be torn apart to get the chambers ready for the next occupants. The corpses are thrown out—wet with sweat and urine, covered with excrement, menstrual blood. Children's bodies fly through the air. . . . Two dozen workers use hooks to pry open mouths and look for gold. . . . Others search genitals and anuses for gold, diamonds, and valuables. Wirth [an SS-guard] motions to me: Just lift this can of gold teeth, this is only from today and the day before! . . . .

From an eyewitness account of mass gassings, in *Vierteljahrshefte für Zeitgeschichte*, (1953), Vol. I, pp. 190–91.

anized mass murder seemed too monstrous even for Hitler. Britain did issue a declaration describing the deportations in December 1942, and Churchill pressed for air attacks on the rail lines leading to Auschwitz. But the great distances to the target, the military demands of the bomber offensive and of the Normandy invasion, and the bureaucratic sabotage of his subordinates prevented action.

Churchill did not resort in this case to the public threat with which he had greeted rumors in early 1942 that Hitler contemplated using poison gas against Britain's Soviet ally. Then Churchill had promised reprisals: a deluge of mustard gas from the air upon Germany. That all too credible threat had deterred Hitler, although the Reich had secretly stockpiled large quantities of nerve gas, a weapon far more powerful than anything in the Allied chemical arsenal. Unlike the Soviet Union, the Jews of Europe were not a state, a British or United States ally. They thus had last call on Allied resources. The victims of Hitler's genocide, like those of Stalin's, perished without even token assistance from that elusive force, world public opinion.

THE HOME FRONT: BUREAUCRACY, PROPAGANDA, TERROR, DEATH

On the home fronts, the war in part followed precedents laid down in World War I and in the Great Depression that had succeeded it. All major belligerents mobilized immense masses of men for war and industry. Women again joined the work force in vast numbers, except in Germany, where the regime's ideology dictated that they remain at home. The Reich filled the gap with up to 12 million Soviet prisoners of war, slave laborers, and foreign workers.

The totalitarian states had conducted themselves even in "peace" as if they were at war. Their economies, even when "capitalist" in formal terms, were largely state-directed even before 1939. War itself provided justification in Germany for ever greater state and Nazi party intervention in the economy and in daily life, and the occasion for ever more intense barrages of lies from Goebbels's "Ministry of Public Enlightenment and Propaganda."

As the ring around Germany grew tighter, terror itself became a key ingredient in the war effort; Hitler was fanatically determined to prevent a repetition of Germany's 1918 political collapse. Civilians who expressed doubts about "final victory" disappeared into Himmler's camps; military personnel guilty of "undermining the will to fight" perished by the thousands on *Wehrmacht* portable gallows. Conversely, Stalin in 1941 and 1942 gave survival priority even over domestic terror. NKVD pressure on the population and the army briefly relaxed. But once the Soviet Union gained the upper hand after 1943, arrests gradually increased once more.

The democracies, as in 1914–18, improvised after 1939 vast bureaucracies to guide public opinion and to ration food, raw materials, and labor. Press, radio, and film became an arm of the war effort. Censorship, often voluntary, normally prevented the publication of news deemed harmful to morale. Photographs of American battle dead rarely appeared. And as in the previous war, public discussion of war aims aroused excessive expectations. At home, especially in Britain, the vehicle of those expectations was planning for a post-war "welfare state" that would banish the misery of the Great Depression. In international politics, the new "United Nations" fulfilled a similiar propaganda function. A new and better League would replace that supposed evil, the balance of power, and secure peace through universal goodwill without excessive effort by the democracies. British and American war propaganda also encouraged a curious unrealism about the allegedly lovable nature and supposed agreement with the principles of the Atlantic Charter of jovial, pipe-smoking "Uncle Joe" Stalin.

Traditional democratic freedoms also suffered partial eclipse, especially for groups that appeared connected with the enemy. Churchill's government rounded up 30,000 German and Italian "enemy aliens" during the great invasion emergency of 1940 and imprisoned them not for offenses committed, but for *suspected* disloyalty. The United States faced an external threat far less immediate than Germans across the Channel. Pearl Harbor nevertheless triggered a hysterical racist clamor against the Japanese-American minority on the West Coast. Roosevelt ordered 112,000 of them deported to the interior; many lost farms and businesses. Deportees of military age put those responsible for this shabby treatment to shame by volunteering to fight. Many served as linguists in the Pacific. Their unit in Europe, the 442nd Regimental Combat Team, terrified the Germans and earned more decorations for valor than any American force of its size and time in combat.

Except for fortunate North America and distant Australia and New Zealand, all major belligerents suffered either occupation or devastation from the air. Many suffered both. That was the most striking difference between the two world wars. In the first, those behind the front had been virtually immune from violent death. In the second, scorched earth and famine, guerrilla warfare and assassinations, reprisals and massacres, and the rain of high explosive, magnesium, white phosphorus, and jellied gasoline from the skies bound "front" and "rear" in shared danger. This was a "total war" far more total than its predecessor.

THE SECOND WORLD WAR, 1941–45

The global war of December 1941 turned swiftly against the Axis. By summer–fall 1942 Germany and Japan were stalled everywhere, from the Don steppe to the South Pacific. Then Allied counterattacks drove the Axis back while air bombardment and submarine blockade wrecked the economies that sustained the Axis forces. As the Allies advanced, the divergences between them became increasingly visible.

The Last Successes of the Axis

While the Germans sought to rebuild the forces shattered in the 1941–42 winter fighting, Japan seized a perimeter from India's western border to Wake Island, west of Hawaii. Hong Kong, the Philippines, Singapore, and the Dutch East Indies rapidly fell to expertly executed air and amphibious operations. Douglas MacArthur, photogenic commander of U.S. forces in the Philippines, retired in March to Australia at Roosevelt's order. His troops fought on until overwhelmed in May. The inglorious surrender on February 15 of over 80,000 British and Empire troops at Singapore—to a smaller Japanese force—was the deathblow to "white" imperial prestige in Asia. By summer 1942 Japan appeared poised to attack India from Burma, while Gandhi inspired a new wave of demonstrations and riots against British rule.

But after a thrust south at New Guinea that led to a first indecisive action between carrier fleets, Japan struck at Midway Island, west of Hawaii. The decipherment of Japanese orders allowed Chester Nimitz, the U.S. theater commander, to lay an ambush. On June 3–6, 1942, the fleets traded air attacks near Midway—and the outnumbered U.S. Navy almost miraculously destroyed four Japanese fleet carriers and their highly trained pilots. The Battle of Midway tore the heart from the Japanese naval air force, and made Japan's far-flung perimeter untenable.

By June 1942, Hitler was himself ready for a last major offensive thrust, toward the oil of the Caucasus region. The *Panzerdivisionen* once again ripped immense gaps in the Soviet front. But as in 1941 Hitler failed to seek one objective and stick to it. As the Soviets crumbled, he ordered simultaneous drives on the Caucasus and on the key Soviet communications point on the Volga, Stalingrad. Both thrusts bogged down. At Stalingrad, the Germans soon found themselves in desperate street fighting in the rubble, where German armor and skill was little use. Bitter Soviet resistance turned Stalin's city into the Verdun of World War II.

Counterattack! Soviet infantry in the ruins of Stalingrad, 1943.

Hitler had lost the strategic initiative in December 1941. He had now lost even the operational initiative; Germany lacked the troops and equipment for wide-ranging offensives. Even in Africa, where Rommel had improvised a modest *Blitzkreig* at the end of a long and precarious supply line, the Germans halted in July 1942 at El Alamein, 75 miles short of Alexandria.

The Allies Strike Back

Allied counterblows soon came. In the Pacific, a Japanese threat to the long and precarious U.S. supply line to Australia provoked a Marine Corps landing at Guadalcanal, at the southern tip of the Solomon Islands. In a savage land, sea, and air battle of attrition that lasted from August 1942 to February 1943 the Marines and the U.S. Army forced the Japanese out. U.S. submarines began a ruthless campaign against Japanese merchant shipping that eventually cut Japan's seaborne empire into isolated fragments.

Rivalry between MacArthur and the Navy dictated a two-pronged thrust back across the Pacific. MacArthur laboriously ascended the Solomons and New Guinea toward the Philippines, to which he had theatrically vowed to return. The Navy, with Marine and U.S. Army landing forces backed by battleship gunfire and carrier aircraft, seized from late 1943 on a succession of blood-stained central Pacific islands: Tarawa, Kwajalein, Eniwetok, Saipan, Guam, Ulithi, Palau. In fall 1944 MacArthur and the Navy joined to invade the Philippines. From Saipan, Tinian, and Guam, the shining new B-29s, the largest and farthest-ranging bombers in existence, could henceforth batter the Japanese homeland.

British and Americans soon drove the Germans from northern Africa. In October–November 1942 the British desert commander, Bernard Montgomery, at last attacked Rommel at El Alamein. Montgomery deliberately fought a 1918-style methodical battle. Weight of fire, not skill, bore down his more nimble opponent. Rommel escaped to face an unexpected attack on his rear after an American-British task force landed in French northern Africa on

November 9, 1942. The slow-footed Allies failed to take Tunis before the Germans, but thereafter methodically laid siege to Rommel and his Italian allies by land, sea, and air. In May 1943 the Axis bridgehead around Tunis collapsed; Hitler and Mussolini lost almost a quarter of a million irreplaceable veterans. The Allies leapt to Sicily in July. As Mussolini's regime crumbled and Italy fled the war, they seized positions south of Rome in September–October 1943.

On the eastern front, the Soviets launched the greatest counteroffensive of all. On November 19, 1942, the Red Army struck from north and southeast of Stalingrad, and encircled 300,000 Germans and German allies in and near the city. Hitler, as was his habit,

ordered implacable resistance on the spot—no withdrawal or breakout, and no surrender. By the end, in February 1943, only 93,000 Germans remained alive to surrender, as food and ammunition ran out. In July 1943 Hitler ventured a last local offensive at Kursk, south of Moscow. Surprise was absent and Soviet antitank guns smashed the Germans in the greatest armored battle in history. Germany had lost even the tactical initiative in the East.

In the Atlantic, the U-boats that had savaged British and U.S. shipping in 1941–42 soon found themselves beleaguered. British microwave radar, British decipherment of the German navy's communications, and the addition of U.S. escorts and airpower to those of Britain won the "Battle of the Atlantic"

The Road to Tokyo Bay   1942–45

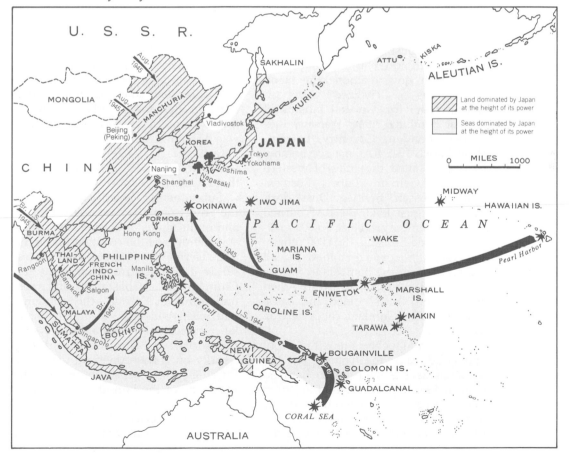

by May 1943. In that month the Germans sank 50 merchant ships at too steep a price: 41 U-boats and crews. The defeat of the U-boats made possible the American build-up in Britain for the coming assault on Hitler's "Fortress Europe."

That beleaguered fortress, as Churchill pointed out in a speech, lacked a roof. Stalin's increasing clamor for an Allied "second front" in Europe impelled Britain to pour vast resources into heavy bomber forces; only in the air could Britain strike directly at Germany. Since German fighters made daylight bombing suicidal, RAF Bomber Command concentrated on night raids. And at night, it emerged by the summer of 1941, British bombers lacked the precision navigation aids needed to hit any target smaller than a German city. The bomber offensive, for lack of alternatives, therefore sought to dislocate the German economy indirectly through what the chief of RAF Bomber Command described with relish as "de-housing" the Germans.

The Reich now paid dearly for having broken down, among the many conventions of "civilized" European warfare that it had violated, inhibitions against bombing cities: Warsaw, Rotterdam, London, Coventry, Belgrad. From March 1942 RAF massed bomber raids devastated the cities of western and central Germany: Lübeck, Rostock, Cologne, Essen, Bremen, Düsseldorf. In July–August 1943, the RAF burned most of Hamburg, killing 50,000 civilians and "de-housing" 800,000 others. The *Luftwaffe*, overcommitted on all fronts, took on the bombers in a bitter struggle of attrition. But fresh Allied aircraft and crews joined the battle faster than the Germans could destroy them.

Hitler and Goebbels took the fall of Stalingrad and the coming of the bombers as the occasion to demand total mobilization for "total war" from the German people. SS terror, loyalty to a still revered *Führer*, and fear of retribution for Germany's war of extermination in the East henceforth kept the German people in the war to the bitter end. War production, thanks to fanatical German efforts and to the mobilization of millions of foreign workers, slave laborers, and prisoners of war, rose until 1944. New "reprisal" weapons, such as the V-1 "buzz-bomb" and V-2 ballistic missile, poured from slave-built underground factories. Jet-propelled fighters, by late 1944, briefly challenged Allied control of the skies. But the Reich failed to overcome the combined forces of the coalition it had created.

That coalition, by fall 1943, had begun to define its war aims. By December 1941, when Churchill's foreign secretary, Sir Anthony Eden, visited Moscow, Stalin had recovered fully from his panic of the previous summer. The Soviet Union was going to survive. Eden discovered, as had Hitler and Ribbentrop before him, that Stalin had ambitions. The Soviet dictator insisted upon retaining the Baltic states that Hitler had delivered to him. That was a violation of the Atlantic Charter promises of self-determination that the Soviet Union had accepted with reservations in September 1941. But Stalin jovially sought to reassure Eden: he was different from Hitler, whose "fatal defect" was that "he does not know where to stop. . . . I can assure you that I will always know where to stop."

Subsequently, Stalin capitalized on the Soviet Union's immense casualties and on its status until June 1944 as the sole member of the coalition that faced large German land forces. Stalin incessantly demanded from Roosevelt and Churchill the establishment of a "second front" in Europe—the front that had existed in 1939–40 and had collapsed thanks in part to Stalin's support for Hitler. Stalin also played masterfully on Anglo-American fears of a Russo-German separate peace that would leave the Western Allies facing Hitler alone. He repeatedly approached Hitler clandestinely with offers of an armistice that would restore the borders of 1939 and the Russo-German quasi-alliance against the Western powers.

Roosevelt and Churchill failed to parry Stalin's diplomacy effectively. They almost apologetically asked Stalin to declare war on Japan, with whom the Soviet Union had contracted a nonaggression pact in April 1941. Stalin fobbed them off with a variety of excuses. Roosevelt, too anxious to please, promised a "second front" in Europe in 1942, a logistical and military impossibility. Partly to placate Stalin, Roosevelt also proclaimed at his January 1943 conference with Churchill at Casablanca that the Allies would accept nothing less than "unconditional surrender" from Germany, Italy, and Japan. A further purpose of that policy, which Roosevelt explicitly derived from the U.S. Civil War tradition, was to prevent a repetition of 1918–19. This time the Western Allies proposed to smash Germany for good and stamp out any "stab-in-the-back" legend or desire for yet another rematch. Stalin responded with an inexpensive gesture: in May 1943 he dissolved the Communist International, which had become superfluous now that he had placed his own men firmly at the head of the International's "fraternal parties."

As with Chamberlain's 1939 guarantee to Poland, Roosevelt's assurances that the "capitalists" would fight Hitler to the bitter end only encouraged Stalin to continue his secret courtship of Hitler. What the Anglo-Americans apparently did not know was that Hitler adamantly refused all compromise; Germany's *Lebensraum* was at stake. Hitler remained willing to strike a deal with the Anglo-Americans—but they demanded Germany's total defeat. Stalin offered Hitler a chance for survival—but Hitler refused to bargain in the East. That deadlock ensured that the war would continue until Germany won, or ceased to exist.

By November–December 1943, when the ill-assorted Allies met for the first "Big Three" conference at Teheran, Stalin held the advantage. British and Americans were stalled in bloody fighting against a handful of German divisions at Cassino, south of Rome; the Red Army was driving back some 2.5 million Germans. Lend-Lease aid, which gave the Red Army the 700,000 U.S. and British trucks that made it capable of the far-ranging offensive thrusts of 1944–45, was no substitute for a large Western ground effort. And the United States drastically weakened its diplomatic position by scaling down its projected army from the 215 divisions planned in 1941 to a mere 89 by early 1944. Roosevelt sought to avoid war-weariness and his own defeat in the 1944 election. But the American decision meant that the Western Allies now *needed* the Soviet Union to defeat Germany, and perhaps even Japan.

Churchill therefore offered preemptive concessions. To give Stalin once again the western border he had secured from Ribbentrop in 1939, the Allies proposed that Poland "move westward" into Germany, whose ultimate dismemberment they agreed on in principle. Stalin, for his part, formally undertook to enter the Pacific war after the defeat of Germany. That was a prize the Anglo-Americans need not have paid for, since the Soviet Union was certain in any event to take booty in Manchuria and Korea after Germany's defeat.

The Reconquest of Europe, 1944–45

Throughout 1943 the Reich had been strong enough to throw into the sea any green American and British troops that might land on the mined and fortified shores of "Fortress Europe." By spring 1944, that had changed. The U.S. Army had acquired in northern Africa and Italy some experience of the Germans and of amphibious landings, the most difficult operation in war. The long-range P-51 Mustang fighters of the U.S. Army Air Corps had secured daylight air superiority over France and

D-Day: Normandy, June 6, 1944.

August he had overrun Paris and was reaching for the German border. Charles de Gaulle, now head of a sizable Free French army, returned to claim the presidency of a new French republic. Even Montgomery, commanding the British and Canadians, showed unexpected speed in pursuit of a thoroughly beaten enemy. For a brief moment Hitler's subordinates despaired of halting the Allies short of the Rhine. In the East, the *Wehrmacht*'s Army Group Center folded up in the face of a massive Soviet summer offensive that advanced over 400 miles, from Smolensk to the outskirts of Warsaw, and cost the Germans half a million troops.

But Hitler himself held on, despite the shock of an assassination attempt on July 20 by a conspiracy of anti-Nazi staff officers. Himmler received the welcome task of purging army and bureaucracy. The Prussian conservatives who had invited Hitler into power and then thought better of it now perished in the concentration camps they had made possible. Goebbels and the NSDAP spurred the German population to fanatical resistance.

Eisenhower reined Patton in and gave Montgomery most of the shrinking stream of supplies reaching the Allied armies from their beachheads and improvised ports. In mid-September Montgomery launched three U.S. and British airborne divisions in a straight line across Holland toward the Ruhr and sent his armored divisions forward to link up. The attack's purpose was transparent and Montgomery's armor was slow. An SS *Panzer* division resting near the Arnhem drop zone crushed the British paratroops and derailed the Allied thrust. Bitter positional fighting amid the minefields and camouflaged bunkers of Hitler's *Westwall* ran on into winter.

Hitler still hoped that a last stunning blow at the Western Allies would break the unnatural coalition and leave him to face Stalin. In the Ardennes, scene of his May 1940 victory, Hitler flung in mid-December 1944 a last offensive at

the western parts of the Reich. Precision heavy bomber attacks on Germany's vital synthetic oil and gasoline plants followed. British decipherment of German signals (code-named ULTRA) gave the Allies forewarning of German operations. Allied deception plans fooled the German command into thinking that the main attack would come near Calais—and might come as far north as Norway.

On June 6, 1944, British and American forces under the supreme command of an American, Dwight D. Eisenhower, landed on the Normandy beaches. Three airborne divisions descended on the German rear. Overwhelming air superiority, Allied logistical mastery, and messy ground fighting resembling that of 1918 expanded the Allied beachhead. Then, in late July, the U.S. First Army broke through at St. Lô and launched the Third Army of George S. Patton around the German western flank. Patton, unlike his cautious superior Eisenhower, understood mobile warfare as well as his German adversaries. By

the Americans, whom he considered soft. His luck was no better than Ludendorff's in 1918, despite a penetration of 50 miles and an SS massacre of U.S. prisoners. The U.S. 101st Airborne division, outnumbered and ringed by German armor, defiantly held the key road junction at Bastogne. Patton spun the Third Army by 90 degrees in mid-winter and within a week struck northward at the German flank. The skies cleared; Allied fighter-bombers hunted the roads clear of German tanks and trucks. This "Battle of the Bulge" consumed most of Germany's reserves of armor, ammunition, and gasoline.

In the East, Stalin had by that point gone far toward the objectives staked out in 1939–40. By late July the great Soviet drive that crushed Army Group Center had seized the Polish city of Lublin. There Stalin established a Communist puppet regime (the "Lublin Committee") like that he had attempted to force on Finland in the 1939 Winter War. On August 1, 1944, as the Red Army approached Warsaw for the second time in a quarter-century, the Polish resistance movement allied

The Road to Berlin   1942–45

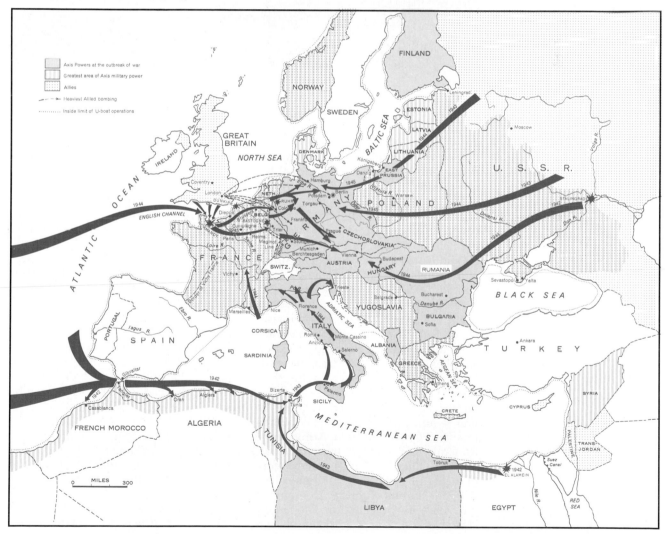

Allied airpower in the Bulge: a supply drop to the 101st Airborne Division at Bastogne, December 1944.

with the Polish government-in-exile in London answered Stalin's bid for political control of Poland. It rose against the Germans inside the city in a desperate effort to liberate the capital before the Red Army and NKVD arrived.

Stalin halted his army across the Vistula River and gave Himmler's pitiless counterinsurgency forces time to crush the Poles in a two-month struggle. The SS eliminated on Stalin's behalf much of the remaining national leadership of Poland. The Soviet dictator met Churchill's protests with denunciations of the Polish resistance as "criminals." He denied to British and American aircraft the use of his airfields to drop supplies to the Poles. Despite pleas from Churchill, Roosevelt refused to use the considerable leverage over Stalin that the great Allied victories in France now gave. And while it marked time in Poland, the Red Army drove Rumania and Finland from the war, overran Bulgaria, and slowly conquered Hungary. Soviet troops seized Belgrade, but the Yugoslav Communist guerrilla army of Josip Broz Tito largely cleared the rest of Yugoslavia of Germans by its own efforts—a fact of much political importance later.

As Stalin carved out a Soviet empire, Churchill made a last attempt to secure a modest measure of independence for eastern Europe. He faced Stalin in the Kremlin in October 1944 and reached an agreement—to which Roosevelt never subscribed—dividing Europe into spheres of influence. By this informal "percentage deal" Stalin conceded Britain a 90 percent preponderance in Greece, where Communist partisans were soon to attack the British and the Greek government that had returned from exile in London. Stalin received a similar preponderance in Rumania and slightly less in Bulgaria. Yugoslavia was to be split "50-50." On Poland, Churchill failed to shake Stalin from his support of the Lublin Poles.

When the "Big Three" met, for the second and last time, in February 1945 at Yalta in the Crimea, Stalin's position was even stronger than it had been the preceding fall. Roosevelt was mortally ill, and even in good health lacked Stalin's relentlessness and mastery of detail. Churchill was now totally dependent on the United States; Britain was financially and militarily exhausted.

Above all, the Red Army now held practically all of Poland. It was advancing into East Prussia amid rape and slaughter of civilians, while the Anglo-Americans were still grinding their way painfully through Hitler's *Westwall* fortifications. Roosevelt's advisers still assumed that they needed Stalin's assistance against Japan, and that they must pay for that assistance with concessions both in Europe and Asia. Finally, Roosevelt himself, although no zealot for world government, assumed that only a new and better League, the United Nations, could prevent a new American retreat into isolationism. The success of the United Nations clearly required Soviet postwar cooperation.

Yalta was thus the masterpiece of Soviet war diplomacy. Stalin had already brushed aside Western objections and had recognized his Lublin Committee as Poland's government. He conceded at Yalta that a few London Poles could enter that government as individuals—and as hostages to the Red Army and NKVD. And he secured a firm commitment to the division of Germany into occupation zones, one for each major ally. He also presumably noted with interest Roosevelt's unguarded remark that United States troops would probably remain in Europe less than two years after the war.

In Asia, Roosevelt capitulated to Stalin's demands for Russia's pre-1904 perquisites and more: railroad rights in Manchuria, the vital warm-water base of Port Arthur, and the annexation of southern Sakhalin and the Kurile islands north of Japan. Roosevelt even accepted the delicate task of securing the acquiescence of Chiang Kai-shek to this renewal of tsarist colonialism. In return, Stalin magnanimously promised to enter the war against Japan three months after Germany's defeat. He pledged Soviet cooperation in founding the United Nations, which eventually came into being at a conference at San Francisco between April and June 1945. Finally, Stalin agreed at

Yalta to a vaguely worded "Declaration on Liberated Europe" that promised free elections in all countries the Allies occupied. Within a month of that promise, Stalin's tanks forced on Rumania a Communist-led government; NKVD roundups in and deportations from Poland intensified. The Western Allies made ineffectual protests.

In early March 1945 Americans and British at last forced the Rhine at several points; it was the Soviet turn to mark time while the Red Army cleared up the Baltic coast. British in the north and Americans to the south swiftly encircled 325,000 German troops in the Ruhr. Patton drove across central Germany toward Czechoslovakia. The U.S. Ninth Army reached the Elbe River, 60 miles from Berlin, two weeks before the Soviets surrounded the city. Two battle-tried U.S. airborne divisions stood ready to descend upon the rubble of Hitler's capital.

But Eisenhower and his superiors in Washington, in the disarray of Roosevelt's last illness and death on April 12, failed to grasp the opportunity to seize Berlin. George Marshall, the U.S. chief

The "Big Three" at Yalta, February 1945.

The Soviet flag rises over the *Reichstag,* April 1945.

tisans who captured the *Duce* shot him "in the name of the Italian people." On May 7 and 9, the *Wehrmacht* capitulated unconditionally to Anglo-Americans and Soviets. Germany, as Hitler had half-promised, had ceased to exist.

Japan in Ashes

As the members of the "anti-Hitler coalition" faced one another across the rubble of central Europe, the United States readied itself for the final assault on Japan. Hundreds of B-29s were now in action. On the night of March 9–10, they turned central Tokyo into a sea of fire and killed between 80,000 and 120,000 civilians. By July 1945 the United States had burned out half of the surface area of urban Japan.

In February–March and April–June, two huge and bloody amphibious landings seized first Iwo Jima and then Okinawa, within fighter range of the Japanese home islands. Japanese pilots, following a tactic tested in the Philippines the previous fall, sought to crash explosive-laden *kamikaze* ("divine wind") aircraft into U.S. carriers, transports, and escorts. They sank 21 U.S. ships and damaged more than 60 others. On land, the Japanese were equally merciless toward themselves and toward the prisoners they rarely took. The Marines replied in kind; only 212 of the 22,000 Japanese on Iwo Jima surrendered successfully. The coming landings on the Japanese home islands, in the view of Truman's advisers, might cost as many as a million U.S. casualties, and many millions of Japanese. The war, U.S. planners assumed, could last until mid-1946.

The Japanese cabinet saw defeat impending. But the army, the decisive force now as earlier, refused to accept defeat. It still held Southeast Asia and much of China, as well as Manchuria, Korea, and Japan. Japanese peace feelers through Moscow, deciphered by U.S. intelligence, suggested the diplomats now sought peace, but feverish Japanese military preparation for a last-ditch defense of the home islands told

of staff, opposed the sacrifice of American lives for "purely political purposes"—an oddly innocent remark, given that war itself is politics "by other means." Marshall and Eisenhower abandoned to the Red Army the symbol of victory over Germany and vital German territory. The United States ignored Churchill's desperate urging that it counter Stalin's all too obvious appetites by meeting the Soviets as far east as possible.

The Red Army took Berlin against fanatical SS and *Wehrmacht* resistance, while Hitler committed suicide on April 30 in his bunker under the Reich chancellory. Mussolini preceded him on April 28; the Italian Communist par-a different tale. And the apparent Allied insistence on "unconditional surrender," which implied the removal of the Emperor, gave the military diehards an apparently unanswerable argument.

It fell to Harry S. Truman, Roosevelt's vice-president and successor, to face this difficult situation. Truman, a man of resolve ("the buck stops here") whose contemporaries underestimated him, entered the presidency with no experience of foreign affairs. He gradually turned against Stalin, but too slowly to affect the outcome in Europe. On July 1, 1945, the U.S. Army, despite further pleas from Churchill, swiftly withdrew from the wide areas it had conquered to the east of the foreordained Western occupation zones.

On July 17, at Potsdam in the center of conquered Prussia-Germany, Truman met Stalin and Churchill at the last wartime conference. Stalin confirmed his promise to enter the war in Asia. He secured half of a scheduled $20 billion in German reparations for the Soviet Union, but pledged in return to deliver food from agricultural eastern Germany to the industrial Western zones. He also demanded a voice in the Ruhr occupation; the Western Allies refused. And he voiced a series of disquieting desires: fleet bases in Greece, a United Nations mandate over the Italian colony of Libya, an interest in French Syria and Lebanon, and a role in the international administration of Tangier. When Churchill congratulated Stalin on his military successes, the Soviet ruler revealed a mild disgruntlement. At least one predecessor in the Kremlin had done better: in 1814 "Tsar Alexander got to Paris." That was an aspiration far beyond anything disclosed to Hitler in the Berlin talks of November 1940.

In the course of the conference, a British election replaced Churchill with the leader of Labour, Clement Attlee. That redoubled the burden on Truman. But Truman had discovered that the United States possessed an asset that Roosevelt had concealed from him—

the still highly secret atomic bomb. Hitler had died before it was ready, but it might speed Japan's collapse. Stalin, informed of it officially for the first time at Potsdam, feigned indifference and expressed the wish that it be used on the Japanese. His own bomb project had begun secretly in 1942, after Soviet intelligence had alerted him to the British, American, and German nuclear efforts.

Truman shared the impatience of most citizens of the democracies. The war must end soon, so that "our boys" could return and happily demobilize. Neither Truman nor his planners explored the possibility of inducing Japan to surrender by siege, without an invasion; that course would require too much time. Nor, despite prompting from some State Department experts, was Truman willing to abandon publicly the demand for "unconditional surrender." That formula had long outlived its supposed usefulness in conciliating Stalin, but it had acquired a life of its own: the public overwhelmingly supported it as a fitting revenge for Pearl Harbor.

Truman and Churchill did attempt to warn Tokyo with a declaration from

Stalin, radiating self-confidence, with Churchill and Truman at Potsdam, July 1945.

The ruins of Hiroshima,
August 1945.

manded continued resistance; most of the high command concurred. To break the deadlock, Suzuki made an unprecedented appeal to Emperor Hirohito, who by ancient but disused custom could in exceptional circumstances decide vital issues.

The Emperor, speaking softly, reproached his military for a wartime performance that had fallen far short of its promises. He insisted that Japan had no choice; it must "bear the unbearable." On August 15, after the suppression of a die-hard military revolt, Japan's god-emperor broadcast to a people who had never before heard his voice and informed them that Japan would end the war. On September 2, 1945, Japan surrendered unconditionally to MacArthur and Nimitz on the deck of the battleship *Missouri,* at anchor in Tokyo Bay.

After six years and a day, the Second World War was over. It had cost the Soviet Union approximately 17 million military and civilian dead. Germany had lost 6.2 million; Poland, 6 million including its Jews; China, perhaps 4 million not counting victims of famine and disease; Japan, 2 million; Yugoslavia 1.7 million; France somewhat over and Italy somewhat under half a million. Britain lost 325,000; the United States escaped with combat losses of only 292,000. Over 50 million people had perished in the most destructive conflict in history. Germany and Japan lay in ruins; tens of millions of destitute refugees, prisoners of war, slave laborers, and concentration camp survivors thronged central Europe. Economic chaos and political vacuum followed the defeat of the Axis in both Europe and Asia.

THE COLD WAR

As in 1918, victory did not bring peace. In bringing order out of chaos the United States and Soviet Union collided. Their ensuing "Cold War" has in most respects continued to the present. Its origins, chronological boundaries,

Potsdam that promised "prompt and utter destruction" unless Japan surrendered and hinted at Allied flexibility on Japan's postwar form of government. The Japanese ignored it. Truman therefore ordered the first two bombs dropped on Japanese industrial cities. He could not "disinvent" the weapon upon which the United States had spent $2 billion. U.S. opinion, from extreme Left to far Right, was in 1945 virtually unanimous in approving its use to end the war. Most thankful of all were the infantry awaiting orders to storm the mined and barbed-wired beaches of the Japanese home islands.

On August 6 and 9, B-29s from Tinian dropped two atomic weapons on Hiroshima and Nagasaki, in southwestern Japan. Roughly 120,000 Japanese perished outright and many died later from long-term radiation injuries. The Hiroshima bomb failed to persuade, but the shock of the Nagasaki bomb and the simultaneous Soviet declaration of war and *Blitzkrieg* in Manchuria produced crisis in Tokyo. The prime minister, Suzuki Kantarō, urged acceptance of the Potsdam declaration before worse followed. The war minister, General Anami Korechika, de-

and nature have provoked bitter ideological debate, at least in the West. But its origins were no mystery. Conflict between great powers of differing aims and interests was neither new nor startling. What was surprising about the Cold War was its long-deferred outbreak. It took two years of ever more brutal Soviet measures in eastern Europe, of Soviet demands and encroachments in divided Germany, and of Soviet pressure on its neighbors on Europe's flanks to provoke the United States to a coherent response.

Before the Cold War: 1945–46

As in 1939–41, Stalin imposed his system on his new territories. As in his destruction of his domestic rivals in the 1920s, he proceeded by stages, keeping his goals deliberately ambiguous. These "salami tactics," as Stalin's man in Hungary, Matyás Rákosi, aptly described them, also owed a debt to Mussolini and Hitler, who had pioneered the technique of "legal" revolution through the power of the state apparatus. Stalin's relative caution, as Rákosi explained to a secret party meeting in May 1945, was a product above all of the need to divide Britain and the United States. If not provoked, Stalin apparently thought, the United States might follow Roosevelt's prediction at Yalta and withdraw its troops from western Europe. That would concede continental hegemony to the Soviet Union.

The Sovietization of eastern Europe therefore proceeded cautiously, in three phases. First came Red Army and NKVD control in 1944–45, then in 1945–47 a slow slicing away of the noncommunist parties. Finally, after the United States showed that it was prepared to stay in Europe and resist, came the creation of one-party communist dictatorships in 1947–49.

In Rumania and Bulgaria, Stalin's proconsuls rapidly imposed Communist-dominated coalition governments. Churchill had in essence conceded both countries to Stalin in the "percent-age deal" and Stalin rightly assumed that action there would not unduly provoke the United States. Stalin was almost equally cavalier in Poland. That unhappy country was his vital land bridge to the Soviet occupation zone in Germany. Inconvenient individuals such as the political leaders of the Polish resistance who surfaced in March 1945 disappeared into NKVD custody. But Stalin was nevertheless careful to

Territorial Adjustments After the Second World War   1945

The boundaries shown on this map date from the beginning of World War II.

■ Axis nations after World War II

▨ Lands which changed hands after World War II

maintain a façade; until 1947 the leader of the London Poles, Stanislaw Mikolajczyk, remained as "second deputy prime minister" in the government of Stalin's Lublin Committee puppets.

Hungary and Czechoslovakia enjoyed relatively free elections in 1945–46. Especially in Czechoslovakia, Stalin did not at first need force. The Czech government-in-exile of President Beneš chose collaboration from the beginning; unlike the Poles, the Czechs had no prior experience of Russian occupation. The Czech Communist Party of Kliment Gottwald achieved a plurality of 38 percent in the 1946 election.

In his zone of Germany, which he rightly regarded, even in ruins, as Europe's greatest power, Stalin applied similar methods. The day after the Red Army hoisted its flag on the remains of the *Reichstag*, a small group of German Communist émigrés under the leadership of the ice-cold and ruthless Walter Ulbricht landed in Berlin from Moscow. The Western Allies at first largely shut down German political activity in their zones and gave priority to the large-scale hunt for war criminals that culminated in trials of the surviving Nazi leaders at Nuremberg in 1945–46. The Soviets shot a few prominent Nazis but gave priority in their zone to the creation of a regime around Ulbricht.

In early 1946, Ulbricht's resurrected German Communist Party cajoled and coerced the much larger SPD organizations in the Soviet zone into a merger that produced a "Socialist Unity Party," the SED. That tactic, which Stalin attempted to apply unsuccessfully through other Communist parties in western as well as eastern Europe, ultimately aimed at a Communist united Germany—a goal Stalin and his associates disclosed to Yugoslav and Bulgarian Communist leaders in early 1946.

Stalin's gradual destruction of non-Communist forces both in the Soviet zone of Germany and elsewhere in east-central Europe was not the only Soviet policy that aroused alarm in the West. Stalin insisted on receiving reparations from the Western zones of Germany without in turn delivering the food from East Germany that he had pledged at Potsdam. He continued to demand a Soviet share in the occupation of the Ruhr while blocking with unacceptable conditions the fitful inter-allied negotiations over a German peace treaty. That provoked the United States, in September 1946, to announce that its occupation force would remain in Germany indefinitely.

On the Soviet Union's borders, Stalin continued to seek gains far beyond those the Red Army had already secured. He pressed the Norwegians for bases on their island outpost of Spitzbergen, and repeatedly demanded bases at the Dardanelles and parts of the Caucasus from Turkey. In Greece, the Communist guerrilla movement that had suffered defeat in December 1944 after attacking the British in Athens renewed the struggle in May 1946. Tito of newly Communist Yugoslavia provided weapons and supplies. Stalin remained in the background but at first made no objection. Communist victory in Greece would isolate Turkey and assure the Soviet Union the foothold in the eastern Mediterranean that Stalin

Göring (left), Ribbentrop (third from left), and associates on trial at Nuremberg, 1945.

had demanded in vain from Britain and the United States.

In three areas Stalin made tactical retreats. In Austria, he refrained from Sovietizing his occupation zone, probably for fear of provoking an *Anschluss* of the Western zones with the Western zones of Germany. In Finland, he contented himself with imposing a military alliance that left Finland's parliamentary institutions intact. That compromise, which rested on Finland's proven willingness to resist Soviet invasion, Finland's political caution, and Sweden's continuing neutrality, has endured. Finally, in March 1946 Stalin suddenly and belatedly agreed to honor his Teheran promise to evacuate the northern parts of Iran that he had occupied in 1941.

That swift—and unique—postwar withdrawal was symptomatic of Stalin's policy. Churchill, out of office but still forceful, had just spoken eloquently under Truman's sponsorship of an "Iron Curtain" that had descended across Europe. U.S. protests over Soviet creation of satellite "republics" in Iran and Churchill's call for a new Anglo-American alliance to block further Soviet expansion apparently made a temporary retreat seem advisable to Stalin. It was his last.

"Containment" against Expansion, 1947–48

Within the ever-disorganized policy machinery in Washington, those who distrusted Soviet intentions gradually gained the upper hand after 1945. Truman, who had remarked in June 1941 that he hoped that Nazis and Soviets would kill each other off, was temperamentally so inclined. But in the absence of Soviet acts of direct hostility to the United States, domestic opinion prevented the translation of sentiment into policy. U.S. wartime propaganda stressing Stalin's amiability and world peace through the United Nations had succeeded too well. That "Uncle Joe" was as merciless though more cautious than Hitler and that no disunited

---

Churchill: "The Iron Curtain"   March 1946

In a speech given at Fulton, Missouri, with Truman in the audience, Churchill sought to educate the American public:

From Stettin in the Baltic to Trieste in the Adriatic, an iron curtain has descended across the Continent. Behind that line lie all the capitals of the ancient states of Central and Eastern Europe. Warsaw, Berlin, Prague, Vienna, Budapest, Belgrade, Bucharest and Sofia, all these famous cities and the populations around them lie in what I must call the Soviet sphere, and all are subject in one form or another, not only to Soviet influence but to a very high and, in many cases, increasing measure of control from Moscow. . . .

The Russian-dominated Polish government has been encouraged to make enormous and wrongful inroads upon Germany, and mass expulsions of millions of Germans on a scale grievous and undreamed-of are now taking place. The Communist parties, which were very small in all these Eastern States of Europe, have been raised to pre-eminence and power far beyond their numbers and are seeking everywhere to obtain totalitarian control. Police governments are prevailing in nearly every case. . . . These are sombre facts for anyone to have to recite on the morrow of a victory gained by so much splendid comradeship in arms and in the cause of freedom and democracy; but we should be most unwise not to face them squarely while time remains. . . . I do not believe that Soviet Russia desires war. What they desire is the fruits of war and the indefinite expansion of their power and doctrines.

From Lewis Broad, *Winston Churchill 1874–1951* (London: Hutchinson & Co., 1951), pp. 574–75.

"United Nations" could repeal the balance of power came as a rude shock.

While the education of the American public proceeded with help from both Churchill and Stalin, the military power of the United States shrank dramatically. The 12.1 million men under arms in August 1945 clamored for release. By June 1946 those vast and battle-hardened forces had dwindled to 3 million, and by June 1947 stood at a mere 1.4 million, most of them without combat experience. Possession of the bomb served on balance as an excuse for complacency. And Stalin's demobilization was far less rapid than that of the United States. By 1948–49 the Soviet armed forces were the largest in the world, with roughly 4 million men. An estimated 30 or more Soviet divisions under unified command in eastern Europe faced a scratch assortment of 2 U.S. and 9 British, French, and Belgian divisions in western Europe. The West lacked a high command, and Soviet tank forces held a crushing edge in numbers and quality.

In the United States, the Republicans achieved majorities in both houses in November 1946 and paralyzed Truman. But to the surprise of the doomsayers, the U.S. economy, which now briefly accounted for half of world industrial production, did not relapse into depression. In the course of the war the United States had finally taken up the role of economic leadership spurned in 1919. At the Bretton Woods Conference of July 1944, the Western powers agreed under U.S. sponsorship to a new international economic order, complete with a World Bank and International Monetary Fund. The Bretton Woods system offered a framework for the expansion of U.S. exports that had not existed between the wars. But a prerequisite for that expansion was the recovery of Europe. By the bitter winter of 1946–47 that recovery was worryingly overdue.

Stalin's appetites and Europe's distress, which might strengthen the large Communist parties in France and Italy as well as checking the expansion of world trade, ultimately impelled Truman to act. Britain furnished the occasion. As in 1919, nationalist revolts from Egypt to India beleaguered its Labour government, which sought at home to implement the long-promised welfare state on the back of a faltering economy. In February 1947 Britain confessed that it could no longer bear the weight of shoring up Turkey and of supporting the Greek government against the Communist partisans. The collapse of the British position in the eastern Mediterranean left a power vacuum. If Truman did not fill it, Stalin clearly would.

On March 12, 1947, after assuring himself of Republican support in Congress, Truman announced the "doctrine" that bears his name. The United States would help Greece, Turkey, and all "free peoples" against "armed minorities or . . . outside pressures." The Republicans, under the leadership of Senator Arthur Vandenberg, enlisted with enthusiasm. But Vandenberg and U.S. public opinion exacted a price. As Vandenberg explained to Truman, Congress would only spend money if Truman "scared hell out of the American people." Truman therefore transformed an essentially pragmatic decision to support two strategic countries into something entirely different: a worldwide ideological struggle between light and darkness. And Truman's choice of words unwittingly placed an intolerable burden on many of America's allies-to-be. To qualify for U.S. aid, they now had to seem virtuous and "free," rather than merely strategically important.

In the short term, Truman succeeded brilliantly. Truman Doctrine aid to Greece and Turkey passed Congress. In June 1947 Truman's new secretary of state, the ex-chief of staff George Marshall, announced a second major initiative. The United States offered to both western and eastern Europe, including the Soviet Union, a massive infusion of economic aid to set the postwar recovery in motion at last. While Congress would never have approved aid to the Soviets, the Marshall Plan's authors left to Stalin the burden of refusal.

A senior state department official, George Kennan, simultaneously supplied a much-needed statement of the Truman Doctrine's underlying rationale. Writing as "Mr. X" in the July 1947 issue of *Foreign Affairs*, Kennan urged a "policy of firm containment, designed to confront the Russians with unalterable counterforce at every point where they show signs of encroaching upon a peaceful and stable world." Containment, Kennan argued, would ultimately foster "either the break-up or the gradual mellowing of Soviet power." He later explained with embarrassment that by "counterforce" he had not necessarily meant the use of force, and that not "*every* point" at which the Soviet Union might seek expansion was equally vital to the United States. But his article, and other semiofficial and official pronouncements from Washington, in theory made U.S. commitments virtually unlimited.

To uphold those commitments, the United States reorganized its armed forces in July 1947, creating a nuclear-armed air force independent of army and navy and a Department of Defense. And America acquired new institutions that until now, alone of the great powers, it had disdained. Permanent peacetime secret services, the Central Intelligence Agency (CIA) for foreign intelligence and "covert action" (1947) and the National Security Agency (NSA) for codebreaking (1952), arose from the debris of the wartime intelligence effort.

Europe Divided

Stalin did not disappoint the framers of the Marshall Plan. Molotov attended the initial conference of the Plan in Paris but soon uttered his characteristic stone-faced "*nyet.*" Stalin commanded his satellites to decline Marshall aid, and ordered the Communist parties of western Europe to oppose the Plan with strikes and riots. The Cominform, a replacement for the defunct Communist International, emerged to enforce ideological discipline.

In the fall and winter of 1947–48 Stalin swiftly completed his "revolution by conquest" in the Soviet Union's new central and eastern European empire. In Hungary, Rákosi arrested key opposition leaders in May 1947. Mikolajczyk fled Poland in fear of his life in October. In December King Michael of Rumania abdicated. In Czechoslovakia, Kliment Gottwald and his Communist party seized control in February 1948 from within the popularly elected government. Jan Masaryck, the protégé of Beneš at the foreign ministry, fell, jumped, or was pushed from a window to his death. Beneš, as in 1938, declined to fight; Gottwald shunted him

aside. The new regimes took the remarkable name of "people's democracies"—Stalin too was a master of packaging dictatorship for the age of mass politics.

The United States, Britain, and France now went ahead rapidly with the reestablishment of economic and political life in their sectors of Germany. When they attempted to include the Western part of Berlin in the creation of a new currency that foreshadowed a West German state, Stalin reacted wrathfully. In June 1948 he violated the wartime interallied agreements providing for free access to Berlin, and blockaded the Western sectors with Soviet tanks.

Truman and his advisers contemplated sending their own few tanks down the *Autobahn*. But in the face of the Soviet Union's crushing ground superiority (roughly 20 Soviet against 2 U.S. divisions in Germany), they opted in characteristic American fashion for an engineering remedy to a political or military problem. To keep alive the same West Berliners that they had bombed three years before, the Allies organized an endless chain of transport

The Berlin airlift, June 1948–May 1949.

aircraft that delivered millions of tons of food, coal, and gasoline. In November 1948, Truman won reelection against all odds. In May 1949 Stalin abandoned the Berlin blockade.

Its effects remained. Stalin's blockade provoked the creation in April 1949 of the North Atlantic Treaty Organization (NATO), the military alliance between the United States and the western European democracies that Wilson had failed to create in 1919. The blockade also impelled the United States and its Allies to hasten the creation of a "Federal Republic of Germany" in the Western zones. The Federal Republic adopted a constitution in May 1949 and held its first election that August. Ulbricht's "German Democratic Republic" arose in response. The two superpowers now confronted one another with unbending hostility from northern Norway to the Turkish Caucasus.

As well as provoking—in the form of NATO—the "unalterable counterforce" Kennan had prescribed, Stalin also failed to Sovietize one key nation in east-central Europe. In early 1948 he attempted to reduce Tito of Yugoslavia to the same subservience as Ulbricht, Gottwald, and Rákosi. When Tito balked, Stalin expelled Yugoslavia from the international Communist movement for "nationalist tendencies." Then he sought to orchestrate a pro-Soviet coup from within the Yugoslav party: "I shall shake my little finger and there will be no Tito." But Tito remained. That first break in the international Communist movement scuttled the Greek insurgency. Stalin had already told the Yugoslavs that it should be "rolled up" as unprofitable now that the United States had made clear its determination in Greece. After the break with Moscow, Tito abandoned the Greek guerrillas; he needed Western economic support to survive.

Increased tension with the United States and the quarrel with Yugoslavia gave Stalin the occasion to tighten further his control at home. An alleged external threat and genuine internal terror went together, as in the 1930s, to force the population to accept the pri-

vation that Stalin's military-economic priorities and crash reconstruction of the wartime devastated areas demanded. In war and aftermath, Stalin deported to Siberia and central Asia millions from nationalities—Crimean Tartars, Volga Germans, and the Baltic and Caucasus peoples—that he accused of collaboration with the German invaders. He vengefully transferred to his own concentration camps all returned Soviet prisoners of war ("In Hitler's camps there are no Russian prisoners of war, only Russian traitors, and we shall do away with them when the war is over.") He demoted prominent military leaders once he no longer needed them, and arrested many whose sole crime was having seen with their own eyes the wealth of the world west of the Soviet borders. The GULAG had suffered a labor shortage after 1941; by 1950 it once more held an estimated 8 to 10 million prisoners.

After war's end, Stalin's lieutenant Andrei Zhdanov began a purge of Soviet writers and scientists that continued even after Zhdanov died a sudden and perhaps unnatural death in 1948. Zhdanov's rival Georgi Malenkov and Yezhov's sinister successor at the NKVD, Lavrenty Beria, subsequently had Zhdanov's former associates in the Leningrad party apparatus liquidated. The gradually intensifying purge, which Stalin extended to the new eastern European satellites, soon took on an overtly anti-Semitic character. "Rootless cosmopolitanism" and "Zionism" were the chief charges under which prominent satellite leaders, many of them of Jewish descent, went to gallows or execution cellars after show trials in 1951–52. Stalin thus applied to the satellites the remedy imposed at home after Kirov's murder in 1934: the removal of all who were not his creatures and the creation of a new ruling class of grateful accomplices.

As Tocqueville had foreseen in the 1830s, America and Russia had each come to "sway the destinies of half the globe." Their confrontation in 1947–49 resulted from and ended a century of ever more destructive European national struggles. Hitler, the most extreme of all nationalist prophets, had invited the superpowers onto the scene. Then he had created a chaos and destruction so vast that at the end only superpowers could master it.

That they proceeded to do and their solutions were mutually exclusive. Here too Tocqueville had seen clearly: "The principal instrument of [America] is freedom; of [Russia], servitude." The democracies of western Europe, despite occasional grumbling, conceded hegemony to Washington. They repeated, against Stalin, the choice Churchill had made in 1940: better to serve as junior partner to another democracy, the United States, than to suffer the domination of a continent-wide slave state. In east-central Europe, Stalin's new multinational empire replaced the Habsburg order that had collapsed in 1918. Supranational American-Soviet confrontation dwarfed and repressed the largely spent forces of European nationalism and froze the borders of 1945. But outside Europe both geography and the alignment of forces were far different. There Stalin failed to discern "when to stop," and nationalism, Europe's most successful export, opened new worlds of violent conflict.

Suggestions for Further Reading

The Second World War

As with World War I, no comprehensive, up-to-date, and readable one-volume history of World War II exists. G. Wright, *The Ordeal of Total War, 1939–1945* (1968), is still a useful survey. J. Lukacs, *The Last European War, September 1939/December 1941* (1976), offers a brilliant synthesis of everything from grand strategy to the intellectual impact of the first two years of war. K. Hildebrand, *The Foreign Policy of the Third Reich* (1973), and A. Hillgruber, *Germany and the Two World Wars* (1981), lay out German strategy and objectives, but see also H. R. Trevor-Roper, ed., *Hitler's Secret Conversations, 1941–1944* (1953), and N. Rich, *Hitler's War Aims* (1973–74). A. Seaton, *The Russo-German War 1941–45* (1971), remains the best one-volume work on BARBAROSSA. G. Fleming, *Hitler and the Final Solution* (1982), and R. Hilberg, *The Destruction of the European Jews* (1961; revised and expanded, 1985), cover the "Final Solution" and Hitler's responsibility for it in chilling detail. M. van Creveld, *Fighting Power* (1982), suggests why the Germans were so difficult to defeat. Among the many excellent books about aspects of the European war, see especially W. Murray, *Luftwaffe* (1984), and M. Hastings, *Overlord: D-Day and the Battle for Normandy* (1984).

Of Hitler's principal enemies only Churchill left memoirs: his wonderfully readable *The Second World War*, 6 vols. (1948–1953), remains the best existing history of the war as seen from London. On Roosevelt and American policy, see R. Sherwood, *Roosevelt and Hopkins* (1950); R. A. Divine, *The Reluctant Belligerent: American Entry into World War II* (1965); and G. Smith, *American Diplomacy in the Second World War, 1941–1945* (revised, 1985). On the Pacific war, see especially A. Iriye, *The Origins of the Second World War in Asia and the Pacific* (1987), and *Power and Culture: The Japanese-American War, 1941–1945* (1981); H. P. Willmott, *Empires in the Balance: Japanese and Allied Pacific Strategies to April 1942* (1982); R. H. Spector, *Eagle Against the Sun: The American War Against Japan* (1985); C. Thorne, *Allies of a Kind: The United States, Britain, and the War Against Japan, 1941–1945* (1978); and R. Butow, *Japan's Decision to Surrender* (1954).

The Cold War

On wartime diplomacy and the origins of the Cold War, H. Feis, *Churchill, Roosevelt, Stalin* (1957), still provides useful narrative; D. S. Gaddis, *The United States and the Origins of the Cold War, 1941–1947* (1972), and V. Mastny, *Russia's Road to the Cold War* (1979), use a wider selection of sources. H. Seton-Watson, *The East European Revolution* (1951, 1956), is still the best overview of the Communist seizure of power in eastern Europe; A. Ulam, *The Rivals: America and Russia Since World War II* (1971), provides a succinct and witty narrative; P. Seabury, *The Rise and Decline of the Cold War* (1967), introduces some of the interpretive issues.

34

The Age of Containment, 1949–1975

*T*he Prague coup and Berlin Blockade marked the beginning of the "classic" Cold War, the fiercest phase of the superpower confrontation that remains the axis of international politics. In Europe, the "war" remained cold. In Asia, by Stalin's choice, cold war became a shooting war in Korea in June 1950. Then military stalemate and Stalin's death in March 1953 ended the most acute period of United States-Soviet hostility.

But truces in Korea and elsewhere in Asia did not end conflict. Anti-Soviet revolts in the satellites and recurrent Soviet threats over Germany marked the post-Stalin "thaw." Superpower tension culminated in 1962 with the attempt of Stalin's successor, Nikita Sergeyevich Khrushchev, to shift the strategic balance by placing nuclear missiles in Cuba. Khrushchev's shamefaced withdrawal and U.S. distraction in Southeast Asia after 1962 inaugurated a period of gradual "détente" or "relaxation of tension," despite wars in the Middle East. The Soviet Union looked on in masterful inactivity as the United States, convulsed at home, ultimately abandoned "containment" in Vietnam in 1972–75.

Unheard-of prosperity in the United States, western Europe, and a resurgent Japan accompanied superpower conflict. American-style material culture—appliances and automobiles, Hollywood films, television serials, and rock and roll—enveloped the world. A new generation arose in the West that remembered neither Depression nor war, and fiercely attacked its elders. A transnational women's movement that originated in France and the United States at last pushed the boundaries of women's rights beyond the vote. For the democracies the age of containment was an age of unprecedented material advance and broadening of wealth. But as in previous ages, the price of change and economic growth was unease and dissatisfaction.

CONFRONTATION IN EUROPE AND ASIA, 1949–53

Stalin's Temptation in Asia

Japan left the Western Allies a difficult legacy. Its slogan of "Asia for the Asians" had been an instrument of Jap-

974

anese colonialism. But that slogan and the inglorious defeat of the British at Singapore in February 1942 had nevertheless mightily encouraged Asian nationalism. Thanks to the "Germany first" strategy, Southeast Asia had enjoyed the lowest priority of all the Allied theaters of war. In August 1945, when Imperial Japan collapsed, the British had only half reconquered Burma. The Guomindang was still hiding in a remote enclave in southeastern China. Indochina and the Dutch East Indies remained under Japanese control. Japan handed that control over not to the former colonial masters, but to armed native movements.

The Dutch ultimately gave up in 1949, under U.S. pressure, and granted Indonesia its independence. In Vietnam, Ho Chi Minh's Communist Party of Indochina assassinated non-Communist nationalist rivals and in September 1945 declared Vietnam's independence from France. The return of French troops led to fierce guerrilla conflict after November 1946.

To the north, the Soviets took Manchuria in their twelve-day war of August 1945 and remained until 1946. They took only half of the former Japanese colony of Korea; the United States, after hard experience in Europe, insisted on dividing that strategically

vital peninsula at the 38th parallel into Soviet and U.S. zones. By 1947–48, two Korean states, one Communist and one with American "advisers," were locked in bitter hostility and intermittent guerrilla warfare. Japan itself fell to the United States alone. Douglas MacArthur, installed in Tokyo as a sort of American Shōgun, contemptuously dismissed Soviet bids to share in the occupation. In the Pacific, unlike Europe, Moscow's contribution to victory had been minimal.

In China, the Guomindang of Chiang Kai-shek and the Chinese Communist Party (CCP) of Mao Zedong (Mao Tse-tung) ended the war as nominal allies. That marriage of convenience inevitably turned to renewed civil war in July 1946. China could not have *two* dictatorships. Truman and his subordinates wavered between attempting to reestablish a Guomindang-CCP coalition, backing the Guomindang, and abstaining. Washington tried all three in succession. Stalin initially sought to maintain a balance between CCP and Guomindang favorable to the Soviet Union, as in the 1920s. But once CCP victory seemed certain he opted for Mao.

In January 1949, Mao's "People's Liberation Army" entered Beijing (Peking). That October Mao proclaimed the People's Republic of China (PRC). Chiang and the remnants of the Guomindang took refuge on Taiwan.

Something resembling a new dynasty, after almost 40 years of war, turmoil, and famine, had replaced the Qing. Mao traveled to Moscow and, after difficult negotiation, signed in February 1950 a "treaty of friendship" with Stalin that promised the return to China of the Manchurian railway and Port Arthur, and allied China and the Soviet Union against Japan.

The "loss" of China and the contemporaneous explosion of a first Soviet atomic bomb in August 1949 created turmoil in the United States. Truman now paid for having "scared hell out of the American people," for having funded resistance to Soviet expansion

The Cold War comes home: McCarthy at work, October 1951.

in Europe by a pledge of aid to opponents of "armed minorities" everywhere. The Republican Right, in the unsavory person of Senator Joseph McCarthy of Wisconsin, out-trumped the president by claiming that he was not anti-Communist enough. McCarthy and his many supporters were convinced of American omnipotence. For them neither Chinese Communists nor Soviets were serious enemies. Only treason at home by U.S. officials could have delivered China to Mao and the "secret" of the atomic bomb to Moscow. They saw above all an internal menace—"Caaamunism" (as McCarthy and his supporters pronounced it) at the State Department and in the academic world of "pointy-headed intellectuals." The public's sudden realization that it faced a Soviet nuclear threat added to the hysteria. The pattern of ideological witch-hunts and populist-isolationist demagogy visible in the 1920s and 1930s reasserted itself. McCarthy's wild charges discredited him in 1954; in the long term he gave resistance to Communism a bad name.

In response to the new situation of 1949–50, Truman decided in the affirmative the contentious issue of whether to build a thermonuclear, or hydrogen, bomb. Stalin, unknown to the Americans, had initiated his own H-bomb research in 1948. The new weapon was orders of magnitude more destructive than the Hiroshima bomb, which had been equivalent to a mere 20,000 tons of high explosive. Truman also called for a review of U.S. defense preparations and strategy; his advisers embodied their conclusions in National Security Council paper NSC-68. It urged a major U.S. conventional as well as nuclear build-up to maintain a balance of power that the Soviet Union's bomb, its ever-growing military, and its alliance with China now threatened.

The recommendations of NSC-68 were politically impractical. The Republicans in Congress persisted in demanding budget cuts while simultaneously damning the administration

for being "soft on Caaamunism." Then Stalin, by an ill-timed display of appetite in Asia that repeated the error of the Berlin Blockade, allowed Truman to counter the Soviet build-up. At the end of 1949 (as Stalin's successor Nikita Khrushchev disclosed in his memoirs) Stalin received Kim Il-Sung, former Soviet Red Army major and chief of the Soviet-sponsored "Democratic People's Republic of Korea." Stalin authorized Kim to attack South Korea. Mao concurred. Stalin supplied weapons, including the T-34 tank that had opened the road to Berlin. On June 25, 1950, Kim's tanks crossed the 38th parallel and rolled the South Korean army up.

Wars in Asia and the Rearmament of Europe

Truman scarcely hesitated. On June 30, 1950, he ordered American ground troops from Japan into combat. Both U.S. control of Japan and the credibility of the U.S. commitment to Europe appeared to be at stake. Like Roosevelt in

Korea   1950–53

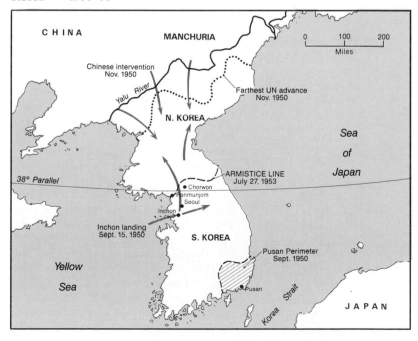

One of Kim Il-Sung's T-34s meets the U.S. Marine Corps (1950).

the Atlantic in 1941, Truman acted without a congressional declaration of war and without congressional opposition. A Soviet walk-out allowed the United Nations Security Council, for the first and last time in its history, to vote with the necessary unanimity to fight in defense of a member. The United States provided supplies and a force that eventually grew to 350,000. South Korea provided up to 400,000, and under the U.N. flag 44,000 troops from 14 nations also served.

The North Koreans, well-trained by their Soviet advisers, stormed south and almost swallowed the peninsula in one gulp. But by early August, with some embarrassment and much air and naval support, an Army, Marine, and South Korean force ground them to a halt around the vital port of Pusan, in the far southeastern corner of Korea. Then MacArthur landed Marines and Army at Inchon, halfway up Korea, cut the North Koreans to shreds, and reached the old border on the 38th parallel. Truman and the United Nations imprudently authorized him to conquer North Korea unless Chinese or Soviet intervention appeared immi-

nent. Containment briefly became "rollback." To MacArthur, who knew neither doubt nor humility, permission to cross the parallel was a blank check. As winter deepened he drove headlong for the Yalu River that divides Korea and China, stringing his forces out on North Korea's icy mountain roads.

Beijing conveyed through a variety of channels the message that it would fight to avoid becoming MacArthur's neighbor. MacArthur disregarded a sudden appearance of Chinese "volunteers" in mid-October. A massive Chinese counteroffensive in mid-November took him completely by surprise, and flung U.N. forces back below the 38th parallel. Only the Marines who walked out from Chosin reservoir near the Yalu—through snow and seven Chinese divisions—emerged with credit from the disaster.

MacArthur, to redeem his reputation, demanded the bombing and blockade of China. Truman relieved him of command in April 1951 for insubordination; in a letter to a Republican congressman, MacArthur had criticized his commander-in-chief by insisting that "in war there is no substitute for victory." Truman and his advisers saw no profit in a wider war against China that would pin down an ever-increasing proportion of U.S. forces and might lead to a direct U.S.-Soviet clash. That would be "the wrong war, at the wrong place, at the wrong time, and with the wrong enemy." The ultimate stakes were western Europe and Japan, the largest non-Communist concentrations of economic power and talent in the world beside the United States. And as in Europe, Washington sought to fill a dangerous economic and political vacuum by encouraging the resurgence of former enemies. In 1952 the United States returned sovereignty to a newly democratized Japan, linked to the United States with military bases and a security treaty.

After MacArthur's defeat, Truman thus fought a "limited war" in Korea. U.S. reinforcements and firepower pushed the Chinese back above the parallel. By July 1951, U.S. and allied forces had inflicted immense casualties and had stabilized the front. Acrimonious truce talks began, while trench raids and nibbling operations continued on Korea's bare and jagged hills. Chinese and North Koreans sought to wear down the resolve of an impatient and pacifically inclined democracy by simultaneously talking and fighting. Stalin willed that the war continue. In January 1951, immediately after MacArthur's catastrophe, he told a secret conclave of satellite Communist leaders that the United States was so feeble militarily that the opportunity for a Soviet stroke against Western Europe would come in the next three to four years. Tying U.S. forces down in Asia served that strategy. In western Europe the Communist parties and their sympathizers mounted a "peace" campaign that played on fears of nuclear annihilation and sought to divide Europe from the United States.

But Stalin was not immortal. He had apparently begun in 1952 to prepare a last purge; the Kremlin doctors, most of them of Jewish extraction, stood falsely accused of plotting to murder the Soviet leadership. Their coming trial, like that of Zinoviev and Kamenev in 1936, promised to unleash a flood of denunciations, arrests, and liquidations. Stalin's associates trembled for their heads. "The Boss" was apparently about to inaugurate yet another round of social mobility, Soviet style.

But on March 5, 1953, Stalin died of a stroke. His heirs inaugurated a "collective leadership" that sought hesitantly to retreat from Stalin's terror within and confrontation without. In the United States, impatience with the Korean stalemate ("die for a tie") carried the Republican candidate, Dwight D. Eisenhower, to victory in the 1952 presidential election. He promised to apply his military experience to ending the war. Stalin's death gave the Communist side flexibility; Eisenhower's expressed willingness to use nuclear weapons in Korea helped concentrate minds in Beijing. On

July 27, 1953, the two sides finally signed an armistice that established the de facto boundary that still separates North and South Korea. After three years and the deaths of a million Chinese, perhaps 2 million Koreans, and 52,246 Americans, the war was over. Only a little over a third of the 10,000 Americans whom the Communists had captured returned alive.

Containment in northeastern Asia had succeeded, but at a price. Part of that price was that after mid-1950 Washington perceived all Communist actions, even unrelated ones, as part of a grand design. Truman deployed the U.S. Navy to shield Taiwan from Mao's forces on the mainland, although Washington had earlier shunned Chiang Kai-shek. The United States looked on approvingly as Britain tamed a Communist insurgency among the overseas Chinese of Malaya. Mao's victory in China impelled Truman in May 1950 to order aid to France in Indochina, a cause of which Washington had earlier disapproved. The North Korean attack impelled Washington to flood Indochina with weapons and funds that amounted to $1 billion a year by 1954.

The French lost. Ho Chi Minh skillfully identified Vietnamese Communism with national resistance to colonial rule. The Vietnamese Communist regular army that Mao's forces trained and equipped in southern China after 1949 showed unparalleled fighting power. U.S. prodding drove Paris to foster non-Communist Indochinese nationalist forces by making promises of eventual independence. More Vietnamese indeed fought on the French side than on Ho Chi Minh's, but few fought as hard. In late 1953 the French staked everything on luring Ho's forces to attack an isolated French outpost in a valley on the Laos border, at Dien Bien Phu. There the excellent artillery that the United States had given Chiang, who had lost it to Mao, who had given it to Ho, trapped the French instead. Dien Bien Phu fell in May 1954. France agreed to withdraw, sub-

Ho Chi Minh ("the Bringer of Enlightenment"), architect of Vietnamese Communism (1954).

ject to a satisfactory truce. The United States, Soviet Union, China, France, and Britain met at Geneva in the first major East-West conference since 1946 and agreed to a cease-fire and the division of Vietnam at the 17th parallel. Laos and Cambodia were to be independent and neutral. The First Indochina War was over.

Contrary to later myth, the Geneva conference did not reach a general agreement that required free elections and reunification of all Vietnam by 1956. The United States rejected elections without United Nations supervision to ensure a fair vote. Nor did Ho's newly minted "Democratic Republic of Vietnam" (DRV), north of the 17th parallel, subscribe to the conference's unsigned face-saving declaration that called for elections. Ho and associates were the least satisfied of the parties at Geneva; they felt that Beijing and Moscow had sold them out by failing to deliver all of Indochina. An unquiet peace nevertheless descended on Asia.

The attack of Stalin's North Korean clients on South Korea thus had worldwide repercussions. It at last roused the United States to attempt to right the military imbalance that its precipitate demobilization in 1945–46 had caused. A rearmed United States and West Germany were the Soviet Union's ultimate rewards for its Korean escapade. The 1950 emergency allowed Truman to persuade Congress to commit to Europe additional U.S. divisions and much military aid. The Germans received back their sovereignty in a peace treaty with the Western powers in 1954 and began rearming in 1955.

Thanks to Stalin's blunder, the United States implemented many of the recommendations of NSC-68. America acquired its first large-scale peacetime draft, a standing military establishment twice the size of that of 1949, and a network of bases that ringed the Soviet Union. By the late 1950s, NATO at last had the forces, both American and German, needed to stop a Soviet armored thrust short of the Rhine. The Soviet Union answered with more armored divisions, intermediate-range nuclear missiles, and an alliance against NATO, founded in 1955, the Warsaw Pact.

THE PERILS OF NIKITA SERGEYEVICH KHRUSHCHEV, 1953–64

In Moscow, Stalin's death apparently prevented a last great purge, a new stage in the totalitarian remodeling of Soviet society. Instead, the Soviet Union fell back into a drab bureaucratic "failed totalitarianism." The messianic claim to remake humanity remained. The will to do so by terror and war henceforth diminished.

"Thaw" at Home and Abroad

Indeed, Stalin's heirs and beneficiaries vied with one another to lead the "thaw" that ensued after March 1953. Lavrenty Beria, master of the security apparatus, moved first. His ministry announced that the confessions of the Kremlin doctors had been fraudulent and extorted by force. That appeared to open the road to the wholesale rehabilitation of millions of other victims of Stalin—and of Beria. Beria's colleagues reacted poorly to their rival's shameless bid for popularity. They coalesced, called on Red Army support, and had Beria shot, possibly in the Kremlin basement. The new "collective leadership," under Georgi Malenkov for the state apparatus and Nikita S. Khrushchev for the Party, then announced implausibly that Beria had been an agent of British intelligence since 1919. Some of Stalin's habits survived him.

Beria's liquidation was nevertheless the last. When the canny Khrushchev displaced Malenkov in 1955, he did no more than demote him. When Malenkov, Molotov, and Stalin's most bloodstained surviving associate, Lazar Kaganovich, combined against Khrushchev in 1957, he merely dismissed them from their Party and government posts. Thanks to Khrushchev, the new Soviet ruling class that Stalin had created at last acquired a degree of job security. Amnesties gradually deflated the GULAG after a series of prisoner revolts.

And Khrushchev, whose deliberately uncouth peasant exterior concealed both shrewdness and a moral courage he had been careful to repress while Stalin lived, soon took on the legacy of his former "Boss." As the Twentieth Party Congress of February 1956 approached, mention of the former "great leader" and "guide of progressive humanity" dropped from the Soviet press. At the Congress, Khrushchev in a secret speech damned Stalin so severely as to place in question the very bases of the Soviet system.

Khrushchev was careful to claim that Stalin's "cult of personality" and his "extreme methods and mass repressions," were an exception, a historical accident that owed nothing to Lenin, much less Marx. But Marx had justified dictatorship and terror. Lenin had authorized terror against the "class enemy" and had erected the dictatorship of a Party that he insisted must be monolithic. Stalin had merely followed that logic to its conclusion and had attempted to make the Party itself monolithic through terror.

Despite its slant, Khrushchev's secret speech contained a wealth of information about the purges, from the technique of extorting false confessions to the startling numbers of victims in the higher ranks of the Party. It soon leaked to the outside world and devastated Communist parties and sympathizers everywhere. Some departed sadly disillusioned with Communism. Others attacked Khrushchev for betraying the faith. In the Soviet Union, as Khrushchev had apparently intended, the speech made a return to Stalin's methods difficult. Dissidents who eventually raised their heads now risked labor camp or punitive psychiatric hospital but rarely immediate death. The "thaw" replaced mass terror with subtle and calculated repression by the reorganized secret police and intelligence service, the Committee for State Security (KGB).

Externally, "de-Stalinization" made Soviet policy less rigid. Khrushchev announced that "war was not fatalistically inevitable" between the "socialist camp" and the Western "capitalist" powers. In a belated attempt to woo rather than terrorize German and European opinion, he agreed to withdraw Soviet forces from Austria in 1955. He visited Tito in 1955 and apologized for Stalin's intemperance against Yugoslavia; the Soviet Union thus recognized that the "Soviet path" was not the sole road to Communism. That was the beginning of a development later described as "polycentrism": the splitting of the formerly monolithic world Communist movement.

But de-Stalinization had limits abroad as well as at home. In the Soviet

---

Khrushchev on Stalin   February 24–25, 1956

Khrushchev sought above all to differentiate between Lenin and Stalin, to present Stalin's terror and "cult of personality" as an accident rather than as a logical consequence of Lenin's party autocracy.

Lenin used severe methods only in the most necessary cases, when the exploiting classes were still in existence and were vigorously opposing the revolution, when the struggle for survival was decidedly assuming the sharpest forms, even including a civil war.

Stalin, on the other hand, used extreme methods and mass repressions at a time when the revolution was already victorious, when the Soviet state was strengthened, when the exploiting classes were already liquidated. . . . It is clear that here Stalin showed in a whole series of cases his intolerance, his brutality and his abuse of power. Instead of proving his political correctness and mobilizing the masses, he often chose the path of repression and physical annihilation, not only against actual enemies, but also against individuals who had not committed any crimes against the party and the Soviet Government.

From Basil Dmytryshyn, *USSR: A Concise History* (New York: Charles Scribner's Sons, 1978), p. 501.

Soviet tanks dominate the streets of Berlin after crushing the East German workers' revolt (June 1953).

The Hungarian uprising, 1956: insurgents burn Russian books and magazines.

Union, the "great patriotic war" of 1941–45 and Stalin's rehabilitation of the Tsarist past had partially merged Great Russian nationalism with Communism. In the satellites, Communism was a Red Army import and nationalism was from the beginning its mortal enemy. The "people's democracies" consequently suffered repeated waves of unrest. In East Berlin, Stalin's death and Ulbricht's imposition of wage cuts in June 1953 triggered a new Kronstadt 1921—a desperate workers' revolt that spread to much of the DDR. The "People's Police" and Soviet armor crushed the workers.

Khrushchev's secret speech led to further ferment. In Poland, workers at Poznán demonstrated against wage cuts in June 1956. Street fighting between workers and troops then triggered a struggle within the Polish Communist Party between Stalinists and "moderates." Street agitation against the regime mounted. But instead of sending tanks, Khrushchev grudgingly accepted assurances from the chief of the "moderates," Wladyslaw Gomulka, that Poland would remain within the Soviet empire. Gomulka then persuaded the population to subside in the name of national survival.

In Hungary, similar events led to tragedy. Rákosi, Stalin's man in Budapest, clung to power until Khrushchev ordered him to resign in July 1956. But his successor was another lesser Stalinist. When Hungary's equivalent to Gomulka, Imre Nagy, at last came to power in late October 1956, the Communist regime was disintegrating in the face of spontaneous revolt. Demonstrators toppled the immense statue of Stalin in Budapest. Communist leaders hid or ran for the Soviet border. A small contingent of Soviet tanks withdrew from Budapest in the face of popular fury. Nagy attempted to persuade Moscow to hold back, while simultaneously seeking to moderate popular demands for a multiparty political system and an exit from the Warsaw Pact.

Nagy failed. Like the Habsburgs whose role he now filled, Khrushchev could not permit the "rollback" of his power by one nationality, lest others follow. Simultaneous disarray in the West over the Suez crisis (see pp. 1013–14) made the decision to act easier. On November 4, 1956, Moscow committed its armored divisions against Budapest and crushed the revolt. In the fighting and aftermath, the Soviets and their collaborators killed thousands of Hungarians; 190,000 refugees fled west. Khrushchev had maintained Stalin's empire by the methods by which Stalin had established it.

The Sino-Soviet Split

To the east, where the Soviet Union faced a new phenomenon, a second Communist great power, such methods were of doubtful use. Stalin had preserved an uneasy ascendancy over Mao even after 1949. Khrushchev and his colleagues could not. Mao was his own Lenin and Stalin; he regarded Stalin's puny successors with poorly concealed contempt. The Chinese also felt slighted by having to carry the military burden of Stalin's Korean misjudgment and vexed at the poor quality and small quantity of Soviet economic aid. They nevertheless bore with Khrushchev, despite de-Stalinization, which Mao read as implicit criticism of his own thriving "cult of personality."

The parting of the ways, the greatest single defeat to Soviet policy since 1941, soon came. In October 1957, in a final bid to keep Beijing a loyal vassal, Khrushchev signed a secret treaty providing China with assistance in developing the atomic bomb. The following year, Mao staked a claim to world ideological leadership of the Communist movement. He launched an economic "Great Leap Forward" complete with collectivization and crash industrialization. The "attainment of Communism in China is no longer a remote future event," the CCP Central Committee trumpeted. That statement was a direct challenge to Moscow, which had not dared promise the rapid attainment of Communism—the blissful end of history amid untold abundance—to its long-suffering subjects. And Mao also challenged the United States by seeking confrontation in the Taiwan straits in the fall of 1958.

In June 1959, Soviet aid to China's nuclear program abruptly ended: Khrushchev had thought better of giving the bomb to his over-mighty and apparently reckless vassal. Soviet military and industrial experts left China. By 1960 the Sino-Soviet split was half public. By the summer of 1963 the two "fraternal parties" were trading mortal insults and mass displays of ritual hatred. Moscow damned Beijing for fanatical rigidity ("dogmatism"). Beijing denounced Moscow for betraying the Marxist-Leninist gospel ("modern revisionism").

From Berlin to Cuba

On the Soviet Union's western front, Khrushchev simultaneously took the offensive. His objective was probably to settle the question of Germany—to end the West's non-recognition of Ulbricht's shaky puppet regime with a German peace treaty and thereby consolidate Soviet control of East Germany and east-central Europe. But Khrushchev's methods lacked subtlety. He had already, in the Suez crisis of 1956, gleefully brandished the Soviet Union's small but growing arsenal of nuclear missiles. In October 1957 the Soviet Union's triumphant launching of the first artificial satellite, *Sputnik*, gave further proof that Soviet military technology could under some circumstances surpass that of the United States. The following month Khrushchev delivered to the West an ultimatum demanding a German peace treaty within six months.

That ultimatum became a rolling one, always extended. The exuberant Khrushchev accompanied it with a drumfire of nuclear threats that punctuated four years of steadily increasing superpower tension. Khrushchev's declared commitment to "peaceful coexistence" did not inhibit him from occasionally predicting in ominous tones the ultimate triumph of Communism: "We will bury you." In September 1959 Khrushchev nevertheless became the first Soviet ruler to visit the United States, for an inconclusive summit with Eisenhower accompanied by acrimonious exchanges with U.S. reporters. After a Soviet anti-aircraft missile knocked down a U-2 high-altitude

The "New Frontier":
Kennedy takes office (1961).

Khrushchev makes a point
(1962).

gan courting Moscow. Khrushchev happily responded during a visit to the United Nations at which he distinguished himself with uncouth shoe-pounding interruptions of a United Nations speech by the British prime minister.

Along with the Cuban problem, Kennedy inherited from Eisenhower a solution: an amateurish CIA-organized invasion of Cuba by anti-Communist Cuban exiles seeking to trigger an uprising against Castro. The landing at the Bay of Pigs on Cuba's south coast began on April 17, 1961. Castro's Soviet tanks swiftly crushed it. Kennedy denied the naval air support that alone could have given the 1,300 lightly armed attackers a chance of survival.

In the aftermath of that delectable humiliation of the "*Yanquis*," Castro consolidated his dictatorship. He took over for his own purposes the pre-existing Cuban Communist Party, secured increased military, police, and economic aid from the Soviet Union, and hastened the export of the most educated and articulate 15 percent of Cuba's population to southern Florida. The Soviet Union acquired a Caribbean satellite, complete with vanguard party, secret police, and GULAG; the United States received in the course of the decade up to a million enterprising new citizens.

Kennedy, sheepish over failure, met Khrushchev at a summit at Vienna in June 1961. There Khrushchev bullied the president unmercifully and apparently emerged with the notion that Kennedy lacked resolve. On August 13, 1961, Khrushchev solved his German difficulties unilaterally. East German forces with Soviet armor behind them sealed East Berlin off from the Western sectors with a massive wall of prefabricated concrete and electrified barbed wire. That closed the last avenue of escape from Ulbricht's "German Democratic Republic," which had lost 3 million citizens to the West in the preceding decade.

Kennedy and other western leaders had no answer to that unexpected So-

reconnaissance aircraft of the CIA over Sverdlovsk in central Russia, Khrushchev aborted the return summit in May 1960 by staging a propaganda circus, complete with personal slurs on Eisenhower.

The 1960 U.S. presidential election brought in a new Democratic administration under the debonair young Boston-Irish grandee, John Fitzgerald Kennedy. That offered Khrushchev new opportunities. Kennedy inherited from Eisenhower a Caribbean problem: Cuba. There a fanatically anti-American revolutionary adventurer, Fidel Castro, had come to power when the military regime of the incompetent Fulgencio Batista collapsed in January 1959. Castro later claimed not entirely implausibly to have been a life-long Marxist-Leninist. He immediately be-

viet stroke, although Kennedy called up U.S. reserve forces as a warning to Khrushchev not to press his luck. Worse followed. Khrushchev ordered nuclear tests that violated both assurances he had given to Kennedy and a moratorium on atmospheric testing to which the nuclear powers had subscribed in 1958. In October 1961 the Soviet Union triumphantly detonated a bomb twice as large as any U.S. competitor, a weapon equivalent in power to 58 million tons of high explosive.

In mid-1962, with Ulbricht's regime at last on the way to consolidation behind barbed wire, the irrepressible Khrushchev launched a spectacular Caribbean gamble. In July he persuaded the Cubans to accept a Soviet garrison of 22,000 troops and technicians, to be armed with at least 48 medium-ranged and 24 intermediate-ranged ballistic missiles capable of striking most of the United States. The 72 missiles would more than double Soviet capacity to deliver thermonuclear weapons to United States targets. A successful *fait accompli* would also open the road for deployment of additional missiles that might give the Soviet Union parity or superiority. And success would shift the psychological superpower balance in favor of the Soviet Union. Khrushchev had evidently failed to learn one lesson of Korea—that the United States, if aroused, might act unpredictably.

By early September 1962, the missile sites were under construction and clearly visible. Khrushchev and his subordinates lied repeatedly to Kennedy: the Soviet Union was merely installing anti-aircraft rockets, not offensive missiles. But on October 14, 1962, photographs from a high-flying U-2 showed patterns already familiar from pictures of intermediate-range missile sites in the Soviet Union. Khrushchev's gamble that he could install the weapons before the United States noticed had failed.

Kennedy and his advisers consulted feverishly. The more militant urged immediate air strikes and an airborne

Berlin divided by concrete and barbed wire: the Berlin Wall.

and amphibious invasion of Cuba. Others pleaded for a predictably futile appeal to the United Nations. Robert McNamara, "boy wonder" of the Ford Motor Company turned Secretary of Defense, claimed with characteristically mechanical logic that the new missiles made little difference to the balance: "a missile is a missile," whether in Cuba or elsewhere. McNamara's analysis showed a peculiar blindness to the devastating effects that Khrushchev's coup, if successful, would have had on U.S. ability to deter further Soviet actions.

Kennedy finally chose a naval blockade; it would give Khrushchev time to climb down without excessive humiliation. But Kennedy also prepared air strikes and invasion, should they be necessary to prevent the 42 missiles already in Cuba from becoming operational. His television announcement on October 22 of a U.S. Navy "quarantine" of Cuba initiated a week of crisis that many in the West feared was the prelude to a "nuclear holocaust." Khrushchev was not that ambitious. When the blockade took effect on October 24, the Soviet ships carrying additional missiles stopped.

The Soviet ballistic missile site at San Cristóbal, Cuba (October 1962).

Khrushchev belatedly admitted having the missiles, but retreated behind the threadbare claim that he had placed them in Cuba to prevent a United States invasion—a threat the Bay of Pigs fiasco had dissipated, and which only revived thanks to the missiles. He offered to withdraw them in return for a U.S. agreement not to invade Cuba. But work on the sites in Cuba continued feverishly; the first missiles were apparently approaching operational readiness.

On October 27 Kennedy therefore sent his brother Bobby, the administration's enforcer, to tell the Soviet ambassador that "the point of escalation was at hand." If Moscow did not agree to withdraw the missiles, the United States would itself remove them. That threat, backed with a strategic nuclear superiority of at least 4 to 1 and by overwhelming air, sea, and ground power in the Caribbean, belatedly persuaded Khrushchev to climb down. The Soviet Union withdrew its missiles. It left behind advisers and a mechanized brigade based near Havana as a praetorian guard for Castro. The United States in turn agreed not to invade Cuba.

Like Stalin's death, the Cuban missile crisis marked the end of a phase in the Cold War. It was the closest that Soviet and U.S. forces had come to fighting since the Berlin blockade—but on that occasion the United States had possessed a nuclear monopoly. In the aftermath of the far more dangerous Cuban crisis, both powers sought to bring their mutual antagonism within bounds. A 1963 treaty banning nuclear tests in the atmosphere and in space was the first result of that effort.

In other respects, the rivals drew divergent lessons from the confrontation. The United States, temporarily reassured about the superpower balance, overcommitted itself in Asia. It also sought to limit nuclear weapons, and by 1969 had by deliberate inaction discarded the superiority that had helped checkmate Khrushchev in Cuba. Nuclear "parity," McNamara and others theorized, would make the Soviets more amenable to arms control and eventual reductions. Thermonuclear weapons, U.S. academics suggested, were so destructive that they had ceased to be usable as weapons. Their only purpose was to deter the use of nuclear weapons by others.

The Soviets took an entirely different view. "You will never be able to do this to us again," a Soviet diplomat grimly informed an American counterpart in the aftermath of the crisis. Khrushchev's colleagues forcibly retired him in October 1964, in part because he threatened the prerogatives of the Party elite, but also for mishandling the missile crisis. The stone-faced new leadership of Leonid Brezhnev and Alexei Kosygin tightened KGB controls at home and increased the Soviet defense budget from an already heavy 10 percent of gross national product in 1965 to 20 percent or more by 1980.

The Soviet Union's accelerating missile programs aimed at nuclear superiority (see Figure 34-1). Unlike Western pundits, the Soviets considered that superiority both militarily meaningful and politically useful. The United States and its allies relied on the U.S. strategic nuclear "umbrella" to hold back superior Soviet ground forces. If the Soviet Union could threaten the United States itself with destruction, the U.S. threat to use nuclear weapons in defense of its overseas allies lost credibility. Superiority would also give the Soviet Union a global reach, and greater latitude in supporting "wars of national liberation" that indirectly sapped the West's position. Finally, the growth of Soviet power would presumably cow the Europeans and Japanese, and separate them politically from the United States.

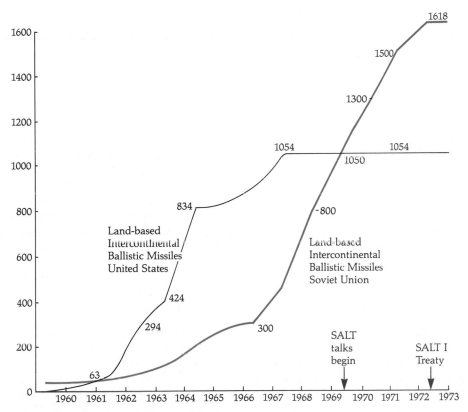

FIGURE 34-1   After Cuba: Missile Power, 1962–72

Adapted from *Le Monde*, November 22, 1972, p. 2.

PEACE AND WAR IN THE SHADOW OF THE COLD WAR

While the superpowers contended, Japan and the once-great powers of Europe enjoyed unprecedented economic growth. Not so the Middle East, where the West ceased after 1945 to fill the vacuum that Ottoman decay had created. The foundation of a Jewish state and the conflicting ambitions of the Arabs led to two generations of bitter wars.

The Mid-Sized Powers in Eclipse

The revival of world trade was the first prerequisite for the recovery of Europe and Japan. In the previous long peace, from 1871 to 1914, world trade had grown by an annual average of 3.4 percent; then the German bid for world mastery had dropped growth to an average of 1 percent per year from 1913 to 1938. But after 1948, over $20 billion in Marshall Plan and other U.S. aid along with the inevitable Korean War boom galvanized the world economy. The Bretton Woods system installed in 1944–47 brought a stability and predictability unknown in the 1920s and 1930s.

The result was stunning growth. From 1950 to 1960, the volume of world trade grew by 6.4 percent each year. Europe and Japan rebuilt under the military protection and economic leadership of the United States. The West German "economic miracle" was the most dramatic in Europe, at 7.7 percent growth per year. France followed, then Italy, which started as a far poorer country. Last, thanks largely to a continuing failure to put its best brains into its economy, came Britain at 2.6 percent.

But despite the aspirations of Europe's technocratic visionaries, no "United States of Europe" emerged. The European Economic Community (EEC) or European Common Market, founded at Rome in 1957, slowly developed a transnational political super-structure and a European Parliament. But its powers remained small indeed. The nation-state remained the principal focus of loyalty. And France crippled the EEC for a decade by checkmating a halfhearted British attempt to enter it in 1963.

Britain after 1945 displayed its usual orderly alternation between Labour and Conservative parties. Labour under Attlee nationalized major industries, thus protecting them from much-needed rationalization and modernization. Government health care and social insurance extended "cradle to grave" security to the entire population. When the aging Churchill returned to power in 1951, he left the welfare state intact but sold off some nationalized industries. His foreign secretary and successor, Anthony Eden, suffered collapse in the Suez crisis of 1956 (see p. 1014), but the reassuring leadership of Harold Macmillan kept the Conservatives in office until 1963–64. Labour then returned under the bland Harold Wilson, Labour's answer to Stanley Baldwin. Both Labour and Conservatives pursued roughly similar policies: the welfare state at home, a "special relationship" with the United States abroad, and retention of as much empire as Britain could hold without debilitating effort.

France, as always, was more lively. The Fourth Republic was roughly similar in political habits and alignments to the Third Republic that died in 1940. The Republic's founders pushed de Gaulle, the savior of his country, into premature retirement in early 1946. He repaid the compliment by damning the political system as "the convolutions of this absurd ballet." His successors halfheartedly waged the Indochina war into which de Gaulle's pro-consuls had blundered in 1945–46. The Fourth Republic's one hour of glory was the 1954–55 premiership of Pierre Mendès-France, who set a deadline for French withdrawal and made it stick.

But the Mendès-France government soon collapsed over the Algerian insurrection against France (see pp. 1015–18)

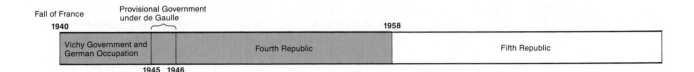

Fall of France	Provisional Government under de Gaulle		1958	
1940				
Vichy Government and German Occupation		Fourth Republic	Fifth Republic	
	1945 1946			

that erupted less than six months after the Indochina settlement. That second great colonial war wrecked the Fourth Republic. The French Right supported NATO, but claimed that Algeria was part of France, despite its Moslem majority. Left-wing opinion and a strong Communist Party opposed NATO but —after some hesitation—favored Algerian independence. Parliamentary deadlock ensued. The army in Algeria was already restless; those who had served in Indochina grimly reproached the politicians for France's long record of defeat. A sense of betrayal impelled the army to swing its support behind de Gaulle's tumultuous return in a quasi-coup in May 1958.

De Gaulle demanded and received from parliament the right to draft a new constitution. His Fifth Republic endured better than its predecessor; de Gaulle as president took stronger powers than any French executive since Napoleon III. De Gaulle used those powers wisely. He led France out of the Algerian war in 1962 without splitting the highly politicized army or provoking the civil war between Right and Left that had seemed imminent in 1958. He gave France unprecedented economic growth. The France of landowning peasants consolidated in the Revolution of 1789 at last became a land of urban workers.

West Germany was Western Europe's most dramatic success. Bonn— the Federal Republic's provisional capital, chosen in the expectation of an eventual move to Berlin—was not Weimar. The constitution of 1949 barred from parliament any party that received less than 5 percent of the vote. That ended the political fragmentation that had helped destroy Weimar. The new presidency, unlike the presidency of Weimar that had made Hitler chan-

cellor, was a purely ceremonial position. And Hitler had through war, terror, and defeat destroyed—along with much else—the conservative elites that had so despised Weimar democracy that they had brought the Nazis to power.

The new Republic's first chancellor was an aged but vigorous former mayor of Cologne and pre-1933 opponent of Hitler, Konrad Adenauer. His party, the Christian Democratic Union/ Christian Social Union (CDU/CSU), was a successor to the Catholic Center party that also appealed to Protestants. It became the mass party of the German urban and rural middle classes and ruled uninterruptedly from 1949 to 1966 in coalition with a small liberal grouping, the Free Democrats (FDP).

The Social Democratic Party (SPD), the only major party survivor from Weimar, opposed the CDU/CSU. After publicly discarding Marxism in 1959, the SPD at last broke the class barrier that had stunted its growth before 1933. Like the CDU/CSU, it appealed to an ever larger and more prosperous middle and working class; it offered "good government" and the welfare state. Under Willy Brandt, a dynamic mayor of Berlin who had passed the Hitler years in political exile, the SPD achieved by 1966 a share of power in coalition with Adenauer's successors in the CDU/CSU. In 1969, in alliance with the FDP, Brandt and the SPD took power in place of the CDU/CSU. West Germany had achieved an orderly alternation between large coherent parties. Antidemocratic fringe groups persisted on the far Right and far Left, but their clamor was infinitely greater than their influence.

Italy also surprised everyone. It achieved stability and unprecedented prosperity. Political parties reemerged

De Gaulle in Algiers (1958).

Two generations of post-war German leaders: Konrad Adenauer (chancellor, 1949–63) and Willy Brandt (1969–74).

after the collapse of Fascism. The Catholic *Popolari*, renamed Christian Democrats, were the largest; they faced small middle-class parties and a Socialist-Communist alliance. Thanks to its collaboration with Mussolini, the monarchy failed to win a majority in a 1946 referendum; Italy became a republic. By 1947–48, as the lines of the Cold War became clear, Italy's politics had set. The shrewd Alcide De Gasperi of the Christian Democrats dominated government. The Communist-Socialist alliance lost heavily in the decisive election of April 1948, which the Christian Democrats fought with massive U.S. and Vatican support and a remarkable platform: "For or Against Christ."

De Gasperi gave way in 1953 to a series of revolving door governments. But more than in France, the "absurd ballet" in parliament cloaked underlying continuity. The Communist Party, western Europe's largest, formed a permanent "disloyal opposition" capable of overthrowing the system if admitted to government. By parliamentary arithmetic, therefore, only a coalition centered on the Christian Democrats could govern. With modifications such as the addition of the Socialists to the coalition in 1963 after they broke with the Communists, that formula gave Italy a government that showed remarkable stability behind a facade of incoherence. And by the late 1980s Italy's gross national product had according to some estimates passed that of the first industrial nation, Britain, and possibly that of France as well. That was an astounding achievement for a society that in 1913 had possessed less than a quarter of Britain's industrial power.

Finally, Japan amazed its American occupiers. MacArthur's democratic revolution from above, the greatest internal upheaval since the Meiji Restoration of 1868, was a success. Drawing on the precedents of the parliamentary 1920s, Japanese politicians created a powerful machine of electoral consensus, the Liberal Democratic party. Its ruling oligarchy achieved and maintained a parliamentary majority based on the votes of Japan's peasantry and urban middle classes. That permanently excluded from power a fragmented opposition that included Communists, Socialists, and a Buddhist political cult. This "half democracy," as Japanese critics described it, provided political stability and fostered spectacular economic growth.

The United States provided other ingredients as well: the technology that U.S. corporations offered their Japanese subsidiaries and markets and raw materials to replace Japan's lost empire in China and Southeast Asia. Direct U.S. aid to Japan after 1954 totalled some $2 billion, but the expenditure by 1970 of over $10 billion in military orders for the wars in Korea and Vietnam was more significant. The goods the U.S. military ordered were predominantly civilian; their production fostered the techniques that Japan used to storm the world's export markets after the mid-1960s. In Japan the United States, even more than in Europe, provided the catalyst for the "economic miracle" of the 1950s and 1960s. But it was the relentless hard work of the Japanese themselves, their highly skilled and educated labor force, that by the 1970s had made Japan the third largest economy in the world after the United States and the Soviet Union.

The New Eastern Question, 1947–73

Hitler failed to kill all the Jews of Europe. Instead, paradoxically and unintentionally, he made possible the first Jewish state since the Roman reconquest of Jerusalem in A.D. 70. His genocide inspired a disgust for Europe in many Jews who survived and provoked a flood of emigration to Palestine. His genocide taught the lesson that only a Jewish state, weapons in hand, could ensure Jewish survival. His genocide discredited anti-Semitism in western Europe and the United States, and inspired guilt in those who had failed to aid the Jews of Europe in time. That unspoken guilt dissipated with time, but it was a powerful source of international support for the creation of a Jewish state.

In the aftermath of Hitler's war, Britain attempted to uphold its 1939 ban on further Jewish immigration to Palestine (see p. 888). British interests in the Arab world—the world of oil— appeared to demand that Britain block the Zionist aspiration to a Jewish state. But by 1945 the 600,000 Jews of Palestine were a third of the population. Many of them had fought for Britain against Hitler. They now resisted Britain as they had resisted the Arabs in the guerrilla conflict after 1936. By 1946 Zionist guerrilla groups, the Irgun, and the "Stern Gang," were at war with both Arabs and British. Chaim Weizmann, the Zionist leader who had secured Balfour's promise in 1917, indefatigably lobbied the powers.

By 1946, Britain's position was untenable. As in Ireland after 1919, the British army could not control a spreading guerrilla war without using methods that no democracy could easily defend. Truman backed the creation of a Jewish state. Even Stalin, who despite his anti-Semitism initially saw the Jews of Palestine as possible allies against Britain, did not oppose it. In 1947 the Labour government therefore thankfully handed over the poisoned gift of Palestine to the United Nations. The U.N. proposed partition along ethnic-religious lines. The Jewish organizations accepted. The Palestinian Arabs and their supporters in the Arab states refused. An Arab "Liberation Army" attacked Jewish communities. In May 1948, as in Greece and India (see pp. 970 and 1012), the exhausted British withdrew.

That left Palestine to anyone that could dominate it. David Ben-Gurion, charismatic veteran of the Jewish settler communities, proclaimed a Jewish state—the state of Israel—on May 14, 1948. The armies of Egypt, Jordan, Syria, Lebanon, and Iraq invaded Palestine with the announced intention of driving the Jews into the sea. Israel, outnumbered and outgunned, fought that "Arab League" to a standstill and drew precarious borders by force. Many Palestinian Arabs heeded calls from their leaders to leave the Jewish areas, in expectation of a swift return with the Arab armies. In some cases Jewish forces drove Arab civilians out. Arab defeat left some 600,000 embittered refugees, and Arab states more committed than ever to expelling the Jews from Palestine.

The core of the new "Eastern Question"—the struggle between the successor states of the Ottoman Empire— was the irreconcilable conflict between the Palestinian Arabs, the Arab states, and Israel. But the antagonism also drew nourishment from a broader and longer-term conflict. The Arabs regarded Israel as yet another intrusion from the West, a successor to the Crusader kingdoms of the twelfth and thirteenth centuries and to the European imperialism of the nineteenth. Israel was a galling symbol of the Islamic world's humiliating weakness, first laid bare by Napoleon's 1798–99 campaign in Egypt. Only Israel's destruction, many Arabs henceforth felt, could restore their own self-respect.

Arab hostility was counterproductive. Relentless external threat welded Israel's disparate inhabitants together and consolidated its parliamentary system under the hegemony of Ben-Gurion's Labor party. Thanks to native ingenuity and money from Jewish organizations abroad, a modern economy took shape. In 1951 the gross national product of Egypt, most prosperous of the Arab states, was three to four times that of Israel; by 1966–67 that ratio had declined to 1.6 to 1.

War gave birth to Israel, a Jewish state, the only democracy in the Middle East. Only war could preserve it, for the Arab League powers refused to recognize the "Zionist entity" as a state and made no secret of their continuing desire to destroy it utterly. Egypt took the lead. Abdel Gamal Nasser, a visionary who dreamed of uniting the Arabs from the Atlantic to the Persian Gulf, emerged as dictator of Egypt after an army coup in 1952. From 1955 on he secured lavish supplies of arms from the Soviet Union.

Twice, in 1956 and 1967, Nasser provoked Israel with Palestinian raids from Gaza and closure of the straits of Tiran that commanded access to Israel's Red Sea port of Eilat. Twice Israel struck first and routed the Egyptians. Indefensible borders and immense numerical odds left Israel no alternative to preemptive war. Nasser's proclaimed desire for a "war of annihilation" suggested that the price of failure would be a new "Final Solution."

In 1956, thanks to the sheepish withdrawal of its British and French allies, Israel had to leave the conquered Sinai to a United Nations "peacekeeping" force that subsequently failed to keep the peace. In 1967, Israel therefore refused to withdraw after victory—and not only from the Sinai and Gaza. Syria and Jordan had joined Egypt in that "Six Days' War" and had lost the west bank of the Jordan River and the strategic Golan heights from which Syrian artillery had routinely shelled the farming settlements of northern Israel. The conquests of 1967 brought strategic security, but also a poisoned gift: a million new Arab inhabitants in the "occupied territories" of the West Bank and Gaza.

The Palestinian "resistance" drew a lesson from the 1967 war: it could not look to the Arab states for victory. In 1968 the "Palestine Liberation Organization" (PLO) and its offshoots therefore launched a campaign of terror against soft targets such as Israeli airliners. Israel replied with air attacks on Palestinian refugee camps and open season on PLO leaders. Israeli reprisals against Jordan moved Jordan's King Hussein to act against the armed Palestinians that constituted a state within his state. In "Black September" 1970 Hussein's highly professional army crushed them. Lebanon, a state too weak to defend itself, became the last stronghold of the PLO.

An embarrassed Soviet Union soon replenished Nasser's arms and manned his radars, anti-aircraft missiles, and fighters. In 1969–70 Nasser and the Soviets waged a "war of attrition" against Israel's forward defenses along the Suez Canal. Negotiations sponsored by the United Nations and United States proved predictably futile. Nasser died of a heart attack in September 1970 after Egypt had suffered 30,000 casualties, and Washington and Moscow—again embarrassed—had together imposed a cease-fire along the Canal. Nasser's successor, Colonel Anwar Sadat, prepared for yet another round against Israel. The increasing economic power of the Arab oil states had begun to isolate Israel from the timid and oil-dependent western Europeans. But this time, instead of a "war of annihilation," Sadat planned a limited attack to take back the east bank of the Canal and bloody the Israelis.

The Soviet Union supplied advanced antiaircraft and antitank missiles by the shipload. But Sadat was careful to distance himself from his patrons, who for their part perhaps feared that too close association with a new Arab war might damage the newly developing "détente" with the United States. In July 1972 Sadat asked for the withdrawal of most of his Soviet "advisers." In 1973, with Egypt's army mobilized and deployed and with Syrian armor drawn up opposite the Golan, Sadat attacked. The date he chose was Yom Kippur, the Jewish Day of Atonement, October 6, 1973.

As Sadat had hoped, Israel's political isolation deterred it from a repetition of the preemptive strikes of 1956 and 1967; the more favorable borders seized in 1967 also induced overconfidence. In 1973 the Israelis thus found themselves compelled to mobilize under Arab attack and to hope for the best. Sadat's carefully planned crossing of the Canal crumbled Israel's thinly held static defenses. Sadat's Soviet antitank missiles broke the first hasty Israeli armored counterattacks. Then the Egyptians ventured too far from the Canal and found themselves fighting a battle of movement which the Israelis dominated with their usual skill and drive. Outnumbered Israeli forces in the Golan routed some 1,000 Syrian and Iraqi tanks and advanced to within artillery range of Damascus. In the south, Israel soon crossed the Canal into Egypt and encircled one of Sadat's two armies. The road to Cairo lay open. Then the superpowers imposed a cease-fire, although not before an unprecedented Soviet threat to commit paratroops in Egypt had provoked a worldwide U.S. nuclear alert.

Militarily the Yom Kippur War was yet another crushing defeat for the Arab cause. But unlike 1967, it was not a total humiliation. Sadat's initial success along the Canal allowed him to claim a moral victory. That made Egypt's position—although not that of the Palestinians or the other Arab states—more flexible, while Israel's near disaster compelled rethinking in Jerusalem. The ultimate result of 1973 was the first break in the wall of Arab hostility surrounding Israel and the transition from war to grudging peace between Israel and Egypt (see p. 1050).

In international terms the Yom Kippur War was nevertheless ominous. It encouraged the oil-producing states of OPEC (Organization of Petroleum Exporting Countries) to more than double the real (inflation-adjusted) price of oil from October 1973 to 1975 while placing a total embargo upon the United States as retribution for its support of Israel. The Europeans cowered. They cut off trade with Israel and, except for Portugal, refused to allow the United States to use NATO bases to support the massive airlift of ammunition that helped the beleaguered Jewish state to survive. Only Holland failed to comply swiftly enough with Arab demands; it suffered both Arab oil embargo and ostracism by its EEC partners. That display of NATO and European disunity inevitably encouraged adversaries of the West to whom events in Southeast Asia had already given heart.

THE AGONY OF CONTAINMENT: AMERICA IN VIETNAM

The United States emerged from its victory in the Cuban missile crisis with a sense that nothing was impossible. Then Kennedy's brilliant rhetoric, the intellectual self-confidence of the aca-

---

Kennedy: "Ask not . . . " 1961

Kennedy's inaugural address contained some of the most stirring phrases ever spoken by an American president. It also unwisely proclaimed a willingness to "pay any price."

Let the word go forth from this time and place, to friend and foe alike, that the torch has been passed to a new generation of Americans, born in this century, tempered by war, disciplined by a hard and bitter peace, proud of our ancient heritage, and unwilling to witness or permit the slow undoing of those human rights to which this nation has always been committed, and to which we are committed today at home and around the world.

Let every nation know, whether it wishes us well or ill, that we shall pay any price, bear any burden, meet any hardship, support any friend, oppose any foe to assure the survival and the success of liberty. . . .

In the long history of the world, only a few generations have been granted the role of defending freedom in its hour of maximum danger. I do not shrink from this responsibility; I welcome it. I do not believe that any of us would exchange places with any other people or any other generation. The energy, the faith, the devotion which we bring to this endeavor will light our country and all who serve it, and the glow from that fire can truly light the world.

And so, my fellow Americans, ask not what your country can do for you; ask what you can do for your country.

From Theodore C. Sorensen, *Kennedy* (New York: Harper & Row, 1965), pp. 245–48.

demic elite that he had drawn into government, and the pressures of domestic politics combined to commit the United States to a second war of containment in Vietnam.

The Illusion of Omnipotence, 1962–68

Containment by war had proved an effective though costly answer to Stalin's adventure in Korea. Against indirect methods, against insurgency, it was less promising. Those familiar techniques were the choice of Ho Chi Minh and his associates. In 1954 they established themselves in Hanoi and consolidated their "Democratic Republic of Vietnam" (DRV) north of the 17th parallel. In 1955–56 they killed as many as 50,000 peasants who resisted collec-

tivization. Above all, they maintained their network of party cadres south of the 17th parallel, in South Vietnam.

There Ngo Dinh Diem, a Catholic anti-Communist from the pre-colonial Mandarin ruling class, established at Saigon a "Republic of Vietnam." Diem's regime rested on the traditional landowning elite and on the Vietnamese army that France had raised to fight the Communists. Eisenhower, after much hesitation, committed the United States to support Diem. If South Vietnam fell to Hanoi and to its apparent backers in Beijing, Eisenhower theorized, other Southeast Asian "dominoes" such as Laos, Cambodia, Thailand, Malaya, and Indonesia would also fall.

The United States had first tolerated France's Indochina war, then after 1950

War in Southeast Asia   1954–88

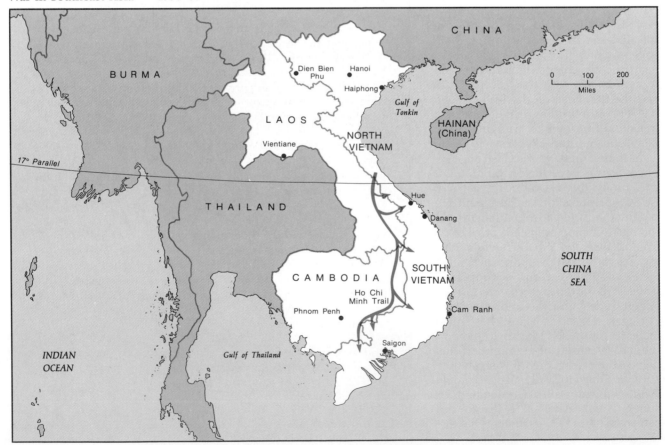

had funded it. After 1954 the United States gradually became France's successor. It failed to foresee the sacrifices that course might entail. Nor did it fully recognize that Vietnam was unlike Korea in two essential ways. Vietnam was not a peninsula, surrounded on three sides by a sea the U.S. Navy owned. And Vietnam was peripheral to the fundamental American goal of maintaining its allies in Europe and Japan.

In January 1959, in deep secret, Ho Chi Minh and his associates on the North Vietnamese central committee decided to resume "armed struggle" in South Vietnam with the aim of annexing it to the DRV. A party army, called "Viet Cong" (Vietnamese Communists) by its enemies, took shape in the South and assassinated over 3,000 Diem administrators or civilians connected with the government between 1961 and 1963. Hanoi announced in December 1960 the creation of a political cover for that army, the "National Liberation Front" (NLF), a "popular front" that included many non-Communists but secretly took its orders from Hanoi. It was important, both to secure wide support in South Vietnam and to delude Western public opinion, that NLF and Viet Cong activities appear to be a Southern revolt against what Hanoi described as the "U.S.-Diem dictatorship."

Diem's regime crumbled in 1962–63. His Catholicism, his autocratic manner, and his sinister brother and police minister Ngo Dinh Nhu alienated the influential Buddhist clergy. Monks burned themselves to death in protests well-publicized on U.S. television. Diem's association with the Americans offended South Vietnam's urban, educated elite. His closeness to the landowners alienated the peasants. The NLF offered the urban elite a romantic nationalism and disingenuous assurances that the Front's victory would mean autonomy for the South. To the peasants the NLF offered land, but made no mention of the fate of the collectivized peasants of the DRV. Viet Cong units

Lyndon Baines Johnson takes the oath of office after Kennedy's assassination, November 22, 1963.

and political cadres established control over ever-wider areas.

Kennedy, an aficionado of spy novels and irregular warfare, raised the 900 advisers he inherited from Eisenhower to over 15,000, including helicopter and fighter-bomber units. That was not enough. When the Buddhist crisis provoked unrest among Diem's generals, Washington tacitly encouraged them. Kennedy made known in Saigon that if Diem did not dismiss Nhu "we must face the possibility that Diem himself cannot be preserved." That was a green light to the Vietnamese military plotters, who overthrew Diem on November 1, 1963. Contrary to Kennedy's intentions, but all too predictably, the coup forces shot Diem and Nhu.

The United States, in the illusion that it could control events in a society of which it was sadly ignorant, thus took total responsibility for the fate of South Vietnam. Kennedy himself died three weeks after Diem, on November 22, 1963, assassinated in Dallas in circumstances that remain unclear. His vice president and successor, Lyndon Baines Johnson of Texas, proved wily and resourceful in his domestic policy. He accomplished what Kennedy had begun, the belated abolition of the "Jim

Crow" segregation laws of the southern United States and the launching of a federal "war on poverty." But Johnson's irresolute attempts to cope with the disaster that he inherited in Vietnam wrecked his presidency.

The impending 1964 presidential election and the legacy of Chinese-American war in Korea made disengagement unthinkable. "Who lost Vietnam?" was a charge that Johnson dreaded as much as Eisenhower and Kennedy before him. Beijing, where Mao and associates were proclaiming a worldwide peasant revolutionary war against the urban capitalism of the West, appeared to loom behind Hanoi. And China appeared all the more menacing after its explosion of its first atomic bomb in October 1964. Withdrawal from Vietnam, the Washington policy elite and press assumed, would weaken the credibility of U.S. guarantees to other allies and unleash a wave of Communist expansion that would engulf "dominoes" from the rice fields of Thailand to the oil fields of Indonesia.

Johnson therefore sought to dissuade Hanoi from pursuing its ambitions in the South. He chose his instruments from the arsenal of the academic armchair strategists that Kennedy had brought from Harvard to Washington—carefully calibrated South Vietnamese commando operations against the DRV and U.S. air strikes at DRV supply routes to South Vietnam. Those operations began in secret in the spring of 1964. Hanoi, undeterred, began sending units of its regular army south.

In August 1964, DRV torpedo boats attacked a U.S. destroyer off North Vietnam shortly after a South Vietnamese raid in the same area. At Johnson's urging, Congress thereupon authorized "the use of armed force" to "prevent further aggression" anywhere in Southeast Asia. Congress later regretted that "Tonkin Gulf Resolution," which gave a broader measure of congressional approval than either Roosevelt or Truman had sought in the Atlantic in 1941 or in Korea in 1950. But

unlike a declaration of war—which Johnson could probably have had in 1964 but did not want—it neither committed the nation as a whole nor defined the enemy.

In the 1964 election Johnson handily defeated the Republican candidate, Barry Goldwater, whom he depicted as an irresponsible warmonger. Then Johnson discovered that massive DRV infiltration down the "Ho Chi Minh Trail" in Laos and the incompetence of the Saigon generals faced the United States with defeat. In March 1965 Johnson therefore began a major air campaign, hopefully named ROLLING THUNDER, to warn off the DRV. That effort delivered by the end of 1967 some 864,000 tons of bombs, far more than the 503,000 tons dropped in the war against Japan. But it delivered them intermittently on targets of secondary importance. Johnson and his advisers had learned from Korea that they must not under any circumstances strike the DRV hard enough to provoke Chinese intervention. The DRV had learned a different lesson: U.S. opinion would not tolerate a long war.

Johnson's use of the military to "send a message" by increments, interspersed with 16 bombing pauses and 70 peace initiatives, hardly impressed Hanoi with American resolve. It also sacrificed aircraft and crews in ever larger numbers. Failure to bring U.S. air power to bear massively and all at once, as Roosevelt and Truman had done against Japan in 1945, allowed Hanoi to acquire from its Soviet and Chinese friends the world's best air defense network. Nor did the bombing have any noticeable effect on the level of fighting in the South.

Ground intervention soon followed Johnson's air war. The North Vietnamese regulars arriving through Laos threatened the demoralized South Vietnamese army with swift destruction. In March 1965 Johnson landed Marines to guard the key airfield at Da Nang on the central coast. In May he committed U.S. Army paratroopers around Saigon. By the end of 1965, almost 200,000 U.S. combat and support troops were again fighting a land war on the Asian mainland alongside troops from South Korea, Australia, and New Zealand.

But the vast army that ultimately reached 543,000 men and women in April 1969 was mostly support troops; of the half million, perhaps 75,000 American infantrymen and 50,000 artillerymen and helicopter crewmen actually fought. The infantry, by comparison with earlier American wars, had everything—excellent weapons, superb communications, crushing air and artillery support, prompt medical evacuation, and rotation back to the United States if they survived their 365 allotted days in Vietnam. What they lacked was a strategy, a means of translating hard-bought battlefield victories into political success. Especially after 1967, they also lacked a sense that the public back in "the World"—the far distant United States—was behind them. Frustration and endless casualties inflicted by unseen enemies sometimes provoked explosions. The most notable was the 1968 massacre of up to 400 Vietnamese civilians by an ill-led battalion of the Americal Division at the hamlet of My Lai 4. Commanders attempted to cover up the atrocity, but once the news leaked the U.S. Army tried those responsible for war crimes.

In Washington, the leadership vacuum persisted. Johnson feared the sacrifice of his domestic "war on poverty"; he therefore attempted to fight cheaply, without the economic mobilization that Truman had demanded and received for Korea. Johnson's repeatedly proclaimed war aim was to force Hanoi to negotiate. That was even less inspiring than "dying for a tie." Nor did the military bureaucracies offer Johnson intelligent choices. The U.S. Navy and Air Force competed to drop ever more bombs on strategically irrelevant targets in and around the North. The Army pursued a war of attrition against the Viet Cong and North Vietnamese in the South. That war maximized *American* attrition.

U.S. intervention nevertheless bought time. Saigon's battlefield performance and political stability slowly improved. In January–February 1968 the victor of Dien Bien Phu, General Vo Nguyen Giap, launched Viet Cong and North Vietnamese forces at the cities of the South. Timed for Têt, the Vietnamese lunar new year, Giap's "General Uprising" was a stinging operational and tactical reverse for Hanoi. U.S. troops held and counterattacked. Saigon's troops, their backs to the wall, stood and fought. Contrary to Giap's expectation, the population of the cities did not join his troops. The Viet Cong and North Vietnamese suffered devastating losses. In many areas of the South, the Têt Offensive led to the collapse of the Viet Cong. Henceforth North Vietnam alone carried the weight of the war and South Vietnam's forces gained a measure of self-confidence. At Hue on the central coast, retreating North Vietnamese took re-

The War of Attrition: Dak To, Central Highlands, 1967

The battle for Hill 875 was over, and some survivors were being brought in by Chinook to the landing strip at Dak To. The 173rd Airborne had taken over 400 casualties, nearly 200 killed, all on the previous afternoon and in the fighting that had gone on all through the night. It was very cold and wet up there, and some girls from the Red Cross had been sent up from Pleiku to comfort the survivors. As the troops filed out of the helicopters, the girls waved and smiled at them from behind serving tables. "Hi, soldier! What's your name?" "Where you from, soldier?" "I'll bet some hot coffee would hit the spot about now." And the men from the 173rd just kept walking without answering, staring straight ahead, their eyes rimmed with red from fatigue, their faces pinched and aged with all that had happened during the night. One of them dropped out of line and said something to a . . . girl who wore a Peanuts sweatshirt under her fatigue shirt and she started to cry. The rest just walked past the girls and the large, olive-drab coffee urns. They had no idea of where they were.

From Michael Herr, *Dispatches* (New York: Avon Books, 1978), p. 169.

Têt, 1968: Marines advance warily through the ruins of Hue.

Johnson had failed to define a war aim. Now he concurred with his critics. Under a rough and profane exterior, the president concealed a fatal desire to be loved. Increasing fire from the press and the growth of raucous demonstrations against the war effort ("Hey, hey, LBJ, how many kids did ya kill today?") deeply wounded him. Subordinates such as Secretary of Defense McNamara had concluded that the war was "unwinnable" because the enemy's commitment to victory was total while their own was not. The Têt fighting and the strong showing of an "anti-war" candidate in the New Hampshire presidential primary broke what little nerve Johnson still retained. Polls nevertheless suggested that many Americans supported "staying the course" if the president would only lead.

On March 31, 1968, Johnson appeared on television and announced three things: that the United States would cease bombing the North except for the area immediately north of the 17th parallel, that the United States would seek to negotiate an end to the conflict, and that he himself would not run for reelection that fall. Assassination brought Johnson to power; he departed by political suicide. His public confession that he thought the war unwinnable changed the terms of debate. Americans henceforth battled over how to leave Vietnam, not over how to win or whether to fight.

Defeat, 1968–75

Johnson's hapless vice president, Hubert Humphrey, lost the 1968 presidential election. Jim Crow took its final revenge on Johnson's domestic policy, for a racist third-party revolt of George Wallace on the Right deprived the Democrats of their usually solid Southern vote. On the Left, violent student demonstrations against Humphrey outside the Democratic Convention in Chicago and the abstention of many "dovish" voters in protest against Johnson's Vietnam policy had a similar

venge for defeat by massacring 2,800 civilians.

Yet out of tactical defeat Hanoi gained strategic victory. The confusion and bloodshed of Têt shocked the American press and television representatives in Saigon. They had sought to cover the war from the comfort and safety of their hotel bars. They interpreted fighting in the cities as a massive U.S. defeat. Walter Cronkite, father-figure of CBS News, intoned funereally that the United States must find an exit.

effect. To the horror of the "doves," the Republican victor was a former associate of Senator McCarthy, Richard M. Nixon.

Nixon had claimed during the campaign to have a "secret peace plan." It remained secret. He did announce in March 1969 the "Vietnamization" of the war and the gradual withdrawal of American troops. He formalized the new policy in July 1969 as the "Nixon Doctrine"—the United States would continue to provide air support and supplies, but would henceforth allow its allies to do their own ground fighting. U.S. troop levels declined from 543,000 in April 1969 to 24,200 in December 1972. To buy time, Nixon in May–June 1970 launched a last offensive thrust, a brief invasion of Cambodia, where up to 300,000 North Vietnamese had set up housekeeping at the southern end of the Ho Chi Minh trail.

Nixon and his devious National Security Adviser, Henry Kissinger of Harvard, may have deluded themselves as well as others that "Vietnamization" would achieve a Korea-style stalemate. More probably they aimed from the beginning at a gradual retreat from Vietnam in the style of the withdrawal from Algeria of de Gaulle, whom Kissinger admired. The principal obstacle was Hanoi: it spurned negotiation. Its delegates to the Paris talks that began in May 1968 demanded instantaneous and total withdrawal by the United States and the dismantling of its ally, the Saigon regime. Hanoi also refused to offer assurances that it would release U.S. prisoners, mostly Navy and Air Force crews, held in its concentration camps. The death of Ho Chi Minh in September 1969 made no difference. The Leninist party he had created lived on.

But by now the international situation that had attended the U.S. plunge into Vietnam had entirely changed. A Communist *Putsch* in Indonesia had failed in 1965; the Indonesian military and Islamic activists had in response massacred perhaps 500,000 Indonesian Communists and sympathizers. *That*

vital "domino" and its oil was not going to fall. As for China, it had ironically ceased to need "containment." Mao had reduced it to chaos with his "Great Proletarian Cultural Revolution" of 1966–69, a cataclysm similar in causes and consequences to Stalin's Great Terror (see p. 912). And the Sino-Soviet split had ripened into a full-scale military confrontation between the two Communist giants along their 5,000 miles of border.

In the spring and summer of 1969 Soviet and Chinese troops fought bitterly on the Ussuri River, north of Vladivostok. A Soviet journalist with close ties to the KGB wrote ominously in the British press that "Marxist theoreticians" were discussing the possibility of full-scale Sino-Soviet war. Soviet spokesmen secretly approached the United States, suggesting that a Soviet strike against China's infant nuclear weapons program would be in the interests of both superpowers. But Nixon sternly warned Moscow off. Kissinger opened a line to Beijing, which he visited in July 1971 for talks with the shrewd Zhou Enlai (Chou En-lai), the second man in China. Kissinger sought

The opening to China: Nixon and Mao (1972).

to exploit Beijing's fears of Moscow to put pressure on Hanoi and to secure from Moscow both arms control agreements and settlement of the still contentious Berlin issue.

In February 1972, Nixon visited Beijing in person and ended the Chinese-American enmity that had endured since war in 1950. Ideology took a back seat to power relationships. The enemy of my enemy—as the Middle Eastern saying has it—is my friend. The U.S. "opening to China" so worried Brezhnev that he agreed to a Nixon visit and gave ground both in Germany and on strategic arms limitation.

Immediately before the Moscow summit of May 1972, Nixon blocked the vital North Vietnamese port of Haiphong with air-dropped mines in reprisal for a failed North Vietnamese offensive aimed at Saigon. The mines and the fact that Brezhnev, like Mao, received Nixon, apparently provoked thought in Hanoi. Nixon's probable victory in the fall 1972 presidential election over the dovish Democrat, George McGovern, made it seem wise to negotiate now. Hanoi therefore dropped its demand for the dismantling of the Saigon regime and agreed to return the U.S. prisoners that had survived its camps.

Then the president of South Vietnam, General Nguyen Van Thieu, raised obstacles. He foresaw abandonment by the United States. Nixon and Kissinger attempted to calm him with secret assurances that the United States would again intervene if Hanoi broke the coming truce. Hanoi sensed American weakness and likewise stalled, even after Nixon's landslide reelection in November. In December 1972 Nixon therefore ordered attacks on vital targets in and around Hanoi with the full firepower of the B-52 heavy bombers of the U.S. Air Force. Nixon's domestic opponents accused him of genocide for this so-called "Christmas bombing" and compared it to Auschwitz and Hiroshima. In actuality Nixon's bombing killed perhaps 1,100 DRV civilians and military, and at last brought Hanoi to

release the United States from the war on terms that did not appear utterly and immediately humiliating.

On January 27, 1973, the DRV representatives signed a peace agreement in Paris that provided for the return of U.S. prisoners, the withdrawal of the U.S. advisers that remained in South Vietnam, and a precarious truce. Publicly, Nixon and Kissinger claimed they had achieved "peace with honor," a phrase rich in historical irony. Privately they apparently hoped for a "decent interval" between U.S. withdrawal and South Vietnamese collapse.

The interval was indecently short. Nixon, like Johnson, aspired to be loved. Incessant personal attacks from his domestic opponents and endless leakages to the press from within his administration warped his sometimes eccentric judgment. During the 1972 election campaign he ordered the "plumbers," a secret White House unit formed to combat leaks, to plant electronic listening devices in the national Democratic party headquarters in Washington's Watergate Hotel. In June 1972, an alert security guard caught the inept "plumbers" breaking and entering. In the spring–summer of 1973 Nixon's frantic attempts to cover up his own role in this "Watergate Affair" collapsed. Televised hearings before Congress left his administration in shambles. On August 9, 1974, he left the presidency by a unique route— resignation to escape impeachment, criminal prosecution, and probable imprisonment.

Internally, the outcome of Watergate was a triumph for the rule of law. Externally, it allowed Congress to seize control of foreign policy, a role the Constitution had not allotted it, and which Congress could not successfully fill. In November 1973 Congress passed over Nixon's veto a "War Powers Resolution" that required congressional approval both before and during the commitment of U.S. forces to combat. Congress drastically cut aid to South Vietnam and to anti-Communist forces in Laos and Cambodia. Fierce congressional opposition paralyzed Nixon's vice president and successor, Gerald R. Ford.

In January 1975 the Politburo in Hanoi took the measure of Congress and of Ford: "Having withdrawn from Vietnam, the United States could hardly return." Hanoi, newly re-equipped with Soviet heavy weapons, prepared a North Korean-style offensive across South Vietnam's northern and western borders. In April 1975, that *Blitzkrieg* crushed the exhausted and demoralized South Vietnamese army with over 700 Soviet tanks. The United States assisted impotently, then organized one last operation: the evacuation from Saigon of all remaining Americans and a few of the many South Vietnamese who had worked for the United States.

On April 30, 1975, Saigon fell to DRV armor. The North annexed the South and renamed Saigon "Ho Chi Minh City." The Second Indochina War was over. It had cost the lives of perhaps 725,000 North Vietnamese, 525,000 South Vietnamese, and 58,000 Americans. Its end brought not peace but immense massacres, millions of refugees, and a Third Indochina War between the Communist victors (see pp. 1044–46).

A "GENERATION OF PEACE"?

As they disengaged from Vietnam, Kissinger and Nixon proclaimed that a new international order was being born. The opening to China would not only extricate the United States from Southeast Asia. It would also open the road to a lasting "détente," or relaxation of tensions, between Moscow and Washington.

Talk of détente was not new. The atmospheric test ban treaty of 1963 was its first monument. Johnson had pursued negotiations and in 1968 had signed with Moscow a nuclear nonproliferation treaty that China and France had rejected in favor of exploding their own hydrogen bombs. Strategic arms

The eve of Saigon's fall: Refugees storm the U.S. embassy to secure places on the last helicopter flights out, April 29, 1975.

talks and a 1968 summit with Brezhnev proved abortive. But in Europe, the West Germans abandoned Adenauer's rigid policy of nonrecognition of Ulbricht's DDR. Willy Brandt of the SPD, upon his entrance into Bonn's governing coalition in 1966, inaugurated a new "eastern policy." Brandt's *Ostpolitik* sought rapprochement both with the DDR and with the nations of eastern Europe upon which Germany had trampled in 1938–45. Extreme versions of *Ostpolitik* looked forward to an end to NATO and the Warsaw Pact, and the reunification of Germany.

As a French intellectual once remarked, Germany's neighbors loved Germany so much that they were delighted to have two of them. *Ostpolitik* was nevertheless a modest success. It suffered a brief setback in August 1968, when the Soviet Union and its Warsaw Pact allies invaded Czechoslovakia to crush the "Prague Spring," a liberalization movement in the Czech Communist party. But embarrassment at Soviet brutality did not long deter Brandt, Johnson, or Nixon from seeking further negotiations.

Brandt became Chancellor of West Germany in 1969, and concluded non-aggression treaties with the Soviet Union, Poland, Czechoslovakia, and the DDR in 1970–73. Kissinger's opening to China helped impel the Soviet Union in 1971 to sign a treaty with the United States, Britain, and France that formally guaranteed Western access to Berlin. In theory that precluded a renewal of Stalin's blockade or of Khrushchev's threats to West Berlin.

Kissinger judged that Brezhnev badly needed reinsurance against Beijing and an infusion of Western technology and money to bolster Soviet economic growth, which had peaked in the 1950s and declined thereafter. Kissinger assumed, in essence, that the West could bribe the Soviets. Economic ties and arms control would in good Cobdenite fashion (see p. 816) enmesh Moscow in a structure of "interdependence." As Kennan had hoped in 1947, the Soviet Union would at last "mellow" and became a status quo power. The need for containment would end, and the world, in Nixon's self-inflating phrase, would enjoy a "generation of peace."

The Soviet view was quite different. Despite Moscow's sensitivity about Kissinger's dalliance with Beijing, the Soviets did not consider China a near-term threat. The vast bulk of Soviet divisions continued to menace western Europe. Brezhnev sought détente as a tool for achieving Soviet objectives, not as an occasion to abandon them. Western money, technology, and grain would shore up his flagging centrally planned economy and upgrade Soviet weapons technology. Détente need not constrain the Soviet Union outside Europe, as the Soviet Union immediately demonstrated by backing Sadat's October 1973 war. Nor did détente mean the end of ideological struggle.

The two greatest monuments of détente, the strategic arms limitation treaty of May 1972 (SALT I) and the Helsinki security treaty of 1975, were thus profoundly ambiguous. SALT I and its accompanying "ABM Treaty" limiting antimissile defenses wrote into international law the quantitative advantage that the Soviet buildup had gained since 1962. The Soviets retained 1,618 land-based and 950 submarine-launched intercontinental ballistic missiles to the 1,054 and 710 of the United States. SALT I limited numbers of mis-

siles only, and placed no restrictions on the "multiple independently targeted" warheads (MIRVs) that soon equipped those missiles. The treaty appeared to make the superpower arms competition more predictable than before, but did little to end it. SALT I's duration was only five years.

The Helsinki treaty of 1975, the final cap on the eastern treaties of 1970–73, was equally problematic. The West, in a Europe-wide conference at Helsinki that included neutral powers, at last conceded legitimacy to Stalin's conquests of 1944–45. In return Moscow offered cultural exchanges, and promises, immediately violated, of respect for human rights and of free movement of people and ideas across the borders of the Soviet empire.

MASS CULTURE AND "COUNTERCULTURE"

Socially and politically, the 1950s were placid times in the West. Pundits prematurely hailed the "end of ideology," the demise of messianic political faiths in the wake of Khrushchev's 1956 revelations. Then worldwide communications, anti-American discontents, a student generation of unprecedented size and affluence, and the twin catalysts of the Vietnam War and the independence struggles in the "Third World" (see pp. 1011–19) created a wave of disturbances unprecedented since 1848.

The Americanization of the World

The growth of the world market in undreamed-of prosperity also meant the rapid worldwide spread of the mass culture of the leading state. Two things speeded that process: the dying British empire's legacy of English as the universal language of commerce, and a new revolution in transportation and communications that paralleled the coming of steam and the telegraph in the nineteenth century. In 1950, almost all intercontinental travel was by ship. By 1960 four-engined jet aircraft had cut the trip from Paris to New York to eight hours; no spot on the globe was more than 24 hours away. By the 1970s satellite television relays provided instantaneous transmission of pictures and sound from anywhere on Earth.

American film and television conveyed sparkling images of affluence and made few intellectual demands on their audience. Suitably dubbed into local languages, they acquired a wide following wherever governments allowed their citizens to view them. They also aroused appetites for wealth and growth that most societies found difficult to satisfy. Even the relatively rich Europeans did not duplicate the credit-card prosperity of the American middle classes until the 1970s.

Along with Hollywood movies and television serials came the gray legions of corporate America, from General Electric to ITT to Coca Cola. They established or widened beachheads for American commerce in Europe, Japan, and the "Third World." That massive expansion of America's cultural and economic visibility aroused a variety of reactions. European business at first gratefully embraced the Marshall Plan and private American investment in Europe. Welcome turned to distrust by the 1960s. U.S. capital export was so massive that Europeans feared losing control of their economies to America's allegedly sinister "multinational corporations." Then the burden of Vietnam undermined U.S. economic performance. Europeans created multinationals of their own and acquired assets in the United States.

Culturally, reaction was likewise mixed. The defeated nations of Germany, Italy, and Japan embraced some elements of American democracy or industrial organization. But especially in Britain, France, and the Islamic world, native traditions resisted fiercely. Britons such as the philosopher and unilateral disarmament crusader Bertrand Russell looked down their noses at what they took to be American provincialism and irresponsibility. Conservative critics, from tra-ditionalist Catholics to stern Gaullists to Shi'ite Moslems, decried "Coca-colonization" and the moral laxity that American wealth allegedly brought. The academic Left, from Mexico City and Tokyo to the cafés of the Left Bank in Paris, turned withering Marxist scorn on America, the leading capitalist state.

Student Revolt and Middle Class Terrorism

After 1945 the United States attempted to create the first society in history in which a majority of citizens had some higher education. In the 1960s much of western Europe began to follow. Rapid university expansion created a shortage of faculty that consigned students to boredom in immense factory-like classrooms. Affluence apparently removed any pressing need to work. Leisure and the outrageous bohemian example of "beat generation" rebels of the 1950s such as the novelist Jack Kerouac fostered the rise in the early 1960s of a youth "counterculture." Its adherents were passionately contemptuous of inherited standards of behavior and dedicated to the joys that contraceptive pills, mind-distorting drugs,

Demonstrators confront military police outside the Pentagon (October 1967).

and the electric guitar had recently made available.

The rebellion of the youthful rich began appropriately enough in the richest country, the United States. In 1964, the University of California at Berkeley exploded in violent confrontation between a rigid central administration and a radical "Free Speech Movement" determined to shock and provoke. Vietnam loomed on the horizon as early as 1963, but it was Johnson's plunge into full-scale war in 1965 that gave the rebels their cause and mass base. College students received draft deferments, but those who graduated or flunked out faced call-up unless they discovered a convenient medical condition.

In these circumstances a "New Left" arose that mocked predictions of an "end of ideology." From 1964–65 on it savaged the American political and academic establishment from the Left with a zeal that recalled the 1950s attacks of Senator McCarthy from the Right. It proclaimed a "second American revolution" against "imperialism" in Vietnam and middle-class society at home. Student insurrections paralyzed Columbia, Harvard, and other campuses in 1967–68. Nixon's 1970 thrust into Cambodia inspired an immense wave of protest.

By then the most determined student radicals had formed a terrorist group that called itself the "Weathermen." The name came from a line of the folk-rock cult figure Bob Dylan: " . . . you don't need a weatherman to know which way the wind blows." The Weathermen sought to "bring the war home," to imitate the "armed struggle" of the Viet Cong and of urban guerrillas such as the Tupamaros in Uruguay (see p. 1031). The most striking Weatherman achievement was the accidental demolition in 1970 of a Greenwich Village townhouse and bomb factory belonging to the parent of a member. And the broader "Movement" deflated swiftly after 1970, thanks to the virtual end of the draft and to the inherent contradiction between Leninist commitment and countercultural hedonism. "Make love not war" also meant making love not revolution. Not "armed struggle" but drugs, sex, rock-and-roll, and imported Buddhist or Hindu mysticism were the most widespread forms of protest against middle-class America.

The American example helped inspire disturbances in Europe far more serious than mere campus revolts. The European rebels were heirs to a tradition of romantic student radicalism stretching back into the nineteenth century. They also drew on the discipline and doctrine of their countries' Communist parties, although they condemned those parties as stodgy. Even more than their American counterparts they found inspiration in the "noble savages" of "Third World" revolutionary movements (see p. 1011).

The Paris "days" of May 1968 turned back the clock to the Paris Commune of 1871; urban insurrection once more appeared practical politics. A student uprising with support from the industrial workers briefly controlled the Left Bank of Paris. Hundreds of thousands marched demanding de Gaulle's overthrow. The general flew in disgust ("reforms yes; bed-messing no") to visit his army and secure the support of the officer corps. He then returned to Paris and rallied the "forces of order" with a television speech that brought millions into the streets singing the "Marseillaise"—a revolutionary anthem transmuted into a call to arms against revolution. The student movement deflated. The Left lost votes in the ensuing election. De Gaulle resigned in 1969 when a referendum went against him, but he resigned in favor of a hand-picked successor. The modern state had again shown its ability to tame upheavals from below.

In Germany, student revolt was in deadly earnest—as it had been under Weimar, where the Nazis had captured the student movement long before they seized the state. Some German "New Left" radicals, Freudian-Marxist in ideology and Stalinist in practice, turned to "armed struggle" in the late 1960s. Their most prominent group, the "Red Army Faction" or "Baader-Meinhof gang," attacked U.S. bases in West Germany and assassinated industrialists, judges, and politicians with ruthless precision. But computerized tracking of suspects eventually demolished the guerrillas. In 1976–77 Andreas Baader, Ulrike Meinhof, and other "Red Army Faction" leaders committed suicide in prison to embarrass "the system." Bombings, assassinations, and revolution by suicide failed to inspire the placid West German "masses" to revolt. After 1979, the German student Left largely abandoned "armed struggle" for ecological and antinuclear protest (see p. 1049).

Italy's student radicals mounted the most determined challenge to the democratic state. Students and industrial workers combined in 1969 to make a deadly serious "hot autumn" of riots, strikes, and factory or university occupations. Throughout the 1970s terrorist groups of ex-students from both leftist and Catholic backgrounds sought to provoke the Italian parliamentary regime into revealing its allegedly "Fascist" nature. Some had received training in KGB-sponsored schools in Czechoslovakia, others with the PLO in Lebanon. Their instrument was the "knee-capping" or assassination of judges, factory managers, journalists, and politicians. In 1978 the terrorist "Red Brigades" kidnapped and killed a former prime minister, the Christian Democrat Aldo Moro. That stroke united Italian opinion against the terrorists and galvanized police and prosecutors. The "Red Brigades" and their offshoots ended in prison. Throughout the West youthful rebellion gave way to middle-class careers.

The Feminist Revolution

Among the movements that flourished in the 1960s alongside student and "countercultural" protest was a renewed and militant feminism. The vote, the Depression, and two world

The power of the state: French police beat Paris students (May 1968).

wars had damped feminist agitation from the 1920s to the 1950s. But in the heady atmosphere of the 1960s, the continuing growth of women's share in the work force—often in poorly paying part-time or temporary jobs—helped ignite protest. The contradiction between women's claims to rights and the facts of male power in the family, at work, and in politics inspired radical theorists, especially in the United States and France. Precursors such as Simone de Beauvoir, France's leading woman intellectual and author of *The Second Sex* (1949), soon appeared insufficiently militant. Beauvoir's elegant and learned analysis of "the slavery of half of humanity" appeared to lack a political program.

Numerous theorists and groups sought to supply one. In the United States, where women entered the labor force earlier and in greater numbers than in Europe, a broad front of women's organizations had arisen by the mid-1960s. It sought to open hitherto male professions to women and to secure "reproductive freedom": the removal of restrictions upon contraception and abortion. This "first wave" of

The new feminism: women march in New York City (1960s).

feminists ranged in its politics from mild liberalism to New Left radicalism. But in practice it took its cue from the Lockean natural rights tradition, as Harriet and John Stuart Mill (see p. 722) had applied it in the nineteenth century—women should enjoy by right the same autonomy as men. To at last assert that autonomy, women now had to learn to compete successfully with men in all fields of human activity. The most radical "first wave" theorists concluded that women's autonomy demanded the destruction of the "patriarchal" family and the liberation of women from childbirth and child rearing.

As the euphoria of the late 1960s subsided, a "second wave" of American feminist theorists began to celebrate—rather than seeking to eliminate—women's differences from men. The new "woman-centered" school had counterparts in western Europe and was related to the "equal but different" tradition of the nineteenth century (see p. 722). It asserted the superiority of women's nature, which was allegedly more intuitive, warm, compassionate, "nurturing," peace-loving, and practical than that of the purportedly cold, calculating, competitive, violent, power-mad male. It dismissed masterful women leaders from Margaret Thatcher of Britain to Indira Gandhi of India (see pp. 1026 and 1050) as victims who had in effect become men. It proclaimed that women were a "sex class" whose shared nature and experience overrode all ideological, social, national, and racial divisions. "Universal sisterhood" would inaugurate a new and purely female culture that would ultimately save humanity. Ironically, that vision caught on just as ideological, social, ethnic, and racial divisions fractured the women's movement—and as a counteroffensive by fiercely antifeminist "pro-family" women sought to roll it back.

But despite internecine struggles and external opposition, the feminist revolt had decisive consequences. In the United States and western Europe, it spurred reforms that gave women a greater measure of formal equality than ever before. It inspired the creation of institutions such as day-care centers that helped to free women to join the work force in ever greater numbers. Above all, it provided middle-class women with encouragement to pursue careers equivalent to those of men, encouragement that their mothers had lacked. Demographically, the consequence was later marriages and fewer children. Emotionally, the attempt to "have it all," to pursue a career and raise a family, sometimes provoked intolerable strain. Men inevitably proved slow to adjust to the equality in practical matters that the new "two-career family" demanded. But change was nevertheless perceptible. The feminist revolution brought closer to reality than ever before the nineteenth-century ideal of equality between the sexes.

Protest within the West was merely one sign of the passing of the "age of containment." The Middle East explosion of 1973 revealed the full extent of Western disunity. The ensuing swift escalation of oil prices struck a stinging blow to the world economy. U.S. foreign policy succumbed temporarily to paralysis as Congress sought to demolish the "imperial presidency" that it blamed for Vietnam. Geographic and strategic circumstances had favored containment in Korea, at a price. The agony of containment in Vietnam hastened the end of America's strategic dominance over the Soviet Union and of its economic edge over Japan. By the mid-1970s the pundits saw a new age of another kind emerging. Détente, they proclaimed, had ended the Cold War. In place of superpower conflict they discerned a growing international class struggle between rich and poor states.

Suggestions for Further Reading

The Superpower Conflict

Few intelligent syntheses cover the post-1945 period. Recent events arouse too much retrospective passion and carry too heavy a weight of current hopes and fears. Sources are simultaneously too wide and too shallow. Much remains buried in the archives, especially the Soviet archives. A. Ulam, *The Rivals: America and Russia Since World War II* (1971), is nevertheless excellent on the central U.S.-Soviet conflict. P. Seabury, *The Rise and Decline of the Cold War* (1967), is acute on that conflict's nature and dimensions. R. Aron, *The Imperial Republic: The United States and the World, 1945–1973* (1974), is both brilliant and detached; F. Schurmann, *The Logic of World Power* (1974), is less detached but full of unusual insights. On the Soviet Union, see first the inside views of M. Djilas, *Conversations with Stalin* (1962), and (with caution) N. Khrushchev, *Khrushchev Remembers* (1974). A. Ulam, *Expansion and Coexistence* (1968–) and *Dangerous Relations: the Soviet Union in World Politics, 1970–1982* (1983), are characteristically well-argued and delightfully written. D. Holloway, *The Soviet Union and the Arms Race* (1983), is indispensable. F. Fejtö, *A History of the People's Democracies* (1971), intelligently covers eastern Europe from Stalin to Brezhnev. For the Cuban missile crisis, see especially G. Allison, *Essence of Decision* (1971).

The Mid-Sized Powers

W. Laqueur, *Europe Since Hitler* (1970), offers a masterful synthesis both of events and of European political and intellectual trends; on the latter, see also J. F. Revel, *The Totalitarian Temptation* (1977). M. Schaller, *The American Occupation of Japan* (1985), traces the process that put Japan back on the road to supremacy in East Asia; E. O. Reischauer, *The Japanese Today* (1988), offers a sympathetic picture of postwar Japan. H. C. Hinton, *Three and a Half Powers: The New Balance in Asia* (1975), places Japan in its international context.

The Middle East

The Middle East arouses even more passion than the Cold War; no reliable narrative history of the area since 1945 exists. L. C. Brown, *International Politics and the Middle East* (1984), is a fine introduction to how it got the way it is. P. Mansfield, *The Middle East: A Political and Economic Survey* (1980), is a useful handbook. Y. Harkabi, *Arab Strategies and Israel's Response* (1977), offers one Israeli view; for Arab difficulties both with Israel and with the modern world, see especially F. Ajami, *The Arab Predicament: Arab Political Thought and Practice Since 1967* (1981). W. Laqueur, *Confrontation: The Middle East War and World Politics* (1974), remains the best book on the Yom Kippur War.

From Korea to Vietnam

Few dispassionate accounts of America's wars of containment exist, but see D. Rees, *Korea: The Limited War* (1964), and G. Lewy, *America in Vietnam* (1978). R. E. M. Irving, *The First Indochina War: French and American Policy, 1945–54* (1975), surveys the antecedents; W. J. Rust, *Kennedy in Vietnam* (1985), contains new material on the early years and the coup against Diem. G. Race, *War Comes to Long An* (1972), is indispensable on the Viet Cong. M. Herr, *Dispatches* (1978), conveys the atmosphere of Vietnam with unparalleled skill. P. Braestrup, *Big Story* (1977), describes with candor and irony the role of the U.S. press. H. Summers, *On Strategy* (1982), is a not always successful attempt to figure out what went wrong. For détente and the opening to China, see A. Ulam, *Dangerous Relations: The Soviet Union in World Politics, 1970–1982* (1983), and (with caution) H. Kissinger, *White House Years* (1979) and *Years of Decision* (1982).

Students and Feminists

The transnational student revolt still awaits its historian. D. Caute, *The Year of the Barricades: A Journey Through 1968* (1988), and R. Johnson, *The French Communist Party Versus the Students* (1972), are nevertheless useful. On the women's movement, see especially J. Mitchell and A. Oakley, *What is Feminism?* (1986); C. Duchen, *Feminism in France* (1986); and H. Eisenstein, *Contemporary Feminist Thought* (1983).

35
The "Third World"

*U*nder the shadow of superpower conflict, "new nations" arose in unprecedented numbers in the years after 1945. The collapse of the European empires under the pressure of that most successful of European exports, nationalism, ultimately produced over 120 states. Most adhered neither to the Soviet empire nor to the group of developed nations of western Europe, North America, and the Pacific that were allied to the United States.

The new states were for the most part poor compared to the developed West. That was their most noteworthy common characteristic. Theorists inevitably sought to lump them together. Alfred Sauvy, a French economic historian, coined in 1952 the name that stuck: the "Third World." Sauvy took his terminology from 1789, from the Abbé Sieyès. The "Third World" was allegedly "ignored, exploited, despised, like the Third Estate." That analogy suggested a conclusion: it was the duty of the "Third World" to follow the revolutionary example of France's Third Estate, and to launch a global revolution against the capitalist "First World."

In the ensuing 30 years, theorists of "Third World" revolution elaborated political myths on that theme. Marxist-Leninist voices from the Soviet bloc, soon known as the "Second World," cheered them on. The economic development of the West, prophets of revolution intoned, was responsible for "Third World" poverty. The "Third World," they insisted, should rise and smite the West, or compel it to give "reparations" that would raise the "Third World" to a developed world standard of living.

Neither revolution nor massive transfers of assets occurred. The "Third World" was neither united nor particularly militant, except verbally at the United Nations. "Third World" states fought one another more readily than they did developed countries. Internal bloodshed between tribal, religious,

The "Third World"
assembled—the Bandung
Conference of "non-aligned"
African and Asian states,
1955.

and social groups took precedence over struggle against the "imperialist" West or "North." And after 1979, the Soviet Union's massacres of Afghans (see p. 1044) showed many in the "Third World" that the West was far from being the most ruthless "imperialist" force in the contemporary world.

By the late 1980s, the "Group of 77," chief lobbying organization of "Third World" nations, had begun to accept Western contentions that states bear responsibility for their own fates and that the chief sources of economic development—or its absence—were internal. Simultaneously, dissatisfaction began to grow with the term itself, for "Third World" lumped together states radically different in history, culture, politics, economic structure, and wealth. The bankruptcy of the concept—the collapse of the notion of a unified "Third World" or southern hemisphere with interests implacably opposed to those of the West or "North"—has slowly opened the way for dispassion-

ate analysis of the sources of economic development and of the sharp historical and cultural differences between "Third World" states. The process of "decolonization" that gave birth to most "Third World" states is one place to begin that analysis.

DECOLONIZATION: IDEOLOGICAL "WINDS OF CHANGE"

The force of ideas was the most powerful of the "winds of change" that swept over the colonial empires in the two decades that followed Britain's defeat at Singapore in 1942. Nationalism, the secular religion of the nation-state, had arisen spontaneously in the "Third World" whenever native elites sought to resist Western power by acquiring Western ideas. From China to Ghana, nationalism offered an ideology to replace the old beliefs and communities that Western power had shattered in the nineteenth century. The creation of nation-states, independent and sovereign externally and focus of *all* loyalties internally, would wipe out the humiliation that Western domination had brought, provide a sense of belonging, and help nationalist intellectuals to power and wealth. That social function, indeed, was a mighty reason for nationalism's dramatic success. As in Europe, the cult of the nation-state rewarded well those who served it. At best they became the new rulers, borne to power on a wave of popular enthusiasm. At worst they could make a living as bureaucrats and schoolteachers, building the state or molding the new generations to its faith.

Some areas took to the new dispensation more readily than others. The states of East Asia were cultural units of long standing. That facilitated their conversion into nation-states on a pattern resembling Europe. In the Islamic world, loyalties were simultaneously too wide and too narrow to fit the new pattern easily. "Arab unity," "Islamic solidarity," or "Islamic revolution" coexisted uneasily with centuries-old tribal, religious, and linguistic-ethnic rivalries. In Latin America, the oldest group of "new nations" other than Holland and the United States, the persistence of stratification by blood—Creole, Indian, black—meant that the elites were often closer to their counterparts in neighboring states than to their own peasants. And in black Africa, state borders bore little relationship to the ethnographic map.

As an ideology of revolt against the West, nationalism inevitably had competitors, of which Marxism-Leninism was the most popular. In formal terms it was an ideology of class war, but outside Europe it often merged in practice with nationalism. As Sun Yat-sen had recognized (see p. 889), nationalism and Leninist organizational techniques were a powerful combination. In the "Third World" as in the Soviet Union, Marxism-Leninism provided the legitimation for all-dominating "cults of personality" and for unlimited power for Party elites. The resulting regimes were the most brutally regimented and fiercely nationalist regimes in history: China, North Vietnam, North Korea, Cuba, Ethiopia. And those strange progeny of the European traditions of nationalism and Marxism were nationalist with a difference. They paradoxically belonged to the "socialist camp," to a multinational empire based on the denial of the importance of nationalism. Only China, Yugoslavia, and Albania ultimately developed Marxist-Leninist nationalisms *against* Moscow.

A variety of "pan-movements" likewise competed with nationalism. The Islamic world gave birth to two mutually contradictory ones—Arab nationalism and pan-Islamism. Arab nationalism, whose chief manifestation was the Arab League of States with its periodic meetings and communiques, proved weak indeed. Pan-Arab sentiment, even if wielded by charismatic figures such as Gamal Abdel Nasser, failed to unify the Arab world politically. Its religious counterpart, pan-Islamism, suffered from even greater weaknesses. Of the more than 800 million adherents of Islam only a quarter are Arabs; the remainder, from Senegal through Iran, Pakistan, and India to Indonesia and the Philippines, include such a wide variety of linguistic and ethnic groups that common action even in the United Nations has rarely proved possible. Islam itself, like Christianity, also has built-in divisions, above all hostility between the minority Shi'ites—10 percent of all Moslems—and the majority Sunni (see p. 220). South of Islam, "pan-Africanism" gave birth in 1963 to an inappropriately named "Organization of African Unity"; the organization has persisted but unity has been absent.

A final contender was—for lack of a better term—"Third Worldism"—the ideology that proclaimed the division of humanity into a rich and oppressive capitalist "North" and an innocent victimized agrarian "South." In 1955, at Bandung in Indonesia, 29 African and Asian states met and inaugurated a series of "Third World" conclaves that promoted the notion of "non-alignment" in the Cold War and made increasingly insistent demands that the West atone for its "imperialist" past.

"Third Worldism," as it developed in the 1960s and 1970s, was a heady mixture. First of its ingredients was the notion that the reduction of the "Third World" to poverty had been the precondition of Western development and wealth. Second came a romantic faith in revolution and its supposed modernizing effects; that faith rested in part on a misreading of the history of the Soviet Union. The third component of "Third Worldism" was psychological, the invention of Frantz Fanon, a French–West Indian intellectual who joined the Algerian rebels and wrote an impassioned work, *The Wretched of the Earth* (1961), that sold millions of copies to the professors and students of Western universities. Fanon celebrated violence, not merely as a means to a political end, but as a good in itself. He proclaimed bloodshed "a cleansing force," a psychotherapy for the oppressed. The final component of "Third Worldism" was the claim that the "Third World" itself was a cohesive unit, that its internal solidarity against "imperialism" overrode divisions of language, tribe, religion, or culture. Those were powerful myths, but they proved less powerful than the cult of the nation-state.

DECOLONIZATION: VIOLENT BIRTH OF THE "THIRD WORLD"

The collapse of the colonial empires was foreordained once the colonized peoples revolted. The empires that remained after World War II had extraordinarily narrow demographic bases. Britain, with roughly 41 million inhabitants in 1939, dominated an empire of over 500 million. The empires of France, Holland, Belgium, and Portugal were less disproportionate in size to the European powers that held

Fanon on Violence

Fanon theorized that violence liberated minds as well as bodies. He predicted prematurely that the masses, initiated politically through violence, would not tolerate post-colonial regimes under "demagogues," "opportunists," or "magicians."

At the level of individuals, violence is a cleansing force. It frees the native from his inferiority complex and from his despair and inaction; it makes him fearless and restores his self-respect. Even if the armed struggle has been symbolic and the nation is demolished through a rapid movement of decolonization, the people have the time to see that the liberation has been the business of each and all and that the leader has no special merit. . . . When the people have taken violent part in the national liberation they will allow no one to set themselves up as "liberators." They show themselves to be jealous of the results of their action and take good care not to place their future, their destiny or the fate of their country in the hands of a living god. Yesterday they were completely irresponsible; today they mean to understand everything and make all decisions. Illuminated by violence, the consciousness of the people rebels against any pacification. From now on the demagogues, the opportunists and the magicians have a difficult task. The action which has thrown them into a hand-to-hand struggle confers on the masses a voracious taste for the concrete. The attempt at mystification becomes in the long run practically impossible.

From Elie Kedourie, ed., *Nationalism in Asia and Africa* (New York: Meridian Books, 1970), p. 536.

them. But even there colonial rule rested on the continuing willingness of the colonized to submit and collaborate.

Overwhelming European power, the power of the Maxim gun, had produced submission and collaboration in the past. But now the correlation of forces had changed. The rise of the Soviet Union and of Mao's China, and their widening reach, gave colonial nationalists powerful allies. The dependable Soviet AK-47 assault rifle, copied from a German weapon of 1943–44, became the Maxim gun of *de*colonization. Economic growth and Western schooling produced native intellectuals who sought ways both peaceful and violent to induce the colonizers to go.

The partition of British India, 1947: Moslem refugees on a road near New Delhi strewn with Moslem dead.

These intellectuals created nationalist mass movements far better adapted to reconquering independence than the precolonial order had been retaining it. In Europe, the vast bloodletting of the two world wars and the economic unprofitability of many colonies persuaded most European democracies to let their empires go once native nationalists mounted a serious challenge.

British decolonization began first and lasted longest, thanks to the size and bizarre variety of Britain's possessions. In relative terms British decolonization was the least traumatic, thanks to London's empiricist willingness to concede, graciously or not, what it no longer had the power to withhold. Ireland went first in 1921–37 (see pp. 886–87). Its leader, the ex-rebel Eamon De Valera, was the first of many nationalist leaders whose road to power passed through British jails.

In the aftermath of World War II, Britain found itself even more beleaguered than in 1919–21. Mohandas Gandhi—fortunately for India—had failed to drag down British rule in 1942 with the Japanese at the gates. But after 1945 the Labour government of Clement Attlee had no alternative but to quit India; it lacked the troops and money to hold down by force a subcontinent of over 400 million inhabitants. Two mass movements fought Britain and each other: Gandhi's Congress Party and Mohammed Ali Jinnah's Moslem League. Congress claimed all India, by right of Hindu nationalism; the Moslem League claimed a Moslem-inhabited "Pakistan" around Karachi and in Bengal, east and west of the Hindu majority. By March 1947, in the words of a subordinate of Britain's last viceroy, the Indian empire was "a ship on fire in mid-ocean with ammunition in the hold." In August 1947 Britain simply left; the excellent British-trained armies of the two successor states, India and Pakistan, fought over the province of Kashmir. Hindu and Moslem populations on the wrong side of the partition lines fled for their lives. Independence brought 15 million refugees and 500,000 to 750,000 dead in religious-ethnic massacres.

Possession of India had impelled Britain to acquire Ceylon, Burma, Malaya, and the north coast of Borneo; the end of empire in India led London to concede independence to Burma and Ceylon (later Sri Lanka) in early 1948. Britain stayed on until 1957 in Malaya and Singapore, thanks to the Communist insurgency based on Malaya's overseas Chinese minority. Britain conceded independence to its possessions in Borneo in 1963, and retained only Hong Kong, which it pledged in 1984 to transfer to China in 1997.

In the Middle East, whose oil was essential to Britain and western Europe, London attempted to hang on until the mid-1950s. It gave up its thankless task in Palestine in 1948 and in 1945 left Egypt. It held only the irreducible minimum: the crucial base of Cyprus, the oil states of the Persian Gulf, and a zone around the Suez Canal that connected the oil with Europe. But soon the sad tale of 1882 repeated itself—with a different outcome. Like the Khedive before him, Britain's Egyptian client King Farouk succumbed to a nationalist officers' revolt. After Farouk's departure for the French Riviera in 1952, a charismatic figure on the model of Arabi Pasha took command, Colonel Gamal Abdel Nasser.

Nasser set himself the task of unifying "the Arabs" from Morocco to Iraq. He sought as first steps to evict Britain from the Canal and to lead the Arab destruction of Israel. In June 1956, weary of terrorist attacks on British sentries, Britain evacuated the Canal Zone. Nasser thereupon confiscated the canal from its European owners while simultaneously challenging Israel with guerrilla raids from the Gaza strip and provoking the United States

South and East Asia since the Second World War

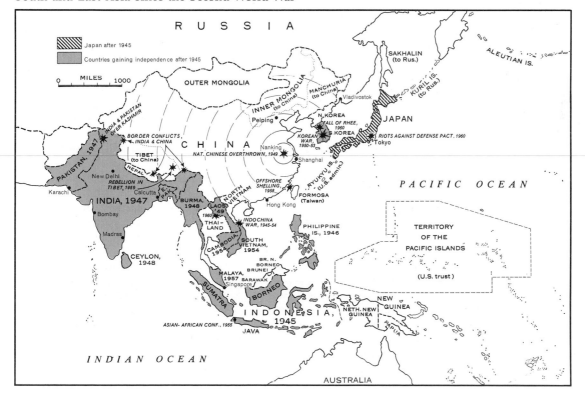

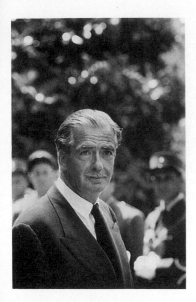

The antagonists of 1956: Anthony Eden (above) and Gamal Abdel Nasser (below).

by arms purchases from the Soviet Union. Anthony Eden, Churchill's wartime foreign secretary and successor, took up the challenge: Nasser was another Hitler. Had he not written a booklet, *Philosophy of the Revolution* (1953)? Was the Suez Canal in 1956 not the Rhineland in 1936? (But in 1936 Eden himself had merely thought Hitler's action "deplorable.") The French, mired in war against the Algerian insurrection and convinced that Nasser the pan-Arab was behind it, were happy to cooperate.

British and French airborne and amphibious forces, in secret cooperation with Israel's land thrust in the Sinai, landed at the Mediterranean end of the canal on November 5–6, 1956. But Eden, thanks to his own pigheadedness and to the ambiguity of Eisenhower's Secretary of State, John Foster Dulles, failed to understand that Washington sought to conciliate "Arab nationalism" and would not tolerate a Franco-British reconquest of Egypt. A U.S. attack on the stability of the British pound caused Eden to panic and withdraw. The French, fuming at British pusillanimity, resentfully followed.

The Suez fiasco allowed Nasser to claim victory, although his army had suffered its usual rout and Cairo was defenseless. Suez, a British military victory, ended Britain's prestige in the Middle East as defeat at Singapore had done in Asia. Coups against British-backed regimes in Iraq, unrest in Jordan, and an incipient civil war between Moslems and Maronite Christians in Lebanon followed in 1958. Iraq bloodily left the British orbit; British paratroops and U.S. Marines briefly landed in Jordan and Lebanon to maintain "stability." In Cyprus, a campaign by Greek guerrillas after 1954 led to Britain's departure in 1959–60. The successor to that struggle was a low intensity war within Cyprus between the Greek majority and the Turkish minority that ended only in 1974, with a Greek coup that provoked a Turkish invasion and the forcible partition of the island.

If the 1940s was for Britain the decade of decolonization in southern Asia and the 1950s that of the Middle East, the 1960s was the decade of Africa and the Caribbean. Harold Macmillan, Eden's successor, spoke grandly in January 1960 of the "wind of change" sweeping the continent. In the next five years, in a remarkable "scramble for Africa" in reverse, Britain and France gave their tropical empires away. In 1956–57 Britain had already conceded independence to the Sudan and to Ghana and the Gold Coast in West Africa. Independence for Nigeria, black Africa's richest and most populous "new nation," came in 1960. The principal retarding force was London's concern about the white settler population in Rhodesia, whose interests it attempted to serve by an abortive Central African Federation. The nationalists of Zambia and Malawi refused to accept the continuance of white privileges and brought the federation down by breaking away in 1964. In 1965 the whites of Rhodesia unilaterally declared their independence of Britain, defied Harold Wilson's Labour government and the United Nations, and fought to preserve their control over the black majority. That proved impossible; negotiations ultimately transformed Rhodesia into black-ruled Zimbabwe in 1978–79.

South of Rhodesia, the Union of South Africa under Boer leadership had achieved virtual independence after World War I, but its politics remained balanced precariously between English-speakers, pro-British Boers, and unreconstructed backwoods *Trekboers*. In 1948 the latter came to power, and imposed in law a rigid system of racial oppression called *Apartheid* ("apartness") that had largely existed in fact. The Boers met black demonstrations such as that at Sharpeville in 1960 with firepower. In 1961 South Africa withdrew from the British Commonwealth rather than listen to further criticism of its peculiar institutions.

Britain took the decisive final steps in its abandonment of empire in the late 1960s and early 1970s. The crucial base at Aden at the entrance to the Red Sea went in 1967, after a bloody guerrilla war by Arab tribal "Marxists." Soviet ships at anchor replaced those of the Royal Navy. Aden mutated into a "People's Democratic Republic of Yemen," complete with AK-47 massacres at Politburo meetings. And in 1971 Britain in essence handed over its oil-bearing clients in the Gulf, from Kuwait in the north to the United Arab Emirates in the south, to the mercy of the Shah of Iran (see pp. 1051–52).

All that remained of the British empire were a few small Caribbean, Atlantic, and Pacific islands along with outposts whose populations feared independence would lead to annexation by covetous neighbors: Hong Kong, Gibraltar, the Falkland Islands off Argentina, and Belize in Central America (which received independence in 1981). The Commonwealth, to which many of Britain's ex-colonies continued to belong, became a debating society.

France did not give up as easily as Britain. Its second colonial empire, acquired after defeat by Germany in 1870–71, was a symbol of national vitality. French schoolteachers had zealously propagated the political myth of France's "civilizing mission" in Africa and Indochina. French politicians, Right, Center, and Left, refused to give their empire up. De Gaulle inaugurated the failed reconquest of Indochina after 1945. Socialists such as prime minister Guy Mollet, who dispatched the task force to Suez, sought at least to hold Algeria. The French army, miserably defeated in 1940, committed its soul to victory in Indochina. It had failed at Dien Bien Phu (see p. 979). The survivors of Indochina returned in 1954 convinced that the Fourth Republic's politicians had stabbed the army in the back: *"On nous a fait le coup"* ["they shafted us"].

In November 1954, Algerian insurgents who took the name of the National Liberation Front (FLN) attacked

The Collapse of the British Empire

1947 India
1948 Ceylon [later Sri Lanka], Burma, Palestine
1956 Sudan
1957 Ghana, Gold Coast, Malaya
1960 Cyprus, Nigeria, British Somaliland [joined ex-Italian Somalia]
1961 Sierra Leone, Cameroons, Tanganyika, Kuwait
1962 Jamaica, Trinidad and Tobago, Uganda
1963 Kenya, Zanzibar [joined Tanganyika to form Tanzania, 1964], Singapore, North Borneo, Sarawak [joined Malaya to form Malaysia; Singapore broke away in 1965].
1964 Malawi, Malta, Zambia
1965 Gambia
1966 Guyana, Botswana, Lesotho, Barbados
1967 Aden, Leeward Islands, Windward Islands
1968 Mauritius, Nauru, Swaziland
1970 Fiji
1971 United Arab Emirates, Bahrein, Qatar

French settlers and police stations. That inaugurated a war that was both colonial and civil, a war that destroyed the Fourth Republic and created an Algerian nation. For Algeria was not simply a colony. Alongside 140,000 Jews and a swiftly growing Moslem population of 9 million lived slightly over a million European settlers, the *"pieds-noirs"*: privileged immigrants from France, Spain, Italy, Malta. Administratively, Algeria was part of France.

France reacted to the Algerian revolt by reinforcing its army there, bombing Moslem villages, and cutting its commitments elsewhere. It conceded independence to Tunisia and Morocco in 1956. The FLN, with some arms from outside but more self-help, soon found a winning strategy. At Philippeville in August 1955, FLN guerrillas and Arab crowds killed some 70 *pieds-noirs*; the French obligingly killed over 1,200 Moslems in reprisals. FLN assassination teams sought out and eliminated all Moslems who maintained contacts

The Sharpeville massacre, 1960: blacks flee the guns of the South African police.

with the French. FLN enforcers cut off the noses of Moslems who smoked tobacco, a French monopoly. The FLN divided the European and Moslem communities with a river of blood; that was the prerequisite for its own domination of the Algerian "camp."

By 1955–56, the two communities were at war. *Pieds-noirs* launched vengeful "rat-hunts" against any and all Moslems, even those entirely unconnected to the insurgents. FLN time-bombs shredded young Europeans in the cafés of the once pleasant city of Algiers. To end the bloodshed, the Fourth Republic abdicated to the army. In January 1957 it called in the *paras,* the army's pride, and made them secret policemen. In the ensuing "Battle of Algiers" the paratroops cordoned the Arab quarters into blocks, swept up suspects at random, tortured them with electric shock and water, and gradually ran the FLN bomb networks to earth. Many thousands of Algerian suspects simply "disappeared."

Torture won the "Battle of Algiers" but helped lose the war. In France, intellectuals of the Left but also of the Center and Right denounced the army. Officers resigned in disgust. FLN spokesmen abroad and states sympathetic to the FLN—including the United States—denounced French methods. And the civilian ministers who had ordered the army to win by any and all methods were already seek-

ing negotiations with the FLN. The army had vowed that *this* time it was going to win; if winning required removal of the politicians before they "betrayed" the army, so be it. In May 1958, amid a proliferation of *pied-noir* and military plots, the armed forces commander in Algeria, General Raoul Salan, demanded the recall to power of Charles de Gaulle.

De Gaulle came once more to save France. But to the chagrin of the army and of the *pieds-noirs,* he soon gave signs of a hidden agenda. In 1958–59 the army crushed what remained of the FLN in the countryside and sought to win Moslem loyalty with promises of "integration." More Moslems, indeed, fought for France than against it. But the FLN maintained its political structures and its claim to represent the Moslem majority. And it began to dawn on French opinion that winning through "integration" would mean a large and ever-growing Moslem presence in the French parliament; the Moslem birth-rate was ten times that of the *pieds-noirs.* De Gaulle, with perfect timing, said the magic word in a speech of September 1959: "self-determination."

Pieds-noirs and army reacted with fury. In 1961 the high command in Algiers, the *paras,* and the Foreign Legion rose against de Gaulle as they had risen against the Fourth Republic. De Gaulle held fast, appealed by radio to the half million draftees in Algeria, and convinced the generals that they were isolated. The Algiers *Putsch* collapsed. In 1962, despite a *pied-noir* terrorist campaign against the army itself and a rising in the European quarter of Algiers, de Gaulle achieved a negotiated settlement. In effect he conceded independence unconditionally, and left the *pieds-noirs* to choose "the suitcase or the coffin." Most chose the suitcase.

The Algerian war was traumatic for France, and still more for the Algerians who suffered by far the largest portion of the war's million or so casualties. It was a graphic illustration of the lengths to which communities driven by nationalism will go to defend or assert control of territory. It also decolonized France. In the course of the war, de Gaulle conceded independence to almost all of France's colonies in sub-

Africa and Southwest Asia in 1988

Saharan Africa: Guinea in 1958, and Cameroun, Chad, the Central African Republic, Congo-Brazzaville, Dahomey, Gabon, Ivory Coast, Mali, Niger, Senegal, and Togo in 1960.

The lesser empires of Holland and Belgium passed more quietly than did that of France. The Dutch found a "Republic of Indonesia" barring their return to the East Indies in 1945. Its leader was Achmet Sukarno, a charismatic nationalist who had collaborated with the Japanese to gain Indonesian independence. Four years of intermittent negotiations and "police actions" by the Dutch armed forces ultimately led under U.S. pressure to an agreement in November 1949 that granted independence, except for the Dutch territory of West Irian (the Dutch half of New Guinea), which Sukarno seized from the Dutch in 1962–63.

The Belgians gave the most spectacular example of irresponsible decolonization. Their Congo empire, which the Berlin Conference of 1884–85 had graciously assigned to King Leopold, had long been a by-word for relentless brutality. Its rubber plantations,

worked by native forced labor, were the subject of international protest even before World War I. And the Belgian state, which took the colony over from Leopold's private Congo Company, did far less than other colonizers to create a Western-educated elite. When the approaching independence of the neighboring French Congo (Congo-Brazzaville) inspired nationalist riots, the Belgians panicked, packed, and left in mid-1960. The Belgian-officered Congolese army mutinied. A multi-cornered civil war and massacres of both tribal enemies and whites followed. Belgian mining companies hired mercenaries to hold the copper-rich province of Katanga. It required four years and 20,000 United Nations troops to restore even a semblance of order. The victor was ultimately the head of the Congolese army, Joseph Mobuto, who established a corrupt but durable dictatorship in 1966, and changed the country's name to Zaire.

Portugal's colonies were the first European seaborne empire; they were also the last. The Portuguese military-clerical dictatorship of Antonio Salazar (1932–68) lost Indian enclaves such as Goa to an unprovoked Indian attack in 1961. In Africa—in Angola, Mozambique, and the west African minicolony of Guinea-Bissau—Portugal elected to fight. The resulting commitment of 150,000 troops from the early 1960s until 1974 bled Portugal's already backward economy. In the end, Salazar gave way to a less effective successor. The Portuguese army, politicized by its long struggle in Africa, overthrew the government in Lisbon in 1974 and dismantled Portugal's empire.

A bloody scramble followed. Indonesia invaded the Portuguese island of East Timor, and in subjugating it killed up to a third of its almost 700,000 people. In Angola, Portugal's withdrawal led to the flight of most remaining whites, economic collapse, civil war between rival groups, and the intervention of the Soviet Union, Cuba, and South Africa (see p. 1040). In Mozam-

Chaos in the Congo, 1963: government paratroopers chase a mutinous policeman.

bique the Marxist-Leninist *Frelimo* ("Front for the Liberation of Mozambique") of Samora Machel took power. In Guinea-Bissau, the Lisbon-educated Amilcar Cabral, the most skillful of Portugal's adversaries, built a movement that grasped independence in 1973–74 without a civil war. But by then Cabral himself had already perished by assassination, a victim of rivalries within his own movement. As he had foreseen, the real test of his movement—as of the rulers of all "new nations"—came after independence.

RICH AND POOR

The new nations, for the most part, were and remain desperately poor in relative terms. In the 1960s, at independence, the poorest had annual per capita levels of gross national product (GNP)—the best indicator of a society's aggregate wealth or poverty—of 100 or less 1965 dollars. That compared unfavorably with Britain's level in 1700, before industrialization, of roughly 300 1965 dollars. Only Japan, with a per capita national product in the 1870s of a mere $74 (1965) was significantly lower than the West at the beginning of its industrialization.

Was widespread "Third World" poverty a consequence of Western wealth, as "Third Worldist" theoreticians have maintained? Little evidence supports that view. The West had been rich, inquisitive, and technologically sophisticated *before* its expansion. The capital and markets that fuelled Britain's development, and still more that of Britain's European competitors, were overwhelmingly internal. The West found the "Third World," with the exceptions of India, China, and Japan, already poor and weak. And India and China failed to match the growth rates of the West after 1800 not because of Western colonial occupation—which was not complete in India until the 1850s and was confined to coastal enclaves in China—but because

they failed to develop machine power on their own.

Europe's world supremacy was a byproduct not a cause of its industrial revolution, a byproduct of Europe's increasing mastery over nature and of the vast disparity in *power* that mastery created. Europeans rarely disdained plunder, but plunder extracted from the conquered played a minor role in Europe's growth; from 1492 to the late seventeenth century, Spain seized more plunder than any other state, but its economy became ever more poor and backward compared with those of the Netherlands and Britain.

If Western wealth was not a major cause of "Third World" poverty, might not colonial occupation itself have set the "Third World" back? A variety of "Third Worldist" theorists have argued that colonialism, by creating dependent economies based on commodities such as gold, silver, copper, tobacco, sugar, rubber, grain, and livestock, distorted the economic growth of the "Third World." The critics have maintained that without European interference, "Third World" growth would have been both better balanced and more rapid than it has been. They have also argued that colonialist "cultural imperialism" or "deculturation" of the "Third World" has discredited traditional cultures without offering adequate replacement. The consequent cultural and psychological disorientation, they have suggested, is itself a cause of slow growth.

Neither hypothesis is verifiable, since Europe *did* intervene and the native states did collapse under its impact. But the evidence from what actually happened speaks against it. Eighty years or less—the typical period of colonial domination in Africa—is a short time indeed for domination to have produced the fundamental changes that the critics allege. One of the very poorest states, Ethiopia (1985 per capita GNP of $110), only suffered occupation for six years, from 1936 to 1941. The Italians massacred Ethiopians with a will, but had no time for serious economic exploitation or "deculturation." And most "Third Worldist" critics, while drawing inspiration from Marx, appear to have forgotten that Marx hailed British rule in India as the triumphant "annihilation of old Asiatic society, and the laying of the material foundations of Western society in Asia." Marx, wrong-headedly or not, saw colonialism as the *precondition* for sustained economic growth in much of the non-Western world.

But, the critics have replied, has the West not throttled "Third World" growth after independence through continuing "neocolonialism," through a relationship of "informal empire" with dependent "Third World" economies? Again, the evidence suggests the contrary. In the nineteenth century, it was precisely the most dependent economies, those most closely tied to Britain's "informal empire" of trade and overseas investment—the United States, Argentina, Canada, Australia, New Zealand—that developed fastest. In the late twentieth century the fastest-developing "Third World" economies have been those most oriented toward the world economy dominated by the "First World" industrial democracies.

States such as Indonesia and Malaysia (with oil) or Brazil (without it) have forged ahead between 1965 and 1985 at annual per capita growth rates of over 4 percent. South Korea, Taiwan, and the Chinese-populated mini-states of Hong Kong and Singapore, at between 6 and 8 percent a year, have made the most spectacular gains of all. Even in Africa, some states that have started poor have made remarkable advances: Cameroons and Congo-Brazzaville had per capita growth rates over the 1965–85 period of over 3 percent. Conversely, Argentina, which in 1900 appeared poised to be another Australia or New Zealand, has stagnated since the 1914–18 collapse of Britain's "informal empire." By 1985 Argentina's per capita GNP had dipped below that of South Korea, which had been desperately poor at the turn of the century.

The fortunes of states naturally vary with those of the world economy. Booms, such as the one that bore world trade upwards from the 1950s until the "oil shock" of 1973, benefit almost all states. Downturns such as the savage declines that followed 1973 and the renewed disruption of oil supplies in 1979 (see p. 1060) disproportionately affect the very poorest, which depend on imported oil but have few exports with which to pay for that oil. The peculiar cure the rich offered after 1973 was, if anything, worse than the disease— "petrodollar recycling." The OPEC states took payments for oil in dollars. They deposited their immense profits in U.S. or European banks. The banks, oblivious to risk, then happily lent those "petrodollars" at high interest rates to "Third World" countries. The

Losers . . .

At least 16 countries achieved a negative per capita growth rate from the 1960s to the 1980s; in other words, they got steadily poorer.

	Population (millions)	Annual per capita GNP (1985 $)	1965–85 growth in annual per capita GNP	Life expectancy at birth	Literacy (percent) (1982–84)
Uganda	14.7		−2.6	49	52
Chad	5.0		−2.3	45	17
Ghana	12.7	380	−2.2	53	30
Zaire	30.6	170	−2.1	51	46
Niger	6.4	250	−2.1	44	10
Nicaragua	3.3	770	−2.1	59	66
Madagascar	10.2	240	−1.9	52	53
Zambia	6.7	390	−1.6	52	54
Liberia	2.2	470	−1.4	50	24
Somalia	5.4	280	−.7	46	60
Jamaica	2.2	940	−.7	73	76
Senegal	6.6	370	−.6	47	10
C. African Rep.	2.6	260	−.2	49	20
Bolivia	6.4	470	−.2	53	63
El Salvador	4.8	820	−.2	64	65
Chile	12.1	1430	−.2	70	94

Source: World Bank, *World Development Report 1987* (New York: Oxford University Press, 1987), pp. 202–203.

"Third World" countries in turn spent the money as much for prestige projects as for oil. Their resulting debts rose daily by compound interest and amounted to $1.25 trillion by 1988. "Petrodollar recycling" ominously resembled the reparation—war debt—U.S. loan merry-go-round of the 1920s. It also suggested that Western bankers and their regulators were deeply ignorant of the history of international debt—a history of repudiation.

As an alternative to loans, "Third World" critics and Western development economists have suggested large-scale gifts from the rich. Unfortunately, little empirical evidence suggests that massive infusions of capital would help. The West did not develop as a result of capital pumped in from outside. The post-1945 economic growth of nations as disparate as Germany and Japan suggests that capital is unimportant compared to human capital. In the "Third World" itself, Ethiopia received $2.26 billion in Western aid between 1979 and 1985, and got steadily poorer. The Sudan received $5.35 billion from 1979 to 1985—80 percent of its 1985 GNP—with similar results. Aid goes almost inevitably not to the peoples of the "Third World" or to their entrepreneurs, but to their ruling bureaucracies, the very organizations whose policies arguably prolong poverty. Even large amounts of aid have failed to make many poor countries capable of exporting to pay for their imports. Much aid has instead funded magnificent and useless new capitals, super-highways for the cars of single-party elites, and bankrupt steel mills rising like "cathedrals in the desert."

Perhaps growth or its absence is chiefly a function of the *internal* conditions within "Third World" states and economies, rather than of their subordinate position in the world market or of their shortages of capital. Perhaps political, social, and economic traditions, the extent of literacy, and the policies of "Third World" governments themselves are predominantly responsible for growth or its absence. Exploring the validity of that hypothesis requires dividing the "Third World" into its cultural, political, and economic components.

Winners . . .

Some economies, despite a position of "dependence" on the larger economies of the "First World," have made gains that range from considerable to spectacular.

	Population (millions)	Annual per capita GNP (1985 $)	1965–85 growth in annual per capita GNP	Life expectancy at birth	Literacy (percent) (1982–84)
Botswana	1.1	840	8.3	57	35
Singapore	2.6	7420	7.6	73	84
South Korea	41.1	2150	6.6	69	90+
Lesotho	1.5	470	6.5	54	60
Hong Kong	5.4	6230	6.1	76	75
Hungary	10.6	1950	5.8	71	98.9
Jordan	3.5	1560	5.8	65	71
Oman	1.2	6730	5.7	54	20
North Yemen	8.0	550	5.3	45	15
Indonesia	162.2	530	4.8	55	62
China	1040.3	310	4.8	69	65
Malaysia	15.6	2000	4.4	68	65
Brazil	135.6	1640	4.3	65	76
Yugoslavia	23.1	2070	4.1	72	90.5
Syria	10.5	1570	4.0	64	47
Tunisia	7.1	1190	4.0	63	62
Thailand	51.7	800	4.0	64	82

Source: World Bank, *World Development Report 1987* (New York: Oxford University Press, 1987), pp. 202–203.

NEW STATES AND OLD: THE "THIRD WORLD" DIVIDED

The "Third World" contains at least five major groups of states: the Chinese cultural area, the Islamic Middle East, South Asia, Latin America, and Africa south of the Sahara. Politically, "Third World" states range from Right authoritarian military regimes, such as those of South Korea or Chile, through attempted democracies, such as the Philippines after 1986, to hermit "socialist" states such as Burma, to the Marxist-Leninist dictatorships of the "second Soviet empire" (see pp. 1040–41). Economically, "Third World" states range from market economies with some government direction (South Korea, Singapore, Ivory Coast) through "African socialist" experiments (Tanzania, Ghana), to "de-Stalinizing" socialist economies (China and possibly Vietnam), to Stalinist centralized economies (North Korea, Cuba). These characteristics intersect in manifold ways, and help account for the wide diversity of outcomes.

Confucian East Asia

Culturally, China has influenced its neighbors—Vietnam to the south and Korea and Japan to the northeast—from the beginning of recorded history. The Confucian pattern that China exemplified placed a high value on literacy, hierarchy, the subordination of the individual to the group. Those qualities made densely populated rice-growing economies work. At least in nineteenth-century China, that pattern may initially have retarded growth by its very success and durability. Japan, which rose to the Western challenge most readily, was always less Confucian than China, thanks to its hereditary warrior ruling caste. China and its neighbors, highly developed cultures with an ethos of literacy, duty, and relentless hard work, were nevertheless best equipped for economic growth of all the non-Western world.

But politics imposed differing outcomes. In Japan, small size helped in the consolidation of a modern state; a fortunate combination of centralization (the Tokugawa Shogunate and the traditions of the Imperial house) and decentralization (the "feudal" domains) gave innovators both their political vehicle for change and their opportunity to seize power. In China, the empire's unwieldiness, the rigidity of its Manchu rulers, and its initial choice of armed resistance rather than accommodation to the "barbarians" all conspired

to produce collapse, according to the recurring historical pattern discerned by the Chinese themselves. The immense Taiping rebellion of the 1850s and 1860s prefigured the far greater upheaval of the twentieth century: four decades of devastating civil war, Japanese invasion, and war in Korea with the United States (1911–53).

Mao Zedong (Mao Tse-tung) and his Party mobilized the peasantry by appealing to land hunger and roused the urban intellectuals by offering a vehicle for nationalism. That was a winning combination. But Mao, intoxicated with revolutionary messianism, soon sought to pioneer in economic development as he had in the adaptation of Marxism-Leninism to a peasant society. In two disastrous experiments, the "Great Leap Forward" (1958–59) and the "Great Proletarian Cultural Revolution" (1966–69), he almost destroyed both the Chinese economy and his own party. "Politics in command!" was Mao's guiding principle; the death by famine of up to 27 million in the "three lean years" of 1959–61 was the result. The forcing of China's peasantry into "communes" and a crash industrialization based on amateur back-yard blast furnaces reduced the economy to a shambles. After that débâcle, Mao's comrades sought to remove him from power while retaining him as a living symbol of the Revolution and of the Party's legitimacy.

But Mao did not resign himself to being thus embalmed and placed on display like the dead Lenin. With the help of Jiang Qing (Chiang Ch'ing), the former Shanghai film actress who had become his second wife, and of the Red Army political leader Lin Biao (Lin Piao), Mao took power back in 1966 through a coup in Beijing (Peking). He then launched an all-out struggle in the provinces against his own Party and government bureaucracy. The stake as Mao conceived it was the continuation of the Revolution: "There were two possibilities. There could be a continued development of the Revolution towards communism. The other possi-

The cult of Mao: National Day celebrations, 1966.

bility was that youth could negate the Revolution and do bad things: make peace with imperialism [the West] . . . and take a stand beside the small percentage of counter-revolutionaries still in the country."

The "Great Proletarian Cultural Revolution" enthused Western student radicals; to China it brought chaos. Groups of youthful fanatics, the "Red Guards," attacked foreigners, high Party figures, government bureaucrats, and one another. The economy again threatened to disintegrate. Another 10 to 20 million may have perished from Red Guard purges, internecine fighting, and malnutrition. The army ultimately restored order while Mao's associates such as the durable Communist mandarin, Zhou Enlai (Chou En-lai), sapped the power of the radicals. Mao himself lost his grip with increasing age and died in 1976. But his work, as one successor summed it up in the mid-1980s, had been catastrophic: "We have wasted twenty years." Only in the late 1970s did China begin to "de-Maoize" and show its economic potential (see pp. 1046–47).

North Korea and Vietnam, although they began under foreign rule rather than under informal domination, followed China's pattern. The Communist "monarchy" of the aged Kim Il-Sung, who in 1984 appointed his son, Kim Jong-Il, as his successor, remains one of the world's most closed and Stalinist states. Its only noteworthy product is military power and its primary export is weaponry and advice on war and terrorism to states as far afield as Iran, Zimbabwe, Grenada, and Nicaragua; North Korean military advisers currently serve in 34 countries. Vietnam, after its 1975 conquest of the South, attempted to impose the Stalinist pattern already proven a failure in the North. The result was economic regression (see p. 1046). A younger generation of leaders came to power in 1986 and announced a sort of NEP (see p. 909): a grudging latitude for private enterprise "within the socialist system."

Why Maoism?

Lu Xun (Lu Hsün, 1881–1936), China's greatest twentieth century short-story writer and social critic, wrote bitter pages in the 1920s that suggest some of the ingredients of Mao's success.

It has never been granted to the Chinese people that they are human beings; at best, they have been raised to the level of slaves, and this is still the case today. In the past, they were often lower than slaves. The Chinese masses are neutral; in time of war they do not know what faction they belong to, and in fact they belong to any faction. Come the rebels: considering the people as being the government's, they loot and murder. Comes the regular army: instead of recognizing its own, it loots and murders too, as if the people belonged to the rebels. At this point, the only wish of the population is to find a Master, a Master who would deign to accept them as his people—no, not even that—who would deign to accept them as his cattle. The people would be ready to eat grass if necessary; all they ask is that the Master point out in what direction they must trot. . . .

As a rule, after each period of anarchy, when chaos reaches its climax, some personality appears—more powerful, more clever, more cunning (sometimes a foreigner)—to unify the empire and grant it some measure of order. . . .

In the end, the simplest and most adequate way of describing the history of China would be to distinguish between two types of periods: (1) the periods when the people wish in vain to enjoy a stable slave condition; and (2) the periods when the people manage to enjoy a stable slave condition. The alternation of these two states is what our old scholars called "the cycle of chaos and order."

From Simon Leys (Pierre Ryckmans), *Chinese Shadows* (New York: Penguin Books, 1978), pp. 200–201.

In contrast, the non-Communist states of Chinese-influenced East and Southeast Asia have prospered mightily. Malaysia, politically Malay but with an economy under the control of its large overseas Chinese minority, has grown at a per capita rate of over 4 percent. Thailand, the one South or Southeast Asian state to avoid colonial occupation, has grown at a comparable rate, thanks to its Chinese minority and relatively literate population. It benefited both from an infusion of dollars during

The Red Guards, vanguard of Mao's revolution against his own party.

the Vietnam War and a subsequent boom in Pacific trade. In Korea, Japanese colonialism (1905–45) and the patronage of the United States helped provide South Korea with an industrial infrastructure and a Western-educated and technologically expert elite capable of swiftly emulating Japan. Politically, South Korea enjoyed enforced stability. The harsh domination after 1948 of a Harvard-educated politician, Syngman Rhee, gave way in 1960–61 to 25 years of military dictatorship. In 1986–87 the new middle class that Korea's industrialization created began forcefully demanding political rights. The military loosened its grip and permitted an election; the military candidate won but promised an increasing measure of democratization. A similar absence of democracy has attended the spectacular per capita growth rates of culturally Chinese and economically capitalist Taiwan, Hong Kong, and Singapore. They outstripped all other contenders including Japan, and suggest in miniature the world-shaking potential of China itself should its ruling Party irrevocably place "economics in command."

The Islamic Middle East

Major cleavages divide the independent states of the Middle East. The most important are (1) between categories of regime, (2) between states aligned with the West or with the Soviet Union, and (3) between states with oil and states without. In addition, cleavages between tribes and between branches of Islam have both split states from one another and divided them internally.

Three main types of regime exist. First come the traditional monarchies and sheikdoms, based on Bedouin or other tribal loyalties—Saudi Arabia, Morocco, Jordan, and the Gulf states from Kuwait to Oman. Egypt, Iraq, and Libya originally belonged to that category, but their monarchies succumbed to military coups in 1952, 1958, and 1969, respectively. The second category is the secular states—Egypt, Syria, Iraq, Tunisia, Algeria, Libya. The Turkey of Kemal Atatürk—military-dominated and dedicated to introducing Western technology and ideas—provided an initial model. Like Turkey, most such states have attempted to make the state the chief motor of economic development. Most have claimed to embody an "Arab socialism" that in practice meant deadening bureaucratic controls that engendered corruption and black markets. Finally, a third model, a revolutionary "Islamic Republic" based on Shi'ite Islam, arose in Iran after 1979 (see pp. 1051–53). It has so far remained unique.

In their external relations, the Middle Eastern states have tended to profess "non-alignment." In practice, they have tilted toward the United States or the Soviet Union; despite much discussion of cleavages between "North" and "South," it is the East-West conflict that has divided the world most deeply. Status quo states such as the traditional monarchies have normally favored the United States. Roosevelt took over Britain's patronage of Saudi Arabia and its oil in 1944–45, and that relationship has endured. Morocco, under its durable monarch King Hassan II (1961–), has usually maintained ties with Washington, as have moderate secular states such as the Tunisia of Habib Bourguiba (1956–87) and the

Egypt of Anwar Sadat after he broke with Moscow in 1976. Algeria, "nonaligned" in rhetoric but less so in practice, has also tended to tilt toward Western Europe and the United States, its customers for gas and oil. Iran until its 1978–79 revolution posed as a bulwark of Western influence in the Gulf— to mask its monarch's megalomaniacal ambitions.

Iran excepted, the Soviets have tended to draw to themselves the most expansionist of Middle Eastern states— Nasser's Egypt, Libya after the revolution of Colonel Muammar Qaddafi in 1969, the Syria of the merciless Hafiz al-Assad (1970–), the Iraq of his equally remorseless counterpart Saddam Hussein (1979–), and the "People's Democratic Republic of Yemen." Lavish provision of arms, the Soviet Union's only major industrial export, and numerous military and "police" advisers have cemented these ties. Soviet influence has nevertheless sometimes been transient. Moscow's position in the region has yet to recover from its loss of Egypt in 1972–76.

After internal politics and external alignments, the possession of oil likewise divides the Middle Eastern states into two classes. Saudi Arabia, Libya, Algeria, Iran, Iraq, Kuwait, the Gulf sheikdoms, and even Egypt after its recovery of Sinai in 1982 have enjoyed to a greater or lesser extent the bounty of oil. After 1973, when the Arab and other oil-producing states combined into the OPEC cartel and more than doubled the real price of oil in a year, that bounty increased markedly. But the newly rich have yet to convert their oil wealth into modern economies. Saudi Arabia and the sheikdoms have small populations that as yet show insufficient willingness to surrender their desert traditions. Secular states with oil sometimes have too little of it, as in Egypt or Algeria. Others smother initiative beneath layers of bureaucracy or attempt to ban enterprise entirely, as in Qaddafi's Libya.

Religious and ethnic fractures likewise divide the Islamic Middle East. Iran after its 1978–79 revolution emerged as the world's only Shi'ite state; religion and Persian nationalism combined to set it at odds with its Sunni Arab neighbors. Iraq, although Arab in population, is mostly Shi'ite in religion; the cleavage between Shi'ite and Sunni is a major source of internal weakness although Arab nationalism partially offsets it. Turkey, Iraq, and Iran contain sizable and militant minorities of Kurds, a mountain warrior people who boast that "Kurds have no friends." Syria contains large Christian communities and its officer corps and rulers are Alawites, a small Shi'ite sect that ruthlessly dominates a Sunni majority.

In Lebanon, five major communities contend. The last census (1932) showed that 29 percent of the population was Maronite Christian, 22 percent Sunni Moslem, 20 percent Shi'ite Moslem, and 7 percent Druze, a heretical and combative Moslem sect. The French, on their departure in 1946, left Lebanon a parliamentary regime that gave the presidency to the Maronites, the prime ministership to the Sunni, and the office of army chief of staff to the Druzes.

Traditional monarchs and secular rulers: King Faisal of Saudi Arabia (1964–75) and (below, left to right) a 1970 encounter between Gaafar Mohammed Nimeiri of the Sudan (1969–85), Muammar Qaddafi of Libya (1969–), and Nasser of Egypt (1954–70).

But the relative weights of the communities soon changed, and a fifth group, the Palestinian refugees, took a hand. By 1984, the Shi'ites made up an estimated 31 percent of the population, the Maronites stood second at 25 percent, the Sunni third at 20 percent, and the Druzes had declined to 6 percent. In 1975 a bid for more power by the rapidly growing Shi'ites helped start a religious-ethnic civil war that still continues.

Finally, nationalism divides the Middle Eastern states, despite the common "Arab" character that all except Iran and Turkey share. Efforts at union between states, such as Nasser's attempt to absorb Syria into a "United Arab Republic" (1958–61) or Quaddafi's federations with Egypt (1972–73), Tunisia (1974), and Morocco (1984–86), have all failed. The rulers of Syria had no desire to become a mere province of Egypt. They possessed their own national consciousness and sense of mission, the creation of a "Greater Syria" that includes Lebanon and Palestine. Nasser also failed to subjugate North Yemen between 1962 and 1968 despite massive Egyptian use of Soviet tanks and mustard gas.

The multiple divisions between sects, tribes, and states have tended to stunt the Middle Eastern states both politically and economically. And the state machines and armies of the Islamic secular states have also proved the classic ground for assassinations and coups. In the absence of settled political traditions and long-established legitimacy, as elsewhere in the "Third World," power grows out of the barrel of a gun. Those who have the guns and the smattering of Western technical knowledge needed to use them have seen no reason why they should not command the state and direct the national economy. The resulting one-party regimes range from the merely inefficient (Egypt, Tunisia, Algeria) to the terrifying (Syria, Libya, Iraq); Hafiz al-Assad of Syria and his Soviet advisers chose to deal with Sunni unrest in 1982 by shelling flat much of the town of Hama and killing perhaps 30,000. The traditional monarchies tend on balance to be less aggressive, less oppressive, and better economic performers than the secular states. But their stability comes from their traditions, the very traditions that economic development undermines. No stable order to replace the defunct Ottoman Empire is in sight, and the rise of Islamic militance has generated new and savage conflicts.

South Asia

The lands of southern Asia are disparate. Four of them, India, Pakistan, Bangladesh (East Pakistan until 1971), and Sri Lanka (Ceylon until 1972) are historically closely linked. They are the ultimate successors, after the British interlude, to the Mughal empire. To the east lies Burma, a borderland between southern Asian and Chinese culture. Indonesia, dominated by Islam, and the Philippines, a compound of Malay, Islamic, Spanish, and U.S. influences, are unique, but their village-based societies are similar in many ways to the pattern of southern Asia. They are Asian but not Confucian.

India and Pakistan have remained locked in struggle since 1947–48. Pakistan, split between the dominant Punjab to the west and East Bengal to the east, failed to consolidate itself. India, under Gandhi's violent successor, Jawaharlal Nehru, quarreled with China over border areas in Tibet in 1961–62; the Chinese army gave the Indians a sharp and persuasive rebuff. Fighting between India and Pakistan erupted once more in 1965–66, and the Soviet Union, seeking favor with India as a counterweight to Mao's increasingly hostile China, brokered a compromise. In 1970–71 the East Bengalis sought autonomy; the generals who ruled West Pakistan answered with massacres. Under Nehru's combative daughter, Indira Gandhi (unrelated to Mohandas Gandhi either by blood or political philosophy), India intervened and swiftly dismembered Pakistan.

East Bengal became independent Bangladesh and soon passed under the rule of its army. India was now supreme on the subcontinent, a status confirmed by its explosion in 1974 of what it whimsically termed a "peaceful nuclear device." Pakistan countered India's weapon with clandestine development of its own "Islamic bomb." The acquisition of Western nuclear fuel technology through espionage and China's alleged gift in the early 1980s of a tested bomb design have perhaps given Pakistan a temporary edge.

Despite continuing interstate strife and periodic religious-ethnic massacres ("communal violence") within India and Pakistan, economic growth has been steady although slow. In per capita terms, India grew between 1965 and 1985 at a rate of 1.7 percent per year, Pakistan at 2.6 percent; only Bangladesh, among the world's poorest states, stagnated at .4 percent. In the north Indian plain, new strains of rice and wheat and the entrepreneurship of India's Sikh minority made an agricultural "Green Revolution" that promised India eventual self-sufficiency in food. A powerful industrial economy, although bound with doctrinaire "socialist" red tape, has arisen around cities such as Bombay. A small but growing minority of India's 800 million people live at "First World" levels.

Pakistan, except for brief interludes in the 1950s and 1970s, remained a military dictatorship, but India persisted in the parliamentary traditions derived from Britain. Indira Gandhi's attempt at dictatorship in 1975–77 collapsed amid universal condemnation, although she returned with a majority in 1980 after promising not to repeat the experiment. Her downfall was the Sikh minority, whose extremists sought an independent Sikh state, "Khalistan," carved from the Punjab, India's agricultural heart. When heavily armed Sikh militants seized the Sikh Golden Temple at Amritsar in 1984, Indira Gandhi evicted them with the Indian army and much bloodshed after negotiations failed. Sikhs assassinated Mrs.

Mohandas Gandhi enjoying a joke with his disciple and successor Jawaharlal Nehru (prime minister 1947–64).

Gandhi in retaliation; Hindus then killed many thousands of Sikhs living in Hindu areas. Mrs. Gandhi's son and successor, Rajiv Gandhi, third of the Congress Party dynasty that Nehru founded, has as yet failed to pacify either the Sikhs or the numerous other disaffected communities in India's patchwork of languages and cultures.

To the south, Sri Lanka showed great promise. Its peoples were 60 per-

Indira Gandhi (prime minister 1966–77, 1980–84), daughter of Nehru and architect of India's hegemony in South Asia.

cent literate; its agricultural export economy grew rapidly until the 1960s. Then nationalism caught up with it. Alongside the majority Sinhalese, Buddhist in religion and 70 percent of the population, lived a Tamil minority of Hindu religion that had originally immigrated from southern India. Under British rule, the two communities had lived in relative peace, but the creation of an independent sovereign state brought with it a struggle for mastery over that state. Within a decade of independence, Sinhalese politicians had imposed Sinhalese as the official language. Sinhalese ideologues proclaimed their alleged superiority as descendants of conquerors from the north in the sixth century B.C.

The Tamils, an enterprising group that dominated commerce and the professions, responded first with riots and then, after 1983, with guerrilla war and demands for a separate Tamil state around the city of Jaffna in northern Sri Lanka. A cycle of terror and reprisal similar to that in Algeria after 1954 locked Sinhalese and Tamil nationalisms into seemingly irreconcilable conflict over the same territory. Indian army intervention in 1987 to broker a peace goaded the "Tamil Tiger" guerrillas to savage attacks on the Indians and to further massacres of Sinhalese civilians. Despite the war, Sri Lanka maintained a growth rate from 1980 to 1985 of 5.1 percent, but economic growth can scarcely survive further large-scale bloodshed.

Further east, Burma retreated into resentful isolation; in 1962 its most durable leader, General Ne Win, proclaimed a non-aligned "Burmese Road to Socialism" that has led to poverty for all except bureaucrats and black marketeers. Indonesia, further south, enjoyed the massive advantage of oil. Sukarno ruled until 1965–68 and squandered that wealth on palaces, monuments, and mistresses. His successor, General Suharto, took power in the aftermath of the failed Communist coup of 1965 and the immense massacre of Communists that followed. His

regime began to realize Indonesia's economic potential, thanks to close economic ties with Japan.

The Philippines suppressed a Communist insurgency after independence in 1947, then succumbed to military dictatorship under General Ferdinand Marcos (1965–86). Marcos's power disintegrated after 1983, when his associates arranged the assassination of a key opponent, Benigno Aquino. With the backing of key army figures, the Catholic Church, U.S. opinion, and the overwhelming majority of articulate Filipinos, the dead man's widow, Corazon Aquino, took power in a largely bloodless "people power" uprising after Marcos sought to steal the 1986 election. Aquino faces economic stagnation and a second and exceedingly bloody Communist insurgency begun during the Marcos years. Despite the restoration of something resembling parliamentary democracy, the prospects for stability appeared poor.

The Three Latin Americas

The "new nations" that arose in Latin America between 1811 and 1839 had few of the advantages of their Dutch and American predecessors. Spain had imposed a centralized bureaucratic pattern that prevented the Creoles, native-born of Spanish descent, from developing experience in self-government—in contrast to the pattern of British "white" colonies from North America to Australia. Narrow landed oligarchies ruled alongside a disproportionately powerful land-owning Church. And Spain had imposed on its colonial economies a pattern similar to that in politics—centralized controls and ruinous taxation that stunted enterprise. Anarchy and despotism, economic stagnation or regression in most cases followed independence (see p. 775).

But not all of the new states suffered the same misfortunes. Latin America is almost as divided as the Islamic Middle East or the "Third World" itself. With the exception of miscellaneous small states such as Guyana and Suriname, the British and Dutch ex-colonies between Venezuela and Brazil, Latin American states fall into three principal categories. First are those with a Creole or European majority: Costa Rica, Argentina, and Uruguay. They began as classic settler economies: Europe transported to the New World. They thrived in the nineteenth century on commodity exports such as coffee, beef, hides, wool, and grain. But as elsewhere, politics intervened.

Costa Rica's parliamentary regime rests on a base of prosperous small landowners, and has maintained an enviable degree of stability and prosperity since the late 1940s. Not so Uruguay. A drop in commodity prices and

Central and South America in 1988

distended bureaucracies and state industries that employed a third of Uruguay's workers brought stagnation and massive inflation by the 1960s. A Marxist urban guerrilla movement, the "Tupamaro National Liberation Front," arose among disaffected children of the upper classes. It sought to destroy parliamentary democracy by provoking the state to violent reprisals that would "unmask" its supposed "true nature" as the organ of repression of domestic "capitalism" and foreign "neocolonialism." The Tupamaros duly brought down the parliamentary regime in 1973–74. The military dictatorship that followed erased the guerrillas with torture and "disappearances." Parliamentary democracy perished, but implacable Rightist dictatorship, not Marxist millennium, replaced it. Civilian government returned hesitantly in 1985.

Argentina traveled a road similar to Uruguay's, but even more savage. Its settler population was overwhelmingly Spanish and Italian, with large German, British, French, and Jewish communities; in 1900 the country had appeared poised to become another Australia. But the Great Depression ended what little political stability it enjoyed. Oligarchic military regimes gave way in 1944–46 to the populist dictatorship of Colonel Juan Perón, admirer of Mussolini and husband of the charismatic Eva (Evita) Duarte, patron saint of Argentina's "shirtless" dispossessed. An army coup destroyed Perón's regime in 1955, but his "Social Justice" [Justicialista] party lived on as Argentina's most powerful political force. Too weak and disunited to overthrow the military, it was strong enough to make Argentina ungovernable until the army wearily permitted Perón to return to power in 1973. Then Perón died in 1974. His third wife, Isabel Martínez Perón, a former cabaret dancer, sought to rule with counsel from the Perónist party and her astrologer. Inflation and a Tupamaro-style Leftist insurgency reduced Argentina to shambles.

In 1976 the military again seized power, and destroyed the guerrillas with torture and mass murder, dumping planeloads of drugged prisoners into the South Atlantic. Between 5,000 and 20,000 suspects "disappeared." The military killed with such abandon that fear of retribution thenceforth locked it into power. Only the inglorious defeat of its 1982 attempt to seize the Falkland Islands from Britain (see p. 1050) led to retreat, and to elections that returned as president a genuine democrat, Raul Alfonsín. Alfonsín had slightly better luck than his predecessors in dominating the Perónists and in spurring an economy crippled by state ownership and bureaucratic sloth. But Argentina's growth rate in GNP per capita from 1965 to 1985 has been .2 percent annually, scarcely better than no growth at all.

The second category of Latin American states, after those with European populations, are the ex-colonies of Spain with an Indian or *mestizo* majority. Of these Chile has the largest Creole population, at 25 percent; there and in most of the remainder, from Bolivia through Central America to Mexico, large *mestizo* or Indian groups remain permanently excluded from a share in power. In Peru and Bolivia, between 30 and 55 percent of the population consists of Indians who speak Quechua or Aymara rather than Spanish; literacy in many of these states is relatively low.

They have nevertheless traveled diverse paths. Mexico and Ecuador, thanks in part to oil, have enjoyed relatively high rates of growth since the 1950s, although the patronage needs and populist rhetoric of Mexico's ruling "Institutional Revolutionary Party" (PRI) have tended to stultify the economy with state-owned industries and unpredictable nationalizations. Colombia has also prospered in relative terms, despite a long-running "*violencia*" or permanent civil war between political parties, Leftist guerrillas, and cocaine lords. Panama, part of Colombia until the United States moved in to build the Canal, has prospered as a banking and shipping center despite the corrupt and oppressive rule of its "National Guard."

Oil did not save Venezuela, nor copper Chile. Venezuela's rulers for much of the twentieth century have been generals, of whom the most conspicuous and brutal were Juan Vincente Gomez (1908–35) and Marcos Peréz Jiménez (1952–58). Thereafter a succession of weak parliamentary regimes nationalized more and more of the economy; the drop in oil prices after 1982 drove Venezuela into negative per capita growth. The government of Chile, the oldest stable parliamentary regime on the continent, collapsed in 1973. Its politics had long been deadlocked between a Marxist Left, a Catholic Christian Democratic center, and a conservative Right. In 1969 the candidate of the Left, Salvador Allende, took power as president on the strength of a plurality of 36.3 percent, less than two points ahead of his closest rival. Despite undertakings to the contrary given to opposition parties that represented a majority of Chileans, Allende attempted to transform in a "socialist" direction an economy largely based on copper mining and inefficient protected industry. He also ostentatiously received Fidel Castro. Both the Nixon administration and the Chilean middle classes objected.

Allende's policies produced 323 percent inflation in 1972–73 and economic paralysis. Politically, he remained intent on a Marxist revolution for which he had no mandate; enthusiasts from all over Latin America and Europe flocked to Chile. In September 1973, with the support of the Right and even of some Christian Democrats, the armed forces rocketed and stormed the presidential palace, and rounded up the Left. Allende apparently killed himself with a treasured machine pistol, a gift of Castro. Allende's supporters accused Kissinger and the CIA of complicity in the coup; Washington had subsidized political opponents of

Allende and had attempted in 1970 to provoke the army against him. But no firm evidence of U.S. involvement in 1973 surfaced, despite lengthy congressional investigation. The generals and admirals who overthrew Allende had a domestic mandate.

Their leader, the uncompromising Augusto Pinochet, soon converted that mandate into one of Latin America's most ruthless dictatorships; the military shot between 3,000 and 10,000 Leftists in the months after the coup. Too late, the Christian Democrats and moderate Rightists realized that Pinochet, like Allende, considered himself a man with a mission—the extirpation rather than the establishment of Marxism. Pinochet has endured. The opposition remained too divided and too fearful of the remnants of the Marxist Left to present a credible alternative to dictatorship. Despite the dictatorship's dismantling of protective tariffs, Chile's growth rate has been a mere .5 percent per year from 1965 to 1985.

To the north, in Bolivia and Peru, military regimes predominated until the early 1980s. The Peruvian military ruled from 1968 to 1980 and adopted "Third Worldist" notions of economic development; it nationalized banks and foreign firms. The result was prolonged stagnation. The ensuing civilian government has done little better, and in addition faces an implacable insur-

Argentina, 1973–83: the military, then Perón (above), the military again, and finally Alfonsín (below).

Two Chilean motorcades:
Allende with Castro (1971)
and Pinochet (1986).

gency of Quechua-speaking Indians and university-educated Maoists that calls itself the *Sendero Luminoso*, the "Shining Path" to revolution. Bolivia too acquired a civilian government in the 1980s, but shows little sign of stability. The Central American states of Honduras, Guatemala, El Salvador, and Nicaragua are among the poorest in Latin America. Revolution and insurgency, explored in the next chapter, are both product and cause of the negative per capita growth rates of Nicaragua and El Salvador.

Finally, the largest of all Latin American states is in a category of its own—

Brazil. Its ethnic mixture, a unique compound of Portuguese, Africans, Italians, Germans, Slavs, East Indians, Japanese, Chinese, and native Indians, defies categorization; blacks remain at the bottom of the social scale, but color lines are less exclusive than in Spanish America. Above all, the New World society that Portugal established left far more room for local and individual initiative than in Spanish America. The result was a society that displays the extremes of wealth and poverty common both in Latin America and in other "new nations." But despite that maldistribution, an ever-growing foreign debt of over $100 billion, and political turmoil that led to army rule between 1964 and 1985, Brazil has prospered. Its per capita growth rate from 1965 to 1985 was 4.3 percent, one of the highest in the "Third World." Its industries have achieved considerable export success. Unfortunately the civilian rule restored in 1985 has yet to take hold convincingly. Galloping inflation, staggering external debt, and political incoherence may yet slow or halt development.

The Sorrows of Africa

No wretchedness in Latin America compares with that found from the fringes of the Sahara southwards. Of the sixteen states of over a million population with negative per capita growth rates between 1965 and 1985, eleven are in Africa south of the Sahara. Of the poorest states in terms of per capita annual GNP, most are African; a few others—Vietnam, Cambodia, Laos, and Afghanistan—probably belong in the same category, but reliable statistics are lacking.

African penury is no accident; Africa's states were poorest at independence. All suffer from a variety of disabilities. Literacy is sometimes below 10 percent. Those who acquire it, either from government or missionary schools, thereby isolate themselves from their society. Traditional animist cults, based on magic, do not prepare

their adherents to function in the cold "disenchanted" world of cause and effect, profit and loss. Islam, Africa's fastest growing religion, carries with it a hostility to the "Christian" West that often extends to Western economic ideas. And the Christian teaching missionaries who remained after independence have often had other priorities than economic development.

States for the most part follow the boundaries drawn by figures such as Bismarck, Lord Salisbury, and Leopold of Belgium, lines that cut across both tribal zones and customary economic units. Black Africa's traditional political units, empires such as those of the Ashanti or the Zulus, tended to expand rapidly for several generations, then crumble from lack of cohesion; they offered little precedent for the creation of nation-states on the European pattern. Economies tend to be subsistence agriculture or export-oriented monoculture. Only Nigeria with its massive oil reserves and the largest population in black Africa, Botswana with its diamonds, and Rhodesia and South Africa with their European economies based on the labor of the black majority ap-

Mengistu Haile Miriam of Ethiopia, exemplar of Lenin's definition of dictatorship: "a power that is not limited by any laws, not bound by any rules, and based directly on force."

The Poorest of the Poor

	Population (millions)	Annual per capita GNP (1985 $)	1965–85 growth in annual per capita GNP	Life expectancy at birth	Literacy (percent) (1982–84)
Ethiopia	42.3	110	.2	45	35
Bangladesh	100.6	150	.4	51	23
Burkina Faso	7.9	150	1.3	45	7
Mali	7.5	150	1.4	46	10
Bhutan	1.2	160		44	5
Mozambique	13.8	160		47	14
Nepal	16.5	160	.1	47	20
Malawi	7.0	170	1.5	45	25
Zaire	30.6	170	−2.1	51	46
Burma	36.9	190	2.4	59	78
Burundi	4.7	230	1.9	48	25
Togo	3.0	230	.3	51	18
Madagascar	10.2	240	1.9	52	53
Niger	6.4	250	2.1	44	10
Benin	4.0	260	.2	49	11
C. African Rep.	2.6	260	−.2	49	20

Source: World Bank, *World Development Report 1987* (New York: Oxford University Press, 1987), pp. 202–203.

Mobutu in 1965, shortly after taking power.

peared sure-fire economic prospects in the 1960s. Most black African states immediately worsened their economic plight by ill-conceived "socialist" measures. Compelling peasants to sell to the state at a fixed price that is sometimes below the cost of production has deprived Africa's farmers of incentives to farm. Much of the continent, self-sufficient in food at independence, now imports it. And food price subsidies for the largely nonproductive urban populations have swelled both their numbers and government debts.

Some states appeared poor prospects from the beginning. Uganda and the Central African Republic succumbed to terrifying dictatorships by former sergeants, Idi Amin Dada and Jean-Bedel Bokassa. Amin killed up to 300,000 between 1971 and 1979. He left the country in a shambles from which it has yet to recover. The states of the Saharan fringe, Mali, Burkina Faso, Niger, Chad, and the Sudan have suffered grievously from a combination of drought and of population pressure on their fragile semi-desert environment.

Ethiopia, east and south of the Sudan, suffered both from drought and from the backward-looking monarchy of Haile Selassie until its overthrow in 1974. His successors, the Marxist-Leninist zealots of the *Derg* ("Provisional Military Administrative Council"), proved far more terrifying than the aged "Lion of Judah." In 1977–78, amid purges and massacres, a Lieutenant Colonel Mengistu Haile Mariam emerged in command of state and army. With Soviet aid he sought implacably to subjugate the Eritreans, the people of the former Italian colony that the United Nations had conceded to Ethiopia on condition that its inhabitants enjoy autonomy. Mengistu also pursued a Stalinist program of collectivization ("villagization") that ruthlessly dispossessed and displaced millions of peasants. Since 1977, war, collectivization, and drought between them have killed more Ethiopians and Eritreans than did Mussolini. The Marxist regimes of Angola and Mo-

Bombed-out remains of a colonial-era house in Nigeria.

zambique, like that of Ethiopia, pressed nationalization and collectivization schemes with similar economic consequences, although less drastic human ones.

Other states adopted forms of "African socialism" less extreme than that of Ethiopia, but with little better results. Ghana achieved independence under Kwame Nkrumah, who styled himself "the Redeemer," established a dictatorship, took on East German and Chinese advisers, and cut a bold figure at "non-aligned" meetings until his removal by Ghana's army in 1966. Economically, Ghana fell steadily further behind its similar but more "capitalist" neighbor, the Ivory Coast; Ghana currently vegetates under the dictatorship of a former air force lieutenant. Tanzania's attempt at a village collectivism that supposedly drew on roots in traditional African culture proved an unmitigated economic disaster, in contrast to the relative success of its "capitalist" northern neighbor, Kenya. Zambia's nationalization of industries and land in the 1970s, along with drought, produced negative per capita growth.

Guinea-Bissau's one-party "socialist" dictatorship and self-inflicted economic failures have exasperated even those most patient of givers of development aid, the Swedes.

Among black Africa's largest and most populous states, Nigeria and Zaire have also proved disappointments. Nigeria's British-style parliamentary regime did not survive the strains of tribalism and of religious conflict between the Arab Moslem north and the black Christian and animist south (a conflict also found in the Sudan). An attempt by the Ibo people of southeast Nigeria to create an independent "Biafra" in 1967–70 met with defeat in a pitiless civil war that left over a million dead. Subsequently, the military ruled until a brief parliamentary interlude in 1979–83 that ended in disorganization and yet another coup. Nigeria's oil wealth prompted ambitious development projects and the building of a new capital—a frequent symbolic gesture of national integration and state power, from St. Petersburg, to Washington, to Brasilia, to Islamabad (Pakistan). But bureaucratic controls and the corruption they generate have slowed growth. As for Zaire, it profited from its great mineral wealth far less than Nigeria has profited from its oil. United Nations and Belgian military intervention helped Mobutu to survive numerous challenges from the provinces. His dictatorship also proved adept at borrowing from Western banks and at spending the money on prestige projects and its own perquisites.

Finally, Rhodesia-Zimbabwe and South Africa, the European economies in Africa, have expanded. Defeat in 1978 did not mean "the suitcase or the coffin" for Zimbabwe's whites. The Marxist victor, Robert Mugabe, pursued a unique course; he encouraged the white minority to remain provisionally and run the economy. But the Boers of South Africa refused to contemplate surrender (see p. 1056). Despite a slowdown produced by international embargoes and sanctions directed against their structure of racial domination, their economy continues to function. It still produces the modern weapons—including possibly nuclear weapons—needed to preserve the supremacy of the "white tribe" of southern Africa.

FUTURES FOR THE "THIRD WORLD"

The history of the "Third World" since 1945 can suggest a variety of conclusions, depending on the observer. The widely differing growth rates of "Third World" states over many years nevertheless make clear that subordination to more powerful economies is hardly a cause of stagnation or regression. The states that sought to *withdraw* from the world market—Burma, Vietnam, Cambodia, Uganda, Ethiopia, and "African socialist" experiments such as Tanzania and Ghana—have done worst. The miseries of those "enslaved by capitalism" are small indeed compared to the miseries of those not "enslaved" by it.

For good or ill development has meant "capitalist development." Private wealth often produces savage contrasts between extremes of luxury and misery. But it is also the only force that has so far powered sustained economic growth. Capitalist development raised the West from poverty; even Marx celebrated it for that. Even the societies over which Stalin and Mao once presided now look to capitalism for economic inspiration (see pp. 1046 and 1063). And sustained capitalist development appears to require guarantees of rights against the state, rights that many "Third World" regimes are reluctant to concede.

The central obstacles to "Third World" development are thus politics and ideology. Most "Third World" single-party elites fiercely distrust private wealth because it is a form of power not under their own control. They have taken easily to forms of Marxism, which provides ready-made legitimation for dictatorship ("their own, naturally," as the anarchist Bakunin once put it; see p. 716). And if rapid development requires the abandonment of arbitrary power and of cherished myths, it also demands political stability. The coup d'état, the dominant form of political change in much of the Middle East, Africa, and Latin America, encourages the unhappy middle classes of those regions to export rather than invest productively what little capital they possess.

Rapid development also requires an economic revolution to end the tariffs and bureaucratic controls that throttle growth from Peru to Tanzania. It requires a relatively free market in agricultural goods to give the peasants incentive for "green revolutions" on the Indian model. It demands and produces both widespread literacy and swift and dislocating cultural change. The "Third World" faces daunting tasks. But the examples of Europe, of Japan, and of much of East Asia show that societies whose rulers give them the opportunity can make the perilous leap from poverty to wealth.

Suggestions for Further Reading

General Works

No adequate survey of the post-1945 "Third World" exists; few reliable or readable works cover even parts of it. G. Chaliand, *Revolution in the Third World* (1978), offers a brief and lively guided tour that is now in some respects dated. It nevertheless provides an interesting critique—from the Left—of "Third Worldist" ideology, and an excellent analysis of the wide cultural differences within the "Third World." See also C. Rangel, *Third World Ideology and Western Reality* (1986). The World Bank's annual *World Development Report* offers comprehensive statistical data with which to test generalizations about the "Third World." E. Luttwak, *Coup d'Etat: A Practical Handbook* (1969, 1979), is a valuable contribution to understanding the "Third World's" dominant method of political change.

Decolonization

No large-scale comparative history of decolonization exists. E. Monroe, *Britain's Moment in the Middle East, 1914–1956* (1963); A. Williams, *Britain and France in the Middle East and North Africa, 1914–1967* (1968); W. R. Louis, *The British Empire in the Middle East, 1945–1951* (1984); and A. Horne, *A Savage War of Peace: Algeria 1954–1962* (1977), are useful on the Middle East and North Africa. B. N. Pandey, *The Break-up of British India* (1969), and *South and Southeast Asia, 1945–1979* (1980), ably covers south and Southeast Asia.

"Third World" Diversity

For the varied cultures of the "Third World" and for post-1945 events there, see—for East Asia—H. C. Hinton, *Three and a Half Powers: The New Balance in Asia* (1975); S. Leys, *Chinese Shadows* (1978), and *The Chairman's New Clothes: Mao and the Cultural Revolution* (1981). On South Asia, see Pandey (listed above) and J. M. Brown, *Modern India: The Origins of an Asian Democracy* (1985). V. S. Naipaul, *India: A Wounded Civilization* (1977), offers pessimistic cultural criticism; N. Maxwell, *India's China War* (1970), is an instructive case study in Indian foreign policy. On the Middle East, D. Pipes, *In the Path of God: Islam and Political Power* (1983), is useful on the force of ideas; P. Mansfield, *The Middle East: A Political and Economic Survey* (1980), imparts basic facts. On Latin America, see especially L. E. Harrison, *Underdevelopment Is a State of Mind: The Latin American Case* (1985); P. Sigmund, *The Overthrow of Allende and the Politics of Chile, 1964–1976* (1977); C. Rangel, *The Latin Americans: Their Love-Hate Relationship with the United States* (1986); and V. S. Naipaul, *The Return of Eva Perón* (1980). On Africa, M. Meredith, *The First Dance of Freedom: Black Africa in the Post-War Era* (1984), provides a sophisticated overview; S. J. Unger, *Africa: People and Politics of an Emerging Continent* (1986), offers an informed popular account; C. Young and T. Turner, *The Rise and Decline of the Zairian State* (1985), provides a depressing case study.

36
The End of the Twentieth Century

The 1975 Helsinki security treaty brought little security. The détente that Nixon and Kissinger had sold to a war-weary Congress as harbinger of a "generation of peace" soon revealed itself as oversold. Soviet military power continued to grow. The Soviet Union acquired a second Soviet empire of "Third World" clients far beyond the "Yalta line" of 1945. In Asia, American withdrawal from Vietnam removed war from U.S. television screens but did not end war; China at last sought to shake off Mao's legacy; Japan's industries stormed the world's markets. Europe suffered stagnation, unemployment, and disorientation reminiscent of the interwar years. In the Middle East, an "Islamic Revolution" swept Iran in 1978–79, generating war and new and potent strains of terrorism. In Lebanon, Israel, southern Africa, and Central America conflicts between or within states exploded or festered. Simultaneous inflation and stagnation battered the world economy. The United States, uncontested world economic leader from 1945 to the 1970s, gradually ceased to lead. And slow economic growth diminished the two superpowers relative to nimbler long-term contenders for superpower status: Japan, Europe, and ultimately China.

In the realm of knowledge, the last half of the century was a period of staggering advance and growing bewilderment about the foundations and purposes of science and scholarship. The geometric expansion of human knowledge brought fragmentation; no single intellect could fully grasp more than a small range of subjects. The gap between high and popular culture inherited from the late nineteenth century further expanded, just as the West's popular culture swept the non-Western world with tides of unprecedented intensity. In this disoriented condition, with world population expanding almost asymptotically, the world prepared to meet the third millennium of the Western era.

THE COLLAPSE OF DÉTENTE, 1975–80

Détente was almost stillborn. Its centerpiece, the SALT I treaty of May 1972, soon attracted criticism as an "unequal treaty" that locked in Soviet nuclear superiority, especially after the Soviet Union developed multiple warhead (MIRV) missiles with unexpected speed. Even nuclear "parity" with the Soviet Union deprived the European and Asian allies of the United States of their traditional strategic "umbrella" against Soviet ground superiority. Few in Europe now expected Washington to risk incineration to defend Hamburg or even Bonn against Soviet armor.

Soon after SALT I the "correlation of forces" tipped further in Moscow's favor. The 1973 Yom Kippur War and Arab oil embargo revealed western Europe's pusillanimity; Nixon self-destructed; Congress turned on the "imperial presidency" and sought to reduce the executive branch to impotence; North Vietnam's final victory in April 1975 suggested that the United States was paralyzed. Simultaneously, major opportunities opened for the Soviet Union in both Europe and Africa.

The April 1974 Portuguese military revolution had a strong Marxist flavor. Many in Portugal's officer corps had sought to understand their enemies in Africa through the study of Marxism-Leninism, and had returned converted. They joined with Portugal's small but ruthlessly Stalinist Communist party in turning the revolution toward the creation of a "People's Republic." The Soviet Union supplied money and advice. But in Portugal the "salami tactics" that had prevailed in eastern Europe ultimately failed, for lack of Red Army backing. Portugal's Socialist party won the 1975 elections with aid from western Europe and the United States. Then it mobilized supporters in the military and consolidated Portugal's first parliamentary democracy.

In Africa, the Soviets entered close relations with newly independent Mozambique. But it was in Angola that they most decisively crossed the "Yalta line." When Portugal departed in November 1975, Soviet aircraft, logistical support, and rubles delivered 12,000 Cuban troops to aid the Marxist-Leninist MPLA ("Popular Movement for the Liberation of Angola") against rivals that enjoyed U.S., Zairean, Chinese, and South African backing. The MPLA established itself as the internationally recognized government of Angola; the U.S. Congress cut off support to the non-Communist guerrillas. But the intervention of the Soviet Union's Cuban "Gurkhas" (as a liberal Democratic Senator described them) did not end the war. The guerrillas of UNITA ("National Union for the Total Independence of Angola") fought on into the 1980s with South African and ultimately U.S. aid. Cuba in response raised its commitment to as many as 50,000 troops and advisers.

Further north, the Soviet Union opened other bridgeheads into the "Third World." It consolidated its foothold at Aden, cemented a close relationship with Somalia by acquiring a base at Berbera, and looked with favor on the approaches of Somalia's rival, Mengistu Haile Mariam of Ethiopia. In 1977–78, Mengistu received over $1 billion in Soviet arms, Soviet and Cuban advisers, and a Cuban armored brigade under the command of the former deputy commander-in-chief of Soviet ground forces. Cubans and Soviets won a war in the Ogaden desert against Mengistu's Somali neighbors, who subsequently gravitated toward the United States. Mengistu failed to crush resistance in Eritrea but at least held Eritrea's cities. After further

On loan to the Soviet Union: Cuban infantry in Angola, 1976.

purges and amid general famine, Mengistu in 1987 proclaimed a Communist "People's Democratic Republic of Ethiopia."

Rapid growth of Brezhnev's navy, which filled out a base network from Cuba to Cam Ranh Bay in Vietnam, complemented disquieting signs of Soviet activism. Most alarming of all was the swift buildup of Soviet conventional and nuclear forces aimed at western Europe. The most important decision of Leonid Brezhnev's long tenure as Soviet leader (1964–82) was to raise the percentage of Soviet GNP spent on the military from roughly 10 percent in 1965 to between 20 and 25 percent by the late 1970s—figures that approximated those of Nazi Germany in 1938–39. On top of its numerical advantage of 2 to 1 or better in deployed divisions, main battle tanks, and artillery, the Soviet Union began to catch up with the West in the sophistication of its armored fighting vehicles, aircraft, and electronics. Détente helped. It allowed the Soviet Union to procure Western high technology openly as well as clandestinely. It encouraged Western bankers and governments to extend lavish credits to the Soviet Union and its satellites. Those credits in essence subsidized Brezhnev's armaments.

In the nuclear arena, the rapid modernization of Soviet strategic forces proceeded within the limits of SALT I. In 1974 Kissinger and Ford signed an agreement with Brezhnev at Vladivostok on the framework for negotiating a SALT II treaty. Then revulsion against Watergate swept the Republicans from office in the 1976 presidential election. Ford's successor, James E. ("Jimmy") Carter, peanut farmer and man of the people, initially shocked the Soviets with a proposal to depart from the Vladivostok framework by *reducing* rather than simply limiting the superpower strategic arsenals. He also irritated the Kremlin mightily by initiating a worldwide crusade for "human rights" that included the rights of Soviet dissidents and Jews. Moscow

Carter and Brezhnev in Vienna for the signing of SALT II, June 1979.

found too late that others took seriously the promises it had made in the 1975 Helsinki treaty. Arms negotiations nevertheless eventually resumed on the old basis; in June 1979 Carter and Brezhnev signed a SALT II Treaty at Vienna. It was apparently less one-sided than SALT I: the SALT II limit of 2,250 intercontinental delivery systems applied equally to both sides. But SALT II still preserved a major Soviet advantage, the 308 massive ten-warhead SS-18 missiles that in theory could by themselves destroy the entire U.S. land-based missile force.

And in theater nuclear forces, which SALT II did not touch, the imbalance was far worse. From 1978 onward the Soviet Union had deployed an entirely new class of intermediate-range ballistic missiles, the three-warhead SS-20. These truck-mounted behemoths were easily hidden, reasonably accurate, and could hit Iceland, Portugal, Japan, and China from deep within the USSR. They also could fire with a minimum of preparation, a valuable quality if Soviet commanders, as their doctrine dictated, should seek to launch a preemptive attack. By 1979 the Soviet Union

The struggle for Afghanistan: the Red Army (above) against the Afghan resistance (below).

dium-range nuclear missiles that would be entirely separate from the U.S. intercontinental arsenal. In theory, the new weapons—464 ground-launched cruise missiles and 108 Pershing II medium-range ballistic missiles—would deter Soviet nuclear or conventional threats. They would also allow Europe to retaliate against SS-20 strikes without necessarily provoking escalation into all-out thermonuclear war. The United States simultaneously offered to negotiate with Moscow a balanced and verifiable agreement limiting all theater nuclear weapons.

That offer did not interest Brezhnev. The Soviets knew that ratification of SALT II was in increasing difficulty in the U.S. Senate, and apparently judged that Carter's embarrassment in Iran after November 1979 (see p. 1052) would paralyze the United States. Washington could thus wield neither carrot nor stick; Moscow saw little reason to resist temptation. On December 27, 1979, KGB commandos and Soviet paratroops descended on Kabul, the capital of Afghanistan, while up to 100,000 Soviet troops rumbled across the Afghan borders.

had deployed 120 SS-20s and no limit appeared in sight; NATO had nothing even remotely similar.

At that point the Europeans reluctantly responded under the leadership of Willy Brandt's successor, the SPD's irascible "Iron Chancellor," Helmut Schmidt. In December 1979 the NATO powers requested the deployment in western Europe of a force of U.S. me-

Afghanistan and the Persian Gulf

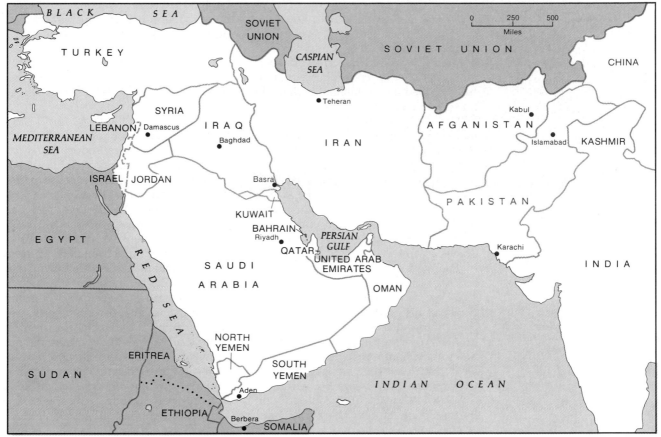

That latest and most violent expansion of Soviet power, like its predecessors, was an outgrowth of events not entirely of Moscow's making. In 1978 a Marxist-Leninist Afghan party, the "Democratic People's Party of Afghanistan" (DPPA), had overthrown the five-year-old Afghan republic. That regime had already maintained close relations with the Soviet Union; its DPPA successor invited thousands of additional Soviet advisers and provoked the independent-minded and devoutly Islamic Afghan tribes with talk of secularism and land "reform." By spring 1979 a powerful insurgency was underway; it drew on Afghanistan's proud nineteenth-century tradition of ferocious resistance to both Britain and Russia. A factional struggle within the DPPA replaced its original leader with Hafizullah Amin, a blood-thirsty figure whom Moscow regarded as untrustworthy.

That development and the spreading revolt apparently helped provoke the drastic measures of December 1979: a KGB assassination of Amin and Red Army occupation of Afghanistan. Moscow's new man, Babrak Karmal, had no more luck in dominating the countryside than his predecessors. Unlike the United States in Vietnam, the Soviet Union had to make do with an auxiliary army of a mere 30,000 Afghans, a force so unreliable that it normally fought only with Soviet tanks watching it from the rear. Despite initial disappointments, the Soviets soon revealed that they saw other vistas beyond Afghanistan itself. At Shindand in southwestern Afghanistan they built an immense air base that threatened Iran and the Gulf.

To make good that threat, however, the Soviet Union still had to pacify Afghanistan. Remorseless artillery and air bombardments and numerous deliberate massacres of civilians by ground troops killed over a million Afghans in a few years, and pushed perhaps 5 million of Afghanistan's 16 million inhabitants over the southern borders into Pakistan and Iran. Air-dropped Soviet mines—some camouflaged to resemble toys—maimed guerrillas and civilians alike. But the Afghans, thanks in part to CIA aid through Pakistan that eventually included advanced antiaircraft missiles, gradually whittled down the Soviet advantage.

The West showed less fortitude than the Afghans. Carter indeed reacted. In 1977 he had denounced the foreign policy of his predecessors for its allegedly "inordinate fear of Communism"; he now confessed that the Kabul coup had taught him more about Soviet policy in a few days than he had learned in the previous three years. He withdrew the SALT II Treaty from consideration by the Senate; it now stood no chance of ratification, although in general both powers continued to observe its limits. He slapped an embargo on the grain sales to the Soviet Union that had flourished with détente. He announced a boycott of the 1980 Moscow Summer Olympics. Above all, on January 23, 1980, he sought to deter further Soviet expansion by announcing a "Carter Doctrine"—any attempt "by any outside force to gain control of the Persian Gulf region will be regarded as an assault on the vital interests of the U.S.A., and such assault will be repelled by any means necessary, including military force."

Both Europe and the U.S. farm voter recoiled in horror from Carter. Canada and Argentina supplied the Soviet Union with the grain it required to make good yet another of its thumping crop failures. Europe and especially West Germany sought to preserve their new-found ties to the Soviets and to

ignore the Afghans, inconvenient inhabitants of a far away country. Superpower détente had nevertheless died on the road to Kabul.

WAR AND PEACE IN ASIA

The Third Indochina War

North Vietnam's conquest of the South in March–April 1975 produced predictable results. Hundreds of thousands of Saigon adherents disappeared into "re-education camps." There many thousands died. Hanoi abolished what was left of the "National Liberation Front" in 1976 and boasted that its world-famous "Front" had been nothing but a front. Northern cadres ruled from "Ho Chi Minh City." Northern bureaucrats sought to stamp the South's economy into the same Stalinist mold as that of the North.

In Cambodia, the Khmer Rouge showed themselves even more implacable than their North Vietnamese patrons. The Khmer Rouge leaders, Pol Pot (born Saloth Sar), Ieng Sary, and Khieu Samphan had imbibed their Maoism at Left Bank cafés while studying in Paris in the 1940s and 1950s. There they acquired a utopian goal of a kind common among uprooted intellectuals: the forging of a unique "Cambodian Road to Socialism" through the eradication of the old society and the severance of all ties between Cambodia and the outside world.

Pol Pot and his associates followed that road with pitiless consistency once they took over Cambodia in the wake of North Vietnam's victory. In a few days in April 1975 they forcibly emptied Phnom Penh, a capital city containing perhaps 3 million inhabitants and refugees; many starved. The teenage peasant zealots of the Khmer Rouge sought out and killed all Cambodians with an education and anyone whose adherence to the collectivized and "ruralized" new order seemed less than total. Cambodia's population had stood in 1970 at perhaps 8 million. By

1980 the population of "Democratic Kampuchea" had fallen to between 5.5 and 6.5 million. Perhaps 750,000 of the 1.5 to 2.5 million missing people had fled across the minefields to Thailand; the rest had died.

World opinion showed its characteristic impotence. Many in the West at first denied the evidence of torture, massacre, and starvation brought by refugees, or blamed the United States—rather than North Vietnam—for hav-having involved Cambodia in war and thus opened the road for Pol Pot. The Khmer Rouge practice of "autogenocide" played no part in their downfall; what destroyed Pol Pot and his associates was their fierce nationalist resentment against their former patrons in Hanoi. In 1977 the Khmer Rouge clashed with Vietnamese troops and shelled Vietnamese villages along the Cambodia-Vietnam border; division-size battles followed. In December 1978 over 100,000 Vietnamese troops with both Soviet and captured U.S. armor and aircraft launched a *Blitzkrieg*

Bones of victims of the Khmer Rouge, Tonle Bati, Takeo Province, Cambodia.

that crushed the Khmer Rouge armies and occupied Cambodia.

That "Third Indochina War" did not remain entirely isolated. China had long looked askance on Hanoi's close ties with Moscow. Hanoi reciprocated. In 1978 it began the expulsion of Vietnam's 900,000 to 1.2 million overseas Chinese. That brutal measure and the

Vietnamese "boat people" after being refused permission to land in Malaysia (1979).

invasion of Cambodia prompted a brief Chinese attack on North Vietnam in February–March 1979. China's inexperienced army did badly and Hanoi's friends in Moscow apparently cautioned Beijing against pressing the attack. Vietnam successfully imposed a colonial regime on Cambodia, complete with hundreds of thousands of Vietnamese settlers. Up to 200,000 Vietnamese troops stayed on indefinitely to fight Khmer Rouge and anti-Communist Cambodian guerrillas. And Moscow fastened on Vietnam itself a semicolonial relationship, with advisers, bases, and 60,000 or more Vietnamese deported to Siberia to do manual labor.

Vietnam itself languished economically except for the black markets of the South; the collectivised North suffered near-famine in 1988. In the decade after 1975, 1 to 1.5 million "boat people" risked death from drowning or Thai pirates rather than remain. At first the refugees were largely ethnic Chinese or Saigon adherents; they soon included disillusioned NLF officials and innumerable ordinary Vietnamese. Hanoi's victory imposed on Indochina endless misery and yet another endless war.

"We can never again undertake . . . radical leftist nonsense": Hu Yaobang (left) and Deng Xiaoping, 1983.

The "De-Maoization" of China

Beijing (Peking) traveled a different road from either Hanoi or Moscow. From 1971 to 1976 the Maoist radicals around Jiang Qing (Chiang Ch'ing), Mao's wife, gradually lost influence. Marshall Lin Biao (Lin Piao), Mao's chief support in the army, mysteriously died in 1971 amid rumors he had attempted a coup. In 1973, Deng Xiaoping (Teng Hsiao-P'ing), the most canny of the Party leaders who had attempted to cage Mao in the early 1960s, achieved rehabilitation. Zhou Enlai (Chou En-lai), who had conducted the delicate negotiations with Kissinger and Nixon, appeared dominant as Mao's health and attention span declined. But in January 1976, Zhou died before Mao. Spontaneous demonstrations of grief by hundreds of thousands of ordinary Chinese provoked Jiang Qing and her radical "Gang of Four" to strike before they lost control. They again disgraced Deng Xiaoping; then Mao died in September 1976 and the radicals lost their principal support. Mao's designated successor was Hua Guofeng (Hua Kuo-feng), a Maoist but no radical. When Hua discredited himself with yet another overambitious program to modernize China, opponents both within the Party and outside it attacked.

With the apparent connivance of Hua's opponents, urban intellectuals posted slogans and essays on a "Democracy Wall" in Beijing. From within the Party, Deng Xiaoping exploited that unrest to oust Hua in 1980–81. In the saddle at last at the age of 76, Deng purged Maoist extremists and suppressed democratic dissidents impartially. He also pressed a radical "de-Maoization" of China's economy. Peasants received the right to sell surpluses from their private plots in free markets. Factory managers gained a measure of freedom from central planning. Opposite Hong Kong, "free enterprise zones" arose to attract foreign investors. The industries of Shanghai prospered mightily. China's GNP growth after 1981 surged to over 10 percent per year.

The Party relaxed its grip on the economy with notable reluctance. It failed to relax politically. Deng's chosen successor, Hu Yaobang (Hu Yao-pang), raised expectations among intellectuals. He denounced Mao for having ruled China as a "feudal-monarchist state" and insisted "that from now on we cannot afford to mess things up, we can never again undertake such radical leftist nonsense as 'take class struggle as the key link' and 'better to have socialist weeds than capitalist seedlings.' We can never again afford internal chaos, or we will cause our own collapse and poverty." The Beijing *People's Daily* made the startling announcement that "if we continue to use certain Marxist principles, our historic development will surely be impaired."

In December 1986 the students of China took the new leadership at its word, and demonstrated massively for democratic freedoms. The police gradually contained the demonstrations. Deng sacrificed Hu Yaobang, while Party zealots campaigned against the contagion of "bourgeois liberalism." But Deng nevertheless held to his economic policies, despite inflation and other pains of rapid growth. He also supervised an orderly transfer of power in the middle ranks of the Party and army from the veterans of the "Long March" of the 1930s to a younger and perhaps less dogmatic generation. But whether economic revolution can in the long run coexist with Party autocracy remains to be seen.

Japan Triumphant

While the United States floundered in Indochina, Japan became the "workshop of Asia." Its gross national product swelled from roughly 13 percent of that of the United States in 1965 to 34 percent in 1985. Its economic structure, thanks to Japan's narrow, poor, and mountainous land, rested overwhelmingly on industry. With almost no oil, few minerals, and a pampered uncom-

---

Democracy Wall: A Chinese Dissident Speaks   1978

Wei Jingsheng was the most daring of those who wrote on the wall in Beijing; he is rumored to have recently died in prison. His 1978 essay, "Democracy, the Fifth Modernization," shows the bitterness of the generation that suffered the full force of Mao's "Great Proletarian Cultural Revolution:"

Today, it is perfectly irrelevant to try to determine the balance account of Mao Zedong's achievements and mistakes. . . . The question which the people should now be asking is this: without Mao Zedong's personal despotism, could China ever have fallen as low as we see her today? Or are we to believe that Chinese people are stupid, or lazy, or devoid of any desire to improve their lot? We know very well that this is not the case. Then what happened? The answer is obvious: the Chinese have taken a path they should never have entered; if they followed it, it is because a despot, who knew how shrewdly to peddle his trash, simply took them for a ride. . . .

German fascism, of stinking memory, was actually called "national socialism." It too was led by a tyrant; it too told the people to tighten their belts; it too deceived the people, assuring them: "You are a great nation!" Above all, it too suppressed basic democracy, because it clearly saw that democracy was for it the greatest danger, the most frightful enemy. Stalin and Hitler could shake hands and sign the famous German-Soviet pact, and on this basis the German and Russian peoples were condemned to suffer slavery and misery. Do we, too, need to continue suffering such slavery and misery? If we wish to break away from it, there is only one way: democracy. In other words, if we want to modernize our economy and science and defense and the like, we must first modernize our people.

From Simon Leys, *The Chairman's New Clothes: Mao and the Cultural Revolution* (London: Allison and Busby Limited, 1981), pp. 260–61.

---

petitive agriculture, Japan inevitably concentrated investment in its factories. As in the United States, automobiles and electrical devices led the way. Unlike the industries of the United States, those of Japan immediately targeted export markets from the United States to Southeast Asia to Europe; to import food and oil, Japan had to export. By the mid-1970s Japan had conquered the U.S. market for television sets and was making inroads in automobiles. By the early 1980s even manufacturers of the United States' most innovative product, the computer chip, were complaining of "unfair" Japanese competition; Europe reacted with similar hostility.

Despite such howls of xenophobic protest, Japanese success was not the product of chicanery. It was the result of 30 years of relentless hard work and attention to detail by Japanese management and by Japan's highly educated and dedicated work force. And Japan, despite its transformation in 1983–86 into the world's greatest creditor—displacing the United States from the position it had occupied since 1914–18—had great vulnerabilities. So great was its dependence on foreign trade that a downturn on the scale of 1929 and after could lay its society waste. Thanks to the pacifist constitution that MacArthur had imposed in 1947 Japan also remained virtually disarmed, unable to defend either itself, its oil lines to the Persian Gulf, or the vast East Asian "co-prosperity sphere" it had at last acquired under U.S. protection. Nor did its neighbors want it rearmed. Beijing, which in 1978 signed a "Peace and Friendship Treaty" with Tokyo directed against Moscow's "hegemonism" and military buildup in Northeast Asia, repeatedly reminded its Japanese partner of the immense massacres that had attended Japan's attempt to conquer China in 1937–45.

Under Yasuhiro Nakasone, who discharged the office of Japanese prime minister with more than usual forcefulness from 1982 to 1987, Japan began to take a role in world economic councils befitting its new status. It grudgingly committed itself to opening its domestic markets, although the absurd restrictions that forced the Japanese consumer to pay over five times the world market price for rice remained in place. It pledged to loosen up by consuming and importing more and saving and exporting less. It hesitantly broke the 1 percent of GNP ceiling on military spending to which it had adhered since the 1950s. Japan's new position as the world's second largest economy, behind the United States but probably ahead of a humiliated Soviet Union, posed the question of how much longer it would or could remain a military-political pygmy.

WESTERN EUROPE IN SEARCH OF ITSELF

Western Europe, although it grew mightily, likewise failed to fill the world role to which its economic power entitled it. The superpower struggle had dwarfed and repressed Europe's nationalisms, but they retained enough vitality to prevent Europe from acting as a unit. Britain attempted to maintain its "special relationship" with its wartime ally, the United States, although it finally joined the European Common Market (EEC) in 1973. France under de Gaulle cemented a "Paris-Bonn axis" designed to keep the West Germans from drifting off eastwards in search of national reunification, and took a high independent line against the United States. As the Soviets achieved nuclear "parity," de Gaulle supplemented the weakened American "umbrella" over western Europe with a French bomber and nuclear missile *force de frappe* under France's sole control. In 1966–67 he withdrew with much fanfare from NATO's combined military command and closed U.S. logistical bases in France. That belated revenge for America's sabotage of the 1956 Suez landing deprived NATO's West German front line of vital lines of communications. France remained in formal terms a NATO member, but its refusal to coordinate war planning and force structure with its allies made it doubtful that French help would reach the battlefield in time if the Soviets attacked. Finally, West Germany under Willy Brandt (1966/69–74) and Helmut Schmidt (1974–82) pursued *Ostpolitik* toward East Germany and the Soviet Union so assiduously that Paris and even Washington began to fear secretly for Bonn's long-term loyalty to the Western alliance.

The EEC rarely rose above indecorous squabbles over budgets and its bloated subsidies to its farmers. It failed even in its initial economic goal, the elimination of trade barriers between member states and the creation of a European market that would give the continent's industries the economies of scale needed to rival the United States. (Bold steps in that direction are scheduled for the 1990s, and transnational satellite television advertising may yet create a true European market where governments have so far failed.)

In the 1973–75 oil crisis, the EEC states acted with astounding disunity. Each nation hastened to make a separate peace with OPEC, whereas a coordinated EEC-USA-Japan policy of joint oil buying and rewards and punishments might have cracked the oil cartel. And détente also opened the coffers of western Europe to the Soviet Union. It precipitated a rush to sell modern industrial plants—some with military uses—to the Soviet bloc and to make western Europe dependent on the lavish supplies of cheap Siberian natural gas that Moscow happily offered.

The end of superpower détente naturally came as a shock. The combination of direct Soviet aggression against Afghanistan and NATO's decision to deploy U.S. missiles to counter Moscow's ever-increasing force of SS-20s led to a wave of trepidation more intense than anything since the Korean War. Much of European opinion by now so feared Moscow that it concentrated its protests against the United States. The American missiles, the protesters announced, were designed to provoke a war that would incinerate Europeans but not Americans.

Protest was strongest in West Germany. There a leftist environmentalist party, the "Greens," offered the children of affluence a vision of an "alternative" anticapitalist future. The other Green appeal was a fierce German nationalism directed primarily against

alleged U.S.—rather than Soviet—"colonization" of divided Germany. The protesters proclaimed above all the nobility of fear: *"Ich habe Angst"* ("I am afraid") was a favorite slogan. Protest failed. Elections in 1983 confirmed the British Conservatives in office and in West Germany gave victory to the CDU/CSU, which favored deployment. When the missiles began arriving in 1983–84 the world did not end as the protesters had predicted. Protest largely ended instead. But the Green and left-SPD vision of a magically denuclearized Europe redeemed through German reunification continued to exert a powerful destabilizing pull.

Two additional factors further intensified tension in western Europe after 1979. Carter, crippled by his mishandling of revolutionary Iran (see p. 1052), lost the 1980 presidential election to a former film actor, Ronald Reagan. Most Europeans perceived Reagan as a vague and aging Hollywood "cowboy" with an itch to obliterate both Europe and what Reagan imprudently referred to as Moscow's "Evil Empire." And that empire simultaneously suffered yet another of its periodic crises.

Of all the satellites, Poland had plunged most deeply into debt during détente. Misconceived industrial investments and rising inflation struck at the living standards of Poland's downtrodden workers, whose riots had toppled Gomulka in 1970 as they had toppled his predecessor in 1956. In summer 1980 Polish workers at Gdansk—once known as Danzig—went on strike, a class struggle against a Marxist-Leninist state. Poland's intellectuals and the Catholic Church, the historic vehicle of Polish nationalism, backed the strike. Against all precedent the workers won the right to replace the Party-run sham unions with an independent national trade union, *Solidarnosc* ("Solidarity"). The demoralized Polish Communist Party lost control even of the press, and began to disintegrate. The largest and most strategically vital of all the satellites appeared about to turn against Moscow, with unforeseeable repercussions in East Germany, Czechoslovakia, and Hungary.

Brezhnev and his associates found the answer in a Polish general. Moscow placed the Polish Communist Party in receivership in the hands of Wojciech Jaruzelski, a prim and ruthless military figure with a long record of absolute obedience. In December 1981 Jaruzelski crushed Solidarity with riot police and army, while Soviet tank forces in East Germany, Poland, and European Russia prepared to back him up. Jaruzelski placed the Polish people before a grim choice: acceptance of his dictatorship, or a Soviet intervention that would endanger national survival. Solidarity persisted underground and Polish workers henceforth scarcely even pretended to work, but Jaruzelski and Moscow had won.

Angst and economic interest prevented any concerted Western reaction such as a cutoff of credit to the Soviet bloc. Bonn found the Polish affair an embarrassment to West Germany's increasingly close trading ties to the Soviet Union; many West Germans secretly despised all Poles and saw little reason to suffer for Gdansk. As Jaruzelski's coup unfolded, Helmut Schmidt met happily with Erich Honecker, Ulbricht's successor as leader of East Germany, and sent birthday greetings to Brezhnev. France and Britain took a less benign view of Brezhnev's actions. But no unified Western or even European policy emerged; Reagan's trade sanctions against the Soviet Union and Poland were a solitary gesture.

And Europe's disunity persisted. In April 1982 the Argentine generals, in an act of folly, invaded the British-inhabited Falkland Islands without provocation. The EEC initially balked when Margaret Thatcher, the formidable Conservative prime minister of Britain, requested economic sanctions against Argentina. Europe only swung behind Britain once it became clear that Thatcher—a prime minister from the

mold of Pitt, Disraeli, and Churchill—was determined to reconquer the islands. (That feat the British armed forces swiftly and elegantly accomplished despite severe logistical and operational constraints; Argentine officers normally spent their careers torturing suspects in basements rather than training for war.) In the Middle East, European or Western unity likewise rarely prevailed except in the negative sense that European governments ritually carped at Israel in order to maintain their own flow of oil.

All except Thatcher deplored Reagan's April 1986 air strikes—in response to a particularly bloody series of terrorist attacks (see p. 1055)—against Qaddafi's Libya. France even refused overflight rights for U.S. aircraft. And when in 1987 the United States deployed large naval forces to maintain order along Europe's oil lines in the Persian Gulf, the allies initially held back. Europe's economic power, like that of Japan, far outweighed its ability or will to bring power to bear.

ISLAMIC WORLD REVOLUTION AND ENDLESS WAR

In the Middle East a brief relaxation followed the Yom Kippur War of October 1973. Anwar Sadat of Egypt definitively cast his lot with the United States in 1976. In 1977 he broke with all precedent and flew to Jerusalem in search of peace with Israel; Egypt was war-weary and in dire economic straits. At a 1978 summit meeting at Camp David near Washington, Carter pushed Israel's master of evasion, Menachem Begin, into a peace agreement underwritten with lavish U.S. aid for both Egypt and Israel. In March 1979 Egypt and Israel signed a treaty that ended 30 years of war. The Arab League in reply boycotted Egypt, the largest Arab state. Despite Sadat's assassination by Islamic militants in October 1981, Israel returned the last slice of Sinai to Egypt in 1982. One border in the Middle East was provisionally at peace. Simultaneously a new phase of the "Eastern Question," one in which Moslems fought one another rather than Israel, was opening.

"Death to America": Revolution in Iran

Sadat succumbed to a widespread upsurge of religious militance of which he himself had provided the most trenchant summary: "This is not Islam, this is madness." The source of that "madness" was twofold: the Islamic world's impotence in the face of nineteenth- and twentieth-century Western power, and the failure of the secular states of the Middle East, states such as Egypt, to catch up with the West or even defeat the Jewish state, the West's Middle Eastern outpost. The trigger of that "madness" was the 1978–79 revolution that convulsed Iran.

Shah Mohammad Reza Pahlavi, "King of Kings" and ruler of Iran from 1941 to 1979, was a man of large ambitions. After a CIA-sponsored return in 1953 to the throne from which anti-Western nationalists had briefly displaced him, he sought to use Iran's oil wealth to bring his subjects by forced marches into the twentieth century. Land reform, secular education, and the partial emancipation of women particularly outraged the powerful landowning Shi'ite clergy. In 1963 one of the clergy's most influential figures, the Ayatollah Ruhollah Khomeini of the holy city of Qum, condemned the Shah and all his works. Khomeini went first to jail and then into exile. There he ceaselessly reviled the Shah as an "unclean" tool of the "satanic" West.

The Shah for his part relied increasingly on his secret police, the dreaded SAVAK. He faced the same dilemma as other "modernizing" autocrats. The introduction of Western ideas and economic practices soon created an intelligentsia that rejected the autocracy—just as those same ideas and reforms shrank or alienated the traditional sectors of society on which the autocracy

Sadat, Carter, and Begin clasp hands at the signing of the Israeli-Egyptian peace treaty, March 26, 1979.

rested. The Shah nevertheless pressed on. With Kissinger's encouragement he took over from Britain the role of lord of the Gulf after 1971. That year he also sponsored an immense celebration at Persepolis of the 2,500th anniversary of the Persian empire, which he evidently hoped to recreate. In 1973–74 he led OPEC's assault on the world economy, and used Iran's fabulous oil profits to buy the latest in tanks, ships, and aircraft from the United States and Europe.

Crowds greet the Ayatollah Khomeini upon his return from exile to Tehran, February 1979.

But the Shah failed to spread the profits from the oil boom widely enough to defuse the resentments of his urban lower classes. His apparent sponsorship of the invasion of Iran by European and U.S. goods and customs, from alcohol to "licentious" advertising to women in tailored blue jeans, aroused outrage among the devout. The intelligentsia deplored his refusal to concede parliamentary government. In January 1978 the clergy led riots at Qum against the regime. Disorder spread across all Iran. The Shah, ill with cancer and irresolute, failed to use the army vigorously while his conscript soldiers still remained loyal. In the Teheran riots of September 1978 the army began to crack. Khomeini's unarmed zealots taunted the troops to make them martyrs; the troops deserted or shot sergeants and officers. The Shah's nerve shattered along with a cherished illusion—that his people loved him. In January 1979 he fled.

Khomeini arrived from Paris—a stern medieval figure alighting from a jumbo jet—to sweep a feeble provisional government from office. He soon purged the officer corps and established a form of government never before seen, a theocratic "Islamic Republic" under the rule of Shi'ite clergy. Student militants, revolutionary committees, "Revolutionary Guards," and the shaven-headed zealots of the Hezbollah ("the Party of God") enforced political conformity. They also ruthlessly reimposed Islamic dress on Iran's women. Teheran crowds enthusiastically chanting "Death to America" filled Western television screens. When Carter allowed the dying Shah to visit New York in October 1979 for cancer treatment, Khomeini's "Islamic students" violated the customary niceties observed between states, and seized the U.S. embassy in Teheran and its staff of over 50.

Khomeini may not have originated the embassy coup, but he swiftly exploited it. What better way to mobilize domestic support, dramatize the Islamic Revolution abroad, and humiliate the "Great Satan" America than to hold its diplomats hostage? The Iranians had learned from North Vietnam, which had tied American negotiators in knots over the release of U.S. prisoners. The American television networks rose to the occasion. Soon each evening news broadcast began with an announcement of the number of days the hostages had been imprisoned.

That placed intolerable pressure on Carter in an election year. He warned Iran that harm to the hostages would have serious though unspecified consequences. He also failed to set a deadline for their release. Iran's position between the Soviet Union and the Gulf deterred him from military action, lest Moscow use U.S. intervention as a pretext to expand its Afghan bridgehead toward the warm waters. In April 1980 Carter launched an ineptly planned rescue mission that broke down in the Iranian desert; fierce interservice rivalry and Carter's eccentric insistence on the *minimum* use of force had made failure likely. The hostage crisis decided the 1980 election. Reagan won by

Khomeini: Islamic World Revolution

Holy war means the conquest of all non-Moslem territories. War will perhaps be declared after the formation of an Islamic government worthy of the name. . . . It will then be the duty of all adult ablebodied men to volunteer for this war of conquest whose final goal is to make Koranic law supreme from one end of the earth to the other. But the entire world should know that the universal supremacy of Islam [will] differ considerably from the hegemony of other conquerors. . . .

To ensure the unity of the Moslem nation, to liberate the Moslem homeland from the domination or influence of the imperialists, we have no alternative but to form a truly Islamic government and to take all possible steps to overthrow the other tyrannical pseudo-Islamic governments put in place by the foreigner, and having attained that goal, to install *the* universal Islamic government.

From Ayatollah Khomeini, *Principes politiques, philosophiques, sociaux et religieux* (Paris, Éditions Libres-Hallier, 1979), pp. 22, 28.

a landslide in part because he promised stern action. Iran packed the hostages onto an Air France jet as the new president took the oath of office in January 1981.

The Gulf War

By then Khomeini had other concerns than the "great Satan." After seizing power he repeatedly called for Islamic upheavals throughout the Middle East. Among his preferred targets was Saddam Hussein, Sunni ruler of the Shi'ite majority of neighboring Iraq. The Iraqi regime, apparently thinking that Iran's military power had disintegrated in revolutionary chaos, replied to Khomeini's threats with an armored thrust at Iran's oilfields in September 1980. Iran's 3 to 1 advantage in population soon began to tell. This was no war of maneuver between sophisticated opponents, but a tropical Somme 1916, a demolition derby of military ineptitude.

In early 1982 Iraq lost the oilfields. By 1985–86 it was close to losing Basra, its second city after Baghdad. Iranian "Revolutionary Guards," many of them adolescents with plastic "keys to Paradise" furnished by the clergy in their knapsacks, pressed the attack at immense cost. "Fountains of blood" ran red at Teheran cemeteries in macabre commemoration of the fallen. Endless war, an "Islamic" successor to SAVAK, and mass executions silenced opponents and doubters.

Iraq responded to defeat by appealing to other Arab regimes for aid against the Persian Shi'ite menace. If Iraq foundered, Kuwait and Saudi Arabia might follow. Iran secured clandestine assistance from Israel, which perhaps mistakenly considered Saddam Hussein a worse threat than Khomeini. Israel also struck the only serious blow in history against the proliferation of nuclear weapons when its F-16 fighter-bombers destroyed Iraq's French-built nuclear reactor in June 1981.

As Iran advanced, Iraq in desperation expanded the war by air and sea. It drenched Iranian troops and Kurdish villages with mustard gas, nerve gas, and hydrogen cyanide. Its air force struck at Iranian cities and at the oil exports that financed Iran's war. Iran in reply attacked international shipping bound for the ports of Iraq's Gulf allies and launched heavy missiles at Baghdad in the manner of Hitler's V-2 bombardment of London in 1944. Iraqi missiles in turn flattened entire blocks in Teheran and Qum. In 1987, after an Iraqi air attack gutted a U.S. Navy frigate by mistake, Washington responded to an appeal from Kuwait to escort its tankers. Britain, France, and Italy gradually committed or reinforced flotillas of their own. In April 1988 the Iranians imprudently challenged the U.S. fleet, and lost much of their navy in a flurry of U.S. cruise missiles. The Western flotillas hemmed Iran in, while Iraqi counter-offensives forced a bitterly resentful Khomeini to accept a ceasefire in July–August 1988. The war had cost up to 2.7 million dead and wounded.

The Agony of Lebanon

The Iranian revolution also enlivened events in Lebanon, where as mentioned in Chapter 35 a multicornered civil war had raged in 1975–76 between the private armies of Lebanon's principal communities, the Maronite Christians, the Sunni Moslems, the Shi'ite Moslems, the Druzes, and the Palestinians; Syrian intervention had imposed a troubled ceasefire. In April 1981 the civil war resumed in earnest. In May–June 1982 Palestinian bombardments of northern Israel and the shooting of Israel's ambassador in London furnished Israel the occasion for an attempt to stamp out the PLO in Lebanon. Israel's forces brushed Syria aside, evicted the PLO "state within a state" from Beirut, Lebanon's unhappy capital, and briefly installed a Maronite ally as president of Lebanon. His assassination by car-bomb in September 1982 provoked the Maronite militias, with the apparent approval of some in the Israeli command, to massacre up to 2,000 Palestinian civilians in the Sabra and Chatila refugee camps in West Beirut.

Israel withdrew from the Beirut area in 1983. Even before it left, Reagan sought to prop up the Maronite-dominated Lebanese central government with Marines in the manner of Eisenhower in 1958. The 1,600 Marines landed along with French paratroops and small British and Italian forces. They soon found themselves beleaguered by Syrian and Iranian-backed Shi'ite and Druze militias. Washington ordered naval and air bombardments of the Marines' tormentors, while entertaining a woolly-headed notion that U.S. forces were in Lebanon as "peace-keepers." Sloppy security by the Marines and the French led swiftly to disaster. In October 1983 suicide truck-bombs penetrated the Marine and French perimeters and killed 241 Marines and 58 French paratroopers. Washington fumed impotently, unable to identify the bombers; subsequently it shelled and bombed Shi'ite, Druze, and Syrian positions. Marines and allies withdrew sheepishly in February–March 1984.

That left the mastery of Lebanon to Syria, if it could conquer it. Damascus sought first to destroy all armed Palestinians not loyal to itself. Yasser Arafat, the chief political leader of the Palestinian movement, escaped with his life. Many of his followers perished. Syria then moved into Beirut itself amid all-out struggle between Christian and Moslem militias. While the Syrians mopped up the few remaining armed Palestinians, Shi'ite and Druze militias allied to Syria massacred Palestinian civilians in the refugee camps in the style of the Maronites in 1982.

Syria remained precariously in control of northern and central Lebanon, despite friction with Iranian-backed Shi'ite elements. Israel's forces, under constant car-bomb attack, withdrew in 1985 to a narrow "security zone" along Israel's northern border. The war— now as before largely a war of Arab against Arab—entered a static phase broken only by assassinations, car-

Yasser Arafat, durable leader of the PLO.

bombs, and the taking of Western hostages.

Terrorists on Television

The hostage-taking, which provisionally reached a peak in 1985–86, was only one aspect of a widespread phenomenon of the 1970s and 1980s: terrorism. The term, despite its baggage of emotion, has two commonsense meanings. Its first and oldest form is the assassination by revolutionaries of rulers or key officials. Its exponents have included the *Narodnaya Volya* plotters who killed Tsar Alexander II in 1881, the Bosnian Serb assassins of Archduke Francis Ferdinand at Sarajevo in 1914, and the middle-class urban guerrilla groups of the European student Left of the 1970s. Their purpose was to terrorize those in power, to weaken existing regimes by striking directly at the persons and authority of the rulers. The "propaganda of the deed" spread the gospel of revolution and might perhaps provoke the target regimes to indiscriminate reprisals that would undermine their legitimacy.

But by the late 1960s technology opened other possibilities, especially to groups like the PLO, whose "revolution by exile" was incapable of mounting a sustained guerrilla campaign inside Israel itself. Worldwide jet travel and instantaneous satellite television offered both soft targets and a new order of magnitude of potential publicity. Why attack the rulers or citizens of a target state? They were too well defended, especially if that state was Israel. Why not instead massacre citizens of other states, especially the Americans, whose government funded and supported Israel? The "cause" would thereby receive free worldwide television coverage; as Madison Avenue taught, there was no such thing as *bad* publicity. And in the "struggle for Palestine," Palestinian militants insisted, no bystanders were innocent.

Thus the "new terrorism," *indiscriminate violence for media effect*, was born. By definition, it was effective only against states with free presses and television networks, such as the industrial democracies. And Arafat's PLO and offshoots such as the "Popular Front for the Liberation of Palestine" were its most fervent practitioners. Until 1982 their finishing schools in Beirut and elsewhere trained terrorist cadres from the West German "Red Army Faction," the Japanese "Red Army," the Irish Republican Army, and a bizarre assortment of other groups. Some repaid the Palestinians; in 1972 Japanese Red Army terrorists killed 25 civilians at Lod airport in Israel.

The PLO's eviction from Beirut did not end Lebanon's role as terrorist world capital. The Syrians helped sponsor the Iranian-backed Lebanese Hezbollah ("the Party of God") that probably delivered the car-bombs to the Marines and the French. In 1985 Syria and the Libya of Muammar Qaddafi between them apparently promoted hijackings by Lebanese Shi'ites of a TWA flight and by Palestinians of an Italian cruise ship, the *Achille Lauro*. In both cases the hijackers singled out and killed Americans; the Palestinians pushed a Jewish American invalid overboard in his wheelchair. The U.S. networks, heedless of political consequences and intent only on "scooping" their rivals, provided instant interviews with the hijackers or their bosses. Attacks on U.S. and French civilians in western Europe accompanied the hijackings throughout 1985 and early 1986.

Finally, in April 1986, the Reagan administration bombed Libya in reprisal and barely missed Qaddafi himself. Most Europeans and some Americans disapproved. Many predicted an intensification of terrorist violence in response. Instead, Qaddafi suffered a nervous breakdown, soon reinforced by the inglorious rout of forces he had sent to conquer his southern neighbor, Chad. Syria sought to ingratiate itself with Washington. Washington's new approach produced a lull in Middle Eastern terrorism.

Terrorists on television: a U.S. airliner held hostage at Beirut airport, June 1985.

What it did not do was resolve the hostage issue. After 1983 numerous Americans and Europeans had disappeared in Lebanon and reappeared on videotapes delivered to Western news organizations, reading propaganda from Shi'ite captors and lamenting their governments' refusal to give in to terrorist demands. In 1985–86 Reagan sought with Israeli encouragement to ransom the captured Americans by secretly selling planeloads of anti-tank missiles to the terrorists' Iranian sponsors.

But 2,008 antitank missiles bought only two hostages. Reagan's aides realized too late that the crafty Iranians had "snookered" them (in the words of Reagan's chief of staff). A Lebanese magazine disclosed this "arms-for-hostages" deal in November 1986 and inaugurated a Watergate-style crisis in Washington complete with televised congressional hearings. It soon emerged that profits from the arms sale had gone to the Nicaraguan *"Contra"* rebels (see p. 1058) in apparent violation of a congressional ban. By default Reagan's advisers settled on a sound course: to ignore the hostages and thus deprive terrorists of any leverage over U.S. policy or incentive to take more hostages.

The Struggle for Israel

The turmoil that followed the Iranian Revolution and Lebanese war did not spare Israel itself. Intervention in Lebanon initially appeared a masterstroke that virtually destroyed the PLO. Then the long occupation of hostile southern Lebanon and the consequent attrition began to tell. A weary Menachem Begin retired in 1983. His eventual successors, an ill-assorted coalition of Israel's Right and Center, sought to cut losses by withdrawal. The Gulf War concentrated the energies of Arabs against Persians and of Sunni against Shi'ite; it appeared to give Israel a breathing space. But by 1987 Jerusalem had begun to ponder the possibility that the eventual victor might sweep away the few moderate and pro-Western regimes in the region, possibly including Sadat's successor in Egypt, Hosni Mubarak.

Worse still for Jerusalem, PLO defeat did not mean the end of Palestinian militance. Israel had from the beginning been a demographic time bomb. The several hundred thousand Palestinians who remained within Israel's borders in 1948–49 had a higher birth rate than the Jewish settlers. The subsequent spread under Israeli sponsorship of antibiotics and modern medical techniques further increased Palestinian fertility and decreased infant mortality. By the 1980s, the Arab population of Israel was twice as prolific as the Jewish population. And Israel acquired a further 1 million Arabs on the West Bank of the Jordan and in the Gaza Strip through the great victories of 1967. By the mid-1980s, 3.6 million Jews faced 2.1 million Arabs within the post-1967 borders of "greater Israel." Existing trends, if continued, will give the Arabs close to a majority by 2005. And rapid population growth increases the demographic weight of the young, the most easily aroused and least tolerant segment of any population.

The Palestinians showed little intention of waiting until 2005; they wanted Palestine—*all* of Palestine—now. In December 1987, the young of the occupied Gaza Strip took on Israel's police and army with rocks and fire bombs. "The Uprising" was a protest against Israel but also against the indifference of the Arab states, preoccupied with the Gulf War. The Israelis, initially badly outnumbered, replied with live ammunition and killed scores of demonstrators. Protest spread from Gaza to the West Bank. The Arabs within Israel's original 1948–49 borders had shown considerable loyalty to a Jewish state that had brought them prosperity; they now joined their fellow Arabs for the first time in political general strikes. Israel's conquest of Palestine had apparently united Palestinians as well as Jews. A no-quarter struggle between the Jewish state and the nationalist aspirations of the Palestinians had apparently begun.

CONFLICTS ON THE PERIPHERY

Besides wars in the Middle East, other struggles between or within small powers punctuated the 1980s. The two most serious, at least potentially, were those in South Africa and Central America.

The Struggle for Mastery in South Africa Resumed

The Boers had long suffered from the same demographic trends that threatened the Jewish state. But the Boer position was far worse than that of the Israelis. In 1951 less than 3 million whites had faced less than 10 million blacks and mixed-race citizens in South Africa. By the late 1980s that gap had widened to 5 million against 30 million. Projections suggest that whites will reach about 7 million in 2050, while blacks and mixed-race will ascend to almost 100 million.

But demography offered only chilling foreboding for the future. In the present, two waves of disturbances in the black townships in 1976 and 1984–

Israel in 1988

LEBANON

SYRIA

Haifa

Mediterranean Sea

Tel Aviv-Yafo

ISRAEL

Jordan River

WEST BANK

Jerusalem

Gaza

Dead Sea

JORDAN

EGYPT

Israeli-administered territory

Gulf of Aqaba

SAUDI ARABIA

87 served notice on the Boers that their adamant refusal to give rights to the black majority had generated ever-growing opposition. The Boer reply was to kill perhaps 3,000 and imprison as many as 25,000, including children. In the face of international pressure, the South African government of Pieter W. Botha also announced a variety of cosmetic changes to its system of racial domination, *Apartheid*. It sought with some success to play off its black opponents, the African National Congress and United Democratic Front, against tribal elements such as the armed Zulu movement *Inkatha*. The result was much bloodshed between blacks.

Pretoria also launched numerous raids into neighboring African "frontline" states, which South Africa dominated economically as well as militarily. Fighting with the Cubans in Angola continued sporadically. Internal unrest and external pressure failed to shake Boer control or cripple the economy, which rested on black labor. The exclusion of Western news cameras from the black townships in 1985–86 won the Boers an external breathing space. But the struggle for mastery between the "white tribe" and its subject populations continued, with potential for full-scale war in southern Africa.

"The Revolution Has No Frontiers": Central America

South of Mexico and north of Panama lie the three unhappy republics of Nicaragua, El Salvador, and Guatemala, along with Costa Rica, Honduras, and Panama. In the 1970s, outside forces combined with indigenous politics, economics, and demography to produce upheaval.

The trigger was Nicaragua. There a dynasty of dictators, the Somoza family, had ruled since 1936 as heir to a series of U.S. Marine interventions that Nicaraguan political factions had invoked to crush their domestic opponents. The first Somoza (Anastasio Somoza García, 1936–56) consolidated his power by presenting himself to Washington as a force for stability. He also assassinated his former ally, Augusto Sandino, a local guerrilla saint of vaguely Leftist leanings who had taken up arms against U.S. Marine intervention in 1927 when it failed to put his own faction in power. The second Somoza dictator (Anastasio Somoza Debayle, 1967–79) carried on the family tradition after a pseudo-constitutional interlude. But youthful opponents from the Nicaraguan moneyed elite sought military and political training in Havana and Moscow. In the 1960s they created a guerrilla movement, the "Sandinista National Liberation Front" (FSLN) with Cuban advice and arms.

The second Somoza began to lose his grip in the mid-1970s. His excessive greed alienated the middle classes. He offended the urban poor by pocketing international relief money sent after a 1972 earthquake partially leveled Managua, the capital. He provoked spontaneous uprisings by assassinating a key opponent in 1978. After his National Guard proved both brutal and ineffectual, Carter urged Somoza to go; he duly fled to Miami in July 1979. Middle-class support and arms shipped from Cuba put the revolution over the top. The Sandinistas promised free elections, political pluralism, nonalignment in foreign policy, and the preservation of a mixed economy. Then they seized control of the victorious revolution through salami tactics.

Elections did not materialize until 1984, after the FSLN had largely suppressed its domestic opponents with arrests and *turbas divinas*, "divine mobs" of youthful fanatics. Nor was the external alignment of the FSLN long in doubt. Within days of Somoza's flight, key Sandinista leaders visited Castro. Within a month the new regime had clinched relations with Moscow, Bulgaria, and Libya. It acquired ties to the PLO and North Korea. Cuban and Soviet-bloc advisers poured into Managua. The FSLN created a propaganda machine that proclaimed America as "the enemy of all humanity." Shipments of Soviet-bloc arms arrived not only for the "Sandinista Armed Forces" (as the new party-army styled itself) but also for insurgencies kindled or rekindled in El Salvador and Guatemala. The revolution, in the slogan of Nicaragua's new ruling class of FSLN *comandantes,* "had no frontiers" [*"la revolución no tiene fronteras"*].

In Guatemala that proved untrue. The Guatemalan army fought back with pacification methods pioneered by the French in Algeria and with home-style massacres of Indian peasants. Washington disapproved and cut off aid, but without effect. At least 12,000 perished; the insurgents shrank from 6,000 in 1980 to 3,000 by 1987. The Guatemalan army handed over power to a civilian government in 1985. The Salvadoran insurgents, with lavish arms supplies from Cuba through Nicaragua, did rather better than their Guatemalan counterparts until 1984, when a Social Democrat, José Napoleón Duarte, won the presidential election. Duarte sought with some success to damp down "death squad" assassinations by the Salvadoran Right; massive U.S. assistance improved the combat performance of the Salvadoran army. The guerrillas dwindled from roughly 10,000 in 1980 to 4,000 in 1987.

The United States also reacted to Sandinista hostility and to the prospect of a Marxist-Leninist state with thousands of Cuban and Soviet-bloc advisers close to Mexico's southern border and to the Panama Canal. In 1981 Reagan halted U.S. economic aid (which amounted to $128 million) to post-revolution Nicaragua; a condition of aid had been that the Sandinistas not supply Marxist insurgents in El Salvador. Reagan soon turned to sterner measures, CIA-organized insurgents known as the *Contras* ("counter-revolutionaries"), recruited from veterans of the Somoza forces, from middle-class opponents of the Sandinistas, and from the Nicaraguan peasantry.

Reagan also struck fear into the Sandinistas by landing troops on the small Caribbean island of Grenada in Octo-

ber 1983, after the leaders of Grenada's Marxist-Leninist "New Jewel Party" (which had seized power in 1979) unexpectedly began shooting one another. Washington found Grenada's close ties to Cuba and the Soviet Union disquieting and feared that U.S. citizens on the island might become hostages. The Grenadans greeted U.S. forces as liberators; Washington soon withdrew in favor of an apparently stable Grenadan parliamentary regime. A Marxist-Leninist dictatorship had fallen—a unique event. The regime's captured archives revealed fierce totalitarian aspirations, an apparently insatiable appetite for weapons, and close ties to the Soviet Union, East Germany, Cuba, Nicaragua, Bulgaria, North Korea, and the PLO.

Along with that apparent portent for Managua came increasing economic strain. *Contra* attacks and military expenditure drained Managua's budget, but Nicaragua's economic regression in the 1980s was above all the result of Stalinist economic experimentation by the FSLN. The regime sought to undermine or expropriate private enterprise in favor of *comandante*-run state businesses and collective farms. Nicaragua's currency-earning exports of coffee and other commodities fell by 50 percent. Living standards dropped to the dirt-poor levels of the 1950s. The regime also created a new form of class division. The Sandinista ruling class had access to special hard currency stores like those serving the Soviet elite. The common people made do with increasingly empty supermarket shelves.

To survive, the Sandinista leaders took the struggle to Washington. To American audiences the *comandantes* gave lavish assurances—assurances contradicted by their words and actions at home and by the frequent ill-timed visits to Moscow of their fatigue-clad supreme leader, Daniel Ortega Saavedra. The Sandinistas protested that only the "*Contra* war" prevented them from fulfilling the promises of political pluralism and non-alignment they had broken in 1979–80, before the *Contras* existed.

Beginning in 1982, Congress sought to leash the *Contras* by rationing or blocking funds and arms. Reagan's National Security Council secretly kept supplies flowing by diverting through Swiss bank accounts the profits from the arms transactions with Iran. The revelation after November 1986 of that clandestine attack on Congress's constitutional power of the purse—and the deep revulsion that most Americans felt against Iran—temporarily made Reagan a "lame duck." That gave the five Central American powers an opening, under the leadership of President Oscar Arias of Costa Rica, to negotiate in July–August 1987 their own "peace plan" to end the region's wars.

The plan's most striking initial success was to win Arias a Nobel Peace Prize. The Salvadoran insurgents broke off talks with Duarte; low-level violence continued in Guatemala. The Sandinistas complied with few of the Arias plan's provisions, which included the restoration of political and press freedoms in Nicaragua. Managua also announced plans to raise the size of the Sandinista armed forces—after the defeat of the *Contras*—to 600,000 regular and reserve troops by 1995. That force would be twice as large as that of Mexico, a country with 24 times Nicaragua's population.

Disclosure of Managua's military plans did not prevent Congress from again cutting off *Contra* aid in February–March 1988. Simultaneously, a Sandinista offensive against *Contra* sanctuaries in Honduras provoked Reagan to dispatch U.S. paratroops to that country for a brief show of force. The *Contras* feared abandonment by Washington, the Sandinistas invasion, continued protracted war, and possible abandonment by Moscow. Both parties therefore compromised on a provisional truce. The Sandinistas apparently hoped that the *Contras* would disintegrate, while the *Contras* looked to

Daniel Ortega (center, in dark glasses) returning to Nicaragua from his trip to Moscow, February 1984.

the United States for renewed aid should Sandinista sabotage wreck the Arias plan. Concurrently, collapse threatened two other pillars of Washington's Central American policy. Duarte of El Salvador contracted a terminal cancer while his party, discredited by corruption, lost control of parliament to the murderous far Right. The brutish ruler of Panama, General Manuel Antonio Noriega, fell afoul of Washington for allegedly renting airfields to U.S.-bound cocaine smugglers. Reagan's subordinates applied economic sanctions that shattered Panama's economy but failed, at least in the short run, to weaken the general's grip on power. Reagan left intractable problems "south of the border" to his successors.

THE WORLD ECONOMY ADRIFT

One backdrop to the crises of the 1970s and 1980s was the steady erosion of the relative economic power and world economic leadership of the United States. In 1945 the United States had commanded perhaps half of world industrial production, for Germany and Japan lay in ruins and the western Soviet Union was devastated. In 1953 the United States share was 44.7 percent; by 1980 it had fallen to 31.5 percent. U.S. production rose steadily in absolute terms, but its relative position—like that of nineteenth-century Britain—inexorably deteriorated.

That deterioration was in a sense an immense U.S. success. The dollar and gold-based Bretton Woods international currency system of 1944, U.S.-sponsored tariff reduction agreements, the Marshall Plan, and the example of the science-based industry of the United States between them propelled the world economy into the greatest spurt in history. The growth of other powers, especially West Germany and Japan, inevitably cut the U.S. share of world production. But economic and foreign policy trends accelerated that relative deterioration and began by the 1970s to compromise the authority of the United States as leader of the world economy inherited from Britain.

Worldwide defense commitments and the overseas investments of U.S. multinational corporations between them generated a persistent balance of payments deficit; from 1950 to 1969 an average of $1.3 billion more left the United States each year than entered. Lyndon Johnson's attempt to fight the Vietnam War painlessly on credit helped provoke a decade of steadily rising inflation. Domestic inflation in turn worsened the balance of payments deficit. Imports, to which the U.S. consumer was becoming pleasantly addicted, cost more dollars than before. And European banks were awash in unwanted "Eurodollars." That oversupply generated unbearable pressure on the Bretton Woods structure of fixed exchange rates based on gold.

In 1971, Nixon briefly clamped wage and price controls on the U.S. economy to check inflation, and devalued the dollar. A second devaluation followed in 1973. By March 1973 the world economy rested on "floating" exchange rates that fluctuated according to demand. The dollar remained the international currency of first and last resort, but "hard" currencies such as West German marks, Swiss francs, and Japanese yen acquired a major role, especially after the EEC created a mark-based European Monetary System in 1979. U.S. leadership was giving way to an oligarchy of the rich.

But western Europe and Japan were ill-equipped to share in world leadership. The more than doubling of the real price of oil in 1973 and again in 1979–80, after Khomeini's revolution and the Gulf War cut Iran's production, helped force the world economy into two recessions (1973–75, 1981–82) more painful than anything since the Great Depression. Unemployment, "stagflation," and oil dependence after 1973 enfeebled the EEC and slowed even Japan.

The United States thus continued to lead by default, through dubious innovations such as the "petrodollar recycling" that piled high the pyramids of international debt. But in the 1980s yet another round of economic irresponsibility in Washington further compromised its leadership position. Reagan came to office apparently convinced that massive tax cuts would so stimulate the economy that federal tax revenues would actually increase and thus balance the budget—a bizarre theory that his vice president, George Bush, had once derided as "voodoo economics." In addition, Reagan inherited a rising military budget from Carter and had pledged to match Brezhnev's buildup.

Unlike Carter, Reagan refused to tell the voters that they must pay for more defense. His first drastic tax cut passed Congress on a wave of bipartisan enthusiasm. The economy expanded steadily after 1982 but tax revenue did not increase as predicted. Reagan therefore loaded the costs of a rebuilt 600-ship navy and numerous new weapons systems onto the national debt, which doubled from $1 trillion in 1981 to $2.1 trillion in 1986. Congress declined to court unpopularity by raising taxes or by cutting into the middle-class social programs that cost even more and grew even faster than the military budget.

"Guns and butter" on credit in the 1980s had effects as dramatic as Johnson's similar attempt to fight in Vietnam while creating a "Great Society" at home. Foreign lenders came to Reagan's rescue by buying Treasury bonds in billion-dollar gulps. Foreign buyers snapped up U.S. corporations. But the inflow of capital was not a free lunch. Foreign buying of dollars to pay for investments in the United States raised the dollar's value sharply against other currencies. That rise in turn increased the price and lessened the competitiveness of U.S. exports. The consequent decline in exports further worsened the balance of payments deficit, as did the ever-increasing interest payments owed to the foreign lenders. The need to continue borrowing to "roll over" an ever-larger debt meant that the United States lost control over its domestic interest rates, which had to remain higher than those abroad to keep foreign investors from taking their money elsewhere. High interest rates in turn made it harder for U.S. industry to invest in the modern plant that it desperately needed to compete in the world market. Finally, the debt binge converted the United States from a net creditor to a debtor for the first time since 1914–18. In 1983–85 Japan took the place of the United States as the world's greatest creditor.

Worse followed. Financial mores had grown loose indeed in the 1970s and 1980s; the shadow of 1929 was far distant. Suspect "financial instruments" proliferated; "junk bonds"—aptly named—financed corporate takeovers and stock manipulation. New financial "products" such as stock index futures—a casino game requiring a 10 to 15 percent down payment and the rest on loan—introduced massive instabilities. Billions in unrepayable "Third World" or eastern European debt undermined U.S. and European banks. Technology opened new frontiers of speed and insecurity. Computers and instantaneous communications welded the world's stock, currency, and commodity exchanges into a seamless 24-hour world market. Instant financial information and fund transfer sent trillions of dollars, marks, yen, and lesser currencies sloshing from market to market, seeking the small exchange rate differences that meant profit. Automatic stock and futures trading driven by computer programs made market hiccups into jagged ascents or hair-raising plunges. The abandonment in the name of free enterprise and efficiency of many post-1929 restrictions on banks and financial institutions further decreased the world economy's margin of safety.

The most dramatic symptom of instability was the giddying rise of the stock market, from a Dow Jones average of below 2,000 in early 1987 to 2,722 by August. In October the Dow broke, and on October 19 it dropped a chilling 508 points. The market lost 36 percent of its August paper value: over half a trillion dollars in assets vaporized. Markets around the world followed;

The crash of '87: Black Monday, October 20, 1987.

only Tokyo stabilized swiftly after a severe drop. The value of the dollar against other currencies followed the markets downward. The jerry-built structures of "Third World," corporate, and consumer debt creaked ominously. But unlike 1929, the U.S. domestic economy remained relatively strong. A cheaper dollar increased U.S. prospects of exporting and thus paying its debts, but also raised the specter of an international devaluation contest of the type that helped deepen the Great Depression (see pp. 885–86). Here too, Reagan left a difficult legacy to his hand-picked successor, George Bush.

THE SUPERPOWERS IN DECLINE

The Soviet Empire

The "Crash of '87" was a visible and outward sign of the relative decline of the United States. The Soviet Union's relative decline was equally if less dramatically demonstrated when its leadership began after 1985 to seek to present a new and softer image to the West. Technological lag, economic stagnation, and the drain of empire apparently dictated a new effort at détente.

Brezhnev's world-spanning navy, his expanding "second Soviet empire" in Africa and Southeast Asia, his intervention in Afghanistan had suggested limitless ambition. But ambition costs. By the mid-1980s, the annual bill for Afghanistan, Cuba, Vietnam and its Cambodian and Laotian empire, Nicaragua, Ethiopia, and other minor dependencies ran into the tens of billions of dollars. Soviet military procurement at last ceased to grow in the early 1980s; the Soviet economy was flagging. Its annual rate of increase fell inexorably from roughly 5 percent in the 1950s to negative growth by the early 1980s. Détente had brought Western loans and technology, but its main consequence was a debt mountain of Brazilian proportions. Central planning,

an uninspired work force ("they pretend to pay us, we pretend to work"), and military expenditure that may have reached 20 percent or more of GNP by 1980 crippled the economy. Rudimentary medical services, a rising industrial accident rate, intense pollution, astounding levels of vodka consumption, and widespread hopelessness made the Soviet Union the only industrialized society in history to experience a long-term *decline* in the life expectancy of its population. Male life expectancy dropped from 65 in 1965 to an estimated 61 or worse in 1981; that of Soviet women from 73 in the early 1970s to 69 in 1985.

And the Soviet Union—Europe's last multinational empire—did not escape the demographic trends that sapped its former rivals. By 1970 only 51 percent of the Soviet population were Great Russians, the ruling nationality. The subject peoples, especially the Moslems of Central Asia, were growing at rates of up to three times that of the peoples of European Russia. Great Russians probably ceased to be a majority in the early 1980s, although they remained the largest single group within the Soviet Union. Nationalist unrest in Soviet Central Asia and the Caucasus accompanied the shift in numbers; demonstrations erupted whenever KGB pressure relaxed. The intervention in Afghanistan apparently provoked resentment and unreliability among Soviet Moslem troops—a portent for the future.

Two transitional figures succeeded Brezhnev upon his death in 1982. Yuri Andropov, long chief of the KGB, came to power at age 68 amid KGB-inspired rumors in the West that he was a "closet liberal" who loved Glenn Miller's music. He reinforced Soviet forces in Afghanistan. After Andropov's death in early 1984 the colorless Konstantin Chernenko briefly held power, then died. In March 1985 the Politburo chose a far younger man, Mikhail Gorbachev. Molotov's pupil and heir at the foreign ministry, Andrei Gromyko, reportedly put Gorbachev over the top

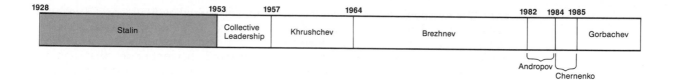

1928		1953	1957	1964		1982	1984	1985	
Stalin		Collective Leadership	Khrushchev	Brezhnev				Gorbachev	

Andropov   Chernenko

by remarking that he had a nice smile and iron teeth.

Gorbachev proceeded cautiously at first, but in 1986–87 announced a massive program of economic reforms. *"Perestroika"* or *"restructuring"* was to limit central planning, introduce some market mechanisms, and eliminate the technological lag that in the long run imperiled both the Soviet economy and Soviet military power. A Gorbachev speech in late 1987 mentioned favorably Lenin's temporary economic retreat, the NEP (see p. 909) and repeated some of Khrushchev's strictures against Stalin. Subsequently the Party allowed mention of Leon Trotsky and rehabilitated Bukharin, who had dared to question Stalin's crash industrialization and collectivization. In the realm of culture and politics, the ambiguous accompaniment of *"perestroika"* was *"glasnost"*—"publicity"—usually mistranslated in the West as "openness." And in foreign policy, Gorbachev appeared far more willing than his predecessors to give as well as take at the arms control negotiating table; the Soviet Union needed a breathing space. Gorbachev also bid for a rapprochement with China, despite stiff Chinese preconditions that included Vietnamese withdrawal from Cambodia. In May 1988 he also began to withdraw Soviet troops from Afghanistan.

But Gorbachev's attempt to launch a new NEP faced numerous contradictions. Domestically, greater economic freedom meant market discipline: bankruptcies, unemployment, and inflation. It also meant an end to the Party's monopoly over the economy. It might ultimately mean following China's example in questioning collectivization, one crippling Stalin policy that Gorbachev initially defended. Finally, economic restructuring required help

from a Soviet people long accustomed to merely "pretending to work." The appeal by the Communist autocracy for support from its citizens, like the similar appeals of earlier Russian autocrats, was likely to call forth forces ultimately hostile to the autocracy itself. That was precisely the complaint of strong groups within the Party and the state bureaucracy; eastern European satellite leaders also became increasingly distraught.

In foreign policy, Gorbachev faced daunting challenges. On the arms control front, he gained successes in 1986–87. He charmed Western opinion by agreeing to consider Reagan's START ("STrategic Arms Reduction Talks") proposal for a 50 percent cutback in strategic warheads. That sudden Soviet interests in cuts was in part a product of Gorbachev's need to remedy Soviet economic stagnation. But it was even more a result of Reagan's "Strategic Defense Initiative" (SDI or "Star Wars"), a proposed space-based antimissile shield that might cancel Soviet advantages in heavy missiles and potentially in theater nuclear forces as well. Gorbachev sought to trade Soviet

Nice smiles and iron teeth: Mikhail Gorbachev meets Margaret Thatcher (1985).

missile reductions for restrictions on "Star Wars" that would induce Congress to kill the U.S. program. Reagan held fast. His stubbornness, more that any other factor, brought the Soviets to the bargaining table with realistic proposals.

START did not bear immediate fruit. The two leaders met at Reykjavik in Iceland in November 1986 for an ill-prepared summit that derailed amid utopian discussions of the total elimination of nuclear weapons in ten years. That thoroughly alarmed the NATO allies, for it suggested that Washington sought to leave them naked in the face of Soviet conventional superiority. In a treaty signed in Washington in December 1987, Gorbachev accepted the same U.S. terms for an intermediate-range missile agreement that his predecessors had contemptuously rejected. "Star Wars" and the defeat of the protesters in western Europe had evidently changed Moscow's views. In the December 1987 treaty the United States agreed to scrap its Pershing II and European cruise missiles. The Soviet Union undertook to destroy both SS-20s and medium-range missiles. Both sides accepted "on-site" inspection provisions unprecedented since the Versailles restrictions placed upon Germany. Cynics, especially in Europe, suggested that the agreement made western Europe safer for Soviet armor.

The prospect of theater-force reductions therefore led to renewed NATO demands for a "mutual and balanced" reduction in conventional forces, an issue on which Soviet negotiators had tied the West in knots during the 1970s. Whether agreed "balanced" reductions were possible, given that an ocean divides the United States from Europe whereas the Soviets need only cross a border, was unclear. That Gorbachev, unlike Brezhnev, appeared set on lessening the burden of arms and of the Afghan war on the Soviet economy was a hopeful sign. But any such Soviet retreat would inevitably encourage demands for independence throughout the empire that Stalin and Brezhnev had acquired.

Whether Gorbachev could—or even proposed to—abandon that empire was uncertain. And no Western expert could say whether or how long Gorbachev would remain in power, whether his reforms would succeed, and to what extent they were a genuine attempt to change the Communist autocracy of Lenin and Stalin into something milder. Optimists in the West proclaimed that containment had succeeded, that the "mellowing of Soviet power" that George Kennan had predicted in 1947 was now finally at hand. Skeptics dismissed *glasnost* and *perestroika* as "an improved lie, a new temporary façade," and pointed to the still unshaken structures of the Soviet power-state and to the eastern European empire that Gorbachev could hold only by force. And pessimists foresaw that if Gorbachev indeed prevailed, his reformed and dynamic Soviet Union would bear an ominous resemblance to the Imperial Germany of 1890–1914.

The "Imperial Republic"

That other "weary titan," the United States, also seemed in need of a measure of *perestroika* by the 1980s. Like Great Britain after 1890, its commitments after 1965 appeared to be outrunning its resources. Military expenditure itself was probably not a crushing burden, if paid for by taxation rather than debt. The United States spent considerably more as a percentage of GNP on arms during the prosperous Eisenhower years than under Reagan. In the 1980s its economy also grew faster than those of its European allies, despite the greater proportion of U.S. GNP spent on defense. But military research increasingly diverted too large a proportion of U.S. scientific and engineering talent into extreme "leading edge" military applications, leaving too few good technical minds to translate innovation into consumer products. And cultural and economic trends skewed the civilian economy. The dubious joys of stock manipulation and corporate takeovers injected too much talent into highly paid parasitic occupations such as corporate law and investment banking. Fear of takeovers in turn drove U.S. firms to pursue short-term profits rather than treading the Japanese road of long-term conquest of markets through consumer satisfaction.

Worst of all, the United States—like nineteenth-century Britain—failed to invest in its schools. By the 1980s its inner-city public education systems had virtually collapsed. Its suburban middle-class schools taught curricula whose vacuousness provoked laughter in Europe and Japan, where relentless and advanced instruction in mathematics, chemistry, physics, expository writing, history, geography, and foreign languages was standard fare. Teaching in America had become a low-paying and low-prestige job that demoralized the few talented and learned individuals it still attracted. A work force that contained a rising proportion of functional illiterates threatened U.S. economic growth, just as the United States led the world into the "information age" of computer technology.

In the realms of domestic politics and foreign policy, the United States suffered from numerous maladies. The collapse of education brought with it a loss of "collective memory." U.S. history—much less that of Europe or Asia—went virtually untaught. Generations graduated or failed to graduate with only hazy notions of the principles upon which their government rested, of the workings of its political process, and of the world beyond its borders. Understandably, only a declining proportion of the population bothered to vote.

Simultaneously, television and computerized opinion polling dramatically altered politics. They made "image" all-important and converted all but the strongest leaders into followers. The cycle of presidential politics became a relentless and debilitating four-year grind, thanks to television and to "reforms" that expanded the role of presidential primaries in small unrepresentative states. Presidents rarely survived long in office. Kennedy, Johnson, Nixon, Ford, and Carter all lasted less than six years. That in turn gave U.S. foreign policy a perilous see-saw quality that perplexed and alarmed both allies and adversaries. Europeans sometimes suggested that parliamentary government, in which the executive also led the legislature, produced greater coherence and continuity than the U.S. system, in which the same party rarely controlled the presidency and Congress simultaneously. But many European parliamentary systems failed the test; few European prime ministers rivalled Margaret Thatcher.

A variety of challenges confronted Washington in its weakened condition. America faced further arms-control negotiations with a Gorbachev whose "charm offensive" ultimately aimed at detaching West Germany from NATO. It faced continued turmoil in Central America and dangerous instabilities in the domestic and world economies. It faced a growing clamor at home that it divest itself of at least a few of the immense responsibilities—from the North Cape of Norway to the Persian Gulf to the "demilitarized zone" between the Koreas—shouldered after 1945, when its relative economic strength had been far greater than in the 1980s. Like the Soviet Union, the United States needed a breathing space.

But the informal empire acquired after 1945 was difficult to shed. The United States had paid dearly—at Pearl Harbor and on the hard road to Berlin and Tokyo Bay—for its flight from responsibility after 1919. Almost half a century after 1945, Europe and Japan still appeared unready to shoulder the burdens which the United States had taken on in its own interest, but also in theirs. To maintain the "American empire" unwillingly acquired against Hitler and Stalin appeared increasingly costly and thankless. To give it up was unsafe.

TOWARD THE TWENTY-FIRST CENTURY

Broad and swift scientific and technological advance paralleled the expansion of the world economy under the umbrella of U.S. power after 1945. Simultaneously, the proliferation of knowledge in myriads of highly specialized scientific and scholarly subdisciplines posed a threat already visible

in the nineteenth century—that educated people, each locked in the jargon of their specialties, would cease to speak a common language. Especially in the social sciences and humanities, skepticism about the possibility of establishing truth corroded all established standards. And as the Americanization of the world through television proceeded, high culture retreated into a cloistered existence in the universities.

The Thrust of Science and Technology

"Command science," the systematic government mobilization of scientific knowledge for a specific purpose, came into its own after 1945. The Manhattan Project had shown the way. Its successors were the postwar programs of the great powers that created thermonuclear bombs, or atomic reactors to generate electricity and power submarines and surface ships.

By the 1980s reactor accidents had lessened enthusiasm for nuclear power. A reactor at Three Mile Island in Pennsylvania partially melted in 1979; its containment vessel held and only small amounts of radioactivity reached the atmosphere. The Soviets did not believe in containment vessels or redundant control systems. When their ill-designed reactor at Chernobyl in the Ukraine exploded and burned in 1986, fire and fallout killed at least 31 and contaminated livestock, milk, and crops from Lapland to Portugal. Oil-poor powers such as France and Japan nevertheless pressed on self-confidently with massive nuclear power programs.

Command science was also the instrument of the conquest of space—a dream entertained since the seventeenth century, but now suddenly practical. The Soviet effort that launched *Sputnik* in 1957 put Yuri Gagarin into Earth orbit in 1961. Kennedy responded with a pledge to put an American on the moon by the end of the decade. The National Aeronautics and Space Administration (NASA),

Success and failure: Neil Armstrong walks on the moon, July 1969. Opposite: Space Shuttle *Challenger* explodes after launch, January 1986.

which Eisenhower established after *Sputnik*, assembled the largest community of scientific talent ever mobilized for a specific purpose, and spent up to $40 billion. On July 20, 1969, Neil Armstrong of the United States became the first human to walk on the Moon. The Soviet Union stuck closer to Earth; its space program was and remained military in inspiration and priorities.

After its moon triumph NASA bet virtually its entire shrinking budget on one program, the reusable "space shuttle." The explosion after launch of the shuttle *Challenger* in January 1986 therefore paralyzed both civilian and military space programs, including the launch of satellites to monitor Soviet compliance with arms-control agreements or provide early warning of attack. Subsequent investigations of NASA disclosed slovenly engineering and blind mismanagement. A U.S. space station (and perhaps orbiting "Star Wars" installations) may materialize in the 1990s. The Soviet Union already operates a small space station and holds all records for length of stay in space. A Mars landing is technologically feasible but budgetary constraints will probably delay it until after the year 2000.

Command science, despite its magnitude and its many "spin-offs," was only a small part of the continuing scientific and technological revolution. During and after World War II, new materials came into their own. Plastics and glass fiber increasingly replaced steel and other metals. Composites of plastic and boron or carbon fiber, lighter and stronger than steel, became available in the 1970s. Titanium, almost 50 percent lighter than steel and with a higher melting point than aluminum, found innumerable uses in supersonic jet aircraft, nuclear reactors, and submarines.

But the most spectacular advances, a wave of innovation as potentially powerful as the "second industrial revolution" of steel, chemicals and electricity, came in electronics and biology. Semiconductors, materials such as germa-

nium and silicon that conducted current only hesitatingly at room temperature, had been a subject of curiosity since primitive germanium diodes had figured in early radio receivers. In 1947 William Shockley, John Bardeen, and Walter H. Brattain of Bell Laboratories invented the transistor, the first semiconductor amplifying device. By the early 1960s the transistor had evolved into the integrated circuit or "chip," innumerable microscopic transistors, linked in complex patterns, imprinted on silicon wafers.

The arrival of the transistor coincided with the birth, speeded by wartime cryptographic needs, of the new discipline of computing. Its theoretical roots reached back into the nineteenth century; its two leading theoreticians were Alan Turing (1912–54) of Cambridge, who played a leading role in Britain's decipherment of the *Wehrmacht*'s supposedly uncrackable codes, and the Hungarian refugee physicist-mathematician John von Neumann (1903–57) of Princeton. By the 1960s their successors had created theories, computer languages, and machines capable of the unimaginably complex and rapid calculations needed to model thermonuclear explosions, solve engineering problems through simulation, predict the paths of space vehicles, guide missiles and robots, and store and manipulate ever-greater masses of information.

From 1959 to the 1980s, chips and therefore computers doubled in computing power each year. The cost per transistor decreased over 20 years by a factor of over *1 million*. That pace of advance shows no signs of slowing. As chip fabricators have approached the apparent limits that silicon places on computer speed, those limits have receded, while other faster materials such as gallium arsenide have emerged. The discovery in 1986–87 of an entirely new class of ceramics that offer no resistance to electricity at relatively high temperatures may make possible a further qualitative leap in computer speed—as well as loss-free transmission of electrical power, vehicles miraculously levitated with superconducting electromagnets, and innumerable applications as yet unforeseen. The invention in the 1960s of lasers, devices that generated focused light of a single frequency, added to the potential of semiconductors. Lasers offered innumerable applications from surgery to weaponry, and allowed the transmission of information over long distances at densities far exceeding the limits of electrical or microwave circuits.

Potentially even more powerful than semiconductors and lasers were the new techniques of molecular biology. In 1951–53 James D. Watson of the United States and Francis H. C. Crick

of Britain jointly deciphered the "double helix," the complex molecular structure of deoxyribonucleic acid or DNA, the material in which cells encode their genetic information. That research led eventually to the beginnings of an understanding of evolution at the molecular level, and to the manipulation of plant and animal genes to make bizarre hybrids that crossed species lines. The mapping of the entire human genetic code—all 100,000 genes, each consisting of 1,500 subunits—appeared a realistic prospect by the end of the century.

Molecular biology opened immense possibilities for good, for the eradication of most diseases and the understanding and possible slowing of aging. It provided the most powerful weapons for fighting the great viral pandemic of the 1980s and 1990s, AIDS ("Acquired Immune Deficiency Syndrome"). The virus, against which conventional medical techniques were almost as powerless as those of the Middle Ages against the Black Death, spread above all through sexual intercourse and the sharing of unsterilized heroin hypodermics. By the late 1980s it threatened millions of victims, especially in Africa, the United States, and Europe.

But together with hope and life, the new biology also appeared to offer death and transfiguration through biological weapons of unprecedented subtlety and power, and through "human perfectibility" in a quite literal sense by the genetic re-engineering of the human species. Nuclear weapons had given humanity a chance to annihilate itself, but also the long European peace after 1945. Molecular biology held out the prospect both of healing and of a new kind of annihilation, the transformation of humanity into something less or more than human.

The Disintegration of Scholarship and High Culture

In the realm of ideas, specialization and the triumph of the relativism that had flourished since the Enlightenment furthered the fragmentation that had already been visible as the twentieth century began. Especially in the Anglo-Saxon countries, philosophers largely abandoned speculation. The new "analytical" philosophers scorned metaphysics—the exploration through imagination of the nature of existence. They sought instead what Bertrand Russell (1872–1970), an early leader of the analytical school, described as the "unattainable ideal of impeccable knowledge." The close examination of language and meaning through logic and mathematics was their method. Their quest led them to narrow increasingly the domain of truth in order to establish certainty.

Ultimately they so narrowed the domain of truth that it vanished. The reclusive Ludwig Wittgenstein (1889–1951), perhaps the greatest of twentieth-century philosophers, abandoned all attempts to describe the world and retreated acerbically into the analysis of language. His taunt that "the belief in the causal nexus is superstition" denigrated all forms of knowledge about nature and human affairs. But as Wittgenstein's eighteenth-century precursor David Hume had pointed out, the philosopher's study was the place for skepticism. Survival in the hard outside world that Wittgenstein shunned still required "superstitions" such as cause and effect.

On the Continent, after Heidegger, traditional forms of philosophy still prospered. The Left Bank sage Jean-Paul Sartre (1905–80) was Heidegger's principal heir. After 1945, Sartre's "existentialism" became a cult phenomenon from Paris to San Francisco that endured until the 1960s. Its basis was Heidegger's call for "authenticity" and his denial of a rational foundation for values. For Sartre, individuals were utterly free to choose their values. Any denial that such freedom existed was inauthentic, was an evasion of responsibility, was "bad faith." But Sartre offered no advice on what values to choose, for advice would constrict freedom and constitute "bad faith." He merely commanded choice, for only

heroic choice was "authentic." Heidegger had chosen Nazism. Sartre, whose only gestures against Nazism had been literary, chose Marxism. He described it as the "unsurpassable philosophy of our time."

French intellectual fashions change as rapidly and wield as powerful an influence throughout the West as the hemlines of Paris designers. After the collapse of the May 1968 student revolt that Sartre's doctrines of heroic commitment helped inspire, new preoccupations became dominant. The most important was an intellectual tendency known as "structuralism." It had originated in linguistics between the world wars and thence spread to anthropology, literary criticism, history, sociology, psychoanalysis, and philosophy. Its lowest common denominator was the claim that the *structure* of a language, myth, or literary or historical "text" was a more fundamental characteristic than other attributes such as origins, history, purpose, or content.

In linguistics, its point of origin, structuralism was largely the product of the insights of the Swiss scholar Ferdinand de Saussure (1857–1913), who suggested that meaning was a product of oppositions or differences between the "signs" that made up language. Meaning was thus entirely relative. "Signs" had meaning only by virtue of their structural relationship to other "signs." An influential American, Noam Chomsky (1928–), added a fruitful conjecture of his own—*all* languages shared a common "deep structure" that grew out of the structure of the human mind itself. Chomsky's apparent biological determinism clashed with his politics; a combative Left-utopian, he rejected the "capitalist" West and implicitly demanded faith in the perfectibility of humanity, a perfectibility doubtful indeed if the human mind was as "hard-wired" as Chomsky the linguist assumed.

Structuralism—though many of its practitioners disclaimed the label—migrated from linguistics through anthropology to a variety of other fields. Its greatest anthropological figure,

The sage of Paris: Jean-Paul Sartre.

Claude Lévi-Strauss (1908–) investigated the myths of Brazilian and American Indians as clues to the structures of the "primitive mind." Structure was primary, content far less important; meaning existed only as part of a structure. Critics such as Roland Barthes (1915–80) carried similar notions into literary criticism. The literary "text" became a subject for a decipherment or "deconstruction" that deliberately ignored the "text's" author, historical context, literary excellence or lack of it, and commonsense meaning. For the structuralist critic, the interpreter not the author gave meaning. That doctrine allowed the interpreter to give a "text" any meaning at all. And the implication that all "texts" were of equal value frequently produced bizarre results. Structuralist critics examined with deep seriousness works that few non-structuralists even considered literature.

Historians, beginning in France, took a Lévi-Straussian interest in the "collective mentalities" of past social groups. Analysis of social or intellectual "structures" began to supersede narrative. The study of long-term change—climatic, economic, and demographic—triumphed for a time over short-term "event history" and the history of ideas. Devotees of economics subjected small portions of the past to "cliometric" statistical examination. Historians increasingly though not always wisely borrowed methods from sociology and psychology. Marxism revived. For the first time in history, historians wrote works incomprehensible to the educated public.

Structuralism and the disciplines it influenced mirrored the disorientation of the age. If *all* truths were relative, tolerance even of bizarre claims was the highest virtue. In the humanities and social sciences few dared affirm that some "truths" were less relative than others and that the test of all generalizations was confrontation with empirical evidence. The natural sciences proved more resistant to bewilderment; experimentation imposed discipline and mathematics still offered an unparalleled means of describing nature.

In the arts, disintegration was almost total as the century drew toward its end. In the visual arts the last undisputed master was Pablo Picasso (1881–1973). Creativity nevertheless remained high, although experiments such as the "pop art" of the 1960s that took its images from American advertising sometimes suggested otherwise. In architecture the "international style" persisted although sometimes adorned with "post-modernist" classical flourishes. In music, few composers after Igor Stravinsky (1882–1971) and Sergei Prokofiev (1891–1953) commanded mass audiences. Dissonance and disjointed rhythms bored or repelled all

"Pop art": Andy Warhol, *100 Cans* (1962).

The anonymous crowd: a Tokyo subway in the 1980s.

except specialists. Symphony orchestras and opera companies made do with the time-honored works of nineteenth-century giants such as Beethoven or Wagner. In literature, especially in the United States, poetry and the serious novel fled to academia to be embalmed in "creative writing" courses. Even Paris began to flag as a fountainhead of novelty. Soviet-bloc dissident and emigré writers, along with those of Latin America, showed more life than their European or American counterparts. Western high culture increasingly lacked the vitality and self-confidence of earlier ages.

THE WIDENING AND NARROWING OF THE WEST

As the century drew to a close, Western ideas dominated the globe as never before. In the nineteenth century, the zenith of the West's relative power, its culture had only touched the surface of non-European societies. By the late twentieth century, instant communications relentlessly drove forward the economic and cultural integration of

the world. That process generated fierce reactions, above all from Islam. The Western conception of government resting on and limited by the rights of the governed—*democratic government*—found few successful imitators. But the extension of the West's scientific and industrial revolution to all of humanity appeared likely to continue. As James Watt's partner had boasted of the new steam-engines, "I sell, Sir, what all the world desires to have—power." Power over nature and over the conditions of human existence was what the West offered those willing to learn. That temptation has so far proved almost irresistible.

But the West has also narrowed in relative terms. By the 1980s the birth rate of Europe from France to the Urals had fallen to roughly equal the death rate. The United States continued to grow, but at a rate lower than ever before. Not so the other continents. China, despite draconian post-Mao laws against unlicensed births, checked its growth rate only slightly as it passed the 1 billion mark. South Asia continued a relentless rise. Africa's population expanded at a pace faster than that of any other continent, although the AIDS pandemic threatened to slow it in the 1990s. World population was 4 billion in 1975 and will almost certainly surpass 6 billion by the year 2000. Thereafter either economic development will reduce birth rates or natural catastrophes, overcrowding, environmental degradation, epidemics, and wars will increase death rates. Most projections suggest that world population will level off between 8 and 9 billion late in the twenty-first century. Of that 8 to 9 billion, Asia will have 5 billion, Africa and the Americas will have over a billion each, and Europe will have less than a billion. The West's share of the human species is contracting as the West's influence as the "mainstream of civilization" expands to embrace all humanity.

Suggestions for Further Reading

The Superpowers in the 1970s

As the present approaches, perspective vanishes and reliable works become ever more sparse; *The New York Times* and *The Economist* (London) offer a better guide to world events than the innumerable jargon-ridden books by policy gurus. J. Keegan and A. Wheatcroft, *Zones of Conflict: An Atlas of Future Wars* (1986), offers a military and political geography of current antago- nisms. A. Ulam, *Dangerous Relations: The Soviet Union in World Politics, 1970–1982* (1983), remains excellent on superpower relations. On the Carter interlude, see the criticisms of J. Muravchik, *The Uncertain Crusade: Jimmy Carter and the Dilemma of Human Rights Policy* (1982), and the praise of G. Smith, *Morality, Reason, and Power: American Diplomacy in the Carter Years* (1986).

Europe and East Asia

W. Laqueur, *A Continent Astray: Europe, 1970–1978* (1979), and the very pessimistic J. F. Revel, *How Democracies Perish* (1985), survey western European disunity and wishful thinking. Nguyen Van Canh, *Vietnam Under Communism, 1975–1982* (1983), describes the fate of South Vietnam after the departure of the United States. The Khmer Rouge revolution still awaits its his- torian, but see F. Ponchaud, *Cambodia Year Zero* (1978), and W. Shawcross, *The Quality of Mercy: Cambodia, Holocaust, and Modern Conscience* (1984). On China, I. C. Y. Hsü, *China Without Mao: The Search for a New Order* (1983), analyzes post-Mao change; T. Terzani, *Travels in Forbidden China* (1986), suggests its limits.

Conflicts on the Periphery

On the Middle East and Islamic militance, see especially D. Pipes, *In the Path of God: Islam and Political Power* (1983); S. Bakhash, *The Reign of the Ayatollahs* (1984); G. Sick, *All Fall Down: America's Tragic Confrontation with Iran* (1985); and I. Rabinovich, *The War for Lebanon, 1970–1983* (1984). W. Laqueur, *The Age of Terrorism* (1987), places 1970s and 1980s terrorism in perspective. G. Chaliand, *Report from Afghanistan* (1982), provides useful background on the Afghan war. On Central America, S. Christian, *Nicaragua: Revolution in the Family* (1986), gives a *New York Times* eyewitness view. Those curious about the regime the United States overthrew in Grenada should consult its English-language internal documents: P. Seabury and W. McDougall, eds., *The Grenada Papers* (1984).

The View from the 1980s

On the superpowers, see for the Soviet Union H. Carrère d'Encausse, *Decline of an Empire* (1981); and *Confiscated Power: How Soviet Russia Really Works* (1982), as well as D. Holloway, *The Soviet Union and the Arms Race* (1983), and M. Voslensky, *Nomenklatura* (1984). All suggest reasons for caution about the prospects and potential consequences of Gorbachev's reforms. G. Wills, *Reagan's America: Innocents at Home* (1987), comments sardonically on the Reagan phenomenon; D. Ravitch, *What Do Our 17-Year-Olds Know?* (1987), documents America's educational collapse; P. Kennedy's highly readable and informative *The Rise and Fall of the Great Powers: Economic Change and Military Conflict from 1500 to 2000* (1987), offers long-term perspective. For intellectual developments since World War II, see especially J. A. Passmore, *A Hundred Years of Philosophy* (1968), and *Recent Philosphers* (1985); R. N. Stromberg, *After Everything: Western Intellectual History Since 1945* (1975); and the merciless G. Himmelfarb, *The New History and the Old* (1987).

Illustration Credits

Line Art Credits

Figure 24-3   (p. 683)
   From Eric Pawson, *The Early In-dustrial Revolution.* Copyright ©
   1979, Harper and Row.

Figure 25-1   (p. 720)
   From Theodore S. Hamerow, *The Birth of a New Europe.* University
   of North Carolina, Chapel Hill,
   NC. Copyright © 1983.

Figure 31-1   (p. 885)
   From Charles P. Kindleberger,
   The World in Depression, 1929–39.
   Copyright © University of Cali-fornia Press, Berkeley, 1973.

Index